LET'S GO:
Ireland

"Its yearly revision by a new crop of Harvard students makes it as valuable as ever."
—*The New York Times*

"Value-packed, unbeatable, accurate, and comprehensive."
—*The Los Angeles Times*

"A world-wise traveling companion—always ready with friendly advice and helpful hints, all sprinkled with a bit of wit." —*The Philadelphia Inquirer*

"Lighthearted and sophisticated, informative and fun to read. [Let's Go] helps the novice traveler navigate like a knowledgeable old hand."
—*Atlanta Journal-Constitution*

"All the essential information you need, from making a phone call to exchanging money to contacting your embassy. [Let's Go] provides maps to help you find your way from every train station to a full range of youth hostels and hotels."
—*Minneapolis Star Tribune*

"Unbeatable: good sight-seeing advice; up-to-date info on restaurants, hotels, and inns; a commitment to money-saving travel; and a wry style that brightens nearly every page."
—*The Washington Post*

▨ Let's Go researchers have to make it on their own.

"The writers seem to have experienced every rooster-packed bus and lunar-surfaced mattress about which they write."
—*The New York Times*

"Retains the spirit of the student-written publication it is: candid, opinionated, resourceful, amusing info for the traveler of limited means but broad curiosity."
—*Mademoiselle*

▨ No other guidebook is as comprehensive.

"Whether you're touring the United States, Europe, Southeast Asia, or Central America, a Let's Go guide will clue you in to the cheapest, yet safe, hotels and hostels, food and transportation. Going beyond the call of duty, the guides reveal a country's latest news, cultural hints, and off-beat information that any tourist is likely to miss."
—*Tulsa World*

▨ Let's Go is completely revised each year.

"Up-to-date travel tips for touring four continents on skimpy budgets."
—*Time*

"Inimitable.... Let's Go's 24 guides are updated yearly (as opposed to the general guidebook standard of every two to three years), and in a marvelously spunky way."
—*The New York Times*

Let's Go Publications

Let's Go: Alaska & The Pacific Northwest
Let's Go: Britain & Ireland
Let's Go: California
Let's Go: Central America
Let's Go: Eastern Europe
Let's Go: Ecuador & The Galápagos Islands
Let's Go: Europe
Let's Go: France
Let's Go: Germany
Let's Go: Greece & Turkey
Let's Go: India & Nepal
Let's Go: Ireland
Let's Go: Israel & Egypt
Let's Go: Italy
Let's Go: London
Let's Go: Mexico
Let's Go: New York City
Let's Go: Paris
Let's Go: Rome
Let's Go: Southeast Asia
Let's Go: Spain & Portugal
Let's Go: Switzerland & Austria
Let's Go: USA
Let's Go: Washington, D.C.

Let's Go **Map Guide:** Boston
Let's Go **Map Guide:** London
Let's Go **Map Guide:** New York City
Let's Go **Map Guide:** Paris
Let's Go **Map Guide:** San Francisco
Let's Go **Map Guide:** Washington, D.C.

LET'S GO

The Budget Guide to
Ireland

1997

Ryan Hackney
Editor

Emily J. Stebbins
Associate Editor

St. Martin's Press ❦ New York

HELPING LET'S GO

If you want to share your discoveries, suggestions, or corrections, please drop us a line. We read every piece of correspondence, whether a postcard, a 10-page e-mail, or a coconut. All suggestions are passed along to our researcher-writers. Please note that mail received after May 1997 may be too late for the 1998 book, but will be retained for the following edition. **Address mail to:**

> Let's Go: Ireland
> 67 Mt. Auburn Street
> Cambridge, MA 02138
> USA

Visit Let's Go at **http://www.letsgo.com,** or send e-mail to:

> Fanmail@letsgo.com
> Subject: "Let's Go: Ireland"

In addition to the invaluable travel advice our readers share with us, many are kind enough to offer their services as researchers or editors. Unfortunately, the charter of Let's Go, Inc. enables us to employ only currently enrolled Harvard-Radcliffe students.

Contents

Stuck for cash? Don't panic. With Western Union, money is transferred to you in minutes. It's easy. All you've got to do is ask someone at home to give Western Union a call on US 1 800 3256000. Minutes later you can collect the cash.

WESTERN UNION | MONEY TRANSFER®

The fastest way to send money worldwide.

Maps

Acknowledgments

Our gratitude to IHH, An Óige, Bus Éireann, and Iarnród Éireann for generously assisting our researchers in the field. Thanks to Elena Olaya for housing four years of researchers. Jake managed us with a wisdom that will serve him well as the big boss. Dan and Mike taught us all those computer tricks we've learned to love, and fixed our mistakes. Thanks to the London boys for a scintillating crunch and for those tasty curry chips. Shamrocks to Amara, Alex, Kevin, Lauren, Tom, Sarah, and Rachel for proofing in a time of need. We could always count on Heather, Danny, Carolyn, and Brian to give us the facts, give them with style, and make us laugh. **—RAH & EJS**

As always, thanks must go to Chaka, without whom none of this would have been possible. Emily's brilliance for formatting and actual comprehension of such things as cross-referencing saved this book from my inadequacies; I will always defer to her in matters of disco and bagging on Cromwell. Thanks to Corey for stories, Allison for past wisdom, Kevin for his show of Irish camaraderie, and Jessica, Leah, Andrew, Bruce, Liz, and Jake for staffing a right proper B&I Room. Thanks to Mom, Dad, Amy, Phil, and Madeleine for being a wonderful family of partially Irish heritage. Finally, my thanks to Casey for basically everything, but more specifically for her exquisite understanding of Sophocles. **—RAH**

Thanks to Ryan for his love of pirates, his hatred of Cromwell, his patience while I learned how to pronounce Irish place names, and most of all for seeing the lawn while I saw blades of grass. Jake answered all the hard questions easily, and kept the B&I room in an eternal state of yo. Thanks to Andrew for his box of boom and fonkay collection, and to Jessica for putting up with it. Thanks to Leah for her funny accents and a soft Hard GI shoulder to cry on. Bruce: good luck with your Solitaire game, but you'll never be as good as Liz. Thanks to Mom, Dad, Michael, Matthew, Sean, and my grandparents for your boundless love and support. You are always in my heart. And finally to Kevin for your patience, your understanding, and most of all your love: I would be lost without you. I.N.C., **—EJS**

Editor	Ryan Hackney
Associate Editor	Emily J. Stebbins
Managing Editor	John R. Brooks
Publishing Director	Michelle C. Sullivan
Production Manager	Daniel O. Williams
Associate Production Manager	Michael S. Campbell
Cartography Manager	Amanda K. Bean
Editorial Manager	John R. Brooks
Editorial Manager	Allison Crapo
Financial Manager	Stephen P. Janiak
Personnel Manager	Alexander H. Travelli
Publicity Manager	SoRelle B. Braun
Associate Publicity Manager	David Fagundes
Associate Publicity Manager	Elisabeth Mayer
Assistant Cartographer	Jonathan D. Kibera
Assistant Cartographer	Mark C. Staloff
Office Coordinator	Jennifer L. Schuberth
Director of Advertising and Sales	Amit Tiwari
Senior Sales Executives	Andrew T. Rourke
	Nicholas A. Valtz, Charles E. Varner
General Manager	Richard Olken
Assistant General Manager	Anne E. Chisholm

Researcher-Writers

Heather Clark *Donegal, Antrim & Derry,*
Down & Armagh, Belfast, Isle of Man

Researching Ireland for an unprecedented third time, Heather roared through the pubs of the North and Northwest with a fervor and vivacity unseen since Cuchullain. She knew good trad when she heard it and a good sunrise when she saw it. She let nothing get in her way, not even the worst Troubles in 25 years. Dodging roadblocks, she made her way to the whimsical Isle of Man, feeding kippers to Manx cats along the way. Many people offered help and friendship; Heather wishes to say *"Go rabh mah agut!"* to John and Fiona, Peter Fitzgerald, Eamon Jordan, Neil and John McGrory, Arnie, Rosie, Aileen, Rita, Finbar, Martin, Laurie, Brian, Christy, Molly, Podge, and Eamon. This book won't soon see another one like Heather.

Daniel Herlihy *Clare, Galway, Sligo, Leitrim,*
Cavan, Monaghan, Fermanagh & Tyrone

This native son returned to his homeland to give it the sort of going-over only a Corkonian could. A brilliant middle-distance runner, Danny rambled swiftly in his trusty car. Shrugging off the insults of bilingual sheep, he subjected hostel and pub owners throughout the West to his razor-sharp research. Neither verdant paths nor the effects of drugs in the Irish countryside were able to hide when he was in town. Bringing his biological acumen to bear on the genetic composition of regional dog populations, he always uncovered startling results. A born poet, Danny said it all and said it well. Danny was trustworthy and solid; when he's a doctor, his patients will appreciate that as much as we did.

Carolyn Magill *Dublin, Wicklow, Meath & Louth,*
Kildare, Carlow, Wexford & Waterford

Conquering castles, savoring pints, and biking just about anywhere, Carolyn remade the Southeast in her own cheerful image. Always diligent and always ascertaining exactly when last year's researcher had had a few too many, she revealed a rare genius for outcharming the Irish. Her boots weren't made for walking, but she did so anyway. In her rare free moments, she attended the Magill family reunion in Co. Cork and researched Irish politics. Despite the attention of numerous admirers, she still found time to send back dolmen-sized batches of fantastic copy. Using her rugby-honed stamina and swiftness, she finished the Dublin Pub Crawl in an unprecedented *single day*. Beat that, Joyce.

Brian Saccente *Cork, Kerry,*
Limerick, Tipperary

Master linguist and teeny-bopper fave, Brian left a string of broken hearts from Kerry to Tipperary. Undaunted by dolphins, shamrock-emblazoned berets, or tacky royalty, Brian took on the Southwest with a scathing pen and a lively wit. Despite nonexistent transportation and high seas, he made it to Skellig Michael Island anyway. Always our James Bond, Brian cleverly resisted the seductive wiles of the beautiful Californian. Sort of. Not one to fool around, he always gave us the straight *cac capaill.* We may not have always understood what he told us (i.e. when it was in a language we didn't know) but whatever it was, it was good. Rather than return home after his exhaustive work, Brian stayed on to further hone his Irish skills.

Bruce Gottlieb *London*

Andrew Nieland *London*

$\mathcal{E}$scape to ancient cities and

 journey to exotic islands with

$\mathcal{CNN}$ Travel Guide, a wealth of valuable advice.

Host Valerie Voss will take you

to all of your favorite destinations,

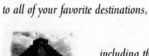 *including those off the beaten path.*

Tune - in to your passport to the world.

SATURDAY 12:30 PM ET
SUNDAY 4:30 PM ET

About Let's Go

Back in 1960, a few students at Harvard University banded together to produce a 20-page pamphlet offering a collection of tips on budget travel in Europe. This modest, mimeographed packet, offered as an extra to passengers on student charter flights to Europe, met with instant popularity. The following year, students traveling to Europe researched the first, full-fledged edition of *Let's Go: Europe*, a pocket-sized book featuring honest, irreverent writing and a decidedly youthful outlook on the world. Throughout the 60s, our guides reflected the times; the 1969 guide to America led off by inviting travelers to "dig the scene" at San Francisco's Haight-Ashbury. During the 70s and 80s, we gradually added regional guides and expanded coverage into the Middle East and Central America. With the addition of our in-depth city guides, handy map guides, and extensive coverage of Asia, the 90s are also proving to be a time of explosive growth for Let's Go, and there's certainly no end in sight. The first editions of *Let's Go: India & Nepal* and *Let's Go: Ecuador & The Galápagos Islands* hit the shelves this year, and research for next year's series has already begun.

We've seen a lot in 37 years. *Let's Go: Europe* is now the world's bestselling international guide, translated into seven languages. And our new guides bring Let's Go's total number of titles, with their spirit of adventure and their reputation for honesty, accuracy, and editorial integrity, to 30. But some things never change: our guides are still researched, written, and produced entirely by students who know first-hand how to see the world on the cheap.

HOW WE DO IT

Each guide is completely revised and thoroughly updated every year by a well-traveled set of 200 students. Every winter, we recruit over 120 researchers and 60 editors to write the books anew. After several months of training, Researcher-Writers hit the road for seven weeks of exploration, from Anchorage to Ankara, Estonia to El Salvador, Iceland to Indonesia. Hired for their rare combination of budget travel sense, writing ability, stamina, and courage, these adventurous travelers know that train strikes, stolen luggage, food poisoning, and marriage proposals are all part of a day's work. Back at our offices, editors work from spring to fall, massaging copy written on Himalayan bus rides into witty yet informative prose. A student staff of typesetters, cartographers, publicists, and managers keeps our lively team together. In September, the collected efforts of the summer are delivered to our printer, who turns them into books in record time, so that you have the most up-to-date information available for *your* vacation. And even as you read this, work on next year's editions is well underway.

WHY WE DO IT

At Let's Go, our goal is to give you a great vacation. We don't think of budget travel as the last recourse of the destitute; we believe that it's the only way to travel. Living cheaply and simply brings you closer to the people and places you've been saving up to visit. Our books will ease your anxieties and answer your questions about the basics—so you can get off the beaten track and explore. Once you learn the ropes, we encourage you to put Let's Go away now and then to strike out on your own. As any seasoned traveler will tell you, the best discoveries are often those you make yourself. When you find something worth sharing, drop us a line. We're Let's Go Publications, 67 Mt. Auburn St., Cambridge, MA 02138, USA (e-mail: fanmail@letsgo.com).

HAPPY TRAVELS!

How to Use This Book

The more you know about Ireland, the happier you'll be when you get there. Our **Essentials** chapter is designed to maximize your happiness. **Planning Your Trip** has information on everything you did and didn't think of asking, from customs to packing to health. It also contains a section on the specific concerns of women, minorities, gays, lesbians, people with disabilities, families, and older travelers. **Getting There** and **Getting Around** help travelers navigate a path through the maze of planes, ferries, rails, and buses. Tips for hiking, biking, and (reservedly) hitching are also included.

An **Introduction** explains the basics of Irish history, literature, sports, and food. The **Northern Ireland** introduction overviews the history and current events of the region and, most importantly, it suggests how to stay out of trouble. The counties and towns in the Republic are organized clockwise around the coast, beginning with Dublin. Northern Ireland does the opposite: its towns are listed from southeast to northwest. We finish with stopovers: the **Isle of Man** is an intriguing country with few tourists and lots of Manx cats, while **London** is a curious anomaly with fewer Manx cats, but more pubs and clubs. A glossary at the back of the book decodes Irish words and slang. If you need to find something, check the index.

Within listings we organized information in order of its probable usefulness, starting with strictly practical matters, followed by where to stay, where to eat, where to drink, and what to see. Our listings are placed in our perceived order of **value.** There are a few things we felt it unnecessary to say in every town: every large town in Ireland makes a good base for exploring the surrounding countryside, and every mountain and tower, when you get to the top, offers a new view.

We suggest you use our listings in this way: read the **town introductions** and decide whether they interest you. Once there, find a place to stay, stash your stuff, get a map, and go find whatever you came to Ireland for. Don't try to make too rigid of an itinerary—the best adventures happen unannounced. Aim for a mixed experience: sample the exciting nightlife of Dublin or Galway, experience the charm of smaller towns like Dingle or Kilmore Quay, and admire the stunning natural beauty of places like the Beara Peninsula or Sperrin Mountains.

It's important when using our books to realize that our choices for listings are based on what we believe represents good value, not just low price. Traveling on a budget can be as good or better than luxury travel, but travelers who become obsessed with saving money may sacrifice the quality of their experience. It's also important to know that while *Let's Go* researchers strive to leave no stone unturned, there are just too damn many stones for us to include them all. Use this book to start your journey, get your bearings, then go find your own stones to turn. *Let's Go* is an enabling device, not a bible. The best way to see Ireland is to head out on your own, meet the Irish people, and talk to them. They know the secrets and treasures of their towns that can make your trip truly memorable. A great adventure awaits; have fun, and let us know about it when you're done.

A NOTE TO OUR READERS

The information for this book is gathered by *Let's Go*'s researchers during the late spring and summer months. Each listing is derived from the assigned researcher's opinion based upon his or her visit at a particular time. The opinions are expressed in a candid and forthright manner. Other travelers might disagree. Those traveling at a different time may have different experiences since prices, dates, hours, and conditions are always subject to change. You are urged to check beforehand to avoid inconvenience and surprises. Travel always involves a certain degree of risk, especially in low-cost areas. When traveling, especially on a budget, always take particular care to ensure your safety.

ESSENTIALS

PLANNING YOUR TRIP

▓ When To Go

Traveling is like comedy—timing is everything. Traveling during the low or off season (mid-Sept. to May) has its benefits: airfares are less expensive, and you won't have to fend off flocks of fellow tourists. The flip side is that many attractions, hostels, B&Bs, and tourist offices close in winter, and in some rural areas of west Ireland, local transportation drops off significantly or shuts down altogether. Most holidays and festivals occur during the summer months (see **Holidays**, p. 468). At any time of the year, the infamous Irish climate is a force to be reckoned with.

WEATHER

The weather in Ireland and Northern Ireland is subject to frequent changes but few extremes, with an average temperature in the low to mid-60s (°F) in summer and in the low 40s (°F) in winter. A bright and cloudless morning sky is often followed by intermittent drizzle and mist throughout the afternoon. Count on feeling chilly and wet at least once a day. The east and south coasts are the driest and sunniest places, while western Ireland is wetter and cloudier.

Spring is the driest season in Ireland, especially on the east coast. May and June are the sunniest months, particularly in the south and southeast, and July and August are the warmest. December and January have the worst weather of the year: wet, cold, and cloudy. It also gets dark early in winter months; kiss the sun good night at 3pm or so. The average annual maximum and minimum temperatures for Dublin are 8°C (47°F) and 1°C (35°F) for January, 20°C (67°F) and 11°C (51°F) for July. For more information, see the **Climate Chart** (p. 467).

TIME ZONE DIFFERENCES

Ireland and the U.K. are on Greenwich Mean Time (GMT), which sets its clock: one hour earlier than (most of) continental Europe; five hours later than Sheldon, VT (EST); six hours later than Baton Rouge, LA (CST); seven hours later than Tombstone, AZ (MST); eight hours later than Fresno, CA (PST); nine hours later than Alaska; 10 hours later than Hawaii; eight, 9½, and 10 hours earlier than Australia; and 12 hours earlier than Auckland, New Zealand.

▓ Useful Information

GOVERNMENT INFORMATION OFFICES

Irish Tourist Board (Bord Fáilte): In the **U.S.:** 345 Park Ave., New York, NY 10154 (tel. (800) 223-6470 or (212) 418-0800; fax 371-9052). In **Canada:** 160 Bloor St. E., Suite 1150, Toronto, Ont. M4W 1B9 (tel. (416) 929-2777; fax 929-6783). In the **U.K.:** 150 New Bond St., London W1Y 0AQ (tel. (0171) 518 0800; fax 493 9065). In **Australia:** Level 5, 36 Carrington St., Sydney NSW 2000 (tel. (02) 299 6177; fax 299 6323). Ask for the *Caravan and Camping Guide,* which lists Bord Fáilte-approved B&Bs and campgrounds and prices.

Northern Ireland Tourist Board: Head Office: 59 North St., Belfast, BT1 1NB, Northern Ireland (tel. (01232) 231221; fax 240960). In **Dublin:** 16 Nassau St., Dublin 2 (tel. (01) 679 1977; CallSave (0800) 282662; fax (01) 679 1863. In the **U.S.:** 551 Fifth Ave., Suite 701, New York, NY 10176 (tel. (800) 326-0036 or (212) 922-

0101; fax 922-0099). In **Canada:** 111 Avenue Rd., Suite 450, Toronto, Ont. M5R 3J8 (tel. (416) 925-6368; fax 961-2175). In the **U.K.:** British Travel Centre, 12 Lower Regent St., London SW1Y 4PQ (tel. (0171) 839 8417; fax 839 6179. From elsewhere overseas, contact any British Tourist Office for Northern Ireland info. Ask any tourist board for free brochures as well as *Where to Stay in Northern Ireland 1996*, a list of all B&Bs and campgrounds and their prices, (US$10, UK£4), and *Where to Eat in Northern Ireland 1996* (US$7, UK£2.50). You can also find them at the British Travel Bookshop (tel. (800) 677-8585).

Isle of Man Tourist Information: Sea Terminal Building, Douglas IM1 2RG, Isle of Man (tel. (01624) 686766; fax 627443).

All Ireland Information Bureau: In **London:** British Travel Centre, 12 Lower Regent St., London SW1Y 4PQ (tel. (0171) 839 8417; fax 839 6179; open Mon.-Fri. 9am-6:30pm, Sat.-Sun. 10am-4pm). In **Australia:** All Ireland Board, 36 Camington Street, Sydney, NSW 2000 (tel. (02) 299 6177; fax 299 6323).

TRAVEL ORGANIZATIONS

Council on International Educational Exchange (Council), 205 East 42nd St., New York, NY 10017-5706 (tel. (888) COUNCIL (268-6245); fax (212) 822-2699; e-mail info@ciee.org; http://www.ciee.org). A private, nonprofit organization, Council administers work, volunteer, and academic programs around the world. They also offer identity cards, including the ISIC and the GO25, and a range of publications, including the magazine *Student Travels* (free). Call or write for more information.

Federation of International Youth Travel Organizations (FIYTO), Bredgade 25H, DK-1260 Copenhagen K, Denmark (tel. (45) 33 33 96 00; fax 33 93 96 76; e-mail mailbox@fiyto.org), is an international organization promoting educational, cultural, and social travel for young people. Member organizations include language schools, educational travel companies, national tourist boards, accommodation centers and other suppliers of travel services to youth and students. FIYTO sponsors the GO25 Card.

International Student Travel Confederation, Herengracht 479, 1017 BS Amsterdam, The Netherlands (tel. (31) 20 421 2800; fax 20 421 2810; e-mail istcinfo@istc.org; http://www.istc.org). The ISTC is a nonprofit confederation of student travel organizations whose focus is to develop, promote, and facilitate travel among youth and students. Member organizations include International Student Rail Association (ISRA), Student Air Travel Association (SATA), ISIS Travel Insurance, and the International Association for Educational and Work Exchange Programs (IAEWEP). Sponsor of the ISIC. Their web site lists all ISIC discounts.

USEFUL PUBLICATIONS

Adventurous Traveler Bookstore, P.O. Box 1468, Williston, VT 05495 (tel. (801) 860-6776; fax 860-6607 or (800) 282-3963; e-mail books@atbook.com; http://www.gorp.com/atbook.htm). Specializes in outdoor adventure travel books and maps including *Best Irish Walks* (US$13), *Ireland by Bike* (US$15), and *Trout and Salmon Rivers of Ireland* (US$25). Free 40-page catalogue upon request. Their World Wide Web site is a great place to browse.

Bon Voyage!, 2069 W. Bullard Ave., Fresno, CA 93711-1200 (tel. (800) 995-9716, from abroad (209) 447-8441; e-mail 70754.3511@compuserve.com). Annual mail-order catalogue offers a wide range of products to suit all travel needs and styles. Books, travel accessories, luggage, electrical converters, maps, videos, and more. All merchandise may be returned for exchange or refund within 30 days of purchase, and prices are guaranteed (lower advertised prices will be matched and merchandise shipped free).

The College Connection, Inc., 1295 Prospect St. Suite A, La Jolla, CA 92037 (tel. (619) 551-9770; fax 551-9987; e-mail eurailnow@aol.com; http://www.eurailpass.com). Publishes *The Passport,* a booklet listing hints about every aspect of traveling and studying abroad. This booklet is free to *Let's Go* readers; send your request by e-mail or fax only. The College Rail Connection, a division of the College Connection, sells railpasses and flights with student discounts.

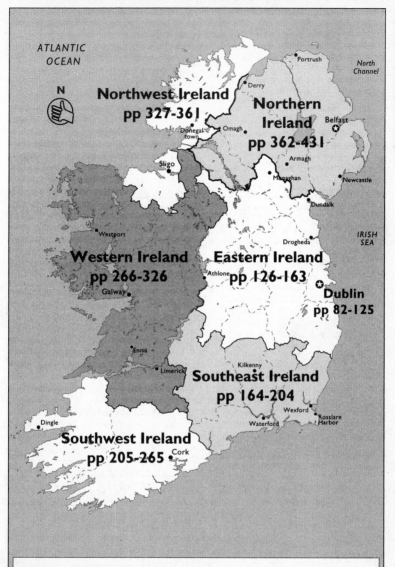

ATLANTIC
OCEAN

N

Northwest Ireland
pp 327-361

Northern Ireland
pp 362-431

Western Ireland
pp 266-326

Eastern Ireland
pp 126-163

Dublin
pp 82-125

Southeast Ireland
pp 164-204

Southwest Ireland
pp 205-265

North Channel

IRISH SEA

Portrush · Derry · Omagh · Donegal town · Sligo · Belfast · Armagh · Monaghan · Newcastle · Dundalk · Westport · Drogheda · Athlone · Galway · Ennis · Limerick · Kilkenny · Wexford · Rosslare Harbor · Waterford · Dingle · Cork

Map of Chapter Divisions

Eastern Ireland
Counties: Monaghan, Cavan, Louth, Meath, Longford, Westmeath, Offaly, Laois, Kildare, and Wicklow.

Southeast Ireland
Counties: Tipperary, Kilkenny, Carlow, Wexford, and Waterford.

Southwest Ireland
Counties: Cork and Kerry.

Western Ireland
Counties: Limerick, Clare, Galway, Roscommon, Leitrim, and Mayo.

Northwest Ireland
Counties: Sligo and Donegal.

Northern Ireland
Counties: Derry, Antrim, Tyrone, Fermanagh, Armagh, and Down.

The World At a Discount

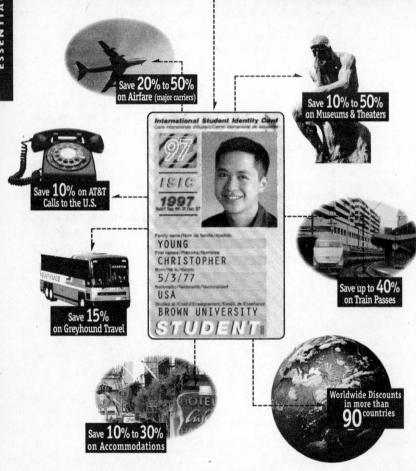

Save **20%** to **50%** on Airfare (major carriers)

Save **10%** to **50%** on Museums & Theaters

Save **10%** on AT&T Calls to the U.S.

Save up to **40%** on Train Passes

Save **15%** on Greyhound Travel

Save **10%** to **30%** on Accommodations

Worldwide Discounts in more than **90** countries

The International Student Identity Card
Your Passport to Discounts & Benefits

With the ISIC, you'll receive discounts on airfare, hotels, transportation, computer services, foreign currency exchange, phone calls, major attractions, and more. You'll also receive basic accident and sickness insurance coverage when traveling outside the U.S. and access to a 24-hour, toll-free Help Line. Call now to locate the issuing office nearest you (over 555 across the U.S.) at:

Free 40-page handbook with each card!

1-888-COUNCIL (toll-free)

For an application and complete discount list, you can also visit us at **http://www.ciee.org/**

Council

CIEE: Council on International Educational Exchange

Forsyth Travel Library, P.O. Box 480800, Kansas City, MO 64148 (tel. (800) 367-7984; fax (816) 942-6969; http://www.forsyth.com). A mail-order service that stocks a wide range of city, area, and country maps, as well as guides for rail and ferry travel in Europe. Also sells rail tickets and passes, and offers reservation services. Call or write for a free catalogue, or visit their web site.

Hippocrene Books, Inc., 171 Madison Ave., New York, NY 10016 (tel. (212) 685-4371, orders (718) 454-2366; fax 454-1391). Free catalogue. Publishes travel reference books, travel guides, foreign language dictionaries, and language learning guides which cover over 100 languages.

Passport to Ireland, a catalog good for hundreds of two-for-one entry to attractions in Ireland, is available from **Irish Books and Media** (tel. (800) 229-3505).

Specialty Travel Index, 305 San Anselmo Avenue, Suite 313, San Anselmo, CA 94960 (tel. (415) 459-4900; fax 459-4974; e-mail spectrav@ix.netcom.com; http://www.spectrav). Published bi-annually, this is an extensive listing of "off the beaten track" and specialty travel opportunities, including a variety of adventures in the Irish outdoors. 1 copy US$6, 1-year subscription (2 copies) US$10.

Superintendent of Documents, U.S. Government Printing Office, P.O. Box 371954, Pittsburgh, PA 15250-7954 (tel. (202) 512-1800; fax 512-2250). Publishes *Your Trip Abroad* (US$1.25), *Health Information for International Travel* (US$14), and "Background Notes" on all countries ($1 each). Postage included in all prices. Open Mon.-Fri. 7:30am-4:30pm.

Transitions Abroad, 18 Hulst Rd., P.O. Box 1300, Amherst, MA 01004-1300 (tel. (413) 256-3414; fax 256-0375; e-mail trabroad@aol.com). Invaluable magazine lists publications and resources for overseas study, work, and volunteering. Also publishes *The Alternative Travel Directory,* a comprehensive guide to living, learning, and working overseas (US$20; postage US$4).

INTERNET RESOURCES

Like everything else in the 90s, budget travel is moving rapidly into the information age. With the growing user-friendliness of personal computers and Internet technology, much of this information can be yours with the click of a mouse. There are many ways to access the **Internet.** Most popular are commercial 'net providers such as **America Online** (tel. (800) 827-6394) and **Compuserve** (tel. (800) 433-0389). Many employers and schools also offer gateways to the Internet, often for free (unlike corporate gateways). For 'net-surfing budget travelers, the most useful parts of the Internet are the World Wide Web and Usenet newsgroups.

The World Wide Web

Increasingly the Internet forum of choice, the **World Wide Web** provides its users with graphics, sound, and textual information. This and the huge proliferation of **web pages** (individual sites within the World Wide Web) have made the Web the most active and exciting of Internet destinations. It is also the newest path from corporate advertisers to the minds of the masses; be sure to distinguish between what is good information and what is marketing. Another large difficulty with the Web is its lack of hierarchy (it is a web, after all). The introduction of **search engines** (services that search for web pages under specific subjects) has aided the search process some. **Lycos** (http://a2z.lycos.com) and **Infoseek** (http://guide.infoseek.com) are the two of the most popular. **Yahoo!** is a slightly more organized search engine; check out its travel links at http://www.yahoo.com/Recreation/Travel. Here are some of our favorite spots to begin budget travel web surfing:

Ireland Pages

Ireland's National Tourism Database (http://www.touchtel.ie/first) has information on camping, hostels, castles, and more; accessible by county and region.

Northern Ireland Tourist Board (http://www.interknowledge.com/northern-ireland) includes information on the Giant's Causeway, the Glens of Antrim, Lough Erne, fishing, and golfing.

ESSENTIALS

Northern Ireland Information Centre (http://www.nireland.com) links you to information on current events, politics, education, religion, and other cultural and social aspects of Northern Ireland.

The Backpacker Guide Ireland (http://www.irelands-web.ie/tourism/bpguide/ire/index.htm) allows you to book hostels on-line, among other things.

West Connemara Tourism Development (http://www.mayo-ireland.ie/ConnConc.htm) is your gateway to the history, business, and culture of the Connemara region of Cos. Mayo and Galway.

General Globe-Trotting Info

Dr. Memory's Favorite Travel Pages (http://www.access.digex.net/~drmemory/cyber_travel.html) is a great place to start surfing. Dr. Memory has links to hundreds of different web pages of interest to travelers.

Rent-A-Wreck's Travel Links (http://www.rent-a-wreck.com/raw/travlist.htm) are, surprisingly, very good and very complete.

Big World Magazine (http://boss.cpcnet.com/personal/bigworld/bigworld.htm), a budget travel 'zine, has a web page with great links to travel pages.

The CIA World Factbook (http://www.odci.gov/cia/publications/95fact) has tons of vital statistics on Ireland and Northern Ireland, including an economic overview and an explanation of the system of government.

Shoestring Travel (http://www.stratpub.com) is a budget travel e-zine, with feature articles, links, user exchange, and accommodations information.

The Student and Budget Travel Guide (http://asa.ugl.lib.umich.edu/chdocs/travel/travel-guide.html) is just what it sounds like.

Let's Go lists relevant web sites throughout different sections of the Essentials chapter. Finally, web sites come and go very rapidly. Thus, as with normal travel, it is important for you to explore on your own in cyber-travel as well.

▓ Documents & Formalities

Be sure to file all applications several weeks or months in advance of your planned departure date. Remember that you are relying on government agencies to complete these transactions, and a backlog in processing could spoil your plans. When you travel, always carry two or more forms of identification, including at least one photo ID. A passport combined with a driver's license or birth certificate usually serves as adequate proof of your identity and citizenship. Many establishments require several IDs before cashing traveler's checks. Never carry all your identification in the same place; you risk being left entirely without ID or funds in case of theft or loss. Also, carry half a dozen extra passport-size photos that you can attach to the sundry IDs or railpasses you will eventually acquire. If you plan to be in Ireland or Northern Ireland for a long time, register your passport with an embassy or consulate. Students should consult **Youth, Student, & Teacher Identification** (p. 11).

U.S. citizens seeking general information about documents, formalities, and travel abroad should request the booklet *Your Trip Abroad* (US$1.25) from the **Superintendent of Documents** (see **Useful Publications,** p. 5).

EMBASSIES & CONSULATES

Ireland: In the **U.S.:** Irish Embassy, 2234 Massachusetts Ave. NW, Washington, D.C. 20008 (tel. (202) 462-3939); consulates at: 345 Park Ave., 17th floor, New York, NY 10154 (tel. (212) 319-2555); Wrigley Building, Rm. 911, 400 N. Michigan Ave., Chicago, IL 60611 (tel. (312) 337-1868); 44 Montgomery St., #3830, San Francisco, CA 94104 (tel. (415) 392-4214); 535 Boylston St., Boston, MA 02116 (tel. (617) 267-9330). In **Canada:** 170 Metcalfe St., Ottawa, Ont. K2P 1P3 (tel. (613) 233-6281). In **Australia** and **New Zealand:** 20 Arkana St., Yarralumla ACT 2600, Australia (tel. (06) 273 3022; fax 273 3741).

Britain: In the **U.S.:** British Embassy, 3100 Massachusetts Ave. NW, Washington, D.C. 20008 (tel. (202) 462-1340); consulates at 845 Third Ave., New York, NY 10022 (tel. (212) 745-0200); Suite 2700, Marquis One Tower, 245 Peachtree Center Ave., Atlanta, GA 30303 (tel. (404) 524-5856); 400 N. Michigan Ave., Suite 1300, Chicago, IL 60611 (tel. (312) 346-1810); First Interstate Bank Plaza, Suite 1990, 1000 Louisiana, Houston, TX 77002 (tel. (713) 659-6270); and 11766 Wilshire Blvd., Suite 400, Los Angeles, CA 90025-6536 (tel. (310) 477-3322). Call the Embassy for additional consulates. In **Canada:** British Tourist Authority, 111 Avenue Rd. Suite 450, Toronto, Ontario M5R 3J8 (tel. (416) 925-6326; fax 961-2175). In **Australia:** British High Commission, Commonwealth Ave., Yarralumla, Canberra, ACT 2600 (tel. (06) 270 6666). In **New Zealand:** British High Commission, 44 Hill St., Wellington ‡ (tel. (04) 472 6049).

ENTRANCE REQUIREMENTS & VISAS

Citizens of the U.S., Canada, the U.K., Australia, New Zealand, and South Africa need a valid **passport** to enter Ireland or Northern Ireland and to reenter their own country. You may be denied entrance if your passport expires within six months, and returning to the U.S. with an expired passport may result in a fine. A **visa** is an endorsement that a government stamps into a passport which allows the bearer to stay in that country for a specified purpose and period of time (about a month, to be spent within six months to a year from the date of issue). Most visas cost US$10-70. Citizens of the U.S., Canada, the U.K., Australia, New Zealand, and South Africa may enter both the Republic of Ireland and Northern Ireland without a visa.

When entering the country, dress neatly and carry **proof of your financial independence** (such as an airplane ticket to depart, enough money to cover your living expenses, etc.). The standard period of admission is three months to Ireland, six months to Northern Ireland. To stay longer, you must show evidence that you can support yourself for an extended period of time, and a medical examination is often required. Admission as a visitor from a non-EU nation does not include the right to work, which is authorized only by the possession of a work permit (see **Alternatives** to **Tourism,** p. 21). Entering either Ireland or Northern Ireland to study does not require a special visa, but immigration officers will want to see proof of acceptance by an Irish or Northern Irish school.

For more information, send for *Foreign Entry Requirements* (US$0.50) from the **Consumer Information Center,** Pueblo, CO 81009 (tel. (719) 948-3334), or contact the **Center for International Business and Travel (CIBT),** 25 West 43rd St. #1420, New York, NY 10036 (tel. (800) 925-2428 or (212) 575-2811 from NYC), which secures visas for travel to and from all countries at a variable service charge.

PASSPORTS

In order to help prove your citizenship and facilitate the issuing of a new passport if you lose the original document, photocopy the page of your passport that contains your photograph and identifying information (especially your passport number) before you leave. Carry this photocopy in a safe place apart from your passport and leave another copy at home. Consulates also recommend that you carry an expired passport or an official copy of your birth certificate in a part of your luggage separate from other documents. You can request a duplicate birth certificate from the Bureau of Vital Records and Statistics in your state or province of birth.

If you do lose your passport, it may take weeks to process a replacement, and your new one may be valid only for a limited time. In addition, any visas stamped in your old passport will be irretrievably lost. If this happens, immediately notify the local police and the nearest embassy or consulate of your home government. To expedite its replacement, you will need to know all information previously recorded and show identification and proof of citizenship. Some consulates can issue new passports within two days. In an emergency, ask for temporary traveling papers that will permit you to return to your home country.

United States Citizens may apply for a passport valid for 10 years (5 years if under 18) at any federal or state **courthouse** or **post office** authorized to accept passport applications, or at a **U.S. Passport Agency,** located in Boston, Chicago, Honolulu, Houston, Los Angeles, Miami, New Orleans, New York, Philadelphia, San Francisco, Seattle, Stamford, or Washington, D.C. Refer to the "U.S. Government, State Department" section of the telephone directory, or call a local post office for addresses. Parents must apply in person for children under age 13. Citizens must apply in person for their first passport, if under age 18, or if their current passport is more than 12 years old or was issued before their 18th birthday. Citizens must submit: proof of U.S. citizenship (a certified birth certificate, certification of naturalization or of citizenship, or a previous passport); identification bearing their signature and either their photograph or physical description (e.g. an unexpired driver's license or passport, student ID card, or government ID card); and two identical, passport-size (2in. by 2in.) photographs with a white or off-white background taken within the last six months. It will cost US$65 (under 18 US$40). Passports can be **renewed** by mail or in person for US$55. Processing takes two to four weeks. Passport agencies offer **rush service** for a surcharge of US$30 with proof of departure within 10 working days (e.g., an airplane ticket or itinerary). Abroad, a U.S. embassy or consulate can usually issue a new passport, given proof of citizenship. Passports lost or stolen in the U.S. may be reported in writing to Passport Services, U.S. Department of State, 111 19th St., NW, Washington, D.C., 20522-1705 or to the nearest passport agency. For more info, contact the U.S. Passport Information's **24-hour recorded message** (tel. (202) 647-0518).

Canada Application forms in English and French are available at all **passport offices, post offices,** and most **travel agencies.** Citizens may apply in person at any one of 28 regional Passport Offices. Canadian citizens residing abroad should contact the nearest Canadian embassy or consulate. Along with the application form, a citizen must provide: citizenship documentation (an original Canadian birth certificate or a certificate of Canadian citizenship); two identical passport photos taken within the last year; any previous Canadian passport; and a CDN$60 fee (paid in cash, money order, or certified check) to Passport Office, Ottawa, Ont. K1A OG3. The application and one of the photographs must be signed by an eligible guarantor (someone who has known the applicant for two years and whose profession falls into one of the categories listed on the application). Processing takes about five business days for in-person applications and three weeks by mail. Children under 16 may be included on a parent's passport, though some countries require children to carry their own passports. Passports are valid for five years and are non-renewable. If a passport is lost, Canadians must be able to prove citizenship with another document. For additional info, call (800) 567-6868 (24hr.; from Canada only); the Passport Office in Quebec at (819) 994-3500; (416) 973-3251 in Toronto; (514) 283-2152 in Montréal. Refer to the booklet *Bon Voyage, But...* for further help and a list of Canadian embassies and consulates abroad (free from any passport office).

Australia Citizens must apply for a passport in person at a post office, passport office (in Adelaide, Brisbane, Canberra City, Darwin, Hobart, Melbourne, Newcastle, Perth, and Sydney), or Australian diplomatic mission overseas. An appointment may be necessary. Parents may file an application for unmarried children under 18. Application fees vary. In Australia, call 13 12 32 toll-free.

New Zealand Application forms for passports are available in New Zealand from travel agents and Department of Internal Affairs Link Centres, and overseas from New Zealand embassies, high commissions, and consulates. Completed applications may be lodged at Link Centres and at overseas posts, or forwarded to the Passport Office, PO Box 10-526, Wellington, New Zealand. Processing time is 10 business days from receipt of a correctly completed application. An urgent passport service is also available. The application fee for an adult passport is NZ$80 in New Zealand, and NZ$130 overseas for applications lodged under the standard service.

South Africa Citizens can apply for a passport at any Home Affairs Office. Two photos, either a birth certificate or an identity book, and a SAR80 fee must accompany a completed application. Passports are valid for 10 years. For further information, contact the nearest Department of Home Affairs Office.

CUSTOMS: ENTERING

It is illegal to bring into the **U.K.** or **Ireland** any controlled drugs, obscene material, fireworks, meat, or plant or vegetable material (including fruit and bark). All animals brought into the country are subject to a six-month quarantine at the owner's expense. Neither country limits the amount of currency brought in, though Ireland places restrictions on the amount taken out: no more than £150 in Irish currency, plus no more than the value of IR£1200 in foreign currency.

Republic of Ireland Citizens or visitors arriving in Ireland from outside the EU must declare everything obtained outside the EU or duty- and tax-free in the EU in excess of the following allowances: 200 cigarettes, 100 cigarillos, 50 cigars, or 250g tobacco; 1L liquor or 2L wine; 2L still wine, 50g perfume, or 250mL toilet water; and anything in excess of IR£142 (IR£73 if under 15 years of age) of other goods. These allowances also apply to duty-free purchases within the EU, except for the last category, which then has an allowance of IR£73. No additional duty or tax will be charged on goods obtained duty and tax paid in another EU country, provided that the goods are for personal use. Travelers under 17 are not entitled to any allowance for tobacco or alcoholic products. For more information, contact The Revenue Commissioners, Dublin Castle (tel. (01) 679 27 77; fax 671 20 21; e-mail taxes@ior.ie; http:\\www.revenue.ie) or The Collector of Customs and Excise, The Custom Houses, Dublin 1.

Northern Ireland Citizens or visitors arriving in the U.K. from outside the EU must declare any goods in excess of the following allowances: 200 cigarettes, 100 cigarillos, 50 cigars, or 250g tobacco; still table wine (2L); strong liqueurs over 22% volume (1L), or other liqueurs including fortified or sparkling wine (2L); perfume (60mL); toilet water (250mL); and UK£136 worth of all other goods including gifts and souvenirs. You must be over 17 to import liquor or tobacco. These allowances also apply to duty-free purchases within the EU, except for the last category, which then has an allowance of UK£71. Goods obtained duty and tax paid for personal use within the EU do not require further customs duty. For more info, contact Her Majesty's Customs and Excise, Custom House, Nettleton Road, Heathrow Airport, Hounslow, Middlesex TW6 2LA (tel. (0181) 910-3744; fax 910-3765).

CUSTOMS: GOING HOME

Upon returning home, you must declare all articles acquired abroad and pay a duty on the value of those articles that exceed the allowance established by your country's customs service. Keeping receipts for purchases made abroad will help establish values when you return. It is wise to make a list, including serial numbers, of any valuables that you carry with you from home; if you register this list with customs before your departure and have an official stamp it, you will avoid import duty charges and ensure an easy passage upon your return. Be especially careful to document items manufactured abroad. Goods and gifts purchased at duty-free shops abroad are not exempt from duty or sales tax at your point of return. "Duty-free" merely means that you need not pay a tax in the country of purchase.

United States Citizens returning home may bring US$400 worth of accompanying goods duty-free and must pay a 10% tax on the next US$1000. You must declare all purchases, so have sales slips ready. Goods are considered duty-free if they are for personal or household use (this includes gifts) and cannot include more than 100 cigars, 200 cigarettes (1 carton), and 1L of wine or liquor. You must be over 21 to bring liquor into the U.S. If you mail home personal goods of U.S. origin, you can avoid duty charges by marking the package "American goods returned." For more information, consult the brochure *Know Before You Go,* available from the U.S. Customs Service, Box 7407, Washington, D.C. 20044 (tel. (202) 927-6724).

Canada Citizens who remain abroad for at least one week may bring back up to CDN$500 worth of goods duty-free once per calendar year. Canadian citizens or residents who travel for a period between 48 hours and six days can bring back up to CDN$200 with the exception of tobacco and alcohol. You are permitted to ship all goods except tobacco and alcohol home under this exemption as long as you declare them when you arrive. Citizens of legal age (which varies by province) may import in-person up to 200 cigarettes, 50 cigars, 400g loose tobacco, 400 tobacco sticks, 1.14L wine or alcohol, and 24 355mL cans/bottles of beer; the value of these products is included in the CDN$500. For more information, write to Canadian Customs, 2265 St. Laurent Blvd., Ottawa, Ontario K1G 4K3 (tel. (613) 993-0534).

Australia Citizens may import AUS$400 (under 18 AUS$200) of goods duty-free, in addition to the allowance of 1.125L alcohol and 250 cigarettes or 250g tobacco. You must be over 18 to import any of these. There is no limit to the amount of Australian and/or foreign cash that may be brought into or taken out of the country. However, amounts of AUS$5000 or more, or the equivalent in foreign currency, must be reported. All foodstuffs and animal products must be declared on arrival. For information, contact the Regional Director, Australian Customs Service, GPO Box 8, Sydney NSW 2001(tel. (02) 2132000; fax 2134000).

New Zealand Citizens may bring home up to NZ$700 worth of goods duty-free if they are intended for personal use or are unsolicited gifts. The concession is 200 cigarettes (1 carton) or 250g tobacco or 50 cigars or a combination of all three not to exceed 250g. You may also bring in 4.5L of beer or wine and 1.125L of liquor. Only travelers over 17 may bring tobacco or alcoholic beverages into the country. For more information, consult the *New Zealand Customs Guide for Travelers,* available from customs offices, or contact New Zealand Customs, 50 Anzac Ave., Box 29, Auckland (tel. (09) 377 35 20; fax 309 29 78).

South Africa Citizens may import duty-free: 400 cigarettes; 50 cigars; 250g tobacco; 2L wine; 1L of spirits; 250mL toilet water; and 50mL perfume; and other items up to a value of SAR500. Amounts exceeding this limit but not SAR10,000 are dutiable at 20%. Certain items such as golf clubs and firearms are subject to a higher duty. Goods acquired abroad and sent to the Republic as unaccompanied baggage do not qualify for any allowances. You may not export or import South African bank notes in excess of SAR500. Persons who require specific information or advice concerning customs and excise duties can address their inquiries to the Commissioner for Customs and Excise, Private Bag X47, Pretoria 0001. This agency distributes the pamphlet *South African Customs Information,* for visitors and residents who travel abroad. South Africans residing in the U.S. should contact the Embassy of South Africa, 3051 Massachusetts Ave., NW, Washington, D.C. 20008 (tel. (202) 232-4400; fax 244-9417) or the South African Home Annex, 3201 New Mexico Ave. #380, NW, Washington DC 20016 (tel. (202) 966-1650).

YOUTH, STUDENT, & TEACHER IDENTIFICATION

Student and youth IDs can get you a lot of discounts on airfares to Ireland, trains and buses within Ireland, and admission to sights. The **International Student Identity Card (ISIC)** is the most widely accepted form of student identification. Flashing this card can procure you discounts for sights, theaters, museums, and accommodations, although the savings on train, ferry, and airplane travel are greater. Present the card wherever you go, and ask about discounts even when none is advertised. It also provides accident insurance of up to US$3000 with no daily limit. In addition, cardholders have access to a toll-free Traveler's Assistance hotline whose multilingual staff can provide help in medical, legal, and financial emergencies overseas.

Many student travel offices issue ISICs, including Council Travel, Let's Go Travel, and STA Travel in the U.S.; Travel CUTS in Canada; USIT in Ireland; and members of the International Student Travel Confederation (ISTC) around the world (see **Travel Organizations,** p. 2). Request a copy of the *International Student Identity Card Handbook,* which lists available discounts by country. You can also write to Council for a copy. The card costs US$18 and is valid from September to December of the following year. Applicants must be at least 12 years old and degree-seeking students of a secondary or post-secondary school. Because of the proliferation of phony ISICs, many airlines and some other services require other proof of student identity, such as your school ID card and/or a signed letter from the registrar attesting to your student status and stamped with the school seal.

The **International Teacher Identity Card (ITIC)** offers similar but limited discounts, as well as medical insurance coverage (US$19). For more info on these handy cards consult the organization's new web site (http://www.istc.org).

Federation of International Youth Travel Organizations (FIYTO) issues a discount card to travelers who are under 26 but not students. Known as the **GO25 Card,** this one-year card offers many of the same benefits as the ISIC, and most organizations that sell the ISIC also sell the GO25 Card. A brochure that lists discounts is free when you purchase the card. To apply, you will need a passport, valid driver's license, or copy of a birth certificate; and a passport-sized photo with your name printed on the back. The fee is US$16, CDN$15, or UK£5. For information, contact Council in the U.S. or FIYTO in Denmark.

DRIVING PERMITS & INSURANCE

You may use an American or Canadian driver's license for one year in Ireland and the U.K., provided you've had it for one year. If you plan a longer stay, you must officially have an **International Driving Permit (IDP)**, though most car rental agencies don't require it. Your IDP must be issued in your own country before you depart and be accompanied by a valid driver's license from your home country. Some travel agents offer the card. U.S. license holders can obtain an IDP (US$10), valid for one year, at any **American Automobile Association (AAA)** office or by writing to the main office: AAA Florida, Travel Agency Services Department, 1000 AAA Drive (mail stop 28), Heathrow, FL 32746-5080 (tel. (407) 444-4245; fax 444-4247). Canadian license holders can obtain an IDP (CDN$10) from any **Canadian Automobile Association (CAA)** branch office, or by writing to CAA Central Ontario, 60 Commerce Valley Drive East, Thornhill, Ontario L3T 7P9 (tel. (416) 221-4300).

■ Money

CURRENCY & EXCHANGE

US$1 = IR£0.62	IR£1 = US$1.61
CDN$1 = IR£0.45	IR£1 = CDN$2.21
UK£1 = IR£0.96	IR£1 = UK£1.04
AUS$1 = IR£0.48	IR£1 = AUS$2.08
NZ$1 = IR£0.42	IR£1 = NZ$2.36
SAR 1 = IR£0.14	IR£1 = SAR 7.26
US$1 = UK£0.64	UK£1 = US$1.55
CDN$1 = UK£0.47	UK£1 = CDN$2.13
AUS$1 = UK£0.50	UK£1 = A$2.01
NZ$1 = UK£0.44	UK£1 = NZ$2.27
SAR 1 = UK£0.14	UK£1 = SAR 6.99

> The information in this book was researched during the summer of 1996. Inflation and the Invisible Hand may raise the prices we list by 10%. In the chapters on the Republic of Ireland, the symbol £ denotes Irish pounds. In the chapters on Northern Ireland, the Isle of Man, and London, it denotes British pounds.

Legal tender in the Republic of Ireland is the Irish pound (or "punt"), denoted £. It comes in the same denominations as the British pound (called "sterling" in Ireland) but has been worth slightly more in recent years. British small change is no longer accepted in the Republic of Ireland. The Irish punt is difficult to convert abroad.

Legal tender in Northern Ireland and the Isle of Man is the British pound. Northern Ireland has its own bank notes, which are identical in value to English, Scottish, or Manx notes of the same denominations. Although all of these notes are accepted in Northern Ireland, Northern Ireland bank notes are not accepted across the water. Remember to swap your Northern Ireland pounds for Bank of England notes before you leave. UK coins now come in logical denominations of 1p, 2p, 5p, 10p, 20p, 50p, and £1. An old "shilling" coin is worth 5p, a "florin" 10p. "Quid," popular slang for pounds sterling, derives from *cuid,* which serves as both the singular and the plural cases in Irish. Therefore the plural of quid is "quid," not "quids."

Most banks are closed on Saturday, Sunday, and all public holidays. Ireland and Northern Ireland enjoy "bank holidays" several times a year. Banks in Ireland are usually open Monday to Friday 9am-4pm, though some close later on Thursday. Usual weekday bank hours in Northern Ireland are Monday to Friday 9:30am-3:30pm. Some close for lunch; some close early or late one day per week.

Follow the fluctuation of exchange rates for several weeks before your trip. If the trend is toward a stronger pound, exchange a significant amount of money at the beginning of your trip. It is more expensive to buy foreign currency than to buy domestic: pounds will be less costly in Ireland than at home. However, converting some money before you go will allow you to avoid airport exchange lines. Generally, you should bring enough Irish currency to last the first 24-72 hours of a trip (exchanging currency will be difficult over a weekend or holiday). Observe commission rates closely and check newspapers to get the standard rate of exchange. Banks generally have the best rates, but sometimes tourist offices or exchange kiosks are better. A 5% margin between buy and sell prices (be sure that both are listed) is a fair deal. Since you lose money with every transaction, convert in large sums (unless the currency is depreciating rapidly), but not more than you'll need.

If you stay in hostels and prepare your own food, expect to spend anywhere from US$16-35 per person per day; transportation (and beer) will increase these figures. Planning a travel budget with a daily allowance is a good idea. Don't sacrifice your health or safety for a cheaper tab. Personal checks from home almost certainly will not be accepted.

TRAVELER'S CHECKS

Traveler's checks are generally the safest means of carrying funds. Several agencies and many banks sell them, usually for face value plus a 1% commission. **American Express, Visa,** and (in Ireland) **Thomas Cook** checks can be sold, exchanged, cashed, and refunded at virtually every bank in Ireland and Northern Ireland, sometimes without a commission. Traveler's checks are accepted at the majority of B&Bs, shops, and restaurants, though many smaller establishments only take cash. Traveler's checks are less readily accepted in small towns than in cities with large tourist industries. Nonetheless, there will probably be at least one place in every town where you can exchange them for local currency. If you're ordering your checks, do so well in advance, especially if large sums are being requested.

Always keep a few extra pounds handy in case of theft or loss. Buying checks in small denominations is usually safer—otherwise, after a small purchase, you'll still be carrying around a large amount of cash. Each agency provides refunds if your checks are lost or stolen, and many provide additional services such as toll-free refund hotlines, emergency message relay services, and stolen credit card assistance. (You may need a police report verifying the loss or theft.) To expedite the refund process in the event of theft or loss, keep your check receipts separate from your checks and store them in a safe place or with a traveling companion. Record check numbers when you cash them and leave a list of check numbers with someone at home, and ask for a list of refund centers when you buy your checks. Keep a separate supply of cash or traveler's checks for emergencies. Countersign your checks only when you're prepared to cash them and have your passport handy.

If you will be visiting other countries in addition to Ireland and Northern Ireland, you should buy your checks in U.S. dollars. Few currencies are as easily exchanged worldwide, and you will save yourself the cost of repeatedly converting currency. If you are staying exclusively in Northern Ireland, you might wish to buy your checks in British pounds. In Northern Ireland, most branches of the Bank of Ireland and of Ulster Bank and some branches of other banks will not charge a commission when changing traveler's checks if you show a student ID. The following companies offer checks in U.S. dollars or British pounds—often in both:

American Express: For general information or to report stolen cheques, call (1800) 626000 in Ireland; (800) 221-7282 in the U.S. and Canada; in the U.K. (0800) 521313; in New Zealand (0800) 441068; in Australia (008) 251902). Elsewhere, call U.S. collect (801) 964-6665. Dublin travel office: tel. (01) 677 2874.
Interpayment: In the U.S. and Canada: (tel. (800) 221-2426). In the U.K.: (tel. (0800) 515884 or (0800) 895078). In Ireland: (tel. (01733) 318949) to the U.K.

(charges can be reversed). Sells Visa traveler's checks, cashable at any **TSB** or Barclays branch. No commission.

Citicorp: Call (800) 645-6556 in the U.S. and Canada; in the U.K. (0181) 297 4781; from elsewhere call U.S. collect (813) 623-1709. Sells both Citicorp and Citicorp Visa traveler's checks. Commission is 1-2% on check purchases. Checkholders are automatically enrolled for 45 days in the Travel Assist Program (hotline (800) 250-4377 or collect (202) 296-8728) which provides travelers with doctor, lawyer, and interpreter referrals as well as check refund assistance and general travel information. Citicorp's World Courier Service guarantees hand-delivery of traveler's checks when a refund location is not convenient.

Thomas Cook MasterCard: Call (800) 223-9920 in the U.S. and Canada; from the U.K. call (0800) 622101 free or (01733) 502995 collect or (01733) 318950) collect; elsewhere call U.S. collect (609) 987-7300. Commission 1-2% for purchases. Try buying the checks at a Thomas Cook office for potentially lower commissions. No commission if you cash checks at a Thomas Cook Office.

Visa: Call (800) 227-6811 in the U.S.; in the U.K. (0800) 895492; from anywhere else in the world call (01733) 318949; a pay call, but the charges can be reversed. Any kind of Visa traveler's check can be reported lost at the Visa number.

CREDIT CARDS

In Ireland, **credit cards** are accepted in all but the smallest businesses. Credit cards are also invaluable in an emergency. Depending on the issuer, credit cards may offer an array of other services, from insurance to emergency assistance—some even cover car rental collision insurance. For cash advances, credit card companies get the wholesale exchange rate, which is generally 5% better than the retail rate used by banks. All such machines require a **Personal Identification Number (PIN),** which credit cards in the United States do not usually carry. You must ask your credit card company to assign you one before you leave. Keep in mind that MasterCard and Visa have different names elsewhere ("EuroCard" or "Access" for MasterCard and "Carte Bleue" or "Barclaycard" for Visa).

In the Republic, **Visa** and **MasterCard/Access** are accepted at some **Bank of Ireland** ATMs and at all **Allied Irish Bank (AIB)** ATMs. Both banks, and **Trustee Savings Bank (TSB),** accept Visa and Mastercard at their foreign exchange desks during opening hours. In Northern Ireland, **First Trust, Northern, Bank of Ireland,** and **Ulster Bank** accept Visa cards at their ATMs. **MasterCard** (tel. (800) 999-0454) and **Visa** (tel. (800) 336-8472) are issued in cooperation with individual banks and some other organizations.

American Express (tel. (800) CASH-NOW (227-4669); outside the U.S. call collect (904) 565-7875) has a hefty annual fee (US$55) but allows AmEx holders to draw up to US$1000 every 21 days (no service charge, no interest) from their checking accounts and cash personal checks at offices in Cork, Galway, Killarney, Limerick, and Waterford. AmEx also offers Express Cash withdrawals (up to US$1000 in a 7-day period) from over 100,000 ATMs worldwide which are automatically debited from the Cardmember's specified bank account or credit line (2% transaction fee for each cash withdrawal with a US$2.50 minimum). Unless using the AmEx service, avoid cashing checks in foreign currencies; they usually take weeks and a US$30 fee to clear. If you lose your card, call (1800) 709907 from Ireland. From abroad call U.S. collect (301) 214-8228) for U.S. Assist, a 24-hour hotline offering medical and legal assistance in emergencies. Benefits of the American Express Travel Service include assistance in changing airline, hotel, and car rental reservations, sending mailgrams and international cables, and holding client mail at an AmEx office.

CASH CARDS

Cash cards, or ATM (Automated Teller Machine) cards, are widespread in Ireland, but international network connections are hard to make. In general, credit cards are more reliably accepted at ATMs than personal bank cards. The two international money networks you should know about are **Cirrus** (U.S. tel. (800) 4-CIRRUS (424-

7787)) and **Plus** (U.S. tel. (800) 843-7587). Depending on your bank, you will be charged US$1-2 to withdraw from abroad.

In the Republic, Cirrus cards will usually meet with more success in ATMs, as the Plus network is not quite as extensive. AIB and Bank of Ireland ATMs are better connected than those at TSB. **Halifax Bank** has ATMs that are on the Plus network; the bank has branches only in a few major cities in Northern Ireland. **Isle of Man Bank** and **Barclays** have branches in most towns on the Isle of Man. Isle of Man Banks' ATMs accept Visa, MasterCard, Plus, and Cirrus system cards; Barclays' ATMs accept Visa, Plus, and Cirrus. TSB ATMs on the Isle of Man accept Visa and MasterCard.

GETTING MONEY FROM HOME

Money can be wired abroad through international money transfer services operated by **Western Union** (tel. (800) 325-6000). Credit card transfers do not work overseas; you must send cash. The rates for sending cash are generally US$10 cheaper than with a credit card. The money is usually available in the country you're sending it to within an hour, although in some cases this may vary.

In dire emergencies, U.S. citizens can have money sent via the State Department's **Overseas Citizens Service, American Citizens Services,** Consular Affairs, Public Affairs Staff, Room 4831, U.S. Department of States, Washington, D.C. 20520 (tel. (202) 647-5225; at night and on Sun. and holidays (202) 647-4000; fax 647-3000; http://travel.state.gov). For a fee of US$15, the State Department will forward money within hours to the nearest consular office, which will then disburse it according to instructions. Often the quickest way to have the money sent is to cable the State Department through Western Union, depending on the circumstances.

VAT (VALUE-ADDED TAX)

Both Ireland and Northern Ireland charge value-added tax (VAT), a national sales tax on most goods and some services. In Ireland, the VAT ranges from 0% on most food and clothing to 12% in restaurants to 21% on other items, such as jewelry, cameras, and appliances. The British rate (applicable to Northern Ireland and the Isle of Man) is 17.5% on many services (such as hairdressers, hotels, restaurants, and car rental agencies) and on all goods (except books, medicine, and food). Prices stated in *Let's Go* include VAT unless otherwise specified. Refunds are available only to non-EU citizens. In Ireland, VAT refunds are available on goods purchased in stores displaying a "Cashback" sticker (ask if you don't see one). You will receive a voucher with your purchase which you must fill out and present at the Cashback service desk in Dublin or Shannon airports. Purchases greater than £200 must be approved at the customs desk first. Your money can also be refunded by mail, which takes six to eight weeks. Visitors to Northern Ireland and the Isle of Man can get a **VAT refund** through the Retail Export Scheme. Ask the shopkeeper from whom you buy your goods for the appropriate form, or get one at the airport, which customs officials will sign and stamp when you take your purchases through customs in your carry-on baggage. Once home, send the form and a self-addressed, Northern Irish-stamped envelope to the shopkeeper, who will then send your refund. In order to use this scheme, you must export the goods within three months of purchase.

TIPPING

Many restaurants in Ireland figure a service charge into the bill (some even calculate it into the cost of the dishes themselves). The menu almost always indicates whether or not service is included. For those restaurants that do not include a tip in the bill, customers should leave 10-15%. The exact amount should truly depend upon the quality of the service (as isn't usually the case in America). The one hard and fast rule is that no tip should be less than 50p.

Tipping is less common for other services, especially in rural areas, but always very welcome. Porters, parking-lot attendants, and hairdressers are usually tipped, cab drivers less so. Hotel housekeepers will welcome a show of appreciation, but B&B owners may actually be insulted by a tip. And above all, never tip the **barman.**

DISCOUNT CARDS

The Irish government offers a **National Heritage Card,** which allows free access to the 31 national parks, monuments, and gardens maintained by the Office of Public Works (OPW). You can purchase the card in the Republic at any site overseen by the OPW, and it can quickly pay for itself, especially if you see more than five sites (IR£15, seniors £10, students £6).

All U.S. travelers to Northern Ireland or other British countries should consider joining the **Royal Oak Foundation,** the U.S. membership affiliate of the **National Trust.** The National Trust is a British charity dedicated to preserving "places of historic interest or natural beauty" in the U.K. Royal Oak membership or membership in one of their fellow Trusts in Commonwealth countries will allow you free entry to over 340 trust sites and properties open to the public. A handbook with brief descriptions of National Trust properties in England, Wales, and Northern Ireland is included with membership (individual UK£26, family UK£48). Membership is annually renewable at a cost of US$40 for an individual and US$65 for a family.For more, U.S. and Canadian residents should contact the Royal Oak Foundation, 285 W. Broadway #400, New York, NY 10013-2299 (tel. (800) 913-6565 or (212) 966-6565). All others should contact the National Trust's Membership Department, P.O. 39, Bromley, Kent, BR1 1BR, England (tel. (0181) 315 1111).

■ Safety & Security

PERSONAL SAFETY

Ireland and Northern Ireland are safer for the traveler than most other European countries, but theft or harassment can easily occur. To avoid unwanted attention, try to **blend in** as much as possible. Walking directly into a pub or shop to check your map beats checking it on a street corner—better yet, look over your map before leaving your hostel. Find out about unsafe areas from tourist offices, the manager of a reputable hotel or hostel, or a local whom you trust. Especially when traveling alone, be sure that someone at home knows your itinerary, and never say that you're traveling alone. Both men and women may want to carry a small **whistle** to scare off attackers or attract attention. When walking at night, stick to busy, well-lit streets and avoid dark alleyways. Do not attempt to cross through parks, parking lots, beaches, or any other large, deserted areas. Whenever possible, *Let's Go* warns of unsafe neighborhoods and areas. If you feel uncomfortable, leave as quickly and directly as you can.

If you are using a **car,** be sure to park your vehicle in a garage or well-traveled area. **Sleeping in your car** is one of the most dangerous ways to get your rest. If your car breaks down, wait for the police to assist you. If you must sleep in your car, do so as close to a police station or a 24-hour service station as possible. Sleeping out in the open can be even more dangerous. For more information, see **By Car,** p. 40.

A good self-defense course will give you more ways to react to different types of aggression, but it might cost you more money than your trip. **Model Mugging,** a national organization with offices in several cities, teaches an effective, comprehensive self-defense course to women and men. Contact Lynn S. Auerbach on the East Coast (tel. (617) 232-7900); Alice Tibits in the Midwest (tel. (612) 645-6189); and Cori Couture out West (tel. (415) 592-7300). Course prices vary from US$400-500. Community colleges frequently offer self-defense courses at more affordable rates.

FINANCIAL SECURITY

Keep your money to yourself: carry as little as possible, don't count it in public, and never carry a wallet in your back pocket. If you carry a purse, buy a sturdy one with a secure clasp, and carry over your shoulder and across your body, away from the street with the clasp against you. For backpacks, buy some small combination padlocks which slip through the two zippers, securing the pack shut. A **money belt** is the best way to carry cash; you can buy one at most camping supply stores or through the Forsyth Travel Library (see **Useful Publications,** p. 2). The best combination of convenience and invulnerability is the **waistpouch,** a nylon, zippered pouch with a belt that should sit inside the waist of your pants or skirt. A **neck pouch** is equally safe, although far less accessible. Refrain from pulling out your neck pouch in public; if you must, be very discreet. Avoid keeping anything precious in a fanny-pack (even if it's worn on your stomach): your valuables will be highly visible and easy to steal. Be wary on public transportation, in city crowds, public telephone booths, busy bus and train stations, money-changing establishments, and other tourist-infested areas. Keep some money separate from the rest to use in an emergency or in case of theft. Label every piece of luggage both inside and out.

Be particularly watchful of your belongings on **buses** and **trains** (for example, carry your backpack in front of you where you can see it). Don't check baggage on trains (especially if you're switching lines), and don't trust anyone to "watch your bag for a second." Lockers at bus and train stations are safe, but you'll need your own padlock. Never leave your belongings unattended; even the most demure-looking hostel (convents included) may be a den of thieves. If you feel unsafe, look for places with either a curfew or a night attendant. Wherever you stow your belongings, try to keep your valuables on your person: consider this an iron-clad rule in the dorm-style rooms of some hostels. Even a trip to the shower can cost you a wallet or a camera. At night, sleep with your worldly goods under your pillow or in another safe place, and put the straps of your bag around the leg of your bed. Remember, if you can't bear to have something stolen, lost, or broken, leave it at home.

Travel Assistance International by Worldwide Assistance Services, Inc. provides its members with a 24-hour hotline for emergencies and referrals. Their year-long frequent traveler package ($226) includes medical and travel insurance, financial assistance, and help in replacing lost documents. Call (800) 821-2828 or (202) 828-5894, fax 828-5896, or write to 1133 15th St. NW, Suite 400, Washington, D.C. 20005-2710. More complete information on safety while traveling may be found in *Americans Traveling Abroad: What You Should Know Before You Go,* available at booksellers across the U.S.

DRUGS AND ALCOHOL

If you are caught with any quantity of **illegal** or **controlled drugs** in Ireland or Northern Ireland, you will be arrested and tried under Irish or British law or be immediately expelled from the country. Your home government is powerless to shield you from the judicial system of a foreign country. If you are imprisoned, consular officers can visit you, provide you with a list of local attorneys, and inform your family and friends, but that's all. The London-based organization **Release** (tel. (0171) 729 9904) advises people who have been arrested on drug charges; that's about all they can do. If you carry **prescription drugs** while you travel, it is vital to have a copy of the prescriptions themselves readily accessible at country borders.

▓ Health

In the event of sudden illness or an accident, dial **999,** the general **emergency** number for the Republic of Ireland, Northern Ireland, and the Isle of Man. It's a free call from any pay phone to an operator who will connect you to the local police, hospital, or fire brigade. "Late-night pharmacy" is an oxymoron, although pharmacies in larger Irish cities often have a rotating late-night schedule. After 6pm, you'll often have to go to a local hospital for medical assistance, even for aspirin. Public bathrooms exist only in larger cities and may cost 10-20p; you're better off stepping into a pub. Street signs, **bathrooms** (*fir* means "men," *mná* means "women"), and other public messages might show up in Irish alone.

Common sense is the simplest prescription for good health while you travel: eat well, drink and sleep enough, and don't overexert yourself. Travelers complain most often about their feet and their gut, so take precautionary measures. Drinking lots of fluids can often prevent dehydration and constipation, and wearing sturdy shoes and clean socks, and using talcum powder can help keep your feet dry. Make sure your shoes are comfortable before you leave, or blisters will ruin your trip. To minimize the effects of jet lag, "reset" your body's clock by adopting the time of your destination immediately upon arrival.

BEFORE YOU GO

In case of an accident, your **passport** should list any information needed: the names, phone numbers, and addresses of anyone you would wish to be contacted, all allergies or medical conditions you would want doctors to be aware of (diabetes, asthma, corrective lenses, etc.), and insurance information. If you wear **glasses** or **contact lenses,** carry an extra pair and know your prescription. Allergy sufferers should find out if their conditions are likely to be aggravated by the Irish flora (or wool), and obtain a full supply of any necessary medication before the trip, since matching a prescription to a foreign equivalent is not always easy, safe, or possible. Carry up-to-date, legible prescriptions or a statement from your doctor, especially if you use insulin, a syringe, or a narcotic. While traveling, be sure to keep all medication with you in carry-on luggage.

For minor health problems, a compact **first-aid kit** should include bandages, aspirin or other pain killer, antibiotic cream, a thermometer, a Swiss Army knife with tweezers, moleskin, a decongestant for colds, motion sickness remedy, medicine for diarrhea or stomach problems, sunscreen, insect repellent, and burn ointment.

Those with medical conditions (e.g. diabetes, allergies to antibiotics, epilepsy, heart conditions) may want to obtain a stainless steel **Medic Alert** identification tag (US$35 the first year, and US$15/year thereafter), which identifies the disease and gives a 24-hour collect-call information number. Contact Medic Alert at (800) 825-3785, or write to Medic Alert Foundation, 2323 Colorado Avenue, Turlock, CA 95382. Diabetics can contact the **American Diabetes Association,** 1660 Duke St., Alexandria, VA 22314 (tel. (800) 232-3472), to receive copies of the article "Travel and Diabetes" and a diabetic ID card, which carries messages in 18 languages explaining the carrier's diabetic status.

For up-to-date health data and information, the **United States Centers for Disease Control and Prevention** maintains an international travelers' hotline (tel. (404) 332-4559; fax 332-4565; http://www.cdc.gov). Or write directly to the Centers for Disease Control and Prevention, Travelers' Health, 1600 Clifton Rd. NE, Atlanta, GA 30333 for the booklet *Health Information for International Travelers* (US$14), an annual global rundown of disease, immunization, and general health advice. For more general health information, contact the **American Red Cross,** which publishes a *First-Aid and Safety Handbook* (US $15) available for purchase by writing to or calling the American Red Cross, 285 Columbus Ave., Boston, MA 02116-5114 (tel. (800) 564-1234). In the U.S., the American Red Cross also offers many first-aid and CPR courses, which are well-taught and relatively inexpensive. **Global Emergency Medical Services (GEMS)** provides 24-hour international medical assistance and support coordinated through registered nurses who have on-line access to your medical information, your primary physician, and a worldwide network of screened, credentialed, English-speaking doctors and hospitals. Subscribers also receive a pocket-sized, personal medical record that contains vital information in case of emergencies. For more information call (800) 860-1111, fax (770) 475-0058, or write: 2001 Westside Drive, Suite 120, Alpharetta, GA 30201.

ON-THE-ROAD AILMENTS

You can minimize the chances of contracting a disease while traveling by taking a few precautionary measures. If you are bitten by an animal, be concerned about

rabies. Clean your wound thoroughly and seek medical help immediately to find out whether you need treatment. The danger of rabies is greatest in rural areas.

Ticks—responsible for Lyme and other diseases—can be particularly dangerous in rural and forested regions all over Europe. Brush off ticks periodically when walking, using a fine-toothed comb on your neck and scalp. Do not try to remove ticks by burning them or coating them with nail polish remover or petroleum jelly. Topical cortisones may help relieve the itching.

The cold, wet climate is a far greater danger than heat in Ireland, especially if you will be hiking. Overexposure to cold brings the risk of **hypothermia,** when body temperature drops rapidly, resulting in the failure to produce body heat. Warning signs are easy to detect and may include shivering, poor coordination, slurred speech, exhaustion, fatigue, hallucination, or amnesia. *Do not let hypothermia victims fall asleep* if they are in the advanced stages—their body temperature will drop more and if they lose consciousness they may die. Seek medical help as soon as possible. To avoid hypothermia, keep dry and stay out of the wind. Wear wool, especially in wet weather—it retains insulating properties even when soggy. Polypropylene also dries quickly when wet, allowing you to stay warm; however, nearly all other fabrics make you colder when wet. If you have hypothermia, remove all wet, non-wool clothing (especially all cotton). Make warm and protective clothing a priority. Dress in layers, and remember that you lose most of your body heat through your head, so carry a wool hat with you and your body will thank you.

WOMEN'S HEALTH

Women traveling in unsanitary conditions are vulnerable to urinary tract and bladder infections, common and severely uncomfortable bacterial diseases which cause a burning sensation and painful and sometimes frequent urination. Drink tons of vitamin-C-rich juice, plenty of clean water, and urinate frequently, especially right after intercourse. Untreated, these infections can lead to kidney infections, sterility, and even death. If symptoms persist, see a doctor. Women are also more susceptible to vaginal thrush and cystitis, two treatable but uncomfortable illnesses. Tampons and pads are sometimes hard to find when traveling, and certainly your preferred brands may not be available, so take supplies along. Some women also use diaphragms or cervical caps to trap menstrual flow temporarily. Refer to the women's health guide *Our Bodies, Our Selves* (published by the Boston Women's Health Collective) for more information on women's health on the road.

BIRTH CONTROL & ABORTION

Contraception has been legal in the Republic of Ireland for over a decade, and condoms are now widely available in pharmacies and in vending machines in some pubs and nightclubs. Women on the pill should bring enough to allow for possible loss or extended stays and should bring a prescription, since forms of the pill vary a good deal. If you use a diaphragm, be sure that you have enough contraceptive jelly on hand. Though condoms are increasingly available, you might want to bring your favorite national brand before you go; availability and quality vary.

Abortion is illegal in Northern Ireland and the Republic, though recent referenda allow women to receive information about abortions and to travel from Ireland to Britain expressly to obtain an abortion. Women's centers, listed in major cities, can provide advice; remember that some are funded by the Catholic Church. For more information, see **abortion** (p. 66). The **U.K. Family Planning Association** can provide you with information on contraception and abortion in Britain; write to 2-12 Pentonville Road, London N1 9FP (tel. (0171) 837 5432; fax (0171) 837 3026). The **United States abortion hotline** (tel. (800) 772-9100; Mon.-Fri. 9:30am-12:30pm, 1:30-5:30pm), 1436 U St. NW, Washington, D.C. 20009 can direct you to organizations which provide information on the availability of and techniques for abortion in other countries. Or contact your embassy to receive a list of ob/gyn doctors who perform abortions. For general information on contraception, condoms, and abortion worldwide, contact the **International Planned Parenthood Federation,** European Regional Office, Regent's College Inner Circle, Regent's Park, London NW1 4NS (tel. (0171) 486-0741, fax 487-7950).

AIDS, HIV, STDS

All travelers should be concerned about **Acquired Immune Deficiency Syndrome (AIDS),** transmitted through the exchange of body fluids with an infected individual (HIV-positive). *Never* share intravenous drug, tattooing, or other needles or have sexual intercourse without using a latex condom lubricated with **spermicide (nonoxynol-9).** Casual contact (including drinking from the same glass or using the same eating utensils as an infected person) is not believed to pose a risk.

For more information on AIDS, call the **U.S. Center for Disease Control's** 24-hour hotline at (800) 342-2437 (Spanish 800-344-7332, daily 8am-2am). In Europe, write to the **World Health Organization,** attn: Global Program on AIDS, 20 Avenue Appia, 1211 Geneva 27, Switzerland (tel. (22) 791 21 11), for statistical material on AIDS internationally. Or write to the **Bureau of Consular Affairs,** CA/P/PA, Department of State, Washington, D.C. 20520.

Sexually transmitted diseases (STDs) such as gonorrhea, chlamydia, genital warts, syphilis, and herpes are a lot easier to catch than HIV, and can be just as deadly. Condoms may protect you from certain STDs, but oral or even tactile contact can lead to transmission.

■ Insurance

Beware of unnecessary coverage—your current policies might well extend to many travel-related accidents. **Medical insurance** policies, especially those from universities, often cover costs incurred abroad, although **Medicare's** foreign travel coverage is valid only in Canada and Mexico. Canadians are protected by their home province's health insurance plan up to 90 days after leaving the country; check with the provincial Ministry of Health or Health Plan Headquarters for details. Your **homeowners' insurance** (or your family's coverage) often covers loss of travel documents (passport, plane ticket, railpass, etc.) up to US$500.

The **International Student Identity Card (ISIC)** and **International Teacher Identity Card (ITIC)** provide US$3000 worth of accident and illness insurance and US$100 per day up to 60 days of hospitalization. They also offer up to $1000 for accidental death or dismemberment, up to US$25,000 if injured due to an airline, and up to US$25,000 for emergency evacuation due to an illness. The cards also give access to a toll-free Traveler's Assistance hotline (in the U.S. and Canada tel. (800) 626-2427; from abroad call collect (713) 267-2525) whose multilingual staff can provide help in medical, legal, and financial emergencies overseas. To supplement ISIC's insurance, **Council** (see **Travel Organizations,** p. 2) offers the inexpensive Trip-Safe plan with options covering medical treatment and hospitalization, accidents, baggage loss, and charter flights missed due to illness; **Council Travel** and **STA** also offer more comprehensive and expensive policies. **American Express** cardholders receive automatic car rental insurance (liability only) and travel accident insurance on flight purchases made with the card (customer service (tel. (800) 528-4800). Also see **Travel Organizations,** p. 2, or **Money,** p. 12.

Insurance companies usually require a copy of the police report for thefts, or evidence of having paid medical expenses (doctor's statements, receipts) before they will honor a claim, and may have time limits on filing for reimbursement. Always carry policy numbers and proof of insurance. Check with each insurance carrier for specific restrictions and policies. Most carriers listed below have 24-hour hotlines.

Access America, 6600 West Broad St., P.O. Box 11188, Richmond, VA 23230 (tel. (800) 284-8300; fax (804) 673-1491). Covers trip cancellation/interruption, on-the-spot hospital admittance costs, emergency medical evacuation, sickness, and baggage loss. 24-hr. hotline.

Travel Assistance International, by Worldwide Assistance Services, Inc., 1133 15th St. NW, Suite 400, Washington, D.C. 20005-2710 (tel. (800) 821-2828 or (202) 828-5894; fax 828-5896; e-mail wassist@aol.com). TAI provides members with a 24-hr. free hotline for travel emergencies and referrals. Their Per-Trip (from US$52) and Frequent Traveler (from US$226) plans include medical, travel, and financial insurance, translation, and lost document/item assistance.

Travel Guard International, 1145 Clark St., Stevens Point, WI 54481 (tel. (800) 826-1300 or (715) 345-0505; fax 345-0525). Comprehensive insurance programs starting at US$44. Programs cover trip cancellation and interruption, bankruptcy and financial default, lost luggage, medical coverage abroad, emergency assistance, accidental death. 24-hr. hotline.

Travel Insured International, Inc., 52-S Oakland Ave., P.O. Box 280568, East Hartford, CT 06128-0568 (tel. (800) 243-3174; fax (203) 528-8005). Accident, baggage loss, sickness, trip cancellation and interruption, travel delay, and default insurance. Covers emergency medical evacuation and automatic flight insurance.

■ Alternatives to Tourism

STUDY

It's not difficult to spend a summer, a term, or a year studying in Ireland or Northern Ireland. Enrolling as a full-time student is more difficult. The requirements for admission can be hard to meet unless you attended an EU secondary school. American students must pay full fees—EU students go free, so Americans are a welcome source of funds—and places are few, especially in Ireland. Local libraries and bookstores are helpful sources for current information on study abroad and the Internet has a study abroad web site at **www.studyabroad.com/liteimage.html. Council** sponsors over 40 study abroad programs throughout the world. Contact them for more information (see **Travel Organizations,** p. 2). The following organizations and programs can also deluge you with information:

Coláiste Dara: Indreabhán, Co. Galway, Ireland (tel. (091) 83480). 3-week intensive Irish-language summer courses in the Connemara *gaeltacht,* 15mi. west of Galway City (IR£280). Homestays with Irish-speaking families included.

Oideas Gael: Gleann Cholm Cille, Co. Donegal, Ireland (tel. (073) 30248; e-mail oidsgael@iol.ie). Offers week-long courses from April until Aug. Irish language and cultural activity courses. The program offers courses at various levels, including the option of being in a bilingual activity such as hillwalking, setdancing, painting, archaeology, and weaving.

Trinity College Dublin: offers a 1-year program of high-quality undergraduate courses for visiting students. Write to The Office of International Student Affairs, Arts Building, Trinity College, Dublin 2, Ireland (tel. (01) 608 2011; fax 677 1698).

University College Dublin: Newman House, 86 St. Stephen's Green, Dublin 2, Ireland. Offers the **Semester in Irish Studies** (tel. (01) 475 4704) every fall semester for college juniors and seniors of all majors with solid academic records. Courses in Irish history, literature, politics, and folk culture. Its **International Summer School** (tel. (01) 475 2004; fax 706 7211) offers a 2½-week course in July on Irish tradition and contemporary culture for students over 17.

Irish Studies Summer School: Seona MacReamoinn, Ireland in Europe, 19/21 Aston Quay, Dublin 2 Ireland (tel. (01) 677 8117; fax 677 8908; e-mail smacreamoinn@usit.ie). From North America, contact: Ireland in Europe Summer School, USIT, New York Student Centre, 895 Amsterdam Ave. New York, NY 10025 (tel. (212) 663-5435; fax 663-5513). On the campus of Trinity College Dublin; offers 2-week courses in Irish civilization in June, July, and Aug. (£790).

University College Cork: Overseas Students Information Office, University College, Cork, Ireland (tel. (021) 902543; fax 903118). 10,000 students are living large in Ireland's college town. Call or write for application and information.

University College Galway: International Office, Galway, Ireland (tel. (091) 750304; fax 525051; e-mail intl@ucg.ie). Offers 1-year and 1-semester opportunities

Start Speaking a Foreign Language Today!

With the LANGUAGE/30 Courses
Learn while biking, driving, exercising... anytime, anywhere!
The perfect course for travelers. Only $16.95

Enhance your travels by communicating in the language of the country you're visiting! Recommended for beginners, business travelers, vacationers or as a refresher course. Based on the widely acclaimed method developed for U.S. Government personnel, these **revised and expanded** courses feature:

- Two Audio cassettes and Phrase Book
- Basic conversational phrases include Greetings, Personal Needs, Transportation, Business, Health and Emergency Terms, and more.
- Native Voices with authentic pronunciation
- Phrases spoken in English & target language, so tapes may be used without Book
- Introduction by world-famous linguist Charles Berlitz
- Basic Grammar Section, Pronunciation Hints, **updated** Social Customs, Vocabulary Index, Phonetic Pronunciation and Foreign Scripts
- Phrase Book can be used separately as a handy, pocket-size reference guide.

33 Languages Available

Arabic	Hebrew	Norwegian	Swedish
Chinese (Mandarin)	Hindi	Persian (Farsi)	Tagalog (Piliplno)
Czech	Hungarian	Polish	Thai
Danish	Indonesian	Portuguese	Turkish
Dutch	Irish	Romanian	Vietnamese
Finnish	Italian	Russian	Yiddish
French	Japanese	Serbo-Croatian*	
German	Korean	Spanish	
Greek	Latin	Swahili	*Serbo-Croatian not revised.

To order: Send Check or Money Order for $20.95 ($16.95+$4.00 S&H), payable to LET'S GO/EDUCATIONAL SERVICES. Please specify shipping address and language(s).
SAVE... order additional courses at $16.95 each, and still pay only $4.00 shipping!

CD-ROM COMPUTER PROGRAMS also available. Call or write for catalog.
LET'S GO/EDUCATIONAL SERVICES, 1725 K Street, N.W., #408, Washington, D.C. 20006
TELE: (202) 298-8424, Ext. 130

for junior year students who meet the college's entry requirements. **Summer school** courses offered July-Aug. include Irish Studies, Culture, Education, and Creative Writing.

British Information Services: 845 Third Ave., 10th Floor, New York, NY 10022 (tel. (212) 752-5747; http://britain.nyc.ny.us). Gives information on study in Britain. Write for their free pamphlet, *Study in Britain,* which is updated annually.

Beaver College Center for Education Abroad: 450 S. Easton Rd., Glenside, PA 19038-3295 (tel. (800) 755-5607; fax (215) 572-2174; http://www.beaver.edu/cea). Operates summer-, semester- and year-long programs at 12 universities in Ireland and 35 institutions in Britain; applicants must have completed three full semesters at an accredited university. Call for brochure.

Inter-Study Programs: 42 Milsom St., Bath U.K. BA1 1DN (tel. (01225) 464769; in the U.S. call (800) 663-1999 or (617) 391-0991). Offers semester- and year-long programs in Britain and Ireland. Handles all details between program institution and your home institution, including housing and credit transfer.

WORK & VOLUNTEERING

There are precious few jobs in Ireland, even for the Irish. If you are not a citizen of an EU or British Commonwealth nation, you will have difficulty finding a paying job that you can legally take. Officially, you can hold a job in European countries only with a **work permit.** Your prospective employer must obtain this document, usually demonstrating that you have skills that locals lack. Visitors between the ages of 17 and 27 who are citizens of British Commonwealth nations (including Canada, Australia, and New Zealand) may work in Northern Ireland during their visit without work permits if the employment they take is "incidental to their holiday." Other Commonwealth citizens with a parent or grandparent born in the United Kingdom may apply for a patriality certificate, which entitles them to live and work in the U.K. without any other formalities. If you do not fit into any of these categories, you must apply for a work permit to be considered for paid employment in Northern Ireland or the Isle of Man. Contact your British Consulate or High Commission for details before you go, and the Department of Employment when you arrive. Regulations in Ireland are even stricter (and unemployment even higher).

If you are a full-time student at a U.S. university, one easy way to get a job abroad is through work permit programs run by the **Council on International Educational Exchange (Council)** and its member organizations (see **Travel Organizations,** p. 2). For a US$225 application fee, Council can procure work permits valid for four months in Ireland or for six months in Northern Ireland (and a handbook to help you find work and housing). Offices in Ireland and Britain will help with finding accommodations, openings, and connections.

Many books list work-abroad opportunities. In order to avoid scams, educate yourself using **publications** from the following sources:

Office of Overseas Schools, A/OS Room 245, SA-29, Dept. of State, Washington, D.C. 20522-2902 (tel. (703) 875-7800). Teaching jobs abroad.

Transitions Abroad Publishing, Inc., 18 Hulst Rd., P.O. Box 1300, Amherst, MA 01004-1300 (tel. (800) 293-0373; fax (413) 256-0373; e-mail trabroad@aol.com). Publishes a bimonthly magazine listing all kinds of opportunities and printed resources for those seeking to study, work, or travel abroad. They also publish *The Alternative Travel Directory,* a truly exhaustive listing of information for the "active international traveler." For subscriptions (U.S. US$20 for 6 issues, Canada US$26, other countries US$38), contact them at *Transitions Abroad,* Dept. TRA, Box 3000, Denville, NJ 07834.

Vacation Work Publications, 9 Park End St., Oxford OX1 1HJ (tel. (01865) 24 19 78; fax 79 08 85). Publishes a wide variety of guides and directories with job listings and information for the working traveler. Opportunities for summer or full-time work in countries all over the world. Write for a catalogue.

Check your local library for *The Directory of American Firms Operating in Foreign Countries* (1996; US$200) and *The Directory of Foreign Firms Operating in the United States* (1995; $150), published by **World Trade Academy Press,** Suite 509, 50 E. 42nd St. New York, NY 10017-5480 (tel. (212) 752-0329). Helpful resources for those wishing to work abroad.

Volunteering is often the most viable (and realistic) option for those wishing to spend time in Ireland without being a tourist. Given rates of employment, visitors will have a difficult time finding a paying job that will compensate for travel and living expenses. The following organizations can provide more information:

The Archaeological Institute of America, 656 Beacon Street, Boston, MA 02215-2010 (tel. (617) 353-9361; fax (617) 353-6550), puts out the *Archaeological Fieldwork Opportunities Bulletin* (US$11 non-members) which lists over 250 field sites throughout the world. This can be purchased from Kendall/Hunt Publishing, 4050 Westmark Drive, Dubuque, Iowa 52002 (tel. (800) 228-0810).

Council (see **Travel Organizations,** p. 2) offers 2- to 4-week environmental or community service projects in over 30 countries around the globe through its Voluntary Services Department (US$250-750 placement fee). Participants must be at least 18 years old.

Service Civil International Voluntary Service (SCI-VS), 5474 Walnut Level Rd., Crozet, VA 22932 (tel. (804) 823-1826; fax 823-5027; e-mail sciivsusa@igc.apc.org). Arranges placement in workcamps in Europe (ages 18 and over). Local organizations sponsor groups for physical or social work. Registration fees US$50-250, depending on the camp location.

Volunteers for Peace, 43 Tiffany Rd., Belmont, VT 05730 (tel. (802) 259-2759; fax 259-2922; e-mail vfp@vermontel.com; http://www.vfp.org). A non-profit organization that arranges for speedy placement in over 800 workcamps in more than 60 countries in Europe, including Ireland and U.K. Most complete and up-to-date listings provided in the annual *International Workcamp Directory* (US$12). Registration fee US$175. Some workcamps are open to 16- and 17-year-olds for US$200. Free newsletter.

Willing Workers on Organic Farms (WWOOF), Postfach 615, CH-9001 St. Gallen, Switzerland (e-mail fairtours@gn.apc.org) distributes a list of names of organic farmers who offer room and board in exchange for help on the farm. Be sure to include an international postal reply coupon with your request.

LONGER STAYS

Unemployment in Ireland is widespread, especially in rural areas. If looking for a job, it's likely you'll have better luck in cities. Check the *Irish Independent* and the *Irish Times* for employment and apartment listings. Also, you might try the kiosks at Trinity College or University College. Council's work program will help with job-placement and housing (see above). For more info on long-term accommodation, see **Home Rentals and Exchange,** p. 46, and **Longer Term Stays,** in Dublin, p. 95.

■ Specific Concerns

WOMEN TRAVELERS

Women exploring on their own inevitably face additional safety concerns. Always trust your instincts: if you'd feel better somewhere else, move on. You may want to consider staying in hostels which offer single rooms with locks on the inside or in religious organizations that offer rooms for women only; avoid any hostel with "communal" showers. Stick to centrally located accommodations and avoid late-night treks or tube rides. **Hitching** is never safe for lone women, or even for two women traveling together.

Your best answer to verbal harassment is no answer at all (a reaction is what the harasser wants). Wearing a conspicuous wedding band may help ward off over-friendly individuals. Don't hesitate to seek out a police officer or a passerby if you are being harassed. Memorize the **emergency number** in Ireland—it's **999** and free—and carry change for the phone and enough extra money for a bus or taxi. Carry a whistle or an airhorn on your keychain, and use it in an emergency. These warnings and suggestions are not meant to discourage women from traveling alone. Keep your spirit of adventure, but don't take unnecessary risks.

Socially, Ireland is still conservative, especially in rural areas, so women should not be surprised if they encounter attitudes that strike them as sexist. The **sexism** in Ireland, according to many, translates into an annoying, and sometimes comical, display of concern for women travelers. Irish men are often surprised at the independence displayed by women traveling solo. Women who have hitched report that the same men who offered them lifts have cautioned them against hitchhiking. For some **women's organizations,** see listings under Dublin (p. 90). The following resources and books are useful:

Handbook For Women Travelers: by Maggie and Gemma Moss. Encyclopedic and well-written. UK£9 from Piaktus Books, 5 Windmill St., London W1P 1HF (tel. (0171) 631 0710).

Women Going Places: a women's travel and resource guide emphasizing women-owned enterprises. Geared towards lesbians, but offers advice appropriate for all women. US$14 from Inland Book Company, 1436 W. Randolph St., Chicago, IL 60607 (tel. (800) 243-0138) or order from a local bookstore.

A Journey of One's Own: by Thalia Zepatos (Eighth Mountain Press, US$17). Interesting and full of good advice, plus a specific and manageable bibliography of books and resources.

OLDER TRAVELERS

Senior citizens are eligible for a wide array of discounts on transportation, museums, movies, theaters, and concerts. In *Let's Go: Ireland,* the discounts on admission fees listed for students are generally also valid for seniors. The terms "concessions" and "OAPs" (old-age pensioners) indicate discounts for seniors. In the Republic, citizens on social welfare are entitled to free rail and bus travels. Unscrupulous foreigners who look old and Irish often try to slip by. Generally, proof of senior citizen status is required for many discounts listed, so prepare to get carded. The following organizations and publishers may be useful:

AARP (American Association of Retired Persons), 601 E St., NW, Washington, D.C. 20049 (tel. (202) 434-2277). Members 50 and over receive benefits and services including the AARP Motoring Plan from AMOCO (tel. (800) 334-3300), and discounts on lodging, car rental, and sight-seeing. Annual fee US$8 per couple; lifetime membership US$75.

Elderhostel, 75 Federal St., 3rd floor, Boston, MA 02110-1941 (tel. (617) 426-7788; fax 426-8351; http://www.elderhostel.org). For those 55 or over (spouse of any age). Programs at colleges, universities, and other learning centers in over 50 countries focus on varied subjects lasting one to four weeks.

Pilot Books, 103 Cooper St., Babylon, NY 11702 (tel. (516) 422-2225). Publishes a large number of helpful guides including *The International Health Guide for Senior Citizens* (US$5, postage US$2) and *The Senior Citizens' Guide to Budget Travel in Europe* (US$6, postage US$2). Call or write for a complete list of titles.

BISEXUAL, GAY, & LESBIAN TRAVELERS

Attitudes in Ireland and Northern Ireland range from tolerant to aggressively hostile. As is true elsewhere, people in rural areas may not be as accepting as those in big cities. Public displays of affection (PDA) in Ireland and most of U.K. might bring you verbal harassment. Even in cities, however, you may end up double-checking the address to be sure you've entered a gay pub. Visitors will be delighted, however, by the age mix in pubs. There is less ageism in Ireland, and much less attitude. Women are sometimes welcome, sometimes not; there are almost no women-only clubs. *Gay*

Community News covers mostly Irish gay-related news. Its listings page covers most gay locales in all of Ireland. *Let's Go: Ireland* has gay pub and nightlife listings, as well as phone numbers for gay information. Check out our coverage of Belfast, Dublin, Cork, London, and Belmullet, Co. Mayo. In Ireland, the age of consent for anyone is 17 (see p. 67). Below are several resources for the BGL traveler:

Are You Two...Together? A Gay and Lesbian Travel Guide to Europe: a travel guide with anecdotes and tips for gays and lesbians traveling in Europe. Includes overviews of regional laws relating to gays and lesbians, lists of gay/lesbian organizations, and establishments catering, friendly, or indifferent to gays and lesbians. Random House, US$18. Covers London (not Ireland).

Ferrari Guides, PO Box 37887, Phoenix, AZ 85069 (tel. (602) 863 2408; fax 439-3952; e-mail ferrari@q-net.com). Gay and lesbian travel guides: *Ferrari Guides' Gay Travel A to Z* (US$16) and *Ferrari Guides' Inn Places: US and Worldwide Gay Accommodations* (US$16). Available in bookstores or by mail order.

Gay Europe (Perigee Books, US$14): a gay guide providing a quick look at gay life in countries throughout Europe, including restaurants, clubs, and beaches. Intros to each country cover laws and gay-friendliness. Available in bookstores.

Gay's the Word, 66 Marchmont St., London WC1N 1AB (tel. (0171) 278 7654). The largest gay and lesbian bookshop in the U.K. Mail order service available. No catalog of listings, but they will provide a list of titles on a given subject. Open Mon.-Sat. 10am-6pm, Thurs. 10am-7pm, Sun. 2-6pm.

International Gay Travel Association, Box 4974, Key West, FL 33041 (tel. (800) 448-8550; fax (305) 296-6633; e-mail IGTA@aol.com; http://www.rainbow-mall.com/igta). An organization of over 1100 companies serving gay and lesbian travelers worldwide. Call for lists of travel agents, accommodations, and events.

Spartacus International Gay Guides: published by Bruno Gmunder, Postfach 110729, D-10837 Berlin, Germany (tel. (030) 615 00 30; fax 615 91 34). Lists bars, restaurants, hotels, and bookstores around the world catering to gays. Also lists hotlines for gays in various countries and homosexuality laws for each country. Available in the U.S. from bookstores (US$33).

DISABLED TRAVELERS

Ireland is not wheelchair-accessible. Ramps, wide doors, and accessible bathrooms are less common than in the U.S., even in cities such as Dublin. Advance booking is strongly recommended; if you notify a bus company of your plans ahead of time, they will have staff ready to assist you. Those with disabilities should also inform airlines and hotels of their disabilities when making arrangements for travel; some time may be needed to prepare special accommodations. Not all train stations are wheelchair-accessible. Guide dogs are always conveyed free, but both the U.K. and Ireland impose a six-month quarantine on all animals entering the country and require that the owner obtain an import license (consult a British or Irish Consulate). Write to the British Tourist Authority or Bord Fáilte for free handbooks and access guides. Other helpful sources of information are:

American Foundation for the Blind, 11 Penn Plaza, New York, NY 10011 (tel. (212) 502-7600), open Mon.-Fri. 8:30am-4:30pm. Provides information and services for the visually impaired. For a catalogue of products, contact **Lighthouse** (tel. (800) 829-0500).

Facts on File, 11 Penn Plaza, New York, NY 10001 (tel. (212) 967-8800). Publishers of *Disability Resource,* a reference guide for travelers with disabilities (US$45 plus shipping). Available in bookstores or by mail order.

Graphic Language Press, P.O. Box 270, Cardiff by the Sea, CA 92007 (tel. (619) 944-9594). Publishers of *Wheelchair Through Europe* (US$13). Comprehensive advice for the wheelchair-bound traveler. Specifics on wheelchair-related resources and accessible sites in various cities throughout Europe.

Mobility International, USA (MIUSA), P.O. Box 10767, Eugene, OR 97440 (tel. (514) 343-1284 voice and TDD; fax 343-6812). International Headquarters in Brussels, rue de Manchester 25 Brussels, Belgium, B-1070 (tel. (322) 410 6297; fax 410

6874). Contacts in 30 countries. Information on travel programs, international work camps, accommodations, access guides, and organized tours for those with physical disabilities. Membership US$25 per year, newsletter US$15. Sells the periodically updated and expanded *A World of Options: A Guide to International Educational Exchange, Community Service, and Travel for Persons with Disabilities* (US$14, nonmembers US$16). In addition, MIUSA offers a series of courses that teach strategies helpful for travelers with disabilities.

Moss Rehab Hospital Travel Information Service (tel. (215) 456-9600, TDD 456-9602). A telephone information resource center on international travel accessibility and other travel-related concerns for those with disabilities.

Society for the Advancement of Travel for the Handicapped (SATH), 347 Fifth Ave., #610, New York, NY 10016 (tel. (212) 447-7284; fax (212) 725-8253). Publishes quarterly travel newsletter *SATH News* and information booklets (free for members, US$13 each for nonmembers) with advice on trip planning for people with disabilities. Annual membership US$45, students and seniors US$25.

KOSHER & VEGETARIAN TRAVELERS

There are lots of veggie options in the land of the potato. *Let's Go* lists vegetarian restaurants wherever we find them, and lists vegetarian entrees in carnivorous restaurants. Many Irish will be mystified by requests for kosher food. If you are strict in your observance, consider preparing your own food on the road. National tourist offices often publish lists of kosher and vegetarian restaurants.The following organizations can offer advice on how to meet your specific dietary needs while traveling.

The European Vegetarian Guide to Restaurants and Hotels (US$14, plus US$1.75 shipping): available from the Vegetarian Times Bookshelf (tel. (800) 435-9610, orders only).

The International Vegetarian Travel Guide (UK£2): last published in 1991. Order back copies from the Vegetarian Society of the U.K. (VSUK), Parkdale, Dunham Rd., Altringham, Cheshire WA14 4QG (tel. (0161) 928 0793; fax 926 9182). Call or send a self-addressed, stamped envelope for a listing of other titles.

The Jewish Travel Guide (US$12, postage US$1.75): lists synagogues, kosher restaurants, and Jewish institutions in over 80 countries. Available from Ballantine-Mitchell Publishers, Newbury House 890-900, Eastern Ave., Newbury Park, Ilford, Essex, U.K. IG2 7HH (tel. (0181) 599 88 66; fax 599 09 84). Available in the U.S. from Sepher-Hermon Press, 1265 46th St., Brooklyn, NY 11219 (tel. (718) 972-9010; US$14 plus US$2.50 shipping).

MINORITY TRAVELERS

The island of Ireland's 5 million people (3.5 million in the Republic, 1.5 million in the north), are overwhelmingly white and Christian. Ireland's Jewish community of 1800 people receives few racist attacks. Although the Irish do not perceive themselves as racist, they have never had to address racial diversity on a large scale. Media coverage and attitudes can sometimes take an unconsciously racist slant. Darker-skinned travelers may be the subjects of unusual attention, especially in rural areas, but comments or stares are more likely to be motivated by curiosity than ill-will.

TRAVELING WITH CHILDREN

Children enjoy Ireland; they should, considering how they get fussed over by enraptured strangers. Children will especially enjoy Ireland's many folk parks. Children under 16 are generally charged one-half the adult price on trains and buses, and three-quarters the adult price for admission to sights.

When deciding where to stay, remember the special needs of young children; if you pick a B&B, call and make sure it's child-friendly. If you rent a car, make sure the rental company provides a car seat for younger children. Consider using a papoose-style device to carry your baby on walking trips. Be sure that your child carries some sort of ID in case of an emergency or if he or she gets lost. Arrange a reunion spot in case of separation when sight-seeing. You may also want to refer to:

Backpacking with Babies and Small Children (US$10): published by Wilderness Press, 2440 Bancroft Way, Berkeley, CA 94704 (tel. (800) 443-7227 or (510) 843-8080; fax 548-1355).

Take Your Kids to Europe: by Cynthia W. Harriman (US$14). A budget travel guide geared towards families. Published by Mason-Grant Publications, P.O. Box 6547, Portsmouth, NH 03802 (tel. (603) 436-1608; fax 427-0015; e-mail charriman@masongrant.com).

Travel with Children: by Maureen Wheeler (US$12, postage US$1.50). Published by Lonely Planet Publications, Embarcadero West, 155 Filbert St., #251, Oakland, CA 94607 (tel. (800) 275-8555 or (510) 893-8555, fax 893-8563; e-mail info@lonelyplanet.com). Also P.O. Box 617, Hawthorn, Victoria 3122, Australia.

■ Pack Light

Pack according to your type of travel (multi-city backpacking tour, week-long stay in one place, etc.) and the temperate drizzle of Ireland. If you don't pack lightly, your back and wallet will suffer. Before you leave, pack your bag, strap it on, and walk uphill on hot asphalt for the next three hours. It's a good idea to lay out only what you absolutely need, then take half the clothes and twice the money. Remember that you can find almost anything you might need in Ireland and the U.K.

LUGGAGE

Backpack: If you plan to cover most of your itinerary by foot, you'll need a sturdy backpack. Some packs convert into more normal-looking suitcases. Many packs are designed specifically for travelers, while others are for hikers; consider how you will use the pack before purchasing one or the other. The pack should have a strong, padded hip belt to transfer weight from your shoulders to your hips. Avoid excessively low-end prices—you'll pay later. Quality packs cost US$150-420.

Suitcase/trunk/other large or heavy luggage: Fine if you plan to live in one or two cities and explore from there, but a bad idea if you're going to be moving around a lot. If you do decide that it best suits your needs, make sure it has wheels and consider how much it weighs even when empty. Hard-sided luggage is more durable and doesn't wrinkle your clothes, but is heavier. Soft-sided luggage should have a PVC frame, a strong lining to resist bad weather and rough handling, and its seams should be triple-stitched for durability.

Shoulder bag: If you are not backpacking, a lightweight duffel bag inside your luggage will work well for dirty clothes while you store purchases in your luggage.

Daypack, rucksack, or courier bag: Bringing a smaller bag in addition to your pack or suitcase lets you leave your big bag in the hostel while you go sightseeing. It can be used as an airplane carry-on: keep the absolute bare essentials with you.

Moneybelt or neck pouch: Guard your money, passport, railpass, and other important articles in either one of these, and keep it with you *at all times.* See **Safety and Security** (p. 16) for more info on protecting you and your valuables.

CLOTHING & FOOTWEAR

Clothing: Choose your clothing with the infamous Irish weather in mind. If you plan to camp, pay a little more for a lightweight poncho that unbuttons to form a groundcloth. Make sure the poncho will cover both you and your pack. Ordinary "rainproof" materials will not suffice in the eternal drizzle of the Emerald Isle. Invest in good quality rain gear that breathes and covers your upper *and* lower body; Gore-Tex® or another specialized material will make your life infinitely more comfortable. A good rain poncho runs US$20-40. Summertime is hardly warm—a wool sweater comes in handy even in mid-June. Packing more than one pair of shorts is needlessly optimistic; you will rarely see Irish locals (other than children) wearing shorts. Sweatshirts and jeans soak up rain like a sponge.

Walking shoes: Not a place to cut corners. Well-cushioned **sneakers** are good for walking, though you may want to consider a good water-proofed pair of **hiking boots.** A double pair of socks—light silk or polypropylene inside and thick wool outside—will cushion feet, keep them dry, and help prevent blisters. Bring a pair of flipflops for protection against the foliage and fungi that inhabit some hostel showers. Talcum powder in your shoes and on your feet can prevent sores, and moleskin is great for blisters. Whatever kind of shoes you choose, break them in before you leave.

MISCELLANEOUS

Only Noah had a complete list, but this one will supply most needs: umbrella, resealable plastic bags (for damp clothes, soap, food, shampoo and other spillables), alarm clock, waterproof matches, sun hat, moleskin, needle and thread, safety pins, sunglasses, a personal stereo with headphones, pocketknife, plastic water bottle, compass, string (makeshift clothesline and lashing material), towel, padlock, whistle, rubber bands, toilet paper, flashlight, cold-water soap, earplugs, insect repellant, electrical tape (for patching tears), clothespins, maps, tweezers, garbage bags, sunscreen, and vitamins. Some items not always readily available or affordable on the road: deodorant, razors, condoms, and tampons. It is always a good idea to bring along a **first-aid kit** (see **Health,** p. 18).

Sleepsacks: If planning to stay in **youth hostels,** make the requisite sleepsack yourself (instead of paying the linen charge). Fold a full size sheet in half the long way, then sew it closed along the open long side and one of the short sides.

Contact lenses: Travelers who heat-disinfect their contact lenses should note that their machines will require a small converter (about US$20). Consider switching temporarily to a chemical disinfection system, though first check with your lens dispenser to see if it's safe to switch. Finding your own brand of saline and cleaner may be difficult and expensive. Either bring your own, or wear glasses.

Washing clothes: *Let's Go* attempts to provide information on laundromats in the Practical Information listings for each city, but sometimes it may be in your best interest to just use a sink. Bring a small bar or tube of detergent soap, a rubber squash ball to stop up the sink, and a travel clothes line.

Electric current: In most European countries, electricity is 220V AC, enough to fry any 110V North American appliance. Visit a hardware store in the U.S. or Ireland for an adapter (which changes the shape of the plug) and a converter (which changes the voltage). Don't make the mistake of using only an adapter (unless appliance instructions explicitly state otherwise), or you'll melt your radio.

Film: is expensive just about everywhere. Bring lots of film from home and, if you will be seriously upset if the pictures are ruined, develop it at home. Non-serious photographers may want to consider bringing a **disposable camera** or two rather than an expensive permanent one. Be aware that, despite disclaimers, airport security X-rays *can* fog film, so either buy a lead-lined pouch, sold at camera stores, or ask the security to hand inspect it. Always pack it in your carry-on luggage, since higher-intensity X-rays are used on checked luggage.

GETTING THERE

■ Budget Travel Agencies

Students and people under 26 ("youth") with proper ID qualify for enticing reduced airfares. These are rarely available from airlines or travel agents, but instead from student travel agencies which negotiate special reduced-rate bulk purchases with the airlines, then resell them to the youth market. Return-date change fees also tend to be low (around US$25 per segment through Council or Let's Go Travel). Most flights are on major airlines, though in peak season some agencies may sell seats on less reliable chartered aircraft. Student travel agencies can also help non-students and people over 26, but probably won't be able to get the same low fares.

Council Travel (http://www.ciee.org/cts/ctshome.htm), the travel division of Council, is a full-service travel agency specializing in youth and budget travel. They offer railpasses, discount airfares, hosteling cards, guidebooks, budget tours, travel gear, and student (ISIC), youth (GO25), and teacher (ITIC) identity cards. U.S. offices include: Emory Village, 1561 N. Decatur Rd., **Atlanta,** GA 30307 (tel. (404) 377-9997); 2000 Guadalupe, **Austin,** TX 78705 (tel. (512) 472-4931); 273 Newbury St., **Boston,** MA 02116 (tel. (617) 266-1926); 1138 13th St., **Boulder,** CO 80302 (tel. (303) 447-8101); 1153 N. Dearborn, **Chicago,** IL 60610 (tel. (312) 951-0585); 10904 Lindbrook Dr., **Los Angeles,** CA 90024 (tel. (310) 208-3551); 1501 University Ave. SE, **Minneapolis,** MN 55414 (tel. (612) 379-2323); 205 E. 42nd St., **New York,** NY 10017 (tel. (212) 822-2700); 953 Garnet Ave., **San Diego,** CA 92109 (tel. (619) 270-6401); 530 Bush St., **San Francisco,** CA 94108 (tel. (415) 421-3473); 4311½ University Way, **Seattle,** WA 98105 (tel. (206) 632-2448); 3300 M St. NW, **Washington, D.C.** 20007 (tel. (202) 337-6464). **For U.S. cities not listed,** call (800) 2-COUNCIL (226-8624). Also 28A Poland St. (Oxford Circus), **London,** W1V 3DB (tel. (0171) 437 7767).

STA Travel, 6560 Scottsdale Rd. #F100, Scottsdale, AZ 85253 (tel. (800) 777-0112 in the U.S.; fax (602) 922-0793). A student and youth travel organization offering discount airfares, railpasses, accommodations, tours, insurance, and ISICs. Over 100 offices worldwide including: 297 Newbury Street, **Boston,** MA 02115 (tel. (617) 266-6014); 429 S. Dearborn St., **Chicago,** IL 60605 (tel. (312) 786-9050); 7202 Melrose Ave., **Los Angeles,** CA 90046 (tel. (213) 934-8722); 10 Downing St., Ste. G, **New York,** NY 10003 (tel. (212) 627-3111); 4341 University Way NE, **Seattle,** WA 98105 (tel. (206) 633-5000); 2401 Pennsylvania Ave., **Washington, D.C.** 20037 (tel. (202) 887-0912); 51 Grant Ave., **San Francisco,** CA 94108 (tel. (415) 391-8407), **Miami,** FL 33133 (tel. (305) 461-3444). In the U.K., 6 Wrights La., **London** W8 6TA (tel. (0171) 938 47 11); 10 High St., **Auckland** (tel. (09) 309 97 23); 222 Faraday St., **Melbourne** VIC 3050 (tel. (03) 349 69 11).

Let's Go Travel, Harvard Student Agencies, 67 Mt. Auburn St., Cambridge, MA 02138 (tel. (800) 5-LETS GO (553-8746) or (617) 495-9649). Railpasses, HI-AYH memberships, ISICs, ITICs, FIYTO cards, guidebooks (including all of the *Let's Go* books and Map Guides), maps, bargain flights, and a complete line of budget travel gear. All items available by mail; see the catalogue inside this book.

Campus Travel, 52 Grosvenor Gardens, London SW1W 0AG (http://www.campus-travel.co.uk). 41 branches in the U.K. Student and youth fares on plane, train, boat, and bus travel. Flexible airline tickets. Discount and ID cards for youths, travel insurance for students and those under 35, and maps, guides, and travel suggestion booklets. Telephone booking service: in Europe call (0171) 730 3402; in North America call (0171) 730 2101; worldwide call (0171) 730 8111; in Manchester call (0161) 273 1721; in Scotland (0131) 668 3303.

Council Charter, 205 E. 42nd St., New York, NY 10017 (tel. (212) 661 0311; fax 972 0194). Offers a combination of inexpensive charter and scheduled airfares from a variety of U.S. gateways to most major European destinations. One-way fares and open jaws (fly into one city and out of another) are available.

CTS Travel, 220 Kensington High St., W8 7RA (tel. (0171) 937 3366 for travel in Europe, 937 3388 for travel worldwide). Student/youth travel and discount flights. Tube: High St. Kensington. Open Mon.-Fri. 9:30am-6pm, Sat. 10am-5pm. Also at 44 Goodge St., W1P 2AD (tel. (0171) 637 4199). Tube: Goodge St.

Educational Travel Centre (ETC), 438 North Frances St., Madison, WI 53703 (tel. (800) 747-5551; fax (608) 256-2042; e-mail edtrav@execpc.com). Flight information, HI-AYH cards, Eurail, and regional rail passes. Write for their free pamphlet, *Taking Off.*

Travel CUTS (Canadian Universities Travel Services Limited), 187 College St., Toronto, Ont. M5T 1P7 (tel. (416) 979-2406; fax 979-8167; e-mail mail@travelcuts). Canada's national student travel bureau and equivalent of Council, with 40 offices across Canada. Also at 295-A Regent St., **London** W1R 7YA (tel. (0171) 637 3161). Discounted domestic and international airfares open to all; special student fares to all destinations with valid ISIC. Issues ISIC, FIYTO, GO25, and HI hostel cards, as well as railpasses. Offers free *Student Traveller* magazine, as well as information on the Student Work Abroad Program (SWAP).

Unitravel, 117 North Warson Rd., St. Louis, MO 63132 (tel. (800) 325 2222; fax (314) 569 2503). Offers discounted airfares on major scheduled airlines from the U.S. to Europe, Africa, and Asia.

USIT Youth and Student Travel, 19-21 Aston Quay, O'Connell Bridge, Dublin 2 (tel. (01) 602 1200; fax 671 2408). In the U.S.: New York Student Center, 895 Amsterdam Ave., New York, NY, 10025 (tel. (212) 663 5435). Additional offices in Cork, Galway, Limerick, Waterford, Maynooth, Coleraine, Derry, Athlone, and Belfast. Offers low cost tickets and flexible travel arrangements all over the world. Specializes in youth and student travel. ISIC, GO25, and EYC (under 26) cards.

■ By Plane

The **airline industry** attempts to squeeze every dollar from customers; finding a cheap airfare in their deliberately mysterious and confusing jungle will be easier if you understand their systems. Call every toll-free number and don't be afraid to ask about discounts. Have several knowledgeable **travel agents** guide you; better yet, have an agent who specializes in the region(s) in which you will be traveling. Travel agents may not want to spend time finding the cheapest fares (for which they receive the lowest commissions), but if you travel often, you should definitely find an agent who will cater to you and your needs, and track down deals in exchange for your frequent business. **TravelHUB** (http://www.travelhub.com) can help you search for travel agencies on the web.

Students and "youth" (people under 26) should never pay full price for a ticket. Seniors can also get great deals; many airlines offer senior traveler clubs or airline passes and discounts for their companions as well. Sunday newspapers often have travel sections that list bargain fares from the local airport. Special deals may also be advertised in the ethnic press. Australians should consult the Saturday travel section of the *Sydney Morning Herald.* Outsmart airline reps with the phone-book-sized *Official Airline Guide* (check your local library; at US$397, the tome costs as much as some flights), a monthly guide listing nearly every scheduled flight in the world (with prices) and toll-free phone numbers for all the airlines which allow you to call in reservations directly. *The Airline Passenger's Guerrilla Handbook* (US$15; last published in 1990) is a more renegade resource. On the Web, try the **Air Traveler's Handbook** (http://www.cis.ohio-state.edu/hypertext/faq/usenet/travel/air/handbook/top.html) for very complete information on air travel.

Most airfares peak between mid-June and early September. Mid-week (Mon.-Thurs. morning) roundtrip flights run about US$40-50 cheaper than on weekends. Traveling from hubs such as New York, Atlanta, Dallas, Chicago, Los Angeles, San Francisco, Vancouver, Toronto, Sydney, Melbourne, Brisbane, Auckland, or Wellington will win a more competitive fare than from smaller cities. Return-date flexibility is usually not an option for the budget traveler; traveling with an "open return" ticket can be pricier than fixing a return date and paying to change it. Whenever flying internationally, pick up your ticket well in advance of the departure date, have the flight confirmed within 72 hours of departure, and arrive at the airport at least three hours before your flight.

COMMERCIAL AIRLINES

The commercial airlines' lowest regular offer is the **APEX** (Advance Purchase Excursion Fare); specials advertised in newspapers may be cheaper, but have more restrictions and fewer available seats. APEX fares provide you with confirmed reservations and allow "open-jaw" tickets (landing in and returning from different cities). Generally, reservations must be made seven to 21 days in advance, with seven- to 14-day minimum and up to 90-day maximum stay limits, and hefty cancellation and change penalties (fees rise in summer). Book APEX fares early for peak season travel; by May you will have a hard time getting the departure date you want.

Even if you pay an airline's lowest published fare, you may waste hundreds of dollars. For the adventurous or bargain-hungry, there are other, perhaps more inconvenient or time-consuming options, but before shopping around it is wise to find out the average commercial price in order to measure just how great a "bargain" you are being offered. A final caveat for the budget conscious: don't get so caught up in the seemingly great deals. Always read the fine print; check for restrictions and hidden fees. Amazingly cheap fares do exist, but there's still no such thing as a free lunch. Major Irish and British destinations are Belfast, Shannon, Dublin, Cork, (via London or Shannon), Edinburgh, and London.

TICKET CONSOLIDATORS

Ticket consolidators resell unsold tickets on commercial and charter airlines at unpublished fares. Consolidator flights are the best deals if you are traveling: on short notice (you bypass advance purchase requirements, since you aren't tangled in airline bureaucracy); on a high-priced trip; to an offbeat destination; or in the peak season, when published fares are jacked way up. There is rarely a maximum age or stay limit, but unlike tickets bought through an airline, you won't be able to use your tickets on another flight if you miss yours, and you will have to go back to the consolidator to get a refund, rather than the airline. Keep in mind that these tickets are often for coach seats on connecting (not direct) flights on foreign airlines, and that frequent-flyer miles may not be credited.

Consolidators come in three varieties: wholesale only, who sell only to travel agencies; specialty agencies (both wholesale and retail); and **"bucket shops"** or discount retail agencies. Private consumers can deal directly only with the latter, but you have access to a larger market if you use a travel agent, who can also get tickets from wholesale consolidators. Look for bucket shops' tiny ads in weekend papers (in the U.S., the *Sunday New York Times* is best).

Be a smart and careful shopper. Among the many reputable and trustworthy companies are, unfortunately, some shady wheeler-dealers. Contact the local Better Business Bureau to find out how long the company has been in business and its track record. Although not necessary, it is preferable to deal with consolidators close to home so you can visit in person, if necessary. Ask to receive your tickets as quickly as possible so you have time to fix any problems. Get the company's policy in writing, and insist on a **receipt** that gives full details about the tickets, refunds, and restrictions, and record who you talked to and when. It may be worth paying with a credit card (despite the 2-5% fee) so you can stop payment if you never receive your tickets. Beware the "bait and switch" gag: shyster firms will advertise a super-low fare and then tell a caller that it has been sold. Although this is a viable excuse, if they can't offer you a price near the advertised fare on *any* date, it is a scam to lure in customers—report them to the Better Business Bureau. Ask also about accommodations and car rental discounts; some consolidators have fingers in many pies.

For destinations worldwide, try **Pennsylvania Travel,** Paoli, PA (tel. (800) 331-0947); **Cheap Tickets,** offices in Los Angeles, CA, San Francisco, CA, Honolulu, HI, Overland Park, KS, and New York, NY (tel. (800) 377-1000); **Moment's Notice,** New York, NY (tel. (718) 234-6295; fax 234-6450), air tickets, tours, and hotels; US$25 annual fee. For a fee, depending on the number of travelers and the itinerary, **Travel Avenue,** Chicago, IL (tel. (800) 333-3335) will search for the lowest international airfare available and give you a rebate on fares over US$300. To Europe, try **Rebel,** Valencia, CA (tel. (800) 227-3235) or Orlando, FL (tel. (800) 732-3588); or **Discount Travel International,** New York, NY (tel. (212) 362-3636; fax 362-3236).

Kelly Monaghan's *Consolidators: Air Travel's Bargain Basement* (US$7 plus US$2 shipping) from the Intrepid Traveler, P.O. Box 438, New York, NY 10034 (e-mail intreptrav@aol.com), is an valuable source for more information and lists of consolidators by location and destination. Cyber-resources include **World Wide** (http://www.tmn.com/wwwanderer/WWWa) and Edward Hasbrouck's incredibly informative **Airline ticket consolidators and bucket shops** (http://www.gnn.com/gnn/wic/wics/trav.97.html).

STAND-BY FLIGHTS

Airhitch, 2641 Broadway, Third Floor, New York, NY 10025 (tel. (800) 326-2009 or (212) 864-2000) and Los Angeles, CA (tel. (310) 726-5000), adds a certain thrill to air travel. Complete flexibility on both sides of the Atlantic is necessary; flights cost US$169 each way when departing from the Northeast, US$269 from the West Coast or Northwest, and US$229 from the Southeast and Midwest. The snag is that you buy not a ticket, but the promise that you will get to a destination near where you're intending to go within a window of time (usually 5 days) from a location in a region you've specified. You call in before your date-range to hear all of your flight options for the next seven days and your probability of boarding. You then decide which flights you want to try to make and present a voucher at the airport which grants you the right to board a flight on a space-available basis. This procedure must be followed again for the return trip. Be aware that you may only receive a refund if all available flights which departed within your date- and destination-range were full. There are several offices in Europe, so you can wait to register for your return; the main one is in Paris (tel. (1) 47 00 16 30).

Air-Tech, Ltd., 584 Broadway #1007, New York, NY 10012 (tel. (212) 219-7000, fax 219-0066) offers a very similar service. Their Travel Window is one to four days; rates to and from Europe (continually updated; call and verify) are: Northeast US$169; West Coast US$249; Midwest/Southeast US$199. Upon registration and payment, Air-Tech sends you a FlightPass with a contact date falling soon before your Travel Window, when you are to call them for flight instructions. Note that the service is one-way (you must go through the same procedure to return), and that *no refunds* are granted unless Air-Tech fails to get you a seat before your Travel Window expires.

Read all the fine print in your agreements with either company—a call to The Better Business Bureau of New York City may be worthwhile. Be warned that it is difficult to receive refunds, and that clients' vouchers will not be honored if an airline fails to receive payment in time.

CHARTER FLIGHTS

The theory behind a **charter** is that a tour operator contracts with an airline (usually one specializing in charters) to fly extra loads of passengers to peak-season destinations. Charter flights fly less frequently than major airlines and have more restrictions, particularly on refunds. They are also almost always fully booked, and schedules and itineraries may change or be cancelled at the last moment (as late as 48hr. before the trip, and without a full refund); you'll be much better off purchasing a ticket on a regularly scheduled airline. As always, pay with a credit card if you can, and consider traveler's insurance against trip interruption.

Try **Interworld** (tel. (305) 443-4929); **Travac** (tel. (800) 872-8800) or **Rebel**, Valencia, CA (tel. (800) 227-3235) or Orlando, FL (tel. (800) 732-3588).

Eleventh-hour **discount clubs** and **fare brokers** offer members savings on European travel, including charter flights and tour packages. Research your options carefully. **Last Minute Travel Club,** 1249 Boylston St., Boston, MA 02215 (tel. (800) 527-8646 or (617) 267-9800), and **Discount Travel International** New York, NY (tel. (212) 362-3636; fax 362-3236), are among the few travel clubs that don't charge a membership fee. Others include **Moment's Notice** New York, NY (tel. (718) 234-6295; fax (718) 234 6450), air tickets, tours, and hotels; US$25 annual fee and **Travelers Advantage**, Stamford, CT, (tel. (800) 835-8747; US$49 annual fee); and **Travel Avenue** (tel. (800) 333-3335; see **Ticket Consolidators,** above). Study these organizations' contracts closely; unwanted overnight layovers are possible.

WITH OUR RAIL PASSES YOU'LL HAVE UP TO 70% MORE MONEY TO WASTE.

With savings of up to 70% off the price of point to point tickets, you'll be laughing all the way to the souvenir stand. Rail passes are available for travel throughout Europe or the country of your choice and we'll even help you fly there. So all you'll have to do is leave some extra room in your suitcase. To learn more call **1-800-4-EURAIL** (1-800-438-7245). *Rail Europe*

COURIER COMPANIES AND FREIGHTERS

Those who travel light should consider flying to Europe as a **courier.** The company hiring you will use your checked luggage space for freight; you're only allowed to bring carry-ons. You are responsible for the safe delivery of the baggage claim slips (given to you by a courier company representative) to the representative waiting for you when you arrive—don't screw up or you will be blacklisted as a courier. You will probably never see the cargo you are transporting—the company handles it all—and airport officials know that couriers are not responsible for the baggage checked for them. Restrictions to watch for: you must be over 18, have a valid passport, and pro-cure your own visa (if necessary); most flights are roundtrip only with short fixed-length stays (usually one week); only individual tickets are issued (but a companion may be able to get a next-day flight); and most flights are from New York. Roundtrip fares to Western Europe from the U.S. range from US$250-400 (off season) to US$400-550 (in summer). **NOW Voyager,** 74 Varick St. #307, New York, NY 10013 (tel. (212) 431-1616), acts as an agent for courier flights worldwide, primarily from New York. Try **Halbart Express,** 147-05 176th St., Jamaica, NY 11434 (tel. (718) 656-5000), or **Discount Travel International,** (tel. (212) 362-3636).

Check your bookstore or library for handbooks such as *Air Courier Bargains* (US$15 plus US$3.50 shipping, from the Intrepid Traveler, P.O. Box 438, New York, NY 10034). *The Courier Air Travel Handbook* (US$10 plus US$3.50 shipping) explains how to travel as an air courier and contains names, phone numbers, and contact points of courier companies. It can be ordered directly from Bookmasters, Inc., P.O. Box 2039, Mansfield, OH 44905 (tel. (800) 507-2665).

If you really have time to spare, **Ford's Travel Guides,** 19448 Londelius St., Northridge, CA 91324 (tel. (818) 701-7414; fax 701-7415) lists **freighter companies** that will take passengers worldwide. Ask for their *Freighter Travel Guide and Waterways of the World* (US$16, plus US$2.50 postage if mailed outside the U.S.).

FLIGHTS FROM BRITAIN

Airplanes fly between Dublin, Shannon, Cork, Kerry, Galway, Knock, Sligo, and Waterford (in Ireland); Belfast and Derry (in Northern Ireland); Gatwick, Stansted, Heathrow, Luton, Manchester, Birmingham, Liverpool, and Glasgow airports (in Brit-ain); and Ronaldsway on the Isle of Man. British Airways, Aer Lingus, British Midlands, Manx Air, and Ryan Air are some of the companies offering service on these routes. **British Midland Airways,** Belfast office: Suite 2, Fountain Centre, College St. Belfast BT1 6ET (tel. (01232) 241 188); Dublin Office: Nutley Bldg., Merrion Rd., Dublin 4 (tel. (01) 283 0700; reservations 283 8833), flies about eight flights per day to London Heathrow. **British Airways,** Belfast office: Reservations Office, Fountain Centre, Col-lege St., Belfast 1 (tel. (0345) 222 111), flies about seven flights per day Monday through Saturday, Sunday six per day. Prices range from UK£70-105 return, but can drop from time to time. Call and inquire about specials. Flights from London to Bel-fast generally take 1¼hr. **Manx Airlines** (tel. (01) 260 1588) flies from Luton to Kerry, and Cardiff, Jersey, and the Isle of Man to Dublin. Book as early as you can to get the cheapest fare. The Air Travel Advisory Bureau, 28 Charles Square, London N16ST, England (tel. (0171) 636 50 00) will put you in touch with the cheapest carriers out of London for free.

■ By Train

In May 1994, the **Channel Tunnel** (Chunnel) was completed, physically connecting England and France. **Eurotunnel** is the name of bi-national Franco-British company that built and owns the Chunnel. Eurotunnel's **Le Shuttle** service carries passengers with cars, buses, or campers. Car passenger service opened in 1994, coach service in March 1995. Starting in the spring of 1995, **Eurostar** hit the scene, barreling passen-gers from the Continent to the Isles and vice versa. Eurostar operates rather like an airline, with similar discounts, reservations, and restrictions. While France, Brit, Brit-

France, Eurail, and Europasses are not tickets to ride, they are tickets to a discount, as is being a youth. Call (800) EUROSTAR (3876 7827) to purchase your ticket. In the U.K., call (01233) 617575 for more information. Service runs from Paris's Nord Station to London's Waterloo Station (10/day; 3hr.; £83.50, £167 return; ages 11-26 £45, £90 return). Discounts are available with various international rail passes; call **Rail Europe Inc.** (800) 438-7245 for info on rates and fares.

■ By Ferry

Ferries are popular and usually more economical than flights. Boats run from Fishguard Harbour and Pembroke Dock in south Wales to Rosslare in southeast Ireland; from Holyhead in north Wales to Dún Laoghaire (dun-LEER-ee) and nearby Dublin; and from Stranraer, Scotland, to Larne, Northern Ireland. Some people ask car drivers to let them travel as one of four free passengers that a set of wheels gets. Ferry passengers from the Republic are taxed an additional IR£5; from England to Éire, there's a tax of UK£5. **An Óige (HI) members** receive a 25% discount on fares from Irish Ferries. **ISIC cardholders** receive a 15% discount from Irish Ferries and an average 15% discount (variable among four routes) on StenaLine ferries. Almost all sailings in June, July, and August are "controlled sailings," which means that you must book the crossing ahead of time (a day in advance is sufficient). Low season on ferry prices runs March to May and October to December; mid-season is June to mid-July and September, while high season is mid-July to August. **All prices listed below are for 1996 and exclude £5 government travel tax.**

Irish Ferries has offices at: 2-4 Merrion Row, **Dublin** 2, or 16 Westmoreland St., Dublin 2 (reservations tel. (01) 661 0511, fax 661 0743; holidays tel. (01) 661 0533, fax 661 0732); St. Patrick's Bridge, **Cork** (tel. (021) 504 333); **Rosslare Harbour** (tel. (053) 33158); **Holyhead,** Wales (tel. (01407) 760222); and **Pembroke,** Wales (tel. (01646) 684161). Their after-hours information line in Ireland is (01) 661 0715; in England (0161) 236 3936. E-mail info@irish-ferries.ie; http://www.iol.ie/ irishferries.

Brittany Ferries, Tourist House, 42 Grand Parade, **Cork** (tel. (021) 277801; fax 277262). Office open Mon.-Fri. 9am-5:30pm, Sat. June-Oct. 9am-noon, Jan.-May 9am-5pm. Call for free brochure listing schedule.

Stena Line, Head Office, Charter House, Park St., Ashford, Kent TN24 8EX, England (tel. (01233) 647047). Other offices: 15 Westmoreland St. **Dublin** (tel. (01) 280 8844); **Dun Laoghaire Travel Centre** (tel. (01) 204 7777); **Rosslare Harbour** (tel. (053) 33115); Tourist Office, Grand Parade, **Cork** (tel. (021) 272965); Tourist Office, Arthurs Quay, **Limerick** (tel. (061) 316259). For 24-hr. recorded information, call **Ferry Check** (tel. (01) 204 7799).

BRITAIN TO IRELAND

Assorted bus tickets that include ferry connections between Britain and Ireland are also available as package deals through ferry companies, travel agents, and USIT offices. Contact Bus Éireann for info (see **By Bus,** p. 38).

To Dublin

Irish Ferries sails from Holyhead, North Wales, to Dublin (2/day; 3¼hr.; £20-29, students and seniors £18-26). Bikes travel free.

Stena Line ferries go from Holyhead, North Wales, to Dún Laoghaire, a Dublin suburb. Aboard the HSS ("the biggest fast ferry in the world"; 4-5/day; 99min.; £26-32, students and seniors £23-28); aboard the Superferry (2/day; 3½hr.; £22-30, students £19-26). Bikes free. Direct **train** service from London's Euston Station to Dun Laoghaire via Sealink takes about 9hr. by ferry or 8hr. by HSS (£39-59).

To Rosslare Harbour

Irish Ferries leaves Pembroke, Wales for Rosslare Harbour (2/day; 4hr.; £20-29, students and seniors IR£18-26). Bikes free.

Stena Line ferries leave Fishguard, South Wales for Rosslare Harbour. Board the Superferry (2/day; 3½hr.; IR£20-30, students and seniors IR£18-26); or the Stena Lynx (2-4/day; 99min.; £24-36, students and seniors £23-32). Bikes free. Direct **train** service from London's Paddington Station to Rosslare Harbour via Sealink takes about 9½hr. by Superferry and costs £55-66.

To Cork

Cork-Swansea Ferries, 52 South Mall, Cork (tel. (021) 271 166), run to Swansea, Wales (1/day (except Tues.) at 9am; IR£29, students and seniors IR£23, bikes IR£7).

Slattery's travel agency, based in Tralee at 1 Russell St. (tel. (066) 21611) runs a combined bus/ferry deal which amounts to very cheap transport to London (IR£42 single, IR£56.50 return).

Ferries to Cork from France and England dock at **Ringaskiddy Terminal,** 9 mi. south of the city. The 20-minute city bus from the ferry terminal to the Cork bus station, or vice versa, costs about IR£3.

To Belfast & Larne

Hoverspeed SeaCat leaves Stranraer and arrives in Belfast (July-Aug. Thurs.-Sun. 5/ day, Tues.-Wed. 4/day; June and Sept. daily 4/day; 1½hr.; UK£24-31, seniors and students UK£16-22, ages 4-15 UK£14-20, under 4 free, bikes £5; for bookings tel. (0345) 523523; outside the U.K. tel. (01232) 313543). A Flexibus shuttle runs into Belfast. For pedestrians, the hovercraft is faster than ferries, comparable in price, and gets you to Belfast rather than dumping you in industrial Larne; drivers, however, may save as much as UK£40 by taking the ferry rather than the Seacat.

Stena Line ferries leave Stranraer, Scotland, and arrive in Belfast. Voyage aboard the HSS (5/day; 1½hr.; £22-26, students and seniors £11-13); or the Superferry (4-8/ day; 3hr.; £22-24, students and seniors £11-12). Bikes free.

P&O Ferries (central office (0990) 980888) run between Cairnryan, Scotland, and Larne. (1/day; Tues. 14.50, seniors and children £10; Wed.-Thurs. £18, seniors and children £14; Sat. £21.50, seniors and children £14.)

To Ireland via the Isle of Man

You can easily combine a ferry across the Irish Sea with a stopover on the Isle of Man. An advantage of this route is that you can ferry into Dublin and ferry out of Belfast at no extra charge. The **Isle of Man Steam Packet Co.** (Belfast tel. (01232) 351009; Douglas tel. (01624) 661661, fax 661065) charges IR£20-28 one way, students UK£15-28, bikes free; the principal ports are Heysham and Liverpool.

FRANCE TO IRELAND

· **Irish Ferries** sail from Le Havre, Cherbourg, and Roscoff, France, to Cork and Rosslare Harbour. (Le Havre-Rosslare 2-3/week, 20hr.; Cherbourg-Rosslare 1-2/week, 17½hr.; Le Havre-Cork June-Aug. 1/week, 21hr.; Roscoff-Rosslare late May to mid-July, 2/week, 15hr.; Roscoff-Cork June-Aug. 1/week, 15hr.) Prices are the same for all sailings: single fares range from IR£87 (students £82) in mid-July down to IR£60 (students IR£55) in Oct.-April. **Eurail passes** grant passage (not a seat, not a berth, just the right to be on the ferry) on ferry services between Rosslare and Cherbourg/ Le Havre.

Brittany Ferries sail to Cork from Roscoff and St. Malo. (Roscoff-Cork: March-Sept. 1-2/week, 14hr.; St. Malo-Cork: May-Sept. 1/week, 18hr.) One-way tickets range from IR£58 in mid-July to IR£38 in March-May and Sept. 11-day return fares cost IR£9-16 more than the one-way fare; Super APEX returns, which must be purchased 21 days before departure, offer discounts on return fares.

THE CONTINENT TO ENGLAND

Stena Line ferries across the channel between France (Calais, Diappe, and Cherbourg) and England (Dover, Newhaven, and Southampton). Sealink ferries are the most frequent and take 1½ hours (1/hr. from Dover to Calais; fares vary, floating

UNIVERSITY COLLEGE CORK
National University of Ireland. Founded 1845

T.E.F.L. IN IRELAND
The Language Centre offers extensive and intensive courses leading to internationally recognised qualifications for teaching English including DAELS, CNNTE, UCLES/RSA CTEFLA, CEELT and DTEFLA.
It also has year-round and summer courses in English for foreigners.

For details contact: *Language Centre,*
University College,
Cork, Ireland
Tel.: +353 21 904090/904102
Fax: +353 21 278150

Recognised by the Department of Education as an English Language Year-Round School for the teaching of English as a Foreign Language

around UK£24 one way, high season). Other routes between the Continent and England include Bergen, Norway, to Newcastle (on **Scandinavian Seaways** tel. (01255) 240240); Esbjerg, Denmark, to Harwich or Newcastle (Scandinavian); Gothenburg, Sweden, to Harwich or Newcastle (Scandinavian); Hamburg, Germany, to Harwich or Newcastle (Scandinavian); Amsterdam, the Netherlands, to Newcastle (Scandinavian); Hook of Holland, Belgium, to Harwich (Sealink).

■ By Bus

Supabus (run by **Bus Éireann,** the Irish national bus company) offers connecting service from Bristol and London to Cork, Waterford, Tralee, Killarney, Ennis, and Limerick, and from Cardiff and Birmingham to Cork, Waterford, Ennis, and Limerick. Prices range from £38 to £59 (youth and students £35-55) for night service and from £39 to £57 (youth and students £36-53) for day service (the higher fares apply July-Aug.). Tickets can be booked through USIT, any Bus Éireann office, Irish Ferries, Stena Line, or any Eurolines (tel. (01582) 404511) or National Express office in Britain (tel. (0990) 808080). Inconvenient arrival and departure times mean that you won't be sleeping very well. Supabus connects in London to the immense **Eurolines** network, which in turn connects with many European destinations. Contact the Bus Éireann General Inquiries desk in Dublin (tel. (01) 836 6111) or a travel agent. Take an **express bus** to London from over 270 destinations in Europe with Eurolines (U.K.) Ltd., 52 Grosvenor Gardens, Victoria, London SW1 0AU (tel. (0171) 730 8235). (London to Paris: UK£33; return UK£44.)

ONCE THERE

■ Embassies & Consulates

United States: American Embassy **Dublin,** 42 Elgin Rd., Ballsbridge, Dublin (tel. (01) 668877). Consulate General **Belfast,** Queens House, 14 Queens St., Belfast BT1 6EQ (tel. (01232) 328239).

Canada: Canadian Embassy, Canada House, 65 St. Stephens Green, **Dublin** 2 (tel. (01) 478 1988; emergencies call 285 1246). Canadian High Commission, Macdonald House, 1 Grosvenor Sq., **London** W1XC 0AB (tel. (0171) 258 6600).

Great Britain: British Embassy, 29 Merrion Rd., **Dublin** 4 (tel. (01) 269 5211).

Australia: Fitzwilton House, Wilton Terrace, **Dublin** 1 (tel. (01) 676 1517).

New Zealand: New Zealand Embassy, New Zealand House, Haymarket, **London** SW1Y 4QT (tel. (0171) 930 8422).

South Africa: South African High Commission, South Africa House, Trafalgar Sq., **London** WC2N 5DP (tel. (0171) 930 4488; fax 451 7284).

■ Getting Around

Fares on all modes of transportation are either "single" (one way) or "return" (roundtrip). "Period returns" require you to return within a specific number of days; "day return" means you must return on the same day. Always keep your ticket with you. Unless stated otherwise, *Let's Go* always lists single (one way) fares. Roundtrip fares on trains and buses are rarely more than 30% above the one-way fare, and are sometimes identical.

Roads between Irish cities and towns have official letters and numbers ("N" and "R" in the Republic, "M," "A," and "B" in the North), but most locals refer to them by destination ("Kerry road," "Tralee road"). Signs and printed directions sometimes give only the numbered and lettered designations, sometimes only the destination. Most signs are in English and Irish; some destination signs are only in Irish. Old black and white roadsigns give distances in miles; new green and white signs are in kilometers. Speed limit signs are always in miles per hour.

BY TRAIN

Iarnród Éireann (Irish Rail) branches out from Dublin to larger cities, but there is limited service. For schedule information, pick up an *InterCity Rail Travellers Guide* (50p), available at most train stations. By far the most useful travel pass for students on trains and buses in Ireland is the **TravelSave stamp,** available at any USIT with an ISIC card and IR£8. Affixed to your ISIC card, this stamp decreases single fares by 50% on national rail and allows you to break your journey to visit at any stop on the way to your final destination (valid for one month). It also provides 15% discounts on bus fares (except on fares less than IR£1). A **Faircard** can get anyone under 26 up to 50% the price of any InterCity trip. Those over 26 can get the less potent **Weekender card** (up to a third off, Fri.-Tues. only). Information is available from Irish Rail information office, 35 Lower Abbey St., Dublin 1 (tel. (01) 836 6222).

While the **Eurailpass** is not accepted in Britain, it *is* accepted on trains (but not buses) in Ireland. Fares for 1996 were as follows: **Eurailpass** 15 days US$522, 21 days US$678, one month US$838; **Youthpass** (for those under 26) 15 days US$418, one month US$598, two months US$798. For groups, the **Eurail Saverpass** allows unlimited first-class travel for 15 days for US$452, 21 days US$578, or one month US$712 per person in groups of two or more (3 or more April-Sept.). **Eurail Flexipasses** allow limited first-class travel within a two-month period: 10 days US$616, 15 days US$812; **Youth Flexipasses,** (for those under 26) are US$438 or US$588, respectively. It's not cost-effective to buy a Eurailpass unless you plan to travel on the Continent as well. The pass is good for travel on Irish Ferries from Rosslare to Cherbourg or Le Havre.

It is easiest to buy a Eurailpass before you arrive in Europe; contact Council Travel, Travel CUTS, or Let's Go Travel (see **Budget Travel Agencies,** p. 29), any of many other travel agents, or **Rail Europe, Inc.,** 226-230 Westchester Ave., White Plains, NY 10604 (tel. (800) 438-7245, fax (800) 432-1329 in the U.S.; and (800) 361-7245), fax (905) 602-4198 in Canada; http://www.raileurope.com), which publishes the free *Europe on Track,* providing up-to-date information on all pass options and rail travel in Europe. They sell railpasses and point-to-point tickets.

Northern Ireland Railways (Belfast tel. (01232) 899411, BritRail service tel. (01232) 230671) is not extensive but covers the Northeastern coastal region well. The major line connects Dublin to Belfast (6/day; 2½hr.; UK£14.50, UK£21.75 return). When it reaches Belfast, this line splits, with one branch ending at Bangor and one at Larne. There is also rail service from Belfast and Lisburn west to Derry and Portrush, stopping at three towns between Antrim and the coast. British Rail passes are not valid here, but Northern Ireland Railways offers its own discounts. A valid **Northern Ireland Travelsave** stamp (UK£5.50, bought at the Student Travel Office, 13b The Fountain Centre, College St., Belfast, and affixed to back of ISIC) will get you 50% off all trains and 15% discounts on bus fares over UK£1 within Northern Ireland. The **Freedom of Northern Ireland** ticket allows unlimited travel by train and Ulsterbus, and can be purchased for seven consecutive days (UK£30, children UK£15) or as a one-day pass (UK£9, children UK£4.50).

BY BUS

Buses in the Republic of Ireland reach many more destinations and are less expensive than trains, but are less frequent, less comfortable, and slower. The national bus company, **Bus Éireann,** operates both long-distance **Expressway** buses, which link larger cities, and **Local** buses, which serve the countryside and smaller towns. The invaluable bus timetable book (80p) is available at Busáras Station in Dublin and at many tourist offices. A myriad of **private bus services** are faster and cheaper than Bus Éireann. *Let's Go* lists these private companies in areas they service. Most of these services link Dublin to one or two towns in the west. In Donegal, private bus providers take the place of Bus Éireann's nearly nonexistent local service.

Bus Éireann's discount **Rambler** tickets mostly aren't worth buying; individual tickets often provide better value. The **Rambler** ticket offers unlimited bus travel within Ireland three out of eight consecutive days (IR£28), eight out of 15 consecutive days (IR£68), or 15 out of 30 consecutive days (IR£98). A combined **Irish Explorer Rail/Bus** ticket good for unlimited travel eight out of 15 consecutive days on rail and bus lines is available for £90. Purchase these from Bus Éireann at the main tourist office in Dublin, Store St., Dublin 1 (tel. (01) 836 6111; in Cork tel. (021) 508188; in Limerick tel. (061) 313333; in Waterford tel. (051) 879000; in Galway tel. (091) 562000). You can also contact the Irish Rail information office, 35 Lower Abbey St., Dublin 1 (tel. (01) 836 6222).

Ulsterbus, Laganside, Belfast (tel. (01232) 320011), runs throughout the North, where there are no private bus services. Coverage expands in summer, when open-top buses cover a northeastern coastal route, and full- and half-day tours leave for key tourist spots from Belfast. Pick up a regional timetable (25p) at any station. Again, the bus discount passes won't save you much money: a **Freedom of Northern Ireland** bus pass offers travel for one day (UK£9, under 16 UK£4.50), seven consecutive days (UK£30, under 16 UK£15). The **Emerald Card** offers travel for eight out of 15 consecutive days (£105, children £53) or 15 out of 30 consecutive days (£180, children £90). The Emerald card allows unlimited travel on: Ulsterbus; Northern Ireland Railways; Bus Éireann Expressway, Local, and City services in Cork, Limerick, Galway, and Waterford; and Intercity, DART, and Suburban Rail Iarnród Éireann services.

BY CAR

The advantages of car travel speak for themselves. Disadvantages include high gasoline prices, the unfamiliar laws and habits associated with driving in foreign lands, and the fact that in Ireland, as in Britain, **they drive on the left.** Be particularly cautious at roundabouts (rotary interchanges)—give way to traffic from the right. Irish drivers fly along narrow, twisting, pot-holed, poorly-lit back roads. You will need to drive more slowly and more cautiously than you would at home, especially at night.

In both countries, the law requires drivers and front-seat passengers to wear seat belts. In Northern Ireland, rear-seat passengers are also required to buckle up—these laws are enforced. In Ireland, children under 12 are not allowed to sit in the front seat of a car. Children under 40 lbs. should ride only in a specially designed carseat, which can be obtained for a small fee from most car rental agencies.

In the Republic of Ireland, roads numbered below N50 are "primary routes," which connect all the major towns; roads numbered N50 and above are "secondary routes," not as well-trafficked but still well-signposted. Regional "R-roads" are rarely referred to by number. Instead, the road takes the name of its destination. The general speed limit is 55mph (90km/h) on the open road and either 30mph (50km/h) or 40mph (65km/h) in town. There are no major highways.

Northern Ireland possesses exactly two major highways (M-roads or motorways) connecting Belfast with the rest of the province. The M-roads are supplemented by a web of "A-roads" and "B-roads." Speed limits are 60mph (97km/h) on single carriageways (non-divided highways), 70mph (113km/h) on motorways (highways) and dual carriageways (divided highways), and usually 30mph (48km/h) in urban areas. (Speed limits are always marked at the beginning of town areas. Upon leaving, you'll see a circular sign with a slash through it, signalling the end of the speed restriction.) Speed limits aren't rabidly enforced; remember, though, that many of these roads are sinuous and single-track—use common sense.

Hiring (renting) an automobile is the least expensive option if you plan to drive for a month or less, but the initial cost of renting a car and the price of petrol will astound you in Ireland. People under 21 cannot rent, and those under 25 often encounter difficulties. Major rental companies include **Avis, Budget Rent-A-Car, Murrays Europcar, Hertz, Kenning, McCausland,** and **Swan National.** Prices range from IR£100 to IR£300 (plus VAT) per week with insurance and unlimited mileage. For insurance reasons, renters are required to be over 21 and under 70-75. **Europe by Car,** however, will rent to younger people if the paperwork is done in advance, in the U.S. Some plans require sizable deposits unless you're paying by credit card. Make sure you understand the insurance agreement before you rent; some require you to pay for damages that you may not have caused. Automatics are around 20-25% more expensive to rent than manuals (stick shifts). Try **Budget Rent-A-Car,** 151 Lower Drumcondra Rd., Dublin 9 (tel. (01) 837 9611; £45/day).

Most credit cards cover standard insurance. If you rent, lease, or borrow a car, you will need a **green card** or **International Insurance Certificate** to prove that you have liability insurance. Obtain it through the car rental agency; most of them include coverage in their prices. If you lease a car, you can obtain a green card from the dealer. Verify whether your auto insurance applies abroad; even if it does, you will still need a green card to certify this to foreign officials. If you have a collision, the accident will show up on your domestic records if you report it to the company.

You may use an American or Canadian driver's license for one year in the U.K. and Ireland, provided you've had it for one year. If you plan on staying for a longer duration, you will need an **International Driver's Permit** (see p. 12). The **Irish Automobile Association** is on 23 Suffolk St., Rockhill, Blackrock, Co. Dublin (tel. (01) 677 9481), off Grafton St. They honor most foreign automobile memberships (24-hr. breakdown and road service tel. (1800) 667788; toll-free in Ireland).

BY BICYCLE

Much of Ireland's and Northern Ireland's countrysides are well suited for cycling by daylight; many roads are not heavily traveled. (Single-digit N roads in the Republic, and M roads in the North, are more busily trafficked; try to avoid them.) Even well-traveled routes will often cover highly uneven terrain. Begin your trip in the south or west to take advantage of prevailing winds. Bikes can go on some trains but not all:

inquire at the information desk. Bikes are allowed on Bus Éireann at the driver's discretion (if the bus isn't crowded) for a fee of £3-5, but drivers don't always make you pay. It's a pain to bring a bike on an airplane, and each airline has different rules. *Let's Go* lists bike shops and bike rental establishments wherever we can find them. In cities, it is often standard policy to waive the cash deposit if one pays for the rental with a credit card.

Irish Cycle Hire, Mayoralty St., Drogheda, Co. Louth (tel. (041) 41067, 43982, or 42338; fax 35369), has offices in Dublin, Cork, Killarney, Dingle, and Donegal. They also own **Viking Rent-a-Bike** and **Railbike,** so they have many depots. The Drogheda office, which is the office to contact with any question, is open from 9am to 6pm. Other offices are open from May to October daily 9am to 6pm. All charge IR£6 per day, IR£30 per week, with IR£30 deposit. Helmets and pannier bags are available for rent at IR£5 per week each. Bikes come with lock pump and repair kit. One-way rental (renting in one location and dropping off in another) is possible for IR£7. ISIC card holders get a 10% discount (also inquire about a 10% discount for *Let's Go* users, especially in Drogheda).

Rent-A-Bike, 58 Lower Gardiner St., Dublin (tel. (01) 872 5399), rents 18-speed cross-country and mountain bikes for IR£7 per day, IR£30 per week, plus IR£30 deposit. The shops will equip you with locks, patch kits, pumps, pannier bags, handlebar bags, and helmets for IR£5 extra. You can return your bike at a different depot for about IR£5. You can also buy a used bike at the Dublin shop and sell it back four months later for half price. Rent-A-Bike depots are located in Dublin; Isaac's Hostel, Cork; An Óige Hostel, Limerick; Shannon Airport; Great Western Hostel, Galway; and Scotts Garden, Killarney. All bookings should be made through the head office in Dublin (open Mon.-Sat. 9am-6pm, plus Sun. 9am-6pm in summer).

Raleigh Rent-A-Bike rents for IR£7 per day, IR£30 per week, plus IR£40 deposit. The shops will equip you with locks, patch kits, and pumps, and for longer journeys, pannier bags (IR£5/week). Their **One-Way Rental** plan allows you to rent a bike at one shop and drop it off at any of 66 others for a flat charge of IR£12. Reservations should be made through the main office at **C. Harding for Bicycles,** 30 Bachelors' Walk, Dublin 1 (tel. (01) 873 3622; fax 873 3622). A list of Raleigh dealers is available at most tourist offices and bike shops. You might also contact **Raleigh Ireland Limited,** 10 Raleigh House, Kylemore Rd., Dublin 10 (tel. (01) 626 1333).

Many small local dealers and hostels also rent bikes; rates are usually IR£6 to £9 per day and IR£25 to £35 per week. Tourist offices sell *Cycling Ireland* (with map, IR£1.50); you should also check a travel bookstore for other Irish cycling guides if you plan to do much long-distance riding. Mountaineers Books (tel. (800) 553-4453) sells *Ireland by Bike: 21 Tours* for US$15 (plus US$3 shipping). If you are nervous about striking out on your own, **CBT Bicycle Tours** (tel. (800) 736-2453 or (312) 404-1710; fax 404-1833) in the U.S. and Canada offer bicycle tours through the U.K. and Ireland that are geared toward the college-aged. They also arrange discounted airfares for their participants. You can take your bike on the **train** for IR£6, and on the **bus** for a variable charge, but bus transport is entirely at the driver's discretion. You'll have better luck getting your bike on a bus if you depart from a terminal, not a wayside stop. If the bus is full, however, you may be out of luck completely. Adequate **maps** are a necessity; Ordnance Survey maps (1" to 1mi.) or Bartholomew maps (½" to 1mi.) are available in most bookstores in Ireland and the U.K., and in good ones in the U.S. The **Northern Ireland Tourist Board** (see **Government Information Offices,** p. 1) distributes leaflets on various on-road biking routes in Northern Ireland and provides addresses of bike rental establishments, many of which rent mountain bikes.

ON FOOT

Ireland's mountains, fields, and heather-covered hills make walking and hiking an arduous joy. The **Wicklow Way,** a popular trail through mountainous Co. Wicklow, has hostels designed for hikers within a day's walk of each other. The best hillwalking maps are the Ordnance Survey ½"-to-1-mi. series; IR£3.70 each. Consult *Dublin and* *the Wicklow Mountains—Access Routes for the Hillwalker* (IR£2.80), and the tourist office's pamphlet *Walking in Ireland* (IR£1.50).

The **Ulster Way** encircles Northern Ireland with 560 mi. of marked trails. Less industrious trekkers are accommodated by frequent subdivisions. Plentiful information is available on the numerous paths that lace Northern Ireland. For the booklet *The Ulster Way* (£2), contact the **Sports Council for Northern Ireland,** House of Sport, Upper Malone Rd., Belfast BT9 5LA (tel. (01232) 381 222). If you're planning a hike through the Mourne Mountains, contact the **Mourne Countryside Centre,** 91 Central Promenade, Newcastle, Co. Down BT33 ODJ (tel. (013967) 24059).

If you're not feeling too adventurous, you can try **Tír na nÓg Tours,** 57 Lower Gardiner St., Dublin 3 (tel. (01) 836 4684), which offers guided backpacking tours of Ireland. The six-day tours zip along the south and west coasts, and the tour price includes breakfast, admission to visitors centers, and hostel accommodations along the way. Tours leave weekly throughout the year (IR£149).

BY THUMB

> *Let's Go* strongly urges you to consider seriously the risks before you choose to hitch. We do not recommend hitching as a safe means of transportation, and none of the information presented here is intended to do so.

No one should hitch without careful consideration of the risks involved. Not everyone can be an airplane pilot, but almost any bozo can drive a car. Hitching means entrusting your life to a random person who happens to stop beside you on the road and risking theft, assault, sexual harassment, and unsafe driving. Hitching in Ireland has a glowing reputation, but it does have sobering risks: two German tourists were recently murdered while hitching in Western Ireland, and a woman hitcher was raped outside Carrickfergus, Northern Ireland.

In spite of this, the gains are many. Favorable hitching experiences allow you to meet local people and get where you're going, especially in rural areas, where public transportation is sketchy. Consider this section akin to handing out condoms to high school students: we don't endorse it, but if you're going to do it anyway, we'll tell you some ways to make it safer and how to do it right.

The **decision to pick up** a hitcher can be a difficult one for a driver, so a smart hitcher will do everything possible to make it a comfortable decision. Your success as a hitcher will depend partly on **what you look like.** Successful hitchers travel light and stack their belongings in a compact but visible cluster. Most Europeans signal with an open hand, rather than a thumb; many write their destination on a sign in large, bold letters and draw a smiley-face under it. Drivers prefer hitchers who are neat and wholesome. No one stops for anyone wearing sunglasses. **Where you stand** is vital. Experienced hitchers stand where drivers can stop, return to the road without causing an accident, and have time to look over potential passengers as they approach. Hitching on hills or curves is hazardous and unsuccessful; try traffic circles and access roads to highways. In the Practical Information section of many cities, we list the bus lines that take travelers to strategic points for hitching out.

You can get a sense of the amount of traffic a road sees by its letter and number: in the Republic, single-digit N-roads (A-roads in the North) are as close as Ireland gets to highways, double-digit N-roads see some intercity traffic, R-roads (B-roads in the North) generally only carry local traffic but are easy hitches, and non-lettered roads are a hitcher's **purgatory.** In Northern Ireland, hitching (or even standing) on motorways (M-roads) is illegal: you may only thumb at the entrance ramps—*in front* of the nifty blue and white superhighway pictograph (a bridge over a road).

Safety issues are always imperative, even for those who are not hitching alone. If you're a woman traveling alone, don't hitch. A man and a woman are a safer combination, two men will have a harder time, and three will go nowhere. Hitchhiking at night can be particularly dangerous; experienced hitchers stand in well-lit places, and expect drivers to be leery of nocturnal thumbers. Couples may avoid hassles with male drivers if the woman sits in the back or next to the door. Avoid getting in the back of a two-door car, and never let go of your backpack. When you get into a car, make sure you can get out in a hurry. If you ever feel threatened, insist on being let off, regardless of where you are. If the driver refuses to stop, act as if you are going to open the car door or vomit on the upholstery.

If you are hitching a **long distance** or to a remote spot with an intervening town between your present and desired location, you would do well to make your sign for the intervening town rather than your final destination. Shorter lifts are easier to pick up because it's easier for the driver and because more cars will be going to the nearby spot than to the distant one. Once you're picked up, if the driver is going to your final destination, then she or he will almost certainly take you the entire way. If the driver is not going the entire way, then you've at least covered some of the distance and probably put yourself in a better location for hitching the rest of the way.

■ Accommodations

Bord Fáilte (bored FAHL-tshah; meaning "welcome board") is the Republic of Ireland's tourism authority. Actually a government department (and a fairly important one), its system for approving accommodations involves a more-or-less frequent inspection and a fee. Approved accommodations get to use Bord Fáilte's national bookings system and display its icon, a green shamrock on a white field. Bord Fáilte's standards are very specific and, in some cases, far higher than what hostelers and other budget travelers expect or require. Unapproved accommodations can be better and cheaper than their approved neighbors, though, of course, *some* unapproved places are real dumps. Most official tourist offices in Ireland will refer *only* to approved accommodations; some offices won't even tell you how to get to an unapproved hostel, B&B, or campground. Most tourist offices will book a room for IR£1-3 fee, plus a 10% deposit. **Credit card reservations** can be made through Dublin Tourism (tel. (01) 605 7777; fax 605 7787).

HOSTELS

A Hosteler's Bill of Rights

There are certain standard features that we do not include in our hostel listings. Unless we state otherwise, you can expect that every hostel has: no lockout, no curfew, a kitchen, free hot showers, secure luggage storage, and no key deposit.

For those out for friends and a unique experience minus the expense, hostels are the place. These generally feature dorm-style accommodations with large rooms and bunk beds; some allow families and couples to have private rooms. Some have kitchens and utensils for your use, storage areas, laundry facilities, and bike rentals. They're not all fun, games, and laundry though: some close during daytime "lock-out" hours, have curfews, or impose a maximum stay. In Ireland more than anywhere else, senior travelers and families are invariably welcome. Some hostels are strikingly beautiful (a few are even housed in castles), while others are little more than run-down barracks. You can expect every Irish hostel to provide blankets, while you have to provide a sheet or sleepsack. Hostels listed are chosen based on location, price, quality, and facilities.

Hostelling International is the largest such organization. A membership in any national HI affiliate allows you to stay in HI hostels in any country. Nonmembers may ask at hostels for an "International Guest Card." When they visit a hostel, an overnight fee plus one-sixth of the annual membership charge buys one stamp; a card with six stamps is proof of full HI membership. In Ireland, the HI affiliate is **An Óige,** which operates 37 hostels countrywide. Many An Óige hostels are in remote areas or small villages and seem designed mostly to serve hikers, long-distance bicyclists, anglers, and others who want to see nature rather than meet people. The North's HI affiliate is **YHANI** (Youth Hostel Association of Northern Ireland). It operates only nine hostels, all comfortable. Many HI hostels have curfews and lockouts (midday hours when everyone has to leave the building), though they're not always strict about them; almost all have laundry facilities and kitchens. Some HI hostels exist only from March to November, April to October, or May to September. The annually-updated *An Óige Handbook* (IR£1.50) lists, locates, and describes all the An Óige and YHANI hostels in both countries; its standard pricing system isn't always followed by all the hostels it lists.

In Ireland, the two significant non-HI, non-governmental hostel organizations recently merged to form **Independent Holiday Hostels (IHH).** The 137 IHH hostels have no lockout or curfew, accept all ages, require no membership card, and have a mellow atmosphere; all are Bord Fáilte-approved. Pick up a free booklet with complete descriptions of each at any IHH hostel. Get in touch with IHH by writing via the IHH Office, 57 Lower Gardiner St., Dublin 1 (tel. (01) 836 4710).

Lastly, if you have Internet access, check out the **Internet Guide to Hostelling** (http://hostels.com). Reservations for HI hostels may be made via the International Booking Network (IBN), a computerized system which allows you to book to and from HI hostels (more than 300 centers worldwide) months in advance for a nominal fee. Credit card bookings may be made over the phone—contact An Óige or YHANI for more details.

Hostelling Membership

An Óige (Irish Youth Hostel Association), 61 Mountjoy St., Dublin 7 (tel. (01) 830 4555; fax 830 5808; http://www.touchtel.ie). One-year memberships IR£7.50, under 18 IR£4, family IR£7.50 for each adult with children under 16 free. Prices from IR£4.50-9.50 a night. 37 locations.

Youth Hostels Association of Northern Ireland (YHANI), 22 Donegall Rd., Belfast BT12 5JN, Northern Ireland (tel. (01232) 315435; fax 439699). Prices range from UK£6.50-10. Annual memberships UK£7, under 18 UK£3, family UK£14 for parents with any number of children.

Hostelling International-American Youth Hostels (HI-AYH), 733 15th St. NW, Suite 840, Washington, DC 20005 (202-783-6161; fax 783-6171; http://www.taponline.com/tap/travel/hostels/pages/hosthp.html). HI-AYH maintains 34 offices and over 150 hostels in the U.S. One-year memberships US$25, under 18 US$10, over 54 US$15, and US$35 for family cards.

Hostelling International-Canada (HI-C), 400-205 Catherine St., Ottawa, Ontario K2P 1C3, Canada (tel. (613) 237-7884; fax 237-7868). Canada-wide membership/customer service line (800) 663-5777. One-year membership fee CDN$25, under 18 CDN$12; 2-yr. CDN$35; lifetime CDN$175.

Youth Hostels Association of England and Wales (YHA), Trevelyan House, 8 St. Stephen's Hill, St. Albans, Hertfordshire AL1 2DY, England (tel. (01727) 855215; fax 844126). Enrollment fees are UK£9.30, under 18 UK£3.20, UK£18.60 for both parents with children under 18 enrolled free, UK£9.30 for 1 parent with children under 18 enrolled free, UK£125.00 for lifetime membership.

Scottish Youth Hostels Association (SYHA), 7 Glebe Crescent, Stirling FK8 2JA (tel. (01786) 45 11 81; fax 45 01 98). Membership UK£6, under 18 UK£2.50.

Australian Youth Hostels Association (AYHA), Level 3, 10 Mallett St., Camperdown NSW 2050 (tel. (02) 565 1699; fax 565 1325; e-mail YHA@zeta.org.au). Memberships AUS$42, renewal AUS$26; under 18 AUS$12.

Youth Hostels Association of New Zealand (YHANZ), P.O. Box 436, 173 Gloucester St., Christchurch 1 (tel. (643) 379 9970; fax 365 4476; e-mail hostel.operations@yha.org.nz; http://yha.org.nz/yha). Annual membership fee NZ$24.

Hostel Association of South Africa, P.O. Box 4402, Cape Town 8000 (tel. (21) 419 1853; fax 216937). Membership SAR45, students SAR 30, group SAR120, family SAR90, lifetime SAR225.

BED & BREAKFASTS

"Bed-and-breakfast" means just that: a bed in a private room in a small place, often a private home with extra rooms, whose price includes a breakfast of some sort. Irish B&Bs are most savory. Singles run about IR£12-20, doubles IR£20-34. "Full Irish breakfasts"—eggs, bacon, sausage, bread, cereal, orange juice, and coffee or tea—are often filling enough to get you through until dinner. Remember that attitudes in rural Ireland can be quite conservative. An unmarried couple traveling together may encounter some raised eyebrows, but usually no real problems. B&Bs displaying a shamrock are officially approved by the Irish Tourist Board, Bord Fáilte. For accommodations in Northern Ireland, check the Northern Ireland Tourist Board's annual *Where to Stay in Northern Ireland* (UK£4), available at most tourist offices.

HOME RENTALS AND EXCHANGE

Barclay International Group, 152 West 52nd Street, New York, NY 10022 (tel. (800) 845-6636 or (212) 832-3777; fax 753-1139), arranges short-term apartment rentals in Ireland and the U.K. All pads have kitchens, telephones, TV, and concierge and maid service. Rentals start at US$500/week in the off season. Recommended for families with children, business travelers, or Kosher or vegetarian travelers, as the apartments tend to be cheaper than comparably-serviced hotels.

Europa-Let/Tropical Inn-Let, 92 North Main St., Ashland, OR 97520 (tel. (800) 462-4486 or (541) 482-5806; fax 482-0660; e-mail Europa-Let@WaveNet), offers over 100,000 private rental properties (castles, villas, apartments, chalets, etc.) with fully equipped kitchens in 29 countries including Ireland and the U.K. Customized computer searches allow clients to choose properties according to their needs and budget. Europa-Let is also the U.S. agent for Auto Europe car rental.

fair tours, CH-9001 St. Gallen, Switzerland (e-mail fairtoursşgu.apc.org) is a home exchange program for environmentally conscious travelers, providing them with an opportunity to avoid large-scale commercial tourism. Personal matching service. Send two international reply coupons for further information.

▓ Camping & the Outdoors

Camping brings you closest to the land, the water, the insects, and continued financial solvency. Ireland is gratifyingly well endowed with sites. Most campsites are open from April to October, though some stay open year-round. While a few youth hostels have camping facilities (the charge is usually half the hostel charge), most campsites are privately owned and designed for people with caravans rather than people with tents. You can legally set up camp only in specifically marked areas unless you get permission from the owner on whose land you plan to squat. It is legal to cross private land by **public rights of way;** any other use of private land without permission is considered trespassing. Remember, **bogs are flammable.**

Camping in State Forests and National Parks is not allowed in Ireland, nor is camping on public land if there is an official campsite in the area. It is also illegal to light fires within 2km of these forests and parks. Designated caravan and camping parks provide all the accoutrements of bourgeois civilization: toilets, running water, showers, garbage cans, and sometimes shops, kitchen and laundry facilities, restaurants, and game rooms. In addition, many have several caravans for hire at the site. Northern Ireland treats its campers royally; there are well-equipped campsites throughout, and spectacular parks often house equally mouthwatering sites.

USEFUL PUBLICATIONS

A variety of publishing companies offer hiking guidebooks to meet the educational needs of novice or expert. For information about camping, hiking, and biking, write or call the publishers listed below to receive a free catalog.

Sierra Club Bookstore, 85 2nd St., 2nd floor, San Francisco, CA 94109 (tel. (415) 977-5600 or (800) 935-1056; fax 923-5500). Books include *The Sierra Club Family Outdoors Guide* (US$12) and their *Annual Outing Catalog* (US$2).
The Mountaineers Books, 1001 SW Klickitat Way, Ste. 201, Seattle, WA 98134 (tel. (800) 553-4453 or (206) 223-6303; fax 223-6306; http://mbooks@mountaineers.org). Many titles on hiking (the *100 Hikes* series), biking, mountaineering, natural history, and conservation.
Wilderness Press, 2440 Bancroft Way, Berkeley, CA 94704-1676 (tel. (800) 443-7227 or (510) 843-8080; fax 548-1355). Publishes over 100 hiking guides including *Backpacking Basics* (US$11), and *Backpacking with Babies and Small Children* (US$11).

CAMPING EQUIPMENT

Purchase equipment before you leave. This way you'll know exactly what you have and how much it weighs. Whether buying or renting, finding sturdy and light equipment is a must. Spend some time examining catalogs and talking to knowledgeable salespeople. Mail-order firms are for the most part reputable and cheap—order from them if you can't do as well locally.

Most of the better **sleeping bags**—made of down (warmer and lighter, but miserable when wet) or synthetic material (cheaper, heavier, more durable, and warmer when wet)—are rated according to the lowest outdoor temperature at which they will still keep you warm. Buy according to the climate of the area you'll be camping in and hiking through. Prices vary widely, but US$65-100 for a summer synthetic, US$135-200 for a three-season synthetic, US$150-225 for a three-season down bag, and US$250-550 for a down sleeping bag usable in the winter are reasonable for good bags. **Sleeping bag pads** include foam pads (US$13 and up for closed-cell foam, US$25 and up for open-cell foam) or air mattresses (US$25-50) to cushion your back and neck (and, if you're camping in a colder region, to insulate you from the ground). A good alternative is the **Therm-A-Rest,** which is part foam and part air-mattress and inflates to full padding when you unroll it.

Your major considerations in selecting a **tent** should be shape and size. The best tents are free-standing with their own frames and suspension systems. They set up

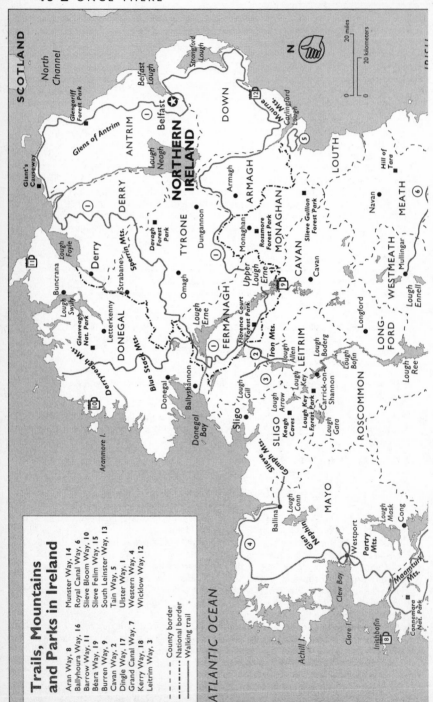

Trails, Mountains and Parks in Ireland

Aran Way, 8
Ballyhoura Way, 16
Barrow Way, 11
Béara Way, 19
Burren Way, 9
Cavan Way, 2
Dingle Way, 17
Grand Canal Way, 7
Kerry Way, 18
Leitrim Way, 3

Munster Way, 14
Royal Canal Way, 6
Slieve Bloom Way, 10
Slieve Felim Way, 15
South Leinster Way, 13
Tain Way, 5
Ulster Way, 1
Western Way, 4
Wicklow Way, 12

- - - County border
-··-··- National border
——— Walking trail

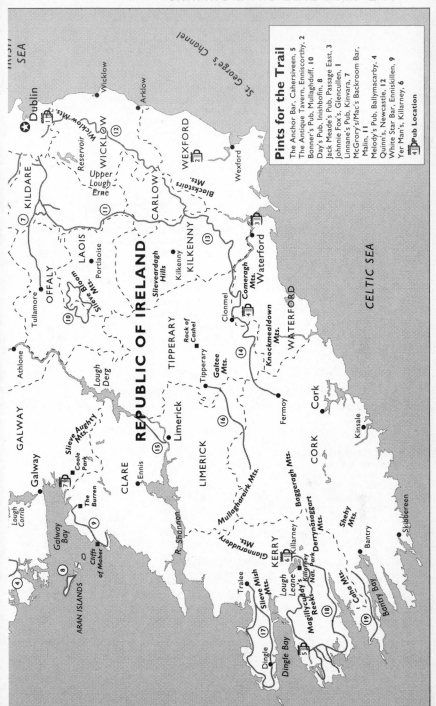

Pints for the Trail

The Anchor Bar, Cahersiveen, 5
The Antique Tavern, Enniscorthy, 2
Bonner's Pub, Mullaghduff, 10
Day's Pub, Inishbofin, 8
Jack Meade's Pub, Passage East, 3
Johnnie Fox's, Glencullen, 1
Linnane's Pub, Kinvara, 7
McGrory's/Mac's Backroom Bar, Malin, 11
Melody's Pub, Ballymacarby, 4
Quinn's, Newcastle, 12
White Star Bar, Enniskillen, 9
Yer Man's, Killarney, 6

🍺 Pub Location

quickly and require no staking (though staking will keep your tent from blowing away). Low profile dome tents are the best all-around. When pitched, their internal space is almost entirely usable, which means little unnecessary bulk. As for size, two people *can* fit in a two-person tent but will find life more pleasant in a four-person tent. If you're traveling by car, go for a bigger tent; if you're hiking, stick with a smaller tent that weighs no more than 3.5 lbs. Good two-person tents start at about US$135; US$200 for a four-person, but you can often find last year's version for half the price. Seal your tent's seams with waterproofer, and make sure it has a rain fly.

Other necessities include: battery-operated **lantern** (*never* gas), plastic **ground-cloth** for the floor of your tent, **nylon tarp** for general purposes, **waterproof back-pack cover** (although you can forego the cover by storing your belongings in plastic bags inside your backpack), **"stuff sack"** or plastic bag to keep your sleeping bag dry. When camping in autumn, winter, or spring, bring along a **"space blanket,"** a technological wonder that helps you to retain your body heat (US$3.50-13; doubles as a groundcloth). Plastic **canteens** or water bottles keep water cooler in the hot sun than metal ones do, and are virtually shatter- and leak-proof. Large, collapsible **water sacks** will significantly improve your lot in primitive campgrounds and weigh practically nothing when empty, though they can get bulky. Bring **water-purification tablets,** for when you can't boil water. **Campstoves** are essential (Coleman, the classic, starts at about US$30). Consider GAZ-powered stoves, which come with bottled propane gas that is easy to use and widely available in Europe. **Waterproof matches, a lighter, a swiss army knife, insect repellent,** and **calamine lotion** are also essential camping items.

Shop around locally before turning to mail-order firms; this allows you to get an idea of what the different items actually look like (and weigh), so that if you later decide to order by mail you'll have a more exact idea of what it is you're getting. The mail-order firms listed below offer lower prices than those you're likely to find in stores, and they can also help you determine which item you need.

Campmor, P.O. Box 700, Saddle River, NJ 07458 (tel. (800) 526-4784; http://www.campmor.com). Has a wide selection of name brand equipment at low prices. One-year guarantee for unused or defective merchandise.

Eastern Mountain Sports (EMS), One Vose Farm Rd., Peterborough, NH 03458 (tel. (603) 924-7231), has stores from Colorado to Virginia to Maine. Though slightly higher-priced, they provide excellent service and guaranteed customer satisfaction on most items sold.

Recreational Equipment, Inc. (REI), 1700 45th St. E, Sumner, WA 98390 (tel. (800) 426-4840; http://www.rei.com). Stocks a wide range of the latest in camping gear and holds great seasonal sales. Many items guaranteed for life (excluding normal wear and tear).

L.L. Bean, Casco St., Freeport, ME 04033-0001 (U.S. and Canada tel. (800) 221-4221, International tel. (207) 865-3111; U.S. fax 797-8867, Canada and International (207) 878-2104). High quality equipment and outdoor clothing, and chock-full of information. Call or write for their free catalogue. The customer is guaranteed 100% satisfaction on all purchases. Open all the time.

SAFETY & WILDERNESS CONCERNS

The three most important things to remember when hiking or camping: stay warm, stay dry, stay hydrated. If you are going on any hike longer than 1 mi., you should pack enough equipment to keep you alive should disaster strike. This includes raingear, warm layers (not cotton) especially hat and mittens, a first-aid kit, high energy food, and water. Always check weather forecasts and pay attention to the skies. If possible, let someone know that you are going hiking: a friend, your hostel, a park ranger, or some local hiking organization. Above all, do not attempt a hike beyond your ability—you will be endangering your life.

Extreme cold is a far greater danger than heat in Britain and Ireland, especially for hikers. A bright blue sky can turn to sleeting rain before you can say **"hypothermia,"**

which can occur even in July, especially in rainy or windy conditions or at night (see **Health,** p. 17). If on a day hike and weather turns nasty, turn back. If on an overnight, start looking immediately for shelter. Never rely on cotton, the "death cloth," for warmth. Instead wear synthetic materials designed for the outdoors such as pile fleece jackets and Gore-Tex® raingear, or wool which stay warm when wet.

Another major concern is safe water. Many rivers and lakes are contaminated with *giardia,* a bacteria which causes gas, painful cramps, loss of appetite, and violent diarrhea. To protect yourself, bring your water to a rolling boil for at least five minutes, or purify it with iodine tablets. A portable water purification system works well also. A good guide to outdoor survival is *How to Stay Alive in the Woods,* by Bradford Angier (Macmillan, US$8). See **Health** (p. 17) for information on basic medical concerns and first-aid.

Don't trample vegetation by walking off established paths. Campers are asked to make small fires using only dead branches or brush; using a campstove is the more cautious (and efficient) way to cook. Don't cut vegetation, and don't clear new campsites. Make sure your campsite is at least 150 ft. from any water supply. If there are no toilet facilities, bury human waste at least 4 in. deep and 150 ft. or more from any water supplies and campsites. Always pack your trash in a plastic bag and carry it with you until you reach the next trash can.

■ Keeping In Touch

MAIL

Sending Mail To Ireland

Mail can be sent internationally through **Poste Restante** (the international phrase for General Delivery) to any city or town; it's well worth using and much more reliable than you might think. Mark the envelope "HOLD" and address it, for example, "Kevin <u>BURKE,</u> Poste Restante, Dublin, Ireland." The last name should be capitalized and underlined. The mail will go to a special desk in the central post office, unless you specify a post office by street address or postal code. As a rule, it is best to use the largest post office in the area; sometimes, mail will be sent there regardless of what you write on the envelope. When possible, it is usually safer and quicker to send mail express or registered. When picking up your mail, bring your passport or other ID. If the clerks insist that there is nothing for you, have them check under your first name as well.

In the Republic, there are no postal codes, except in Dublin, where there are 24 widely ignored ones. Northern Ireland uses the British system of six-character codes. *Let's Go* lists post offices in the Practical Information section for each city and most towns. Generally, letters specifically marked "airmail" are faster than postcards and provide more writing room than **aerogrammes,** printed sheets that fold into envelopes and travel via airmail, available at post offices. Most post offices will charge exorbitant fees or simply refuse to send Aerogrammes with enclosures. Airmail letters between the Republic and American cities average 10-14 days, between Northern Ireland or the Isle of Man and America 6-10 days. If regular airmail is too slow, there are a few faster, more expensive, options. Federal Express (tel. (800) 463-3339) can get a letter from New York to Dublin in two days for a whopping US$28.50. By Uncle Sam's Express Mail, the same letter would arrive in two to three days and would cost US$21.

Surface mail is by far the cheapest and slowest way to send mail. It takes one to three months to cross the Atlantic, appropriate for sending large quantities of items you won't need to see for a while. It is vital, therefore, to distinguish your airmail from surface mail by explicitly labeling "airmail" in the appropriate language. When ordering books and materials from abroad, always include one or two **International Reply Coupons (IRCs)**—a way of providing the postage to cover delivery. IRCs should be available from your local post office (US$1.05).

American Express offices throughout the world will act as a mail service for card-holders if you contact them in advance. Under this free **"Client Letter Service,"** they will hold mail for 30 days, forward upon request, and accept telegrams. Again, the last name of the person to whom the mail is addressed should be capitalized and underlined. Some offices will offer these services to non-cardholders (especially those who have purchased AmEx Travelers' Cheques), but call ahead to make sure. We list AmEx office locations for most cities; a complete list is available free from AmEx (tel. (800) 528-4800) in the booklet *Traveler's Companion.*

TELEPHONES

Calling Ireland

When calling overseas, remember time differences so as not to wake B&B proprietors in the wee hours. Dial your country's international access code (011 for the USA and Canada, 0011 for Australia, 00 for New Zealand); then the country code (44 for Britain, Northern Ireland, and the Isle of Man; 353 for the Republic of Ireland); then the regional telephone code, *dropping the initial zero,* and, finally, the local number. The phone code for the Isle of Man is 01624. *Let's Go* lists telephone codes in Practical Information sections, except when covering rural areas where more than one telephone code may apply (in those cases we list the telephone code, in parentheses, together with the number, out of parentheses). For example, when calling from the U.S. to order books from Fred Hanna's in Dublin (telephone code 01), dial 011-353-1-677-1255. Regional telephone codes range from two to six digits, and local telephone numbers range from three to seven digits.

Calling Home

From The Republic of Ireland

Operator (not available from card phones): 190.
Directory inquiries (for the Republic and the North): 1190.
Directory inquiries for Britain: 1197.
Telecom Éireann information number: (1800) 330 330.
International operator: 114.
International access code: 00.

Using Irish pay phones can be tricky. Public phones come in two varieties: coin phones and card phones. Public coin phones will sometimes make change (it depends on which order you insert coins) but private pay phones ("one-armed bandits") in hotels and restaurants do not—once you plunk in your change, you can kiss it goodbye. In any pay phone, do not insert money until you are asked to, or until your call goes through. The frightening pip, pip noise that the phone makes as you wait for it to start ringing is normal, and can last up to 10 seconds.

Local calls cost 20p on standard pay phones; "one-armed bandits" can charge 30p or whatever they please. Local calls are not unlimited—one unit pays for four minutes. News agents sell **callcards** in denominations of £3.50, £7.50, or £15; they're essential for international calls. For calls direct-dialed to the U.S. during the cheapest hours, one card unit lasts eight seconds, so a 100-unit (£15) card lasts for 13.3 minutes. Talk fast. Card phones have a digital display that ticks off the perilous plunge your units are taking. When the unit number starts flashing, you may push the eject button on the card phone; you can then pull out your expired calling card and replace it with a fresh one. If you try to wait until your card's units fall to zero, you'll be disconnected, which is a bummer. Eject your card early, and use that last remaining unit or two for a local call.

To make **international calls** from the Republic of Ireland, dial the international access code (00); then the country code (see **Appendix,** p. 467); area code (dropping the initial zero); and local number. Alternatively, you can access an Irish international operator at 114. Note that to call the North from the Republic, you dial (08) plus the regional phone code (*without* dropping the initial zero) plus the number. International calls from the Republic are cheapest during **economy periods.** The low-rate period to North America is Monday through Friday 10pm to 8am and Saturday and Sunday all day; to EU countries it's Monday through Friday 6pm to 8am and Saturday and Sunday all day; to Australia and New Zealand call Monday through Friday 2 to 8pm and midnight to 8am and Saturday and Sunday all day. There are no economy rates to the rest of the world. Long distance calls within the Republic are also cheapest Monday through Friday 6pm to 8am and Saturday and Sunday all day.

From Northern Ireland, The Isle of Man, & London
   Operator: 100.
   Directory inquiries: 192. **Other inquiries:** 191.
   International operator: 155.
   International directory assistance: 153.
   International access code: 00.

The pay phones in Northern Ireland and the Isle of Man charge 10p for local calls. A series of harsh beeps warns you to insert more money when your time is up. The digital display ticks off your credit in 1p increments so you can watch your pence in suspense. Only unused coins are returned. You may use all remaining credit on a second call by pressing the "follow on call" button (often marked "FC"). Phones don't accept 1p, 2p, or 5p coins. The dial tone is a continuous purring sound; a repeated double-purr means the line is ringing. Northern **Phonecards,** in denominations of £2, £5, £10, and £20, are sold at post offices, newsagents, or John Menzies stationery shops. The £5 and higher denominations provide extra credit. Phone booths that take cards are labeled in green; coin booths are labeled in red. Many phone booths take cards in Belfast, Derry, and other developed areas; in the rural North, they're rare. In Belfast, card phones labelled in green and blue take phonecards, credit cards (Visa or MasterCard/Access), or change. Bright blue **Mercury** phones are scattered about the Belfast city center. They take cash or credit cards (Visa or Mastercard/Access). International calls are cheaper on these phones. Card phones are common on the **Isle of Man,** where Manx Telecom **Smart Cards** come in £2, £3, £5, and £10 denominations, with 10% extra credit free. These cards are available at post offices and newsagents.

   To make **international calls** from Northern Ireland or the Isle of Man, dial the **international access code (00);** the country code for where you're calling (see **Appendix,** p. 467); the area/city code (dropping the initial zero); then the local number. **Reduced rates** for most international calls from Northern Ireland and the Isle of Man apply Monday through Friday 8pm to 8am, and weekends all day. Rates are highest Monday through Friday 3 to 5pm. The low-rate period to Australia and New Zealand is daily midnight to 7am and 2:30 to 7:30pm. Rates to the Republic of Ireland go down Monday through Friday 6pm-8am and weekends.

Calling Card Calls
A **calling card** is another, cheaper alternative. Your local long-distance phone company will have a number for you to dial while traveling (either toll-free or charged as a local call) to connect instantly to an operator in your home country. The calls (plus a small surcharge) are then billed either collect or to a calling card. AT&T provides **AT&T Direct** service from Britain and Ireland; by calling a toll-free number in Ireland or the UK you can access a U.S. operator who will help you place a collect call (US$5.75 surcharge) or charge it to your AT&T calling card (US$2.50 surcharge). Rates run about US$1.75-1.85 for the first minute plus about US$1 per additional minute. The people you are calling need not subscribe to AT&T service. If you are in the North, if no one else can help, and if you can find one, use a Mercury phone; it is generally cheaper to make a connection by Mercury than by British Telecom. To reach the long-distance companies listed below when calling from a Mercury phone, dial (0500) instead of (0800).

EMERGENCY

Dial **999** anywhere in Ireland, Northern Ireland, the Isle of Man, or London for police, fire, or ambulance; no coins are required. Police in the Republic of Ireland are called *garda* (GAR-da), plural *gardaí* (gar-DEE).

OTHER COMMUNICATION

Domestic and international **telegrams** are slower than phone but faster than post. Fill out a form at any post or telephone office; cables to North America arrive in one or two days. Telegrams can be quite expensive, so you may wish to consider **faxes** for more immediate, personal, and cheaper communication. Major cities have bureaus where you can pay to send and receive faxes.

If you're spending a year abroad and want to keep in touch with friends or colleagues in a college or research institution, **electronic mail (e-mail)** is an attractive option. With a minimum of computer knowledge and a little planning, you can beam messages anywhere for no per-message charges. Befriend college students as you go and ask if you can use their e-mail accounts, or look for bureaus that offer access to e-mail for sending individual messages. Search through http://www.easynet.co.uk/pages/cafe/ccafe.htm to find a list of cybercafés around the world.

Let's Go Picks

These are the places we loved, the places we'd like to stay for two months instead of two days, and the friends we'd like to bump into. But subjective is as subjective does: how about a Readers' Picks '98? Send us a postcard of the best of your travels.

Best pubs: Yer Mans, Killarney (see p. 242), turf fires and Guinness in jam jars. **Kelly's,** Portrush, a town institution with 11 bars and three discos. **Mac's Backroom Bar,** Culdaff (see p. 360), serious *craic* and consistently authentic music. **The Shamrock,** Falcarragh (see p. 349), possibly the best Saturday trad session in Ireland. **Cruises Pub,** Ennis (see p. 275), tasty food, memorable music, copious *craic*. **Phil Carrol's,** Clonmel (see p. 179), will write your name in the foam on your pint. **Mulligan's,** Dublin (see p. 98), serves the best pint you can get in a pub, anywhere.

Best restaurants: RiverGod Cafe, Dingle (see p. 256), huge, tantalizing sandwiches. **Escape,** Bray (see p. 125), heaps of creative vegetarian cuisine. **La Sabbia,** Bundoran (see p. 336), cheap and impeccable eats, cosmo cool atmosphere. **Franco's,** Enniskillen (see p. 387), this bistro's pizzas amaze.

Best museum/castle/monastic ruins: Cloghan Castle, Banagher (see p. 161), all antique furniture, all with a story, and acres of delightful Jacob's sheep. **Skellig Michael Island** (see p. 250), otherworldly monastery full of birds. **King House,** Boyle (see p. 326), interactive exhibits and touching displays. **Enniscorthy Castle,** Enniscorthy (see p. 191), three towers overlooking the Slaney, the one-stop museum on nationalism in Wexford. **Blasket Center,** Dunquin (see p. 258), brings to life the lost culture of the Blaskets. **Tower Museum,** Derry City (see p. 423), vivid presentation of the city's rich, troubled history. **Ulster American Folk Park,** Omagh (see p. 425), fantastically extensive chronicle of Ulster emigrants and descendants.

Backpacker's bests: Wicklow Mountains (see p. 126), from Enniskerry to Glendalough—mountains, cascades, and monastic ruins. **Killarney National Park** (see p. 243), gorgeous trails around mountains and lakes. **Glenveagh National Park** (see p. 350), fresh forest glens and Ireland's two tallest mountains. **Aughinish Peninsula** (see p. 285), gorgeous views of the Burren across Galway Bay's crashing waves.

Best beaches: Velvet Strand, Malahide (see p. 121), real sand, just a DART away from Dublin. **Allihies,** Beara Peninsula (see p. 238), wild Beara beach action—majestic and unspoiled. **Culdaff Strand,** Culdaff (see p. 360), the glorious Inishowen beach is stunning at sunrise. **Enniscrone Strand,** Enniscrone (see p. 321), a mile of beach all to yourself with seaweed baths close by.

Best places to stay: Wicklow Bay Hostel, Wicklow (see p. 133), cheery family-run hostel on the sea, just off the Wicklow Way. **Maria's Schoolhouse,** Union Hall (see p. 225), beautiful building, peat fire, and rare comfort. **Screag an Iolair Hill Hostel,** Crolly (see p. 347), Neolithic stone circles and trad. **Wild Haven Hostel,** Achill Sound Town (see p. 317), just like home, maybe better. **Mr. & Mrs. Augustin Claffey,** Clonmacnoise (see p. 160), lambskin rugs and rocking chairs in a 156-year-old cottage.

Researcher's picks: Birr (see p. 160), extremely friendly, under-touristed town. **Inishbofin Island** (see p. 308), quiet, amiable, great pubs, and away from everything. **Dingle Town** (see p. 255), lovely seaside town with romance in the air. **Donegal Gaeltacht** (see p. 346), gorgeous, unspoiled region that shows what the rest of Ireland used to be. **Drogheda** (see p. 142), cathedrals, nightlife, and Neolithic tombs, all near Dublin. **Skibbereen** (see p. 226), laid-back gateway to Beara with bohemian flair. **Glencolmcille** (see p. 342), Irish-speaking village in a starkly beautiful valley. **Kinvara** (see p. 284), right by the Burren, music as good as Doolin but without the tourists.

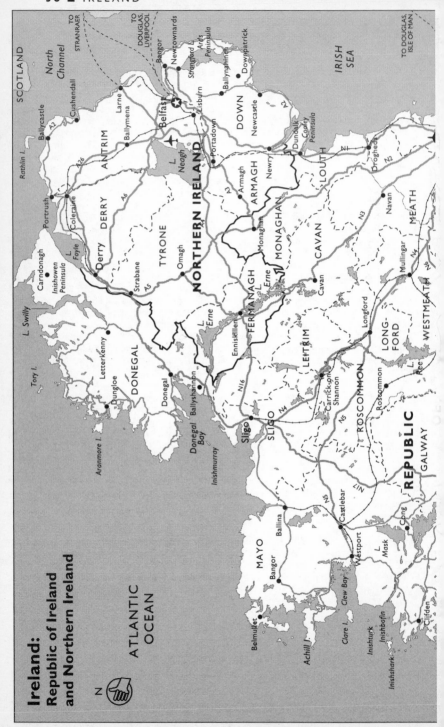

Ireland:
Republic of Ireland
and Northern Ireland

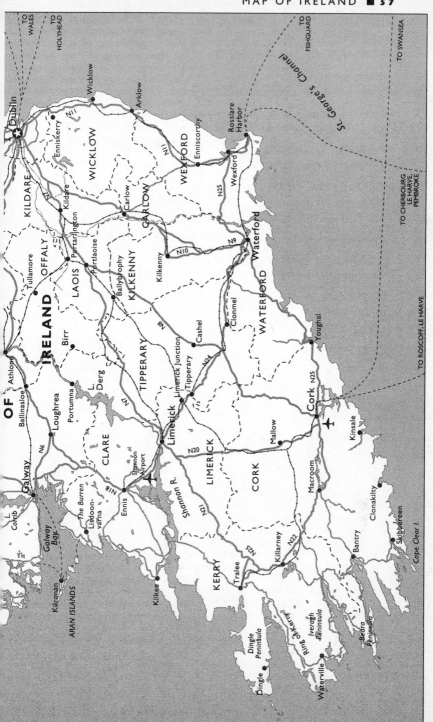

IRELAND (ÉIRE)

It can be hard to see Ireland through the mist of stereotypes that surrounds the island even on the clearest of days. Although much of the country is still rural and religious, there is also a developing urban culture with links to Great Britain and the Continent. Traditional musicians roam Western pubs, while rockers try hard in Dublin, Cork, and Galway. The Irish language lives both in coastal villages and in national magazines. Literature in English—especially poetry—thrives on this highly-educated island. Long hiking trails, roads, and cliff walks make a chain of windy, watery, spectacular scenery around the coast from Wexford all the way up to Inishowen, while Dublin diffuses its uniquely Irish modernity and sophistication to everything within its orbit.

Though the chapters in *Let's Go: Ireland* don't perfectly mirror these divisions, it helps to know that Ireland is traditionally thought of in four provinces: **Leinster,** the east and southeast; **Munster,** the southwest; **Connacht,** the province west of the river Shannon; and **Ulster,** the North, six of whose nine counties make up Northern Ireland. You shouldn't have to go out of your way in any of the four to encounter either Ireland's past—its castles, medieval streets, monasteries, legends, language, and music—or its equally exciting present.

■ History

Travel in this nation with a strong sense of past will be more rewarding for those who take time to learn its history. *Let's Go* can provide only a very compressed account. Mark Tierney's *Modern Ireland* is a clear and comprehensive narrative covering the period from 1850 to 1968; *The Oxford History of Ireland* is a good source on earlier periods; and R.F. Foster's hefty tome *Modern Ireland: 1600-1972* is authoritative and interesting if you know a little already.

PRE-CHRISTIAN IRELAND (TO 350 AD)

The first major civilization in Ireland culminated in the **Neolithic** mound builders (4500-2500 BC). These mysterious, industrious, and agrarian people left Ireland dotted with cairns, dolmens, and passage-tombs. Beakers (perhaps for drinking mead) and stone henges (circles) of a religious/astronomical bent also appeared around 2500 BC with advances in copper working.

Bronze arrived in Ireland circa 2000 BC, perhaps with Celtic invaders. The island's culture radically changed over the next 700 years. The megaliths and henges disappeared, more weapons and fortifications emerged, and a new warrior aristocracy took control and began furiously hurling weapons at each other and into rivers and bogs as part of a new weapons and water cult. The last two centuries of the Bronze Age (900-700 BC) saw an unprecedented flowering of Irish culture. Ireland in the **Irish Golden Age,** dominated by hierarchical warrior-nobles, held a central position on Atlantic trade routes stretching from Gibraltar to Sweden. Few artifacts remain from the **Irish Dark Age** (700-300 BC), which was followed by the **Celtic Iron Age.** Complex artwork (later seen in Christian texts like the *Book of Kells*) shows a Continental influence. The heroism prominent in the *Táin* (see **Legends and Folktales,** p. 69) and other Irish epics, was inspired by this period.

The Roman armies who conquered England didn't think Ireland worth invading. The society they chose to leave alone was ethnically Celtic, spoke Old Irish, lived in small farming settlements, and organized itself under a loose hierarchy of regional chieftains and provincial kings. The most famous of these were the **Ulaid of Ulster,** chariot warriors who dominated La Tène culture from their capital near Armagh.

EARLY CHRISTIANS AND VIKINGS (350-1200)

A series of hopeful missionaries Christianized Ireland in piecemeal fashion. The foremost of these missionaries, **St. Patrick,** was taken here as a boy slave. He escaped to England and returned (without church permission) to do God's work, landing probably in southeast Co. Down in the early 5th century. St. Patrick's exploits are legendary, but many are inventions of Armagh churchmen, who used the claim that their local saint had gone on to convert the rest of the island to justify their claims to authority over the entire Irish Church.

As barbarians overran the Continent, monks fled to island safety. The enormous and hierarchical **monastic cities** of the 6th to 8th centuries later earned Ireland the name, the "island of saints and scholars." From their bases in Armagh, Durrow, Derry, Kells, Clonmacnoise, Iona (in Scotland), and elsewhere, the monastics recorded the old epics, wrote long religious and legal poems in Old Irish and Latin, and illuminated gospels. The *Book of Durrow* and the *Book of Kells* now sit in exhibits at Trinity College. Monastic cities allied themselves with up-and-coming chieftains: Armagh owed its prominence in part to the Uí Néill (O'Neill) clan, which gradually spread from Meath into central Ulster.

Vikings raided every coastline in Northern Europe, making no exception for Ireland. Those who tired of pillaging founded larger towns in the South, such as Limerick, Waterford, and Dublin. Settled Vikings allied themselves with local chieftains, injected Scandinavian words into Irish, and left the southeast littered with Viking-derived place names, like Wexford *(Wæsfjord).*

The first decade of the new millennium saw the rise of High King **Brian Ború** of the warlike Dál Cais clan of Clare, who challenged the Uí Néill clan for control of Ireland and finally took Armagh in 1005. The Battle of Clontarf in 1014 set Leinstermen and Vikings against Brian Ború's clan. The Dál Cais won, but Brian died in battle, leaving Ireland divided. Brian's successors, including **Rory O'Connor** and **Dermot Mac-Murrough,** skirmished over who was the true "High King." Dermot made the mistake of asking English Norman nobles to help him reconquer Leinster. **Richard Fitzgilbert de Clare (Strongbow)** was too willing to help. Strongbow and his Anglo-Normans arrived in 1169 and cut a bloody swath through south Leinster. Dermot died in 1171. Strongbow married Dermot's daughter, Aoife, and seemed about to proclaim an independent Norman kingdom in Ireland. King Henry III sent English troops to Waterford, which proved unnecessary. By the time they arrived, Strongbow had sent a message to Henry, in which he affirmed his loyalty and offered to govern Leinster on England's behalf.

FEUDALISM (1200-1607)

Thus began the English hold over Ireland. The next 200 years saw Ireland carved up into feudal counties and baronies, some held by the Norman-descended "Old English," some held by surviving Gaelic lords. The Old English areas, concentrated in Leinster, had more towns and more trade, while Gaelic Connacht and Ulster remained more rural. England controlled **the Pale,** a fortified domain around Dublin. Old English and Irish fiefdoms used similar castles, ate similar foods, appreciated the same poets, and hired the same mercenaries. This cultural cross-pollination worried the English crown, who sponsored the notorious 1366 **Statutes of Kilkenny.** These decrees banned English colonists (dubbed "more Irish than the Irish themselves") from speaking Irish, wearing Irish styles of dress, or marrying the native Irish, and forbade the Irish from entering walled cities (like Derry). The harsh statutes had little effect. Gaelic lords kept taking land from English ones. Feudal skirmishes and economic decline lasted until the rise of the "Geraldine Earls," two branches of the FitzGerald family who fought for control of south Leinster. The victors, the **Earls of Kildare,** were virtual rulers of Ireland from 1470 to 1534.

When Henry VIII broke with the Catholic Church, the Old English and the Gaelic lords stayed Catholic. The Old English wished to remain loyal both to Catholicism and to the Crown. **Thomas FitzGerald** of Kildare sent a missive to Henry VIII stating this position. Henry responded as if to an armed rebellion, and destroyed the power of Kildare. A newly convened Dublin Parliament declared Henry head of the Protestant **Church of Ireland,** whose membership remained minuscule. Feudal warfare continued for decades. A FitzGerald uprising in Munster in 1579 was harshly suppressed, planting the idea in English heads that Irish land had to be directly controlled by Protestants if it were to be considered safe and loyal. **Hugh O'Neill,** an Ulster earl, raised an army of thousands in open rebellion in the late 1590s. Gaelic lords supported him, but the Old English lords were divided. The King of Spain promised naval assistance which arrived in Kinsale Harbour in 1601, then sat there with Spanish soldiers still on their boats as armies from England demolished O'Neill's forces. His power broken, O'Neill and the rest of the major Gaelic lords fled Ireland in 1607 (the **Flight of the Earls**). The English used their military advantage to take control of the land and to parcel it out to Protestants.

PLANTATION & CROMWELL (1607-1688)

The English project of "planting" Ireland with Protestants and dispossessing Catholics of their land was most successful in Ulster, where Scottish Presbyterians (the Scots-Irish), joined the expected mix of adventurers and ex-soldiers. King Charles's representative in Ireland, Lord Wentworth, pursued a policy with few supporters outside England, closing off the South to the Scots and confiscating more land than there were Protestant takers. The dispossessed people revolted in Ulster in 1641, under a loose group of Gaelic-Irish leaders who were soon joined by **Owen Roe O'Neill,** who had returned from the Continent to lead the insurrection. The Catholic Church backed the rebels, who advanced south and in 1642 formed the **Confederation of Kilkenny,** an uneasy alliance of Church, Irish, and Old English lords. Some members of the last group considered themselves loyal to the King while rebelling against his treasonous viceroy. The arrival of the English Civil War complicated the tangle of interests: the English in Ireland were split between Parliamentarians and King's men, the Church envoy and Owen Roe O'Neill had different goals, and the Old English were still divided. Long negotiations between the Confederates and the King's envoy, Ormond, ended with **Oliver Cromwell's** victory in England and his arrival in Ireland at the head of a Puritan army.

Anything Cromwell's army did not occupy it destroyed. Catholics were massacred and whole towns were razed as the Confederate army and Ormond's Royalists melted away. Entire tracts of land were confiscated and given to soldiers and other Protestant adventurers. The native Irish landowners could go "to hell or Connacht," i.e., they could own land only in remote and soil-poor provinces. In practice, the richest landowners found ways to stay, while the smaller farmers were uniformly displaced. The net result was that by 1660, the vast majority of land was owned, maintained, and policed by imported Protestants.

THE PROTESTANT ASCENDANCY (1688-1801)

Again, 30 years later, English political change meant Irish bloodshed. The closet-Catholic **James II,** driven from England by the "Glorious Revolution" of 1688, came to Ireland with his army, intending to conquer first this island, and then the other. Jacobites (James's supporters) and Williamites (supporters of new, Protestant King William III) fought each other all over Ireland, with a siege in Derry ending in Williamite victory. The **Battle of the Boyne,** another Williamite win which drove James into exile again, led to the disastrous **Battle of Aughrim** and to the war's end in the **Treaty of Limerick,** which ambiguously promised Catholics civil rights that were never delivered. The unenforceable **Penal Laws** (enacted 1695-1704) attempted to limit Catholics economically and banned the public practice of their religion.

The newly secure Anglo-Irish elite built their own culture in Dublin and the Pale with political parties, garden parties, talk, and architecture second only to London. The term **"Ascendancy"** was coined to describe a social elite whose distinction depended upon Anglicanism. Within this exclusive social structure, thinkers such as **Bishop George Berkeley** and **Edmund Burke** rose to prominence. **Jonathan Swift** campaigned against dependency upon England by criticizing reliance upon imported manufacturing and tirelessly pamphleteering on behalf of both the Protestant Church and the rights of the Irish people. Swift was an early proponent of the limited nationalism developed by Irish Parliamentary "patriots" like **Henry Grattan** and **Henry Flood,** who wanted their Anglo-Irish state (under the King, and excluding Catholics) free from the authority of the English Parliament. **Trinity College** flourished as the quintessential institution of the Ascendancy. Meanwhile, displaced peasants filled Dublin's poorer quarters, creating horrific slums.

The Penal Laws made life difficult for priests, but did not prevent the growth of a Catholic, Gaelic-descended merchant class in places like Galway and Tralee. Early in the 18th century, Catholics exercised their religion furtively, using hidden, big, flat rocks **(Mass rocks)** when altars were unavailable. Denied official education, Gaelic-Irish teens learned literature and religion in **hedge schools,** hidden assemblies whose teachers were often fugitive priests. The hedge schools later became a powerful symbol of the poor Irish of the 18th century. Typically, landlords were Anglo-Irish Protestants and their tenants Gaelic-Irish Catholics. The cultural divide made brutal rents and eviction policies easier for some landlords to adopt, while secret agrarian societies, like the **Defenders,** formed to defend peasant holdings.

The American and French Revolutions inspired ideas of independence. The **United Irishmen** began as a radical Ulster debating society. When war between England and Napoleon's France seemed likely, the United Irishmen were outlawed. They reorganized as a secret society, linking up with the Defenders. Their Protestant leader, **Theobald Wolfe Tone,** had hoped for a general uprising to create an independent, non-sectarian Ireland. His followers had less abstract ideals, erupting in May of 1798 in a bloody rising of peasants and priests. **Vinegar Hill,** near Enniscorthy, saw the rebels' celebrated last stand. A month later, French troops under General Humbert arrived in Co. Mayo and managed to hold territory there for about a month before meeting utter destruction. (French soldiers were held as prisoners of war and shipped home; Irish soldiers were executed.)

By relaxing anti-Catholic laws, England had hoped to make Irish society less volatile, but Wexford's rebels spooked the British into abolishing Irish "self-government" altogether. The 1801 **Act of Union** abolished the Dublin Parliament and created "The United Kingdom of Great Britain and Ireland." Wolfe Tone committed suicide in captivity, while other United Irishmen escaped to France, building a secret network that would eventually link up with the Fenians (see p. 62).

O'CONNELL (1801-1841)

The mad gaiety of Dublin vanished. The new government dotted the coastline with **Martello towers:** simple, defensible lookout towers designed to defend against another French invasion. The Anglo-Irish gentry collapsed as agrarian violence continued. English and Continental visitors to Ireland were aghast at its rural poverty.

Union meant Ireland could now send representatives to the British parliament, and the electoral reforms of the 1810s and 20s lowered the property qualifications to the point where many Irish Catholic small farmers had the vote. They voted for **Daniel O'Connell,** whose election to Parliament in 1829 essentially forced Westminster into repealing the remaining anti-Catholic laws, one of which would have barred him from taking his seat. O'Connell acquired the nickname "The Liberator." At first, his efforts within the Parliament unlocked more money to improve Irish trade, living conditions, and health care, but when the unsympathetic Tories took power, O'Connell began to convene huge rallies in Ireland, showing popular support for his goal of repealing the Act of Union. Romantic Nationalism, imported from Germany and Italy, pervaded the intellectual air, and some felt O'Connell had not gone far enough.

"Young Ireland" poets and journalists, like **John Mitchel** (whom Yeats quoted: "Send war in our time, O Lord"), wanted independence, not repeal, and would work for it through violence. They tried a revolt in 1848. No one noticed or cared, since much of Ireland was starving.

FAMINE (1841-1870)

The only crop capable of providing enough nutrients per acre to support 19th-century Ireland's population was the potato. From 1845-47 a new fungal disease made increasing amounts of the crops blackened and inedible. Famine ensued, exacerbated by English economists, who advised the government not to tamper with free markets (i.e., divert crops meant for export) even to feed the starving poor. Some landlords were known for their efforts to help the displaced famine victims; others were notorious for their cruelty. Famine lasted roughly from 1847 to 1851. When the corpses were buried, rural Ireland had been devastated. Of the 1841 population of eight million, an estimated 1.5 to 3 million people had died. Another million had emigrated to Liverpool, London, Australia, and especially America. Depopulation in Connacht was particularly severe, while the number of Dublin poor swelled.

The remaining Irish peasants completely reorganized. The bottom layer of truly penniless farmers had been eliminated. Men married late, eldest sons inherited whole farms, and unskilled younger sons were as likely as not to leave Ireland. The **Encumbered Estates Act** began the 50-year process of removing the landlord class. This was continued by a series of Land Acts and by the **Congested Districts Board,** converting Ireland by 1900 into a nation of conservative, religious, culturally uniform, Catholic smallholders (except for Dublin and northeast Ulster). The widening net of railroads—more extensive than today—improved rural standards of living.

Young Ireland leftover **James Stephens** (not the poet) founded the **Irish Republican Brotherhood** or **IRB (the Fenians)** in 1858. The IRB, and its counterpart American organization, were secret societies aimed at the violent removal of the British. Fenian violence in 1867 made William Gladstone, among others, notice the Irish discontent. He became Britain's Prime Minister a year later under the slogan "Justice for Ireland." Justice consisted in disestablishing the minority Protestant Church of Ireland and battling over land reform. Combining agrarian thinkers, Fenians, and the Home Rule Party's new leader, **Charles Stewart Parnell,** the **Land League** of the 1870s pushed for reforms with O'Connell-style mass meetings.

PARNELL & CULTURAL NATIONALISM (1870-1914)

Isaac Butt founded the Irish Home Rule Party in 1870. Its several dozen members adopted "obstructionist" tactics—making long dull speeches, introducing endless amendments, and generally trying to keep the rest of Parliament angry, bored, and ineffective until they saw fit to grant Ireland autonomy. **Charles Stewart Parnell** was a charismatic, Protestant aristocrat with an American mother and a hatred for every-

---

Potatoes! The Story Behind the Starch

In the 19th century, potatoes literally sustained life for peasants on small and land-poor farms in west and southwest Ireland. A dietary staple, potatoes are the only cheap food that can support life as a sole diet. The rural peasants relied almost exclusively upon them for nourishment. On average, an adult ate about seven pounds of potatoes per day. Although dozens of smaller blights and crop failures had already befallen during the earlier 19th century, the Great Famine of 1845 was far harsher. Called a "Malthusian apocalypse," the Famine dealt a devastating blow to rural communities dependent upon the crop, wiping out rural population and prompting waves of emigration. Blighted by an invisible fungus, *phytaphthera infestans,* infected potatoes blackened and decayed, forming an inedible soft mass of potato ooze. One rural newspaper suggested: "Cut off diseased parts and steam or boil into a mash with bran and salt. When warm it is nourishing for pigs and cattle, but tainted potatoes cold are apt to disagree."

thing English. Backed by Parnell's invigorated Irish party, Gladstone introduced a Home Rule Bill, which was defeated. Parnell gained more esteem when letters linking him to an infamous Fenian crime (the **Phoenix Park Murders;** see **Phoenix Park,** p. 111) turned out to be forgeries. But, in 1890 allegations that Parnell was having an affair were proven true: the scandal split the Home Rulers, and all of Ireland, into Parnellites and anti-Parnellites.

While the parliamentary movement split, civil society grew. Many groups, and many journals, tried to revive or preserve what they took to be essential "Gaelic" culture. Some were blatantly racist. The **Gaelic Athletic Association** tried to replace English sports with hurling, camogie, and Gaelic football and the **Gaelic League** spread the use of the Irish language. The IRB infiltrated these organizations, seeing them as means to a future mobilization. The quarrelsome **Arthur Griffith,** who advocated Irish abstention from British politics, called his tiny movement and little-read newspaper by the catchy name **Sinn Féin** (shin fayn, meaning "Ourselves Alone"). **James Connolly** led strikes in Belfast, while **James Larkin** spearheaded the enormous Dublin general strike of 1913, a short-term defeat which nevertheless established large trade unions in Ireland. From 1910-13 Northern Protestants, moved by anti-Catholic bigotry as well as by loyalty to Great Britain, had joined mass rallies, signed a Covenant, and organized themselves into the quasi-military **Ulster Volunteer Force (UVF)** to resist Home Rule. Nationalists led by **Eoin MacNeill** followed their example in 1913 by creating the **Irish Volunteers,** which the IRB correctly saw as a potential revolutionary force.

THE EASTER RISING (1914-1918)

In summer 1914, Irish Home Rule seemed imminent—the House of Commons had already passed a Home Rule Bill—and Ulster seemed ready to go up in flames. Neither happened; WWI intervened. Home Rule party leader **John Redmond,** also an Irish Volunteer leader, urged the Volunteers to enlist in the Army; 600,000 Irish people and 170,000 Volunteers did. An 11,000-member guard remained in Ireland, led officially by MacNeill, who knew nothing of the revolt which the Volunteers' other leaders (all IRB members) were planning. If there was one architect of what followed, it was poet and schoolteacher **Padraig Pearse,** who won his co-conspirators over to an ideology of "blood sacrifice." If, Pearse believed, a small cabal of committed men might die violently and in public as martyrs for Ireland, then the entire nation would mobilize and win its independence.

Pearse was right. The rump Volunteers conducted a series of unarmed maneuvers and parades throughout 1915-16, leaving Dublin Castle convinced of their harmlessness, while the Volunteers' secret IRB leaders planned a shipment of German arms to be used in a nationwide revolt on Easter Sunday 1916. The arms arrived a day too early and were never picked up, and the British captured the man who was to meet the shipment, **Sir Roger Casement,** and hanged him. The week before Easter Sunday, those in the IRB faction who had planned the Rising showed MacNeill a forgery which purported to be a Dublin Castle order for the suppression of the Volunteers. At the same time, they told him about the arms shipments. Realizing he had been in the dark for two years, but thinking that inaction risked the destruction of the Volunteers, MacNeill gave orders for the Easter Sunday mobilization. On Saturday he learned that the Castle order had been forged and that the arms had been captured, and inserted in the Sunday papers a plea ordering all Volunteers *not* to mobilize.

MacNeill and most IRB leaders had been thinking in terms of military success, which at that point was clearly impossible, but the Pearse cabal wanted blood sacrifice. On Sunday the Pearse group met and decided to have the uprising anyway on the following Monday, though it could only be organized in Dublin. Pearse, James Connolly, and others seized the General Post Office on O'Connell St. and a few other public buildings, read aloud a "Proclamation of the Republic of Ireland," and held out for five days of firefights across downtown Dublin. Dubliners initially saw the Easter rebels as criminal annoyances, since their only tangible accomplishment was massive property damage.

IRELAND (ÉIRE)

The British martial-law administration in Dublin transformed popular opinion by turning **Kilmainham Gaol** into a center of martyrdom. Over 10 days in May, 15 "ringleaders" received the death sentence, among them Pearse, Pearse's brother (executed primarily for being Pearse's brother), and James Connolly, who was shot while tied to a chair because his wounds prevented him from standing. **Eamon de Valera** was spared because the British wrongly thought him an American citizen. By June the public mood was sympathetic to the martyrs—and increasingly anti-British. In 1917 the Volunteers re-formed under master spy and IRB bigwig **Michael Collins** and Cathal Brugha. Under de Valera and Collins, the **Sinn Féin** party, which everyone thought had had some link to the Rising (which it hadn't), became the political voice of military Nationalism. When in 1918 the British tried to introduce a military draft in Ireland, the public turned overwhelmingly to Sinn Féin, repudiating the nonviolent plans of the Home Rule party.

INDEPENDENCE & CIVIL WAR (1919-1922)

Extremist Volunteers became known as the **Irish Republican Army (IRA),** which functioned as the military arm of the new Sinn Féin government. The **War of Independence** was fought between the new government and the British, who reinforced their police with the **Black and Tans,** demobilized soldiers whose nickname came from their patched-together uniforms. The IRA's guerrillas were notorious for committing atrocities, but the tactics of the Blacks and Tans were even worse. The British, under Prime Minister Lloyd George, understood that they had to get out of Ireland. Secret and hurried negotiations produced the **Anglo-Irish Treaty,** which recognized a 26-county state, since the North had by this time set up its own Protestant and Unionist government. The Treaty also imposed on Irish officials a tortuous oath of allegiance to the King of England, but not to the British government.

The Sinn Féin, the IRA, and the population split on whether to accept the Treaty. Collins said yes, de Valera said no. The representative parliament voted yes, and the capable Collins government began the business of setting up a nation, with treasury, tax collection, a foreign ministry, and an unarmed police force (the *Garda Síochana*). The part of the IRA that had opposed the treaty included **General Rory O'Connor,** who occupied the Four Courts in Dublin and took a pro-Treaty Army general hostage. Collins' government attacked the Four Courts. Two years of **civil war** followed, tearing up the countryside and dividing the population. The pro-Treaty government won. A dwindling minority of anti-Treaty IRA officers fled deeper into Munster, but Collins was assassinated before the end of 1922.

THE DE VALERA ERA (1922-1960)

W.T. Cosgrave and his party Cumann na nGaedheal (which evolved into today's **Fine Gael** party) headed the first stable Free State administration until 1932. His government restored civil order, and brought **electrical power** to much of the West by damming the Shannon River. The anti-Treaty voters at first supported abstentionist Sinn Féin. Eamon de Valera broke with Sinn Féin and with the IRA in 1927, founding his own political party, **Fianna Fáil,** to participate in government and oppose the Treaty nonviolently. Fianna Fáil won the 1932 election, and de Valera held power for much of the next 20 years. His ideal Ireland was a nation of deeply Catholic small farmers. Accordingly, Fianna Fáil's economic program broke up the remaining large landholdings and imposed high tariffs. The tariffs produced a trade war with Britain which battered the Irish economy until 1938. IRA hard-liners trickled out of jails in the early 30s and resumed violence, heckling Cumann na nGaedheal meetings. The **Blueshirts** formed around Eoin O'Duffy to oppose the IRA, and became a pseudo-Fascist organization with mass rallies and military-style discipline. By 1936 the Blueshirts had been suppressed and the IRA outlawed. The episode bolstered support for de Valera but tarnished the new state's public image.

In 1937 de Valera and the voters approved what is still the **Irish Constitution.** It begins "In the name of the most Holy Trinity," declares the state's name to be Éire, and establishes the legislative structure. The legislature consists of two chambers. The **Dáil,** the powerful lower house, is comprised of 166 seats directly elected in proportional representation. The less important upper house (the **Seanad** or Senate), has 60 members which are chosen by electoral colleges. Both offices are five-year terms. The **Taoiseach** (Prime Minister) and **Tánaiste** (Deputy Prime Minister) lead a Cabinet, while the **President** (Douglas Hyde was the first) is the ceremonial head of state, elected to a seven-year term. Article 2 says the state's authority extends over "the whole island of Ireland," but article 3 admits that it doesn't, "pending the reintegration of the national territory." The original Constitution referred to the special role of the **Catholic Church** in Ireland. Though Ireland remains overwhelmingly Catholic, the "special position" clause was deleted by a constitutional amendment in 1972.

Ireland was neutral during WWII. Some Irish (especially Northern Nationalists) supported the Nazis on the grounds that they, too, were fighting England, though far more Irish citizens (around 50,000) served in the British army. **"The Emergency,"** as the war was known, meant strict rationing of basic foodstuffs and severe censorship of newspapers and letters. Éire expressed its neutrality in such a way as to effectively assist the Allies; for example, downed American or British airmen were shipped north to Belfast, while downed German pilots were detained in P.O.W. camps. After the firebombing of Belfast in 1941, Northerners cheered the arrival of Dublin's fire brigade. De Valera demonstrated what he thought neutrality meant by delivering official condolences to the German ambassador on the death of Hitler—the only head of government in the world to do so.

A Fine Gael government under John Costello had the honor of officially proclaiming "the Republic of Ireland," but was plagued with problems. The balance between the Church and its political role needed to be defined in almost uniformly Catholic Ireland. The Republic's Nationalism proved to be unabashedly Catholic. This position created many controversies between the new coalition government and the Church, one of which was the proposed reforms of the health care plan. **Dr. Noel Browne,** appointed as Minister of Health to the Dáil, proposed a "Mother and Child Scheme" to improve a health bill passed by the Fianna Fáil in 1947 and before Browne took office. Emphasizing a need to clarify the position of women in the health scheme, Browne suggested additions to the health bill which made it a state maternal plan operating without a means test: free maternity care to all mothers, childcare up to the age of 16, and an education plan. Browne's plan was innovative, but was criticized for containing aspects of a socialized medical care system reminiscent of the British National Health Service. It was indicted by the Catholic Church for running counter to Church teachings "in direct opposition to the rights of the family and of the individual and...liable to very great abuse."

The last de Valera government, in the late 50s, and its successor under **Sean Lemass** finally boosted the Irish economy by ditching protectionism in favor of attempts to attract foreign investment. In place of the skirmishes—verbal and military—over Constitutional issues that had dominated the 20s, Irish politics had become a contest between two ideologically similar parties who vied with each other to provide local benefits and constituent services.

RECENT HISTORY & CURRENT ISSUES (1960-1996)

The 1960s brought Ireland into unprecedented contact with the outside world, which meant economic growth and a slowdown in emigration. Government developed the economy, improved education, and bolstered tourism. In 1967, the government introduced free secondary education; in 1968, it introduced free university education for those below a certain income level. Tourism became a major industry: Shannon Airport and Bord Fáilte grew big and professional. Ireland entered the European Economic Community (now the **European Union**) in 1972. In 1969, the Troubles in the North disturbed everyone but didn't alter the Republic's political or economic trends. While politicians still expressed nationalist sentiments, few Irish citizens cast votes based on Northern events (see **History and Politics,** p. 362).

Entering a European community and welcoming international visitors inevitably produced a more secular Ireland. **Garret FitzGerald** revamped Fine Gael partly under that banner. During the late 70s and early 80s, he and **Charlie Haughey,** Fianna Fáil's leader, alternated as Taoiseach, producing a bewildering set of economic programs and initiatives periodically interrupted by scandal and events in the North. The **Fianna Fáil** seemed to be caught up always in a more rhetorical Ireland than a pragmatic one. The party emphasized its conception of a United Ireland, but actually made little concrete progress to realistic improvements. Recession in the mid-80s inspired a new wave of emigration and produced more complex economic problems for the party. FitzGerald had the honor of signing the 1985 **Anglo-Irish agreement,** which gave Éire an official (but not legal) role in Northern negotiations. EU membership and EU funds are crucial to Ireland's economy, and greater involvement in the Continent's culture and economy saves the Irish from having to choose between isolation and Great Britain.

In September of 1993, Ireland elected a coalition between Fianna Fáil and the newer, smaller, leftist **Labour Party.** The latter's enormous success in the November '92 election surprised even the party leaders, who had not yet fielded a full slate of candidates. Newly elected Taoiseach **Albert Reynolds** declared that stopping violence in Northern Ireland was his highest priority. Almost miraculously, Reynolds announced the August 1994 cease-fire agreement with **Gerry Adams** and the IRA.

When faced with the appointment for President of the High Court of Ireland, Reynolds ignored the party's coalition with the Labour Party, Tánaiste and Foreign Minister **Dick Spring** of the Labour Party, and their requests for a liberal appointee. When Reynolds appointed conservative Attorney General **Harry Whelehan** as President of the High Court on November 11, 1994, the Labour ministers walked out of the Cabinet Room. Whelehan had been heavily criticized for his lack of action in a case involving an allegedly pedophiliac priest, **Father Brendan Smyth.** Other scandals in the Church implicated the conservative government for protecting priests from legal charges of sexual misconduct and abuse. During the week following the appointment, Fine Gael, led by **John Bruton,** introduced a no-confidence motion against the government in Parliament. Reynolds attempted to defend his appointment of Whelehan, but was secretly pressuring him to resign. When this failed, Reynolds claimed he had been purposely misled by Whelehan. Dick Spring announced that he had discovered that Reynolds himself had withheld information regarding the Father Smyth case. Reynolds was forced to resign. The Labour Party formed a new coalition with Fine Gael, and John Bruton became Taoiseach in mid-December.

Social reform under the Labour Party and its coalition government continues to gather momentum. Although the **women's movement** has been historically tied to political activism, it has become a bona fide movement of its own. The surprise election in 1991 of President **Mary Robinson** was a public turning point in the Republic's progressive liberalism when a forward-looking activist was elected to a typically figurehead position. Robinson, the first woman and first non-Fianna Fáil candidate elected, has taken a vigorous approach in elevating her office above the purely ceremonial role it had lapsed into.

This new liberalism seemed threatened when Ireland's High Court horrified many people in February, 1992, by ruling temporarily that a 14-year-old girl (called **X** in court papers) who said she had been raped could not leave the country to obtain an **abortion.** In 1983 voters had approved, by almost 2:1, a constitutional amendment endorsing "the right to life of the unborn." In November, 1992, voters still said no to legalizing abortion, but did approve a measure to provide "right to information." In March, Parliament voted to affirm the bill, and in May, 1995, the abortion information law won final approval from the High Court, making it legal for centers to give advice on where to go abroad for a safe clinic. Counselors can now arrange for counseling before and after the procedure, and for medical records of women to be forwarded to the physicians involved. Over 5000 Irish women per year travel abroad to seek abortions. Contraception has been legal for over a decade.

A November 24, 1995 referendum legalized **divorce** by a margin of 50.3% to 49.7%, the closest vote in Irish history. The newly passed **Divorce Bill,** which closely follows the terms of the referendum, allows divorce if spouses have lived apart for four years with "no reasonable prospect of a reconciliation." Legislators trod shaky ground when drafting the bill, attempting not to alienate the near-half of the electorate which voted no. The vote highlights the distance between rural and urban Ireland—60% of urban voters backed divorce, while only 43% of rural voters did—and the more significant generation gap—66% of people under 34 and 55% of ages 35 to 49 voted yes, while 57% of ages 50 to 64 and 75% of people over 65 voted no. Ireland was the last Western nation to legalize divorce, but progressivism has clearly wrought changes over the past 10 years. In 1986 two out of three voters chose to keep divorce illegal. This year, despite appeals from Pope John Paul II and Mother Theresa, the 92% Catholic nation did not blindly follow the lead of the Church. The Irish government came under fire for its pro-divorce advertising campaign, which the High Court found to be illegal. The Court did not find, however, that the constitutional wrongdoing had influenced the result of the referendum.

The **gay and lesbian rights** movement is slowly gaining legal ground. In 1980, the first legal challenge to laws against homosexuality was brought before the High Court. Lawyer Mary Robinson (who would be President) represented David Norris, a gay lecturer of Trinity College who challenged the essentially tacit laws. Losing in both the High Court and the Supreme Court, Robinson and Norris appealed to the European Court of Human Rights in Strasbourg. Ireland's government claimed that since the laws were not enforced, there was no need to change them. In 1988, however, the European court ordered Ireland to change its laws.

In June, 1993, the age of consent between gay men was set at age 17. The **Employment Equality Bill,** passed in June, 1996, bans workplace discrimination on grounds including sexual orientation. The proposed **Equal Status Bill** will outlaw discrimination in all public places on bases including sexual orientation and membership of the travelling community. Some publicans and hoteliers fear that they will be unable to bar criminals, drug pushers, or drunkards from their establishments. The Bill, originally set to be published early in 1996, had not been passed by July, 1996, despite statements from politicians promising swift action. The **Refugee Bill,** published in

Travellers

Travellers, Ireland's distinct itinerant population, traditionally roamed the countryside peddling tinware and handmade crafts, trading horses and donkeys, and performing seasonal labor. Post-WWII industrialization eliminated the demand for their wares and services as roads, transportation, and machines improved. Many migrated to urban areas in the 50s, while others still live in rural areas in caravans along the roadsides, in fields, or in "halting sites."

There are an estimated 4000 traveller families (often of as many as 12 children) in Ireland today. Many are concerned with securing safe housing, as many halting sites lack services such as water, sewer, and electricity. Travellers have infant and adult mortality rates twice that of "settled" Irish, an average life expectancy of 50, and many are illiterate since few participate in public education.

Many "settled" Irish stereotype travellers as criminal, intemperate, and lazy, and vigilante groups try to keep travellers out of their neighborhoods by constructing roadblocks and burning caravans. In the "new Ireland," however, travellers can no longer be ignored. Pressure from such groups as the Irish Traveller Movement prompted the government to create a task force on travellers which recently unveiled a five-year plan to provide 3100 accommodation units. The National Union of Journalists deemed offensive labels of travellers such as "tinkers" or "knackers" in reporting. Travellers are routinely denied service in pubs, and 32 hotels recently refused to host a traveller wedding reception, but the passage of the Equal Access Bill (p. 67) would curb discrimination. Travellers may now file job-discrimination claims under the Employment Equality Bill (p. 67).

November of 1995, has a provision enabling foreigners persecuted because of their sexual orientation in their home country to apply for refugee status.

Dublin especially has developed a large and relatively open gay scene, and colleges are becoming more aware of gay issues. A pamphlet offering advice to third-level students about "coming out" at college was recently distributed nationwide, and Galway RTC became the first in Ireland to establish a gay officership and to form a student group. The Centre for Women's Studies at Trinity College Dublin offered for the first time an introductory course to lesbian and gay studies.

As more Irish young people spend time abroad and as more international travelers spend time here, the culture's conservatism slowly cracks. The short-term result is an enormous generation gap and growing disparity between rural and urban areas. The "new Ireland" is an oft-used term, but few can agree on its meaning as the country continues to cringe under stress between a historically sectarian religious fervor and an increasingly secular (and European) human rights movement. Recent scandals in the Catholic Church betray public confidence, and an increase in violent crime highlighted by the murders of **Veronica Guerin** (a leading journalist who exposed powerful crime rings) and Garda Detective **Jerry McCabe** leave many longing for the old, safe days. After the Whelehan appointment and the Father Smyth case, the new government is particularly cautious. However, the hopes for solidarity of a politically and religiously unified Ireland seem to be abandoned.

■ Archaeology

Since the Romans never tore up the countryside, more Stone, Bronze, and Iron Age remains are visible in Ireland than in most European countries. Ireland's real prehistoric past is as complicated as its legendary one, with many waves of invaders and settlers distinguishable by their styles of pottery, weaponry, and burial.

Dolmens are T-shaped or table-shaped groups of three or more enormous stones, with one big flat stone as the roof or tabletop. They might have been used for a number of things, but the best recent guess is that they're a kind of shrine. **Passage graves,** stone-roofed, ornamented, underground hallways, lead past series of rooms containing corpses or cinerary urns. **Stone circles** look like rings of pint-sized gravestones. They mark spots of religious importance, show up on top of passage graves, and sometimes track heavenly paths.

The late Bronze and Iron Age peoples built **ring forts** around their villages, made of stone or of earth. **Souterrains,** underground chambers, were used for storage or for hiding from marauders and were built both inside and outside the ring forts. A **clochán** is a mortarless beehive-shaped stone hut. Mysterious and smaller freestanding monuments are the **ogham** stones, property-marking obelisks which usually record a man's name and that of his father in a non-Latin script made up of dots and slashes. These stones date from the early Christian period. The highest concentration of remains is probably in the Burren, Co. Clare, whose limestone moonscape kept later settlers out. The most famous, best-studied sites are the Hill of Tara and the passage graves of Brú na Bóinne, in Co. Meath.

Missionaries and monks brought new kinds of simple structures: the short *oratories* gave way to viking inspired **round towers,** dozens of which survive. A few now charge admission, but most are just sitting out there in fields and forests, in various states of disrepair. **High crosses,** or **Celtic crosses,** have a circle near the top, which made the cross more palatable to sun-worshipping pagans. These stone crucifixes are as tall as or taller than a human being, and have elaborate carvings on their sides which sometimes illustrates Bible stories or legends of saints.

■ The Irish Language

Irish is a Celtic language closely related to Scottish Gaelic and Manx and more distantly to Breton and Welsh. (Only foreigners call the Irish language "Gaelic.") Irish is spoken exclusively in only a few isolated parts of Ireland, called **gaeltachta.** Some prominent areas are on the Dingle Peninsula, on Cape Clear Island, in the Aran Islands, around the Ring in Co. Waterford, in Connemara in Co. Galway, and in patches of Co. Donegal. Even in the *gaeltachta,* all but a few elderly people *can* speak English—they'd just rather not. Ulster, Munster and Connacht each have dialects of Irish. Ulster Irish, like Donegal's traditional music, has been altered by contact with Scotland and Scottish Gaelic.

In 1600 there were as many speakers of Irish worldwide as of English. The Anglophones had more money and better armies; over the next 250 years more Irish speakers had to learn English to conduct business. Their children and grandchildren grew up speaking English only. Mid-19th-century British efforts to introduce systematic schooling in rural areas resulted in the further spread of English. The Famine hit Irish-speaking areas hardest, and the number of Irish speakers continued to decline.

The **Gaelic League,** founded by **Douglas Hyde** in 1893, was created to inspire enthusiasm for Irish among people who didn't grow up speaking it. The League aimed to spread the everyday use of Irish as part of a project to de-Anglicize the island, just as the Gaelic Athletic Association aimed to overpower English sports. Placing political importance in cultural nationalism, Hyde believed that political revolution could wait and cultural change was the most important thing, although many Gaelic Leaguers disagreed. Gaboodles of adults whose first language was English took to the study of Irish, and the League ballooned, becoming almost trendy. Writers who were bilingual from birth, like **Flann O'Brien,** enjoyed Douglas Hyde's famous mispronunciations. O'Brien's *An Béal Bocht* ("the poor mouth") satirized these new language enthusiasts.

The revolutionaries of 1916 and the political leaders of the 20s were almost without exception excited about reinvigorating the Irish language, and tried to use government to strengthen it: the civil service exam included an Irish test, and there were attempts to require all elementary schools to teach in it. The new policies were resented, and eventually overlooked. Preoccupied with economic development, the people and governments of the postwar Republic ignored Irish for years. The *gaeltachta* shrank, though a government department was "maintaining" them.

The last 15 years have seen more controversy over the fate of Irish. A book called *The Death of the Irish Language* used statistics and demographics to prove that there would soon be no Irish-speakers left. Its author and his methods were immediately attacked by people from other disciplines. While long-term trends in most *gaeltachta* still point to de-population and dispersal, the movement for more Irish-language media and educational requirements should help. There's already a Connemara-based Irish radio station, and agitation for Irish-language TV continues. Schoolchildren of all ages in the Republic are required to take extensive Irish courses, and all Irish universities require a knowledge of the language for admission. Voluntary elementary schools that teach all subjects in Irish are gaining some adherence in urban areas, both in the Republic and among Northern Catholics. A growing movement of **Irish-language summer camps** offer a heavy dose of culture and patriotism (see **Study,** p. 18). You may hear younger English-speakers break into Irish briefly for privacy's sake, although many teens and twenty-somethings resent being forced to learn a language that is essentially useless in the broad, EU market in which they are now immersed. The Irish books read in Irish schools can be a wistful, antiquated series of autobiographies uncharacteristic of the modern Irish-literature community, which produces dozens of novels, poetry collections, and critical essays every year.

In Éire, all government documents must contain both Irish and English. See the **Glossary** (p. 472), for a list of Irish words and phrases.

■ Legends & Folktales

Scholars have been arguing for decades about which of Ireland's legends, folktales, and epics record actual events, and which ones are just good yarns. The vast repertoire includes fairy tales, war stories, revenge tales, and many tales of cattle raids. (Cattle was the ancient Celts' most marketable commodity—slaves and women were valued in cows.) Each story had many "authors" and passed orally down through many generations before someone (most likely a medieval monk) wrote it down. The books we have now often compile surviving bits and pieces of different versions. The Christian monks sometimes altered especially pagan details as they recorded the tales, or created tales of historical saints by appropriating stories of pre-Christian heroes or gods. The legends aren't incredibly accurate as a record of historical events, but they do give an exciting picture of ancient Irish culture: defensive about property (especially cows), warlike, sport-loving, and heavy-drinking.

The stories of the **Túatha de Danann** may have developed to explain the burial mounds left behind by the pre-Celtic Stone Age culture. The Túatha de Danann are a race of beings somewhere between gods and men who live underground, emerging occasionally to aid their descendents, fight with the mortals, and seduce (or when all else fails, abduct) mortal beauties.

The long, famous **Book of Invasions** (*Leabhar Gabhála Éireann*) claims to be a historical record of the cultures and armies that have invaded Ireland, from Noah's daughter, Cesair, up to the Celts. The tales locate the Irish peoples' ancestry in the Greek islands. Nemed, a Scythian, became lost at sea after pursuing a mysterious tower of gold which rose out of the waves. After a year and a half of wandering, he and his ships landed in Ireland, until the next wave of settlers arrived...and the next, and the next, in wave upon wave of invasions (hence the name). Three clans of Nemed's descendants survived: one settled in the northern Greek islands, studied druidic arts, and became the Túatha de Danann. Another group was enslaved in Greece but eventually escaped, returned to Ireland as the **Fir Bolg,** and fought the Túatha de Danann. Each of the early waves of invaders had to deal with the fierce and mysterious indigenous people, the Formorians. These stories aren't the oldest Irish legends, but they do claim to have taken place first.

The earliest tales of the Túatha de Danann describe them as ordinary warriors and chieftains—only when fighting other races do their supernatural powers arise. Poets living in the chieftains' households invented the art of verse satire. These poets, and sometimes ordinary folk, have the power to curse and lay a *geis,* a magic compulsion or prohibition. When the Túatha de Danann retreat to the Other World, leaving Éire to the Celts, the Celtic heroes acquire some of the gods' ways and skills.

Several "cycles" or collections of tales narrate the entire life story of a hero. One of the largest is the **Ulster Cycle,** the adventures of King Conchobar of Ulster and his clan, the **Ulaid.** His archenemies are Queen Medbh of Connacht and her husband Ailill. Ulster and Connacht are continually raiding each other and exacting revenge. (In reality, the Laigin of Leinster were the arch-enemies of the Ulaid.) Ulster's champion is **Cú Chulainn** (COO-hullin), the king's nephew, whose adventures begin at the age of five. Cú Chulainn falls in love with Emer, whose father disapproves. He sends Cú Chulainn to train with the Amazonian warrior Scathach, hoping that the Amazon will kill his potential son-in-law. Instead, she teaches him the arts of war and shows him how to wield the Gae Bolga, the sun-god's destructive spear.

The central tale of the Ulster Cycle is the **Táin bo Cuailnge** (Cattle Raid of Cooley). In the tale, Medbh and Ailill's bedtime banter turns to comparing their possessions (as it often does), and Queen Medbh is alarmed to discover that her husband is richer than she is—by one bull. Determined to surpass him, she decides first to borrow, and then to steal, the most famous bull in the country, the Donn of Cooley. She assembles an army to capture the bull and invades Ulster when all the Ulster warriors are disabled by the curse of Queen Macha (see, **Queen Macha,** p. 401). Only the 17-year-old Cú Chulainn is immune. He strikes a deal with the Queen, and fights her warriors in single combat one by one for an entire season. He beats them all, but the Connacht soldiers invade anyway and capture the Donn. The Ulstermen recover, invade Connacht, and recapture their bull. In the process the Donn escapes and kills Aillil's bull. On its triumphant return, however, the Ulster animal's heart bursts, and it dies.

Other cycles include **Tales of the Traditional Kings,** and the **Cycle of Finn, Ossian, and their Companions.** Finn McCool, or Fionn MacCumaill, leads a group of heroes that includes his son, Ossian, and his grandson, Oscar. In some stories, he is

Irish Wakes: in the midst of life we are in death.

The purpose of a wake was to pray for the dead and to sympathize with the relatives of the dead person the night before the actual funeral. Besides mourning, the wake gave the family time to make sure the person was actually dead. For centuries in Europe, a wake was also a "waking" of the dead where the deceased would be given a final party in his or her honor. With the rise of Christianity, the wild wake died out on the continent but persisted in Ireland until the end of the last century. A typical Irish wake began solemnly enough as women would say prayers over the body and keen in sorrow. But a wake was also a huge social occasion with games, storytelling, drinking, eating, and more drinking. Throughout the night, the deceased would be treated as if alive—a drink would be placed by their casket and card games were invented so the dead could be dealt a hand. As the evening wore on and the guests got drunker and rowdier, the corpse might be taken from the casket and danced with in turn. Wild wakes were not intended to show disrespect for the dead or the clergy (who strongly forbade them). Rather an Irish wake was a deeply rooted custom of celebrating life in the house and keeping death waiting at the doorstep.

more or less a mercenary. In others, he is a king or a giant with supernatural powers and saves Ireland from monsters. In the **Pursuit of Diarmuid and Gráinne,** Finn has grown old and unattractive, but is betrothed to the young Gráinne. She meets him, has no wish to marry him, and decides to elope with Diarmuid, one of Finn's younger companions. Diarmuid refuses, but Gráinne lays a *geis* on him to flee with her. Whenever Finn catches up to the couple, Diarmuid deliberately kisses her, driving her betrothed into a jealous frenzy. After 16 years of pursuit, Finn seems willing to be reconciled: he invites Diarmuid to help hunt a famous wild boar. Having left his trusty spear at home, Diarmuid finds the creature impervious to all his weapons. The boar gores him. Diarmuid dies, and Gráinne marries Finn. Various forests and caves throughout Ireland claim to have been places at which Diarmuid and Gráinne rested during the pursuit.

Literati (including W.B. Yeats) have periodically compiled Ireland's **folktales.** Some stories involve the *sí (*sometimes spelled *sidhe*), who are residents of the Other World underground or undersea. **Leprechauns** are a late, degenerate version of the *sí,* who themselves are supposedly the disempowered remnants of the Túatha de Danann. Other stories are simply about ordinary folks and their pranks and troubles. For more myths and tales, try *Folktales of Ireland,* edited by Sean O'Sullivan; Yeats's *Fairy and Folk Tales of Ireland, Ancient Irish Tales,* edited by Cross and Slover, or *The Irish Literary Tradition,* by J.E.C. Williams and P.K. Ford.

■ Literature

BEFORE 1600

In early Irish society, language was equal to action. What the bard (directly from the Irish *baird*) sang about battles, valor, and lineage was the only record a chieftain had by which to make decisions. Descending from Druidic tradition, poetry and politics were so intertwined that the *fili*, trained poets, and *breatheamh,* judges of the Brehon Laws, were often the same people. The poet-patron relationship was fairly simple and symbiotic—the poet sang long praise poems about his lord and in return received his three meals and a roof above his head.

Toward the end of the first millennium, the oral tradition of the bards ceded some ground to the monastic penchant for writing it all down. The monastic settlements of pre-Norman Ireland compiled enormous annals of myth, legend, and history. Divorced from the courts and their poetic economy, the monks created lasting monuments to old Irish prose. An established pagan tradition and the introduction of Christianity created a beautiful tension in Irish literature between recalling old bardic forms and incorporating a new worldview. This tension, it could be argued, exists in Irish literature to this day and is expressed fully in *Sweeney Astray,* the story of a pagan king who turns into a bird after being cursed by a monk. After the Norman incursions and the decline of the monasteries, feudal courts run by the Old English competed with Gaelic ones in hiring and maintaining traditional poets.

1600-1800

After the Battle of Kinsale, in 1601, a group of Irish writers, of whom **Geoffrey Keating** was the most famous, predicted an imminent collapse of Irish language and culture. A majority of the works written in Irish at this time lament the state of Ireland and draw heavily on the traditional trope of Ireland as a captive woman. **Daíbhí Ó Bruadhair's** "The Shipwreck" laments the Treaty of Limerick. **Aogan Ó Rathaille** and **Eoghan Rua Ó Sulleabhain** were two of the period's increasingly despairing and impoverished poets. Ireland in the early 1700s had enough bilingual readers to support "macaronic" works like **Seán Ó Neachtain's** *The Story of Eamon Cleary,* whose unusual, often punning effects depended on a mixture of English and Irish. Joyce would later copy such techniques.

Jonathan Swift (1667-1745), for decades the Dean of St. Patrick's Cathedral in Dublin, towered above his Anglo-Irish contemporaries with his mix of moral indignation, bitterness, and wit. Besides his masterpiece, *Gulliver's Travels,* Swift wrote political pamphlets and essays decrying English exploitation (and defending the Protestant Church of Ireland). "A Modest Proposal" satirically suggests that the overpopulated and hungry native Irish sell their children as food. After his death, Swift's works dominated the Irish literary scene for the second half of the 18th century.

1800-1880

The Act of Union (1801) was a death knell for Irish writing, since the Anglo-Irish gentry could no longer afford to support the arts. Still, **Maria Edgeworth** *(Castle Rackrent),* **Gerald Griffin, John Banim,** and **William Carleton** wrote realistic, still-read novels about the gentry and peasantry which attempt to define the nature of rural Irish society. Many of these books depict peasants plotting against their selfish and rich Irish masters up in the mansion. Almost as soon as these novelists died, however, their works were rejected by the **Young Ireland** movement, which decided that these writers had given in, both in language and in form, to the demands of English writers and critics. The books were, essentially, too middle-class and perpetuated a false stereotype of Irish peasants.

While there was a proliferation of both poets and literary journals, few poets could eke out a living by writing alone. (**William Allingham,** for example, wrote poetry and acted as a customs agent.) Even fewer poets became famous. In order to survive, many joined groups so that their work would be published in journals, but had to conform their views and objectives to those of the group. Others remained distinct from any classification but thereby relinquished any chances for fame.

Through original writings and frequent translations, three main attitudes toward poetry and language evolved in Ireland. The first tried to soften nationalist sentiment with a Victorian respectability—**Thomas Moore** wrote popular lyrics along these lines. Another vein of poetry adopted a militant attitude, propounding outright rebellion against English language, culture, and politics in order to maintain the Irish versions. Poets of this type often wrote for *The Nation,* a Dublin-based periodical. One of the main contributors to the journal was **James Clarence Mangan,** a poet and prolific translator. Unfortunately, his knowledge of Irish was far from perfect, which resulted in rather creative translations. A third group of poets tried to find a middle way by merging English words and an Irish spirit or essence. A Belfast Unionist, **Samuel Ferguson,** used poetry and energetic translations to link Irish and Catholic with English and Protestant to form a single, shared identity.

The Famine greatly affected approaches to literature in Ireland. Two Irish economists, in analyzing the tragedy, made major advances in political economy. **Isaac Butt**

Maria Edgeworth (1768-1849)

Maria Edgeworth (1768-1849) was the major figure in the Irish literary world after Swift and before Shaw and Yeats. A contemporary of Jane Austen, Edgeworth's early didactic works are greatly influenced by her father's rational and utilitarian way of thinking. Her later works, which depict regional life, were largely determined by his decision to relocate to the family land in Ireland (rural Edgeworthstown, Co. Longford.), which revealed the life of provincial, Irish peasants to Maria. Her most famous and lasting work, published anonymously in 1800, was titled *Castle Rackrent, An Hibernian Tale: Taken from the Fact, and from the Manners of the Irish Squires, Before the Year 1782*. The central concern is the responsibility of landowners to their tenants.

Much of Edgeworth's extensive body of mostly historical fiction is typical of its age. She began her career with ideas about the connection between moral worth and social position. Some stories reveal a subtle romantic preoccupation with the achievement of personal integrity through solitude. But her innovations and the anomalies in her writing add a twist to an author otherwise representative of her era. Edgeworth was a woman in the midst of men. She, with her family, moved to Ireland when most people went the other way. She also realized, as few at this time did, that there existed a British social reality, not entirely separable into England and Ireland. Finally, Maria Edgeworth paved the way for future literary journals by raising the question of a compromise between the modern and the antiquarian. This legacy, more than any other, substantially determined the concerns of later writers, including those of the Revival.

argued against the falsity of a Union which claimed political unity but refused unified economic aid. **John Elliot Cairnes** blasted the idea of *laissez faire*, which he claimed was only applicable to those countries whose economic organization and division of land imitated those in England.

The "Young Ireland" group, which originally coalesced around **Thomas Davis,** drifted farther toward the left after the Famine. Davis, an idealist, wanted to reform a unified Irish cultural identity reliant on the Irish language. But he failed to realize that Irish culture was intertwined with both politics and economy. Thus his theories seem to ignore the centrality of the Famine, alienating both readers and authors. The Famine induced Irish authors to put economic questions ahead of political affairs, and political affairs ahead of cultural concerns. But their blatantly political poems were rather shallow and obvious, suitable for the outrage which immediately followed the Famine. The future Irish Revival would reverse this artistic trend.

The late 19th century saw the removal of a number of talented authors to England. Many emigrated because it was easier to make a living by writing in London than in Ireland. Dublin-born **Oscar Wilde** moved to London and set up as a cultivated aesthete to write one novel and several sparklingly witty plays, including *The Importance of Being Earnest*. Prolific playwright **George Bernard Shaw** (1856-1950) was also born in Dublin but moved to London in 1876 where he became an active socialist. Never forgetting his Irish roots, Shaw used it in the service of socialist ideals, as in *John Bull's Other Island*, which depicts the increasing hardships of the Irish peasant laborer. Shaw himself identified much of his writing as Irish, in form if not always in content: "When I say I am an Irishman I mean that my language is the English of Swift and not the unspeakable drivel of the mid-19th century newspapers." Shaw won the Nobel Prize for Literature in 1925 for a body of work which includes *Arms and the Man, Candida, Man and Superman*, and *Pygmalion*.

1880-1939

Following on the heels of these literary movements and counter-movements, a vigorous and enduring effort known today as the **Irish Literary Revival** took over the scene. The Irish poetic and dramatic traditions were reconceived. For almost an entire century, Irish writers' central concern had been a reaction, either cultural or political, against England. It became the task of literature to discover the real Ireland (not always in reference to England), whether Gaelic or Anglicized (or both).

Interest in the Irish language suddenly revived. **Peig Sayers'** *Peig,* a mournful book about growing up on the Blaskets, was written during the revival and is still read in high schools today. This memoir, like others written by Blasket Islanders, mourns the decline of Gaelic culture and language.

The Irish Literary Revival began with attempts to record peasant stories. By means of the old tales and traditions, a new elite would create a distinctively Irish literature in English. The writers of the Revival considered their own works to be chapters in a book of Irish identity—it was just such "Irishness" that literature was supposed to reveal. Affected by the revivalists, and by the Sligo of his boyhood, **William Butler Yeats's** (1865-1939) early poems create a dreamily rural Ireland of loss, longing, and legend. His early work from *Crossways* (1889) to *In the Seven Woods* (1904), won Yeats worldwide fame and the Nobel Prize.

The turbulence of 1914, 1916, and after enabled Yeats to recreate himself as a poet of difficulty, power, and violence. "Easter 1916" described the sudden transformation the Easter rebels brought to the Irish national self-image: "All changed, changed utterly/ A terrible beauty is born." With his friends and his longtime unrequited love Maud Gonne caught up in rebel activity, Yeats was finally forced into marriage with George Hyde-Lees. Yeats then bought and renovated a stone tower, Thoor Ballylee. The tower became a symbol in an idiosyncratic and mystical system which appears in his last two decades of poems. From *The Tower* (1928) to the posthumous *Last Poems* (1939) Yeats was at his of peak of verbal invention.

Yeats's lifelong friend and colleague, **Lady Augusta Gregory** (1852-1932), wrote 40 plays as well as a number of translations, poems, and essays. She began her career by collecting the folktales and legends of Galway. Soon, the Abbey Theatre Movement became her main concern. While helping other playwrights revise, Gregory discovered her own skill as a writer of dialogue. Her comedies, including *Spreading the News* and *The Rising of the Moon,* were most successful. A combination of reality and myth-making marks Gregory's work. By the end of the 19th century, Gregory was a staunch nationalist and spent many of her last years defending the codicil in her son's will which left his collection of art to Ireland.

The **Abbey Theatre Movement,** spearheaded by Yeats and Lady Gregory, aimed "to build up a Celtic and Irish school of dramatic literature." But conflict almost immediately arose between various contributors. Was this new body of drama to be written in verse or prose and in the realistic or the fantastic and heroic mode? Ideally, the plays would be written in Irish, but practically they needed to be written in English. A sort of compromise was found in the work of John Millington Synge, who wrote English plays that were perfectly Irish in essence. Padraic Colum wrote in plainer language about more timely issues and emotions. Finally, Sean O'Casey achieved a synthesis of urban realism and heroic poetry.

Playwrights resonated with their audiences by writing with an ear for English as it is spoken by people who grew up hearing Irish. **John Millington Synge** (1871-1909) spent much of his early years traveling and living in Paris. He was a multi-faceted man who "wished to be at once Shakespeare, Beethoven, and Darwin." During one of his many stays in Ireland, Synge met Yeats, who advised that he look for inspiration on the Aran Islands. This advice, which Synge followed in 1898, led him to write *The Aran Islands,* a documentary of life on the islands. His experiences also gave him the subject matter for writing his black comedy *The Playboy of the Western World,* which destroys the pastoral myth about Irish peasantry and humorously portrays a rural society divided into classes. The play's first production instigated riots. **Sean O'Casey,** (1880-1964) a later playwright who also knew how to use Irish-English, created a similar uproar with *The Plough and Stars.* The play depicts the Easter Rebellion, and nationalism, in an unflattering light and sentimentalizes the urban poor. O'Casey eventually emigrated to England.

James Joyce (1882-1941) attacked the myth of the timeless, classless country peasant by a different tactic. This most famous of Irish authors was born and educated in

Dublin, but spent much of his time after 1904 on the continent. One of his earlier works, *A Portrait of the Artist as a Young Man,* comes nearest to autobiography. *Dubliners,* a collection of linked short stories which results in a novelesque work, is his most accessible writing. Most of the stories describe movement out of the city as being liberating, in contrast to most urban literature. *Ulysses,* Joyce's revolutionary novel, appeared in 1922. It minutely chronicles one day in the life of the antihero, Leopold Bloom, a middle class man living his life in a stagnating Dublin. Its structure follows that of Homer's *Odyssey*—hence the title. Joyce's last book, *Finnegans Wake,* is so dependent on allusions and puns that some people find it unreadable. Those who can make sense of it often see it as his masterpiece.

Yeats ignored everyday life and suffering in Ireland in pursuit of a deeper vision. The Northern Protestant poet **Louis MacNeice** (1907-1963) compensated with a lyric persona both humane and skeptical. He took no part in the sectarian politics. His "Valediction" masterfully attacks an idealized Ireland. **Patrick Kavanaugh** also debunked a mythical Ireland in poems such as "The Great Hunger." Other poets wrote works in which technical elegance was the redeeming feature. They attempted to combine the popular ballad with aesthetics (the archaic and the modern), an effort which failed largely because there was no appropriate language. Poets like **Patrick Pearse, Padraic Colum, Seamus O'Sullivan,** and **Thomas MacDonagh** tried their hand at various language and forms, but none seemed totally suitable for the uniquely Irish dilemma between past and present, Gaelic and English.

The year 1929 brought the **Censorship of Publications Act,** which severely restricted the development of Irish literature. This Act was part of an Irish Ireland movement, provincial and Catholic in its beliefs. After the heroism of the Civil War and Republicanism, Ireland had suddenly become conservative. In the journal which he edited, the poet **AE** fought against such repression and tried to retain pre-Civil War idealism. He saw the prevailing conservative and Catholic social climate as one of reaction to the romanticism of the pre-Civil War period. But rather than giving in to such provincialism, he envisioned and propounded a broad cultural synthesis which would include various cultures and religions, not just those which Ireland's new government accepted.

1939-THE PRESENT

Samuel Beckett, a Trinity graduate who fled Ireland for Paris and never came back, is thought of as the last product of Irish modernism. His three novels (*Molloy, Malone Dies,* and *The Unnameable*), world-famous plays (*Waiting for Godot, Endgame),* and bleak prose poems convey a deathly pessimism about language, society, and life. Unsurprisingly, Beckett's influence has been felt most outside Ireland.

Reviving the notion, first developed by AE, of the writer as social critic, **Seán O'Faoláin** founded *The Bell* in 1940, which he insisted would espouse no restrictive ideology. In the artistic vein of the time, the *Bell's* editor pleaded for "honesty" and "realism." O'Faoláin wanted to search for Ireland wherever he could, not just in a Catholic and Gaelic nationalism.

At the same time, the short story was becoming a popular, successful, and sophisticated art form in Ireland. More palatable and often more comprehensible than the contemporary works of Beckett, these stories frequently took the common lives of Irish men and women as their theme, depicting individual liberty and energy as victims of oppressive provincialism. **Frank O'Connor, Bernard McLaverty, Sean O'Faolain,** and **Edna O'Brien** all achieved some overseas recognition for their short stories. **Flann O'Brien** let loose an unrestricted literary inventiveness which earned him an international reputation that has lasted to this day. Unlike other writers of the time, he set almost all his work in Dublin. O'Brien tried to provide a comic answer to Joyce and to set himself in opposition to a cultural and linguistic lethargy: *At Swim-Two-Birds* is a book-length prank in which an author's characters conspire to keep the author asleep so that the characters can do what they please.

Poets went largely unrecognized; most became introverts and happily succumbed to provincialism. One of the rare exceptions, **Padraic Fallon** (1905-1974), continued to combine political and religious topics in his poetry but avoided the plague of nationalism, as did **Charles Donnelly.** The idea of the existence of a common humanity became the inspiration in his poetry. While many poets, like Louis MacNiece, condemned Ireland's neutrality in WWII as cowardice, others remained entirely nationalist and unconcerned with anything but Ireland itself.

Stimulated by O'Brien, the Irish novel developed. **Brian Moore's** *The Emperor of Ice Cream* is an appealing coming-of-age story set in wartime Belfast, and **Roddy Doyle** wrote the trilogy which led to the films *The Commitments* and *The Snapper.*

After 1950, Irish poetry suddenly began to free itself from a stifling provincialism. This movement involved an increased contact with the continent: playwright **Brendan Behan** and poet **John Montague** both went to Paris. Yet Irish writing was still unsure of its place in the world, signaled by an increased obsession with the father-son relationship. Living in the backwash of the Revival and the Civil War, these new Irish poets questioned their inheritance. The answer that presented itself was a new version of Ireland that was a parody of the old one.

But the same problems persisted. Authors were still trying to bridge the gap between Gaelic and Anglo-Irish themes and languages. As an affirmation of the former, Irish language poetry revived. **Michael Hartnett** began to write solely in Irish. **Nuala ní Dhomhnaill** is a living poet whose public readings are generally bilingual. In contrast to the pessimism non-speakers associate with the Irish language, her work brings refrigerators, feminism, and smart bombs into proximity with the *Sí.* The younger poet **Biddy Jenkinson** refuses to authorize any translation of her work into English, although it has been rendered into French. The preeminent Irish-language novel is **Máirtín Ó Cadhain's** *Cré na Cille* (Churchyard Clay), which is a dialogue between corpses in a graveyard.

Others, like **Máirtín Ó Direáin** (a modernist writer) and **Seán Ó Riordain,** tried to incorporate the English modes into the Irish tradition. **Derek Mahon** saw the poet as an anthropologist (rather than a student of Gaelic inheritance or of Republicanism). He was interested in the common elements that humans of all cultures share. Most contemporary poetry is intensely private. Although some poets (**Padraid Fiacc** and **Tom Paulin**) are directly political and almost propagandistic, most treat the issue from a distant, mundane, every-day perspective. **Frank Ornsby,** for example, writes poetry devoid of political conflict that celebrates the rituals of domestic life.

Born in rural Co. Derry, **Seamus Heaney,** who won the Noble Prize for Literature in 1995, is the most prominent living Irish poet. Concentrating on bogs and earth, Heaney writes in an anti-pastoral mode. His fourth book, *North* (1975), tackles the Troubles head-on. He was part of the **Field Day movement,** led by Derry poet and critic **Seamus Deane,** which produced what was billed as the definitive anthology of Irish writing (although it's come under heavy fire for its relative lack of women writers). Heaney's contemporary, who also writes in a non-political vein, is **Paul Muldoon,** whose tools are a corrosive self-skepticism, supple couplets, and a terrific ear for weird rhymes. Influenced by MacNeice and Auden, Muldoon reflects the cosmopolitan consciousness of Ireland's new wave of high cultural aspirations. Yet his rhymes and forms show the influence of the Irish language. **Ciaran Carson** uses Muldoon-like ironies in long-lined poems that tell stories about the working-class culture of Belfast and the rural North. **Eavan Boland** is one of the few modern Irish poets who has attempted to capture the experience of middle-class, suburban women. **Medbh McGuckian** is one of few modern, successful female Irish authors.

The Field Day Movement also gave its name to a successful theater company. Native playwrights include politically conscious **Frank McGuinness** and **Brian Friel,** whose *Dancing at Lughnasa* was a Broadway hit. Important critics and essayists are **Conor Cruise O'Brien,** a former diplomat who writes about history, literature, politics—hell, everything. **Denis Donoghue's** *We Irish* is a vigorous, skeptical lit-crit grab-bag. For the provocative **Declan Kiberd,** Ireland is a "postcolonial" society more like India than like England.

■ Music & Film

Irish traditional music is alive and well, as is Irish folk music, but the two can mean different things. "Folk music" often means singing with acoustic guitar accompaniment, whether it's Irish (the Clancy Brothers, Christy Moore, Luka Bloom) or not (Joni Mitchell). "Traditional music" or "trad," on the other hand, means the centuries-old array of dance rhythms, cyclic melodies, and embellishments which has passed down through generations of traditional musicians. It can be written down, but that's not its primary means of transmission. Indeed, a traditional musician's training consists largely of listening and imitating others. The tunes and forms (hornpipe, reel, etc.) are the skeletons around which the players in a trad session build the music. The same tune will produce a different result every session.

TRADITIONAL MUSIC

Irish traditional music is encountered in mainly two forms. It is often heard as impromptu sessions in pubs in the evenings or can be found in recordings, which are becoming more numerous. Well-known recording artists include **Altan, De Danann,** and the **Chieftains.** Trad music is also, though rarely, performed at concerts. *Let's Go* lists many pubs with regular trad sessions, but you'll find the best music by asking local trad enthusiasts. Pubs in Cos. Clare, Kerry, Galway, and Sligo are especially strong. If you want a guarantee that you'll hear lots of traditional music, find a *fleadh*. These are big gatherings of trad musicians whose officially scheduled sessions often spill over into nearby pubs. **Comhaltas Ceoltóirí Éireann**, the national traditional music association, organizes *fleadhs*. Write or call them at 32 Belgrave Sq., Monkstown, Co. Dublin (tel. (01) 280 0295).

For centuries the most common way to "listen" to trad music was to dance to it. This isn't true anymore. Spontaneous traditional dancing is fading fast, replaced by formal, rigid competitions where traditional dancers are graded, like ballroom dancers. *Céilís,* where attendants participate in traditional Irish set-dancing, do still take place occasionally in many Irish towns, but are planned in advance.

The instruments with which Irish trad music is most frequently played are the fiddle, the simple flute, the concertina or hand-held accordion, the tin whistle, and the *uilleann* pipes (elbow pipes). These pipes are similar to bagpipes, but pumped with a bellows held under the arm and are more melodic than the Scottish instrument. To play traditional music well requires tremendous practice and skill, though the techniques have little in common with those of European classical music; it's often said that training in one is an impediment to playing the other. The harp, Ireland's national symbol, is rarely encountered in live trad music now, since it's big and hard to lug around. It is, however, still frequently heard in recordings.

The *bodhrán*, (BOUR-ohn) a hand-held Goldstein drum, wasn't seen as a legitimate instrument until the 60s, when the influential **Sean Ó Riada** of the Chieftains introduced it in an effort to drive rock and jazz drumming out. Today, the *bodhrán* has skillful specialists. It is played either with both ends of a stick or with the bare hand. To observers, it looks easy, but playing it well takes practice and patience.

Purists get in heated arguments about what constitutes "traditional" singing. A style of unaccompanied vocals called *sean-nós* ("old-time") is more talked about than heard, though everyone says it sounds great. This style of nasal singing descends from the ancient practice of keening. It requires the vocalist to sing each verse of a song differently, either by using embellishments or varied techniques or different sounds, like clicks. Sessions in pubs will sometimes alternate fast-paced traditional instrumental music with guitar- or mandolin-accompanied folk songs.

FOLK & ROCK MUSIC

In Ireland there is surprisingly little distinction between music types—above all a fine musician is a fine musician and uses material from a variety of sources. This cross-pollination produces fabulous live music and a number of successful folk musicians who draw on traditional elements. Chief among this group, the inspiring and hugely popular **Christy Moore** has been called the Bob Dylan of Ireland. The ballads and anthems that Moore made popular now form something of a pub-singalong canon—hardly a late-night session goes by without someone's moving rendition of "Ride On," "City of Chicago," or the lament "Irish Ways and Irish Laws." Other popular groups include Christy's old bands, **Moving Hearts** and **Planxty**.

This lack of distinction between different genre has had mixed results. **Van Morrison's** inspirations included American soul and blues. Submerging them into Celtic "soul," he managed to make them his own. **Horslips** became hugely popular in the 70s by trying to merge trad and rock forms, but wound up shuffling uneasily between the two. **Thin Lizzy** tried to Gaelicize early heavy metal, while a succession of groups, like **Clannad,** started out trad and slowly became bad rockers. The **Saw Doctors** and **Lir** live life on the edge of the rock/trad duality. Maybe the best hybridizers were the **Pogues,** London-based Irishmen whose famously drunken, punk-damaged folk songs won a wide international audience. New York-based Irish emigres **The Black 47** recently tried for Poguish success by fusing trad with rap.

The worldwide punk rock explosion, which began in the late 1970s, had brilliant effects in Belfast, where **Stiff Little Fingers** spit forth three years of excellent anthems (followed by 10 years of bad hard rock). Most Northern punks rebelled against their over-serious parents by emphasizing the fun part of rock and roll. They tried to create, through their songs, the de-politicized youth culture that had existed in England and America since the 50s. Starjets, Rudi, Protex, Big Self, and the silly Radio Stars emphasized this approach in Belfast, but its most successful advocates were Derry's **Undertones.**

Punk was slower to happen in Dublin, though the **Boomtown Rats** (fronted by future Live Aid guy Bob Geldof) tried. A bit later, so did **U2:** from the adrenaline-soaked promise of 1980's *Boy,* the band slowly ascended into the rock stratosphere. Now, abandoned by their older, loyal fans who fell in love with their early rock style, U2 plays to media- and techno-inspired TV screens as in *Zooropa.* The smartest Irish popsters of the 80s, bands like the **Slowest Clock** and the folky **Stars of Heaven,** went almost nowhere commercially, while plenty of U2-derived bands have raced up and down British and American charts on the basis of their perceived Celtic aura. Distortion-masters **My Bloody Valentine** started in Ireland, though like the Pogues, or John Lydon, or U2, they moved to London before becoming significant. **Sinéad O'Connor** used Gaelic themes and reeling fiddles in at least one of her hits, "I Am Stretched on Your Grave." **The Golden Horde** are a talented, unpretentious punk band who still perform. Lately, the lowercase **cranberries** (from Limerick) have hit big in the U.S. New risers in the U.S. folk/rock scene are **Mary Black, the Chieftains,** and **Sharon Shannon.** Meanwhile, the rock press has christened Cork a hot spot; its flagship bands, the **Frank and Walters** and the **Sultans of Ping F.C.,** are not exactly revolutionary, but a hubbub of new 'zines and clubs in Cork, Dublin, and the Southeast may herald a more inventive, post-U2 era in Irish rock.

FILM

Hollywood has known about Ireland's untouched expanses of green, appealing small towns, and comparatively low labor costs since the early 70s, when movies set elsewhere were sometimes made here. In the last five-odd years, however, the Irish government has begun to encourage a truly Irish film industry. An excellent art cinema has opened in Dublin, and there's an office two blocks away to encourage budding moviemakers. Based on novels by Roddy Doyle, *The Commitments* (directed by an American, Alan Parker) and *The Snapper* made audiences snap their fingers and weep with stories of kids from the depressed North Side of Dublin who form a band to play American soul music. *The Crying Game's* tight plot, tortured hero, IRA theme and ballyhooed surprise-middle (well, slightly below-middle) won it huge audiences as well as critical praise. Some claim that it would have won an Oscar had it been released by a major American studio rather than by a private distributor. The film took place entirely in England and Northern Ireland. Its director, **Neil Jordan,** resides near Dublin. More recently, Irish writers and studios have produced **Widow's Peak** and **In the Name of the Father,** in which Daniel Day-Lewis expressed the Troubles in Northern Ireland. **Circle of Friends** chronicles a typical love story, circa 1950, while trying simultaneously to comment on Irish rural and political life.

Last year's **Dublin Lesbian and Gay Film Festival,** held during the first week of August, was the biggest in its three-year history, with 21 features and shorts shown in the Irish Film Centre. The **Dublin Film Festival** also had a strong showing of gay-and lesbian-themed films, including **Ballot Measure 9, Stonewall,** and **L'Attraction.**

▓ Media

Ireland supports eight national **dailies** with a combined circulation of around 1.5 million. The largest of these are the *Irish Independent* and the *Irish Times.* The *Independent* tends to be conservative, while the *Times* is liberal. *The Herald* is an evening daily with a tabloid format which tends to be more moderate. There are five or so national Sunday papers. The *Sunday Business Post* gives the latest on the corporate world. **Tabloids** such as the *Daily Mirror,* the *Irish Sun,* the *Irish Star,* and the *Sporting News* offer low-level coverage with an emphasis on stars, scandals, and sports, and the occasional topless picture. A large number of regional papers offer more in-depth local news; the largest is the Cork *Examiner.*

The national radio and television service is **Radio Telefís Éireann (RTE).** Most of the country has cable service with access to the BBC and other independent British channels. Satellite stations are available via cable in Dublin and Cork. Televisions are in 96% of Irish households, while 70% have a telephone.

▓ Sports

Ireland is mad for two sports: hurling and football. For many Irish, these games are the reason that spring changes into summer. Beer bellies are burned off over the last mile or two to the stadium and welded back on again after the game, win or lose. All 32 counties take place in the knockout rounds of the two sports' "All Ireland" Championships, but only two make it to either final in September. Many a day would be wasted trying to find a farmer, businessman, or sheep unaware of his or her county's progress. Attending a pub the day of that county's game will leave you happy, deaf, drunk, and counting down the days to the next round. Most traditional Irish sports, such as Gaelic football, hurling, and rugby, are modern developments of contests fought between whole clans or parishes across expanses of countryside.

Hurling, Éire's national pastime, is best imagined as a blend of lacrosse and field hockey. This fast and dangerous-looking game is first recorded to have been played in the 13th century. The game is named after the stick with which it is played, called a "hurley," or *caman.* The hurley is like a hockey stick with a shorter and wider blade and is used to hit the ball along the ground or overhead. Sides of 15 members each try to score a "point" by hitting the ball over the 8 ft.-high crossbar of the goalposts. A "goal" is worth three points, and is scored by hitting the ball under the crossbar. The ball, or *sliothar,* is leather-covered and can be caught for hitting but not thrown. The ball may be carried or juggled along on the stick.

Gaelic football is the Irish version of American football. Leagues exist mainly in Ireland and the United States. At each end of the field is a set of goalposts, but below the crossbar there is a net resembling a soccer net. One point is scored for putting the goal over the crossbar between the posts, three for netting it. The ball is shorter and fatter than the American football, and can be dribbled, punched, or kicked, but not thrown. Teams of 15 each play two 30-minute periods.

▓ Pubs and Food

The pub is in a sense the living room of the Irish household. Locals of all ages, from every social milieu, head to the public house for conversation, food, singing and dancing, and lively *craic* (crack), an Irish word meaning simply "a good time." Though the clientele of the average public house is predominantly male, female travelers can feel comfortable here, especially on the weekends in urban areas when students swarm the town. People aren't normally looking for much other than communal talk and drink. You might have your ears talked off, however, especially by amateur *seanachaí* (SHAN-ukh-ee), traveling storytellers. In the evening, some pubs host traditional music. Local and traveling musicians, toting fiddles, guitars, *bodhráns* (a shallow, one-sided drum), and whistles, drop in around 9:30pm to start impromptu trad sessions.

Pubs in the Republic are generally open Monday to Saturday from 10:30am to 11:30pm (11pm in winter), and Sunday from 12:30 to 2pm and 4 to 11pm (closed 2-4pm due to Holy hours). Pubs in the North tend to be open Monday to Saturday from 11:30am to 11pm, and Sunday from 12:30 to 2:30pm and 7 to 10pm. Some pubs close for a few hours on weekday afternoons as well, particularly in rural areas. Pub lunches are usually served from Monday to Saturday, 12:30 to 2:30pm, while soup, soda bread, and sandwiches are served all day. Children are often not allowed in pubs after 7pm. The legal drinking age in Ireland and Northern Ireland is 18 (and not likely to be checked).

Beer is the default drink in Irish pubs. Cocktails are an oddity found mainly in American-style bars and discos, and most pubs stock only a few token bottles of wine. Beer comes in three varieties: **lagers** (blond, fizzy brews served cold, a bit weaker than ales or stouts), **ales** (slightly darker, more bitter, and sometimes served a bit warmer than lagers), and **stouts** (thick, dark-ruby colored, and made from roasted barley to impart an almost chocolaty flavor). **Guinness** stout inspires a reverence otherwise reserved for the Holy Trinity. Known variously as "the dark stuff," "the blonde in the black skirt," or simply "I'll have a pint, please," it's a rich, dark brew with a head thick enough to stand a match in. It's also far better in Ireland than anywhere else. For a sweeter taste, try it with blackcurrant or cider. Stout takes a while to pour properly (usually, 3-4min.), so quit drumming the bar and be patient. **Murphy's** is a similar, slightly sweeter, stout brewed in Cork, as is **Beamish**, a tasty "economy" stout. **Smithwicks** ale (Smiddicks; a hoppy, English-style bitter) and **Harp** lager (made by Guinness) are both popular domestic brews. You might be surprised by the many pubs serving Budweiser or Heineken here, and the number of young people quaffing such imported lagers. In general, the indigenous brews are far worthier. Beer is served in imperial **pint glasses** (about 20oz.) or half-pints (called a "glass"). If you ask for a beer you'll get a full pint, so be loud and clear if you can only stay (or stand) for a half. Or just take the pint and drink faster. A pint of Guinness costs anywhere from £1.90 to 2.30.

Irish whiskey (which Queen Elizabeth once declared her only true Irish friend) is sweeter and more stinging than its Scotch counterpart, spelled "whisky". (Irish whiskey is distilled three times, while Scotch whisky is distilled only twice.) Irish whiskey is also served in larger measures than you might be used to. Dubliners are partial to **Powers,** drinkers in Cork enjoy **Paddy,** and **Bushmills** is the favorite in the North. **Jameson** is popular everywhere. **Irish coffee** is sweetened with brown sugar and whipped cream and laced with whiskey—allegedly invented at Shannon Airport by a desperate bartender looking to appease cranky travelers on a layover, though others place the drink's origin in San Francisco. **Hot whiskey** (spiced up with lemon, cloves, and brown sugar) can provide a cozy buzz, as will the Irish version of **eggnog** (brandy, beaten egg, milk, and lemonade). In the west, you may hear some locals praise "mountain dew," a euphemism for **poitín** (po-CHEEN), a lethal (and illegal) distillation sometimes given to cows in labor that ranges in strength from 115 to 140 proof. Bad *poitín* can be very dangerous indeed.

Food in Ireland can be fairly expensive, especially in restaurants. The basics—and that's what you'll get—are simple and filling. "Takeaways" (take-out) and "chippers" (fish 'n' chips shops) are quick, greasy, and very popular. For variation, try chips with gravy, potato cakes (flat pancakes made of potato flakes), or the infamous spiceburger (a breaded, spiced patty of fried breadcrumbs). Many **pubs** serve food as well as

A Spot of Tea

There's more to drinking tea in Ireland than quenching thirst or politely washing down unwanted cabbage. After a couple of sips, even the gray rain is a pleasant hue. Pulses are raised as local scandals unfold over a pot of the hot stuff. Friends meet for a cup and laugh about the old times and the nosey old-timers. The good tea-makers are well-loved, and the bad...well, they're lonely.

drink, and **pub grub** is a good option for a quick and inexpensive meal. Typical pub grub includes Irish stew (meat, potatoes, carrots, and onions), burgers, soup, and sandwiches. *Colcannon,* "ploughman's lunch," and Irish stew, usually £4, are probably the essential Irish dishes.

Another alternative is to do your own **shopping.** Soda bread will keep for about a week and is delicious. Irish dairy products are addictive. Seafood can be a bargain in some small towns: smoked mackerel is splendid year-round and Atlantic salmon is freshest around July. Regional specialties include *crubeen* (tasty pigs' feet) in Cork, and *coddle* (boiled sausages and bacon with potatoes) in Dublin. Wexford berries in the Southeast are luscious May through July.

In **Northern Ireland,** you'll find similar culinary offerings, along with a few regional specialties. Meal portions tend to be large, fried, and inevitably canopied with potatoes. A hearty Ulster Fry (fried eggs, fried bacon, fried sausage, fried potato bread, and fried tomatoes) at breakfast will tide you over until the main midday meal, and tea is often substituted for dinner around 6pm. Every town has a few tempting bakeries selling pasties (PASS-tees, meat or vegetable wrapped in a pastry) and traditional soda bread. For a listing of Northern restaurants and pubs that serve food, check *Where to Eat in Northern Ireland,* available at most tourist offices.

County Dublin

Dublin and its coastal suburbs form one economic and commercial unit, all of which can be reached by DART (Dublin Area Rapid Transit) and suburban rail. All these towns, except Bray, are in County Dublin—the administrative unit that encircles the capital. Cityfolk hop out to the suburbs on weekends, while suburbanites rush to the capital in search of nightlife. Fast and modern Dublin dispels many preconceptions about "backward" Ireland, but the country's greener and more traditional side hides just a DART ride away. Dublin's suburbs are no less distinctive than Ireland's romanticized rural villages (though they are more crowded), and some towns—notably Howth and Bray—boast patches of unsurpassed beauty.

GETTING AROUND COUNTY DUBLIN

By Bus

The lime-green **Dublin Buses,** *Bus Átha Cliath* in Irish, are fantastically useful once you figure them out. The buses, sporting "db" logos, run from 6am to 11:30pm to comprehensively cover the city of Dublin and its suburbs north to Balbriggan, Rush, Malahide, and Donabate, west to Maynooth and Celbridge, and south to Blessington, Dún Laoghaire, and Bray. A **NiteLink** service runs express routes to the suburbs (Thurs.-Sat. midnight, 1, 2, and 3am; £2.50, no passes valid). Tickets for the NiteLink are sold from a van parked on the corner of Westmoreland and College St., next to the entrance to Trinity College. Dublin has a new **wheelchair-accessible** bus service around the downtown area called **OmniLink** (Mon.-Sat. 8am-11pm; 30p).

Buses are cheap (55p to £1.25) and extensive, but some routes run infrequently (8am-6pm generally every 8-20min., every 30-45min. other times). A majority of bus routes end or begin at the city center, or *An Lár,* defined by the streets around O'Connell Bridge. The yellow bus timetables along the quays have insets of the city center which indicate route termini by printing the route number inside a box. It's easiest to figure out bus routes by using the *Map of Greater Dublin* (£4.10) in conjunction with the accurate **Dublin Bus Timetable** (£1.20; also good for finding termini in city center). Both are available from newsagents and the **Dublin Bus office,** 59 O'Connell St. (tel. 873 4222 or 872 0000 Mon.-Sat. 9am-6pm; open Mon. 8:30am-5:30pm, Tues.-Fri. 9am-5:30pm, Sat. 9am-1pm), which also has free pamphlets detailing each route.

Travel passes were not designed for the casual traveler. Except for the 10 Journey bus pass, all have time limits that require constant use of transport to be worth their price. The **One Day Travel Wide** (£3.30, Dublin buses only), the **One Day Bus/Rail** (£4.50, valid on buses, DART, and rail service anywhere between Kilcoole, Balbriggan, and Maynooth), and the **Four Day Explorer** (£10, 4 days of everything you get with the One Day Bus/Rail) are your pass options. Passes should be inserted into the scanner on the right side of the bus entrance. With a **CIE card** from the Dublin bus office (£2; a Dublin address is required, but the street address of a hostel will work), tourists can also buy a **weekly adult bus pass** (valid Sun.-Sat.; £11 within £1.10 fare-range, all zones £14) or a **weekly adult bus/rail pass** (valid Sun.-Sat.; £14.50). With a CIE card *and* a TravelSave stamp on their ISIC cards, **students** can buy weekly bus passes for £9, all zones £10. Newsagents with the Dublin Bus "db" logo in the window sell these passes but only the Dublin bus office sells the CIE card. Individuals or groups may want to consider the transferable (anybody can use the same book) **10 Journey ticket books,** which allow 10 trips of the same price (55p, 80p, £1, £1.10, or £1.25) and produce savings of 50p to £2.

By Train

The electric **DART** trains run frequently up and down the coast to serve the suburbs. From Connolly, Pearse, and Tara St. Stations in the city center, the DART shoots all the way south to Bray and north to Howth. DART trains are inevitably faster and more predictable than comparable bus rides. The DART runs every 15 minutes from 6:30am to midnight (75p-£1.60). Tickets are sold in the station and must be presented at the end of the trip. The orange trains of the **suburban rail** network continue north to Malahide, Donabate, and Drogheda, south to Wicklow and Arklow, and west to Maynooth. These trains leave from Connolly Station, though the southern line also stops at Tara St. and Pearse Stations. Trains to Kildare leave from Heuston Station. Trains are frequent on weekdays, less so on Sunday.

▩ Dublin

In a country known for its relaxed pace of life and rural quietude, Dublin is fast, urban, and energetic. The Irish who live outside of Dublin worry that it has taken on the characteristics of big cities everywhere: crime and a weakness for short-lived international trends. Perhaps they also fear the rapid social change in the city. The truth is that Ireland is changing, and that Dublin, holding close to one-third of the country's population in its environs, is at the forefront of those changes. Dublin, growing fast from both rural and international immigration, fosters progress in music, culture, and an active gay and lesbian population. The old Ireland is certainly present—castles, cathedrals, and fine old pubs saturate the city. The friendliness of the Irish people, the love of good *craic,* and the willingness to befriend a stranger, although sometimes hidden beneath a veneer of urban bustle, is always ready to burst out, whether while waiting for a bus or over a round of Guinness. While not cosmopolitan in the same sense as London or Paris, Dublin has a degree of urban sophistication, manifested in its vibrant theater, music, and literary productions, that shows it to be taking its place among the great cities of modern Europe.

Dublin has been a port since the winter of 840-41, when Vikings built this longship port downstream from the older Celtic settlement of Áth Cliath. After a few years of visiting, the Vikings set up a permanent town, Dubh Linn ("Black Pool"), around the modern College Green. The Viking Thingmote, or hill of assembly, stood there as administrative center for both Viking powers and the Norman Pale until William III's victory at the Battle of the Boyne in 1690. During the ensuing Protestant Ascendancy (p. 60), the Irish Parliament House sprang up near the old Viking center along with a Protestant English culture still evident in the architecture of Dublin's tidy Georgian squares.

The capital of Ireland since the late 17th century, Dublin has seen a blending of cultures which has produced an extraordinary intellectual and literary life. From Swift and Burke to Joyce and Beckett, Dublin has produced so many great writers that virtually every street contains a literary landmark. The city's public life, which takes place on the streets, in open markets, and behind inviting pub doors, is vibrant with both Irish and English energies. There are pubs for every mood, and the music scene inside is world-renowned. Dublin may not embody the "Emerald Isle" that the tourist brochures promote, but it charms and excites in its own urban way.

TO & FROM THE TRANSPORTATION HUBLIN

Rail lines, bus lines (both official and private), and the national highway system radiate from Ireland's capital. Major highways N5 and N6 lead to N4. N8, N9, and N10 all feed into N7, pumping buses and cars into Dublin's vehicular sphere. Because intercity transport is so Dublin-centric, you may find it more convenient in the long run to arrange your travel in other parts of the Republic while you're in the capital. To get the best deals, check in with USIT (p. 27) for a TravelSave stamp if you intend to take buses or trains and ask around for private bus lines. Refer to the **Essentials** section for sea (p. 31) and air travel (p. 27) into the capital.

From the Airport or Ferry Port

From **Dublin Airport** (tel. 844 4900), Dublin bus #41, 41A, or 41C (every 20min.; £1.30) takes travelers to Eden Quay in the city center. Alternatively, **Airport Express**

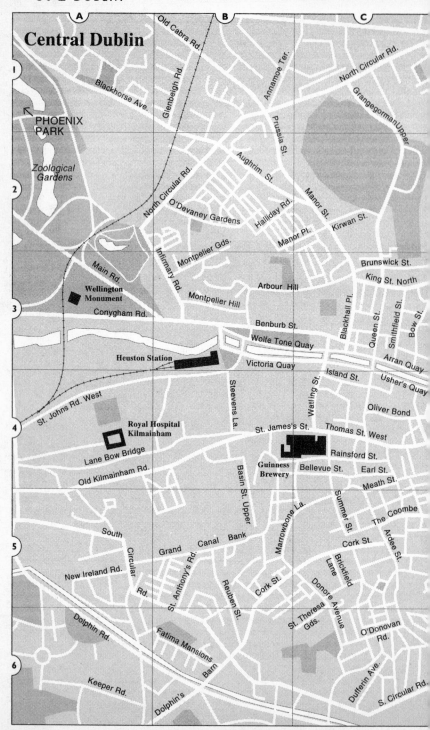

Central Dublin

PHOENIX PARK

Zoological Gardens

Blackhorse Ave.

Old Cabra Rd.

Glenbeigh Rd.

Annamoe Ter.

North Circular Rd.

Grangegorman Upper

Prussia St.

Aughrim St.

Manor St.

North Circular Rd.

O'Devaney Gardens

Halliday Rd.

Manor Pl.

Kirwan St.

Brunswick St.

Montpelier Gds.

Arbour Hill

King St. North

Main Rd.

Infirmary Rd.

Montpelier Hill

Blackhall Pl.

Queen St.

Smithfield St.

Bow St.

Wellington Monument

Conygham Rd.

Benburb St.

Wolfe Tone Quay

Arran Quay

Heuston Station

Victoria Quay

Island St.

Usher's Quay

St. Johns Rd. West

Steevens La.

Watling St.

Oliver Bond

Royal Hospital Kilmainham

St. James's St.

Thomas St. West

Lane Bow Bridge

Guinness Brewery

Rainsford St.

Old Kilmainham Rd.

Bellevue St.

Earl St.

Meath St.

Basin St. Upper

Marrowbone La.

Summer St.

The Coombe

South Circular Rd.

Grand Canal Bank

St. Anthony's Rd.

New Ireland Rd.

Cork St.

Cork St.

Ardee St.

Brickfield Lane

Donore Avenue

Dolphin Rd.

Reuben St.

St. Theresa Gds.

O'Donovan Rd.

Fatima Mansions

Barn

Dufferin Ave.

Keeper Rd.

Dolphin's

S. Circular Rd.

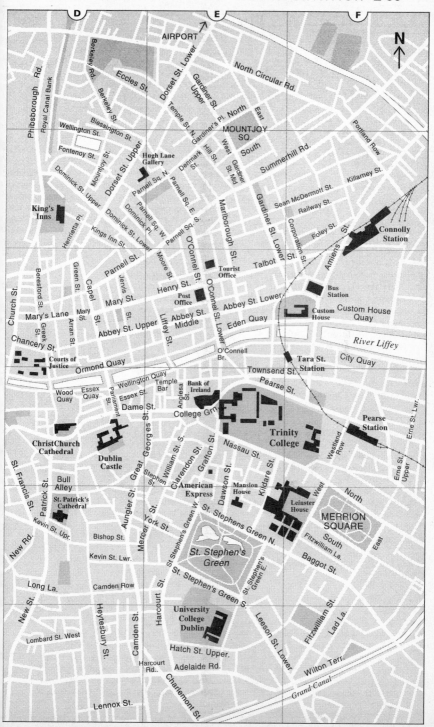

Buses (tel. 704 4222; Mon.-Sat. 6:40am-11pm, Sun. 7:10am-11pm; every 15-30min.; £2.50) will bring you to Busáras Central Bus Station and sometimes continue to Heuston Station. A cab from the airport to the city center costs £12-14. Several cab companies offer wheelchair-accessible cabs (call ahead).

B&I ferries dock at the mouth of the River Liffey, just outside central Dublin. Buses #53 and 53A run from there past Alexandra Rd. and arrive near the Custom House (80p). **Stena-Sealink** ferries arrive in Dún Laoghaire (p. 121), from which the DART shuttles weary passengers to Connolly Station, Pearse Station, or Tara St. Station in the city center (£1.30). Buses #7, 7A, and 8 go from Georges St. in Dún Laoghaire to Eden Quay (£1.30).

By Train

Most inter-city trains arrive at **Heuston Station** (tel. 703 2132), just south of Victoria Quay, well west of the city center (a 20-min. walk from Trinity College). Any Dublin bus heading east—and several pass by every minute—will take you into the city. Buses #26, 51, and 79 go specifically to the city center. To facilitate **train and bus connections,** bus #90 (every 10min.; 60p) makes the circuit of Dublin's three train stations and its bus station.

The other major rail terminus is **Connolly Station,** Amiens St. (tel. 836 3333), located just north of the Liffey and close to Busáras Bus Station and several hostels and B&Bs. Buses #20, 20A, and 90 will take weary souls south of the river, but it's faster to walk. **Pearse Station,** just east of Trinity College on Pearse St. and Westland Row, receives southbound trains from Connolly Station. Both Connolly and Pearse are also DART stations serving the north and south coasts (see **Getting Around County Dublin,** p. 82). **Luggage storage** is available at Heuston and Connolly Stations (items £1/day; open at Heuston Mon.-Sat. 7:15am-8:35pm, Sun. 8am-3pm and 5-9pm; at Connolly Mon.-Sat. 7:40am-9:30pm, Sun. 9:15am-1pm and 5-10pm).

Irish Rail, *Iarnród Éireann* in Irish, 35 Lower Abbey St. (tel. 836 6222), spews data on its own InterCity services as well as on DART, suburban trains, international train tickets, and ferries. (Open Mon.-Fri. 9am-5pm, Sat. 9am-1pm; phones open Mon.-Sat. 9am-6pm, Sun. 10am-6pm.) Trains run **from Connolly** to: Belfast (Mon.-Sat. 8/day, Sun. 3/day; 2-2½hr.; £15); Sligo (Mon.-Sat. 4/day, Sun. 3/day; 3hr. 20min.; £12); and Wexford/Rosslare (Mon.-Sat. 3/day, Sun 2/day; 3hr.; £10, students £7). Trains **from Heuston** make tracks for: Cork (Mon.-Sat. 4/day, Sun. 3/day; 3¼hr.; £32); Galway (Mon.-Sat. 4/day, Sun. 2/day; 3hr.; £14, Fri.-Sat. £24); Limerick (Mon.-Sat. 9/day, Sun. 6/day; 2¾hr.; £25); Tralee (Mon.-Sat. 3/day, Sun. 2/day; 4hr.; £33.50); and Waterford (Mon.-Sat. 4/day, Sun. 3/day; 2¾hr.; £11.50).

All fares in *Let's Go* listings are for adult, one-way tickets, unless otherwise noted. Student fares (with ISIC and TravelSave stamp) are generally 50-70% of the adult fare. All lines, except those to Cork and Limerick, boast cheaper return (round-trip) promotion fares, for which the restrictions, often on days of travel, vary from line to line. Unlike bus tickets, train tickets sometimes allow travelers to break a journey into stages yet still pay the price of a single-phase trip. 24-hour "talking timetables" recite info on trains to: Belfast (tel. 855 4477), Cork (tel. 855 4400), Galway/Westport (tel. 855 4422), Killarney/Tralee (tel. 855 4466), Limerick (tel. 855 4411), Sligo (tel. 855 4455), Waterford (tel. 855 4433), and Wexford/Rosslare (tel. 855 4488).

By Bus

Bus Éireann, the national bus company, covers the entire island. Its inter-city buses to Dublin arrive at **Busáras Central Bus Station,** Store St. (tel. 836 6111), directly behind the Customs House and next door to Connolly Station. **Luggage storage** is in the station (Mon.-Sat. 8am-7:45pm, Sun. 10am-5:45pm; £1.50/item, £2/rucksack/day). Buses run from Busáras to: Belfast (7/day, Sun. 3/day; 3hr.; £10, students £8.10); Cork (4/day, Sun. 3/day; 4½hr.; £12, students £8.50); Derry (5/day, Sun. 3/day; 4½hr.; £10, students £8.50); Dingle (2/day, Sun. 1/day; 7hr.; £16, students £9.50); Donegal Town (5/day, Sun. 3/day; 4¼hr.; £10, students £8); Galway (8/day, Sun. 4/day; 4hr.; £8, students £6.50); Killarney (2-5/day, Sun. 3/day; 6hr.; £14, students £9);

Limerick (8/day; 3¼hr.; £10, students £7.50); Rosslare Harbour (6/day, Sun. 5-6/day; 3hr.; £9, students £6.50); Shannon Airport (6/day, Sun. 5/day; 4½hr.; £10, students £8); Sligo (3/day; 4hr.; £8, students £7); Tralee (5/day; 6hr.; £14, students £9); Waterford (8/day; 2¾hr.; £6, students £5); Westport (3/day, Sun. 1/day; 5½hr.; £11, students £8.50); and Wexford (6/day, Sun. 5-6/day; 2¾hr.; £7, students £6). **Private bus companies** typically run one or two buses per day between Dublin and some other destination. They usually run more frequently than Bus Éireann and cost less, but it's maddeningly hard to find info on them. **PAMBO** (Private Association of Motor Bus Owners), 32 Lower Abbey St. (tel. 878 8422), can provide you with the names and numbers of private bus companies which service your intended destination (open Mon.-Fri. 10am-5pm). Private bus lines from Dublin to other cities are listed in *Let's Go* under **Getting There** for those cities.

By Thumb

Hitchers into Dublin generally ask drivers to drop them off at one of the myriad bus and DART stops outside the city. Hitchers out of Dublin ride a bus to the city outskirts where the motorways begin. Buses #25, 25A, 66, 66A, 67, and 67A from Middle Abbey St. travel to Lucan Rd., which turns into N4 (for Galway and the West). To find a ride to Cork, Waterford, and Limerick (N7), hitchers usually take bus #51, 51B, or 69 from Fleet St. to Naas (NACE) Rd. Wicklow, Wexford, and Rosslare are along N11, for which hitchers take bus #46 or 84 from Eden Quay or #46A from Fleet St. to Stillorgan Rd. N3 heads to Donegal and Sligo, and can be reached on bus #38 from Lower Abbey St. or #39 from Middle Abbey St. to Navan Rd. Buses #33, 41, and 41A from Eden Quay to Swords send hitchers on their way to the North, Belfast, and Dundalk (on N1).

ORIENTATION

The **River Liffey** cuts central Dublin in half from west to east. The better food and more famous sights reside on the South Side (of the river), though plenty of hostels and the bus station sprout up on the grittier North Side. Beware that several main streets in Dublin undergo a name change every few blocks. Tourists should ask directions frequently and buy a map with a street index. Dundrum publishes the invaluable, color-coded *Handy Map of Dublin* (£4). The streets running alongside the Liffey are called quays (KEYS); their names change every block. Each bridge over the Liffey also has its own name, and all streets change names as they cross the river. If a street is split into "Upper" and "Lower," then the "Lower" part of the street is always closer to the mouth of the Liffey.

The core of Dublin is circumscribed by North and South Circular Rd. Almost all the sights are located within this area, and you can walk from one end to the other in a half hour. **Trinity College Dublin (TCD)** functions as the nerve center of Dublin's activity, drawing legions of bookshops and student-oriented pubs into its orbit. Heading west from TCD, Dame St. leads to **Temple Bar.** Dublin's version of Soho, this area is Dublin's liveliest nightspot with excellent pubs and trendy nightclubs. Its eclectic array of funky restaurants and a set of art museums and workshops ensure that Temple Bar draws a crowd throughout the day as well.

Back at TCD, **Grafton St.** runs south and turns into Harcourt St. after it reaches **St. Stephen's Green.** This is where you'll find the more expensive, tourist-oriented shops and restaurants. Important north-south arteries on the south side of the Liffey are **South Great Georges St.** (west of Grafton St.) and **Wexford St.** East of Grafton St., Kildare St. connects Trinity College and St. Stephen's Green. Grafton St. becomes Westmoreland St. at TCD and then **O'Connell St.** as it crosses the River Liffey over O'Connell Bridge. Merchandise and services on the north side of the Liffey are more affordable than their southern counterparts. **Henry/Talbot St.** is a pedestrian shopping zone that runs perpendicular to O'Connell near the General Post Office (GPO). The **North Side,** home to Dublin's working class, has the reputation of being a rougher area, but generally this region is not as dangerous or run-down as some would have you believe. You should, however, avoid walking in unfamiliar areas at night, especially if you're alone.

PRACTICAL INFORMATION

Tourist Information: Main Office, Dublin Tourist Centre, Suffolk St. (tel. 605 7748). From Connolly Train Station, walk left down Amiens St. to the Quay, and right past Busáras until you come to O'Connell Bridge. Turn left over the bridge and walk past TCD; Suffolk St. will be on your right. The Centre is in a converted church. Accommodation service with £1 booking fee and 10% deposit; £2 charge to book outside Dublin. The king among billions of pamphlets is the *Map of Greater Dublin* (£4.10). American Express maintains a branch office with currency exchange here (tel. 605 7709). Bus Éireann and Stenalink have representatives on hand to provide info and tickets. Argus Rent-a-Car has a desk here and a free list of car rental agencies is also available. Open Sept.-June Mon.-Sat. 9am-5:30pm; July-Aug. Mon.-Sat. 9am-8:30pm, Sun. 11am-5:30pm.

Branch Offices: Dublin Airport, open mid-June to mid-Sept. daily 8am-10:30pm; mid-Sept. to mid-June 8am-10pm. **Dún Laoghaire Harbour,** Ferry Terminal Building, open daily 10am-9pm (subject to ferry arrivals), **Tallaght,** The Square Towncentre, open daily 9:30am-5pm, and **Baggot Street,** open daily 9:15am-5:15pm. All telephone inquiries are handled by the central office. (Tel. 605 7748. Credit card reservations tel. 605 7777. General info on Dublin tel. (1550) 112233 within Ireland or tel. 605 7799 from overseas.) Use one of these branches if possible; each is well staffed and well stocked, but not as crowded as the main branch.

Northern Ireland Tourist Board: 16 Nassau St. (tel. 679 1977 or (1800) 230 230). More extensive info on the 6 northern counties than the Dublin Tourism Centre. Open Mon.-Fri. 9am-5:30pm, Sat. 10am-5pm.

Temple Bar Information Centre: 18 Eustace St. (tel. 671 5717). Heading away from Trinity College, make a right off Dame St. where it intersects both Eustace and Great George's St. They have info on the artsy Temple Bar, better arts information than the Dublin Tourist Office offers, and more time to answer questions. The center publishes the useful, bimonthly *Temple Bar Guide* (free) and distributes *Gay Community News* (free). Open June-Sept. Mon.-Fri. 9am-7pm, Sat. 11am-7pm, Sun. noon-6pm; Oct.-May Mon.-Fri. 9:30am-6pm, Sat. noon-6pm.

Community and Youth Information Centre: Sackville Pl. (tel. 878 6844), corner of Marlborough St. A library with a wealth of resources on careers, culture, outings, travel and tourist information, accommodations (no bookings), camping, sporting events, counseling, and referrals. Bulletin boards advertise youth and special-needs groups. Open Mon.-Wed. 9:30am-6pm, Thurs.-Sat. 9:30am-5pm.

Budget Travel: USIT (Irish Student Travel Agency), 19-21 Aston Quay (tel. 679 8833), near O'Connell Bridge. The place to seek Irish travel discounts. ISIC, HI, and EYC cards; TravelSave stamps £7. Big discounts, especially for people under 26. They even book hostels. Open Mon.-Fri. 9am-6pm, Sat. 11am-4pm.

An Óige Head Office (Irish Youth Hostel Association/HI): 61 Mountjoy St. (tel. 830 4555), corner of Wellington St. Follow O'Connell St. north, continuing through all its name changes. Mountjoy St. is on the left. Book and pay for HI hostels here. Package bike and rail tours. The *An Óige Handbook* (£1.50) lists all HI hostels in Ireland and Northern Ireland. Membership £7.50, under 18 £4. Open Mon.-Fri. 9:30am-5:30pm; April-Sept. also Sat. 10am-12:30pm.

Embassies: United States, 42 Elgin Rd., Ballsbridge (tel. 668 8777). **Canada,** 65 St. Stephen's Green South (tel. 478 1988; emergencies, call 285 1246). Open Mon.-Fri. 10am-noon and 2-4pm. **Britain,** 29 Merrion Rd. (tel. 269 5211). Open Mon.-Fri. 9am-1pm and 2-5pm. **Australia,** Fitzwilton House, Wilton Terrace (tel. 676 1517). Open Mon.-Thurs. 10am-12:30pm and 2-3:30pm, Fri. 9am-noon. **New Zealand's** embassy is in London: New Zealand House, Haymarket, London SW1Y 4QT. From Ireland, dial 00 44 (171) 930 8422. **France,** 36 Ailesbury Rd. (tel. 269 4777). Open Mon.-Fri. 9-11am and 2-4:30pm. **Germany,** 31 Trimleston Ave. (tel. 269 3011 or 269 3123). Open Mon.-Fri. 9am-noon. **Italy,** 63 Northumberland Rd. (tel. 660 1744). Open Mon.-Fri. 10am-12:30pm. **Japan,** 22 Ailesbury Rd. (tel. 269 4244). **Spain,** 17A Merlyn Pk. (tel. 269 1640; after hours, call 269 2131). Open Mon.-Fri. 9am-3pm.

Banks: Best exchange rates are in banks. **Bank of Ireland,** 6 Lower O'Connell St. (tel. 872 9799); **ATM. AIB (Allied Irish Bank),** 10 Lower O'Connell St. (tel. 873 0555); **ATM.** Both open Mon.-Wed. and Fri. 10am-4pm, Thurs. 10am-5pm.**TSB (Trustees' Savings Bank),** 12 Lower Abbey St. (tel. 878 6266). Open Mon.-Wed. and Fri. 9:30am-5pm, Thurs. 9:30am-7pm. Bureaux de change also in the General Post Office and in the tourist office main branch.

American Express: 116 Grafton St., Dublin 2 (tel. 677 2874), up the street from Trinity College gates. Traveler's Cheque refunds (tel. (1800) 626000). Client mail held; currency exchange (no commission for AmEx Traveler's Cheques). Open Mon.-Sat. 9am-5pm, also June-Sept. Sun. 11am-4pm. Also in the tourist office on O'Connell St. (tel. 878 6892).

Phones: Telecom Éireann (inquiries and phonecard refunds, tel. 671 4444). A fleet of **public pay telephones** docks in the General Post Office (phones open Mon.-Sat. 8am-8pm, Sun. and holidays 10:30am-6:30pm). Another anchors at the Gaiety Centre, on South King St. across from St. Stephen's Green (open Mon.-Fri. 9:30am-5pm). Both locations have a cargo of phone books covering all of Ireland.

Directory Inquiries: tel. 1190, no charge.

Buses: Inter-city buses (see **By Bus,** p. 86) and intra-city buses (see **Getting Around County Dublin,** p. 82) are covered above.

Trains: (see **By Train,** p. 83).

Ferries: Bookings in Irish Rail office (below). Ferries from England, Wales, and the Isle of Man are covered in Essentials (see **by Ferry,** p. 31). Ferry port to Dublin transport is covered above (see **From the Airport or Ferry Port,** p. 83).

Iarnród Éireann (Irish Rail): 35 Lower Abbey St. (tel. 836 6222). Info and bookings on trains and ferries. Open Mon.-Fri. 9:15am-5pm, Sat. 9:15am-12:45pm; phones open Mon.-Sat. 9am-6pm, Sun. 10am-6pm.

Taxi: National Radio Cabs, 40 James St. (tel. 677 2222). **Co-op Taxi** (tel. 677 7777 or 676 6666). **Central Cabs** (tel. 836 5555) and **City Group Taxi** (tel. 872 7272) have wheelchair-accessible taxis (call in advance). All are 24-hr. services. Fares start at £1.80; 80p/mi.; £1.20 call-in charge.

Car Rental: Argus, 59 Terenure Rd. East, Dublin 6 (tel. 490 4444; fax 490 6328). Offices also in the tourist office on O'Connell St. and in the airport. From £38/day, £225/week for ages 26-64. Special arrangements for drivers 23-26 or 64-70.

Bike Rental: (see **By Bike,** p. 36). **Raleigh Rent-A-Bike,** Kylemore Rd., Dublin 10 (tel. 626 1333). Limited one-way rental system (£12 surcharge; deposit credit card) includes C. Harding (below). Bikes £7/day, £30/week; deposit £40. In Dublin, the best selection and advice comes from **C. Harding for Bikes,** 30 Bachelor's Walk (tel. 873 3622; fax 873 3622) open Mon.-Sat. 8:30am-6pm. Other Raleigh dealers include **McDonald's Cycles,** 38 Wexford St. (tel. 475 2586) and **Little Sport,** 3 Merville Ave., off Fairview Rd. (tel. 833 2405). **Rent-A-Bike,** 58 Lower Gardiner St. (tel. 872 5931 or 872 5399; fax 836 4763). Cross-country and mountain bikes £7/day, £30/week; deposit £30. For £5 extra, you can return the bike to other locations. Panniers, helmets, and child seats £5/week. Bike repair. Sells bikes for about £100, buys them back for half-price within 6 months. Cycling holidays for £82/week staying in An Óige hostels, £135/week staying in B&Bs. Open Mon.-Sat. 9am-6pm. **RailBike,** Heuston Station, affiliated with **Irish Cycle Hire** (tel. (041) 41067). £6/day, £30/week; helmets £5/week, pannier bags £5/week; deposit £30. Return the bike to RailBike depots in the main rail stations.

Bike Repair and Storage: Square Wheel Cycleworks, Temple Lane South (tel. 679 0838), off Dame St. below the Well-Fed Café. Excellent advice on bicycle touring, expert repair, and supervised bicycle park (20p/hr., 40p/half-day, 60p/day, £2.50/week). Open Mon.-Fri. 8:30am-6:30pm. **C. Harding,** 30 Bachelor's Walk (tel. 873 2455), has bike storage north of the Liffey and a repair service (50p/4hr., £1/day, £3.50/6 days for students; overnight parking £1.50). Open Mon.-Sat. 8:30am-6pm. Turn right off O'Connell St. before the bridge.

Luggage Storage: In the central bus and train stations (see **To & From the Transportation Hublin,** p. 83).

Newsagent: Read Newsagent, 24 Nassau St. (tel. 679 6011; fax 671 1684). Photocopying 2p/page. Go ahead, xerox the phone book. Cheap stationery. Foreign newspapers and periodicals. Open Mon.-Fri. 8:30am-6:30pm, Sat. 9am-6:30pm.

COUNTY DUBLIN

Library: New Central Library, ILAC Centre, Moore St. (tel. 873 4333). Video and listening facilities and a children's library. Telephone directories on shelves for EU countries and on microfilm for U.S. and Canada. Open Mon.-Thurs. 10am-8pm, Fri.-Sat. 10am-5pm.

Laundry: The Laundry Shop, 191 Parnell St. (tel. 872 3541). Closest to Busáras and North Side hostels. Wash £2.20, dry £1.30, soap 50p. Open Mon.-Sat. 8:30am-6pm. **All-American Launderette,** Wicklow St. (tel. 677 2779). £3.50 wash and dry, £4.60 serviced, powder 50p. Open Mon.-Sat. 8:30am-7pm, Sun. 10am-6pm.

Bisexual, Gay, and Lesbian Information: Gay Switchboard Dublin, Carmichael House, North Brunswick St., Dublin 7 (tel. 872 1055). Info on meetings, outdoor groups, and nightlife. Open Sun.-Fri. 8-10pm, Sat. 3:30-6pm. **Lesbian Line** (tel. 872 9911) open Thurs. 7-9pm. **LOT (Lesbians Organizing Together),** 5 Capel St. (tel. 872 2770). Library and drop-in center Tues. and Thurs. 10am-5pm. **National Gay and Lesbian Federation (NGLF),** the Hirschfeld Centre, 10 Fownes St. (tel. 671 0939), behind the Central Bank. Deals mostly with legal disputes and publishes *Gay Community News,* a free monthly publication covering all of Ireland. Get it here or at the Temple Bar Information Centre (see above).

AIDS Resource Centre: 14 Haddington Rd. (tel. 660 2149), off Baggot St. Advice, counseling, and HIV testing. Also operates the **Gay Men's Health Project,** Tues. and Wed. 8-9:30pm (no appointment necessary). **Dublin AIDS Alliance,** 53 Parnell Sq. (tel. 873 3799), offers counseling and info on HIV. **AIDS Helpline** (tel. 872 4277) open Mon.-Fri. 7-9pm, Sat. 3-5pm.

Hotlines: Samaritans, 112 Marlborough St. (tel. (1850) 609 090 or 872 7700), for the depressed, lonely, or suicidal. 24-hr. **Rape Crisis Centre,** 70 Lower Leeson St. (tel. 661 4911; weekends after 5:30pm tel. 661 4564). **Women's Aid** (tel. (1800) 341 900 or 860 0033). Open Mon.-Fri. 10am-10pm, Sat. 10am-6pm. **Dublin Well Woman Centre,** 73 Lower Leeson St. (tel. 661 0083 or 661 0086), a professional health center for women. **Cura,** 30 South Anne St. (tel. 671 0598), Catholic-funded support for women with unplanned pregnancies. **Alcoholics Anonymous,** 109 South Circular Rd., Dublin 8 (tel. 679 5967). **Narcotics Anonymous** (tel. 830 0944), 24-hr. phone service for those fighting drug addiction.

Pharmacy: O'Connell's, 55 Lower O'Connell St. (tel. 873 0427). Open Mon.-Sat. 8:30am-10pm, Sun. 10am-10pm. Convenient to city bus routes. **Temple Bar Pharmacy,** 21 Essex St. East (tel. 670 9751), offers the usual plus a range of homeopathic treatments. Open Mon.-Sat. 9am-7pm.

Hospital: Meath Hospital, Heytesbury St. (24-hr. tel. 453 6555, 453 6000, or 453 6694). Buses #16, 16A, 19, 19A, 22, 22A, and 55 run here. **Mater Misericordiae Hospital,** Eccles Street, off Dorset St. Lower (tel. 830 1122). Served by buses #10, 22, 38, and 120. **Beaumont Hospital,** Beaumont Rd. D9 (tel. 837 7755). Served by buses #27A, 51A, 101, and 103. **St. James Hospital,** James St., Dublin 8 (tel. 453 7941). Buses #17, 19, 19A, 21A, 78A, and 123 stop here.

Emergency: Dial 999; no coins required. **Garda:** Dublin Metro Headquarters, Harcourt Sq. (tel. 732 222). Store St. office (tel. 873 2222 or 478 1822), Fitzgibbon St. office (tel. 836 3113). **Garda Confidential Report Line:** tel. (1800) 666 111.

Post Office: General Post Office (G.P.O.), O'Connell St. (tel. 705 7000), near the tourist office. Big. Dublin is the only city in Ireland with postal codes (24 of them). Even-numbered postal codes are for areas south of the Liffey, odd-numbered are for the north. The numbers increase with distance from city center. *Poste Restante* pick-up at the bureau de change window closes 15min. early. Open Mon.-Sat. 8am-8pm, Sun. 10am-6:30pm. **G.P.O. Postal Code:** Dublin 1.

Phone Code: 01.

ACCOMMODATIONS

Dublin has a host of marvelous accommodations, but the ever-flowing glut of visitors ensures that real dumps stay open as well. Reserve well ahead to be sure that you've got a bed, particularly during Easter weekend, bank-holiday weekends, and July to August. Private hostel rooms and B&B singles are especially hard to come by. The tourist offices books local accommodations for £1, but they only deal in Bord Fáilte-approved B&Bs and hostels, which aren't necessarily better than unapproved ones.

Dublin hostels that pay the fee to be plugged into Bord Fáilte's system are Avalon House, An Óige, Isaac's, Kinlay House, the Marlborough Hostel, Morehampton House, and Goin' My Way/Cardijn House. Tourist officials may turn strangely mum if you mention any of the others.

Phoenix Park may tempt the desperate, but impromptu camping there is a bad idea. If the *garda* or park rangers don't get you to leave, the threat of thieves and drug dealers should. Dublin is big—the accommodations listed here are not the only ones. If these are full, consult Dublin Tourism's annually-updated *Dublin Accommodation Guide* (£3), or ask hostel and B&B staff for referrals.

Hostels

Hostels abound north of the River Liffey and east of O'Connell St. The hostels south of the river fill up fastest. Most are independent (unconnected to An Óige/HI). Dorm prices range from £6.25 to £12 per night. **Reserve ahead** in the **summer** and in **weekends** throughout the year, especially for private rooms. Call as early as possible, even if it's a few hours before you'll arrive. **The Old School House Hostel** in Dún Laoghaire (p. 122) is a hosteler's alternative to busy city life. All hostels listed below have 24-hour reception.

The Brewery Hostel, 22-23 Thomas St. (tel. 453 8600). Follow Dame St. past Christ Church through its name changes (High and Cornmarket). Prime location next to Guinness and a 10-min. walk to Temple Bar. Furniture and facilities are brand new; sturdy beds with orthopedic mattresses provide hotel-like comfort. Family-run, exceptionally friendly, fun staff. Barbecue area and patio make it easy to meet other hostelers. All rooms w/bath. Carpark. TV lounge area w/VCR and full kitchen/dining area (w/microwave) open 24hr. 10-bed dorm £8. 6- to 8-bed dorm £10. 3- to 4-person room £12/person. Single £17. Breakfast buffet w/cereal. Free tea/coffee available all day. Free luggage storage. Laundry £2 wash and dry.

Ashfield House, 19/20 D'Olier St. (tel. 679 7734). Great location around the corner from TCD, one block east of Westmoreland St. Opened in 1996, this hostel boasts new beds with real (i.e. thick) mattresses and bright, airy rooms. From time to time the traffic is noisy, so request a quiet room if necessary. All rooms w/bath. Bureau de change. Wheelchair accessible (elevator). Full kitchen (w/microwave) open 24hr. Dorm June-Sept. £10, March-May and Oct. £9, Nov.-Feb. £7.50. 6-bed dorm £11.50, £10, and £9.50 respectively. 4-bed dorm £13, £12, and £11 respectively. Triple £39, £36, and £33 respectively. Twin £36, £32, and £30 respectively. Breakfast. Free luggage storage. Serviced laundry £4/load.

Avalon House (IHH), 55 Aungier St. (tel. 475 0001; fax 475 0303). South Great Georges St., off Dame St., becomes Aungier St. The rooms are a joy to return to: groovy comforters and terracotta decor, though beds are a trifle short. Co-ed showers, toilets, and dorms (all non-smoking). 4-bed dorms are split-level: the 2 beds on each level are connected by a circular stairway. The result is B&B-level privacy at dorm prices. Bike rack. TV room. Coffee bar (open 9:30am-midnight; entrees about £2). Smallish kitchen w/microwave open 7:30-10am and noon-10:30pm. 24-bed dorm July-Aug. £10.50, Sept.-June £7.50. 4-bed dorm July-Aug. £11.50, March-June and Sept.-Oct. £11, Nov.-Feb. £9. Double £27, £26, and £22 respectively. Add £2 for rooms w/bath. **Wheelchair-accessible room** £13.50/person. Breakfast included. Towels 50p. Safety deposit boxes w/£5 deposit.

Kinlay House (IHH), 2-12 Lord Edward St. (tel. 679 6644; fax 679 7437), the continuation of Dame St. Protestant country boys who came to work in the city once slid down the beautifully carved oak banisters in the lofty entrance hall. Today, tired backpackers trudge upstairs to collapse on comfortable beds or on soft couches in the TV room. It's located in hip 'n' happening Temple Bar, but a neat key-card system keeps the happenings outside. Bureau de change. Wake-up calls. Lockers. 10-bed dorm £9.50. 4- to 6-bed dorm £12, w/bath £13. Single £18. Twin £27, w/bath £28. Oct.-June prices £1 cheaper. Breakfast and towel included. Free luggage storage. Bike storage and rental £7/day. Laundry £4.

Strollers, 58 Dame St. (tel. 677 5614 or 677 5422; fax 839 0474). In the middle of Temple Bar action, about halfway between Trinity College and Dublin Castle,

Strollers wins the award for best-located hostel in Dublin. It's also close to the top for luxury. Truly restful beds in bright, spotless, non-smoking rooms induce visions of sugar plums. Two minor drawbacks: loud traffic and smallish rooms. Wheelchair accessible. 8-bed dorm £11. Quads £13/person. Double £30. Breakfast and discounts at the attached café (dinners £5; open daily 9am-11pm). Live music 4 nights/week; no cover.

Abraham House, 82 Gardiner St. Lower (tel. 855 0600; fax 855 0598). Tired travelers fall into the low, soft bunks (extra-long beds optional) and heave a sigh of relief in large, open rooms. Gallons of hot water. Kitchen with microwave. 10-bed dorm July-Sept. £10.50, Oct.-June £7. 6- to 8-bed dorm 50p more. Quads July-Sept. £11.50, March-June and Oct. £11, Nov.-Feb. £9. Singles £18, £16, and £13 respectively. Twin £13.50, £13, and £11 respectively. Rooms w/bath add £1.50, £1, and £2 respectively. Light breakfast and towels included.

Marlborough Hostel (IHH), 81 Marlborough St. (tel. 874 7629 or 874 7812; fax 874 5172), directly behind the O'Connell St. tourist office. Large and light rooms with super-comfy beds. Barbecues in the backyard garden in summer. Bike shed. Kitchen with microwave. Common room with peat fire. Check-out 10:30am. 4- to 10-bed dorm £7.50. Single £14. Double £22. Continental breakfast included. Sheets 50p. Laundry 50p.

Isaac's (IHH), 2-4 Frenchman's Lane (tel. 874 9321), first right off Lower Gardiner St. walking up from the Custom House. Floor upon floor of rooms attractively decorated with framed prints and floral comforters. Youthful staff and guests mingle in the bustling, inexpensive café and outdoor patio on the ground floor. Drawback: this hostel is huge—some rooms are more comfortable, spacious, and cleaner than others. Bed lockout 11am-5pm. 12- to 14-bed dorm £7. 6- to 8-bed dorm £8.50. Twin £31. Single or triple room £18.50/person. Rates 70p-£1 cheaper Jan.-April and Oct. Continental breakfast £1.25, Irish breakfast £2. Lockers (in rooms) 50p deposit. Fills up a week in advance for Fri. and Sat. nights.

M.E.C., 42 North Great Georges St. (tel. 872 6301 or 872 5707), off Parnell St. This grand Georgian building was first built as the home of the Archbishop of Dublin, then served as a convent until 1987. The beautiful stairway and the lovely, high ceilings reveal the building's potential, but the interior also belies the building's age. The beds are long and a little soft, but the neighborhood is refreshingly quiet. Kitchen and 24-hr. TV lounge. 8- to 16-bed dorm £8.50. Single £13.50. Double £21. Quad £34. Weekly rate July-Aug. £45, Sept.-June £35. Sheet and pillow £1. Free luggage storage and carpark.

Dublin International Youth Hostel (An Óige/HI), 61 Mountjoy St. (tel. 830 1766 or 830 1396). O'Connell St. changes names three times before reaching the turn left onto Mountjoy St. A convent with stained-glass windows and confessional boxes converted into an institutional, 420-bed hostel. Large rooms, squeaky wooden bunks. Guard possessions closely; it's not the nicest neighborhood. Secure parking. Currency exchange. 24-hr. kitchen. Dorm £9, non-members £9.50. 4- to 6-bed dorm £10/person. Twin £24. Prices £2 cheaper Oct.-May. Breakfast w/ cereal included. Café w/cheap meals (£3.50) and packed lunches (£2). Luggage storage 50p. Sheets £1. Self-service laundry £4.

Globetrotter's Tourist Hostel (IHH), 46 Gardiner St. Lower (tel. 873 5893). Comfortable beds top each other in high bunks. Most excellent bathrooms. Groove to Percy Sledge in the funky dining room. July to mid-Sept. £12/person, mid-Sept. to June £10/person or £25 for 3 nights (not applicable July-Aug.). Breakfast w/cereal. Safety deposit boxes £1.50. Free luggage storage.

Morehampton House Tourist Hostel, 78 Morehampton Rd., Donnybrook (tel. 668 8866; fax 668 8794). Although it's a bit out of the way (10-min. bus ride, 20-min. walk from city center), this refurbished Victorian building provides comfortable accommodations. Take buses #10, 46A, and 46B. Luggage storage. Bike park and rental. Kitchen, TV room, and laundry. 10-bed dorm £8. 6- to 8-bed dorm £11. Double £30. Prices £1-2 cheaper Oct.-May. Add £2 for rooms w/bath.

Baggot University Centre, 114 Baggot St. (tel. 661 8860). Sean and Moira Fitzgerald make their hostel a welcoming place. The mattresses are thin and some rooms get overcrowded, but breakfast is unique for Dublin hostels: yogurt, fresh brown bread, and orange juice. Carpark. Small self-catering kitchen. 5- to 8-bed dorm £10.50. Double £25. Free luggage storage.

If you're still without a room, you may want to try **Gogarty's Temple Bar Hostel,** 18-21 Anglesea St. (tel. 671 1822; £14/dorm in summer), or **Goin' My Way,** 15 Talbot St. (tel. 878 8484 or 874 1720; £7/dorm). Either way, you get what you pay for. Also worth considering is university housing, freed up in the summers. These tend to be modern, comfortable, and expensive. **Dublin City University,** Glasnevin (tel. 704 5736) can be reached by bus #11, 13, or 19A from city center. (Single in 2-room suite w/kitchenette and bathroom is £17/night, £90/week, £60/week for 2-4 weeks. Twin room £24/night, £100/week. Rooms available June 18-Sept. 22.) Other options are **USIT,** which operates University College Dublin dorms in Belfield (tel. 269 7111), and **University of Dublin** dorms in Rathmines (tel. 497 1772).

Bed & Breakfasts

A blanket of quality B&Bs covers Dublin and the surrounding suburbs. Those with a green shamrock sign out front are registered, occasionally checked, and approved by Bord Fáilte. B&Bs without the shamrock haven't been inspected but may be better-located and cheaper. B&B prices stretch from £12 to £25 per person. Near the city center, inexpensive B&Bs cluster along Upper and Lower Gardiner St., on Sheriff St., and near the Parnell Sq. area. These B&Bs are rarely warm, welcoming places; exceptions are listed below.

Neighborhood B&Bs are often spare rooms in a house that has emptied of children. They tend to be close to the city: Clonliffe Rd., Sandymount, and Clontarf are no more than a 10- or 15-minute bus ride from Eden Quay. Suburbs offer more calm and a greater chance of finding decent B&Bs, especially for those without a reservation: B&Bs in Howth (p. 117) and Dún Laoghaire (p. 122) are just as accessible (by DART) to Dublin as many of the B&Bs listed below. Maynooth (p. 136) and Malahide (p. 120), reached by suburban rail, are also good places to stay. Aside from the regions covered below, B&Bs within the city limits are also to be found in large numbers in Raheny (Dublin 5), Drumcondra (Dublin 9), Templeogue (Dublin 6W), and Santry Rd. (Dublin 9, close to the airport). Dublin Tourism's annually updated *Dublin Accommodation Guide* (£3) lists all approved B&Bs and their rates.

Gardiner Street

The B&Bs in this area can be a budget-traveler's purgatory. Many travelers arrive late at night and, knowing no better, are plundered here. Choose wisely, or choose a suburban B&B. Lower Gardiner St. and Upper Gardiner St. are within walking distance, but buses #41, 41A, 41B, and 41C from Eden Quay are convenient for the farther parts of the road. Those who are walking should head north up O'Connell St. and take a right onto Parnell St. to reach Gardiner St.

Glen Court, 67 Gardiner St. Lower (tel. 836 4022), 1 block west of Busáras, 2 blocks east of O'Connell. An old Georgian house with high ceilings and a potential that the beds and furniture don't match, but it's clean, cheap, and well-located. Single £16. Double £28. Triple £39. Quad £44.

Leitrim House, 34 Blessington St. (tel. 830 8728), on the final stretch of what was O'Connell St. after it crosses Mountjoy St. Leitrim House is 1 block past the false teeth repair shop. Bus #10 drops you off nearby at the top of Mountjoy St. Lilac walls and flowers on the windowsill result in flowery and pleasant-smelling rooms. Reliquaries in the parlor strike a contrast. Mediocre beds. Pampering proprietor really makes the place. £13/person.

Parkway Guest House, 5 Gardiner Place (tel. 874 0469). The rooms are plain but comfortable, and the location, just off Gardiner St. but without the noisy traffic, is excellent. Friendly, young proprietor offers discerning advice on restaurants and pubs and could talk for hours about Irish sports (his hurling scars brand him an authority). Single £17. Double £32. w/bath £34.

Marian Guest House, 21 Upper Gardiner St. (tel. 874 4129). Guests have enjoyed the antique marble fireplaces in this old building for decades and also revel in the delightful rooms (all w/TV). Call ahead. June-Oct. £15/person, Nov.-May £14.

Clonliffe Road

This respectable lower-middle class neighborhood seems to have a grandmotherly figure behind every door. An ideal place to stay if you're planning to attend an event at Croke Park, or if you want to listen to the concerts there for free (cutting-edge rockers Tina Turner, Bryan Adams, and Bon Jovi played here in summer 1996—try to contain your excitement). Take bus #51A from Lower Abbey St. or take a 20-minute walk from the city center: up O'Connell St., right on Dorset St., across the Royal Canal, and finally right onto Clonliffe Rd.

Mrs. M. Ryan, 10 Distillery Rd. (tel. 837 4147), off Clonliffe Rd., on the left if you're coming from city center. Yellow paint trims this gingerbread-like house, attached to #11. Pink-haired in '93, blonde in '94, and platinum in '95, the grandmotherly proprietor looked pretty normal in 1996. She welcomes all with firm beds and warm comforters. £12/person, single £14.

Mrs. Kathleen Greville, Mona B&B, 148 Clonliffe Rd. (tel. 837 6723). Firm beds and clean rooms kept tidy by a warm proprietor who is also an avid sports fan. Fresh homemade bread, tea, and cakes are always on hand to welcome guests. Single £17. Double £30. Open May-Oct.

Mrs. Brid Creagh, St. Aiden's B&B, 150 Clonliffe Rd. (tel. 837 6750). The healthy plants, nonsmoking rooms, and green, gurgling fountain are bound to remind you of home. £15/person. Open April-Sept.

Sandymount

Slightly farther away (1¾mi. south of city center), Sandymount is a peaceful, middle-class seaside neighborhood near Dublin Port, south of city center. Take bus #3 from O'Connell St. or take the DART to Landsdowne Rd. or Sandymount stops (10min.).

Mrs. R. Casey, Villa Jude, 2 Church Ave. (tel. 668 4982), off Beach Rd. Bus #3 or DART (Lansdowne Rd. stop). Mrs. Casey has nourished 7 children and countless others with her homemade bread and strapping Irish breakfasts. The parlor over-flows with family photos, fresh flowers, and lace doilies. Every room is immaculate and TV-equipped. £13/person.

Mrs. Bermingham, 8 Dromard Terrace (tel. 668 3861). Bus #3 from O'Connell St. or DART to Sandymount stop. Old-fashioned rooms, one with a bay window over-looking the garden, and a TV in the sitting room. Soft beds with great, fluffy com-forters. Owner is lots of fun. Single £15. Double £26, July-Aug. £28.

Mrs. Dolores Abbot-Murphy, 14 Castle Park (tel. 269 8413). Friendly owner is as sweet as candy. Each cheerful room has a TV. The dining room adds elegance to every meal. £14/person, w/bath £16. Open May-Oct.

Clontarf and Malahide Rd.

Clontarf Rd. runs along Dublin Bay across from the Dublin Port facility north of the city center. Behind it rise the startlingly pretty hills of Howth. Houses with addresses in the 200s face directly onto the Irish Sea; those with addresses in the 90s face it through a maze of smokestacks. Sea breezes and a waterfront park almost make up for the lively sight of car ferries chugging into dock. Take bus #30 from Lower Abbey St. to Clontarf Rd. (15min.).

Mrs. Carmel Drain, Bayview, 265 Clontarf Rd. (tel. 833 9870). Palm tree in the front yard. Mrs. Drain made the sheepskin rugs scattered throughout the house with sheep from her brother's farm. Bay view, indeed, with mountains too. Ortho-pedic beds and tea and biscuits in each room. £15/person, w/bath £16.50.

Ferryview Guest House, 96 Clontarf Rd. (tel. 833 5893). Thick carpets, fluffy com-forters, friendly family—you won't want to leave. Nautical objects abound in the cheerful, non-smoking rooms. Single £16. £15/person, w/bath £16.50.

Mrs. M. Dunwoody, 19 Copeland Ave. (tel. 833 9091), between Malahide Rd. and Howth Rd. Easy access to buses and a location 10min. closer to the city than other B&Bs in the area. A doll collection resides in the elegant dining room. Nonsmoking rooms. Single £17.50. Double £28, w/bath £33.

Mrs. Patricia Barry, Bayview, 98 Clontarf Rd. (tel. 833 3950). Recently refurbished, fresh, airy rooms. Beds have pink bows on them. Piano in sitting room. Super showers. £16/person, w/bath £17.

Mrs. Geary, 69 Hampton Ct. (tel. 833 1199). Comfortable rooms made special by friendly proprietors. Hampton Ct. connects Vernon St. with Castle St. off Clontarf Rd. £14, w/bath £16.50.

Camping

Most campsites are far from the city center, but camping equipment is available in the heart of the city. **The Great Outdoors,** Chatham St. (tel. 679 4293), off the top of Grafton St., has an excellent selection of tents, backpacks, and cookware. (10% discount for An Óige/HI members. Open Mon.-Wed. and Fri.-Sat. 9:30am-5:30pm, Thurs. 9:30am-8pm). **O'Meara's,** 26 Ossory Rd. (tel. 836 3233), off North Strand Rd., sells camping equipment and rents tents. (£25/week. Open Mon.-Thurs. and Sat. 10am-1pm and 2-6pm, Fri. 10am-9pm, Sun. 2:30-5:30pm.) **Mary St.,** the continuation of Henry St. (off O'Connell St.), has several shops with affordable equipment.

Backpackers EuroHostel, 80/81 Lower Gardiner St. (tel. 836 4900). Not really a campsite, but a big room behind the hostel has mattresses where diehard budget travelers can camp out (£4) and still use all of the hostel facilities. No toilet seats, few showers—by no means plush.

Comac Valley Caravan & Camping Park, Corkagh Park, Naas Rd., Clondalkin (tel. 462 0000; fax 462 0111). Peaceful, modern campground accessible by buses #77, 77A, 49, and 65 (30min. from city center). Foodshop, laundry, and kitchen facilities; electricity included. Lounge with cable TV. Caravans £7-8.50. Tents £2-3.50 plus £1/adult, 50p/child.

Shankill Caravan and Camping Park, (tel. 282 0011). Buses #45, 45A, 46, and 84, from Eden Quay, and the DART all run to Shankill. Middle-aged travelers in campers alternate with shrubs and tents. Not the ideal accommodation for seeing Dublin. The views of the hills and the 20-min. walk to the beach are much more convenient. £4.50-5.50/tent plus £1/adult, 50p/child. 8-min. shower 50p.

North Beach Caravan and Camping Park, Rush (tel. 843 7131 or 843 7602). Bus #33 from Eden Quay (runs every 45min.) and the suburban train rush here. Peaceful, beach-side location in a quiet town just outside of Dublin's sphere of influence. Kitchen; indoor beds for emergencies. £3.50, children £1.75. Electricity £1. No dogs allowed.

Long-term Stays

Solo travelers expecting to spend several weeks in Dublin may want to consider a bedsit, or sublet. Long stays are often most economical when sharing the cost of renting a house or apartment with others. Rooms in outer-city locations like Marino and Rathmines fetch about £32-50/week (ask whether electricity, phone, and water are included). B&Bs sometimes give reduced rates (£70/week) for long-term stays but are often reluctant to do it in the summer. Dublin's countless university students are often looking for roommates, usually for the summer but also on a weekly basis. The most up-to-date, comprehensive postings of vacancies are at USIT, 19-21 Aston Quay. Trinity College has a **noticeboard** near the guard's desk. Also check in the Student Union and the main entrance to TCD (Trinity College).

A group looking to rent a house or apartment for a few months should consult the *Dublin Accommodation Guide* (£3), which lists affordable abodes (£45-100/week/person). Ballsbridge (Dublin 4) and Rathmines (Dublin 6) are popular, up-scale neighborhoods with pubs, restaurants, and stores of their own. Classified ads in the two main daily newspapers, the *Irish Times* and the *Irish Independent,* can also help in finding cheap housing, often at weekly rates. If you want someone else to do the legwork, **Relocators,** 38 Dame St. (tel. 679 3511), opposite the Central Bank, arranges accommodation in Dublin and the suburbs. The company has set deals with land-lords to get reduced rates on flats, apartments, B&Bs, and Irish cottages. Bedsits may be as little as £25/week, but a service charge of £45 is required. (Open Mon.-Fri. 9am-7:30pm, Sat. 10am-4:30pm, Sun. 11am-3:30pm.)

FOOD

Dublin's **open-air markets** sell fresh and cheap fixings with interesting colors and smells. Vendors with thick east-coast accents hawk fruit, fresh Irish strawberries, flowers, and the occasional chocolate bar from their pushcarts. The frenzied **Moore St. Market,** lined with butcher shops, is the city's main trading center (open Mon.-Sat. 9am-5pm). Moore St. runs between Henry St. and Parnell St. The **Thomas St. Market,** along the continuation of Dame St., is a calmer alternative for fruit and vegetable shopping (open Fri.-Sat. 9am-5pm). The **Festival Market,** at the corner of Nicholas St. and Back Lane off High St. (just past Christ Church), is better known for inexpensive clothing and jewelry than for produce (open Fri.-Sun. 9am-5pm).

The cheapest **supermarkets** around Dublin are the **Dunnes Stores,** which are at St. Stephen's Green Shopping Centre, ILAC Centre, off Henry St., and on North Earl St., off O'Connell St. (All open Mon.-Wed. and Fri.-Sat. 9am-6pm, Thurs. 9am-8pm.) **Quinnsworth** supermarkets are also widespread. There are so many grocery stores around that it's quite easy to find basic supplies. The **Runner Bean,** 4 Nassau St. (tel. 679 4833), vends wholefoods, homemade breads, and veggies, fruits, and nuts for the squirrel in you (open Mon.-Fri. 8am-6pm, Sat. 9am-6pm). **Down to Earth,** 73 South Great Georges St. (tel. 671 9702), stocks health foods, herbal medicines, and a dozen varieties of granola (open Mon.-Sat. 10am-6pm). **Padania Gastronomic Emporium,** corner of Crow and Cecilia St., Temple Bar (tel. 679 2458), offers "the largest selection of exclusive Italian delicacies in Ireland." Cook this food in hostel kitchens and watch your popularity increase three-fold.

Temple Bar

This neighborhood is ready to implode from its mass of inexpensive and creative eateries. The Temple Bar has more ethnic diversity in its restaurants than the combined counties of Louth, Meath, Wicklow, and Longford (probably Offaly, too). For an area marketed to tourists, the prices are surprisingly reasonable. Be sure to pick up a **Temple Bar Passport** for a 5-10% discount at area stores and restaurants (available at the Temple Bar Information Centre, Eustace St., and most hostels).

The Well Fed Café, 6 Crow St. (tel. 677 2234), off Dame St. Inventive vegetarian dishes served by a worker's cooperative in a stripped-down, bohemian atmosphere. Peace and protest posters on the walls; idealists and disenchanteds at the tables. Adverts for indie band gigs and leaflets for liberal causes in lobby. Popular with the gay community. Brown bread and soup £1, main courses £2.40-2.70, apple pie with cream 80p. Open Mon.-Sat. noon-8pm. Wheelchair accessible.

Bad Ass Café, Crown Alley, off Temple Bar (tel. 671 2596). Burned down in 1994 but, like phoenixes, Bad Asses rise from the ashes. Colorful, exuberant atmosphere. The food fits right in. Besides, Sinéad O'Connor once worked here, so you can't go wrong. Lunch £3-5. Medium pizza £5.15-7.75. Student menu (with ISIC): coleslaw, scone and butter, "magic mushrooms," medium pizza, beverage (£5.75). Open daily 9am until "late" (past midnight).

Old New Orleans, 3 Cork Hill (tel. 670 9785), across from Dublin Castle. The least expensive Cajun restaurant in town, it's spicy enough to satisfy even expatriate Louisianians. High booths ensure privacy amidst the candlelit tables. If the mood is right, Liam may read your palm with eerie accuracy. Vegetarian jambalaya £5.45, cajun chicken salad £3.50. Open Mon.-Fri. noon–midnight.

Poco Loco, 32 Parliament St. (tel. 679 1950), between Grattan Bridge and City Hall. Proprietor Neasa O'Riordan asks country music stars using *Let's Go* to please visit her when in Dublin. Excellent Tex-Mex in Ireland—who knew? Enchiladas, burritos, chimichangas, or tacos £4.75, combo of 2 £6. Where else can you get Dos Equis? Open Mon.-Fri. noon-midnight, Sat. 5pm-midnight, Sun. 5-10pm.

La Mezza Luna, 1 Temple Lane (tel. 671 2840), corner of Dame St. Stars and half-moons twinkle from a midnight-blue ceiling. The food is celestial, too. You can't upstage *paglia*—smoked ham with a mushroom, cream, and wine sauce (£5.50). A spicy *pasta pomodoro* (£4) fills diners to the brim. For dessert, *tiramisú* (£3). Open Mon.-Sat. 12:30-11pm, Sun. 4-10:30pm.

Gallaghers, 20/21 Temple Bar (tel. 677 2762). Trilingual menu (English, French, and Italian) reflects diverse selection. Place to come for a 3-course meal (lunch £5, dinner £10). Several vegetarian dishes. Open daily 11am-midnight.

Gogarty's Hotel Café, 18-21 Anglesea St. (tel. 671 1822). Much more reasonable price-wise to eat than to stay here. Big breakfast £3, pastas £3.50, sandwiches £1.30, Irish dish of the day £3.50. Open daily 8am-8pm.

Trinity College, Grafton Street, Christ Church

Leo Burdock's, 2 Werburgh St. (tel. 454 0306), uphill from Christ Church Cathedral. Luckily the steps of the Cathedral are nearby—Burdock's is take-out only, and eating Burdock's fish and chips is a religious experience from which walking shouldn't distract. Dubliners' pick for best fish and chips in the universe. Haddock or cod £2, large chips 95p. Open Mon.-Fri. 12:30-11pm, Sat. 2-11pm.

Chez Jules, 16a D'Olier St. (tel. 677 0499). Always pumping with people of all ages; fun atmosphere. Mainly seafood and pasta dishes. Special 3-course lunch £5, 3-course dinner £10. Mussels in garlic £5.75, veggie dish of the day £5.75. Open Mon.-Fri. noon-3pm and 6pm-11pm, Sat. 1-4pm and 6-11pm, Sun. 5-10pm.

Marks Bros., 7 South Great Georges St. (tel. 667 1085), off Dame St. Thick sandwiches (£1.30-1.70) and high salads for starving artists and punks. 3 levels allow for solitary contemplation of James Joyce or of the causes of social stratification. Very popular among gays. Just for fun, tally up the total number of pierced body parts among the waitstaff. Legendary cinnamon buns 40p, choice of 10 herbal teas 50p, salads 95p. Open Mon.-Sat. 10am-5pm.

Metro Café, 43 S. William St. (tel. 679 4515). New wave café with a fine coffee selection and homemade breads. Simple but scrumptious. Ciabatta (Italian roll) £3, caesar salad £3.50, cappuccino w/cinnamon 85p. Open Mon.-Sat. 8am-8pm.

Harrison's, Westmoreland St. (tel. 679 9664). Romance that special someone without spending a fortune: 3-course meal for £7 served 5-7pm on candlelit tables as piano music floats through the air. Prices still reasonable after that: vegetable roulade £6.50, seafood medley £5.80. Open daily noon-10:30pm.

Bewley's Cafés (tel. 677 6761). 4 locations. A Dublin institution frequented by a delightful crowd of Dublin characters. Dark wood paneling, marble table tops, and mirrored walls complete the look. Wildly complex pastries (£1); outstanding coffee. Meals are plain but inexpensive. Branches at: 78 Grafton St., the largest (open Sun.-Thurs. 7:30am-1am, Fri.-Sat. 7:30am-2am); 12 Westmoreland St., once frequented by James Joyce (open Mon.-Sat. 7:30am-9pm, Sun. 9:30am-8pm); 13 South Great Georges St. (open Mon.-Sat. 7:45am-6pm); and Mary St., past Henry St. (open Mon.-Wed. 7am-9pm, Thurs.-Sat. 7am-2am, Sun. 10am-10pm).

Cornucopia, 19 Wicklow St. (tel. 677 7583). This vegetarian horn of plenty overflows with huge portions. Sit down for a serious meal (vegetable and bean curry w/ rice and salad £4.45) or just a snack (large lentil soup £1.50) and people-watch. Open Mon.-Wed. and Fri. 9am-8pm, Thurs. 9am-9pm, Sat. 9am-6pm.

The Stag's Head, 1 Dame Court (tel. 679 3701), via an alleyway off Dame St. at Stanley Racing #28. Marked by a Stag's Head logo in tile on the sidewalk. A great pub with even better grub. Boiled cabbage and potatoes £4.25, chicken and mushroom pie with chips and vegetables £4.50, sandwiches £1.30. Food served Mon.-Fri. 12:30-3:30pm and 5:30-7:30pm, Sat. 12:30-2:30pm.

Wed Wose Café, Exchequer St. off South Great Georges St., near the bwock-wong wed-bwick mawket. Ecwectic decor, cwamped seating, and good cheap food. "Mega-bweakfast" (double bacon, egg, sausage, toast, tomato, white pudding, beans, and fwied bwead) £3; steak sandwich on Fwench bwead, veggie burgers £3.25; sandwiches £1.50. Open Mon.-Sat. 7am-7pm.

La Cave, 28 South Anne St. (tel. 679 4409), off Grafton St. An underground wine-bar replete with Frenchness. Elegant, romantic, soothing. Wines served by every measure. On Sunday nights, poets, musicians, and aesthetes gather for readings and repartee. Cheese plate £4.50 (enough for a meal), vegetarian couscous £5.50, beef braised with Dijon mustard £5.50, *table d'hôte* (complete meal; say "TAH-bluh DOTE" to fit in) £12.50. Open daily 12:30-3pm and 6pm-2am or later.

North of the Liffey

Eating here is undoubtedly less interesting than it is south of the river. O'Connell St. sports blocks of neon fast-food chains, and side streets are filled with fish-and-chips shops and newsagents stocking overpriced groceries. Your options are limited.

The Winding Stair Bookshop and Café, 40 Lower Ormond Quay (tel. 873 3292), near Bachelor's Walk. Café overlooking the river shares 2 floors with bookshelves. Contemporary Irish writing, periodicals, and soothing music decrease the pace even more. Big Greek salad £2.60, sandwiches £1.50, soup and bread £1.60. Open Mon.-Sat. 10:30am-5:30pm.

Flanagan's, 61 O'Connell St. (tel. 873 1388). "A well-regarded establishment whose tourist trade occasionally suffers from being too close to a McDonald's," describes Tom Clancy in *Patriot Games*. Close, but better. Veggie dishes £6, calzone £4.90. Special deals at pizzeria upstairs: (12" 2-topping pizza £4.25; garlic bread, salad, 12" pizza and tea £6). Open daily 8am-midnight.

Clifton Court Hotel, Eden Quay (tel. 874 4535). Excellent pub grub served in a convivial atmosphere. Trad music nightly at 9pm, no cover. Chicken and mushroom *vol au vent* £5, salmon steak £6.45. Open daily noon-9pm.

PUBS

"Good puzzle would be cross Dublin without passing a pub," wrote James Joyce. A local radio station once offered £100 to the first person to solve the puzzle. The winner explained that you could take any route—you'd just have to visit them all on the way! While smaller Irish towns pack everyone into a few gloriously generic pubs, Dublin's size allows for shapes, styles, subcultures, and specialties. Dublin is the place to hear Irish rock. It is not, however, the best place for traditional music. The *bodhrán* is present, but it's much easier to find in the west. Beware of pubs that advertise "traditional" music but mean traditional American country or folk. Check *In Dublin, Hot Press,* or the *Event Guide* for pub music listings, or ask around.

Many heated debates begin from the postulation that Guinness tastes slightly different from every tap. In-depth *Let's Go* research suggests that the Guinness Hop Store, attached to the Guinness Brewery (see p. 107), serves the city's best, while Mulligan's, the former world champ, keeps its hold on second place. Responsible visitors do their part to contribute to this growing field of research. The **Jameson Literary Pub Crawl** (tel. 454 0228) traces Dublin's liquid history in reference to the literary history. The tour spews snatches of info and entrancing monologues. (Meet at The Duke, 2 Duke St. June-Aug. Mon.-Sun. 7:30pm, Mon.-Sat. 3pm, and Sun. noon; May and Sept. Mon.-Sun. 7:30pm; Oct.-April Fri.-Sat. 7:30pm, Sun. noon. £6, students £5.) The **Let's Go Dublin Pub Crawl Map** aids in discovering the city. The number following each pub listing is the key to its location on the map itself.

Temple Bar & Vicinity

The Brazen Head [7], 20 Lower Bridge St. (tel. 679 5186), off Merchant's Quay. Dublin's oldest pub, established in 1198 as the first stop after the bridge on the way into the city. The courtyard is quite the pickup scene on summer nights.

The Stag's Head [20], 1 Dame Court (tel. 679 3701). From Dame St., the entrance is next to #28, Stanley Racing, and is marked by "Stag's Head" written in tile on the sidewalk. Beautiful Victorian pub with stained glass, mirrors, and brasswork. Shiny. Huge whiskey kegs on the walls. Truly excellent grub.

Mulligan's [13], 8 Poolbeg St. (tel. 677 5582), behind Burgh Quay off Tara St. Big rep as the best pint of Guinness in Dublin, outside the brewery itself. This is a sit, smoke, and talk sort of pub. The crowd consists mainly of middle-aged men. Hang out here to get a taste of the typical Irish pub: low-key and nothing fancy.

Out on the Liffey [6], 27 Upper Ormond Quay (tel. 872 2480). Peter Hosford, Mr. Gay Ireland 1996, calls this "a typical Dublin pub that happens to be gay." Dark wood paneling and small alcoves add to the friendly, relaxed atmosphere.

COUNTY DUBLIN

Dublin Pub Crawl

The White Horse, 1
Lanigan's, 2
The Grattan, 3
Slattery's, 4
Hughes', 5
Out on the Liffey, 6
Brazen Head, 7
Mother Redcap's
Tavern, 8
Whelan's, 9
Chocolate Bar, 10
O'Donoghue's, 11
Kennedy's, 12
Mulligan's, 13
The Buttery, 14
The Palace, 15

Oliver St. John
Gogarty, 16
The Porter House, 17
The George, 18
The Globe, 19
Stag's Head, 20

International Bar, 21
Davy Byrne's, 22
Café en Seine, 23
Sinnott's, 24
McDaid's, 25
Break for the Border, 26

Oliver St. John Gogarty [16], corner of Fleet St. and Anglesea St. (tel. 671 1822). Lively and convivial atmosphere in a traditionally decorated pub. Named for Joyce's nemesis and onetime roommate, who appears in *Ulysses* as Buck Mulligan. Trad sessions nightly 7:30pm (no cover) and good food. Always crowded. Open until 1am Thurs. and Fri., until midnight Sat.

The Porter House [17], 16-18 Parliament St. (tel. 679 8850). Dublin's only micro-brewery brews 6 different kinds of porter, stout, and ale, including Wrasslers 4X Stout, "Michael Collin's favorite tipple—a stout like your grandfather used to drink." If you're up for it, try *An Brainblásta*—7% alcohol by volume.

Whelan's [9], 25 Wexford St. (tel. 478 0766), continue down South Great Georges St. A bit of a walk away from everything. Nightly music makes it one of the hot spots for live rock in Dublin. They know it, and have a "21 and over" policy. Nightly Irish indie rock or blues (cover £2-4). Late club Sat. at 11:30pm.

Mother Redcaps Tavern [8], Back Lane (tel. 453 8306), near Christ Church. In a spacious former shoe factory, convenient to Burdock's (see **Food**, p. 96). Tradi-tional music Tues. and Thurs., folk and ballads Wed., various live artists Fri. and Sat. (10pm-12:30am). Show off your musical talents at open trad sessions Sun. 12:30pm and 9pm. At the separate bar upstairs, Fri. and Sat. nights bring big names in trad music (and a cover, £5-6).

The Palace [15], 21 Fleet St. (tel. 677 9290), behind Aston Quay. A classic neigh-borly Dublin pub has old-fashioned wood paneling and cramped quarters that encourage *craic*. The favorite pub of many a Dubliner.

The Globe [19], 11 South Great Georges St. (tel. 671 1220). Music issues forth from the Roman busts on the walls. Frothy cappuccino and Guinness fuel the hip, young clientele of this café/pub. It is indeed pretentious, and yet so relaxed that you can appreciate the modernist paintings next to the bust of Julius Caesar. **Ri Ra** night-club attached. Nightly 11pm-2:30am. Ri Ra cover £6, £4 w/concession.

The George [18], 89 South Great Georges St. (tel. 478 2983). Dublin's first gay bar. Young, fashion-conscious crowd. Mostly gay men. Lesbians welcome any time but most come Wed. nights. Late bar Wed.-Sat. until 2am. Upstairs, **The Block** is a bar and nightclub for gay men (Fri.-Sat.).

Grafton Street & Vicinity

Davy Byrne's [22], 21 Duke St. (tel. 671 1298), off Grafton St. "Nice quiet bar. Nice piece of wood in that counter. Nicely planned. Like the way it curves there." Come see what Joyce meant in *Ulysses*. The many comfortable seats may not bring epiph-any about why Joyce considered this a "moral pub," but they do enhance the enjoy-ment of pints. Lively, middle-aged crowd.

McDaid's [25], 3 Harry St. (tel. 679 4395), off Grafton St., across from Anne St. Writer Brendan Behan frequented this cheery place. Old books adorn the walls, inspiring conversations of love and honor among the young Dubliners in the crowded downstairs and more spacious upstairs areas; occasional rock gigs.

The International Bar [21], 23 Wicklow St. (tel. 677 9250), off Grafton St. on the corner of South William St. Excellent improv comedy on Mon. nights and stand-up comedy on Wed. nights. All other nights blues (performances 9pm; cover charge £3.50). Sun. 12:30pm, ballads and traditional Irish music (no cover).

The White Horse [1], 1 Georges Quay (tel. 679 3068). For those mornings when you just *need* a pint with your muesli, the White Horse opens at 7:30am every day. It's a small, simple bar, frequented by regulars who come for the trad and rock (starts around 9:30pm; no cover). Low-key—yet to be invaded by tourists.

Sinnott's [24], South King St. (tel. 478 4698). Classy crowd of 20-somethings gather in this loud pub that feels more like a club (without the dancing). Open noon-2am daily.

The Chocolate Bar [10], Hatch St., corner of Harcourt St. (tel. 478 0225). No spe-cial attractions like music or a literary past, but hugely popular. Young, lively group of clubbers drink here until **The Pod,** the attached nightclub, opens.

Break for the Border [26], Lower Stephen's St. (tel. 478 0300). With a restaurant, bars, and a nightclub, this "entertainment complex" is always buzzing. Sun.-Tues. late bar and DJs, Wed.-Sat. live rock and dance music. Open noon-2am.

Baggot Street & Vicinity

O'Donoghue's [11], 15 Merrion Row (tel. 676 2807), between St. Stephen's Green North and Baggot St. Original home of The Dubliners, a renowned Irish band. Every night new hopefuls attempt to break through into the traditional Irish music scene (9:30pm in summer, 9pm in winter; no cover). Outdoor seating and two floors accommodate the multi-generational crowd which may have trouble standing as the night unfolds.

Café en Seine [23], 40 Dawson St. (tel. 677 4151), is built to impress. A café with dainty pastries occupies the front of the shop. A very long bar stretches through a high-ceilinged hall hung with tapestries and zany paintings. A large crowd of mixed ages packs in, unconcerned that the Seine is not at all nearby.

Kennedy's [12], 31 Westland Row (tel. 676 2998), on the southeast corner of Trinity College campus. Boisterous TCD hangout. Jolly musicians gather to play informal sessions (June-Sept. Thurs. and Sat.; Oct.-May Tues., Thurs., and Sat.).

The Buttery [14], Trinity College. Dark, smoky, and crammed with students, even at 3pm. This pub offers no extras. People come here to talk and drink. Watch out for the notorious Colm MacPhaídin. Open Mon.-Fri. noon-11pm.

North of the Liffey

Fibber MaGee's, 80 Parnell St. (tel. 874 5253). A big pub full of a young crowd dancing to indie rock. You can rest your pint on tree-stump tables outside. The antithesis of a "classy" pub, Fibber's has pints for only £1.65 from 10:30am-5pm every day and pints for only £1.80 every Wed. evening. Local rock bands play on Sat. afternoons (cover £3). Open until 2am every night, so you can avoid the dreaded 11:30pm bar call. Prices go up to £2/pint after the other pubs close.

Lanigans [2], Clifton Court Hotel, Eden Quay (tel. 874 3535). Imagine a pub with Irish folk singers that actually attracts more Dubliners than tourists: this happy pub is it. Live music nightly at 9pm breaks down any generational barriers as people of all ages enjoy the *craic.*

The Grattan [3], 165 Capel St. (tel. 873 3049), on the corner of Little Strand St. Cushy blue velvet seats envelop international ears attuned mostly to jazz, but also blues, folk, rock, and "Australian mad convict rock." Separate rock venue upstairs (cover £2) often features French rock bands whose mettle draws a Euro-slick, urbane crowd. Music starts 9pm.

Slattery's [4], 129 Capel St. (tel. 872 7971). The pub best known for traditional Irish music and set dancing. Rock and blues, too. Music nightly 9pm: trad downstairs (free), rock and blues upstairs (cover £2-4).

Hughes [5], 19 Chancery St. (tel. 872 6540), behind the Four Courts. A delightful venue for trad (nightly, no cover) and set dancing (Mon. and Wed. 9pm).

The Flowing Tide, 8 Abbey St. Lower (tel. 874 0842). Eclectic mix of regulars, students, and patrons and actors of the Abbey Theatre. Ground floor attracts an older, artsy crowd while the **Neptune Bar** downstairs fills with Dublin students. Pints of Guinness 10p less than the area norm.

O'Casey's Off-license, (tel. 874 4294), around the corner from the Flowing Tide. For those who want a break from the pub scene without a break from the brew.

TOURS

Self-Guided Walking Tours

Dublin is definitely a walking city. Most major sights lie within a mile of O'Connell Bridge. The tourist office sells *Visitor Attractions in Dublin,* which lists the main sights (£2), and many info-stuffed brochures that describe self-guided walking tours (£1 each). **The Cultural Trail,** starring James Joyce and Sean O'Casey, zips among the Four Courts, the Custom House and King's Inn, the Municipal Gallery, and the Dublin Writers' Museum. It touches on most of the important historical and political sights. The **Old City Trail** begins on College Green and weaves its way through the Liberties, the markets, and Temple Bar. It's mostly a gathering of "here-once-stoods," which seldom have any relation to each other. The **Georgian Heritage Trail** is more tangibly gratifying. This theme-walk connects some of the better preserved Georgian streets, terraces, and public buildings south of the Liffey. Lastly, the disturbingly wor-shipful **Rock'n'Stroll Trail** brochure, accompanied by a cassette tape, makes a circuit of significant sights in Dublin's recent musical history, labelling each with a plaque. Sinéad O'Connor's waitressing job at the Bad Ass Café and U2's Windmill Lane Stu-dios are its highlights. For Joyce fans, the tourist office provides a *Ulysses* map of **Dublin** (50p) that details some of Leopold Bloom's haunts. It retraces Bloom's literary actions, beginning with kidneys for breakfast. The entire walk inevitably takes 18 hours (including drinking and debauching).

Guided Walking

If you lack the discipline to follow a self-guided walking tour in its entirety (oh Danny boy, the pubs, the pubs are calling...), you should consider a guided one. Generally tours last about two hours, but entertaining anecdotes and continuous movement preclude boredom. The **Historical Walking Tour** (tel. 845 0241) is a two-hour crash course in Dublin's history from the Celts to the present, stopping at nine points of his-torical interest and laying great emphasis on the "gritty" lives of ordinary Dubliners. (June-Sept. Mon.-Sat. at 11am, noon, and 3pm; Sun. also at 2pm; Oct.-May Sat.-Sun. at noon. Meet at Trinity's front gate. £5, students £4.) The witty and irreverent **Trinity College Walking Tour** also touches on Dublin's history, but it concentrates on Uni-versity lore. (June-Sept. 10am-4pm. Leaves every 15min. from the Info Booth inside the front gate; ½hr. £5, students £4, includes admission to the Old Library and the Book of Kells.)

Dublin Footsteps (tel. 496 0641 or 845 0772) runs an "early morning" tour of Dub-lin's main attractions (meets at the Grafton St. Bewley's, Mon.-Sat. 10am), as well as tours along literary and medieval lines. (Mon.-Sat. literary tour 11am; medieval tour 2:30pm; 2hr.; £5. Tours meet at Bewley's Café on Grafton St. Free coffee to finish the tour.) Those yearning for guidance in the matters of *céilí* and Guinness should try the **Traditional Music Pub Crawl,** which meets at Oliver St. John Gogarty's on the corner of Fleet St. and Anglesea St. (May-Oct. Sat.-Thurs. 7:30pm; £6, students £5). **The Lit-erary and Historical Performance Tour** puts its suffering guides into period cos-tume as they make the sight seeing circuit (pre-booked groups only; call Mark tel. 478 0191; £5, students £4.50).

Bus Tours

Bus tours don't give the personal feel for the city of a walking tour, but are much eas-ier on the feet. The **Dublin City Sightseeing Tour** (tel. 873 4222) stops at Dublin's major sights, including the Writers Museum, TCD, and the Guinness Brewery, and allows you to get on or off all day (April-Sept. daily departs every ½hr. from 9:30am-5pm; driving time 1hr. 50min.; £5). The **Dublin Grand Tour** (tel. 872 0000), covers a larger area and includes more sights, but does not stop (departs every ½hr. from 9:30am-5pm; 2½hr.; £8). Both tours depart from the Dublin Bus office on 59 O'Con-nell St. Tours often change, so call Dublin Bus for the latest offering.

SIGHTS

South Side

Trinity College & Nearby

Trinity College (tel. 677 2941) sprawls within its ancient walls in the very center of Dublin, between Westmoreland St. and Grafton St., fronting on the block-long traffic circle now called College Green. Pearse St. runs along the north edge of the college, Nassau St. to its south. Inside, stone buildings, a cobblestone walk, and spacious green grounds give the campus an illusory seclusion and allow for the occasional white-suited game of cricket. The British originally built Trinity in 1592 as a Protes-tant religious seminary "to civilize the Irish and cure them of Popery." The college became part of the accepted path which members of the Irish Anglican upper class trod on their way to high government and social position. The Catholic Jacobites who briefly held Dublin in 1689 used it as a barracks and prison, but for the next 100 years it was a focus of Anglo-Irish society. Jonathan Swift, George Berkeley, Robert Emmett, Thomas Moore, Edmund Burke, Oscar Wilde, Samuel Beckett, and Robin Garvey are just a few of the famous Irish Protestants who studied here. Until the 1960s, the Catholic church deemed it a cardinal sin to attend Trinity. Once the church lifted the ban, the size of the student body more than tripled.

The 1712 **Old Library** holds Ireland's finest collection of Egyptian, Greek, Latin, and Irish manuscripts, including the **Book of Kells.** Around 800 AD, Irish monks squeezed multicolored ink from insects to make the famous *Book,* a four-volume edition of the Gospels. Each page holds a dizzyingly intricate lattice of Celtic knotwork and scrollwork into which animals and Latin characters are interwoven. In 1007 the books were unearthed in Kells, where thieves had apparently buried them. In order to enhance preservation, only two volumes are on display. One page is turned each month. For your own amusement, you could ask the Trinity librarians why they won't return the *Book of Kells* to the town of Kells. Trinity owns other illuminated books, like the *Book of Durrow,* Ireland's oldest. Some of these are periodically put on display. Tourists viewing the *Book* should also check out the ever-changing science and history exhibits. Upstairs, in the Library's Long Room, are "Ireland's oldest harp"—the Brian Ború harp (the designer model for Irish coins), and one of the few remaining 1916 proclamations of the Republic of Ireland. (Library open Mon.-Sat. 9:30am-5:30pm, Sun. noon-5pm. Admission £3, students £2.25.) The line to see the *Book of Kells* is often lengthy, and visitors are herded onward by fastidious librarians. Ignore the pressure and pause to ponder away.

In Trinity's Davis Theatre, the **Dublin Experience** movie takes visitors on a 45-minute historical tour of Dublin, reminiscent of grade-school educational films. (Daily 10am-5pm, on the hour. Admission £2.75, students £2.25. Combination ticket to Library and Dublin Experience £5.50, students £4.25.) **The Douglas Hyde Gallery** (no tel., but they do have paintings of fire and skulls), on the south side of campus, exhibits the works of modern Irish artists (open Mon.-Sat. 10am-5pm; free). During the academic year, TCD bulges with events and activities, which are listed on bulletin boards around campus. Concerts and plays are posted at these points.

Staring down Trinity from across College Green is a monolithic, Roman-looking building, the **Bank of Ireland** (tel. 677 6801). Built in 1729, it originally housed the 18th-century Irish Parliament, a body that represented the Anglo-Irish landowning class (whose kids attended TCD across the road). Its members envisioned a semi-independent Irish "nation" under the British crown and made up of the privileged Protestants of the Pale. After the Act of Union, the British sold the building to the bank on the condition that the bank blot out any material evidence of the legislature. The enormous curved walls and pillars were erected *around* the original structure to make the whole look more impressive. The bank inside is actually much smaller. Tourists can still visit the former chamber of the House of Lords. There, beneath a huge antique chandelier, is the gold mace of the old House of Commons. The last Speaker of the House refused to hand the mace over, saying he would keep it until an Irish assembly returned. Also on display is Maundy Money: special coins once given to the poor on the Thursday before Easter, and legal tender only for that day. (Open during regular banking hours Mon.-Wed. and Fri. 10am-4pm, Thurs. 10am-5pm. Guided tours Tues. 10:30am, 11:30am, and 1:45pm; 45min. Free.)

South of College Green (away from the Liffey) run the three or so blocks of **Grafton Street,** off-limits to cars and ground zero for shopping tourists and residents alike. This crowded pedestrian street provides some entertaining observations, but nothing much to do or even to buy (most things are too expensive). Upstairs at the Bewley's Grafton St. branch is the **Bewley's Museum,** located in the coffee chain's former chocolate factory. Tea-tasting machines, corporate history, and a display on Bewley's Quaker heritage are among the fun curiosities (open daily 10am-7pm; free).

Merrion Square & St. Stephen's Green

South of Trinity College at Leinster St., with Kildare St. at its back and Merrion Square in front, **Leinster House** provides chambers for the present-day Irish parliament. It holds both the *Dáil* (DOIL), which does most of the government work, and the *Seanad* (SHAN-ad), the less powerful upper house. Together these two houses make up the parliament, called (in Irish) *An tOireachtas* (on tir-OCH-tas). When the *Dáil* is in session, visitors can view the proceedings by contacting the Captain of the Guard (tel. 678 9911; passport is necessary for identification). The *Dáil* meets, very roughly, Wednesday through Friday from January to July (10:30am-5pm). The Captain's office also conducts some tours of the *Dáil's* galleries (Sat. 10:30am-12:45pm and 1:30-4:50pm). Leinster House was once the house of the Duke of Leinster. When he built it, most of the urban upper-crust lived north of the Liffey. By erecting his house so far south, he was able to front it with an enormous lawn. The first Irishman to ride in a balloon ascended in 1785 from this same lawn. The airman had neglected to bring enough ballast, however, and drifted out over the Irish Sea, where well-aimed gunfire from the Dún Laoghaire barge brought him down.

Near Leinster House, a passel of museums pop up. The **National Museum,** Kildare St. (tel. 677 7444), focuses on legendary ancient Ireland and the equally heroic Easter Rising. One room gleams with the Tara Brooch, Ardagh Chalice, and other Celtic goldwork. Another, devoted to the Republic's founding years, offers plenty of historical information for the curious and shows off the bloody vest of James Connolly to pique the interest of the morbid. Connolly made a name for himself as a leading exponent of socialism in Ireland before he took part in the Easter Rising. After the rebellion, Connolly was condemned to death by the British. Other chambers collect musical instruments and, oddly, Japanese ceramics. (Open Mon. 10am-9pm, Tues.-Wed. 2-9pm, Thurs.-Fri. 10am-5pm, Sat. 10am-1pm. Free.)

Connected to the National Museum, the **Natural History Museum** (tel. 677 7444) specializes in stuffed Irish wildlife. They present a mounted Great Irish Elk, Ireland's noble, extinct beast. They've got leeches and tapeworms, too (safely mounted). The collection is large and contains tons of info, but everything is in need of organization and preservation (same hours as the National Museum; free).

Down the street on Merrion Sq., the **National Gallery's** 2400 canvases (tel. 461 5133) include paintings by Brueghel, Goya, Rembrandt, and El Greco. The works of Irish artists comprise a major part of the collection. Portraits of Lady Gregory, Eliza O'Neill, James Joyce, George Bernard Shaw (who willed a third of his estate to the Gallery), and William Butler Yeats (by his father, John Butler Yeats) stare at one another in the four-story staircase. (Open Mon.-Sat. 10am-6pm, Thurs. 10am-9pm, Sun. 2-5pm. Free.) Nearby, the **National Library** (tel. 661 2523) chronicles Irish history and exhibits literary objects in its entrance room. (Library open Mon. 10am-9pm, Tues.-Wed. 2-9pm, Thurs.-Fri. 10am-5pm, Sat. 10am-1pm. Free, but academic reasons needed to obtain a library card and entrance to the reading room.)

Dublin may remember its Viking conquerors more fondly than its British ones, but the British had much more influence on the appearance of the capital today. **Merrion Square** and **Fitzwilliam Street** (near the National Museum) are plum full of Georgian buildings and their elaborate rows of colored doorways. W.B. Yeats moved from 18 Fitzwilliam St. to 82 Merrion Sq. Farther south on Harcourt St., playwright George Bernard Shaw and Dracula's creator, Bram Stoker, were once neighbors at #61 and #16, respectively. **#29 Lower Fitzwilliam Street** (tel. 702 6165) tries to give tourists an impression of late-18th-century Dublin domestic life. The National Museum has stuffed the Georgian house with period furniture, elegant drapes, and Irish crafts. Though the house hardly depicts the realistic 18th-century life of any social class, some of the objects make for interesting viewing (open Mon.-Sat. 10am-5pm, Sun. 2-5pm; admission £2.50, students £1).

The prim Georgian townhouses continue up **Dawson Street,** which connects St. Stephen's Green to Trinity College, one block west of Leinster House. A few small and endearing churches line this street, as does **Mansion House,** home to Lord Mayors of Dublin since 1715. The house's various façades and additions give it an interesting but eclectic appearance. The Irish state declared independence here in 1919. The Anglo-Irish truce (not the Treaty) was signed here in 1921.

Kildare, Dawson, and Grafton St. all lead south from Trinity to **St. Stephen's Green.** The 22-acre park was a private estate until the Guinness clan bequeathed it to the city. The park today is constantly in use and has become a real center for activity. It's crowded with arched bridges, an artificial lake, flowerbeds, fountains, gazebos, pensioners, punks, trees, couples, strollers, swans, ducks, more trees, and a waterfall. On sunny days, half of Dublin seems to fill the lawns. During the summer, even the ducks enjoy the outdoor theatrical productions near the old bandstand. (Gates open Mon.-Sat. 8am-dusk, Sun. 10am-dusk.)

Edging the green, **Newman House,** 85-86 St. Stephen's Green South (tel. 706 7422 or 706 7419), was once the seat of University College Dublin, the Catholic answer to Trinity. The poet Gerard Manley Hopkins spent the last years of his life teaching classics at the new college. Joyce's years here are chronicled in *Portrait of the Artist as a Young Man.* Inside Newman House, the range of restored rooms has less kitsch than those at #29 Fitzwilliam. (Open June-Sept. Tues.-Fri. 10am-4pm, Sat. 2-4:30pm, Sun. 11am-2pm. Admission £1, students 75p.)

The **George Bernard Shaw House,** 33 Synge St. (tel. 475 0854), lies between Grantham St. and Harrington St., off Camden Rd. and near the Grand Canal Bridge. It is of interest both as a period piece and as a glimpse into Shaw's childhood. Mrs. Shaw held recitals, sparking little George's interest in music, and kept a lovely Victorian garden, sparking George's interest in landscape painting. So how did he get into socialism in London? (Open May-Oct. Mon.-Sat. 10am-1pm and 2-6pm, Sun. 11:30am-1pm and 2-6pm. Admission £2.20, children £1.10. Joint ticket with Dublin Writer's Museum and the James Joyce Museum £6, children £5. If it's too wet to walk, take bus #15, 16, 19, or 22 from O'Connell St.)

The **Irish Jewish Museum,** 3-4 Walworth Rd., off Victoria St. (tel. 676 0737), lies even farther from the city center. South Circular Rd. runs to Victoria St., and from there the museum is signposted. A restored, former synagogue that houses a large collection of artifacts, documents, and photographs chronicling the history of the Jewish community in Ireland from 1079—five arrived and were duly sent away—through the massive waves of European migrations. The most famous Dublin Jew is probably Leopold Bloom, hero of *Ulysses.* He's covered here, too. (Open Sun. 10:30am-2:30pm or by appointment. Donation requested.)

Temple Bar, Dame Street, & Cathedrals

West of Trinity College between Dame St. and the Liffey, the **Temple Bar** neighborhood wriggles with activity. Narrow cobblestone streets link up cheap cafés, hole-in-the-wall theaters, rock venues, and used clothing and record stores. The Irish transport authority intended to demolish the neighborhood and replace it with a seven-acre transportation center. As the transport authority acquired Temple Bar properties, they decided to lease the land (and make a profit) for the short term, until they had acquired all the necessary property. However, the artists and other transient types who moved into Temple Bar started a brouhaha about being forced into homelessness. In 1985 they circulated petitions and saved their homes and businesses from the rapacious transit project.

Government-sponsored Temple Bar Properties has since spent over £30 million to build eight arts-related tourist attractions in the Temple Bar. Though deadlines have been postponed until 1996, work continues on an expansion of the existing Temple Bar Art Gallery, a Children's Cultural Centre, a Photography Centre with school and gallery, and a Multi-Media Centre for video and high-tech arts. Among the cultural attractions are the **Irish Film Centre** (tel. 679 3477); four contemporary art galleries; **The Ark** (tel. 670 7788), a cultural center aimed at seven- to fourteen-year-olds; and the **Temple Bar Music Centre** (tel. 677 7349). Call each venue directly, or consult the Dublin Event Guide (tel. 677 7349).

South of the Temple Bar across Dame St. awaits another inviting, unpretentious shopping district. The **Dublin Civic Museum,** South William St. (tel. 679 4260), seems a bit out of place in the middle of all those shops. The pint-size, two-story townhouse holds photos, antiquities, and knick-knacks relating to the whole range of Dublin life, from the comparatively small-toed Vikings to the shoes of Patrick Cotter, the 8'6" "giant of Ireland." Another of the original 1916 proclamations of the Republic is held here. Photos of the 1907 Dublin Exhibition show a reconstructed Somalian village, complete with real Somalians, that was shipped in to Dublin. Disturbing. (Open Tues.-Sat. 10am-6pm, Sun. 11am-2pm. Free.)

At the west end of Dame St. where it meets Parliament St. and Castle St., sits **Dublin Castle** (tel. 677 7129). King John built the castle in 1204 on top of an old Viking fort. For the next 700 years Dublin Castle was the seat of British rule in Ireland and the office of the British Governor General. The present Dublin Castle structure actually dates mostly from the 18th and 19th centuries. The Birmingham Tower was once a prison. Fifty insurgents died at the castle's walls on Easter Monday, 1916. Since 1938 the presidents of Ireland have been inaugurated here. The State Apartments, once home to English viceroys, now entertain EU representatives and foreign heads of state. If they're not entertaining state visitors when you get there, you can entertain the notion of a tour. (State Apartments open Mon.-Fri. 10am-12:15pm and 2-5pm, Sat.-Sun. and holidays 2-5pm, except during official functions. Admission £1.75, students £1. Rest of castle is free.) The Visitors Centre exhibits photos of many of Dublin's architectural showpieces and of the Castle itself. Next door, the **Dublin City Hall** boasts an intricate inner dome and statues of national heroes like Daniel O'Connell. Designed as the Royal Exchange in 1779, it is open to the public.

Dublin's ecclesiastical beauties line up west of the Castle. All are owned by the Church of Ireland, none by the Catholic Church. As Ireland is overwhelmingly Catholic and the Anglo-Irish aristocracy (which had the funds to support the ornate churches) no longer exists, the cathedrals and churches are now considered works of art more than centers of worship.

Christ Church Cathedral (tel. 677 8099) looms at the end of Dame St., uphill and across from the Castle. Sigtyggr Silkenbeard, King of the Dublin Norsemen, built a wooden church on this site in 1038. Strongbow rebuilt it in stone in 1169. Further additions were made in the following century and again in the 1870s. Stained glass sparkles above the raised crypts (one of them supposedly Strongbow's own). The cathedral's cavernous crypt once held shops and drinking houses. Now, cobwebs hang down from the ceiling, fragments of ancient pillars lie about like bleached bones, and a mummified cat is frozen in the act of chasing a mummified mouse. (Open daily 10am-5pm except during services. Choral evensong Sept.-May Thurs. 6pm. Admission £1.) Christ Church also hosts **Dublinia** (tel. 679 4611), a charming re-creation of medieval Dublin with life-size reconstructions of a merchant's house and of Wood Quay c. 1200. Less than charming is the buboe-covered mannequin in the Black Death display. (Open May-Sept. daily 10am-5pm; Oct.-April 11am-4pm. Admission £4, students and children £2.90; includes admission to Christ Church.) Bus #50 and 50A from Aston Quay, or your feet, will carry you here.

From Christ Church, Nicholas St. runs south and downhill, becoming Patrick St. and encountering **St. Patrick's Cathedral** (tel. 475 4817). The body of the church dates to the 12th century, though many parts date from Sir Benjamin Guinness's 1864 remodeling job. Measuring 300 ft. from stem to stern, it's Ireland's longest church. St. Patrick, who brought Christianity to Ireland and drove out all the snakes, allegedly baptized converts in the park next to the cathedral. Artifacts and relics from the Order of St. Patrick show up inside. Jonathan Swift, who wrote *Gulliver's Travels,* spent his last years as Dean of St. Patrick's. Sir Walter Scott said of his visit to St. Patrick's that "one thinks of nothing but Swift there...The whole cathedral is practically his tomb." His crypt rises above the south nave. (Open Mon.-Fri. 9am-6pm, Sat. 9am-5pm, Sun. 10-11am and 12:45-3pm. Admission £1.20, students 50p.)

Marsh's Library, St. Patrick's Close (tel. 454 3511), beside St. Patrick's Cathedral, is Ireland's oldest public library. A peek inside reveals its elegant wire alcoves, or "cages." The library has an extensive collection of early maps. Swift said of the library's founder, Archbishop Marsh, that "no man will be either glad or sorry at his death." (Open Mon. and Wed.-Fri. 10am-12:45pm and 2-5pm, Sat. 10:30am-12:45pm. £1 donation expected.)

Farther west, along High St., stands **St. Audoen's Church** (Church of Ireland), the oldest of Dublin's parish churches, founded by the Normans. Papal Bulls were read aloud here during the Middle Ages (open Sat.-Sun. 2:30-5pm). There is also a totally separate, Catholic St. Audoen's Church. **St. Audoen's Arch,** built in 1215 next to the church and now obscured by a narrow alley, is the only gate that survives from Dublin's medieval **city walls**. During the 16th century, walls ran from Parliament St. to the Dublin Castle, along the castle walls to Little Ship St. and along Francis St. to Bridge St., then along the Liffey.

Guinness Brewery & Kilmainham

From Christ Church Cathedral, follow High St. west (away from downtown) through its name changes to Cornmarket, Thomas, and then James to reach the giant **Guinness Brewery,** St. James Gate (tel. 453 6700; fax 454 6519). **The Hop Store,** on Crane St. off James St., is Guinness's sneaky way of perpetuating the legend of the world's best stout. The building still smells of the hops that were stowed there for 200 years. Farsighted Arthur Guinness signed a 9000-year lease at the original 1759 brewery nearby. There are exhibits on the historical and modern processes of brewing, a short promotional film, and art exhibits on the top floor that showcase local talent. Best of all is the bar, where visitors get two complimentary glasses of the dark and creamy goodness. This stuff is rumored to be the best Guinness in Dublin and hence, according to Dublin logic, the world's best beer. But is it really "good for you?" (Open June-Sept. Mon.-Sat. 9:30am-5pm (last admission), Sun. 10am-4:10pm (last admission); Oct.-May Mon.-Fri. 10am-3:50pm (last admission). Admission £3, students £1.50.) Buses #21A, 7, and 78A head here along the quays.

The Royal Hospital and Kilmainham Gaol lie farther to the west, a 20-minute walk from the city center. The **Royal Hospital Kilmainham** began in 1679; it wasn't a "hospital" in the modern sense, but an old-age home for retired or disabled soldiers. The façade and courtyard copy those of Les Invalides in Paris; the baroque chapel looks cool too (tours Sun. noon-4:30pm and by request; £1). Since 1991 the hospital has held the **Irish Museum of Modern Art** (tel. 671 8666), whose capacious, brightly colored galleries might just as well be showing art in New York, Oakland, or Auckland; the museum project took some heat over its avant-garde use of this historic space. Modern Irish artists are intermixed with others as the gallery builds up a permanent collection. (Call for changing exhibits, artist talks, or concerts. Museum and building open Tues.-Sat. 10am-5:30pm, Sun. noon-5:30pm. Free. Guided tours Wed. and Fri. 2:30pm, Sat. 11:30am.)

"The cause for which I die has been rebaptized during this past week by the blood of as good men as ever trod God's earth," wrote Sean MacDiarmada in a letter to his family, while he was awaiting his execution for participation in the 1916 Easter Rising. He, along with most of the rebels who fought in Ireland's struggle for independence from 1792 to 1921, was imprisoned at **Kilmainham Gaol** (tel. 453 5984). Today the former prison is a museum which traces the history of penal practices over the last two centuries. The jail's last occupant was Éamon de Valera. The tour, which lasts 1½ hours, begins in the prison chapel, where Easter Rebel Joseph Plunkett was married to his betrothed hours before his execution. The reception was a subdued affair. (Open late-April to Sept. daily 9:30am-6pm; Oct. to mid-April Mon.-Fri. 1-4pm, Sun. 1-6pm. Admission £2, students and children 60p.) Take bus #51, 63, 69, 78A, or 79 from the city center to both the Museum and the Gaol.

Distant Sights

For a beautiful view of Dublin and the action of Dublin Port, take bus #1 from the O'Connell St. stop outside the tourist office to its terminus at the Powerstation. Go around the station, past the dump, past the rocks, and onto the South Wall. The road extends 2 mi. into Dublin Bay with the darling Poolbeg Lighthouse at the end, built in 1761. On a windy day, the long walk can feel like a boat ride.

COUNTY DUBLIN

Drimnagh Castle, Long Mile Rd. (tel. 450 2530), behind the school. A partially restored 12th-century Norman keep. Open Wed. and Sat.-Sun. and bank holidays noon-5pm and other times by arrangement. Admission £1.50, students £1.

Chester Beatty Library and Gallery of Oriental Art, 20 Shrewsbury Rd. (tel. 269 2386 or 269 5187), take DART to Sandymount, bus #5, 6, 6A, 7A, or 8 from Eden Quay, or #10 from O'Connell St. If you're into Arabic calligraphy in illuminated copies of the Koran, you'll go nuts here. Strong Turkish collection of manuscripts and paintings. Also Biblical papyri from 200 AD, Japanese snuff bottles, and Chinese rhinoceros horn cups. Free. Guided tours Wed. and Sat. 2:30pm. Open Tues.-Fri. 10am-5pm, Sat. 2-5pm.

Museum of Childhood, 20 Palmerstown Park (tel. 973 223), take bus #13 or 14 from College Green. A private collection of dolls and toys from the 1700s to the present, including the oldest doll in Ireland. Utterly charming. Dollhouse kitchens have tiny mice and rats. Tanya's Crystal Palace is a big dollhouse of 20 rooms filled with tiny brass beds, porcelain sinks, and typewriters. Open Sun. 2-5:30pm. Last admission 4:45pm. Admission £1, students and children 75p.

Pearse Museum, St. Edna's Park, Grange Rd. (tel. 934 208). Bus #16 from O'Connell St. See Patrick Pearse's study and learn about his work as educator, writer, and revolutionary. Also features the Nature Study Centre with a self-guided tour. Free. Open May-Aug. daily 10am-5:30pm; Sept.-Oct. and Feb.-April 10am-5pm; Nov.-Jan 10am-4pm. Closed daily 1-2pm.

North Side

O'Connell St. & Parnell Square

Rising from the river to Parnell Square, **O'Connell Street** is the commercial center of Dublin, at least for those who can't afford to shop on Grafton St. It's also said to be the widest street in Europe, though it's hard to imagine anyone traveling to Madrid with a yardstick to compare. In its Joycean heyday, it was known as Sackville Street. The name was changed in honor of "The Liberator" after independence. Smaller avenues leading off of O'Connell St. retain the old name. The center traffic islands are monuments to Irish leaders: Parnell, O'Connell, and James Larkin, who organized the heroic Dublin general strike of 1913. O'Connell's statue faces the Liffey and O'Connell Bridge; the winged women aren't angels but Winged Victories, though one has a bullet hole in a rather inglorious place.

Farther up the street, the newer statue of a woman lounging in water is officially the Spirit of the Liffey or "Anna Livia," unoffically and scathingly called "the floozy in the jacuzzi," "the whore in the sewer," (in Dublin, that rhymes too), or "Anna Rexia." The even newer statue of Molly Malone, of ballad fame, on Grafton St. gets called "the tart in the cart." Decide for yourself whether Dubliners are mocking the city, the monument-making mentality, or simply women in general with this series of popular nicknames. One monument you won't see is Nelson's Pillar, a tall freestanding column which remembered Trafalgar outside the GPO for 150 years. The IRA blew it up in 1966 in commemoration of the 50th anniversary of the Easter Rising; Nelson's English head now rests in the Dublin Civic Museum.

The **General Post Office** presides over O'Connell St. Not just a fine place to send a letter, the Post Office was the nerve center of the 1916 Rising. Patrick Pearse read the Proclamation of Irish independence from its steps. When British troops closed in, mailbags became barricades. Outside, some bullet nicks can still be seen; inside, a glass case exhibits pennies fused together by the British army's incendiary bombing. A few blocks up O'Connell St., turn right on Cathedral St. to find the inconspicuous **Dublin Pro-Cathedral,** the city's center of Catholic worship, where tens of thousands once gathered for Daniel O'Connell's memorial service. "Pro" means "provisional"—Dublin Catholics want Christ Church Cathedral returned.

Overlooking the park, the **Hugh Lane Municipal Gallery,** Parnell Sq. North (tel. 874 1903 or 874 1904), confines modern art within the Georgian walls of Charlemont House. When Lane offered to donate his collection of French Impressionist paintings to the city, he did so on the condition that the people of Dublin contribute to the gallery's construction. Because his collection and the architect chosen to build the

North Dublin Sights

Abbey Presbyterian
(Findlater's Church), 1
Bank of Ireland, 2
Belvedere House, 3
Brazen Head Hotel, 4
Christ Church Cathedral, 5
Custom House, 6
Four Courts, 7
Garden of Remembrance, 8
General Post Office, 9
King's Inns
(Constitutional Hill), 10
Mountjoy Square
(Gardiner St., Charles St.), 11
Pro-Cathedral (St. Mary's), 12
Rotunda Hospital, 13
St. George's Church, 14
St. Mary's Abbey, 15
St. Mary's Church, 16
St. Michan's Church, 17
Trinity College, 18

gallery were foreign, Dubliners refused to lend their support. Yeats lamented their provincial attitudes in a string of poems. Lane's death aboard the *Lusitania* in 1915 raised decades of disputes over his will, which were resolved by a plan to share the collection between the gallery in Dublin and the Tate Gallery in London. (Open Tues.-Fri. 9:30am-6pm, Sat. 9:30am-5pm, Sun. 11am-5pm. Free.)

Next door, the **Dublin Writers' Museum,** 18 Parnell Sq. North (tel. 872 2077; fax 872 2231), introduces visitors to the city's rich literary heritage. Rare editions, manuscripts, and memorabilia of Beckett, Brendan Behan, Patrick Kavanagh, Sean O'Casey, Frank O'Connor, Swift, Shaw, Wilde, and Yeats blend with caricatures, paintings, and an incongruous Zen Garden. (Open June-Aug. Mon.-Fri. 10am-7pm, Sat. 10am-5pm, Sun. 11:30am-6pm.; Sept.-May Mon.-Sat. 10am-5pm. Admission £2.75, under 18 £2. Combined ticket with either Shaw Birthplace or James Joyce Tower £4.35, children £3.75; ticket for all 3 £6, students £5.) Adjacent to the museum, the **Irish Writer's Centre,** 19 Parnell Sq. North (tel. 872 1302), is the administrative nerve center of Ireland's writing community, providing working and meeting space for today's aspiring Swifts. Frequent poetry and fiction readings present current writings to the public. The center is not a museum, but if you ring the doorbell you can go in for information about Dublin's literary happenings.

Just past Parnell Sq., the **Garden of Remembrance** eulogizes the martyrs who took the GPO. A cross-shaped pool is plugged at one end by a statue representing the mythical Children of Lir, who turned from humans into swans. They proclaim, in Irish, their faith in a vision of freedom: "In the winter of bondage we saw a vision. We melted the snows of lethargy and the river of resurrection flowed from it."

One block east of Parnell Sq. East lies the new **James Joyce Centre,** 35 North Great Georges St. (tel. 873 1984), up Marlborough St. across Parnell St. If you only visit one of Dublin's many Joycean institutions, this restored 18th-century Georgian house should be it. Run by his nephew, this museum features documents, photos, and manuscripts which make Joyce come alive. Feel free to mull over his works in the library or the tearoom, whose walls are lined with a *Ulysses* mural depicting each of the book's chapters. Call for info on lectures, walking tours, and Bloomsday events. (Open Mon.-Sat. 9:30am-5pm, Sun. 12:30-5pm. Admission £2.50, students £1.75, children 70p.)

Along the Quays

East of O'Connell St. at Custom House Quay, where Gardiner St. meets the river, is one of Dublin's architectural triumphs, the **Custom House.** It was designed and built in the 1780s by James Gandon, who gave up the chance to be St. Petersburg's state architect to settle in Dublin. The building's expanse of columns and domes suggests the mix of Rome and Venice that the 18th-century Anglo-Irish wanted their city to become. Carved heads along the frieze represent the rivers of Ireland; the Liffey is the only woman of the bunch. Several quays to the west, on Inn's Quay, stands another of Gandon's works, the **Four Courts;** from the quay or across the river, the building is monumentally impressive, but back and sides reveal 20th-century ballast. On April 14, 1922, General Rory O'Connor seized the Four Courts on behalf of the anti-Treaty IRA; two months later, after provocations, the Free State government of Griffith and Collins attacked the Four Courts garrison, starting the Irish Civil War. The building now houses the highest court in Ireland.

Mummies! Just up Church St., the dry atmosphere has preserved the corpses in the vaults of **St. Michan's Church,** which inspired Bram Stoker's *Dracula*. Of particular interest in this creepy place of death is a 6'6" crusader (dead) and the hanged, drawn, and quartered bodies of two of the 1759 rebels (very dead). (Open Mon.-Fri. 10am-12:45pm and 2-4:45pm, Sat. 10am-12:45pm. Admission £1.20, under 16 50p. Church of Ireland services on Sundays at 10am.) Farther north, uphill at the top of Capel St., the **King's Inns** on Henrietta St. were Gandon's last major building; from a cobblestone yard, two wings with pediments enfold a dome. Lawyers bark inside.

The **Irish Whiskey Corner,** Bow St. (tel. 872 5566), is located in a whiskey warehouse off Mary St. Learn how science, grain, and tradition come together to create the golden fluid with "the coveted appellation, whiskey." The film recounts the rise, fall, and spiritual renaissance of Ireland's favorite spirit. The experience ends with a glass of the Irish whiskey of your choice. Feel the burn. (Tours Mon.-Fri. 3:30pm, May-Oct. additional tours 11am and 2:30pm, and 3:30pm on Sat. Admission £3 including whiskey tasting.) From O'Connell St., turn onto Henry St. and continue straight as the street becomes Mary St., then Mary Lane, then May Lane; the warehouse is on a cobblestone street on the left.

Distant Sights

Take bus #10 from O'Connell St. or #25 or 26 from Middle Abbey St. west along the river to **Phoenix Park,** Europe's largest enclosed public park. The "Phoenix Park murders" mentioned in *Ulysses* happened in 1882; the Invincibles, a tiny nationalist splinter group, stabbed the Chief Secretary of Ireland, Lord Cavendish, and his Under-Secretary, 200m from the Phoenix Column. A British Unionist journalist forged a series of letters purporting to link Parnell to the murderers; when the fakes were exposed, Parnell's stock rose even further. The Phoenix Column, a Corinthian column capped with a phoenix rising from flames, is something of a pun—the park's name actually comes from the Irish *Fionn Uísce,* meaning "clean water." The 1760-acre park incorporates the President's residence *(Áras an Uachtaraín),* the U.S. Ambassador's residence, cricket pitches, polo grounds, and grazing red deer and cattle. The deer are quite tame and not to be missed; they usually graze in the thickets near Castleknock Gate. The park is peaceful during daylight hours, but unsafe at night. Nearby, the **Dublin Zoo** (tel. 677 1425) is one of the world's oldest zoos. It contains 700 animals and a discovery centre which features the world's biggest egg. (Open June-Aug. Mon.-Sat. 9:30am-6pm, Sun. 10:30am-6pm; Sept.-May Mon.-Fri. 9:30am-4pm, Sat. 9:30am-5pm, Sun. 10:30am-5pm. Admission £5.50, students £4, children £3, family £15.) Bus #10 from O'Connell St. passes the zoo.

Casino Marino, Malahide Rd. (tel. 833 1618), is a cute architectural gem and house of tricks. You can certainly gambol here, but you can't gamble; it's a casino only in the sense of "small house," built for the Earl of Charlemont in 1758 as a seaside villa. Funeral urns on the roof are chimneys, the columns are hollow and serve as drains, the casino has secret tunnels and trick doors, and the lions standing guard are actually made of stone. Speaking of tricks: since then, the house's ocean view has vanished! (Open mid-June to Sept. daily 9:30am-6:30pm, Oct. daily 10am-5pm, Nov. and Feb.-April Sun.-Wed. noon-4pm. Admission £2, students £1.50, children £1. Take bus #20A or B from Eden Quay, or #27 or 27A from Lower Gardiner St.)

ENTERTAINMENT

Be it Seamus Heaney or the Pogues you fancy, Dublin is equipped to entertain you. The *Dublin Event Guide* (free; available at tourist info offices and Temple Bar restaurants) comes out every other Friday with ads in the back, slightly fawning reviews in the front, and reasonably complete listings of museums and literary, musical, and theatrical events in between. Hostel staff are often good, if biased, sources of info. *In Dublin* (£1.50) comes out every two weeks with feature articles and listings for music, theater, art exhibitions, comedy shows, movie theaters, and gay and lesbian info (listings include place, date, time, and price).

Music

Dublin's music world attracts performers from all over the country. Pubs are the scene of much of the musical action, since they provide musicians with free beer and a chance to play. There is often a cover charge of £2-3 on better-known acts. *Hot Press* (£1.50) has the most up-to-date music listings, particularly for rock. Its commentaries on the musical scene are usually insightful, and its left-leaning editorials give a clear impression of what the Dublin artistic community is thinking. *In Dublin* comes out less often and thus isn't quite so up-to-the-minute, but its listings are more comprehensive and it has a wider range of information. Record store clerks and habitués are valuable founts of knowledge on the current Irish rock scene. Tower Records on

Wicklow St. has reams of leaflets. Bills posted all over the city also inform of coming attractions. Scheduled concerts tend to start at 9pm, impromptu ones even later.

Traditional music is not a tourist gimmick, but a vibrant and important element of the Irish culture and the Dublin music scene. Both natives and foreigners can clap hands and stomp to the beat. Some pubs in the city center have traditional sessions nightly, others nearly so: **Hughes', The Brazen Head, Slattery's, Oliver St. John Gogarty, McDaid's, The International Bar, Mother Redcaps Tavern,** and **O'Donoghue's** are all good choices for trad (see **Pubs,** p. 98). Traditional dancing or music are nightly events at **Comhaltas Ceoltóirí Éireann** (co-UL-tus), 32 Belgrave Sq., Monkstown (tel. 280 0295). From the Seapoint DART stop, Alma Rd. runs to Monkstown Rd. Belgrave Sq. is three blocks down on the left.

Big deal bands frequent the **Baggot Inn,** 143 Baggot St. (tel. 676 1430). U2 played here in the early 80s (some people are still talking about it). **Whelan's,** 25 Wexford St., the continuation of South Great George's St. (tel. 478 0766), is one of the hottest spots. Their posters cover the entire town. **An Béal Bocht** often hosts rock acts (see **Theater,** below). Big, big acts play to huge crowds at **Tivoli Theatre** (Francis St., tel. 454 4472), and will not only be well-publicized but also quite often sold out. **The Waterfront Rock Bar,** Sir John Rogerson's Quay (tel. 677 8466), was the big pub featured at the end of *The Commitments.* ("Tour of Irish Rock" nightly 8pm. Open Sun.-Thurs. until 11:30pm, Thurs.-Sat. until late.)

Country and western twang at **Brazen Head,** at **Barry's Hotel,** 1 Great Denmark St. (tel. 874 6943), or at the American-style **Bad Bob's,** 32 East Essex St. (tel. 677 5482). Customers mellow at **Rudyard's Wine Bar,** 15 Crown Alley (tel. 671 0846), to the sound of live jazz sessions Friday and Saturday night at 9pm. **McDaid's,** 3 Henry St. (tel. 679 4395), hosts acts on Mondays and Tuesdays at 8:30pm. On the North Side, **The Grattan,** 165 Capel St. (tel. 873 3049), hosts jazz on Wednesdays.

The **National Concert Hall,** Earl's Fort Terrace (tel. 671 1533), provides a venue for classical concerts and performances. July and August bring nightly shows (8pm; tickets £7-10, students half-price). A summer lunchtime series makes a nice break from work on occasional Tuesdays and Fridays (tickets £2.50-3). Programs for the National Symphony and smaller local groups are available at classical music stores. Sunday afternoon jazz is a common phenomenon. *In Dublin* has listings. The biggest names in rock and pop play at **Croke Park,** Clonliffe Rd. (tel. 836 3152).

Dance Clubs

In recent years, clubs have displaced rock venues as the home of Dublin's nightlife. As a rule, these spots open at 10:30 or 11pm, but the action gets moving only after 11:30pm when the pubs close. Clubbing is not the least expensive evening entertainment, since the cover runs £4-8 and pints are a steep £2-2.50. Most clubs close at 2 or 3am, but a few have been known to last until daybreak at 6am. To get home after Dublin Bus shuts down at 11:30pm, dancing fiends can take the **NiteLink bus** (Thurs.-Sat. midnight-3am hourly; £2.50), which runs designated routes to Dublin's outer city and its suburbs from the corner of Westmoreland and College St. Otherwise, taxi stands are located in front of TCD, on Aston Quay, and Abbey St. Lower. Be prepared to wait 30-45 minutes on Friday and Saturday nights.

Club Paradiso, at the Irish Film Centre (tel. 677 8788), has an appropriately cinematic decor. IFC members only (see **Cinema,** p. 114 for membership info and directions). Open 11:30pm-late. Cover £4.

UFO, upstairs at Columbia Mills, Sir John Rogerson's Quay. A mind-bogglingly intense club.

The Mission, Crowe St., is one of Dublin's hottest and newest clubs. Funky atmosphere attracts a refreshing mix of clubbers whose ages span two decades.

Pod, 35 Harcourt St. (tel. 478 0225), sports a colorful, Spanish-style decor that promotes the convivial, relaxed atmosphere.

The Kitchen, The Clarence Hotel (tel. 662 3066). Serious clubbers congregate.

Temple of Sound, in the Ormond Hotel on Ormond Quay, pumps out serious dance grooves on Thurs.-Sun. nights. Open 8:10pm-late. Cover £3-8.

Rí-Rá, 1 Exchequer St. (tel. 668 0995), in the Central Hotel, is a social epicenter for cool modern people but is open to anyone. Open daily 11pm-2:30am. Cover £6, concession £4.

The Turk's Head (tel. 679 2606), beneath the bar on Parliament St., will remind you of bygone days with its choice selection of 70s and 80s classics. Open nightly 10:30pm-2am. Sun.-Wed. free, Thurs. £3, Fri.-Sat. £5.

Gay & Lesbian Dublin

Dublin's progressive (for Ireland) thinking translates into an acceptance that was exemplified by the peaceful success of PRIDE, an annual, week-long festival celebrating gay identity in July. This accepting attitude has encouraged the development of a small but lively gay scene, punctuated by organized events. *Gay Community News* offers the most comprehensive and up-to-date information on gay life and nightlife in Dublin (free; available at Books Upstairs Bookstore, Temple Bar Information Centre, and the Well Fed Café). *In Dublin*'s gay page lists pubs, dance clubs, saunas, gay-friendly restaurants, bookshops, hotlines, and organizations. The listings are comprehensive but sometimes outdated. Copies of *Out* and *Advocate* magazines, when they exist, can be found at Eason's bookstore. Visit **Books Upstairs,** 36 College Green (tel. 679 6687), for your copy of the pricey *Irish Scene Gay Guide* (£7), which lists gay hotlines and venues throughout Ireland, or *The English Gay Times,* a monthly magazine that addresses social and political issues.

Gay Switchboard Dublin is a good resource for events and updates. It also sponsors a hotline (tel. 872 1055; Sun.-Fri. 8-10pm, Sat. 3:30-6pm). **Lesbian Line** offers similar services (tel. 661 3777; open Thurs. 7-9pm). **The National Gay and Lesbian Federation,** Hirschfield Centre, 10 Fownes St. (tel. 671 0939), in Temple Bar, publishes *Gay Community News* and offers counseling on legal concerns. It is not an info service but can provide advice. The lesbian community meets at **LOT** (Lesbians Organizing Together), 5 Capel St. (tel. 872 7770). The drop-in resource center and library is open Tuesdays through Thursdays 10am to 5pm. **Outhouse** is a gay community and research centre hoped to be established by 1997 (mailing address P.O. Box 4767, Dublin 2). Ask NGLF for more information. Tune into local radio FM103.8 for a gay talk show, **Out in the Open** (Tues. at 10pm).

Out on the Liffey is Dublin's best gay pub (see **Pubs,** p. 98). **The Front Lounge,** Parliament St. (tel. 679 3369), is a classy pub that stays open until 1am on Thursdays and Fridays. Gays, lesbians, and straights comfortably enjoy each other's company. **The George** hosts a disco called **The Block** Thursday through Sunday nights.

Most gay dance venues occur one night per week:

The Trinity, Nassau St., across from Trinity College, boogies on Sat. nights.

Stonewall, at the Barracks, is further away from the city center but larger and livelier. Dancing, a video screen, and pool tables make this club worth the trip. Bus #19, 19A, or 22, Griffith College, South Circular Rd. Cover £3.

The Furnace, 1-2 Aston Place, hosts **Get Out** the second Sun. of every month. Cabaret, dancing, and performances ensure a full-house and great *craic.*

The Playground, Temple of Sound, Ormond Hotel, Upper Ormond Quay (tel. 872 1811). Trendy clubbers head here on Sun. and bank holidays. Cover £5.

Freedom, at the Mission, Eustace St., livens it up on Mon. with music from the 70s and 80s. Gay staff. Open 11pm until late. Cover £3.

Pull, at the Kitchen, Essex St., draws in an artsy crowd of gays and lesbians. Open Mon. 11pm-2:30am. Cover £4.

Gosh, at Ri Ra, 1 Exchequer St., hosts serious, well-dressed gays and lesbians. Open Mon. 11pm-2:30am. Cover £6, with concession £4.

Lucky Lips, Irish Film Centre, Eustace St., lures lesbians on the last Fri. of every month. Described by the *Irish Scene Gay Guide* as a "cross-over between a sweaty café bar and a banging house party." Don't miss it.

Theater

Dublin's curtains rise on a full range of mainstream productions, classic shows, and experimental theater. Showtime is generally 8pm. Dame St. and its Temple Bar alleyways are home to a few companies. The rest are scattered within a 10-minute radius of O'Connell Bridge.

Abbey Theatre, 26 Lower Abbey St. (tel. 878 7222), was founded by Yeats and his collaborator Lady Gregory in 1904 to promote Irish cultural revival and modernist theater, which turned out to be a bit like promoting corned beef and soy burgers—most audiences wanted one or the other. J.M. Synge's *Playboy of the Western World* was first performed here in 1907. The production occasioned storms of protest and yet another of Yeats' political poems. Today, the Abbey, like Synge, has become respectable. As part of the National Theatre, it receives government funding. Box office open Mon.-Sat. 10:30am-7pm. Tickets £8.50-13.50; student standby 1hr. before show Mon. and Thurs., £6.

Peacock Theatre, 26 Lower Abbey St. (tel. 878 7222), downstairs, is more experimental. The usual evening shows plus occasional lunchtime plays, concerts, and poetry (£8, students £5). Box office open Mon.-Sat. at 7:30pm for that night's performance only; advance booking at the Abbey Theatre box office.

Gate Theatre, 1 Cavendish Row (tel. 874 4045), produces everything from Restoration comedies to Irish classics. Box office open Mon.-Sat. 10am-7pm. Tickets £10-12; student standby £6 Mon.-Thurs. at curtain time.

Project Arts Centre, 39 East Essex St. (tel. 671 2321), presents not just theater but all the performing arts, including avant-garde theater, dramatic readings, comedy, and dance. Box office open daily 10am-6pm; tickets £8, concessions £6. The free gallery hosts rotating visual arts exhibitions (open same time as box office).

Gaiety, South King St. (tel. 677 1717), provides space for modern drama, ballet, pantomime, and the Dublin Grand Opera Society. Box office open Mon.-Sat. 11am-7pm; tickets £7.50-12.50.

Olympia Theatre, 72 Dame St. (tel. 677 7744). Old standbys like *The Sound of Music.* Box office open Mon.-Sat. 10am-6:30pm; tickets £8-15; ½-price student standby after 7pm.

Andrews Lane Theatre, Andrews Lane (tel. 679 5720), off Dame St. Dramatic classics, old and new—Shakespeare, Molière, Brecht.

An Béal Bocht, 58 Charlemont St. (tel. 475 5614), hosts traditional Irish-language theater Wed. at 9pm (£5).

City Arts Centre, 23-25 Moss St. (tel. 677 0643), parallel to Tara St. off George's Quay. Avant-garde exploration of sexual and political issues (£6, students £4).

Samuel Beckett Theatre, Trinity College (tel. 478 3397). Inside the campus. Hosts anything that happens to pass, from drama to dance, done by students or professionals.

Cinema

Ireland's well-supported film industry got a kick in the pants with the arrival of the **Irish Film Centre,** Eustace St., in Temple Bar (tel. 679 3477 or 679 5744). The IFC mounts tributes and festivals, including a gay and lesbian film festival in August and a French film festival in October. A variety of classic and European arthouse films appear throughout the year. You must be a "member" to buy tickets. (Weekly membership £1; yearly membership £10, students £7.50; membership must be purchased at least 20min. before start of show; each member can buy only 4 tickets per screening. Matinees £2; 5pm showing £2.50; after 7pm £4, students £3.) Other artsy cinemas are the **Lighthouse Cinema,** 107 Fleet St. (tel. 873 0438; shows every night; £2 before 5pm, £3.50 after), and **The Screen,** D'Olier St. (tel. 671 4988 or 872 3922). First-run movie houses cluster on O'Connell St., the quays, and Middle Abbey St. The **Savoy,** O'Connell St. (tel. 874 6000), and the **Ambassador,** O'Connell St. (tel. 872 7000), and **Virgin,** Parnell St. (tel. 872 8400) offer the widest selection of new releases, primarily American films.

Events

The tourist office's *Calendar of Events* (£1; info on events throughout Ireland) and *Dublin Events Guide* (free; biweekly) describe Dublin's many festivals, provincial parades, mayor's balls, concerts, dances, and art shows. Ask about *fleadhs,* traditional day-long musical festivals. The **World Irish Dancing Championships** are held in late March or early April. The **Festival of Music in Irish Houses,** held during the second and third weeks of June, organizes concerts of period music in local 18th-century homes. The **Dublin Film Festival** (tel. 679 2937) in March features Irish and international movies and a panoply of seminars. The **Temple Bar Blues Festival** is a three-day blues extravaganza in mid-July. Bluesmen come from all over. Past guests have included Robert Cray and B.B. King. The Commitments would play here if they hadn't tragically disbanded. (Contact Temple Bar Information Centre for information, tel. 671 5717; most acts free; program guides available in July.)

St. Patrick's Day (March 17) occasions enormous parades, drunken carousing, and closed banks. Pubs offer special promotions, contests and extended hours. Don't expect corned beef and cabbage for dinner though—that's more of an Irish-American tradition.

Dublin returns to 1904 each year on **Bloomsday,** June 16, the day on which the action of Joyce's *Ulysses* takes place. Festivities are held all week long. The **Joyce Centre** (tel. 873 1984) sponsors a mock funeral and wake, a lunch at Davy Byrne's, and a breakfast with Guinness, all as part of its Bloomstime program. On the day itself, a Messenger Bike Rally culminates in St. Stephen's Green with drink and food. Many bookstores have readings from *Ulysses.* Some of the better ones are Books Upstairs and Fred Hanna's (p. 116). Check out the June issue of *In Dublin* and the *Dublin Event Guide* for year-to-year details.

The **Dublin Theatre Festival** in late September and early October is a premier cultural event. Tickets may be purchased all year at participating theaters and at branches of the Irish Life Building Society (main office on Lower Abbey St., tel. 704 2000). As the festival draws near, tickets are also available at the Festival Booking Office, 47 Nassau St., Dublin 2 (tel. 677 8439; tickets £8-14, £2 less for students; student standby tickets £3-5).

Sports & Recreation

Dubliners, probably because they have more to distract them, aren't as sports-centered as their country cousins tend to be. Sports are still a serious business, though, as attested to by the frequency of matches and events. The seasons for **Gaelic football** and **hurling** (the national sports of Ireland) run from mid-February to November. Both are games of skill, stamina, and strength that have evolved from ancient origins. Action-packed and often brutal, these games are entertaining for any sports-lover. Provincial finals take place in July, national semifinals in August (hurling on the 1st Sun., football on the 2nd and 3rd Sun.), and All-Ireland Finals in September. Games are played in Croke Park and Phibsborough Rd. (tickets available at the turnstiles; All-Ireland Finals tickets sell out quickly). Home games of the Irish **rugby** team are played in Lansdowne Road Stadium (Oct.-March). **Camogie** (women's hurling) finals also take place in September. For sports information, check the Friday papers or contact the Gaelic Athletic Association (tel. 836 3232). **Greyhound racing** continues all year. Meets start at 8pm and end around 10pm (Mon. and Sat. at Shelbourne Park, tel. 668 3502; Tues., Thurs., and Fri. at Harold's Cross, tel. 497 1081). **Horses** race at Leopardstown Racetrack, Foxrock, Dublin 18 (tel. 289 2888).

SHOPPING

Dublin is not really a center for international trade, and consumer goods are generally expensive. Your time may be better spent in pubs and castles. That said, if something is made anywhere in Ireland, you can probably find it in Dublin. Stores are usually open from 9am to 6pm Monday through Saturday, with later hours on Thursdays (until 7-8pm). Tiny shops pop up everywhere along the streets both north and south of the Liffey, but Dublin's major shopping is on **Grafton St.** and **Henry St.** On pedestrianized Grafton St., well-dressed consumers crowd into boutiques and restaurants, and buskers aplenty lay out their caps for money. **St. Stephen's Green Shopping Centre** is, well, a mall. Nearby, Lord Powerscourt's 200-year-old townhouse on Clarendon St., now the **Powerscourt Townhouse Centre,** has been converted into a string of chic boutiques carrying Irish crafts. **Georges St. Market Arcade** on South Great Georges St. near Dame St. will suit the more casual shopper. The arcade includes a number of vintage clothing, jewelry, and used record stalls as well as a fortune teller. (Nose-piercing with stud, £1.50. Open Mon.-Sat. 8am-6pm, Thurs. until 7pm.) **Wild-Child,** 61 South Great Georges St. (tel. 475 5099), has Dublin's largest selection of vintage and secondhand goods, including clothes, jewelry, accessories, make-up, and posters (open Mon.-Sat. 10am-6pm, Thurs. until 7pm).

Teens and barely-twenties buy their used clothes and punk discs in the **Temple Bar.** Be sure to use your **Temple Bar Passport,** which entitles you to discounts at stores and restaurants (available at hostels or the Temple Bar Info Centre, 18 Eustace St.). Across the river, Henry St. and Talbot St. sport shops for those on a tighter budget. **Henry St.,** off O'Connell, has cheaper goods, in price and quality, to suit a less finicky clientele. **ILAC,** another mall, lurks just around the corner on Moore St. (behind a rainbow facade), where street vendors sell fresh produce at very low prices. **Clery's** (tel. 878 6000) on Upper O'Connell St. is Dublin's principal department store. They pride themselves on quality goods to meet every need (open Mon.-Wed. and Fri.-Sat. 9am-5:30pm, Thurs. 9am-8pm).

Young couples have long planned to "meet under the Clery's clock." Perhaps they should also plan a trip to **Condom Power,** 57 Dame St. (tel. 677 8963), where a wide selection of prophylactics awaits (open Mon.-Sat. 9:30am-6pm, Thurs. until 8pm). If you want wool but don't have the sheep, **Dublin Woolen Co.,** Ha'penny Bridge, 41 Lower Ormond Quay (tel. 677 0301), has the best values in its selection of sweaters and tweeds (open Mon.-Sat. 9:30am-6pm, July-Aug. Sun. 1:30-5:30pm).

Dublin's Literary Shopping

Fred Hanna's, 27-29 Nassau St. (tel. 677 1255), across from Trinity College at Dawson St. Dublin's best-known, and with reason. Second-hand books mingle with new ones under the watchful eye of an intelligent staff. Any questions about contemporary Irish writing are best answered here. Open Mon.-Sat. 9am-5:30pm.

An Siopa Leabhar, 6 Harcourt St. (tel. 478 3814). Varied selection of Irish historical and political books, as well as tapes and books on traditional music. Specializes in literature and resources in Irish.

Winding Stair Bookstore, 40 Ormond Quay (tel. 873 3292), on the North Side. Three atmospheric floors of good tunes, great Liffey views, and cheap café food. Used books, contemporary Irish literature, and literary periodicals. Open Mon.-Sat. 10:30am-6pm.

Books Upstairs, 36 College Green, near Trinity Gate (tel. 679 6687). Dublin's alternative bookshop. Extensive sections on gay literature and women's studies. The principal distributor for *Gay Community News.*

Waterstone's, 7 Dawson St. (tel. 679 1415), off Nassau St. Five floors of well-stacked books and an informed reference staff. Open Mon.-Fri. 9am-8:30pm, Sat. 9am-7pm, Sun. noon-7pm.

Hodges Figgis, 56-58 Dawson St. (tel. 677 4754). Part of an English chain, this large bookstore has a good selection for those with eclectic tastes. Open Mon.-Fri. 9am-7pm, Sat. 9am-6:30pm, Sun. noon-6pm.

Eason's, 40-42 Lower O'Connell St. (tel. 873 3811). Lots of serious tomes and an extensive "Irish interest" section (*Let's Go: Ireland* £13.65). Wide selection of local and foreign magazines and newspapers. Special bargain section in the basement. Open Mon.-Sat. 8:30am-6:15pm.

Sinn Féin Bookshop, Parnell Sq. West (tel. 872 6100 or 871 6932). IRA paraphernalia, shirts, and rebel songs on tape. Open Mon.-Sat. 11am-5pm.

Records, Tapes, & CDs

Besides **Tower** (tel. 671 3250), the megastores in Dublin are **HMV,** 65 Grattan St. (tel. 679 7817), and **Virgin,** 14 Aston Quay (tel. 677 7361). Most stores have roughly an equal selection of cassettes and CDs. Cassettes run from £6-12, CDs from £11-16.

Claddagh Records, 2 Cecilia St., Temple Bar (tel. 677 0262), between Temple Lane and Crow St. Best selection of traditional Irish music and a good variety of music from other countries and cultures. Open June-Sept. daily 10:30am-5:30pm; Oct.-May 12:30-5:30pm.

Freebird Records, 1 Eden Quay (tel. 873 1250), on the North Side facing the river. Slick, crowded basement shop below a newsstand proves its name with a good selection of indie rock, probably Dublin's best. Proprietors are refreshingly honest about which local bands they actually like. Open Mon.-Sat. 10:30-6pm.

Comet Records, 5 Cope St., Temple Bar (tel. 671 8592). Much like Freebird, but smaller and open later. More info on current groups and gigs, used LPs, and new indie CDs. Punk, metal, techno, and t-shirts, too. Open Mon.-Sat. 10am-6:30pm.

Smile, 59 South Great Georges St. (tel. 478 2005). Good selection of American soul and jazz. Also has a wall of used books, some of which expound on rock. "Shoplifters will be reincarnated as snails," they warn. Don't let it happen to you, sluggo. Open Mon.-Sat. 10am-6pm.

NORTH OF DUBLIN

The suburbs north of Dublin are randomly scattered around the rocky coast and inland regions. Tract houses and factories crowd ancient castles and beach resorts. DART and suburban rail are by far the best way to travel (single tickets are never more than £1.50). Buses, however, can be confusing and unreliable. The best beach in Dublin is said to be the one at Dollymount, nicknamed the **Velvet Strand.** It's within walking distance of Malahide: to reach it, get off the train at Portmarnock, one stop before Malahide. If time allows for only one suburban jaunt, heather-crammed, peninsular Howth is the incontestable choice. If monastic ruins and historical monuments are what you're looking for, check out the towns of the Boyne Valley, a little further north. Any of these towns can be seen in an afternoon, and all share Dublin's undiscriminating **phone code, 01.**

■ Howth

Only 9 mi. from Dublin, and quite DARTable, hilly Howth gives a quick look at Ireland's highlights—scenery, pubs, history, literature, a castle, an abbey, and fresh fish, all in one town. Howth, dangling off the mainland, looks out to sea from the north shore of Dublin Bay. Fish are central to the Howth life. The food chain here proceeds from fishing boat to open-air vendor to hungry traveler.

The easiest way to reach Howth is by **DART.** Take a northbound train to the end of the line (6/hr.; 30min.; £1.10). **Buses** bound for Howth leave from Dublin's Lower Abbey Street. Bus #31 goes to the center of Howth (near the DART station; 1-2/hr.) and #31B climbs Howth Summit. Orient yourself with the *Guide to Howth Peninsula*, a hand-drawn map of Howth with sights and walking trails clearly labeled. It's posted at the harbor entrance, across from the St. Lawrence Hotel.

Financial transactions occur at **Bank of Ireland,** 1 Main St. (tel. 839 0271; open Mon.-Fri. 10am-4pm, Thurs. until 5pm; **ATM**). The **post office,** 27 Abbey St. (tel. 831 8210), also exchanges currencies. **C.S. McDermott's Pharmacy,** 5 Main St. (tel. 832 2069), does the obvious (open Mon.-Sat. 9am-6pm, Sun. 10:30am-1pm).

ACCOMMODATIONS

Howth's B&Bs and the convenience of the DART (which doesn't service all of Dublin's suburbs) make it a fine base for hopping to Dublin. Prices don't vary much from one establishment to the next.

Glenn Na Smol (tel. 832 2936), on the left at the end of Nashville Rd. off Thormanby Rd. This is a full-service B&B. Mrs. Rickard's satellite dish pulls in MTV and CNN for the benefit of the post-literate, while a generous supply of books suits wormier guests. Lip smackin' homemade bread with fresh rhubarb jam and huge bathrooms. £17/person w/bath.

Highfield (tel. 832 3936), 20-min. walk up Thormanby Rd. Highfield's sign is obscured by its hedges, but it's on the left as you go up the hill. Honeysuckle tumbles onto the lawn during the spring and summer. Inside, beautiful floral prints spill onto the bedspreads and wallpaper. Comfortable lounge with cable TV. £17.50/person, all w/bath.

Hazelwood (tel. 839 1391), in the Thormanby Woods estate off Thormanby Rd. Hazelwood offers peace and quiet in an already demure town. Firm, comfortable beds. £17.50/person, all w/bath.

FOOD & PUBS

Quash your monstrous traveler's appetite with fabulous pizza and sundaes at **Porto Fino's,** Harbour Rd. (tel. 839 3045), *tagliatelli* and salmon £4.50; pizzas £3.50-5; veggie stir-fry £5 (open Mon.-Fri. noon-10:45pm (last order), Sat.-Sun. 1-10pm). **Caffé Caira,** Harbour Rd. (tel. 839 3823), is a better-than-average chippy, and its tables soothe the Howth youth (burgers or fish £2-3, chips 95p). Hungry shoppers run to **Spar Supermarket** on St. Laurence Rd. off of Abbey St. (open Mon.-Sat., 8am-10pm). Book a seat in advance (or stand and regret it) to hear traditional music at **Ye Olde Abbey Tavern,** Abbey St. (tel. 832 2006 or 839 0282; music Tues.-Sun. 9pm; cover £3). If you're not up for battling the crowd at the Tavern, the **Lighthouse,** Church St. (tel. 832 2827), offers a mellower atmosphere and has trad (Wed.-Thurs. and Sun. 9pm).

SIGHTS

Maud Gonne, Yeats's unyielding beloved, described her childhood in Howth in *A Servant of the Queen:* "After I was grown up I have often slept all night in that friendly heather…From deep down in it one looks up at the stars in a wonderful security and falls asleep to wake up only with the call of the sea birds looking for their breakfasts." A one-hour **cliff walk** rings the peninsula and trails through just such heather and past the nests of thousands of seabirds. A cairn reputed to be the grave of Griffan (the last pre-Christian King) interests pagan enthusiasts. The cleft in Puck's Rock marks the spot where the devil fell when St. Nessan waved a Bible at him. To get to the trail head from Howth, turn left at the DART and bus station and follow Harbour Rd. around the corner and up the hill (about 20min.). The footpath begins where the cul-de-sac ends, at the top of this long, long hill. The trail is not only unmarked but also uncleared in places. Regardless, the views, and especially the springtime blooms of the slopes, are inspiring. For the less hearty, bus #31B cruises from Lower Abbey St. in Dublin to the cliffs' summit.

The town of Howth itself occupies this long hill. The ruins of **St. Mary's Abbey** stand peacefully surrounded by a cemetery at the bend in Church St. The walls and arches of this 13th-century abbey are still quite sound. The courtyard, cordoned off, is nevertheless visible. You can get the key from the caretaker, Mrs. O'Rourke, at 13 Church St. The more modern **Howth Harbour** bustles with working fishermen. A strip of fresh fish shops lines West Pier. Thursday nights, when fishing boats come in, are the best times to buy.

Just offshore, **Ireland's Eye** once provided both religious sanctuary and strategic advantage for monks, as attested to by the ruins of **St. Nessan's Church** and one of the coast's many **Martello towers,** both located on the island. The monks eventually abandoned their refuge when pirate raids became too frequent. The island's long beach is now primarily a bird haven. **Frank Doyle & Sons** (tel. 831 4200) jet passengers across the water. Their office is on the East Pier, towards the Lighthouse. (15-min. roundtrip £3, children £2. Call ahead to schedule departure times.)

Howth has its own castle on the outskirts of town. To reach **Howth Castle,** take a right on Harbour Rd. as you leave the DART station. The castle turn-off, ¼ mi. down the road, is marked by signs for the Deer Park Hotel and the National Transport Museum. The castle itself is a patchwork of different architectural styles, which gives its exterior an awkward charm. The castle is a private residence (not open to the public) belonging to the St. Lawrence family, which has occupied it for four centuries.

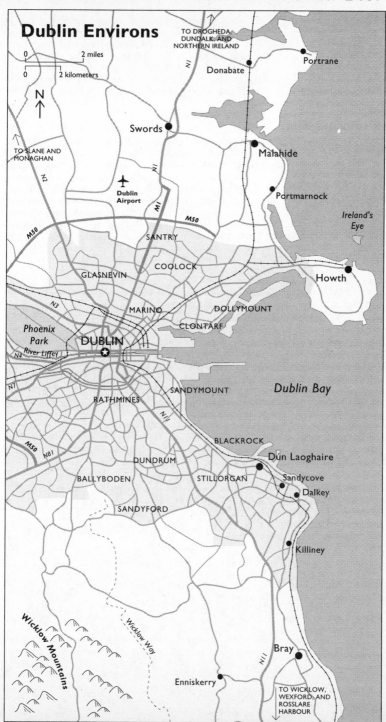

Dublin Environs

0   2 miles
0   2 kilometers

N ↑

TO DROGHEDA, DUNDALK, AND NORTHERN IRELAND

TO SLANE AND MONAGHAN

Portrane

Donabate

Swords

Malahide

Dublin Airport

Portmarnock

M50

SANTRY

Ireland's Eye

COOLOCK

GLASNEVIN

Howth

MARINO

DOLLYMOUNT

CLONTARF

Phoenix Park

DUBLIN

River Liffey

Dublin Bay

SANDYMOUNT

RATHMINES

BLACKROCK

Dún Laoghaire

DUNDRUM

Sandycove

STILLORGAN

Dalkey

BALLYBODEN

SANDYFORD

Killiney

Wicklow Way

Wicklow Mountains

Bray

Enniskerry

TO WICKLOW, WEXFORD, AND ROSSLARE HARBOUR

> ### Monstrous, Thick, Impenetrable Structures
> Martello towers, named after Cape Mortella in Corsica, are short, thick, cylindri-
> cal, and almost impenetrable structures. The English, upon encountering them
> in Corsica, decided to copy these brilliantly defensive towers. Being British, they
> felt free to improve on the name. Paranoid generals constructed these squat edi-
> fices all along the coasts, awaiting a Napoleonic assault that never came.

You might try knocking if your surname is O'Malley. In 1575, the pirate queen Grace
O'Malley paid a social call but was refused entrance on the grounds that the family
was eating. Not one to take an insult lightly, Grace abducted the St. Lawrence heir
and refused to hand him back until she had word that the gate would always be open
to all O'Malleys at mealtimes.

At the end of the road on which the castle perches is the **National Transport
Museum** (tel. 848 0831), an amiable collection of old buses, cars, and trucks. (Open
June-Aug. Mon.-Fri. 10am-6pm, Sat.-Sun. 11am-6pm; Sept.-May Sat.-Sun. noon-5pm.
Admission £1.50, children 50p.) Farther up the hill, the path leads around the Deer
Park Hotel to the fabulous **Rhododendron Gardens.** The ending of Joyce's *Ulysses* is
set "among the rhododendrons at Howth Head." At the top of the forested path, you
emerge into an astounding floral panorama overlooking Howth, Ireland's Eye, and
Dublin to the South. The flowers bloom in June and July (always open; free).

■ Malahide

Eight miles north of Dublin, rows of prim and proper shops smugly line the main
street in Malahide, a perennial coastal contender in Ireland's cutthroat Tidy Town
competition. The gorgeous parkland and castle at Malahide Demesne partially justify
the town's pride. Bus #42, which leaves from behind the Custom House (Beresford
Place) in Dublin, drives right up to the park entrance. Suburban rail to Malahide
leaves Connolly, Tara, and Pearse stations infrequently (£1.10). You can even take the
DART to Sutton Station (one stop before Howth) and then take bus #102 to Malahide
(Mon.-Sat. 3/hr.). Turn left from the rail station onto Coast Rd. to reach Malahide's
center and all its facilities at a four-way intersection between Church Rd. and New St.
called "The Diamond." Malahide distributes brochures and maps at the **Citizens
Information Centre** (tel. 845 0627), located behind the library on Main St. Ask for
the *Malahide Tourist Guide,* which has a town map.

Accommodations & Food Malahide hosts a number of inexpensive B&Bs
along Coast Rd. and its tributaries, particularly along Biscayne St. (20-min. walk from
the Diamond). Since Malahide is only a 10-minute drive from the airport (bus #230
runs back and forth throughout the day, £1.10), it's convenient for travelers without
the energy to drag themselves to Dublin. **Aishling,** Mrs. Noreen Handley, 59 Biscayne
(tel. 845 2292), one block off Coast Rd., has pink carpets and curtains, and firm, comfortable beds. Hairdryers! Big breakfast includes fruit, yogurt, and homemade bread
(£15/person, w/bath £16; open March-Nov.). **Pegasus,** Mrs. Betty O'Brien, 56 Biscayne (tel. 845 1506), impresses with welcoming, well-appointed rooms that boast
elegant channel views. The full Irish breakfast includes smoked kippers for the dar-
ing. For those un-schooled in Irish *haute cuisine,* kippers are herring cooked in tea
(£15/person, w/bath £16; open March-Nov.). Most of the restaurants around the Diamond are greatly overpriced. **The Grove,** Grove Rd. (tel. 845 2208), has a friendly
pub atmosphere with better-than-average pub grub (roast chicken £5, prawn salad
£4, scampi £5). Trad nightly.

Sights Left off Main St. (a 10-min. walk heading north, past the railroad tracks),
Malahide Demense envelops **Malahide Castle** (tel. 846 2184; fax 846 2537), the
town's main attraction. The castle luxuriates in 250 acres of sweeping lawns and
densely foliated paths. Oliver Cromwell, always one for soothing angry emotions,

commented that here, and nowhere else, would he tolerate living on Irish soil. Now publicly owned, the well-preserved mansion houses a collection of Irish period furniture and part of the National Portrait Collection inside its regal walls. The Malahide Demesne also surrounds a church, a playground, and stunning botanical gardens. (Castle open April-Oct. Mon.-Fri. 10am-5pm, Sat. 11am-6pm, Sun. 11:30am-6pm; Nov.-March Mon.-Fri. 10am-5pm, Sat.-Sun. 2-5pm. Demesne/Park open daily June 10am-9pm; July-Aug. 10am-8pm; Oct. 10am-7pm; Nov.-Jan. 10am-5pm; Feb.-March 10am-6pm. No tours 12:45-2pm. Admission £2.85, students £2.30. Combined Malahide Castle and Newbridge House (Donabate) ticket £4.60, students £3.60.)

Between Malahide and **Portmarnock** (2mi. down the coastal road toward Dublin) lies the **Velvet Strand.** This stretch of soft, luxurious beach makes a fantastic stop on a sunny day, and can hold its own with any Caribbean beach.

■ Near Malahide: Donabate

In Donabate, 4 mi. north of Malahide, the 18th-century **Newbridge House** (tel. 843 6534 or 846 2184) is surrounded by a 350-acre park. The half-hour walk from the rail station, clearly marked, is as worthwhile as the house itself, as it takes you past the gardens of Donabate and through a lush tree-lined field. The rolling grass in the park is a favorite spot for family and school outings and a great spot for your picnic. The Archbishop of Dublin erected the mansion in 1737. It lacked electricity until the makers of the movie *The Spy Who Came in From the Cold* wired it up in the 1960s. Three rooms in particular should not be missed: the **kitchen** will blow your microwave-and-toaster preconceptions clear out of the water, the **private museum** is an attic full of very English, very eccentric collections (moth and ostrich eggs), and **Tara's Palace** is a luxurious 14-room, pre-Barbie dollhouse. (Open April-Sept. Tues.-Fri.10am-1pm and 2-5pm, Sat. 11am-1pm and 2-6pm, Sun. 2-6pm; Oct.-March Sat-Sun. 2-5pm. Admission £2.60, students £2.30, children £1.45. Newbridge House and Malahide Castle combination ticket £4.60, students £3.60.) **Smyth Pub** (tel. 843 6053), across from the station, serves pub grub to weary travelers (sandwich £1.20, salad plate £2.50). To get to Donabate, either take the infrequent bus #33B from Eden Quay, or, preferably, take the suburban rail from Connolly, Tara St., or Pearse Station in downtown Dublin (£1.20; go one stop beyond Malahide).

SOUTH OF DUBLIN

The suburb/beach/port hybrids from Dún Laoghaire to Killiney form a nearly unbroken chain of snazzy houses and bright surf. The whole area is technically the "Borough of Dún Laoghaire." The individual cities are best thought of as neighborhoods within this larger town. A set of paths called the "Dún Laoghaire Way," "Dalkey Way," and so on, connects the towns by what, someone has decided, is the best walking route. The separate parts combine into a whole trail that is 3 mi. long. Getting from one town to the other is easy enough as long as you stay within 10 blocks of the sea, on the path or not. For those who don't want to invest the shoe leather, the DART also makes for great (and less exhausting) coastal views between Dalkey and Bray. An entertaining ramble would begin with a ride on bus #59 from the Dún Laoghaire DART station to the top of Killiney Hill and proceed along the path through the park and down into Dalkey. The **phone code** brays 01.

■ Dún Laoghaire

As Dublin's major out-of-city ferry port, Dún Laoghaire (dun-LEER-ee) is the first peek at Ireland for many tourists. Fortunately it is a pleasant, well-developed town and a good spot to begin a ramble along the coast south of Dublin. The **tourist office** (tel. 280 6600) in the ferry terminal is a gold medal office, accustomed to dealing with delirious travelers and equipped with copious maps and pamphlets on all of Dublin and the Borough of Dún Laoghaire. Bring flowers for the helpful staff. (Open June-Sept. daily 10am-9pm; Oct.-Dec. Mon.-Sat. 10am-9pm; Jan.-March Mon.-Sat. noon-9pm; April-May Mon.-Sat. 9am-9pm.) Ferry travelers can change money at the **bureau de change** in the ferry terminal, or they can wait for the **Bank of Ireland** on Upper George's St. (open Mon.-Wed. and Fri.10am-4pm, Thurs. 10am-5pm, and at ferry arrival times; **ATM**). From the tourist office, Royal Marine Rd. climbs up to the center of town. George's St., at the top of Marine Rd., holds most of Dún Laoghaire's shops, many in the **Dún Laoghaire Shopping Centre** at the intersection (open Mon.-Wed. and Sat. 9am-6pm, Thurs.-Fri. 9am-9pm). Patrick St., which continues Marine Rd.'s path uphill on the other side of George's St., offers cheap eateries (open early and late, according to the ferry schedules). Reach Dún Laoghaire on the DART south from Dublin (£1.10) or on buses #7, 7A, 8 or 46A from Eden Quay.

ACCOMMODATIONS

Dún Laoghaire is so close to Dublin via DART that it is a convenient town from which to visit the city while avoiding the rigors of staying in the capital itself. As the port for the Stena-Sealink ferries, Dún Laoghaire is prime breeding ground for B&Bs, some more predatory than others.

Old School House Hostel (IHH), Elbana Ave. (tel. 280 8777), signposted on Elbana Ave. right off Royal Marine Rd. Full-service hostel sports a TV lounge, an eager 24-hr. staff, and a friendly atmosphere. Café enhances hostel life. Safety deposit boxes at reception and innovative lockers built into the beds. 24-hr. kitchen. Wheelchair access. 6-bed dorm £8. Double £22. Quad £36. Add 50p for rooms w/bath. Sheets included; towels £1. Laundry £2/wash, £1/dry. Rent **bikes** £7/day, £30/week; deposit £50.

Marleen, 9 Marine Rd. (tel. 280 2456). Fall off the DART or ferry, and you'll be here—great location on the first block of Marine Rd. just west of the harbor. Friendly owners, TV and tea facilities in every room. £17/person.

Avondale, 3 Northumberland Ave. (tel. 280 9628). Next to Dunnes Stores. A crimson carpet leads honored guests to pampering rooms with high ceilings and big beds. Single £18. Double £32.

Ariemond, 47 Mulgrave St. (tel. 280 1664). The rooms are a bit dark, but the beds are firm and comfy. £16/person, w/bath £18.

FOOD & PUBS

Stock up on provisions at **Quinnsworth Supermarket** (tel. 280 8441) in the Dún Laoghaire shopping center (open Mon.-Wed. and Sat. 9am-6pm, Thurs.-Fri. 9am-9pm) or at fruit stands and delis. Fast-food restaurants and inexpensive coffee shops line George's St. **The Coffee Bean,** 88b Upper George's St. (tel. 280 9522), virtually rolls customers out, filled to the brim with quiche (£3.75), soup and brown bread (£1.20), and scrumptious desserts (£1-1.50). A full Irish breakfast is served until noon (£2.45; open Mon.-Sat. 8am-6pm). **Bits and Pizzas,** Patrick St., gives a good return for your money (lunch special: pizza, cole slaw, and tea £4; open Mon.-Sat. noon-6pm). Normally pricey **de Selby's,** 17/18 Patrick St. (tel. 284 1761), will give you a free dessert if you prove that it's your birthday. The restaurant (also an art gallery) is named for the mad scientist in Flann O'Brien's novels (sirloin steak sandwich £6.50, hot veggie platter £8; open Mon.-Sat. 5:30-11pm, Sun. noon-10pm).

The Purty Kitchen, Dunleary Rd. (tel. 284 3576), is a lively pub. Upstairs, the **Purty Loft** livens Dún Laoghaire weekends with groovy disco action (cover £3-6). From the harbor, turn right down Crofton Rd. (a 15-min. walk; the pub is actually closer to the Monkstown DART station than Dún Laoghaire's). **Smyth's Pub,** Callaghan's Lane (tel. 280 1139), at the corner of George's St., is a pleasant old pub with tasty pub entrees (hot open sandwiches £2.50, roast stuffed chicken £4) and some cozy snugs. Live music (contemporary or trad) Thursday through Sunday nights.

SIGHTS

The **harbor** itself is a sight, filled with yachts, boat tours, car ferries chugging to Wales, and fishermen on the west pier. On a clear day, grab a picnic and head down to the piers to soak up the ambience, the sun, or the fishy smells. Samuel Beckett's *Krapp's Last Tape* is set on one of the piers.

Otherwise, try the **National Maritime Museum,** Haigh Terrace (tel. 280 0969). From the tourist office, turn left on Queen's Rd. to the stone steps which lead up to Haigh Terrace. The museum is in the Mariners' Church. A giant lens has been moved here from its home in the Bailey Lighthouse in Howth. In the center of the museum stretches a longboat (akin to a rowboat) sent by revolutionary France to support the United Irishmen in 1796. (Open May-Sept. Tues.-Sun. 1-5pm; April-Oct. Sat.-Sun. 1-5pm. Admission £1.50, children 80p.)

■ More DARTable Fun

SANDYCOVE

Upper George's St. continues from Dún Laoghaire into dandy Sandycove. Restaurants and grocers gather on the street here, as they do farther north. Sandycove is pretty enough in a Victorian way, but its real allure is the **James Joyce Tower,** Sandycove Ave. West (tel. 280 9265). From the Sandycove DART station, go left at the green house down Islington Ave., then right along the coast to Sandycove Point; or take bus #8 from Nassau St. in Dublin to Sandycove Ave. West. The museum is in a Martello tower (see **Monstrous, Thick, Impenetrable Structures,** p. 120). James Joyce stayed in the tower for six days in August 1904 as a guest of Oliver St. John Gogarty, a Dublin surgeon, poetic wit, man-about-town, and the tower's first civilian tenant. Unfortunately, Gogarty's other guest was an excitable Englishman with a severe sleepwalking problem. One night, as the foreigner paced, Gogarty shouted "leave him to me" and fired his shotgun into a row of saucepans. Joyce took the hint and left in the morning. A month later he escaped to the continent with Nora Barnacle. Part I of *Ulysses* is set in and near the tower, with Gogarty portrayed by Buck Mulligan, the Englishman played by "an Englishman," and Joyce, alias Stephen Daedalus, meditating on the wine-dark sea from the gun platform at the top of the tower. Another scene takes place at the Forty Foot Men's Bathing Place (below).

Sylvia Beach, Joyce's publisher, opened the tower as a museum in 1962. The two-room museum contains Joyce's death mask, his bookshelves, some of his correspondence, clippings of Ezra Pound's rave reviews, and lots of editions of *Ulysses,* including one illustrated by Henri Matisse. One letter to Italo Svevo mentions a briefcase "the color of a nun's belly." Genius! Upstairs, the Round Room reconstructs Joyce's bedroom; from the gun platform, you can stand in his shoes to see "many crests, every ninth, breaking, plashing, from far, from farther out, waves and waves." (Open April-Oct. Mon.-Sat. 10am-1pm and 2-5pm, Sun. 2-6pm; Nov.-March by appointment. Admission £2.20, seniors and children £1.90.)

At the foot of the tower lies the infamous **Forty Foot Men's Bathing Place.** A wholesome crowd with plenty of toddlers splashes in the shallow pool facing the road. But behind a wall, on the rocks below the battery and adjacent to the Martello Tower, men traditionally skinny-dip year-round—they don't even seem to mind that they're tourist attractions. The pool rarely contains 40 men, or even 20. Instead, the name derives from the *Fortieth* regiment of British *foot* soldiers, who made it their own semi-private swimming hole. Joyce's host, Oliver St. John Gogarty, once took the plunge here with a reluctant George Bernard Shaw in tow.

KILLINEY

"Europe was exhausting. Everything's at the top of a hill," joke the Kids in the Hall. You won't be laughing if you take the DART to Killiney (kill-EYE-nee), a posh suburb that's really just a DART stop on the beach, not an actual town (it does make a great start for a walk along the coast). Do yourself a favor and take bus #59 from the Dún Laoghaire DART station to its terminus on Killiney Hill. On foot from the Killiney DART station, you'll have to turn right on Station Rd. and climb up the countless flights of a pedestrian stairpath.

The easiest route is to get off at the Dalkey DART stop. Pick up the Heritage map of Dun Laoghaire for details on the seven area walks and historical anecdotes. From Castle St. take a left onto Dalkey Ave. and proceed to climb Dalkey Hill, which leads to **Killiney Hill Park.** From the obelisk at the top, the views are breathtaking—that dark smudge on the horizon is called Wales. A path runs from the obelisk to Dalkey Hill. The **wishing stone** is on the way. If you walk around each level from base to top and then stand facing Dalkey Island and make a wish, it's bound to come true. Beware that this works only if you walk in a clockwise direction; in earlier times, women wishing to acquire the power of witchcraft walked naked in a counter-clockwise direction. The Heritage guide states that "visitors should not do this on Killiney Hill!"—sorry to disappoint. The path slips off Dalkey Hill onto Torca Rd. Up the road on the left, **Shaw's Cottage** was the home of George Bernard Shaw during a fraction of his childhood. Steps descend from Torca Rd. to coastal Vico Rd., which runs to Dalkey. Killiney itself has a bonny beach. **Groceries,** for refreshment after the hard climb, are sold across from the Killiney Hill Park entrance next to atmospheric **Druid's Chair Pub** (tel. 285 7297), where you can down a pint in calm surroundings before making the final commitment to trek to the obelisk.

BRAY

Bray is a beach town where Dubliners find refuge. If you're looking for rural Irish charm, you won't find it here, but Bray is the southernmost point on the DART and a jumping off point to Co. Wicklow's mountainous treats. The **tourist office** (tel. 286 7128) is the first stop south of Dublin which can give you info on Co. Wicklow. The office is adjacent to the Heritage Centre, downhill on Main St. next to the Royal Hotel. Pick up a history trail brochure (free; open June-Sept. Mon.-Sat. 9:30am-5:30pm; Oct.-May Mon.-Sat. 10am-5pm). **Scotman's Hut,** 5 Albert Walk (a pedestrian alley by the station; tel. 286 9178), is the ideal Army-Navy store for hikers, providing equipment for those Wicklow hikes (open Mon.-Sat. 9:30am-6pm). David's Market in the DART station rents **bikes** for those who snub their noses at the bus to Enniskerry (tel. 287 6989; £4/4hr., £10/day; deposit £20). Bray is a 45-minute DART ride from Connolly Station (£2.50 return). Bus #45 also leaves Dublin's Burgh Quay for Bray, and bus #84 leaves from Eden Quay. Bray has good connections to Enniskerry, Co. Wicklow. Bus #85, from the DART station in Bray to Enniskerry (£1), runs more frequently than the Enniskerry-Dublin bus.

Bray's history since the Neolithic Age is on display in a small but well-designed **Heritage Centre** on Main St. near the Royal Hotel (in the same building as the tourist office; admission £1, seniors, students, and children 50p). Joe Loughman, local historian and phone repairman, gathered the center's artifacts by exchanging them with the local populace for working phones. The floor is a giant map of Bray (tel. 286 7128; open same hours as tourist office). Along the **Esplanade,** grim amusement palaces and B&Bs cater to a dwindling crowd of Dublin beachgoers. Low-confidence gamblers can try 2p slot machines in the **Fun Palace** on the seafront. Kiddie rides, dodgems, and computer games promise to entertain children on rainy afternoons (tel. 286 4450; open daily 10am-7pm).

Enough with these silly amusements; climb the rocky outcrop that is **Bray Head** and glory over the Irish Sea. The trailhead is clearly marked at the end of the promenade. **Brandy Hole,** a cave at the foot of Bray Head, was once a smugglers' warehouse. Inland, the ruins of **Raheen A Cluig,** a 13th-century Augustinian church, look very small and very old. The climb to Bray Head takes a good 45 minutes.

Seafront **B&Bs** line the Strand. The cheaper ones are on Convent Ave. and Sidmonton Ave., both off the Strand. **St. Judes,** Convent Ave. (tel. 286 2534), entices customers with a comfortable atmosphere and colorful comforters (£14/person; open June-Sept.). **Sans Souci,** Meath Rd. (tel. 282 8629), next to Convent Ave., helps travelers forget their worries in well-decorated rooms. Only the luckiest guests get to sleep in the bed that once cushioned Sting's bones (July-Aug. £16/person, w/bath £18; low season £2 less).

The shelves overflow with groceries at **SuperQuinn** market on Main St. north of the tourist center (open daily 8am-6pm). The surrounding shopping center also houses fruit stands and sandwich shops. On the Strand, **Porter House** (tel. 286 0668) serves food until 8pm (subs, nachos, or filled potato £2.50, steak sandwich £5.75) and boasts what is "probably the largest selection of beers in Ireland"—Chimay, Grolsch, and (if you honestly crave American beer) Rolling Rock. Trad on Wednesday, Friday, and Sunday nights; nightly in summer. The best meal in town is waiting for you at **Escape,** Albert Ave. (tel. 286 6755), where heaping portions of creative vegetarian dishes please any appetite. Lunches around £4, dinner special £5.25. New menu daily (open Mon.-Sat. noon-10:30pm, Sun. noon-8:30pm).

EASTERN IRELAND

Woe to the unfortunate tourist whose exposure to eastern Ireland is limited to what she or he sees out of the window on a bus headed to the west. Although less-frequented by foreign visitors, the eastern towns offer many interesting and unique places to visit. Where else but Kildare can you find a horse farm run according to the laws of metaphysics or a theme-park based on bogs? The mountains of Wicklow offer spectacular views. Tired hikers can rest along the beaches of the nearby shoreline. The tiny lakeland towns of Co. Monaghan, really a part of the Fermanagh Lake District, hold surprises like Hare Krishna Island. Standard tourist attractions in this region are the monastic city at Clonmacnoise and the ruins in Co. Meath. Counties Meath, Louth, Wicklow, and Kildare all hold goodies fit for daytrips from Dublin.

County Wicklow

Mountainous Co. Wicklow allows wilderness fans to lose themselves on deserted back roads, zoom down seesaw ridges by bicycle, and still be back in Dublin by nightfall. Wild as parts of it are, the whole county is in the capital's backyard. All its major sights are accessible by one bus or another from downtown Dublin, but traveling within the county is often best done by bike or car. The Wicklow Way hiking trail is an excellent reason for your feet to come to the county, and the remains of the monastic city of Glendalough are certainly worth a visit.

Ninth-century Vikings settled at present-day Wicklow and Arklow and used them as bases while raiding Glendalough and other monasteries. Norman invaders in the 1100s followed the same pattern, building defences on the coast while leaving the mountains to the Gaelic O'Toole and O'Byrne clans. English control was not fully established until the 1798 rebellion, when military roads and barracks were built through the interior so that the British Army could hunt down the remaining guerrillas. The mountains later produced a mining industry in the southern part of the county. Bray *is* in Co. Wicklow, but since it's on the DART, *Let's Go* covers it under South of Dublin (see **Bray,** p. 124).

WICKLOW MOUNTAINS

Over 2000 ft. high, covered by gorse and heather and pleated by rivers rushing down wooded glens, the Wicklow summits are home to grazing sheep and a few villagers. Glendalough, in the midst of the mountains, draws a steady summertime stream of coach tours from Dublin. The towns of Enniskerry, Ashford, Rathdrum, Avoca, and Blessington, all in the Wicklow Mountains, are on the tourist trail and are covered separately below. The area is a bit difficult to navigate, so get a map. Bray, Wicklow Town, Arklow, and Rathdrum all have free maps in the tourist offices.

■ Glendalough

In the 6th century, St. Kevin had a vision telling him to give up his life of ascetic isolation and found a monastery. Evidently reasoning that if you've got to be a monk, you'd might as well be a monk in one of the most spectacularly beautiful valleys in Ireland, he founded Glendalough (GLEN-da-lock, meaning "glen of the two lakes"). During the great age of the Irish monasteries—563 to 1152 AD—monastic schools were Ireland's religious and cultural centers, attracting pilgrims from all over Europe

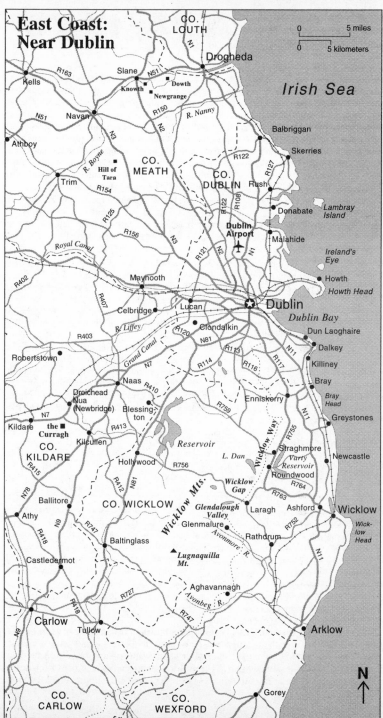

East Coast:
Near Dublin

EASTERN IRELAND

0   5 miles
0   5 kilometers

Irish Sea

CO. LOUTH

Drogheda

Kells
R163
Slane
N51
Knowth
Dowth
Newgrange
R150
R. Nanny
Navan
N51
N3
Athboy
R. Boyne
Hill of Tara
CO. MEATH
Trim
R154
R125
R156
Royal Canal
R402
Maynooth
R407
Balbriggan
Skerries
R122
CO. DUBLIN
Rush
R108
R122
Donabate
Lambray Island
Dublin Airport
Malahide
Ireland's Eye
Howth
Howth Head
Celbridge
Lucan
Clondalkin
Dublin
R403
R. Liffey
Grand Canal
N3
R121
N2
N1
Dublin Bay
Dun Laoghaire
Dalkey
Killiney
Bray
R120
N81
R113
R114
R116
R117
N11
Robertstown
N7
Naas
R410
Droichead Nua (Newbridge)
Blessington
R759
Enniskerry
Bray Head
Greystones
Kildare
the Curragh
CO. KILDARE
Kilcullen
R413
R415
R412
N81
Hollywood
Reservoir
R756
L. Dan
Wicklow Way
R755
Straghmore
Varty Reservoir
Roundwood
Newcastle
Ballitore
N78
Athy
N9
R418
Castledermot
R747
Baltinglass
CO. WICKLOW
Wicklow Mts.
Wicklow Gap
Glendalough Valley
Glenmalure
Avonmore R.
Laragh
Ashford
R764
R763
Wicklow
R752
Wicklow Head
Lugnaquilla Mt.
Rathdrum
Aghavannagh
Avonbeg R.
R727
R747
Carlow
N9
Tullow
R418
Arklow
N11
N
Gorey
CO. CARLOW
CO. WEXFORD

to the "land of saints and scholars." Supported by lesser monks who farmed and traded, the privileged brothers inscribed and illuminated religious texts and collected precious jewels and relics for the glory of God.

Practical Information Glendalough town consists of the monastic site, a tiny **tourist office** (open Tues.-Sat. 10am-1pm and 2-6pm, Sun. 11am-1pm and 2-6pm), a hostel, and an over-priced hotel/restaurant—all within a ¼ mi. radius. For more affordable food, B&Bs, and groceries, travelers should depend on **Laragh** (LAR-a), a village 1 mi. up the road (signposted, 10-min. walk from the Wicklow Way; 15mi. from Powerscourt, 7mi. from Roundwood). Most pilgrims to Glendalough come by car; a few hike the Wicklow Way into town. The rest catch the private **St. Kevin's Bus Service** (tel. (01) 281 8119). The buses run from St. Stephen's Green West, Dublin (Mon.-Sat. at 11:30am and 6pm, Sun. 11:30am and 7pm; £5, £8 return). They also leave from Bray, just past the Town Hall (Mon.-Sat. 12:10 and 6:30pm, Sun. 12:10 and 7:30pm; £6 return). Buses return from the glen in the evening (Mon.-Fri. 7:15am and 4:15pm, Sat. 9:45am and 4:15pm, Sun. 9:45am and 5:30pm). In Laragh, the bus leaves from the phone booth across from the post office. **Bus Éireann** also runs tours to Glendalough daily from April to September (except on Mon., Tues., and Thurs. in March, and not on Tues. or Thurs. in Oct.). Buses leave Busáras Station in Dublin at 10:30am, travel along the coast, pass through Avoca, stop in Glendalough, and return to Dublin by 5:45pm. The driver is the tour guide, and admission fees are included in the cost (tel. (01) 836 6111 for booking; £15, children £8). **Wicklow Tours** (tel. 67671) runs a van to Rathdrum (Avondale) and Wicklow daily (departs from Glendalough hotel Mon.-Sat. 11:25am, 1:55 and 4:25pm, Sun. 11:45am, 2:25 and 4:55pm; to Wicklow £5 return; to Rathdrum £3 return). **Mary Gibbons** (tel. (01) 283 9973) offers an afternoon tour of Powerscourt Gardens and Glendalough leaving from Dublin (leaves Suffolk St. tourist office Tues., Thurs., and Sat.-Sun. 12:45pm, returns at 6pm; £16/person includes admission fees). **Hitching** is unpleasant, since almost all the cars going to Laragh and Glendalough are filled with nervous tourists. Hitchers do make it as far as the juncture of N11 with Glendalough's R755 by starting at the beginning of N11 in southwest Dublin (see **To and From the Transportation Hublin,** p. 83). In Laragh, **bike rental** is available from the **post office/video rental store** (tel. 45236; £6/day, £24/week; deposit £20; open daily 9am-10pm). The **phone code** wakes for matins at 0404.

Accommodation, Food, & Pubs The **Glendalough Hostel (HI/An Óige)** (tel. 45342) lies five minutes up the road past the Glendalough visitors center. The dorms are cramped and the beds squeak, but the view is scintillating. Arrangements made for groceries. Rooms range from a 24-bed dorm to private rooms with a bunk-bed. (Dorm £6, Oct.-May £5. Breakfast £2. Sheets 85p. Bikes £3/half-day, £6/day. Lockout noon-5pm; midnight curfew; unguarded luggage storage all day; kitchen open 7:30-10am and 5-10pm.) In **Laragh,** the **Wicklow Way Hostel** (tel. 45398) is relatively new and has sturdy, somewhat lumpy beds and warm comforters (sheets 50p). The attached coffeehouse serves inexpensive breakfasts. Kitchen with microwave open 7am-10pm; lounge with TV (co-ed dorm £6; private room £10/person; double £25). The older, more cramped **Old Mill Hostel** (tel. 45577) offers beds 10 minutes down the road (signposted). (Dorm £6.50, private room £9.50/person. Camping £4.50/person. Secure luggage storage, no lockout or curfew, kitchen facilities.) B&Bs abound in Laragh. One of the most welcoming is **Gleannailbhe,** next to the post office (inquire there; tel. 45236). Tea/coffee facilities, TV lounge, and choice of breakfasts (£14/person, w/bath £16).

In Glendalough, **Mrs. Holden** pours tea and butters hot scones (£1.60) in her house across from the Glendalough hotel. Coffee and sandwiches (£1.90) are served as well (follow the "TEAS" signs; open March-Nov. daily 10am-5:30pm). In Laragh, **Patsy** offers the same services a bit cheaper (sandwich or scone and tea £1.50; open daily 9am-9pm). The **Laragh Inn** (tel. 45345) piles plates high with hot edibles (open

Climbing a Stairway to Kevin

Kevin was apparently an angelically beautiful man who wasn't interested in women. A lascivious princess named Kathleen made advances on Kevin, forcing him to move his hermitage to Glendalough. Still she pursued him, so he withdrew to his cave near the Upper Lake. The princess scoured the area until Kevin's dog gave him away. Kathleen followed the dog to Kevin's cave, where she found him asleep and began to take advantage of the situation. Kevin awoke and angrily flung Kathleen into the lake, off the rocky ledge now called "Lady's Leap." She drowned. Kevin felt guilty, lived a life of atonement, and prayed that none might ever drown in the lake again. Lest this tale lead one to judge harshly this pious man, those that recount this legend add that "Kevin may not have had much time for women, but many legends have grown up concerning his kindness to the animals that inhabited Glendalough."

noon-9pm; entrees £5-7). The attached **Bridge Bar** attracts hostelers and locals alike with its ballad sessions (Sat.-Sun. 10pm; no cover).

Sights Today only the **visitors center** (tel. 45352) and a handful of tourist trappings mark the ancient monastic spot. The center shows a 20-minute film on the history of monasteries and conducts guided tours of the local ruins. (Open daily June-Aug. 9am-6:30pm; Sept. to mid-Oct. 9:30am-6pm; mid-Oct. to mid-March 9:30am-5pm; mid-March to May 9:30am-6pm. Admission £2, students and children £1. Wheelchair accessible.)

The present ruins were only a small part of the monastery in its heyday, when wooden huts for low-status laborer monks were plentiful. Monks once hid in the 100-ft. **Round Tower,** built in the 10th century as a watchtower and belltower. The entrance is 12 ft. from the ground. When Vikings approached, the monks would climb the inside of the tower floor by floor, drawing up the ladders behind them. **St. Kevin's Cross** is an unadorned high cross. A high cross is a crucifix merged with a ring representing the sun, a pagan symbol. Early proselytizers hoped that combining the two would make Christianity more palatable to the pagan Irish. The **Cathedral,** constructed in a combination of Greek and Roman architectural styles, was at one time the largest in the country. **St. Kevin's Church** is also jokingly known as St. Kevin's Kitchen because its stone roof and round tower give the appearance of a chimney for cooking. Built in the 11th century, it was used as a church until the 16th century. It lay derelict until the 19th century, when locals once again used it as a church until the newer St. Kevin's Church was built a mile away.

The **Upper and Lower Lakes** are a rewarding walk from the monastic site, across the bridge and to the right. A five-minute walk, the Lower Lake is serene. Near the spectacular Upper Lake, a half-hour walk from the site, **St. Kevin's Bed** is the cave where he prayed. Local chieftains are buried in a church nearby. Legend says that when St. Kevin prayed, his words ascended in a vortex of flame and light which burned over the Upper Lake's dark waters with such intensity that none but the most righteous monks could witness it without going blind. Although many tales recount the piety of St. Kevin, others show that not even he was perfect.

■ The Wicklow Way

The lonely mountain heights reach westward and upward. They are negotiable by foot, bike, or horse along many established trails. The 70-mi. Wicklow Way, Ireland's first and best-known long-distance path, starts a few miles south of Dublin and progresses south along the crests all the way to Clonegal in Co. Carlow. Parts of it are well-graded and even paved. Though the path is well-marked with yellow arrows, hikers should get the Ordnance Survey's *Discovery Series #56* for hiking in the northern part of the county and *Discovery Series #62* for hiking in south Wicklow. The latter covers the trail to Aghavannagh and has descriptive text on the reverse. Both are free in bookstores and tourist offices. The *Wicklow Way Map Guide* is more colorful but expensive and not much more informative (£4.50). Since the path is mostly out of sight and hearing range of the lowlands, traveling alone can be risky. It's a bad idea to drink water from the streams en route, and it is *illegal* to light fires within 1 mi. of the forest.

The northern 45 mi. of the path (from Dublin to Aghavannagh) are the most popular, have the best scenery, and offer better access to hostels. To reach the northern end of the path, take bus #47B from Hawkins St. in Dublin's city center to its terminus at Marlay Park in Rathfarnham, a Dublin suburb. Bus #47 also stops nearby. It takes three days to hike the northern section (assuming 7-8hr./day of hiking). The entire trail takes six days. Bikers cover virtually the same mileage by sticking to roads—it is not advisable to take a bike on the way itself.

From its start in Marlay Park the Wicklow Way piggybacks on **Kilmashogue Forest Trail,** which gives great views of Dublin and the distant Mourne Mountains. Farther on, the trail passes the 400-ft. **Powerscourt Waterfall** in Enniskerry. Unfortunately, you have to pay to get a close look, but the view is worth it. (Open mid-May to mid-Oct. daily 9:30am-7pm; late Oct. to early May 10:30am to dusk. Admission £1.50, seniors and students £1, under 16 80p.) The Knockree hostel is between the trail and Enniskerry, while the Glencree hostel is off the trail in the opposite direction from Knockree and Enniskerry. A "Greatest Hits" excerpt of the Wicklow Way would start in Enniskerry and end in Glendalough. Between the two, the trail climbs to the summit of **White Hill** (2073ft.), from which you can see the mountains of North Wales on a clear day. Soon after White Hill, the trail passes Annamoe, where a road and trail lead to Ashford, Devil's Glen, and the Tiglin Hostel (see **Ashford,** p. 132).

The trail then descends to Roundwood, a stop for **St. Kevin's Bus** (see **Glendalough,** p. 126), and runs alongside the Glenmacnass Rd. to Glendalough's impressive monastic ruins. The trail rises to visit **Poulanass Waterfall.** It then climbs a forest track towards **Mullacor,** which at about 2300 ft. is the highest point of the Way, and drops into **Glenmalure,** with another hostel and Mt. Lugnaquilla nearby. The trail crosses another mountain ridge and tiptoes across the **Dun River** over an iron bridge, 1½ mi. southeast of the hostel at Aghavannagh. A detour east off the way between Glendalough and Aghavannagh leads to bus and rail stations in Rathdrum.

Past Aghavannagh, the trail makes smaller climbs amid mellower scenery, ending in Co. Carlow with views of antenna-topped Mt. Leinster. Long-distance hikers can connect here to the **South Leinster Way.** Bus Éireann serves the southern section of the Wicklow Way at Aughrim, Tinahely, Shillelagh, and Hackettstown.

An Óige prints a list of suggested stages for a six-day walk along the Way, with mileage and expected walking time. Get it from any of An Óige's Wicklow hostels or from their main office, 61 Mountjoy St., Dublin. Walking times between the hostels are: Tiglin to Glendalough, five hours; Rathdrum to Aghavannagh, four hours; Aghavannagh to Glenmalure, five hours; Aghavannagh to Glendalough, seven hours. Other trails meander every which way through the Wicklovian wilderness.

ACCOMMODATIONS

Several hostels lie within 5 mi. of the Wicklow Way; these fill up in July and August. For An Óige hostels, book ahead through the An Óige Head Office, 61 Mountjoy St., Dublin (tel. (01) 830 4555); call other hostels directly. The hostels are listed north to south. **Wicklow Way, Old Mill,** and **Glendalough hostels** are reviewed under Glendalough (p. 128).

Knockree (An Óige/HI), Lacklan House, Enniskerry (tel. (01) 286 4036; on the Way), is a reconstructed farmhouse 4mi. from the village and 2mi. from Powerscourt Gardens/Waterfall. From Enniskerry, take the left fork road leading from the village green, take a left at Buttercups Newsagent, and begin a steep walk, following signs for Glencree Drive. Alternatively, take the DART to Bray and bus #85 to Enniskerry, which drops you off 2mi. from Knockree. Simple, single-sex dorms.

Spacious kitchen and dining area w/fireplace. Lockout 10:30am-5:30pm (unless it's raining). Dorm £5.50, Oct.-May £4.50.

Tiglin (An Óige/HI), a.k.a. **Devil's Glen,** Ashford (tel. (0404) 40259; 5mi. from the Way), near the Tiglin Adventure Centre. 50 beds in a very basic accommodation. From Ashford, follow the Roundwood Road for 3mi., then follow the signs for the Tiglin turnoff on the right-hand side, a hilly 8mi. from Powerscourt (see **Ashford,** p. 132). Dorm £5.50, Oct.-May £4.50.

Wicklow Way Hostel (tel. (0404) 45398; on the Way), dorm £6.

Glendalough (An Óige/HI; tel. (0404) 45342; 1½mi.), dorm £6, Oct.-May £5.

Glenmalure (HI/An Óige), Grennane (no phone; 2mi.). From Dublin, take bus #65 from Eden Quay, which brings you to Donard (3mi. to Ballinclea Youth Hostel and 7mi. by mountain track to Glenmalure). Intimate country-cottage feel, maybe because it's the only habitation in sight. The Avonbeg River provides excellent fishing for brown trout and water for washing and cooking, which is handy since the hostel doesn't have running water or electricity. West of Glenmalure is an army range in the Glen of Imaal where military exercises are conducted. Stay out. Dorm £5.50, Oct.-May £4.50. Open July-Aug. daily; Sept.-June weekends only.

■ West Wicklow

Other Wicklow Mountain hostels are west of the tallest peaks in less spectacular but even less populated territory. Don't plan to hike here from the Wicklow Way, since you would have to pass through the Irish Army's target practice in the Glen of Imaal. Two buses every day run from Busarus in Dublin to Baltinglass. The Baltinglass **tourist office** in Weavers Sq. (tel. (0508) 81615) dispenses West Wicklow hiking info (open July-Sept. Mon.-Sat. 9am-5pm; Oct.-June Mon.-Fri. 9am-1pm and 2-5pm).

Baltyboys (An Óige/HI), a.k.a **Blessington Lake Hostel,** Blessington (tel. (045) 867266). A reconstructed old schoolhouse with excellent fishing and Russborough House nearby (see **Blessington,** below). Basic bunks in co-ed dorms. Hot showers. Lockout 10am-5pm. Dorm £5.50, Oct.-May £4.50. Open March-Nov. daily; Dec.-Feb. Fri. and Sat. nights.

Ballinclea (An Óige/HI), Donard (tel. (045) 404657), near forest and Blessington Lake, but cut off from Glenmalure Hostel by the Army range in Glen of Imaal. Simple, clean accommodations. From Dublin's Eden Quay, try taking bus #65 to Donard (Sat.-Sun. 1/day; £1.10). Dorm £5.50, Oct.-May £4.50. Open March-Nov. daily; Dec.-Feb. Fri.-Sat. nights.

Rathcoran House (IHH), Baltinglass (tel. (0508) 81073; fax (01) 453 2183). A safer hiking destination from the western Wicklow hostels (since you won't have to make a huge detour around the Army). Easy access via Tullow to N81 road between Dublin and Wexford makes this a good stopping or ending point for West Wicklow hikers. Bus Éireann runs to Dublin or Waterford twice daily via Baltinglass. Dorm £7.50. Double £17. **Camping** £3.50/person. Open May to mid-Sept.

BLESSINGTON

Since the Liffey was dammed to make a reservoir for Dublin's teeming, thirsty masses, Blessington in West Wicklow has become a popular recreation center. A pretty lakefront embellishes art-filled **Russborough House** (tel. (045) 65239; fax (045) 65054) built in 1741 for Joseph Leeson, a member of the old (Anglo-) Irish parliament. The architect was Richard Cassells, who is also responsible for Dublin's Leinster House and many of Trinity College's Georgian marvels. As at Powerscourt and Castletown, the design is Palladian, its central block flanked by colonnades and wings. Lavish trim is spread throughout the inside of the house like icing across a too-sweet cake. The house also holds paintings by Goya, Velasquez, and Rubens. The National Gallery of Ireland sometimes mounts exhibits here. The house is 2½ mi. down the main road toward Ballymore. (Open June-Aug. daily 10:30am-5:30pm; April-May and Sept.-Oct. Sun. 10:30am-5:30pm. 45-min. tour of main rooms and paintings £3, students £2, ages 12-18 £1. Half-hour tours of the bedrooms £1.)

Turn to the Blessington **tourist office,** in the town square (tel. (045) 65850) for ideas on outdoor pursuits (open June-Aug. Mon.-Sat. 10am-1pm, 1:30-6pm, Sun. 10am-6pm). The **Baltyboys Hostel (An Óige/HI)** a.k.a. **Blessington Lake Hostel,** Blessington (tel. (045) 67266), provides cozy accommodation (see above).

From Dublin's Eden Quay, Blessington is served by **bus** #65 (1/hr.; £1.10). On Saturday and Sunday, one bus continues on to Donard and the Ballinclea Hostel there. **Bus Éireann** passes through Blessington on its Dublin/Waterford route (3/day), connecting it with Baltinglass and its hostel. Blessington is on N81, which undulates from Dublin to Enniscorthy via Tullow. R410 road connects Blessington to Naas, from which N7 leads to nicer Kildare.

WICKLOW COAST

The natural sights and uncrowded towns of Wicklow coast seem a world away from urban Dublin. As a route to the southeast, it lacks the heavy-hitting historical sites of the inland route through Glendalough and Kilkenny, but its natural offerings are more intriguing.

ASHFORD

Ashford, 6 mi. northwest of Wicklow on N11 (26mi. south of Dublin), provides access to both mountains and ocean. On Friday mornings the town trades goods and cattle at its **marketplace.** The **Mount Usher Gardens** (tel. (0404) 40116 or 40205), on N11, encompass 20 acres of well-pruned rare trees, shrubs, flowers, and bees along the River Vartry. (Open mid-March to Oct. daily 10:30am-5:20pm. Admission £3, students and seniors £2.) Gardeners will recognize Mount Usher as a prime example of a Robinsonian garden. This style stresses informality and natural design. Paths weave through the flora along a stream that is ornamented with cute miniature suspension bridges, splashing weirs, waterfalls, and subsidiary brooks. Two miles beyond Ashford on the road to Roundwood, imps may be hiding in the thickly wooded **Devil's Glen.** The glen is a chasm dug by the River Vartry's 100-ft. waterfall, which tumbles into the **Devil's Punchbowl.** The 1½-mi. turn-off is on the Glendalough-Ashford Rd., not far from Tiglin.

Tiglin National Adventure Centre (tel. (0404) 40169; fax 40701), just 3½ mi. from Ashford off the same road, challenges any takers. Experts teach mountaineering, rock climbing, canoeing, and kayaking. Courses may include mountain biking, snorkeling, and full board in two- to four-person dorm rooms. Weekend courses run Friday night to Sunday afternoon and cost £75-90 (including room and board). The course is also offered at a daily rate of £30; cost-cutting eco-tourists could combine days at Tiglin with nights at the Tiglin Hostel and meals at the grocers in Ashford.

Across the gravel path the **Tiglin Hostel (An Óige/HI),** a.k.a. the **Devil's Glen Hostel** (tel. (0404) 40259), is a simple, not pampering, accommodation. Lockout noon-5pm (June-Sept. £5.50, Oct.-May £4.50). Book through An Óige's head office in Dublin (tel. (01) 830 4555). From the hostel, a scenic five-hour hike over Bookey's Bridge ultimately ends up in Laragh, next to Glendalough (maps available at hostel). **Bus Éireann** passes through Ashford on its route from Dublin to Wicklow (to Dublin or Wicklow 8/day, Sun. 6/day; £4.30, student £2.60).

■ Wicklow Town

Wicklow Town is touted both for its coastal locale and for its usefulness as a departure point into the Wicklow Mountains. Older Wicklovians are chatty and friendly while the town's black-clad youth strive for urbanity. Wicklow also boasts an unusual level of ethnic diversity (for Ireland). While the town itself doesn't have any extraordinary charms, a few hours spent biking along the nearby coastal road can pleasantly occupy an afternoon. Long, skinny Main St. snakes past the Grand Hotel and the grassy triangular plot by the tourist office to its terminus in Market Square.

Practical Information The **tourist office**, Fitzwilliam Sq. (tel. 69117; fax 69118), on Main St., can fill you in on the Wicklow Way and other county attractions. Their book and map selection, which includes *Let's Go: Ireland*, is excellent (open June-Aug. Mon.-Sat. 9am-6pm; Sept.-May Mon.-Fri. 9:30am-1pm and 2-5:30pm). An **AIB** conducts business on Main St.; **ATM. Trains** run to Dublin's Connolly Station and to Rosslare (Mon.-Sat. 4/day, Sun. 2/day; to Dublin £4). The station is a 15-minute walk east of town via Church St. **Bus Éireann** leaves for Dublin from both the street uphill from the Billy Byrne monument and from the Grand Hotel at the other end of Main St. (Mon.-Sat. 9/day, Sun. 7/day; £3.50 return). **Wicklow Tours Ltd.** (tel. 67718) runs a van from the Bridge Tavern, Bridge St., to Rathdrum (Avondale) and Glendalough (July-Aug. Mon.-Sat. 10:35am, 1:05 and 3:35pm, Sun. 10:45am, 1:35 and 4:05pm; £5; to Glendalough £4, £6 return). **Dolan's Bus Service** (tel. 67420) runs buses daily (8:30am-11:30pm) from Newcastle, 12 mi. north of Wicklow Town, down the coast to Silver Strand and then Brittas Bay. **Bikes** may be rented from **Wicklow Hire** on Abbey St., the continuation of Main St. (tel. 68149; open Mon.-Sat. 8:30am-5:30pm; £6/day, £25/week; deposit £30; pump and lock included). Wicklow's **phone code** got its teeth knocked out at 0404.

Accommodations Travelers will be content in almost any of the many B&Bs on Patrick Rd., uphill from Main St. and past the church. Wicklow Town can now accommodate hostelers in the **Wicklow Bay Hostel,** the Murrough (tel. 69213). From Fitzwilliam Sq., head toward the river, cross the bridge, and walk left until you see the big building called "Marine House." Family-run, this former beer-bottling factory is a cheery, spacious hostel with firm beds, spectacular sea views from the roof, tea/coffee available all day, 24-hour full kitchen, and TV lounge. (Dorm £7.50; mid-Sept. to June double £16, July to early Sept. £18. Irish breakfast £3, continental breakfast £1. Open March-Oct.) It takes a bit of energy to hike up Patrick Rd. to friendly Mrs. H. Gorman and son's **Thomond House,** Upper Patrick Rd. (tel. 67940). A veranda, panoramic views, and rooms as comfortable as your own are certainly worth the 15-minute walk. (£14/person, w/bath £18. If you call from Wicklow Town, Mrs. Gorman will pick you up. Open March-Oct.) The **Bridge Tavern,** Bridge St. (tel. 67718), has lots of hairy cats, snooker tables downstairs, and good value for its standard rooms (£12.50/person, w/bath £17.50).

Two **campgrounds** are both 7 mi. south of Wicklow off the Wexford Rd. (N11). **Johnson's** (tel. 48133; high season £6, low season £5; plus £1/person) and **River Valley** (tel. 41647; high season £6, low season £5; plus £1/person) are similar. Both are open March-Sept.; both charge 40p for showers. From Wicklow, turn right off N11 at Doyle's pub. Johnson's is 1 mi. down the road, River Valley 2½ mi.

Food & Pubs Main St., like Main streets everywhere, is lined with greasy takeaways and fruit stands. **Fresh Today,** Main St. (tel. 68322), stocks stacks of fruits and vegetables that are, of course, fresh (open Mon.-Sat. 8:30am-6:30pm). **Quinnsworth,** Church St. offers an even wider selection of nutriments. The **Coffee Shop,** Fitzwilliam Sq. (tel. 68006), will provide a quick shot of caffeine before your hike and furnish you with salads (85p), sandwiches (£1.50), and baked goods. Plant yourself in **Pizza del Forno,** Main St. (tel. 67075), to enjoy your choice of a variety of foods (3-course lunch £4.25, sandwiches £1, pizzas £4.50, unique desserts £1.70-4; open daily 10am-11:30pm).

A number of pubs offer musical evenings for the delectation of Wicklow's residents. Every Thursday through Sunday night (in summer; off season Thurs. only), the **Bridge Tavern** on Bridge St. (tel. 67718), resounds with traditional music. It's also known to have informal squeezebox sessions on Wednesday and Saturday nights in the summer to calm the nerves of the snooker players in the back. Those not satisfied with listening should visit **Mulvihill's,** Market Sq. near the monument (tel. 68823).

The comfortable little bar advertises that "roving bards are welcome," has plenty of seats for listeners, and throws its own sessions Thursday through Monday. Check the fence opposite the tourist office in Fitzwilliam Sq. for lists of concerts and events in town.

Sights True to its name, **Market Square,** at that end of Main St. farthest from the train station, holds open-air markets and displays a pike-less monument to local hero Billy Byrne, a Protestant landowner who fought against the Crown in the 1798 rebellion. At the other end of Main St., an **abbey** keeps company with the remnants of a 13th-century **Franciscan Friary.** The abbey was founded at the same time as Black Castle and destroyed along with it. It was subsequently rebuilt and became a place of retirement for both Normans and native Irish, who considered it neutral ground. The first left past Market Sq. leads to **Black Castle.** Though only a few wind-worn stones remain, the promontory on which it was built elevates you to a great vantage point above the sea and meadows. The Normans built the castle in 1169; the local O'Byrne and O'Toole clans immediately attacked and finally destroyed it in 1301. The staircase cut into the seaward side of the remains is reputed to access a tunnel to the nearby convent.

A cliff trail leads to **St. Bride's Head,** where St. Patrick landed on Travilahawk Strand in 432 AD. The local population greeted him by knocking the teeth out of one of his companions, who was later assigned to convert the locals in Wicklow. The trail itself is only slightly less threatening, leading past cannons before arriving at St. Bride's Head. It takes about one hour to walk there. The heights of the cliff walk provide smashing views.

Beaches stretch south of Wicklow to Arklow. The closest ones to Wicklow are **Silver Strand** and **Jack's Hole.** The most popular is crowded **Brittas Bay,** midway between Wicklow and Arklow, where you can buy ultra-cheap crabs in summer. At the Billy Byrne monument, Wicklow Town's Main St. becomes Summer Hill (the coastal road), which will lead you to sun and sand. In the last week of July, Wicklow hosts its **Regatta Festival,** the oldest such celebration in Ireland. The two-week festival features a race of barges made of barrels and timber, and includes the street music, drama performances (£3), and extended bar hours requisite for true Irish fun. Contact the tourist office (tel. 69117) for more information.

■ Near Wicklow Town

RATHDRUM

Rathdrum, perched above the steep wooded valley of the Avonmore river, is picture-postcard pretty. The **International Cartoon Festival** (tel. (0404) 46183 or 46811) makes this small town a popular destination on the first weekend in June. International and local cartoonists come to Rathdrum to exhibit and draw for the public and to hold workshops for budding artists (exhibition £1, related events free). Live entertainment, face-painting and a contest for the best-dressed dog inspire zany antics. The festival never stops at the **Cartoon Inn** (tel. (0404) 46774), on Main St., a pub with wacky cartooned walls and a lip-smackin', belly-ticklin' lunch. The **tourist office** (tel. (0404) 46262) in the center of town will encourage you to stay and spend the money it can exchange for you. (Open Mon.–Fri. 9am-5:30pm, Sat.-Sun. 9am-6pm in summer.) There are a number of B&Bs around Rathdrum, but the cheapest option is **The Old Presbytery Hostel** (tel. (0404) 46173), a very clean and new hostel built from an old Presbyterian monastery (6-bed dorm £9/person, single £10; wheelchair accessible). Book your room early for the festival, or plan to stay in nearby Arklow.

AVONDALE HOUSE

The best reason to visit Rathdrum is nearby **Avondale House** (tel. (0404) 46111), the birthplace and main residence of political leader Charles Stewart Parnell. The former home is now a Parnell museum where restorers have turned the clocks back to circa-

1850 decor. The walls are decked with political cartoons and transcriptions of Parnell's love letters to Kitty O'Shea. The 20-minute biographical video is a well-produced and genuinely interesting glimpse into Parnell's life and his role in the development of Irish independence.

Flora fanatics will faun over the 500 acres of **forest** and parkland which surround the house and spread along the west bank of the Avonmore River. In 1904, the government of Ireland purchased Avondale's land for its first silvicultural experiment; they wanted to figure out how best to reverse Ireland's severe deforestation. The plots of trees stretch out around the **Great Ride,** a grassy expanse that winds its way among the diverse tree species of Avondale's grounds. Otters play hide-and-go-seek on the river's muddy banks. Avondale House is on the road from Wicklow Town to Avoca, 1 mi. after Rathdrum, and before the Meeting of the Waters. From Rathdrum, take Main St. heading towards Avoca and then follow the signs. (House and forest open Mon.-Fri. 10am-5pm, Sat.-Sun. 11am-5pm, winter daily 11am-4pm. Admission £2.50, students £1.50.)

▓ Arklow

Arklow has a long and fishy history—for the past two millennia it has made its living by fishing and shipping. While its museum and factories educate visitors on town industries, the calm Avoca River ripples past Dubliners who choose Arklow for their weekend getaways. When St. Kevin visited the town in the 5th century, he blessed the town's fishermen, guaranteeing prosperity. A more tangible blessing was bestowed later by the Anglo-Irish government which built a modern harbor in the 18th century. Arklow blossomed into a strapping and well-known port and shipbuilding center. The town flops along Main St., parallel to the Avoca River. The harbor, beaches, and potteries are farther east of town center.

The Arklow **tourist office** (tel. 32484), really a trailer parked in the town center, is at the end of St. Mary's Rd. and Main St. (open all year Mon.-Sat. 9:30am-1pm, 2-5:30pm). **Bank of Ireland** (tel. 32004) and **AIB,** with **ATMs,** are on Main St. **Trains** run to Arklow from Dublin on their way to Rosslare (Mon.-Sat. 4/day, Sun 2/day). **Bus Éireann** passes through Arklow on its way to Rosslare and Wexford (Mon.-Sat. 5/day, Sun. 3/day). **Black's Bike Shop,** Upper Main St. (tel. 31898), repairs and rents bikes (£8/day, £37/week, £20 deposit. Open May-Oct. Mon.-Sat. 9:30am-6pm; winter hours vary). Arklow is 40 mi. south of Dublin on the N11 (Dublin/Wexford road). The **phone code** is a fishy 0402.

Accommodations & Food Those who can't resist Arklow's siren call head to Coolgreany Rd., which houses a passel of B&Bs. Turning right off Station Rd., Main St. becomes first Upper Main St. and then Coolgreany. **Vale View** (tel. 32622) boasts huge bedrooms and good, firm beds; kudos to the glass-roofed "honeymoon suites" (single £19; double £28, w/bath £32). **Dunguaire** (tel. 32774) is another comfortable B&B, with a good view of the green countryside from the spacious dining room (single £16; double £28, w/bath £32).

The **River Walk Restaurant** (tel. 31657), on the shore of the Avoca River, serves hearty fare at low prices (full breakfast all day for £3.75, chicken curry and rice £3.60; open daily 9am-10pm). For fast food in the wee hours of the morn, Arklow heads to the **Roma Grill** (tel. 32480) on Upper Main St. (curries, kebabs, burgers £1-2; open Mon.-Wed. 11am-12am, Thurs.-Sun 11am-3am). Across the street, **The Green Pepper** (tel. 39889) vends all kinds of produce (open 9am-6pm).

Sights Located about one mile from town, the north and south **beaches** are both safe for swimming, but grey and rocky. A walk along the Avoca River is lovely, but why walk when you can paddle? Paddleboats, rowboats, and canoes can be hired next door to the River Walk Restaurant (£2/person for ½hr.).

The seafoam-green **Arklow Maritime Museum** froths on St. Mary's Rd. between the train station and the Catholic Church. If you like ships, set sail for this one-room museum, which is nearly all that remains of Arklow's maritime past. Inform your curiosity about John Tyrrell and Sons, who have been building ships in Arklow for 130 years. A piece of the first transatlantic cable, laid by an Arklow captain, is proudly displayed (open daily 10am-1pm and 2-5pm; admission £2, students £1).

St. Savior's Church, Upper Main St. (tel. 32439, Rev. David Moynan), at the roundabout, is a beautiful building with an international reputation for campanology (bell-ringing). The ringers sound their stuff on Sunday mornings. This area of Ireland produces the raw materials for ceramics, and Arklow is known for its finished products of all types, from bathroom ceramics to vases (the warehouse is next to the beach for those sun-bathing/redecorating days). **Arklow Pottery,** on the South Quay, was established in 1934 and remains the largest manufacturer of tableware in Ireland. (Factory open Mon.-Fri. 9am-5pm, Sat.-Sun. 10am-5pm; factory tours Mon.-Fri. Booking tel. 31101; individuals can join pre-booked groups. Free). The Arklow and Wicklow Vale **pottery outlets,** along the quays, sell glassware and ceramics straight from the kiln.

County Kildare

The towns immediately west of Dublin in Co. Kildare are still well within the city's orbit: the best sights—Kildare's horses and Lullymore's Peatland World—are easily seen as daytrips from Dublin. Only a bit farther from Dublin, though, the towns become shockingly tiny communities. The County is linked to Dublin by more than just highways—half of Kildare was included in the Pale, the region of English dominance centered around Dublin. From the 13th to the 16th century, the FitzGerald Earls of Kildare had effective control over all of eastern Ireland. Today, mansions and the big-money Irish Derby evoke Kildare's former prominence.

▓ Maynooth

Maynooth (ma-NOOTH) is sandwiched between Carton House on one end of Main St. and Maynooth Castle and St. Patrick's College the other. Between them, they make Maynooth a dignified and religiously significant sandwich. Maynooth was originally founded on fear: King George III granted permission for this first Catholic seminary in Ireland to open in 1795 out of concern that priests educated in Revolutionary France (the only other option) would acquire dangerous notions of independence. He later said that opening St. Patrick's "cost me more pain than the loss of the colonies." The Maynooth Seminary was the only site for training Irish Catholic priests for much of the 19th century. Although other centers exist today, many of today's priests, both in Ireland and abroad, are still ordained at this National Seminary.

The **Citizens Information Centre,** Main St. (tel. 328 5477), is not a tourist office but answers questions about the area (open Mon.-Fri. 10am-4pm). **Buses:** #66 runs directly to Maynooth from Middle Abbey St., Dublin (2/hr.; 50min.; £1.50); #67A, also from Middle Abbey St., takes the long way through Celbridge (2/hr.; £1.50). Suburban **trains** run from Connolly Station in Dublin (Mon.-Sat. 14/day; Sun. 4/day; 30min.; £1.60). Maynooth is 12 mi. west of Dublin on N4. **Hitchers** from Dublin stand on Chapelizod Rd., between Phoenix Park and the Liffey, or even farther west where the same street becomes Lucan Rd. The copycat **phone code** is Dublin's 01.

Accommodations, Food, & Pubs The **Leinster Arms,** Main St. (tel. 628 6323), is primarily a pub, but it's also a great B&B value for groups. Guests pay a flat £22 per room, with or without bath. Reserve ahead in summer, especially for the room with an attached kitchen. The pub downstairs serves both snacks and entrees for the kitchenless (vegetables £2.50, entrees about £5; open daily 10:30am-10pm). **St. Patrick's College** rents out singles and doubles in student apartments. (Mid-June

to Sept.; B&B £15/person; contact Bill Tinley at the conference center, tel. 708 3726).
Enjoy light lunch fare at **Elite Confectionery,** Main St. (tel. 628 5521; soup of the day
85p, salad 80p, cheesecake £1; open Mon.-Sat. 8:30am-6:30pm).

Sights **Maynooth Castle** was built in 1176 by Maurice FitzGerald and dismantled
in 1647. The powerful family controlled their vast domains from here. The edifice
now lies in ruins in a sun-dappled field right off Main St. Pick up the key from Mrs.
Saults at 9 Parson St., the road across from the castle, to become the sole, if temporary, resident of this castle. Hundreds of noisy birds take off when you climb the staircase into the roofless Great Hall (open whenever Mrs. Saults is home; free).

Next to the castle, **St. Patrick's College,** Ireland's oldest Catholic seminary, draws
in the tourists with interesting architecture and alluring, lush gardens. The **Visitors
Centre,** on the left after passing through the arch, displays Christian artifacts and
offers tours of the college (tel. 708 3576; open Mon.-Sat. 11am-5pm, Sun. 2-6pm;
tours £1.50, students £1). The arch leads into a world all its own that consists of the
oldest swimming pool in Ireland (built in 1903), a cypress-shaded garden, and the
Ecclesiastical Museum (tel. 628 5222). The museum contains a spectrum of priestly
paraphernalia and an impressive collection of 19th century scientific instruments,
including the induction coils of Dr. Nicholas Callan, their inventor. The unifying
theme is unclear (open Tues. and Thurs. 2-4pm, Sun. 2-5pm; free). Farther inside the
arch grow the gorgeous gardens created in 1995 for the seminary's bicentennial.

At the other end of Maynooth's main drag, the Georgian **Carton House,** set at the
end of a long, beautifully landscaped drive, impresses visitors with its imposing
facade. Still privately owned, the house isn't open to the public.

■ Near Maynooth: Celbridge

The *raison d'être* of Celbridge (SELL-bridge) is **Castletown House** (tel. (01) 628
8252; fax 627 1811). The estate's driveway extends for a full ½ mi., spilling past its
entrance gates to become the town's Main St. The grounds overlook the Liffey and
are ideal for picnics; the shaded, bubbling creek is popular with young lovers. William Conolly, once the Speaker of the Irish House of Commons, built himself this magnificent home, thus touching off a nationwide fad for Palladian architecture. Edward
Lovett Pearce, who also designed the Parliament House/Bank of Ireland in Dublin
(see **Trinity College & Nearby,** p. 102), finished the house after Conolly's death.
From a central block, two wings and rows of colonnades stretch out in graceful arcs
to hide the stables behind. Inside, sumptuous furnishings and baroque wallpaper (to
match the grand colonnades) show off the luxurious life-styles of the rich and
obscure Anglo-Irish gentry. Of particular note are the print room (the only one of its
kind surviving in Ireland) and some garish chandeliers in the den. The **devil** allegedly
visited the dining room one afternoon for tea, but no evidence of hoof-prints remains.
Outside, the Obelisk, also known as **Conolly's Folly,** is merely an unruly stack of
arches and towers conceived as a make-work project during the severe winter of
1739. Americans may be surprised that the original plans for the Washington Monument looked like this, only bigger. (Open April-Sept. Mon.-Fri. 10am-6pm, Sat. 11am-
6pm, Sun. 2-6pm; Oct. Mon.-Fri. 10am-5pm, Sun. 2-5pm; Nov.-March Sun. 2-5pm.
Tours £2.50, students £1.)

Down Main St. from the House's entrance, **Celbridge Abbey** provides another
opportunity for picnicking. The abbey and its gardens are maintained by mentally-
handicapped people, whom the Abbey houses and employs. The elegantly manicured gardens spread out behind the house, laced with two trails which tell stories
about Jonathan Swift. There's also a neat model railway (abbey open March-Oct.
Tues.-Sun. noon-6pm; admission £1.50, students £1). Purchase picnic supplies for
both dinner and lunch on the two lovely lawns at **Damien's Londis Supermarket,**
Main St. (tel. (01) 628 8506; open Mon.-Sat. 8:30am-8pm, Sun. 9am-6pm). **Quinn's
Salad Bar,** also on Main St., serves light and vegetarian fare (sandwiches £1, salads
£2.50). **Buses** #67 and 67A run to Celbridge from Middle Abbey St., Dublin. #67A

stops in Maynooth along the way. The suburban rail also has an infrequent service to Celbridge from Dublin's Heuston Station.

■ Kildare Town

Kildare Town is like many a 12-year-old lass—it's still in its horse phase, and is likely to remain so for a long time. Purebreds are the lifeblood of the town. Racehorses are beautiful, elegant creatures, as anyone who's attended the Irish Derby well knows. Kildare seems imbued with some of their nervous energy and natural grace, especially in contrast with the town's mule-like neighbors. While Kildare's present religion centers around horses, its past was more influenced by Christianity. It grew around a church founded here in 480 AD by St. Brigid. The town's original name— *Cill Dara,* meaning "Church of the Oak"—derives from a story that Brigid founded the Church next to an oak tree that she saw in a vision.

Practical Information The Kildare **tourist office,** in the Square (tel. 522 6960), has a ferocious enthusiasm for local pubs (open June-Sept. Mon.-Sat. 10am-1pm and 2-6pm). Kildare is well-connected by **train** to Dublin's Heuston Station (Mon.-Sat. 30/day, Sun. 12/day; 40min.; £3.50) and also by **Bus Éireann** to Dublin (1/hr.; 1½hr.). Dublin-bound buses from Cork and Limerick also stop in Kildare. Kildare lies on the N7 (the Dublin-Limerick Rd.). Bikers will hate the N7—it's fast, has huge, scary, monster trucks, and one lane in each direction, so that cars must pass each other using the road shoulder/bicycle lane. To avoid the highway, rent a **bike** in Kildare at **Kieran's Bike Shop** on Claregate St. and take the back roads. The **phone code** is a galloping 045.

Accommodation, Food, & Pubs Accommodation in Kildare isn't very forthcoming. Toward the Stud on the outskirts of town, **Fremont,** Tully Rd. (tel. 521604), has firm beds, well-decorated rooms, and a quasi-rural setting (on the way to the Japanese Gardens) that allow visitors to dream of racehorses (single £17, double £30). In town, the **Lord Edward Guest House B&B,** Dublin St. (tel. 522389), is more hotel than B&B, with professional staff and a TV in every room. Organists are welcome to jam on the organ in the lobby (single £18, double £30). **The Shell House** (tel. 521293), on the Dublin Rd. is worth a stop just to gawk. Once a thatched cottage with a bizarre form of weatherproofing, one of the conditions of sale was that the shells that cover all the outside walls of the house must be maintained. They are arranged to form pictures of local attractions, like the round tower and cathedral steeple. Inside, the beds are firm, the showers are hot, and the breakfast is light (single £14, double £28).

Good pubs are plentiful. **The Silken Thomas,** the Square (tel. 522232), has locally renowned food, ranging from bar snacks (smoked salmon sandwich £3.75) to serious entrees (8oz. steak £8.50). Lunch, lounge, and dinner menus variously served between 11am and 10pm. The pub's name isn't a euphemism, but a reference to "Silken Thomas" FitzGerald, who raised a revolt against the British in Dublin in 1534. **Li'l Flanagan,** in the back of the Silken Thomas (tel. 522232), is a small, delightfully scruffy, old-time pub. (Trad sessions at 9:30pm on Mon., Wed., Thurs., and Sun. nights, rock and easy listening on Fri. and Sat. nights; no cover.) **Nolan's,** the Square (tel. 521528), is a low-key pub that served as a hardware store for several years. Sadly, the saws are gone, but they make up for it with trad sessions on Tuesday through Thursday nights (no cover).

Sights Kildare is a town with a lot of character, as evidenced by the bustling square at the center of town and the close-knit patrons of its pubs. The **Round Tower,** originally built in the 10th century, stands testimony to Kildare's rich cultural heritage. This is one of the few round towers in Ireland that visitors can actually enter and climb—most of the others have no floors inside. (Open Mon.-Sat. 9am-1pm and 2-5pm, Sun. 2-5pm. Admission £1, children 50p.) **St. Brigid's Cathedral** lies in the shadow of the tower. The cathedral, an imposing building with old stonework, rests on the site where St. Brigid founded one of Ireland's first churches in 480 AD. She was one of the first powerful women in the Christian church, even holding power over bishops. Next to the church is **St. Brigid's Fire Temple,** a site of pagan rituals that Brigid repossessed for Christianity. Only women were allowed to tend the fire, which burned continually for 1000 years. There is an unadorned high cross on the site. Its uncarved surface indicates great age. (Cathedral open May-Oct. Mon.-Sat. 10am-1pm and 2-5pm, Sun. 2-5pm. Free tours of the Cathedral are available upon request.)

The **Irish National Stud,** "where strength and beauty live as one," about 1 mi. from Kildare in Tully (tel. 521617), does its best to make the town's horse fever contagious. (Don't use the gold and wrought-iron gates on the Dublin Rd.; instead, follow the plentiful signs for the turnoff from the main road.) Colonel William Hall-Walker, the mystical son of a Scottish brewer, started to breed thoroughbreds at Tully in 1900. Every time a foal was born, the Colonel would cast its horoscope; if it was unfavorable, the foal would be sold, regardless of how well it was bred. The "system" has proved remarkably successful. Astrology aside, the whole place is still eccentric. The horses quaff naturally sparkling mineral water from the Tully River; its water is carbonated and has 260 parts per million of calcium, which is said to promote good bone formation. Hall-Walker stressed that the moon and stars should exercise their maximum influence on the horses, so skylights were incorporated into the roofs of all stables. Lantern roofs in the stallion boxes, built after Hall-Walker's death, continue his policy.

As the sights lose any practical purpose, things grow steadily weirder. The small **Irish Horse Museum** is housed in a converted groom's house and stallion boxes. It tells the history of the horse from its eohippus origins to modern times, most vividly with the skeleton of Arkle, Ireland's greatest steeple chaser. A noble horse, even in death. **The Japanese Gardens,** also part of the Stud, are beautiful and truly bizarre, like a walk-through boardgame. Devised by Hall-Walker and built by two Japanese gardeners between 1906 and 1910, the gardens purport to tell "the story of the life of man" on a guided-by-numbers trail. (Irish National Stud, Irish Horse Museum, and Japanese Gardens open Feb. 12 to Nov. 12 daily 9:30am-6pm. Joint admission £5, students and seniors £3, under 12 £2.)

■ Near Kildare Town

THE CURRAGH

Entertainment in Kildare is understandably equinocentric. Between Droichead Nua/Newbridge and Kildare on N7 lies **The Curragh,** 600 acres of what are perhaps the greenest fields in Ireland. Thoroughbred horses graze and train, hoping one day to earn fame and money at The Curragh racecourse (tel. (045) 541205), which hosts the **Irish Derby** (DAR-bee) on the first Sunday in July. The race, sponsored by horse-crazy Budweiser, is Ireland's premier sporting and social event and one of the most prestigious races in the world. The atmosphere on race day is grand—everyone dresses like royalty. The Derby race itself is at 4pm. Other races are held from late March to early November (Irish Rail timetable lists dates; trains stop at The Curragh on racedays. Admission £9 to Derby, £7.50 to other events; students and seniors get 50% off by purchasing tickets at the Enquiries booth, opposite the racecourse's VIP entrance.) The Curragh was once a headquarters for the British military presence in pre-1916 Ireland. In the important but hushed-up "Curragh mutiny" of 1914, British army officers (who wrongly thought they were about to be ordered north) stated that they would rather be fired than act against the Unionists.

PEATLAND WORLD & LULLYMORE

When times get tough in the bogs, the boglanders know who to turn to—their friend peat. Nine miles from Kildare in Lullymore campy **Peatland World** (tel. (045) 60133 or 60193) explains this phenomenon. Located in the immense Bog of Allen, Peatland World is comprised of a museum and a natural history gallery. The natural history part expounds on the ecological diversity of the bogs and some of its eco-friendly post-peat-production uses. The museum explains the evolution of turf production from community activity to big business, with some attention to the "social impact of turf" over the centuries. On display are bog-preserved prehistoric artifacts, a model of an Irish cottage with a turf fire, and trophies from turf cutting competitions. The museum displays their achievements: a model of a peat briquette factory and a peat-fueled power station, as well as a range of peat-based products, including a cosmetics line and clothing. (Open Mon.-Fri. 9:30am-5pm. Admission £2, students £1.50, children £1.) Those bitten by the bog bug should certainly take a bog tour on the West Offaly Railway (see **Near Athlone: Clonmacnoise,** p. 159).

Anyone interested in early-Christian Ireland should not miss **Lullymore Heritage Park** (tel. (045) 560353). Surrounded by bogland and farms, the park offers a realistic depiction of Irish life in the pre-famine years and shows relics and ruins from Lully-more's 5th-century heyday. Included is a recipe from a famine soup kitchen: one ox-head with tongue, 28lbs. of turnip, 3½lbs. onions, 7lbs. carrots, 21lbs. of peameal, 14lbs. of Indian cornmeal, and 28 gallons of water (open Mon.-Fri. 10am-6pm, Sat.-Sun. 2-6pm; 1-hr. tour; admission £2, students £1.50, children £1). To reach Lully-more from Kildare, take Allenwood Rd. to Rathangan Rd. It's a tricky hitch; you're best bet is to go by bike. Buses drive to nearby Allenwood from Dublin (6/day, Sun. 3/day; 1¼hr.).

Meath & Louth

Meath is a quiet, peaceful county, which makes it an appropriate home for the crypts of ancient, creeping terror that lurk among its hills. In pre-Norman times, after the builders of these crypts had faded into stony memory, Meath was considered Ireland's fifth province. In pre-Christian times, since it contained Tara, it was the political and spiritual center of Ireland. Vikings sailing up the Boyne built Drogheda, which today serves as a base for exploring the county's pleasantly morose charms. Farther north in Co. Louth, the Cooley Peninsula, almost an island, contains hills and water for bikers and sailors to enjoy. When going to Cooley, the boat trip is much more enjoyable and interesting than the dull land routes.

BOYNE VALLEY

Among the towns, highways, back lanes, and furrows of the Boyne Valley are the richest sets of archaeological remains anywhere in Ireland. Slane and Trim have some of the best-preserved medieval castles (and a rock festival or two). The Celtic Hill of Tara and the neolithic tomb-mounds of Newgrange, Knowth, and Dowth puzzle professional archaeologists and amaze more casual visitors. Every so often the valley's farmers plow up weapons or artifacts from the 1690 Battle of the Boyne.

Buses from Dublin and Drogheda hit the major Boyne towns, but many famous sights are miles off the main roads, and service between towns is spotty. The several N-roads that criss-cross the valley make it easy to hitch, but the grand tour requires a fair degree of hiking. Bikers will find the terrain between the sights welcoming: mostly flat, with hills gentle enough to conquer without stopping but steep enough to boost one's ego. Bus fares from Dublin range from £3-6 return. Several tours herd visitors through the circuit of sites. **Celtic Twilight** (tel. (088) 54787) offers a full sight-seeing "Tour of the Royal Meath" (June-Aug. Sun.; £12). The coach leaves the Nassau St. entrance to Trinity College Dublin at 10am and returns to Dublin at 5:30pm. **Sightseeing Tours** (tel. (01) 283 9973) visits Newgrange and Knowth on its

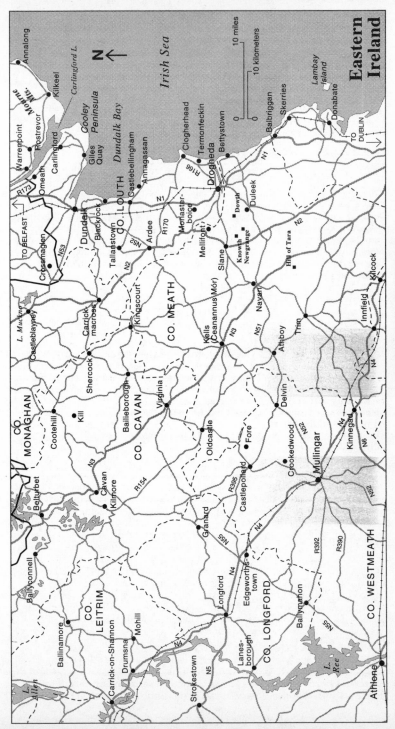

Eastern Ireland

N

Irish Sea

10 miles
10 kilometers

Annalong
Kilkeel
Mourne Mts.
Warrenpoint
Rostrevor
Omeath
Carlingford
Carlingford L.
Cooley Peninsula
Giles Quay
Dundalk Bay
Clogherhead
Termonfeckin
Bettystown
Balbriggan
Skerries
Lambay Island
Donabate
TO DUBLIN

R173
CO. LOUTH
Castlebellingham
Annagassan
Drogheda
N1
R166
Dunleer
Dowth
Duleek
N2

TO BELFAST
Crossmaglen
N53
Dundalk
Blackrock
Tallanstown
Ardee
N52
N2
R170
Monaster-boice
Mellifont
Slane
Knowth ■ Newgrange
Hill of Tara
Navan
N1

L. Muckno
Castleblayney
Carrick-macross
Kingscourt
CO. MEATH
Kells (Ceanannus Mór)
N3
N51
Athboy
Trim
Innfield
Kilcock
N4

CO. MONAGHAN
Shercock
Ballieborough
Virginia
CO. CAVAN
Oldcastle
Fore
Delvin
N52
N4
Kinnegad
N6

Cootehill
Kill
N3
Crookedwood
Mullingar
N52

Belturbet
Cavan
Kilmore
R154
Castlepollard
R395
CO. WESTMEATH
R392
R390

Ballyconnell
Granard
N55
N4
Delvin

Ballinamore
CO. LEITRIM
Mohill
Longford
Edgeworths-town
Ballymahon
N55

Ballinamore
Drumsna
Carrick-on-Shannon
N4
Lanes-borough
CO. LONGFORD
L. Ree

L. Allen
Strokestown
N5
Athlone

Boyne Valley tour. The bus leaves the Dublin Tourist Office on O'Connell St. (June-Sept. daily at 1:20pm, return at 6pm; £14).

■ Drogheda

Founded by Vikings in 911, Drogheda (DRA-hed-a) once rivaled Dublin as a center of trade and Armagh as a center of worship. It's still a busy port. Despite suburban development, old walls linger at unexpected points throughout the town. Most of the city is north of the River Boyne and is connected to the south side by St. Mary's Bridge. Most of the sights in Meath are within biking distance of Drogheda.

PRACTICAL INFORMATION

Tourist Office: Donore Rd. (tel. 37070), in the bus station off Dublin Rd. Offers the *Cultural Map of Drogheda* (60p), which covers practical information, and *Drogheda* (£1), a historical summary with a better map and a walking tour. Open June-Sept. Mon.-Sat. 10am-1pm and 2-5:30pm.

Banks: AIB, West St. (tel. 36523). Open Mon.-Wed. and Fri. 9:30am-5pm, Thurs. 9:30am-7pm; **ATM. TSB,** West St. (tel. 38703). Same hours.

Trains: Station is east out of town on the Dublin Rd.: follow John St. south of the river. Station inquiries (tel. 38749). To Dublin (Mon.-Sat. 8/day, Sun. 3/day; ½hr.; £7.50, £9.50 return) and Belfast (Mon.-Sat. 5/day, Sun. 3/day; 2hr.; £11).

Buses: leave from the bus station on John St. (tel. 35023). Inquiries desk open Mon.-Fri. 9am-6:30pm, Sat. 8:30am-1:30pm. Buses go to: Athlone (Mon.-Sat. 2/day, Sun. 1/day; 2½hr.; £9); Belfast (Mon.-Sat. 4/day, Sun. 3/day; 2hr.; £8); Dublin (Mon.-Sat. 16/day, Sun. 7/day; 50min.; £4.80); Dundalk (Mon.-Sat. 11/day, Sun. 6/day; 40min.; £4.40); Galway (Mon.-Sat. 2/day, Sun. 1/day; 4½hr.; £12); and Mullingar (Mon.-Sat. 2/day, Sun. 1/day; 2hr.; £7.50).

Taxi: Lawrence St. (tel. 38439).

Bike Rental: Bridge Cycles, North Quay (tel. 34526), is the best place to rent bikes. £6/day, £30/week; deposit £30. Helmet rental £5. Open Mon.-Sat. 9am-1pm and 2-6pm. 10% discount with ISIC card, another 10% discount if you mention you got their name out of *Let's Go.* It's affiliated with the head office of **Irish Cycle Hire,** Mayoralty St. (tel. 37422 or 41067), off North Quay.

Hospital: Our Lady of Lourdes, Cross Lanes (tel. 37601).

Emergency: Dial 999; no coins required. **Garda:** West Gate (tel. 38777).

Post Office: West St. (tel. 38157). Open Mon.-Sat. 9am-5:30pm.

Phone Code: 041.

ACCOMMODATIONS

Drogheda's accommodations, like most everything in the town, are north of the River Boyne. **Harpur House,** William St. (tel. 32736), is a small hostel in a big townhouse. Follow Shop St. up the hill, continue up Peter St. and take a right onto William St.; the hostel is on the right. The house is old and it shows, but the rooms are airy and the beds are not bunks. Simple B&B rooms provide additional privacy. (9-bed dorm £7, w/full breakfast £10; B&B £15/person. Kitchen facilities; no curfew.) Buses from Harpur House do half-day sightseeing tours of the Boyne Valley (£10). A well-kept and backpacker-friendly B&B, **Abbey View House,** Mill Lane (tel. 31470) defines courtesy. Head west on West St. and take the first left after it crosses over to Trinity St. Sitting pretty right next to the River Boyne, the house has parking, bikes, canoes, a tunnel to Monasterboice, and big rooms with patchwork quilts (£14/person). High ceilings and elegant wallpaper make **St. Laurence's Lodge,** King St. (tel. 35410), seem more like a hotel than the old Christian Brothers school that it is. The rooms are pleasant, with firm beds, tea-makers, and TVs (£17/person, single £20; all w/bath).

FOOD & PUBS

Groceries can be found on West St. at Dunnes Stores and Quinnsworth. (Both open Mon.-Tues. and Sat. 9am-6:30pm, Wed. 9am-8pm, Thurs.-Fri. 9am-9pm.)

A Little Mouthful, corner of Shop St. and North Quay (tel. 42887), provides anything but. They serve hot meals (lasagna £3.20), full breakfast all day (£2.50), and salads (£2.70). But don't leave without trying their delicious homemade bread (sandwiches £1.55-2.90) or pastries (75p). Open Mon.-Sat. 8:30am-6pm.

The Pizzeria, Peter St. (tel. 34208). All kinds of Italian specialities. Very popular, so make reservations or arrive before 9pm if you want a seat (13 types of pizza, £5.40; steaks and pasta £5-9). Open Mon.-Tues. 6-11pm, Thurs.-Sun. 6-11pm.

Birdie Mac's, West St. (tel. 33861), serves everything from bus snacks (potato wedges £2) to full meals (prawn and shellfish pasta £5, steak sandwich £5.50). Food served daily 3-9pm; live music Thurs.-Fri. and Sun. 9:30pm.

The Copper Kettle, 1 Peter St. (tel. 37397), just up from the junction with West St., this seems like a hole-in-the-wall café. The offerings are simple but scrumptious (white coffee 60p, scones 25p). Open Mon.-Sat. 9:30am-5:30pm.

As the largest town in the area, Drogheda has a pretty active nightlife. Start at **Peter Matthews,** 9 Laurence St. (tel. 37371), also known as McPhail's; dark wood engulfs you at this very old, very likable pub (live rock and blues Thurs.-Sun. nights). **The Weavers,** West St. (tel. 32816), is renowned for its lunchtime and dinner grub. There's more wood and darkness here, hosting a well-dressed business-type clientele (DJs spin top 40 tunes Fri.-Sun. nights; no cover). **Carberry's,** Back Strand, is the only place in town with trad music (Thurs. and Sun. nights), in a friendly, smoky environment. There are rumors that it never closes.

Drogheda has a happening disco that draws dancers from miles around. **The Earth,** Stockwell Lane (tel. 30969), is a Flintstones-meet-techno sort of place, with fossils embedded in the walls and bar, rock-oriented bathrooms, and not a single straight wall. (Open Thurs.-Sun. 11pm-2:30am. Cover £5, £3 w/concession before midnight and Sun. Techno-dance music is on Fri. and Sat. night, Thurs. and Sun. are more oriented towards 70s disco style.)

SIGHTS

Encounter a blackened shriveled head in the imposing, neo-Gothic **St. Peter's Church** on West St. (open 8:30am-8:30pm). Built in the 1880s, the church safeguards what's left of the martyred saint Oliver Plunkett. Pious visitors light candles and pay homage. Plunkett is at the end of the left-hand aisle, along with the door of his London prison cell. Archbishops of Armagh sometimes lived in Drogheda until the 18th century. Most of the town's medieval churches (at one time there were as many as seven) were sacked or burned by Cromwell, a deeply religious man.

At the end of West St. stand the four-story, round, twin towers of **St. Laurence Gate,** a 13th-century fortification outside the walls of the town, which is no less impressive for the fact that it never really faced a serious attack. At the top of the hill on St. Peter's St., the mossy **Magdalen Steeple,** dating from 1224, is all that remains of the Dominican Friary that once stood on the spot. The **Droichead Arts Centre,** Stockwell St. (tel. 33946; fax 42055), displays artwork and runs a theater which shows locally produced and traveling shows (open Mon.-Sat 10am-5pm; gallery free). On Saturday mornings, an open-air market is held in Bolton Square, as it has been every week since 1317. The **Millmount Museum** (tel. 33097) occupies a Martello tower on the southern hill overlooking Drogheda's center. It displays artifacts from the Civil War period, antique household appliances, and a geological collection (open April-Oct. Tues.-Sat. 10am-6pm; admission £1.50, children 75p). In early August, Drogheda holds the **Drogheda Folk Festival,** a three-day festival of traditional music and drinking. On Old Abbey La., south of West St., are the few remains of the 5th-century **Priory of St. Mary,** perched among the urban refuse of the modern town.

■ Near Drogheda

The Battle of the Boyne raged at **Oldbridge,** 5 mi. west of Drogheda. On July 1, 1690, Protestant forces under William of Orange (William III of England) defeated the Irish Catholic armies supporting the ousted Stuart king of England, James II, who fled the country weeks later. Though the Catholic armies fought for a year, the battle gave William control of Dublin, and James's flight made it clear that English Protestants would continue to control at least the eastern half of Ireland. Catholics, and English Jacobites, remembered the Battle of the Boyne as a momentous tragedy for centuries; the Ulster Protestants made it an occasion for celebration. Calendar reform has moved the battle's "anniversary" to July 12, Orange Day, when Protestant militants march all over Northern Ireland.

▓ Brú na Bóinne

The area southeast of the town Slane—*Brú na Bóinne* (brew na BO-in-yeh, "the Palace of the Boyne")—is saturated not with palaces, but with prehistoric tombs: Newgrange, Knowth, Dowth, and 37 more. All the tombs were made by an indigenous pre-Celtic neolithic culture with mind-boggling engineering talents. The tombs are older than the pyramids and Stonehenge; in July or August, you may grow old yourself waiting in the long lines to see them, especially at Newgrange (the earlier in the day you arrive, the less you'll have to wait). But the prehistoric architectural ingenuity will prove worth the wait. All of Brú na Bóinne is very well signposted: all three of the passage-tombs are reached from the turnoff on N51, 3 mi. from Slane and 7 mi. from Drogheda. Follow the turnoff road for about ½ mi., then take a right at the intersection for Knowth, a left for Newgrange and Dowth. The road is very well travelled, and hitchers report an easy trip to and from the tombs. Follow signs for Slane (west down West St.) and then Dowth for a more scenic (but equidistant) route. Hitchers should stick to the well-traveled Slane Rd. until they come to the intersection where signs direct you to Knowth and Newgrange. Bikers in search of the easiest ride should follow the road to Dowth on their way to the tombs and take the Slane Rd. back to Drogheda. The **phone code** here, as in Celtic times, is 041.

NEWGRANGE

Newgrange (tel. 24488; fax 24798), the most spectacular, most restored, and most visited of the sites, is the prime example of a passage-tomb. Built by a highly organized religious society over 5000 years ago using stones carted from Wicklow 40 mi. away, Newgrange is covered with elaborate patterns and symbols mystifying to archaeologists. The inner chamber's roof was cobbled together without the use of mortar, and has stood since around 3200 BC. The 30-minute tour is one part information and 10 parts wild speculation (do the drawings represent "the triumph of life over death" or are they "art for art's sake?"), but it's the only way to see the inside of the one-acre tomb. The highlight of the tour is the recreation of the moment which actually occurs five days each year around the winter solstice, when the sun's rays enter at just the right angle to illuminate the inner chamber. Though this function was only recently discovered, the natives have told stories for thousands of years of how the people of the mound could "stop the sun." Watch for antique graffiti, left by visitors to Newgrange since the rediscovery of its passage in 1699. Bring a windbreaker or a warm sweater; it gets chilly inside even in summer. (Tours begin every 20min. daily, June-Sept. 9:30am-7pm, Oct. 10am-5pm, Nov.-Feb. 10am-4:30pm, March-April 10am-5pm, May 9:30am-6pm. Last tour 45min. before closing. Admission £3, seniors £2, students £1.25.) The **tourist office** (tel. 24274) is in Newgrange (just before the entry to the site, near the parking lot; open April-Oct. daily 10am-7pm). Make it up to your children or companions bored with Newgrange by taking them next door to **Newgrange Farm.** More than a coffee-shop (open daily in summer), this farm houses animals that visitors are welcome to feed and pet.

KNOWTH & DOWTH

One mile west of Newgrange is the less frantic, and less restored, site of **Knowth** (rhymes with "mouth"). Knowth was inhabited continuously from 3000 BC until the Battle of the Boyne, so that the site today is a mishmash of Stone Age tombs, early Christian subterranean refuge tunnels, and Norman grain ovens. Among those who made use of the mounds were the "beaker people." These mysterious people were not muppets, but pre-Celtic tribes known only for their drinking flasks. They may have worshipped mead. The tour here is more informative and entertaining than that at Newgrange, and it's usually less crowded. Because people lived on top of the tomb for so many years, it's unsafe to go inside, but guests are welcome to crawl through short, underground tunnels. Though there is no tourist office, the admission office sells booklets about Knowth's history (Tel. 24824. 30-min. tours May to mid-June daily 10am-5pm; mid-June to mid-Sept. 9:30am-6:30pm; mid-Sept. to Oct. 10am-5pm. Admission £2, students £1.) One mile east of Newgrange is **Dowth** (rhymes with "Knowth"), the third of the great passage tombs. Dowth is not open to the public, but follow signs past it anyway to take the more scenic and less traveled route back to Drogheda. Everyone will enjoy the subtle humor of farmer Willie Redhouse who can take you on a tour of his 400-acre farm, pausing by a chuckling river and prehistoric mounds on his property. Newgrange tours may attribute such grassy wonders to religious origins, but Willie invites more imaginative speculation: where else would leprechauns bury their gold and the tooth fairy store everyone's teeth? (Open daily July-Aug. daily 10am-5pm; April-June and Sept. Sun.-Fri. 10am-5pm. Admission £2.25.)

■ Sailing Up the Boyne

MELLIFONT ABBEY & MONASTERBOICE

Two of what were once the most important monasteries in Ireland crumble 5 mi. north of Drogheda. Turn off of Drogheda-Collon Rd. at Monleek Cross and follow signs for either one. The more interesting of the two, **Mellifont Abbey** (tel. (041) 26459), has served as a grand setting for many of Ireland's tragedies. Founded in 1142 by St. Malachy, a friend of Bernard of Clairvaux, Mellifont was the first Cistercian abbey in Ireland. The 1152 Senate of Mellifont saw the end of the independent Irish monastic system, as a papal legate divided Ireland into four bishoprics with Armagh as primate and confiscated the monasteries' tithes. Consequently, the monastic centers declined, along with the traditions of scholarship within their walls. Three years later, Cistercian pope Adrian IV issued a bull giving the English King authorization to "correct" Ireland, which served as approval for the Norman invasion of the 1170s.

The last of the O'Neills, who once ruled Ulster, surrendered to the English here in 1603 and then skipped Ireland for the Continent. Most of the grandeur of the place has disappeared as well, though a glimpse remains at the **old lavabo,** where monks once cleansed themselves of sins and grime. This bath of past ages will give you an idea of the original structure's impressiveness. (Open May to mid-June daily 10am-5pm; mid-June to mid-Sept. daily 9:30am-6:30pm; mid-Sept. to Oct. daily 10am-5pm. Last admission 45min. before closing. Admission £1.50, students 60p.)

Just off N1, the monastic settlement of **Monasterboice** (MON-ster-boyce; always open; free), is well-known for its 9th century high crosses and round tower. Founded in 520, the monastery was one of Ireland's most wealthy until it was sacked and burned by Vikings in 1097. **Muiredach's Cross,** the first one you'll see upon entering, is one of Ireland's best examples of a high cross. A frenzy of sculpted Bible scenes, from Eve tempting Adam to the Judgement Day, cover the cross, the top of which is carved in the shape of a reliquary. Standing nearly 7 yd. high, the timeworn West Cross is the tallest High Cross in Ireland.

HILL OF TARA

From prehistoric times until at least the 10th century, Tara was the political and sometime religious center of Ireland. The hill is home to a Stone Age tomb, an Iron Age fort, and the principal late Celtic royal seat—the combination has guaranteed Tara's popularity with tourists and archaeologists alike. As the seat of the powerful Uí Néill family, control of Tara theoretically entitled their warlord to be High King. Ownership of the hill was understandably disputed until the 10th century, but the arrival of St. Patrick (traditionally in 432, more likely closer to 400) deposed Tara from its position as the Jerusalem of Ireland. Tara's symbolic importance remains even in modern times; in 1843, Daniel O'Connell gathered a million people here for a Home Rule rally. The overlapping of bronze age, high king, and early Christian civilizations at Tara has confused historians and archaeologists for centuries, and today the historical function of many of the hill's structures remains unknown.

The enormous site is about halfway between Dublin and Navan on the N3. Take any Navan-bound **bus** from Dublin (13/day, Sun. 5/day; 1hr.) and ask the driver to let you off at the turnoff; it's about 1 mi. straight uphill to the site. The actual buildings—largely wattle, wood, and earthwork—have long been buried or destroyed; what you'll see is mostly a set of concentric and overlapping earthen rings and walls, whose traditional names correspond to the buildings the mounds were thought to cover. The whole history of Tara decamps at the **visitors center** (tel. (046) 25903), in an old church at the site. Aerial photos of Tara, essential for making sense of the place, are displayed here. The center shows a good 20-minute flick about Tara's history, complete with warrior-kings, pagan priestesses, and scary sound effects. After the film, an excellent guided tour (25min.) circles the site. The full site encompasses 100 acres of many smaller mounds and ring forts, though you'll likely see only the sites at the top of the hill. (Visitors center open May to mid-June daily 10am-5pm, mid-June to mid-Sept. 9:30am-6:30pm, mid-Sept. to Oct. 10am-5pm. Mounds always open. Admission £1, seniors 70p, students and children 40p.)

■ Trim

A series of enormous, well-preserved Norman castles and abbeys that thrill even the most jaded tourist overlook this charming town on the River Boyne. It's definitely worth a trip from Dublin. Trim's **tourist office** on Mill St. (tel. 37111; open all year daily 9:30am-6pm) has a meaty amount of information on Meath, and the useful self-guided walking tour of Trim (60p). The **Bank of Ireland** surveys Market St. (tel. 31230; open Mon. 10am-4pm, Tues.-Fri. 10am-5pm). **Bus Éireann** stops on Castle St. in front of the castle en route to Dublin (6/day; £5 return) and Athlone (1/day). Trim's **phone code** is a slim, vivacious 046.

Accommodations, Food, & Pubs A handful of B&Bs makes a night in Trim an enticing possibility. The **White Lodge,** Lackanash New Rd. (tel. 36549; follow High St. to Navan Rd. and take the first right), has spacious, well-decorated rooms with TVs (single £20; double £28, w/bath £32.) In the heart of town pumps **Brogan's,** High St. (tel. 31237), a pub that does hotel-like B&B (£15/person). Floral comfort blooms in **O'Briens,** Friars Park (tel. 31745), off Dublin Rd. The rooms are both spacious and neat (single £14; double £28, w/bath £30).

The **Pastry Kitchen,** Market St. (tel. 36166), puts sturdy breakfasts and luscious pastries and breads on the table (breakfast £2.20, served all day; open Mon.-Sat. 7:30am-6pm, Sun. 10am-6pm). **The Abbey Lodge,** Market St. (tel. 31549), presents a tremendous plate of roast stuffed chicken with fries and veggies (£3.50) with your pint. **McCormack's,** across from the Castle on Castle St. (tel. 31963), may show cricket on TV, but it's all Irish on Sunday nights when the *bodhrán,* tin whistle, and a fiddle or two liven things up (cover £1). **The Bounty,** across the Bridge St. bridge (tel. 31640), is bedecked with spinning wheels, old umbrellas, and bulls' horns. On Emmet St., the bustling **Emmet Tavern** (tel. 31378) fills stomachs with its carvery.

Sights When Norman invader Hugh de Lacy first built **Trim Castle** in 1172, he couldn't know that 822 years later Mel Gibson would sack the place in the making of *Braveheart*. He was, however, aware that the unruly O'Connors of Connacht trashed the place a year later. A new castle, the one which Mel would later attack, was constructed in the 1190s. King John of England dropped by long enough to rename it **King John's Castle**. For a few hundred years, the castle was an important fortification for all of Meath and defended a walled town with separate gates and battlements. Richard II housed the young Prince Hal here in 1399, perhaps as a hostage to use against his then-rebellious father, Henry IV. The castle, which says it's the largest in Ireland, stands above the center of town and can be easily reached through the gate on Castle St. **Walking tours** offer access to parts of the castle (others are still undergoing renovations; July-Aug. daily 9:30, 11am, 2, and 6pm; £2).

For more spicy Trim history, the **Meath Visitors Centre** (tel. 37227), next to the tourist office, educates and frightens with a multi-media presentation, an exhibit, and an excellent, dramatic slideshow (decapitations, the villainous Hugh de Lacy, and hideous plague rats—maybe Trim isn't so charming after all. Open Mon.-Sat. 9:30am-6pm. Admission £2, seniors £1.25, children 70p.)

Across the picturesque river stand the 12th-century remains of **St. Mary's Abbey,** destroyed by Cromwell's armies. You can still see the **Yellow Steeple** (so called because of the yellowish gleam it gives off at twilight), the only remains of the holy sisters' old place (once home to "Our Lady of Trim," a miracle-performing statue). In front of the Yellow Steeple is what's left of **Talbot's Castle,** a 15th-century manor built by John Talbot, Viceroy of Ireland. The manor (built on the site of an old Augustinian abbey) has a very British air: Queen Elizabeth wanted it to be the country's first university, but it ended up as just a school. Outside the two ruins lies the **Sheep Gate,** the only surviving medieval gate of the once walled town. You can rid yourself of unwelcome warts at the **Newtown Cemetery,** far behind the Castle, by putting a pin between two tomb figures wrongly known as the **Jealous Man and Woman.** The name comes from the sword between them, which conventionally signified not resentment, but chastity. When the pin rusts (which shouldn't take long in this country) your warts will disappear.

Butterstream Gardens, ½ mi. out of town on Kildalkey Rd. (tel. 36017), is one of Ireland's most frequently honored private gardens; in the summer of 1995, it was graced by the helicopter of Prince Charles as one of the few sights in Ireland that the gardener-prince demanded to see (open May-Sept. daily 11am-6pm; admission £3). For one week each June (usually the last), the **Scurlogstown Olympiad Town Festival** fills Trim with horse fairs, carnival rides and traditional music concerts.

BEYOND THE VALLEY OF THE BOYNE

■ Kells (Ceanannas Mór)

The name of Kells is known far and wide, thanks to a book which wasn't even written there. The monastery at Kells was founded by St. Columcille (also known as St. Columba) in 559, before the saint went on to found the more important settlement of Iona on an island west of Scotland. It was at Iona that the famous *Book of Kells,* an elaborately decorated Latin gospels, was started. It came to Kells in some form of development in 804 when the Columbans fled Iona. In 1007, the book was stolen, its gold cover ripped off, and the pages buried under sod and recovered two months later. It remained in Kells until 1661, when Cromwell carted it off to Trinity College, where it is now recovering. Kells is trying to get the book back, which Trinity finds amusing. Even without the book, Kells can boast of some of the best-preserved monastic ruins in Ireland, including an oratory, a round tower, and five high crosses.

EASTERN IRELAND

Most maps refer to Kells in Irish, as *Ceanannas Mór*. **Bus Éireann** stops outside of O'Rorke's Bar on Castle St. on its way to Dublin (Mon.-Sat. 17/day, Sun. 8/day; 1hr.; £6 return). **AIB** bank is on John St. (tel. 40610; fax 41222; open Mon. 10am-5pm, Tues.-Fri. 10am-4pm), while the **post office** (tel. 40127) is on Farrel St. (open Mon.-Sat. 9am-5:30pm). Kells's **phone code,** 046, hasn't been swiped by Trinity. Yet.

Accommodations, Food, & Pubs   Kells can boast the area's only real hostel. **Kells Hostel,** on the Dublin-Donegal Rd. (tel. 40100; fax 40680), has a real jacuzzi and squash courts. The gym downstairs offers a special £2 per session rate for hostelers. The dorms are clean and spacious, and beds are almost always available except on Slane Castle Concert weekend. Check in at Monaghan's Bar next door to the hostel. (Dorm £5.50, Sept.-May £5; 6-bed dorm £6.50. Sheets 50p; self-service laundry £2. Snooker table available in the common room for 50p.) **Camping** is available behind the hostel, with full use of the indoor hostel facilities (£3/person). **Latimor House** (tel. 40133), ½ mi. down the Oldcastle Rd., does B&B in a pretty, rustic setting. The house is full of antiques and the beds are firm with thick comforters. Relax to the lowing of the cows on the distant hills (single £14, double £28; from Market Sq., go down Cross St. and take the first right onto Canon St.).

After the cemeteries, stop in for a drink and some great grub at **O'Shaughnessey's,** Market St. (tel. 41110), everyone's favorite eating and drinking center (pizza £3.25, sandwiches £1.20). Trad session come to the pub on Wednesday nights, and balladeers do their thing on Friday, Saturday, and Sunday nights (music around 10pm; no cover). **Penny's Place** (tel. 41630) is a pink paradise on Market St., serving sensational scones (35p; open Mon.-Sat. 9am-6pm).

Sights   Despite its centuries-long tradition as a center of Christian learning, the monastery at Kells kept getting burned down by rival monasteries. The current church, with the exception of the 12th-century belltower, dates only to the 1700s. Inside **St. Columba's Church** (tel. 40151) there's a replica of the Book; upstairs, copies of selected pages are enlarged for your viewing pleasure. The door should be open during daylight hours; if not, ask at the gate outside. Wander around and you'll find four large **high crosses,** some better preserved than others, scattered on the south and west side of the church and covered with Bible scenes. The 100-ft.-high **round tower** sheltered the monks, the relics of St. Columcille, and (less successfully) would-be High King Murchadh Mac Flainn, who was murdered there in 1076.

The most satisfying of the sights, however, is **St. Columcille's House,** on Church Lane, where the *Book of Kells* may have been finished. When facing the gates of the Church yard from Market St., walk up the lane on the right of the yard; you can't miss the only 8th-century house on the block. The key is available from Mrs. Carpenter, 100 yd. down the hill from Columcille's house on Church Lane. The place looks almost exactly as it would have in St. Columcille's day, except that the present aboveground door was originally part of a secret underground passageway from the churchyard—the original entrance began 8 ft. above the present ground level. Climb the ladder to the three tiny attic rooms for a glimpse of the sleeping quarters: they're alright for a monk, but not so fit for the entire families which lived here in the centuries before this one.

A town **Heritage Centre,** John St., includes an audio-visual presentation of the town's history, as well as the Market Cross, a high cross that served as a whipping and hanging post for the Fenian rebels of 1798. The Market Cross was originally in the town square, but trucks had this nasty tendency of running into it. The center will also contain a replica of the *Book of Kells,* which will be a relief to the tourists who invariably come here looking for it. If the center isn't open, don't despair; **Monaghan's Pub,** off the Dublin Donegal Rd. (tel. 40100), also has a copy displayed in their entryway. The best time to see it is early July, when the town holds a nine-day **Kells Heritage Festival** of traditional music, dancing, and rock.

Two miles down Oldcastle Rd., within the People's Park, is the **Spire of Lloyd,** a 150-ft.-high viewing tower erected by the old Headfert landlords. (Open Tues.-Fri.

2:30-5pm, Sat. 3:30-6pm, Sun. 2-6pm. Admission £1, children 50p.) From the top, behold spectacular Irish countryside and Northern Ireland in the distance. Next to the Spire is the **Graveyard of the Poor,** where the area's huge pauper population buried their dead in mass graves. The plot was a chaotic cow pasture until a few years ago, when the town scraped together the money to restore it. Now the grass is cut regularly and there's a high sign which reads: "1838-1921, Erected to the poor interred here during the operation of the English Poor Law System. R.I.P." Tours available on request; contact Father Gallogly (tel. (046) 42208).

Several historical sites are within the near vicinity of Kells, but bus service through most of the area is nonexistent. The best way to see the area is **Shamrock Experience,** a backpacker-oriented tour that covers the Spire of Lloyd, the town of Oldcastle, and the neolithic tomb of Lough Crew, an excavated tomb of comparable size and age to Newgrange. (Contact Shane at Kells Hostel tel. 40100. Tours available upon request; £5 half-day, £7 full day (includes the Fore Abbey). The tour involves walking, so bring good shoes.)

■ Dundalk

If you want to see the Cooley Peninsula, it's better to stay *on* it, rather than look *at* it from Dundalk. Located at the mouth of Dundalk Bay, the very Republican town of Dundalk has information on the rest of Co. Louth and Cooley Peninsula, but it has little to attract tourists other than a youthful atmosphere. Enriched by the presence of a regional college, Dundalk hosts a hopping pub and nightclub scene.

Practical Information The **tourist office,** Jocelyn St. (tel. 35484), hands out free maps marked with the city's few sights. They have the helpful, wide-ranging, and free *100% Proof,* a guide to the pubs of Cos. Laois, Louth, Meath, and Westmeath, heaps of information on Carlingford Lough, and Patrick Kavanagh greeting cards (open Mon.-Fri. 9:30am-1pm and 2-5:30pm). From the bus stop on Clanbrassil St., walk past the square and turn left onto Crowe St.; the tourist office is on the right after the library. The **National Irish Bank** (tel. 32156) is on Earl St. (open Mon. 10am-5pm, Tues.-Fri. 10am-4pm). **Trains** (tel. 35521) pass through the Dundalk station, Carrickmacross Rd. en route to Belfast (Mon.-Sat. 7/day, Sun. 3/day; 1hr.; £7) and Dublin (Mon.-Sat. 4/day, Sun. 3/day; 1hr.; £9.50). **Buses** stop at the Bus Éireann station, Long Walk (tel. 34075), and run to Belfast (Mon.-Sat. 7/day, Sun. 3/day; 90min.; £6), and Dublin (Mon.-Sat. 15/day, Sun. 7/day; 90min.; £8). Take a **taxi** home from the nightclub—they run until 5am on weekends (tel. 33296 or 33333; 24-hr. service tel. 74777; £3 minimum, about £1/mile). The **Bike Shop,** 11 Earl St. (tel. 33399), sells used bikes and rents new ones for £8 per day with a £30 deposit (open Mon.-Fri. 9am-1pm and 2-6pm, Sat. 9am-6pm). N1 highway zips south to Dublin and north to Belfast, becoming A1 at the border. **Hitching** is less safe and much more difficult in and around Dundalk than elsewhere in the Republic. The **post office** (tel. 34444; open Mon.-Tues. and Thurs.-Sat. 9am-5:30pm, Wed. 9:30am-5:30pm) is on Clanbrassil St. The **phone code** is the meaning of life, 042.

Accommodations, Food, & Pubs If you must stay in town, **Oriel House,** 63 Dublin St. (tel. 31347), is inexpensive and serviceable with dark but comfortable rooms (£12/person). **Glen Gat House,** 18/19 The Crescent (tel. 37938), adjacent to the train station, is nicer but more expensive (£15/person).

Most restaurants cluster on Clanbrassil St. None will amaze you, but there are plenty of cheap options. The **Imperial Hotel Coffee Shop,** Park St. (tel. 32241), serves sandwiches (£1.70), quiche, and lasagna to hungry night owls (open daily 8am-10pm). **Seanachaí,** 12 Park St. (SHAWN-na-kee; tel. 35050), has lots of traditional music and character. The locals' pub, **Windsor Bar,** on Dublin St. (tel. 38146), is convenient to Oriel House and serves particularly good bar food. **Mr. Ridley's Nightclub,** 91 Park St. (tel. 33329), plays 70s music (open Mon. and Thurs.-Sun. until

2:15am). The less trendy congregate at **Tivoli,** at the Imperial Hotel, Park St. (tel. 32241; open Thurs.-Sun. 10pm-2:30am; cover £6).

Sights **St. Patrick's Cathedral,** Francis St. (tel. 34648), hides an ornate Gothic interior behind a dark facade of gray stone. It was modeled after King's College Chapel in Cambridge (open daily 7:30am-5pm). Next door, your footsteps will echo in the **Louth County Museum** (tel. 26578), which exhibits "Louth's industrial legacy"—perfect for that research paper on Louth's tractors (open Tues.-Sat. 10:30am-5:30pm, Sun. 2-6pm; admission £1). Standing seven stories high, the **Seatown Windmill** was once one of the largest in Ireland, but the wind has been taken out of its sails: they were removed in 1885. Balmy beaches beckon from **Blackrock,** 3 mi. south of the R172. Ulsterbus runs tours of the Mournes from Dundalk (late June to late Aug. Mon.-Sat.; £14; call 43075 for info).

COOLEY PENINSULA

There are numerous trails in the surrounding mountains and Carlingford Lough has the warmest waters in the northern half of the island. The area is steeped in intriguing historical myths. It was the setting for part of the most famous Irish epic, the *Táin bo Cuailnge,* or "The Cattle Raid of Cooley" (see **Legends and Folktales,** p. 69). Although little material evidence remains of these legendary feats, the medieval settlements, built about 1300 years after the epics supposedly took place, are remarkably well preserved. According to proud locals, Little Cooley Peninsula is the "best bit of Ireland," unjustifiably overlooked by tourists and Bord Fáilte. Come during one of Carlingford's festival days and see for yourself what everyone else is missing. Cooley's **phone code** is a cool 042.

■ Carlingford

Situated at the foot of Slieve Foy (the highest of the Cooley Mountains), the coastal village of Carlingford has changed remarkably little since its heyday in the 14th, 15th, and 16th centuries. The town's past is still visible in historic stone cottages and crumbling medieval fortifications. **The Holy Trinity Heritage Centre,** Church Yard Rd. (tel. 73454), housed in a former Church of Ireland, shows a short video and sells an informative map of "Medieval Carlingford" for £1. If they're giving a tour of the town, you can join in for £2.50. (Call for bookings; open Mon.-Fri. 10am-1pm and 2-4:30pm, Sat.-Sun. 1-6pm; July-Aug. also Sat.-Sun. 11am-7pm. Admission to center £1.) An **AIB** (tel. 73105) opens its doors on Newry St. (open Tues. and Thurs. 10:30am-12:30pm and 1:30-2:30pm). **Buses** (tel. 34075) stop along the waterfront on their way to Dundalk (Mon.-Sat. 5/day; 40min.; £3.20) and Newry (Mon.-Sat. 2/day; 40min.; £3.50).

Accommodations, Food, & Pubs At the **Adventure Centre and Hostel,** Tholsel St. (tel. 73100), the friendly staff shows adventurers along long twisty corridors to rather dark rooms with wooden bunks and locker-room-style bathrooms with hot, hot showers. (8-bed dorm £7, 4-bed dorm £8, double £18. Sheets £1.50. Open Feb.-Nov.; all year to groups.) If there's a group staying at the Centre, meals are available (breakfast of cereal and juice £2.50, lunch £3.50, dinner £5.50). **B&Bs** in Carlingford tend to be posh and expensive. You can dance the hora all the way to the nondenominational B&B **Shalom,** Ghan Rd. (tel. 73151), signposted from town center. All rooms have TV, hotpot, and bathroom (£16/person). **Carlingford House** (tel. 73118), well-posted from town center, has stately rooms (£17.50/person). Otherwise, head to the Omeath Youth Hostel (see **Around the Peninsula,** below).

   McKevitt's, down the street from the hostel, sells expensive groceries (tel. 73109; open Mon.-Thurs. and Sat. 9am-6pm, Fri. 9am-8pm, Sun. 2-6pm). Pub grub and good *craic* pile up at **Carlingford Arms,** Newry St. (tel. 73418). Look for daily dinner specials. Various music plays here weekends. **PJ's Anchor Bar,** across the street from the hostel (tel. 73106), is barely larger than a breadbox, but tight quarters induce close friendships. In good weather, the backyard provides a refreshing and less crowded alternative. Inside, publicans proudly display the clothes of the leprechaun caught in the hills several years ago.

Sights & Events **King John's Castle,** by the waterfront, is the largest and most foreboding of Carlingford's five medieval remains. Built in the 1190s and named for King John, who visited in 1210, the castle is usually locked. If renovations are complete, you might be able to finagle the key out of the Heritage Centre staff. **Taaffe's Castle,** towards town along the quay, was built in the 16th century as a merchant house on what was then the waterfront. You can't go in—now, as then, the castle is privately owned. In a tiny alley off Market Square, the turret-laden 16th-century **Mint** is fenestrated with five ornate limestone windows. At the end of the street, one of the old 15th-century town gates—**the Tholsel**—survives, leaving only a narrow path underneath for cars. Most impressive (and most accessible) is the mammoth **Dominican Friary** at the south end of town. The recently renovated ruins are open for exploration. You can pretend that you're a Dominican friar and that Cromwell is oppressing you. The **Adventure Centre,** Tholsel St. (tel. 73100), gives instruction in canoeing, windsurfing, kayaking, and sailing (all £28/day, children £17/day). Peadar Elmore's *MV Slieve Foy* (tel. 73239) goes **deep-sea fishing** (£15/person).

The village seems to have about as many annual festivals as it does houses. The **Leprechaun Hunt** in late May is a race through the hills to find 50 hidden "leprechauns," statuettes with tags marked £25, £50, or £100. The hunt actually was created by the legendary P.J. (see PJ's Anchor Bar, above) who is still remembered fondly as the man who almost convinced people that leprechauns existed. The winners get to keep the money. A mid-June **fleadh** manipulates traditional music and dancers; and **Cooley Vintage Day,** August 1, is a country fair with horses. The late-August **oyster fest** supposedly increases everyone's virility for a week; it definitely makes for a great lunch. The season ends on Heritage Day in late September with a **medieval banqueting weekend** that brings on parades, costumes, and indigestion, and a weekend **folk festival** that draws musicians from all over the Republic.

Cavan & Monaghan

The teeny towns of Co. Cavan and Co. Monaghan make fine stopovers on the way to the Northwest or to Northern Ireland's Fermanagh Lake District, especially since crossing the border has now become so easy and painless. Tourists are a rare breed in these counties—Hare Krishna Island, in particular, is a great place to avoid them.

BELTURBET

The sleepy little town of **Belturbet** overlooks the River Erne from a hill and has its own little citizen-run **Tourist Information Office,** along the main street (tel. (049) 22044; open summer Mon.-Fri. 9am-9pm, Sat. 11am-9pm, Sun. 2-9pm; call for winter hours) on the main street. Stop in at **The Seven Horses,** Main St. (tel. (049) 22166), for a pint of the blonde in the black among wagon wheel chandeliers, furry hides, and stuffed pheasants. Belturbet still reels from the long-awaited opening of the £30 million Shannon-Erne waterway. For the first time in 125 years you can travel from Belturbet to Carrick-on-Shannon by boat. **Turbet Tours** (tel. (049) 22360) sail the *Erne Dawn* from Belturbet to Ballyconnell. The 2½-hour trip either bores or inspires, depending on how you feel about water. Take the first right after Mrs. McGreevy's B&B—the marina is right down the road. (To Ballyconnell: April to mid-Sept. Tues. and Thurs. 11am, 1:30pm, Sat. 3pm. To Crom: Mon., Wed. and Fri. 3pm. £5 for either trip.) If you plan on spending the night in the area, the hostel in Ballyconnell is worth finding. If it's full, Mrs. McGreevy's **Erne View House,** Bridge St. (tel. (049) 22289), makes for a quiet night's sleep. (£16/person w/bath, double £27). Belturbet comes alive, believe it or not, the week of August 1 during the **Festival of the Erne,** when 20 women seek the title "Lady of the Erne."

Near Belturbet

Take the Killashandra and Crossdoney Rd. south of Belturbet and follow the signs to the hamlet of **Garthrotten,** where plain nature trails lace **Killykeen Forest Park** (tel. (049) 32541) and anglers cast their lines into lakes. It would take an imaginative mind to find adventure here, but it is a fine spot for a picnic (park always open). The ruin of the **O'Reilly Clan Castle** stoically resists crumbling into Lough Oughter. **On Yer Bike Tours** visits sites and scenery on wheels and by boat, June through September. They arrange bikes, admission fees, and refreshments (6-person min.; 8-hr. tour £19.80/person). They also rent bikes out (£5/day, £25/week; deposit £30; for either service contact Michael (tel. (049) 22219)).

HARE KRISHNA ISLAND & BALLYCONNELL

Sandville House Hostel (tel. (049) 26297) promises tremendous views and solitude around Ballyconnell. Its remote location, 3 mi. south of town, will guarantee isolation. Vent excess energy on the makeshift soccer field or volleyball court before settling by the fireplace in the converted barn. Call from Belturbet or Ballyconnell for pick-up by one of the friendly staff (dorm £5; open March-Nov.).

Folks at the hostel can tell you all about the Hare Krishnas. Better yet, why not visit the Krishnas yourself at the extraordinarily un-Irish **Hare Krishna Island** (Inis Rath). Their presence here isn't just coincidence. Since the 6th century, the islands of Lough Erne have played host to various groups of Christian and pagan devotees. A 10-minute rowboat adventure takes you to an island gloriously stocked with deer, swans, peacocks, and rabbits. The only requirement for guests is an open mind to experience the Krishna way of life: waking up at 4am for prayers, dancing, readings, meditation, and recitation of the Hare Krishna mantra. The rest of the day is filled with services, chores, and indulging in *prasadam,* food specially prepared and offered to Krishna. But don't take more than you can eat, since Krishna etiquette requires leaving no food on your plate. Says one Krishna, "you'll never forget us." Boat pickup from Ballyconnell or Maguiresbridge—phone from either town and they'll pick you up if possible. If not, **Cabra Cars** (tel. (049) 23323) charges £10 from Sandville Hostel to the jetty and about £6 from Maguiresbridge. Reserve one day in advance; overnight guests are preferred. Lodging and food are free. From Northern Ireland, call (01365) 721512. From the Republic, call (08 01365) 721512.

▓ Monaghan Town

Monaghan (MOH-nah-han) is indifferently pleasant—it's a busy market town in the center of the country, encircled by loads of tiny, egg-shaped hills called drumlins—but there is nothing here worth going out of your way to see. From Church Sq., walk up the Market St. hill to find the **tourist office.** (Tel. 81122. Open June-Sept. Mon.-Fri. 9am-6pm, Sat. 9am-5pm, Sun. 10am-2pm; Oct.-May Mon.-Sat. 10am-1pm and 2-5pm.) For **banks** try **AIB,** the Diamond, where the **ATM** accepts Visa. The **bus station** (tel. 82377; open daily 9am-9pm), north of Market Sq., runs buses to Dublin (7/day; 2hr.; £6, students £5) and Belfast (Mon.-Sat. 5/day; 1½hr.; £4.90, students £3.50). **Tommy's Taxis,** (tel. 84205), can scoot you farther afield. You might be able to rent bikes at **Clerkin's Cycles Shop,** Park St. (tel. 81113; £15/week; open Mon.-Wed. and Fri.-Sat. 8:30am-1pm and 2-6pm). Just north of Church Sq. lies the **post office,** Mill St. (Tel. 82131. Open Mon. and Wed.-Fri. 9am-5:30pm, Tues. 9:30am-5:30pm, Sat. 9am-1pm and 2-5:30pm.) Chant the **phone code:** 047.

Accommodations, Food, & Pubs   The best accommodation and only hostel/camping in the area is in Castleblayney (see p. 153). If you want to stay in town,

Ashleigh House, 37 Dublin St. (tel. 81227), has rosy rooms decorated with floral prints, and breakfast that is "whatever you want" (single £14, w/bath £18; double £26, w/bath £30). Two doors down, **Argus Court,** 32 Dublin St. (tel. 81794), provides basic, no frills B&B (single £13; double £24; economy double £22).

    Genoa Restaurant, 61 Dublin St. (tel. 82205), combines a coffee shop with fast food offerings to the beat of a jukebox. (Ice-cream soda 85p, pizza margherita £3. Coffee shop open Mon.-Sat. 10am-7pm, Sun. noon-7pm. Fast food open Mon.-Sat. noon-12:30am, Sun. noon-1:30am). **Pizza D'Or,** 23 Market St., behind the tourist office (tel. 84777) is a town institution; it stays open until after the discos close (small veggie pizza £4.55; open Mon.-Thurs. 5pm-1am, Fri.-Sun. 5pm-3:30am). Monaghan has a **SuperValu supermarket,** on Church Sq. (tel. 81344; open Mon.-Wed. 9am-7pm, Thurs. 9am-8pm, Fri. 9am-9pm, Sat. 9am-6pm). **The Squealing Pig,** The Diamond (tel. 84562), with its young crowd, barn-like wooden floor, and large-screen TV, gets the vote for the most popular pub in town.

Sights In the center of town, the **Monaghan County Museum,** Hill St. (tel. 82928), across from the tourist office, painstakingly chronicles Co. Monaghan's history. A 14th-century Cross of Clogher titillates (open Tues.-Sat. 11am-1pm and 2-5pm; free). Extremely thorough and specific, the **St. Louis Heritage Centre,** Market Rd. (tel. 83529), occupies the red-brick building in the convent school grounds. The center traces the Saint Louis Order of nuns. Past sisters' hairshirts and cutlery are on display, while Barbie dolls model the evolution of nun fashion. (Open Mon.-Tues. and Thurs.-Fri. 10am-noon and 2:30-4:30pm., Sat.-Sun. 2:30-4:30pm. Admission £1, children 50p. Wheelchair accessible.)

■ Near Monaghan: Castleblayney

Twenty miles southeast of Monaghan, Castleblayney challenges sports enthusiasts and hikers at the **Lough Muckno Leisure Park** at the end of the town's main street. The park consists of 900 acres of forests and trails around Lough Muckno, as well as a hostel, an adventure center, camping facilities, and Hope Castle Bar and Restaurant. Situated in a stoic stone building, the **Lough Muckno Leisure Park Adventure Centre (IHH)** (tel. (042) 46356), welcomes grungy backpackers to clean, airy, efficiently run accommodations (dorm £7, w/continental breakfast £9, w/full Irish breakfast £12; no self-catering). **Camping** space is also available (open St. Patrick's Day weekend to mid-Oct.; £4/tent plus £1/person). The **Adventure Centre** offers both land and water activities for the energetic (open June-Sept. Tues.-Fri. 2-7pm, Sat.-Sun. noon-7pm; windsurfing £20/4hr., tennis £2/hr.).

    Fast food at **Barney's,** Main St. (tel. (042) 40120) is the best of the town's few options (chicken breast at £1.80; open Mon.-Sat. noon-1am, Sun. 3pm-1am). Or pack a picnic at **Spar Supermarket** on Main St. **Gunner Brady's,** Main St. (tel. (042) 40053), is a hopping place for pints. (Food available Mon.-Sat. noon-7pm. Daily specials £3.50. Traditional music on Thurs. nights, live bands Fri.-Sun.).

    Lucky windsurfers may get blown (over land) to **Clones,** a petite town 20 minutes southwest of Monaghan on the N54 (serviced by the Monaghan-Cavan bus route) where lovely lace is plentiful. The Clones Lace Guilde, 10 Fermanagh Terrace (tel. (047) 51729 or 51051) has recently opened the **Canal Stores,** on the Cavan Rd. You can admire old lace, buy new lace, and even see the stuff being made.

Westmeath, Offaly, Laois, & Longford

With the exception of spectacular Clonmacnoise and the intriguing bog, these central counties are passages rather than destinations. Co. Westmeath, with nineteen lakes, is sometimes called the Land of Lakes and Legends—it's something like Minnesota, but smaller. Farming and fishing are the only occupations in Co. Westmeath. Farther south in famously soggy Co. Offaly, small towns civilize the peatland with rabid consumer culture. Co. Laois (LEESH) gets a lot out of its central location. Its county capital, Portlaoise, boasts a central mail sorting facility, shopping centers, a peat-powered generator with cooling towers, and a prison. The Slieve Bloom Mountains, between Mountrath, Kinitty, and Roscrea, are unfairly neglected, but info is available in Birr. And no, we didn't forget forlorn Co. Longford: it's mostly harmless.

■ Mullingar

Plum in the center of Co. Westmeath, Mullingar is an ideal base for exploring the county's few attractions by day and for discoing at night. The fishing and boating on Lough Ennell and Lough Owel are just minutes away, while Sligo and Galway, for which destinations passage through Mullingar is also necessary, are farther away.

Practical Information The **tourist office** (tel. 48650; fax 40413) is far from town, ½ mi. down the Dublin Rd. (open June-Aug. Mon.-Fri. 9am-6pm, Sat. 10am-1pm and 2-6pm; Sept.-May Mon.-Fri. 9:30am-5:30pm). The **Chamber of Commerce Tourist Information Centre** (tel. 44044 or 44285), in Market Sq., corner of Pearse and Mount St., is more convenient than the tourist office and almost as well-stocked with info, including the monthly *Calendar of Events* (open Mon.-Fri. 9:30am-5:30pm; also May-Sept. Sat.-Sun. 10am-4pm). **TSB,** Oliver Plunkett St., has the longest hours of area banks (open Mon.-Wed. and Fri. 9:30am-5pm, Thurs. 9:30am-7pm). From the **train station** (tel. 48274), follow the road to the green bridge and turn right onto Dominick St. to reach the town center (station open 6:30am-8:30pm; **luggage storage** £1/item). **Trains** chug to Dublin (Mon.-Sat. 5/day, Sun. 3/day; 1½hr.; £7) and Sligo (Mon.-Thurs. and Sat.-Sun. 4/day, Fri. 5/day; 2hr.; £8.50). **Bus Éireann** carries customers to: Athlone (3/day; 1hr.); Dublin (5/day; 1½hr.); Galway (1-2/day; 3hr.); and Sligo (7/day (3 of which leave from the train station); 2½hr.). **O'Brien's Bus Co.** (tel. 48977) sends buses to Dublin (Mon.-Sat. 5/day, Sun. 3/day; £9.50 return). Bus Éireann stops at Miss Fitz's Hair Salon on Castle St.; O'Brien's buses stop in front of the post office on Dominick St. **Bingo** happens in the community center Sun. 8pm. The **post office,** Dominick St. (tel. 48393), is open Mon.-Sat. 9am-5:30pm. The **phone code** of Lakes and Legends is 044.

Accommodations, Food, & Pubs Palm trees shade the fish pond at **Grove House,** Grove Ave. (tel. 41974). From Oliver Plunkett St., turn right onto Dominick Pl., which leads directly to the front door. Fluffy pillows and cheery rooms glow in the owners' genuine warmth (£14/person, w/bath £15; single £15; open Feb.-Nov.). Call ahead for rooms and access to the private sauna at **Auburn B&B,** Auburn Rd. (tel. 40507). Head down Mount St. and turn left onto Sunday's Well Rd. The B&B is opposite the park (£12.50/person, w/bath £15). The **Midland Hotel,** Mount St. (tel. 48381), hides rooms above the ground-floor pub (£15/person).

The **Kitchen Fare Deli,** Mount St. (tel. 41294), is a great place to munch on delicious, lunch-sized, meat-filled salads (60p) and fruit scones (45p; open Mon.-Thurs. 7:30am-6pm, Fri.-Sat. 7am-11pm, Sun. 11am-4pm). **The Greville Arms Hotel,** Pearse St. (tel. 48563), feeds restaurant meals at coffee-shop prices to Mullingar residents in

Midlands and Boglands

a luxuriously red pub (deep fried filet of plaice £4.10; open daily 9am-7pm). The most youthful and popular pub in town is **Hughes'** (tel. 48237), on the corner of Pearse and Castle St. Candlelit trad sessions draw big crowds on Wednesday nights (variety of music Fri.-Sat.; no cover). **The Final Fence,** Oliver Plunkett St. (tel. 48688), hosts "Kamikaze Drinking Night" as well as a nightclub on Friday to Sunday nights (starts at 11pm; cover £5).

Sights The modest **Market House Museum** (tel. 48152) on the corner of Pearse St. and Mount St. above the Chamber of Commerce Tourist Information Office, displays a peculiar array of weaponry and Iron Age implements. (Open by appointment mid-July to mid-Sept. Mon.-Fri. 2:30-5:30pm.) Crowned with not one, but two spires, the **Cathedral of Christ the King** dominates the end of Mary St. The names of the 52 bishops who have presided over the diocese of Meath since 1117 AD are listed inside. An **ecclesiastical museum** (tel. 44625), also inside, displays wooden penal crosses and the vestments of St. Oliver Plunkett, Ireland's most recently canonized saint. (Cathedral and museum open Thurs. and Sat.-Sun. 3-4pm or by appointment. Admission £1.) South across the canal bridge, an immediate right and then a left will lead to the **Military Museum** at Colomb Barracks (tel. 48391). It's chilling to learn that some Irishmen privately fought for the Nazis in WWII out of pure hatred for England (open by appointment, call for scheduling; free). If you've been wondering, "How did Mullingar get its name?" or "What was James Joyce doing here?" then you should join a **Forgotten Heritage Guided Walking Tour,** which departs from the information center in Market Sq. (Tel. (044) 44044. Tours leave Mon., Tues., Thurs., and Fri. 10:30am and 2:30pm; 1hr. £1, students 50p.)

Anglers and aquaphiles can **rent boats** at **Lough Owel** (call Mrs. Doolan at tel. 42085) or **Lough Ennell** (call Eileen Hope at tel. 40807). Prices for both are the same: £10 per day, £20 per day for boat with engine. **Sam's Tackle,** Castle St. (tel. 40431) sells fishing gear and maggots (£1.60/pint; open Mon.-Sat. 9:30am-6pm).

■ Near Mullingar

THE FORE TRAIL

Heading north of Mullingar, the Fore Trail first follows N4 to Coole, then turns east onto R395 and finally swoops back down to Mullingar on R394. The first stop on the trail is 6 mi. north of Mullingar. Here, in the little village of **Multyfarnham,** monks observe their vows of chastity at a 15th-century **Franciscan friary.** Life-size wooden figures depict the stations of the cross in a peaceful garden, where the trees whisper softly to the birds. **Boats** are for hire from Tommy Newman (tel. (044) 71111; £9/day), and hiking trails also lace the area. Four miles north along N4 brings travelers on the trail to **Coole,** home of the 200-year-old Georgian mansion, **Turbotstown House** (privately owned; open May-Sept.) Some of the Midlands' famous **bogs** border Coole on the west. To the east is romantic, turreted **Tullynally Castle** (tel. (044) 61159), 1 mi. before Castlepollard. The largest castle in Ireland still used as a family home, Tullynally's Gothic Revival towers are surrounded by 30 acres of gardens. Black Australian swans swim proudly in the garden pond. (Castle open mid-June to mid-Aug. daily 2:30-5:30pm. Gardens open May-Sept. daily 2-6pm. Castle and gardens £3.50, students £2; gardens only £2, students £1.)

The lakeshore town of **Fore** could be Glendalough with a little marketing. Fore was known for its seven wonders: water that flows uphill, water that won't boil, a tree that won't burn, a tree with only three branches (the Holy Trinity), a monastery that should have sunk into the bogs, a mill without a source of water to turn it, and a saint encased in stone (he vowed never to leave his cell). Fore's monastery was founded in 630 AD by St. Fechin and rebuilt during the 11th, 13th, and 15th centuries. Today, it is the most extensive set of Benedictine ruins in Ireland. St. Fechin's Church, in the graveyard, is the oldest standing building (all always open; free). Fore Abbey can be reached from Kells with **Shamrock Experience** tours (tel. (046) 40127;

see **Kells,** p.147). The Fore Trail continues along R395 to R394, then turns south to reach Collinstown Village. From the village, the trail turns east onto the Kells Rd. toward **Delvin,** where a golf course abuts the ruins of the 12th-century castle which once marked the western boundary of the British-controlled Pale (site always open; free). Returning to R394 along the Kells Rd., the trail carries on to **Crookedwood,** where a well-preserved 14th-century church sits in front of a ring fort (always open; free). The trail continues south until it returns to Mullingar.

THE BELVEDERE TRAIL

The **Belvedere Trail,** which covers the area south of Mullingar, follows N52 to N6 and then takes the Kilbeggan Rd. back to Mullingar. Four miles south of Mullingar, the 18th-century **Belvedere House and Gardens** (tel. (044) 42820) pompously promenade along the shore of Lough Ennel. The house seems to strive for imperial grandeur, with Roman gods frescoed along the ceiling. Robert Rochford, Lord Belvedere, for whom the house was built, also commissioned an Italian architect to create the fake and expensive "ruins" of a nonexistent abbey. His purpose was to obstruct his own view of his brother's superior rose garden. The ruin is now called, in his dishonor, "the Jealous Wall." (Open April-June and Sept. daily noon-4:30pm; July-Aug. daily noon-6pm. Admission £1, students 50p.)

As the trail turns off N52 and onto N6, it passes by **Tyrellspass Castle** (tel. (044) 23105), an Irish stronghold that Cromwell tried to eradicate. The castle itself was built in 1411 and lay in disrepair until its restoration in 1979 (open daily 10am-6:30pm). Following N6 (the Dublin-Galway Rd.) east, **Kilbeggan** appears at the next major intersection. This small town is home to **Locke's Distillery** (tel. (0506) 35118), a former firewater factory converted into a museum. The huge vats and 19th-century steam engine are impressive, but what makes a visit here worthwhile are the zany anecdotes about the workers' experiences on the job (when you make whiskey for a living, you're bound to have adventures). (Open April-Oct. daily 9am-6pm, Nov.-March daily 10am-4pm. Admission £2, students £1.50, children £1.) From Kilbeggan, the trail turns right, heading northeast to **Lough Ennell,** a major bird sanctuary favored by trout fishermen (for permits, call the Wildlife Service, tel. (044) 42771). On the shore of the lough await **Lilliput House** and **Jonathan Swift Park.** The park offers walking trails and fishing piers, but, sadly, no miniature mansion. According to local legend, Swift conceived *Gulliver's Travels* during a visit to Lough Ennell in the 1720s. Shortly after its publication in 1726, the area around the park was renamed Lilliput in his honor (grounds always open; free). The Belvedere Trail continues northeast and returns to Mullingar along N52. A short detour from the trail (west from Kilbeggan along N6) brings you to the town **Moate,** where **Dún na Si** (on Mt. Temple Rd., tel. 81183) has traditional *céilí* around an open fireplace (Sept.-June first Fri. of the month; July-Aug. weekly).

▨ Athlone

The geographical center of Ireland, Athlone lies at the crossroads of the Galway-Dublin Rd. and the River Shannon. Its location makes it a travel hub and its rich history makes it worth a look. If you have a car, Athlone is a great headquarters for touring the rest of Ireland. The river rushes through town and flares into Lough Ree to the north. The right bank holds Church Street's shops and greasy chippies, while the left bank is home to the three traditional components of an Irish town—the market square, the cathedral, and the castle. The river divides Athlone between two counties and two of the ancient provinces of Ireland—Co. Roscommon and Connacht on the left of the Shannon, Co. Westmeath and Leinster on the right.

Practical Information The **tourist office** in the castle (tel. 94630) has free copies of the *Athlone and District Visitors Guide* and *Athlone Alive* (open June-Aug. Mon.-Sat. 9am-6pm; mid-April to May and Sept.-Oct. Mon.-Sat. 9:30am-5:30pm). **Bank**

of Ireland (tel. 75111), and **AIB** (tel. 72089) adorn Church St.; both have **ATMs.** Athlone's **train and bus depot** (tel. 73322) is on Southern Station Rd., which loops off Church St. **Trains** leave for Dublin (8/day; 2hr.) and Galway (4/day; 1hr.). **Buses** shuttle off to: Dublin (8/day.; 2hr.; £7); Galway (9/day, 8/Sun.; 1½hr.; £7); Tullamore (1/day); Rosslare (1/day; £14); Cahir (1/day; 3hr.); and Dundalk (1/day; 3hr.; £10). The **laundromat,** Pearse St. (tel. 92930), washes and dries for £4 per load. The **Athlone Youth Resource Centre,** Northgate St. (tel./fax 78747) offers info and secretarial services (Mon.-Fri., 10am-5:30pm). The **post office** is on Barrack St. (tel. 83544; open Mon.-Tues. and Thurs.-Sat. 9am-5:30pm, Wed. 9:30am-5:30pm). Athlone's **phone code,** 0902, has a golden voice.

Accommodations The brand new **Athlone Holiday Hostel** (tel. 73399, ath-hostl@iol.ie) is a conveniently located (next to the train station) and comfortable place to stay. It has a 24-hour reception and a common area with TV, a pool table, and murals depicting Irish legends, painted by a local artist. (10-bed dorm £8, w/full breakfast £10. Sheets and towel included. Laundry. Showers 50p. **Bikes** £8/day. Kitchen and spacious dining area open 8am-11:30pm. Access to receive and send e-mail.) B&Bs inhabit Irishtown Rd. and its continuation towards Dublin. Closer to town is Mrs. Devaney's **Shannon View,** 3 Sean Costello St. (a section of Church St.; tel. 78411), which offers crisp rooms with big beds and TVs (£13/person). Across the river on Pearse St., **Higgins** (tel. 92519) has motel-like rooms over the pub, each with bath and TV (single £16, double £30). Across from the castle, **The Thatch** (tel. 94981) also provides B&B, all with bath. Beware that this street gets especially noisy as pubs close (£15/person). Three miles northeast on N55 (Longford Rd.), **Lough Ree Caravan and Camping Park** (tel. 78561) awaits. Follow turnoff signs for Lough Ree (open May-Sept.; £2.50/person).

Food & Pubs The shelves overflow at the **Quinnsworth Supermarket,** Athlone Shopping Centre, Dublin Rd. (tel. 72465; open Mon.-Wed. and Sat. 9am-6pm, Thurs.-Fri. 9am-9pm.) **The Left Bank,** Bastion St. (tel. 94446), serves delicious meals and homemade desserts. (Smoked salmon salad £5, steak sandwich £5. Lunch Mon.-Sat. 10:30am-5:30pm; dinner Mon.-Sat. 6pm-10pm.) **The Crescent Restaurant** (tel. 73456) at the hostel, serves fresh meals in a café atmosphere. (Veggie pasta £4, pies £1.20. Open daily 8am-7pm, July-Aug. closes 10:30pm.) **Beez Rock Diner,** in the Court off Church St. (tel. 75536) serves American diner food in a 50s hep cat den. (Veggie burger £1, lamb and chips £2.60. Open Mon.-Wed. 10am-1am, Thurs.-Sat. 10am-4am, Sun. 11:30am-4am.) **The Hooker Tackle Shop,** Custume Place (tel. 74848), provides fishing equipment for catching your own dinner; if you're unlucky, a pint of maggots is only £2.50.

The Westmeath Independent has entertainment listings. **Sean's Bar,** Main St. (tel. 92358), behind the castle, goes traditional five nights per week, and features various instruments including the accordion, banjo, bungalow, and fiddle. It traces an ancestry back to 1654; ask for the history lesson. Dim and wood-paneled, the **Keg,** Barrack St. (tel. 93031), hosts musicians (Fri.-Sat. nights) and Irish dancing (Thurs.). The crowd at **The Palace Bar** (tel. 92229) gathers for trad (Tues., Sat., and Sun. nights; beware—on other nights it can be empty). **BoZo's Club,** at Conlon's on Dublingate St., honks its nose with delight (Thurs.-Sun. 11:30pm-2am. £5 cover but look for concessions in pubs—you shouldn't pay more than £3).

Sights The course of English history took a pivotal turn at the 1691 **Siege of Athlone,** when William's army captured the Leinster half of town and laid the smaller Connacht half under siege. The Jacobites broke down the bridge and prevented its repair to stop the English advance. The jig was up after the Williamites fired 12,000 cannonballs into the Connacht half of town, forded the river, and stormed the castle. **The Athlone Castle Visitor Centre** (tel. 72107 or 92912) tells the story with stiff models and a noisy 45-minute audio-visual show. The local museum, inside the castle, has a 1000-year-old chunk of butter, Bronze Age instruments, and other oddities.

O Johnny Boy, the Pipes, the Pipes Are Calling...

John McCormack, Athlone's native son, is considered one of the finest tenors of the early 20th century. From his choir boy days in Athlone, McCormack went on to Dublin where he won first prize at *Feis Ceiol*, the National Irish Music Festival. The honor springboarded McCormack to Italy where he trained extensively for the opera. At 22, McCormack made his operatic debut in London as Luriddu in Pietro Masiagni's *Cavallina Rusticana*. Although a marquee name in opera, McCormack endeared audiences around the world with the Irish folk songs he invariably included in his recitals. McCormack often compared himself to old Irish minstrels. His variety of tone and enunciation while conveying meaning was a natural gift, nurtured by growing up around traditional Irish singing. After 1914, McCormack sang principally in concert and for those new-fangled phonograph records. In 1919, he became a U.S. citizen, but soon returned to his native Ireland and was made a papal count by Pope Pius XI. Although he retired in 1938, McCormack made charity appearances until his death in 1945.

(Open May-Sept. daily 10am-6pm, multimedia show 1-4:30pm. Admission £2.50, students £1.75; museum only, half-price.) Poking around Athlone Castle, with its grand Shannon views, is free (castle open May-Sept. daily 9:30am-6pm). For more Athlone history, **Athlone Town Walks** gives the inside scoop (about 1½hr., £1.50. Call Mary at 72466 or Jean at 75184 to arrange a tour).

Take a free tour of the **Athlone Crystal Factory,** 28 Pearse St. (tel. 92867), which is what Waterford Crystal would be if it had only one glass-cutter; covet goods in the small factory shop (open Tues.-Fri. 10am-6pm). For river fun, **Rossana Cruises** (tel. 92513) sails up the Shannon to Lough Ree. Boats leave from the strand, across the river from the castle (2/day; 1½hr.; £4.50, students £4, under 16 £3.50). For a faster trip, **Hovercraft Tours,** Monksland (tel. 92658 or 74593), shows you Lough Ree at 40 mph (from £5; departs every ½hr. from Hudson Bay Hotel).

Athlone celebrated its tercentenary of the siege with a festival and reenactment in 1991, and the last week in June still brings the **Athlone Festival** each year. The tourist office and many local businesses have the schedule of events, which include parades, exhibits, and free concerts. Aspiring singers head to Athlone in late autumn for the **John McCormack Golden Voice** opera competition, named for Athlone's most famous tenor. Contact Athlone Chamber of Commerce (tel. 73173) for info.

■ Near Athlone: Clonmacnoise

If Clonmacnoise were anywhere near the beaten path, it would be Glendalough with fantastic river views. Instead, Clonmacnoise is a huge detour, but the monastic city and the perfect accommodation nearby are worth the trip. To locals it is a graveyard, to historians a fantastically preserved ancient monastery, and to tourists the hot-spot of the bogs. St. Ciaran (KEER-on) founded Clonmacnoise in 545 on the eastern (Leinster) shore of the Shannon. His settlement grew into a city and an important scholastic center. Monks wrote the precious *Book of the Dun Cow* here around 1100. It was supposedly written on vellum from St. Ciaran's cow; this Dun Cow traveled everywhere with Ciaran and produced milk for the whole monastery. The monks' *Annals* record a vision of manned ships passing through the air above the city in 748 AD; Seamus Heaney's *Seeing Things* retells the sighting.

The site itself is impressive for its lonely grandeur, with crumbling buildings rising amid hills, bog, river, and sheep. The **cathedral** was destroyed by Vikings and rebuilt by monks several times; the current structure dates from about 1100. The last High King of Ireland, Rory O'Connor, was buried inside in 1198. **O'Connor's Church,** built in 1000, still has Church of Ireland services on the fourth Sunday of the month at 10am. A ¼-mi. walk from Clonmacnoise is the peaceful **Nun's Church.** Follow the path through the main site and bear left. The chancel, arc, and doorways are finely detailed—the best Romanesque architecture in Ireland.

The **visitors center** (tel. (0905) 74195) craves attention for its wheelchair-accessible displays. A number of **high crosses** and a 20-minute audio-visual show dazzle and educate. Groups should call ahead for guided tour bookings (included in entrance fee). Entrance to the ruins is through the visitors center. (Open daily, except Christmas. June to early-Sept. 9am-7pm; mid-March to May and mid-Sept. to Oct. 10am-6pm; Nov. to mid-March 10am-5pm. Admission £2.50, students £1.75.) The earlier in the day you visit, the more peaceful your visit will be. The **tourist office,** at the entrance to the Clonmacnoise car park (tel. (0905) 74134), gives local info and sells Kenneth MacGowan's excellent *Clonmacnoise* (£2.50), a guide to the monastic city (open June-Aug. daily 9am-6pm, April-May and Sept.-Oct. 10am-6pm).

The best accommodation awaits at **Mr. and Mrs. Augustin Claffey** (tel. (0905) 74149), on the Shannonbridge Rd. near town. The couple restored the cottage across the road—it's white, with red trim windows and a peat roof, and dates from 1843. Charm is added by two double beds and a lambskin rug in the bedroom, peat fire in the sitting room, and a large modern bathroom, plus cooker and refrigerator. One lucky couple spent their honeymoon here. The price? £10 per person. Reserve far in advance. Another good spot is **Kajon House** (tel. (0905) 74191), past the Claffeys on the Shannonbridge Rd. (£14/person, all w/bath). Pitch a tent in the field next to the house (£2/person; local farmers also often permit camping). Along with a great bog views, Kajon House offers fresh scones to all guests. It also dishes up Kajon cooking for breakfast and dinner (omelette and chips £4.75).

If you have a car, the easiest way to reach Clonmacnoise from either Athlone or Birr is on N62 to Ballynahoun and then follow the signs. A **Minibus Service** (tel. (0902) 74839), departs from the front of the Athlone Castle (Mon.-Fri. 11am), runs to both Clonmacnoise and the Clonmacnoise and West Offaly Railway, and returns around 4pm. (Special visits to Clonmacnoise can be arranged at other times, call for info. Adults £15, students £10, includes price of admission to both sights.) The Athlone Holiday Hostel (tel. (0902) 73399) also arranges visits. Clonmacnoise is reachable by bike, but it's 14 mi. of hilly terrain. Hitchers first get a lift to Ballynahoun on the heavily trafficked N62, and then get a ride from there to Clonmacnoise. It might also be possible to hitch a ride on a boat traveling down the River Shannon.

■ Birr

William Petty labelled Birr *"Umbilious Hiberniae"*—loosely translated, Birr is Ireland's bellybutton. Its central location in Ireland gives it navel, not naval, qualities. The tired Georgian houses along Birr's tree-lined malls contrast with the dramatic scale of the castle and its gorgeous gardens. Visitors can use Birr as a base for touring the country, making short daily trips to major cities (only 2hr. to Dublin and Cahir; 1½hr. from Waterford and Limerick) and nearby historic sites.

Birr makes a decent starting point for an expedition into the Slieve Bloom mountains to its east. The well-informed **tourist office** is on Rosse Row, across from the entrance to Birr Castle (tel. 20110; open May-Sept. daily 9:30am-1pm and 2-5:30pm). Ask for *Info Sheet #26F: The Slieve Blooms.* Unfortunately, Birr is still 9 mi. from Kinitty, which lies at the base of the mountains. If you don't have a car, your best bet would be to bike there—not enough cars go by to make hitching worthwhile. **AIB** bank (tel. 20069) offers an **ATM** in Emmet Sq. To Limerick take the Riverstown Rd., to Cashel the Roscrea Rd., to Cloghan Castle (see below) the Banagher Rd., to Athlone the Tullamore Rd. **Bus Éireann** runs to: Dublin (Mon.-Sat. 3/day, Sun. 1/day; 2hr.; £9); Cahir (1/day; 2hr.; £12); and Athlone (1/day; 50min.; £5). **P.L. Polan,** Main St. (tel. 20006), rents **bikes** at the corner of Wilmer Rd. (£7/day, £30/week, deposit £40; open Mon.-Wed. and Fri.-Sat. 9:30am-6:30pm). When in Birr, the Earl of Rosse's **phone code** is 0509.

Accommodations, Food, & Pubs Birr has a new and very comfortable place to stay at **Spinners Town House,** Castle St. (tel./fax 21673). It offers firm beds, amicable owners, and a bistro downstairs. The decor is modern, displaying the artwork and crafts of local artists. (7-bed dorm w/continental breakfast £10; single £16; double w/Irish breakfast £25, w/bath £30. Baby-sitting and laundry services available.) The Irish are known for their hospitality, and **Kay Kelly** defines it. Her B&B (tel. 21128) rests atop the toystore on Main St. and boasts comfortable rooms and a playground out back. Mrs. Kelly offers the best advice in town on Birr's pubs and restaurants (single £15, double £28). The highly recommended but cheap **Kong Lam** cooks up Chinese take-away at the end of O'Connell St. (chicken fried rice £3.50). A crowd of mixed ages gathers to watch sports and listen to music at **Craughwell's** on Castle St. (tel. 21839).

Sights You're welcome to tread on the Earl of Rosse's front lawn at **Birr Castle** (tel. 20056), which remains his private home. A babbling brook, a tranquil pond, the tallest box hedges in the world, and acres of lush woods and gardens make Birr Castle a stand-out even among Ireland's mighty castles. Don't miss the immense telescope, whose 72-in. mirror was the world's largest from 1845-1917. The third Earl of Rosse used this very instrument to discover that nebulae could be resolved into separate star systems beyond our galaxy; the fourth Earl used it to measure the heat of the moon. The castle hosts zany summer exhibitions. (Grounds open daily 9am-1pm and 2-6pm, exhibitions open May-Oct. daily 2:30-5:30pm. Admission April-Oct. £3.20, students £1.60; Nov.-March £2.60, students £1.30.) The castle itself opens for special occasions, like plays and concerts (tel. 20056 for info; tickets £10-20).

In town the **Slieve Bloom Environmental Display Centre,** Railway Rd. (tel. 20029), is in the Outdoor Pursuits Centre (from Emmet Sq., follow signs for Roscrea to reach Railway Rd.). The center explains the flora and fauna of the Slieve Blooms and also functions as a museum for the tiny town of **Kinitty.** (See *Slieve Bloom Mountains* pamphlet for more info. Open July-Sept. Mon-Fri. 10am-6pm, Sat-Sun. 2:30pm-6pm. Free.) The blasted 19th-century factory by Elmsgrove Whiskey was once the R. and J. Wallace Distillery; in 1889 the distillery caught fire and coated the Camcor River with floating, flaming whiskey. **Birr Vintage Week,** which takes place in mid-August, involves a parade, a car rally, an antique and art fair, and much dressing-up, especially in Georgian costume.

■ Near Birr: Banagher

Eight miles north of Birr lies the serene town of **Banagher.** On the banks of the River Shannon, this fishing village is renowned for its marina, traditional pubs, and nearby wildlife reserve. The latter, known as the **Callows** (literally: wet grasslands), is home to the endangered corncrake and numerous other species of birds. Opened in 1996, the **Crank House Hostel** (tel. (0509) 20124) provides comfortable, if simple, accommodations. The attached coffee shop serves inexpensive dishes (soup and homemade bread £1.35, pastries 40p, mushroom crepes £4.30; open daily 9am-6pm). It offers an equipped kitchen, secure luggage and bike storage, and **bureau de change.** (6- to 8-bed dorm £7.) **Houg's,** Main St. (tel. (0509) 51893), is an authentic traditional pub whose nightly music (9:30pm) brings in locals and visitors alike.

The best reason to visit Banagher is 13th-century **Cloghan Castle** (tel. (0509) 51650). If the 9th-century chapel, the 90-ft. defensive fortress, and the 13 centuries of documented history are not enough to get you to visit, the amazing collection of antique furniture and rare artifacts inside should do the trick. Among the rarities are William Pitt's snuff box, a morning star, and 300-year-old four-poster beds and chests. You might think that the man tending sheep and the woman gardening are the hired help, but look again. They're probably Mr. and Mrs. Thompson, who own and live in the castle. (45-min. tours June-Sept. Wed.-Sun 2-6pm or by request. £3.50, students and seniors £3, children £1.50. B&B £40/person.) To get to the castle from town center, turn left at the small road opposite the chemist. At the Lusmagh Church continue straight and take the second right, opposite a stone windmill. The castle is 1 mi. down

SLIEVE BLOOM MOUNTAINS

Though only 2000 ft. at their highest, the Slieve Bloom Mountains (shleeve bloom) give the illusion of great height. None of this mucking around with foothills—the mountains burst up from plains within a parallelogram formed by Birr, Roscrea, Portlaoise, and Tullamore. **Ard Erin** ("highest in Ireland"), was once mistakenly thought to be the tallest peak in Ireland. **The Slieve Bloom Way** is a circular walking trail that passes mountain bogs, Ard Erin, waterfalls, and heaps of scenery. The trail is marked along the way by signs which explain the features that make this area a geological nirvana. From these peaks all of Ireland is at your feet. The tourist office in Birr makes the best pre-mountain stop. Hikers will need directions from *The Slieve Bloom Way (Info Sheet # 26F)*, theoretically available in any Bord Fáilte office, but definitely available in Birr. The office sells the Ordnance Survey's map *Slieve Blooms Sheet #54. New Irish Walk Guides,* found in bookstores, has more info on Bloom walks. The **Slieve Bloom Environmental Display Centre** discusses the regional flora and fauna, as well as local history. Remember, bogs are highly flammable: it is illegal to light fires anywhere on the Way. **Mountrath,** southeast of the mountains in Co. Laois, and **Kinitty,** to the northeast in Co. Offaly, make good springboards for hiking. It's possible to trek from one to the other.

ROSCREA

Picturesque Roscrea poses 10 mi. south of Birr. Among the shops and pubs on its narrow, winding streets are the remains of several medieval wonders. **St. Cronan's Monastery,** now divided in two by Church St., sports a finely worked Romanesque gable, a well-preserved high cross, and a round tower, which had 20 ft. lopped off its height in 1798. On Castle St., a 13th-century **castle** surrounds the **Damer House,** the best preserved example of Queen Anne architecture in Ireland—with an amazing vaulted ceiling—and home to the spectacular Bog Butter, a 1000-year-old chunk of butter rescued from the bog. The **Roscrea Heritage Centre,** located in the castle (tel. (0505) 21850), is the closest thing in town to a tourist office; in addition to tours of the castle, it has the useful and free *Roscrea Heritage Walk* map. (Walk takes about 1hr. Open June-Sept. daily 9:30am-6pm, Oct.-May Sat.-Sun. 10am-5pm. Castle tours £2.50, students £1.) Fragments of the 15th-century **Franciscan friary** surround the parish church on Abbey St.

Bank of Ireland (tel. (0505) 21877) on Castle St. sports an **ATM.** Groceries abound at **Quinnsworth** in the Roscrea Shopping Centre, Castle St. (open Mon.-Wed. and Sat. 9am-7pm, Thurs.-Fri. 9am-9pm). **Bus Éireann** stops in front of Christy Maker's pub on Castle St. (to Dublin, 3/day, 2hr.; to Limerick, 3/day, 1hr.). **Mick Delahunty's,** Main St. (tel. (0505) 22139), offers pub grub (kebabs £3), and trad (Thurs., Sat., and Sun. nights). Next door, the aptly named **Yellow House B&B** (tel. (0505) 21772) offers a warm reception and decent beds (£12.50/person, w/bath £15). **The White House,** Castle St. (tel. (0505) 21516), offers elegant rooms. Mrs. Fogarty will take good care of you (£13/person, w/bath £15).

PORTLAOISE

Portlaoise (port-LEESH) is a decent-sized town with multi-stop shopping for people on their way to the Slieve Bloom Mountains and points west. Nearby, set in the middle of all that farmland, the **Rock of Dunamase** is worth a look. Take Stradbally Rd. east 4 mi.; the Rock is on the left (follow the sign to Athy/Carlow at the big, red Catholic church). The Rock is a truly ancient fortress (it was recorded by Ptolemy), and passed between Irish and Viking hands many times over the years. The mound still bristles with fortifications. The Rock is a fantastic vantage point for viewing the Slieve Bloom Mountains (always open; free).

Back in town, the **tourist office** on Lawlor Ave. (tel. (0502) 21178) can provide you with *The Slieve Bloom Way (Info Sheet # 26F)* (free) to help you plan your hike.

Facing uphill on Main St., Lawlor Ave. is the street on your left parallel to Main. (Open Mon.-Fri. 10am-6pm, July-Aug. also Sat.) **AIB** bank (tel. (0502) 21349) graces Lawlor Ave. with an **ATM.** The **train station** (tel. (0502) 21303) hides in a tall gray building at the curve in Railway St. (open daily 7:30am-9pm). **Trains** run to Dublin and to points south (Dublin 8/day; 1hr.; £10.50). **Bus Éireann** stops at Egan's Hostelry on Main St. between Dublin and Cork (to Dublin: 10/day; 1½hr.; £9). Buses feel free to leave 10 minutes early. There's a **laundromat** in the mini-mall across from the public library (wash and dry £4; open Mon.-Sat. 9am-6pm). The regional **post office** (tel. (0502) 22339) enthusiastically sorts mail inside the shopping center on Lawlor Avenue (open Mon.-Fri. 9am-5:30pm, Sat. 10am-1pm and 2-5pm).

Walk left at the top of Main St. to reach the most economical accommodations, **O'Donoghue's B&B,** Kellyville Park (tel. (0502) 21353), a large, hotel-like B&B with flower gardens and new beds (single £18; double £30, w/bath £34). **Dowlings,** half way up Main St. on the left (tel. 22770), offers the best deal on fresh meals: veggie soup £1.40, roast chicken & chips £3. (Open Mon.-Thurs. 8:30am-6pm, Fri. and Sat. 8:30am-7pm, Sun. 10am-6pm.) **Sally Gardens,** on Main St. (tel. (0502) 21658), is the pub of choice in this small town. Frequent impromptu session and live music Monday to Thursday ensure that there's always good *craic* in Portlaoise.

EASTERN IRELAND

SOUTHEAST IRELAND

Southeast Ireland is the country's sunniest region. It also reveals the most foreign influence, since the Vikings, and then the Normans, made it their power base. Irish people take holidays on the beaches along the south coast, from cozy Kilmore Quay to tidy Ardmore. Waterford has the resources and the grit of a real city. Wexford is a charismatic town, packed with historic sites and convenient to many of the Southeast's finest attractions. Cashel has a superbly preserved cathedral complex. Ring is the region's sole *gaeltacht*. Heading to the south coast from Dublin, you can take in the rocking nightlife of a route through Carlow, Kilkenny, and Waterford, or enjoy the pretty coastal path through Glendalough, Wicklow, Enniscorthy, and Wexford.

Carlow & Kilkenny

■ Carlow Town

Contemporary Carlow is a small, busy town with surprisingly good nightlife. Despite its seemingly placid appearance, Carlow has hosted several of the most gruesome historic battles between Gael and foreigner due to its position on the southern edge of the Pale. During the 1798 rising, 417 Irish insurgents were ambushed in the streets of Carlow; they are buried in the gravel pits of Graiguecullen, across the River Barrow from Carlow. Part of the gallows from which they were hanged is now displayed in the county museum. Carlow sits on the eastern side of the River Barrow, on the N9 (the Dublin-Waterford road).

The Carlow **tourist office,** College St. off Tullow St. (tel. 31554), is worth a shot; it's in the Chamber of Commerce office, in front of the cathedral. Request the oversized *Visitor's Guide to County Carlow* for its decent map of the town (free) and be on your way (open Mon.-Fri. 9:30am-12:45pm and 2-5:30pm; June-Aug. also Sat. 10am-2pm and 3-5:30pm). **Trains** run from Dublin's Heuston Station on their way to Waterford (Mon.-Thurs. and Sat. 4/day, Sun. 3/day; 1¼hr.; £11). **Bus Éireann** bounces from Carlow to: Athlone (1/day; 2¼hr.); Dublin (Mon.-Sat. 6/day, Sun. 4/day; 1¾hr.); and Waterford via Kilkenny (6/day; 1¼hr.). **Rapid Express Coaches,** Barrack St. (tel. 43081), runs a bus from Tramore-Waterford-Carlow-Dublin and back (Mon.-Fri. 7/day, Sun. 5/day). From the **train station,** it's a 15-minute walk to the center of town; head straight out of the station down Railway Rd., turn left onto the Dublin Rd., and make a left at the Court House onto College St. Rent **bikes** from **Coleman Cycle,** 19 Dublin St. (tel. 31273; £7/day, £30/week; deposit £40; open Mon.-Sat. 8am-8pm). The **phone code** took part in a gruesome battle in 0503.

Accommodations Located on the banks of the River Barrow and offering bright rooms with comfortable beds, the **Otterholt Riverside Hostel** (tel. 30404; fax 41318) is by far the best place to stay in Carlow. It's ½ mi. from the center of town on the Kilkenny Rd., but on the bus to or from Kilkenny you can request a stop at RTC, the college across the street (4- to 6-bed dorm £6; single £9; sheets £1, laundry £3). A hostel closer to town is **Verona,** Pembroke Rd. (tel. 31700 or 31846). Walking over the Dublin St. Bridge, Pembroke Rd. is the first right off Burrin St. If you can overlook the torn carpet, you'll appreciate the location (2- to 4-bed dorm £7; bike shed; open June-Sept.). B&Bs in the area tend to be expensive, but **Redsetter Guest House,** 14

Dublin St. (tel. 42837), next to the Royal Hotel, is reasonable. It's modern and right in the center of town (£15/person, w/bath £18). Other inexpensive B&Bs lie along the Kilkenny Rd., 2 mi. from the town center.

Food & Pubs **Muffins,** 115 Tullow St. (tel. 43455), serves meals and tea in a mild-mannered setting (jumbo breakfast £2.85, pizza £1.55; open Mon.-Sat. 8:30am-6pm). **Scragg's Alley,** 12 Tullow St. (tel. 42233 or 40407), has hearty food (soup and roll £1.20, BBQ ribs £3; lunch served daily noon-2:30pm). For groceries, **L&N Superstore,** Tullow St., has a huge range (open Mon.-Sat. 9am-6pm). Turn to the **Health Store,** Tullow St. (tel. 40118), for your goat's milk needs (open Mon.-Sat. 9:30am-1:15pm, 1:45-5:30pm).

Carlow grooves at **Scragg's Alley,** where pub-goers can hear live rock and traditional sessions Thursday and Saturday nights, and find a nightclub with plenty of attitude Fridays through Sundays starting at 11pm. When An Emotional Fish played here the cover was £7.50, but it's usually free. **Tully's,** 149 Tullow St. (tel. 31862), is friendly and offbeat, with occasional live bands—squirm in the seats made out of church pews for a religious drinking experience. **The Owl,** 56 Dublin St. (tel. 43156), sings ballads on Saturdays to a crowd reclining on the red crushed velvet. **Racey Burne's** attracts an older crowd who enjoy trad Thursday to Sunday nights (tel. 31790). **O'Loughlin's,** 53 Dublin St. (tel. 32205), is dark and velvety, with typewriters strewn about; no music, but a lively, young crowd.

Sights A large and very heavy thing lies just outside of town. The **Brownshill Dolmen** has the largest capstone in Europe, weighing over 100 tons. It brings to mind a large, stone UFO. Follow Tullow St. through the traffic light and straight through the roundabout; the dolmen is 2 mi. away in a field on the right.

Turn right at the end of College St. onto Tullow St. and continue on to Castle St.; a left onto Mill Lane will take you around to **Carlow Castle,** behind the storefronts on Castle St. The castle is closed to the public, though you can get up very close without going through the locked gates. As an English stronghold, the castle was frequently attacked; during the 14th century, Carlow was considered so unsafe that English officers had to be paid danger money to live in town. The castle's ruined condition (two towers remaining from an original four) can be blamed on one Dr. Middleton, who intended to convert the castle into an asylum but wanted to enlarge the windows and thin the walls. He used dynamite to make his modifications. Oops.

The Carlow Museum, Haymarket (tel. 40730), through the carpark behind Town Hall, looks like somebody's attic. An old bar and blacksmith shop are tritely reconstructed; on the plus side, there's an informative exhibit on the 1798 massacre (open Tues.-Fri. 11am-5pm, Sat. and Sun. 2-5pm; admission £1, students 50p).

The best time to visit Carlow is during the first two weeks of June, when the town hosts **Eigse** (egg-sha, meaning gathering), a 10-day festival of the arts. Artists from all over Ireland come to present visual, musical, and theatrical works; some events require tickets. Call the Eigse Festival office (tel. 40491) for more info.

▨ Kilkenny Town

> There once were two cats from Kilkenny,
> Each thought there was one cat too many.
> So they fought and they fit,
> And they scratched and they bit,
> 'Til excepting their nails and the tips of their tails,
> Instead of two cats there weren't any.

Touted as the best-preserved medieval town in Ireland, Kilkenny Town (pop. 20,000) is the modern incarnation of a Norman commercial center established in 1169. Following the British occupation of Ireland, it was said that the town's separate English and Irish communities scratched and hissed like "Kilkenny cats." Even today Kilken-

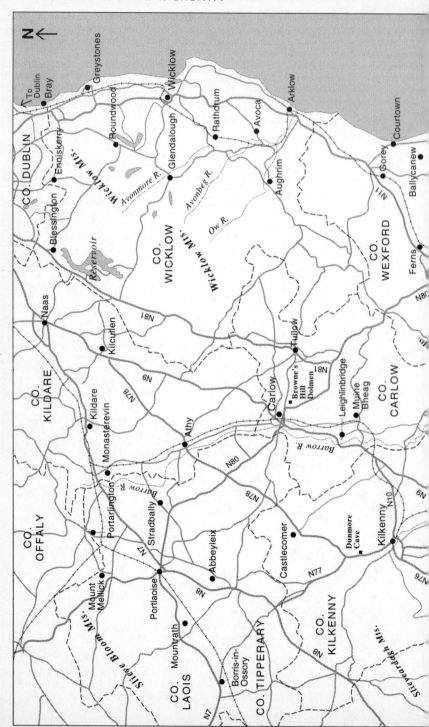

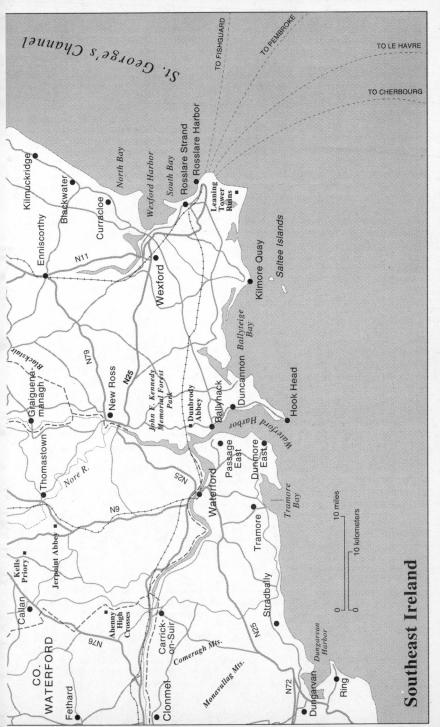

St. George's Channel

TO FISHGUARD

TO PEMBROKE

TO LE HAVRE

TO CHERBOURG

North Bay

Wexford Harbor

South Bay

Rosslare Strand

Rosslare Harbor

Kilmuckridge

Blackwater

Curracloe

Leaning Tower Ruins

Enniscorthy

N11

Wexford

Kilmore Quay

Saltee Islands

Blackstair

Graiguena-managh

N79

New Ross

N25

John F. Kennedy Memorial Forest Park

Dunbrody Abbey

Ballyhack

Duncannon

Ballyteige Bay

Hook Head

Waterford Harbor

Thomastown

Nore R.

Passage East

Dunmore East

Kells Priory

Jerpoint Abbey

N9

Waterford

N25

Tramore Bay

Callan

Ahenny High Crosses

N76

Carrick-on-Suir

Tramore

Stradbally

10 miles

10 kilometers

CO. WATERFORD

Fethard

Clonmel

Comeragh Mts.

Monavullag Mts.

N25

N72

Dungarvan

Dungarvan Harbor

Ring

0

Southeast Ireland

nians call the Parliament St. area "Irishtown." But during the English Civil War, the Old English and the native feudal lords found common cause in Catholicism. Between 1642 and Cromwell's invasion in 1649, they created the short-lived independent government called the Confederation of Kilkenny. Disagreements soon followed this attempt at cooperation; the two factions only joined administratively in 1844. Today, the town luxuriates in its affluence, evident in the boutiques and stately homes that line its pristine streets. Visitors find both excitement and history in Kilkenny, in which ancient architecture houses rocking nightlife and nine churches line the same streets as 78 pubs.

ORIENTATION & PRACTICAL INFORMATION

The Castle dominates Kilkenny from the Parade. If you arrive at McDonagh Station, turn left on John St. and continue straight to reach The Parade. The town's main activity takes place in the triangle formed by Rose Inn St., High St., and Kieran St.

Tourist Office: Rose Inn St. (tel. 51500; fax 63955). Free maps. Demand the free *Kilkenny City and County Guide*. Open June-Sept. Mon.-Sat. 9am-6pm, Sun. 11am-5pm; Oct. Mon.-Sat. 9am-1pm and 2-5:30pm; Nov.-Feb. Tues.-Sat. 9am-1pm and 2-5:15pm; March-April Mon.-Sat. 9am-1pm and 2-5:15pm.

Banks: AIB, The Parade (tel. 22089), at the intersection with High St. Open Mon. 10am-5pm, Tues.-Fri. 10am-4pm; **ATM. TSB,** High St. (tel. 22969). Open Mon.-Wed. and Fri. 9am-5:30pm, Thurs. 9am-7pm.

Trains: Everything stops at **McDonagh Station,** Dublin Rd. (tel. 22024). Open Mon.-Sat. 8am-8pm, Sun. 10am-noon, 3-5pm, and 6:30-8:30pm. Always staffed, though ticket window opens only around departure times. Kilkenny is on the main Dublin-Waterford rail route (Mon.-Sat. 4/day, Sun. 3/day; to Dublin, 2hr., £9; to Waterford, 45min., £5; to Thomastown (south), 15min., £3).

Buses: McDonagh Station, Dublin Rd. (tel. 64933). Buses leave for: Clonmel (Mon.-Sat. 5/day, Sun. 3/day); Cork (3/day; 3hr.); Dublin (Mon.-Sat. 5/day, Sun. 4/day; £9); Galway (mid-June to mid-Sept. daily); Rosslare Harbour (mid-June to mid-Sept. daily); Thomastown (1/day); and Waterford (daily 5/day). **Buggy's Buses** (tel. 41264) run from Kilkenny to Castlecomer, 2/day (except Sun.) with stops at Dunmore Cave (20min.; £1), and the An Óige hostel (15min.; £1).

Hitching: Hitchhikers take N10 to Waterford, the Freshford Rd. to the N8 to get to Cashel, and N16 to go towards Dublin. Be patient. It's a virtue.

Taxi: K&M Cab (tel. 61333). £3 max. within the city.

Bike Rental: J.J. Wall Cycle, Maudlin St. (tel. 21236). £5/day, £25/week; deposit £30. Open Mon.-Sat. 9am-5:30pm.

Laundry: Brett's Launderette, Michael St. (tel. 63200). Wash and dry £5.70. Open Mon.-Sat. 8:30am-8pm. Last wash 7pm.

Pharmacy: Several on High St. Different one open Sun. according to a rotation system; check any pharmacy's door for the current one. Open Mon.-Sat. 9am-6pm.

Hospital: St. Luke's, Freshford Rd. (tel. 21133). Continue down Parliament St. to St. Canice's Cathedral, then turn right and take the first left to Vicar St.

Emergency: Dial 999; no coins required. **Garda:** Dominic St. (tel. 22222).

Post Office: High St. (tel. 21879). Open Mon.-Sat. 9am-5:30pm.

Phone Code: 056.

ACCOMMODATIONS

B&Bs average £14-16. Call ahead in summer, especially on weekends. Waterford Rd. and more remote Castlecomer Rd. have the highest concentration of beds.

Kilkenny Town Hostel (IHH), 35 Parliament St. (tel. 63541), is always brimming with activity as people bustle about in the kitchen, lounge on couches, and socialize on the front steps. Directly across from popular pubs and next to the brewery. Clean, light, and bare rooms. Friendly, non-smoking environment. Kitchen (7am-11pm) w/microwave. Cyclist maps available. Check-out 10:30am. 6- to 8-bed room

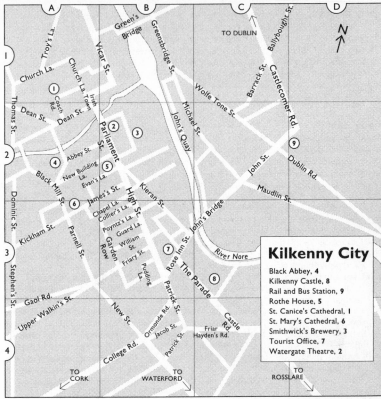

Kilkenny City

Black Abbey, **4**
Kilkenny Castle, **8**
Rail and Bus Station, **9**
Rothe House, **5**
St. Canice's Cathedral, **1**
St. Mary's Cathedral, **6**
Smithwick's Brewery, **3**
Tourist Office, **7**
Watergate Theatre, **2**

£6. 4-bed room £7. Laundry (wash and dry) £3. Sheets 50p. Call ahead in summer. Sept.-June: 50p discount to *Let's Go* readers.

Ormonde Tourist Hostel, Johns Green (tel. 52733), opposite the train station. More privacy and better bathroom facilities than the IHH, but a 10- to 15-min. walk from the best nightlife and attractions. 24-hr. kitchen w/microwave. Dorm £7. 4-bed room £8. Single £10, w/bath £12. Laundry £4.

Foulksrath Castle (An Óige/HI), Jenkinstown (tel. 67674). Awesome 16th-century castle 8mi. north of town on N77 (Durrow Rd.). Turn right off N77 at signs for Connahy, ¼mi. down on the left. Buggy's Buses (tel. 41264) run from The Parade, Kilkenny to the hostel Mon.-Sat. at 11:30am and 5:30pm, leaving the hostel for Kilkenny Mon.-Sat. 8:25am and 3pm (20min.; £1.50). Under renovation in 1996, this castle promises to be one of the nicest hostels in Ireland by 1997. TV room. Kitchen open 8am-10pm. Dorm £5.50. Laundry £4. Sheets £1.

Bikes and Beds, 49 John St. (tel. (087) 448537). Cramped quarters, but rate includes continental breakfast. Free luggage storage. 24-hr. kitchen. Dorm £6.

Philomena Heffernan, Dean St. (tel. 64040). Immaculate and comfortable rooms at low rates. A sign warns that the house is guarded by an attack housewife, but don't worry, she's actually rather charming. £9/person. Single £12 w/o breakfast. Bank holiday weekends £17.50. Add £3 for breakfast.

Fennelly's B&B, 13 Parliament St. (tel. 61796), above the pub. Large, clean, floral rooms. Bathtub! Single July-Aug. £20, Sept.-June £15. Double £27, w/bath £35.

The Deanery, 6 Dean St. (tel. 52822), above the Deanery café. Big beds in small rooms make sleeping easy, walking tough. TV in most rooms. £15/person w/bath.

Bregagh House B&B, Dean St. Handsome wood furniture and floral comforters; three stuffed quails. £13.50, w/bath £15.50; July-Sept. add £2. **Camping** amid flowers in their giant backyard, with access to showers and toilets (£5).

Nore Valley Park, (tel. 27229), 6mi. south of Kilkenny between Bennetsbridge and Stonyford, signposted from Kilkenny. A class act, with hot showers, laundry, and TV room. Hikers £2/person. Open March-Oct.

FOOD

The biggest grocery selection is in the **Super Quinn** (tel. 52444), in the new Market Cross shopping center off High St. (open Mon.-Wed. and Sat. 9am-6pm, Thurs.-Fri. 9am-9pm). Alternatively, stock up on supplies at the immense **Dunnes Supermarket,** several steps away from the tourist office (open Mon.-Wed. and Sat. 9am-6pm, Thurs.-Fri. 9am-9pm, Sun. and Bank holidays noon-6pm). **Shortis Wong Delicatessen,** John St. (tel. 61305), sells noodles, spices, and canned, exotic, and baked foods (open Mon.-Sat. 9am-7pm, Sun. 10am-2:30pm).

M.L. Dore, High St. (tel. 63374), near Parliament St. A combo deli, restaurant, and bureau de change. Customers buried under copious ham (roast chicken dinner £4). Open Mon.-Sat. 8am-11pm, Sun. 8am-10pm; evening meals 5:30-10pm.

P.J. Crotty, 92 High St. (tel. 21099). Cafeteria-style restaurant with stunning sandwiches, breakfast, and pastries. Irish breakfast £3, cottage pie £3, caramel sundae £1. Open Mon.-Sat. 8:30am-6pm.

Italian Connection, 38 Parliament St. (tel. 64225). Gourmet Italian food in a mahogany setting colored with carnations. Lunch specials daily (noon-3pm). All pastas £6, pizzas £4-6, lasagna £4. Open daily noon-11pm.

Edward Langton's, 69 John St. (tel. 65133). Voted the country's best pub food 3 times, but with a huge new addition, Langton's seems more like a hotel lounge than an Irish pub. Lunch menu (daily noon-3pm): roast chicken £5.50, veggie quiche £3.25. Dinner menu (daily 4:30-11pm) reaches double digits.

Lautrec's Wine Bar, 9 St. Kieran St. (tel. 62720). Tex-Mex and wine even after pubs have closed. Veggie crepe £3, pizza £4, steak fajita £4. Open Mon.-Sat. 5:30pm-1am, Sun. 5:30-11pm.

PUBS

Kilkenny is known as the "oasis of Ireland." The Smithwicks here is sublime. Enjoy.

Pump House Bar, 26 Parliament St. (tel. 63924), remains a favorite among locals and visitors (many hostelers). Live rock music Mon.-Thurs. Always packed.

Cleere's Pub, 28 Parliament St. (tel. 62573). Thespians converge for nightly poetry readings, improv comedy, and trad and folk sessions. Tickets for some acts cost £3-5, discounts for students.

Fennelly's, 13 Parliament St. (tel. 64337), hosts an older crowd in its homey confines. Trad sessions Fri. and Sun. nights during July and Aug.

Kyteler's Inn, St. Kieran St. (tel 21064). This historical pub has a witch in the basement and butcher-blocks for tables. Mixed ages gather for food and *craic* in a relaxed atmosphere. The wine cellar dates back to 1324. Trad 6 nights/week in summer; enjoy drinks in the beergarden. Late-night Thurs.-Sun. transfer yourself next door to **Neru's,** a happening nightclub (cover £5; open 11:30pm-2am).

Maggie's, St. Kieran St. (tel. 62273), hosts trad music on Tues. nights and live contemporary on Wed. Usually a younger crowd.

Caisleán Uí Cuain, 2 High St. (tel. 65406), at the intersection with the Parade. Yuppies enjoy high-grade pub grub in a classy lounge (Greek salad £4.50; lunch served 12:30-3pm). Traditional music Mon. nights and Sun. afternoons.

SIGHTS

All of central Kilkenny is a sight—most of the buildings have preserved their medieval appearance. **Tynan Walking Tours** (tel. 65929) offers an hour-long introduction to Kilkenny's history. Tours depart from the tourist office on Rose Inn St. (mid-March to

Oct. Mon.-Sat. 6/day, Sun. 4/day; £2.50, students £2). At the **City Scope Exhibition** (tel. 51500), upstairs at the tourist office, a miniature, detailed model of the city shows the changes in Kilkenny's life and housing through the years. But the *real* city is right outside. (30-min. show Mon.-Fri. 9am-12:45pm, 2-6pm; Sat. 9am-12:45pm, 2-5:30pm; Sun. 11am-1pm, 2-5pm. Admission £1, students 80p.)

Thirteenth-century **Kilkenny Castle**, The Parade (tel. 21450), housed the Earls of Ormonde from the 1300s until 1932. A walk inside evokes images of swishing velvet robes and clashing swords. Many rooms have been restored to their former opulence; ogle the Viking-shipesque Long Room and the portraits of English bigwigs. In the basement, the **Butler Gallery** mounts modern art exhibitions. This level also houses a **café** in the castle's kitchen and shelters the castle's ghost, the spirit of a girl burned at the stake by the bloodthirsty townsfolk. The formal flower garden and park adjoining the castle are beautifully maintained. (Castle and gallery open June-Sept. daily 10am-7pm; Oct.-March Tues.-Sat. 10:30am-5pm, Sun. 11am-5pm; April-May daily 10:30am-5pm. Access by guided tour only. Admission £3, students £1. Gardens open daily 10am-8:30pm; free.) **The Kilkenny Design Centre** (tel. 22118) fills the castle's old stables with fine but expensive Irish crafts. (Open April-Dec. Mon.-Sat. 9am-6pm, Sun. 10am-6pm; Jan.-March Mon.-Sat. 9am-6pm.)

A Tudor merchant house built in 1594, **Rothe House,** Parliament St. (tel. 22893), is now a small museum of local archaeological finds and Kilkennian curiosities. The tour introduces you to the lifestyles of the 16th-century rich and famous. The Rothes were Kilkennian bigwigs, serving as sheriffs and mayors. Exhibits show frightening dinner sporks. (Open April-Oct. Mon.-Sat. 10:30am-5pm, Sun. 3-5pm; Nov.-March Sat.-Sun. 3-5pm. Admission £1.50, students £1.)

Kilkenny is well-endowed with religious architecture. The finest is 13th-century **St. Canice's Cathedral** on Dean St.; the stone-step approach from Irishtown is lined with fragments of old sculpture from the cathedral itself, which was sacked by Cromwell's merry men(aces). The name "Kilkenny" itself is derived from the Irish *Cill Chainnigh,* meaning "Church of St. Canice." Inside the church, medieval tombstones are embedded in the floor and walls. (Open daily 10am-6pm, except during services. Cathedral free, donation requested.) The 100-ft. tower, near the south transept, is a relic of the earlier 6th-century Church of St. Canice. For an additional 70p, you can climb the series of six steep ladders inside for a panoramic view of the town and its surroundings. The **Black Abbey**, off Abbey St., was founded in 1225 and got its name from the black habits of its Dominican friars. Within the heavy stone structure, a fiery modern stained-glass window contrasts with older, subtler ones. Nearby **St. Mary's** stands testament to the incredible religious faith of the Irish people. The townspeople built the cathedral in 1849, during the darkest of the Famine days.

It is rumored that crafty 14th-century monks brewed a light ale in St. Francis' Abbey; appropriately, the abbey's yard now contains the **Smithwicks Brewery** on Parliament St. The abbey is in ruins, but its industry survives. Smithwicks Brewery offers an audio-visual show and ale tasting. Smithwicks itself is a tasty brew (naturally best in Kilkenny), but the company also profanes the abbey by brewing Budweiser there. (Tours July-Aug. Mon.-Fri. 3pm; tourist office distributes free tickets.)

ENTERTAINMENT

The Kilkenny People is a good source for arts and music listings. **The Watergate Theatre,** Parliament St. (tel. 61674), puts on traditional Irish plays. (Tickets usually £5, students £3. Booking office open daily 10am-8pm.)

The last week of August is **Kilkenny Arts Week,** which has a daily program of concerts, recitals, poetry readings, and exhibitions by some of Ireland's top artists. Admission varies for individual events (free-£7; student tickets available); a week-long ticket costs £75, before July 31 £65 (student discounts available). Buy tickets from Kilkenny Arts Week at Rothe House, Parliament St. (tel. 63663), or the tourist office. Kilkenny's population increases by 10,000 in early June for the **Cat Laughs** (tel. 51254), a week-long festival that hosts Irish, English, and American comedians.

■ Near Kilkenny Town

THOMASTOWN & JERPOINT ABBEY

Thomastown, a tiny community perched on the Nore River, is picturesque but manages to be genuinely interesting anyway. The visual arts are abundant here, fueled by the two arts schools in town. For **tourist information,** ask for the free pamphlets at **Wrapped Up** or next door at **Barrett's Pharmacy** (tel. 24216; open Mon.-Sat. 9am-6:30pm, Sun. 10am-noon). **Bus Éireann** stops by Kavanagh's between Waterford and Kilkenny (7/day, Sun. 4/day). **Gary's Minibus** (tel. 24102) can take you to points of historical interest. **Simon Treacy Hardware** rents **bikes** (tel. 24291; £5/day, £25/week), and sells fishing tackle (open Mon.-Sat. 9am-6pm). **Supervalu,** around the corner on Marshes St., is open Mon.-Wed. 8am-7pm, Thurs.-Fri. 8am-9pm, and Sun. 8am-12:30pm. Thomas goes to town with a **phone code** of 056.

An amazing lunch can be had at the serene **Watergarden** (tel. 24690) on Ladywell St. (follow signs from Market St.). Members of the Camphill Community, an organization which supports and employs the mentally-handicapped, serve tasty food in a cozy café (vegetable lasagna £3; open 9am-6pm). The gardens in the back are lovely. **O'Hara's** pub (tel. 24597), with 200-year-old walls and fireplaces, was Chris O'Donnell's favorite watering hole while filming *Circle of Friends* in nearby Inistioge. Upstairs, Mrs. O'Hara offers **B&B** in comfortable, newly decorated rooms with bath and TV. Kitchen access (single £18, double £32).

At one end of Market St. rests the remains of **St. Mary's,** a church built in the early 13th century. Among the gravestones lies a rare stone with ancient Ogham writing, as well as part of a Celtic cross and the weathered effigy of 13th-century man. At **Jerpoint Glass** (tel. 24350), Keith Leadbetter lets visitors watch as he sculpts glass.

Jerpoint Abbey (tel. 24623), founded in 1180, is 1½ mi. toward Waterford. It is one of the most beautiful Cistercian ruins in Ireland, with remarkable etchings and tombs. Numerous other remains dot the landscape surrounding Thomastown. Most are on private land, but local farmers usually don't object to visitors exploring them.

DUNMORE CAVE

North of Kilkenny, on the road to Castlecomer, lurks the massive **Dunmore Cave** (office tel. (056) 67726), known as "the darkest place in Ireland." It contains fascinating, varied limestone formations. Recently unearthed human bones show that 40 people died underground here in 928 AD, hiding from marauding Vikings. (Open mid-June to mid-Sept. daily 10am-7pm; mid-Sept. to Oct. daily 10am-6pm; Nov.-Feb. Sat.-Sun. 10am-5pm; mid-March to mid-June Tues.-Sat. 10am-5pm, Sun. 2-5pm. Last admission 45min. before closing. Admission £2, students £1.) There is no direct public transport to the cave, but **Buggy's Buses** (tel. (056) 41264) runs a bus between Kilkenny and Castlecomer that passes nearby (4/day; ask ahead of time to stop here). Or take N78 (Dublin Rd.) from Kilkenny; the turn-off for the cave, on the right, is after the split with N77 (Durrow Rd.).

County Tipperary

Trek south from Kilkenny Town or west from Waterford City to reach the medieval remains in south Tipperary, where Clonmel, Cahir, and Cashel bolster a plethora of castles and cathedrals. North Tipperary is a long way from the beaten tourist track, and for good reason—its acres are fertile, but fascinating only to farmers. From Cashel, keep going west until you reach Co. Kerry, or drop down south for a walk in the underrated Comeragh, Galtee, or Knockmealdown Mountains on your way to Co. Cork. Although Lismore is actually located in Co. Waterford, it is covered under Co. Tipperary with the nearby Knockmealdown Mountains.

■ Tipperary Town

Good-bye to Piccadilly/Farewell to Leicester Square.
It's a long way to Tipperary/And my heart lies there.

If the song is right, then you've come a long way for nothing. Tourists who don't know better go out of their way to see Tipperary, assuming that the famously-named town is as exciting as the WWI marching song. But "Tipp Town," as it's affectionately known, is primarily a market town for the region's fertile Golden Vale farming region. Compared with the sun-dappled beauty of the surrounding area, Tipp Town itself is depressing.

Skip Tipp and head for the nearby **Glen of Aherlow**. The **tourist office** on James St., just off Main St. (tel. 51457), is a useful resource for trips into the nearby mountains. (Open May-Oct. Mon.-Sat 10am-6pm; Glen of Aherlow walking trail maps 50p.) An **AIB** is on Main St. (open Mon.-Wed. and Fri. 10am-4pm, Thurs. 10am-5pm; **ATM**). The **post office** hides on Davis St. (open Mon.-Fri. 9am-5:30pm, Sat. 9am-noon and 1-5:30pm). Tipp's **phone code** marches into war whistling "062."

The best B&B in Tipp is the aptly named **Central House B&B,** 45 Main St. (tel. 51117), which has a welcoming owner and spacious rooms—one boasts a four-poster brass and wrought-iron bed frame (£15/person, w/bath £16). Other B&Bs are on the Emly Rd. about ½ mi. from town. Walk west down Main St. and continue straight. **The Brown Trout,** Abbey St. (tel. 51912), on the corner of the road to the Glen of Aherlow, has surprisingly reasonable prices (filet of plaice £5) considering its chandelier, spanky red tablecloths, and multiple sets of flatware (open daily 12:30-3pm and 6-9:30pm). You'll find hearty Irish food at the **Butler's Pantry** (tel. 51788), down Main St. just before the turnoff for Clonmel Rd. Meals come served in a diner-like atmosphere complete with vinyl booths. (Roast chicken £3.50. Open Mon.-Fri. 9:30am-8pm, Sat. noon-3pm, Sun. noon-6pm.) For simple bistro fare you're sure to get lucky at the **Seamróg**, Davis St. (Tel. 33881. Mushroom omelette £4. Open March-Oct. Mon.-Sat. 8am-8pm, Sun. 4-8pm; Nov.-March Mon.-Sat. 8am-6pm.) Fortunately, there is a full-scale **SuperValu** on Main St. (open Mon.-Wed. and Sat. 9am-6pm, Thurs. and Fri. 9am-9pm). Youth congregate in the **Underground Tavern,** James St., which looks a bit like an old winery with wine barrels that now function as tables (rock and pop Thurs. and Sat.-Sun.). **Corny's Pub,** Davitt St. (later it becomes Limerick Rd., and even later Church St.) Tipp's oldest tavern, plays nightly trad that attracts an older crowd.

■ Cashel

Truly magical when seen from a distance, the commanding **Rock of Cashel** rises above the town of Cashel. The dark limestone hill bristles with an elaborate complex of medieval buildings 300 ft. above the plain. In town, the efficient **tourist office** shares space with the Heritage Centre in the recently renovated Cashel City Hall, Main St. (Tel. 62511. Open July-Aug. daily 9:30am-8pm; March-June daily 9:30am-5:30pm; Sept.-Feb. Mon.-Sat. 9:30am-5:30pm, Sun. noon-5:30pm.) **McInerney's,** Main St. (tel. 61366), next to SuperValu, rents bikes (£7.50/day, £30/week; open Mon.-Sat. 9am-6pm). **AIB**, Main St., does currency exchange and has an **ATM.** (Open Mon.-Wed. and Fri. 10am-12:30pm and 1:30-4pm, Thurs. 10am-12:30pm and 1:30-5pm.) The **post office** (tel. 61418) is also on Main St. (open Mon.-Fri. 9am-1pm and 2-5:30pm, Sat. 9am-1pm). The **phone code** rocks the Cashel at 062.

Cashel lies inland between Waterford and Cork, tucked behind a series of mountain ranges on N8 from Cork to Dublin. **Bus Éireann** (tel. 62121) leaves from Alice's Bistro on Main St., serving: Dublin (4/day; 3hr.; £9, students £6.50); Cork (4/day; 1½hr.; £8, students £5.30); Limerick (4/day; £8.80, students £5); and Cahir (4/day; 15min.; £2.40, students £2). Bus transport to Waterford is available via Cahir. Hitching to Cork or Dublin along N8 is a breeze; thumbing west to Tipp and Limerick on N74 is also feasible.

SOUTHEAST IRELAND

Accommodations Contributing greatly to the town's appeal as a backpackers' base, Cashel is graced with two excellent hostels. The **Cashel Holiday Hostel (IHH)**, 6 John St. (tel. 62330), just off Main St., is extremely comfortable, with spacious bedrooms named after famous Irishmen and women, a gorgeous light-bathed kitchen crowned with a glass pyramid skylight, and an informative, gregarious staff. Their hints on the area's natural and archaeological sights have been known to keep backpackers in Cashel for an extended stay. (4- to 8-bed dorm £6; 4-bed dorm w/bath £7.50; private room £8.50/person. Laundry £3.50. Key deposit £3.) **O'Brien's Farmhouse Hostel,** off Dundrum Rd. (tel. 61003; from town, make the first left after the abbey), is truly stunning with its spotless rooms, fluffy beds, and unbelievable location. Roll out of bed to one side, and the shadowy abbey looms outside the window, roll to the other side, and the rock towers on the horizon. (6-bed dorm £6, private room from £9. **Camping** £3.50/person. Wash and dry £5.) The Rock attracts a fair number of tourists to Cashel, a fact reflected in the high quality (and high price) of local B&Bs. Just steps from the Rock on Moor Lance is **Rockville House** (tel. 61760), which does credit to its outstanding location with crisp bedrooms (£13/person w/ bath).

Food & Pubs You can get anything you want at **Alice's Bistro,** 105 Main St. (tel. 62170), where an omelette and chips cost £4 (open daily 12:30-10:30pm). **The Bake House** (tel. 61680), across from the Heritage Centre on Main St., is the town's best spot for scones, coffee, and light meals (open Mon.-Sat. 8am-9pm, Sun. 10am-7pm). **The Spearman Restaurant,** 97 Main St. (tel. 61143), offers a delicious but costly break from the brown-bread diet. (Sandwiches £1.60; dinner prices higher. Open daily noon-2:30pm and 6-9:30pm; May-Sept. 10am-10pm.) **Pasta Milano,** Lady's Well St. (tel. 62729), will be a relief for those who miss Italian restaurants *à la tacquée*, complete with drippy candles, fountains, and Greco-Roman statues. Extensive and affordable menu (*tagliatelli* with spinach and mushrooms £6; open daily noon-midnight). **SuperValu Supermarket,** Main St., offers the biggest selection of groceries (Mon.-Sat. 8am-9pm, Sun. 9am-6pm), while **Centra Supermarket** on Friar St. is open latest (daily 7am-10:30pm).

Good *craic* and nightly music entice locals to the best pub in Cashel, **Feehan's,** Main St. (tel. 61929; trad bands Tues.-Wed., trad session Thurs., Take a Chance Fri.-Mon.). **O'Sullivan's,** across the street at 9 Main St. (tel. 61858), serves popular pints. Staid and well-appointed, **Dowling's,** 46 Main St. (tel. 62130), attracts a mixed crowd with trad music on Wednesdays.

Sights The elevated **Rock of Cashel** is a huge limestone outcropping dominated by a complex of secular and ecclesiastical buildings on top. The Rock itself has a number of legends, some historically substantiated and others of dubious origin, attached to it (see **The Legendary Rock,** below). On the Rock, **Cormac's Chapel,** a majestic, dual-towered structure, was consecrated in 1134. The interior displays ornate Romanesque carvings and a richly decorated sarcophagus, once thought to be in the tomb of King Cormac. A highlight of Cashel's illustrious history was the reported burning of the cathedral by the Earl of Kildare in 1495. When Henry VII demanded an explanation, the Earl replied, "I thought the Archbishop was in it." Henry made him Lord Deputy. The 13th-century **Cashel Cathedral** survived the Earl, and though its vaulted Gothic arches no longer buttress a roof, the cathedral is unequalled in its grandeur. Beside the Rock, the 90-ft. **round tower** is the oldest part of the Rock, probably dating from just after 1101. The museum at the entrance to the castle complex preserves the 12th-century **St. Patrick's Cross.** Kings of Munster were crowned on the site marked by the *croix faux.* Much of the Rock is off-limits. (Tel. 61437. Rock open mid-June to mid-Sept. daily 9am-7:30pm; mid-March to mid-June 9:30am-5:30pm; mid-Sept. to mid-March 9:30am-4:30pm. Last admission 40min. before closing. Admission £2.50, students £1.) Far from the madding crowd and down the cow-

The Legendary Rock

The seat of Munster's Kingship since the days of the ancient Éire (about 1-700 AD), the Rock was held for centuries by the Eóganacht (later MacCarthy) clan. They challenged the "High Kings" at Tara until subordinated to the Dál Cais king (Brian Ború's brother) in 859. Although Brian retained the title "King of Cashel," his real power was consolidated along the Shannon. (In legend, St. Patrick visited Cashel to baptize a fictional Eóganacht king, and accidentally pierced the king's foot with his pointy pastoral staff. The king didn't complain, thinking the injury part of the ceremony.) Cashel didn't become an ecclesiastical center until after 1101, when King Muirchertach O'Brien donated the site to the Church, thus ensuring the loyalty of the Irish church and rendering the Eóganacht powerless at the same time. Over the next few centuries, local political and ecclesiastical powers subsequently added to the construction on the Rock, creating a Gothic cathedral crammed between a round tower and a Romanesque chapel which, incredibly enough, fails to look incongruous.

path from the Rock, **Hore Abbey** looms silently. The last Cistercian monastery established in Ireland, its ruins are open, free, and afford a striking view of the Rock.

The small but brilliantly executed **Heritage Centre,** on Main St. (tel. 35362), features exhibitions (both permanent and temporary) including "Rock: From 4th to 11th century" and "Rock: 12th-18th century" with temporary exhibitions on such themes as Hore Abbey, Cashel Palace, and "Life in Cashel." (Open July-Aug. daily 9:30am-8pm; March-June daily 9:30am-5:30pm; Sept.-Feb. Mon.-Sat. 9:30am-5:30pm, Sun. noon-5:30pm. Admission £1, student 50p.) In Cashel proper, the **GPA-Bolton Library** (tel. 61944), on John St. past the hostel, displays a musty collection of books and silver formerly belonging to an Anglican archbishop of Cashel, Theophilus Bolton. The collection harbors ecclesiastical texts and rare manuscripts, including a 1550 edition of Machiavelli's *Il Principe* and the first English translation of *Don Quixote.* (Open Mon.-Fri. 11am-4:30pm. For a tour, call tel. (062) 61232; £2.50, students £1.50.) The **Brú Ború Heritage Centre** (tel. 61122), at the base of the Rock, performs Irish traditional music, song, and dance to international acclaim (performances June 15-Sept. 15 Tues.-Sat. at 9pm; £5). Five miles west of Cashel on Tipperary Rd. stand the ruins of golden **Althassel Abbey,** a 12th-century Augustinian priory founded by the Red Earl of Dunster.

▨ Cahir

Cahir (CARE) comes from the Irish word "Cathair," meaning "city." The name is false advertising—it's more a busy square than a city. The town's two prominent sights, Cahir Castle and the Swiss Cottage, can be explored in a few hours. Those planning to spend some time in the area should consider basing themselves in more scenic and hostel-blessed Cashel.

Practical Information The well-signposted **tourist office,** Castle St. (tel. 41453), knows surprisingly little about the mountains surrounding the town, but they do sell invaluable, if expensive, maps. (Open mid-April to Sept. Mon.-Sat. 9:30am-6pm; July and Aug. Sun. 11am-5pm.) **Trains** leave from the station off Cashel Rd., just past the church, for Limerick and Rosslare (Mon.-Sat 2/day). **Bus Éireann** runs from the tourist office to: Limerick via Tipperary (Mon.-Thurs. and Sat. 4/day, Fri. 5/day; 1hr.; £7.30, students £4.30); Waterford via Clonmel (Mon.-Thurs. and Sat. 5/day, Fri. 6/day; 1¼hr.; £7.70, students £4.30); Cork (4/day; 1½hr.; £7, students £5); Dublin (Mon.-Sun. 4/day; 3hr.; £10, students £7.50); and Cashel (15min.; £2.50). **Hitchers** to Dublin or Cork station themselves on N8, which involves a 20-minute hike from the center of town. Those hoping to hitch to Limerick and Waterford wait just outside of town on N24 (Limerick/Waterford Rd.) which passes through the town square. Backpackers can stow their bags for a time, for free, at the **Crock O'**

Gold (across from the tourist office). If you want to call someone, you should cahir that the **phone code** is 052.

Accommodations, Food, & Pubs There are two hostels in the countryside, relatively close to Cahir. **Lisakyle Hostel (IHH)** (tel. 41963), 1 mi. south of Cahir on Ardfinnan Rd., is the more accessible of the two. Though the place is beautiful outside, the accommodations are truly rustic and the beds are thin (dorm £6, private £8; camping £4). Reserve a bed with the hostel's superfriendly owners at **Condon's Shop** on Church St., across from the post office. Condon's will also arrange lifts to the hostel from the trains, buses, or from town. The **Kilcoran Farm Hostel (IHH)** (tel. 41906 or (088) 539185) promises to be an education in rural living, with vocal sheep out back and an impressive collection of rusting farm tools. All rooms, singles or doubles, go for £7 per person. Free bikes, and free rides from Cahir. From Cahir, take Cork Rd. for 4 mi., turn left at the Top Petrol Station, go ¼ mi., then veer right at the T-shaped junction. The closest B&B to Cahir is **Killaun**, a ¼-mi. hike from town along the Clonmel Rd. (tel. 41780). Comfortable, airy rooms and a friendly hostess (£14/ person, w/bath £16).

The best bet for groceries is **SuperValu Supermarket,** Bridge St., across the bridge from the castle (tel. 41515; open Mon.-Wed. 9am-6:30pm, Thurs. 9am-8pm, Fri. 9am-9pm, Sat. 9am-7pm). The **Italian Connection,** Castle St. (tel. 42152), serves bountiful plates of pasta (£5) on red tablecloths (open daily noon-11pm). **The Castle Arms,** Castle St. (tel. 42506), serves up economical grub in an atmosphere that could only be called "pub" (chicken curry £3.75). Though unluxurious, the **Shamrock Lounge,** 15 Castle St. (tel. 41423), offers a three-course lunch, with coffee, for only £5. Decidedly more posh and a local favorite is the **Galtee Inn** (tel. 41247), where lunch entrees cost £4.85 (lunch noon-3pm, dinner 5-10:30pm).

For an innocuous-looking town that panders to tourists, Cahir has a bizarre biker following. Consequently, it fosters a number of biker bars. Compare tattoos at **Black Tom's** (tel. 42539), on the Limerick Rd. past SuperValu, a favorite among Tipperary's leather set that features occasional live rock on weekends. **J. Morrissey,** on Castle St. across from the tourist office (tel. 42123), holds traditional sessions every Tuesday night. **Galtee Inn,** Church St. (tel. 42147), and the **Castle Arms,** across from the tourist office on Castle St. (tel. 42506), attract fewer Harleys and more well-dressed ex-yuppies and older locals. They probably drive mopeds.

Sights Cahir defines itself, physically and metaphysically, by **Cahir Castle** (tel. 41011), one of the larger and better preserved castles in Ireland. It is exactly what every tourist envisions a castle to be—heavy, wet, and gray—which must be why so many tourists come to reinforce their preconceptions. Climb the towers for an unparalleled view of the tourist office and parking lot. Built in the 13th century, the Castle has a long history of being attacked: in 1599, the Earl of Essex pounded a cannonball into one of its walls; in 1650, Cromwell, ever the considerate correspondent, wrote a letter to the Castle demanding its immediate evacuation. The family freaked, packed up, and fled. Cromwell never came. Note the 10,000-year-old preserved head of the long-extinct Irish Elk. The noble beast's antlers span nearly an entire wall. (Open mid-June to mid-Sept. daily 9am-7:30pm; April to mid-June and mid-Sept. to mid-Oct. 10am-6pm; Nov.-March daily 10am-1pm and 2-4:30pm. Admission £2, students £1. Last admission 45min. before closing.)

The broad River Suir that flows into Waterford Harbour is still a mere stream in Cahir. The wildly green **river walk** follows it from the tourist office to the 19th-century **Swiss Cottage** (tel. 41144; 30-min. walk from town) and beyond. Consisting of a charming jumble of architectural styles, the luxurious house approximates an aristocratic conception of the simple life. (Access by guided tour only; open May-Sept. daily 10am-6pm; April Tues.-Sun. 10am-1pm and 2-5pm; March and Oct.-Nov. Tues.-Sun. 10am-1pm and 2-4:30pm. Admission £2, students £1. Last admission 45min. before closing. No wheelchair access.)

Fishing opportunities abound along the river walk past the Swiss Cottage. Fishing licenses are required. For information and a free fly-tying demonstration, contact celebrated fly-tyer **Alice Conba,** Old Church St. (tel. 42348). Ms. Conba exhibits her framed, individually signed flies and is eager to enlighten individuals about her craft. Her collection includes dry flies, hair-winged salmon flies, and a unique gift idea: "beautifully crafted Fly Brooches."

■ Near Cahir

The **Mitchelstown Caves** (tel. (052) 67246) drip 8 mi. off the Cahir-Cork road in the town of Burncourt, about halfway between Cahir and Mitchelstown. The perfunctory tour lasts only 30 minutes, but that's plenty of time for the subterranean formations to leave you awestruck. The stalactites and stalagmites formed over millions of years from rainwater filtering through the porous limestone. The dripping water deposited bits of rock in rippled, gooey structures. (Open daily 10am-6pm. Admission £2.50, students £2.) Located about 3 mi. from the caves, the tiny village of **Ballyporeen** has the distinction of being home to Ronald Reagan's ancestors, now buried at Templetenny Cemetery in the village. It's a pleasant enough village, if you like supply-side economics.

The **Galtee Mountains** rise abruptly from the flatlands due west of Cahir. The purplish range boasts Galtymore among its peaks, at 3654 ft. Ireland's third-highest mountain. The north climb is most difficult. Serious hikers should invest in one of the excellent Ordnance Survey maps at the tourist office or local bookstore (£4.10). The *New Irish Walk Guides* have maps and routes for the Galtees, along with all the other mountains in the region (available in bookstores). Tourist offices in Tipp Town, Cahir, and Cashel also sell a four-walk series of trail maps. Each contains a map and written directions detailing a "classic" and a less strenuous "family walk" (50p). The walks take in the Glen of Aherlow, Lake Muskry, and Lake Borheen, Glencush and Lake Curra, and Duntry League Hill. Glenbarra is a popular base camp, accessible by driving west from Cahir towards Mitchelstown.

The **Glen of Aherlow (Ballydavid Wood) Youth Hostel (An Óige/HI)** (tel. (062) 54148), 6 mi. northwest of Cahir off Limerick Rd. (signposted) is a renovated old hunting lodge. It makes a good home for cavorting around the Galtees (June-Sept. £6, March-May and Oct.-Nov. £5.50). On occasion, dedicated hikers make the 10-mi. trek across the mountains to the **Mountain Lodge (An Óige/HI),** Burncourt (tel. (052) 67277), a gas-lit Georgian hunting lodge in the middle of the woods. From Cahir, follow the Mitchelstown Rd. (N8) 8 mi., then turn right at the sign for another 2 mi. on an unpaved path (£5.50/person; new showers). The **Kilcoran Farm Hostel** (tel. (052) 41906) also makes a convenient hiking home (see **Cahir,** p. 175). The campsite in the Glen of Aherlow, **Ballinacourty House** (tel. (062) 56230), is excellent. The staff provides detailed information on the Glen. (£7/tent, off season £6, plus £1/person. Meals and cooking facilities available. Open April to mid-Sept.) They also operate a pleasant B&B and restaurant (double £32 w/bath). To reach Ballinacourty House, take R663 off the Cahir-Tipperary Rd. (N24) in the town of Bansha, and follow for 11km. Turn right at the signposted turnoff.

▓ Clonmel

Clonmel (pop. 16,000) derives its name from the Irish *Cluain Meala,* "the honey meadow." This medieval town on the banks of the River Suir (SURE), bordered by the Comeragh Mountains, does have something sweet about it. Locally produced Bulmer's cider fills the air with sweet apple scents in the fall, and the *New York Times* recently declared the town the "optimism capital of Ireland." Clonmel now keeps itself plugging along as the county town of Co. Tipperary as well as the commercial center of its southern half.

ORIENTATION & PRACTICAL INFORMATION

The town's central street runs parallel to the Suir. From the station, follow Prior Park Rd. straight to Parnell St. and turn right. It becomes Mitchell St., O'Connell St., and eventually Irishtown. Businesslike Gladstone St. intersects O'Connell St.

Tourist Office: Sarsfield St. (tel. 22960), across from the Clonmel Arms Hotel. Pick up the excellent *Clonmel and South Tipperary Guide* (free). The 6 "Self-guided walking tours" of Clonmel and the Nire Valley are printed on green and orange waterproof sheets (50p). Open Mon.-Fri. 9:30am-5:30pm, Sat. 10am-2pm.

Bank: AIB, O'Connell St. (tel. 22500). Full services, including **ATM** that accepts all major cash systems.

Trains: Prior Park Rd., a continuation of Gladstone St. farther north of the river. Train information (tel. 21982). Trains chug here (2/day, 4/day in summer) between Limerick and Rosslare Harbour via Waterford. You'll change in Waterford (£6.50, student £3.25) or Limerick Junction (£11, student £5.50) before going anywhere else.

Buses: Bus information available at **Rafferty Travel** on Gladstone St. (tel. 22622). Open Mon.-Sat. 9am-6pm. Buses head to Clonmel from: Cork (3/day; £8, students £4.90); Dublin (3/day; £8, students £6); Galway (Mon.-Fri. 5/day, Sun. 3/day; £12, students £7.50); Kilkenny via Carrick-on-Suir (Mon.-Sat. 4/day, Sun. 3/day; £3.50); Limerick via Tipperary (daily 5/day; £8.80, students £5); Rosslare (2/day £10, students £6); and Waterford via Carrick-on-Suir (Mon.-Sat. 7/day, Sun. 5/day; £5.90, students £3.50).

Pharmacy: Joy's, 68 O'Connell St. (tel. 21204). Open Mon.-Sat. 9am-6pm.

Hospitals: St. Joseph's/St. Michael's, Western Rd. (tel. 21900).

Emergency: Dial 999 (no coins required). **Garda:** Emmet St. (tel. 22222).

Post Office: Emmet St. (tel. 21164), parallel to Gladstone St. Open Mon.-Fri. 9am-5pm, Sat. 9am-1pm.

Phone Code: 052.

ACCOMMODATIONS

Hostel-goers be forewarned: Clonmel is not the most backpacker-friendly town in Ireland. It caters more to a hotel and B&B crowd—the only hostel is well outside of town. Explore Clonmel by day then head to the gorgeous **Powers-the Pot Hostel and Caravan Park,** Harney's Cross (tel. 23085), majestically perched atop the Comeragh Mountains. Following Parnell St. east out of town, turn right at the first traffic light (not N24) crossing the Suir and continuing straight for 5½ mi. of arduous mountain road, to the signposted turnoff. Niall and Jo run the hostel out of their large 19th-century house, offering huge fluffy beds, a bar and restaurant under a thatched roof (dinners £6.50-9.50, breakfast £3.50), and an unparalleled mountain-top view. (Dorm £6. **Camping** £3/person. Laundry; maps and walking guides for the Munster Way; freezing and smoking facilities for anglers. Open May to mid-Oct.)

In Clonmel, the area past Irishtown along the Cahir Rd. and Abbey Rd. is graced with numerous **B&Bs.** The options are relatively extensive, provided you're willing to walk a mile or two to town. In Clonmel proper, gracious **Riverside House,** on New Quay overlooking the Suir (tel. 25781), entertains its guests with large rooms, access to the river, in-room BBC, and Max the Wonderdog (£13.50/person).

FOOD & PUBS

Grocery shopping is a surreal experience at **Crazy Prices** on Gladstone St. (tel. 27797; open Mon.-Tues. 9am-7pm, Wed.-Fri. 9am-9pm, Sat. 9am-6pm). **The Honey Pot,** Abbey St. (tel. 21457), sells health foods and bulk grains. Organic vegetable sellers parade their wares here on Fridays (open Mon.-Sat. 9:30am-6pm).

Catalpa, Sarsfield St. (tel. 26821), next to the tourist office. This Italian restaurant is so good that diners sometimes fall into a coma of bliss after tasting the Penne Arrabiata (£4.40). Unconsciousness is safe here, though—the building used to be both

THE MUNSTER WAY ■ 179

a bank vault and an RIC barracks during the war for independence. Open Tues.-Sat. 12:30-2:30pm and 6:30-11pm.

Tom Skinny's Pizza Parlor, 4 Gladstone St. (tel. 26006). Pizza made fresh right before your eyes. Try the unbelievable lunch special; £4.30 gets you a small 2-topping pizza, tea or coffee, and soup or ice cream. Open daily noon-midnight.

Angela's Wholefood Café, Abbey St. (tel. 26899), on a side street off of Mitchell St. Well-prepared and healthy wholefood served on country pine tables. Tomato and spinach flan with salad £3.80. Open Mon.-Sat. 9am-5:30pm.

Niamh's (NEEVS), Mitchel St. (tel. 25698). Locals love this cozy and efficient deli/ restaurant. Niamh, herself, is just plain funny. Hot lunches, sandwiches, and Irish breakfast served all day. Pita the Great £2.60. Open Mon.-Sat. 9am-5:45pm.

Tierney's, O'Connell St. (tel. 24467), winner of the **Munster Pub of the Year, 1994,** is resplendent with wood panelling and polished brass. This may be the clubbiest, most luxurious pub in Ireland. With a restaurant upstairs and meals served all day, it feels less like a pub than a cushy club. The town's most popular pub for the trendy, younger set, is **Phil Carrol's,** on Parrel St. (don't blink, you might miss it; tel. 25215). Known to have the best pint in town, on which the barman can write your name in Guinness foam. **Mulcahy's,** Market St. (tel. 22825), is by far the biggest and most elaborate pub in town. On Thursday to Sunday nights, they host **Danno's,** the disco. (Cover £5, cheaper with concessions, women free before midnight on Thurs.) The Clonmel Arms also hosts a disco, **The Riveroom** (tel. 21233; Thurs.-Sat., cover £2-5). Check the *Nationalist* for entertainment listings.

SIGHTS

Guided tours of Clonmel leave Town Hall (Parrel St.) at 2:30pm and take in all the major historic sights of town (£2). An audio-visual presentation is given at town hall, weekdays at 11:30am (£1). The walking tour and the presentation cover sights in Clonmel such as the **West Gate,** straddling the west end of O'Connell St., which was built in 1831 on the site of the old west gate by a rich, nostalgic citizen. **Old St. Mary's Church,** Irishtown, built in 1204, has an 84-ft. octagonal bell tower and stained-glass windows. In the 1800s, **Hearn's Hotel** on Parnell St. was the nexus of Clonmel Mayor Bianconi's huge horsecart business, which competed successfully with the train in the 1850s. The **Franciscan Friary,** on Abbey St. between Parnell St. and the Quay, has housed the tomb of the Lords of Cahir since the 13th century though most of the current structure dates from the 1880s. Several walks in the area and in the nearby Nire Valley are described in the tourist office's glossy leaflets *Clonmel Walk #1* and *#2* (50p each) and the fat *Clonmel and South Tipperary* (free). See **Comeragh Mountains,** p. 180, for day hike info.

Tipperary S.R. County Museum, Parnell St. (tel. 25399), has an art gallery and traveling exhibitions with no real relevance to Clonmel. More intriguing is the gallery upstairs, which concentrates on somewhat esoteric facets of local history—including relics of Carrick-on-Suir's prodigious cyclist Sean Kelly (open Tues.-Sat. 10am-1pm and 2-5pm; free).

■ The Munster Way

The Munster Way footpath starts in Carrick-on-Suir, hits Clonmel, skirts the Comeragh Mountains, and hits the Knockmealdowns full-force. It currently ends at the Vee Gap, 8 mi. north of Lismore. The best **maps** to use are sheets 74 and 75 of the 1:50,000 Ordnance Survey series. In addition, the *East Munster Way Map Guide* (£4), available at the Clonmel tourist office and at Powers-the-Pot Hostel, provides a written guide and an accurate but less detailed map (as an added bonus, it points out all the pubs along the way!). Powers-the-Pot is the best information center for hiking in and around the Comeragh and Knockmealdown Mountains.

CARRICK-ON-SUIR

Most people stop in Carrick-on-Suir to break up the journey from Rosslare or Waterford to the southwest, or as a starting point for forays into the Comeraghs. Carrick is blessed with grand views of both the mountains and the Suir on which it sits. The **tourist office** (tel. 640200) is at the **Heritage Centre,** a one-room museum that relates the history of Carrick through artifacts and pictures. A town map costs £1 (open June-Sept. 10am-5pm; Oct.-May Mon.-Fri. 10am-5pm; museum £1, students 50p). The **AIB** on Main St. has an **ATM** (open Mon. 10am-5pm, Tues.-Fri. 10am-4pm). **Buses** stop in Carrick on their way from Waterford to Clonmel (4/day). **OK Sports** rents **bikes** (£7/day, £40/week). Carrick's **phone code** is a Suir thing at 051.

The **Gables** (tel. 641400), on Main St., is a B&B the size of a small hotel. This former convent now has plain rooms and a spacious lounge with TV and pool tables (£13/person w/bath, single £15). Buy groceries at **Supervalu** (tel. 640803) on Main St. (open Mon.-Wed. and Sat. 8:30am-7:30pm, Thurs.-Fri. 8:30am-9pm, Sun. 9am-6pm). **Europa** (tel. 41115) serves food until 1:30am weeknights and until 3:15am on Saturdays (pizzas £2.60-5.50, chicken curry £3). The **Carraig Hotel** (tel. 641455) offers pub grub (lunches £4.50), and folk music on Monday nights. It also houses **Club Shaba,** a happening disco with a £5 cover. Ladies free before midnight on Fridays and two can go for the price of one on Sundays. **Jimmy Fahey's,** New St. (tel. 641985), attracts a crowd with live music in its beergarden every weekend.

Ormond Castle, Main St. (tel. 640787), is a stately Elizabethan manor house. Original wooden beams and stucco paneling date from the time of "Black Tom" Butler, 10th Earl of Ormond and a favorite of Queen Elizabeth. It was whispered that he was the Virgin Queen's "Black Husband." (Tours June-Aug. daily 9:30am-6:30pm, Sept. 10am-5:30pm; ½hr.; £2.50, students and children £1.50.) The **Carrick Bridge** has linked the banks of the river Suir for 500 years. The **Town Clock,** built in 1783, has an unusual salmon weathervane. The intricately carved **Ahenny High Crosses,** which date from the 8th-century, lie ½ mi. down Cregg Rd. The **Tipperary Crystal Factory** (tel. 641188), founded by renegade Waterford workers, offers tours and an outlet shop 3 mi. towards Clonmel on the Waterford-Clonmel Rd.

COMERAGH MOUNTAINS

The Comeragh "mountains" are more like large hills; not even the highest peaks are very steep. The ground is almost always soft and wet. Hiking boots are obviously best, but most of the terrain is manageable in sneakers. If you'd rather expend your energy admiring the view instead of trying to avoid the mud, consider doing the Comeragh Mountains on horseback (inquire in Clonmel). The technical term for the mountain hollows so common in the mild Comeraghs is "cwms" (KOOMS). Borrowed from the Welsh, it's the only word in the English language without a vowel.

Nire Valley Walk #1 to *12* (50p each at the Clonmel tourist office, Powers-the-Pot Hostel, and the Ballymacarby Tourist Office) are excellent waterproof maps explaining Comeragh day hikes from Clonmel. For more extensive hikes, begin from **Powers-the-Pot Hostel,** ½ mi. off the Munster Way (see **Clonmel,** p. 177). Other trails begin nearby and pass through the village of **Ballymacarby,** on the Clonmel/Dungarvan Rd. (R671), where the tourist info center dispenses local info and plenty of hiking guides for the Comeraghs (tel. (052) 36455; open June-Aug. 9am-6pm daily). "Ballymac," as the locals call it, is also home to a fantastic watering hole, **Melody's Pub** (tel. (052) 36169), where trad can be heard on Tuesday and Wednesday nights (they've got horse trekking too; ask at the bar). The best B&B is **Choc-na-Rí** (tel. (052) 36239). Follow the signs from the village, the B&B is approximately 3 mi. outside of town (£20/person).

The best **map** for exploring the Comeraghs is sheet 75 of the ordnance series. There is another map and guide, the *Walking Guide to the Comeragh Mountains and the Nire Valley,* but it will put you out a steep £8, and experts say it contains several inaccuracies. If you want to wing it, head east from Powers-the-Pot and follow the ridges south. The land is mostly open, and in good weather it's relatively hard to get lost (still, make sure that someone knows you're out there).

KNOCKMEALDOWN MOUNTAINS

Straddling the Tipperary/Waterford border 12 mi. south of Cahir, the Knockmealdown Mountains rise in a rippling wave. *Knockmealdown Walks 1* to *4* (50p) are available at local tourist offices, including offices in Clonmel and Clogheen. All four start at Clogheen (though walks 2 and 4 assume transportation to nearby carparks that mark the true beginnings of these walks). As an alternative, many hikers prefer to begin in the town of **Newcastle,** where tiny, but locally renowned **Nugent's Pub** stands. For guided tours, contact Helen McGrath at (052) 36359. Tours are given on Sundays, and depart at noon from the Newcastle Car Park (£5/person, other days available on request). If you are winging it, the best **map** to use is sheet 74 of the ordnance survey series. Sights to head for include the spectacular **Vee Road** south from Clogheen, which erupts with purple rhododendrons on its way to **Knockmealdown Gap.** Just before the **Vee,** in the town of Graigue, stop in at **Ryan's Pub,** a charming little thatched building in the middle of a farm yard. At the pass of the Knockmealdown Gap about two-thirds of the way to the top of the gap, the pines give way to heather and bracken, and a parking lot marks the path up to the top of **Sugarloaf Hill.** The walk takes about an hour and affords a panorama of patchwork fields on a clear day. From there, you can continue on to the Knockmealdown Peak, the highest in the range at 2609 ft. Beautiful (and supposedly bottomless) **Bay Loch,** on the road down to Lismore, is the stuff of legend. The affable and decidedly unofficious **tourist office** in Clogheen (tel. (052) 65258; across from the Vee Rd. turnoff) is generous with local maps and lore (open Mon.-Sat. 10am-6pm). Descending from the gap to Lismore, the left fork to Cappoquin (R669) will bring you to **Mount Melleray Youth Hostel (An Óige/HI)** (tel. (058) 59390; £5.50/person; open June-Sept.). The idyllic **Kilmorna Farm Hostel** in Lismore (tel. (058) 54315) makes a far more luxurious if somewhat less convenient base for hiking in the range (see **Lismore,** below). Five minutes from the village on Cahir Rd., **camping** is available in **Clogheen** at **Parsons Green** (tel. (052) 65290), which is part gardens and part campsite, offering river-walks, boat rides, pony rides, and a petting farm (£5/2-person tent; kitchen; laundry £2).

LISMORE

The disproportionate grandeur of Lismore's castle and cathedral reminds visitors that in the 8th century, the endearingly small town was a thriving center of monastic learning. Lismore, Co. Waterford, still straddles the aptly named Blackwater River at the end of Vee Rd., across the Knockmealdowns from Cahir. Lismore's extremely helpful **tourist office** (tel. (058) 54975) is in the Interpretive Centre (open June-Aug. Mon.-Sat. 9:30am-6pm, Sun. noon-5:30pm; April-May and Sept.-Oct. Mon.-Sat. 9:30am-5:30pm, Sun. noon-5:30pm). **Bus Éireann** stops at O'Dowd's Bar on West St. and runs to: Dungarvan (Mon., Thurs., Sat. 2/day; ½hr.); Waterford (Mon.-Sat. 1/day, Fri. 2/day; 1¼hr.); and Cork (Fri. 1/day; 1¼hr.). The best way to get to Lismore is by foot or by bike over the Vee or along the Blackwater River. **Hitching** to Dungarvan is also relatively easy. To get to Cork, hitchers first ride east to Fermoy, then south on N8.

Swathed in foliage and standing over the Blackwater River, **Lismore Castle** is stunning. Once a medieval fort and bishop's residence, the castle was extensively rebuilt and remodeled in the 19th century into a romantic's ideal of a castle. In 1814, the Lismore Crozier and the *Book of Lismore,* priceless artifacts thought to have been lost forever, were found hidden in the castle walls. A former home of Sir Walter Raleigh, the castle was also the birthplace of 17th-century scientist Robert Boyle (of PV=nRT fame). The castle is privately owned (occasionally accommodating guests at about £10,000/week). Fred Astaire's brother-in-law was a member of the family who currently owns the castle, so when Fred wasn't too busy cutting the rug somewhere, he was known to fish along the river in front of the castle. Admire the castle from the bridge over the Blackwater River, because its gardens are not worth their admission fee. (Lismore Castle Gardens tel. (058) 54424; open daily 1:45-4:45pm. Admission £2.50, under 16 £1.50.) The bridge is also the starting point for the shady **Lady Louisa's Walk** along the tree-lined Blackwater.

Locals whisper that a secret passage connects the castle to the Protestant **Lismore Cathedral,** Deanery Hill. Although built in 1633 (by Boyle's father Richard), the west wall incorporates grave slabs from Lismore's 10th-century imminence. The cathedral also contains Ireland's only example of an Edward Burne-Jones stained glass window. Outside the cathedral, notice the large number of tombs sealed with stone slabs in the ageing graveyard. This reflects Lismore's infamous past as a center for bodysnatching; the slabs ensured that the stiffs wouldn't be stolen. Lismore's **Interpretive Centre** (tel. (058) 54975), in the town square, includes a video presentation and a cursory exhibit highlighting the 1000-year-old *Book of Lismore* (open same hours as tourist office; admission £2.50, students £2). Included in the admission price is a guided tour of the town (£1.50 for the tour without the audio-visual presentation, £1 for a self-guided tour booklet). Oenophiles can taste the unsung virtues of the **West Waterford Vineyards** (tel. (058) 54283), 5 mi. from Lismore off Dungarvan Rd. The Vineyard produces a dry white wine in addition to seasonal fruit wines such as pear or strawberry (open daily 10:30am-8pm).

One mile from Lismore, the **Kilmorna Farm Hostel** (tel. (058) 54315) competes with the castle in luxury. The 18th-century coach house and stables were converted brilliantly (gingham curtains, fluffy duvets, and solid wood beds built by a local craftsman). They offer a common room with TV and a perfectly appointed kitchen. The working farm provides fresh groceries and supports cows, chickens, and no fewer than six dogs. (3- to 6-bed dorm £8; double £18. Breakfast £3.50. Laundry £3.50.) From town, walk up Chapel St. (to the left of the Interpretive Centre), take the first left, and follow the signs (or call for a lift). Cheerful rooms open up behind unpromising doorways in the **Red House Inn** (tel. (058) 54248), across from the Interpretive Centre on Main St. (£12.50/person, £10 w/out breakfast). Stock up on supplies at **Londis,** Main St. (tel. (058) 54279; open Mon.-Wed. and Sat. 9am-6:30pm, Thurs. 9am-7:30pm, Fri. 9am-8:30pm). **Eamonn's Place,** Main St. (tel. (058) 54025), is the best spot for a standard, substantial meal, which can be eaten in their gorgeous stonewalled beergarden. (Lunch entrees £3.50; open for lunch Mon.-Fri. 12:30-2pm, dinner Mon.-Sun. 6-9pm). The **Red House Inn** (tel. (058) 54248) has occasional traditional sessions on Fridays, much anticipated by Lismore's younger crowd. **Madden's Bar,** East Main St. (tel. (058) 54148), pleasantly serves pints in a history-rich pub.

Wexford & Waterford

Geography makes Co. Wexford the front door to Ireland for anyone coming from France, Wales, or England. Ireland's invaders—from Vikings to Normans to modern backpackers—have begun their island conquering business in Co. Wexford. Naturally, with so many people passing through, Wexford has been particularly prone to foreign influences. Christianity arrived here with St. Iba, after St. Declan but before St. Patrick. Co. Wexford and Co. Waterford also witnessed one of Ireland's most pivotal historic tales—Dermot MacMurrough's invitation to Strongbow to take his daughter and the land. Regardless of all the strangers passing through her ports, some of Co. Wexford's residents retain the Irish language. Co. Wexford has mellow beaches, a splendid variety of pubs in Wexford Town, and more sun than any other part of the country. The beaches spread out just a few miles from businesslike Rosslare Harbour and pop up again at the county's southwest edge, along Waterford Harbour and Tramore. Antiquities are not as rampant in Co. Waterford as in other parts of Ireland; rather, the county is dedicated to the production of industrial and agricultural goods. The commercial and cultural core of the Southeast is Waterford City, where thriving crystal and sootier industries create an urban environment worlds apart from the sheep-speckled fields of the inner county. Waterford, with its fine hostels and urban amenities, makes an ideal base for exploring the Southeast.

Slí Charman, (SHLEE KAR-man) a.k.a. "An tSlí," is a pathway that runs 135 mi. along Wexford's coast from the Co. Wicklow border through Rosslare and Wexford to Waterford Harbour. The path usually climbs along cliffs but sometimes borders paved roads. Trekking the whole way is not as rewarding as hiking the Wicklow Way, but short stretches of the path offer a good dose of stormy seascapes. Maps hang out at Bord Fáilte offices in Waterford, Tramore, Wexford, Rosslare, New Ross, Enniscorthy, and Arklow. Major roads in the region are the east-west N25 (Rosslare-Wexford-New Ross-Waterford), the north-south N11 (Wexford-Enniscorthy-Arklow-Dublin), and the N30 from Enniscorthy to New Ross.

■ Rosslare Strand and Harbour

The sole purpose of Rosslare Harbour is to receive or bid farewell to Ireland's visitors and voyagers. A bit of terminology: Rosslare Harbour refers to the over-equipped village from which the ferries to France, England, and Wales depart, Rosslare Town is the less important town between Rosslare Harbour and Wexford on N25, and Rosslare Strand is the beach near Rosslare Town. Ferries from Rosslare Harbour run daily to Britain and almost as frequently to France. Shops in town open and close with the arrivals and departures of the ferries, and B&Bs swamp N25 between Wexford and Rosslare Harbour. While the town of Rosslare Harbour is best seen from the porthole of a departing ferry, many Irish know the value of sunny beach towns like Rosslare Strand and Kilmore Quay. If you have to spend time in Rosslare Harbour, spend it at the beach south of the harbor. Hitchhiking anywhere around the ferry port can be very difficult. Neither locals surfeited with tourists nor a foreign family of four in an overstuffed car are likely to pick you up. Some hitchers try to convince a driver whose car has fewer than the allowed four passengers to take them on the ferry as part of their allotment—possible, but unlikely.

PRACTICAL INFORMATION

Tourist Office: The Rosslare area has two tourist offices: one manic-panic office in the ferry terminal and another office 1mi. from the harbor on the Wexford Rd. in Kilrane. The **ferry office** (tel. 33623) runs on ferry time. TravelSave stamps, but no ISIC cards. Open daily 6:30-9:30am and 11am-8:30pm or 1-8:30pm, depending on ferry arrival times. The **Kilrane office** is more sedate (tel. 33232). Open May to mid-Sept. daily 11am-8:30pm.

Bank: Currency exchange at the **Bank of Ireland** (tel. 33304), on the main road. Open Mon.-Fri. 10am-12:30pm and 1:30-4pm; no ATM.

Ferries: Trains and buses often connect with the ferries. Bus Éireann and Irish Rail have desks in the terminal (tel. 33592; open daily 6:30am-9:45pm). There is also a bureau de change in the ferry port. **Stena Sealink** (tel. 33115, recorded info 33330; fax 33534; office open daily 9am-5pm), **Irish Ferries/Britain and Ireland line** (tel. 33158; fax 33544), and **Sea Lynx** (office open daily 7am-10pm) all operate from the ferry port. For info on ferries from Rosslare Harbour to England and France see **Getting There** (p. 31).

Trains: Trains run from the ferry port to: Dublin (Mon.-Sat. 3/day, Sun. 2/day; 2hr.; £10); Limerick (Mon.-Sat. 2/day; 2¾hr.; £13); Waterford (Mon.-Sat. 3/day; 1¼hr.; £8.80); and Wexford (Mon.-Sat. 3/day, Sun. 2/day; 20min.; £2.50).

Buses: Buses run to: Galway, Killarney, and Tralee via Waterford (Mon.-Sat. 4/day, Sun. 3/day; £6); Cork (Mon.-Sat. 4/day, Sun. 3/day; £12); Limerick (3/day; £12); Waterford (Mon.-Sat. 4/day, Sun. 3/day; £6); Dublin (Mon.-Sat. 6/day, Sun. 5/day; 3hr.; £10); and Wexford (Mon.-Sat. 10/day, Sun. 8/day; 20min.; £3.50). Buses stop outside the ferry port at J. Pitt's Convenience Store in Kilrane, and at the new Catholic church in Rosslare Harbour.

Taxis: It'll cost you, but you can call **Paddy's Taxis** (tel. 33533).

Emergency: dial 999; no coins required.

Post Office: In the **SuperValu,** between produce and checkout (tel. 33207). Open Mon.-Fri. 9am-1pm and 2-5:30pm, Sat. 9am-1pm. Bureau de change.
Phone code: And then the burning she-goat shrieked "053."

ACCOMMODATIONS

The nature and function of Rosslare Harbour makes accommodations here inevitably predatory (though convenient). Exhausted ferry passengers fill up both good and mediocre beds, while the better places to stay (down the Strand, in Kilmore Quay, and in Wexford) go untenanted. In Rosslare, more than anywhere in Ireland, take the Bord Fáilte shamrock as a measure of quality—there is a noticeable difference between approved and non-approved B&Bs on N25.

Mrs. David Power (tel. 31243). Its only drawback is the 1½mi. separating it from the harbor. It's on the left-hand side of N25, marked only by a sign reading "Self-catering accommodations £5" and by belligerent cows across the road. A hostel in a converted farmhouse that would do most B&Bs proud, with comfy bunks, tea-makers, and a radiator to keep you toasty warm. July-Aug. £7.50/person (£5/person after the first 2 people); Sept.-June £5/person. Shower £1.

Rosslare Harbour Youth Hostel (An Óige/HI), Goulding St. (tel. 33399; fax 33624). At the top of the steps on the hill opposite the ferry terminal, walk right, and then left around the far corner of the Hotel Rosslare. It's off Rosslare Harbour's one street. Offers weak showers, cramped bunks, and a collection of continental youth. Not the nicest hostel in Ireland, but you only have to stay one night. Officially check-in is at 5:30pm, curfew at midnight; be aware that the curfew is strict, late stragglers may bang on the door to no avail. June-Aug. £6.50; Sept.-May £5.50. Sheets 85p. MC, Visa accepted.

Clifford House, Christine Delaney (tel. 33226), on the main road. Climb the steps from the harbor and turn left. At the end of the street turn left again. Bright, comfortable rooms with a beautiful view of the beach. Single £14, w/bath £16.

Marianella B&B (tel. 33139), off N25 across the road from The Anchor Restaurant. Rosemarie Sinner's house doesn't have a great view, but the airy rooms are some of the best on the highway. Cookies and tea laid out in every room. £14/person, w/ bath £16. £5 supplement for a single. Spacious family room available.

Mrs. O'Leary's Farmhouse, Killilane, in Kilrane (tel. 33134). Signposted from the N25, it's ½mi. up N25, then 2mi. west. Set on a gloriously rural 100-acre farm, Mrs. O'Leary's place is a holiday unto itself. A grassy lane leading to a secluded private beach. Mrs. O'Leary will pick you up if you call her from the ferry or the train station. Single £15. Double £28, w/bath £32.

Mrs. J. Foley, 3 Coastguard Station (tel. 33522). Down a gravel walkway between the Great Southern Hotel and the Tuskar Hotel. Offers, simply enough, a bed (2- or 4-person room) and breakfast (continental). Homemade bread is the highlight. You get what you pay for. Noon check-out. £8/person. **Camping** £2/person.

Rosslare Holiday Caravan and Camping Park, Rosslare Strand (tel. 32427 or 45720), is opposite the Bay Bar, 5mi. from the ferry. Take N25 (Wexford Rd.) for 1½mi., turn right at Chushen's Bar in Tagoat, then turn right at the third junction (another 2mi.). The park has a pretty beach setting and is a notch above closer campsites. Wheelchair accessible. Hairdryers, irons, and kitchen. Laundry £2. Showers 50p. Electricity £1.80. £2.50/hiker or cyclist. Caravan £7.50.

FOOD

The restaurants in Rosslare Harbour are expensive, thus the **SuperValu supermarket** (tel. 33107) is popular with the hostel crowd. A tastefully laid out grocery store with a nice selection, the SuperValu is opposite the Rosslare Harbour Youth Hostel on the only road in town (open Mon.-Wed. and Sat. 8am-6pm, Thurs.-Fri. 8am-7pm, Sun. 9am-1pm). Good things come to those who wait (and to those who trek a mile down the road toward Kilrane). There, on the left approaching from Rosslare Harbour, **The Anchor Restaurant** (tel. 33366) serves family-style fare on wooden tables and dishes up inexpensive take-out. Their special supper (soup, entree, vegetables, tea or coffee, and dessert) is a bargain at £6. (Open daily 7am-11pm.)

■ Near Rosslare Harbour

OUR LADY'S ISLAND

Five miles south of Rosslare Harbour and 7 mi. east of Kilmore Quay in Broadway, Our Lady's Island is actually connected to the mainland. The peninsula contains the ruins of an Augustinian priory and a 15-ft. **Leaning Tower** (tilted at a sharper angle than that overrated thing in Italy). The most remote site on the peninsula, **St. Vauk's at Carnsore Point,** is worth the penance. Each year (Aug. 15-Sept. 9) a group of pilgrims flocks around the holy island, where three girls once saw the Virgin Mary appear. The pilgrims are joined by birds of a religious bent, many of whom inhabit one of the world's largest **tern nesting sites,** where more than 2000 pairs of terns breed. The best time to see them is in summer, when they constantly catch fish for their chicks; most breeds head for Africa in winter. From Rosslare Harbour, bikers and walkers should head north on N25, turn left in Tagoat, and follow the signs for Broadway. Camp at **St. Margaret's Caravan and Camping Park** (tel. (053) 31169), by the beach (£2.50/cyclist or hiker, £7 caravan; open June-Aug.).

KILMORE QUAY

Thirteen miles southwest of Rosslare on Forlorn Point, the small fishing village of Kilmore Quay charms with its thatched, white-washed seaside cottages and its beautiful beaches. **Information** about Kilmore Quay can be had at the **Stella Maris Community Centre** (tel. 29922), open throughout the year. The village berths its **Maritime Museum** (tel. 29655) in the lightship *Guillemot* (a lightship is a floating lighthouse). The tour, offered in English, French, and German, encompasses both Irish naval history and the history of the town. One of the highlights is the set of dramatic photos of a 1989 storm, whose 50-ft. waves devastated the community. (Open June-Sept. daily noon-6pm; admission £1, students and children 50p.) **Kilmore Seafood Festival** (tel. 26959) runs in mid-July, with loads of cheap seafood, music, and dancing. In English, French, and German, the **phone code** is 053.

Kilmore Quay also sends boat trips out to the two **Saltee Islands,** formerly a pagan pilgrimage site and now Ireland's largest bird sanctuary with a winged population nearing 50,000. These puffin palaces and razorbill refuges are owned by Prince Michael Salteens, who bears no likeness to the cracker. A narrow ridge of rock connects the smaller island to the mainland. This land bridge, called **St. Patrick's Bridge,** was once used for driving cattle to the island for pasture. (Judging by the width of the road, they must have been thin cows.) When running, boats leave the mainland each morning, stranding you for picnics, ornithology, and bonding with gray seals until 4:30pm. **Declan Bates** (tel. 29684) sails daily during summer months, weather permitting. Times and rates vary—call for more information. **Dick Hayes** (tel. 29704) offers to bring you aboard for deep-sea angling and reef-fishing. Call in advance. Bike rental is available at the aptly-named **Kilmore Quay Bike Hire** (tel. 29781), at Island View House (£7/day, £30/week). **Bus Éireann** runs between Wexford Town and Kilmore Quay (Wed. and Sat. only, 2/day; 30min.; £3.60 return). From Rosslare Harbour, take the Wexford Rd. to Tagoat and turn left; from Wexford, take the Rosslare Rd. and turn right 4 mi. from town, at Piercetown.

Kilmore imbibes at **The Wooden House** (tel. 29804), a friendly local pub with a (predictably) nautical decor and live entertainment on Fridays and Saturdays. Pub grub is also marine-themed (seafood platter for two £10). The overachieving pub also offers **B&B.** Small, low-ceilinged rooms with whitewashed walls copy ship cabins, right down to the salty sea breeze (£12/person, June-Aug. £15). **Curlew Cottage** (tel. 29772) provides B&B in a 300-year-old thatched roof house (£12.50/person). For scads of very fresh seafood (fried scampi £4.25), take yourself across from the Maritime Museum to the **Silver Fox** (tel. 29888).

One mile from town up the Wexford Rd., between Kilmore Quay and Kilmore Town, the **Kilturk Independent Hostel** (tel. 29883) shelters weary souls. An old schoolhouse enlivened by a coat of new paint, the hostel has an impressive kitchen, funky TV lounge, and a new café (open 7am-9pm in summer), but no secure luggage storage (9-bed dorm £5.50; private rooms £7/person; wheelchair accessible.) The hostel arranges fishing trips and tours of the islands daily (£10). Bus Éireann stops at the hostel by request on its way from Wexford to Kilmore Quay.

■ Wexford Town

Thin, winding streets leading to fishing boats tied along the quay give Wexford Town a quiet, small-town, southern European appearance that belies its prominence on the map and in the history books. In 1169, the Normans conquered the Viking settlement of *Wæsfjord* ("harbor of the mud flats") and built their characteristic fortifications. Narrow passages, cutting from Main St. down to the quays, survive as a testament to their efforts. Henry II spent Lent of 1172 in Selskar Abbey, doing penance for the murder of Thomas à Becket. Oliver Cromwell, trying to instill fear in the nationalist population and hence deter future insurrections, ravaged the town in 1649 and slaughtered over 300 people in the centrally located Bull Ring. In 1798, the rebellion sparked by revolutionary activities around the world found its bloodiest expression in Wexford. Today, the only reminders of this violent past are a statue of **the Pikeman** and the stories of invasions and tortures at the Westgate Tower. Spared many of the ravages of industrial development, Wexford retains the charm of an Irish town but offers the lifestyle and facilities of a city.

ORIENTATION & PRACTICAL INFORMATION

Wexford presents a sleepy face to anybody on the quays, but curvy Main St. is more lively. It runs one block inland, parallel to the quays. Redmond Square, with the train station, anchors the north end of Main St. The Bull Ring, at the city center, connects North and South Main St. The Twin Churches punctuate the skyline of an otherwise huddled harbor city. The Franciscan Friary, tall and inviolate, stands at the top of the hill, surveying the older city and train station to its right.

Hitching around Wexford Town can be quite rewarding. Hitchhikers to Dublin (N11) stand at the Wexford Bridge off the quays; those bound for Rosslare head south along the quays to Trinity St.; hitchers heading to Cork, New Ross, or Waterford continue down Westgate and turn left onto St. Ita's Terrace (N25). Take note: the N11 and the N25 are merged near the city, so be sure to specify either the Dublin Rd. (N11) or the Waterford Rd. (N25). Hitchers find the most success thumbing before noon; the early bird gets the ride.

Tourist Office: Crescent Quay (tel. 23111), in the Chamber of Commerce building. Centuries of sailors have sharpened their knives on the windowsills of the building, as the scars and blemishes attest. The free *Junior Chamber Guide to Wexford* offers a nifty map of the city. Open mid-June to Sept. Mon.-Sat. 9am-6pm, Sun 10am-5pm; Oct.-June Mon.-Sat. 9am-1pm and 2-6pm.

Travel Office: O'Donohoe Travel, Commercial Quay (tel. 22788). Sells ferry, rail, and airplane tickets. Not a specialist in budget or discounted travel, just the biggest travel agency in town. Open Mon.-Fri. 9:30am-5:30pm, Sat. 9:30am-1pm and 2-5pm. The nearest **USIT** office is in Waterford.

Banks: Bank of Ireland, Custom House Quay (tel. 23022). Open Mon. 10am-5pm, Tues.-Fri. 10am-4pm; **ATM. TSB** bank, 73/75 Main St. (tel. 41922). Open Mon.-Wed. and Fri. 9:30am-5pm, Thurs. 9:30am-7pm.

Trains: North Station, Redmond Sq. (tel. 22522), is a 5-min. walk along the quays from Crescent Quay. Booking offices open around departure times. When the office is closed, buy tickets on the train. Someone is on duty to answer questions from 7am until last departure. Trains hustle to Dublin (Mon.-Sat. 3/day; Sun. 2/day; 3hr.; £10) and Rosslare Harbour (Mon.-Sat. 4/day; Sun. 3/day; 30min.; £3).

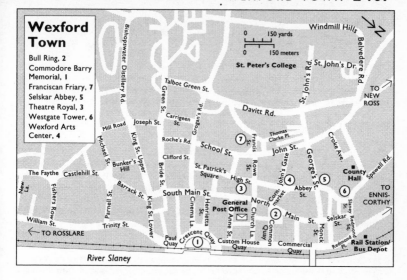

Wexford Town

Bull Ring, **2**
Commodore Barry Memorial, **1**
Franciscan Friary, **7**
Selskar Abbey, **5**
Theatre Royal, **3**
Westgate Tower, **6**
Wexford Arts Center, **4**

Buses: Arrive in and depart from the train station. Buses run to Dublin (daily 5/day; 2½hr.) and to Rosslare Harbour (Mon.-Sat. 7/day, Sun. 5/day; 20min.). Buses to and from Limerick connect with Irish Ferries and Stena-Sealink sailings (daily 2/day). From mid-July to Aug., buses run directly to Galway and other points west.

Taxi: Jim's Cabs, 2 Slaney St. (tel. 47108). 24-hr., £2.50 max. fare within the city.

Bike Rental: Wexford enjoys a glut of bicycle shops. **The Bike Shop,** North Main St. (tel. 22514), £5/day, £3/half-day, £30/week; drop-off points offered at no extra charge; deposit £20, £40 with drop-off. Open Mon.-Sat. 9am-6pm. **Hayes Cycle Shop,** 108 South Main St. (tel. 22462), Raleigh touring bikes £7/day, £30/week; deposit £40. Fishing tackle also available. Open Mon.-Sat. 9am-6pm. **Dave Allen Cycles,** 84 South Main St. (tel. 22516), £6/day, £30/week; deposit £20. Open Mon.-Sat. 9am-6pm.

Laundry: My Beautiful Launderette, St. Peter's Sq. (tel 24317), up Peters St. from South Main St. Get kissy with Daniel Day Lewis, or enjoy TV, videos, and complimentary tea or coffee while you wait. Wash £1.60; 2-min. dryer 50p; soap 30p. Showers, too (£1). Open Mon.-Sat. 10am-9pm. Sundays and holidays, access via video store next door, 3-8pm.

Pharmacy: Seven pharmacies along Main St. rotate Sunday and late hours; all open Mon.-Sat. 9am-1pm and 2-6pm.

Hospital: Wexford General Hospital, New Town Rd. (tel. 42233), on the N25.

Emergency: Dial 999; no coins required. **Garda:** Roches Rd. (tel. 22333).

Post Office: Anne St. (tel. 22587). Open Mon.-Tues. and Thurs.-Sat. 9am-5:30pm, Wed. 9:30am-5:30pm.

Phone Code: 053.

ACCOMMODATIONS

The nearest hostels are about 10 mi. away in Rosslare and Kilmore; staying in a B&B in Wexford Town proper is a more convenient way to see the city. Many B&Bs compete for customers along N25 (Rosslare Rd.), Bayview Drive off the Dublin Rd., or St. John's Rd. off Georges St. Wexford's B&Bs are generally good; if the ones listed are full, ask the proprietors for recommendations.

The Selskar, corner of N. Main and Selskar St. (tel. 23349). Ideal location. Clean rooms, spacious lounge areas with TV. For breakfast, help yourself to cereal, toast, and juice and use the kitchen area to prepare your own food. Free access to washer and dryer. £15/person.

Carraig Donn, Mrs. Daly, New Town Court (tel. 42046), off the New Town (a.k.a. Waterford) Rd. Call from the center of town for Mrs. Daly to pick you up or trek the 15-min. walk from Main St. The ideal grandmother presents large rooms and Brady Bunch decor. Single £15. Double £28. Wheelchair accessible.

Nancy Edwards, 51 St. Ita's Terrace (tel. 24597), on the New Town (Waterford) Rd. Exquisite hospitality. Bright rooms with large beds. Single £13. Double £24.

Ferrybank Caravan and Camping Park (tel. 44378 or 43274). On the eastern edge of town, across from the Dublin Rd. Take the bridge and continue straight to the camping site. Beautiful ocean view, clean area. Swimming pool! £3.50/1-person tent, £5/2-person tent. Showers 75p. Laundry £1.50. Open Easter-Oct.

FOOD

Groceries galore! **L&N Superstore** (tel. 22290), on Custom House Quay, and **Crazy Prices** (tel. 24788), on Crescent Quay, are typical, large supermarkets. **Dunnes Store** (tel. 45688) has a wide selection of meats and sells clothes, too (fondly recall Wal-Mart). (All open Mon.-Wed. 9am-6pm, Thurs.-Fri. 9am-9pm.) **Greenacres,** 56 North Main St. (tel. 24788), contains deli meats, exotic fruit, and a baby-changing facility; a step above the average grocery store.

Tim's Tavern, 51 South Main St. (tel. 23861). Pub grub elevated to *haute cuisine.* Tim's has won national awards for dishes like avocado, pear, and crab (£5.50), crab in garlic butter (£7), and lamb cutlets (£5). Tim's presents similar food (more veggies, more sauces, more expensive) for dinner. Lunch served daily noon-3pm, dinner 6-9:30pm. Traditional music Wed. and Sat. nights at 9:30pm.

La Cuisine, North Main St. (tel. 24986). Bakery and restaurant with a Parisian feel due to racks of delicious baguettes and a chatty, café atmosphere. Makes a mean chicken sandwich (£1.20) and tart apple tarts (£1). Open Mon.-Sat. 9am-6pm.

Michael's Restaurant, N. Main St. (tel. 42196). Even Mikey likes it here (lamb cutlet £4, veggie burger £3.25). Open daily 11am-11pm.

PUBS

The Centenary Stores, Charlotte St. (tel. 24424). "The Stores," a pitch-dark back room of a former warehouse with high ceilings and brick walls, is the popular hangout for twentysomethings. Excellent trad on Sun. morning as well as Tues. and Wed. nights. Blues and folk on Mon. night. Thurs.-Sun a DJ spins dance music 11pm-2am.

O'Faolain's, 11 Monk St. (tel. 23877). The friendliest and liveliest of Wexford's pubs; a crowd of all ages mingles here without generational strife. The place croons trad music on Sun. morning and Mon. night, mixed music on Sun. and Tues. nights, and ballads on Thurs. night.

The Yacht, Monk St. (tel. 22338). Across from O'Faolain's, the happening crowd here enjoys live music nightly. Trad Sun. and Tues. nights, popular songs and classics all other nights.

Mooney's, Commercial Quay (tel. 21128). Lunch served daily noon-2pm. New bar with fieldstone walls and high ceilings. Disco music every night in summer at 11:30pm. Open until 1am Fri. and Sun. nights. Though it's a rich man's world, at Mooney's there's never any cover.

SIGHTS

The historical society runs free **walking tours** on random nights, departing from White's Hotel at 8:15pm; call the hotel (tel. 22311) for scheduled tours. *Welcome to Wexford* (free from the tourist office) details a 45-minute self-guided walking tour. **Westgate Heritage Tower** (tel. 46506) also offers walking tours of Wexford (no regular schedule—call ahead to book a tour, or join a booked group; £2.50/person; 1½-2hr.)

The remains of the Norman **city wall** run the length of High St. to its north. At the intersection of High St. and Westgate St., **Westgate Tower** is the only one of the wall's six original towers that still stands. You can even see the barred and blackened cell that served as a lock-up for renegades. The tower gate now holds the **Westgate Heritage Centre** (tel. 46506). The audio-visual show dramatically recounts the history of Wexford. The fire and cannon special effects will blow your mind. (Open April-Dec. Mon.-Sat. 9am-5pm, last admission 4:30pm, also June-Sept. Sun. 2-6pm; admission £1.50, students £1.) Next door, the **Selskar Abbey,** site of King Henry II's extended penance, now acts as a windowbox for lush wildflowers. The dark and frightening tower stairwell leads up to a precarious view of the town and the bay. (Enter through the tall, narrow wicket gate next to the center; open same hours as the center.)

The northern half of the city is studded with ancient buildings and monuments; southern Wexford Town, built on recent landfill, will have to wait a few years to be deemed historic. Separating North and South Main Streets, an open area marks the **Bull Ring.** Bullfights were inaugurated in 1621 by the town's butcher guild as a promotional device. The mayor got the hide while the poor got the meat. "The Pikeman," a statue of a stalwart peasant fearlessly brandishing a sharp instrument, commemorates the 1798 uprising (see **The Protestant Ascendancy,** p. 60). **Crescent Quay** held ship repair yards until the early 1900s. The statue facing the sea is Commodore John Barry, Wexford-born founder of the U.S. Navy. The bottom of the quay is reputed to be cobblestoned, though nobody has gone down to check. **The Friary Church** in the Franciscan Friary, School St., houses the "Little Saint." This creepy effigy of young St. Adjutor shows the wounds inflicted by the martyr's Roman father. Franciscan monks have lived in town since 1240—keep a lookout for peaceful fellows in brown robes.

ENTERTAINMENT

The Wexford People (85p) lists events for all of Co. Wexford; the events section comes after "Farm Scene." The very active **Wexford Arts Centre,** in the Cornmarket (tel. 23764 or 24544), presents free visual arts and crafts exhibitions; evening performances of music, dance, and drama also take place in the center throughout the year. "Open mike" night, June through August on Wednesdays at 9pm, features poetry readings and songs (admission £2; box office open Mon.-Sat. 10am-6pm). Crouched backstage in an inconspicuous building on High St., the **Theatre Royal** produces performances throughout the year, specializing in the acclaimed **Wexford Festival Opera** during the last two weeks in October. For these festivities, three obscure but deserving operas are rescued from the artistic attic and performed in an intimate setting. For info on the opera festival or regular performances, contact the Theatre Royal, High St. (Tel. 22400; box office tel. 22144. Open Mon.-Fri. 11am-5pm. Opera tickets £36-48, available from early June; afternoon, late-night, and lunchtime concerts and operatic scenes £5-10.)

■ Near Wexford Town

The surrounding attractions are spread-out, so unless you have a car you might want to bike it. Otherwise, **Whitty's Cabin minibus service** (tel. 22221), on Trimmer's Lane West, runs buses from the tourist office to: the Irish National Heritage Park (departs Mon.-Sat. 10am and 1:30pm, Sun. noon and 2pm; £6 return); Johnstown Castle Gardens (departs Mon.-Sat. 11am, Sun. 2:30pm; £6 return); and both (departs Mon.-Sat. 11am, Sun. noon; £10 return).

The **Irish National Heritage Park** (tel. (053) 41733), in **Ferrycarrig,** is 3 mi. north of Wexford off N11. In the interests of education, the park regales visitors with 9000 years of replicated Irish culture, from the Stone Age to the arrival of the Normans. The park-like site features a 20-minute film and full-scale replicas of: a dolmen (Stone-Age tomb), stone circles (Copper-Age planetariums), a cist burial, an *ogham* stone, a Viking ship, typical Irish homesteads, places of worship, and a Norman round tower. With everything so nicely packaged, who needs Ireland? The exhibits are even outside, so that you can experience the Irish rain (open March-Nov. daily 10am-7pm, last admission 5pm; admission £3.50, students £3).

The **North and South Slobs** are messy, but in a delightful way: "slob" is the term for the cultivated mudflats to the north and south of Wexford Harbour that are protected from flooding rivers by dikes. The Slobs are internationally famous for the rare geese who winter there at the **Wexford Wildfowl Reserve** (tel. 23129). Ten-thousand of Greenland's white-fronted geese (one-third of the world population) descend on the Slobs from October to April, cohabiting with other rare geese, some from as far as Siberia and Iceland. Summer is a more mellow time for the Slobs, as most of its residents then are ordinary Irish birds. Excitement derives from the herons and grebes mating along the channels and streams. The **Reserve Centre** will help visitors spot specific species (open mid-April to Sept. daily 9am-6pm, Oct.-April 10am-5pm; free). The Reserve is on the North Slob, 2 mi. north of Wexford town. Take the Castlebridge/Gorey Rd. to well-signposted Ardcavan Lane.

■ Enniscorthy

Fourteen miles north of Wexford Town, the welcoming hilltop town of Enniscorthy perches above the River Slaney. The town is exceptionally conscious of its Republican history: in 1798, rebels led by a local priest held the British at bay for 12 days before suffering defeat at nearby Vinegar Hill. Enniscorthy was one of the only towns to join Dublin's 1916 Easter Rising—and the last to surrender. During the Irish Civil War that followed, Irishmen fought each other on Enniscorthy's streets. Today, Enniscorthy sprawls across the river. Its comelier west side incorporates a cluster of historic buildings, including a 13th-century Norman castle with an eclectic museum inside. This introduction into the political conflicts of Ireland's past may be a sobering experience—but the 20 or so pubs within walking distance ensure that it doesn't need to be.

Practical Information The town **tourist office** (tel. 34699) is in the castle off Castle Hill Rd (Directions? It's the big gray castle. Open mid-June to mid-Sept. Mon.-Sat. 10am-6pm, Sun. 2-5:30pm). **AIB** Bank (tel. 33184) dispenses cash (**ATM**; open Mon.-Wed. and Fri. 9:30am-4pm, Thurs. 9:30am-5pm). **Trains** running between Dublin and Rosslare stop in Enniscorthy (Mon.-Sat. 3/day, Sun. 2/day; to Dublin 2hr., £7.50; to Rosslare Harbour 50min., £4.50). The railway station is across the river from the main shopping area. Take your first left after the bridge on Slaney Drive. **Buses** leave from the Bus Stop Shop on Templeshannon Quay, opposite the castle, running south through Wexford and north through Ferns (10min. from Enniscorthy). N11 motorway passes straight through Enniscorthy, heading north to Arklow, Wicklow, and Dublin, and south to Wexford. The **post office,** Abbey Quay (tel. 33545), is off Mill Pack Rd. The **phone code** is a Grand Old 054.

Accommodations, Food, & Pubs From Market Sq., take the first right on Main St., then left onto Bohreen Hill to find Mrs. Ann Carroll's **Don Carr House,** Bohreen Hill (tel. 33458). Don Carr comes equipped with two sumptuous sunrooms, high ceilings, and bouncy beds (£13/person, w/bath £15). At **Aldemar,** Summerhill (tel. 33668), Mrs. Agnes Barry's hospitality and pleasant company justify the 10-minute walk from Main St. (£13/person; open June-Sept.). The award for best location goes to **Murphy's** (tel. 33522) on Main St. Walking up the hill toward town, Murphy's is on your left, just past Market Square. The rooms are clean but small (£13/person, w/bath £15). The nearest hostels are in New Ross and Courtown; the latter makes a good stopover for the Dublin-bound. The **Anchorage Hostel,** Poulshone, Courtown Harbour (tel. (055) 25335), is a former B&B with great beaches nearby (£7/person, double £12; open May-Oct.).

Food eagerly awaits you on the shelves at the **L&N Supermarket** (tel. 34541) in the shopping center on Mill Park Rd., off Abbey Sq. (open Mon.-Wed. and Sat. 9am-6pm; Thurs.-Fri. 9am-9pm), or at the various pubs. Vegetarians or those seeking home-baked goodies should try **The Baked Potato,** 18 Ratter (tel. 34085), where food is hot and inexpensive (vegetarian lasagna, £3; open Mon-Sun. 9am-6pm).

Killeen's, Slaney St. (tel. 35935), dishes up roast chicken, potatoes, and vegetables for £4. They also have trad sessions on Saturday nights. Twice-awarded "pub of the year," **The Antique Tavern** (tel. 33428) features artifacts from the depths of Enniscorthy's Republican past. No need to fear that they're still in use; no weaponry is allowed. The sign out front explicitly forbids "three card tricksters" and bandits: you know who you are. You can mix with locals at **Murphy's** pub, where not even newcomers are exempt from the good-natured slagging.

Sights The **Walking Tour of Enniscorthy** (tel. 36800) reveals the town's dirty little secrets with a provocative blend of drama and civic pride. Contact Maura Flannery at the **Castle Craft Shop,** across from the castle on Castle Hill Rd. (tel. 36800; fax 36130). Tours, in English, French, or Spanish, leave from the craft shop at noon or 2pm (£2, students £1.50, under 18 £1). The castle itself houses the tourist office, but the **Wexford County Museum** (tel. 35926) constitutes the bulk of the building. The museum chronicles Co. Wexford's collective stream of consciousness rather than any historical narrative. Starting with 13 items in 1960, the curators stuffed the castle from eaves to dungeon with such odd bits as ship figureheads and a collection of the world's police patches. The exhibits feature the original letters and belongings of the principle players of the 1798 and 1916 risings. (Open June-Sept. Mon.-Sat. 10am-1pm and 2-6pm, Sun. 2-5:30pm; Oct.-Nov. and Feb.-May daily 2-5:30pm; Dec.-Jan. Sun. 2-5pm. Admission £2, ages 13-18 £1, children 50p.)

　　St. Aiden's Cathedral, Cathedral St. (continue down Main St.), was built in 1860 under the close personal supervision of architect Augustus Pugin, who littered Ireland's towns with his neo-Gothic creations. During renovations in 1994, Catholic masses were celebrated at the Protestant church down the road, an agreeably ecumenical gesture in a town with a history punctuated by sectarian violence. In Market Square, a statue commemorates Father Murphy who, in 1798, led the town in rebellion. The priest had been something of a Loyalist before an angry mob threatened to burn down his church. He was instantly affected with revolutionary zeal and promptly put himself at the head of the rowdy crowd.

　　Starting on the last weekend in June, eight days of festival and fructose redden Enniscorthy's streets during its annual **Strawberry Fair.** Sports events and a Strawberry Queen are featured. Pub theater performances draw the literati and "Lego Competitions" attract the child in each fair-goer. After all, strawberries, like pints of Guinness, are good for you. The **Blues Festival** in mid-September features

Why Can't We All Just Get Along?

Even though the Anglo-Irish Treaty created deep divisions between pro-Treaty and anti-Treaty nationalists, the extent to which animosity between the two groups existed on the local level is often exaggerated. During the Irish Civil War, a group of Free-Staters (anti-Treaty) captured supporters of the treaty and held them in Enniscorthy Castle. They promised to treat the prisoners kindly if the latter would hand in their weapons and promise never to arm themselves against Free-Staters again. The captors were so impressed with how quickly the prisoners agreed that they let them go. To ensure there were no hard feelings, the Free-Staters treated their former captives to sandwiches and beer at a nearby pub. But Captain Gallagher, the leader of the pro-Treaty forces, heard the story and became enraged at the mockery it made of his cause. He promptly brought more troops to Enniscorthy, forcing the anti-Treaty soldiers to surrender. Another example of nationalist sympathy with their supposed enemies occurred in August of 1922. The IRA seized and occupied St. Ann's, the Protestant church in Enniscorthy. Ever-mindful of all things holy, however, the nationalists vacated the church at scheduled mass times so that the Protestants' religious observances would not be interrupted. The IRA soldiers promptly resumed control of the church after mass ended.

three days of entertainment by locally and internationally renowned musicians. Contact Maura Flannery (tel. 36800) for information.

■ Near Enniscorthy: Ferns

If you don't love the view from the top of **Ferns Castle,** you're in the wrong country, Mack. Green fields dotted with small houses and farms expand for miles. **Ferns,** a tiny village 8 mi. north of Enniscorthy on N11, was once capital of Ireland. The castle, whose profile smiles at you as you enter town, was once a large rectangle with cylindrical towers at the corners; only 1½ towers now remain. The stronghold was built in the 13th century by William Marshall, Strongbow's son-in-law, who locked up his daughter in the cellar to prevent her elopement. (Site always open. Free. To climb around in the tower, get the key from the cool cat of a caretaker, Jim Gettings, 36 Castle View, 100m to the right of the castle.) **Bus Éireann** runs from Enniscorthy, stopping at the bend in Main St. (4/day; 10min.; £2.90).

Down Main St., two sets of ruins skulk in the backyard of the Cathedral of St. Aiden (not to be confused with St. Aiden's Monastery of Adoration, a depressingly modern structure built in 1989). In the graveyard are three **high crosses,** as well as a granite stump which is said to mark the grave of Dermot MacMurrough, King of Leinster. The Romanesque archways of **Ferns Cathedral,** also in the cemetery, actually date from the 10th century. After burning down the original 13th-century building in a fit of pique in 1575, the O'Byrne clan was ordered to rebuild the Cathedral, and their crude reconstruction is what remains today. In a grassy field behind the churchyard are the ruins of **St. Mary's Abbey,** founded by Dermot MacMurrough in 1158 in order to save his much-blemished soul. The abbey helped save his skin as well when he took refuge here in 1167 while awaiting the arrival of his Norman ally, Strongbow. The Abbey's original charter entitled it to a portion of all the beer brewed in Ferns—ballast for the body and the soul—but the good times ground to a halt when Henry VIII shut down the monasteries in 1539. Farther up the Gorey Rd. lie more remains: the 16th-century **St. Peter's Church** and **St. Mogue's Well,** founded in 607 by St. Moling as a real wishing well (all sites always open and free).

■ New Ross

The old center of the city, rising steeply from the shores of the River Barrow, still preserves a faint medieval flavor. The city's more recent past—for a time in the 19th century, New Ross joined forces with Waterford to handle over half of Ireland's shipping—are only slightly more in evidence. Today, New Ross seeks post-industrial happiness in its own small way. Quay St./Mary St. rises up from the bridge; North St., the main drag, becomes South St. as it crosses Mary St.

The New Ross **tourist office,** in the JFK Centre (tel. 421857), overlooks the river traffic from North Quay St. (open Oct.-May Mon.-Fri. 9am-5pm; July-Sept. Mon.-Fri. 9am-8pm; Sat. 10am-8pm, Sun. noon-6pm). **TSB** bank (tel. 422060) is at 17 South St. (open Mon.-Wed. and Fri. 9:30am-5pm, Thurs. 9:30am-7pm). Or exchange money at **A. McDonald's,** Mary St. (open Mon.-Sat. 7:30am-10pm, Sun. 8:30am-10pm). **Bus Éireann** runs from Ryan's on the Quay to: Dublin (Mon.-Sat. 3/day, Sun. 2/day; 3hr.; £8); Rosslare Harbour (3/day; 1hr.; £7); and Waterford (Mon.-Sat. 7/day, Sun. 5/day; 35min.; £3). Wexford and Waterford are the closest places to rent bikes. New Ross is on the N25 (Wexford/Cork Rd.) and the N30 (Enniscorthy/Waterford Rd.). Hitchers can find plenty of rides on either, most in the morning or late afternoon. You can travel in Barrow style on **The Galley** (tel. 421723), which runs daily restaurant cruises from New Ross to Waterford. Eat lunch (April-Oct. at 12:30pm; 2hr.; £11, £5 for cruise only), tea (June-Aug. at 3pm; 2hr.; £5, £4 for cruise only), or dinner (April-Sept. at 7pm; 2-3hr.; £20, £9 for cruise only). The **post office** delivers on Charles St., off the Quay (tel. 421261; open Mon.-Fri. 9am-5:30pm). New Ross's **phone code** asks what you can do for your country at 051.

Accommodations **Mac Murrough Farm Hostel** (tel. 421383) is an idyllic reason to be in (well, near) New Ross. Follow Mary St. uphill to the Abbey and turn left, then take the first right, continuing through the square with a cross in the middle. Take a left at the supermarket, then a right at the Statoil Station; from there, follow the signs for 2 mi. to the hostel. Call if you need to be picked up. The sheep give a rowdy greeting (£6/night; sheets 50p). **Riversdale House,** William St. (tel. 422515), provides comfort and convenience for those who choose to stay in town. Follow South St. all the way to William St., then turn left up the hill. Friendly owners take pride in their commanding view of town (£16/person, single £21, all w/bath).

Food & Pubs **The Sweeney,** Mary St. (tel. 421963), is a cozy deli with a room full of palm trees and a menu full of sandwiches (£1.25), soup and bread (£1.65), and omelettes (£3; open Mon.-Tues. and Thurs.-Sat. 9am-6pm and 6:30-9:30pm, Wed. 9am-2pm and 6:30-9:30pm, Sun. noon-8pm). **M&J Restaurant,** South St. (tel. 421833), serves coffee shop fare (cheese sandwich 80p, full breakfast £3, omelette £2.50; open Mon.-Fri. 8:30am-9pm). **Hanrahan's,** North St. (tel. 421526), is a dark, sports-oriented pub with memorabilia from GAA hurling matches on the wall. The pub is one of the several local businesses bearing this name; in 1690, King James II stayed a night in Hanrahan's Inn while fleeing William of Orange.

Sights New Ross isn't much of a city for museums; most of its historical sights are still being used for practical purposes. The site of the **Tholsel,** South St., originally held a Norse tollbooth (*thol-sel,* "toll stall"). The original structure collapsed in the mid-1700s; the current Tholsel, now the town hall, was built in 1749. Strongbow's grandson founded **St. Mary's Church,** off Mary St., in the 13th century. Even if you don't go in, at least hang out with the crows in the eerily beautiful graveyard. Get the key from Mrs. Culleton, 6 Church St., four doors down from the church. She'll also give you a booklet detailing the significance of the stone structures inside. JFK memorabilia philanders in the tourist office lobby in the **John F. Kennedy Centre,** North Quay. See pictures of Jack being adored by throngs of Wexfordians during his 1963 visit, old parish registers containing the magic name, and a copy of the young JFK's Harvard yearbook entry. (Office open Mon.-Fri. 9am-5pm.) Four miles from New Ross on the N30 (Enniscorthy Rd.), the **Berkeley Costume and Toy Museum,** Berkeley Forest, houses a private collection of English rocking horses, Irish dresses, and 18th-century French and German dolls. (Open May-Sept.; tours 11:30am, 3, and 5:30pm; admission £3, children £1.)

Irish-Americans and Irish locals wanted to further honor the memory of JFK and decided to say it with flowers. They found 4500 different ways, which are displayed in a 400-acre thesaurus of flora, **The John F. Kennedy Arboretum,** 7 mi. south of New Ross on the Ballyhack Rd. (tel. 388171). The park packs preposterous proportions of trees and shrubs (all labeled) and 500 different rhododendrons, all dedicated to the memory of Ireland's favorite U.S. president. A small café doubles as a gift shop and a playground entertains children bored by flowers. (Open May-Aug. daily 10am-8pm, April and Sept. 10am-6:30pm, Oct.-March 10am-5pm. Last admission 45min. before closing. Admission £2, students £1, family £5. Tours £1.50/person.)

■ Waterford City

In 1003 AD, Vikings built Reginald's Tower to defend their longships in *Vadrafjord;* today, the tower overlooks the massive freighters which ply their trades in Waterford's busy harbor. The tower is a perfect symbol for the town, whose ideal position next to one of Ireland's natural ports has made it a military and commercial center for a millennium. Over the years, Waterford, so important to the nation militarily and economically, has endured sieges by Strongbow and Cromwell. Hardy Waterford (pop. 45,000) has lived long and prospered, becoming the center for nightlife and shopping in the southeast while preserving traces of its rich, strife-filled history.

ORIENTATION & PRACTICAL INFORMATION

Waterford shows a mix of narrow, Viking streets and broad English thoroughfares. You can navigate them with **city buses**, which leave from the Clock Tower on the Quay and cost a flat fare of 75p for trips within the city. City bus timetables await at the Bus Éireann office (in the tourist office) or at Plunkett Station.

Tourist Office: 41 Merchant's Quay (tel. 875788). The office is behind a green facade between Hanover St. and Gladstone St. Ask for a map of Waterford and the free, ad-packed *Ireland's South East* guide. *The Waterford Guide* (£1.50) has good county-wide info. Open July-Aug. Mon-Sat. 9am-6pm, Sun. 10am-1pm and 2-5pm; June and Sept. Mon.-Sat. 8am-6pm; Oct.-Feb. Mon-Fri. 9am-1pm and 2-5:15pm; March-April Mon.-Sat. 9am-1pm and 2-6pm.

Budget Travel: USIT, 36-37 Georges St. (tel. 872601; fax 871723). Near the corner with Gladstone St., 1 block east of Barronstrand St. As knowledgeable as the Dublin USIT office. ISIC cards, Travelsave stamps, student fares to London. Deals in daily flights from Waterford to London and in a bus/ferry package to London (see **Getting There,** p.26). Open Mon.-Fri. 9:30am-5:30pm, Sat. 11am-4pm.

Banks: Bank of Ireland, Merchants Quay (tel. 872074); **ATM.** Open Mon. 10am-5pm, Tues.-Fri. 10am-4pm. **TSB,** O'Connell St. (tel. 872988). Open Mon.-Wed. and Fri. 9:30am-5:30pm, Thurs. 9:30am-7pm.

Airport: (tel. 875589). Served by British Airways and Suckling Airlines. Follow The Quay, turn right at Reginald's Tower, then left at the sign. It's 20min. from town.

Trains: JFK's ancestors grew up in Waterford, and the city is still well-connected. Buses and trains leave from **Plunkett Station,** on the other side of the bridge from The Quay (for train info call: Mon.-Fri. 9am-5pm tel. 873401; after hours Mon.-Fri. tel. 873402; Sat. 9am-6pm tel. 873403; 24-hr. recorded timetable tel. 876243). Train station staffed Mon.-Sat. 9am-6pm, Sun. at departure times. Trains chug to: Limerick (Mon.-Sat. 2/day; 2¼hr.; £10); Kilkenny (Mon.-Sat. 4/day; 40min.; £5); Dublin (Mon.-Sat. 4/day, Sun. 3/day; 2½hr.; £11); and Rosslare Harbour (Mon.-Sat. 3/day; 1hr.; £7.50).

Buses: (Bus info tel. 879000). Office open Mon.-Sat. 9am-5:30pm, Sun. 2-5:30pm. Buses from Plunkett Station drive to: Dublin (Mon.-Sat. 8/day, Sun. 6/day; 3½hr.; £6); Kilkenny (1/day; 1hr.; £4.70); Limerick (4/day; 2½hr.; £6); Cork (Mon.-Sat. 7/day, Sun. 5/day; 2½hr.; £9.70); Galway (Mon.-Sat. 4/day, Sun. 3/day; 4¾hr.; £13); and Rosslare Harbour (3/day; 1¼hr.; £7.50).

Hitching: Hitchers place themselves on the main routes, away from the tangled city center. To reach the N24 (Cahir, Limerick), N10 (Kilkenny, Dublin), or N25 (New Ross, Wexford, Rosslare), they head over the bridge toward the train station. For the N25 (Cork), they continue down Parnell St.; others take a city bus out to the Waterford Crystal Factory before they stick out a thumb.

Bike Rental: Wright's Cycle Depot, Henrietta St. (tel. 874411; fax 873440). £7/day, £30/week; deposit £40. Open Mon.-Thurs. and Sat. 9:30am-1pm and 2-6pm, Fri. 9:30am-1pm and 2-9pm.

Luggage Storage: in Plunkett Station. £1/item. Open Mon.-Sat. 7:15am-9pm.

Laundry: Rainbow Laundrette, Thomas St. (tel. 855656). Serviced wash and dry (no self-service) £5.50, £7.50 for two loads. Open Mon.-Fri. 8:45am-6pm, Sat. 9am-5:30pm.

Crisis Lines: Samaritans, 13 Beau St. (tel. 872114). 24-hr. hotline. **Rape Crisis Centre** (tel. 873362). Mon. 10am-noon, Tues.-Wed. and Fri. 10am-noon and 2-4pm, Thurs. 10am-noon, 2-4pm, and 8:30-10pm.

Youth Information Centre: 130 The Quay (tel. 877328). Has information on work, travel, health, and a variety of support groups; they also provide information on gay and lesbian support groups. Photocopy and fax service. Open to all. Open Mon.-Fri. 9:30am-5:30pm.

Hospital: Ardkeen Hospital (tel. 873321). Follow The Quay to the Tower Hotel; turn left, then follow signs straight ahead to the hospital.

Emergency: Dial 999; no coins required. **Garda:** Patrick St. (tel. 874888).

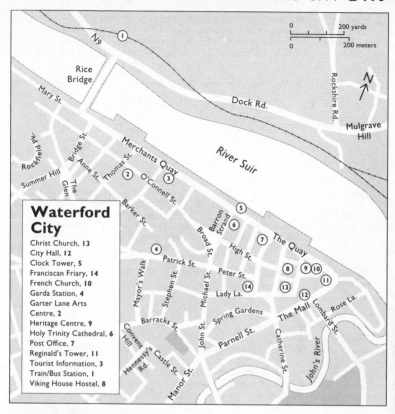

Waterford City

Christ Church, 13
City Hall, 12
Clock Tower, 5
Franciscan Friary, 14
French Church, 10
Garda Station, 4
Garter Lane Arts Centre, 2
Heritage Centre, 9
Holy Trinity Cathedral, 6
Post Office, 7
Reginald's Tower, 11
Tourist Information, 3
Train/Bus Station, 1
Viking House Hostel, 8

ACCOMMODATIONS

We recommend only two hostels in Waterford. If they are full, stay in a B&B or in a hostel in Tramore or Arthurstown. Most B&Bs in the city are unimpressive; those on the Cork Rd. are a better option.

Viking House Hostel (IHH), Coffee House Ln. (tel. 853827; fax 871730). Follow The Quay east past the Clock Tower and 1block past the post office; the hostel is on the right, behind another building. A luxurious hostel in the heart of Waterford, with excellent facilities, good showers, and a large, beautiful lounge. Slightly mushy beds are the only flaw. The friendly and well-informed staff have published guides (10p) on area pubs. Free luggage storage and lockers. Kitchen 10am-10pm. June-Sept. 14-bed dorm £8. 4- to 6-bed room £11. Double £30. Add £1 for room w/ bath and £2 for TV. Prices £1 less March-May and £2 less Oct.-Feb. All w/continental breakfast (cereal not included in dorm rate). Free sheets.

Waterford Hostel, John St. (tel. 850163). Not as big or as nice as Viking House, but clean and comfortable. Kitchen and TV lounge open until midnight. Location next to the city's most popular pubs means you won't have a long stumble home. No curfew. 4- to 6-bed room £7 w/continental breakfast.

Mrs. J. Ryder, Mayor's Walk House, 12 Mayor's Walk (tel. 855427). With a smile that defines "winsome," Mrs. Ryder (and her perennial guests) welcome *Let's Go* readers with advice, biscuits, and an endless pot of tea. Generous, flowery rooms. A 15-min. walk from the train station. Single £13. Double £25. Open March-Nov.

Derrynane House, 19 The Mall (tel. 875179). Winding halls lead to plain, comfortable rooms with good, firm beds and a curious link to Montana. £15/person.

Beechwood, Mrs. M. Ryan, 7 Cathedral Sq. (tel. 876677). Elegant, silky rooms look out on pedestrian street and cathedral. Single £15. Double £26.

Corlea House, New St. (tel. 875764), off Michael St. Small, cozy rooms, each with TV, are topped off by the owner's friendly manner. Single £14. Double £26.

FOOD

Be sure to sample Waterford's contribution to classy cuisine, the *blaa*. Pronounced "blah," this is a floury white roll of Huguenot origins. Besides the *blaa*, Waterford gave the world the modern process of bacon curing. Thank you, Waterford! For cheap groceries, visit **Roches Stores** in the City Square Mall (open Mon.-Wed. and Sat. 9am-6pm, Thurs.-Fri. 9am-9pm). **Treacy's,** The Quay (tel. 873059), has a very large selection for a late-night grocery (even a small deli; open daily 9:30am-11pm). **The Late, Late Shop** (tel. 855376; fax 853223), farther up The Quay, gives you an extra hour to shop but a smaller selection (open daily 7:30am-midnight).

Haricot's Wholefood Restaurant, 11 O'Connell St. The vegetarian and the meat-eater live in harmony with Haricot's tasty, innovative dishes as peacemakers. Seafood pancakes £4.70. Open Mon.-Fri. 10am-8pm, Sat. 10am-5:45pm.

Chapman's Pantry, 61 the Quay (tel. 873833). A combination of a gourmet food-store, bakery, and delicatessen-style restaurant. *Blaas* 13p, meals £2.50-5.50. Open Mon.-Sat. 9am-6pm.

Sizzlers Restaurant, the Quay. This diner serves through the wee hours—here's where you'll find the crowd after the pubs and discos close. Full Irish breakfast £3, burger and chips £3.50. Open Sun.-Wed. 7am-2am, Thurs.-Sat. 24hr.

Gino's, John St. (tel. 879513), at the Apple Market. Busy family restaurant serves pizza made right before your eyes. Reservations recommended on Fri. and Sat. nights. Small pizza (for 1) £2.25 plus 50p/topping. Open daily noon-midnight.

The Reginald, The Mall (tel. 855087). Right behind Reginald's Tower, this bar/restaurant serves rich, delicious food in a classy environment. Dinner is expensive, but lunch is reasonable. Lunch special £5, vegetarian specials £6.45. Lunch daily noon-3pm, dinner 5:30-10:30pm.

Crumbs, Michael St. (tel. 854323). Good food served quickly in a coffee-shop atmosphere. Soup with brown bread £1.20. Open Mon.-Sat. 9am-6pm.

PUBS

The Quays are loaded with pubs, and there are even more as you travel up Broad St. into town. Consult the pub guides at Viking House for more information.

Geoff's Pub, 9 John St. (tel. 874787). The best pub in Waterford in nearly everyone's opinion. Favored by Waterford's budding artists and the slick theater crowd. Wonder at a dark, smoky setting where cappuccino and Camus almost edge out Guinness and *craic.*

T&H Doolan's, George's St. (tel. 841504). Live trad or contemporary music nightly attracts many of Waterford's visitors: Newfies, Taffies, Aussies, and Yanks hang out here in harmony.

The Pulpit, John St. (tel 879184). A hip, young, and charismatic crowd is drawn by the upstairs nightclub, **Preachers.** Open Wed.-Sun. 10:30pm. Cover £3-5.

Mullane's, 15 Newgate St. (tel. 873854), off New St., is famous for its hard-core trad sessions. A sprinkling of the young and a dash of tourists added to the older regular crowd results in the perfect mix. Sessions Tues., Thurs., Sat., and Sun. nights at 10pm—no cover. The pub is all but empty when there isn't a session.

The Wine Vault, High St. (tel. 853444; fax 853494). Drink wine in a classy bistro even after the pubs close. Well-stocked 200-year-old wine cellar downstairs. Over 200 wines available. Jazz and blues sessions on Sat. nights; a glass of house red starts at £1.90. Open Mon.-Wed. until midnight, Thurs.-Sun. until 12:30am.

Muldoon's, John St. (tel. 873693). The late bar is open Thurs.-Sun. 10pm-2am with never any cover. Pizza served until closing (£1.50/slice, whole pizza £3-6).

It's a Delicate Matter

The glass-making process at the Waterford Crystal Factory begins when raw ingredients are fed into pots kept at 1400°F. **Blowers** then huff and puff into a long tube with a globule of molten glass at its end, rotating the tube to create the shape of a vase or a fruit dish. **Cutters** have the design patterns memorized, and cut two-thirds deep into the emerging crystal. Both blowers and cutters apprentice for five years before qualifying for work. **Engravers** have it even tougher—the apprenticeship is ten years. Video game junkies will be excited to learn that good hand-eye coordination is a crucial qualification for potential glass-workers.

SIGHTS

You can cover all of Waterford's sights in a day, but only if you move quickly. The **Waterford Crystal Factory** (tel. 873311), 1 mi. out on N25 (Cork Rd.), is the city's highlight. Forty-minute tours allow you to witness the transformation of molten glass into polished crystal. Many of the people taking the tour intend to buy something sparkly and expensive at its end; don't feel bad if you don't. Admire the finished products—and their outrageous prices—in the gallery. The least expensive item is a crystal heart (£16). (Tours and audio-visual shows every 10min. April-Oct. daily 8:30am-4pm, showroom open 8:30am-6pm; Nov.-March daily 9am-last tour at 3:15pm, showroom open 9am-5pm. Admission £3.50, students £1.75.) Tours are wheelchair accessible. Book ahead via telephone or through the tourist office. Self-guided tour in summer months. City bus route #1 (Kilbarry/Ballybeg) leaves across from the Clock Tower every 30 minutes and passes the factory (75p).

Much of Waterford's history has unfortunately been converted into retail space. Because the city hasn't expanded outward since 1790, Viking, Victorian, and modern structures are piled on top of each other. **Walking Tours of Historic Waterford** (tel. 873711) commence from the Granville Hotel on the Quay (March-Oct. daily at noon and 2pm; £3). The entertaining, one-hour tours are a worthwhile way to get an understanding of Waterford's complex, tortuous history. They also give 25% off admission to Reginald's Tower and the Heritage Centre.

Reginald's Tower, at the end of The Quay (tel. 873501), has guarded the entrance to the city since the 12th century. Its 12-ft. thick Viking walls were almost impossible for invaders to penetrate. Climb the stone spiral staircase for bits of local history and old maps of Waterford, as well as a view of the city. The tower has housed a prison, a mint, and the wedding reception of Strongbow and Aoife. Nearby, a wealth of Viking artifacts snatched from the jaws of bulldozers is now on display at the tiny **Waterford Heritage Centre,** Greyfriars St., off The Quay (tel. 871227). A cross-section of an archaeological dig reveals the course of the town's history, from the floor of a Viking house to Norman-era rubbish to Michael Jackson-era Pepsi cans. (Open March-June and Sept.-Oct. Mon.-Fri. 10am-5pm, Sat. 10am-1pm; July-Aug. Mon-Fri. 8:30am-8:30pm, Sat.-Sun. 8:30am-5pm. Admission £1.50, students £1, children 50p, 25% off with walking tour ticket.)

After your visit to the Heritage Centre, ask at the reception for the key to the ruins and wide-open tombs of the **French Church,** a Dominican monastery built in 1240 AD, at the corner of Bailey's New St. and Greyfriars St. The monastery was given to Huguenot refugees in the 17th century. Many of Waterford's more recent monumental edifices were the brainchildren of 18th century architect John Roberts. The **Theatre Royal** and **City Hall,** both on The Mall, are his secular masterpieces. He designed both the Roman Catholic **Holy Trinity Cathedral** on Barronstrand St. and the Church of Ireland **Christ Church Cathedral** in Cathedral Square (up Henrietta St. from the Quay), thereby making Waterford the only Irish town to have both faiths united by a common architect. Christ Church Cathedral has the rather unique tomb of Bishop Tunes Rice, which shows vermin chewing on his decaying corpse: a gruesome posthumous sermon on the ephemeral nature of human life. Other highlights include a 2000-year-old sword from the Bronze Age, and a 1681 version of the New Testament written in Irish. Scattered throughout town are remnants of the town's medieval **city walls;** the biggest blocks are behind the Theatre Royal on Spring Garden St. and on Patrick St., extending to Bachelor's Walk.

ENTERTAINMENT

The Munster Express (80p), a local newspaper, has entertainment listings. **The Roxy,** O'Connell St. (tel. 855145), is Waterford's hottest nightclub; it also hosts live, occasionally major, acts. The pub downstairs is unremarkable, since the real action begins after pubs close. (Club open Wed.-Sun. 10pm-2am. 70s and 80s rock Thurs. and Sun., acid/house Sat., live bands Fri. Cover £2-5, free if you arrive before 10:30pm on Wed., Sat., or Sun.) **Metroland,** the nightclub at **The Metropole,** Mary St. (tel. 78185), is a giant dance hall. Important gigs are well advertised around town. Speaking of important, **Boyzone** (an Irish NKOTB) played here to kick off their debut single. Hang tough, Boyzone! Check in pubs for more music options.

The **Waterford Show** at City Hall (tel. 358397 or 875788) is an entertaining performance of Irish music, story, song, and dance in a historical setting (Thurs., Sat., and Sun. at 9pm; admission £6; call for reservations). The **Garter Lane Arts Centre,** Garter Lane 2, 22a O'Connell St. (tel. 877153), stages dance, music, and theater in an old Georgian building. In July and August, the Summer Arts and Crafts Fair fills the exhibition space, displaying handmade objects for sale. Down the street at Garter Lane 1, 5 O'Connell St., **screen/space** (tel. 857198) strikes a lowercase balance between art and capitalism. The result is a mix of smart second-run movies and cheap tickets. Information about Waterford's theater scene is available here. (Double features Wed.-Thurs. at 8pm. You must buy a membership in order to buy a ticket: yearly memberships are £2, tickets £1.50.)

■ Waterford Harbour

East of Waterford City, Waterford Harbour straddles the Waterford/Wexford county line. It is here that Oliver "the Snake" Cromwell coined the phrase "by hook or by crook," referring to his plan to take Waterford City by landing either at Hook Head or on the opposite side of the harbor, at Crooke. (Neither plan worked very well—Waterford held out for a very long time and escaped the Cromwellian destruction visited on places like Cork and Limerick.) Both sides of the harbor are host to historic ruins, friendly fishing villages, and gorgeous ocean views. Think of the scenic harbor as A-shaped: on the left slope of the A is popular beach destination Dunmore East while on the right slope is thin Hook Head. The crossbar represents the **Passage East Car Ferry** (tel. (051) 382488 or 382480), which carries coastal explorers between Passage East (6mi. from Waterford City on the west side of the harbor) and Ballyhack on the east side, circumventing a 37-mi. land route between them. From the Quay in Waterford, it's a swell bike ride to Passage East—turn left at the Tower Hotel and follow signs for Passage East and Dunmore East. From Wexford, follow signs for Ballyhack to reach the ferry. (Continuous sailings April-Sept. Mon.-Sat. 7:20am-10pm, Sun. 9:30am-10pm; Oct.-March Mon.-Sat. 7:20am-8pm, Sun. 9:30am-8pm. Pedestrians 80p, £1 return; cyclists £1.50, £2 return.)

DUNMORE EAST

Across Waterford Harbour from the Hook is **Dunmore East,** a tiny town in which fishing and tourism uneasily coexist. **Suirway** bus runs the 9½ mi. from Waterford to Dunmore East (2/day; £1.50). The sandy strand attracts bathers and tanning frogs on the rare days when the sun is shining. At several points, trails descend to the isolated coves below, which are more secluded places to swim. At **Badger's Cove,** facing the docks, dozens of seagulls perch on the rocky cliff face and produce a frightening cacophony of echoing cries. The nests here are possibly the closest seagull nesting site to human habitation. For an even more dramatic view, follow the gravel road past Dock Rd. to see the ocean crashing onto rocky coves. There's no ATM in Dunmore, but **Powers,** the convenience store on Dock Road, has a **bureau de change** (tel.

83202; Mon.-Sat. 9am-9pm, Sun. 10am-7pm). At the end of Dock Rd., behind the pink Harbour House, Irish surfer dudes at the **Dunmore East Adventure Centre** (tel. 383783) will teach you to snorkel, sail, surf, kayak, or ride a horse. Bring a towel and swimsuit; they provide the equipment (£11/½-day, £22/full day, prices £2 higher July-Aug.). The **phone code** has done more at 051.

The elegant **Dunmore Harbour House,** Dock Rd. (tel. 83218), offers budget accommodations. Some rooms have an ocean view at no extra charge. (Dorm £6.50. 4-bed room £8.50. Twin £11. Family rooms June-Aug. £14/adult, £7/child.) If you prefer to treat yourself, stay across the road at **Harbour View B&B** (tel. 383198). Miriam Shipsey doesn't joke about eating off a silver platter; she serves your breakfast on it. Antique china and furniture adorn every room of this 19th-century house (£16/person). Down the road, the **Dunmore Caravan and Camping Park** (tel. 383200) has offices in the Park Shop. The park is packed with trailers, but you can pitch a tent (hikers/cyclists £3, showers 50p). **Lucy's Kitchen** on the Strand (tel. 383350) dishes up take-away food (chickenburger £1.90; open daily 8am-1am). Farther up the road, the **Ocean Hotel Restaurant** (tel. 383136) creatively plays with its food (cream cheese and spinach pancakes £5.50; open Mon.-Sat. 10am-10pm, Sun. 12:30-3pm and 4-9pm). Groceries abound at **Londis Supermarket** (open Mon.-Fri. 8:30am-8:30pm, Sat.-Sun. 9am-8pm). Dunmore gathers at the **Strand Inn** (tel. 383783), where they enjoy the pool table and live music (Mon., Wed., Fri., and Sat.).

PASSAGE EAST

Passage East is just that: from here, people hop on the ferry that crosses the River Suir to the Wexford side. Passage is a small, friendly fishing village oriented around two open squares. Several B&Bs in the village live off the late-night ferry traffic. **Harbour Lights B&B** (tel. (051) 382646), facing the ferry, is lovely, with bare wood floors and wicker chairs in each room (£10/person). Just off the road between Waterford and Passage, travelers often stop at regionally famous **Jack Meade's Pub** (tel. (051) 873187). The pub has been in operation since 1705 and owned by the same family for nearly 150 years. Antiques adorn the walls and a close-knit band of locals claims their own corner, yet frequent entertainment attracts people from all around and a playground keeps kids happy. In September, Passage East has mollusk mania during the annual **Mussel Festival,** which features exhibitions, cooking demonstrations, fishing tips, and mussel-tasting (get your mouth muscles ready for all those mussels). The **Suirway** bus service (tel. (051) 382209) goes to Passage from Waterford (2/day; £1.50); buses depart opposite the tourist office in Waterford.

BALLYHACK

The profile that Ballyhack offers to its cross-channel neighbor (Passage East) is dominated by the 15th-century **Ballyhack Castle** (tel. (051) 389468 or 389164). Built by the Crusading Order of the Knights Hospitalers (a.k.a. the Knights of Malta) in the 1450s, the castle now houses an unimpressive heritage center. A tour of the tower, empty except for cheesy Crusader mannequins, will take no longer than the 10 minutes that you have to wait for the ferry. (Open July-Aug. daily 10am-7pm; March-June and Sept. Wed.-Sun. noon-6pm; admission £1, students 50p.) Next door to the castle in a building marked "The Half Door" is a diminutive but informative **tourist office** (tel. (051) 389468; open June-Aug. Mon.-Sat. 10am-6pm, Sun. noon-6pm). This is virtually the only place to find info on the Waterford Harbour area. Pick up the brochure entitled *The Hook* for a map and brief description of nearby towns. *Historic Hook Head* (£2) is a pricey but thorough guide to the area.

Dunbrody Abbey (tel. (051) 388603), 2 mi. from Ballyhack on the New Ross Rd., is a magnificent Cistercian ruin dating from 1190. Almost wholly intact, this abbey lets you wander through staircases and little rooms that are ideal for a game of medieval hide-and-go-seek. (Open daily 10am-6pm; go through the turnstile on the left side of the road, cross the field, and climb on in. Admission £1.50, children £1, family £3.) Across the road, the **visitors center** (tel. (051) 389468) sits among the ruins of a castle once associated with the Abbey. The center features a doll-house replica of what the castle would have looked like fully-furnished and intact. There is also mini-golf and an unamazing hedge-row maze—it's two feet tall. Bring your hobbit friends. (Open June-Aug. daily 10:30am-6pm; admission £1.)

ARTHURSTOWN

Head south from Ballyhack past the ferry to the beginning of *Slí Charman* (SHLEE KAR-man), a coastal walking path that leads almost all the way to Dublin. Follow the path for just a few minutes until you round the bend to reach **Arthurstown,** which offers accommodations, a pub, and little else. **Supervalu,** on Duncannon Hill, is the only grocery store (open Mon.-Sat. 9am-6pm, Sun. noon-6pm). The only competition is the prepared grub at the **King's Bay Inn,** the local pub (tel. (051) 389173; salmon sandwich £1.70), which also sports a **bureau de change.** The first left coming from Ballyhack, across from Marsh Mere House, is the entrance to the **Arthurstown Youth Hostel (An Óige/HI;** tel. (051) 389441). Once a coast guard barracks, it still has many of the original pine walls and moldings. In summer '96 renovations were stalled indefinitely. Rooms that are available are small but clean. (Curfew 10:30pm. Lockout 10:30am-5pm. Kitchen open 7:30-10am. £6, under 18 £4.50. Open June-Sept.) **Glendine House,** on Duncannon Hill (tel. (051) 389 258), is a large, Georgian-style house surrounded by acres of green grass. The rooms are suitably spacious and beautifully decorated with plush chairs and puffy duvets. You'll recognize it by the horses prancing in the front yard. (June-Aug. £15/person, w/bath £16; Sept.-May £14, w/bath £15. **Camping** on the lawn £5/tent, shower £1.)

DUNCANNON & HOOK HEAD

South of Arthurstown, the sunny and scenic **Hook Head Peninsula** begins. A circuit of the towns, ruins, and sea views of the peninsula is easily accomplished on a bike and eminently enjoyable and enlightening. From Arthurstown, head east on Duncannon Rd. and keep an eye out for the sharp right labeled "Duncannon." One mile will bring you to town.

Duncannon Fort (tel. (051) 325208) perches on the cliffs at the edge of the village. The fort was attacked by the Spanish Armada in 1588, Cromwell in 1649, William of Orange in 1690, and the United Irishmen rebels in 1798. The Irish army took it over and refitted it during World War II, and it served as a summer camp until 1986. The original Elizabethan structures were used right up to the abandonment of the fort in 1945. Today, the tired site is being restored and turned into a museum. The tour is fascinating and brilliant; don't leave Duncannon without taking it. (Open daily mid-June to Aug. 10am-6pm. Tours every hour on the hour. Admission £1, students and children 50p. For info, call Roche's pub, tel. (051) 389188.)

Duncannon Campground (tel. (051) 389193) is ½ mi. from town on the Churchtown Rd. (open March-Oct.; £4-5/tent). **The Strand Stores,** also in Duncannon, sells groceries (daily 9am-10pm). Next door is the **Strand Tavern** (tel. (051) 389109) with a groovy mug collection and a meditative ocean view.

Horse rides on the Hook can be arranged through the **Hook Trekking Centre,** 1 mi. from Duncannon on the New Ross Rd. (call (051) 389166 to schedule; £5/30min., £9/hr.; open daily 9am-6pm). The **Duncannon Festival** runs the first week in July, offering fish, cheap tarts, and other inexpensive delectables. Call Eileen Roche (tel. (051) 389188) for details.

From Duncannon, the **Ring of Hook** road goes down to **Hook Head,** the tip of the peninsula. Welsh missionary St. Dubhan founded the first **Hook Lighthouse** in the 5th century, making it one of Europe's four oldest. The structure has beaconed continuously since then. On the eastern side of the peninsula is **Tintern Abbey** (tel. (051) 62321), founded in the 13th century as a daughter abbey of the Tintern in Wales, of Wordsworthian fame. The Abbey is minutes from the Ballycullane stop on the Waterford-Rosslare train line (open all year; admission £1, students 50p), but service there is limited. **Wexford Festival Tours** (tel. (051) 397124) can arrange for a bus to take you around the Hook to get up close and personal with the sights.

■ Tramore

Tramore has beaches (*Trá Mór* means "big beach"), beautiful coastal views, and great places to stay. Amusements line up along the promenade in classic seaside-resort style. Despite this cheesy section of town, Tramore retains its small-town character and low prices. The **beach** itself is beautiful, wide, and shallow. With its fine accommodations, Tramore makes a sunny alternative to Waterford as a headquarters for your Southeast travels.

The very professional **tourist office,** Strand Rd. (tel. 381572), can help you see past the tourist traps (tourist office open June to mid-Sept. Mon.-Sat. 10am-1pm and 2-6pm). An **AIB ATM** is next to the tourist office. **Bus Éireann** stops on Strand St. en route from Waterford (1/hr., more during rush hour; 20min.; £1.50, £2.25 return). **Flanagan's,** Market St. (tel. 381252), rents **bikes,** but Tramore is so darn hilly that cycling won't be much fun (£7/8hr., £8/day, £35/week, no deposit). Tramore's **phone code** puzzles monkeys at 051.

Accommodations
The Cliff, Church St. (tel. 381363), looks out on the ocean from a prime cliffside location. The view cannot be beat, even with a shillelagh. Technically a YWCA Hostel, its single and double rooms, each with wash basin, come closer to B&B status. The TV lounge seems entirely surrounded by the sea—who needs cartoons? (Co-ed. Resident pooch. No kitchen. £7/night. Sheets £2. Continental breakfast £1.50, full Irish breakfast £3. Book well ahead July-Aug.) The **Monkey Puzzle Hostel (IHH),** Upper Branch Rd. (tel. 386754), is named after an unusual, recently deceased tree. The view isn't as spectacular as from The Cliff and there are four to eight beds per room, but it is well located between the ocean and the main street. Very hospitable owners. (July-Aug. dorm £6.50, double £17; Sept.-May dorm £6, double £16. Laundry £2/wash, £1/dry.)

Tramore is bursting with B&Bs, especially on Church Rd. For a killer view try **Turret House,** Church Rd. (tel. 386342), whose plain rooms are enlivened by the ocean. (Single £16, double £28, w/bath £32; Sept.-May prices £1 lower.) **Venezia,** Church Road Grove (tel. 381412), signposted off Church Rd., is immaculate and glossy, with top-notch, firm beds (£16/person, w/bath £21). **Church Villa,** Church Rd. (tel. 381547), is, appropriately, across the road from Christchurch. TVs in every room add that special something (£13/person, w/bath £15). Family-style **Newtown Caravan and Camping Park** (tel. 381979 or 386189), 1½ mi. from town off the Dungarvan Coast Rd. between the golf course and the **Metal Man,** a monument to shipwreck victims, is the best of several nearby campsites. (Hikers/cyclists £2.50, July-Aug. £3; showers 50p; open Easter-Sept.)

Food, Pubs, and Water
Tourist traps line up next to the amusements and Splashworld; walk into town instead for regionally famous **Cunningham's Fish and Chips,** Main St. (fish and chips £2.10; open daily 5pm-midnight). **The Sea Horse,** Strand St. (tel. 386091), has great pub grub and a friendly atmosphere (salmon and mussels £3.75, cappuccino and specialty coffees; food served noon-9pm). Sate your late-night appetite across the street at **Gav's** (tel. 390171), a groovy diner (veggie omelettes £2.80; open Mon.-Thurs. 8am-4am, Fri.-Sat. 24hr.). **Londis Supermarket** provides groceries right off Main St. (tel. 383471; open Mon.-Sat. 8:30am-7pm). Locals love to be hip and abbreviate their fave watering holes. The **Victorian House ("The Vic"),** Queens St. (tel. 390338), offers trad on Tuesday nights. The younger crowd prefers **The Hibernian ("Hi B"),** at the bottom of Strand St. at the crossroads (tel. 386396; disco 10pm-2am Fri.-Sun. nights; cover £4). Most locals congregate at **O'Neill's** (tel. 381808) on Summer Hill (at the top of Strand St.).

Splashworld, The Promenade (tel. 390176), has heated bubble pools, water slides, and wave machines. (March-Oct. Mon.-Sun. 10am-10pm; Nov.-Feb. Mon.-Fri. noon-8pm, Sat.-Sun. 11am-6pm; £4 for a 2hr. session, students £3.25, children £3.)

■ Dungarvan

The administrative headquarters for Co. Waterford, this busy market town concentrates on business and fishing. At night, the seaside town comes alive with a vibrant pub scene and some of the best boot-stomping trad around. Main St. (also O'Connell St.) runs through the central square; Emmet St. (also Mitchel St.) runs parallel to Main St., one block uphill, and is home to the hostel and a number of B&Bs. The road to Cork veers off Emmet St. at the Garda station. The unreservedly helpful **tourist office,** on the Square (tel. 41741), is a good resource for information about the nearby Ringville *gaeltacht* (open June-Aug. Mon.-Fri. 8am-8pm, Sat.-Sun. 9am-6pm; Sept.-May Mon.-Sat. 9am-6pm). The best villages in West Waterford are inaccessible by bus—bikes can be rented at **Murphy's Cycles,** 68 Main St. (tel. 41376; open Mon.-Sat. 9am-6pm). It's a **Raleigh Rent-A-Bike** depot (£7/day, £30/week; deposit £30). **Bank of Ireland,** on the Square, has a 24-hour **ATM** that accepts all major cash networks, as does **AIB,** just steps away on Meagher St. (Both banks open Mon. 10am-5pm, Tues.-Fri. 10am-4pm). The **post office** sits on Bridge St. just outside the square (tel. 41210; open Mon.-Fri. 9am-5:30pm, Sat. 9am-3pm). **Buses** run east to Waterford (Mon.-Sun. 9/day; 1hr.; £5, students £3), west to Cork (Mon.-Sat. 7/day, Sun. 5/day; £7, students £4), and north to Lismore daily from Davitt's Quay (bus info tel. (051) 79000). The **phone code** in Dungarvan prefers to say 058 in Irish, thank you, *a náid, a cúig, a hocht.*

The **Dungarvan Holiday Hostel (IHH),** on the Youghal Rd. (tel. 44340), just off Emmet St. opposite the Garda Station, used to be a chapel for the Christian Brothers. Dark rooms and tightly packed beds perpetuate the ascetic life (4- to 6-bed dorm £7, double £16; wheelchair accessible). **Santa Antoni,** Mitchel St. (tel. 42923), is appreciably more welcoming with a gregarious owner (single £12, double £22). Two doors down the road, **Amron** (tel. 43337) nearly bursts with the energetic hospitality of its proprietress, who lets out her basic rooms for £12.50.

Ormond's Café, The Square (tel. 41153), a few doors down from the tourist office, serves outstanding desserts and even the meals to precede them in its stone-walled back rooms (quiche £3; open daily 8am-6pm). **An Bialann,** 31 Grattan Sq. (tel. 42825), is a little café with overstuffed vinyl booths and £4.50 quarter-pounders with chips (open daily 9:30am-8:30pm). There's an **L&N Superstore** (tel. 41628) on Main St. (open Mon.-Wed. and Sat. 9am-6pm, Thurs.-Fri. 9am-9pm).

The **Gows,** 13 Main St. (tel. 41149), is probably the best pub in town, even though their sign is upside-down. Absolutely incredible trad sessions (Mon.-Wed.). **Davitt's Pub,** Davitt's Quay (tel. 44900), is huge and usually packed (11pm-2:15am; disco Thurs.-Sun. nights, cover £5). **The Anchor** (tel. 41249), down the quay a bit, is popular among the younger crowd, and hosts trad on Friday nights, live rock on Saturday. **Lady Belle,** Grattan Sq. (tel. 44222), invites you to sing along with the big boys, Tuesday and Friday nights. If you have transportation, try **The Seanachie** ("The Storyteller;" tel. 46285) on N25 to Cork, about 10 mi. from Dungarvan. The food is terrific and terrifically expensive (dinner £12). They pump out marathon trad sessions nightly and all-day *craic.*

The **Dungarvan Museum** (tel. 41231), at the end of Lower Main St. above the library, spares nothing in its breathless and well-mounted story of Dungarvan. From the Ice Age to Vikings, Cromwell, and maritime trade, it's in there (open Mon.-Fri. 2-5pm; free). One-hour **Walking Tours** of medieval and Georgian Dungarvan leave the tourist office two times per day during July and August (£2, students £1.50). **King John's Castle,** presiding over Davitt's Quay, was built around 1200 by none other than King John. The castle has 7-ft.-thick walls but has nevertheless been in various states of disrepair since 1299. It's not yet open to the public, but the Office of Public Works has its hands on it, so it's sure to be a heritage center before long.

There's not much else to see in Dungarvan itself, but deep-sea and in-shore **fishing** is excellent just off the coast—fishermen claim to have caught 16 varieties in a day, including blueshark, conger, and ling. Book a boat at **Gone Fishin',** 42 Lower Main St. (tel. 43514), a professional outfit with plenty of experience guiding less professional anglers to a catch. A deep-sea expedition leaves daily at 9:30am, returning at

> ### Na hÉireannaí agus a dTeanga
> ### (The Irish and Their Language): The Picture Today
>
> The Irish language, *an Ghaeilge,* is one of the oldest living languages in Europe. The oldest vernacular literature and the largest collection of folklore in Europe are in Irish. Still, less than 2% of the Irish people speak the language. In the 1970s, it appeared likely that the language could die out; today the language's future is uncertain.
>
> This decline is partly due to the way the language has been taught for the last 80 years. Antiquated teaching methods and an emphasis on the written language rather than the spoken one nearly killed interest in the language for most Irish students. Usually the least favorite subject in school, students hastened to pass the Irish parts of their leaving certification tests, and to forget the language in favor of the more useful French or German.
>
> The picture has begun to change, however, with the renewed interest in all things Celtic. As Irish students increasingly travel abroad and are often mistaken by continentals as English, they are feeling the need to assert the distinctiveness of their own culture. Adults, who hated Irish in their youth, regret having let it atrophy and are now attending classes. Many parents are sending their children to the increasingly common and chic *gaelscoileanna* (Irish language immersion schools). The Irish language curriculum has also begun to change with the times, as modern novels start to replace antiquated and dry traditional novels which have little bearing on the lives of modern students. By 1997, a new Irish language television station, *Teilifís na Gaeilge,* should be well under way.
>
> Support for the language is not universal. While most Irish do not want to see their language die, they also see the appropriation of needed money to Irish programs as a waste. The paradox leaves the language's fate in the air. Although it will never be the *lingua franca par excellence* of Ireland, Irish is showing signs of life. As Nuala Ní Dhomhnaill, the most revered modern Irish language poet, described it, "[Irish] is the corpse that sits up and talks back." *Gaeilge go Brágh!*

6:30pm (£25, rod and tackle hire £5; open Mon.-Sat. 9am-6pm). **Baumann's,** 6 St. Mary St. (tel. 41395), dispenses fishing tackle, licenses, and a wealth of inside info.

Dungarvan is home to a number of annual festivals. *Féile na nDéise* takes over the town during the first weekend in May, and fills the streets with free trad. Valentine's weekend, in mid-February, brings the **Dungarvan Jazz Weekend,** guaranteed to have you hummin' the blues (or the greens; this is Ireland). The **Motorsport Weekend** pulls in vintage and race car enthusiasts who compete in hill-climbing races (mid-July).

■ Near Dungarvan: Ringville

If you make it out to the local **gaeltacht, *An Rinn*** (ahn RINE, anglicized as **Ringville**), 6 mi. down the coast west of Dungarvan, you can treat yourself to the *Féile na nOisirí* (Oyster Festival). Locals and sportsmen from all over Ireland come to compete in oyster shucking and presenting competitions (or maybe they just come for the booze and music, both of which abound). Locals also crown their Oyster Queen (no Oyster-shell evening gown competition involved). Stop in at the best pub in town, *Tigh an Cheoil* (tel. 46455), where their trad sessions (Fri.-Sat.) are famous. (Brush up on your Irish—it's the *teanga an tí* (language of the house) here.)

■ Ardmore

Pastel houses and thatched cottages line Main St., which eventually disappears into the sea. Besides having a great **beach,** Ardmore says it's the oldest Christian settlement in Ireland, and has the ruins to back its claim. St. Declan christianized the area between 350-450 AD. St. Declan's feast day, "Pattern Day," is July 24—a big deal in Ardmore. Ardmore set another record on August 27, 1989, when 704 people wriggled their way into the *Guinness Book of World Records,* making the world's longest human centipede!

The **tourist office** (tel. 94444), in the car park by the beach, is housed in the most interesting building in Ardmore. Shaped like a sandcastle, the tourist office dispenses information about the local beaches, as well as an excellent leaflet outlining a one-hour **walking tour** of town (open Easter-Sept. daily 10am-8pm). Ardmore is a 3-mi. detour off Cork-Waterford Rd. (N25). Hitching from the junction to the town can be slow. Buses run to: Cork (Mon.-Sat. 3/day, Sun. 1/day; 1½hr.; £7.30, students £4.20); Dungarvan (July-Aug. Mon.-Thurs. 2/day; all year Fri.-Sat. 1/day; 40min.; £3.10, students £2); and Waterford (July-Aug. Mon.-Fri. 2/day; all year Sat. 1/day; 2hr.; £7.70, student £4.30). The **phone code** is a wiggling centipede of 024 humans.

Ardmore's tranquil, seaside location has finally been exploited by a hostel, and a beautiful hostel it is. The **Ardmore Beach Hostel,** Main St. (tel. 94501), is brand spanking new and features shiny pine floors, a bright kitchen, and a sunny black patio with beach access. Firm beds and fluffy comforters are marred by the aesthetic desolation of cinder block walls. (Dorm £8, double £20; 50p in winter for heating. Laundry £4.60. Free bike storage.) Ardmore is home to quite a few B&Bs with breathtaking sea views. **Byron Lodge,** Middle Rd. (tel. 94157), has literary aspirations, a large flower garden, and rooms with sunny alcoves. From Main St., take the street that runs uphill between the two thatched cottages (from £13.50/person, w/ bath £16; single £17.50; open Easter-Sept.). The **Cush B&B** (tel. 94474) is a 10-minute walk from town on the Dungarvan Rd. and is another wise choice (single £15.50, double £27). **Camping** in Ardmore is available along the beach at **Healy's** (tel. 94181; look for the caravans; £5/tent for backpackers, £6/tent with a car), but some travelers just pitch their tents in local fields. Ask around in the pubs for pointers.

Ardmore's limited food offerings reflect its size and its tourism role as a daytrip rather than a destination. The local favorite is **Cup and Saucer,** Main St. (tel. 94501), which has a delightful flower garden out back for sunny days (quiche and salad £3.50; open daily 10am-9pm). **Paddy Mac's,** Main St. (tel. 94166), is the Mac Paddy of pub fare. Their smoked salmon on brown bread (£3.75) will make you jump, jump. Rousing trad sessions on Thursday nights and Sunday afternoons in the presence of an encouragingly mixed crowd. **Quinn's Foodstore** (tel. 94250), in the town center, has the best selection of groceries (open daily 8am-10pm). **Riley's** pub has more character than it knows what to do with. Fear not, it may look run-down and abandoned, but it's open and still attracts plenty of older locals. **Keever's Bar,** Main St. (tel. 94141), is also a favorite among the more mature Ardmore crowd.

The free walking tour guide to Ardmore serves as a useful introduction to the town's historic monuments. The **cliff walk** winds along the coast with views of the beach. The **cathedral,** built piecemeal between 800 and 1400, covers the site of St. Declan's monastery. Its west gable is carved ornately with long rows of human figures. The tiny **Beannachán** (oratory) is the oldest building in the graveyard. St. Declan is said to be buried inside, and the faithful avow that soil from the saint's grave cures diseases. The cathedral and its graveyard are marked unmistakably by the 97-ft.-high **round tower**, where strange head-shaped projections suggest ancient head-hunting rites. Farther along the St. Declan pilgrimages, the **St. Declan's Stone** is perched at water's edge (just right from Main St. along the shore). Rumor has it that in the past, locals would wedge themselves under the stone during prayers on Pattern Day…a sort of "penance on the rocks." Down past the Cliff House hotel, at the start of the cliff walk, is **St. Declan's Well,** whose water is said to cure illness and affliction. Inquire at the hotel for directions to the little path leading to the well.

SOUTHWEST IRELAND

Traveling west from Cork City means moving from an English-influenced, 20th-century landscape into one that often looks untouched: the scenery is lush, the fishermen enthusiastic, and the roads lousy. This is the most fertile of the West's scenic coasts. The derelict monuments that once had spiritual significance to ancient civilizations now bestow a sense of timelessness on the open landscape. Life in the Southwest is leisurely and localized—the newly settled foreign expatriates, the remote pubs that stay open until 3am, and the stretches of wild, open, undeveloped land are all tributes to the region's informal and decidedly anti-urban atmosphere. At the same time, as Southwest Ireland gains popularity among foreign blow-ins, its cultural landscape is becoming more cosmopolitan. The area has incorporated new ideas and influences seamlessly into the native patchwork of cultural forces, while somehow managing to retain genuine Irish charm. If you're short on time, spend a day or two in Cork City, try to visit an island or coastal town in West Cork, then zip up to the mountains on one of the three peninsulas. Get to know a few places well rather than doing the typical tourist's whirlwind tour through Cork, Killarney, the Ring of Kerry, and Dingle.

County Cork

County Cork encompasses the full range of Ireland. It is home to both the Republic's second-largest city and some of its most desolate, rocky peninsulas. Eastern Cork's superb harbors made it a prosperous trading center, while its distance from Dublin and the Pale gave the English less leverage over it. Perhaps as a result, Cork was a center of patriotic activity during the 19th and early 20th centuries. Headquarters of the "Munster Republic" that the anti-Treaty forces controlled during the Civil War, the county produced spymaster Michael Collins, as well as the man who assassinated him in 1922. Cork City replaces the old patriotic energies with mercantile and cultural ones, while the sea towns of Kinsale and Cobh gaily entertain tall ships along with stooped backpackers. "West Cork," the southwestern third of the county, was once the "badlands" of Ireland whose ruggedness and isolation rendered it lawless and largely uninhabitable. Ex-hippies and antiquated fishermen have replaced the outlaws, and they do their best to render the villages laid-back and ultra-hospitable. Roaringwater Bay and wave-whipped Mizen Head mark Ireland's land's end. The lonely beauty here is matchless, a stately solitude untrodden by the polyester shamrock-shlock brigades raining down on other parts of Ireland. Ireland's rich archaeological history is particularly visible in Cork. Celtic ring forts, mysterious stone circles, and long-ruined abbeys dot the sheep-speckled hills.

One way to see the county is **The Hostel Hopper Bus** (tel. (028) 28165 for info, 28413 for booking), which runs in July and August and makes one daily round to all IHH hostels in Co. Cork (4/week). You can book through either the above number (8-10am) or a hostel operator. The bus begins in Schull and goes to Killarney and Cork before returning to Schull along the south coast. The route is divided into five zones; £6 per zone, £25 round trip. Luggage and bike transport are available.

■ Cork City

Cork's 146,000 inhabitants are constantly on the move—their vibrancy lends the city a cosmopolitan flair on the scale of a much larger city. Cork is the center for commerce, culture, and nightlife in the Southwest. On weekends, the city springs alive: families stroll the shops along Patrick St. and Oliver Plunkett St., shoppers haggle for goods at the English Market, and young and old alike fill the city's cafés and pubs at night. This youthful energy hides Cork's ancient past. Though it's 400 years older than Dublin (St. Finbarr founded a monastery here around 600 AD), there's almost no history left to be seen. The old city burned down in 1622, Cromwell expelled half its citizens in the 1640s, the English Duke of Marlborough laid siege to it in 1690, slum clearances and an 1853 flood required more new building, and the British torched the city again in 1920 during the Irish War of Independence. In between all these depredations, Cork became fairly prosperous—shipping, butter, and Henry Ford's first European factory kept the town expanding faster than anyone could tear it down. Cork is still growing, but so is its level of unemployment. But never fear—if a city can take fires, floods, cannons, and Cromwell, a bad economy won't be its end. Things have been looking up recently, as new bistros, cafés, shops, and performance centers have sprung up throughout the city.

ORIENTATION & PRACTICAL INFORMATION

Downtown Cork is the tip of an arrow-shaped island in the **River Lee**; most streets downtown were Venice-style canals until the 1700s, when Cork discovered pavement. Plentiful bridges link the island to Cork's residential south side, and to its north side, including the poorer **Shandon** district. Downtown action concentrates on **Oliver Plunkett St., Patrick St., Paul St.,** and the north-south streets that connect them. Heading west from the **Grand Parade, Washington St.** becomes **Western Rd.** and then N22 to Killarney; to the north of the Lee, **MacCurtain St.** flows east into **Lower Glanmire Rd.,** which becomes N8 and N25. Cork is compact and pedestrian-friendly. City buses crisscross Cork and its suburbs; from downtown, catch the buses (and their schedules) at the bus station on Merchant's Quay or on Patrick St., across from the Father Matthew statue. Downtown buses run every 20 to 40 minutes (reduced service on Sunday) from about 7:30am to 11:30pm (70p).

Tourist Office: Tourist House, Grand Parade (tel. 273251), near the corner of South Mall and Grand Parade downtown. Cork area maps sell for £1. The £1 *Tourist Trail* leaflet provides an extensive self-guided walking tour of all the sights. The office also runs free guided walking tours of the city in July and August. Call for schedules. Open May Mon.-Sat. 9:15am-5:30pm; June Mon.-Sat. 9am-6pm; July-Aug. Mon.-Sat. 9am-7pm; Sept.-April Mon.-Sat. 9:15am-5:30pm, Sundays 2-5pm.

Budget Travel Office: USIT, 10 Market Parade (tel. 270900), in the Arcade off Patrick St. Large, helpful travel office sells TravelSave stamps (essential for student discounts on bus and rail travel), Rambler, and Eurotrain tickets. Open Mon.-Fri. 9:30am-5:30pm, Sat. 10am-2pm. USIT has a second office at University College, across from Boole Library (tel. 273901). Open Mon.-Fri. 9:30am-5:30pm.

An Óige/HI (Irish Youth Hostel Association): Cork International Hostel, 1-2 Redclyffe, Western Rd. (tel. 543289). Open 8am-midnight.

Banks: TSB, 4/5 Princes St. (tel. 275221). Open Mon.-Wed. and Fri. 9:30am-5pm, Thurs. 9:30am-7pm. **Bank of Ireland,** 70 Patrick St. (tel. 277177). Open Mon. 10am-5pm, Tues.-Fri. 10am-4pm; self-service Mon.-Fri. 9:30am-5:30pm.

Airport: Cork Airport (tel. 313131). **Aer Lingus** (tel. 311000), **Manx Airlines** (tel. (01) 2601588), and **Ryanair** (tel. 313000) connect Cork to Dublin, the Isle of Man, various English cities, and Paris. A taxi (£5-6) or bus (19/day; £2.50) will deliver you to Cork City. The airport is 5mi. south of Cork on Kinsale Rd.

Trains: Kent Station, Lower Glanmire Rd. (tel. 506766), across the river from the city center in the northeast part of town. Open Mon.-Sat. 7am-8:30pm, Sun. 7am-8pm. Lockers £1. Cork has train connections to: Dublin (Mon.-Sat. 9/day, Sun. 6/day; 3hr.; £32, students £12.50); Limerick (Mon.-Sat. 6/day, Sun. 3/day; 1½hr.; £13, students £6); Killarney (Mon.-Sat. 5/day, Sun. 3/day; 2hr.; £13.50, students £6); and Tralee (Mon.-Sat. 5/day, Sun. 3/day; 2½hr.; £17, students £7).

Buses: Parnell Pl. (tel. 508188), 2 blocks from Patrick's Bridge on Merchants' Quay. Inquiries desk open Mon.-Fri. 9am-6pm; April-Sept. Mon.-Fri. 9am-6pm, Sun. 9am-5pm. **Luggage storage** £1.30/item, 80p/each additional day (open Mon.-Fri. 8:35am-6:15pm, Sat. 9:30am-6:15pm). Bus Éireann goes to all major cities: Bantry (Mon.-Sat. 3/day, Sun. 2/day; 2hr.; £8.80, students £5); Galway (Mon.-Sat. 5/day, Sun. 4/day; 4hr.; £12, students £7.50); Killarney (Mon.-Sat. 7/day, Sun. 5/day; 2hr.; £8.80, students £5); Limerick (Mon.-Sat. 6/day, Sun. 5/day; 2hr.; £9, students £5.30); Rosslare Harbour (Mon.-Sat. 3/day, Sun. 2/day; 4hr.; £13, students £8); Tralee (Mon.-Sat. 7/day, Sun. 5/day; 2½hr.; £9.70, students £6); Waterford (Mon.-Sat. 6/day, Sun. 5/day; 2¼hr.; £8, students £5); Dublin (Mon.-Sat. 4/day, Sun. 3/day; 4½hr.; £12, students £8.50); Belfast (Mon.-Sat. 2/day, Sun. 1/day; 7½hr.; £17, students £13); Sligo (3/day; 7hr.; £16, students £9.50); Donegal Town (1/day; 9hr.; £17, students £10). **Local Bus Info:** Bus Éireann Kiosk, Patrick St., near the bridge (open Mon.-Sat. 7:30am-11:15pm, Sun. 9:30am-11:15pm).

Ferryport: Ferries to France and England dock at **Ringaskiddy Terminal** (tel. 378111) 9mi. south of the city. The 30min. bus ride from the terminal to the bus station in Cork costs £3. For 24-hr. ferry information call (01) 6610715. See **Getting There** (p. 33) for air and ferry details.

Car Rental: Great Island Car Rentals, 47 MacCurtain St. (tel. 503536), £40/day, £90 for 3 days, £160/week for subcompact standard; min. age 25. **Budget Rent-a-Car,** Tourist Office, Grand Parade (tel. 274755), £35/day, £30/day for 3-5 days, £175/week; min. age 21.

Bike Rental: The Bike Store, 48 MacCurtain St. (tel. 505339), across from Isaac's hostel and at the Cork International Hostel on Western Rd. (tel. 543289). Rents mountain bikes and trekking bikes at £7/day, £30/week; deposit £30 (or you can leave your passport or other valid ID). Return at any Rent-A-Bike depot for an extra £5. Open Mon.-Sat. 9am-6pm. **Bike Repair: Geary's Cycles and Surplus Store,** 29 Parnell Pl. (tel. 273467). Open Mon.-Fri. 9:30am-5:30pm, Sat. 9:30am-1:30pm.

Hitching: Hitchhikers headed for West Cork and County Kerry walk down the Western Rd. past both the An Óige hostel and the dog track to the Crow's Nest Pub, or take Bus #8 there. Those hoping to hitch a ride towards Dublin or Waterford stand along Lower Glanmire Rd., on the hill to the train station.

Bookstores: Collins Bookshop, Carey's La. (tel. 271346), between Patrick St. and Paul St. Small, but well-stocked. Open Mon.-Sat. 9am-6pm. **Waterstone's,** 69 Patrick St. (tel. 276522). Monstrously huge. Open Mon.-Thurs. 9am-8pm, Fri. 9am-9pm, Sat. 9am-7pm, Sun. noon-7pm.

Camping Supplies: Outside World and the Tent Shop, Parnell Pl. (tel. 278833), next to the bus station. 2-person nylon tent £14/wk.; deposit £8. Extensive stock of camping supplies, including boots and clothing. Open Mon.-Fri. 9am-6pm, Sat. 9:30am-5pm. **Tents and Leisure,** York St. (tel. 500702). Smaller selection than the above, but bigger (and pricier) tents. 3- to 4-person tent £16/night, family-sized tent £10/night; no deposit.

Laundry: College Launderette, Western Rd. by the University. Large load, full service £5. Open Mon.-Sat. 6am-6pm. **Cork Launderette Service,** 14 MacCurtain St. (tel. 501421). £1/small load, £2/large load, 50p/20min. drying time. Open Mon.-Sat. 9am-8pm.

Pharmacies: Hayes, Conygham, & Robinson, 71-2 Patrick St. (tel. 270977). Open Mon.-Wed. 1-6pm, Thurs.-Fri. 9am-9pm, Sat. 1-6pm. **Regional Late Night Pharmacy,** Wilton Rd. (tel. 344575), opposite the Regional Hospital. Take bus #8. Open Mon.-Sat. 9am-10pm, Sun. 10am-10pm. **Phelan's Late Night,** 9 Patrick St. (tel. 272511). Open Mon.-Sat. 9am-10pm, Sun. 11am-6pm). **Duffy's Dispensing Chemists,** 96 Patrick St. (tel. 272566). Open Mon.-Thurs. 9am-6pm, Fri. 9am-9pm, Sat. 9am-6pm.

Bisexual, Gay, and Lesbian Information: The Other Place, 8 South Main St. (tel. 278470), is a resource center for gay and lesbian concerns in Cork and hosts a gay mixed disco (Fri. and Sat., 11:30pm-2am) and a gay coffee house (Mon.-Sat. 10am-6pm). **The Other Side Bookshop** (tel. 317660) downstairs sells new and second-hand gay and lesbian publications. Open Mon.-Sat. 10am-5:30pm. **Gay Informa-**

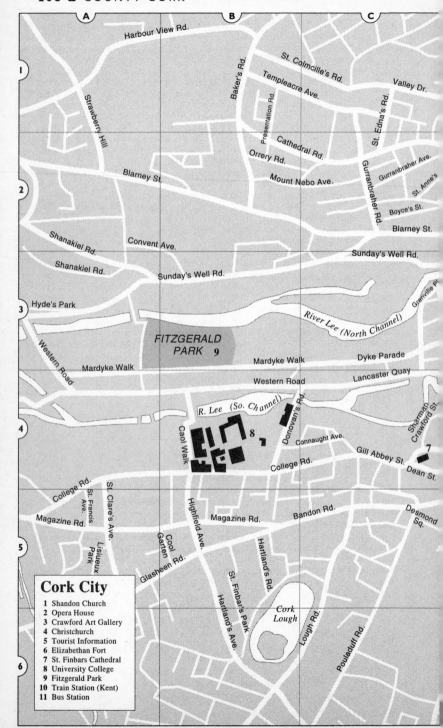

A B C

1

Harbour View Rd.

St. Colmcille's Rd.

Templeacre Ave.

Valley Dr.

Baker's Rd.

Presentation Rd.

Cathedral Rd.

St. Edna's Rd.

Strawberry Hill

Orrery Rd.

Mount Nebo Ave.

Gurranbraher Ave.

St. Anne's

2

Blarney St.

Gurranbraher Rd.

Boyce's St.

Blarney St.

Shanakiel Rd.

Convent Ave.

Sunday's Well Rd.

Shanakiel Rd.

Sunday's Well Rd.

3

Hyde's Park

River Lee (North Channel)

Grenville Pl.

Western Road

FITZGERALD PARK 9

Mardyke Walk

Dyke Parade

Mardyke Walk

Lancaster Quay

Western Road

R. Lee (So. Channel)

Sharman Crawford St.

4

Caol Walk

8

Donovan's Rd.

Connaught Ave.

Gill Abbey St.

7

College Rd.

Dean St.

College Rd.

St. Francis Ave.

St. Clare's Ave.

Magazine Rd.

Highfield Ave.

Magazine Rd.

Bandon Rd.

Desmond Sq.

5

Lisieux Park

Cool Garten

Glasheen Rd.

St. Finbar's Park

Hartland's Rd.

Pouladuff Rd.

Lough Rd.

Cork Lough

Hartland's Ave.

6

Cork City

1 Shandon Church
2 Opera House
3 Crawford Art Gallery
4 Christchurch
5 Tourist Information
6 Elizabethan Fort
7 St. Finbars Cathedral
8 University College
9 Fitzgerald Park
10 Train Station (Kent)
11 Bus Station

tion Cork (tel. 271087) offers a telephone helpline Wed. 7-9pm, Sat. 3-5pm. Lesbian line Thurs. 8-10pm. **Festivals:** The **Irish Gay and Lesbian Film Festival** happens the first weekend in Oct., and the second weekend of May is **Cork Women's Fun** weekend. Contact The Other Place for info.

Hotlines: Rape Crisis Centre, 5 Camden Pl. (tel. 1-800-496496). 24-hr. counseling. **AIDS Hotline,** Cork AIDS Alliance, 16 Peter St. (tel. 276676), open Mon.-Fri. 10am-5pm. **Samaritans** (tel. 271323) offers a 24-hr. support line for depressed or suicidal individuals.

Hospital: Mercy Hospital, Grenville Pl. (tel. 271971). £12 fee for access to emergency room. Or take bus #8 to **Cork Regional Hospital** (tel. 546400).

Emergency: Dial 999; no coins required. **Garda:** Anglesea St. (tel. 313031).

Post Office: Oliver Plunkett St. (tel. 272000). Open Mon.-Sat. 9am-1pm and 2-5:30pm. That special someone would certainly appreciate a post card.

Phone Code: 021. **Directory Assistance:** dial 1190.

ACCOMMODATIONS

Cork's six hostels range from the drearily adequate to the brilliantly beautiful. B&Bs are clustered along Western Rd. near University College and across the Lee on MacCurtain St. and Lower Glanmire Rd., near the bus and train stations.

Campus House (IHH), 3 Woodland View, Western Rd. (tel. 343531). From the Grand Parade turn on Washington St. (Western Rd.) and continue for 15min., or take bus #8. Travelers feel immediately at home in this immaculate and cheerful hostel, replete with comfy beds, fluffy comforters, and excellent showers. An extremely helpful and ebullient staff greets you with Cork info. Reception 8:30am-9:30pm. Dorms £6. Sheets 50p.

Isaac's (IHH), 48 MacCurtain St. (tel. 500011). Follow Patrick St. across the North Channel and take the second right. This large and modern hostel has stunning polished wood floors and exposed brick arches. High-ceilinged rooms feature fluffy beds and plenty of closet space. Conveniently located near the bus and train stations. Wheelchair accessible. 24-hr. reception. Dorm lockout 11am-5pm. 12- to 14-bed dorm £6.25. 6- to 8-bed dorm £7.75. Double from £29. Triple £30. Café open 7:30am-3pm; continental breakfast £1.50, Irish £2.25. Bike rental.

The Cork City Independent Hostel, 100 Lower Glanmire Rd. (tel. 509089). From the train station, turn right and walk 100yd.; the hostel is on the left. Incense hangs in the air of this splendidly offbeat hostel. Small and creaky, but fun. Eclectic artwork created by guests hangs on multicolored walls in the dining room. No lockout, no curfew. Dorm £6. Double £14. Laundry £3.

Sheila's Budget Accommodation Centre (IHH), 3 Belgrave Pl. (tel. 505562), by the intersection of Wellington Rd. and York St. Red and yellow decorating scheme in a quiet building near the train station; why venture to the store when they sell scones at the front desk? Huge kitchen and small backyard with barbecue. Nonsmoking rooms. Reception open 8am-3:30am. Checkout 10:30am. 6-bed dorm £6.50. 4-bed dorm £7.50. Single £15. Double £19. Rooms available w/bath. Sheets 50p. Luggage storage free. Key deposit £1.

Cork International Hostel, An Óige (HI), 1-2 Redclyffe, Western Rd. (tel. 543289), a 15min. walk from the Grand Parade, or take bus #8. Dreary but liveable bunkrooms in a stately brick Victorian townhouse. Currency exchange, bike rental, laundry, hostel vans to Blarney (£2 return), and pool table. Major renovations planned for 1997 include en suite rooms, a coffee shop, and wheelchair access. Check-in 8am-midnight. Dorm £6.50, Sept.-May £5.50. Single £8, Sept.-May £7. Continental breakfast £1.75, 4-course dinner £4-5.50. Sheets 50p.

Kinlay House (IHH), Bob and Joan Walk (the street), (tel. 508966), down the alley to the right of Shandon Church. Located in less-than-luxurious Shandon, Kinlay House is large, welcoming, and well-appointed. Modern and impressive, each room features a free locker and wash basin. Safety deposit box in office. Luggage facilities. Kitchen with microwave. Dorm £7.50. Single £15. Double £22. 10% discount with ISIC. Free continental breakfast. Laundry £3.60.

Fairylawn House, Western Rd. (tel. 543444). The spacious rooms are somewhat bare, but the gardens out front are lovely. Living room with piano. Continental breakfast included. Single £11.50. Double £21.

Garnish House, Western Rd. (tel. 275111). Gorgeous rooms, fluffy comforters, fresh fruit, and flowers in every room, free laundry service, fresh scones when you arrive before 10am. A new complimentary breakfast menu features 26 choices. Prepare to be pampered. Single from £20. Double from £36.

Danny's B&B, St. John's Terrace, Upper John St. (tel. 503606). Cross the North Channel by the Opera House, make a left on John Redmond St., then bear right onto Upper John St. Cork's only gay B&B, Danny's is all luxury, with colorful decorating that one might call "homobaroque." Complimentary breakfast (catering to vegetarians) is served in a cozy nook by the fire. Oversized armchairs, washbasins, TVs, and tea and coffee making facilities in every room. £18/person.

Camping: Cork City Caravan and Camping Park (tel. 961866), southwest of the city center on Togher Rd., ½mi. beyond Lough Rd. Bus #14 runs every 20min. 1-person tent £3.50. Multiple-person tent £5 plus £1/person. Open Easter-Oct.

FOOD

Don't attempt to explore the center of Cork on an empty stomach—intriguing restaurants and cafés are abundant and in close proximity. Particularly appealing are the lanes connecting Patrick St., Paul St., and Oliver Plunkett St. The **English Market** hops with a mesmerizing display of fresh fruit, meat, fish, and cheese. One stand is exclusively devoted to olives and olive oils (accessible from Grand Parade, Patrick St., and Princes St.; open Mon.-Sat. 9am-5pm; Wed. and Sat. are the best days to visit). **Quinnsworth Supermarket** (tel. 270791) on Paul St. is the biggest grocery store in town (open Mon.-Wed. and Sat. 9am-6pm, Thurs.-Fri. 9am-9pm) and the **Quay Co-op** stocks health and specialty vegetarian foods (see listing below). Cork's historic role as a meat-shipping center meant that Corkonians often got stuck eating the leftovers: feet, snouts, and other delectable goodies. Cork's local specialties include *crubeen* (pig's feet), *drisheen* (blood sausage; its texture is a cross between liver and Jell-O), and Clonakilty black pudding (an intriguing mixture of blood and grain). For the less carnivorous, there's a scone around every corner. Herbivores will be tickled green by the number of Cork's vegetarian options.

Quay Co-op, 24 Sullivan's Quay (tel. 317026). A cow's delight. Nary a creature was sacrificed for the scrumptious vegetarian delights served in this alternatively classy establishment. Inexpensive wine list; you can also bring your own (£2 corkage fee). The healthfood store below caters to all your organic/vegan needs. Gay-friendly. Table service Mon.-Sat. 7-10:30pm, store open Mon.-Sat. 9am-6pm.

Gino's, 7 Winthrop St. (tel. 274485), between Patrick and Oliver Plunkett St. Super fresh (and super cheap) pizza made to order (small cheese pie £2.60). A café setting reminiscent of Florence and a selection of *gelato* (Italian ice cream) combine to test the strongest of wills. Open daily noon-midnight.

Paddy Garibaldi's, Washington St. (tel. 272577). Food from an Irish-Italian dream. Paddy's extensive menu and wine list are served in a lively atmosphere beneath cathedral ceilings. Tagliatelli St. Lucia £7. Open daily noon-midnight.

The Bov Bar, 76 Grand Parade. This place is so cool, they don't even have a phone. Chomp on cheap sandwiches (3-decker club with side salad £2) to thumping mood music while you enjoy the fuzzy faux-fur framed artwork on the maroon and mustard-colored walls. Open Mon.-Wed. 11am-7pm, Thurs.-Sat. 11am-4am, Sun. 11am-7pm.

Scoozi, Winthrop Ave. (tel. 275077). Follow the grinning tomato to this intimate brick-and-wood lined establishment. There's no need to ex-scooze yourself for enjoying burgers, pizza, and pasta with wild abandon. Pesto Tagliatelli £5.25. Open Mon.-Sat. 9am-11pm, Sun. 4-10pm.

The Gingerbread House, Paul St. (tel. 276411). Enormous windows, cool jazz, and heavenly breads and pastries—an essential fixture in Cork's café culture. ½ quiche £2.60. Open Mon.-Wed. 8:15am-9:30pm, Thurs.-Sat. 8:15am-10:30pm.

Loon Wah, 8 Cook St. (tel. 276521). Don't let the flowered Victorian wallpaper and curtains fool you, this is indeed a Chinese restaurant. Sit in elegant high-backed chairs and select something delicious from the extensive menu. Beef and chicken dishes start at £5.30. Open 5:30pm-1am, Sat. 5:30pm-2am.

Truffles Restaurant, 6 Princes St. (tel. 270251). A cozy little bistro right off Patrick's St. that won't break your wallet. Small, intimate tables on the second floor look over the busy shopping street below. Lunch and dinner. Burger £3.55. Open Mon.-Thurs. 8am-4pm, Fri.-Sat. 8am-10pm, Sun. 10am-3pm.

Café Paradiso, Western Rd. (tel. 277939). Creative vegetarian entrees and blissful desserts are worth the splurge. Don't miss the superb foccacia served with olive oil. Fresh tagliatelle £7.50. Open Tues.-Sat. 10:30am-10:30pm.

Bully's, 40 Paul St. (tel. 273555). Enjoy sinfully-good Italian specialties while sitting at candle-lit tables surrounded by fiery scarlet walls. Be naughty and indulge! Extensive wine list. Open Mon.-Sat. noon-11:30pm, Sun. 1-11pm.

The Delhi Palace, 6 Washington St. (tel. 276227). Consume like a maharajah without paying the price. Vegetarian dishes around £4, meat dishes around £6. Lunch Thurs.-Sat. 12:30-2:30pm; dinner daily 5:30pm-midnight.

PUBS

Cork's pubs have all the variety of music and atmosphere you'd expect to find in Ireland's second largest city. The city is so crowded with pubs that it seems as though there are more watering-holes than people to fill them. Pubs compete for pint-guzzlers along Oliver Plunkett St., Union Quay, and South Main St. Cork is the proud home of **Murphy's,** a thick, sweet stout that sometimes, and especially in Cork, tastes even better than Guinness. Beamish, a cheaper stout, is also brewed here.

An Spailpín Fánach, 28 South Main St. (tel. 277949). One of Cork's most popular pubs, and probably the oldest (it opened in 1779). The name (Uhn Spal-PEEN FAW-nuhk) means "the wandering potato picker." A mature crowd tucks itself into the brick-walled, wood-trimmed nooks for conversation and great music. Live music (Sun.-Thurs.) ranges from blues to traditional. Pub grub (Irish stew £3.75) served Mon.-Fri. noon-3pm.

Loafer's, 26 Douglas St. (tel. 311612). Cork's sole gay and lesbian pub is jam-packed nightly by men and women of all ages. Close-quartered cruising and fabulous conversation makes this cozy spot a favorite for Cork's BGL community.

The Old Oak, Oliver Plunkett St. (tel. 276165). The hardwood floors and stained glass cathedral ceilings strain to contain the huge mixed crowd that files in here nightly. With live music three to four times a week and never a cover charge, The Old Oak is a Cork favorite.

The Donkey's Ears, Union Quay (tel. 964846). Deceptively quaint, Donkey's Ears is the most "alternative" of the Quay pubs. To ease the pains of a Sunday hangover, a full Irish breakfast (with choice of pint), is served from 4-6pm.

The Lobby, 1 Union Quay (tel. 311113). The largest of the Quay pubs, The Lobby is arguably the most famous venue in Cork. The Lobby has given some of Ireland's biggest folk acts their start. Live music nightly, ranging from traditional music to acid jazz. Cover charge £3-5.

An Phoenix, 3 Union Quay (tel. 964275). Blues on Tues. and rock on Thurs. in this smoky multi-leveled pub. The balcony above attracts a younger crowd, while the wine cask-embedded walls of the lower level contain a more mixed crowd.

Charlie's, Union Quay (tel. 965272). Art by local student artists decks the walls of the smallest of the Quay pubs. Live music ranging from acoustic blues to rock/pop nightly in summer (3-4 times per week during the rest of the year).

The Thirsty Scholar, Western Rd. (tel. 276209), across the street from Jury's Hotel. Steps from campus, this congenial pub is proof that students will walk no farther for a pint than they absolutely have to. Live trad music sessions at various times of the week in summer.

O'Flaherty's, 21-2 Parnell Pl. (tel. 273054). A thirty-something crowd moves to throbbing dance and disco in this large, beautiful bar. Live ballad singing on Tues.,

Wed., and Sun. nights. O'Flaherty's serves above average grub, from scampi to roast stuffed lamb, all under £4.25.

The Western Star, Western Rd. (tel. 543047). The new favorite for UCC students (they actually bus them home at closing), this pub is under new ownership and doing fantastic things. Enjoy the outdoors bar and marquée, a patio by the Lee River, and a huge beer garden in summer. Trad music two nights per week (call for details). Lunch served Mon.-Fri. (baked potato special £2).

SIGHTS

Cork has a smattering of captivating sights that can be reached easily by foot. For guidance, pick up *The Tourist Trail* at the tourist office (£1), or take advantage of one of the free walking tours (ask the tourist office for details).

The Old City

You might start seeing Cork from the center of the old city—Christ Church Lane off the Grand Parade, just north of Bishop Lucey Park. Walk down the lane (keeping the park on your left) and you'll emerge on South Main St., once the city's main drag. On the right is steepleless **Christ Church,** now the Cork Archives (closed to tourists). The church is an emblem of the persistence of Catholicism in Cork; it has been burned to the ground three times since its 1270 consecration, but rebuilt promptly each time, most recently in 1729. Edmund Spenser married Elizabeth Boyle here in 1594, in tribute to which he wrote *Prothalamium* and *Epithalamium.*

Nestled against the church is the small but dynamic **Triskel Arts Centre,** Tobin St. (tel. 272022), the locus of Cork's cultural libido. The Centre maintains a small gallery with rotating contemporary exhibits. It also runs a brilliant café and organizes a wide variety of cultural events (music, film, literature, theatre, and the visual arts; open Mon.-Wed., Fri-Sat. 10am-5:30pm, Thurs. 10am-8pm; free). Continuing south along Main St., you will pass (and no doubt smell) the **Beamish Brewery,** which produces Cork's own budget stout (brewery not open to tourists). Crossing the South Gate Bridge, turn right onto Proby's Quay, in the shadow of St. Finbarr's Cathedral, and then left onto obscure Keyser Lane. At the top of the stairs appears **Elizabethan Fort,** a star-shaped, ivy-covered remnant of English rule in Cork (always open; free). Built in 1601 after the Elizabethan English clobbered Hugh O'Neill's forces at the Battle of Kinsale, the fort's ruins now sequester the Garda station. Climb the stairs just inside the main gate to get to the top and enjoy the fort's strategically valuable view.

Down the street, **St. Finbarr's Cathedral** (tel. 963387) is a testament to the Victorian ideal of Gothic bombast. St. Finbarr allegedly founded his "School of Cork" here in 606, but no trace of the early foundation remains. The present cathedral was built between 1735 and 1870, but its Gothic style makes it appear much older. (Cathedral open daily 10am-5:30pm, Oct.-April daily 10am-1pm and 2-5pm; free.)

Shandon

On the other side of the Lee, North Main St. becomes Shandon St., heart of the Shandon neighborhood. It's less affluent than the rest of Cork but has more neighborhood pride and a cooler accent: "Cork" becomes "Caulk." Walk up Shandon St. until you see Donnelly's Diner on the left; then take a right down the unmarked Church St. and walk straight to **St. Anne's Church** (tel. 505906), Cork's most famous landmark. (Most people call it **Shandon Church,** since the steeple is "Shandon Tower".) The red and white (sandstone and limestone) sides of the steeple inspired Cork's ubiquitous "Rebel" flag; the salmon on top of the church spire represents the River Lee. Like most of Cork, the original church was ravaged by 17th-century pyromaniacal English armies; construction of the current church began in 1722. Four clocks grace the four sides of Shandon's tower. Notoriously out of sync with each other, the clocks have been held responsible for many an Irishman's tardy arrival at work. This trend has earned the Church its endearing nickname, "the four-faced liar." For £1.50, visitors can subject the city to their experiments in bell-ringing (sheet music provided; open Mon.-Sat. 10am-5pm, 4pm in winter). Just opposite the church is the **Shandon Craft**

Centre, Church St., where artisans practice weaving, crystal-cutting, and pottery. The circular **Firkin Crane Centre** (tel. 507487), a performance hall, is next door.

Emmet Place & Western Road

Walk down the other side of the hill, re-cross the north fork of the Lee, and you'll arrive at the monstrous, cement **Opera House,** erected 20 years ago after the older and more elegant opera house went down in flames. The adjacent **Crawford Municipal Art Gallery,** Emmet Pl. (tel. 273377), boasts one of the most important collections of Irish art and features contemporary and avant-garde traveling exhibitions (open Mon.-Sat. 10am-5pm; free).

Cork's other major sights are on the western edge of the city. Coming from the Grand Parade, walk down Washington St., which soon becomes Western Rd. **University College Cork (UCC),** built in 1845, has its main entrance on the Western Rd. Gothic windows, grassy expanses, and long, stony corridors make for a fine, secluded afternoon walk or picnic along the Lee. Tours of the campus tell the story of George Boole, the Cork professor of mathematics (and the mastermind of Boolean logic) upon whom Sir Arthur Conan Doyle based the character of Prof. James Moriarty, Sherlock Holmes's nemesis. (Tours by prior arrangement, £15/group. Campus always open for self-guided touring.) Across the street from the College entrance, signs point to the **Cork Public Museum,** Fitzgerald Park (tel. 270679), set in long public gardens studded with statues and flowers. The museum's exhibits are intriguing and astoundingly esoteric. The splendid gardens of **Fitzgerald Park** justify the walk. (Open April and Sept. Mon.-Sat. 8:30am-8pm; May and Aug. Mon.-Sat. 8:30am-9pm; June and July Mon.-Sat. 8:30am-10pm, Sun. 10am-10pm; Oct.-March Mon.-Sat. 8:30am-5pm; free, 10p on Sun.)

The **Cork City Gaol** is a reconstruction of the gaol as it appeared in the 1800s, and is an easy walk from Fitzgerald Park: cross the footbridge at the western end of the park, turn right on Sunday's Well Rd., then follow the abundant signs. A tour of the jail tells the story of individual Cork prisoners and the often miserable treatment they endured (for punishment, prisoners were forced to run for hours on a "human treadmill" which was used to grind grain). At the end of the tour is a captivating film which explains "why some people turned to crime." (Open daily 9:30am-6pm; winter Mon.-Fri. 10:30am-2:30pm, Sat.-Sun. 10am-4pm; admission £3, students and seniors £2.50, children £1.50; last tour is one hour before closing.)

ENTERTAINMENT

Cork is easy to enjoy. If you tire of drinking, take advantage of Cork's music, dance clubs, theaters, and sports—or just explore the innumerable cafés and bookshops. The nightlife is bustling and always in flux—fashions and hip bands change nightly.

Music & Clubs

Cork bands are big these days: the Sultans of Ping F.C. and the gentler Frank and Walters are two, but you're not likely to hear them in Cork. Popular local bands include Tree House, The Orange Fettishes, Mickey Rourke's Fridge, and L.I.P. What is hip one week, however, can be passé the next. The **Lobby** is a consistently sound choice for live music—pick up a schedule. **Nancy Spain's,** 48 Barrack St. (tel. 314452), is one of the city's most popular venues, often featuring live rock and blues. DJ Thurs.-Sat., nightclub upstairs. Call for live music schedule. Cover £5-6. **Charlie's Bar,** Union Quay (tel. 965272), has live folk, rock, blues, trad, and poetry nightly. See **Pubs** (p. 212) for other venues.

Cork is home to numerous trendy nightclubs that suck up the sloshed and swaying student population once the pubs have closed. Be aware before you fork over your £3-5 cover charge that all close at 2am. Follow the tropical fish to the twin clubs **Club FX** and **The Grapevine,** Gravel Ln. (tel. 271120). From Washington St., make a right on Little Hanover St., then a left onto Gravel Ln. Club FX features two levels with plenty of pulsating lights, while The Grapevine sports an odd, nautical/Mediterranean interior. Both pull in a young college crowd (Wed.-Sun. 10:30pm-2am; cover £3-5).

Zoës, Oliver Plunkett St. (tel. 270870), with its infernal red interior, draws in a similar crowd with a mixture of club music (11pm-2am nightly, cover £3-5). On Thursday and Friday, the adjoining **Black Bush** serves as a late night pub, remaining open until 2am. Ascend the lit staircase at **Klüb Kaos,** Oliver Plunkett St., a new and chic club for pounding dance and techno music nightly (11pm-2am; cover £3-5). **Gorby's,** Oliver Plunkett St. (tel. 270074), features a broader range of music, cover £2-4. **Sir Henry's,** South Main St. (tel. 274391), is arguably the most popular club in Cork, and also the most intense. Prepare to wedge yourself between sweaty, semi-conscious bodies and throb to raging techno (Wed.-Sat., cover £2-11). Head to **City Limits,** Coburg St. (tel. 501206), for a pleasant, mixed-age crowd. No dance music here; DJs spin anything from the 60s to the 90s (Thurs. and Sun. 11pm-2am, Fri. and Sat. are Comedy Nites, 9pm-2am). **The Other Place** (tel. 278470), Cork's only gay and lesbian disco, rocks every Friday and Saturday, 11:30pm-2am. First Friday of the month is ladies night. With a dance floor downstairs and a bar/café upstairs, there's something (and someone?) for everyone. The club attracts the majority of Cork's gay population, especially the younger set, on weekend nights. **The Half Moon Club** (tel. 274308), tucked behind the Opera House on Half Moon St., delights with jazz, blues, and traditional music (Thurs.-Sat.; check Opera House box office for listing; bars open at 11:30pm). Or try the Waterside Hotel's **An Sráidbhaile** (uhn SRAIJ-why-luh), Grand Parade (tel. 274391), for traditional Irish set dancing (June-Sept. 9:30pm-midnight, admission £4).

Theater & Film

Cork's theater scene has been revitalized by the opening of the **New Granary,** Mardyke Quay (tel. 904275), with performances of new scripts by local and visiting theater companies. **Triskel Arts Centre,** Tobin St. (tel. 277300), simmers with avant garde theater and performance art and hosts regular concert and film series. **Everyman's Theatre** (a.k.a. "the Palace"), MacCurtain St. (tel. 501673), stages big-name musicals, plays, opera, and concerts (Brendon Reeley, for one; open Mon.-Sat. 10am-5pm, 7pm on show dates; tickets £6-15). The **Opera House** (tel. 270022) presents an extensive program of dance and performance art (open Mon.-Sat. 10:15am-7pm). For a fix of mainstream American celluloid (and the occasional Irish or art-house flick), head to the **Capitol Cineplex** (tel. 272216), at Grand Parade and Washington St. (£4, matinees £2).

Sports

Cork is sporting-mad. Its soccer, hurling, and Gaelic football teams are perennial contenders for national titles. Be cautious when venturing into the streets on game days (especially during championships)—screaming, jubilant fans will either bowl you down or, worse yet, force you to partake in the revelry. Tickets to big games are £13-15 and scarce, but Saturday, Sunday, and Wednesday evening matches are inexpensive (£1-4) or free. Tickets to these local games can be purchased at the stadium. **Hurling** and **Gaelic football** take place every Sunday afternoon (3pm) from June to September in the Gaelic Athletic Association Stadium in Blackrock (take bus #2); call the GAA (tel. 385876), or consult *The Cork Examiner*. **Grand Central,** Sheare's St. (tel. 273000), features pool, snooker, an arcade, bowling, internet "cyberstations," and a high-speed monorail ride. Open daily 10am-11pm. For more mindless fun, the **Leisure Plex Coliseum** offers 24-hour bowling, pool, snooker, arcade, and Quasar. (Open Mon.-Thurs. 4pm-midnight, Fri.-Sat. noon-4am, Sun. noon-midnight.)

Festivals

The **Cork Choral Festival** (tel. 308308; first weekend in May) fills city churches with international singing groups while the **Cork Folk Festival** (tel. 317271), held in various pubs and hotels, jams in September. Also popular is the **International Film Festival** during the first week of October at the Opera House and the Triskel Arts Centre; documentaries and shorts elbow the features for attention (contact the Triskel Arts Centre, tel. 271711). See the big names for free in local pubs during the three-week-long **Guinness Jazz Festival** in October (call 273946 for information). Book well ahead at all hostels.

■ Near Cork City

BLARNEY (AN BHLARNA)

While sucking down tour bus fumes and standing in line with tourists from around the globe, you may forget why you're in Blarney. The main attraction is, certainly, **Blarney Castle** (tel. 385252), and its terrifically overrated **Blarney Stone.** Not only are the stone's origins obscure (some say it was brought from Jerusalem during the Crusades, others claim it's a chip off the Scottish Stone of Scone), the stone itself is obscure, too; it's just a slab of limestone among others in a castle wall. Tourists don't doubt its magic, though—they lean over backwards to kiss the stone in hopes of acquiring the legendary eloquence bestowed on those who smooch it. The term "blarney" itself, meaning "smooth-talking b.s.," was supposedly coined by Queen Elizabeth I after a series of particularly frustrating negotiations with the devious Irish Lord Dermot MacCarthy, who resided at Blarney Castle. The Irish themselves consider the whole thing a bunch of blarney; they're mostly concerned with the sanitary implications of thousands of people kissing the same rock. More impressive than the stone is the castle itself, built in 1446 as a stronghold for the final generations of independent, Irish-speaking feudal aristocrats. A trip to the top of the castle is rewarding. The view, if you're lucky enough to get one, makes up for the tour group from Tacoma. (Open May Mon.-Sat. 9am-6:30pm; June-Aug. 9am-7pm; Sept. 9am-6:30pm; Oct.-April Mon.-Sat. 9am-sundown. Sundays: summer 9:30am-5:30pm, winter: 9:30am-sundown. Admission £3, seniors and students £2, children £1.)

Two hundred yards from the castle lies the **Rock Close,** a beautifully manicured rock-and-plant garden supposedly built on sacred Druid grounds. After you receive the mystical vibes, walk around the fields and explore the limestone cave near the castle (bring a flashlight, unless you enjoy groping your way in total darkness). The crowds tend to confine themselves to the castle, making the Rock Close and adjacent fields a perfect place for a picnic. The nearby **Blarney House** (tel. 385252), obscures its historical past with modern renovations; a trip to the Laura Ashley shop in Cork would achieve the same degree of authenticity. (Open July-Aug. Mon.-Sat. 12:30-5pm, last admission is 30min. before closing; admission £2.50, students £2.)

Across from the castle is the other main attraction of Blarney, the **Blarney Woolen Mills** (tel. 385280; open April-Oct. daily 9am-7pm, Nov.-March 9am-6pm). The outlet sells Aran sweaters (£25 and up), Waterford crystal, china, and the standard tourist fare; you can also tour the mill (Mon-Sat. 9:30am-5pm; free). On the town square, **St. Helen's Restaurant** (tel. 385571), located above **SuperValu,** serves cheap sandwiches starting at £1.20 (open Mon.-Sat. 9am-6pm) while **The Blarney Stone** (tel. 385482) cooks up Irish specialties (stew with potatoes £4.50; open Mon.-Sat. 10:30am-9:30pm, Sun. 11:30am-9pm). Trad music and pub fare can be had at the **Muskerry Arms** (tel. 385066), music nightly 9:30-11:30pm. Across the square, the **Castle Hotel Restaurant** (tel. 385116) whips up Irish specialties (soup of the day and fresh soda bread £1.50) along with a host of French, Spanish, and Italian food. Open daily 8am-9:30pm, Oct.-March 8am-6pm.

Blarney is 25 minutes from Cork by bus, so there is no reason, practical or otherwise, to stay overnight. Should you fall madly in love with the Blarney Stone after giving it a wet-lickery one, the **Blarney Tourist Hostel** (tel. 385580 or 381430), 2 mi. from town on the Killarney Rd., rents basic and functional beds in a converted farmhouse (£6). **Bus Éireann** runs buses from Cork to Blarney (Mon.-Sat. 16/day, Sun. 10/day; £2.60 return). From July 5 to August 25, they also offer the **Cork Tourist Trail bus,** which trundles from the Cork bus station to the City Gaol, the Ballincollig Powder Mills, Blarney Castle, and back to Cork (Tues.-Thurs. 4/day; £2, children £1). Blarney is a short and pleasant bike ride from Cork. The **phone code** in Blarney is a rock-solid 021.

County Cork
S. Tipperary, W. Waterford

N

CO. TIPPERARY

CO. WATERFORD

Monavullagh Mts

Fethard
R691
R692
Cashel
R687
Clonmel
R678
R671
R676

N8
Cahir
R Suir
Knockmealdown Mts.
Cappoquin
N72
Dungarvan
Dungarvan Harbor
Ring
Mine Head

Tipperary
Glen of Aherlow
Galtee Mts.
Lismore
River Blackwater
Ardmore
Ram Head

Limerick Junction
R665
N8
Youghal
Youghal Bay
N25

CO. LIMERICK
Mitchelstown
10 miles
10 kilometers

Charleville
Ballyhoura Mts.
R637
Shanagarry
Ballycotton Bay
0
0

To LIMERICK
Liscaroll
R578
Fermoy
N8
Midleton
N25
Ballycotton

R580
Nagles Mts.
R626
Carrigtohill
R629

Mallow
N72
R614
Fota
Cobh
Cork Harbor

R619
N20
Cork
Ringaskiddy
Ringabella Bay

Blarney
Crosshaven
R579
Ballincollig
N71

Banteer
R618
R600
Kinsale
Kinsale Harbor
Old Head of Kinsale

Millstreet
CO. CORK
Musheramore ▲
R607
Ballinspittle
R605

Rathmore
Macroom
R602
Bandon
R603
Court-macsherry Bay
Seven Heads

Derrynasaggart Mts.
N22
Crookstown
Timoleague

CO. KERRY
R584
Shanacrane
R588
Clonakilty
Clonakilty Bay
Galley Head

Killarney
N72
R585
Dunmanway
R399
Rosscarbery
Rosscarbery Bay

Mangerton Mt. ▲
Gougane
Crohane ▲
R586
Drimoleague
Leap
Glandore
Union Hall

Lough Leane
R569
SEE KERRY MAP FOR FAR WEST
R593
Skibbereen
R596
Castletownshend

SOUTHWEST IRELAND

COBH (AN CÓBH)

Until the 1950s, Cobh (KOVE) was Ireland's main transatlantic port; for many of the 2.5 million emigrants who left from Cobh harbor between 1848 and 1950, Cobh was the last they saw of their country. Cobh was also the *Titanic*'s last port of call before the "unsinkable" ship struck an iceberg on her maiden voyage, killing 1683 people. Later, when the Germans torpedoed the *Lusitania* during World War I, most survivors and some of the dead were taken back to Cobh in lifeboats, accounting for the town's mass grave of 150 victims. Pick up the "Cobh Tourist Trail" map at the **tourist office** (tel. 813301; down the hill from the train station, on the right; open Mon.-Fri. 9:30am-5:30pm, Sat.-Sun. 11:30-5:30pm). Cobh is best reached by **rail** from Cork (Mon.-Sat. 12/day, Sun. 5/day; 25min.; £2.50 return). Cobh's **phone code** docks at 021.

Should you feel the call of the sea and want to stay in Cobh, try the **Beechmont House Hostel,** Bond St. (tel. 812177). A small but functional hostel, £7.50 per person will also get you breakfast. Pubs, restaurants, and B&Bs face Cobh's harbor from Beach St. **Rumble's Bistro,** 2 Casement Sq. (tel. 812112), across from the *Lusitania* Memorial, cooks quiche (£3.50), pastries, and ethnically diverse entrees (chicken curry, rice, and garlic bread £4). Enjoy delicious scones or a full Irish breakfast (£2.85) while admiring the oil paintings of local Cobh artists at **Kate's Coffee Pot,** 8 Pearse Sq. (tel. 813642; open Mon.-Sat. 7:30am-6pm, Sun. 9:30am-6pm). Alternatively, buy a picnic at **SuperValu supermarket** (tel. 811586) on West Beach and eat it seaside at John F. Kennedy Park, near the waterfront (supermarket open Mon.-Tues. 9am-6pm, Wed.-Fri. 9am-9pm). Cobh's pubs are young and rowdy, reflecting the town's renewed vitality. A young and aloof crowd sits in the smoky atmosphere of Cobh's Euro-café bar, **Rob Roy,** Pearse Sq. The **Rotunda,** 14 Casement Sq. (tel. 811631), across from the *Lusitania* monument, is more sedate, with plush banquettes of crimson velvet.

In remembrance of its eminent, but tragic, history, Cobh recently established a museum called **The Queenstown Story** (tel. 813591), adjacent to the Cobh railway station. The museum's flashy, multi-media exhibits trace the port's eventful history, with sections devoted to emigration, the *Lusitania,* the *Titanic,* and the peak and decline of transatlantic travel (open daily 10am-6pm, last admission 5pm; £3.50, students £2.50). In June 1995, the Cork-Cobh train ran into the museum, hurtling through two walls and the ceiling—not an auspicious start in this accident-prone town. **St. Colman's Cathedral** towers over Cobh. Its ornate Gothic spire dominates the town's architectural landscape and gives a great view of the harbor. Completed in 1915, the cathedral boasts the largest carillon in Ireland, consisting of 47 bells weighing over 7700 pounds. (Cathedral open daily 7am-8pm; free.) The small **Cobh Museum,** housed inside the Scots Church on High Rd., deals almost exclusively with Cobh's maritime history (open Mon.-Sat. noon-5:30pm, Sun. 3-6pm; 50p).

Cobh revels in its aquatic heritage. The tourist office, in fact, occupies the recently restored site of the Royal Cork Yacht Club, reputed to be the world's first yacht club, built in 1854. Today's visitors take advantage of the harbor for all types of water sports. **International Sailing** (tel. 811237) on East Beach rents canoes (£8/3hr.), sailing dinghies (from £22/3hr.) and windsurfers (£18/3 hr.; open daily 9am-6:30pm). **Headline Tackle** (tel. 814184), across the street rents fishing poles and tackle (£5/day; deposit £20; open daily 9am-6pm). The second week in July brings **Seisiún Cois Cuan Festival,** a celebration of traditional Irish music and storytelling. The **Cobh People's Regatta** during the second week of August and the **Deep-Sea Angling Festival** in early September draw crowds to Cobh harbor.

Near Cobh: Fota

Ten minutes from Cobh by rail lies **Fota Island,** home of **Fota Wildlife Park** (tel. (021) 812678), where penguins and giraffes adapt to Ireland's temperate climate. The 70 acre park houses 70 species of animals from South America, Africa, Asia, and Australia—don't be surprised if a kangaroo hops across your path (open March 28-Oct.

28 Mon.-Sat. 10am-6pm, Sun. 11am-6pm; admission £3.60, students £3.20). Adjacent to the Park, the **Fota Arboretum** houses a diverse range of plants and trees, as exotic and unencumbered as the beasts next door (always open; free). Fota is an intermediate stop on the **train** from Cork to Cobh; if you buy a ticket from Cork to Cobh or vice versa, you can get off at Fota and reboard for free.

MIDLETON

A short drive from Cork or Cobh on the main Cork-Waterford highway is **Midleton,** home of the **Jameson Heritage Centre** (tel. (021) 613594). That's Jameson as in Jameson Irish Whiskey. The Centre rolls visitors through a one-hour tour detailing the craft and history of whiskey production; better yet, they give you a glass of the potent stuff at the end. (Open March-Nov 10am-6pm; admission £3.50, children £1.50, family £9.50.) If you want some food to soak up your whiskey, head to the **Midleton Park Hotel,** Old Cork Rd. (tel. (021) 631767). Follow the left fork out of town; various sandwiches £1.60. For some great Italian treats (small pizza Napolitana £3), try **Leonardo's Italian Bistro,** 83 Main St. (tel. (021) 613867). Follow the right fork out of town to get to the **Millwheel Bar** (tel. (021) 632127) which hosts live music on Saturday nights. The highlight of Midleton, however, is its new hostel, **An Stór (IHH)** (tel. (021) 633106). From Main St., turn on Connoly St., then take your first left. The hostel's name means the "the treasure" in Irish. Spanking new, the intimate common room and en suite bedrooms are a find. Sink into the plush carpets (dorm £6, private room £8; sheets £1, towel 50p; laundry £3).

■ Youghal

Thirty miles east of Cork on N25, beach-blessed Youghal (YAWL, or "Y'all" for cute Southerners) can make an excellent daytrip or a stopover on the way to Waterford and points east. If you've seen the movie *Moby Dick* with Gregory Peck, you've seen Youghal—it was filmed here in 1954. Recently the town of 7500 became home to the less glamourous production of carpets and computers.

The helpful **tourist office,** Market Sq. (tel. 92390), on the waterfront behind the clocktower, distributes a useful "tourist trail" booklet (50p), and can steer you to traditional sessions in the town's pubs. (Open June-Sept. Mon.-Fri. 9:30am-7pm, Sat.-Sun. 10am-6pm; Oct.-May Mon.-Fri. 9:30am-5:30pm.) **Buses** stop in front of the public toilets on Main St. (just before it becomes one way), and travel to Cork (Mon.-Sat. 13/day, Sun. 9/day; 50min.; £5.50, students £3.20) and Waterford (Mon.-Sat. 7/day, Sun. 5/day; 1½-2hr.; £8.80, students £5). An alternative to **Bus Éireann** is the private **Rapid Express** service (tel. (058) 41741), which stops in front of the tourist office (3/day, £3 return to Cork). **Hitching** to Cork or Waterford along N25 is viable. Thar she blows—the white whale of a **phone code** is 024.

Hillside, 6 Strand St. (tel. 92468), is a puzzling cross between a hostel and a B&B, but it is by far the cheapest place to stay in town. The owner sold off all the antiques that once graced the house, so now you'll have to make do with knit afghans covering spongy beds (2- to 4-bed room £7.50/person). **Devon View,** Pearse Sq. (tel. 92298), is considerably nicer, if slightly garish, with antique furniture and silver in the dining and sitting rooms, all rooms with bath, TV, and phone (£14/person, £16 single). Gossip holds that a fantastic new hostel should be open in Youghal in time for the '97 season; inquire at the tourist office. Locals report that some travelers set up their tents on the beach for a night.

Y'all came to Youghal at a good time; the gourmet godmother has turned what was once cuisine-challenged into a town with some pretty good eats. Mosey on down to the lavender **Earl of Orrery,** 140 North Main St. (tel. 94359), for some truly magnificent creations, specializing in local seafood. Stick to the lunch specials, as dinners get a little pricey. (Lunch entreé £4-5. Open for lunch noon-3pm; dinner 6-10pm; coffee all day.) On the other side of town on Front Strand (continuation of South Main St.) stands **Jack o'Patsy's Pottery** and **Restaurant** (tel. 92553). Upstairs from this chic pottery shop, a delectable treat awaits in the rafters. Jack o'Patsy's serves artfully prepared pizza and pasta (not to mention delectable desserts and homemade ice cream) on its own handmade dishes. Art and photography adorn the walls as opera fills the air. (*Tagliatelli* with salmon and chili sauce £5. Day menu 9:30am-6pm; dinner 6-10pm.) The **Coffee Pot,** 77 North Main St. (tel. 92523), is extremely popular among locals, serving pastries, soup, and light meals (soup and brown bread £1.45; open daily 9:30am-7:30pm). Should Youghal not tempt the tastebuds, there's the **Super-Valu** in the town center near the tourist office (open Mon.-Thurs. 9am-6pm, Fri. 9am-9pm, Sat. 9am-8pm).

Local youth converge nightly on the blue and orange **Yawl Inn,** North Main St. (tel. 93024), to fill up on pints and thumping techno. **The Nook,** next door (tel. 92225), is arguably the most popular and pleasantly mixed pub in town. Other good pubs include **Moby Dick's,** Market Sq. (tel. 92756), across from the tourist office, and the **Central Star,** North Main St. (tel. 92419), where mature locals gather to play darts and make weekend sing-a-longs memorable experiences.

Enjoyably informative historical **walking tours** of the town (1½hr.) leave from the tourist office (tel. 92390; June-Aug. Mon.-Sat. at 11am and 3pm; £2.50, students £1.50). The huge **Clockgate** (built in 1777) straddles the narrow, crowded Main St. From here you can see the old city walls, built on the hill sometime between the 13th and 17th centuries. The tower served as a prison and a low-budget gallows (prisoners were hanged by the windows). Off North Main St. on Church St., two remarkable buildings stand side-by-side: **St. Mary's Church** and **Myrtle Grove.** St. Mary's Church is possibly the oldest operating church in Ireland, parts of it dating back to the original Danish-built church constructed in 1020. The sight itself, including a holy yew tree, has been in continual use as a center of spirituality since the time of the Druids. Myrtle Grove was the residence of Sir Walter Raleigh when he served as Mayor here from 1588-89. Pay due respect to the corner of the garden where he is said to have planted the first Irish potatoes. (Not open to tourists.)

For an encapsulated exhibition of Youghal's history since the 9th century, (which involves a lot less walking), drop by the tourist office's **Heritage Centre** (open the same hours as the tourist office; admission £1, students 50p). Across the street from the tourist office and up a little alley is **Fox's Lane Folk Museum** (tel. 92390). Dedicated to illustrating the history and social context of "domestic bygones" between 1850 and 1950, the museum's collection has been lovingly and singlehandedly assembled over 30 years. (Open Tues.-Sat. 10am-1pm and 2-6pm, Sun. 2:30-6pm. Last tour at 5:30pm. Admission £2, students £1.)

The **Busking Festival** takes over town during the first weekend of August, filling the streets with puppet theater, street theater, nightly open-air music, and plenty of food. Though overly popular with the tour-bus geriatric league, **Ceolta Sí** (KYOL-ta SHEE; "fairy music") reaps the talent of local youth in an enjoyable semi-professional program of traditional dance, music, and storytelling (Thurs. in July and Aug. at 8:30pm; £3, students £1.50).

WESTWARD HO!

From Cork City, there are two routes to Skibbereen and West Cork: an inland route, and a coastal route beginning in Kinsale. Two major **bus routes** depart from Cork City and serve West Cork: a coastal bus runs from Cork to Skibbereen, stopping in Bandon, Clonakilty, and Rosscarbery. An inland bus travels from Cork to Bantry, stopping in Bandon and Dunmanway (both 3/day, Sun. 2/day). Charming hitchers are reported to have no problems in these parts.

■ The Inland Route

Cyclists and hitchers wishing to save time or avoid crowds should consider one of the inland routes from Cork to Skibbereen, Bantry, the Beara, or Killarney, instead of the coastal N71 through Clonakilty. Popular routes are Cork-Macroom-Killarney, Cork-Macroom-Ballingeary-Bantry/Glengarriff, and Cork-Dunmanway-Bantry/Skibbereen. The views at sunset through the Shehy Mountains around Dunmanway and Ballingeary win glowing praise.

South of Macroom on R587, **Dunmanway** is less a town than a single busy main square. **Bus Éireann** voyages from Cork to Dunmanway (4/day, Sun. 2/day; £6.30) and from Dunmanway to Glengarriff via Bantry (3/day, Sun. 2/day). Buses leave in front of The News Basket on the square. The best place to stay (and the best reason to come to Dunmanway) is the **Shiplake Mountain Hostel (IHH)** (tel. (023) 45750), in the hills 3 mi. from town. Call for a ride from Dunmanway, or follow Castle St. (next to the Market Diner) out of town towards Coolkelare until you see the hostel sign, then turn right. Quaint Shiplake commands a view of the lakes and mountains, does pub runs, rents bicycles (£3/day), and cooks the best hostel food in Ireland. Interesting greenhouse-like shower facilities. A cute and extremely popular gypsy caravan (trailers painted in bright colors) behind the hostel accommodates couples or families. (Dorms £5.50; caravan £7/person; **camping** £3.50/person. Wholefood groceries available; prepared meals £2.50-5.) Back in town, **An Toísín** pub, Main St. (tel. (026) 45076), 200 yd. from the square, rings with live music on the weekends. Good pub stops are made at the dark-green **Southern Bar** (tel. (026) 45265), Clonakilty Rd., on the left side of the road as you leave town, or the **Arch Bar** (tel. (026) 45155). For those late-nighters, Dunmanway's most popular club, **Gatzby's** (tel. (026) 55275), offers dance music until 2am.

Northwest of Dunmanway on R584, **Ballingeary** and the quiet, very basic **Tig Barra Hostel (IHH)** make a good base for exploring **Gougane Barra Forest,** the **Shehy Mountains,** or your budding interest in the Irish language. Ballingeary is in the heart of one of West Cork's *gaeltachts,* and Tig Barra's owner is a native speaker (tel. (026) 47016; hostel £5.50; **camping** £3/person; laundry £2; open mid-March to Sept.). The mountains around Dunmanway and Ballingeary erupt with hiking and biking possibilities. Either hostel will give details.

■ Kinsale (Cionn tSáile)

Big-boated anglers, swimming parties, and gourmets salivating before Kinsale's famed **Good Food Circle** (of 12 expensive restaurants) fill the town with money every summer as its population temporarily quintuples. Luckily, Kinsale's best attractions—its pubs, its forts, and its seaside location—don't discriminate by class.

Kinsale has held a grimmer role in history than its pleasant present suggests. Elizabethan English armies destroyed the native Irish followers of Ulster chieftain Hugh O'Neill in the 1601 Battle of Kinsale while O'Neill's supposed Spanish allies watched the action from ships stationed nearby. Some historians blame Spanish duplicity while others point to poor military communications. In any case, the Brits won, leading to decisive British control over Munster and Leinster and to the Flight of the Earls. (See **History: Feudalism**, p.60.) Kinsale was legally closed to the Gaelic Irish for almost two centuries after the English victory. In 1688, the freshly deposed King James II of England, trying to gather Catholic Irish support for a Jacobite invasion of Scotland, entered Ireland at this very spot; for his efforts, James had a fort named after him. The attention of the outside world turned to Kinsale again in 1915, when the *Lusitania* sank just off Old Head of Kinsale.

Orientation & Practical Information Kinsale is a half-hour drive southwest of Cork City on R600—an easy daytrip. The city lies at the base of a U-shaped inlet. Facing the tourist office, Charles Fort and the Scilly Walk (SILL-ee, silly) are to the left; the piers, Compass Hill, and James Fort are to the right; the town center is behind you. The **tourist office,** Emmet Pl. (tel. 772234, Dec.-Feb. 774026), in the black-and-red building, gives out free maps and sells postcards and guidebooks (walking tours begin outside, £3; open March-Nov. Mon.-Sat. 9:30am-6pm; June-Aug. Mon.-Sun. 9:30am-7pm). **Bank of Ireland,** Pearse St. (tel. 772521), provides VISA-friendly, 24-hour **ATM** services (open Mon. 10am-5pm, Tues.-Fri. 10am-4pm). Rent **bikes** at **Deco's Cycles,** 182 Main St. (tel. 774884), for £6 per day (fishing poles £10/24-hr.; open June-Aug. Mon.-Sat. 9am-6pm, Sun. 10am-6pm; Sept.-May Mon.-Sat. 9am-6pm). **Buses** between Cork and Kinsale stop at the Esso station on the Pier (Mon.-Sat. 6/day, Sun. 4/day; £3.60, students £2.20). The **phone code** can sail at 021.

Accommodations Although Kinsale caters to an affluent tourist crowd with hotels and plush B&Bs, there are two hostels just outside of town. The **Castlepark Marina Centre** (tel. 774959), sits across the harbor, a half-hour walk away from Kinsale: walk south along the harbor from the bus depot, turn left on Duggan Bridge, turn right and walk along the other side of the harbor. Ferries leave from the Trident Marina for the hostel in peak season (call hostel for schedule). This ancient stone-faced building shares the same rocky peninsula as James Fort and offers marvelous views of Kinsale. Rooms are large, airy, and bright, with bay windows that open out onto the harbour. Beach access and no curfew. (Dorm £8. Laundry services £3/load. Security-box access 50p. Open March-Nov.) Castlepark's newly-opened restaurant features intimate tables and a gourmet menu (baked goat's cheese £4.75). Closer to town, **Dempsey's Hostel (IHH),** Cork Road (tel. 772124), offers adequate rooms in a plain house. Industrial kitchen (dorm £5; sheets 50p; shower 50p). In town, the **Yello Gallery,** 43 Main St. (tel. 772393), provides affordable B&B (£10/person, shared bath). Reasonable, if not retro, accommodations can also be found at **O'Donnovan's B&B** Guardwell Rd. (tel. 772428; £14/person, w/bath £16). The **campground** nearest to Kinsale is **Garrettstown House Holiday Park** (tel. 778156), 6 mi. west of Kinsale on R600, in Ballinspittle. (Open April 29-Sept. 30; 2-person tent £4.50, family tent £5.50, £1 less in June and Sept. Buses run there Thurs. 3/day, Fri. 1/day and Sun. 1/day; Sun. bus runs June 23-Aug. 18 only.; ½hr.)

Food & Pubs Kinsale is Ireland's gourmet food capital—locals claim it's the only town in Ireland that has more restaurants than pubs. The **Good Food Circle** has 12 restaurants which uphold both Kinsale's well-deserved culinary reputation and its reputation for tourist-scalping expense. The budget-conscious fill their baskets at the **SuperValu,** Pearse St. (tel. 772843; open Mon.-Sat. 9am-9pm, Sun. 10am-9pm).

   Café Palermo, on Pearse St. (tel. 774143), serves delicious Italian food and sinful desserts, like Death By Chocolate (fresh pasta lunch £4-5; open daily 10am-11pm). **1601,** Pearse St. (tel. 772529), helps the pub grub-deprived—try the Battle Burger, named after the Battle of Kinsale, £5. All-Irish cabaret Mon. nights.

   The **Spaniard** (tel. 772436) rules over the Kinsale pub scene from the hill on Scilly Peninsula (follow the signs ¼mi. to Charles Fort). Stone walls, dark wood paneling, low-beamed ceilings, and a bar the length of the Shannon (lively trad sessions Wed., other nights vary). **The GreyHound,** Market Sq. (tel. 772889), attracts a young crowd, while **1601** (see above) serves traditional music along with chips. Downhill from The Spaniard, and farther on the Scilly Walk, **The Spinnaker** (tel. 772098), presides over the harbor and plays loud American rock. Those who make the walk to Charles Fort are rewarded with the inviting **Bulman Bar** (tel. 772131), a picturesque spot for liquid iron therapy—Ireland's own black gold, Guinness.

Sights The half-hour trek up **Compass Hill** south from Main St. rewards with a view of the town and its watery surroundings. More impressive is the view from Charles Fort (tel. 772263), a classic 17th-century star-shaped fort that remained a British naval base until 1921. (Sack the fort mid-June to mid-Sept. daily 9am-6pm; mid-April to mid-June and mid-Sept. to mid-Oct. Mon.-Sat. 9am-5pm, Sun. 9:30am-5:30pm; admission £2, students and children £1; guided tours on request.) Reach Charles Fort by following Scilly Walk, a sylvan path along the coast.

In 1915, the *Lusitania* sank off the Old Head of Kinsale, a promontory south of the town of Kinsale; over 1000 civilians died. As it turned out, a German torpedo was to blame, and the resulting furor helped propel the United States into World War I. Hearings on the *Lusitania* case took place in the Kinsale Courthouse, now a low-key but interesting **Regional Museum,** Market Sq. (tel. 772044), which is home to the "Holy Stone" of Kinsale. (Sporadic hours; call ahead; admission 50p.) Just beyond Market Sq., the west tower of the 12th-century **Church of St. Multose** (patron saint of Kinsale) and its ancient graveyard bewitches visitors; the old town stocks still stand inside (tel. 772220; open daylight hours; free). **Desmond Castle,** Cork St., a 15th-century custom house, served as an arsenal during the 100-day Spanish occupation in 1601. It was put to use in the 18th century as a prison for salty French and American soldiers (open June-Sept. daily 9am-5pm; £1, students 40p).

Across the harbor from **Charles Fort,** the ruins of star-shaped **James Fort** delight with secret passageways and panoramic views of Kinsale (always open; free). To reach the fort, follow the pier away from town, cross the bridge, then turn left. After exploring the ruins and the rolling heath, descend to Castlepark's hidden arc of beach, behind the hostel. Rent windsurfing equipment, kayaks, and dinghies from the **Kinsale Outdoor Education Centre** (tel. 772896); 5-day training courses in sailing, canoeing, kayaking, and windsurfing. Full-day deep-sea fishing trips can also be arranged at **Castlepark Marina** (tel. 774959; £25/person, £5 rod rental).

■ Coastal Route

From Kinsale, southerly R600 sits watch over farming valleys before hugging the coast and wide, deserted beaches on the way to Timoleague and Clonakilty. From Cork, N71 carries buses and cars to Bandon and then on to Clonakilty.

Six miles east of Clonakilty along watery R600, **Timoleague** slumbers on the Ardigheen Estuary. **Buses** from Cork rarely stop here (Mon.-Fri. 1/day, 2/day on school days) and traffic from Kinsale is light. Timoleague's main attraction is its shell of a **Franciscan Abbey** founded in 1240 (always open; free). Ravaged by English armies throughout the 1600s, the abbey was abandoned by frustrated monks in 1696. Now it hosts an overgrown and desolate graveyard. Floodlights keep the ghosts away at night. Down the road past the town church are the unimpressive remains of **Timoleague Castle,** built in 1215. Smell flowers or pick your own raspberries at the well-tended **Castle Gardens,** more fun than the castle itself (open June-Aug. Mon.-Sat. 11am-5:30pm, Sun. 2-5:30pm; admission £2, students £1.50).

The most compelling reason to visit tiny Timoleague is the stately hostel and restaurant **Lettercollum House** (tel. (023) 46251), perched on a hill above the village. The 19th-century mansion was recently used as a convent. High ceilings, huge oil portraits by artists-in-residence, and a garden give this hostel an air of grandeur. The huge kitchen and slim pine beds are pluses (dorm £6.50; private room £8, w/bath £12; open mid-March to Oct.). Lettercollum House's **restaurant,** in the chapel of the old convent, is lit by stained glass windows. Specializing in organic vegetarian and non-vegetarian meals, the eatery is an award-winning delight (open daily in summer 7:30pm to close, Sun. lunch served beginning at 1:30pm; lunch £11, dinner £13.50, enquire about vegetarian prices). **Dillon's** (tel. (023) 46390) beckons the after-dinner crowd with delicious desserts (créme caramel), good tunes (folk and jazz), and the nectars of Éire on tap (open Mon.-Sat. noon-11:30pm, food until 9:30pm, Sun. 12:30-2pm and 4-9pm). Camping is available at **Sexton's Caravan and Camping Park** (tel. (023) 46347), 2 mi. from town on Clonakilty Rd. (£4.50/tent).

■ Clonakilty

Once a linen-making town with a workforce of over 10,000 people, Clonakilty (pop. 3000; the slick crowd says "Clon") lies between Bandon and Skibbereen on N71. Military leader, spy, and organizational genius Michael Collins was born near Clonakilty in 1890; a bit earlier, so was Henry Ford. Like Kinsale, tidy Clon is a vacation spot whose animated streets and vibrant pub scene rival its natural attraction, Inchydoney Beach. Clon is known for its live music, which can be sampled in its pubs nightly. On the last weekend in August, the **Country and Bluegrass Festival** literally takes over the streets. Winner of the **Entente Florale '95,** Clon is coming up roses with flower-boxes adorning nearly every window in town. The **tourist office** (tel. 33226) vacations at 9 Rossa St. (open June-Sept. Mon.-Fri. 9am-6pm, Sat. 9am-1pm). **Buses** from Skibbereen (3/day; £4.30, students £2.60) and Cork (Mon.-Fri. 6/day, Sat.-Sun. 3/day; £5.90, students £3.70) stop in front of Lehane's Supermarket on Pearse St. Clon's **phone code** of 023 is a sausage-like concoction of blood and grains.

Accommodations, Food, & Pubs The brand-new **Clonakilty Hostel,** Emmet Square (tel. 33557), one block past the Kennedy Gardens, is a welcome addition to town. Sparkling clean, this hostel sports a beautiful kitchen and comfortable new beds. (Wheelchair accessible, 24-hr. reception. No curfew. Dorm £7, double £18.) Just east of town, try Mrs. McMahon's **Nordav,** 70 Western Rd. (tel. 33655), a right turn after the museum. Set back from the road behind a well-groomed lawn and splendid rose gardens, this B&B features enormous, en suite rooms with TVs; some rooms with private kitchen and terrace (£15/person). **Ashville,** on Clark St. (tel. 33125), is less luxurious but closer to town (open March-Sept.; £13/person). **Desert House Camping Park** (tel. 33331) is ½ mi. southeast of town on a dairy farm. Follow the signs (open May-Sept.; £5/family tent, 50p/person; £4/small tent; showers 50p).

Clon is famous (or notorious) for its **black pudding,** a sausage-like concoction made from blood and grains, but it offers other culinary options. **Fionnuala's Little Italian Restaurant,** 30 Ashe St. (tel. 34355), attempts to please with candles in wine bottles that illuminate your antipasto (£1.50-3.50; open daily 5-10pm). **The Copper Kettle,** Pearse St. (tel. 33456), serves pastries and simple sandwiches (£1-3, open daily 9am-6pm), while **Jade Garden,** MacCurtain Hill (tel. 34576), will treat you to surprisingly excellent Chinese take-away (chicken chow mein £3.20; open Sun.-Thurs. 5pm-1am, Fri.-Sat. 5pm-1:30am). **The Doorstep,** 1 Western Rd. (tel. 34863), offers a pleasant country setting and tasty sandwiches (smoked chicken £2.50; open Mon.-Sat. 10am-7pm). Brown-bag it at **Lehane's Supermarket,** Pearse St. (open Mon.-Thurs. 8am-6:30pm, Fri.-Sat. 8am-9pm, Sun. 9am-1:30pm).

There's music aplenty in Clonakilty. The most popular pub is **De Barra's,** Pearse St. (tel. 33381), with folk and trad nightly all year. Though the pub is huge (3 rooms, 2 bars, and a beer garden), come early if you want to sit down; in this town of pubs, De Barra's is the center of action. Around the corner, **Shanley's,** 11 Connolly St. (tel. 33790), juggles folk and rock nightly in summer and winter; national-level stars have played here. **An Teach Beag** (tel. 33250), nestled behind O'Donovan's Hotel on Recorder's Alley, features traditional music and storytelling sessions nightly at 9:30pm. For a game of darts or pool, stop by **Bernie's Bar,** Rossa St. (tel. 33567).

Sights To fill the hours before the pubs pick up, join the locals at **Inchydoney Beach,** billed as one of the nicest beaches east of Malibu. Arrive in the morning, before everyone else does. (Camping here is permitted, but uncommon.) You can walk the 3 mi. to Inchydoney or rent a bike at **Healy's Bikes,** Rossa St. (£5/day or £25/week; open daily 9am-6pm), or **MTM Cycles,** 33 Ashe St. (tel. 33584; £6/day or £30/week). On Inchydoney Rd. you'll pass the **West Cork Model Village** (tel. 33224), where 1940s-era West Cork has been replicated in miniature, complete with model railways and smokestacks. (Open daily 11am-5pm, phone for special summer hours. Admission £2.50, students £1.50.) Back in town, the **Clonakilty Museum,** Western Rd., displays the first minute book of the Cloghnikilty Corporation (dated 1675) and other historical Clon minutiae. (Open May-Oct. Mon.-Sat. 10:30am-5:30pm and Sun. 2:30-5:30pm. Admission £1, students 50p.) Then explore the ancient **Templebryan Stone Circle** or the **Lios na gCon Ring Fort,** 2 mi. east; the ring fort has been "fully restored" based on clues its excavators dug up.

■ Clonakilty to Skibbereen

A subtly beautiful countryside lurks between Clonakilty and Skibbereen. Pastures give way to forests and heaths too rocky or too hilly for farming. Sleepy towns dot the hills, each with a few rows of pastel houses, a couple of pubs, and a B&B or two. This combination of rugged vitality with quiet beauty is quintessential Co. Cork. As long as you're in the area, stop by **Connolly's Bar** (tel. 33215), in Leap, reputed to host the best music in West Cork.

ROSSCARBERY

Eight miles west of Clonakilty, Rosscarbery sits by the sea along N71. From town, head east along the coast road to reach the **beaches** and the **Galley Head Lighthouse.** Built in 1641, **Castlefreke Castle,** 1½ mi. east of town off the coast road, housed generations of Carberys until the 1950s, when Lord Carbery renounced his family and moved to Kenya. Today it's the centerpiece of a public park.

West of Rosscarbery, off the Glandore Rd. (R597) in the Rowry River valley, lie the charred ruins of a 17th-century mansion called **Coppinger's Court** (always open; free). A mile farther along the Glandore Rd., the famous **Drombeg Stone Circle** (150 BC) is a well-preserved example of West Cork's recumbent stone circles. Archaeologists speculate that the horizontal ("recumbent") stone was used for human sacrifice; excavators unearthed one gruesome corpse here in the 1950s.

UNION HALL & CASTLETOWNSHEND

Just across the water from the picturesque but unexciting hamlet of Glandore, the fishing village of **Union Hall** was once a hangout for Jonathan Swift and family. Now it's home to the legendary hostel **Maria's Schoolhouse (IHH)** (tel. (028) 33002). Formerly the Union Hall National School, Maria's is resplendently redecorated and refitted. Cathedral ceiling and peat fire in the huge common room, funky pastels in the bedrooms—this hostel is reason enough for a detour en route to Skibbereen. (Dorm £7, w/bath £9; double £30. Breakfast £4.50. Laundry £4. Canoeing lessons £5/hr. Wheelchair accessible. Open March-Sept.) To get to Maria's, turn right in the center of Union Hall, left at the church, and proceed ½ mi. (or call Maria for a lift). Back in town, **Dinty's Bar** (tel. (028) 33373) plays live music on weekends, while **Nolan's Bar** (tel. (028) 33589) supplies civilized gossip. **Casey's Bar** (tel. (028) 33590) provides a waterside patio beergarden on which to enjoy your smoked fish chowder with soda bread (£2.50). Pterodactyl teeth and dinosaur droppings reside in the **Ceim Hill Museum** (tel. (028) 36280). The museum's proprietress, who is both more interesting and older than most of her exhibited items, found these and other prehistoric artifacts in her backyard (open daily 10am-7pm; admission £2).

From Union Hall, the most scenic route to Skibbereen is via **Castletownshend,** an Anglo-Irish hamlet that makes its way down to the sea. On the way, you'll pass **Rineen Forest** and **Raheen Castle,** built around 1580 using the latest grouting technique (a grisly mortar of blood, horsehair, sand, and lime). The castle is almost intact, except for the cannonballs which Cromwell's army embedded in its walls. **Knockdrum Fort,** just west of town, is a typical ring fort. Celts built the tribal center in the early Iron Age and then fortified it with walls and ditches. In Castletownshend itself, you can defend the **Townshend Castle** (tel. (028) 36100; open Sun.-Fri. 2:30-6:30pm; admission £2). **Mary Ann's Bar and Restaurant** (tel. (028) 36146) serves yummy, cream-laden bar food and seafood dishes (avocado and clambake £6.50).

SKIBBEREEN & THEM ISLANDS

From Clonakilty on, the population starts to thin out. Mountains rise up inland, rocky ridges replace smooth hills, and sunset-laden shoals proliferate as Ireland's southern coast starts to look like its west. Crossroads along N71 link mellow tourist towns and hardworking fishing villages. "Blow-ins," refugees from urban America and Northern Europe, have settled in the area by the hundreds. They are usually kick-back expats who appreciate the quiet pace and extraordinary scenery of the southwest but have shaped its culture to their own tastes. Trad music thrives in these small towns, attracting long-time locals and artsy expats alike.

The islands in the stretch of ocean between Baltimore and Schull may be the wildest, remotest human habitations in all of southern Ireland. High cliffs stagger into the sea in which many a ship has found a watery grave. The O'Driscoll clan of pirates informally ruled the bay for centuries, sallying into the Atlantic for raids, off-loading brandy (gold too, if they felt like it) from Spanish galleons, then speeding home through secret channels among the islands. Though all nine O'Driscoll castles stand in ruins, the clan still dominates the area. During the last weekend in June, O'Driscolls from Ireland and abroad assemble in Baltimore to elect a clan chieftain and to revel for three days. Those in Baltimore who are not named O'Driscoll regard the gathering as something of a joke, but a good party nonetheless.

■ Skibbereen

The biggest town in West Cork unites blue-collars and blow-ins within its varied landscape: there are as many hardware stores here as cafés. When Algerian pirates attacked Baltimore in 1631, the scared survivors moved north, establishing Skibbereen as a sizable settlement. The town is now the gateway for land-lubbers to Roaringwater Bay and the Beara Peninsula and consequently something of a tourist haunt. The best day to visit is Friday, when farmers tote in plants, fresh produce, and pies for the weekly **market** (1:30pm in summer, 2:30pm in winter). Or, bid at the weekly **cattle market** on Wednesdays on Bridge St., held from 11am-4pm.

Practical Information & Orientation Comely Skibbereen is L-shaped, with Main and Bridge Streets comprising the height and North St. the base, while the clock tower, Tourist Office, and stately "Maid of Erin" statue compose the junction. **Buses** stop in front of Calahane's Bar, Bridge St. (the continuation of Main St.), connecting to: Baltimore (June-Sept. Mon.-Sat. 4/day; £2.10); Cork (Mon.-Fri. 5/day, Sat. 3/day, Sun. 2/day; £8.80); and Clonakilty (Mon.-Fri. 3/day, Sat. 2/day; £4.40). **Hitchers** stay on N71 to go east or west, but switch to R595 to go south.

Tourist Office: Town Hall, North St. (tel. 21766). Open Mon.-Sat. 9:15am-5:30pm. May close later in summer; call for details.

Banks: AIB, 9 Bridge St. (tel. 21388; **ATM** accepts VISA). **Bank of Ireland,** Market St. (tel. 21700). Both open Mon.-Fri. 10am-4pm, Wed. until 5pm.

Bike Rental: Roycroft Stores, Ilen St. off Bridge St. (tel. 21235). Open Mon.-Wed., Fri.-Sat. 9am-1:10pm, 2:15-6pm, Thurs. 9am-1pm. £7/day, £30/week. Return bike to Schull or Rolf's Hostel or the Diving Center in Baltimore, £1.

Laundry: Bubble and Suds Laundry, 18 North St. (tel. 22621). Open Mon.-Sat. 10am-6pm. Small wash and dry £3.10. **Hourihane's Laundrette,** Ilen St. (tel. 22697), behind Busy Bee fast food. Complete services £3.50/load.

Hospital: tel. 21677.

Emergency: Dial 999; no coins required. **Garda:** tel. 21088.

Post Office: The Square. Open Mon.-Sat. 9am-5:30pm.

Phone Code: 028.

Accommodations The **Russagh Mill Hostel and Adventure Center (IHH)** (tel. 22451) is a brand-new hostel about 1 mi. outside of town on Castletownshend Rd. Set in a renovated 200-year-old mill, this hostel offers huge common rooms, with the defunct mill machinery still in place. (Special rates on outdoor activities such as canoeing, rock climbing, and hill walking. Dorm £7; private room £10/person.) Tucked among the rolling hills 4 mi. from town, the glorious **Mont Bretia B&B** (tel. 33663) is just a step from heaven in its light and airy old farmhouse. Gay and lesbian friendly, this B&B offers cozy rooms with fluffy bathrobes, free bikes and maps of local sights, and delicious vegetarian food. Call first for directions or a lift from Leap or Skibbereen (£15/person; dinner £6.50, 2-course dinner £8). If Mont Bretia is full, try a B&B in town. **Ivanhoe,** North St. (tel. 21749), offers big beds and bathrooms (£13/person). **Bridge House,** Bridge St. (tel. 21273), offers the utmost in Victorian accommodations with canape beds, satin-laced rooms, and the biggest bathtub in West Cork (£15/person, offers vegetarian breakfast option).

Food & Pubs Cafés cluster on Main St. and North St., making a handful of inviting options. **O'Donovan's,** 12 Bridge St. (tel. 21163), has a window full of yummy baked goods. Scone-lovers munch their colossal brown ones on the terrace out back (hot lunch £4). Ever-versatile, the **Stove,** Main St. (tel. 22500), serves copious breakfasts and Irish specialties for lunch (full Irish breakfast £3; open Mon.-Sat. 8am-6pm). **Wine Vaults,** Main St. (tel. 22743), provides excuses for a mid-day pub stop—delicious sandwiches, pizzas, and salads (brunch £2-3; food served noon-12:30pm and 5-8pm). Follow the live music and the crowds here in the evenings, when locals and tourists mingle for slightly alternative *craic.* **Bernard's,** Main St. (tel. 21772), behind O'Briens Off License, offers above-average pub grub in this large, beautiful, bar/restaurant (Irish stew £6; food served noon-9pm). Skib's **SuperValu market** (tel. 21400) dispenses bargains (open Mon.-Sat. 9am-6:30pm).

Kearney's Well, 52-53 North St. (tel. 21350), attracts a young, lively crowd with live music at least three nights per week. Traditional music is generally featured on Friday and Sunday nights. **Seán Óg's,** Market St. (tel. 21573), hosts contemporary folk and rock on Friday and Saturday nights, and features an outdoor beer garden.

Sights The **West Cork Arts Centre,** North St. (tel. 22090), across from the town library, hosts about 12 exhibits per year by Irish artists and craftsfolk. It also draws poetry readings, concerts, dance performances, and other cultural events to West Cork. Get wired into the local arts scene with a copy of *Art Beat,* a guide to the arts in West Cork, available at the Centre (gallery open Mon.-Sat. 11am-6pm; free). The **gardens** at nearby **Liss Ard Experience** (tel. 22368) promise to "induce new perceptions of light and sky." Designed as a unique attempt at conservation, the nonprofit organization's 50 acres of gardens include a waterfall garden, a wildflower meadow (with over 100 species of butterfly), and the surreal "Irish sky garden," designed by American artist James Turrell. The hefty admission fee (£12, students £8), includes a lunch at the Liss Ard's café. The **Creagh Gardens** (tel. 22121), 3½ mi. west of town on the Baltimore Rd., are less mysterious. Here, a woodland setting constrasts with well-maintained gardens (open daily 10am-6pm; admission £2, children £1). At the end of July, Skibbereen celebrates **Welcome Home Week** and **Maid of the Isles Festival,** featuring free street entertainment and culminating in the crowning of a local girl as "Maid of the Isles."

■ Baltimore

The tiny fishing village of Baltimore (pop. 200) and its harbor serve as the point of departure for Sherkin Island and Cape Clear Island. In the center of the village stand the stone remains of *Dún na Sead* ("The Fort of the Jewels"), a 16th-century O'Driscoll castle. The O'Driscoll family congregates here to elect a chieftain and to stage a family gathering, complete with live music, jammed pubs, and inebriated Irishmen. Artists, like seagulls, congregate in Baltimore in spring and fall for bright, dramatic seascapes. Baltimore's main road head's past town (with the pier on your right) for about 1 mi. to the **Beacon,** a phallic white lighthouse perched on a magnificent cliff with views over the ocean and across to Sherkin Island.

The **tourist office** (tel. 20441), 50 steps up from the ferry depot, is non-Bord Fáilte and keeps sporadic hours. The craft shop next door, **Islands Craft,** dispenses helpful information on Sherkin and Cape Clear, including historical accounts of the islands and the more basic ferry schedules (open June Mon.-Sat. 11:15am-7pm; July-Aug. daily 11:15am-7pm; Sept. 1-15 Mon.-Sat. 11:15am-7pm). Inquire at **Algiers Inn** (tel.

20145) for information about deep-sea angling. A number of wrecks offshore await divers willing to brave the icy waters. To arrange dives or rentals, contact the **Baltimore Diving & Watersports Centre** (tel. 20300), down the road from Rolf's (full set of equipment w/wetsuit £20/day, £70/week, boat trips from £12). **Buses** run to and from Skibbereen (June-Aug. Mon.-Sat. 5/day, Sun. 4/day; Sept. daily 4/day; £2, £2.75 return; the post office has a full schedule in its window). Notoriously bloodthirsty pirates assert that 028 is the **phone code.**

Accommodations, Food, & Pubs A visit to Baltimore requires a stay at **Rolf's Hostel (IHH)** (tel. 20289), run by a charming German family in a 300-year-old complex of stone farmhouses, five minutes from town off the Skibbereen road. Comfortable pine beds (brass in the private rooms) and a dining room with stunning views (and delicious food) are hard to resist. (Dorms £6, double £20. **Camping** £3.50/person. Laundry £3.15. Bike rental £6/day.) Rolf's also serves delicious pasta, fresh fish, and Malaysian munchies (main courses £4-6). **Café Opus,** next door, offers an exquisite menu, elegant ambiance, and rotating art exhibits for those who want to splurge a bit (main courses £9.50-11.50). The **Lifeboat Restaurant** (tel. 20143) in the post office building serves cheap soup, sandwiches, and pizza in a glassed-in room on the harbor's edge (entrees £3.50-4.75; open daily 10am-8pm). Stock up on food for the islands at **Cotter's** (tel. 20106; open daily 9:30am-7:30pm, 9:30am-9:30pm in peak season). All of Baltimore's pubs offer food. **Declan McCarthy's** (tel. 20159) is the liveliest pub, with trad and folk three to four nights in summer (no cover). The comfortable stools and tables outside **Bushe's Bar** (tel. 20125) are prime spots for scoping out the harbor, while cozy **Algiers Inn** (tel. 20145) draws a younger crowd (fish and chips £5, food served Mon.-Sat. 5:30-9:30pm).

Sights Once equipped with bicycles or lifts, explorers head east to circle **Lough Ine** (lock EYE-na), Northern Europe's only salt-water lake, where clear rapids change direction with the tide. Originally a fresh-water lake, the lough was inundated when sea levels rose after the last ice age. It is now a stomping ground for marine biologists, since it shelters dozens of sub-tropical species. A 30-minute ascent through the moss-strewn **Knockomagh Wood** (adjacent to the Lough; trails leave from the carpark) affords a view of nine towns and the Mizen Head.

■ Near Baltimore

SHERKIN ISLAND

Just a hop on the ferry from Baltimore, Sherkin Island offers stunning, cliff-enclosed beaches, wind-swept heath, and a sense of unhurried ease. **Ferries** depart from Baltimore (June-Sept. 7/day, Sept.-May 3/day; £4 return). Ferry schedules are posted outside the visitor information office (see **Baltimore** p. 227) or call Vincent O'Driscoll (tel. 20125) for information.

If you're looking for isolation, **Island House,** on the main road, 10 minutes from the ferry landing (tel. 20314), is ideal. An old farmhouse with colorful bedspreads, high ceilings, large and airy rooms, and the occasional strain of cool jazz, it offers mesmerizing views from rustic (charming, if not exactly modern) rooms (£14/person; open April-Sept.). **Cuina House** (tel. 20384), behind the Jolly Rodger, offers modest accommodations a little closer to the pier (£14/person). **Murphy's Bar** (tel. 20116), close to the ferry landing and next to Dún-na-Long ruins, serves a mean pint with expansive views of the bay. By the summer of 1997, the bar should be joined by a full restaurant (call ahead). The amiable **Jolly Rodger,** across the street (tel. 20379), has spontaneous live music sessions nearly every night in summer. The **Abbey,** on the main road (tel. 20181), is the only food store on the island and it stocks only the basics (open summer Mon.-Sat. 9am-6pm, Sun. noon-6pm).

When you get off the ferry, you'll encounter the ruins of a 15th-century **Franciscan abbey** founded by Fineen O'Driscoll (not Fineen "the Rover"—who comes later).

Vengeful troops from Waterford sacked the abbey in 1537 to get back at the O'Driscolls for stealing Waterford's wine. The ruins are currently undergoing renovation and are closed to the public. Sacked in the same raid, **Dún-na-Long Castle** ("fort of the ships"), which was also built by our favorite buccaneer clan, lies in ruins north of the abbey, behind Murphy's Bar (castle always open; free). Stay straight on the main road from the ferry dock and you'll pass the blue-green **Kinnish Harbour** and Sherkin's yellow one-room schoolhouse, where the island (pop. 90) educates its children. The beaches on Sherkin are sandy, gradually sloped, and great for swimming. **Trabawn Strand, Cow Strand,** and the bigger **Silver Strand** are all on the west side of the island (follow the main road and bear right after Island House B&B). The defunct **lighthouse** on Horseshoe Harbour stares across the channel toward the unsightly Beacon. This spot affords some of the best views on the island.

CAPE CLEAR ISLAND (OILEÁN CHLÉIRE)

Before the Famine, Cape Clear Island supported a completely self-sufficient population of 1200. Today, the population stands at approximately 150. During the summer, however, the island's population nearly quadruples with college students who come here to brush up on their Irish—the native tongue of a sizeable portion of the island's residents. The main industry is still farming. The landscape of patchwork fields separated by low stone walls hasn't changed much since the Spanish galleons stopped calling here hundreds of years ago.

Ferries run to and from Baltimore (May Mon.-Fri. 2/day, Sat.-Sun. 1/day; June and Sept. daily 2/day; July-Aug. Mon.-Sat. 3/day, Sun. 4/day; Oct.-April Mon.-Thurs. and Sat.-Sun. 1/day, Fri. 2/day; £5; £8 return). Call Capt. Conchúr O'Driscoll (tel. 39135) for more information. Ferries to the island **from Schull** leave daily, in June at 2:30pm, in July and August at 10am, 2:30, and 4:30pm. Another ferry from Baltimore cruises via Heir Island to Schull (May and Sept. 1/day; June-Aug. 3/day; £6), call Ciarán O'Driscoll (tel. 39153) for information.

Once you get to the Cape, life is leisurely and hours are approximate. The island's stores and pubs keep flexible hours and B&Bs arise and decline according to the residents' inclination to host guests. For an updated version of opening hours, as well as general island information, check the bulletin board at the end of the pier. The island's grocery store, **An Siopa Beag** (tel. 39119), stocks the essentials in a white building a few hundred yards to the right as you walk down the pier (open Mon.-Sat. 10am-1pm, 2-5pm, and 7:45-8:45pm; Sun. 2-5pm). The island **co-op** (tel. 39119) doubles as an information office (open Mon.-Fri. 9:30am-1pm and 2-5pm, Sat. 3-4pm, Sun. 12:45-1:45pm and 2:45-3:45pm). **Cistin Chéire** (tel. 39155) serves sandwiches, soup, and pastries harbor-side (open daily 11am-8:30pm).

What the Cape Clear pub scene lacks in variety it makes up for in stamina. Cape Clear Island has no resident authorities to regulate after-hours drinking, and if any have the impudence to sail over from the mainland, their lights give revellers plenty of time to close up shop. The island's 150 people support two pubs. **The Night Jar** (tel. 39102) opens at noon and is liveliest in the afternoon and early evening, while **Club Chléire** (tel. 39184), above the café, has live sessions most weekend nights, which often last until 4am or later.

The **An Óige Hostel (HI)** (tel. 39144) is about 10 minutes from the pier, keeping left on the main road. Though spartan and a little sullen, the hostel invokes the real estate mantra, "location, location, location." Situated only steps from the south harbor, it lets you fall asleep in front of an open fire to the song of the crashing waves right outside the window. (June-Sept. £6/person; April-May and Oct. £5/person. Sheets 60p. Reception open 8:30-10:30am, 5-9:30pm.) Inarguably more hospitable is **Cluain Mara** (tel. 39153), off a right turn from the yellow general store on the main road. The gracious Irish-speaking family offers large rooms and comfortable beds (£14/person, w/bath £15). A self-catering apartment across the road is also available for £20, posing an attractive alternative to the hostel for groups (bed space for 3). The island's **campsite** (tel. 39136) is a five-minute walk from the harbor: go up the main road, turn right at the yellow general store, then continue, bearing left. Located on the south harbor, campers get the same breathtaking views as hostelers (open June-Sept.; £2.70/person, under 15 £1.50).

About a 25-minute walk up a bone-shatteringly steep hill is the island's **Heritage Centre,** which is half a room containing everything from a butterfly collection to items recovered from shipwrecks. Maps of the island (20p) decipher the code of numbered posts marking the archaeological and historical sites. (Open June-Aug. Mon.-Sat. 2-5:30pm. Admission £1.80, students £1, under 18 50p.) On the road to the center, **Cleire Goats** (tel. 39126) sells **goat's milk ice cream** for a mere 65p and even raises the animals responsible. Should you find yourself *really* attracted to the beasts, Cleire Goats offers a two- or five-day goat keeping course. Past the center, a right turn leads to the **windmills** which generate three-quarters of the island's electricity. On a misty day you'll hear the eerie noise of their motion long before you see them. Cape Clear also shelters gulls, stormy petrels, cormorants, and ornithologists. The **bird observatory,** the white farmhouse on North Harbour, is one of the most important in Europe. Cape Clear hosts an annual **International Storytelling Festival** (tel. 39157) during the first weekend of September, featuring puppet workshops, music sessions, and a weekend's worth of memorable tales.

THE MIZEN HEAD PENINSULA

If you've made the mistake of skipping Cape Clear Island, you'll have to pass through Ballydehob on the land route to Schull, Crookhaven, and Mizen Head. Ballydehob is only worth a stop for a pint. Otherwise spend your time exploring craggy tips and secluded beaches along the peninsula. Schull is a more ideal destination, with a great hostel and excellent eateries. The **phone code** masts the Mizen at 028.

SCHULL

A jovial seaside hamlet 45 minutes from Cape Clear by ferry or 4 mi. west of Ballydehob by road (R592), Schull (SKULL) makes the best base for exploring the Mizen Head Peninsula. Intermittent ferries connect Schull to Cape Clear and to Baltimore. Contact Capt. O'Driscoll (tel. 39135 or 39153) for ferry schedules and rates. The Schull **tourist office** on Main St. (next to the Courtyard) dispenses information on Schull and the rest of the peninsula (open June-Aug., call the Schull Backpackers Lodge (tel. 28681) for current hours). The **bus** to Cork and Goleen (3/day) stops in front of Griffin's Bar on Main St. From June to September, there is also bus service between Schull and Killarney (1/day). Inquire at the Backpacker's Lodge for information on school bus service between Schull and Bantry. Either sing half-clothed on a street corner or get cash at **AIB,** 3 Upper Main St. (tel. 28132), which has a 24-hour **ATM** that accepts VISA (open Mon.-Fri. 10am-12:30pm and 1:30-4pm).

Schull's appeal for budget travelers is immeasurably enhanced by the opening of the **Schull Backpackers' Lodge (IHH),** Colla Rd. (tel. 28681). A brand-new wooden lodge, the hostel is bright and immaculate, with fluffy comforters, a sparkling kitchen, and the best showers in West Cork (dorm £7; 4-bed room £8 (peak season); double £20, w/bath £24; laundry £4). **Adele's B&B,** Main St. (tel. 28459), warms you up with small fireplaces and dark wooden floors (£12.50/person w/continental breakfast). Three miles from town on the way to Goleen, **Jenny's Farmhouse** (tel. 28205) offers friendly, quiet B&B (£10/person; call for possible pick-up in Schull).

Schull is known for its cosmopolitan shopping and eateries. The town is a treat for scone and brown bread connoisseurs. **Adele's Restaurant** (tel. 28459) bakes decadent cakes and pastries and dishes up tasty soups, salads, and sandwiches (£2) in a proper tea room (open May-Oct. for lunch and tea daily 9:30am-7pm, dinner Wed.-Sun. 7-10pm). Not to be outdone, the multi-talented **Courtyard,** across the street (tel. 28390), bakes eight types of bread (70p-£1.10/loaf) and sells a variety of gourmet foods, wholefoods, soups, and sandwiches. Plentiful dinners, with such specialties as warm goat's cheese salad with sun-dried tomatoes and basil (£5.85) are served daily

(6-9pm). On weekends, the adjacent **pub** features traditional music, jazz, and blues. *Céilí* dancing on Tuesday nights (food served Mon.-Sat. 9am-6pm). **The Bunratty Inn** (tel. 28341), up the hill on Main St., concocts some of West Cork's best pub fare (smoked salmon and local cheese £5.50; food served Mon.-Sat. noon-7pm, Sun. 12:30-2pm). The **Bunratty Inn** and **An Tigín** (tel. 28337) host live folk and rock on summer nights. **The Galley Inn** (tel. 28733) features a mean bowl of soup for £1.50, as well as rollicking tunes Thursday nights and long weekends. Finally, before leaving, stock up for Mizen forays at one of Schull's **grocery stores** on Main St.: **Spar Market** (tel. 28236; open daily 7am-9pm) or smaller **Hegarty's Centra,** across the street (tel. 28520; open Mon.-Sat. 8am-10pm, Sun. 9am-9pm).

Schull's location on the Mizen Peninsula makes it an ideal base to explore the walking trails that snake along the water and up the nearby hills. Inquire at the Backpacker's Lodge for maps and information. Southern Ireland's only planetarium, the **Schull Planetarium,** Colla Rd. (tel. 28552), offers extraterrestrial diversions (open June-Sept. Tues., Fri., and Sat. 2-5pm; additional days July-Aug. Wed. and Thurs. 2-5pm and 7-9pm; admission £1, star show £2.50). A calm harbor near numerous shipwrecks makes Schull a diver's paradise. The **Watersports Centre** (tel. 28554) rents dinghies, windsurfers, wetsuits, and diving gear (open Mon.-Sat. 9:30am-6:30pm). They offer some of the cheaper rates on the bay, so take advantage of them if you're set on taking to the sea. Terrestrial types can rent bikes at **Freewheelin',** Cotter's Yard, Main St. (tel. 28165; bikes £8/day or £45/week; open Mon.-Sat. 10am-noon). Bikes can also be picked up and returned at Schull Backpacker's Lodge.

FARTHER ON: MIZEN HEAD

The Mizen becomes more scenic and less populated the farther west one goes from Schull. Depending on when you go, Mizen can be mobbed on sunny Sunday afternoons, as beach-goers and sun-worshippers pack sandy beaches. **Bus Éireann** only goes as far as Goleen (2/day; inquire in Schull or Ballydehob for schedule). Hitching can only be rewarding if it is high-traffic season for camping—but a perfect daytrip to Mizen Head can be made by bike (which must be rented at Schull). Most reliable is **Betty's Bus Hire** (tel. 28410) which will take you on a tour of the Mizen via the scenic coast road (£8, £7.50 student). The tour includes bits of local history and admission to the **Mizen Vision** (see below). Betty leaves from Schull's at 10:30am on Saturday, Sunday, Wednesday, and Thursday; flexible return times.

The block-long town of **Goleen** seems to move at half-pace. At **Heron's Cove B&B** (tel. 35225), £16.50 rents a modern room with a view of the cove (and a balcony and a TV). The **restaurant** downstairs lovingly serves seafood (crab sandwich £4.50; May-Sept. daily noon-9:45pm).

From Goleen, the slightly longer but worthwhile coast road roams to Barley Cove and Mizen Head. **Crookhaven,** a 1-mi. detour, is perched at the end of a peninsula. It's a haven for Euroyachts which swarm to the village every summer. At the end of Crookhaven Pier, **O'Sullivans** (tel. 35319) serves sandwiches, desserts, and cold pints on the water's edge (salmon sandwich £2.50). The **Crookhaven Inn** (tel. 35309) serves similar fare in a lovely outdoor café overlooking the bay (open daily 11am-11:30pm). **Barley Cove Caravan Park** (tel. 35302), 1½ mi. from Crookhaven, offers camping to a sea of cooler-sporting, satellite-disked campers. (£6/tent, £3 if you bring your own, £1/extra person from July to mid-Aug. Showers 50p. Mini-market and laundry available. **Bikes** £5/½-day, £8/day; deposit £20 for campers or £40 for non-campers. Open May 7-Sept. 11.) A cheaper (it's free) and infinitely more romantic option is to camp *near* the **Barley Cove Beach,** a gorgeous ¼-mi. of sand whose warm, shallow coves satisfy bathers who won't brave the frigid sea.

Three miles past Barley Cove, Ireland ends at spectacular **Mizen Head,** whose cliffs rise to 700 ft. **The Mizen Head Lighthouse,** built in 1909, was recently automated and electrified, and the buildings nearby were turned into a mediocre museum, the **Mizen Vision** (tel. 35115). To get to the museum (it's on a small island), you'll have to cross a harrowing suspension bridge. The museum assembles lighthouse paraphernalia and sheds light on the solitary lives of lighthouse-keepers, all set to the sound of seagulls and sea-surf amplified by loudspeakers. The admission fee, though not justified by the exhibits, pays off with the view outside. (Open June-Sept. daily 10:30am-5:30pm; Oct.-May call 32553. Admission £2, students £1.50.)

BEARA PENINSULA

Untold numbers of visitors traveling up and down Ireland's southwest coast skip the Beara altogether. This region has much of the majesty of the Ring of Kerry and a more profound sense of tranquility. The spectacular **Caha** and **Slieve Miskish Mountains** march down the spine of the peninsula, separating the Beara's rocky southern coast from its lush northern coast. West Beara remains remote—travelers traverse the treacherous few single-track roads of the stark Atlantic coastline, dodging mountains, rocky outcrops, and the occasional herd of sheep. For unspoiled scenery and solitude the Beara is superb; if you're looking for pubs, people, and other signs of civilization, you might be happier on the Iveragh or Dingle Peninsulas. The dearth of cars west of Glengarriff makes cycling the Beara a joy (weather permitting), but hitchhikers may find themselves admiring the same views for longer than their sanity can bear.

■ Bantry

According to the *Book of Invasions*, the first human beings landed in Ireland just a mile from Bantry. Bantry's second "invasion" is more generally agreed upon by historians—English settlers seized Bantry and drove out the 17th-century Irish. Irishman Theobald Wolfe Tone tried to return the favor by attacking the town in 1796. A day or two in civilized Bantry may pay off with a cruise round the bay, a visit to Wolfe Tone Square on Saturday afternoon, or an expedition to the Armada exhibit.

PRACTICAL INFORMATION

Bantry is settled at the east end of Bantry Bay. Sheep's Head stretches due west, while journeying north then west will bring you to the Beara Peninsula. Hitchers, cars, and bicyclists stay on N71 to get in or out of town.

> **Tourist Office:** Wolfe Tone Sq. (tel. 50229). Open June-Sept. Mon.-Sat. 9am-6pm.
> **Banks: AIB,** Wolfe Tone Sq. (tel. 50008); has **ATM. Bank of Ireland,** Wolfe Tone Sq. (tel. 51377); both open Mon.-Wed. and Fri. 10am-4pm, Thurs. 10am-5pm.
> **Buses:** Buses stop outside of Lynch's Pub in Wolfe Tone Sq., several doors from the tourist office toward the pier. **Bus Éireann** heads to: Cork and Bandon (Mon.-Sat. 3-5/day, Sun. 2-4/day; £8.80); Glengarriff (Mon.-Sat. 3/day, Sun. 2/day; £2.25).

Now That's Creative Writing!

The Beara Peninsula is bleak and unspoiled, but it was here that the first humans supposedly set foot on Ireland. Before the first invaders, the Milesians, landed in about 2000 BC, they actually had to bring the land into existence. According to *The Book of Invasions,* the Milesians were pressured into composing (quite literally) the land. It was necessary for their bard, Amergin, to chant the land into existence before they could set foot on shore:

> *I am wind on sea*
> *I am wave in storm*
> *I am sea sound*
> *I am hawk on cliff*
> *A word of art*
> *A piercing point that pours out rage*
> *The god who fashions fire in the head*
> *Who if not I?*

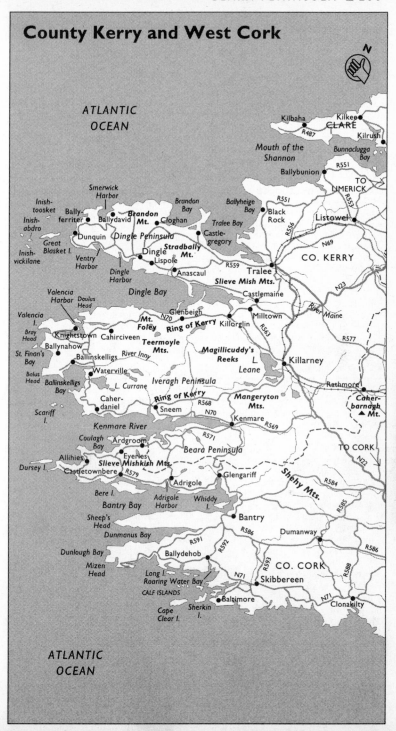

County Kerry and West Cork

ATLANTIC
OCEAN

Kilbaha
R487
Kilkee
CLARE
Kilrush

Mouth of the
Shannon
Bunnaclugga
Bay

Ballybunion
TO
LIMERICK
R551

Smerwick
Harbor

Brandon
Bay

Ballyheige
Bay
Black
Rock

R551

Listowel

CO. KERRY

Inish-
tooket
Inish-
abdro
Bally-
ferriter
Ballydavid
**Brandon
Mt.**
Cloghan

Tralee Bay
Castle-
gregory

N69

Great
Blasket I.
Dunquin
Dingle Peninsula
Dingle
**Stradbally
Mt.**

R556
R553

N23

Inish-
vickilane
Ventry
Harbor
Lispole
Anascaul

R559
Tralee

Dingle
Harbor

Slieve Mish Mts.
Castlemaine

Valencia
Harbor
Daulus
Head
Dingle Bay
Glenbeigh
Milltown

Valencia
I.
Bray
Head
**Mt.
Foley**
N70
Ring of Kerry
Killorglin
River Maine

R577

Knightstown
Cahirciveen
**Teermoyle
Mts.**
R563
Killarney

Ballynahow
St. Finan's
Bay
Ballinskelligs
River Inny
**Magillicuddy's
Reeks**
L.
Leane

Bolus
Head
Waterville
L. Currane
Iveragh Peninsula
Rathmore

Ballinskelligs
Bay
Ring of Kerry
R568
Sneem
**Mangeryton
Mts.**
**Caher-
barnagh
▲ Mt.**

Scariff
I.
Caher-
daniel
N70
Kenmare
R569

Kenmare River
R571

Coulagh
Bay
Ardgroom
Beara Peninsula
TO CORK
N22

Allihies
Eyeries
Slieve Mishkish Mts.
Castletownbere
R579
R584
R585

Dursey I.
Adrigole
Glengarriff
Shehy Mts.

Bere I.
Adrigole
Harbor
Whiddy
I.

Sheep's
Head
Bantry Bay
Bantry
Dumanway
R586

Dunmanus Bay
R591
R586
R588

Dunlough Bay
Ballydehob
R592
R593
CO. CORK
N71

Mizen
Head
Long I.
Roaring Water Bay
N71
Skibbereen

CALF ISLANDS
Baltimore
Clonakilty

Cape
Clear I.
Sherkin
I.

ATLANTIC
OCEAN

June-Sept. only, buses go to: Skibbereen (2/day); Clonakilty (1/day); Killarney via Kenmare (2/day); and Schull (1/day). **Berehaven Bus Service** (tel. 70007) stops in Bantry on the way to and from Cork (p. 237).

Bike Rental: Kramer's, Glengarriff Rd., Newtown (tel. 50278). Open Mon.-Sat. 9am-6pm, Sun. 9am-5pm. £6/day; deposit license, credit card, or passport.

Laundry: The Wash Tub, Wolfe Tone Sq. Wash and dry £3.50; open Mon.-Sat. 10am-6pm. There's nothing nicer than crisp, clean trousers.

Pharmacy: Coen's Pharmacy, Wolfe Tone Sq. (tel. 50531). Open Mon.-Tues. and Thurs.-Sat. 9:30am-1pm and 2-6pm, Wed. 9:30am-1pm.

Hospital: Bantry Hospital, Dromleigh (tel. 50133), ¼mi. past the library.

Emergency: Dial 999; no coins required. **Garda:** Wolfe Tone Sq. (tel. 50045).

Post Office: 2 William St. (tel. 50050). Open Mon.-Tues. and Thurs.-Sat. 9am-5:30pm, Wed. 9:30am-5:30pm.

Phone Code: 027.

ACCOMMODATIONS

Bantry Independent Hostel (IHH), Bishop Lucey Place (tel. 51050). Walk out of town up the Glengarriff Rd. (Marino St.), take the left fork and walk ¼mi. to this cozy little hostel nestled among the trees. The best hostel in Bantry, it has hot and plentiful showers and a kitchen with a microwave. 6-bed dorm £6.50. Private room £8/person. Open mid-March to Oct.

Harbour View Hostel, Harbour View (tel. 51313), to the left of the fire station along the water. Basic hostel accommodations on the bay. Dorm £6.50, £5.50 in winter. Double £15, in winter £12.

Eagle Point Camping and Caravan Park, Glengarriff Rd. (tel. 50630), 4mi. from town in Ballylickey. This spacious campground occupies its own private peninsula and is so well-kept that the lawns look as if they've been vacuumed. Private beach and tennis courts. Laundry, TV room, free showers (but no equipment for hire). £3.50/person. Open May-Sept.

FOOD & PUBS

Bantry has numerous inexpensive lunch restaurants. For an evening meal, pub fare at the **Snug** or the **Wolfe Tone** may be the best value. **SuperValu** is on New St. (open Mon.-Thurs. 9am-6pm, Fri. 9am-9pm, Sat. 9am-5pm), while **Essential Foods** on Main St. stocks health food (open Mon.-Sat. 10am-1pm and 2-5:30pm).

The 5A Café, Barrack St. Serves savory vegetarian selections at laughably low prices to a kick-back café crowd (Thai salad £5). Open Mon.-Sat. 10am-4:30pm, also Thurs.-Sat. 6-10pm.

O'Siochain, Bridge St. (tel. 51329). Solid, well-prepared food in a coffee house atmosphere. Sandwiches £1.50, pizza and entrees £3.50-5. Open daily 9am-10pm.

O'Connor's, Wolfe Tone Sq. (tel. 50221). Eight variations on the mussel theme. Satisfy your seafood cravings at lunch (mussels and pasta £5; dinner prices much higher). Open daily noon-9:30pm, bar/lunch menu available until 5pm.

The Steak House, Wolfe Tone Sq. (tel. 50025). As the name implies, vegetarians need not apply. Decent prices (chicken Kiev £6.50; open daily 10am-12:30am).

Bantry nightlife has kicked into overdrive thanks to **1796** (tel. 52008; a.k.a. the Bantry Folk Club), Wolfe Tone Sq. They play live music most nights, hosting both nationally known musicians and impromptu sessions. Food served noon-9pm; spaghetti w/garlic bread £4.50. **The Wolfe Tone,** Wolfe Tone Sq. (tel. 50900), has music (Tues. and Thurs.-Sun. in summer) and cooks excellent pub grub (sandwiches £1.35-4). **The Snug,** Wolf Tone Sq. (tel. 50051), aside from being an exceedingly popular pub, also serves up grub at great prices (beef burgers £4.50). **J.J. Crowley's** (tel. 50029) offers country and ballads every summer weekend. As any good seaside town should, Bantry sports its **Anchor Bar,** New St. (tel. 50012); this one is garnished with a working miniature lighthouse. For those looking for a little techno with their seafood,

Amadeus (tel. 50062), in the Bantry Bay hostel, draws a young dancing crowd on Friday and Saturday nights, 11:30pm-1:30am.

SIGHTS

The town's highlight is undoubtedly **Bantry House** (tel. 50047), a Georgian manor with an imposing garden overlooking Bantry Bay. The tired mansion is in a sad state internally, but the House contains some impressive art and furnishings. The former seat of the four Earls of Bantry (and the current residence of the same, though now less wealthy, family), the House was transformed into a hospital during Ireland's Civil War and again during the "Emergency" (neutral Éire's term for World War II). Much more impressive than the house are the manicured gardens and the view of the bay from the grand lawn. The long and shaded driveway to the house is a 5-min. walk from town on Cork Rd. (Open mid-March to Oct. daily 9am-6pm. Garden £1 contribution, house and garden £5, students £3.50.)

Next door to Bantry House is the **1796 Bantry French Armada Exhibition Centre** (tel. 51796). In 1796 Theodore Wolfe Tone, whose last two names now grace streets from Kells to Sligo, arranged for 50 French ships to sail to Ireland and aid his anti-British insurrection. A storm fatefully intervened: 40 ships turned back and 10 sank, of which one, recovered in 1985, is reconstructed at the Armada Centre. The Centre focuses on Wolfe Tone's general revolutionary activities and the revolutionary trend at the time. The museum's proximity to Bantry House is historically ironic, given that Richard White, owner of Bantry House at the time of the Armada's sailing, was instrumental in rallying British resistance to the threatened invasion. (Open March-Nov. daily 10am-6pm. Admission £3, students £1.75.)

Bantry is home to the **West Cork Chamber Music Festival** during the last week of June. The heart of the festival is the **RTE Vanburgh String Quartet,** who have invited artists such as Barry Douglas, Véronique Dietschy, and the Parisii String Quartet. Last year's festival, held at Bantry House, also featured a reading by Seamus Heaney. Call box office for general inquiries (tel. 61105).

Sea trips circumnavigate the harbor or drop you at **Whiddy Island,** a prime spot for repressed ornithologists. Trips leave from the pier hourly (tel. 50310; run July-Sept. daily 10am-6pm; £4 return). For two weeks in August (usually beginning on the second weekend), the **Bantry Bay Regatta** employs the best sailors in Ireland. Festivities abound; ask around for details.

Sheep's Head is the empty space on your map west of Bantry. Largely ignored by the heavy-footed herd of tourists stampeding through Skibbereen, Bantry, and Glengarriff, this narrow finger of land is best explored on a daytrip by bike or on foot. Hitchers may find it difficult to get a ride to or from the peninsula, since it's the most sparsely populated of West Cork's peninsulas. Cyclists head west along the cove-filled southern shore and return by the barren and windswept northern road, while hikers explore the spine of hills down the middle. Inquire in Bantry for directions.

Sheep's Head itself is marked by the requisite lighthouse and its spectacular (and untouristed) cliff-top vistas. If you're lucky, you might see the tide change in Bantry Bay, where incoming breakers meet the outgoing tide and create a mini-maelstrom. For a snack on the way out, try the highly recommended **Tin Pub** in **Ahakista,** on the southern road—the corrugated iron "shack" serves yummy sandwiches. You can also try the nearby Japanese restaurant, **Shiro** (tel. 67030).

▧ Glengarriff & Garinish

Glengariff identifies itself as a "gateway" to the Beara peninsula. If you're wise (or already well-stocked with Guinness paraphernalia), proceed quickly through this touristy gateway. Glengariff is graced with two friendly **tourist offices.** The large, privately run office is in "the village" next to the public bathrooms and offers the typical shamrock schlock (open daily 9am-6pm). The smaller Bord Fáilte office is on Bantry Rd. (tel. 63084), next to the Eccles Hotel (office open June-Aug. Mon.-Sat. 10am-1pm and 2:15-6pm). **Bus Éireann** runs to Glengarriff from Bantry (Mon.-Sat. 3-5/day, Sun. 2-3/day; 25min.; £2.25). Another route runs between Killarney and Glengarriff via Kenmare (June to mid-Sept. Mon.-Sat. 2/day; Kenmare 45min.; £3.70; Killarney 1¾hr.). Buses stop in front of Casey's Hotel on Main St. **Berehaven Bus Service** (tel. 70007) also runs buses to Cork (Mon.-Sat. 3/day, Sun. 2/day; 2¾hr.) and Bantry (Mon. 2/day, Tues. and Thurs.-Sat. 1/day). The **phone code** flowers 027.

Accommodations, Food, & Pubs There has been a recent proliferation of "hostels" (often private houses stocked with beds and billed as cheaper, if less private, alternatives to the town's B&Bs; no IHH or An Óige) in Glengarriff. A 20-minute walk from town on the Kenmare Rd., the **Glengarriff Independent Hostel** is the best option—a stark but spotless dorm costs £6. Smaller and closer to town along the Kenmare Rd., the **Hummingbird Rest** (tel. 63195) offers cramped, private rooms for £5 per person. A 10-minute walk from town toward Bantry passes **St. Anthony's B&B,** Bantry Rd. (tel. 63109); a basic B&B puts you out only £11. In the center of town, **Maureen's,** Main St. (tel. 63201), offers comfortable rooms (£13.50, w/bath £14.50). Two **campsites, Dowling's** (tel. 63154) and **O'Shea's** (tel. 63140), are neighbors on the Castletownbere Rd. 1½ mi. from town (both open mid-March to Oct.; £5/tent). Sandwiches and tempting pastries can be found at **The Coffee Shop,** Main St. (tel. 63073; cake slice £1.65), while **Johnny Barry's** (tel. 63315) and **The Blue Loo** (tel. 63167), both on Main St., serve standard pub grub.

Sights Glengarriff's proximity to the lush **National Forest** is its kindest attraction, where hiking trails allow you to meander among giant rhododendrons and moss-strewn evergreens. Walking trails in the area range from pebbled walks for the most sedentary, scone-eating tourists to rugged climbs for serious hikers. *Let's Walk Around Glengarriff,* available at hostels in town and at the tourist office, outlines several walks in the park, but more intense hikers should pick up maps at the tourist office in town. For the truly committed, Glengarriff is a good starting point for the newly opened 130-mi. **Beara Way** walking path.

The town's popularity, however, really results from **Garinish Island,** formerly a rocky outcrop inhabited only by gorse bushes. Now, a million hours of labor and countless boatloads of topsoil later, it's an exotic flower garden! Three ferry companies along the main Bantry Rd. overcharge—a return trip is a steep £5 (students £4); prices are somewhat negotiable, especially from September to June. Garinish's **Latinate Garden,** also known as Illnacullin, blooms and flourishes with the seasons and offers an expensive view of the peninsula's mountains. (Open daily July-Aug. Mon.-Sat. 10am-5:30pm, Sun. 11am-6pm; April, June, and Sept. Mon.-Sat. 10am-5:30pm, Sun. 1-6pm; March and Oct. Mon.-Sat. 10am-4:30pm, Sun. 1-5pm. Admission £2.50, students £1.50.) Boats usually leave every 10 to 20 minutes, depending on the weather and the crowd. Nearby, **Lake Eskenohoolikeaghaun** ("Lake of Twelve Cows") wins Ireland's longest-name contest. Glengarriff's water gets more attention for its fishing than its aesthetic value. Upper and Lower Lough Avaul are stocked with brown and rainbow trout, but you need a fishing permit to catch 'em. Barley Lake, nearby rivers, and the ocean, do not require permits. For more details, pick up the free *Fishing in Glengarriff* and ask around by the piers.

The breathtaking **Healy Pass** branches north off east-west R572 near Adrigole; it's a narrow, winding road which takes you through the green and rocky Caha Mountains to Lauragh. The **Glanmore Lake Youth Hostel (An Óige/HI)** (tel. (064) 83181) makes a good base for hiking or fishing in the little-explored mountains near Lauragh. The prim and immaculate hostel is housed in a stately former schoolhouse with great mountain views. (Dorm £5.50, £4.50 in low season; open Easter-Sept.) Follow signs from town; it is located 3 mi. from Lauragh on a dead end road.

■ Castletownbere

In contrast to Glengarriff, the fishing town of Castletownbere is an unpretentious relief. This largest town on the Beara Peninsula reverberates daily with the sounds of ferry engines, cars, and wind over the world's second-largest natural harbor, Bere-haven Bay. During the summer, the town supports street musicians, festivals, and long-distance cyclists who stop here for a pint. The summer culminates with the regatta at the **Festival of the Sea** during the first weekend in August. Winters show the town's true calling—working hard for the fruit of the sea.

Practical Information The bathroom-sized **tourist office,** behind O'Dono-ghue's by the harbor, gives away heaps of maps (open June-Sept. Mon.-Sat. 11am-5pm). The **ATM** at the **AIB** on Main St. (tel. 70015) accepts VISA (open Mon. 10am-12:30pm and 1:30-5pm, Tues.-Fri. 10am-12:30pm, and 1:30-4pm). **Bus Éireann** oper-ates a summer service between Castletownbere and Killarney, via Kenmare (June 26-Sept. 2 Mon.-Sat. 2/day; £8.80, students £5). **Berehaven Bus Service** (tel. 70007), heads to Bantry via Glengarriff (Mon. 2/day, Tues.-Sat. 1/day; Glengarriff 45min., £2.70; Bantry 1½hr., £4) and to Cork (Thurs. only; 3hr.; £8) from the parking lot next to O'Donoghue's. Two **minibus** services leave Cork for Castletownbere Mon.-Sat. 6pm and Sun. 8pm: phone **Harrington's** (tel. 74003) or **O'Sullivan's** (tel. 74168) for mandatory reservations (both buses £8). **Bike hire** is available at **SuperValu** on Main St. (tel. 70020; open Mon.-Sat. 9am-7pm, Sun. 9am-1pm; £7/day; deposit £20). The **phone code** for Castletownbere and Bere Island is a grizzly 027.

Accommodations, Food, & Pubs Two miles west of town on Allihies Rd., just past the fork to Dunboy Castle, the **Beara Hostel** (tel. 70184) offers comfortable beds in a pleasantly rural setting (dorm £6, private room £7.50/person; **camping** £3.50). **Seapoint B&B** (tel. 70292), about 1 mi. outside of town towards Glengariff, has spectacular views and spotless, spacious rooms. Gay and lesbian friendly (£16/person w/local wholefood breakfast; laundry £5). **Castletown House,** Main St. (tel. 70252), above the Old Bank Seafood Restaurant, offers lovely rooms and lots of info (£13, w/bath £15).

Four miles farther, and a good deal more isolated, is the euphoria-inducing **Gar-ranes Farmhouse Hostel (IHH)** (tel. 73147). This luxurious and intimate cottage perched above the sea has a view to inspire meditation (dorm £6, double £16). Stay on the Allihies Rd.; if you hit a fork in the road, you've gone too far. Phone ahead to confirm that all the space hasn't been gobbled up by the Buddhist center next door and to arrange a possible lift from town. Next door to the Garranes Farmhouse Hostel is the **Dzogchen Buddhist Centre,** where dabblers and devotees alike practice medi-tation. There are no drugs or altered states involved. The aim is to awaken "Buddha Nature"—to free yourself from transient angers and passions and convert them into compassion. You can attend a **meditation session** every Saturday at 8pm and most other evenings in summer.

Seafood spawns in almost all of Castletownbere's restaurants. **The Old Bakery,** Main St. (tel. 70790), serves up killer pizzas (12" w/2 toppings, £6) in a charming building that used to be a bakery. Live trad and jazz Friday nights. **Jack Patrick's,** Main St. (tel. 70319), serves enormous fish platters (open Mon.-Sat. 10:30am-9pm). Across the street, **Niki's** (tel. 70625) expands the seafood options with creativity (open daily 10am-3pm and 7-9:30pm). For the less gourmet, the **Hideaway Take-Away,** Main St. (tel. 70386), serves up reasonable food fast and fresh (fish and chips £2.10; open Mon.-Sat. 5pm-12:30am, Sun. 1pm-12:30am). **SuperValu,** Main St. (tel. 70020), sells the largest selection of foodstuffs (open Mon.-Sat. 9am-9pm, Sun. 9am-6pm). The most popular pub in town is **MacCarthy's,** Main St. (tel. 70014), which serves food all day (all sandwiches under £2), and live trad and ballads on the weekends. **O'Dono-ghue's** pub, Main St. (tel. 70007), on the square, lures a younger catch with its pool table and sunny (or starry) tables outside. **Lynch's,** Main St. (tel. 70363), is also popu-lar, hosting sporadic live music in summer.

Sights Castletownbere's seat at the foot of awe-inspiring **Hungry Hill** (3414ft.) makes it a fine base for day trips up the mountain (inquire in the tourist office for details). In addition, the huge harbor is a joy for watersport enthusiasts. **Beara Kayaks** (tel. 70692) offers one- and two-hour classes in Castletownbere, Bere Island, Glengariff, and Schull (£5/hr., all equipment included; call for bookings).

Two miles southwest of Castletownbere on the Allihies Rd., **Dunboy Castle** shelters two separate ruins. Cows roam the crumbling Gothic-style halls of its 18th- and 19th-century mansion, and ¾ mi. past the gate stand the ruins of the 14th-century O'Sullivan Bere fortress (pedestrians and cyclists 50p). The road that runs past the castle soon becomes a shady trail that passes a number of sheltered coves perfect for swimming, as long as you don't mind jellyfish.

■ Near Castletownbere: Bere Island

Cape Clear Island it isn't, yet. While Bere Island's proximity to the mainland and its dedication to shipping may disturb its tranquility, the island still offers fantastic views of the Beara peninsula and is undergoing a three-year beautification process. Two **ferries** chug to Bere Island. **Murphy's Ferry Service** (tel. 75004) leaves from the pontoon 3 mi. east of Castletownbere off the Glengarriff Rd. but lands you much closer to the island's "center," Rerrin Village (daily 4/day; £4 return, students £3). The other company, **Bere Island Ferry** (tel. 75009), leaves from the center of Castletownbere but drops you inconveniently on the western end of the island (June 21-Sept. 2, 5/day, Sun. 4/day; £3 return). A *Let's Go* researcher was stranded here for hours when her ferry from the island left half an hour early; tell the ferryman on which boat you plan to return.

Bere Island used to be a British naval base—forts and military remnants are still scattered around the island. The Irish Army now uses the island for training. These days, **Glenan's Sailing School** (tel. 75012), founded by the Irish and French during the *résistance,* rules the waters with week-long courses (£170/week, inclusive of food, equipment, and accommodations). If you plan to stay the night, you've no other choice than to dock at **Mrs. Sullivan's Harbour View B&B** (tel. 75011), a ½-hr. walk from the Bere Island Ferry on the west end of the island (£14/person, w/bath £16). Call for a lift, or ask an islander for one at **Kitty Murphy's Café** (tel. 75004). This wonderful little bistro serves the only affordable food on the island. Kitty herself may be the best, friendliest source of information on the Bere. **Murphy's Shop**, next door, or the **Hotel Bere Island** (tel. 75018), actually a pub and a store located east of Mrs. Sullivan's, will fill all of your grocery needs. Next door to the café, **Desmond Sullivan's** will pamper you in the Guinness department.

■ The Rest of the Ring

Past Castletownbere, the Beara Peninsula stretches out with craggy knolls, cliff-lined coasts, and desolate villages. The stark isolation of this part of the Ring is both an attraction and a frustration for hitchers. While green-polyester-clad tourists are hard to find, so too are drivers. Hitchers report the mid-afternoon beach traffic during July and August yields the most success. Otherwise, rent a cycle.

Teeny **Allihies** dangles west of Castletownbere, along R575. The town consists of one street on the Atlantic, ensconced by the Slieve Mountains. **The Village Hostel (IHH),** Main St. (tel. (027) 73014), formerly Bonnie Brae's, next to the very red O'Neill's pub, is an excellent base for exploring the nearby coastline. Robin's egg-blue walls, sun-drenched kitchen, and warm showers take the desolate edge off of Allihies. (Dorm £6, double £16. **Camping** £3/person. Laundry £3.50. Open May-Sept.) One mile south of the village (and well-marked by signs) lies the spare **Allihies Youth Hostel (An Óige/HI)** (tel. (027) 73014), which threatens to compound the sense of bare isolation in Allihies (dorm £5.50, under 18 £4; sheets 60p; open June-Sept.). **O'Neill's Bar and Restaurant** (tel. (027) 73008), next to the Village Hostel, offers a varied menu of pub grub (curried chicken paprika £5.50). **The Atlantic,** Main

St. (tel. (027) 73072), prepares modest seafood right off the boat (plaice £6; open daily 9am-10pm). **O'Sullivan's** (tel. (027) 73004) sells everything necessary for a first-class picnic on Dursey and even rents bikes to get you there (open daily 9am-9pm; mountain bikes £7/day). Allihies' four pubs cater mostly to locals. Usually one pub—seemingly chosen by tacit consensus among the villagers—is quite lively each night. **O'Neill's** is a safe bet, and so is **The Lighthouse.** The **Oak Bar** hosts trad music every Thursday night.

The blunt northern head of the peninsula is choked with architectural fossils. Children's gravestones crumble outside the **Celtic Church,** 2 mi. from Allihies, and marked on some maps and signs as Point Nadistiert. The collapsing entrance to a series of caves stands nearby. **Mass rocks** dot the fields surrounding the village, and the shafts of abandoned **copper mines** dot Allihies' upper slopes. Evidence of a booming mid-19th-century mining industry, the mines are fenced off. **Ballydonegan Strand** is just short of town on the Castletownbere Rd. More pristine and secluded are the white sands of **Garnish Strand,** across from the post office on the Dursey Rd. The **Windy Point House** (tel. (027) 73017), at the cable car a few minutes away, sustains scone-deprived beachgoers and tempts some to stay the night with its amazing views of Dursey Sound (sandwiches under £2; B&B £12, w/bath £15).

The best scenery on the Beara is on **Dursey Island,** reached by Ireland's only cable car (tel. (027) 73017). The car makes the 10-minute aerial trip continuously Monday to Saturday 9-11am, 2:30-5pm, and 7-8pm; Sunday hours vary (£2.50 return). The English Army laid waste to Dursey Fort in 1602 after raiding the unarmed garrison and callously tossing many soldiers over the cliffs to their doom. The whole of Dursey Island is best seen by bike, but call ahead to ensure that there is room for your bike on the cable car. A trip to the western tip provides a stunning view of the sea and a chance to observe the island's much-vaunted migrant bird flocks. There is no accommodation on the island, but camping is legal. Besides, the island's nine residents could use the company.

Ten miles to the northeast of Dursey Island via some of the most barren land and some of the most exciting road in Ireland lies the colorful hamlet of **Eyeries.** Head to the **beach** here; or ask for directions to **Ballycrovane,** where the tallest *ogham* stone in Ireland (17ft.) stands (it's on private property but well-signposted). Five minutes east of the village, the **Ard Na Mara Hostel** (tel. (027) 74271) makes you feel like a friend of the family (dorm £6, private room £7; laundry £3).

The only other thing to see on the northern side of the Beara—except for mountains, forests, and sea—are the **Derreen Gardens** (tel. (064) 83103), where you can lose yourself in the mossy tunnels that run through evergreens and massive rhododendrons. (½mi. north of Lauragh on the coast road. Open daily April-Sept. 11am-6pm. Admission £2.50.) Heading east past Eyeries, you pass through **Ardgroom,** a small village with…drum roll please…a good pub. **The Holly Bar** (tel. (027) 74082) hosts live trad on Fri. and serves up a mean bowl of seafood chowder (£3).

County Kerry

Various places in Co. Kerry claim to be Europe's westernmost inhabited land. They're all wrong (the honor goes to Hellisandur, Iceland), but the ubiquitous mistake reveals something about Co. Kerry. Consisting of a string of towns, forests, mountains, and peninsulas so far from the Continent, Co. Kerry can believe in its own version of European commerce and geography. The county is so removed from Dublin's metropolitan orbit that when its residents think about the big, bad city, they think of Cork. Famous for its natural beauty, the county can subsist economically from the tourism trade along the Ring of Kerry. If you spend enough time, you may come to agree that the world worth seeing is bounded by the River Shannon and the Beara Peninsula.

The Iveragh Peninsula (colloquially equated with the Ring of Kerry road) has the lake-filled Killarney National Park at its base, Bray Head near its tip, and noxious tour buses traveling between the two. Even so, the views are incomparable. The Dingle Peninsula is slightly less visited: narrow roads protect Slea Head, the West Dingle (*Corcha Dhuibhne) gaeltacht,* and the Blasket Islands from tour bus madness. Summer bus transport throughout Kerry is all too available. In the off season, public transportation grows sparse along coastal routes.

■ Killarney

Package tourists just love Killarney. But, if you can dodge the blue-haired brigade from Boise, and slide by the *shillelagh* vendor, Killarney has a lot to offer serious travelers. A lively town with plenty of entertainment options, and delicious food, Killarney is also home to one of Ireland's most treasured natural parks. With some of the most splendid inland scenery in Ireland, Killarney National Park offers refuge from the folks with the big cameras and belt buckles.

ORIENTATION & PRACTICAL INFORMATION

Killarney packs into three crowded major streets. **Main St.,** in the center of town, begins at the Town Hall and the tourist office, then becomes High St. **New St.** and **Plunkett St.** both intersect Main St. New St. heads west to the Knockreer Estate and toward Killorglin. Plunkett St. becomes College St. and then Park Rd., heading east to the bus and train stations. East Avenue Rd. begins by the train station, bends, then becomes Muckross Rd. en route to the Muckross Estate and Kenmare.

Tourist Office: Main St., in the Town Hall (tel. 31633). Exceptionally helpful and deservedly popular. Open July-Aug. Mon.-Sat. 9am-8pm, Sun. 9am-1pm and 2:15-6pm; June and Sept. Mon.-Sat. 9am-6pm, Sun. 10am-5pm; Oct.-May Mon.-Fri. 9:15am-5:30pm, Sat. 9:15am-1pm.

Banks: TSB, 23/24 New St. (tel 33666). Open Mon.-Fri. 9:30am-5pm, Thurs. until 7pm. **AIB,** Main St., next to the tourist office (tel. 31922). Open Mon.-Fri. 10am-4pm, Wed. until 5pm. **ATM,** Main St., accepts MasterCard/Access and Visa.

American Express: International Hotel (tel. 35722), around the corner from the tourist office. Moneygrams, Traveler's Cheques, and client mail service. Open Mon.-Fri. 9am-9pm, Sat.-Sun. 10am-7pm. Winter: Mon.-Fri. 9am-5pm (tentative).

Trains: Killarney Station off East Avenue Rd. (tel. 31067), near the intersection with Park Rd. past the Great Southern Hotel. Open Mon.-Sat. 7:30am-12:45pm and 1:45pm-6:10pm, Sun. ½hr. before train departures. Trains flee to: Cork (daily 5/day; 1½hr.; £13.50, students £6), Dublin (4/day; 3½hr.; £33.50, students £12.50), Galway (3/day; 6hr.; £30, students £12), and Limerick (Mon.-Sat. 4/day, Sun. 3/day; 2hr.; £15, students £6.50). No trains leave after 6:30pm.

Buses: off East Avenue Rd. (tel. 34777), across from the Great Southern Hotel. Open daily in summer 8:30am-5:50pm, in winter 8:30am-4pm. Buses travel to: Cork (6-7/day; 2hr.; £8.80, students £5); Dingle (3-6/day; 2hr.; £8.80, students £5); Dublin (3-4/day; 6hr.; £14, students £9); Galway (5-7/day; 7hr.; £13, students £8); Limerick (4-5/day; 2hr.; £9.30, students £5.60); and Sligo (2-3/day; 7½hr.; £17, students £10). From June-Sept., buses leave Killarney for the **Ring of Kerry Circuit** (Mon.-Sat. 2/day, Sun. 1/day), which stops in Killorglin, Glenbeigh, Kells, Cahersiveen, Waterville, Caherdaniel, Sneem, and Moll's Gap. (£9.70, students £6. A return, which allows you to get on and off as often as you wish, is £8.50 for students.) A bus to Cahirsiveen does the northern half of the Ring of Kerry (summer Mon.-Sat. 4/day, Sun. 2/day; 1½hr.; £7.30, students £4.20). The **Dingle/Slea Head tour** (Mon.-Fri. 1/day) stops in Inch, Annascaul, Dingle, Ventry, Slea Head, Dunquin, and Ballyferriter (£9.70, students £6). A charge of about £5 is levied for carrying bikes; ask driver ahead to ensure there's space.

Bike Rental: Crafts and Curios Rent-a-Bike, High St. (tel. 32578), next to Neptune's Hostel. £5/day, £25/week. Free panniers, locks, and park maps. 10% discount w/ISIC (daily rates). Open daily 8:30am-8pm.

Laundry: J. Gleason's Launderette (tel. 33877), next to Spar Market on College St. £4.50/load. Open Mon.-Wed. and Sat. 9:15am-6pm, Thurs.-Fri. 9:15am-8pm.
Pharmacy: Sewell's Pharmacy, corner of Main and New St. (tel. 31027). Open Mon.-Sat. 9am-6:30pm. No snake-bite kits, but that's usually not a problem here.
Hospital: District Hospital, St. Margaret's Rd. (tel. 31076). Follow High St. 1mi. out from town center.
Emergency: Dial 999; no coins required. **Garda:** New St. (tel. 31222).
Post Office: New St. (tel. 31288). Open Mon.-Sat. 9am-5:30pm.
Phone Code: 064.

ACCOMMODATIONS

It's easy to find a cushy B&B in Killarney. The town is also home to some excellent hostels—six lie within easy walking distance of the town center, while three are in rural settings near the National Park. Camping is not allowed in the National Park.

The Railway Hostel, Park Rd. (tel. 35299), across the street from the bus and train stations. Big and bright hostel with skylights, excellent beds, and a pool table. The Railway Hostel is surprisingly friendly for its large size. 4- to 12-bed dorm £6.50. Double £16-20. Bikes £5/day.

Neptune's (IHH), Bishop's Lane (tel. 35255), the first walkway off New St. on the right. Large and clean with good showers and solid mattresses. 6- to 8-bed dorms £6. 4-bed dorms £7.50. Double £16. 10% discount to ISIC cardholders. Laundry £3.50. Sheets 50p. Lockers £1. Free tour booking. Bikes £5/day.

Bunrower House (IHH), Ross Rd. (tel. 33914). Follow Muckross Rd. out of town and take a right onto Ross Rd. at the Esso station. The hostel is about ¾mi. down the road, on the left. Free mini-bus to and from train and bus stations. Like its sister hostel, the Súgán, the "Bun" has a common room with peat fire, spacious bunkrooms, sky-lit toilets, outstanding showers, and a golden retriever. Dorm £6. Double £17. Sheets 50p. **Camping** in the quiet yard is the closest you can legally get to sleeping in Killarney's big National Park (£3.50).

The Súgán (IHH), Lewis Rd. (tel. 33104), 2min. from the bus or train station; turn right, then left onto College St. Lewis Rd. is the first right. Late nights spent in the stone common room with a glowing turf fire, candlelight, and groovy music give the hostel an incomparable ambiance. Small, ship-like bunk rooms blur the distinction between intimacy and claustrophobia. 4- to 8-bed dorm £6. Hostelers can enjoy a superb 3-course dinner in the restaurant downstairs for £7.

Atlas House, Park Rd. (tel. 36144). A 10-min. walk from town. College St. past the bus station until it turns into Park Rd. At the first traffic light, make a left. Atlas House bills itself as "budget accommodation" rather than a hostel. Situated in a huge, spanking new building, the hostel will comfort those suffering Holiday Inn withdrawal. Big kitchen, and a luxurious sitting room with satellite TV. Dorm £7.50-9. Double £24, w/bath £27. Triple £34.50. Continental breakfast included.

The Four Winds Hostel (IHH), 43 New St. (tel. 33094). Situated in town but very close to the entrance to the National Park, the Four Winds is large, liveable, and handy, though its cinder-block architecture makes it a little dreary. Large dorm £6. Small dorm £7.50. Double £17. Breakfast £3.50. Laundry £4.

Aghadoe Hostel (An Óige/HI) (tel. 31240). In Aghadoe, 3mi. west of town on the Killorglin Rd., this hostel occupies a stone mansion with magnificent views of the mountains. Grandiose and comfortable, the hostel offers outdoor activities, including canoeing, climbing, and day-long classes on Celtic heritage, storytelling, and local lore (£20, includes lunch). Reception 8:30am-10:30pm. Midnight curfew. Free van to and from bus and train stations. Dorm June-Sept. £6.50, Oct.-May £5. Café food £1.50-3.50. Laundry £2.50. Bikes £6/day.

Peacock Farms Hostel (IHH) (tel. 33557). Take Muckross Rd. out of town and turn left at Muckross Village, just after the hotel. Take that road 2mi. and follow the signposts—if you think you are nearly there, you haven't gone far enough. As a less taxing alternative, call for a ride from the bus station. Overlooking Lough Guitane and surrounded by Killarney's slopes, this hostel is home to a family of peacocks and a collection of homing pigeons. Skylights, hand-painted showers, and comfy rooms. Wheelchair accessible. Dorms £5. Open May-Sept.

Black Valley Hostel (An Óige/HI) (tel. 34712), 12mi. from town on the Gap of Dunloe Rd. This was one of the last places in Ireland to receive electricity. Buy food in town or eat at the hostel. This spare but spotless hostel is conveniently located on the Kerry Way. Midnight curfew. Dorm £6, off season £5. Linen 80p.

Fossa Caravan and Camping Park (tel. 31497), 3½mi. west of town on the Killorglin Rd. Kitchen, laundromat, tennis courts, shop, and restaurant. £3.50/person. Laundry £1.50, 50p/20-min. dry. Showers 50p. Open mid-March to Oct.

Flesk Caravan and Camping (tel. 31704), 1mi. from town on Muckross Rd. £3.25/cyclist or hiker. Laundry £1.50, 50p/dry. Showers 50p. Open March-Oct.

FOOD

Food in Killarney is affordable at lunchtime, but prices skyrocket as the sun sinks. **Quinnsworth**, on New St., is the town's grocer (open Mon. 9am-8pm, Tues.-Wed. 9am-7:30pm, Thurs.-Fri. 9am-9pm, Sat. 9am-7pm). A number of fast-food joints and take-aways stay open until 2-3am nightly to satisfy the post-Guinness munchies.

No. 12, 12 High St. (tel. 36744). Lunch or dine on eclectic cuisine from around the world to strains of jazz. Vegetarian-friendly. Thai salmon fishcakes £7. Open Tues.-Sun. noon-10pm.

The Súgán, Lewis Rd. (tel. 33104). Delicious and generous vegetarian-friendly dinners are a bargain for those staying at the hostel upstairs. Main courses (for nonhostelers) £7. Dinner served daily 6-9:30pm.

An Taelann, Bridewell Lane (tel. 33083), on the left off New St. Fair but creative vegetarian dishes with an international flair. Lunch £1.50-4.30, dinner entrees £8.

Robertino's, 9 High St. (tel. 34966). Eat bruschetta and antipasti in the company of plaster Greco-Roman goddesses. Pasta £7, pizza £7. Open daily 12:30-4pm and 5-10:30pm. **Allegro's,** next door, is run by the same owners (pizza £5-6.50).

Claret's, 10 College St. (tel. 36467). What Claret's loses in the way of atmosphere, it gains in affordability. Seemingly the only place in town that offers appetite-sized portions. Spaghetti Carbonara £4.25. Open daily 9am-10pm.

PUBS

The battalions of jig-seeking tourists make it hard to find a decent pub in Killarney, but a few have managed to withstand the rising tide of Shamrock-mania. During the summer, traditional music can be heard nightly around town.

Yer Mans, Plunkett St. (tel. 32688). Uncontestedly the best pub in town, it is frequented by a young, mixed crowd who actually live in Killarney. On request, Guinness is served in jam jars (£1.25), and Yer Mans is the only pub in Ireland licensed by Guinness to do so. Trad most nights in summer, singer/songwriter nights every other Fri. If you arrive before 10:30pm, you can stay in their alter-ego club, **Rudy's,** without paying the cover charge.

Fáilte Bar, College St. (tel. 33404). A large, relaxed crowd gathers at this dark and woody pub. Singer/songwriter sessions every night (trad Mon.-Tues. from 9pm).

Buckley's Bar, College St. (tel. 31037). Tourist-tolerant drinkers warm themselves by the peat fire. Lack of atmosphere compensated for by some of the best trad in Killarney, nightly from 9:30pm.

Mustang Sally's, Main St. (tel. 35790). A young crowd flocks to the loud rock music, some of it live, which scares away the tourists.

O'Connor's Traditional Pub, 7 High St. (tel. 32496). Tourists and locals mingle in this upbeat and comfortable pub. Trad on Mon. and Thurs. nights.

SIGHTS & ENTERTAINMENT

Congested with pubs, souvenir shops, and disoriented foreigners, Killarney's charm is elusive. The glories of Killarney are to be discovered in the National Park just beyond city limits. The neo-Gothic **St. Mary's Cathedral** on New St. seats 1400 and boasts three altars, one the size of a tennis court, inside its rough limestone exterior (always open; free). Killarney's festivals are worth anthropological exploration: locals take them quite seriously and come out *en masse*. In mid-March, Killarney hosts the **Guinness Roaring 1920s Festival,** in which pubs, restaurants, and hostels bust out in jazz, barbershop singing, and flapper regalia. In mid-May and mid-July, horses gallop around the race course on Ross Rd., competing in the **Killarney Races** (tickets available at gate; £3-5). The **Killarney Regatta** in July draws rowers and spectators to Lough Leane. **Gaelic football matches** are held in Fitzgerald Stadium on Lewis Rd. most Sunday afternoons and some weekday evenings (Kerry's fanatical rivalry with Cork comes to a head when Cork's team comes to town).

Several **nightclubs** around Killarney simmer from 10:30pm until 1:30 or 2am. Most charge £4-5 cover but often offer discounts before 11pm. **Rudy's Nightclub,** above Yer Mans on Plunkett St. (tel. 32688), plays alternative music (Tues., Thurs., Fri., Sat., and Sun. evenings) for Killarney's ruthlessly hip element. **Revelles,** East Avenue Rd. (tel. 32522), in the East Avenue Hotel, clogs with rave and club kids on Friday through Sunday nights, while **Scoundrels** in the Eviston House Hotel on New St. (tel. 31640) attracts a slightly older crowd. (Mon. 60s-80s, Tues.-Thurs. mixed music, Fri. dance, Sat.-Sun. mixed and often live music. Always a discount before 11pm. Closes 1:30am.) Check the *Killarney Advertiser* (free) for happenings around town and the *Kingdom* (70p) for county events.

■ Killarney National Park

Scooping a series of glens and strewing about ice-smoothed rocks and precarious boulders, the Ice Ages had a dramatic impact around Killarney. The 37-sq.-mi. park, stretching west and south from Killarney towards Kenmare, incorporates a string of forested mountains and the famous **Lakes of Killarney:** huge **Lough Leane (Lower Lake),** medium **Middle (Muckross) Lake,** and smallest **Upper Lake,** 2 mi. southwest and connected by a canal. Ireland's last indigenous herd of red deer, numbering about 850, roams the glens that surround the lakes.

Although the Kenmare Rd. curves along the southeastern shores of the lakes, hitchhiking is both difficult and unnecessary. The park's major scenic spots are only a few miles apart and connected by plenty of well-paved paths ideal for walking or mountain biking. But, be forewarned, these paths are also frequented by droves of horse-drawn buggies. There's more *cac capall* (Irish for what's left on a road after dozens of roughage-eating horses have traveled it) than any sane person would want to see (or smell) in a lifetime. Don't attempt to explore the park without one eye on the road and one eye on a decent map. Maps from the Killarney tourist office or the **Information Centre** behind Muckross House (tel. 31440; open daily June-Sept. 9am-6pm) may suffice for outings along most trails, but serious hikers should buy the 1:25,000 Ordnance Survey map.

The most frequented destinations are the **Ross Castle/Lough Leane** area, **Muckross House** on Middle Lake, and the **Gap of Dunloe,** which is bordered on the southwest by Ireland's highest mountain range, **Macgillycuddy's Reeks** (most of the peaks are under 3000ft.). The Gap of Dunloe is a full-day excursion, but the others are close to town and can be managed in several hours or stretched over a full day, depending on your mode of transport. Hikers and bikers should take the necessary precautions whether traveling alone or in groups (see **Camping,** p.41).

The best way to see almost all of the park in one day is to bike to the Gap of Dunloe (see below for more details). If, however, a 14-mi. bike excursion strikes you with trepidation, there are several short, well-marked, and well-paved walking trails closer to the Killarney side of the park. The park is also a perfect starting point for those who plan to walk the 129-mi. **Kerry Way,** essentially the Ring of Kerry on foot. The first (or last) leg of the walk, the **Old Kenmore Road,** passes through the spectacular Torc and Mangerton Mountains, and can be managed in one day (from Killarney, follow the Kenmare Rd. 4 mi. and turn left just beyond the main entrance to Muckross House—the path leaves from the carpark on this side road). If you plan to hike the rest of the Kerry Way, take a good map, pack lightly, and do not attempt the trail from October to March, when rains make the uneven terrain dangerous. The Killarney

SOUTHWEST IRELAND

bookstore sells a *Kerry Way* guide, with topographic maps of the Way. Also available are excellent 1:50,000 Ordnance Survey maps of the Iveragh that include minor roads, trails, and archaeological points of interest. Unfortunately, the maps are expensive (£4.60) and far from waterproof.

ROSS CASTLE & LOUGH LEANE

From town, **Knockreer Estate** is a short walk down New St. The original mansion housed the Grosvenor family (of National Geographic fame) and, before that, the steadfastly Catholic Earls of Kenmare. The current building, dating only from the 1950s, is unimpressive but still gives great views of the hills. You can drive to **Ross Castle** (turn right on Ross Rd. off Muckross Rd.; tel. 35851), but the numerous footpaths from Knockreer are more scenic (a 1-mi. walk). The castle, built in the 14th century by the O'Donoghue chieftains, was the last one in Munster to hold out against Cromwell's army. In the last two decades the castle has been completely renovated, and it shows: the limestone is clean, the wood beams fresh. Admission to the castle is by guided tour only, which are preoccupied with the O'Donoghue clan's vaguely paranoic, and ultimately futile, measures to repel intruders. (Open daily June-Aug. 9am-6:30pm, May 9:30am-5pm, Sept. 9am-6pm, Oct. 9am-5pm. Admission £2.50, students £1. Last admission 45min. before closing.) Past the castle, paths lead to the wooded and relatively secluded **Ross Island**—not an island at all, but a peninsula shaped like a lobster claw stretched out into Lough Leane. Ross Island is the sight of the green-colored **copper pools.** It is thought that copper has been mined here for over four millennia.

The view of Lough Leane and its mountains from Ross Island is great, but the best way to see the area is from the water. Two **waterbus services,** Pride of the Lakes (tel. 32638) and Lily of Killarney (tel. 31068), leave from behind the castle for lake cruises every 30 to 60 minutes daily in summer (£5/person). You can hire your own rowboats by the castle (£2/hr.), or take one of the many **motorboat trips** (tel. 34351) to Innisfallen Island (£3/person), to the **Meeting of the Waters** (£5/person; through Lough Leane and Muckross Lake), or to the **Gap of Dunloe** (£7/person, £10 return; through Lough Leane, Muckross Lake and Upper Lake).

On the **Innisfallen Island** are the stoic remains of **Innisfallen Abbey.** St. Finian the Leper founded the abbey around 600 AD. The abbey was eventually transformed into a university during the Middle Ages (High King Brian Ború was educated here). The *Annals of Innisfallen,* now entombed at Oxford, recount world and Irish history. Written in Irish and Latin by 39 monastic scribes, the annals were supposedly finished when the last scribe put pen to parchment in 1326. At the abbey's center is a yew tree: yew and oak groves were sacred to the Druids, so abbeys were often built in and around them. Now the abbey walls are crumbling. The separate Augustinian abbey is so ruined it's barely recognizable. (Both ruins always open; free.)

MUCKROSS HOUSE & ABBEY

The remains of **Muckross Abbey,** built in 1448, lie 3 mi. south of Killarney on Kenmare Rd. Cromwell graciously tried to burn it down, but enough still stands to demonstrate the grace of the part-Norman, part-Gothic cloisters (always open; free).

From the abbey, signs direct you to **Muckross House** (tel. 31440), a massive 19th-century manor whose garden blooms brilliantly in early summer. The grand and proper house (completed in 1843) reeks of aristocracy, commanding a regal view of the lakes and mountains. Upon first visiting Muckross House, the philosopher Bishop George Berkeley proclaimed: "Another Louis XIV may make another Versailles, but only the hand of the Deity can make another Muckross." (Open July-Aug. daily 9am-7pm, Sept.-June daily 9am-6pm.) **Muckross Traditional Farms** lie outside the House. Traditional cottages recreate rural life in early 20th-century Co. Kerry. The view is spectacular, and the expansive lawns are perfect for a mid-afternoon nap or picnic. The gorgeous flora is typical of sub-tropical climes. (Same hours and prices as the house. Joint ticket £4, students £2.)

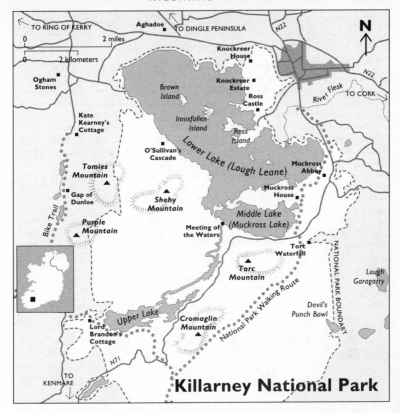

To Ring of Kerry
Aghadoe   To Dingle Peninsula   N22
0   2 miles
0   2 kilometers
Knockreer House
Ogham Stones
Knockreer Estate
Ross Castle
River Flesk   To Cork
Brown Island
N22
Kate Kearney's Cottage
Innisfallen Island
Ross Island
O'Sullivan's Cascade
Lower Lake (Lough Leane)
Muckross Abbey
Tomies Mountain
Muckross House
Gap of Dunloe
Shehy Mountain
Middle Lake (Muckross Lake)
Bike Trail
Purple Mountain
Meeting of the Waters
Tort Waterfall
NATIONAL PARK BOUNDARY
Lough Garagarry
Torc Mountain
Devil's Punch Bowl
National Park Walking Route
Upper Lake
Cromaglin Mountain
Lord Brandon's Cottage
N71
To Kenmare
Killarney National Park

From Muckross House, it's a 2-mi. stroll to the **Meeting of the Waters;** walk straight down the front lawn and follow the signs. The paved path is nice, but the dirt trail through the **Yew Woods** is more secluded (but not accessible to bikes). The Meeting of the Waters is the natural sight that is intended to justify a trip, but the real focus for tourists is **Dinis Cottage** (tel. 31954), serving homemade pizza, drinks, and pastries (open June-Sept. daily 10am-6pm). If you're coming from the cottage, the roaring influx of water straight ahead is Upper Lake, while the forks to the left and right lead to Middle Lake and Lough Leane. The path returns you to the main (Kenmare/Killarney) road, from which it's about a mile to **Torc Waterfall** (turn left, toward Killarney). A short walk through the mossy woods brings you to the cascading 60-ft. drop. Following the trail past the waterfall, you can make your way up **Ford Mountain,** which affords dramatic views of the lakes.

GAP OF DUNLOE

There are many ways to see the Gap, perhaps the best scenery and daytrip in the park. There are plenty of organized trips to the Gap which can be booked from the Killarney tourist office (£13/person). These trips, designed to be combination walking tour and boat-trip, bus visitors to the foot of the Gap, effectively cutting the 7-mi. from Killarney. Walking the Gap in this direction, however, means walking the often steep mountain pass *uphill.* Far better, and somewhat less expensive, is to attack the Gap by bike from the opposite direction. Take a **motorboat** trip to the head of the Gap (£7; £6 if booked at the tourist office), which will leave you and your bike at **Lord Brandon's Cottage** (tel. 34730). Grab a bite to eat (sandwiches £1-3), or just relax and enjoy the scenery of the Upper Lake (open June-Sept. daily 10am-6pm). The 1½-mi. stretch before arriving at the head of the Gap is a steep uphill climb, but well-rewarded by the 7-mi. downhill coast through the park's most breathtaking scenery that lies beyond.

At the foot of the Gap, you'll pass **Kate Kearney's Cottage** (tel. 44116). "Kate Kearney" was an independent mountain-dwelling woman famous for brewing the near-poisonous *poitín* (moonshine). Now her former home is a pub and a restaurant sucking in droves of tourists. (Open daily 9am-midnight; restaurant open until 9pm. Live trad often.) On the 8-mi. ride back to Killarney (bear right after Kate's, turn left on the road to Fossa, turn right on Killorglin Rd.) you will pass the entirely ruined **Dunloe Castle,** an Anglo-Norman stronghold which Cromwell's bloodthirsty armies demolished. There is also a set of *ogham* stones (c. 300 AD) bearing a form of writing unique to the early Christian period in Ireland (see **Archaeology,** p. 59).

RING OF KERRY

The Southwest's most gorgeous peninsula once embodied the tough, romantic spirit of Ireland. Today it is the epitome of package tourism. Legions of visitors, drawn by a ferocious publicity onslaught, board buses and pay exorbitant fees for brief real-life glimpses of what they've already seen on travel brochures. On the other hand, the publicity isn't entirely duplicitous; find a good hostel in a small town on a windy day by the sea, and you may find some serious bliss.

The term "Ring of Kerry" is often used to describe the entire Iveragh Peninsula, but it more correctly refers not to a region, but to a set of roads: N71 from Kenmare to Killarney, R562 from Killarney to Killorglin, and the long loop of N70 west and back to Kenmare. Stay away from the prepackaged private bus tours based out of Killarney. **Bus Éireann** does a more practical summer circuit through all the major towns on the Ring (daily 2/day), since you can get off anywhere and anytime you like. (Unfortunately, you will have to pay in increments for the trip, since they don't offer one single Ring package that allows you to get on and off. You can, however, pay the roundtrip fare, get off the first bus, and then pick up the later bus, as long as it's all done in one day.) Generally, towns on the Ring fill up between noon and 6pm as the buses move through, but the native color returns by evening as the crowds return to Killarney. Buses travel around the Ring counterclockwise, from Killarney to Killorglin, west along Dingle Bay, east along Kenmare River and north from Kenmare to Killarney. Some people advise bikers to travel against tour bus traffic. Biking is best in the afternoon and during other non-prime tour bus times.

■ Kenmare

Kenmare's central location subjects it to a fast-moving flow of sightseers: most people traveling through the Ring of Beara and the Ring of Kerry pass through the town. Kenmare makes an ideal, if slightly touristy, base for exploring the peninsulas. The town is attractive and colorful, dotted with tasteful craft shops and appetizing restaurants alongside the less appealing leprechaun pot holder vendors. Even if its charm is marred by plastic shamrocks, Kenmare is more palatable than larger and more densely touristed Killarney to the north.

ORIENTATION & PRACTICAL INFORMATION

Kenmare's streets form a triangle: Henry St. is the lively base, while Main St. and Shelbourne St. form the other two sides. Main St. flows into the Square, which contains a lovely park, and then becomes N71 to Moll's Gap and Killarney; N70 to Sneem and the Ring of Kerry also branches off this road. From Kenmare, cunning travelers take N70 west, not N71 north, to do the Ring clockwise and avoid tour bus traffic.

Tourist Office: The Square (tel. 41233). Open May-Sept. Mon.-Sat. 9am-6pm; July-Aug. daily 9am-7pm. Ask those questions about Kerry's agricultural exports.

Bank: AIB, 9 Main St. (tel. 41010). Open Mon.-Fri. 10am-12:30pm and 1-4pm, Wed. 10am-12:30pm and 1-5pm; **ATM** accepts Visa.

Buses: Leave from Brenan's Pub on Main St. to: Killarney (Mon.-Sat. 3/day, Sun. 2/day; 1hr.); Tralee (Mon.-Sat. 3/day, Sun. 2/day; 2hr.); Sneem (June-Sept. Mon.-Fri. 2/day; 35min.); and Cork via Bantry (June-Sept. 2/day; 4hr.).

Bike Rental: Finnegan's, (tel. 41083), on the corner of Henry and Shelbourne St. £6/day, £35/week. Open Mon.-Sat. 9:30am-6:30pm.

Laundry: The Pantry Launderette, Market St., just off the Square. Wash and dry £4.50. Open Mon.-Fri. 10am-1pm and 2-6pm, Sat. 10am-1pm and 2-3pm.

Pharmacy: Sheahan's, Main St. (tel. 41354). Open Mon.-Sat. 9am-6pm.

Hospital: off the Old Killarney Rd. (tel. 41088). Follow Henry St. past the Square.

Emergency: Dial 999; no coins required. **Garda:** Shelbourne St. (tel. 41177).

Post Office: Henry St. (tel. 41490), at the corner of Shelbourne St. Open Mon.-Fri. 9am-1pm and 2-5:30pm, Sat. 9am-1pm.

Phone Code: 064

ACCOMMODATIONS

Fáilte Hostel (IHH), corner of Henry and Shelbourne St. (tel. 41083). Not the white building that says "private hostel" but the one across the street. Spacious and comfortable, but unluxurious. The hostel features a common room with a VCR, ideal for a rainy day. Huge kitchen with an antique coal burning stove to satisfy adventurous cooks. Dorm £6.50. Double £18.

La Brasserie, Henry St. (tel. 41379). Situated above the bistro of the same name, La Brasserie offers surprising luxury and a great location, while being the best B&B bargain in town. £12/person. Irish or continental breakfast included.

Keal Na Gower House B&B, the Square (tel. 41202). Sleep comfortably within earshot of a brook in this small B&B; one room with bathtub, the other two with brook views. Single £16. Double £30.

Ring of Kerry Caravan and Camping Park, Sneem Rd. (tel. 41366), 2½mi. west of Kenmare. Overlooks mountains and bay. £3.50/person. Open May-Sept.

FOOD & PUBS

Good food is plentiful, if pricey, in Kenmare. Stick to the smaller cafés for the lowest prices. **SuperValu** is on Main St. (tel. 41307; open Mon.-Thurs. 8am-8pm, Fri. 8am-9pm, Sat. 8am-7pm, and Sun. 8:30am-5pm). **The Pantry** on Henry St. (tel. 42233) sells wholefoods and organic produce (open Mon.-Fri. 9am-8pm, Sat. 10am-6pm).

Mickey Ned's, Henry St. (tel. 41591). A young crowd wolfs down decadent cakes and open-faced sandwiches in this bustling café. All is homemade; turkey sandwich £1.60. Open Mon.-Sat. 9am-5:30pm.

Virginia's Restaurant, Henry St. (tel. 41021). Sit back and enjoy the relaxed atmosphere of this well-attended little restaurant. Dinner specials offer great deals. Vegetarian menu. Filet of cod £5, ice cream 60p/scoop.

La Brasserie Bistro, Henry St. (tel. 41379). Reasonably priced meals all day long in a spacious dining area. Penne with garlic bread £5. Open daily 9am-9pm.

An Leath Phingin, 35 Main St. (tel. 41559). Italian masterpieces served up in an old stone townhouse. They even make their own pasta and smoke their own salmon. Splurge a little, it's well worth it. 10" pizza £6-9.50. Open daily 6-10pm.

Kenmare's pubs attract a hefty contingent of tourists. Native Guinness guzzlers, however, hear too much good music to quibble over polyester. **Ó Donnabháin's,** Henry St. (tel. 42106), is a favorite among natives, with a pleasant beergarden out back. **Murty's,** New Rd. (tel. 41453), just off Henry St., hosts live bands (Wed., Fri., and Sat. nights). This huge pub also features disco (Thurs. and Sun. nights). **Brennan's,** Main, St. (tel. 41011) serves great pub grub (BBQ Thai chicken £4.50), and live music (3-4 nights/week). **Crowley's,** Henry St. (tel. 41472), asks: "When you've got frequent trad sessions, why bother with interior decorating?"

SIGHTS

There are plenty of good hikes in the country around Kenmare, but few sights in the town itself. The ancient **stone circle,** a two-minute walk from The Square down Market St., is the largest of its kind in Southwest Ireland (55ft. diameter) and worth a visit (admission £1). The new **Kenmare Heritage Centre** shares a building with the tourist office and focuses on the town's prowess for lacemaking as well as the general history of Kerry and Kenmare (same hours as the tourist office; cassette self-tour £2, students £1.50). Invented in 1862 by the lacemaking nuns at the Kenmare convent as a source of revenue to alleviate poverty in the town, the Kenmare techniques were once on the cutting edge of lace. Local artisans are working to resurrect the craft. **Demonstrations** take place in the lace center above the tourist office (open Mon.-Sat. 10am-1pm and 2-6pm; free).

Seafari Cruises (tel. 83171) explores Kenmare Bay and its colonies of otters, seals, and whales, daily, departing from the pier (follow the Glengarriff Rd. and turn right just before the bridge). Cruises last 1½-2hr. and cost £9.50, students £8. You can fish at the **Ardtully Castle Salmon Fishery** on Roughty Rd. (£10/day, £30/week. For permits contact Mr. John O'Hare, 21 Main St. Open daily 9am-7pm.)

■ Sneem

Tourists make Sneem their first or last stop along The Ring, and the town has adapted to please them. Sneem's first claim to fame came with Charles de Gaulle's visit to the town in 1969, which is commemorated with a monument that locals call "de Gaulle's Stone." More recently, Sneem won Ireland's 1987 Tidy Town competition, and 10 years later it still defines itself by the honor. Ever been to Legoland? More grass, fewer plastic bricks.

Sneem's **tourist information center** (tel. 45270) is across the street from Murphy's Pub (open daily 11am-6pm). The Ring of Kerry **bus** leaves for Killarney via Kenmare from the Square (June-Sept. daily 2/day; 1hr.; £5.50, students £2.80). Rent a bike to explore Sneem at **M. Burns' Bike Hire,** North Sq. (tel 45140), £5 per day, £28 per week (open 9:30am-8pm). If Sneem's **phone code** took out a personal ad, it would read "Slim, attractive **064** likes long walks, leather, and Sneem."

Sneem's only hostel, the **Harbour View Hostel** (tel. 45276), ¼ mi. from town on the Kenmare Rd., used to be a motel and still looks like one—comfortable ranch-style units (with hairdryers!) scattered in a gravel lot. Visit the hostel's on-premises pub, **Davey's Bar,** for a pint that's only a hop, skip, and drunken stumble from your room (dorm £6; private room £7.50/person; **camping** £3). Occupying a former stone convent, **Woodvale House,** Pier Rd. (tel. 45181), just off the Square, has charming rooms with mountain views (£16/person). They also offer picturesque **camping** next to the sculpture garden by the river (£3/person) and laundry (wash £2.50, dry 50p/ ¼hr.). Three doors up from the Texaco station, the unmistakably blue **Homestead** (tel. 45179) is friendly and all dolled up with Irish lace (£13).

Check out the **Riverain Restaurant** (tel. 45245) for low-fat and vegetarian meals with a view of the river. (Early-bird 3-course dinner £9; open May-Sept. noon-9:30pm.) The **Sacre Coeur Restaurant** (tel. 45186) dishes up seafood at reasonable prices. The lunch and snack menus offer the best value (open prawn sandwich £4; open April-Oct. 12:30-3pm and 5-9:30pm). On the north side of town, **The Village Kitchen** (tel. 45281) serves up seafood and sandwiches in a comfortable café setting (sandwiches under £2; open 9:30am-8:30pm). For the best fish and chips on the Ring, gallop down to **The Hungry Knight,** North Sq. (tel. 45237). The **Blue Bull** (tel. 45382), next to the wool shops on the Square, is a pub noted for its seafood (pub grub £3-5, served noon-8:30pm) and hosts traditional and country music (July-Aug. Mon. and Fri.). The **Green Linnet** pub, across the bridge on the Caherdaniel Rd. (tel. 45224) reverberates to eclectic beats Thursday and Saturday nights.

Don't miss Sneem's **sculpture park** near the church along the river. Local artisans have created odd cone-shaped houses out of local stone. The park also features a stone panda from China, a steel tree from Israel, the Goddess of Isis from Egypt, and the famous and ever-funny "de Gaulle's Stone." (Always open; free.) **The Silver Sea-Horse Trekking Centre** (tel. 45276) offers local horse-back riding trips, equipment, and free collection from your hostel or B&B (£10/hr., call 24hr. ahead of time). Frankie Jim leads **boat trips** from the pier (gear provided; tel 82904), and Jackie O'Shea offers **deep-sea angling** trips from Rossdohan Pier (tel. 45369).

■ Caherdaniel

Tiny Caherdaniel has little to attract the Ring's drove of travel coaches—it's just a hamlet with two pubs and a stretch of gorgeous white beach. The new **tourist office** is located 1 mi. east of town at the **Wave Crest Camping Park** (open daily 8am-10pm). Information can also be had at **Mathius Adams Junk Shop**, in the center of town (tel. 75167). The **bus** stops in Caherdaniel at the junction of the Ring of Kerry Rd. and Main St. Buses go to Sneem and Killarney (June-Sept. 2/day; Sneem ½hr., £2.90, students £1.70; Killarney 1½hr., £7.30, students £3.80). Caherdaniel's **phone code,** 066, is looking for a committed partner who enjoys Thai and tennis.

The brand new **Traveller's Rest Hostel** (tel. 75175), with its turf fire in the kitchen and small but comfortable rooms upstairs, looks and feels more like a B&B than a hostel. Not for the pastel-phobes out there; pink and yellow abound in this flower-box haven (dorm £6.50; private room £8/person). The **Caherdaniel Village Hostel** (tel. 75277), across the street from Skellig Aquatics, resides in the first English police building to be deserted in the 1923 Revolution. (Climbing trips and diving holidays for experienced divers arranged; inquire about rates. Dorm £6. Open Feb.-Nov.) One-quarter mile west of town on the Ring of Kerry Rd. is the intimate seven-bed **Carrigbeg Hostel** (tel. 75229), which features expansive views of the surrounding hills and the beach and bay. (Dorm £6. Laundry £3. Call for free lift from Caherdaniel.) Campers get their beauty sleep 1 mi. east of town on the Ring of Kerry Rd. at **Wave Crest Camping Park** (tel. 75188), overlooking the beach. (£3.50/cyclist or hiker. Showers 50p. Open April-Sept.).

Donnelly's Restaurant (tel. 75355) serves the most affordable food in town, and the most incredible Bailey's cheesecake on the planet. (Quiche Lorraine £5, all sandwiches £2; open daily 9am-9:30pm.) The **Courthouse Café** (tel. 75422) has both a sit-down menu and take-away. (Sandwiches under £2, open daily 11am-10pm, take-away until 1am.) **Freddy's Bar** (tel. 75400) sells groceries (open daily 8:30am-9pm) and serves pints to locals. In summer, the bright yellow **Blind Piper** (tel. 75126) attracts a lively crowd with trad sessions on Tuesday nights.

To reach **Derrynane Strand,** the soul of Caherdaniel, follow the signs from the center of town to Derrynane House. The strand here is one of Ireland's finest, with 2 mi. of white sand. **Derrynane House** (tel. 75113), just up from the beach, was the cherished residence of Irish patriot Daniel "the Liberator" O'Connell, who won Catholic Emancipation in 1829. Inside the house, look for the dueling pistol that O'Connell used to kill challenger d'Esterre, and the black glove he wore to church for years afterwards to mourn his victim. The half-hour film on O'Connell presents an engrossing and refreshingly multi-faceted image of the acerbic barrister. (Open May-Sept. Mon.-Sat. 9am-6pm, Sun. 11am-7pm; March, April, and Oct. Tues.-Sun. 1-5pm; Nov.-Feb. Sat.-Sun. 1-5pm. Admission £2, students and children £1. Last admission 45min. before closing.)

Offshore lies a shipwreck rumored to have been a smuggling ship financed by Maurice "Hunting Cap" O'Connell, Daniel's uncle. If you can dive, it's worth a look. Contact **Derrynane Sea Sports** (tel. 75266) or **Skellig Aquatics** (tel. 75277) for rental information. If you can motivate yourself for several miles of uphill hiking or pedaling to get there, the pre-Christian **Staigue Fort** (tel. 75288), west of town, will make you feel tall and powerful. The largest and one of the best-preserved forts in Ireland, Staigue Fort stands high on a hill overlooking the sea below. Skip the **heritage center** devoted to the fort, which runs the danger of being a rip-off tourist attraction. (Open Easter-Oct. daily 10am-9pm. Admission £2, students £1.50.)

■ Waterville

Waterville suffers both presently and historically from a dearth of quaintness, but it's got a damn fine beach. Originally, Waterville was planned as a cluster of summer homes for wealthy English vacationers. That "Miami retirement village" feeling isn't helped any when the bus-tourists (who are all retired from Miami) fill the streets at midday. But when the buses leave and the fumes clear, one is left with Waterville's gently lapping waves and the sun setting over the hills on the other side of the beach. Nearby, tiny towns like Ballinskelligs and Portmagee provide departure points for the ultra-remote monastic remains of Skellig Michael.

The **tourist office** soaks up sea spray across from Butler Arms Hotel on the beach (open Mon.-Fri. 9am-7pm, Sat. 10am-6pm; mid-Sept. to late June Mon.-Fri. 9am-5pm). The Ring of Kerry **bus** (June-Sept. 2/day) stops in Waterville in front of the Bay View Hotel on Main St., with service to: Caherdaniel (20min.; £2.20); Sneem (50min.; £4.30); and Killarney (2hr.; £8.60). In the off season, **Dero's** (tel. (064) 31251) fills in with a Ring of Kerry bus all its own (1/day; £10; reservations required). **Bus Éireann** travels to Cahersiveen Monday to Friday at 8:20am (also Sat. from June-Sept.). The Bay Area's **phone code,** 066, loves the beach.

The grand stone edifice that is now the **Waterville Leisure Hostel (IHH)** (tel. 74644) has all the amenities you could ask for: VCR, pool table, huge kitchen, spacious dining room. Bear right at the fork at the Butler Arms Hotel, walk three minutes up the hill, and make a left at the sign. (Dorm £6, double £20. Laundry £2 wash, 30p/3-min. dry. Wheelchair accessible.) Back in the town center facing the beach is funky **Peter's Place.** Cozy and full of surprises, Peter's candles and peat fires are always burning. Peter is a *seanachaí* (Irish storyteller), spinning yarns that are the best reason to come to Waterville. (Dorm £5, **camping** £3.) Should both hostels be full, **The Huntsman** (tel. 74124) offers gorgeous seaside B&B accommodations at the right price (£13 w/bath).

Across from the Butler Arms Hotel is the self-described "purple passion house of food," **An Corcán** (tel. 74711). Serving up delectable little numbers, An Corcán is intimate and affordable (lasagna £3.75; open daily 8am-10:30pm). Up the hill from the tourist office, the **Beach Cove Café** (tel. 74733) offers café cuisine and take-away overlooking the beach (fish and chips £2.35). The **Lobster Bar and Restaurant,** Main St. (tel. 74255), is worth a visit just for the icon outside—a giant lobster clutching a Guinness—though the pub food isn't bad (fisherman's soup and bread £2.50; open pub hours). The Lobster is the liveliest pub in town, with a pool table and live music on weekends. The **Bay View Hotel Restaurant and Bar** (tel. 74510) serves a 3-course tourist dinner for £7. The hotel also has a disco on Friday nights (cover £3). **Mick O'Dwyer's** (tel. 74248) does the disco thing (Wed. and Sat. 11pm-1:30am; cover £3). Charlie Chaplin's old haunt is the **Fishermen's Bar** (tel. 74205), which is linked to the Butler Arms Hotel (trad Thurs. and Sat.; open July-Sept.).

Two miles from town, **Lough Currane** lures anglers, boaters, and divers with its numerous picnic-friendly islands and its submerged castle ruins. **Waterville Boats** (tel. 74255) rents rowboats (£10/day) and fishing poles (£5/day).

The Irish-speaking hamlet of **Ballinskelligs** isn't worth a special trip, but if you're there to catch a boat, check out the ruins near the pier of the **Ballinskelligs Monastery,** the crumbling twin of the Skelligs Rocks monastery. It was here that the monks moved from their lofty heights to start Europe's first "university." If you do decide to spend the night in Ballinskelligs, the quiet **Prior House Youth Hostel (An Óige/HI)** (tel. 79229) overlooks the Bay and offers basic hostel accommodations (June-Sept. £5.50; April and May £4.50). Two miles south of Ballinskelligs, **Bolus Head** affords great views of the Skelligs and the bay on clear days.

■ Skellig Michael

Eight miles offshore the Iveragh Peninsula, the **Skellig Rocks** (and their centuries old, dry-stone, vertigo-inducing 650 steps) break the ocean's surface. The nearly completely white Little Skellig appears to be snow-covered. As your boat swings down-wind of the island, however, it becomes clear from the stench that the white substance is not snow, but the inevitable consequence of the thousands of gannets living there. The island bird sanctuary is not open to the public, but the larger Skellig Michael makes an exciting (if expensive) trip. Christian monks founded an austere monastery in the 6th century along the craggy faces of the 714-ft. high rock which George Bernard Shaw once called "not after the fashion of this world." Their beehive-like dwellings are still intact. The old steps and walls on the reef of the island now shelter 40,000 gannets, petrels, kittiwakes, and the ever-adorable puffins.

The fantastic and stomach-churning **ferry voyage** takes up to 1½ hour, depending on where you begin; from Ballinskelligs, it's only 45 minutes. Mrs. Walsh (tel. 76155) sails from Reenard Pier near Cahersiveen (£15), Joe Roddy (tel. 74268) and Sean Feehan (tel. 79182) depart from Ballinskelligs (£20), and Michael O'Sullivan and Mr. Casey (tel. 74255) leave from Portmagee (£20). Roddy and O'Sullivan will give you a lift from Waterville, and Casey will pick you up from your hostel in Cahersiveen. The boats run mid-March to October, depending on the weather; phone ahead for reservations and to confirm that the boats are operating. They usually leave between 9:30am and noon and land for at least two hours on the island. The grass-roofed **Skellig Experience** visitor center (tel. 76306) is just across the Portmagee Bridge on Valentia Island. Videos and models engulf visitors in virtual Skellig. The video is a good diversion on a rainy day, provided you ignore the dramatic rhetorical questions. (Open daily April-Sept. 10am-6pm; admission £3, students £2.70.)

■ Cahersiveen

Perhaps because it's the Iveragh Peninsula's biggest town, Cahersiveen (car-si-VEEN) hasn't allowed foreigners to drag it down or gloss it up. It's a businesslike place serving the prosaic needs of its full-time residents. After Waterville and Sneem, Cahersiveen's hustle may come as a relief. And with nearly 30 pubs, there's certainly no shortage of nightlife.

Practical Information Cahersiveen's official **tourist office** is housed in the former barracks on the road to Ballycarbery Castle (tel. 72589; open Mon.-Sat. 10am-6pm). A **craftshop** in the old Protestant church on Main St. is another source of local information (tel. 72996; open May-Sept. daily 9:30am-7pm). Main St. is home to **AIB** (tel. 72022; open Mon. 10am-5pm, Tues.-Fri. 10am-3pm; Visa-friendly **ATM**) and **Bank of Ireland** (tel. 72122; open Mon. 10am-5pm, Tues.-Fri. 10am-4pm, closes for lunch 12:30-1:30pm). The Ring of Kerry **bus** stops in front of Banks Store on Main St. (June-Sept. daily 2/day) and continues on to: Waterville (25min.; £2.70); Caherdaniel (1½hr.; £3.10); Sneem (2hr.; £6.30); and Killarney (2½hr.; £9). One bus route heads directly east to Killarney (Mon.-Sat. 1-2/day). Cahersiveen's **post office** is on Main St. (tel. 72010; open Mon.-Fri. 9:30am-1pm and 2-5:30pm, Sat. 9:30am-1pm). Cahersiveen's **phone code** gives a care at 066.

Accommodations The **Sive Hostel (IHH),** (pronounced like "hive") 15 East End, Main St. (tel. 72717), hosts mighty *craic*. Comfortable and remarkably friendly, Sive has free live music by the resident songwriter/warden and great sunsets from the third-floor balcony. (Dorm £6, double £15. Camping £3. Laundry £2 wash, £2 dry.) Behind its charming bay window and flowerpot facade, newly opened **Mortimer's Hostel,** Main St., competes with Sive for the town's friendliest hostel honors. Whereas the Sive's rooms are more comfortable, Mortimer's features a great garden which often hosts post-pub-run bonfires (dorm £6, £1 key deposit.) At the west end of town, the **Mannix Point Caravan and Camping Park** (tel. 72806) adjoins a waterfront nature reserve, facing across the water toward the romantic ruins of **Ballycarbery Castle.** Mannix Point's common area (complete with turf fire) feels like a relaxed hostel. It's one of the best camping parks in the country. Camping fee includes hot showers and use of a cooker-less kitchen—bring your own stove (£2.75/person; open mid-March to mid-Oct.).

Food & Pubs Generous **Grudle's,** Main St. (tel. 72386), serves huge slices of cakes and pies, as well as vegetarian dishes for those who find it easy being green (vegetable curry £4; open daily 9am-10pm). The gloriously decorated **Teach Chulann** (tel. 72400), which serves expensive gourmet delights by evening, offers an equally exquisite but affordable lunch menu by day (marinated chicken breast sandwich £4; open noon-3pm and 6-10pm). **Shebeen** (tel. 72361), near the Sive Hostel on Main St., gives great pub grub (vegetable pizza £4.50; open daily 9:30am-10:30pm). The **Point Bar,** Reenard Point (tel. 72165), located by the pier, is famous for fresh fish. After a few pints at this endearing pub, people don't seem to mind the interruptions of the Valentia ferry (fresh fish £5-9; open daily 10:30am-midnight).

Cahersiveen still has several **original pubs** on Main St.—common in rural Ireland during the first half of this century, these establishments were a combination of watering hole, general store, blacksmith, leather shop, and farm goods store. The **Anchor Bar** (tel. 72049), towards the west end of Main St., is one of the best. Don't come before 10pm, and be sure to take your drink into the kitchen for an unforgettable night. **Mike Murt's** (tel. 72396) seethes with pure Irish character. Come here to chat with the locals during the afternoon, but be prepared to tell your life story to the entire pint-clutching ensemble. The warm and newly renovated **Central Bar** (tel. 72441) is a favorite with laid-back natives and features a charmingly effervescent hostess. You may have to sing a few songs with the crowd. For live music, the **East End Bar,** the **Shebeen** (tel. 72361), and **Teach Chulann** (tel. 72400) are your best bets. Since trad sessions are often spontaneous, ask around town for pointers.

Sights Every schoolchild in Ireland knows that Cahersiveen is the birthplace of Daniel O'Connell. The Catholic Church in town that bears his name is the only one in Ireland named for a layperson. O'Connell, the "Liberator," is celebrated at a new **Heritage Centre** (tel. 72589) housed in the town's former guard barracks (see tourist office, above). The center is an engrossing introduction to the life of O'Connell, complete with sections devoted to the Famine and Irish rebellions under British rule (open Mon.-Sat. 10am-6pm, Sun. 1-6pm; admission £2.50, students £1.50). Two miles northwest of the town (signposted from downtown), the ruins of the 15th-century **Ballycarbery Castle,** once held by O'Connell's ancestors, commands great views of mountains and sea. Two hundred yards past the castle turnoff lie two well-preserved stone forts. **Leacanabuaile Fort** lets you walk atop its 10-ft.-thick walls while **Cahergal Fort** encloses a 10th-century beehive hut.

■ Valentia Island

Valentia Island makes an appealing respite from the Ring of Kerry pilgrimage. Valentia lacks much of the Atlantic starkness of Cape Clear or Sherkin Island, but it offers accessibility instead (connected to the mainland by a land bridge). Valentia Island is archaeologically and historically rich. The first transatlantic telegraph cable infused Valentia with cable operators and allowed some of the island's families to work at cable stations around the globe. Valentia Island hosts two restaurants that are deserving of a special, if expensive, visit.

Ferries depart from Reenard Point, 3 mi. west of Cahersiveen off the Ring of Kerry road. Ferries run often, but there's no set schedule; ask at the Point Bar in Reenard or the Royal Pier Bar on the island (going rates are £3-4 return). In addition, a regular car ferry is planned for the spring and summer of 1997, and fares should be in the neighborhood of £2-3 each way. A bridge ties Valentia to the mainland at Portmagee, 10 mi. west of Cahersiveen, but hitching there is difficult. To get to Portmagee, go south (from Cahersiveen) or north (a longer trip from Waterville), then west on R565. Hardcore bikers can also make a worthwhile trip following the "loop" (Waterville to Ballinskelligs, Portmagee to Knightstown to Cahersiveen). The island's **phone code** wires 066.

The ferry drops you off at **Knightstown,** the island's population center, where the monstrous **Royal and Pier Hostel (IHH)** (tel. 76144) looms before you. The once-luxurious hotel, built for Queen Victoria's one-night stand on the island, retains little of its aged grandeur and even less of its mattresses' firmness. The adjoining pub offers pub grub from noon-9pm, while the hostel restaurant offers complete Irish breakfast (dorm £6, private room £7.50; breakfast £4; laundry service £4). The **Valentia Island Hostel (An Óige/HI)** (tel. 76154), in the old (very old) coast guard station sign-posted off the main road, provides only the bare necessities (£5.50/person; reception 5-9pm, lockout 10am-5pm; open June-Sept.). Knightstown's smattering of B&Bs are more inviting. A few blocks up the hill from the pier, **Altazamuth House** (tel. 76300) may lack complexity, but with crisp taste and rich pine undertones, it is worthwhile (£14/person). **Spring Acre** (tel. 76141), across from the pier has bedrooms with enormous waterfront windows (£15/person w/bath).

The **Gallery Kitchen** (tel. 76105), on the main road in town, serves creative meals amid scandalous sculptures and drawings of half-clothed people (fresh pasta £6.50; open daily 1-4pm and 6:30-9:30pm). Two miles from Knightstown (on the road to the Quarry), the **Lighthouse Café** (tel. 76355) may be the best reason to visit the island. It serves comforting meals and desserts in a candlelit cottage overlooking Valentia lighthouse (open Mon.-Thurs. 10am-7pm, Fri.-Sun. 8am-midnight).

The road from town to the **old slate quarry** offers some of Valentia's best views across Dingle Bay. The quarry supplied the slate that roofed the Paris Opera House and the British Parliament, and is now the site of an astoundingly tacky "sacred grotto." Bring a flashlight to explore the quarry's dark recesses. At the opposite end of the island, you can hike up to the ruins of a Napoleonic lookout tower at **Bray Head,** with views to the Skelligs. On the way there, you'll pass the turnoff for **Glanleam Subtropical Gardens** (tel. 76176), a smaller and less-manicured version of Garinish Island (open daily 11am-5pm; admission £2.50, students £1.50).

▓ Killorglin

The Ring of Kerry traditionally commences in Killorglin, though this should be your last stop if driving behind gigantic tour buses isn't your cup of tea. Thirteen miles west of Killarney, Killorglin lives in the shadow of Iveragh's mountain spine and of the tourism generated by them. But if you are traveling clockwise around the Ring on N70, stop at the **Quarry in Kells** (tel. 77601). This restaurant/craft shop/convenience store comes with magnificent views and dark green benches. The shop is particularly inviting to haggard bikers cycling against hurricane-like winds (open daily 8am-8pm, restaurant 9am-6pm). Killorglin's hibernation is interrupted every year from August 10-12, when it holds the riotous **Puck Fair,** a livestock festival culminating in the crowning of a particularly virile he-goat as King Puck. The pubs stay open for 72 straight hours to refresh the exuberant musicians, dancers, and singers. Be fore-warned, the town's hostel and B&Bs operate on a first-come, first-served basis during the Puck Fair. During the rest of the year residents show off their mountains, enter-tain the Ring crowd, and plan the next fair.

The spiffy **tourist office** (tel. 61451) is on the corner of Iveragh Rd. and Upper Bridge St., beside the library (open May-Sept. Mon.-Sat. 9:30am-6pm, Sun. 10am-3pm). **AIB** (tel. 61134) is on the corner of Main St. and New Line Rd. (open Mon. and Wed.-Fri. 10am-4pm, Tues. 10am-5pm). The omnipresent Ring of Kerry **bus** stops in Killorglin next to the tourist office. (June-Sept. 3/day; Cahersiveen 50min., £5; Water-ville 1¼hr., £5.90; Sneem 3hr., £8.80.) The eastbound bus from Cahersiveen goes more directly to Killarney (Sept.-June Mon.-Sat. 3/day, July-Aug. Mon.-Sat. 4/day; Sun. 2/day). Rent a **bike** at **O'Shea's** on Main St. (tel. 61919; open Mon.-Sat. 9am-6pm; £6/day, £30/week). Clothes sparkle at **Starlite Cleaners,** Bridge St. (£5/load; open Mon.-Sat. 9am-6pm). The **post office** (tel. 61101) is on Main St. (open Mon.-Fri. 9am-5:30pm, Sat. 9am-1pm). The **phone code,** 066, is a virile he-goat.

Laune Valley Farm Hostel (IHH), 1½ mi. from town off the Tralee Rd. (tel. 61488), is bright, beautiful, and hosts a local farm population of cows, chickens, dogs, and ducks (save your table scraps for the ducks). Fresh milk and eggs from the farm are for sale. (Dorm from £6; double from £16, some w/bath. **Camping** £3.50/person. Wheelchair accessible.) **The Manner Inn,** Iveragh Rd. (tel. 61317), features large rooms (£13/person; w/bath £17.50), a pub downstairs (*céilí* on Tues. nights, Sun. live music and set dancing), and a nightclub on Sat. nights (10:30pm-1:30am; free for residents, £4 cover for non–residents; over 21 only). **Orglan House** (tel. 61540), atop a small hill on the Killarney Rd., proffers grand views from immaculate rooms and relieves you from brown bread delirium with its delicious breakfasts (£14/person, w/bath £16). **Laune Bridge House** (tel. 61161), a few doors down from Orglan, opens its florid and comfortable rooms (£16/person w/bath). Commune with RV people at **West's Caravan and Camping Park** (tel. 61240), 1 mi. east of town on the Killarney Rd. Pool table, tennis (racket 75p), and fishing (rod £3) are available. (July 9-Aug. 20 £3.50, off season £3; open Easter-Nov.)

The **Bianconi Restaurant** on Lower Main St. (tel. 61146) is pricey and somewhat touristy, but the salads are famous, and the à la carte menu offers some reasonable choices. (Cheese souffle £4.50; open Mon.-Sat. 11am-9pm, Sun. 12:30-2pm and 5:30-9pm.) Sacrificing ambiance, good budget food can be had at the **Starlite Diner,** the Square (tel. 61299). Burgers are all under £3, and a complete breakfast can be had for £4 (open daily 9:30am-11pm). Across from the tourist office hunkers **Bunker's** (tel. 61381), a pink-faced restaurant/café/take-away. Their regal purple pub lies next door. The live music wraps up at 11:30pm (café open 9:30am-11pm; restaurant open 6pm-10:30pm).

A young local crowd flocks to the **Old Forge,** Main St. (tel. 61231) to satisfy all their Guinness needs in this lively stone pub. Live trad Monday to Thursday, live rock on Fridays, and a disco on Saturday. An older and more subdued crowd watches football at the **Laun Bar,** Lower Main St. (tel. 61158), which hosts folk sessions on Thursday nights. For those who like to sing once they've had a few, there's **Nick's Piano Bar,** Lower Main St. (tel. 61219).

The **Cappanalea Outdoor Education Centre** (tel. 69244), 7 mi. southwest of Killorglin off the Ring of Kerry Rd., offers canoeing, rock-climbing, windsurfing, sailing, hillwalking, fishing, and orienteering. (Open daily 10am-5pm. Any activity £10/half-day, £17/day. Overnight programs with accommodations available. Book a few days in advance.) **Cromane Beach** is only 4 mi. west of town (take New Line Rd.—it branches off Main St. south of the Square). Five miles off the Killarney Rd., the 16th-century **Ballymalis Castle** lies on the banks of the River Laune in view of Macgillycuddy's Reeks. Frustrated golfers can play a round at the **Killorglin Golf Club** (tel. 61979, 1½mi. from town on the Tralee Rd.), whose green fees are much more affordable than those in Killarney (18-hole-green fees £12, half-set of clubs £5).

DINGLE PENINSULA

The Dingle Peninsula has some beautiful beaches, and, as the tourist industry realizes this, it's getting more crowded by the day. Slieve Mish and the flat farming country of East Dingle are a bit dull. More exciting and convenient for backpackers is Dingle Town, the rising nightlife capital of the region. The coast to the west of town combines striking scenery with *gaeltacht* communities. Tradition is still very much alive on the peninsula: hand-built *curraghs* ply the waters around Brandon Bay and Blasket Sound. Dingle's *bohareens* (side roads) are best-explored by bike—the entire western circuit, from Dingle out to Slea Head, up to Ballydavid, and back, can easily be covered in a day. The Cloghane/Brandon area in the north remains most free of foreigners; Slea Head, Dunquin, and the Blasket Islands are the most inspiring spots. Maps available in area tourist offices describe **The Dingle Way,** a walking trail which circles the peninsula. While Dingle Town is well-connected to Killarney and Tralee, public transport within the peninsula is scarce. **Buses** to towns in South Dingle peninsula run daily in July and August, but only two or three times per week the rest of the year. There is no bus service to towns on the northern side of the peninsula from Dingle Town. Hitchers along the **Connor Pass** find unspoiled hamlets. For detailed bus information, call the Tralee station (tel. (066) 23566).

▓ Dingle Town

For now, *craic* in Dingle is still authentic, but the word is out about the fabulous pubs, the breathtaking views, the smart cafés, and the too-cute dolphin, Fungi, who charms the whole town from his permanent residence in Dingle Bay. Hostels, restaurants, and souvenir shops are all multiplying with the tourists. If Dingle plays its cards right, it could follow the lead of Galway. If not...Killarney's shamrock berets loom. Scour the deserted parts of the peninsula for vistas and *ogham* stones, then come here in the evening for *craic* and quality time with your publican.

ORIENTATION & PRACTICAL INFORMATION

Dingle lies in the middle of the south coast of Dingle Peninsula. R559 heads east to Killarney and Tralee and west to Ventry, Dunquin, and Slea Head. A narrow road north through the Connor Pass branches to Stradbally and Castlegregory.

Downtown Dingle approximates a grid pattern, though it's just a bit more confusing than you'd expect. The lack of street signs in English complicates matters. Strand St. and Main St. parallel Dingle Harbour, while the Mall, Dykegate St., and Green St. run perpendicular to the shore, uphill from Strand St. to Main St. On the eastern edge of town, Strand St., the Mall, and Tralee Rd. converge in a roundabout.

Tourist Office: Corner of Main St. and Dykegate St. (tel. 51188). Great if you like lines. Brainwashed by Bord Fáilte. Open April-Oct. Mon.-Sun. 9am-6pm.

Banks: AIB, Main St. (tel. 51400). Open Mon. 10am-12:30pm and 1:30-5pm, Tues.-Fri. 10am-12:30pm and 1:30-4pm. The **ATM** accepts most major cards. **Bank of Ireland,** Main St. (tel. 51100). Same hours.

Buses: Bus stop on Ring Rd. is behind Garvey's SuperValu. Bus information is available from the Tralee bus station (tel. (066) 23566). **Bus Éireann** rushes out of Dingle to Ballydavid (Tues. and Fri. 3/day; £3.15 return); Dunquin and Ballyferriter (summer Mon. and Thurs. 4/day, Tues.-Wed. and Fri.-Sat. 2/day, Sun. 1/day; £2.30); Killarney (June-Sept. Mon.-Sat. 3/day, Sun. 2/day; 1½hr.; £7.30); and Tralee (June-Sept. Mon.-Sat. 6/day, Sun.5/day, Oct.-May Mon.-Sat. 6/day, Sun. 4/day; 70min.; £5.90). From June-Sept. 2 additional buses a day (Mon.-Sat.) tour the south of the peninsula from Dingle.

Bike Rental: Paddy's Bike Shop, Dykegate St., rents the best bikes in town. £5/day, £25/week. Open daily 9am-7pm. **The Mountain Man,** Strand St. (tel. 51868), £6/day, £21/week. See hours below.

Camping Equipment: The Mountain Man, Strand St. (tel. 51868). Open July-Aug. daily 9am-9pm, Sept.-June daily 9am-6pm. No tent rental.

Laundry: Níolann an Daingin, Green St. (tel. 51837), behind El Toro. Open Mon.-Sat. 9am-5:45pm. Medium wash and dry from £5.50.

Pharmacy: O'Keeffe's Pharmacy Ltd. (tel. 51310). Open Mon.-Wed. and Fri.-Sat. 9:30am-6pm, Thurs. 9:30am-1pm, Sun. 9:30am-12:30pm.

Emergency: Dial 999; no coins required.

Garda: the Holy Ground (tel. 51522), across from Tig Lise.

Post Office: Upper Main St. (tel. 51661). Just the place for mailing Fungi postcards. Open Mon.-Fri. 9am-1pm and 2-5:30pm, Sat. 9am-1pm.

Phone Code: 066.

ACCOMMODATIONS

There are plenty of hostels in Dingle, though some are a fairly long walk from town. You'll need your own transport to reach the ones east of town. B&Bs along Dykegate St. and Strand St. and hostels in town tend to fill up fast in summer; call ahead.

Rainbow Hostel (tel. 51044), 15min. west of town on Strand Rd. (at the corner of Dunquin Rd., bear right and inland), and worth the hike. Irish folk legend Christy Moore knows the owner and bunks at this fabulously hip hostel when in Dingle. The huge wood-paneled kitchen is a gourmand's dream. Free lifts to and from town. Dorm £6. Double £16. **Camping** £3. Laundry £3. Bikes £6/day. Angling trips £10/3hr. Dolphin trips £6/person. Massages £20/1¼hr.

Grapevine Hostel (tel. 51434), Dykegate St., off Main St. Smack in the middle of town and just a short stagger from Dingle's finest pubs, the Grapevine features close but comfortable en suite bunk rooms. The common room has a peat fire, CD player, and dangerously cushy chairs. Dorm £6.50.

Ballintaggart Hostel (IHH) (tel. 51454), a 25-min. walk east of town on the Tralee Rd. Ballintaggart is set on the grand estate where the Earl of Cork poisoned his wife in an upstairs room (which her ghost supposedly haunts). Gloriously renovated, it has enormous bunk rooms, an enclosed cobblestone courtyard, a crystal chandelier, and a pasta/pizza restaurant (main course £4-6). Free shuttle to town. Groceries. Kitchen locked after 10pm. 10- to 12-bed dorm from £6. 4-bed dorm £7. Private room from £11/person. **Camping** £3.50. Laundry service £4. Bike hire £6/day. Horse treks £10/1½hr. Wetsuits £10/3hr.

Marina Hostel, Strand St. (tel. 51065), across from the pier. Central location, intimate quarters, and helpful staff. Dorm £6. Double £16. **Camping** £3. Laundry £3.

An Caladh Spáinneach, Strand St. (tel. 52160; un KULL-uck SPINE-uck). This new hostel offers basic rooms across from the marina. Open June-Sept. Dorm £6, weekends £7.

Lovett's Hostel, Cooleen Rd. (tel. 51903), turn opposite the Esso Station past the roundabout, right on the bay. A decent choice if the other hostels are full. Sept.-June dorm £5, double £13. July-Aug. dorm £6, double £14. Laundry £2 (no dryer).

Phoenix Hostel (tel. 66284), on the Dingle-Killarney Rd. (R561), 4mi. west of Castlemaine, east of Dingle. Attached wholefood café serves interesting vegetarian and Asian food (2-course meal £5.50 for hostelers; open daily 9am-midnight). Funky, relaxed country house with Indian tapestries and spiritually elevating books (not to mention a bathtub). Inquire about the belly-dancing lessons. Pub runs. 6-bed dorm £7. Double £22. **Camping** £3.50. Breakfast £2.50. Laundry £4. Sheets £1. Bikes (reserve evening before) £6/day.

The Marina Inn B&B, Strand St. (tel. 51660), upstairs from the pub. Very basic rooms are a bargain. Double with breakfast £20.

Avondale House, Dykegate St. (tel. 51120). Charming Mrs. Houlihan uses homemade brown bread and jam to draw guests back to her centrally located home year after year. Irish or vegetarian breakfasts. From £14.50/person.

Kirrary House, (tel. 51606), across from Avondale House. With good cheer and pride, Mrs. Collins puts guests up in her delightful rooms. £16/person w/bath.

FOOD

Dingle is home to enough eateries to satisfy even the most famished Fungi fans. **SuperValu supermarket,** The Holy Ground (tel. 51397), stocks a SuperSelection of groceries and juicy tabloids (open Mon.-Sat. 9am-9pm, Sun. 9am-6pm). **An Grianán** on Dykegate St., near the Grapevine Hostel, offers a selection of crunchy wholefoods and an organic vegetable and cheese deli counter (open Mon.-Sat. 9am-6pm).

The RiverGod Café, (tel. 51825), next to the roundabout. All ye hungry travelers, bow down to the god of culinary delights. Possibly the best food value in Kerry, the RiverGod serves huge sandwiches on baguettes, at prices even pilgrims can afford (from £3.50). The mysterious *Holy Sauce* is an extra-spicy treat. Sushi Bar planned for 1997. Vegetarian dishes on request. Open 1-9:30pm, closed Wed.

Adam's Pub and Restaurant, Main St. (tel. 52133). A favorite among budget-conscious locals who feast on cheap main courses (marinated steak sandwich £4) and homemade desserts. Open Mon.-Sat. noon-8:30pm.

An Café Liteartha, Dykegate St. (tel. 51388), across the street from the Grapevine hostel. This café/bookstore was one of the first Irish-language cafés in the Republic, and Irish-speakers still frequent the place. Open Mon.-Fri. 10am-5:30pm, Sat.-Sun. 11am-5:30pm. Bookstore open until 6pm.

An Sméara Dubha, off Strand St. (tel. 51465). Vegetarian meals are artfully assembled in this cozy bistro. Main courses £8 (lentil lasagna). Open 6-10pm.

Café Ceol, Green St., opposite the church and behind Dick Mack's pub. Outside seating, exotic wholefoods, and great live traditional music (which usually starts at 7:30pm) will keep you here for hours and hours. Dinner entrees £7-9. Open daily 1-4pm and 6:30-9:30pm, later when there's music. During the day, try one of the sweet or savory crepes at **Cul an Tí** downstairs. (Open daily 11am-5pm.)

Greany's, Bridge St. (tel. 51694). Hearty, heavy seafood in tight quarters. Colossal sandwiches and excellent chips. Scampi £7. Open daily 9am-10pm.

PUBS

Though only 1500 people live in Dingle permanently, the town has 52 pubs. In theory, every inhabitant could hoist a pint simultaneously without anyone having to scramble for a seat. Many pubs are beginning to cater to tourists, but the town still produces copious *craic*. The *Dingle Storytelling Pub Crawl* (tel. 52161) presents a literary tour of Dingle's pubs and "other sacred sights." Tours meet outside the post office on Main St. (July-Aug. Thurs.-Mon. 7-8:30pm; £3/person, £5/couple).

An Droichead Beag, Lower Main St. (tel. 51723), also referred to by its English name, "The Small Bridge." This most popular pub in town is nearly always crowded, but still unleashes the best trad in town, nightly in summer.

O'Flaherty's Pub, Holy Ground (tel. 51983), a few doors up from the traffic circle. Memorable, varied jam sessions most nights in this well-decorated pub. The word is out about the great atmosphere; get here by 9pm if you want a seat.

Dick Mack's, Green St. (tel. 51070), opposite the church. A leather bar—"Dick Mack's Bar, Boot Store, and Leather Shop," that is. The proprietor leaps between the bar and his leathertooling bench. Shoeboxes and whiskey bottles hang from the walls. The soft lighting and quiet atmosphere encourage conversation.

Danno's, Strand St. (tel. 51855). Recent refurbishments contribute to aesthetic enjoyment. A mixed crowd comes to its pub and restaurant (penne creole £4.75).

Murphy's, Strand St. (tel. 51450). The Lost Generation sidles up to the super-long bar in this pub by the marina. Trad and ballads nightly.

McCarthy's, Upper Main St. (tel. 51205), across the street and a few doors up from the post office. Quiet, intimate, undiscovered pub. Good *craic* when there's music (Thurs.-Sat.). Thurs. is no-smoking night.

Jack Neddy's, on the corner of Green St. and Strand St. Defines "unpretentiousness"—the sign outside the green-trimmed building says simply "Bar." Frequented by locals who, if you're lucky, will break into a spontaneous singing chorus.

SIGHTS

Fungi the Dolphin swam into Dingle Bay one day in 1983 with his mother, and the pair immediately became local celebrities. Dolphins are common in the bay, but Fungi particularly liked it around Dingle, cavorting with sailors and swimmers, flirting with TV cameras, and jumping in and out of the water for applause. Mom has died, but egomaniacal Fungi remains fond of humans. Wetsuited tourists incessantly swarm around him, while much of the tourist industry here sinks or swims with the delightful dolphin. **Boat trips** to see the dolphin leave from the pier constantly in summer. Most cost around £6 and guarantee that you'll see the dolphin. In the evening (after 6pm) when Fungi isn't following boats, he often hangs out in a little cove east of town. To get there, walk two minutes down the Tralee Rd., turn right at the Skellig Hotel, and then follow the beach away from town. On the other side of a stone tower, the small beach will probably be packed with Fungi-seekers. You can rent a **wetsuit** from Flannery's (tel. 51967), just east of town off the Tralee Rd. (£14/2hr., £22 overnight), or just jump in as you are. Ballintaggart Hostel rents suits cheap to its guests (see **Accommodations,** above).

Deep-sea angling trips (tel. 51337) leave daily in summer at 10am and 6pm from the pier. Full (£40, lunch included) and half-day (£15) sailing also available (book ahead at tel. 59882). For a closer look at marine matters, **Dingle Ocean World,** Strand St. (tel. 52111), features 160 species of fish, a 160,000L tank with a walk-through tunnel, and a petting-zoo tank where rays and skates swim up to have their fins scratched. One *Let's Go* researcher was so thrilled by this that his squeals of delight almost created a scene. (Open July-Aug. 9:30am-9:30pm; April-July and Aug.-Sept. 10am-6pm; in winter, daylight hours, closed Mon. Admission £4, students £3.)

The Dingle area has some interesting historical sites. The information office at the Mountain Man sells *The Easy Guide to the Dingle Peninsula,* which details walking tours, cycling tours, local history, and includes a map. **Sciúird Archaeology tours** (tel. 51606) take you from the pier on a three-hour whirlwind bus tour of the area's ancient spots (3/day; £6.50/person; book ahead). The same company also coordinates historic walking tours of Dingle Town (2/day; £2.50/person).

Summer festivals periodically turn the town into a carnival. The **Dingle Races** (second weekend in August) are geared more for children than for horses, while the **Dingle Regatta** (usually the third Sunday in August) pulls in salty mariners.

■ West Dingle

DUNQUIN (DÚN CHAOIN) & SLEA HEAD

Glorious **Slea Head** inspires with jagged cliffs and crashing waves. *Ryan's Daughter* and parts of *Far and Away* were filmed around here, and it's easy to see why. Green hills, interrupted by rough stone walls and sheep, lead down to plunging cliffs chiseled away by the sea. There's plenty of space on the head to **camp,** though in high season you'll have some neighbors. For some, the too-cute **Enchanted Forest Cafe** is so cheesy, it should come with crackers. Others may be delighted by the hundreds of teddy bears. Downstairs, a satisfying lunch can be had with breathtaking views of the Head (brown bread sandwiches from £2.10, teddy bear scones £1.10). Upstairs, the teddy-bear orgy of a museum creatively depicts the four seasons and Celtic pagan holidays (admission £2, under 12 £1).

The road from broad horseshoe-shaped **Ventry Beach** out to Slea Head passes dozens of Iron Age and early Christian stones and ruins. **Dunbeg Fort** (admission £1, students 80p) and the **Fahan Group** (admission £1) of beehive-shaped stone huts (known as oratories) built by early monks cluster on hillsides over the cliffs. The view alone from Dunbeg is worth the admission.

North of Slea Head, the scattered settlement of **Dunquin** consists of stone houses, a pub, and plenty of spoken Irish, but no grocery store. Stock up in Dingle or in Ballyferriter if you're going to stay here or on Great Blasket. **Kruger's** (tel. 56127), purportedly the westernmost pub in Europe, features pub grub (chicken Kiev £5.65), frequent spontaneous music sessions, and fantastic views. Its adjacent **B&B** has basic but comfortable rooms (£14/person). Along the road to Ballyferriter, **An Óige Hostel (HI)** (tel. (066) 56121) provides adequate and clean bunkrooms and a spacious, window-walled sitting and dining room which looks out onto the sea. (June-Sept. £6.50, Oct.-May £5.50. Lockout 10:15am-5pm; midnight curfew; showers closed 9am-5:30pm. Breakfast £1.75. Sheets 60p.) Two miles past Dunquin, about halfway to Ballyferriter, **Tig Áine** (tel. 56214), a gallery and café, charms visitors with views of the cliffs. Stop in for scones and tea, or enjoy the huge and affordable dinners made with home-grown vegetables (vegetable stirfry and salad £5).

The stunning architecture of the **Blasket Centre** (tel. (066) 56371), across from the youth hostel, enhances the museum's outstanding exhibits. Writings and photographs of the Great Blasket authors re-create the lost era of the islands. The museum also presents exhibits on the past richness and current status of the Irish language. (Open July-Aug. daily 10am-7pm, Easter-June and Sept. to mid-Oct. daily 10am-6pm. Admission £2.50, students £1. Last admission 45min. before closing.)

The Last Islander

The famous autobiographers of the Blasket Islands described 19th and early 20th century Irish life on the island and voiced concern over the possible eradication of Irish culture. By 1953, most of Great Blasket's residents were old, with the exception of a 19-year-old who represented "the future" to everyone else on the island. He came down with meningitis during weather so severe that no boats could leave for the mainland's hospital. The sea calmed down only two days after his death. By the end of that year, everyone had moved to the mainland.

BLASKET ISLANDS (NA BLASCAODAÍ)

The Blaskets comprise six islands: Beginish, Tearaght, Inishnabro, Inishvickillane, Inishtooskert and Great Blasket. Ferries sail to Great Blasket, now occupied by a handful of isolation-seeking summer residents. Evacuated in 1953, the Blasket Islands have famously come to stand for the elegiac vision of an antiquated *gaeltacht* culture, once inhabited by poet-fishermen, proud but impoverished and aging villagers, and memoirists reluctantly warning that "after us, there will be no more." Blasket writers themselves, in English and Irish, helped produce and publicize that vision. The well-known memoirs *Twenty Years a-Growing* (Maurice O'Sullivan), *The Islander* (Thomas O'Crohan), and *Peig* (Peig Sayers, recently published in English) are obscure in America but required (and often dreaded) reading for Irish students. Mists, seals, and occasional fishing boats may continue to pass the Blaskets, but the simpler ways of life exemplified there are gone forever.

Days on somnolent Great Blasket are long and meditative: wander through the mist down to the white strand, follow the grass paths of the island's 10 mi. circumference, explore the stone skeletons of former houses in the village, and observe the puffins and seals that populate the island. Those spending the night can enjoy fresh fish and wholefood dinners in the **café** near the old village for £5—the portions are massive (the seaweed is choice; open daily 10am-6pm when there are customers). **Campers** can pitch their tents anywhere for free. There's no hot water, food (other than in the café), or electricity, so if you plan to stay, stock up on supplies in Dingle or Ballyferriter. Keep in mind that if the weather is bad, the boats don't run—people have been stuck here for two weeks during gales. **Boats** for the Blaskets depart from Dunquin May to September daily, every hour from 10am to 6pm, weather and ferry operator's mood permitting (tel. (066) 56455; £10 return). A shuttle bus runs from Dingle to the Blasket ferry and back (2/day; £10; call 56422 for details). **Sail cruises** departing from Dingle Town encircle and stop on the Great Blasket. (10am usual departure. Full day including lunch £30/person; half-day cruise (no stop on islands) £15/person. Call 59882 for bookings and information.)

BALLYFERRITER (BAILE AN FHEIRTÉARAIGH)

Ballyferriter is West Dingle's closest approximation to a town center. In contrast to the Blasket Centre, which eulogizes the almost extinct Irish oral tradition, Ballyferriter (an authentic *gaeltacht*) stands as a testament to the language's continued existence—even the Guinness signs are in Irish. The views aren't as spectacular as at Slea Head, but the town is a lively center of Irish culture and language.

Many people are lured to Ballyferriter by the musical strains and prosaic voices inside **Peig's Pub**, Main St. (tel. (066) 56433), where there are frequent trad sessions in the evenings. Peig's makes a welcoming spot for an appetizing meal (including vegetarian options; daily specials £5.50). Across the street, **Murphy's** (tel. (066) 56224) serves pub food. **Ócatháin** occasionally lures local musicians on weekends.

The largest grocery in town is **Ollmhargadh Market** (tel. (066) 56157), in the town center (open in summer daily 9am-10:30pm, winter daily 9am-8pm). Five minutes outside town on the Dunquin Rd., the simple **An Cat Dubh** (Black Cat Hostel; tel. (066) 56286) crosses your path in a tacky but friendly sort of way—Lord, deliver us from clashing pastel paisley. (£6/person. **Camping** £3/person.) The B&B next door, **An Spéice** (tel. (066) 56254), provides quiet rest (£13/person, w/bath £14).

Back in town, the **Heritage Centre** (tel. (066) 56333) brims with photos and text relating to the area's wildlife, archaeology, and folklore (open June-Sept. Mon.-Fri. 10am-noon and 2-4pm; admission £1). The Heritage Centre is a noble attempt at making the area's history accessible, but the actual ancient sites aren't far. From Ballyferriter, follow the signs to **Dún An Óir** (the Fort of Gold), an Iron Age fort where, in 1580, the English massacred over 600 Spanish, Italian, and Irish soldiers who openly supported the Irish Catholics' rebellion against Queen Elizabeth. From the main road, signposted roads branch to **Riasc,** a puzzling monastic site with an engraved standing slab, to the **Dillon Stone** (a monument erected by early British settlers; Protestants flock there every year on January 7), and to Ballydavid.

■ North Dingle

A winding cliffside road runs north from Dingle via the 1500-ft. **Connor Pass** and affords tremendous views of the valleys and the bays beyond. Buses won't fit on the road, but private automobiles squeeze through the pass. A slight detour west on the north side of the Connor Pass (watch for the signs) leads to the quiet hamlet of **Cloghane.** From here you can hike north along the scenery-splashed main road to **Ballyquin Strand** and **Brandon Point** or west (and up) to 3127-ft. **Mt. Brandon** and its surrounding lakes (follow the signs west from Cloghane). **The Saint's Road** to the summit was cleared by St. Brendan. It may have been easy for someone who crossed the Atlantic in a leather boat, but for most people it's quite a hike. Climb on the west side from Ballybrack, or try the more impressive ascent from the Cloghane side, which begins between Brandon Point and Cloghane (watch for signs).

Back toward Tralee in **Stradbally,** narrow beds proliferate in the friendly **Connor Pass Hostel (IHH)** (tel. (066) 39179; £6/person; open mid-March to Nov.). The hostel makes a good base for hikes in the **Slieve Mish Mountains** to the east. The 2713-ft. ascent to **Cáherconree** culminates with views of the peninsula, the ocean, and the Shannon Estuary. Stradbally is also an excellent base for the **Loch a'Duín** nature and archaeology walk. Inquire at **Tomásin's Pub** (tel. (066) 39179) across the street from the hostel, for info packets (£3). The pub also serves mean grub (fillets of plaice £7; lunch noon-4:30pm, dinner 6-9:30pm). In summer, swimmers escape on daytrips to the huge, empty strands west of the hostel.

If you're intent on exploring north Dingle, **Castlegregory** may make a better base—there's a tourist office and a grocery store here. The small but informative **tourist information centre** (tel. (066) 39422) is open from 10am to 8pm (off season until 5pm). **Spar Market** (tel. (066) 39433) is open daily 8:30am to 9pm. The quiet **Lynch's Hostel** (tel. (066) 39128) is the better of the two hostels in town (2- to 4-bed dorm £6; **bikes** £6/day, £36/week). If you're stuck, try **Fitzgerald's Euro-Hostel** (tel. (066) 39133) above the pub (dorm £5.50, single £10; showers 50p). Small **Milesian Restaurant,** Main St., hosts frequent poetry readings in a charming farmhouse. Ever-changing menu with cheap vegetarian options (lamb curry £6; open Easter-Nov. 10am-10pm, weekends in winter). **Ferriter's Pub** (tel. (066) 39494) plays trad and ballads on Wednesdays and weekends. **Ned Natterjack's** (named for the rare and quite vocal Natterjack toad that resides in this area), presents trad on Wednesdays in summer; various live rock Thursday to Sunday.

From Castlegregory, head north up the sandy **Maharees Peninsula** where you can play a round of golf at the **Castlegregory Golf Club** (tel. (066) 39444; £12), rent windsurfers from **Focus Windsurfing** (tel. (066) 39411; from £8/hr., with wetsuit), or swim at numerous strands. A **bus** to Tralee runs erratically (July-Aug. Mon., Wed., Sat. 2/day; Tues. and Thurs. 2/day; all year Fri. 3/day; £3.80).

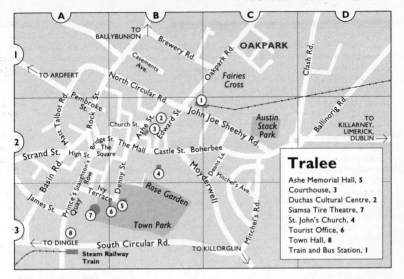

Tralee

Ashe Memorial Hall, **5**
Courthouse, **3**
Duchas Cultural Centre, **2**
Siamsa Tire Theatre, **7**
St. John's Church, **4**
Tourist Office, **6**
Town Hall, **8**
Train and Bus Station, **I**

NORTH KERRY

■ Tralee

While tourists tend to identify Killarney as the core of Kerry, residents correctly see Tralee (pop. 20,000) as the county's economic center. The commerce and industry frequently make visitors, fresh from Dingle or the Ring, perceive Tralee as an unwelcome return to urban reality. But there's plenty for tourists to do here these days: local effort and buckets of EU development funds have gone towards building new, splashy attractions. Precious minutes are most wisely spent at Kerry the Kingdom museum, the folk theater next door, and the radiant rose gardens. Although Tralee has its touristy aspects, the pubs, restaurants, and shops exist primarily for locals.

ORIENTATION & PRACTICAL INFORMATION

Tralee's streets are hopelessly knotted; find the tourist office immediately and arm yourself with a free map. The main street in town—variously called the Mall, Castle St., and Boherboy—is a good reference point.

Tourist Office: Ashe Memorial Hall, at the end of Denny St. (tel. 21288). From the station, go into town on Edward St., right on Castle St. and left onto Denny St. The staff is extremely kind and helpful. Open Mon.-Sat. 9am-7pm, Sun. 9am-6pm; off season Tues.-Sat. 9am-5pm.

Banks: Bank of Ireland, Castle St. Open Mon. 10am-5pm, Tues.-Fri. 10am-4pm. **AIB,** corner of Denny and Castle St. Open Mon. 10am-5pm, Tues.-Fri. 10am-4pm. Both have **ATMs** that accept most major credit cards.

Trains: Edward St. and John Joe Sheehy Rd. (tel. 23522). Ticket office open sporadically. Phone inquiries taken Mon.-Fri. 9am-12:30pm and 1:30-5:30pm. Trains tie Tralee to: Cork (Mon.-Sat. 5/day, Sun. 3/day; 2½hr.; £17, students £7); Killarney (Mon.-Sat. 5/day, Sun. 4/day; 40min.; £5.50, students £3.50); Galway (3/day; £33.50, students £12.50); Dublin (Mon.-Sat. 4/day, Sun. 3/day; 4hr.; £33.50, students £12.50); Waterford (Mon.-Sat. 2/day; 4hr.; £33.50, students £12.50); and Rosslare Harbour (Mon.-Sat. 2/day; 5hr.; £33.50, students £12.50).

Buses: Edward St. and John Joe Sheehy Rd. (tel. 23566). Station open Mon.-Sat. 8:30am-6pm, Sun. 11am-6pm; 5:10pm close in winter. Buses run to: Cork (Mon.-Sat. 6/day, Sun. 4/day; 2½hr.; £9.70, students £6); Dingle (July-Aug. Mon.-Sat. 9/day, Sun. 6/day; Sept.-June Mon.-Sat. 4/day, Sun. 2/day; 1¼hr.; £5.90, students £3.70); Killarney (June-Sept. Mon.-Sat. 14/day, Sun. 8/day; Oct.-May Mon.-Sat. 5/day, Sun. 6/day; 40min.; £4.40, students £2.80); Limerick (Mon.-Sat. 5/day, Sun. 4/day; 2¼hr.; £9, students £5.30); and Galway (Mon.-Sat. 5/day, Sun. 4/day; £13, students £8).

Airport: Kerry Airport (tel. 64644), off N22 halfway between Tralee and Killarney. Manx Airlines (tel. (01) 260 1588) flies to London for at least £105 return (7-day advance purchase required).

Taxi: Kingdom Cabs, 48 Boherboy (tel. 27828). Cabs park on Denny St. at the intersection with the Mall and charge £1/mile, less for longer distances.

Bike Rental: O'Halloran, 83 Boherboy (tel. 22820). Sometimes, you've just got to ride. £5/day, £25/week. Open Mon.-Sat. 10am-6pm.

Camping Equipment: Landers, Courthouse Lane (tel. 26644), has an extensive selection. No tent rental. Open Mon.-Sat. 9am-6pm.

Laundry: The Laundry, Pembroke St. (tel. 23214). Open Mon.-Fri. 9am-6pm.

Hotlines: Samaritans, 44 Moyderwell (tel. 22566), 24hr.

Pharmacy: Kelly's Chemist, the Mall (tel. 21302), indulges your pharmaceutical fancies. Open Mon.-Fri. 9am-8pm, Sat. 9am-6pm.

Hospital: Tralee County General Hospital, off Killarney Rd. (tel. 26222).

Emergency: Dial 999; no coins required. **Garda:** High St. (tel. 22022).

Post Office: Edward St., off Castle St. (tel. 21013). Open Mon. and Wed.-Sat. 9am-5:30pm, Tues. 9:30am-5:30pm.

Phone Code: 066.

ACCOMMODATIONS

While Tralee is neither especially charming nor picturesque, it boasts six good hostels. A number of pleasant B&Bs line Oakpark Rd., while a smattering of others sit on Boherboy, by the traffic circle.

Finnegan's Hostel (IHH), 17 Denny St. (tel. 27610). At the end of the city's most dignified street, this majestic 19th-century townhouse contains part of the old town castle. The hostel's location is brilliant, as is its common room: grand doorways, oriental rugs, and velvet furniture. Spacious, wood-floored bunk rooms are named after Ireland's literary heroes. Dorm £6.50. Double £18.

Collis-Sandes House (IHH) (tel. 28658). Near-perfect, but far from town. Follow Edward St./Oakpark Rd. 1mi. away from town, taking the first left after Halloran's Foodstore and following signs to the right. This stately stone mansion, built in 1857, has beautiful high ceilings, stained glass, and a coat of arms. Hostel hosts a folk/blues weekend the last week of July. Free lifts to town. Wheelchair accessible. Dorm £6-7. Double from £16. Breakfast from £1. Laundry £2.50, wash or dry. Bike and walking tours (bikes £7/day, £30/week; £40 deposit); tour £8/day.

Seán Óg's Hostel, Church St. (tel. 28822). Walk up Barrack Ln., the pedestrian walkway off the Mall opposite Denny St., and make the first right. Small, downtown hangout with a cozy, warm sitting room and a skylit kitchen. Dorm £6.50. Double £18. Triple £21.

Lisnagree Hostel (IHH), Ballinorig Rd. (tel. 27133), on the left fork just after the traffic circle before the Maxol garage (follow Boherboy away from town), ½mi. from town and close to the bus/train station. Small, relaxed hostel perfect for families or couples. 4-bed dorm from £6.50. Doubles from £16. Laundry £4.

Atlas House, Castle St. (Boherboy; tel. 20722). More like a Holiday Inn than a hostel. Satellite TV, large kitchen, continental breakfast included. Non-smoking rooms. 8-bed dorm £7.50. 4-bed dorm £9. Twin from £24.

Kelly's Hostel, Princes Quay (tel. 20551), across from Siamsa Tíre. Centrally located, this small family-run hostel makes you feel at home with basic but cozy rooms. Outside patio. Dorm £6.50. Private room £8.50/person.

Dowling's Leeside, Oakpark Rd. (tel. 26475). About ½mi. from town center on Edward St./Oakpark Rd. Pamper yourself at this cheerful B&B, decorated with country pine antiques and cushy chintz chairs. Glass-enclosed dining room makes breakfast bright. Flowers outside, but no lace in sight. Single £16. Double £30.

FOOD

Tralee's culinary landscape has definitely improved over the past few years. A number of new restaurants have appeared on the scene, as well as legions of fast-food joints. For the chefs, there's a **Quinnsworth Supermarket** (tel. 22788) in the Square (open Mon.-Tues. 9am-7pm, Wed.-Fri. 9am-9pm, Sat. 9am-6pm) and a health food store/bakery, **Sean Chara** (tel. 22644), across the street (open Mon.-Wed. and Sat. 9am-6pm, Thurs. 9am-8pm, Fri. 9am-9pm). **Counihans Newsagent** on the corner of Prince's St. and Ivy Terrace sells expensive groceries until 11pm.

Finnegan's, below the hostel on Denny St. (tel. 27610). Savor the delicacies prepared in this candle-lit, shadowy bistro. A fireside meal could last for hours. Dinners are in the upper range of budget eats, but large and tasty (entrees £7-14).

The Old Forge, Church St. (tel. 28095), next to Seán Óg's Hostel. A Tralee institution, with authentic Irish fare. Beef and Guinness casserole £6.75, Irish breakfasts £3.50. Open July-Sept. Mon.-Sat. 9am-10pm; Oct.-June Mon.-Sat. 9am-6pm.

Brat's Place, Milk Market La. (pedestrian walkway off the Mall). Substantial, conscientiously prepared vegetarian food uses mostly local and organic ingredients. Specializes in low-cal, low-fat, and gluten-free meals. Potatoes, spinach, and goat cheese £4. Delicious desserts £1-1.50. Open Mon.-Sat. 12:30-3pm.

The Skillet, Barrack La. (tel. 24561), off the Mall. If the pizza doesn't exhilarate you, the photos of Mt. Everest will (the owner was on the first Irish expedition to climb it). Pizzas £3 (lunch only). Chicken curry and chips £7, lunch £4. Open daily 9am-10pm; closed Sun. in winter.

Roots, 76 Boherboy (tel. 22665). An ever-changing menu of vegetarian food, in gargantuan portions (£3-4). Open Mon.-Fri. 11am-3pm, also Wed.-Fri. 7-9pm.

Pizza Time, (tel. 26317), next to Quinnsworth on the Square. Pizza £3.50-8. Open every day of the week, even when the rest of Tralee is closed. Open Mon.-Thurs. and Sun. noon-1am, Sat.-Fri. noon-3am.

PUBS

Baily's Corner Pub, (tel. 23230), corner of Ashe and Castle St. This mellow pub hosts outstanding trad sessions Tues. nights. Kerry's Gaelic football legacy hangs on the walls while real-life players drink at the bar, along with an older crowd.

Paddy Mac's, the Mall. Another Tralee favorite with many a trad session, compensating for its lack of physical charm. Trad on Tues. and weekends.

Val O'Shea's, Bridge St. (tel. 21559). Extremely popular among natives, Val's draws in a mixed crowd for *craic* and conversation, but no live music.

The Old Market Place (tel. 29888), next to Abbeygate Hotel. This huge and brand-new pub displays vintage knick-knacks in lit showcases and features live music most nights of the week. Trad with dancing on Sun.

Abbey Inn, the Square (tel. 22084). Tough crowd comes to hear live rock and reggae. Bono swept here! When U2 played here in the early 80s, the manager made them sweep the floors to pay for their drinks because he thought they were so bad. Open until 1am Mon., Thurs., and Fri. (cover £2 those nights).

SIGHTS

Ireland's second-largest museum is **Kerry the Kingdom,** Ashe Memorial Hall, Denny St. (tel. 27777). Named one of Europe's top 20 museums in 1994, the Kingdom marshals all the resources of display technology to tell the story of Co. Kerry from 8000 BC to the present. Though the rise and fall of the Kerry Gaelic football league gets disproportionate attention, some temporary exhibits are world-class. "Geraldine Tralee" downstairs is a reconstruction of Tralee in 1450 seen from a small moving cart. You even get the old city's stench for part of the ride! (Open March-July and Sept.-Oct. Mon.-Sun. 10am-6pm; Aug. Mon.-Sat. 10am-7pm, Sun. 10am-6pm; Nov.-Dec. Mon.-Sat. 2-5pm. Admission £4.20, students £3.75.)

Across from the museum, the **Roses of Tralee** bloom each summer in Ireland's second-largest town park. The gardens, designed in 1987, could convert even floraphobes into rose sniffers. The gray carpeting in **St. John's Church,** Castle St., dampens the echo and the Gothic mood, but the stained glass is worth a look.

The building on the Prince's Quay traffic circle that looks like a cross between a Gothic castle and a space-age solarium is actually Tralee's new £4.5-million **Aquadome** (tel. 28899). Inside, a wave pool, river rapids, and speedy waterslide are all substantially warmer than the Atlantic. Whirlpools, steam room, sauna, and a gym (admission £4 (July £6), students £3 (July £5); open daily 10am-10pm).

Just down Dingle Rd. (N86/R559) is the **Blenneville Windmill and Visitor Centre** (tel. 21064). Blenneville's is the largest operating windmill in Britain or Ireland, and you can climb to the top. Recalling Blenneville's status as Kerry's main port of emigration during the Famine, a small **museum** focuses on the "coffin ships" that sailed from Ireland during the Famine (open April-Oct. daily 10am-6pm; admission £2.75, students £2.25). The restored **Tralee & Dingle Railway** (tel. 21064) runs the 3km between the aquadome and the Blennerville complex. Trains leave the aquadome every hour on the hour, and leave the windmill on the half hour (runs 10am-5:30pm except 2nd Sun. and Mon. of each month; £2.75, student £2.25).

ENTERTAINMENT

The **Siamsa Tíre Theatre** (tel. 23055), at the end of Denny St. next to the museum, is Ireland's national folk theater. It mounts brilliant summer programs depicting traditional Irish life through mime, music, and dance. (Productions July-Aug. Mon.-Sat.; May-June and Sept. Mon.-Thurs., and Sat. Shows start at 8:30pm. Box office open Mon.-Sat. 9am-10:30pm. Tickets £9, students £8.) The **Dúchas Cultural Centre,** Edward St., puts on dance and music (July-Aug. Tues. 8:30pm; £4).

Less culturally elite entertainment is available in Tralee's two nightclubs. The **Brandon Hotel,** Prince's St. (tel. 23333) discos on Wednesdays and Fridays through Sundays. **Horan's,** Boherboy (tel. 21933), blasts country-western and disco on Thursday through Sunday nights. Both stay open until 1:45am (cover £4-5).

Lovely Irish lasses from around the world come to town during the last week of August for the **Rose of Tralee International Festival.** A maelstrom of entertainment surrounds the event, a personality competition to earn the coveted title, "Rose of Tralee." Rose-hopefuls or spectators can call the Rose office, in Ashe Memorial Hall (tel. 21322). For local goings-on, check *The Kerryman* (85p).

■ Near Tralee

Take Fenit Rd. (R558) out of town for views of the Tralee Bay and the Dingle Peninsula and for the new **Fenit Sea World** aquarium (tel. 36544). Eels and prawns frolic in huge tanks of native sea life, much of it captured just off the pier (open daily 10am-8pm (6pm close in off season); admission £4, students £3). Beyond the pier, deserted beaches stretch for miles. From the aquarium, a tangle of backroads (or take R551 from Tralee) lead to **Ardfert,** where St. Brendan the Navigator founded his **monastery** in the 6th century. The Office of Public Works has taken over the crumbling structures, but you can still explore a few of them for free. If you're curious, go inside for a guided tour, but the "museum" isn't worth the price (tel. 34711; center open daily 9:30am-6:30pm; admission £1.50, students 60p). Ardfert's real gem is the never-ending **Banna Strand** (watch for the signs from town center or anywhere along Tralee-Ardfert Rd.). A monument remembers Roger Casement, an Irish nationalist put ashore here by a German U-boat in mid-April 1916, returning from his mission to secure German arms for an Irish rebellion. He showed up a day too late—the British had discovered the shipment. He was captured and hanged.

Twelve miles from Tralee in **Castleisland** on Limerick Rd. (N21), visitors can amuse themselves with stalactites and stalagmites in the **Crag Cave** (tel. 41244). Divers discovered the one million-year-old limestone cave in 1983 (there was no terrestrial entrance until humans blasted one). Now a good portion of its 6 mi. is open to guided tours. (Open mid-March to Oct. 10am-6pm, July-Aug. 10am-7pm. Admission £3, students £2.50 w/ID.)

TARBERT

Anyone traveling between Co. Kerry and Co. Clare should take the 20-min. **Tarbert-Killimer car ferry** (tel. (065) 53124), thus avoiding the 85-mi. land detour via Limerick. (Sailings April-Sept. Mon.-Sat.7:30am-9:30pm, Sun. 9:30am-9:30pm; Oct.-March Mon.-Sat. 7:30am-7:30pm, Sun. 10:30am-7:30pm. Boats sail every hour on the half hour and return on the hour from Clare. £2/passenger or cyclist, £3 return, £7/car including passengers.) There's also a hostel in Tarbert, the **Nest** (tel. (068) 36165). A simple place with a garden in the backyard, the Nest is a stone's throw off the Foynes Rd. (Dorm £6. **Camping** £4. Open June-Aug.)

Tarbert's **tourist office** is in the 1831 **Bridewell Jail and Courthouse** (tel. 36500), a small but interesting look at Irish prison history (admission £3, students £2; tourist office and exhibit open April-Oct. 10am-6pm). A few hundred meters from the ferry stands **Tarbert House** (tel. (068) 36198), the home of the Signeur Leslie of Tarbert since 1690. The house is full of period pieces and priceless art, but has lost much of its grandeur. (Open 10am-noon and 2-4pm; admission £2, student rates available; tours given by Mrs. Leslie herself).

From mid-June through September, **Bus Éireann** travels from Tralee to Galway and Doolin via the Tarbert-Killimer ferry (Mon.-Sat. 3/day, Sun. 2/day; Galway to Tralee £13, students £8). During the rest of the year, the nearest bus stop to Killimer is in Kilrush, 8 mi. north, with connections to Milltown Malbay and Ennis (late June to late Aug.). Mid-afternoon hitchers in Killimer will have an easy time finding rides to Kilrush with workers from nearby Moneypoint, who get off work at 4:30pm.

WESTERN IRELAND

Dubliners will tell you to get out of their dirty old town, and that the west is the "most Irish" part of Ireland. Yeats would agree: "For me," he said, "Ireland is Connacht." For less privileged Irish, Connacht has sometimes meant poor soil, starvation, and emigration. When Cromwell uprooted the native Irish landowners in Leinster and Munster and resettled them west of the Shannon, he was giving them a raw deal. The West was also hardest-hit by the potato famine—entire villages emigrated or died. Today, each western county has less than half of its 1841 population. But from Connemara north to Ballina, hikers, cyclists, and hitchhikers enjoy the isolation of boggy, rocky, or brilliantly mountainous landscapes.

Galway City is a different story, a successful port that's now a boomtown for the young. The rest of Co. Galway draws summer tourists to its rugged scenery and Irish-speaking villages. To the south, the barren moonscape of the Burren, the Cliffs of Moher, and a reputation as the center of the trad music scene attracts travelers to Co. Clare. Western Ireland's gorgeous desolation, tragic history, and enclaves of traditional culture are now its biggest attractions.

Limerick & Clare

The Dál Cais (later O'Brien) clan invaded Clare around 744 AD, ruthlessly exterminated the natives, who were called the Corcu Modruad, and prepared themselves for a 300-year rise to power and high-kingship. Cos. Limerick and Clare are substantially less violent today. The poverty of Western Ireland is most visible in Limerick City but is alleviated a bit by Shannon Airport. Geology defines Co. Clare: fine sands glisten on the beaches of Kilkee, limestone slabs higher than some skyscrapers mark the Cliffs of Moher, and 100 sq. mi. of exposed limestone form Ireland's weirdest landscape, the Burren.

■ Limerick City

Although grimy industry and unemployment have kept it sagging, the Republic's third largest city is in the middle of a multi-year face-lift. Limerick has gotten a lot of bad press over the years, much of which is undeserved. It's true, Limerick is not the prettiest city in Ireland, but it is a vibrant university town with a top-notch museum and a number of spectacular historic sights. The recent elimination of the Shannon stopover rule, which required all North American flights to touch down at Shannon, ensured that Limerick will not soon be a major tourist center, but the city can still be a pleasant place to spend a few nights. Delightful 18th-century Georgian architecture in the classier parts of town and a burgeoning quay development along Limerick's two rivers point towards a brighter future.

The Vikings settled around Limerick in 922, presaging a millennium of turbulent hullabaloo. The O'Brien's also lived here, until the Normans came near (12th century), and then English oppression grew. During the English Civil War, Limerick was the last stronghold of Royalist support against Cromwell's army. When the city finally did break, it took Cromwell's commander, Henry Ireton, with it. Forty years later, the Jacobites made their last stand here against the Williamites. The battle resulted in the infamous Treaty of Limerick, a promise of limited civil rights for Catholics that the English had no intention of keeping (see **The Protestant Ascendancy,** p. 60). The treaty became a sore point in British-Irish relations for the next 150 years. Later, this unpromising terrain became a center of manufacturing: the world's first mass-pro-

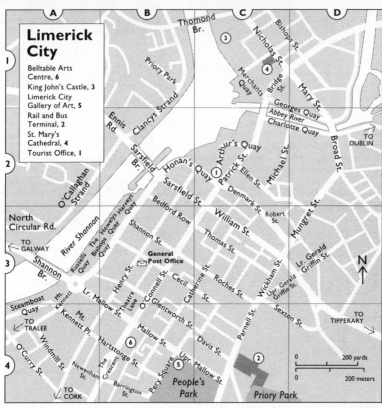

Limerick City

Belltable Arts
Centre, 6
King John's Castle, 3
Limerick City
Gallery of Art, 5
Rail and Bus
Terminal, 2
St. Mary's
Cathedral, 4
Tourist Office, 1

duced clothing rolled off a Limerick assembly line. Eyes turned towards Limerick in April 1919 when a workers' soviet chose the eve of the War of Independence to lead a general strike.

ORIENTATION & PRACTICAL INFORMATION

Limerick's streets form a grid pattern, bounded by the River Shannon on the west and by the Abbey River on the north. **O'Connell St.** fosters most of the city's activity in its few blocks. Following O'Connell St. north, cross the Abbey River to reach King's Island, which is dominated architecturally by St. Mary's Cathedral and King John's Castle. The city itself is easily navigable by foot, but to reach the suburbs, catch a **city bus** (65p) from Boyd's or Penney's on O'Connell St. (buses run Mon.-Sat. 8am-11pm; 2/hr., Sun. 1/hr.). Buses #2, 5, and 8 access the University, while bus #6 follows Ennis Rd.

> **Tourist Office:** Arthurs Quay (tel. 317522), in the space-age glass building. From the station, walk straight down Davis St., turn right on O'Connell St., then left just before Arthurs Quay Mall. Excellent, free city maps. The tourist office also houses a bureau de change and a Bus Éireann info booth. Open July-Aug. Mon.-Fri. 9am-7pm, Sat.-Sun. 9am-6pm; March-June and Sept.-Oct. Mon.-Sat. 9:30am-5:30pm; Nov.-Feb. Mon.-Fri. 9:30am-5:30pm, Sat. 9:30am-1pm.
>
> **Budget Travel Office: USIT,** O'Connell St. (tel. 415064), across from Ulster Bank. Issues ISICs and TravelSave stamps. Open Mon.-Fri. 9:30am-5:30pm, Sat. 10am-1pm. Also located at University of Limerick (tel. 332073).

American Express: Ivernia Hall, 97 Henry St. (tel. 313066). AmEx Traveler's Cheques redeemable, commission-free. Client mail service.

Trains: Colbert Station, just off Parnell St. (tel. 315555). Enquiries desk open Mon.-Fri. 9am-6pm, Sat. 9:30am-5:30pm. Trains from Limerick go to: Dublin (Mon.-Sat. 10/day, Sun. 5/day; 2hr.; £25, students £10); Waterford (Mon.-Sat. 2/day (winter 1/day); 2hr.; £17, students £7); Rosslare (Mon.-Sat. 2/day; 3½hr.; £23, students £9.50); Ennis (2/day; £5.50, students £3.50); Cork (7/day, Sun. 6/day; 2½hr.; £13.50, students £6); Killarney (Mon.-Sat. 4/day, Sun. 3/day; 2½hr.; £15, student £6.50); and Tralee (4/day, Sun. 3/day; 2¼hr.; £15, student £6.50).

Buses: Colbert Station, just off Parnell St. (tel. 313333 or 418855; 24-hr. talking timetable tel. 319911). Open June-Sept. daily 8:45am-6pm; Oct.-May Mon.-Sat. 8am-6pm, Sun. 3-7pm. Most buses leave from the station, but some depart from Penney's or Todd's downtown on O'Connell St. Limerick sends buses to: Cork (6/day; 2hr.; £9, students £5.30); Dublin (Mon.-Fri. 8/day, Sun. 5/day; 3hr.; £10, students £7.50); Galway via Ennis (7/day; Ennis 1hr., £5, students £3.20; Galway 2hr.; £9, student £5.30); Killarney (Mon.-Sat. 6/day, Sun. 3/day; 2½hr.; £9.30, students £5.60); Sligo (4/day; 6hr.; £14, students £8.50); Tralee (6/day; 2hr.; £9, students £5.30); Waterford (Mon.-Thurs. and Sat. 5/day, Fri. 6/day, Sun. 5/day; 2½hr.; £9.70, students £6); and Wexford and Rosslare Harbour, with some departures timed to meet the ferries (4/day; 4hr.; £12, students £7.50).

Luggage storage: in Colbert Station. Lockers £1/day, 24-hr. limit.

Bike Rental: Emerald Cycles, 1 Patrick St. (tel. 416983). £7/day, £30/week; deposit £40. £12 for return at other locations. Open Mon.-Sat 9:15am-5:30pm. **McMahon's Cycleworld,** 25 Roaches St. (tel. 415202). £7/day, £30/week.

Laundry: Speediwash Laundrette & Dry Cleaners, 11 Gerard St. (tel. 319380). £1.50 wash, 20p/5-min. dry; £5 serviced wash. Open Mon.-Sat. 9am-6pm.

Camping Equipment: River Deep, Mountain High, 7 Rutland St., off O'Connell (tel. 400944). Open Mon.-Thurs. and Sat. 9:30am-6pm, Fri. 9:30am-9pm.

Pharmacy: Arthurs Quay Pharmacy, Arthurs Quay Centre (tel. 416662). Open Mon.-Wed. 9am-7pm, Thurs.-Fri. 9am-9pm, Sat. 9am-6pm.

Emergency: Dial 999. **Garda:** Henry St. (tel. 414222), at Lower Glentworth St.

Post Office: Main office on Lower Cecil St. (tel. 315777), just off O'Connell St. Open Mon. and Wed.-Sat. 9am-5:30pm, Tues. 9:30am-5:30pm.

Phone code: 061.

ACCOMMODATIONS

For a city of its size, Limerick is strangely lacking in hostels. At present there are two, with a third eagerly anticipated for early 1997 (inquire at tourist office). What Limerick does offer is budget accommodation geared towards term-time university students. These dorm-like establishments are usually institutionally sized and in very good condition, but are slightly more expensive and less homey than the average hostel. Limerick is not the place to find cozy cottage hostels with peat fires ablaze. For those seeking refuge from the bustle of the city, Ennis St. is a B&B bonanza, with most priced around £16 per person.

Barrington Hostel (IHH), George's Quay (tel. 415222), near St. Mary's Cathedral. From the station, make a right on Parnell St. and follow it over the Abbey River. After a left on George's Quay, the hostel is on the right. Barrington compensates for its large size by offering relatively private dorms. Colorful murals soften the urban edge. Offers 2 kitchens, a restaurant during peak season, and a gorgeous front garden. 4-bed dorm £6.50. 3-bed dorm £7. Single £9. Twin/double £15. Prices £1 less if booked along with bus ticket from Shannon Airport. Laundry £5.

An Óige Hostel (HI), 1 Pery Sq. (tel. 314672). From Colbert Station, walk straight down Davis St. to the monument and turn left onto Percy Sq. A pleasant, old Georgian house and a super-cheerful warden help to ease the usual An Óige restrictions and dreariness. Metal bunks in rooms with splendid views of People's Park. Midnight curfew, no lockout. 12- and 14-bed dorm June-Sept. £6.50, Oct.-May £5.50. Sheets £1.

Westbourne Holiday Hostel (IHH), Courbrack Ave. off Dock Rd. (tel. 302500). From Colbert Station, make a left on Parnell St., then a right on Upper Mallow St. by the park. Follow Mallow St. to the traffic circle, make a left and continue for about 1mi. The hostel is on the left after the Shell Station. This student housing masquerading as a hostel is stunning, if a little far from the city center. No bunks, carpeted hallways, a huge kitchen and dining room, and a lounge and TV. 3-bed dorm £6.50/person. Single £10. Double £16. Continental breakfast included. Linen £1. Laundry £1 wash, £1 dry.

Parklodge Holiday Hostel, Dublin Rd. (tel. 400404). Follow signs to Dublin from O'Connell St.; at N24, N7 roundabout, stay on Dublin Rd. Hostel is about 200yd. farther on your left. Or take Bus #2, 5, or 8 from Boyd's on William St. This "hostel" feels more like a roadside motel, complete with faux cherry closets and traffic outside. No dorms. Single £9, £11 w/linen, £13 w/B&B. Twin £15.50, £18 w/linen, £22 w/B&B. Group rates available.

Clyde House, St. Alphonsus St. (tel. 314357), right off Henry St. Budget student accommodations/hostel in a clean but institutional setting. Dorm £7.50. Single £15.50. Double £26. Triple £36.75. Quad £46. No common kitchen, self-catering units are from £1 extra.

St. Anthony's, 8 Coolraine Terrace, Ennis Rd. (tel. 452607), 1mi. from city center. Pleasant rooms look out onto a flourishing garden. Homemade brown bread and jam await in the morning. *Let's Go* special: £12.50/person, w/bath £15/person.

FOOD

Limerick probably has more fast-food joints than all the truck stops in Ohio combined, but there are also some top-notch eateries with reasonable prices. Otherwise, stock up at Quinnsworth **Supermarket** in Arthurs Quay Mall (open Mon.-Wed. 9am-7pm, Thurs.-Fri. 9am-9pm, Sat. 9am-6pm) or at **Eats of Eden,** Henry St. (tel. 419400), a well-stocked health food store (don't miss the apples; open Mon.-Fri. 9am-6pm, Sat. 9am-5:30pm).

Pierre Victoire, Rutland St. (tel. 400822). With high ceilings and long, stately windows, this French bistro has a unique combination of atmosphere and gourmet value. A 3-course lunch special will set you back £4.90 (dinner costs more). Open Mon.-Sat. noon-3pm and 6-11pm.

The Green Onion Café, 3 Ellen St. (tel. 400710), just off O'Connell St. Crimson-sponged walls etched with musings surround diners. Excellent bistro fare at egalitarian prices (brie and sundried tomatoes £4). Stick to the lunch menu; dinners sky-rocket in price. Open daily noon-10pm.

Moll Darby's, 8 Georges Quay, (tel. 411511), just across the Abbey River. Delicious and artfully prepared international cuisine is served up in this popular quay-side restaurant. *Ragout* of tomato and bacon *tagliatelli* £7. Open daily 6-11pm.

O'Grady's Cellar Restaurant, O'Connell St. (tel. 418286). Crimson walls and faux thatched cottages abound in this cozy little subterranean place. Chicken Maryland £6, 3-course tourist dinner menu £8. Open daily 8:30am-11pm.

Dolmen Gallery and Restaurant, Honan's Quay (tel. 417929), across from the tourist office. Enjoy vegetarian stir-fry (£4) or other daily specials while critiquing the current exhibit. Decadent afternoon tea (£3.50, daily 3-5:30pm) includes enough sweets to last a week. Open Mon.-Sat. 10am-5:30pm.

Java's, 5 Catherine St. (tel. 418077). Flavored coffees, herbal teas, and desserts please the late-night crowd in this coffeehouse with tie-dyed walls. Hot chicken sandwich £4. Open daily 8am-4am.

PUBS

Traditional music is played nightly around town. You can pick up the tourist office's Guinness guide to Irish music for schedules or you can opt for one of the local gig "Guides" for more detailed information and local gossip. A large student population ensures plenty of more raucous options.

Nancy Blake's, Denmark St. (tel. 416443). One of the best pubs in town, and insanely popular. A mature crowd packs itself into the large store rooms while the younger set revels in the outdoor "outback." Trad inside every Sun.-Thurs., rock and blues outside nightly, live bands Fri., Sun., and sometimes Wed.

Doc's, Michael St. at the corner of Charlotte's Quay in the Granary (tel. 417266). Spacious, interesting pub in a former warehouse with arched brick ceilings. Large outdoor beergarden, complete with palm trees and waterfalls, is invariably packed with tumescent youth. Bands on Wed. and Thurs., DJ on Sun. nights.

Locke Bar, George's Quay (tel. 413733). Hip, but without the grunge baggage of Doc's or the Henry Cecil pub. Pleasant, quay-side seating with festive Christmas lights! Owner Richard Costello, who used to play rugby for Ireland's national team, now plays trad music Sun. and Tues. nights.

Feathery Bourkes, Henry St. (tel. 400852). Popular isn't the word. Perhaps "£1 a bottle" might better suit this huge and crowded pub. Outdoor beergarden with frequent summertime BBQ. Disco Thurs.-Sun. (free before midnight; £2 after).

Tom Collins, Cecil St. (tel. 415749). There's no music here, since it would interrupt the pub's true calling. Described as a "palace of conversation" for "all walks of life" by a local novelist, you'll meet all types of talkative folk here. Even the mayor is a frequent visitor. Unsuspecting American tourists have come here, asking for a "Tom Collins" (you know, the cocktail). They fetched the owner.

The White House, not 1600 Pennsylvania Ave, but the corner of O'Connell and Glentworth St. (tel. 412377). An older and artsy crowd gathers at this relaxed pub. Trad sessions often arise in a burst of *bodhrán* and spontaneity.

SIGHTS

Shannonside Walking Tours (tel. 311935) and **Limerick City Bus Tours** (tel. 313333) leave the tourist office (Mon.-Fri. June-Aug. at 11am and 2:30pm). Tours focus primarily on the old English city on King's Island, including St. Mary's Cathedral and King John's Castle (walking tour £3.50, students £2.50; bus tour £5). The tours skip the area around the Daniel O'Connell monument on **O'Connell St.,** which is dominated by red-brick Georgian townhouses with brightly painted, stately doorways. The consistently elegant, if slightly decrepit, buildings are indicative of careful town planning during the late 18th and early 19th centuries. The buildings contrast sharply with the discordant architecture on Lower O'Connell St.

A few decades after the Normans invaded Ireland and displaced the O'Brien dynasty from the Limerick area, Norman King John ordered a castle built for protection. **King John's Castle,** on Nicholas St. (tel. 411201), still defends Limerick, although the ranks of prospective invaders have dwindled significantly. Walk across the Abbey River and take the first left after St. Mary's Cathedral. Today, the castle's presence is more educational than physically impressive, with well-prepared exhibits supplying a survey of history from the Vikings to the present. The importance of military strength becomes obvious outside, where the **mangonel** is displayed. Easily recognizable from its use in *Monty Python and the Holy Grail,* the mangonel used to catapult pestilent animal corpses into enemy cities and castles. (Open daily 9:30am-5:30pm, last admission 4:30. Admission £3.60, students £1.95.)

Close by is the rough exterior of **St. Mary's Cathedral** (tel. 416238), built by the O'Briens in 1172. On the side of the altar, fold-down seats called "misericordia," are built into the wall. Their elaborate carvings depict the struggle between good and evil. They are called *misericordia,* Latin for "acts of mercy," for good reason—they were places to rest the holy arse during long services in which sitting was prohibited. The cathedral hosts the fascinating *Son et Lumiere,* a surreal, and slightly irreverent sound and light show telling the history of Ireland from the late stone age to the present. (Church open Mon.-Sat. 9am-1pm and 2-5pm. Light shows Mon.-Fri. at 9:15pm. Admission £2.50, students £1.50.) Across the river, in the city proper, Irish paintings can be critiqued for free at the **Limerick City Gallery of Art,** Percy Sq. (tel. 310633; open Mon.-Wed. and Fri. 10am-1pm, Thurs. 2-6pm, Sat. 10am-1pm; free). More modern and abstract art decks the walls at the **Belltable Arts Centre,** O'Connell St. (tel. 319866; open Mon.-Sat. 9am-6pm; free).

The fascinating **Hunt Museum,** Custom House, Rutland St. (tel. 312833), is due to reopen in January of 1997 at this new location. The museum houses the largest collection of medieval, stone age, and iron age artifacts outside the national museum in Dublin, as well as a clay copy of the most "perfect" of Leonardo da Vinci's four "Rearing Horses." The impressive collection is appreciably enhanced by an excellent guided tour (call ahead to arrange times). Should you venture to the University, stop by the **National Self-Portrait Collection** (tel. 333644) which displays itself in Plassey House (open Mon.-Fri. 10am-5pm; free).

ENTERTAINMENT

Limerick has a nightclub scene worthy of the Republic's third-largest city. Most social events seem to congregate according to word of mouth, but a few nightclubs are safe bets. **Doc's** (see **Pubs,** above) revels with a rave-like disco Thursday through Sunday nights. **Baker's Place,** Dominick St. (tel. 418414), a few doors down from the Clock Tower on Davis St., has live music nightly, with a club pumping music Tuesday through Sunday nights. **The Works,** on Bedford Row next to the Cinema, has a club operating nightly. **Ted's,** O'Connell St. (tel. 417412), provides a classier alternative nightly (no sneakers). Cover charges range from £3-6 depending on the night. Watch out for concession stubs in the pub.

The **Belltable Arts Centre,** 69 O'Connell St. (tel. 319866), stages excellent, big-name productions year round (box office open Mon.-Sat. 9am-6pm and prior to performances; tickets £5-7). The **Theatre Royal,** Upper Cecil St. (tel. 414224), hosts any large concerts that come to town. Phone or ask at the tourist office for current offerings. The **University Concert Hall** on the university campus (tel. 331549) attracts opera, dance, and classical and traditional music (tickets £8-14). Greyhounds race every Monday, Thursday, and Saturday night at the Market's Field on Mulgrave St. (several blocks up William St.). Races start at 8pm and cost £3. The free **Limerick Events Guide,** at the tourist office, has details on all events.

■ Near Limerick: Adare

Adare's well-preserved medieval architecture and meticulous rows of thatched cottages have earned it a reputation as one of the prettiest towns in Ireland. With that distinction came busloads of tourists. An older, well-heeled set crowds the town's award-winning restaurants and grand hotels, sometimes making the backpackers stopping here for the monuments feel out of place. Adare (from *Áth Dara,* or "Ford in the Oak") is worth a day trip, but it can get boring after a few hours. The **tourist office** (tel. (061) 396255) is located on Main St. (Open June-Sept. Mon.-Fri. 9am-7pm, Sat.-Sun. 9am-6pm; earlier closings in spring and fall; open weekends in winter 9am-6pm.) **Buses** travel to Adare from Limerick (Mon.-Sat. 6/day; Sun. 7/day; 20min.; £3.50) and Tralee (Mon.-Sat. 6/day, Sun. 7/day; 1¾hr.).

Although there is no hostel here, Adare is B&B central. Many people touring the Shannon region, or awaiting flights at the airport, prefer to stay here rather than in Limerick. Good choices include **Riversdale,** Manorcourt, Station Rd. (tel. (061) 396751; double £28, w/bath £30), and the charming160-year-old cottage **Murphy's Cross** (tel. (061) 396042), 1½km outside town in the Killarney Rd. (single £16; double £28, w/bath £32). Food is generally expensive in Adare. **The Blue Door** (tel. (061) 396481), a 200-year-old thatched cottage with roses blooming outside, offers reasonable lunches (quiche and salad £5) and pricey dinners (open daily 10am-9:30pm). A similar lunchtime value can be found at **The Arches Restaurant** (tel. (061) 396246), where a main course and coffee is £6.50. Pub grub awaits those who wish to eat after 2pm with their funds unpillaged. **Pat Collin's Bar,** Main St. (tel. (061) 396143), is the best bet for sandwiches and soups. **Shean Collin's Bar,** around the corner, hosts live music Tuesday and Saturday nights during the summer.

The medieval Fitzgerald family endowed Adare with several thriving monasteries of three monastic orders. The monasteries' ruins attest to the small village's more illustrious history. The **Trinitarina Abbey,** which survives on Main St., was established in the 13th century by an order of monks who liberated Christian prisoners during the Crusades. Renovated in the 19th century, the priory now serves as the town's Catholic Church. Farther on Main St. toward Limerick, the **Augustinian Priory** (14th century) stands similarly restored. The **Franciscan Friary,** adjacent to the grounds of Adare Manor, lies in crumbling disarray. The 13th-century **Desmond Castle** is slightly farther down Main St. on the banks of the River Maigue. The castle has been declared a national monument but has been closed to the public due to its present condition. Back in the village, the **Adare Heritage Centre,** in the same building as the tourist office (tel. (061) 396666), traces Adare's history, filled with earls, knights, and lords named "Fitz" (open daily 9am-7pm; admission £2, students £1). Five miles from Adare, nature trails wind through the 600-acre **Curraghchase Forest Park.** The **Adare Jazz Festival** kicks off in mid-March. **Horse trials** and **country fairs** are scheduled in the area around Adare in March, May, and October.

■ Lough Derg

Lough Derg, the lake region northeast of Limerick, plays host to affluent middle-aged tourists, or "cruisers," who navigate their private boats upriver from Limerick to the small towns of Killaloe, Mountshannon, and Portumna. Younger, land-based travelers are much rarer here than they are farther west. Archaeological attractions are not the draw; visitors come to the lake for swimming, windsurfing, and other recreational activities. The **Lough Derg Way** walking path starts in Limerick, follows the western bank of the Shannon up to Killaloe, then crosses over to Ballina. The trail traces the eastern shore of the lake beneath Arra Mountain, where Fintan the White, consort of Cesair, survived the flood (see **Legends and Folktales,** p. 69). His refuge is marked by the Neolithic tombs known as the "Graves of the Leinstermen."

Killaloe and Mountshannon lie along the Lough Derg Drive northeast of Limerick. Public transport virtually ignores Mountshannon and Killaloe, though buses sometimes do venture forth from Limerick (3/week; £3.50). Hitchhikers report an easy time getting to Killaloe from Limerick or from Dublin Rd. (from Dublin Rd., hitchers station themselves on R494 and hitch to Ballina, just across the river). Thumbing farther north to Mountshannon may require a bit more patience.

KILLALOE

Fifteen miles out of Limerick along the Lough Derg Drive and just south of the lake itself, Killaloe's (KILL-a-loo) rolling hills and nautical orientation feel distant from the industry of the big city. Old churches and oratories remember Killaloe's 7th-century function as a religious center, when St. Lua (*Molua* in Irish) and St. Flannan made it their home. High King of Ireland Brian Ború lived here too (from 1002-1014), at Kincora. A Catholic church stands on the ruins of his former residence.

The **tourist office** (tel. 376866), in Lock House on the Killaloe side of the bridge, can provide free maps of town, and information on several rural walks around Killaloe (open June-Sept. daily 10am-6pm). Main St. is home to an **AIB** bank (tel. 376115; open Mon. and Wed.-Fri. 10am-4pm, Tues. 10am-5pm) and, farther uphill, the **post office** (tel. 376111; open Mon.-Fri. 9:30am-12:30pm and 1:30-5:30pm, Sat. 9:30am-12:30pm). Brian Ború declared the **phone code** to be 061.

You can make Killaloe a daytrip from Limerick, but several nice B&Bs near town make it a pleasant stopover. **Kincora House,** across from Crotty's Pub (tel. 376149), is very hospitable and will serve you a healthy breakfast on request (£16/person). Super-fresh seafood makes the **Dalcassian,** Main St. (tel. 376762), near the cathedral, a local favorite (open daily 11am-5pm and 6-9:30pm; dinner entrees £7-9; bar menu until 5pm). Another immensely popular pub, serving up fantastic trad (Thurs. and weekends) and gourmet treats in an outdoor beergarden (pasta *matriciana* £7.25), is **Crotty's Courtyard Bar** (tel. 376965). Next to the bridge in Ballina, **Molly's** serves elevated pub grub (Irish stew £4) and pleasant lake and river views (and *al fresco* pints if the weather allows; food served from 12:30-9pm). Check out the **Seanachaoi**

Pub (tel. 376913). The Irish name means "storyteller," and its owners will be telling plenty a tale about this pub. Originally from Oregon and Alaska, they won the Seanachaoi in the Guinness *Win Your Own Pub in Ireland '96* contest. The best place to stock up for a picnic is **McKeogh's** (tel. 376249), on Main St. in Ballina (open Mon.-Wed. 9am-7:30pm, Thurs.-Fri. 9am-9pm, Sat. 9am-8:30pm, Sun. 9:30am-1pm).

At the base of the town on Royal Parade lies **St. Flannan's Cathedral,** built between 1195 and 1225 and still in use. Inside the Cathedral, the Thorgrim Stone is written in Scandinavian Runic characters and again in the Irish monks' *ogham* script as a prayer for the conversion of Thorgrim, a Viking, to Christianity. This occurrence of Runic writing with accompanying *ogham* inscription is particularly rare. Market Sq. may have once held Brian Ború's palace of Kincora. The other candidate for the coveted site-of-Ború's-palace award is the abandoned fort known as **Beal Ború,** 1½ mi. out of town toward Mountshannon, and unfortunately not much to see. Behind the tourist office, a **heritage center** occupies itself with the legendary Ború (open Mon.-Sun. 10am-6pm; admission £1.50, students 70p). In mid-July, Killaloe recognizes its most famous ex-resident with **Féile Brian Ború,** four days of music, watersports, and various Ború-revering activities.

Lough-related activities abound in Killaloe. The **Derg Princess** leaves from across the bridge in **Ballina,** Co. Tipperary, for relaxing, if not informative, one-hour cruises (tel. 376364; £5). Two **boat rental** companies, **Whelan's** (tel. 376159) and **Haskett** (a.k.a. Killaloe; tel. 376693), station themselves across from the tourist office and rent out motorboats for fishing or cruising (£10/first hr., £5/every hr. after). A boat (and a bit of navigational prowess) will allow you access to **Holy Island.** A couple of miles north of Killaloe, you can indulge in an afternoon of watersports at the **University of Limerick Activity and Sailing Centre** (tel. 376622; windsurfing £8/hr.; canoeing £3/hr; sailboats from £10/hr.).

■ Limerick to Ennis

Fifteen miles west of Limerick off Ennis Rd. (N18) along the north shore of the river, **Shannon Airport** sends jets to North America and Europe (tel. (061) 471444; Aer Lingus info tel. (061) 471666). The airport has spawned unsightly industrial development (and much-needed employment) in the coastal areas west of Limerick. Until a couple of years ago, all transatlantic flights to Ireland were bound by Irish law to stop first at Shannon. Bus Éireann hits the airport from Limerick (Mon.-Sat. 22/day, Sun. 13/day; 45min.; £3.50, students £2.50) and Dublin (5/day; 4½hr.; £10, students £8). To reach Ennis, Galway, Westport, Tralee, and Killarney, you'll have to catch connecting buses from Limerick station. **Car rental** opportunities abound. The cheapest is **Thrifty** (tel. (061) 472649; £35/day (3-day min. rental), £190/week; min. age 23; call ahead).

BUNRATTY

Eight miles northwest of Limerick along the Ennis Rd., **Bunratty Castle** and **Bunratty Folk Park** (tel. (061) 361511) amalgamates a collection of historical attractions brought here from all over Ireland. Bunratty Castle says it's Ireland's most complete medieval castle, with superbly restored furniture, tapestries, stained-glass windows, and a historically significant virginal. The castle derives much of its popularity from the medieval feasts that it hosts nightly for deep-pocketed tourists. Local lasses, dressed in period costume, serve much wine and meat to would-be chieftains (5-course meal w/wine £30/lord or lady). The folk park took root in the Bord Fáilte-approved 60s, when builders at Shannon Airport couldn't bear to destroy a quaint cottage in order to build a new runway. Instead, they moved the cottage to Bunratty. Since then, reconstructions of turn-of-the-century houses from all over Ireland and a small village of old-fashioned stores (now catering to modern tourist tastes) have been added. (Open July-Aug. daily 9:30am-7pm; Sept.-June 9:30am-5:30pm. Last admission 1hr. before closing. Castle closes at 4:15pm. Admission £4.75, students

£2.30.) Try not to visit in mid-afternoon during the high season, as the thick queue of tourists on the narrow castle stairways is annoying and treacherous. The Bunratty complex also claims one decent but still tourist-friendly pub. The first proprietress at **Durty Nelly's** (founded 1620) earned her name by serving Bunratty soldiers more than just beer. Buses between Limerick and Shannon Airport pass Bunratty (see **Limerick to Ennis,** above).

■ Ennis

Twenty miles northwest of Limerick, movin' and groovin' Ennis (pop. 16,000) is home to narrow, high-walled streets and bustling crowds. Makeshift stands vend fruit along the river, and pubs shake with trad music on weekends. Ennis will never pack in the tourists with its scenery, but it has its share of historical goodies. An enjoyable route through the region would head through Ennis and then southwest to Kilkee and the sea or northwest to the Cliffs of Moher, Doolin, and the Burren.

PRACTICAL INFORMATION

Tourist Offices: Ennis Tourist Office, O'Connell Sq. (tel. 41670), in the Upstairs Downstairs shop, will exuberantly answer your queries and provide information on buses and trains. (Open June-Sept. daily 9am-9pm; Oct.-May Mon.-Sat. 9am-6pm, Sun. 10am-6pm. **Shannon Region Tourist Office** (tel. 28366), ½mi. from the bus station on Clare Rd., looks like a rest stop on a highway and seems designed to serve the car-equipped. From the station, take a left and follow Clon Rd., then take a left onto Clare Rd. They'll book rooms for you in B&Bs, hostels, and hotels (local bookings £1, national £2). Open June-Sept. daily 9am-7pm; Oct.-May Tues.-Sat. 9am-6pm.

Banks: Bank of Ireland, O'Connell Sq. (tel. 28615). Open Mon.-Tues. and Thurs.-Fri. 10am-4pm, Wed. 10am-5pm; **ATM. AIB,** Bank Pl. (tel. 28089). Open same hours; **ATM.**

Trains: next to the bus station. **Station** (tel. 40444) open Mon.-Sat. 7am-5:30pm, Sun. 15min. before departures. Trains leave for Dublin via Limerick (Mon.-Sat. 2/day, Sun. 1/day; £16, students £9.50). You're better off catching the train from Limerick, where 8-13/day leave for Dublin.

Buses: The **station** (tel. 24177) is a 10-min. walk from the town center on Station Rd. Open Mon.-Fri. 7:15am-5:30pm, Sat. 7:15am-4:45pm. To: **Limerick** (12/day, Sun. 7/day; 50min.; £5, students £3.50); **Galway** (6/day; 1¼hr.; £7.30, students £4.30); **Dublin** via Limerick (5/day; 4hr.; £10, students £8); **Cork** (7/day, Sun. 5/day; 3hr.; £10, students £6); **Kilkee** (2-3/day; Sun. 1/day, July-Aug. 2/day; 1hr.; £6.90, students £4.20); **Doolin** (3/day, Sun. 1/day; 1½hr.; £5.50, students £3.50); **Shannon Airport** (Mon.-Fri. 13/day, Sat. 9/day, Sun. 10/day; 40min.; £3.50, students £2.50). Also a **West Clare line** (Mon., Sun. 2/day): Lisdoonvarna, Ennistymon, Lahinch, Miltown Malbay, Doolin, Kilkee, and Kilrush. The crowded **post bus** runs from the post office to Liscannor and Doolin on the coast. (Mon.-Sat. 2/day; Ennis to Doolin £2.50, students £1.) Arrive early to get a seat.

Bike Rental: Michael Tierney Cycles and Fishing, 17 Abbey St. (tel. 29433). Rentals and repair. Tierney helpfully suggests routes through the hilly countryside. £3.50/afternoon, £7/day, £30/week; deposit £20. Open Mon.-Sat. 9:30am-6pm. **Irish Cycle Hire/Railbike,** Ennis Train Station (tel. (041) 41067). £6/day, £30/week; deposit £30. Open daily 9am-8pm.

Luggage Storage: in the bus station on Station Rd., off O'Connell St. Lockers for 50p. Coaches for £100,000. Open Mon.-Sat. 7:30am-6:30pm, Sun. 10am-7:15pm.

Pharmacy: O'Connell Chemist, Abbey St. (tel. 20373). Open Mon.-Sat. 9am-6pm, Sun. 11am-1pm. **Michael McLoughlin** (tel. 29511), in Dunnes Supermarket, O'Connell St. Open Mon.-Wed. 9am-6pm, Thurs.-Fri. 9am-9pm, Sat. 9am-6pm.

Samaritans: tel. (1850) 609090. 24hr.

Emergency: Dial 999; no coins required. **Garda:** tel. 28205.

Post office: Bank Pl. (tel. 21054). Open Mon.-Tues. and Thurs.-Fri. 9am-5:30pm, Wed. 9:30am-5:30pm, Sat. 9:30am-2:30pm.

Phone code: 065.

ACCOMMODATIONS, FOOD, & PUBS

Right on the river, across Club Bridge from Abbey St., the **Abbey Tourist Hostel (IHH),** Harmony Row (tel. 22620), is a 300-year-old labyrinth. The hostel itself is clean and comfortable, but the showers can be erratic. (Reception open 9:30am-10:30pm. July-Aug. dorm £5.50, private room £7/person; Sept.-June dorm £5, private room £7. Sheets 50p, laundry £2.50.) **Derrynane House** (tel. 28464), in the Square, will put a roof over your head right in the middle of town (£16/person, all w/bath). Dinner and pubs go hand in hand, but there are a few alternatives. **Dunnes supermarket** (tel. 40700) lurks on O'Connell St. (open Mon.-Tues. 9am-6:30pm, Wed.-Fri. 9am-9pm, Sat. 9am-6:30pm, Sun. noon-6pm). The **Food Emporium,** Abbey St. (tel. 20554), does deli favorites (sandwiches £1.10). **Considine's,** Abbey St. (tel. 29054), serves huge, salad-surrounded sandwiches (£3.50) and tempting chicken plates (£4.50). **Derrynane House** (see above) cooks up satisfying, belt-loosening breakfasts between 9am and noon (Irish breakfast £2.50). **Cruises Pub,** next to the Friary on Abbey St. (tel. 41800), stuffs its customers with griddle scones and muffins with cream and jam (60p) or the special Atlantic shrimp sandwich (£4; music nightly in summer). **Brandon's Bar,** O'Connell St. (tel. 28133), serves huge plates of spuds, meat, and veggies (entrees £3.50) alongside its pints. **Brogan's,** O'Connell St. (tel. 29859), is your supplier of Irish stew (£5.50) in the afternoon or early evening. It becomes packed and smoky in the evening as young people flock here. Ennis has its fair share of dark and woody pubs serving dark and frothy pints, the darkest and woodiest being **The Usual Place,** 5 Market St. (tel. 20515).

SIGHTS

Ennis's four main streets—O'Connell St., Abbey St., Bank Pl., and Parnell St.—meet in **O'Connell Square,** where a lofty statue of Daniel O'Connell watches over his hometown. The original O'Connells were Catholic landowners dispossessed by Cromwell. Almost 200 years later in 1828, Ennis residents elected Catholic barrister Daniel O'Connell to represent them at Westminster. The Protestant-only parliament refused him his seat because he would not renounce his religion. The resulting political uproar led to Catholic Emancipation in the U.K. (1829) and thrust O'Connell into the role of "the Liberator," the leader of Catholic Ireland for the next 20 years. A 10-minute walk from the town center on the Mill Rd. leads to the **Maid of Erin,** a life-size statue remembering the "Manchester Martyrs," three nationalists hanged in Manchester in 1867.

Abbey St. leads northeast to the ruined and roofless 13th-century **Ennis Friary** (tel. 29100), famous for the slender panes and peaked points of its east window. In 1375 the seminary housed and taught 350 Franciscan monks and 600 students. It was one of Ireland's most important pre-Reformation theological schools. Inside, depictions of the Passion adorn 15th-century **McMahon tomb.** (Open mid-May to Sept. daily 9:30am-6:30pm; admission £1, students 40p.) Across from the Friary, a block of sandstone inscribed with part of Yeats's "Easter 1916" remembers the Easter Rising.

A few doors from the Abbey House Hostel on Harmond Row, **de Valera Library and Museum** (tel. 21616) adds a door from the Spanish Armada to its collection of the ex-Taoiseach's stuff, which includes his private car. IRA weapons and Land League banners recall Ennis's political life. (Museum and library open Mon. and Thurs. 11am-5:30pm, Tues.-Wed. and Fri. 11am-8pm; free.) Saturday is **Market Day** in Market Sq. All conceivable wares are sold below a statue of crafty Daedalus.

CLARE COAST

Those traveling between Co. Kerry and Co. Clare should take the 20-minute **Tarbert-Killimer car ferry** across the Shannon estuary, avoiding an 85-mi. drive via Limerick City (see **Tarbert,** p. 265). (Sailings April-Sept. Mon.-Sat. 7:30am-9:30pm, Sun.

9:30am-9:30pm; Oct.-March Mon.-Sat. 7am-7pm, Sun. 10am-7pm. Boats sail every hour on the half hour and return on the hour from Clare. £2/passenger or cyclist, £3 return; £7/car (including passengers), £10 return.) While waiting for the ferry, you can visit the restored **Tarbert Bridewell,** where lifelike dummies re-enact the life of Thomas Dillon and fellow prisoners. (April-Oct. daily 10am-6pm, admission £3, students £2, seniors and children £1.60.)

■ Kilrush

The route to the Clare Coast from either Tarbert or Limerick passes through Kilrush (pop. 2900), a pleasing market town with some history and some beguiling forest trails. Home to the Coast's only marina, Kilrush has a close connection with the sea. You can hear the town's bitter memories of the Great Famine on "Kilrush in Landlord Times," a self-guided cassette tour (£2) of the town's history, available at the **Kilrush Heritage Centre,** Town Hall, Market Square (tel. 51577; open May-Sept. Mon.-Sat. 9:30am-5:30pm, Sun. noon-4pm). You can change money at the **AIB** and its **ATM,** Frances St. (tel. 51012; open Mon. 10am-5pm, Tues.-Fri. 10am-3pm). **Bus Éireann** (tel. 24177 in Ennis) stops in Market Sq. on its way to Ennis (Mon.-Sat. 3-5/day, Sun. 2-3/day) and Kilkee (Mon.-Sat. 2-4/day, Sun. 1-2/day). Bike hire is available at **Gleesons,** Henry St. (tel. 51127), which is affiliated with **Raleigh rent-a-bike** (£30/week). **Duffy's Chemist** (tel. 551029), on Frances St., has what you need (Mon.-Sat. 9am-6pm, Sun. 11am-1pm). The **post office** is on Frances St. (open Mon.-Sat. 9am-5:30pm). Telephones here favor a **phone code** of 065.

    Katie O'Connor's Holiday Hostel (tel. 51133), next to the AIB on Frances St., provides a friendly kitchen and a thoughtful fire. Before you go to bed, read the history of your room; it dates back to 1795 (dorm £6.50, private room with 4 beds £25; sheets 50p). You can stock your larder at the **SuperValu** (tel. 51885) across the street. **Crotty's Pub,** Market Square (tel. 52470), welcomes the weary traveler with trad music on Tuesday nights.

    In town, a monument facing the Town Hall remembers the Manchester Martyrs. Just outside of town on the Ferry road, the dirt paths of the **Kilrush Forest Park** promise adventure, romance, and an ultimate return to town. They may not deliver, but they're pretty and not so long that you can't backtrack to town. Kilrush's real attraction, however, is offshore **Scattery Island,** where monastic ruins, deserted churchyards, and a round tower stand tall. Boats depart for the unspoiled island regularly from June through September (4-5/day, depending on the tide) and irregularly at other times. **Tours** of the island may be booked through the tourist office or transport can be arranged with Gerald Griffen (tel. 51327) or Martin Brennan (tel. 52031). The 15-minute journey costs £3.50 for a day return. On the mainland, at Merchant's Quay, the **Scattery Island Centre** (tel. 52139) explains the island's history and ecology (open mid-June to mid-Sept. daily 9:30am-6:30pm; free).

■ Kilkee

In Kilkee, on the southwest tip of Clare, three rows of Victorian houses built by lovers of great scenery line the coastal road. Gorgeous cliffs rise high on eroded islands where farms lay hundreds of years ago. Irish, not foreign, holiday makers crowd the plastic storefronts and fill the deafening arcades and fine white beaches in the summer. The lively pub scene tempts tourists and locals alike, but the solitary **Westend Cliff Walk** will remain etched in your memory. You'll never forget it. Never!

    The **tourist office** pops up in the central square across from the Stella Maris Hotel (tel. 56112; open June-Sept. daily 10am-6pm). The **ATM** at the **Bank of Ireland,** O'Curry St. (tel. 56053), puts cash in your pocket. (Open Mon. 10am-12:30pm and 1:30-5pm, Tues.-Fri. 10am-12:30pm and 1:30-4pm.) **Bus Éireann** (tel. 24177, in Ennis) scrapes by twice a day for Ennis and Limerick and three times per day for Galway and Cork. All buses stop outside Kett's Bar. Rent **bikes** and get your greens from **Rosarie's** (tel. 56622) on O'Curry St. (£6/day, £32/week; deposit £20; open May-Sept.

County Clare

WESTERN IRELAND

daily 9am-11pm). **Williams,** opposite the post office on Circular Rd, also rents bikes (£6/day; a Raleigh dealer). The **post office** (tel. 56001) is on Circular Rd. (open Mon.-Fri. 9am-5:30pm, Sat. 9am-12:30pm). Kilkee's **phone code** chirps 065.

The welcoming **Kilkee Hostel (IHH),** O'Curry St. (tel. 56209), is so clean that you won't mind if your toothbrush falls on the floor. The family-run place creates an atmosphere of fellowship between travelers. (Dorm £6. Sheets 50p, laundry £3. **Bikes** £6/day.) **Duneam House B&B** (tel. 56545) sits atop high cliffs on the coastal road to the left of the bay. Beautiful view outside, smiling faces inside (double £32).

If your greatest ambitions are to eat and lounge on Irish beaches, you could live your whole life between the beach and O'Curry St. A **Central Stores supermarket** vends victuals on the corner of O'Curry St. and Circular Rd. (open summer Mon.-Thurs. 9am-8:30pm, Fri.-Sun. 9am-9pm; winter daily 9am-8pm). **Country Cooking Shop** specializes in desserts for the decadent traveler. Adjoined **Pantry** (tel. 56576) is a café/restaurant run by the same folks (Irish breakfast £3; chicken, leek, and vegetable pie £4; open June-Sept. daily 8:30am-9:30pm). **Eats & Treats,** O'Curry St. (tel. 56866), serves snacks to hungry beach bums (nachos £2.90, bagel with cream cheese £1; open June-Oct. daily 9am-8pm; Nov.-May Fri.-Sun. 9:30am-6:30pm). **Purtills,** O'Curry St. (tel. 56900), is a full restaurant—a rare breed in these parts. (Chicken kebabs £6.50. Open Easter-Sept. daily 6-10pm; Oct.-March Sat.-Sun. 6-10pm.) Kilkee's pub crawl is famously fun. The **Strand Hotel** is a good start, and then on to **Michael Martin's Pub** (opposite the tourist office). If you're still standing (get up!), the **Central Bar** (tel. 56103), **Richie's,** and the **Myles Creek Pub** (tel. 56670), all on O'Curry St., offer quality pub time. After last call, pubgoers head to **Waterfront** (tel. 56838), a nightclub above the amusement center at the end of O'Curry St. Music sounds out between 11pm and 2am (cover £3).

The **Westend Cliff Walk** begins to the left of the seafront and climbs easily up to the top of cliffs. Poets can bring their notebooks, but it will take much scribbling to capture this sea-hewn beauty with words. Two sets of **Diamond Rocks** lie on the coast: the original is a slippery kelp-coated mussel bed next to the harbour—locals come out with nets at low-tide; the "new" Diamond Rocks are a collection of quartz rocks farther up the coast. A gravel path from the car park leads to the original rocks. Four **"Pollock Holes"** provide natural rock pools for swimming (the fourth is a men's nudist bathing spot).

The path out to the (new) Diamond Rocks leads into **Loop Head Drive,** which passes through small villages, ruined farmhouses, and plenty of pasture to **Loop Head** itself, at the very tip of Co. Clare. Only a lighthouse and four electrical fences stand between the road and the crashing water at the foot of the cliffs. The Loop Head Drive passes through Carrigaholt village, 7 mi. south of Kilkee on the Shannon Estuary. Boat trips geared for **dolphin sighting** "with 100% success" shove off from here into waters where approximately 60 bottlenosed dolphins have made their home (tel. (088) 584711; admission £8, under 14 £4).

▓ Kilkee to Doolin

MILTOWN MALBAY

Once you've enjoyed Kilkee and the sea, only small towns stand between you and the awesome Cliffs of Moher. Most of the people who stop and stay in these towns are looking for golf courses, in large supply here. Miltown Malbay, 20 mi. north of Kilkee on coastal N67, wakes up for the first week of July, when the **Willie Clancy School of Traditional Music** lets fly one of Ireland's larger musical celebrations. People from all corners of the globe flock here in the thousands to their pre-booked accommodations.

The **tourist office,** Main St. (tel. 84730), is happy to see you (open June-Sept. Sun.-Mon. 10am-6pm, Tues.-Sat. 10am-6:30pm). The **Bank of Ireland** (tel. 84018) is across the street next to O'Friels bar (open Mon.-Wed. and Fri. 10am-12:30pm and 1:30-4pm, Thurs. 10am-12:30pm and 1:30-5pm). **Byrne's** on Ennis Rd. (tel. 84079) rents and repairs **bikes** and has a limited supply of camping equipment. (Bikes £7/day, £30/week; deposit £40; open Mon.-Sat. 9:30am-6:30pm.) **Marie Kelly's Pharmacy** is on Main St. (tel. 84440; open Mon.-Sat. 9:30am-6pm except Wed., when it is open until 7pm). Miltown-Malbay's **phone code** booms 065 on its *bodhrán*.

Miltown pubs are praised for their trad sessions. **Cleary's** (tel. 84201) has trad music on Thursday nights, while **Wilson's** (tel. 84189) hosts both trad and folk nightly. **Clancy's** (tel. 84077) and **The Lark's Inn** (tel. 84308) also join the action (trad Fri. and Sun. nights). **Mary's Place Restaurant & Pizzeria** (tel. 84551) on Ennis Rd. is a little bit of heaven in Miltown. (Fresh salmon bisque with bread £2; 9" 5-topping pizza £4. Open July-Aug. Mon.-Sat. 10am-8pm, Sun. noon-8pm; Sept.-June Mon.-Sat. 10:30am-6pm.) **Spar Supermarket & Bakery,** Main St. (tel. 84093; open Mon.-Sat. 9am-9pm, Sun. 9am-1:30pm) sells super groceries. Halfway between Miltown and the beaches at Spanish Point, **Three Corner View** (tel. 84362) has rooms (£12/person). The affordable **Station House** (tel. 84008) at the old railway station has huge beds and is run by friendly twins (£12.50/person).

LAHINCH & LISCANNOR

Golfers cluster in a triad of towns north of Miltown Malbay on N67, near Liscannor Bay. Tiny **Lahinch,** a seaside resort, calls itself "the St. Andrews of Ireland." The wide beach below the town attracts a large summertime beach population and offers a pleasant evening's walk. A **tourist office,** Waterworld Complex (tel. 81730), can help you out (open June-Sept. daily 10am-7pm). The nearest **bank** and **ATM** are in **Ennistymon,** about 2 mi. east. Change your currency in the **bureau de change** around the corner at the top of Main St. (tel. 81743; open Mon.-Sun. 9am-10pm). The **post office** (tel. 81001) is on Main. St. (open Mon.-Fri. 9am-1pm and 2-5:30pm, Sat. 9am-1pm). The **phone code** gracefully putts 065.

Clean bunkrooms, friendly staff, and a waterfront location score a hole-in-one at **Lahinch Hostel (IHH)** (tel. 81040) on Church St. in the town center. (Dorm £6, 4-bed room £7. Sheets free, laundry £2.) The **Lahinch Caravan & Camping Park** on N67 (tel. 81424) rents **bikes** (£7/day; open daily 9am-9pm) and has plenty of space for **camping** (£3/tent; open Easter-Sept.). **Mrs. O'Brien's Kitchen,** Main St. (tel. 81020), serves stomach-soothing breakfast all day and hosts a wine bar from 9pm to 1am for those seeking an alternative to the usual pub scene (open March-Sept. daily 8am-1am). **Kenny's Bar,** Main St. (tel. 81433), resounds with ballads, trad, and rock (music Mon.-Thurs. in summer, 3 nights/wk. in winter). **O'Looneys Bar & Restaurant** (tel. 81414), at the top of Main St., serves good food in a crowded, woody interior that looks out at the crashing waves and the surfers they carry.

The 26-mi. **Burren Way** crosses the village of **Liscannor.** These walker- and cyclist-friendly twisting country roads are marked by well-placed signposts that take you to the Cliffs of Moher and Doolin. The lengthy slice of trail from Liscannor to Doolin runs along cliffs sprinkled with wildflowers. John P. Holland, inventor of the submarine, grew up in these parts. The **Village Hostel (IHH)** (tel. 81385) on the main road in Liscannor is somewhat like a submarine with depopulated bunkrooms and a huge, echoing kitchen. (Dorm £6, private room £8/person. Sheets 50p. B&B with packed lunch and dinner £15. **Bikes** £6/day. **Camping** £3.50/person.) The Cliff Top Centre (tel. 81031) on the main road houses a **Spar supermarket** and a **restaurant** (Burren smoked salmon £4.50; open noon-10pm). **Egan's** has fresh food aplenty (large crab sandwich with salad £5) and even more pints. Locals love the little bar that is **Joe McHugh's** (tel. 81163; steak and kidney pie with salad £3.50). Trad music harmonizes nightly in summer, Fridays in winter.

CLIFFS OF MOHER

Visiting the Cliffs of Moher is like seeing a world being created out of Chaos. From the edge of the Cliffs of Moher, you can look 700 ft. straight down into the open ocean. These cliffs are so high that humans actually see gulls whirling below them. Tourists, often filing behind tour guides, cluster where the road ends at the cliffs, though the better views are a bit farther off the road. Occasionally marked paths wander along the cliffs; tourists drop away after the first curve. Wallace Stevens based his wonderful poem "The Irish Cliffs of Moher" on photographs—he'd never been here. You shouldn't miss the chance.

The **tourist office** (tel. (065) 81171) houses a **bureau de change** (open July-Aug. daily 9am-8pm; mid-Feb. to April 10am-6pm, May 9:30am-6pm, and Sept. to mid-Jan. 9:30am-6pm.) **O'Brien's Tower,** built in 1835 as a viewing tower for tourists, marks Clare's first attempt at promoting local tourism, yet adds nothing to the thrilling cliffside view. Cars must pay £1 for use of the parking lot. (Tower open same hours as tourist office; admission 70p, students 50p.) A teashop rejuvenates weary travelers (open same hours as tourist office; soup £1.70). The Cliffs brush against R478 3 mi. south of Doolin. Roads to the cliffs are well-marked. **Bus Éireann** clangs by on the summer-only Galway-Cork route (Mon.-Sat. 3/day). The **Burren Way** and several non-linear bike trails lead more elusively through raised limestone to the cliffs. Hitchers report mixed success in finding rides here.

▓ Doolin

Ireland sees Doolin ("Fisherstreet" on some maps) much as Europe views Ireland: windy, beautiful, musical, oriented around pubs, and overtouristed. Twenty years ago, Doolin was a blip on the map. Today Dubs and foreigners outnumber residents 10 to 1. And for good reason; all three pubs—McGann's, McDermott's, and O'Connor's—host world-class music. Great *craic* is generally a guarantee.

Doolin is shaped like a barbell, made up of two smaller villages about a mile apart from each other (Martin Breen's *The Doolin Guide and Map* has good info; £3). The **Lower Village** (Fisherstreet) is closer to the shore and the **Upper Village** (Roadford) is farther up the road. A **traveling bank** comes to Doolin's shores every Thursday from 10:30-11:15am, but bureaux de change abound. **Doolin Rent-A-Bike** (tel. 74429) rents bikes (£7/day; deposit £40), runs one- and two-day tours of the Burren (£18/day, including rental; 4 person min.), and repairs the afflicted bike (open April-Oct. daily 9:30am-9:30pm; call Nov.-March). The **post office** (tel. 74209) operates from the Upper Village (open Mon.-Fri. 9am-1pm and 2-5:30pm, Sat. 9am-1pm). Doolin's **phone code** is a musical 065.

A 3-mi.-long, paved, and bicycle-friendly segment of the **Burren Way** links Doolin to the Cliffs of Moher. The steep climb along the road from Doolin to the Cliffs is more than offset by the thrilling glide back down and the anticipation of another night of carousing at the pubs. **Boats** leave the pier on the other end of town for the Aran Islands, but boats from Galway and Rossaveal are cheaper under almost any circumstances (see **Galway City,** p. 286).

ACCOMMODATIONS

The immense popularity of Doolin's pubs has necessarily flooded the area with places to stay. Book ahead at all times.

Aille River Hostel (IHH) (tel. 74260), ¼mi. downhill from the Upper Village, by the river. Small, relaxed hostel with groovy ambiance and the benefit of being a few steps from those pubs of legend, McGann's and McDermott's. Live music almost every night. Warms its stone common-room floor with a stove. Dorm £6, July-Aug. 6.50. Private room £7/person, July-Aug. £7.50/person. **Camping** £3.50. Free laundry! Open mid-March to mid-Nov.

Rainbow Hostel (IHH) (tel. 74415), Upper Village. Small, with rainbow-colored rooms. Cheerful appearance, casual atmosphere. Free 90min. guided walking tours of the Burren for hostelers. Dorm July-Aug. £6.50, Sept.-June £6. Double July-Aug. £14, Sept.-June £13. Laundry £3.

Doolin Hostel (IHH) (tel. 74006), Lower Village. This quiet, modern hostel run by "Paddy," as he is affectionately known to visitors, offers more than the average: a shop, bureau de change, and bus ticket sales. Very clean and comfortable. Buses to

Dublin, Cork, and Galway stop outside their door daily. Free tennis court and rackets. Reception open 8am-9pm. Dorm July-Aug. £6.75, Sept.-June £6; £5 key deposit. Sheets 50p, laundry £2.50. **Bikes** £6/day. MC, Visa.

Westwind B&B (tel. 74227), Upper Village, in the same driveway as the Lazy Lobster. Pleasing to the eye and comforting to the legs. Run by a friendly young couple. Vegetarian or meaty breakfasts are available, as is advice for spelunkers or other Burren explorers. £11/person.

Doolin Cottage (tel. 74762) is run by a friendly young couple and is often used by backpackers when the Aille River Hostel is full. £11/person sharing, £12 w/bath. Open March-Nov.

Campsite (tel. 74458), near the harbor, has a kitchen and laundry. £4/tent plus £1/ person. Showers 50p. Laundry £3.

FOOD & PUBS

Doolin has many excellent but costly seafood restaurants. Luckily, all three pubs serve excellent grub. **The Doolin Deli** (tel. 74633), near O'Connor's in the Lower Village, packs overstuffed sandwiches (£1.30) and stocks groceries (open June-Sept. Mon.-Sat. 8:30am-9pm, Sun. 9:30am-9pm). Positive karma fills the **Doolin Café** (tel. 74429), Upper Village, where meat lovers, vegetarians, and vegans are all fed and cared for. Feast on the Doolin Café Special of local cheeses, cured ham, mixed salad, brown bread, and fruit (£4.50) or snack on a homemade cinnamon fruit scone (55p; open daily June-Sept. 9:30am-2pm and 6-9:30pm, May weekends 6-9:30pm).

People definitely come to Doolin for the pubs. Both O'Connor's and McGann's have won awards in the past for the best trad music in Ireland. **McGann's,** Upper Village (tel. 74133), has music nightly at 9pm in the summer, weekends in winter, and Irish stew in both seasons (£5). The homemade rhubarb tart with cream (£1.50) is deviously delicious. **McDermott's,** Upper Village (tel. 74328), with its warming fireplace, ranks right up there with McGann's (chicken curry and rice £4; music nightly in summer, weekends in winter). Most sessions start at 9:30pm to standing room only in summer. **O'Connor's,** Lower Village (tel. 74168), never stops (music nightly and Sun. afternoons all year). It provides drink, food, and song (garlic mussels and brown bread £4. B&B, tel. 74242, £14/person w/bath).

■ Lisdoonvarna

Lisdoonvarna's relative fame comes from its **Matchmaking Festival,** by far the best known of the several once held all over Ireland. On these occasions, farm boys— their crops safely harvested, but with wild oats still to sow—gathered together to pick their mates (and, one hopes, vice versa). The five-week-long festival still fills the town each September, but today's Irish women tend to stay home and make jokes about the randy bachelors and foreign women who go. The town's other claim to fame is as the title of a Christy Moore song about a massive music festival held here in 1983. During the rest of the year, the pubs range from lively to pathetic. Half-empty posh hotels and innumerable pub names (The Matchmaker, the Lonely Hearts, etc.) testify to thousands of men who thought the town would do for them what they couldn't do for themselves.

The **Lisdoonvarna Tourist Information Centre** (tel. 74630; open May-Oct. 10am-6pm daily) is buried in the Spa Wells Shop (signposted from town center). **Bus Éireann** stops at the corner just up from Burke's on either side of the road. Rent **bikes** at **Burke's Garage,** the Square (tel. 74022; £6/day, £30/week; deposit £40; open daily 9:30am-7pm). A few miles inland amid scrubby hills, Lisdoonvarna weds the R476, R477, and R478 to N67. R478 leads southwest to Doolin and the Cliffs of Moher; N67 heads northeast through the Burren to Ballyvaughan. Plenty of unmarked bike paths and trails circumvent the roads. The **Laundrette** (tel. 74577) hides in the corner of the carpark across from the Imperial Hotel (open Mon.-Sat. 10am-6pm; small load £4, large load £6). Lisdoonvarna's **phone code** is perky, red-haired, and a pretty sight at 065.

The **Burren Holiday Tourist Hostel (IHH),** Doolin Rd. (tel. 74300), disguises itself in Kincora House with a red and gold carpeted staircase reminiscent of a palatial hotel. A huge mirror by the stairs lets you step out to meet your match looking your best. A turf fire flickers in the cheery pub downstairs, and in the summer traditional set dancing rocks the bar. Delicious meals include Irish stew (£4.50) and various seafood plates (£5). Excellent rental **bikes** £6; **bureau de change** with rates as good as those in town. (Mid-Sept. to June dorm £6.50, double £16; July to mid-Sept. dorm £7, double £17.) Dream of genie under the foot-high, comfy comforters at Mrs. O'Connor's **Roncalli House** (tel. 74115; single £16, double £27; all w/bath). In town, Mrs. Barrett's hospitable **Marchmont House** (tel. 74050) is within stumbling distance of the pubs (single £20, double £30).

Imperial Hotel (tel. 74042) offers a soup and main course special (£4.90) until 9pm (open March-Oct.). The **Family Value supermarket** in the square can also provide your dinner (open daily 8:30am-10pm), but **The Dolmen** (tel. 74760), in the square, is cozier and well-priced (open May-Sept. 9am-9pm). Possibilities for a pint and an earful of music abound. The **Roadside Tavern,** Doolin Rd. (tel. 74494), looks more like an antique shop than a bar, but the nightly trad music gives it away (March-Sept. at 9:30pm; Oct.-Feb. Sat. only). The tavern also serves yummies (soup £1.20; noon-8:30pm). The **Kincora Bar** (tel. 74007), by the Burren Tourist Hostel, has a less cultured interior (high season music daily, set dancing every Thurs. night; off-season music weekends only). Beef stew in Guinness (£4.50) is the best seller on the menu. The large, bright red **Matchmaker Bar** (tel. 74042) could symbolize hell or love, depending on your mood. Far more men than women line the bar here (live music after 9pm, dancing nightly; open March-Oct.).

Festival-goers and others take advantage of Lisdoonvarna's mineral springs at the **Spa Wells Health Centre,** Sulfur Hill Rd. (tel. 74023), ¼ mi. from the center of town. The springs were discovered in the early 1700s, and Lisdoonvarna began to boom. If you can't stay for a bath, at least savor their aromatic sulfur water (30p/glass; electric sulphur bath £10, full massage £18, sauna £5). The **Lisdoonvarna Smoke House** (tel. 74432), between the Burren Holiday Hostel and the center of town, provides a free, seven-minute video crash-course into the mysteries of smoked salmon (open March-Oct. daily 9am-7pm).

■ Corofin

The small village of Corofin, "the crossing place of Finn," enjoys the water of seven lakes and the River Fergus, but is only a few miles from the barren Burren. Tourists, eager to reach Ennis or Doolin, usually overlook Corofin's quiet charm.

The **tourist office** (open June-Sept. daily 10am-6pm) is in the **Clare Heritage Centre,** Church St. (tel. 37955). **Buses** from Ennis to Lahinch pass through Corofin (Mon.-Sat. 1/day). The **post office** is on Main St. (open Mon.-Fri. 9am-1pm and 2-5:30pm, Sat. 9am-1pm). Finn crossed the **phone code** at 065.

The **Corofin Village Hostel and Camping Park,** Main St. (tel. 37683), offers clean, modern facilities plus bend-over-backwards hosts who can arrange bird watching trips. The common room has a piano and a TV. Wheelchair accessible. Campers have separate facilities. (Bureau de change. Dorm £6, private room £7.50. **Camping** £3/hiker or cyclist, £4.50/family tent plus £1/person. Laundry £5. **Bikes** £6/day, £25/week.) **MacNamara's Convenience Store,** Main St. (tel. 37602), caters to light grocery needs (open daily 8am-9pm). **Cahir's Bar** (tel. 37238) is a lively little spot (music 3 nights/week in summer, Sun. nights in winter). The **Corofin Arms** (tel. 37373) also has music (3 nights/week). The **Teác Celide,** on Main St. near the post office, puts Clare heritage into action on Thursday evenings with organized music, song, set dancing, and the obligatory brown bread and tea.

You can find a "microcosm of 19th-century Ireland" at the **Clare Heritage and Genealogical Research Centre,** Church St. (tel. 37955). The Genealogical Centre, across the street, caters to the thousands of people whose ancestors emigrated from Clare. **Dysert O'Dea Castle and Archaeology Centre** (tel. 37722), 1½ mi. south of

Corofin, uncovers the more distant past. The museum, inside a restored 15th-century tower, explains the archaeological features of the surrounding lands (open May-Sept. daily 10am-6pm; admission £1.80). A **history trail,** which stays within 2 mi. of the center, leads you to the sights (about 25). Well-preserved, 12th-century **St. Tola's Cross** is visited by the trail, as is a **battlefield** where in 1318 Conor O'Dea and a few of his friends defeated the intruding Normans and put off English domination for another two centuries. The **Dromore National Nature Reserve** and its peaceful, swan-inhabited lakes are about 8 mi. west of Corofin. Follow signposts to Crusheen and from there to the nature reserve. **Guided tours** are available, but the nature trails allow you to amble at your own pace. Fishing is rampant in the many lakes and rivers around. **Burke's** shop (tel. 37677) can help you out with hiring gillies (fishing guides, £35-40) and boats.

THE BURREN

The Burren begins around Lisdoonvarna when bare limestone pops up amid the grasses and sheep. Limestone plains, spines, and outcroppings dominate this 100-sq.-mi. region. The elaborate moonscape includes rare wildflowers, flat stone pedestals, and jagged hills resembling gray skyscrapers bombed to rubble.

Oliver Cromwell famously complained that the Burren had "no wood to hang a man, no water to drown him, and no earth to bury him"—wonder what his mission was? He was right about the wood—nothing grows above knee-level—but orchids, gentians, and other rare wildflowers proliferate. He missed the boat on the water, though; underground rivers have hollowed out 25 mi. of caves under the earth. The area's crazy geology has spawned its own lingo: *furloughs* (temporary lakes that disappear into the limestone), *clints* (a type of rock outcropping), and *grikes* (cracks in clints) compose much of the terrain. It also has its own species of colored snails, orchids, ferns, and green butterflies. Wild goats and Irish hares patrol and fertilize the area. Geologists have decided that the Burren's layers formed undersea before the last Ice Age, as decaying shells turned to powder and mixed with sediment. Earthquakes brought the rock to the surface and advancing glaciers cracked it open.

Ancient tribes roamed the Burren, building settlements out of the ever-present stone. Since no one bothered to invade the area, these encampments were never attacked or disassembled. The fieldless region is now a field day for paleoarchaeologists. Certain archeological terms are frequently thrown around, notably *dolmen* (a prehistoric burial site marked by a huge upright stone) and *souterrain* (an underground passage used as a pantry or an escape tunnel). The R480 road south from Ballyvaughan through Caherconnell is particularly rich in archaic refuse: the Gleninsheen wedge tomb, the Poulnabrone dolmen, and the Caherconnell stone fort all date from the 3rd millennium BC. At last count, the Burren National Park contained about 120 massive dolmens and wedge tombs and some 500 stone forts.

The way to see the Burren is to walk or cycle in it. George Cunningham's *Burren Journey: West* is worth a look (£3), as is Tim Robinson's meticulous map (£3.60). The Burren Rambler maps (£2) are extremely detailed. Any of the Burren's tourist offices (in Kilfenora, Lisdoonvarna, Corofin, and Ballyvaughan) is bound to stock these. You can grab lesser-quality maps of the region for free at any tourist attraction, hostel, or eatery; the *North Clare Wonderland Cycling Guide* isn't bad. The **Burren Way** and its subsidiary walking trails traverse terrain as sterile as steel and patches of pulverized stone teeming with blue-headed grasses and red-winged butterflies. The 26-mi. trail passes through Ballyvaughan, Ballynalackan, Doolin, and Liscannor. Yellow arrows and the occasional "walking man" signs point the way throughout northwest Co. Clare.

Bus service in the Burren is poor. **Bus Éireann** connects Galway, Kinvara, Ballyvaughan, Lisdoonvarna, and Doolin infrequently—only a couple times per week. Every weekday in summer (June-Oct.), some of those buses continue over the Shannon car **ferry** at Killimer to Killarney and Cork. Bus stops are at the Doolin Hostel in Doolin, Burke's Garage in Lisdoonvarna, Linnane's in Ballyvaughan, and Winkles in Kinvara. Other infrequent but year-round buses run from some individual Burren towns to Ennis (Bus Éireann info: tel. (065) 24177). **Brian's West Clare Shuttle** supplies a door-to-door Galway to Doolin service every morning, with stops at hostels in Fanore and Lisdoonvarna if prearranged. Around noon, Brian arrives in Doolin and then turns around (£5; book ahead at tel. (091) 767801 or (088) 517963). Hitchhiking requires persistence; bikes are the best bet.

▨ Kilfenora

A small town 5 mi. southeast of Lisdoonvarna along R478, Kilfenora calls itself "the heart of the Burren." It's certainly a useful stopover. Tourists, most of them on bicycles, stop here for a pint, some grub, and a walk through the **Burren Centre** (tel. 88030), which explains the formation of the region and shows an excellent film on Burren biology. The adjacent tea room serves cheap lunches. (Open March-May and Oct. daily 10am-5pm; June-Sept. daily 9:30am-6pm. Centre and film £2.20, students £1.60.) A **tourist office** sits next to the Centre (tel. 88198) and sells the helpful *Burren Rambler* map series (£2; open June-Oct. daily 9:30am-6pm). Bicycles stack up at **Howard's Bicycles** (tel. 88127; hourly or daily rental up to £6). The **post office** (tel. 88001) is on Main St. across from the grocery store (open Mon.-Fri. 9am-5:30pm, Sat. 10am-1pm). The **phone code** is a barren 065.

Next to the Centre, Catholic masses are still held in the nave of the **Kilfenora Cathedral** (Sun. 9:45am). The rest of the Cathedral and its graveyard stand open to the sky. The structure itself dates from 1190, but the site has held churches since 1055. (Tours July-Aug. £1, ask at the tourist office.) West of the church is the elaborate **Doorty Cross,** one of the "seven crosses of Kilfenora" built in the 12th century. Though time and erosion have taken their toll, carved scenes of three bishops and Christ's entry into Jerusalem still adorn the Doorty Cross. Odd birds and menacing heads cover its sides. Another cross is railed off in the field just beyond the church.

Kilfenora has only three pubs. **Linnane's** (tel. 88157) feels tourist lethargy in the afternoons, but revives at night with trad sessions (nightly in summer, weekends in winter). Red vinyl covers just about everything at **Nagle's** (tel. 88011; music Fri.-Sun. in summer). **Vaughan's** (tel. 88004) entertains locals with music most nights and set dancing two nights per week in summer. For all those expatriated Texans and Carolinians, Vaughan's has a barbecue Fridays and Sundays 7-9pm (£5). **Ms. Mary Murphy,** Main St. (tel. 88040), runs a comfortably central B&B with snug comforters (£13/person, w/bath; open June-Sept.).

▨ Kinvara & Doorus

Galway Bay's shore makes a sharp turn at **Kinvara,** Co. Galway, a town which considers itself the musical equivalent of Doolin, only without the throngs of tourists. A night on the town will probably leave you in agreement. The view across the bay is best seen from **Dunguaire Castle** (tel. 37108). The narrow, winding staircase weaves its way to a vista of rugged, fundamental beauty. (Open May-Sept. daily 9:30am-5pm; admission £2.35, students £1.30.) East of Kinvara, the landscape quickly fades into the dull farmland of southern Co. Galway. Yeats's summer homes, Coole Park and Thoor Ballylee, stand a bit off N18 between Ardrahan and Gort, tantalizingly close to Kinvara. Unfortunately, no official bus connects Kinvara and Gort, it's a difficult hitch, and it's just too far to walk (see **Near Galway,** p. 295). Bus Éireann hits Kinvara on its Galway-Doolin route (May 27-Sept. 21 Mon.-Sat. 4/day, Sun. 2/day). **Kinvara Pharmacy,** Main St. (tel. 37397), can soothe your blisters (open Mon.-Sat. 9:30am-6pm). The **phone code** for Kinvara and Doorus is a lucky 091.

Johnston's Hostel (IHH), Main St. (tel. 37164), uphill from the Quay, is a relaxing retreat. The gigantic common room was converted from an old dance hall. Upstairs, the colorful, spacious four-bed rooms are blessed with fireplaces. Reputedly the first

Lookin' for Love in All the Wrong Places?

Lonely, single traveler in Ireland seeking mate? Forget Lisdoonvarna; rendezvous with romance at Johnston's Hostel in Kinvara, the happy site of many loves at first sight. Heartbreak hostel it's not—the owner met his American wife here, and an Aussie far from home fell in love with the girl at the desk. Cupid does strike thrice: two other hostel workers met here and were soon smitten. The owner advises, "Don't stay too long, or do." He makes no guarantees, though: at least one employee was unlucky in love in 1995 (but not for lack of trying).

independent hostel in Ireland, it has been hit often by Cupid's arrows (see **Lookin for Love...,** below). (12:30am lockout. Dorm £6; **camping** £3.50. Sheets £1; showers any donation. Open June-Sept.) Mary Walsh's **Cois Cuain B&B** (tel. 37119) reposes in manicured gardens on the Quay (double £32; open May-Sept.).

The **Londis supermarket** (tel. 37508) does its grocery thing on the main road (open daily 9am-9pm). Across the street from the hostel is **Tully's,** where a grocery and bar keep company in smoky surroundings. The acoustics make it a favorite of musicians. **Flatley's** (tel. 637112), also on Main St., is locally renowned for the quality of its weekend trad sessions. The **Café on the Quay** is perfectly named (tel. 678134; mussel platter £5, breakfast served all day; open April-Oct. daily 9am-9:30pm; Nov.-March daily 9am-5pm). Back on Main St., **Partners** (tel. 637503) makes hunger disappear (vegetarian quiche and salad £3.50; open March-Oct. Mon. and Wed.-Sat. 10am-10pm, Sun. 12:30-10pm). **Linnane's Pub** (tel. 78120) is 3 mi. off a signposted road from Kinvara. Music gets the joint jumpin' on Fridays and Sundays. Excellent seafood (baked crab £3.50, fresh lobster £15).

For those with an urge to sail, **Michael Linane** (at the Kinvara inlet) will take groups of four on a tour of the bay and across to the village of **Doorus,** Co. Galway (roundtrip sailing £6/person). Yeats and Lady Gregory stayed here while planning the Abbey Theatre and collaborating on plays. The house they inhabited is now the isolated **Doorus House Hostel (An Óige/HI)** (tel. 637512). The large, well-appointed hostel has an inviting common room with a turf fire. (Dorm June-Sept. £6, Oct.-May £5.) For those not enamored of nature, it's probably best to stay in Kinvara, but for hikers and bikers Doorus is righteous. Toni the warden happily helps hostelers plan their routes. A 10-mi. roundtrip through the **Aughinish Peninsula** offers views of the Burren across the bay accompanied by splashing waves—Irish natural sublime in its prime. More convenient, the **Traught Strand** is just a five-minute walk from the hostel. Campers can pitch a tent in the field nearby and wake to the slosh of surf. The Galway-Doolin **bus** does not pass through Doorus but will stop on request at the turnoff on the Ballyvaughan Rd. (June-Sept. Mon.-Sat. 4/day, Sun. 2/day; Oct.-May Mon.-Sat. 1/day); from there it's a 2-mi. walk.

■ Ballyvaughan

Eight miles west of Kinvara on N67 along the jagged edge of Galway Bay, Ballyvaughan (BAH-lee VUH-han) is bona-fide Burren. Unfortunately, the natural desolation of the Burren is interrupted by the man-made desolation of identical rows of "holiday cottages." Thankfully, Ballyvaughan's pubs rescue the town's aesthetic butt with excellent trad sessions. A friendly **tourist office** (tel. 77105) sits just off the main road on the Lisdoonvarna side of town (open June to mid-Oct. daily 10am-6pm). Monk's Pub provides Raleigh **bike hire** (£7/day, £30/week). Ballyvaughan's **phone code** is a naturally desolate 065.

There's no hostel in Ballyvaughan, but B&B is available at **Gentian Villa** (tel. 77042) on the main road on the Kinvara side of town, where all rooms have a bath (£15/person; open Easter-Oct.). If you insist on a hostel, take the scenic journey to **Fanore,** 8 mi. west of Ballyvaughan on R477 after Black Head. The small **Bridge Hostel** (tel. 76134), on the banks of the river just up from the bridge on the main road, has panache, an open fire, and lovely showers. Graham and Frances can help you plot your path through the midst of the Burren so as not to miss the good stuff. (Dorm £5.50, private room £7.50. **Camping** £3/person. Open March-Oct.) Breakfast (£2.50), homemade brown bread (£1.20), and evening meals (about £3.50) served.

Spar Supermarket (tel. 77077) can sell you fresh bread from their bakery (open June-Aug. daily 8:30am-9pm; Sept.-May daily 9:30am-8pm). **The Tea Junction Café** (tel. 77174) tempts you to ruin your appetite with Marianne's famous chocolate cake (£1.25). Marianne will also provide breakfast and take-away, and remembers the vegetarians (vegetable and bean chili pita pocket £3; open mid-March to Oct. Tues.-Sun. 10am-6pm). **An Féar Gorta** (tel. 77023), by the pier, has a menu appealing to the stomach and the mind. Read *The Legend of the Hag of Loughrask* while you wait for food (smoked salmon and salad £3.80; open June-Sept. 11am-5:30pm).

The Burren Way leads down to the pier and **Monk's Pub** (tel. 77059), which serves seafood specialities (fishcakes with salad £4.50). Music abounds most nights in summer, Friday through Sunday in winter. Back in town, **Greene's** is a small card-playing locals' pub with an older crowd who know where the Guinness runs best. The menu consists of only one daily special (about £5), but the huge helpings are hot from noon to midnight. **O'Brien's** (tel. 77303) has a younger, louder crowd and music four nights per week in the summer (weekends in winter). The food is good, cheap, and plentiful (smoked salmon platter £3; food served noon-8:30pm).

Prehistoric bears once inhabited the two million-year-old **Aillwee Cave** (tel. 77036 or 77067), 2 mi. south of Ballyvaughan and over ¾ mi. deep. The 30-minute tour is all about bears, but you'll be gaping at spectacular rocks and waterfalls. The engineering required to open the cave to the public is almost as impressive as the geology itself— look up when you get outside. (Open July-Aug. daily 10am-6:30pm; mid-March to early Nov. Mon.-Fri. 10am-5:30pm. Admission £4, students £3.)

In town, the **Dállan Gallery** (tel. 77156), located in the same building as the tourist office, is a more civilized attraction. An eclectic range of contemporary work from fabric paintings and metal work to witch dolls are on display (open May-Sept. daily 10am-7pm). One mile out of Ballyvaughan on N67 is the turnoff for **Newtown Castle and Trail** (tel. 77216). The 16th-century home of the O'Loghlens, the princes of the Burren, has been restored. Ancient Clare manuscripts and Bardic Poetry recitals are seen on the hour-long **tour.** Another hour-long guided tour covers about ¾ mi. of beautiful hillside terrain and discusses the geology and archeology of the Burren. A Victorian folly "gazebo" (a children's miniature castle) and an 18th-century military waterworks system are both parts of the latter tour. (Open Easter to early Oct. daily 10am-6pm. Castle or trail tour £2, both tours £3.50.)

County Galway

Lots of people visit both Galway City and the terrain to its west, but they do so for disparate reasons. The city is the world headquarters of *craic*, especially during its many festivals. Land west of Galway, on the other hand, offers peaceful, rugged scenery at its best. Clifden has thriving nightlife; Inishbofin has that as well as a rugged life. Cong, a popular hamlet just over the Mayo border (we cover it under Co. Galway), has grassy natural attractions and stony ruined ones. Avoid east Co. Galway: Ballinasloe may excite farmers, but even the cows wouldn't recommend it.

■ Galway City

From Rosslare to Ballycastle, a message is rising in the Irish travel circuit: "Go west, young person." More and more, this means a trip to Galway, a social city deriving energy from pubs and theaters. The cobblestone lanes fill to bursting during the spring and summer as the crowds of *craic*-seekers mix with the students and hardworking residents (pop. 51,000). The energy finds its true focus by late afternoon, as

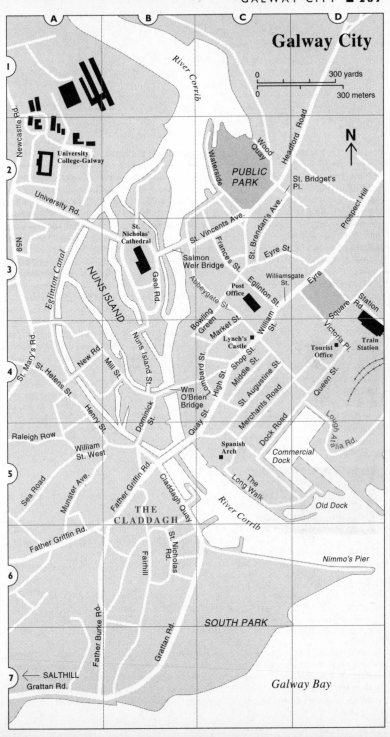

Galway City

River Corrib

0 _____ 300 yards

0 _____ 300 meters

N

Newcastle Rd.

University
College-Galway

University Rd.

N59

Eglinton Canal

NUNS ISLAND

St. Nicholas'
Cathedral

Gaol Rd.

Salmon
Weir Bridge

Wood
Quay

Waterside

PUBLIC
PARK

St. Bridget's
Pl.

Headford Road

Prospect Hill

St. Vincents Ave.

Frances St.

St. Brendan's Ave.

Eyre St.

Abbeygate St.

Post
Office

Eglinton St.

Williamsgate
St.

Eyre
Square

Station
Rd.

Bowling
Green

Market St.

William
St.

Train
Station

St. Mary's Rd.

New Rd.

Mill St.

Nuns Island St.

Lynch's
Castle

Shop St.

High St.

Middle St.

Victoria Pl.

Tourist
Office

Queen St.

St. Helens St.

Henry St.

Dominick St.

Lombard St.

Quay St.

Wm
O'Brien
Bridge

St. Augustine St.

Merchants Road

Lough Atalia Rd.

Dock Road

Raleigh Row

William
St. West

Spanish
Arch

Commercial
Dock

Father Griffin Rd.

Claddagh Quay

The
Long Walk

Old Dock

Sea Road

Munster Ave.

THE
CLADDAGH

River Corrib

Nimmo's Pier

Father Griffin Rd.

St. Nicholas
Rd.

Fairhill

Father Burke Rd.

Grattan Rd.

SOUTH PARK

SALTHILL
Grattan Rd.

Galway Bay

WESTERN IRELAND

the crowds migrate to Galway's myriad pubs. Galway's port and location have made it the hot city in the region for some time. An oligarchy of 14 families of Welsh descent (the "Tribes of Galway") ruled the region until the late 18th century and grew rich from trade with Spain. Under their direction, Galway became the three-way intersection connecting the fertile inland districts to the ships of the European maritime trade and to Connemara. Galway's popular university, its relative wealth, and its proximity to the Connemara *gaeltacht* make it a likely place to find literary and theater culture in both of Ireland's languages. But "high" culture by no means dominates the town. People discuss poems over a pint or see plays in a pub. Many hostels and exciting nightlife make Galway an ideal base for exploring the West.

ORIENTATION & PRACTICAL INFORMATION

Any transport to Galway will deposit you in **Eyre Square,** a central block of lawn and monuments with the train and bus station on its east side. A string of lonely B&Bs begs for business northeast of the square along Prospect Hill. The real town, or the part most want to visit, spreads out south and west of the square. **Williams St.** descends southwest into the cobblestone area around **High, Shop,** and **Quay St.**— Galway's "Left Bank," where most of the food and the pubs are concentrated. A bridge leads over the River Corrib and past Nuns' Island to **Dominick St.,** where hostels and pubs compete. From there, both a path and a road stretch past the quays for a mile or two to Salthill's bayfront arcades. After passing the cathedral, **Abbeygate St.** becomes **University Rd.,** so called because it passes University College Galway. Suburban **Renmare,** 1 mi. east of the center, slumbers peacefully by its bird sanctuary. To reach it from the station, follow the path next to the railway tracks.

    City buses costing 60p leave from Eyre Sq. (D3) at 20-minute intervals. Buses roll to each area of the city: #1 to Salthill, #2 to Knocknacarra (west) or Renmare (east), #3 to Castlepark, and #4 to Newcastle and Rahoon. (Service runs Mon.-Sat. 8am-9pm, Sun. 11am-9pm.) Or walk—it's good for you (just like Guinness). Hitchhikers abound in Galway. Dozens at a time wait on Dublin Rd. (N6), scouting rides to Dublin, Limerick, or Kinvara. Most catch bus #2, 5, or 6 from Eyre Sq. to this prime thumb-stop. University Rd. leads drivers to Oughterard and Clifden via N59.

Tourist Office: Victoria Pl. (tel. 563081), just over 1 block southeast of Eyre Sq. Aran Islands info makes the usual pamphlet mania more exciting than ever. Open May-June daily 8:30am-5:45pm; July-Aug. daily 8:30am-7:45pm; Sept.-April Mon.-Sat. 9am-5:45pm. **Salthill office** (same phone), visible from the main beach. Open June to mid-Sept. daily 9am-5:45pm; July-Aug. 9am-7:45pm.

USIT (Student Travel): Kinlay House, Victoria Place, Eyre Sq. (tel. 565177), across the street from the tourist office. Offers the usual student discounts and sells *Let's Go.* Open June-Aug. Mon.-Fri. 9:30am-5:30pm, Sat. 10am-3pm; Sept.-May Mon.-Fri 9:30am-5:30pm, Sat. 10am-1pm.

Banks: Bank of Ireland, 19 Eyre Sq. (tel. 563181). Open Mon.-Wed. and Fri. 10am-4pm, Thurs. 10am-5pm; **ATM. AIB,** Lynch's Castle, Shop St. (C4; tel. 567041). Exactly the same hours; **ATM.** Salthill: **Bank of Ireland** (tel. 522455). Open Mon.-Wed. and Fri. 10am-4pm, Thurs. 10am-5pm; **ATM.**

American Express: John Ryan's Travel, 1 Williamsgate (tel. 567375). Open Mon.-Fri. 9:15am-5:30pm, Sat. 10am-1pm and 2:15-4pm.

Galway Airport: tel. 75569, in Carnmore.

Trains: Eyre Sq. (tel. 561444). Open Mon.-Sat. 7:40am-6pm. Trains to Dublin (8-10/day, Sun. 3/day; 3hr.; Mon.-Thurs. and Sat. £14, Fri. and Sun. £19, students £9 daily) stop in Athlone (Mon.-Thurs. and Sat. £7, Fri. and Sun. £11, students £4.50 daily); transfer at Athlone for all other lines. **Irish Rail/Iarnród Éireann office:** (tel. 564244 or 561444). Open Mon.-Fri. 9am-5:30pm.

Buses: (tel. 562000). Open July-Aug. daily 8am-8:30pm; Sept.-June Mon.-Sat. 8am-6pm. **Bus Éireann** runs regularly Mon.-Sat., less frequently on Sun. Buses depart Eyre Sq. for: Athlone (11/day, Sun. 8/day; £7, students £5); Ballina (6/day, Sun. 1/day; £9.70, students £6); Belfast (2-3/day, Sun. 1/day; £17, students £12.40); Cork (daily 5/day; £12, students £7.50); Doolin (June-Sept. 4/day; Sun. 2/day; Oct.-May

1/day; £8.20, students £4.60); Dublin (8-9/day, Sun. 7-8/day; £8, students £6.50); Limerick (6-7/day, Sun. 6/day; £9, students £5.30); Rosslare (2/day; £16, students £9.50); Shannon Airport (5/day, Sun. 4/day; £8.80, students £5); Sligo (4-5/day, Sun. 3/day; £10.50, students £6.50); and Westport (3-5/day, Sun. 1/day; £8.80, students £5). Private bus companies specialize in the Dublin-Galway run. **P. Nestor Coaches** (tel. 797144; Mon.-Thurs. and Sun. 2/day, Fri. 7/day, Sat. 5/day; £5 single or day return, £8 open return; leaves from Imperial Hotel, Eyre Sq.) and **Citylink** (tel. 564163; 5/day, last bus at 5:45pm; same prices as Nestor's; leaves from Supermac's in Eyre Sq.) both run back and forth between Galway and Dublin. A **West Clare Shuttle** to Doolin, Lisdoonvarna, and Fanore leaves various Galway hostels on request (June-Sept. daily 1/day; £5). Bus tours of Connemara also available (see **Connemara**, p. 304).

Luggage Storage: in the train station. Backpacks and large bags £2/day, other bags £1/day. Open Mon.-Sat. 7:30am-10pm, Sun. 11am-6:20pm.

Taxis: Big O Taxis, 21 Upper Dominick St. (tel. 585858). **Rice Edward,** 12 Oaklands, Salthill (tel. 22860). **Galway Taxis,** 7 Mainguard St. (tel. 561111), around the corner from McSwiggan's Pub; 24-hr. service. **Hackneys: MGM** (tel. 757888), **Claddagh** (tel. 589000), **Moycullen** (tel. 585818; 24hr.). Call to book; flat rate within city, by the mile outside. There are usually taxis available at Eyre Sq. (D3).

Car Rental: Budget Rent-a-Car, Eyre Sq. (tel. 566376).

Bike Rental: Europa Cycles, Hunter Buildings, Earls Island (tel. 563355), opposite the cathedral. £3/day, £5/24hr., £25/week; deposit £30. Open Mon.-Sat. 9am-6pm, Sun. 10am-2pm and 4-6pm. **Celtic Cycles,** Queen St., Victoria Place (tel. 566606), next to the Celtic Hostel. £7/day, £30/week; deposit £40 or ID; remote dropoff charge £12. Open daily 9am-6pm.

Camping Equipment: River Deep Mountain High, Middle St. (tel. 563968). Open Mon.-Sat. 9:30am-6pm. Reasonably priced backpacks, wetsuits, climbing gear, manuals, and more.

Bookstores: Eason & Son, Ltd., 33 Shop St. (tel. 562284). Huge selection and specials on Irish literature. Open Mon.-Sat. 9am-6:15pm.

Laundry: The Bubbles Inn, 18 Mary St. (tel. 563434). Wash and dry £4; last wash 4:30pm; open Mon.-Sat. 8:45am-6:15pm. **Prospect Hill Launderette,** Prospect Hill (tel. 568343). Wash and dry £4; open Mon.-Sat. 7:30am-7pm.

Youth Information Centre: Ozanam House, St. Augustine St. (tel. 562434). Open Mon.-Fri. 9am-5pm. Also an AIDS resource center.

Bisexual, Gay, and Lesbian Information: P.O. Box 45 (tel. 566134). Lesbian line open Wed. 8-10pm; gay line open Tues. and Thurs. 8-10pm. Call for information on videos and discussion groups.

Rape Crisis Centre: 3 St. Augustine St. (tel. (1 800) 355355).

Hotline: Samaritans, 14 Nuns' Island (tel. 561222). 24-hr. phones.

Pharmacies: Commins, Shop St. (tel. 562924). Open Mon.-Sat. 9am-6pm. **Really's,** 17 William St. (tel. 562332). Open Mon.-Fri. 9am-9pm.

Hospital: University College Hospital, Newcastle Rd. (tel. 524222).

Emergency: Dial 999; no coins required. **Garda:** Mill St. (tel. 563161).

Post Office: Eglinton St. (tel. 562051). Open Mon.-Sat. 9am-6pm. Long lines.

Phone Code: 091.

ACCOMMODATIONS

In the last two years the number of hostels in Galway has nearly tripled. Nevertheless, during weekends and big festivals, finding a nice bed can be difficult. Reserve at hostels or pay the steep price during Galway Arts Week (mid-July) and the Galway Races (late July to early Aug.). Try to arrive in town before 5pm if you can't make reservations in advance. **Woodquay** hostels cluster about five minutes from Eyre Sq. around the Salmon Weir. **Dominick St.** hosts its own fleet on the west side of the River Corrib, and **Eyre Sq.** hostels are closest to the bus and train stations. B&Bs should set you back £12-15 a night per person. Most of them, and a few hostels, are in **Salthill,** 1 mi. away. If you're a club-goer, consider staying in Salthill, where the majority of post-midnight nightlife is. (If you get into town late, you may have to stay in Salthill anyway.) **Renmare** is a sedate Galway suburb with a few B&Bs of its own.

Hostels & Camping

Galway

Great Western House, Eyre Sq. (tel. 561150 or FreeFone 1-800-GALWAY (425929)), across from bus and train station. With its sauna, pool room, and satellite television, Great Western is slightly more expensive than the other hostels but allows weary backpackers a luxurious stay in Galway. In the face of modern, hotel-like amenities, the friendly staff bravely strives to maintain a hostel's atmosphere. 24-hr. reception. Wheelchair accessible. Bureau de change. July-Aug. and bank holidays 8- to 10-bed dorm £8.50, 4-bed dorm w/bath £12.50, double w/bath £31. March-June and Sept.-Oct. £8, £11.50, £29 respectively. Nov.-Feb. £7.50, £10.50, £28 respectively. Free continental breakfast; Irish breakfast £1; packed lunch £3; dinner from £6. Laundry £5. Bikes £6/day.

Quay Street Hostel (IHH), Quay St. (tel. 568644 or 561094). Shop St. becomes Quay St. A dark wooden common room with a fireplace and pleasant dorms add to the unbeatable location in the city center. July-Aug. dorm £7.20; 6-bed dorm £7.50, w/bath £8.50; 4-bed dorm £8.50, w/bath £10, double w/bath £23. Sept.-June £6.90, £7.50, £8.50, £9.50, £23 respectively. Laundry £3.50.

Salmon Weir Hostel, St. Vincent's Ave., Woodquay (tel. 561133). Turn right onto St. Vincent's Ave. off Francis St. (formerly Eglinton St. in Eyre Sq.). Clean, comfortable, and fun-loving. Follow the other guests to the pubs at night. Free tea, coffee, washing powder, and peace of mind. Curfew 2am, 3am in summer. June-Aug. 4-6 bed dorm £7, double £20; May £6.50 and £18 respectively; Sept.-April £6 and £16. Laundry £4. Bikes £5/day, £3.50/½day.

The Galway Hostel, Eyre Sq. (tel. 566959), across from bus and train station. Soft yellow walls and attractive, airy rooms (some with balconies) which look out onto Eyre Sq. Chinese floor tiles, super-clean bathrooms, heaters in rooms. The small kitchen fills fast in this 80-bed hostel. June-Aug. 8-14 bed dorm £6.90; 4-bed dorm £8.90, w/bath £9.90; double w/bath £23.80. Sept.-May £6; £8, £8.90; and £21.80, respectively. Discounted laundry nearby, £3 per load.

Kinlay House, Merchants Rd. (tel. 565244), across from the tourist office. Brand new, spotless, and friendly, but a little sedate. Bring your hiking boots for the trek upstairs to reception. Washcloths, bars of soap, blue duvets, and closet space in airy, uncrowded rooms approach luxury. Awesome medieval mural in dining room. 24-hr. access. July-Sept. and special events 6-bed dorm £8, w/bath £9; 4-bed dorm £10.50, w/bath £11.50; double £26, w/bath £28; single £17. Oct.-June £8, £9; £9.50, £10.50; £24, £26; £16.50, respectively. 10% discount with ISIC. Free continental breakfast. Bureau de change. Laundry £4.

Galway City Hostel, 25-27 Dominick St. (tel. 566367). A relaxing hostel down the road from the city's main streets, this tall building entices you to relax with it on the riverbank. June-Sept. dorms £6.50, 4-bed dorm £8, double £20. Oct.-May dorms £5.50, 4-bed dorm £7, double £16. Laundry £2.50. Sheets 50p.

Celtic Tourist Hostel, Queen St., Victoria Pl. (tel. 586606 or 521559 at night), around the corner from the tourist office. Sit back, relax, and look out the big windows in the sitting room. Big kitchen. Large dorms can get crowded. Microwave and VCR. July-Aug. dorm £7, private room £10.90/person. Sept.-June dorm £6, private room £9.90/person. Sheets £1. Bikes £7/day.

The Westend, Upper Dominick St. (tel. 583636), across from the Arch View Hostel. Artsy travelers in flannel shirts or flowery skirts enjoy storytellers, jugglers, and musicians in an deeply mellow atmosphere. Old house with creaking floorboards (best when barefoot) and free tea and coffee. Bus service from train. Curfew 3am. July-Aug. dorm £7, private room £10/person. Sept.-June dorm £5, private room £8/person.

Corrib Villa (IHH), 4 Waterside (tel. 562892). Just past the courthouse, about 4 blocks from Eyre Sq. down Eglinton St. Spacious, old Georgian house is rumored to get a little chilly when the weather turns poor, but worth a look if the others are full. Curfew 3am. July to mid-Sept. £6.50. Mid-Sept. to June £5.50.

Salthill

The Grand Holiday Hostel (IHH), Promenade (tel. 522150). Bus #1 from Eyre Sq. runs here. Once a hotel, always well-vacuumed. Fresh and tidy rooms overlooking the sea conspire to make your holiday grand. July-Aug. dorm £7, double £20. Sept.-June dorm £6.50, double £18. **Strawberry Fields Café** (tel. 526919), on the ground floor, serves American food (breakfast £2.50; open 7am-10:30pm). Laundry £3; sheets 50p. Currency exchange. Bikes £6/day.

Stella Maris (IHH), 151 Upper Salthill (tel. 521950). Bus #1 from Eyre Sq. Mega-blue hallway, reminiscent of the sea, leads to 2-, 4-, or 6-bed rooms. Large common room looks out onto the real sea. Staff on duty 24hr. June-Aug. dorm £6.50, double £17. Sept.-May dorm £5.50, double £15. Sheets 50p. Bikes from £3/day.

Camping: Salthill Caravan and Camping Park (tel. 522479). On the bay, ½mi. west of Salthill. Crowded in summer. £3/hiker or cyclist. Open April-Sept.

Bed & Breakfasts

St. Martin's, 2 Nuns' Island (tel. 568286), on the west bank of the river at the end of Dominick St. (visible from the Bridge St. bridge). Gorgeous riverside location with a grassy lawn. In summer £16/person, off season £15/person.

Brasstacks, Diana Walsh, 3 St. Helen's Street (tel. 524728). Off Newcastle Rd., a 10-min. walk. Henry St. (right from the end of Dominick St.) becomes St. Helen's St. Amicable comfort. £14/person.

Mrs. E. O'Connolly, 24 Glenard Ave., Salthill (tel. 522147), off Dr. Mannix Rd. Bus #1 from Eyre Sq. is easiest. Excellent B&B for an excellent price. £8.50 w/continental breakfast, £11 w/full Irish breakfast.

Mrs. Ruth Armstrong, 14 Glenard Ave., Salthill (tel. 522069), lies just down the road and serves a full Irish breakfast with friendly chatter (£12-13).

FOOD

Galway is full of students in winter, hence there are plenty of excellent cheap eats. Stick east of the river and near the short blocks around Quay St., High St., Shop St., and Abbeygate St. for good values. **Roches Stores,** Eyre St. (tel. 561211), is a department store and cheap supermarket economically rolled into one (open Mon.-Thurs. and Sat. 9am-5:30pm, Fri. 9am-9pm). **Evergreen Health Food,** 1 Mainguard St. (tel. 564215), offers food from its shelves as well as from a menu (open Mon.-Thurs. and Sat. 9am-6:30pm, Fri. 9am-8pm). Two other stores, **Healthwise** (tel. 568761) and **Honeycomb Health** (tel. 568995), are both on Abbeygate St. On Saturdays, a **market** (8am-1pm) sets up in front of St. Nicholas Church on Market St. Fishers may wander through the pubs all evening, selling cups of fresh mussels (around £1) and other shellfish from the bay. Buy. Eat. Go mussel mad.

The Home Plate, Mary St. (tel. 561475). Expect a wait between noon and 3pm, when the whole city lines up to bat. Colossal servings include a humongous beverage for washing down big mouthfuls. Some take-away available. Vegetarian fajita £2.90, BIG sandwiches £2. Open Mon.-Sat. 10am-8pm.

The Couch Potatas, Upper Abbeygate St. (tel. 561664). Visitors to Ireland really should experience the potatoes. "Hawaii 5-0" is a baked potato with ham, cheese, pineapple, and onion (£4). Spuds & butter £1.75. Crowded at lunchtime with all types. Open Mon.-Sat. noon-10pm, Sun. 1-10pm.

McDonagh's, 22 Quay St. (tel. 565001). A world-class chippy. Certificates, newspaper clippings, and magazine articles line the wall to prove its popularity. The pride and joy of the collection is an official recognition from the former Soviet fleet naming this the best chipper at any port of call. Especially crowded after the pubs close. Cod fillet and chips £3.20. Open Mon.-Sat. noon-midnight, Sun. noon-11pm. Restaurant (open daily noon-11pm) is pricier than take-away.

Fat Freddy's, Quay St. (tel. 569381). Everyone under 25 goes here. And since everyone in Galway is under 25, it's always ridiculously crowded. But jeepers, that pizza is tasty. Eccentric mix of Italian dishes and chowder. Best pizza in Western Ireland. Large cheese pizza £4.80. Open daily noon-10:30pm.

Java's, Upper Abbeygate St. (tel. 567400). A carbon copy of the great Seattle coffee-house, even to the stamped cards that give every 10th drink free. Galway's somber-eyed youth sit here for hours in the afternoon, reading and smoking, smoking and talking. After midnight, loud, drunken intellectuals drive the sober ones to seek solitude elsewhere. 32 kinds of coffee (90p), 25 of tea (75p). Salad and sandwiches of fewer varieties. Open Mon.-Sat. 9am-4am, Sun. noon-4am.

The Runner Bean, Mary St. (tel. 569292). Surrounds every meal of the day with a lemon-colored casual setting. House special breakfast £2.25 (served 9am-noon), seafood chowder £2. Open Mon.-Sat. 8am-10:30pm, Sun. 9am-10:30pm.

Scotty's Casual Gourmet, 1 Middle St. (tel. 566400). Scotty casually beams you downstairs to foot-long subs and fresh salads. Spicy pastrami and Swiss sub £2.50. Open Mon.-Sat. 7:30am-5:30pm.

Food for Thought, Lower Abbeygate St. (tel. 565854). Coffeeshop and wholefood restaurant serves a variety of interesting vegetarian dishes (£2.50) and mind-bogglingly big sandwiches from £2. Open Mon.-Fri. 8am-7pm, Sat. 8am-6pm.

Hungry Grass, 15 Cross St. (tel. 565719). This Paris-style café with tables on cobblestones outside will have you thinking with a French accent. Chocolate Fudge croissant 95p.

Le Café de Paris, Cross St. Two-level café caters to crepe fantasies. Croissants 45p, omelette with salad and brown bread £1.50. An adjoining bakery also offers sandwiches. Open Mon.-Sat. 8am-9pm, Sun. 10am-7pm.

PUBS

Half the businesses in downtown Galway seem to be pubs. There is an average of five on every block, so there's no excuse for stopping and staying in one that doesn't suit you. Fabulous, fast-paced traditional music usually blazes from several pubs each night. Unfortunately, second-rate musicians exist alongside the good ones. Good and bad versions of rock, guitar-folk, country, blues, and metal also rear their heads. The most talked-about pubs congregate on Dominick St. and Quay St.

The Quays, Quay St. (tel. 568347). Popular with the younger crowd, including large numbers of scamming yuppies and Americans. The massive, multi-floored interior was built with carved wood taken from the balconies and stained glass windows of an old church. Fabulous atmosphere is a bit forced, but good *craic* is generally guaranteed. It's worth a visit simply to see the intriguing interior.

McSwiggan's, 3 Eyre St., Woodquay (tel. 568917), around the corner from Eddie Rockett's. Just as popular with twentysomethings as The Quays. Dark, worn-wood interior with paneled glass. The back of the bar is forever hidden behind unnumbered corners and crannies. The bog-preserved tree sucks in tourists. Good restaurant upstairs. Trad Sat.-Sun. nights.

The King's Head, High St. (tel. 566630), continue down Shop St. Crazy student hangout. Most people who drink here are under 21. All kinds of music nightly. Lunchtime theater Mon.-Sat. 1-2pm, £2. Popular Sun. jazz brunch 12:45-2:15pm.

Roisín Dubh, Dominick St., (tel. 586540), "The Black Rose." Old bicycles and dead branches on the walls. Music varies between trad, rock, and folk. Bigger names appear on Mon. and Tues. nights; cover £5-10.

The Lisheen, 5 Bridge St. (tel. 563804). Outstanding and ceaseless trad nightly and Sunday morning. Musicians and pool shooters welcome.

Taaffe's, Shop St. (tel. 564066). Everyone from tweed-capped men to platform-shoed mods comes here to hear quality trad nightly and during the day on Fri. and Sat. (except Good Friday). Barman claims that there is "no useless bric-a-brac to distract from the job of drinking here."

Busker Browne's, Cross St. (tel. 563377), next to Knockton's. Huge, with 3 bars and 4 floors. The top one is a medieval banquet hall lined with long tables. Be careful not to get so spirited that you throw your bones on the rushes.

The Cellar Bar, Eglinton St. (tel. 563966). The subterranean source for music. Live bands downstairs nightly (9pm).

Seaghan Ua Neachtain (a.k.a. Knockton's), Quay St. (tel. 568820). A dark maze of secret nooks and fireplaces. Mixed crowd interested primarily in the melodious trad which blares out every Mon., Wed., and Fri.-Sat.

SIGHTS

The commercial and cultural Galway overshadows its historic aspects. The tourist office sells the *Medieval Galway Map,* which informs tourists about local history (£3.50), and gives away the free *Junior Chamber Galway Tourist Guide,* whose price reflects its value.

Galway's **Catholic Cathedral,** officially known as the "Cathedral of Our Lady Assumed into Heaven and St. Nicholas," looms above the Salmon Weir Bridge. It's located across the river from most of the city, where Gaol Rd. and University Rd. meet. The boring exterior reveals none of the controversy that assailed its eclectic design 25 years ago. The impressive interior, where circles of Connemara marble intersect with elaborate mosaics, was the main subject of debate. (Excellent tours and mood-setting organ practice, Mon.-Fri. 3:30-5:30pm; also open Sun. for masses.) Closer to the center of town near the Church of St. Nicholas, the tiny **Nora Barnacle House,** 8 Bowling Green (tel. 564743), exposes a few letters and photos relating to James Joyce and his wife. Joyce visited the house in 1909 and 1912. Nora reputedly inspired much of his writing, including *The Dead.* The table where Joyce composed a few lines to Nora draws the admiration of Joyce addicts. (Open mid-May to mid-Sept. Mon-Sat. 10am-1pm and 2-5pm; admission £1.)

Shop St. runs past **Lynch's Castle,** an elegant, 16th century stone mansion with incongruous gargoyles. The Lynch family ruled Galway from the 13th to the 18th centuries. Exhibits inside the edifice analyze the castle's architecture and heraldry and relate a family legend. In the late 1400s, Lynch Jr. killed a Spaniard whom he suspected of liking his girlfriend. The son, sentenced to hang, was so beloved by the populace that not one man would agree to be the hangman. Lynch Sr., the lord of the castle, was so determined to administer justice that he had to hang his own son. The window from which Lynch lynched Lynch Jr. is supposedly the one behind St. Nicholas Church. A skull and crossbones engraved into the glass remembers the just deed. The castle now houses the Allied Irish Bank. (Bank and exhibits open Mon.-Wed. and Fri. 10am-4pm, Thurs. 10am-5pm. Free.)

Many Lynches lie together in their family tomb in the **Church of St. Nicholas,** Market St., behind the castle. The church, full of oddities from many sources, devotes some of its attention to a heritage project. Columbus stopped to pray here before pillaging the New World; a stone marks the spot. Glorious stained glass and relics from the Connacht Rangers provide more distractions. The unnecessary tours cost £1, students 50p. (Open May-Sept. daily 9am-5:45pm; free.)

By the river, the Long Walk makes a pleasant stroll which brings you to the **Spanish Arch,** the only surviving gateway to the old trading town. Built in 1584 as a defensive bastion for the port, this worn, one-story stone curve is revered by townspeople despite its unimpressive stature. The **Galway City Museum** (tel. 567641), in Tower House next to the arch, can show you up the stairs to the top of the arch. A knife-sharpener by a peat fire and some fishy statistics next to the one that didn't get away are the highlights of this small museum. Intriguing old photographs of the Claddagh line the walls. (Open May-Oct. daily 10am-1pm and 2:15-5:15pm; for opening times Nov.-April, check at the tourist office. Admission £1, students 50p.)

Across the river, the neighborhood called the **Claddagh** centers itself around Dominick St. Until the 1930s, this area was an independent, Irish-speaking, thatched-cottage fishing village. The cottages were long ago replaced by stone bungalows, but a bit of the small-town appeal and atmosphere still persists. The famous Claddagh rings, traditionally used as wedding bands, are mass-marketed but still remarkable examples of Celtic metalworking. The rings depict the thumb and forefingers of two hands holding up a crown-topped heart. The ring should be turned around upon marriage: once the point of the heart faces inward, the wearer's heart is attached and no longer available for viewing.

From the Claddagh, the waterfront road leads west to Salthill. The coast here alternates between pebbles and sand; when the ocean sunset turns red, its time for some serious beach frolicking. The *Corrib Princess* sails from Galway's Woodquay on a guided tour of Lough Corrib to the north (tel. 592447; June-Aug. daily 2:30pm and 4:30pm; 90min.; £5). Energetic types can hire a rowboat to visit the ruins of **Menlo Castle,** the burned-down seat of the Blake family.

ENTERTAINMENT

Culture crowds into Galway proper; music of all varieties barrages Salthill's clubs. *The Advertiser* and *Galway Guide* are free and provide listings of events. The **Galway Arts Centre,** 47 Dominick St. (tel. 565886), may be able to inform you (open Mon.-Sat. 10am-5:30pm). The center also hosts rotating art or photography exhibits and frequent workshops on dance, writing, and painting.

The **Druid Theatre Company,** Chapel Lane (tel. 568617), off Quay St., produces four Irish-themed plays each year (box office open Mon.-Sat. noon-6pm, until 8pm on show nights; ticket prices vary; buy tickets at least a week in advance). **The Punchbag Theatre,** Quay Lane. (tel. 565422), tops the Druids by staging five shows a year, both contemporary and traditional—but always Irish (box office open Mon.-Fri. noon-6pm; £8, students £6). For a pint with your play, try **Taylor's Pub,** Upper Dominick St. (£3.50, including lunch) or the **King's Head,** High St. (tel. 566630, 1-2pm; £2). The mostly Irish-language theater **an Taibhdhearc** (TIVE-yark), Middle St. (tel. 562024), has launched quite a few Irish actors into the limelight. Poetry readings and other artsy events share the space with full-blown plays. Some shows are bilingual, giving non-speakers a lyrical earful of Irish language and drama (box office open Mon.-Fri. 10am-6pm, Sat. 1-6pm; prices vary). Along different lines, the Omniplex 7-screen **cinema** (tel. 567800) shows the usual mainstream flicks 5 mi. from town on the Headford Rd.

Between 11pm and midnight, the pubs empty out in Galway proper. The tireless then decide to go dancing. The **nightclub** population is denser in Salthill, but Galway can satisfy the immobile. In the center of town, **Central Park,** 32 Upper Abbeygate St. (cover £4), and **GPO,** Eglinton St. (tel. 563073), both throw crowds into a tizzy. GPO reserves Friday nights for comedy and Sunday for Funky Jazz.

Groups will find a hackney service the best way to get to Salthill. The walk along the waterfront takes about 20-35 minutes, but is not recommended after dark. Salthill's biggest nights are Wednesday, Friday, and Saturday. Those who go on other nights will find the clubs more or less empty. All the clubs charge a £3-6 cover for a sweaty night inside dripping walls; those listed here all lie on Upper Salthill, the main road. A major hot spot, **C.J.'s,** 143 Upper Salthill (tel. 522563), rocks to pop. **The Castle** (tel. 255083) is famous (or infamous) for its raves (cover £4). **The Warwick** plays alternative or blues. The crowd and the music selection are both mixed at **The Oasis Club,** Kings Hill (tel. 22715; cover weekdays £2, weekends £3). Adventurous types head to **Vagabonds** for theme nights, including Irish-only bands, techno, and rave (cover £3.50). **Feet First** bounces to hip-hop on Wednesday nights at Vagabonds. Nightclubs all open between 10 and 11pm, but don't expect them to get going until 11:30pm. Either way, clubbers lose: they can enjoy the pubs and stand in line, or skip the pubs only to find the discos empty. The action stops early, at 2am in summer, 1:30am in winter.

Festivals knock at Galway's door at the rate of about one major event every month. At the **Galway Poetry and Literature Festival,** or the **Cúirt** (tel. 565886), the very highest of the nation's brows gather together in the last week of April. Past guests have included Nobel prize-winner and Caribbean poet Derek Walcott and reggae star Linton Johnston. For twelve crazed days in mid-July the **Galway Arts Festival** (tel. 583800)—the largest of its kind in Ireland—reels in famous trad musicians, rock groups, theater troupes, filmmakers, and comedians. The highlight of the Festival is a colorful and joyous **Macnas Parade.** The town is packed to overflowing for the festival, so be sure to reserve a bed. The same is true of the famous **Galway Races,** which commence at the end of July or beginning of August and last for one week. Those attending the races celebrate horses, money, and stout, not necessarily in that order (tel. 753870; tickets £2 at the gate).

■ Near Galway

COOLE PARK

W. B. Yeats's two best-known residences are about 20 mi. south of Galway near Gort, where N18 meets N66. One is now a ruin and national park, the other is restored to its condition when he lived there. One mile north of Gort on N18 (the Galway Rd.) and well before Ardrahan, **Coole Park** was Lady Augusta Gregory's estate. This friend and theatrical collaborator of Yeats welcomed him to her home many times. Lady Gregory supposedly planted a tree on the grounds every time she received a fee or royalty for her writing. In the picnic area, the famous great copper beech "autograph tree" bears the initials of some of Ireland's most important literary figures: George Bernard Shaw, W.B. Yeats, Sean O'Casey, John Masefield, and Douglas Hyde, Gaelic League founder and first president of Ireland. In Yeats's writing the estate represented the beautiful aristocratic order which the wars of the 1920s and the crass, materialistic industrialists were destroying: "ancestral trees/Or gardens rich in memory glorified/Marriages, alliances and families/And every bride's ambition satisfied." The house itself was ruined by the 1922 Civil War; only the foundations are now visible. The yew walk and garden, however, are preserved as part of a national forest and wildlife park.

Coole Park's **Visitors Centre** (tel. (091) 31804) is in the right place, but it eschews Yeats in favor of local rocks, trees, and furry wildlife. (Open mid-April to mid-June Tues.-Sun. 10am-5pm; mid-June to Aug. daily 9:30am-6:30pm; Sept. daily 10am-5pm. Last admission 45min. before closing. Admission £2, students £1.) A mile from the garden, **Coole Lake** spreads out (always open; free). Yeats watched nine-and-fifty swans here "all suddenly mount/And scatter wheeling in great broken rings/Upon their clamorous wings." They're still there, so Leda, beware!

THOOR BALLYLEE

In 1916, Yeats bought and renovated a 13th- and 14th-century tower, **Thoor Ballylee.** Three miles north of Coole Park a road turns off Galway Rd. and runs a mile down an unfrequented road to Thoor Ballylee. The poet lived there with his family off and on from 1922, but abandoned the tower permanently in 1928. While he was cloistered here writing "Meditations in Time of Civil War," Republican forces blew up the bridge by the tower. In Yeats's account, they "forbade us to leave the house, but were otherwise polite, even saying at last 'Good-night, thank you.'"

Yeats assumed that after his descendants moved out, Thoor Ballylee would "become a roofless ruin that the owl/May build in the cracked masonry and cry/Her desolation to the desolate sky." The **Visitors Centre** (tel. (091) 31436) that now exists there was never in the plans. A film on Yeats's life informs visitors. (Open Easter-Sept. 10am-6pm; admission £2.50, students £2.)

ARAN ISLANDS (OILEÁIN ÁRANN)

The three Aran Islands—Inishmore, Inishmaan and Inisheer—poke up out of Galway Bay 15 mi. southwest of Galway City. Visitors are bewildered by the stark limestone landscapes that drop straight into the sea, prehistoric and historic ruins, and people whose traditions have attracted tremendous attention. Dublin-born writer John Millington Synge met with Yeats in 1894 looking for some creative criticism. Yeats told him to go to the Arans, learn Irish, and write plays about the islanders. Synge did, and became instantly famous (see **Literature: 1880-1939,** p. 73). Robert Flaherty's groundbreaking film *Man of Aran* (1934) added to the islands' fame. All this fame and the islands' reputation for harboring traditional ways of life have stimulated a somewhat mercenary tourist industry.

The flocks of high-season visitors to the Arans give residents of really isolated islands (like Inishbofin and Cape Clear) the willies. During July and August, throngs of curious foreigners surround every monument and pub on Inishmore. Luckily, the empty spaces between the sites (those not accessible by mini-bus) are still deserted. Tourists are rarer on the two smaller islands than on Inishmore. The scenery remains awe-inspiring, regardless of the number of people who see it. The lifestyle also remains traditional—locals still make *curraghs* (small boats made from curved wicker rods tied with string and covered with cowskin and black tar). Some of them retain local styles of dress, footwear, and fishing, and many speak Irish.

If ferries in Galway gave you a headache, here they're twice the trouble. Double-check with fishermen to find out where and when the boats are coming. The **phone code** for all three islands is a craggy 099.

GETTING THERE

Two ferry companies—Island Ferries and O'Brien Shipping/Doolin Ferries—operate boats to the Aran Islands. They reach the islands from three points of departure: Galway (1½hr. to Inishmore), Rassaveal (several miles west of Galway; ½hr. to Inishmore), and Doolin (½hr. to Inisheer). The majority of ferries float to Inishmore, the largest island. Fewer boats dock at Inisheer, the smallest, and the hardest to reach is Inishmaan, the middle one. There is no charge to bring **bicycles** on board.

If the ferry leaves from Rossaveal, the company making the trip will provide a shuttle bus from Galway City to Rossaveal, usually for £3. The hitch is difficult. On the other hand, a boat departing from Rossaveal will always wait at the Rossaveal pier, if necessary, for its own company's bus from Galway to arrive. The closest hostels to Rossaveal are in Inverin and Spiddal (see **Galway City to Clifden** p. 305), but unless you have transport, it's easiest to stay in Galway.

Ferries serving Inishmore are reliable (always leaving daily) and generally on time. Even in the summer, ferries to the smaller islands are less certain. And if they are running, they're liable to leave either port early or late. Don't get stuck the day before your flight for Vermont leaves. The best idea is to formulate firm travel plans and take them to the ferry companies in Galway on a comparison-shopping spree.

Island Ferries (tel. (091) 561767, after hours (091) 72273), is based in the Galway Tourist Office. The *Aran Sea Bird* serves all three islands year-round from Rossaveal. A bus connects Galway with the ferry port (£3 return; departs 1½hr. before sailing time). Ferries leave from Rossaveal for Inishmore (35min.; £15 return, students £12) and to Inishmaan or Inisheer (£18 return, students £16). The *Sea Sprinter* connects Inishmore with Inisheer via Inishmaan (£8 return per island). They also offer a package for students, which includes the bus from Galway, return ferry to Inishmore, one night's accommodation at the Mainistir House Hostel, and continental breakfast (£19).

O'Brien Shipping/Doolin Ferries (tel. (091) 567672 from Galway, (065) 74455 in Doolin, after hours (065) 71710. Year-round service connects Doolin and Galway to the Aran Islands. Galway to any island (return £18, students £15, single £12.50). Doolin to Inishmore (single £10, return £20), to Inishmaan (single £9, return £18), to Inisheer (single £7.50, return £15). Galway-Aran-Doolin (£25, students £20), same price in the other direction, includes inter-island travel.

Aer Árann (tel. (091) 93034), located 19mi. west of Galway at Inverin, flies to the Arans. Reservations are accepted over the phone or in person at the Galway Tourist Office. (All year 4/day; 6min. to Inishmore, serves all three islands; £18, students £15; £35 return, students £29.)

▓ Inishmore (Inis Mór)

Inishmore (pop. 900) is the largest and northernmost of the Aran Islands. Crowds disembark at Kilronan, spread out to lose themselves amid the stone walls and stark

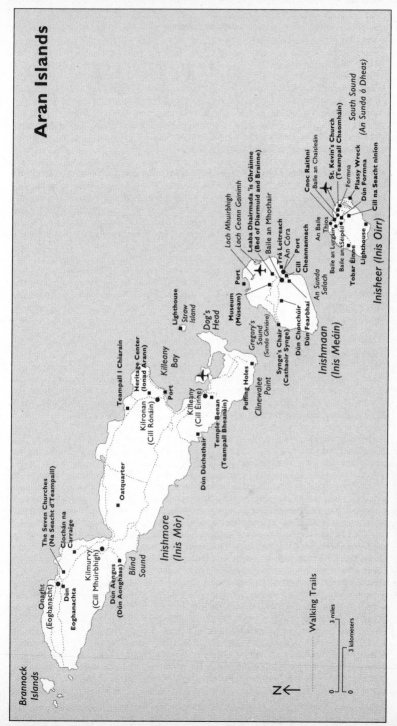

Aran Islands

Brannock Islands

Onaght (Eoghanacht)
The Seven Churches (Na Seacht dTeampaill)
Clochán na Carraige
Dún Eoghanachta
Kilmurvy (Cill Mhuirbhigh)
Dún Aengus (Dún Aonghasa)
Blind Sound

Oatquarter

Inishmore (Inis Mór)

Teampall Chiaráin
Heritage Center (Ionad Árann)
Kilronan (Cill Rónáin)
Killeany Port
Killeany Bay
Dún Dúchathair
Temple Benan (Teampall Bheanáin)
Killeany (Cill Éinne)
Puffing Holes
Clinewalee Point
Dog's Head
Straw Island
Lighthouse

Museum (Museam)
Port

Loch Mhuirbhigh
Loch Ceann Gainimh
Leaba Dhiarmada 'is Ghráinne (Bed of Diarmuid and Gráinne)
Baile an Mhothair

Trá Leitreach
An Córa
Cill Port
Cheannannach

Gregory's Sound (Súnda Ghríora)
Synge's Chair (Cathaoir Synge)
Dún Chonchúir
Dún Fearbhaí
An Sunda Salach

Inishmaan (Inis Medin)

Cnoc Raithni
St. Kevin's Church (Teampall Chaomháin)
Plassy Wreck
Dún Formna
Formna
Cill na Seacht nínion
An Baile Thíos
Baile an Lurgáin
Baile an tSéipéil
Tobar Éinne
Lighthouse

Inisheer (Inis Oirr)

South Sound (An Sunda ó Dheas)

Baile an Chaisleáin

.... Walking Trails

0   3 miles
0   3 kilometers

N

> ### Leaping sheep!
> Many of the stone walls which enclose the fields on the Aran islands have no gates. Farmers must knock down part of the wall to let the animals in or out, and then restack the stones. Their only other alternative would be to train the sheep in the high jump (a future Olympic exhibition event?).

cliffs, and then coalesce again around any major sight. Minivans and "pony traps" traverse the island incessantly, begging anyone on foot to climb aboard and pay up. The landscape resembles that of the Burren in Co. Clare. Dozens of ruins, forts, churches, and "minor sites" (holy wells and kelp kilns) inhabit the island. Exactly 437 kinds of wildflowers rise from the stony terrain.

Practical Information Ferries land in Kilronan (*Cill Rónáin*), where you couldn't possibly get lost. The **tourist office** (tel. 61263) changes money, holds bags during the day (75p), and sells Tim Robinson's meticulous and invaluable map (£3; open May to mid-Sept. daily 10am-7pm). Bikes are great for exploring island paths and can be rented at **Mullen's Aran Bicycle Hire** (tel. 61132; £5/day, £21/week; deposit £5; open March-Nov. daily 9am-8pm). **B&N Bicycle Hire** (tel. 61402) at the base of the Ti Joe Mac Bar/Hostel also rents bikes (£5/day, £20/week; deposit £5; open daily March-Oct. 9am-7pm., Nov.-Feb. 9am-5pm). Strangely enough, bike theft here is a problem: lock it up, hide it, or don't ever leave it. The **Minibuses** roaming the island can be flagged down for a ride (£5 return to Dún Aengus). The buses also organize two-hour tours of the island for about £5. The **post office** (tel. 61101; bureau de change; open Tues.-Sat. 9am-5pm, Mon. 9am-1pm) is up the hill from the pier, past the Spar Market.

Accommodations It's not a bad idea to spend the day on Inishmore and the night in one of the less crowded hostels on the other islands. **Mainistir House (IHH)** (tel. 61169) offers decent hostel accommodations just ½ mi. from Kilronan (from the pier, go uphill and turn right after the supermarket). If staying on the island, it's wise to book in advance. Mainistir deserves its excellent reputation for huge "vaguely vegetarian" dinners (£7), and the common room is a comfortable space to settle after dinner. The rooms are packed, especially during summer. (Dorm £8 w/morning porridge, scones, tea/coffee; single £11.50; double £20. Laundry £4. Bikes £5.) **Dún Aengus Hostel** (tel. 61318), is more personable, but hides 4 mi. west in Kilmurvey, a 10-minute walk from Dún Aengus. (July-Aug. £6/person, Apr.-June and Sept.-Oct. £5; shuttle service included. Laundry £3.)

Bed down in style at Mrs. G. Tierney's ivy-covered **St. Brendan's House** (tel. 61149), across the street from the ocean (April-Oct. £13/person, £11 w/continental breakfast; Nov.-March £10 and £8; tea/coffee facilities in rooms). Three miles west of Kilronan, **Mrs. B. Conneely's Beach View House** (tel. 61141) lives up to its name and more. It also offers views of Dún Aengus and framed versions of the Alps (single £18, double £26; open May-Sept.). **Johnston Hernon's Kilmurvey House** (tel. 61218) offers ready access to Kilmurvey Beach, near Dún Aengus (single £24, w/bath £28; double £27, w/bath £35; open April-Sept.).

Food, Pubs, & Entertainment Spar Market (tel. 61203), past the hostel in Kilronan, seems to be the island's social center (open Mon.-Sat. 9am-8pm, Sun. 10am-6pm). Restaurants tend to be expensive and aren't open in winter. You may want to stick to tea houses, which serve homemade soups and snacks. **Bay View House** (tel. 61260) caters to every budget (open Feb.-Nov.; coffee shop daily 9am-6pm, restaurant daily 6-9pm). **An Seán Chéibh** (tel. 61228), an embellished chippy with outdoor seating, is a short walk left from the harbor (fresh Aran fish £2.90). (Open June-Sept. Mon.-Thurs. 9am-11pm, Fri.-Sun. 9am-1am; March-April and Oct. daily 9am-5pm; May daily 9am-9pm.) Pubs are a way of life here. **Joe Watt's Bar,** east of the harbor on the main road, offers food, music, and conversation to accompany thick pints. The

American Bar (tel. 61303) attracts younger islanders and droves of tourists (music most nights in summer). Traditional musicians occasionally strum on the terrace at **Tí Joe Mac** (tel. 61248). On Friday, Saturday, and Sunday nights in summer, the first steps of a *céilí* begin at midnight at the **dance hall** (cover £3). *Man of Aran* is shown here (summer 3/day; £3).

Sights The sights are crowded while the paths between them are desolate and unmarked (most people travel by minibus; cycling is more fun). The tourist office's £3 maps correspond to yellow arrows that mark the trails, but markings are frustratingly infrequent and can vanish in fog. The trails themselves seem to disappear at times. Anyone exploring the island on foot should bring a compass. The £1.50 brochure called *Inis Mór* is helpful.

The island's most impressive (and best known) monument, dating from the first century BC, is magnificent **Dún Aengus** *(Dún Aonghasa)*, 4 mi. west of the pier at Kilronan. The fort's walls are 18 ft. thick and form a semi-circle around the sheer drop at Inishmore's northwest corner. One of the better-preserved prehistoric forts in Europe, Dún Aengus commands a thought-provoking view of miles of ocean from its hill. Many have been fooled by an imaginary island that appears on the horizon. The vision was so realistic that it appeared on maps until the 20th century. Down the side of the cliff, **Worm Hole** is a saltwater lake filled from the limestone aquifer below the ground. The bases of the surrounding cliffs have been hollowed by mighty waves to look like pirate caves. Two roads lead to the fort from Kilronan, one inland and a more quiet one along the coast. On the way to the fort past **Kilmurvey** *(Cill Mhuirbhigh)*, **The Seven Churches** lie 3 mi. west of Kilronan. These scattered groupings of religious remains stimulate speculation about the island's former inhabitants. The island's best **beach** lies flat at Kilmurvey.

In Kilronan, the new **Aran Islands Heritage Centre** *(Ionad Árann;* tel. 61355) caters to inquisitive tourists who walk uphill from the pier. *Curraghs,* soil and wildlife exhibits, old Aran clothes, and a cliff rescue cart constitute this local effort. (Open April-Oct. daily 10am-7pm; £2, students £1.50.) The **Black Fort** *(Dún Dúchathair)*, 1 mi. south of Kilronan over eerie terrain, is even larger than Dún Aengus and about 1000 years older.

■ Inishmaan (Inis Meáin)

Inishmaan (pop. 300) is where Synge set *Riders to the Sea,* but the island is better known for it's gloomy solitude. The seagulls plead with you to stay a little longer on the cliffs—they seem to need the company. Goats stand on stone walls looking for signs of life in the nearby fields of limestone. For those who find beauty in solitude, a walk along the rocky clifftop is bliss.

At the pier, **An Cora,** a small coffeeshop inside an old Irish cottage, dispenses food and **tourist information** all on one plate (tel. 73010; open Easter-Sept. daily 9am-6pm). The island's tiny village spreads out along the road west of the pier to divide the island in half. B&B and victuals can be had at **Tig Congaile** (tel. 73085), the first house on the right walking uphill from the pier (£12/person). The restaurant concentrates on perfecting seafood (lunch under £5, dinner from £6, soup £1.20; open June-Sept. daily 9am-9pm). A self-catering cottage is available for £150 per week. **Mrs. Faherty** (signs from the pier show the way) also runs a cheerful B&B and fills you up with an enormous dinner (tel. 73012; single £13, double £22; open mid-March to Nov.). A **post office** (tel. 73001), public phone, and **shop** (tel. 73002, open Mon.-Sat. 9am-8pm) constitute the majority of the village. The center of life on the island, Padraig O'Conghaile's thatched **pub,** serves pub grub all day.

The *Inishmaan Way* brochure (£1.50 in Galway or Inishmore tourist office) describes a 5-mi. walking route covering all the island's sights. One mile north of the pier is Inishmaan's safest and most inviting beach, **Trá Leitreach.** It's by no means an easy walk, but a visit to **Synge's Chair** pays off with a view of splashing waves and a unique path system. **Dún Chonchúir,** a 7th-century fort, looks over the entire island.

Near the village of **Baile an Mhothair,** 8th-century **Cill Cheannannach** left its remains on the shore. Islanders were buried here for ages under simple stone slabs, until the mid-20th century. Halfway across the island on the main road hunches what's left of **Synge's cottage,** where the Anglo-Irish author wrote much of his Aran-inspired work, from 1898-1902. A small **museum** in the Knitwear factory (tel. 63009) records island history (in Irish) near Dún Chonchúir. Ferries to the mainland visit the middle island sporadically, which makes getting on and—more importantly—off the island a questionable affair.

■ Inisheer (Inis Oírr)

Someone has described the Arans as "quietness without loneliness," but Inishmore isn't always quiet and Inishmaan can get lonely. Only Inisheer (pop. 300) fulfills the promise of the famous phrase. This smallest (and most commercialized) island is fewer than 2 mi. across in either direction. Islanders and stray donkeys seem to be present in even proportions on this island of labyrinthine stone walls.

Tourist information is cheerfully offered up in English or Irish at the red-gated office near the main pier (tel. 75008; open mid-June to Sept. daily 10am-6pm). Roth-air Inis Oírr (tel. 75033) rents **bikes** of all colors (£5/day, £25/week). See the island from a different perspective with a pony cart **island tour** (tel. 75092). A **post office** resides farther up the island in a white house with green trim (tel. 75001; open Mon.-Fri. 9am-1pm and 2-5:30pm, Sat. 9am-1pm).

The best of the Aran Island hostels is found on Inisheer. The **Brú Hostel (IHH)** (tel. 75024), visible from the pier, is clean and spacious. Upper-level rooms have skylights for stargazing. The hostel organizes *curragh* trips. Call ahead in July and August. (4- to 6-bed dorm £6; private room £8, w/bath £9.50. Irish breakfast £3, continental breakfast £1.50. Sheets 75p, laundry £2.) **Rory's Hostel** (tel. 75077) is a tiny eight-bed stone cottage behind the post office (£5). **Sharry's** (tel. 75024), a well priced B&B, is found behind the Brú Hostel (£12/person). The **Ionad Campála Campground** (tel. 75008) stretches its tarps near the beach for camping aficionados who don't mind chill winds off the ocean (£2/tent, £10/week; showers 50p; open May-Sept.). A list of Inisheer's 17 B&Bs (a lot of B&Bs for one small island) hangs on the window of the small **tourist office** next to the pier.

Marb Gan é (tel. 75049), serves coffee and treats by the pier (homemade soup with brown bread £1.30; open June-Sept. daily 10am-6pm) and even offers B&B (£12/person). **Sharry's Restaurant** (tel. 75024), next door to the Brú Hostel, cooks hearty goodies (full Irish breakfast £3.50, prawn cocktails £2; open June-Sept. daily 8:30am-9pm). **Tigh Ned's** pub lies next to the Brú Hostel and caters to a younger crowd, while the pub at the **Ostan Hotel** (tel. 75020), just up from the pier, is exceptionally crowded, dark, and mellow (roast of the day w/vegetables and potatoes £5, grub served 11am-9:30pm). **Tigh Ruairí** (tel. 75002) is another pub/shop just up the road (shop open July-Aug. daily 9am-8:30pm; Sept.-June Mon.-Sat. 9am-7:30pm, Sun. 10:45am-12:30pm).

The **Inis Oírr Way** covers the island's major attractions in 6½ mi. The first stop is in town at **Cnoc Raithní,** a bronze-age tumulus (stone burial mound) 2000 years older than Christianity. Walking along the An Trá shore leads to the romantic overgrown graveyard of **St. Kevin's Church** *(Teampall Chaomháin).* This St. Kevin, patron saint of the island, was believed to be a brother of St. Kevin of Glendalough. Each year on June 14, islanders hold Mass in the church's ruins in memory of St. Kevin. His grave nearby is said to have great healing powers. Below the church, a pristine sandy beach stretches back to the edge of town. Farther east along the beach, a grassy track leads to **An Loch Mór,** a 16-acre inland lake where wildfowl prevail. Above the lake is the stone ring-fort **Dún Formna.** Continuing past the lake and back onto the seashore is the *Plassy* **wreck,** a ship which sank offshore in 1960 and washed up on Inisheer. From the wreck, look for the Inisheer lighthouse, then head north. The walk back to the center leads through **Formna Village** with its typical Aran old thatched houses, and on out to **Cill na Seacht nInion,** a small monastery with a stone fort. The remains

LOUGH CORRIB ■ 301

of the 14th-century **O'Brien castle,** which Cromwell razed in 1652, sit atop a nearby knoll. On the west side of the island **Tobar Einne,** the Holy Well of patron St. Enda, supposedly has healing powers.

LOUGH CORRIB

Three hundred and sixty-five islands dot Lough Corrib, one for each day of the year. The eastern shores of Lough Corrib and Lough Mask stretch quietly into fertile farmland. The western shores slip into bog, quartzite scree, and the famously rough country in Connemara. The island of Inchagoill, right in the middle of the lough, is the location of the second-oldest existing Christian monuments.

■ Oughterard

Tourists seldom stop here, which adds to the town's appeal. While everyone else hurries to Clifden and the sea, you can stop to sample the lake and islands as an appetizer. Oughterard is attached to Lough Corrib's western flank at the base of the northwesterly Maam Turk Mountains, on N59 between Galway and Clifden.

An independent **tourist office** (tel. 82808) helps out on Main St. (open May-Aug. Mon.-Sat. 9am-7pm, Sun. 10am-2pm; Sept.-April Mon.-Fri. 9am-5pm). The **Bank of Ireland,** Main St. (tel. 82123), holds the only **ATM** between Clifden and Galway (open Mon.-Wed. and Fri. 10am-4pm, Thurs. 10am-5pm). **Bus Éireann** coaches from Galway to Clifden stop in Oughterard (4-6/day, Sun. 2/day; Sept.-June 1/day; ¾hr. to Galway, 2hr. to Clifden). **Hitchhikers** report easy going, at least in summer, between Galway and anywhere west or northwest. **Keogh's Launderette** (tel. 82542), just a few steps from the bank, can help you clean up your act (open Mon.-Sat. 9am-1pm and 2-6pm). **Frances Geoghegan's Pharmacy,** Main St. (tel. 82348), is open Mon.-Tues. and Thurs.-Sat. 9:30am-1:45pm and 2:15-6pm, Wed. 9:30am-1pm. The **post office** (tel. 82201) sends letters from Main St. (open Mon.-Fri. 9am-1pm and 2-5:30pm, Sat. 9am-1pm). 'Scuse me Maam, but the **phone code** is 091.

Accommodations Cranrawer House, Station Rd. (tel. 82388), a 15-minute walk from town, is a newly built, friendly hostel in a quiet spot. (May-Sept. 8- to 10-bed dorm £7.50, 5-bed dorm w/bath £8.50, private room w/bath £9/person. Oct.-April £6.50, £7.50, £8.50 respectively. Camping £5/person. Continental breakfast £2. Laundry £3.50. Key deposit £5. Rowboats £14/day.) **Lough Corrib Hostel (IHH)** (tel. 82866), is found on Camp St. Hostelers enjoy conversations with the funny owner about anything from the sticky fur of koalas to long-neck lamps. (Dorm £5.50. Private room £8. **Camping** £3. Sheets £1. **Bikes** £6, £5 for hostelers. Boat trips to Inchagoill £6; 4 person minimum. Canoe rental £5.50. Fishing rods £3. Open April-Nov.) The **Western Way,** Camp St. (tel. 82475), lets saddle-sore pilgrims hit the hay (single £14, double £25). **Cregg Lodge B&B,** Station Rd. (tel. (095) 82493), knows how to lodge (£14/person, w/bath £16/person; open April-Sept.).

Food & Pubs The selection of eateries covers all tastes. **Corrib County,** Main St. (tel. 82678), serves all three meals, though lunch is most affordable (tuna sandwich £2.60; open April-Oct. daily 8:30am-10pm). Good pub grub, nightly traditional music, and brilliant *craic* hover around the boat hull bar at **The Boat Inn,** the Square (tel. 82196; music nightly in summer, weekends in winter; Irish stew £5; food served 10:30am-10pm). **Power's Bar** (tel. 82712), a few doors down, is a local favorite (music Thurs.-Sun., disco Sat.). **The Angler's Rest,** Main St. (tel. 82203), exudes the grimy, groovy atmosphere of pubbing past. **Keogh's Grocery,** the Square (tel. 82583), sells food, fishing tackle, and hardware. (Open winter Mon.-Sat. 8am-10pm; summer Mon.-Sat. 8am-8pm, Sun. 9am-9pm.) Adjoining **Keogh's Bar** (tel. 82222) encourages people to eat, drink, and be merry (bacon and vegetables £3.50; music Tues.-Sun. nights in summer, Fri.-Sun. off-season).

Sights One mile south of town, a turnoff from N59 leads to 16th-century **Aughnanure Castle** (tel. 82214), where a river red with peat curves around a three-room fortified tower. The secret chamber, feasting hall, and murder hole are highlights of the high-quality tour. The view from the castle roof is tremendous; the key can be borrowed from the ticket booth. (Open mid-June to mid-Sept. daily 9:30am-6:30pm. Admission £2, students £1.) Glann Rd. covers the 9 mi. from Oughterard to the infamous **Hill of Doon,** where the pre-Celtic Glann people annually sacrificed a virgin. The practice supposedly continued in secret until the Middle Ages. The **Western Way Walk** (16mi.) begins where Glann Rd. ends and passes along the lake shore to Maam, at the base of the Maam Turk Mt. range.

Irish contemporary art is on display in town at Peter Conneely's avant-garde **West Shore Gallery** (tel. 82562; open Mon.-Sat. 10am-6pm, 6 exhibits/yr.) In June, Oughterard hosts the **Currach Racing Championships.** Competitors from all over Ireland assemble. Anglers worldwide know of Lough Corrib and the Mayfly bait that miraculously arises from it. The EU designated the lake a "salmonid," meaning that it should be preserved as a special trout and salmon lake. Greg Forde (tel. 82678) can rent you a **fishing boat** (about £25/day). The **Fuschia Craft Shop** (tel. 82644) offers Lough Corrib cruises to Cong (2/day; £10 return, including 1hr. stop on Inchagoill Island) and Inchagoill Island (July-Aug. 2/day; £6 return). Bikes are £3 on either trip.

■ Cong

Cong (pop. 300), Co. Mayo, is a romantic and beautiful town with immediate access to islands in the loughs on either side of it. Opulent Ashford Castle, where the Guinness clan once lived, stands firmly in Cong. Oscar Wilde made fun of it and Ronald Reagan and Jason Priestley slept in it; regardless, it's impressive. John Wayne and Maureen O'Hara shot *The Quiet Man* here in 1951. Obsessed moviegoers come here and quote the whole film. Cong was designated by legend as the site of the First Battle of Moytura between the pre-human Fir Bolg and the god-like Túatha de Danann. Be that as it may, this king of a town holds caves, graves, an abbey, and a unusually dry canal (see **Water, Water, Everywhere...,** p. 304).

PRACTICAL INFORMATION

The town's privately established **tourist office,** Abbey St. (tel. 46542), will point you toward Cong's wonders, listed in the free *Get to Know Cong* (open mid-June to Oct. daily 10am-6pm). *Cong: Walks, Sights, Stories* (£2.50), available from the town's hostels, describes good hiking and biking routes. **Buses** leave for Westport, Ballina (Mon.-Sat. 2/day), Clifden (Mon.-Sat. 1/day), and Galway (Mon.-Sat. 1-2/day) from outside Ryan's Hotel. **O'Connor's Garage,** Main St. (tel. 46008), is the friendliest renter of Raleigh **bikes** (£7/day, £30/week; students £5/day, £30/week; deposit ID. Open daily 9am-9pm.) The **post office** (tel. 46001) is on Main St. (open Mon.-Sat. 9am-1pm and 2-5:30pm). John Wayne starred in *Phone Code: 092.*

ACCOMMODATIONS, FOOD, & PUBS

Both the **Quiet Man Hostel** and the **Cong Hostel,** owned by the same helpful family, are perfect if you're in the mood for a bit of company. Both hostels offer a laundry service that picks up, washes, dries, and folds for £4. Other bonuses include free fishing rods (deposit £20), returnable guidebooks (deposit £2.50), guided tours of *The Quiet Man* locations (£2.50), and free screenings of the film *Un Taxi Mauve,* also made near Cong. No one will stop you from **camping** on Inchagoill Island.

Quiet Man Hostel (IHH), Abbey St. (tel. 46511), across the street from Cong Abbey. Spacious and central. Shows *The Quiet Man* nightly and names its rooms after the movie's characters. Dorm £6. Bike rental £6. Open April-Sept.

Cong Hostel (IHH) (tel. 46089), 1mi. down the Galway Rd. Clean and comfortable. All rooms have skylights. Screening room for nightly *The Quiet Man* showings. Playground, picnic area, and games room. Dorm £6. Double £16. Continental breakfast £2.50, full Irish breakfast £4. Bikes £6. Rowboats £6/2hr., £15/day. **Camping** £3 (separate facilities).

Courtyard Hostel (IHH) (tel. 46203), several miles east of Cong, in Cross. Clean and fresh hostel will show you peace of mind off the beaten track. Dorm £5.50. Private room £6.50. Bikes £5/day. **Camping** £3.

White House B&B, Abbey St. (tel. 46358), across the street from Danagher's Hotel. Smothered in geraniums and ivy. TV and coffee-making facilities in every room. £16/person, off-season £15.

Just across the street from the White House B&B, locals down mammoth meals (roast lamb, vegetables, and potatoes £6) and countless pints at **Danagher's Hotel and Restaurant** (tel. 46494). The most brilliant *craic* in the region occurs here, and youth from the nearby countryside come in for the weekend discos. **The Quiet Man Coffee Shop,** Main St. (tel. 46034), is obsessed with Hollywood. (Soup and sandwich £2.60, milkshake £1.50. Open Easter-Sept. daily 10am-6pm.) Cooks can go crazy at **O'Connor's Supermarket** on Main St. (open daily 9am-9pm).

SIGHTS

From 1852 to 1939, the heirs to the Guinness fortune (later Lord and Lady Ardilaun) lived in **Ashford Castle,** a structure as impressive as the lake on which it sits. Big-deal diplomatic visitors stay in the Castle, now a hotel. *The Quiet Man* was shot on the castle grounds. Oscar Wilde once informed Lady Ardilaun that she could improve her gardens by planting petunias in the shape of a pig. Though lacking such clever designs, the grounds do hold exotic floral delights. A pleasant walk from the castle along Lough Corrib leads to a stone monument, bearing Lady Ardilaun's message to her lost Lord: "Nothing remains for me/What shall remain, is nothing." The castle-hotel is closed to visitors, but you can see the gardens for £3.

A sculpted head of its last abbot keeps watch over the ruins of the 12th-century **Royal Abbey of Cong,** located near Danagher's Hotel in the village (always open; free). The last High King of a united Ireland, Ruairi ("Rory") O'Connor, retired to the abbey for his final 15 years after repeatedly leading Gaelic armies in futile battles against Norman troops. Ironically, centuries later, it was General Rory O'Connor who disunited the 26 counties and sparked the Irish Civil War by seizing the Four Courts in Dublin in 1922. Across the abbey grounds, a footbridge spans the River Cong. Continuing to the left past the **Monk's Fishing House,** the footpath takes you to **caves,** called Pigeon Hole, Teach Aille, and Ballymaglancy Cave, and to a 4000-year-old burial chamber, **Giant's Grave.** (Both hostels have detailed cave maps you can borrow.) Spelunkers have free access to caves, but Kelly's Cave is locked (the key is held at the Quiet Man Coffee Shop). Spelunking safety requires a friend who knows when to expect you back, two flashlights, and waterproof gear.

■ Near Cong: Inchagoill

Inchagoill (INCH-a-gill), a forested island in the middle of Lough Corrib, has been uninhabited since the 1950s. A deserted monastery and two churches, about which very little is known, stand quietly. The two churches hide down the right-hand path from the pier. **St. Patrick's Church,** built in the 5th century, is now only a pile of crumbling stone. The name Inchagoill means "Island of the Foreigners," which suggests that Christians in Ireland were still "foreigners" when the monastery was built. The famous **Stone of Lugna,** supposedly the tombstone of St. Patrick's nephew and navigator, stands 3-ft. high among the stones surrounding the church. The inscription on the stone reads *LIE LUGUAEDON MACCI MENUEH,* or "stone of Luguaedon the

> ### Water, Water Everywhere, and This Canal Did Drink
>
> Clonbur, where **Mount Gable** rises up above the flatness, was the site of a 19th-century engineering disaster. The **Dry Canal** is a deep, empty, 4 mi. groove in the earth just east of Cong off the Galway Rd., near the Cong Hostel and clearly signposted. Locks punctuate the useless canal just as if water were flowing through it. While there is water aplenty in Ireland, not even the leprechauns could make it stay in the ground around Cong, which is composed of porous limestone. The canal-opening ceremony in the 1840s was a surprising failure, as water that was let into the canal from Lough Mask promptly vanished into the absorbent walls. The canal could have been sealed and made useful, but by the 1850s trains had already replaced canals as the most efficient means of commercial transport, leaving the canal as hapless as its engineers.

son of Menueh." The stone is almost certainly the second-oldest inscribed Christian monument in Europe (the oldest are the catacombs of Rome; see *Let's Go: Rome, 1997*). The **Church of the Saint** dates back to the 12th century. Its archway is lined with carved heads. Inchagoill's only current full-time residents are a colony of **wild rats.** They're civilized and proper (i.e. invisible) during the day, but can be surly at night. Would-be campers should take these furry fellows into consideration. **Ed Hickey** at Lough Corrib Hostel in Oughterard can take you out to Inchagoill or bring you back "anytime" (£6 return, 4 person minimum). The *Corrib Queen* (tel. (092) 46029) sails daily from Lisloughrea Quay, on the Quay Rd. in Cong. (June-Aug. 4/day; 1½hr.; £8 return includes a brief, but enlightening tour of the island.)

CONNEMARA

A lacy net of inlets and islands along the coast and a rough gang of inland mountains (with some bogs in between) make up rugged Connemara, the thinly populated western arm of Co. Galway. The land has little agricultural value and was therefore of little interest to Ireland's English occupiers. The Irish subsistence farmers who did settle the land were devastated by the Famine. Connemara may not be the place for farming, but it is ideal for camping, since the coast is dotted with small beaches and almost all of the offshore islands are accessible. Ireland's largest *gaeltacht* stretches along the south Connemara coast, west from Galway City to Carna. The Republic's steps to preserve the use of the Irish language have met with varied results. Corporate development incentives, designed to pump money in and prevent poverty-stricken natives from leaving the *gaeltacht,* have tended only to fill target towns with immigrating English-speaking technicians. Connemara-based Irish-language radio, *Radio na Gaeltachta,* however, has successfully fostered an interest in the language.

As with much of the western coast, the most rewarding way to absorb Connemara is on bike. Consider renting in Galway, then cycling northwest to Clifden via Lough Corrib and Cong, though the roads get a bit difficult toward the end of the ride. A public bus runs from Galway to Clifden via Cong. The three-hour ride passes through the most miraculous parts of Connemara. N59 from Galway to Clifden is the main thoroughfare; R336, R340, and R341 are more elaborate coastal loop roads. Hitchers report that friendly locals can give the best tours.

Buses serve southern Connemara from Galway many times per day (summer up to 8/day) and less often serve northern Connemara (Mon.-Sat. 1/day). **Lally's Coaches** (tel. (091) 562905) gives tours of Connemara that leave from the tourist office in Galway at 10am (return 5:30pm; £10, students £9). **Western Heritage** (tel. (091) 521699) offers a number of different sightseeing tours to Connemara, the Burren, the Cliffs of Moher, and Lough Corrib. Tours take a full- or half-day (£8-10, students £7-9). **Michael Nee** (tel. (091) 51082) runs a private bus service to Clifden and Cleggan, connecting with the 2pm ferry to Inishbofin (operates June-Sept.; £5, £7 return). **Bus Éireann** (tel. (091) 562000) conducts a day tour of Connemara that departs Galway

Railway Station at 9:45am (late June to Sept.; £6). **O'Neachtain's** does full- or half-day guided tours of Connemara (tel. (091) 83188). Tourist offices can give more info on specific tours.

GALWAY CITY TO CLIFDEN

There are two ways to get to Clifden from Galway. The inland route, which passes through Oughterard, Maam Cross, and Recess, is faster unless you stop to take in the misty, mountainous scenery which has even the sheep transfixed in the middle of the road (don't hit the silly, wee beasts). The coastal route weaves in and out of numerous peninsulas and along stretches of beach.

As the landscape gets starker, so do the hostels. **Connemara Tourist Hostel,** Aille, Inverin (tel. (091) 593104), lies 2 mi. west of Spiddal. It's relaxing 'cause hey, there's nothing to do here anyway! (£5.50; midnight curfew). The **Indreabhán Youth Hostel (An Óige/HI)** (tel. (091) 593154) is 5 mi. farther from Spiddal. While the people couldn't be friendlier, the hostel has seen better days (June-Sept. £6.50; Oct.-May £5.50; sheets 75p). The coastal bus from Galway stops at both hostels.

Those continuing along the coast to **Gortmore** and the northern peninsula should make the detour to **Rosmuck,** a small peninsula that juts into Kilkieran Bay. The **cottage of Padraig Pearse** (tel. (091) 574292) squats in a small hillock overlooking the northern mountains. Pearse and his brother spent their summers here learning Irish and dreaming of an Irish Republic. The Republic-come-true declared the cottage a national monument. (Open late May to early Oct. daily 9:30am-1:30pm and 2:30-6:30pm. Admission £1, students 40p.)

The roads and beaches south of Clifden offer opportunity for hours of wandering. Seven miles south along R341, **Ballyconneely** sits on an isthmus near the wonderfully sandy **Coral Strand. Roundstone,** a quiet holiday resort 8 mi. southeast of Ballyconneely, is home to **Roundstone Musical Instruments** (tel. (095) 35808). They are the only full-time *bodhrán* (BOUR-ohn) makers in the world (see **Traditional Music,** p. 77). (Open daily 8am-7pm; Sept.-Feb. Mon.-Fri. 8am-7pm.) Where there are musical instruments, there is music, and if you spend the night, **An galún Taoscta** is where you're likely to find it (trad Wed. nights, session during lunch on Sun.) Afterwards, bang your *bodhrán* in the direction of **Wits End B&B** (tel. (095) 35951; £15/person w/bath).

■ Clifden (An Clochán)

As the region's only community approaching town status, Clifden has become a miniature Killarney: five hostels, tons of tourbuses, and countless bureaux de change are bound to take their toll on any community. In summer you're almost certain to hear more German than English or Irish. The past half-decade has seen Clifden's nightlife rocket from nonexistent to famous. People who would never have left Galway years ago now come here for *craic.* Waterfront buildings provide a scenic backdrop to Clifden Bay, and where the buildings end, the beach begins. Clifden's size, geography, and general cheerfulness makes it the best base from which to explore Connemara. N59 makes a U-turn at Clifden. Most traffic is from Galway, two hours southeast, but the road does continue northeast to Letterfrack and Connemara National Park. Hitchers usually wait at the Esso station on N59.

PRACTICAL INFORMATION

Tourist Office: Market St. (tel. 21163). Open May and Sept. Mon.-Sat. 10am-5pm; June-Aug. Mon.-Sat. 9am-6pm.
Banks: AIB, The Square (tel. 21129). Open Mon.-Fri. 10am-12:30pm and 1:30-4pm, Wed. open until 5pm. **ATM** accepts Visa, MC, Plus. **Bank of Ireland,** Sea View (tel. 21111). Open Mon.-Fri. 10am-12:30pm and 1:30-5pm.
Buses: Buses from Galway run through Oughteraard and then to Clifden (June-Aug. Mon.-Sat. 6/day, Sun. 2/day; Sept.-May 1/day; 2hr.). A summer service runs

between Westport and Clifden (mid-June to August 1-2/day; 1½hr.). **Bus Éireann** leaves from Cullen's Coffeeshop on Market St. **Michael Nee** (tel. 51082) runs a private bus to Galway and Cleggan, leaving from The Square (June-Sept.; to Galway £5, £7 return; to Cleggan June-Sept. 1-2/day, Oct.-May 2/week; £2, £3 return). Inquire at the tourist office.

Taxi: Desmond Morris, Ben View House, Bridge St. (tel. 21256).

Bike Rental: Mannion's, Bridge St. (tel. 21160, after hours 21155). £5/day, £30/week; deposit £10. Open Mon.-Sat. 9:30am-6:30pm, Sun. 10am-1pm and 5-7pm.

Boat Rental: John Ryan, Sky Rd. (tel. 21069). Prices negotiable.

Laundry: Hillview Laundrette, Church Hill (tel. 21836). Open Mon.-Fri. 9am-9pm, Sat. 9am-6pm, Sun. 11am-5pm; wash and dry £3.75.

Pharmacy: Clifden Pharmacy (tel. 21821). Open Mon.-Sat. 9:30am-6:30pm.

District Hospital: tel. 21301 or 21302.

Emergency: Dial 999; no coins required. **Garda:** tel. 21021.

Post Office: Main St. (tel. 21156). Open Mon.-Fri. 9am-5:30pm, Sat. 9am-1pm.

Phone Code: *caoch ólta* after 095 pints.

ACCOMMODATIONS

The Clifden Town Hostel, Market St. (tel. 21076). Great facilities, perfect near-pub location, and a friendly, yet quiet, atmosphere make for a relaxing night. Dorm £6, 3- or 4-bed dorm £7. Private room £8/person. Sheets £1. Bikes £5/day.

Leo's Hostel (IHH), Sea View (tel. 21429). This big old house is feeling its age, but a turf fire, good location, and the astounding "loo with a view" outweigh other considerations. In addition to dorms, there are sleeping huts (wooden tents) and cabins. Double cabin £12; quad hut £5/person. Sept.-June dorm £5.50; private room £6/person. July-Aug. dorm £6; private room £7/person. Bikes £5/day, £4 off-season. Laundry £3. Sheets free. **Camping** £3/person.

Brookside Hostel, Hulk St. (tel. 21812). Owner will painstakingly plot a hiking route for you. Parking available. Wheelchair accessible. Sept.-June dorm £5; July-Aug. £6. Availability and rates of private rooms vary. Laundry £4. Tickets on *M.V. Queen* to Inishbofin £8 return; from Rossaveal to Aran Islands £10 return.

Bayview Hostel, Market St. (tel. 21866), behind King's Garage. Very basic, but what a view! "No niceties," says the owner, and a more colorful man you'll be hard-pressed to meet. Curfew 2am (key available). Microwave. Dorm £5 (Nov.-Feb. £4.50). Private room £6-7/person. Laundry (water and the sun). Bikes £5/day.

Crannmer, Churchill (tel. 21174). Family restaurant has 2 impeccable rooms (w/bath) for post-feast slumber. Coffee/tea facilities. Double £27. Single negotiable.

Kingston House, Mrs. King, Bridge St. (tel. 21470). Spiffy rooms with a partial view of the church. £14/person, w/bath £16. No singles July-Aug.

White Heather House, The Square (tel. 21085). Centrally located, tastefully decorated rooms. Part of the sea is even visible. £15/person w/bath.

Shanaheever Campsite, (tel. 21018), a little over a mile outside Clifden on the Westport Rd. The tranquility of this spot compensates for its distance from the pubs. Games room. Hot showers. Kitchen. Hikers/cyclists £6/tent and 2 people (£3/additional person). Motorists £8/tent and 2 people. Laundry £4.50.

FOOD & PUBS

Finding a good restaurant or café in Clifden requires little effort; fitting the prices into a tight budget is more difficult. **O'Connor's SuperValu,** Market St., may be the best place to score some vittles (open Mon.-Sat. 9am-7pm, Sun. 11am-2pm).

Derryclare Restaurant, The Square (tel. 21440). Dark wood adds class. Lunch specials are a particularly good value (½ dozen oysters £3). Dinner, of course, is priced a bit higher (veggie pizza £6). Open daily 8am-10:30pm.

Mitchell's Restaurant, The Square (tel. 21867). A cozy, candlelit restaurant serving plates for all palates. Smoked salmon salad £5. Open daily 11:30am-10:30pm.

Fogarties Restaurant, Market St. (tel. 21427). More cozy wood—a popular Clifden decorating scheme. Pasta alle Bolognese £5.90. Open daily noon-10pm.

Connemara Kitchen, Market St. (tel. 21054). This delicatessen dishes out snazzy salads and slaw. Egg and spring onion £1.40. Open daily 10am-6pm.

E.J. King's, The Square (tel. 21330). Crowded bar serves incomparable fare on exceptionally old wood furniture. Pork Louisiana (hot!) £6.75. Pub hours.

Drinks and music (5 days/week in summer, weekends in winter) by the huge open fire agree with everyone at **The Central,** Main St. (tel. 21430). Bring your own instruments to frequented favorite **Mannion's,** Market St. (tel. 21780), which has music nightly in summer (Fri.-Sat. in winter). Residents of Clifden congregate at **Lowry's,** Market St. (tel. 21347; nightly music in summer, Sat. in winter). **E.J. King's,** The Square (tel. 21330), is a talking, laughing, shouting pub that rocks the casbah, while **Humpty's** (tel. 21511), across the street, rolls with a younger, rowdier bunch.

SIGHTS AND ENTERTAINMENT

There are no cliffs in Clifden itself, but 10-mi. **Sky Road,** which loops around the head of land west of town, paves the way to some dizzying cliffs and makes an ideal cycling route. One mile down Sky Rd. stands the gate to the ruins of **Clifden Castle,** the former mansion of Clifden's founder, John D'Arcy. Farther out, a peek back at the opposite side of the bay reveals the spot where U.S. pilots Alcock and Brown landed after crossing the ocean in a biplane. One of the nicer ways to acquaint yourself with Connemara is by hiking south to the Alcock and Brown monument, 3 mi. past Salt Lake and Lough Fadda.

Connemara Heritage Tours, Market St. (tel. 21379), led by an inspiring archaeologist, explore the history, folklore, and archaeology of the region (Easter-Oct. daily at 9, 11am, 2, and 7pm; 4hr.; £10, students £8). The same friendly fellow organizes a **tour of Inishbofin** that delves into the island's natural history, archaeology, and geology (leaves from Clifden daily at 11am, return 6:15pm; bus, ferry, and tour £20, students £18). The entrepreneurial archaeologist has also developed a **tour of the Aran Islands** along the same lines (Easter-Oct. leaves Clifden Wed. at 9am, return at 6:30pm; ferry, bus, and tour £26).

Clifden is into art. Two galleries in town, the **Lavelle Art Gallery** (tel. 21882) and **Clifden Art Gallery** (tel. 21788; open May-Oct.), both on Main St., display local artists' works (and sell them to the non-budget traveler). The Lavelle brothers can also relate an interesting story about shoe-gazing. **Irish night** hits Clifden Town Hall every Tuesday at 9pm (July-Aug.), reviving an ancient culture of traditional music, dance, and song. The **Clifden Regatta** floats in during the first weekend in July. The **Clifden Country and Blues Festival,** held the first weekend of September, draws musicians from across the hills and over the seas.

■ Near Clifden: Cleggan

Tiny Cleggan, 10 mi. northwest of Clifden, serves tourists mainly as a useful jumping-off point for the isle of Inishfobin. Like most towns that rely on the sea, Cleggan is a no-nonsense place: people here talk fish, football, and little else. **Omey Island,** just offshore of Claddaghduff a few miles due south of Cleggan, has rolling sandhills and minor ruins for exploration. But this island's true gift is its accessibility—it can be reached on foot at low tide. Bareback riding along the Cleggan Strand makes for more good stories (£10/hour; contact the Master House Hostel).

People come to the airy **Master House Hostel (IHH)** (tel. (095) 44746) and find it difficult to part from the turf fire. Formerly a courthouse, shop, and an eponymous headmaster's residence, the hostel is full of plants and bright wood, but the bathrooms are not the cleanest. (Dorm £6; private room £8/person. **Camping** £3. Irish breakfast £2.50, continental £1.25. Laundry £3; sheets £1. **Bike rental** £5/day, book in advance.) Cleggan lacks a dirt cheap restaurant, but **Oliver's Seafood Bar** (tel. (095) 44640), with seafood (seafood chowder £2), sandwiches, and a currency exchange, leaves enough change to rattle in your pocket. Upscale **Pier Bar** (tel. (095) 44690) is by the quay and serves "sizzling hot" Garlic Prawns with salad and rolls (£7). **Kings Convenience Store** (tel. (095) 44642), farther down the road, provides local tourist information and sells provisions and ferry tickets to Inishbofin on the *M.V. Queen* (£10 return, students £8, bikes free; open May-Sept. daily 9am-9pm, Oct.-April daily 9am-7pm). Transport to Cleggan is limited to an irregular **Bus Éireann** service (1-3/week from Clifden and Galway) or **Michael Nee's** more frequent private bus from Clifden (June-Sept. 1-2/day, Oct.-May 2/week; £2, £3 return).

■ Inishbofin

On the friendly island of Inishbofin (pop. 200), 7 mi. from Cleggan at the western tip of the Connemara, travelers can choose between complete solitude on white beaches or drinking and dancing with seasoned locals. Inishbofin is infinitely less spoiled than the Aran Islands; package tours are still an unrecognized concept here. The island keeps time according to the ferry, the tides, and the sun, and visitors easily slip into a similar habit. A fishing boat which ran aground years ago still lies tilted on its side in the harbor. Inishbofin seems to be part of another world, or at least past known boundaries of our own.

Ferry tickets are sold at the Brookside Hostel in Clifden, the Master House Hostel in Cleggan, and at the Cleggan pier. Two **ferries,** the *M.V. Queen* (Malachy King, tel. 44642) and the *M.V. Dun Aengus* (Paddy O'Halloran, tel. 45806), leave Cleggan Pier for Inishbofin (July-Aug. 3/day, April-June and Sept. 2/day). During the winter months (Oct.-Easter), when the 45-minute crossing is even rougher, only the *Dun Aengus* operates (it's also the island's mail boat). Both charge £10 (£8 for students or hostelers) and carry bikes free. The **phone code** is an unspoiled 095.

Accommodations, Food, & Pubs Probably the best hostel in all Connemara, the **Inishbofin Island Hostel (IHH)** (tel. 45855) is up the hill past the church. The hostel will bless you with pine bunks, a large conservatory, and constantly entertaining views. People come for a night and stay months. (Dorm £6; private rooms from £8/person. **Camping** £3.50/person. Sheets £1; laundry £2.) **The King's House** (tel. 45833), just before the hostel, furnishes B&B in light and airy rooms with views (£13.50/person; **bikes** £7/day). Remote **Horseshoe B&B** sets itself apart on the east end of the island (tel. 45812; £12/person). Close to the pier on the west end, **Day's Pub and Hotel** (tel. 45829) serves food all day (smoked salmon £3.50) and drink at night. The nightlife is unusually vibrant with frequent music during summer (4 nights/week). The small disco at the hotel bulges with a young, well-traveled crowd. **Murray's Pub,** a 15-minute walk west of the pier, is smaller and more sedate, the perfect place for conversation, slurred or otherwise. **Days Shop** (tel. 45829), is behind the pub and has what you'll need for relaxing in the sun or hiking the hills (open Mon.-Sat. 11:30am-1:30pm and 3-5pm, Sun. 11:30am-12:30pm).

Sights A folk tale recalls the instance when two fishermen lit a fire on the island. The flames broke a spell which had been cast to imprison a witch. Upon her release, the witch struck a white cow and it instantly became a rock. Consequently, the island is now called *Inis Bó Finne* ("Island of the White Cow"). It takes roughly three days to thoroughly walk around the island's periphery. The **east end** of the island is more quiet than the harbor and equals its natural splendor. A large, deserted beach lies at the end of the road which leads past the hotel to the eastern side. A trek to the **west end** of the island takes longer but affords more dramatic views of massive coves and blow-holes. Inishbofin is a favorite breeding ground for grey seals (most visible during mating season, Sept. to early Oct.). The island also provides a perfect climate for those trees hospitable to the corncrake, a bird hard to find on the mainland except in Seamus Heaney's poems. The **Connemara Summer School** (tel. 41034), during the first week of July, teaches about the island's ecology.

The menacing **Cromwellian fort** (across Inishbofin Harbour from the pier), was constructed to hold prisoners before transportation to the West Indies. At low tide, the **Bishop's Rock,** a short distance off the mainland, becomes visible. Cromwell once tied a recalcitrant priest to the rock and forced his comrades to watch as the tide washed over him. Basically, Oliver was a jerk. From the northwest tip of the island, a collection of offshore rocks, **The Stags,** are visible. Past the hotel, at the eastern end of the island lie the ruins of a 15th-century Augustinian Abbey. The abbey was built on the site of a monastery St. Colman founded in 667 AD. A few gravestones and a well from the 7th-century structure remain.

■ Clifden to Westport

CONNEMARA NATIONAL PARK

East and northeast of Clifden, the country hunches up into high hills and collapses into squishy, grass-curtained bogs interrupted only by the rare bare rock. The landscape of the Connemara National Park conceals a number of curiosities, including hare runs, orchids, bogs, and roseroot.

Letterfrack hasn't quite achieved town status—it's three pubs at a crossroads on the edge of the national park. The local **bus** stops in Letterfrack on the route from Galway to Clifden via Cong and Leenane (late June to Aug. Mon.-Sat. 11/week; Sept. to mid-June 4/week). A summer-only route goes from Clifden to Westport via Letterfrack (Mon. and Thurs. 2/day; Tues.-Wed. and Fri.-Sat. 1/day). Hitchers report medium waits on the main road (N59), but a lack of cars frustrates thumbers on the byways. Uphill, on the way from town to the park, the **Old Monastery Hostel** (tel. (095) 41132) provides high-ceilinged rooms in a stately 300-year-old house. Downstairs, a cozy café cooks vegetarian buffet dinners (£6) and free organic breakfasts: tea, coffee, and homemade scones (dorm £6, private room £7.50/person; laundry £3; **bikes** £5/day). Good pub grub, seafood, groceries, and pints are available at **Veldon's** (tel. (095) 41046), which also sporadically sponsors music (plowman's platter £5; open June-Aug. daily 9:30am-1:30pm and 2:15-9:30pm; Sept.-May daily 9:30am-1:30pm and 2:15-7pm). **The Bard's Den,** across the intersection (tel. (095) 41042) is lit by a large open fire and skylight (disco Fri. and Sun. in summer).

Outside Letterfrack, **Connemara National Park** (tel. (095) 41054) occupies 7.7 sq. mi. of mountainous, bird-filled countryside. The far-from-solid terrain of the park is composed of bogs with a screen of grass and flowers over it. It's wisest to wear shoes and pants that you won't mind getting dirty, or perhaps even throwing away. Guides lead walks over the hills and through the bogs (July-Aug. Mon., Wed., and Fri. 10:30am; free) and speak on ecological and archaeological subjects (July-Aug. Wed. 8:30pm; free). The **visitors center** excels at explaining bogs, turf, and other ground cover in the park. (Park open May and Sept. daily 10am-5:30pm; June daily 10am-6:30pm; July-Aug. daily 9:30am-6:30pm. Admission £2, students £1.)

The **Snuffaunboy Nature Trail** and the **Ellis Wood Trail** provide half-hour self-guided (guidebook 50p) tours of the park geared toward lovers of flowers, Connemara ponies, and easy hikes. Staff at the visitors center will help plan longer hikes. Experienced hikers often head for the **Twelve Bens** (*Na Benna Beola,* a.k.a. the Twelve Pins), a rugged range that reaches 2400-ft. heights and is not recommended for single or beginning hikers. The Bens are accessed through the park. Trailheads are located behind Diamond Hill. Diamond Hill itself has been climbed so many times (by so many feet that dislodge so much soil and stone) that soil erosion endangers the hill and everything around it. For peat's sake, don't ascend that hill. Hikers base themselves at the **Ben Lettery Youth Hostel (An Óige/HI)** (tel. (095) 51136) in Ballinafad, far away from anything else. (Easter-May and Sept. £5, June-Aug. £6.) The hostel is 8 mi. east of Clifden; the turnoff N59 is west of Roundstone road.

Kylemore Abbey, 4 mi. north of Letterfrack, peacefully shelters a beautiful view. Above the Abbey (a castle and a Gothic church), a rocky path winds upwards, under trees and over streams, towards a ledge with a lookout you'll be loath to leave. A statue with arms aloft welcomes you from your half-hour climb. Below, the Abbey is worth stepping into. Every month from May to October the music of the past is celebrated with a **Gothic Church Concert** (tel. (095) 41145; tickets £6-10). The Abbey

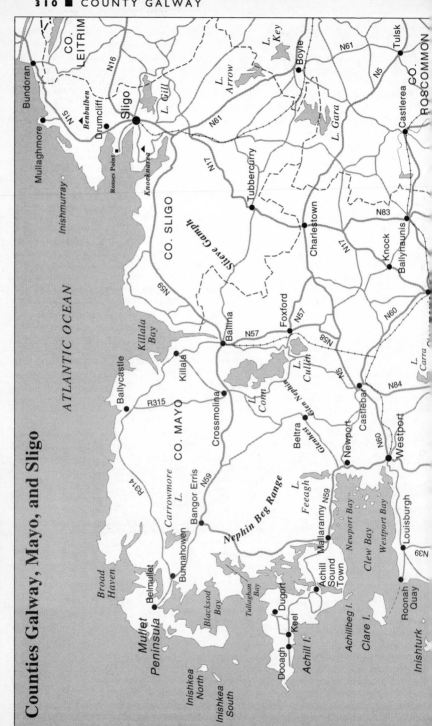

Counties Galway, Mayo, and Sligo

N60
Roscommon
Shannon R.
CO. GALWAY
Moylough
R362
N63
N83
Tuam
N17
N84
Ballinrobe
Cong
Inchagoill
L. Corrib
L. Mask
L. Nafooey
Oughterard
N59
Joyce Country
Partry
Doo L.
Mweelrea ▲
Killary Harbor
Letterfrack
Connemara National Park
Clifden
Connemara
Ballyconneely
Roundstone
Bertraghboy Bay
Mannin Bay
Cleggan
Inishbofin
Inishshark
Gortmore
Rosmuck
Carraroe
Rossaveal
R336
Lettermore I.
Gourna I.
ARAN ISLANDS
Kilronan
Inishmore
Inishmaan
Inisheer
Ballinasloe
Aughrim
N6
N65
Loughrea
Portumna
N41
L. Derg
Mountshannon
Slieve Aughty Mts.
Athenry
N6
99N
Thoor Ballylee
N18
Gort
Claregalway
Oranmore
Kilcolgan
Doorus
Coole Park
Kinvarra
Ballyvaughan
CO. CLARE
The Barren
N67
Lisdoonvarna
Kilfenora
Ennistymon
Doolin
Cliffs of Moher
Liscannor
Lahinch
N18
Galway
Barna
Spiddal
Galway Bay
Ballyvaughan Bay
ATLANTIC OCEAN

N ←

0 ___ 10 miles
0 ___ 10 kilometers

and trail are open year-round daily and the restaurant and craft shop are open from mid-March to November (both open 10am-6pm).

KILLARY HARBOUR

Farther east along N59, Killary Harbour, Ireland's only fjord, breaks through the mountains to the town of **Leenane,** which wraps itself in the skirts of the **Devils-mother Mountain.** *The Field* was filmed here in 1989, and no one in town will ever forget it. The murder scene was shot at Aasleagh Falls. At **Leenane Cultural Centre** (tel. (095) 42323), on the Clifden-Westport Rd., spinning and weaving demonstrations clarify what happens to the wool of the sheep that graze right outside (open April-Oct. daily 10am-7pm; admission £2, students £1). Gemstone and silver jewelry at **Killary Crafts,** across the road from Hamilton's, are the products of a different, but also local, craftsmanship (open April-Sept. daily 10am-8pm). Stop for a pint at **Gaynor's Lounge** (tel. (095) 42261) or at next-door neighbor, **Hamilton's** (tel. (095) 42262). Hamilton's hides behind a tiny shop that is open daily 8:30am-12:30am. It's hard to fight the temptation for an eggburger and chips (£3) from the **Village Grill** (tel. (095) 42253; open daily 10am-10pm). **Bay View House** (tel. (095) 42240), on the northern side of town along N59, boasts a bizarre dining room that was once a chapel (single £20-24, double £29). **Killary Harbour Hostel (An Óige/HI)** (tel. (095) 43417) perches on the very edge of the harbor shore 7 mi. west of Leenane. The hostel has an unsettlingly gorgeous waterfront location. Like Wittgenstein, you can write *Philosophical Investigations* here. A hostel shop sells baked beans and other necessaries. At £6 a night from June-August (March-May and Sept. £5), it's a wonderful bargain. At 5 mi. off N59, it's also inconveniently remote.

County Mayo

Co. Mayo's appeal is largely a result of its distance from well-traveled paths. Bogs, beaches, and big fish fill the county and attract travelers of all sorts. The best scenery is found along the inlets around the Belmullet Peninsula while the best fish swim in Lough Conn and Lough Cullin. Mayo's one big moment in history occurred in 1798, "The Year of the French," when General Humbert landed at Kilcummin. Combining French soldiers, Irish revolutionaries, and Irish rural secret societies into an army, Humbert briefly controlled half the county, from Killala to Castlebar. The English retaliated and won at Ballina and Ballinamuck. The village of Cong, Co. Mayo, is covered under Co. Galway (p. 302).

■ Westport

Westport has an exciting, thriving pub life, plenty of good cafés, and three excellent hostels. Its many conveniences make it an entirely agreeable stop between Connemara and Mayo's islands to the northwest. The town's convenient layout, with a central Octagon and the scenic Mall, was produced by the same English architectural planning that produced stately Westport House. N60 passes through Clifden, Galway, Sligo, and Castlebar on its way to Westport. Hitchers call it an easy route.

ORIENTATION & PRACTICAL INFORMATION

Westport's North Mall and South Mall run parallel to each other, one on each side of the Carrowbeg River. Most of the town extends off South Mall. Perpendicular to it, Bridge St. favors pubs, eateries, and Sunday strolls. Most activity centers on The Octagon (the junction of James St., Peter St., and Shop St.), or at the clock tower at the other end of Shop St., where it meets High, Mill, and Bridge St.

Tourist Office: North Mall (tel. 25711). Open Mon.-Fri. 9am-6pm, Sat. 10am-6pm.

Banks: Bank of Ireland, North Mall (tel. 25522). Open Mon.-Wed. and Fri. 10am-4pm, Thurs. 10am-5pm; **ATM. AIB,** Shop St. (tel. 25466). Open Mon.-Wed. and Fri. 10am-4pm, Thurs. 10am-5pm; **ATM.**

Trains: Trains arrive at the **Altamont St. Station** (tel. 25253 or 25329 for inquiries, Mon.-Sat. 9:30am-6pm), a 5-min. walk east of town on the continuation of the North and South Malls. The train goes to Dublin via Athlone and Castlebar (daily 3/day; Dublin £14, Fri. and Sun. £20).

Buses: For Westport bus info, call the tourist office (tel. 25711). Almost no buses leave Westport on weekends. Buses leave from the Octagon and travel to: Ballina (Mon.-Sat. 1-3/day, Sun. 1/day); Castlebar (Mon.-Sat. 5/day); Louisburgh (Mon.-Sat. 2/day; £4.40); Galway (Mon.-Fri. 2/day; £9.70); Knock (Mon.-Sat 3/day, Sun. 1/day; £6.70); and Belfast via Sligo (Mon.-Sat. 1/day).

Taxis: Brendan McGing, Lower Peter St. (tel. 26319).

Bike Rental: Breheny & Sons, Castlebar St. (tel. 25020).

Laundry: Westport Washeteria, Mill St. (tel. 25261), near the clock tower. £3.50, self-service £2.50, soap 40p. Open Mon.-Tues. and Thurs.-Sat. 9:30am-6pm, Wed. 9:30am-1pm.

Travel Agency: Westport Travel, 4 Shop St. (tel. 25511). USIT prices for students; Western Union Money Transfer point. Open Mon.-Sat. 9:30am-6pm.

Pharmacy: O'Donnell's, Bridge St. (tel. 25163). Open Mon.-Sat. 9am-6:30pm. Rotating Sunday (12:30-2pm) openings are posted on pharmacy doors.

Emergency: Dial 999; no coins required. **Garda:** Fair Green (tel. 25555).

Post Office: North Mall (tel. 25475). Open Mon.-Sat. 9am-5:30pm.

Phone Code: 098.

Disorientation and Impractical Information: Clay Pigeon Shooting (tel. 21926), Liscarney, Leenane Rd. Open daily 11am-dark.

ACCOMMODATIONS

Westport's B&Bs, with their faux-wood headboards, are easily spotted on the Castlebar and Altamont Roads. Most charge £14-16.

Old Mill Holiday Hostel (IHH), James St. (tel. 27045), between The Octagon and the tourist office. There isn't a more pleasant hostel in Western Ireland. Firm pine beds line up in a renovated mill and brewery. The showers are often compared to a second date—hot and full of pressure. Book ahead during festival weeks. Bedroom lockout 11am-1pm; kitchen and common room lockout 11pm-8am. £5, June-Aug. £6.50. Sheets 50p. Laundry £2.

Club Atlantic (IHH), Altamont St. (tel. 26644 or 26717), a 5-min. walk from North or South Mall. This massive, 140-bed complex across from the train station has a pool table, ping-pong, video games, Irish videos, a shop, an elephantine kitchen, and an educational exhibition on Croagh Patrick. June and Sept. dorm £5.90, double £13.80. July-Aug. £6.50, 13.80. Mid-March to May and Oct. £5.50, £11.80. Single £9. Sheets £1. Laundry £2. **Camping** £4. Bikes £6/day, £30/week. Guests can use sauna and swimming pool facilities at the nearby Westport Hotel for £4.

The Granary Hostel (tel. 25903), 1mi. from town on the Louisburgh Rd., near the main entrance to Westport House. A garden and conservatory flank the 150-year-old converted granary. If you don't mind the outdoor shower, you may enjoy a night surrounded by the rugged walls. Dorm £5. Open Jan.-Nov.

Altamont House, Altamont St. (tel. 25226). 30 years of B&B and still going. Roses peep in the windows of spacious rooms. £16/person. Open March-Dec.

FOOD

Gorge on digestives from the **SuperValu supermarket** (tel. 27000) on Shop St. (open Mon.-Wed. 9am-7pm, Thurs.-Fri. 9am-9pm, Sat. 9am-6:45pm). **Country Fresh** (tel. 25377) sells juicy produce (open Mon.-Fri. 8am-6:30pm, Sat. 8am-6pm; closes early on Wed. during winter). The **country market** by the Town Hall at The Octagon vends farm-fresh vegetables, eggs, and milk (Thurs. 10:30am-1:30pm).

McCormack's, Bridge St. (tel. 25619). Pastries, teas, and simple meals on floral tablecloths. Praised by locals as an exemplary teahouse. Daily special, potato, and salad £4.20. Open July-Sept. Mon.-Sat. 10am-6pm; Oct.-June Tues.-Sat. 10am-6pm.

Cafolla, Bridge St. (tel. 25168). Eat in or take away, the food is still incredibly cheap. Plain pizza £1.75, omelettes from £2.20. Open June-Sept. Mon.-Sat. 11am-1am, Sun. noon-11pm; Oct.-May Mon.-Sat. 11am-11pm, Sun. 5-11pm.

The Continental Health Food Shop and Café, High St. (tel. 26679). Enjoy succulent sandwiches (under £3) by the fireplace. Open Tues.-Sat. 10am-6pm.

Bernie's High Street Café, High St. (tel. 27797). Soft light, ecru walls, and healthy plants are comforting. Caesar salad £3.70. Open daily 10am-10pm.

The Urchin, Bridge St. (tel. 27532). A menu full of old favorites. Quiche and salad £3.20. Lunch is affordable, dinner isn't. Open daily 10am-10pm.

PUBS

Westport is blessed with *craic* as good as the food. Search Bridge St. to find a scene or session that suits. In case of a musical or social emergency, call the southwest Mayo **pub hotline** (tel. 27371) for a rundown of music in Westport and Newport.

Matt Molloy's, Bridge St. (tel. 26655). Owned by the flautist of the Chieftains. All the cool people, including his friends, go here. Trad sessions nightly in summer.

O'Malley's Pub, Bridge St., across from Matt Molloy's. Laid-back 20-somethings relax in the dark wood interior.

The West, corner of Bridge St. and South Mall (tel. 25886), on the river. Choose between the light and creamy outside and the dark and woody inside. Friendly Westport youth thrive in both settings. Live rock most nights in summer.

Pete McCarthy's, Quay St. (tel. 27050), uphill from the Octagon. Old, dark, and smoky pub attracts regulars—you know the score. Trad on weekends in summer.

The Towers (tel. 26534), down by The Quay, 1mi. from town center. Fishing nets and excellent grub hook lots of customers. Beef in Guinness, a uniquely Irish specialty, is worth £4.90. Music thrice a week in summer, twice in winter.

SIGHTS

The current commercial uses of **Westport House** (tel. 25430) would horrify its former elite inhabitants, the Marquesses of Sligo. A carnival and the bog-preserved butter in the museum are hardly worth the entrance fee. The zoo and train ride betray an emphasis on entertaining children. (Open May and early Sept. daily 2-5pm; June and late Aug. daily 2-6pm; July to mid-Aug. Mon.-Sat. 10:30am-6pm, Sun. 2-6pm. Admission May-June and Sept. £5, July-Aug. £6; students £3.50.) More interesting and cheaper is the **Clew Bay Heritage Centre** (tel. 26852), at the end of The Quay. The narrow interior crams together a pair of James Connolly's gloves, a sash belonging to John MacBride, and the stunning original photograph of Maud Gonne which graces her biographies. A genealogical service is available. (Open July-Sept. Mon.-Fri. 10am-5pm, Sat.-Sun. 2-5pm; Oct.-June Mon.-Fri. noon-3pm. Admission £1.)

Perfectly conical **Croagh Patrick** rises 2510 ft. over Clew Bay. The summit has been revered as a holy site for thousands of years. Perhaps because of its height, it was sacred to **Lug**, sun god, god of arts and crafts, and temporary ruler of the Túatha de Danann (see **Legends and Folktales,** p.69). St. Patrick prayed and fasted here for 40 days and nights in 441 AD before he banished the snakes from Ireland. The deeply religious climb Croagh Patrick barefoot on the last Sunday in July. Not coincidentally, this date is also Lug's holy night, Lughnasa. Others climb the mountain just for the exhilaration and the view from the top. It takes about four hours total to climb and descend the mountain. Shod climbers start their excursion from the village of **Murrisk,** several miles west of Westport on R395 to Louisburgh. Buses drive to Murrisk (July-Aug. Mon.-Fri. 3/day, Sept.-June Mon.-Sat. 2/day). Pilgrims and hikers also set out for Croagh Patrick along a path from **Ballintubber Abbey** (tel. (094) 30709), several miles south of Castlebar and 19 mi. from Murrisk. Founded in 1216 by King of Connacht Cathal O'Connor, the abbey still functions as a religious center.

■ Near Westport

LOUISBURGH

The wild, mountainous landscapes south of Westport, clearly more exhilarating than the farmlands of inner Mayo, are rocky and barren. **Louisburgh,** a dull town 13 mi. west of Westport on R395, has little to offer fun-seeking tourists except its proximity to Westport and Roonah Point. **Tourist information** is available near the Square at the **Granuaile Heritage Centre** (tel. (098) 66195), which honors Grace O'Malley, 16th-century Pirate Queen of Clew Bay. O'Malley met Queen Elizabeth I here in 1593, and 400 years later President Mary Robinson met Queen Elizabeth II. Wax figures depict Gaelic chieftains, Queen Elizabeth, and the graceful pirate queen. (Open March-May Mon.-Fri. 2-5:30pm, June Mon.-Sat. 10am-6pm, July-Sept. daily 10am-7:30pm, Oct.-Nov. Mon.-Fri 11am-5:30pm. Admission £2.) The many O'Malleys in town willingly relate the spicy version of Grace's life.

Staunton's Pharmacy, the Square (tel. (098) 66139), is the local chemist (open Mon.-Sat. 10:30am-7:30pm, Sun. 12:30-1:30pm). The **post office** exchanges currency on Main St. (open Mon.-Fri. 9am-1pm and 2-5:30pm, Sat. 9am-1pm). **Durkan's Food-store,** Bridge St. (tel. (098) 66394), satisfies appetites (open June-Aug. daily 9am-9pm; Sept.-May Mon.-Sat. 9am-9pm). **Village Tea Shop** (tel. (098) 66577) serves light luncheons to bridge groups (open Mon.-Sat. 11:30am-5pm, Sun. 1-6pm). Its **Aimhirgin Gallery** displays sculpture and ceramics. Bread and beer sustain customers at **Durkan's Weir House,** Chapel St. (tel. (098) 66140; lasagna, salad, and brown bread £5; food served daily noon-10pm). The attached restaurant has fancier food (seafood pancake w/lobster sauce £4; open daily from 6:30pm). Mary O'Malley's **Rivervilla** (tel. (098) 66246) is in Shraugh, ¾ mi. from Louisburgh (signs mark the way). Her riverside farmhouse is open to guests mid-April to October (£14/person). **Old Head Forest Caravan and Camping Park** (tel. (098) 66021 or 66455) helps guests enjoy tennis and clean laundry. (£3/hiker, £3.50/motorcyclist plus 50p/person in a small tent. Caravans and large tents: Mid-May to June and mid-Aug. to mid-Sept. £4.50; July to mid-Aug. £5.50. Open mid-May to mid-Sept.)

Old Head Strand, 2 mi. northeast of town, is one of the finer beaches in the **Clew Bay** area and along the coast, though **Carramore Strand** is closer to town (1mi. away). Mountain-type people will have to travel a bit farther. Fifteen miles south of town, calm **Doolough** ("Black Lake") offers a choice of several heart-pounding climbs up the **Sheffrey Hills, the Mweelrea Mountains,** or **Ben Gorm.** The south end of the lake leads into an enchanted wooded dell which runs into the River Bundarragh. Cars and bikes can head back to Westport on the scenic route, which bends left at the south end of the lough. The loop from Westport to Louisburgh to Killary Harbour and back to Westport covers 40 mi. Cars are few and far between.

CLARE ISLAND

Four miles west of Louisburgh, boats leave Roonah Point for **Clare Island** (pop. 150), a scenic dot in the Atlantic that is less popular than Inishmore or Achill but not as isolated as Inisheer or Inishbofin. The island has a history of bloodthirsty pirates. Grace O'Malley ruled the 16th-century seas west of Ireland from her base on the eastern end of this island. Her notorious galley fleet exacted tolls from all ships entering and leaving Galway Bay, and she even abducted the grandson of Dublin aristocrats when they refused her entrance into their castle (see **Howth,** p.117). Grace was supposedly laid to rest here under the ruins of **Clare Island Abbey** halfway down the beach. Ascending Knockaveen Hill requires little energy; climbing Croaghmore takes more effort, but the reward is greater. You can search for buried treasure on the west coast of the island, where the cliffs of **Knockmore Mountain** (1550ft.) rise vertically out of the sea. Maps and printed directions are available at the tourist office in Louisburgh. **Clare Island Historical Safaris** (tel. (098) 25048) organizes one-day explorations of a megalithic tomb, Bronze Age cooking sites, a 12th-century abbey, and Grace O'Malley's 15th-century castle. (£25/person, including transport and meals; reduced rates for groups; minimum of 6 people for a tour.)

The **Bay View Hostel** (tel. (098) 26307), just up the beach road on the right side of the harbor, offers two deals. A bed costs £7, while a combined hostel and ferry package (*The Very Likely* leaves Roonagh Quay for Clare Island 6/day in summer) costs £15. The hostel also serves lunch between 12:30 and 3:30pm, and an evening meal from 6:30 to 8:30pm. Mrs. O'Malley's **Cois Abhain** (tel. (098) 26216), down by the harbor, will pick you up then give you B&B (single £15, double £26).

Charlie O'Malley's **Ocean Star Ferry** (tel. (098) 25045) crosses the bay from Roonah Quay in 15 minutes (£10 return, bikes free). Since the ferry delivers cargo to the island's permanent residents, it only stops running in the worst storms. (July-Aug. 5/day; May-June and Sept. 3-5/day; call Oct.-April.) **Clare Island Ferry,** (tel. (098) 26307) departs from Westport Harbour (1½hr; £15 return) and Roonagh Point (6/day). The picturesque cruise passes among many tiny islands and under the shadow of Croagh Patrick (daily 9am; leaves Clare Island 5pm).

DELPHI

Three kinds of people go to Delphi: the artistic, the athletic, and the rich. Delphi isn't really a town since it doesn't even have a pub, but this tiny hamlet has rivers and lakes that are perfect for photos, picnics, and fishing (contact the Delphi fishery, tel. (095) 42213 for permits). **The Lodge** sells seclusion to the rich and famous. Locals still fondly remember Prince Charles' visit in 1995. The **Delphi Adventure Centre** (tel. (095) 42307) provides energetic activities and hostel beds. Adventurous types can try surf-skiing, rock climbing, and abseiling, among other activities (£22/day, £14/½-day). Times of kitchen access are limited. The coffeeshop has a pool table and comestibles (soup and brown bread £1.30). You can hire a bike for £7 per day, or you can relax in the sauna for £3. (Dorm £6, double £17. Laundry £5; sheets, pillow, and duvet £2. **Camping** £5.50/2-person tent. Open July-Aug.)

▓ Achill Island

Achill Island is Co. Mayo's most popular holiday refuge and, measuring 15 by 12 mi., Ireland's largest island. Ringed by glorious beaches and cliffs, Achill's interior consists of bog, mountain, bog-like surface, and bog. Hardly an acre of land is cultivable. The island's several towns divide its large tourist trade among them. Keel is most central and convenient to the island's sights, but the best hostel is in Achill Sound Town and the best scenery is in the far west of the island. Recent Nobel-winning novelist Heinrich Böll once lived in Dugort.

Buses run infrequently from Achill Sound Town, Dugort, Keel, and Dooagh to Westport (summer Mon.-Sat. 4/day, winter Mon.-Sat. 2/day; £5.50 return, students £4.30), and to Sligo, Enniskillen, and Belfast (summer Mon.-Sat. 3/day, winter 2/day). **Barton's Transport** (tel. (01) 6286026) runs a weekend return to Achill from Dublin (1/week; 5½hr.; £15). **Hitchers** report relative success during July and August, but cycling is more reliable and just as easy. There's no bank on the island, so change money on the mainland or suffer rates that resemble piracy. The **phone code** emerges from the bog at 098.

ACHILL SOUND TOWN

About 6 mi. south of Achill Sound Town (from the road onto the island take a left at the first crossroads), two sets of ruins crumble near each other. The ancient **Church of Kildavnet** was founded by Dympna when she fled to Achill Island to escape her father's incestuous desires. The remains of **Kildownet Castle,** really a fortified tower house dating from the late 1400s, proudly stand nearby. Grace O'Malley, the swaggering, seafaring pirate of medieval Ireland, once owned the castle (ask at the house next door for the key). The **Atlantic Drive** roams along the south coast from the ruins past beautiful beaches and up to Dooega, Keel, and Dooagh.

The **tourist office** (tel. 45384; open June-Aug. Mon.-Sat. 10am-1pm and 2-5:30pm) is next to Alice's Harbour Inn on the opposite side of the bridge from the main part of town, which holds a **post office** and **bureau de change** (tel. 45141; open Mon.-Fri. 9am-12:30pm and 1:30-5:30pm), a SuperValu **supermarket** (open Mon.-Sat. 9am-6pm), and a **pharmacy** (tel. 45248; open July-Aug. Mon.-Sat. 9:30am-6pm; Sept.-June Tues.-Sat. 9:30am-6pm). **Achill Sound Hotel** (tel. 45245) rents **bikes** (£6/day, £30/week; deposit £30; open daily 9am-9pm).

Achill Sound Town accommodates flocks of tourists at two hostels. The **Wild Haven Hostel** (tel. 45392) is just like home. Painted signs point the way from the main road. Polished floors, antique furniture, and an open turf fire in a cozy sitting room tame the wild haven. (Lockout 11am-3:30pm, except on rainy days. Dorm £7; private room £9/person. **Camping** £4. Breakfast £3.50; candle-lit dinner £10. Sheets £1. **Bikes** £6/day, £30/week.) Just before the bridge to town, the **Railway Hostel** (tel. 45187) is a simple, multi-kitchened, casual family affair at a prime location—a pub is just across the street. (Dorm £6; private room £7/person, all w/bath. Continental breakfast £2.50, full Irish £3.50. Laundry £2; sheets £1. **Bikes** £5/day.) The proprietors can be found at Mace Supermarket, in town. Opposite the Railway Hostel, **Alice's Harbour Inn** (tel. 45138) does more than its share for the tourist industry. The owners allow **camping** and will provide tourist info if the office is closed. The inn also feeds hungry souls (Achill cod w/vegetables and chips £5; food served 10am-10pm). In the summer of 1994, **Eric Clapton,** in the words of locals, was caught "slobbering over a guitar" here during an impromptu jam session.

KEEL & DOOAGH

Keel fades gracefully into its spectacular 3-mi. strand, **Trawmore,** flanked by cliffs and rocks. Two miles north of Keel on the road looping back to Dugort, the **Deserted Village** is populated only by stone houses closely related to early Christian *clocháns*. They were used until the late 1930s as pasture and shelter for fattening cattle. Some of these "booleying" houses are scheduled for restoration. The site is used in the summer months for an **Archaeological Summer School** (call Theresa McDonald, tel. (0506) 21627) which sponsors evening lectures at the Warecrest Hotel (tel. 43153) in Dooagh (mid-July to Aug. Tues. 8:30pm; admission £5).

Pedal out with groceries in your pack from **O'Malley's Island Sports** (tel. 43125; bikes £6/day, £30/week; open Mon.-Sat. 9am-9pm, Sun. 9am-7pm) in the **Spar Supermarket.** The bike can carry you to **Keel Sandybanks Caravan and Camping Park** (tel. 43211), where you can get sand in your tent (July-Aug. £5.50/tent, late May-June and Sept. £4.50). An infinitely more comfortable, though more expensive option, is Mrs. Joyce's **Marian Villa** (tel. 43134), a 20-room hotel/B&B with a veranda that looks onto the sea (from £18/person, all w/bath and TV). A few pints can aid sleep on the less-than-large bunks at the **Wayfarer Hostel (IHH)** (tel. 43266), a large, white building on your right as you enter town. Central location and a short walk to Trawmore Strand. (Dorm £5.50; private room £6.50. Sheets 50p. Microwave. Open mid-March to mid-Oct.)

Drunken inspiration is encouraged at the vinyl **Annexe Inn** (tel. 43268). The pub has pictures of dead sharks and trad sessions nightly in July and August, but only on Saturdays in winter. The large **Mináun View Bar,** across from the caravan park, is legendary for its Republican fervor. Although there are numerous decadent chippies, more nutritious food is available at the **Beehive Handcrafts and Coffee Shop** (tel. 43134) where sweaters alternate with wooden tables (soup and brown bread £1.30; open daily 10am-6:30pm). **Calvey's** (tel. 43158), next to the Spar Supermarket, whips up hearty meals (Chicken Goujons £5; open daily 10am-10pm).

Two miles up the road from Keel in **Dooagh** (DOO-ah), **Corrymore House** (tel. 43333) was one of several Co. Mayo estates owned by the infamous Captain Boycott. His mid-19th-century tenants went on an extended rent strike that turned his surname into the verb. The **Folklife Centre** displays household utensils, furniture, and farm implements from the turn of the century (open daily 10:30am-5pm). Dooagh hosts a music, dance, art, and writing **festival week** (call Dr. Paddy Loneen, tel. 45284) during the first two weeks of August.

The **Abha Teangai Restaurant and Guest House** (tel. 43424) has a number of guises. It is both a vegetarian restaurant (veggie stir-fry £6.30) and a gallery displaying local artists' work (open daily 9am-10:30pm). In August, the art gallery turns into a heritage center, displaying the usual crafty assortment of baskets, *curraghs,* and woven goods. **B&B** is also available here for £12.50. **The Pub,** just a bit farther down the main street, is managed by the beloved mistress of the house. Don Allum, the first man to row both ways across the Atlantic, made his first stop upon landing in Ireland at The Pub. Pictures of Don in the pub will be discussed by old men for years to come: "I knew him well. He had arms like Fionn MacCumhaill..." Four miles into Achill's wild west past Keem Bay, the **Croaghaun Mountains** are the source of the stream on **Achill Head.** The mountains provide bone-chilling views of **Croaghaun Cliffs,** Europe's highest sea-cliffs. The climb to the top of the cliffs from Keem Bay is less strenuous but provides similar views.

DUGORT

A right turn in Achill Sound Town leads to the northern part of the island, where Dugort has slept through the 20th century and may sleep through the 21st as well. The tiny hamlet perches atop a sea-cliff. Mist-shrouded Slievemore Mountain looms to its east. Germans flock here to see the former cottage of Heinrich Böll, now a retreat for artists-in-residence. His favorite pub, the **Valley,** still serves pints to literary pilgrims. Modern-looking cemeteries and abandoned buildings west of Dugort are the result of a futile mid-1800s effort to convert the islanders to Protestantism by sending in Irish-speaking missionaries. On the other side of **Slievemore Mountain** gapes the chambered tomb known as **Giant's Grave** (easily accessible from Dugort). Other megalithic tombs lurk nearby. The main signposted tomb after McDowell's Hotel towards Keel is easiest to find, 1 mi. straight up from the road. It has been eroded away to a sinuous beauty. **Boats** leave for the **seal caves** from the pier at Dugort (up the road from the Strand Hotel) daily at 11am and 6pm.

Seal Caves Caravan and Camping Park (tel. (098) 43262) lies between Dugort Beach and Slievemore Mountain (July-Aug. £2.50/hiker or biker; April-June and Sept. £2/hiker or biker; open April-Sept.). A softer pillow for your head awaits at **Valley House Hostel** (tel. 47204). The 100-year-old house is furnished in a paroxysm of fading splendor with antique furniture, massive windows, and an open turf fire. An in-house pub is the most luxurious of amenities (£6; open Easter-Oct.). The woman who once owned the house was brutally murdered. Her murderer's story became the basis for Synge's *Playboy of the Western World.* The road to the hostel turns left off the main road 2 mi. east of Dugort at the valley crossroads. Nearby, self-proclaimed seafood specialist **Atoka Restaurant** (tel. 47229) feeds hearty portions to applauding locals (entrees £6-12; grilled lamb cutlets £8; open May to late Sept. daily 8:30am-11pm). Those who stay for B&B get a big breakfast, too (£12/person).

■ Mullet Peninsula

Unlike popular Achill Island, the Mullet Peninsula remains desolate and untouristed. Remote **Belmullet** occupies the slender strip of land between Broad Haven and Blacksod Bay, which connects the soggy mainland to an equally soggy but more unusual peninsula. Equestrian trails, guided tours, and walking paths unroll from Belmullet to the sea, where amateur anglers crowd the waters. The farther you get from Belmullet, the wilder the landscape becomes. Small white cottages dot the rugged bogland, while the sea rages on either side of the peninsula (the end of which is a small *gaeltacht*). An infrequent **bus** service runs to the Mullet Peninsula from Ballina. A summer service connects the towns to Dublin (July-Aug. Mon.-Sat. 2/day; Sept.-June Mon.-Sat. 1/day).

The **Erris Tourist Information Centre** (tel. 81500) serves the area well (open June-Sept. daily 9:30am-7:30pm; Oct.-May 9am-5:30pm). The **Bank of Ireland** (tel. 81311) monopolizes peninsula finances (open Mon.-Wed. and Fri. 10am-12:30pm and 1:30-5pm; **ATM**). **Belmullet Cycle Centre, American St.** (tel. 81424), does a good trade in rentals (£6/day; deposit £10; reduction for group rentals; open Mon.-Sat. 9am-6pm). The **Centra Supermarket** (open Mon.-Fri. 9am-7pm, Sat. 9am-9pm) is across Main St. from **Lavelle's Pharmacy** (tel. 81053; open Tues.-Fri. 9:30am-6:30pm, Mon. 11am-1pm, Sat. 10am-8pm). The **post office** is at the end of Main St. (tel. 81032; open Mon. and Wed.-Sat. 9am-5:30pm, Tues. 9:30am-5:30pm).The **Garda** can be reached at tel. 81038. The area's **phone code** is a soggy 097.

Eight miles south of Belmullet, the **Ten Degrees West Hostel and Watersports Centre** (tel. 82111) grants relaxing holidays on remote, windy Elly Bay. It sports bright murals, a young Irish-speaking staff, and a waterfront location. Call ahead during summer months. (Dorm £6. **Camping** £2. Irish breakfast £1.50, dinner £3.50.) To reach Ten Degrees West, cross the bridge and stay on the main road, keeping the sea to your left. Blissfully peaceful **Pollatomish**, between Belmullet and Ballycastle, invites you to its relaxing **An Óige Youth Hostel** (tel. (091) 84511; lockout, midnight curfew; June-Sept. £5.50/person, April-May £4.50; open Easter-Sept.). B&Bs are a bit closer to Belmullet; many provide tackle rooms for fishing. **Nora Walsh, Western Strands Hotel,** Main St. (tel. 81096 or 82254), provides B&B (£11/person w/bath; single £13). **Mill House B&B,** American St. (tel. 81181), near the bridge, offers cute rooms for £12.

The **Curragh Café,** Elly Bay, serves good chips and better Guinness. A jukebox, video games (10p), and disco keep the Irish-American connection alive. **Padden's Family Fare,** Carter Sq. (tel. 81324), is the town's only decent restaurant (entrees £3-5; open Tues.-Sun. noon til late). **Clan Lir,** also popular with the young folk, gets rowdy during football games. Suave international males smoke across the street at **Lavelle's,** reputedly Mayo's only gay pub. Birdwatchers and a youthful crowd flock to the **Anchor Bar,** Barrack St. (tel. 81007), which records ornithological sightings.

Bogseeing package tours assemble at **Turasoireacht Lorrais** (tel. 82292), known in English as the **Erris Tourist Organization.** Pony trekking at the **Duvullaun Riding Centre** is £5 per hour. **Boat trips** can be taken to the islands off the Mullet Peninsula by contacting Josephine and Matt Geraghty (tel. 85741). Most trips visit **Inishkea** and can go to the Achill Islands (daily; off season 3/week; £10 return or single when busy, £12 otherwise; 6-person min.). **The Belmullet Sea Angling Competition** in mid-July (tel. 81076) awards £2 per pound for the heaviest halibut, as well as money prizes for variety, and a life jacket for the best specimen caught. **Watersports** go for reasonable rates at the Ten Degrees West hostel (surfing, windsurfing, sea kayaking, etc. cost £8/½-day, £6/hr.; see above).

▨ Ballina

What Knock is to the Marian cult, Ballina (bah-lin-AH) is to the religion of bait and tackle: hordes of pilgrims in olive green waders invade the town each year during the fishing season, from February to September. Some anglers fish without pause for three days and three nights when the salmon are biting. But the town also has non-ichthyological attractions, such as its hip hostel and the lovely vistas of its river walks. Forward-looking Irish President Mary Robinson grew up in Ballina and refined her political skills in the town's 67 pubs (see **Recent History,** p. 66).

PRACTICAL INFORMATION

Tourist Office: Cathedral Rd. (tel. 70848), along the river next to St. Muredach's Cathedral. Open Easter-Sept. Mon.-Sat. 10am-5:30pm.

Banks: Bank of Ireland, Pearse St. (tel. 21144). Open Mon.-Wed. and Fri. 10am-4pm, Thurs. 10am-5pm; **ATM** accepts Visa, MC; **Irish Permanent Building Society,** Pearse St. (tel. 22777). Open Mon.-Fri. 9:30am-5pm; **ATM** accepts AmEx, Visa, Plus.

Trains: Train Station: Station Rd. (tel. 71818), near the bus station. Open Mon.-Fri. 7:30am-6pm, Sat. 9am-1pm and 3:15-6pm. Service to Dublin via Athlone (daily 3/day; £14, students £10).

Buses: Bus Station: Station Rd. (tel. 71800 or 71825), a 5-min. walk from the town center (turn left out of the station and walk straight). Open Mon.-Sat. 9am-6pm. Buses to: Athlone (1/day; £11, students £6.50); Dublin via Mullingar (3/day; 4hr.; £8, students £4.40); Galway (Mon.-Sat. 9/day, Sun. 5/day; 3hr.; £9.70, students £6); Donegal (Mon.-Sat. 3/day, Sun. 1/day; £10, students £6); Sligo (Mon.-Sat. 3-4/day; 2hr.; £7.30, students £4.20); and Westport (Mon.-Sat. 3/day, Sun. 1/day; 1½hr.; £6.30, students £3.90).

Taxis: Mulherin Taxi Service, the Brook (tel. 21783).

Bike Rental: Gerry's Cycle Centre, 6 Lord Edward St. (tel. 70455). £7/day, £30/week; collection service available. Open Mon.-Sat. 9am-7pm.

Luggage Storage: At bus station, £1.30/piece.

Pharmacy: S. Quinn and Sons Chemist, Pearce St. (tel. 21365). Open Mon.-Sat. 9am-6pm.

Laundry: Moy Laundrette, Cathedral Rd. (tel. 22358). Wash and dry £4.

Emergency: Dial 999; no coins required. **Garda:** Walsh St. (tel. 21422).

Post Office: Casement St. (tel. 21498). Open Mon.-Sat. 9am-5:30pm.

Phone Code: 096.

ACCOMMODATIONS

The Salmon Weir Hostel, Berret St. (tel. 71903), is reason enough to come to Ballina. Glorious, luxurious, harmonious—this hostel has an outdoor patio, fantastic kitchen, and beds that even *smell* clean. Most rooms have river views (beware; the river salmon have terrestrial pretensions. Bed with sleeping bag £6.50, dorm £7.50; private room £9/person. Irish breakfast £3.50, continental £1.80. Laundry £4.50. Bike rental £7/day.) From the bus station, turn right, take your first left (after the small shop), then the first right, and again the first left onto Barrett St. The hostel is on the right. The river, the lake, and seafishing are just a cast away from Ms. Galvin's **Greenhill,** on Cathedral Close behind the tourist office (tel. 27674; £14/person, w/bath £16; Jan.-Nov.). Nearby, Breda Walsh's **Suncraft,** 31 Cathedral Close (tel. 21573) also charges £14/person, w/bath £16. **Belleek Camping and Caravan Park** (tel. 71533) is 2 mi. from Ballina toward Killala on R314, behind the Belleek Woods (£3/hiker with tent; laundry and kitchen; open March-Oct.).

FOOD & PUBS

Aspiring gourmets can prepare for a feast at Quinnsworth **supermarket** (tel. 21056) on Market Rd. Gourmands have it good, too.

Cafolla's, Bridge St. (tel. 21029). Cheap, fast, and almost Italian. Small cheese and tomato pizza £2, veggie kebab £2.65. Open Mon.-Sat. 10am-12:30pm.

Murphy Bros., Clare St. (tel. 22702), past the Cathedral. Excellent bar food (chicken Kiev £4), excellent but expensive restaurant food. Open pub hours.

Jordy's, Pearse St. (tel. 21916). Get caught up in the fishing nets and flowers. Jordy specializes in grilling but can placate vegetarians, too. Vegetarian stir-fry £4.40, Florida burger £2.65. Open Mon.-Sat. 9:30am-midnight, Sun. 11am-midnight.

Tullio's, Pearse St. (tel. 21890). Exudes elegance. Crab claws in garlic butter £4.75. Restaurant open daily noon-3pm and 6-10pm. Bar food noon-10pm.

Brogan's Bar and Restaurant, Garden St. (tel. 21961). Some of the best meat in town, but you have to pay for it. Fisherman's platter £8.50. Food served til 9pm.

Down by the river on Clare St., **Murphy's** (tel. 22702) serves pints to twenty-somethings settled into the dark wood furnishings. **Longneck's** (tel. 22702), a popular disco (Thurs.-Sun. nights) sporting an adobe and sombrero motif, is in the same building. **Hogan's,** O'Rahilly St. (tel. 22527), has a hint of the Victorian in its old pictures and stained glass windows. **Gaughan's** (tel. 21151), across the street, emphasizes its addictive and traditional atmosphere by selling pipe tobacco and snuff. **An Bolg Bui,** just before the bridge on Bridge St. (tel. 22561), is Irish for "the yellow belly." The pub calls itself a "young fisherperson's pub." Along with pouring pints, it displays its talents and fearlessness by organizing fishing trips, tackle, and licenses. **Doherty's,** next door (tel. 21150), revels more exclusively in the angling lifestyle. **The Loft,** Pearse St. (tel. 21881), rocks with all kinds of music nightly in summer, less frequently in winter. Or sink into the **Armada Bar** (see **Sights,** below).

SIGHTS

Christmas comes twice a year here, once in December and once in the second week of July during the **Ballina Salmon Festival** (tel. 71877), which has been swinging since 1964. All of Mayo is hooked for the festival's **Heritage Day,** when the streets are closed off and life reverts to the year 1910. All aspects of traditional Irish life are staged: greasy pig contests, a traditional Irish wake, donkey-driven butter churns, etc. Events center on Wednesday but overflow into the rest of the week.

Trace out walks along the river in the bird-rich **Belleek Woods** (bah-LEEK) around **Belleek Castle,** a fairytale forest with an exquisite bird-to-tree-to-stream ratio. To reach the Beleek Woods entrance, cross the lower bridge near the cathedral on Pearse St. and keep Ballina House on your right. Beleek Castle is an expensive hotel, but its **Armada Bar,** eerily reminiscent of a Spanish galleon, is accessible and affordable. Downstairs, another hotel bar carouses in a medieval banquet hall. Owner Marshall Doran gives tours of the castle and even allows a look at his own fossil collection and **armory museum,** with exhibits dating as far back as the 16th-century (tel. 22400; by appointment only; admission £2).

A nearby dolmen, called "Table of the Giants," dates to 2000 BC. It supposedly marks the burial site of four Maols who murdered Ceallach, a 7th-century bishop of Connacht. They were hanged at Ardaree, then commemorated with the huge rock.

East of Ballina, the lonely **Ox Mountains** are best seen by bike. Dirt and asphalt trails criss-cross their way up the slopes under trees and around tiny lakes. The 70-km **Ox Mountain Drive** traces the scenic perimeter of the mountains, and is pretty well signposted from **Tobercurry** (34km south of Sligo on the N17). Equestrian enthusiasts can ride horses 7 mi. north of Ballina along the road to Sligo, at **Ox Mountain Slopes Ltd.,** Cloonkeeland, Corballa (tel. (096) 36451; pony trekking £8/hour).

■ Near Ballina

ENNISCRONE

Fifteen minutes northeast of Ballina on the scenic Quay Rd. (R297), the gorgeous **Enniscrone Strand** (or Inishcrone) stretches along the east shore of Killala Bay. You'll have a mile to yourself on this long beach. The town itself is small and pleasant. Maura O'Dowd's **Point View House,** Main St. (tel. (096) 36312) serves a home-style dinner (£7) before sending you to a comfortable night's sleep (£14/person w/bath). The **Atlantic Caravan Park** (tel. (096) 36132) puts some grass under your tent (£4) or caravan (£6) and has laundry facilities. **Walsh's Pub,** Main St. (tel. (096) 36110) serves great pub grub all day (herbed mackerel salad £3.75; dinner 6-9pm). This cozy, dark pub also has trad music Wednesday nights. **Harnett's Bar,** Main. St. (tel. (096) 36137) serves good, but pricey, lunch from 1 to 2:30pm (tuna salad £4.50; Beef in Guinness £4.50) amid walls decorated with old matchboxes.

Opposite the long beach, the dreamy, family-run **Kilcullen's Bath House** (tel. 36238) simmers and steams, leaving you weak all over. Steam baths in cedarwood cabinets which leave only the head exposed and cool seaweed baths can relax even the most excitable traveler (no time limits, towels supplied; £6/seaweed bath, £7/steam bath and hot & cold seaweed baths). Post-soak, a tea room with views of the Strand awaits. (Both open June-Aug. 10am-10pm, May and Sept.-Oct. 10am-9pm, Nov.-April noon-8pm.) An **Art Exhibition,** Main Rd., displays paintings of local and Irish scenery (open Mon.-Sat. 10:30am-6pm, Sun. 2-6pm). **Fishing** enthusiasts should contact John McDonagh (tel. 45332) for guidance and equipment.

BALLYCASTLE

Tidy Ballycastle is bordered by rich farmland on one side, by bogs on the other. The town would make a nice set for a tragic love story: stunning beaches for the good stuff, two tantalizing, remorse-inducing churches, and the Ceide (KAY-ja) cliffs for when love sours. R314 crosses Ballycastle on its way west from Ballina to Belmullet; R315 leads due south to Crossmolina. **Tourist information** (tel. 43256) is available from Moy Valley Resources Ltd., Lower Main St. (open Mon.-Sat 10:30am-5pm, Sun. 1-4pm). **Ulster Bank** opens its mini-office Tuesday 10am-noon. **Bus Éireann** has a service to Killala and Ballina (Mon.-Sat. 3/day). The **post office** (tel. 43036) on Main St. will send love letters (open Mon.-Fri. 9am-5:30pm, Sat. 9am-1pm). The **phone code** in this tragic love story is 096.

Accommodations, Food & Pubs Opulent—nay, *palatial*—digs, huge meals, and potpourri under the pillow grace Mrs. Chambers' B&B, **Suantai** (tel. 43040), on the edge of town toward Killala (£15/person w/bath). **Ceide House B&B** and restaurant, Main St. (tel. 43105), offers a double feature that starts with distinctly Mayo cuisine (open daily 9am-9pm) and ends the show in comfortable lodgings (£14.50/person w/bath). A tearoom and bar march side by side to the beat of different drums at **Barrett's** (tel. 43006; open 10:30am-12:30am). **McNamee's Supermarket**, Main St. (tel. 43057), sells peanut butter, jelly, and more; open 9am til late. Forget rebellions and revolutions: at the **Castle Lounge** (tel. 43031), an olive green interior captures the spirit of 1976 (salmon sandwich £1.60).

Sights Apart from the **Catholic Church** in town, any structures of real significance are outside Ballycastle. To see the sights, walk across town toward **Ceide Fields,** turning right at the sign for the fisheries. From there, the road follows a bucolic route to the ocean, passing **Dun Briste** and stoic **Downpatrick Head.** The multi-layered rock formation supposedly broke off from the mainland during a dispute between St. Patrick and a pagan king; Patrick used the geological disturbance as convincing evidence of his God's power. More recently, a car manufacturer helicoptered one of its vehicles upon Dun Briste to make a spectacular TV commercial.

Five miles toward the Mullet Peninsula, the **Ceide Fields** are open to visitors through an **interpretive center** (tel. 43325), which offers exhibits, films, guided tours, and an excavated Stone Age wall. Ancient farming settlements are buried in the bog around the center. The center is architecturally interesting, as it was built around a 5000-year-old Scotch pine that had been dug out of the bog. And if all the muck gets you down, the 350 million-year-old Ceide Cliffs rise high nearby. The excellent film and tour provide the same information. (Open mid-March to May and Oct. Mon.-Sat. 10am-5pm; June-Sept. Mon.-Sat. 9:30am-6:30pm. Tours every hr., film every ½hr. Admission £2.50, students £1. Wheelchair accessible.)

LOWER MOY VALLEY

Ten miles south of Ballina on N26, the massively over-hyped **Foxford Woolen Mills,** Main St. (tel. (094) 56756), were founded by an entrepreneurial nun a century ago. The mill is full of religious icons, and a showroom displays a series of life-like tableaux chronicling the run-of-the-Mill history. (Open May-Oct. Mon.-Sat. 10am-6pm, Sun. noon-6pm; Nov.-April Mon.-Sat. 10am-6pm, Sun 2-6pm. Tours: 3/hr., 1hr. Admission £3, students £2.50.) Between Foxford and Swinford on N57 is the **Carraig Abhainn Farm** (tel. (094) 56444). Follow signposts to "Open Farm." Barn dances, trad music, and farm animals drag in the locals (open Easter-Sept. Mon.-Sat. 10am-6pm, Sun. 1-6pm; admission £2.50).

The general frenzy of fins and hooks continues west of Foxford, across the lakes in the minuscule town of **Pontoon.** The **Tiernan Brothers' North Mayo Angling Centre,** Upper Main St. (tel. (094) 56731, ask for Thomas; open daily 7am-late) may become your spiritual guide. Gillies (guides) for one full day cost £30, but advice is free. **Cooltra Lodge** (tel. (094) 56640), a 14-bed hostel, monopolizes a great location

100 yd. from the Pontoon Bridge at the intersection of Lough Conn and Lough Cullin (dorm £5, private room £6/person; **bikes** £4/day; open June-Sept.).

The miniature **Bellacorick Bog Train** (tel. (096) 53002) departs from its station on N59 between Ballina and Bangor, west of Crossmalina. The 50-min. guided rail tour chugs through blanket bog, Ireland's first windfarm, and the flora and fauna of the Nephin Mountains (open May-Sept. Mon.-Sat. 5/day; £3, students £1.75).

▨ Knock

At 8pm on August 21, 1879, St. Joseph, St. John, and the Virgin Mary appeared at Knock with a cross, a lamb, an altar, and a host of angels. The visions materialized before at least 15 witnesses, who stood in the rain for two hours watching the apparitions and chanting the Rosary. The Catholic hierarchy endorsed the reports, and Knock quickly developed into a major pilgrimage site. The streets overflow with entrepreneurs hawking anything (keychains, ashtrays, Knock-knacks, etc.) emblazoned with the Knock label. While the blatant commercialism may be amusing, the intent and holy atmosphere of the town seems remarkably sincere. To anyone interested in the sociology of religion, Knock proves fascinating.

Knock lies between Galway and Sligo on N17 and makes a good roadside stop for folks hopping between the two. Knock's **tourist office** (tel. 88193) is suitably central (open May-Sept. daily 10am-6pm). Two doors down, the **shrine office** (tel. 88100) hides to the left of the Presbytery and sells Knock literature and official calendars. The *Knock Pilgrim's Guide* (10p) contains a useful map (open June-Oct. daily 9am-8:30pm, Nov. 10am-6pm). **Bank of Ireland** is located in the tourist office building (open May-Oct. Mon. and Thurs. 10:15am-12:15pm; Nov.-April Mon. 10:15am-12:15pm). Testifying to the drawing power of Knock, **Horan Cutríl Airport** (tel. 67222), 11 mi. from the town, near Charlestown, attracts pilgrim cash with direct flights to the U.K. and is the subject of a tune by Christy Moore. **Bus Éireann** stops at either Coleman's or at Lennon's. Buses depart for Dublin (2/day, Sun. 1/day), Westport or Roscommon and Athlone (Sun. 1/day), and Sligo (Sun. 3/day) and arrive from Athlone, Ballina, Castlebar, Galway, Roscommon, Sligo, and Westport (all Mon.-Sat. 2-3/day). The **post office** is in Henegan's by the traffic circle (tel. 88210; open Tues.-Sat. 9am-5:30pm). Knock, knock. Who's there? **Phone code 094!**

"Hostels" in town are for the sick or elderly, but B&Bs abound. Mrs. Carney's **Burren,** on Kiltimagh Rd. (tel. 88362), induces restful slumber (£13.50/person). Campers stay at **Knock Caravan and Camping** (tel. 88223), about ½ mi. from the roundabout on the Claremore Rd (N17). (July-Aug. £5.50/caravan and 25p/person, £3.50/cyclist or hiker; March-June and Sept.-Oct. £5/caravan and 25p/person. Laundry.) Food prices are aimed toward the masses. When bread and water lose their appeal, head for **Beirne's Restaurant** (tel. 88161), on the main road (£6/3-course lunch; open daily noon-6pm). **Ard Mhuire's** (tel. 88459) is an enticing split-level restaurant on Main St. (roast beef, veggies, and potatoes £4.50; open April-Oct. 10am-7:30pm). **Wally's,** Main St. (tel. 88408), burdens you with food and change; nothing on the large menu costs over £2 (burger and chips £1.80; open June-Sept. daily noon-1:30am; Oct.-May daily 6pm-1:30am).

Despite all the pilgrims (a 1979 Papal visit drew a half-million faithfuls), Knock is a tiny, one-street town, and all of the religious sights are clustered along this street. The Apparition supposedly appeared in the **Courtyard of Statues,** next to the **Church of the Apparition**. Numerous healings are said to have occurred in the courtyard. The enormous **Church of Our Lady** holds 20,000 people, but remains peaceful and cozy. Mass times are posted in the processional square (services at 8, 9:30, 11am, noon, 3, and 7pm). Signs everywhere command visitors to keep quiet and off the grass, but the devout can collect holy water at one of 18 automatic dispensers near the statues. The **Knock Folk Museum,** to the right of the basilica (tel. 88100), portrays rural 19th-century life. The eyewitness accounts of the apparition and the old photographs of Irish life are the best reasons to visit. (Open July-Aug. daily 10am-7pm; May-June and Sept.-Oct. daily 10am-6pm; admission £1.50.)

Roscommon & Leitrim

■ Carrick-on-Shannon

Water, water everywhere—and, probably, Guinness to drink. Lough Allen and Lough Key empty into the River Shannon in and around Carrick-on-Shannon. Anglers catch pike; yachtsmen drop in. Natural beauty lures tourists to the Lough Key Forest Park. Two major streets, Bridge and Main, meet at the town's clock tower. The Famine Museum in nearby Strokestown is a moving reminder of the catastrophe endured by western Ireland during the mid-19th century.

PRACTICAL INFORMATION

Tourist Office: the Marina (tel. 20170). Open Sept.-June Mon.-Fri. 9am-1pm and 2-5pm, Sat. 9am-6pm, Sun. 10am-2pm; July-Aug. Mon.-Sat. 9am-1pm and 2-8pm.
Bank: AIB, Main St. (tel. 20055). Open Mon. 10am-5pm, Tues.-Fri. 10am-4pm; **ATM.**
Trains: The train station (tel. 20036), a 10-min. walk southwest of town, sends carriages to: Sligo (3/day; 1hr.; £4) and Dublin (4/day, Sun. 3/day; 2½hr.; £10).
Buses: Buses leave from Coffey's Pastry Case for: Athlone (1/day; 1½hr.); Boyle (3/day; 15min.); Sligo (3/day; 1hr.); and Dublin (3/day; 3hr.).
Taxis: P. Burke, Bridge St. (tel. 21343).
Bike Rental: Geraghty's, Main St. (tel. 21316). £5-7/day, £15-25/week; deposit £20. Fishing tackle £15/week. Open daily 9am-9pm.
Boat Rental: Michael Lynch, Villa Maria, (tel. 20034).
Laundromat: McGuire's Washeteria, Main St. (tel. 20339). Open daily 10am-6pm. Wash and dry £4.50.
Pharmacy: Cox's, Bridge St. (tel. 20158). Open Mon.-Sat. 9am-6pm.
St. Patrick's Hospital: Summerhill Rd. (tel. 20011 or 20287; nights 20091).
Emergency: Dial 999; no coins required. **Garda:** Shannon Lodge (tel. 20021).
Post Office: St. George's Terrace (tel. 20020). Open Mon.-Sat. 9am-5:30pm.
Phone Code: 078.

ACCOMMODATIONS, FOOD, & PUBS

Clean, comfortable bunk rooms, well-fed birds, and a microwave are found at the **Town Clock Hostel (IHH)** (tel. 20068), at the junction of Main and Bridge St. (£5.50, sheets 50p; open June-Sept.). B&Bs border Station Rd. and the manicured lawns of St. Mary's Close. Mrs. Clarke's **Sunnybank,** Station Rd. (tel. 20988), has several luxurious rooms worthy of Robin Leach's nasal commentary (£14/person; open April-Oct.). **Aisling,** St. Mary's Close (tel. 20131), behind the Church of Ireland on Main St., corners the market on cozy abodes. It also pampers guests with a TV and coffee/tea facilities in each room (double w/bath £30; open April-Nov.).

Chung's Chinese Restaurant, Main St. (tel. 21888), cooks up a storm. Order takeaway and save big; eat in and savor the candlelight. (Sweet 'n sour chicken £4.50 take-away, £5.80 eat-in; open Sept.-June Mon., Wed., and Thurs. 6-11pm, Fri.-Sat. 6pm-midnight; July-Aug. Mon.-Thurs. 6-11pm, Fri.-Sat. 6pm-midnight, Sun. 12:30pm-midnight.) To eat at **Coffey's Pastry Case,** Bridge St. (tel. 20929), without sampling the cake is a sin (pizza slice w/choice of 3 salads £2.85; open Mon.-Sat. 8:30am-9pm, Sun. 10:30am-7pm). Wash down great meals to the tune of traditional sessions (every Sat. and Sun. in summer, impromptu sessions in winter) at **Cryan's Pub,** in The Riverside Inn on Bridge St. (tel. 20409). Move in with the Lost Generation and locals in the splendidly furnished **Flynn's Corner Pub,** Main St. (tel. 20003), near the tiny town clock. **Ging's** (tel. 21054), just across the town bridge, boasts a beer garden on the River Shannon. They don't serve food, "just drink—and plenty of it."

SIGHTS

At the intersection of Main and Bridge St., teeny, tiny **Costello Memorial Chapel** is reputedly the second smallest in the world. The **Angling Information Centre,** 2 mi. from Carrick-on-Shannon in Drumsna (tel. 20694), supplies boats (£15/day), tackle, bait, and even info. For more detailed information, the **Angling and Tourism Association** (tel. 20489) is the place. Fishing tackle is sold at **Holt's,** Bridge St. (tel. 20184; open daily 7:30am-10pm).

■ Near Carrick-on-Shannon

STROKESTOWN

Fifteen miles south of Carrick on R368, where it meets N5 from Longford, poses the 18th-century **Strokestown Park House,** on Main St. (tel. (078) 33013). This former family estate of the Mahons has been expansively restored. The family's dark history of Irish blunders includes fighting as mercenaries for Oliver Cromwell, evicting 3006 tenants during the Famine, and subsidizing a number of coffin-ships (the infamous emigration ships). By 1847, the worst year of the Famine, the tenants had had enough oppression and killed Denis Mahon. The house was occupied until 1979. A casual, unforced grandeur remains. Stags' heads, Chippendale bookcases, and velvet curtains seem to naturally belong here, but meager servants' quarters, kitchen, and underground service tunnel reveal the other side of post-feudal oppression.

The **Famine Museum,** located in the old stables next to the house, moves and angers visitors more than anything in the house itself. Photographs and drawings of sallow, wide-eyed, starving tenants depict a world totally different from the one in the Strokestown House. (See **Famine (1841-1870),** p.62.) (Open Easter-Oct. Tues.-Sun. 11am-5:30pm. Museum £3, house £2.50; guided tours are available.)

LOUGH RYNN & LOUGH KEY

The Earls of Leitrim once roamed the 100-acre **Lough Rynn Estate** (tel. (078) 31427), just outside Mohill, 15 mi. east of Carrick on N4 to Dublin. A walled Victorian garden and the turret house overlooking 600 acres of lake are remnants from the past century. A pleasant walking tour will guide you into the beautiful parklands, which include angling spots and the country's oldest monkey-puzzle tree. (Open late April to Aug. daily 10am-7pm; admission £1.50, cars £3.50; tours £1/person, last tour at 4pm.) The **Lough Rynn Caravan Park** (tel. (078) 31054) services campers on the shores of Lough Rynn (£5/tent, £5/caravan; open March-Oct.).

Four miles west of Carrick-on-Shannon on the road to Boyle, the **Lough Key Forest Park** (tel. (079) 62363) bursts with rhododendrons in the springtime. Its 850 acres and 33 forested islands are worth exploring any time of the year. Underground chambers, "bog gardens," and boat tours strew themselves across the shores. Numerous signposts won't let you miss the round tower, fairy bridge, and wishing chair (admission £1; always open). North of the Lough lies the site of Ireland's most important pre-human battle, in which the Túatha De Danann defeated Ireland's indigenous demons, the Formorians (see **Legends and Folktales,** p. 69).

■ Boyle

The last major city on the Dublin-Sligo route, Boyle makes a convenient stop before launching into the **Curlieu Mountains.** Boyle is mostly overlooked by tourists as a destination, but recent developments, such as the excellent King House, have made it an interesting place for a short stay.

PRACTICAL INFORMATION

Tourist Office: Main St. (tel. 62145), inside the main gates of King House. Open May to mid-Sept. 9am-5pm.

Banks: National Irish Bank, at Bridge and Main St. (tel. 62058). Open Mon. 10am-5pm, Tues.-Fri. 10am-3pm; **ATM. Bank of Ireland,** Main St. (tel. 62015). Open Mon. 10am-12:30pm and 1:30-5pm, Tues.-Fri. 10am-12:30pm and 1:30-4pm.

Trains: The **station** (tel. 62027), past the Town Clock on the road to Roscommon, lies on the Dublin-Sligo route. Trains go to Dublin (3/day; 2½hr.; £10, students £7) and Sligo (3/day; 40min.; £4, students £2).

Buses: The stop is outside the Royal Hotel on Bridge St. Services to: Dublin (daily 3/day; 3¼hr.); Sligo (daily 3/day; 45min.); and Athlone (daily 1/day; 1¼hr).

Bike Rental: Sheerin Cycles, Main St. (tel. 62010). A Raleigh agent; £7/day, £30/week; deposit £40. Open Mon.-Tues. and Thurs.-Sat. 9:30am-1pm and 2-6pm.

Taxi: McHughs (tel. 63344).

Pharmacy: Patrick J. Ryan, Patrick and Main St. (tel. 62003). Open June-Sept. Mon.-Sat. 9am-6pm; Oct.-May Mon.-Tues. and Thurs.-Sat. 9am-6pm, Wed. 9:30am-1:15pm.

Emergency: Dial 999; no coins required. **Garda:** Military Rd. (tel. 62030).

Post Office: Carrick Rd. (tel. 62029 or 62028). Open Mon., Wed., and Thurs.-Fri. 9am-5:30pm, Tues. 9:30am-5:30pm, Sat. 9am-1pm and 2-5:30pm.

Phone Code: 079.

ACCOMMODATIONS, FOOD, & PUBS

The best and only hostel in the area is in nearby Carrick-on-Shannon (see p.324). Every visitor to Boyle's **Abbey House,** Abbeytown Rd. (tel. 62385), gets an individually decorated room (£14/person, w/bath £16/person). **Avonlea** (tel. 62538), on the Carrick Rd. just before you enter Boyle, puts up Annes by the dozen (single £15, double £28). The **Lough Key Forest Caravan & Camping Park** (tel. 62212), and its laundry facilities are just a five-minute drive from Boyle on the Carrick Rd. (£7.25/tent, £2.50/hiker or cyclist; open Easter-Aug.).

D. H. Burke, Main St. (tel. 62208) fulfills the duties of a supermarket (open Mon.-Thurs. 9:30am-6pm, Fri. 9:30am-8pm, Sat. 9:30am-7pm). **Una Bhán Restaurant** (tel. 63033), located within the gates of the King House, is the place to go for breakfast and lunch (battered cod, chips, and peas £3.10; open daily 9:30am-6:30pm). **Chung's Chinese Restaurant,** Bridge St. (tel. 63123), has bunches of bean sprouts (open Mon.-Tues. and Thurs.-Sun. 5:30-11pm). **The Royal Hotel,** Bridge St. (tel. 62016), says, "beer today, scone tomorrow." The coffee shop part will feed you (lasagna £2.50; open 10:30am-6pm; lunch served 12:30-3pm) and the bar will comfort you (shepherd's pie £2.10; dinner 6-9pm).

SIGHTS & ENTERTAINMENT

Gothic arches curve over the green lawns of magnificent **Boyle Abbey** (tel. 62604; on A4), built in 1161 by Cistercian monks. The central arched walls, though lacking a roof, are perfectly preserved. (Open mid-June to mid-Sept. daily 9:30am-6:30pm. Admission £1, students 40p. Key available from the caretaker in off season.)

King House, Main St. (tel. 63242), recently reopened its doors and its four Georgian floors to superb historical exhibits. Built by Sir Henry King around 1730 for entertaining VIPs, it served as a family home and as army barracks. The house is now decked out in 3-D displays and excellent interactive exhibits chronicling the history of the "Kings of Connaught." Particularly touching is a letter sent by a prisoner to his mother: "...dreadful news that I am to be shot...But what harm..." King House is also home to the **Boyle Civic Art Collection** of paintings and sculptures. (Open May-Sept. daily 10am-6pm, April and Oct. Sat.-Sun. 10am-6pm. Admission £3, students £2.50. Last admission at 5pm).

New in town, **Frybrook House,** Bridge St. (tel. 62170), lies on the banks of the Boyle River. Built in 1752, this Georgian house has been restored and refurbished to resemble its glory days. Although not as grand as King House, Frybrook has undeniable style. The house is still used as a residence, so only a set of intriguing windows and the bottom floors are open for viewing (open June-Aug. daily 2-6pm; admission £3, students £2.50; tour included).

NORTHWEST IRELAND

The farmland of the upper Shannon gradually gives way to Sligo. Sligo Town, alive and kicking, is surrounded by landscapes and monuments close to the heart of William Butler Yeats. A mere sliver of land connects Co. Sligo to Co. Donegal, the most remote and most foreign of the Republic's counties. Donegal's windy mountains and winding coasts are a dreamlike landscape. Don't leave the country before seeing the inspiring Inishowen Peninsula (Derry, in Northern Ireland, is readily accessible from here). Hitchhikers report that the upper Shannon region is difficult to thumb through and that they often end up relying on trucks. Drivers in Donegal are said to be much friendlier.

County Sligo

If W.B. Yeats had never existed, County Sligo would be merely a pretty coastal stretch of hills, low cliffs, and choppy waves between boggy north Mayo and mountainous Donegal. As it is, the county is something of a literary pilgrimage site. The preadolescent Yeats divided his time between London and Sligo Town. The windswept landmarks near Sligo Bay became symbols and settings for many of his poems. It's easiest (and most exciting) to spend the nights in Sligo Town; everything else can be seen either on daytrips or on the way to Enniskillen or Donegal.

■ Sligo Town

The gray River Garavogue gurgles along, swans and all, through the commercial, industrial, and market center that is Sligo Town (pop. 18,000). As you approach the town by rail, two imposing hills, Knocknarea and Benbulben, loom in the mist beyond train windows like possessive guardians competing for prominence in Sligo's stormy seaside landscape. W.B. Yeats was raised here by his mother's family, the Pollexfens, who owned a mill over the Garavogue. Most of Sligo can (and does) boast of some connection to the poet. The busy Sligo streets flow with a steady stream of people during the day. Sligo evenings bop to the beat of some 70 pubs and discos. Musical offerings range from Gaelic lays to Gaelic rock to Garth Brooks.

ORIENTATION & PRACTICAL INFORMATION

Both trains and buses pull into the same station on Lord Edward St. From the station, take a left and follow Lord Edward St. straight onto Wine St., then turn right at the post office onto O'Connell St., which is the main street. More shops, pubs, and eateries beckon from Grattan, left off O'Connell.

> **Tourist Office:** Temple St. on the corner of Charles St. (B3; tel. 61201). From the station, turn left along Lord Edward St., turn right onto Adelaid St., follow this up the hill past the cathedral and around the corner onto Temple St. to find the Northwest regional office with information on Donegal, Monaghan, Cavan, Leitrim, and Sligo counties. Some freebies, but the bulk of the literature will cost you. Open June Mon.-Sat. 9am-6pm; July-Aug. Mon.-Sat. 9am-8pm, Sun. 9am-2pm; Sept. Mon.-Fri. 9am-8pm, Sun. 9am-1pm; Oct.-May 9am-5pm. There's also an info booth on O'Connell St. in Quinnsworth arcade (open Mon.-Sat. 10am-5:30pm).

Travel Agency: Broderick's Travel, O'Connell St. Arcade (tel. 45221). USIT rates for students. Open Mon.-Sat. 9am-6pm.

Banks: AIB, 49 O'Connell St. (tel. 41085). Open Mon.-Wed. and Fri. 10am-4pm, Thurs. 10am-5pm; **ATM** accepts Visa, MC. **TSB,** 31 O'Connell St. (tel. 45360). Open Mon.-Wed. and Fri. 9:30am-5pm, Thurs. 9:30am-7pm.

Airport: Sligo Airport, Strandhill (tel. 68280). Open daily 9am-8pm.

Trains: McDiarmada Station, Lord Edward St. (tel. 69888; open Mon.-Sat. 7am-6pm, Sun. 20min. before departure) sends trains to Dublin via Carrick-on-Shannon and Mullingar (Mon. 4/day, Tues.-Sun. 3/day; £12, students £9).

Buses: Station (tel. 60066) open Mon.-Thurs. 9:30am-6pm, Fri. 9:30am-7pm, Sat. 9:30am-4:30pm, Sun. 2-5pm. Buses fan out to: Belfast (Mon.-Sat. 3/day; 4hr.; £11.50, students £8.50); Derry (Mon.-Sat. 6/day, Sun. 3/day; 3hr.; £10, students £6); Dublin (3/day; 4hr.; £8, students £7); Galway (Mon.-Sat. 4/day, Sun. 3/day; 2½hr.; £10.50, students £6.50); and Westport (Mon.-Sat. 3/day; 2¾hr.; £9.70, students £6).

Luggage Storage: In the train station; £1.30/piece.

Taxi: Cab 55, tel. 42333; **Finnegan's,** tel. 77777, 44444, or 41111 (for easy dialing if you're drunk); at least £3 in town, 50p/mi. outside.

Bike Rental: Gary's Cycles, Quay St. (tel. 45418), £6/day, £25/week; deposit £30. Open Mon.-Sat. 9am-6pm. **Flanagan's Cycles,** Connelly and High St. (tel. 44477; after hours tel. 62633). £7/day, £30/week; deposit £35. They offer other deposit destinations and do repairs. Open Mon.-Sat. 9am-6pm.

Bike Repair: P.J. Coleman, Stephen St. (tel. 43345).

Boat Rental: Peter Henry (tel. 42530), Blue Lagoon. Rowboat £15/day; w/motor £25/day plus fuel.

Bookstore: Keohane's, Castle St. (tel. 42597). Big and smart. Sells Kirby's *Sligo, Land of Yeats's Desire.* Open Mon.-Sat. 8am-6:30pm, Sun. 8am-1:30pm.

Camping: Out & About, 20 Market St. (tel. 44550). All your outdoor needs met indoors. Open Mon.-Sat. 9:30am-6pm.

Laundry: Gurries, High St. (tel. 69268). Small wash and dry £3-4, large (like 30 pairs of jeans) £10-14. Open Mon.-Sat. 9am-7pm; last wash 4:45pm.

Hotline: Samaritans: tel. 42011. 24hr.

Pharmacy: E. Horan, Castle St. (tel. 42560), at Market St. Open Mon.-Sat. 9:30am-6pm. Local pharmacies post schedules of rotating Sun. openings.

Hospital: General Hospital, the Mall (tel. 42161).

Emergency: Dial 999; no coins required. **Garda:** Pearse Rd. (tel. 42031).

Post Office: Wine St. (tel. 42593), on the corner of O'Connell St. Open Mon. and Wed.-Sat. 9am-5:30pm, Tues. 9:30am-5:30pm.

Phone Code: The unpurged images of day recede, 071.

IMPRACTICAL INFORMATION

Wind Surfing: Sligo Yacht Park, Rosses Point (tel. 77168).

Woodcarver/Storyteller: Michael Quirke, Wine St. (tel. 42724). Open Mon.-Sat. 9am-6pm.

Fork Lift Rental: Meadowbank Industrial Estate (tel. 69890).

Falconry Courses: Michael Devlin (tel. 83211).

Tennis: Ballincar House Hotel (tel. 45361). Private hard court free.

ACCOMMODATIONS

There simply are not enough hostels in Sligo to handle the hordes of invading tourists, especially during the Yeats International Summer School weeks in mid-August. The cheaper options are often overcrowded and chaotic. B&Bs abound five minutes (on foot) out of town on Pearse Rd.

Eden Hill Holiday Hostel (IHH), Pearse Rd. (tel. 43204), entrance via Marymount or Ashbrook. 10min. from town, but worth it. Cozy rooms and a Victorian sitting parlor. An open fire fosters new friendships. Kitchen with 2 microwaves. TV and VCR in common room. Esso station nearby is open 24hr. for munchies. Dorm £6.50. Double £15. **Camping** £3/day. Laundry £2. Bikes £7/day.

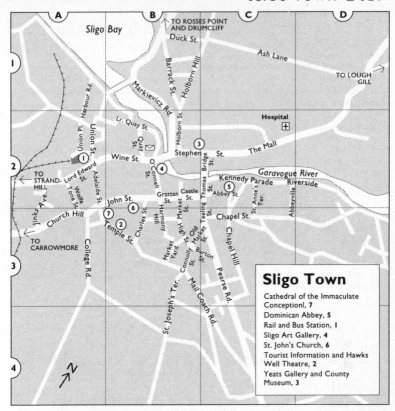

Sligo Town

Cathedral of the Immaculate Conceptionl, **7**
Dominican Abbey, **5**
Rail and Bus Station, **1**
Sligo Art Gallery, **4**
St. John's Church, **6**
Tourist Information and Hawks Well Theatre, **2**
Yeats Gallery and County Museum, **3**

White House Hostel (IHH), Markievicz Rd. (tel. 45160 or 42398), the first left off Wine St. after it crosses the bridge. Just 5min. from the train station, it fills fast. The epitome of a hip hostel, White House has bunks named after the likes of Jimi Hendrix, James Connolly, and Socrates. Call to reserve a woolly blanket and avoid disappointment. Dorm £6.50. Sheets £1. Key deposit £2.

Yeats County Hostel, 12 Lord Edward St., across from bus station. With small rooms it can get a little claustrophobic, but the company is friendly and the TV room home-like. Dorm £6. Key deposit £5.

Knocknarea Holiday Hostel, 5mi. out of town on the Strandhill Rd. (tel. 68777). With the solemn Knocknarea mountain in the back garden and the Atlantic Ocean near the front door, this refreshing hostel offers peace and quiet, excellent views, and plenty of exercise for those walking back from Sligo's pubs. Dorm £7. Laundry £1. Sheets £1. Open May-Oct.

Glenview B&B, 1mi. out of town on the Strandhill Rd. (tel. 62457). Friendly Mrs. Kane keeps 4 fine private rooms. Single £21. Double £32.

Renati House, Upper Johns St. (tel. 62014). Businesslike, spotless, and the cheapest B&B near the tourist office. Single £19, w/bath £21. Double £28, w/bath £32.

Greenlands Campground (tel. 77113 or 45618), on Rosses Point, 5mi. west of town (see below; buses run Mon.-Sat. 4-6/day; £1.65). At the end of Rosses Point Rd., Greenlands flanks the spectacular green land of a golf club. £5/tent, July-Aug. add 50p/person. Laundry free. Open late May to Sept.

Buenos Ayres, Seahill Rd. (tel. 68120), on the other side of the bay near Strandhill, is within earshot of the surf and just off the airport road (buses Mon.-Sat. 4-6/day; £1.60). £5/tent, July-Aug. add 50p/person. Laundry £2. Open Easter to mid-Sept.

FOOD

"Faery vats/Full of berries/And reddest stolen cherries" are not to be found in Sligo today. The demands of international visitors have, however, induced culinary development here. **Quinnsworth Supermarket,** O'Connell St., might sell berries (open Mon.-Tues. 9am-7pm, Wed.-Fri. 9am-9pm, Sat. 9am-6pm). **Tír na nÓg,** Grattan St. (tel. 62752), stocks health foods and, for the sophisticated, wine and cheese balls (open Mon.-Sat. 9am-6pm). Good restaurants are expensive (no poetic justice here).

The Cottage, Castle St. (tel. 45319). Irish-Asian flair (the Irish part is the pine furnishing). Kebabs of sundry varieties for £3.85. Open Mon.-Sat. 9am-6pm.

Kate's Kitchen, Market St. (tel. 43022). Not quite a restaurant, this combination deli/wholefood shop varies its take-away menu each day. French bread with gourmet toppings, vegetarian delights, homemade soups (£1), and fresh sandwiches from £1.15. Open Mon.-Sat. 9am-6:30pm.

Gullivers, Gratten St. (tel. 42030). Slightly upmarket and very classy, with an exterior that calls you in to eat. (pizza £5.15, golden fried fresh plaice £6.30; best bet is the chef's special £4). Open Mon.-Sat. 10am-midnight, Sun. 12:30pm-midnight.

Lyon's Café, Quay St. (tel. 42969). Tucked away upstairs, this cute café brews Bewley's coffee and bakes a selection of cakes. Lasagna salad £3.50. Open Mon.-Sat. 9am-6pm; lunch served 12:30-2pm.

Hargadon Bros., O'Connell St. (tel. 70933). Its reputation precedes it. Be prepared to scramble for a seat (see **Pubs,** below) Veggie lasagna and 2 salads £3. Restaurant open July-Oct. daily 10:30am-5pm; Sept.-June 10:30am-4pm.

PUBS

Sligo loves its pubs. Many pubs have live music during the summer. The weekly *Sligo Champion* (75p) lists events and venues.

Hargadon Bros., O'Connell St. (tel. 70933). Open fires, old Guinness bottles, *poitín* jugs, and dark, intimate nooks—nothing's changed here since 1868. The traditional pub of all traditional pubs, but no music.

McGarrigle's, O'Connell St. (tel. 71193). 18th-century lanterns light the cave-dark wooden interior. Live music Wed. and Thurs.; impromptu sessions other nights.

Shoot the Crows, Castle St., but clean up after yourself. Naked men carouse with snakes on the mural outside: an apt introduction to the epicenter for social gatherings of cool modern people. Music on Tues. and Thurs.

The Bear and Cat, Thomas Bridge St. (tel. 41310), don't really get along, but the pinball machines entertain kids. Cynical not-quite-young people hang out here. Live bands once or twice a week.

Connolly's, Markievicz Rd. (tel. 67377), a few steps from White House Hostel. Oldest pub in Sligo.

McLynn's, Old Market St. (tel. 60743). The *International Pub Guide* ranks McLynn's as the best pub for music in Sligo. Music on Fri. nights.

The Clarence, Wine St. (tel. 42211). Crowds stumble to this nightclub after the pubs close Tues.-Sat. nights. Live band Sat. (cover £3.50). The lounge bar has lounge music on lounging weekends.

SIGHTS

Yeats praised peasants and aristocrats (at least in principle) and disdained modern middle-class merchants and industrialists. Appropriately, most of the Yeatsian sights are at least a mile from the mercantile town center. In town, the 13th-century **Sligo Abbey,** Abbey St., is one of the best preserved of its type. This Dominican friary boasts cloisters and ornate coupled pillars that, though old and disused, can hardly be called ruins. A new staircase now allows visitors to view the equally intriguing upper floors. A defaced monument stone, which until quite recently bore the names of a mother and her child, graces the sacristy. Tradition claims that the mother's descendants, not wanting a public reminder of their forebears' illegitimacy, hired a stonemason to chisel the names away in secret. (Open summer daily 9:30am-6:30pm; last admission 45min. before closing. Admission £1.50, students 60p. If closed, ask for the key from Mrs. McGuinn, 6 Charlotte St.) The oldest of Sligo's churches is the 17th-century **St. John's Church,** on John St. (open Mon.-Sat. 10am-5:30pm; free). Next door, the hulking **Cathedral of the Immaculate Conception** is best visited at dawn or dusk, when the sun's rays stream through dozens of truly magnificent stained glass windows.

The **Yeats Art Gallery,** Stephen St., houses one of the country's finest collections of modern Irish art, including a number of works by Jack Butler Yeats (William Butler's brother) and contemporaries such as Nora McGuinness and Michael Healy. Among the museum's other treasures are some first editions of Yeats and original publications by the Dún Emer Press and Cuala Press. The gems among these are a few illustrated broadside collaborations by Jack and W.B. Yeats. The **Sligo County Museum** preserves small reminders of Yeats: pictures of his funeral and Countess Markievicz's prison apron. (Museum open June-Sept. Mon.-Sat. 10:30am-12:30pm and 2:30-4:30pm, April-May and Oct. Mon.-Sat. 10:30am-12:30pm. Gallery open Tues.-Sat. 10am-noon and 2-5pm. Both free.) The **Sligo Art Gallery** in the Yeats Memorial Building, Hyde Bridge (tel. 45847), hosts traveling exhibitions of Irish art (open daily 10am-5:30pm when there's a traveling exhibit).

ENTERTAINMENT

The Hawk's Well Theatre, Temple St. (tel. 61526 or 62167), beneath the tourist office, presents modern and traditional dramas, ballets, and musicals. The theater also sponsors lectures and conferences (partially linked to the Yeats Summer School). The theater box office is at 6 Union St. (open daily 10am-6pm; £6, students £4). **The Blue Raincoat Theatre Company,** Lr. Quay St. (tel. 70431), produces one-act plays, some, if you can believe this, by Yeats (June-Aug. Mon.-Fri. at 1pm).

A monthly *Calendar of Events,* available and free at the tourist office, elucidates the festivals and goings on in the Northwest region. Late August brings the **Sligo Arts Festival** and its fantastic events to town: traditional music, blues, rock, classical music, short story readings, comedy, and dance (contact the Sligo Arts Festival Office, Wine St.; tel. 69802). For two weeks in August, the internationally renowned **Yeats International Summer School** opens some of its poetry readings, lectures, and concerts to the public. International luminaries such as Seamus Heaney are regular guests. (For an application, contact the Yeats Society, Yeats Memorial Building, Douglas Hyde Bridge, Sligo; tel. 42693, call Mon.-Fri. 10am-1pm and 3-5pm.)

■ Near Sligo Town

LOUGH GILL

Lough Gill is just a short distance southeast of Sligo. From town, take the Enniskillen Rd. and turn off at the Lough Gill signs. Signs from the main road point to **Holywell,** a rather unusual shrine, with a well and waterfall. During the Penal Law years, secret masses were held at this site. If by chance the British Military approached, the congregation would disband and pretend to be enjoying a football game. The main road itself reaches **Dooney Rock,** on the south shore of Lough Gill near Cottage Island. Here, Yeats's "Fiddler of Dooney" made "folk dance like a wave of the sea." An even younger Yeats wrote **"The Lake Isle of Innisfree,"** about an actual island in Lough Gill where "peace comes dropping slow." To see it yourself, descend to the edge of the Lough.

Along the same route lies **Dromahair,** which still shelters Creevelea Abbey. Founded in 1508 as the Friary of Killanummery, its active days ended in 1650 when Oliver "Religious Freedom" Cromwell expelled monks from the confiscated monastery. It has been a burial site since 1721. Dromahair is the farther point of the Lough Gill route. From here, turn left onto R286 to head back to Sligo Town.

NORTHWEST IRELAND

On the route back stands **Parke's Castle** (tel. (071) 64149), a 17th-century planta-tion castle. Originally built for protection from the British, its waterfront location enables a quick getaway across the Lough. (Open mid-April to May Tues.-Sun. 10am-5pm; June-Sept. daily 9:30am-6:30pm; Oct. daily 10am-5pm. Admission £2, students £1.) Two miles before town, a left turn leads to Hazelwood. Yeats walked in this park "among long dappled grass" in "The Song of Wandering Aengus." The sculpture trail makes a particularly interesting walk.

Lough Gill is accessible by boat and by bus. **The Wild Rose Water-Bus** (tel. (071) 64266) offers a number of tours: a Sligo-Parke's Castle-Garavogue-Lough Gill-Sligo trip (daily; 3hr.; £3.50); a Parke's Castle-Innisfree trip (3/day; 1hr.; £3); a Doorly Park (Sligo)-Parke's Castle trip (daily; 1hr.); and a night cruise of the Lough that departs from Parke's Castle (Mon., Wed., and Fri. 9pm). **Lough Gill Tours,** 57 Mountain Close (tel. 642 66), does a tour of the Garavogue and Lough Gill (stopping at Parke's Castle, 3½hr.; £4.50), and Innisfree Island (1hr.; £3.50). In July and August, **John Howe's bus company** (tel. 42747) departs from the Sligo tourist office to guide visitors through Yeats country (3hr.; £5.50-6.50). Information on self-guided **walking tours** is available from the tourist office.

YEATS, YEATS, YEATS

Yeats's body rests in **Drumcliff churchyard,** 4 mi. northwest of Sligo on N15 (Bundo-ran Rd.) under bare Benbulben's head. The poet chose his epitaph: "Cast a cold eye/ On life, on death./Horseman, pass by!" Yeats died in France in 1939. WWII prevented his wife, Georgie, from shipping his body back to Ireland for several years. An engrav-ing marks her tomb, at his feet. Some of Yeats's roots are in the churchyard—one of his ancestors was rector here many years ago. His grave is to the left of the church door (behind the crowd of tourists; always open; free). Just outside, the **Old Stables** (tel. 44946) caters to literary pilgrims' needs with bulging pots of tea and a conve-nient bureau de change (open June-Sept. Mon.-Fri. 9am-6pm, Sun. 1-6pm). **Buses** run from Sligo to Drumcliff (Mon.-Sat. 3/day; in summer Sun. 1/day; 10min.; £2.60 return, students £1.65). **Hitching** is reportedly painless along the 4-mi. stretch of N15. A few miles northeast of Drumcliff, **Glencar Lake** is the subject of more literary excursions. It was mentioned in Yeats's "The Stolen Child." Stunning views of Knocknarea and Benbulben and the smashing Glencar Falls add thoughts of natural beauty to those of literary genius. The lake is marked by a sign about 1 mi. north of Drumcliff on N15.

North of Drumcliff, eerie **Benbulben**—the subject of Yeats's eponymous poem— protrudes from the landscape like the keel of a foundered boat. The climb up the 1729-ft. peak is rather windy, and the summit can be downright gusty. Marks of old turf cuttings on the way up give evidence for one of the mountainside's historic uses. Clear signs guide travelers to Benbulben from the Drumcliff Rd. Ask at the gas station in Drumcliff for detailed directions to trailheads.

Four miles west of Drumcliff is **Lissadell House** (tel. 63150), where poet Eva Gore-Booth and her sister Constance Markiewicz (second in command in the Easter Rising and later the first woman elected to the Dáil) entertained Yeats and his circle. The gaunt house has lost some of its luster, and the carpets are wearing thin, but the Gore-Booth family still lives here and allows tours. Henry Gore-Booth was an Arctic explorer and avid hunter—his harpoons and stag heads create a macho atmosphere that must have given mild-mannered Yeats the willies. Admire the double staircase made of Kilkenny marble and find where Constance Markiewicz scratched her initials on a window pane in the anteroom. (Open June to mid-Sept. Mon.-Sat. 10:30am-12:15pm and 2-4:15pm. Admission £2.15. Grounds open year-round; free.) Take the first left after Yeats Tavern Hostel on the Drumcliff Rd. and follow the signs. Near Lis-sadell and the village of Carney, the excellent food at **Laura's Pub** (tel. (071) 63056), just past Orchard Inn, justifies the prices (chicken Kiev £3.50).

INISHMURRAY & MULLAGHMORE

Mullaghmore, 15 mi. north of Drumcliff, is one of the departure points for faraway **Inishmurray**, a tiny monastic island which looks like a hill fort with no hill. Founded around 600 AD, pounded by Vikings around 800, and finally abandoned in 1948 when the turf supply ran out, the windswept island is now a deserted maze of stone walls and altars. The power of the *Clocha Breaca* (cursing stones) found on the islands can be unleashed on your worst enemies. Be careful of your wish, however, as it will rebound on you if it is unjustified. No regular scheduled ferries go to Inishmurray: to get there you should be rich or find a group of eight to twelve others who want to see the island. Then try boatman **Brendan Merrifield** (tel. (071) 41874), who organizes angling trips or crossings for £100. **Mullaghmore** itself is a beautiful fishing village with two long miles of sheltered beach, a headland, and **Classiebawn Castle,** the former residence of Lord Mountbatten, the Queen's brother-in-law. He was murdered here by the IRA. B&Bs are expensive here, but dinner at **Eithne's Restaurant** (tel. (071) 66407) is worth the splurge. The meal will keep you fed for an entire day or more (open in summer daily, lunch 12:30-3pm, *à la carte* dinner 6:30-10pm). You can feasibly visit Mullaghmore on a daytrip from Sligo but you'll be more comfortable doing so from Bundoran, just 5 mi. away.

CARROWMORE & KNOCKNAREA

A fantastic assortment of passage graves spooks visitors south of Sligo. Just 3 mi. from town, **Carrowmore** is Ireland's largest group of megalithic tombs. More than 60 tombs and stone circles mark the fields, some pre-dating Newgrange (p. 144) by seven centuries. The excellent **interpretive center** (tel. 61534) explains their meaning (open May-Sept. daily 9:30am-6:30pm; admission £1.50, students 60p).

The mountain **Knocknarea** faces Benbulben on the opposite shore of Sligo Bay. Queen Mebdh, or Maeve, the villain of the *Táin bo Cuailnge* (see **Legends and Folktales,** p.69) is reputedly interred in the cairn on the summit. She is buried standing up to face her enemies in Ulster. Her notoriety is evident from the size of the cairn, which is about three times that of Creevykeel. Decades ago, tourists started taking stones from the cairn as souvenirs; to preserve the legendary monument, local authorities created a "tradition" that any unmarried man or woman who brought a stone *up* the mountain to place on the cairn would be married within the year. The plot succeeded; the cairn survives. The stunning mountain also makes a cameo appearance in Yeats's "Red Hanrahan's Song about Ireland"—"The wind has bundled up the clouds high over Knocknarea/And thrown the thunder on the stones for all that Maeve can say."

Knocknarea is a long walk from Carrowmore; walk in the direction away from Sligo from the **Visitors Centre.** Take a right at the church, then the first left to the sign *Mebdh Meirach*. The hour-long walk up the path gets boggy and slippery; walk softly and carry a big stick (or bring a friend to lean on). From Sligo, turn right at the bottom of O'Connell St., and walk straight—for an hour. The reward is a stunning view of the misty bay and heathered hills. Animal enthusiasts will delight in the bilingual sheep (they speak cow) shouting insults at the less intelligent cows and tourists stumbling up the near-vertical path.

County Donegal

Though its name means "fort of the foreigner," tourists are still likely to feel a bit out of place in this most remote and least Anglicized of Ireland's "scenic" provinces. Among Ireland's counties, Donegal is second to Cork in size and second to none in glorious wilderness. There's more forest (that is, less deforestation) than in Connacht, and the coastline alternates glorious beaches with majestic cliffs. The biggest cliffs are around Slieve League. Inishowen makes the best cycling or driving route. In between the larger pockets of civilization, distance from all things English has preserved the biggest *gaeltacht* in the country.

Donegal's decent harbors and their remoteness from London made it a stronghold for Gaels (especially the Northern Uí Néill (O'Neill), Ó Domhnaill (O'Donnell), and McSwain (McSweeney) clans) until the Flight of the Earls. After years of English occupation (though few English actually lived in this barren "wasteland"), Donegal was given to the Irish state in 1920, as its largely Catholic population would have put at risk the Protestant majority that was Northern Ireland's reason for being. Today, cottage industries, fishing boats, and the underwear factory help the county keep body and soul together. The tourist industry has started to pick up as well, but be assured that you'll encounter fewer camera-toting tourists here than anywhere else in the country. One of the best books on any Irish region is J.J. Tohill's *Donegal: An Exploration*, a historical work to complement your travel guide.

GETTING THERE & GETTING AROUND

Donegal has the public transportation to get you where you want to go, but only if you're willing to wait. There are no trains past Sligo and Derry into Donegal, and buses tend to hit smaller towns only once per day, sometimes in the early morning. **Cycling** is always fun, though the distances are large and the terrain is hilly. Most towns, including major towns like Letterkenny, Donegal town, Sligo, and Dungloe, rent bikes. **Hitchers** report very short waits and friendly drivers on the main roads, especially those north of Donegal town. Byways are largely devoid of drivers, but any that pass will usually pick up hitchers who look friendly or really hungry.

Bus Éireann (tel. (01) 366111) connects Dublin with Letterkenny (tel. (074) 21309; Mon.-Sat. 4/day, Sun. 3/day; 4hr.; £10, £13 return), Donegal town (Mon.-Sat. 5/day; Sun. 3/day; 4¼hr.; £10, £13 return), and these two towns with some of the smaller villages in the southern half of the region. **Lough Swilly Buses** (Derry tel. (01504) 262017; Letterkenny tel. (074) 22400) fan out over the northern area, connecting Derry, Letterkenny, the Inishowen Peninsula, the Fanad Peninsula, and western coastal towns as far south as Dungloe. Swilly also offers a **Runabout** ticket good for eight days of unlimited travel (£18, students and children £9). **McGeehan's Bus Co.** (tel. (075) 46101 or 46150) runs to and from Dublin each day, passing through almost every intervening town (Donegal to Dublin £11, £15 return). McGeehan's also runs a hostel bus service that hits all 14 hostels along the coast from Glencolmcille to Dunfanaghy. An eight-day **Rambler** ticket, good for unlimited travel, costs £21 (single fares also available). **John McGinley** (tel. (074) 35201; Dublin tel. (01) 4513804) based in Falcarragh, runs from Dublin to Letterkenny and continues as far as Crolly (Mon.-Thurs. and Sat.-Sun. 2-3/day, Fri. 4/day; to Letterkenny 3½hr., to Crolly 5hr.; £8, £10 return). **Feda O'Donnell** (tel. (075) 48114; in Galway tel. (091) 761656) runs up and down the Donegal coast, connecting northwest Ireland with Galway (from Letterkenny, Mon.-Sat. 2/day, Sun. 3/day; £8, £12 return), and carries bikes for free. Bus prices on the main routes like Letterkenny-Dublin fluctuate due to competition. Private bus companies tend to be more extensive than Bus Éireann, and their drivers more open to persuasion if you want to be let off on the doorstep of a remote hostel.

■ Bundoran

Bundoran, at the mouth of Dobhran River, is the first stop in Donegal when arriving from Sligo or Leitrim. A thriving seaside resort, its hopping nightlife, water sports, and horseback riding attract an overwhelming crowd of partiers. The population of the town swells from 2000 to 20,000 during the summer but the masses of vacationers disappear once you travel a bit farther into the remoter regions of the county.

Information is available from the **tourist office** (tel. 41350) over the bridge on Main St. (open May-Sept. Mon.-Sat. 10am-1pm and 2-6pm, Sun. 10am-1pm). Farther down the street roosts the **post office** (tel. 41224; open Mon.-Fri. 9am-5:30pm and Sat. 9am-

County Donegal

N

10 miles

10 kilometers

0

Portstewart

Coleraine

A37   B66

CO. DERRY

B20

B98

A29

Dungiven

Limavady

CO. DERRY

Sperrin Mts.

B69   A6

A2

Cudaff

Carndonagh

R238

Malin Head

Malin

Slieve Snaght

INISHOWEN PENINSULA

Lough Foyle

Moville

R244

Ballyliffen

Tullagh Pt.

Clonman

R238

Muff

Derry

Fanad Head

Lough Swilly

Buncrana

R239

NORTHERN IRELAND

Strabane

R. Foyle

A5

Fahan

Melmore Head

FANAD PENINSULA

Knockalla Mt.

Portsalon

Glenvar

Inch Island

N13

Newtownstewart

B47

Ulster American Folk Park

B89

Horn Head

ROSGUILL PENINSULA

R248

Carrickart

Carrowkeel

Rathmullan

Ramelton

Gweedore

Gaoth Dobhair

Dunfanaghy

Milford

Glenveagh Nat'l Park

Kilmacrenan/ Cill Mhic Reanan

Letterkenny

N14

N13

Gweebarra Bay

Inishdooey

Inishbofin

Tory I.

Inishbeg

Bloody Foreland

Barbeg An Barra Beg

Gortahork Gort an Choirce

Muckish Mt.

Creeslough

Dunlewy

Errigal Mt.

Derryveagh Mts.

Glenties

Oatran I.

Gartan L.

N56

Blue Stack Mts.

Ballybofey

B72

To Omagh

CO. TYRONE

CO. TYRONE

Castlederg

Aranmore I.

Annagary Anagaire

The Rosses

Dungloe/ An Clochan Liath

Dooey Pt.

Maghery

Crohy Head

Burtonport

Ardara

R250

R262

CO. DONEGAL

Frosses

Mountcharles

Fintown

Baile na Finne

Duchoraidh/ Duncharry

Donegal Town

L. Eske

Rossnowlagh

R232

L. Derg

To Enniskillen

Lower L. Erne

Ballyshannon

Glen Head

Glencolumbkille/ Gleann Cholm Cille

Glengesh Pass Forest

Slieve League

Malin Beg   Malin Bheg

Rathlin O'Byrne I.

Kilcar

R263

Carrick

Teelin

St. John's Pt.

Killybegs

Dunkineely

Donegal Bay

Bundoran

R250

N15

R281

CO. SLIGO

N16

Mullaghmore

Drumcliff

To Sligo

N15

1pm). **AIB** is on Main St. (open Mon.-Wed. and Fri. 10am-4pm, Thurs. 10am-5pm; **ATM**). **Bus Éireann** and **Feda O'Donnell** coaches leave from the bus station on Main St. for Donegal Town and Sligo. The **phone code** whistles 072.

Every other house in Bundoran seems to be a B&B; the cheaper and quieter ones are farther down Main St. away from the bridge. **Homefield Hostel (IHH),** Bayview Avenue (tel. 41288), is a five-minute walk from the Bundoran bus stop: take a left at McGrath's guest house and walk to the top of the hill. More like a four-star hotel than a hostel, quaint Victorian rooms with don't-wake-me mattresses, a spacious sitting room with roaring hearth and huge TV screen, a bistro, friendly, artsy owners, and a great location make this hostel one of the best in Ireland. (Dorm £7. Double w/bath £16-20. Continental breakfast included. Laundry £4. **Bikes** (£6/day, £30/week, £30 deposit), horseback riding, hill walking, fishing, and local tours.) Mrs. McGloin's **Atlantic Guest House,** West End, Main St. (tel. 41403), has splendid views of Donegal Bay from its bedrooms (£15.50/person).

The best restaurant in town, if not in all Donegal, is **La Sabbia,** a first-rate Italian bistro connected to the hostel. Cheap and impeccable food (tomato and basil fettucine £4) is served in a cosmopolitan cool atmosphere tempered by a Donegalian roaring fire and trad. **Conroy's,** at the west end of Main St. (tel. 41280), is fish-licious (fish 'n chips £3). The **Ould Bridge Bar,** on the corner of Main St. and Church St. (tel. 42050), is the locals' favorite, with frequent trad sessions in summer and boots hanging from the ceiling. **Brennans,** on Main St., is a real, old pub experience; it's been in the same family for over 100 years and hasn't changed much. People from all around flock to Bundoran's nightclubs and discos.

Aughross Cliffs ("headlands of the steeds") was once a grazing ground for war horses. A leisurely stroll here past the Northern Hotel affords an impressive view of mighty Atlantic waves on your left. Curious sights include the **Fairy Bridges,** the **Wishing Chair** (so called because the natural stone formation looks like one), and the **Puffing Hole,** where water spouts up volcano-style through a hole in a bed of rock. Farther along are the golden beaches of Tullan Strand, a surfers' mecca. **Fitzgeralds,** Main St. (tel. 41223), reports conditions and provides equipment.

■ Ballyshannon

St. Patrick once offered to make Ballyshannon "a second Rome." Though still pope-less, the town does host the raucous annual **Ballyshannon Folk & Traditional Music Festival** (tel. 51049; tickets on sale after July 29), which attracts about as many people as a papal visit might. The festival itself is on the August bank holiday weekend, but informal sessions begin during the last week of July. Tickets for the entire weekend cost £25 and admit purchasers to performances, afternoon music workshops, and a jammed campsite. During the rest of the year, Ballyshannon twiddles its musical thumbs by the River Erne, which splashes over the Falls of Assaroe (or *Ess Ruaid*) just west of the bridge. Though the falls are one of Ireland's most ancient pagan holy sites (representing the domineering male river flowing into the joyous female sea), there's little to see other than water. Ballyshannon doesn't really offer much more than water(-ing holes); Bundoran is more fun.

Practical Information Ballyshannon's **tourist office** consists of a desk in the Abbey Centre Cinema complex at the end of Tirconaill St. (tel. 51375; open June-Aug. Mon.-Sat. 9am-5pm). Ask here about guided walking tours. The **AIB,** Castle St. (tel. 51169), has an **ATM** (open Mon.-Wed. and Fri. 10am-4pm, Thurs. 10am-5pm). **Buses** leave the depot just beside the bridge (tel. (074) 31008) on their way to Sligo (Mon.-Sat. 11/day, Sun. 5/day; 1hr.; £5.50) and Donegal Town (Mon.-Sat. 10/day, Sun. 3/day; 25min.; £3.20). Call the **police** at 51155. The **post office** (tel. 51111; open Mon.-Fri. 9am-1pm and 2-5:30pm, Sat. 9am-1pm) settles halfway up Castle St. The **phone code** bubbles 072.

Accommodations, Food, & Pubs Ballyshannon lacks a great place to stay, so we recommend staying in Bundoran. **Duffy's Hostel (IHH),** Donegal Rd. (tel. 51535) just outside town, does not have the cleanest kitchen or sheets and the mattresses are rock-hard (£6/person; **camping** £3; open March-Oct.). At **Mullac naSi,** (tel. 52702), Mrs. Nolan-Coyle hospitably houses guests in big, comfortable rooms overlooking Erne Estuary (£16/person); she can also arrange pony trekking.

A Yeats quote graces the door of the **Dead Poets Cafe,** 3 Main St. (tel. 52770), where bookshelves and bronzed tree branches line the forest-green walls. Speak softly. (Large sandwiches £1.25. Open Mon.-Sat. 9am-6pm, Sun. 11am-4pm.) In town across from the roundabout lies **El Gringo,** Allingham Rd. (tel. 51540), which serves up the best fajitas (£8.25) north of the Shannon along with American, Indian, and Italian cuisine. Discos and cabarets on weekends (open Mon.-Fri. noon-2:30pm and 6pm-10pm). **Spar Supermarket** sells groceries at the end of Tirconaill St. (Open Mon.-Thurs. 9am-8pm, Fri.-Sat. 9am-8:30pm, Sun. 11:30am-8pm.) **Finn McCool's,** Main St. (tel. 52677) is the most popular pub in town, with reputedly the best trad sessions around (4 nights/week in summer). Get here early; the pub is tiny and the Guinness bottles take up as much space as the people. **The Cellar,** Bundoran Rd. (tel. 51452), has acoustic sessions on Wednesdays, while Thursdays are the nights for "pints and poems." **Herman's Nite Club,** Main St., rocks Friday to Monday (Fri.-Sun. cover £2; Mon. no cover).

Sights **Allingham's Bridge** connects the town's two halves and honors Ballyshannon's most famous native, the poet William Allingham. He inspired Yeats to study the folklore, mythic beliefs, and ancient traditions of Sligo. Most of the town lies north of the river, where Main St. divides halfway up a hill. This hill, named Mullach na Sídh ("Hill of the Faires") has a panoramic view and is believed to be the burial site of the legendary High King Hugh, who supposedly drowned in the Assaroe Falls. From the left fork of Main St., a left turn past the Imperial Hotel will bring you to **St. Anne's Church,** where Allingham is buried. His grave lies on the south side of the church, marked by a white slab. Back by the river, a fish pass at the power station allows tourists to watch the ancient biological cycle of salmon and trout struggling upstream during spawning season, around June. Distinguishing the sun-god in salmon form—believed to swim past every night after dipping into the western ocean—is a challenge.

Just outside Ballyshannon, the river meanders past the barely visible 12th-century **Cistercian Abbey of Assaroe,** built on an ancient pagan holy site. The Cistercians were brilliant water engineers. They canalized the river to harness its hydraulic power for running a **water mill** which still operates. Restorers have added a neat tea shop (open June-Aug. daily 10:30am-6:30pm; Sept.-May Sun. 1:30-6pm). Outside the mill, a tiny path leads to the **Abbey Well,** blessed by St. Patrick (what hasn't been?). Pilgrims bless themselves with its water each year on August 15 (though they avoid the river, which Patrick cursed). Nearby, a tiny cave harbors a Mass rock which was used during Penal Days and two hollow stones that were used to hold holy water. To reach the cave, take a right after you cross Allingham's bridge and follow the river bank for about 100m. Trails to the caves and the well get quite muddy and slippery. To get to the mill hill from town, continue up the left fork of the main road, past the Thatched Pub. From there, take the second left down a tiny lane.

■ Donegal Town

Most international travelers regrettably begin their tour of Co. Donegal with a stay in Donegal Town. An inevitable stopover between Sligo or Fermanagh and the splendor of the north and west, Donegal Town itself has few natural and historical wonders to offer tourists. However, as far as night life, amenities, bustling social activity, and souvenirs are concerned, this is the place to be. The **International Arts Festival,** held on the last weekend of June, brings such diverse activities as parachuting, theater, storytelling, and traditional music that render the town a summertime center of entertainment. The town is too far south to make a good base for traveling around the rest of Donegal, but its tourist office—by far the county's best—can tell you about more remote destinations along the scenic northern coast.

PRACTICAL INFORMATION

Tourist Office: Quay St. (tel. 21148), south of the Diamond on the Sligo Rd. Brochures on the entire county, as well as a basic, free map of the city; be sure to stop here before heading north. Open July-Aug. Mon.-Sat. 9am-8pm, Sun. 10am-1pm and 2-8pm; Sept.-Oct. and Easter-June Mon.-Sat. 9am-6pm.

Banks: AIB, the Diamond (tel. 21016). Open Mon.-Wed. and Fri. 10am-4pm, Thurs. 10am-5pm; **ATM. Bank of Ireland,** the Diamond (tel. 21079). Open Mon.-Wed. and Fri. 10am-4pm, Thurs. 10am-5pm; **ATM.**

Airport: tel. (075) 48232. Flights to Glasgow.

Buses: Bus Éireann (tel. 21101) runs to Dublin (Mon.-Sat. 6/day, Sun 3/day; 4hr.; £10) via Ballyshannon (25min.; £3) and Galway (Mon.-Sat. 3/day, Sun. 2/day; 4hr.; £13) via Sligo (1hr.; £7.30). Buses stop outside the Abbey Hotel, where timetables are also posted. **McGeehan Coaches** (tel. (075) 46150) ride to Dublin at least once a day. **Feda O'Donnell** (tel. (075) 48114) leaves for Galway daily at 9:45am.

Taxis: tel. 35162.

Bike Rental: C.J. O'Doherty's, Main St. (tel. 21119). £7/day, £30/week; £30 deposit. Open Mon.-Sat. 9am-1pm and 2-6pm. **The Bike Shop,** Waterloo Pl. (tel. 22515). £7/day, £30/week; £40 deposit. Open Mon.-Sat. 9am-6pm.

Laundry: Eleanor's Launderette, Upper Main St. Wash £2, dry 30p/5min.; £1 charge for dry without wash. Open Mon.-Sat. 9am-6pm. Last wash 5:30pm.

Pharmacy: Begley's Chemist, the Diamond (tel. 21232). Open Mon.-Fri. 9am-6pm, Sat. 9am-7pm.

Hospital: tel. 21029.

Emergency: Dial 999; no coins required. **Garda:** tel. 21021.

Post Office: Tirconaill St. (tel. 21030), north of the Diamond. Open Mon.-Sat. 9am-5:30pm.

Phone Code: 073.

ACCOMMODATIONS

Ball Hill Youth Hostel (An Óige/HI) (tel. 21174), 3mi. from town; proceed 1½mi. out of Donegal on the Killybegs Rd., turn left at the sign, and keep moving for another 1½mi. towards the sea. A taxi ride runs about £3-4. An old coastguard station sitting on a cliff, this hostel has light and spacious rooms. Manager Kevin gives hostelers a warm welcome—ask to see the "pagan shrine." Curfew 12:30am. No lockout. 8-bed dorms. May-Sept. £6/person, Oct.-April £4.50/person. 3-course dinner available at nearby Mountcharles Hotel for £5.

Donegal Town Hostel (IHH), 1mi. out on the Killybegs Rd. (tel. 22805). High on a hill overlooking the main road, this hostel has been under new management since July, 1995. The Cunninghams are working hard and it shows: hardwood floors, a large kitchen, and decent bedrooms. Owners will pick up travelers in town. £5.75/person. £2.50 surcharge for leaving after 11am. Sheets 50p. Laundry (wash and powder) £4.50.

Atlantic Guest House, Main St. (tel. 21187). A 17-room guest house with long corridors and an unbeatable location. Each clean room has a TV, coffee/teapot, and sink. £15/person, w/bath £20; prices negotiable in off-season.

Aranmore House, Killybegs Rd. (tel. 21242). Seven clean, white rooms line up like peas in a pod in Mrs. Keeny's large, rhododendron-fortified home, a 5-min. walk from the town center. Open fire in the lounge. Free coffee and tea. Single £14, w/bath £15. Double £28, w/bath £30. Open Easter-Oct.

FOOD & PUBS

Cafés and take-aways compete for tourists' attention on the streets of Donegal, where lost-looking Americans thumb guidebooks. Most eateries inhabit the Diamond and the streets near it. **Foodland Supermarket** (tel. 21016) has cheap groceries (open

Mon.-Thurs. 9am-8pm, Fri. 9am-9pm, Sat. 9am-7:30pm). Nature store **Simple Simon's** (tel. 22687) sells fresh baked goods, local cheeses, and (inedible) crafts from around the world (open Mon.-Sat. 9:30am-6pm).

The Blueberry Tea Room, Castle St. (tel. 22933). Justifiably popular. Looks like Grandma's kitchen with white porcelain geese and teapots. Sandwiches, daily specials, and all-day breakfast (quiche and salad £3.25). Open daily 8am-9pm.

Errigal Restaurant, Main St. (tel. 21428). Local hangout with the cheapest dinner in town—their potatoes are freshly chipped every day. (Fresh fish and chips £2-4, chicken dinner £3.50.) Open Mon.-Sat. 9am-10:30pm, Sun. 3-10:30pm.

Stella's Seafood Bar, at McGroarty's Pub, the Diamond. Serves creative, healthy food using organic vegetables. Dinner is expensive but delicious (shellfish pancakes £11). Lunch is more reasonable (chicken-filled pita, baked potato, and veggies £4). Live trad on Thurs. Open Mon.-Sat. noon-9pm.

Harbour Restaurant, Quay St. (tel. 21702). Fish and chips (£3-4), sandwiches and chips (£2). Hearty steaks and baked potatoes, too! Open daily 11am-9pm.

Donegal puts on a good show at night, especially in the summertime. Pubs have tons of events during the International Arts Festival; keep a sharp lookout for the happening places. During the winter, the trad dries up, but rock and blues still happen on the weekends. **Schooner's,** Upper Main St. (tel. 21671), has the best trad sessions in town, particularly during the summer. **Olde Castle Restaurant Bar,** Castle St., has old stone walls and an medieval-looking hearth to light your fire. **Charlie's Star Bar,** Main St. (tel. 21158), sparkles with live rock, country, and blues most nights a week in summer. **The Abbey Hotel,** the Diamond (tel. 21014), draws tourists to its folk cabaret and to its lively summer disco (July-Aug. Tues. and Sun.). **The Stables,** Castle St. (tel. 21056), confines its trad action to Monday. **The Cellar Bar,** Upper Main St. under the Coach House (tel. 22855), features trad nightly. Confident musicians and singers are also invited to perform. **Nero's Nite Club,** Main St. (tel. 21111), plays the fiddle while Donegal burns (dancing Thurs.-Sat., live bands Sun.).

SIGHTS

Donegal's historic sites don't really explain the masses of visitors crowding its streets, but once you elbow your way around the tourists the few old buildings can be interesting. **Guided tours** (tel. 22312) of the town leave from the chamber of commerce (Mon.-Fri. at 11am and 2pm; £2). **Donegal Castle,** a 15th-century oddity, stands just north of the Diamond, smack in the center of town (castle closed for renovations; will open when U.S. budget is balanced).

A ruined **Franciscan Friary** awaits just a short walk from the tourist office along the river south of town. Thirteen delicate arches and their supporting pillars are all that remain of the original 15th-century cloister. Founded in 1474 by Red Hugh O'Donnell's wife, the friary was abandoned quite unceremoniously in 1608. Four of the monks who fled—Brother Michael O'Cleery, Fearfeasa O'Maolconry, Peregrine O'Duignean, and Padraig O'Cleary—wrote the *Annals of the Four Masters,* the first narrative history of Ireland. The narrative dates back to the time of Noah's grandmother, 40 years before the Great Flood, and continues until 1618 AD. The monks may have written the tome in another, more-ruined monastery near Bundoran, but it has become tradition to claim that they completed the classic of Irish literature in Donegal Town. An obelisk in the center of the Diamond recalls the four holy men, as does **St. Patrick's Church of the Four Masters,** a fine example of stolid, Irish Romanesque architecture about ½ mi. up Main St. (open Mon.-Fri. 9am-5pm; free).

Just south of Donegal Town, 1 mi. out on the Ballyshannon Rd. at the **Donegal Craft Village** (tel. 22225), six craftspeople open their workshops to the public. The work of an Invereske potter (tel. 22053), a batik artist (tel. 22015), a jewelry designer (tel. 21742), an uileann pipe maker (tel. 23311), a jewelry metalworker (tel. 22225), and a porcelain crafter (tel. 22200) make great gift alternatives to the mass-produced leprechauns sold in the Donegal Town stores (workshops open July-Aug. daily 9am-

6pm, Sept.-June Mon.-Sat. 9am-6pm, Sun. 11am-6pm). The **Donegal Drama Circle** presents summer theater at the slightly derelict Old Cinema, Main St., in July and August (tickets £4, students £2). Posters all over town give details.

■ Near Donegal Town: Station Island

Several miles due east of Donegal Town, Co. Donegal's **Lough Derg** (there's another Lough Derg along the Shannon) encircles **Station Island.** One of Ireland's most important pilgrimage sites, Station Island witnesses a three-day barefoot religious ordeal every summer, the subject of Seamus Heaney's long poem *Station Island.* Though St. Patrick never visited Lough Derg, legend has it that he visited nearby Saints Island, where he temporarily descended into Purgatory. The pilgrimage, which can be any three days between June 1 and August 13, involves three days of similarly hellish fasting and circling the island barefoot. "Lough Derg soup" has become an island delicacy; the pilgrims, who aren't allowed to eat, snack on this concoction of boiled water flavored with salt and pepper. Hard-core Catholics scowl at a recent addition to the pilgrim's calendar—a special one-day retreat to the island that some think is too easy.

For budget-traveler pilgrims, **Bus Éireann** visits Lough Derg daily from Whit Sunday to the Feast of the Assumption on its Dublin-Cavan-Enniskillen route. The Galway-Sligo-Lough Derg route runs both ways on Sundays, but only *to* Lough Derg *from* Galway Monday to Saturday (so don't go on Mon., or you'll have to stay the entire week). Regular ferry service picks up pilgrims at the lakeshore. The "Lough Derg Journey" at the **Pettigo Visitor Centre** (tel. (072) 61546) lets you visit the area in virtual reality. Real boat trips can be arranged through the Centre. (Open March-April Sat. 10am-5pm, Sun. 2-5pm; May-Oct. Mon.-Sat. 10am-5pm, Sun. noon-5pm. Boat trips March-April Sat. noon and 3pm, Sun. 4pm; May-Oct. Mon.-Sat. noon and 3pm, Sun. 3pm and 5:30pm. Center £2, students £1.50; center and boat £4, students £3.) Bring nothing but warm clothing and a repentant heart. Contact the Monsignor of Lough Derg, Fr. Mohan, Pettigo, Co. Donegal for more info (tel. (072) 61550).

KILLYBEGS PENINSULA

The road west (N56) along Donegal's southern edge winds within yards of the Atlantic coast and then swerves inland around weather-beaten cliffs and wee villages. The Coast Rd. from Shalwy to Carrick yields a jaw-dropping view; high passes through the heather afford similar aesthetic wonders inland. Although it is not particularly appealing (especially to the nose), **Killybegs,** Ireland's premier fishing port, has some of the only services in the area. An **AIB** is on Main St. (open Mon.-Wed. and Fri. 10am-12:30pm and 1:30-5pm). **Buses** run from Donegal town to Killybegs (Mon.-Sat. 3/day; early July-Aug. 4/day). The early-morning bus on Saturday continues on to Glencolmcille at Rossan Point. **McGeehan Coaches** (tel. (075) 46150) also has a service (at least 1/day) to Donegal and Dublin from most towns on the peninsula. N56 (from Killybegs) is quicker to Glencolmcille, but not as pretty as the northern road. **Cyclists** report rewarding views but hilly terrain. **McGee's Chemist** on Main St. (tel. 31009) sells aspirin and toothpaste (open Mon.-Sat. 9:30am-6pm). The **post office** sits on Main St. (tel. 31060; open Mon.-Fri. 9am-1pm and 2-5:30pm, Sat. 9am-1pm). The Killybegs Peninsula's **phone code** baits its hook with 073.

Killybegs' pubs all have late licenses; last call is at 12:30am (which means no one leaves until 2am). The **Harbour Bar,** across from the pier, is notorious for its late hours. **The Pier Bar,** across the car park (tel. 31096) caters mainly to fishermen but does excellent bar food during the day (outside seating). **The Veronica,** Ireland's largest fishing vessel, is often at port. One mile away off the N56, Mrs. Tully (tel. 31842) puts up guests in her new B&B, **Tullycullion House,** which has panoramic views of Killybegs Harbour (£14/person).

MOUNTCHARLES & ST. JOHN'S POINT

The coastline becomes more rugged and more dramatic farther west, but there's nothing shabby about the eastern towns. In **Mountcharles,** you can go **deep-sea fishing** in Donegal Bay from the Mountcharles Pier (daily 11am-5pm; £20/person; contact Michael O'Boyle at tel. 35257). Ten miles past Mountcharles, a turnoff leads to **St. John's Point,** which has fantastic views across to the Sligo coastline. Another mile past the St. John's turnoff, in **Bruckless,** the **Gallagher's Farm Hostel** (tel. 37057) sits about ¼ mi. off the main road. Mr. Gallagher built the wonderfully clean, well-outfitted hostel himself. He also provides trail info for walks around the gently undulating countryside. Two kitchens (and a third one for campers), a huge fireplace, and a ping-pong table may make you want to stay forever. Separate bathrooms are outside. (Dorm £6. **Camping** £3.50/person. Continental breakfast w/fresh baked scones £3. Laundry (wash and powder) £2.50.)

KILCAR

A stunning 8 mi. along N56 takes shoppers to tiny **Kilcar,** a base for many of the area's weavers. **Studio Donegal** (tel. 38194) sells handwoven tweeds fresh off the loom. Visitors are invited to watch weaving action (open Mon.-Fri. 9am-5pm; also open July-Aug. Sat. 10am-6pm). Downstairs, **Mary's Tea House** cooks up homemade soups and sandwiches (£1.20 each; open Mon.-Fri. 9am-7pm, Sat. 10am-6pm, Sun. 2-4pm). In the same building, the **Northwest Tourism Information Centre** (tel. 38002) consists of an unstaffed desk with brochures (open Mon.-Fri. 9am-7pm, Sat. 10am-6pm, Sun. 2-4pm).

Traditional music fans should visit Kilcar during the **Francie "Dearg" Byrne Memorial Fleadh,** on the third weekend in July. The first week of August sees a street Theatre Festival featuring music, dance, tomfoolery, and *craic.* At the **Piper's Rest,** Main St. (tel. 38205), playful plaques adorn the walls, reminding patrons that "the rooster may crow but the hen delivers the goods." Trad music on Thursday and Saturday nights, but the music sessions are often unplanned, as aspiring musicians can volunteer to perform anytime. **Teelin Harbour Cruises** (tel. 39079 by day, 39117 in the evening) ship out along the Slieve League coast (boat trips July-Aug.; 1½-2hr.; £7/person). Closer to home, **Jim Maloney** of Kilcar (tel. 38316) provides cruises or fishing trips (£6/person); rods and tackle also available for rental.

Several miles farther along the coast road from Kilcar to Carrick, **Dun Ulun House** (tel. 38137) is a luxurious alternative to hostel life. Sleep in a large, flowery bed at night and wake up to continental breakfast in the morning. You may hear Mrs. Lyons's talented daughters perform music. (Dorm beds for £7.50, off-season £6. B&B Sept.-June £12.50/person, July-Aug. £13.50/person, all w/bath. Laundry £5. **Bikes** £6/day, £30/week; £20 deposit.) Farther down the road and five minutes from the beach, Sean at the **Derrylahan Hostel (IHH)** (tel. 38079) welcomes guests like long-lost cousins; don't even *think* about refusing the initial cup of tea. The showers stay hot, the laughter and wit never run dry, and the on-premise grocery shop stays well-stocked. Campers have separate showers and kitchen facilities. (Dorm £5; private room £7/person. **Camping** £3. **Bike** rental.) Call for a pick-up from Kilcar or Carrick. Buses pass daily on the way to Killybegs and Glencolmcille.

CARRICK AND SLIEVE LEAGUE

Smaller than Kilcar, Carrick has little to offer but ready access to **Slieve League,** whose stunning cliffs drop straight into Donegal Bay. In late October and early November, Carrick hosts the annual **Carrick Fleadh,** one of the better music festivals around. Just south of Carrick, Mrs. Maloney, at **Teelin Bay House** (the third B&B on the road to Teelin; tel. 39043), is deservedly famous for the care she bestows upon her guests. It's a bit of a hike but the view just keeps getting better. You'll have to book well ahead (£13/person). **Fishing** is fabulous and rewarding around Carrick. Head for **Salmon Leap,** just south of Carrick (follow signs for Teelin), for the best salmon; the **Glen River** is best for trout.

In clear weather it'd be unconscionable *not* to visit **Slieve League,** a 2000-ft. mountain set in the midst of a precipitous, beautiful coastline which is itself composed of 1000-ft. cliffs. To reach the mountain, turn left halfway down Carrick's main street and follow signs for Teelin. In Teelin, turn right to follow signs for Bunglass; at the end of the road sits a car park with fantastic views. From here, a cliff path heads west along the coast. Farther along (about ½hr. from Bunglass), the clifftop narrows to 2 ft. On one side of this pass—called **One Man's Pass**—the cliffs drop 1800 ft. to the sea. On the other side, the cliffs drop a measly 1000 ft. to a rocky floor. There are no railings, and most people go across on their butts or hands and knees (the less courageous and more sane can take a route slightly inland). After bringing hikers perilously close to death, the path continues all the way along the cliffs to **Rossarrel Point,** near Glencolmcille. The entire Slieve League way usually takes four hours. It's always a good idea to ask a local expert for advice. *Never go to Slieve League in poor weather.* Use extreme caution if you plan to cross the pass. People have died attempting this under poor conditions.

■ Glencolmcille (Gleann Cholm Cille)

Though less dramatic then the mountain paths, N56 is a more convenient route to Glencolmcille (glen-kaul-um-KEEL) at the westernmost point of the peninsula. Named after St. Colmcille, who founded a monastery here, this Irish-speaking town and pilgrimage site sits between two huge cliffs in a starkly beautiful valley of barren rolling hills and sandy coves. Tourists with cars stop in the tiny town center, though a walk along the desolate, wind-swept cliffs to the west of the village will rid you of their presence. Glencolmcille's tiny **tourist office** is on Cashel St. (tel. 30116; open April to mid-Nov. daily 9am-9pm). The town's own folk village has an **exchange bureau** with a better rate than that at the **post office** east of the village center (post office open Mon.-Fri. 7:30am-1pm and 2-5:30pm, Sat. 9am-1pm). **McGeehan's buses** leave from Biddy's Bar to go to Killybegs, Ardara, and Letterkenny daily. **Bus Éireann** has services to Donegal Town. Ask at the hostel or tourist office for details. The **phone code** is a handcrafted 073.

Accommodations, Food, & Pubs The entrance to the **Dooey Hostel (An Óige/HI)** (tel. 30130) is located incredibly in a cave in the side of the hill. Solid bedrock forms one wall of the foyer. To reach the hostel, turn left just past the village and follow the signs about ¾ mi. uphill. Several kitchens grace the hostel (you can have a private lunch here), which houses guests in two- to eight-bed dorms, most with stunning views of the sea (dorm £6, private room £6.50/person; **camping** £3.50/person; sheets £1). To stay past 11am, you must pay a £2.50 fee or book for the next night. Mrs. Ann Ward's **Atlantic Scene** (tel. 30186), near the hostel, lives up to its name. You'll stay up just to admire the view longer (£13; open May-Oct.). There are also B&Bs in the village itself.

The **Lace House Restaurant and Café,** above the tourist office on Cashel St., is half diner, half chipper. Sink into the red vinyl seats and smoke a Dunhill—everyone else is (roast beef, potatoes, and veggies £5; open Easter-Sept. daily 11am-10pm). **An Bradan Feasa** (tel. 30213), at the Cultural Centre, is affordable only at lunchtime (lasagna and salad £4; open Mon.-Sat. 10am-9:30pm). The **teashop** in the Folk Village tempts with sandwiches and Guinness cake (80p). The **grocery shop** on Cashel St.

supplies the basics (open Mon.-Sat. 9:30am-10pm, Sun. 9:30am-1pm and 7-8pm). The village's three pubs have a dark, dusty 1950s Ireland feel to them and lots of trad and folk music in the summer. Look for signs to find out which pub has music on a given night. Small and cozy **Biddy's** is at the mouth of the Carrick Rd. **Roarty's,** farther down Cashel St., has more trad music and a bigger crowd during the summer. **Glen Head Tavern** pours a refreshing afternoon pint.

Sights Glencolmcille's craft movement began in the 1960s as a cure for unemployment. Now, the town is renowned for its handmade products, particularly sweaters, which are on sale at the **Foras Cultúir Uladh** ("The Ulster Cultural Institute"; tel. 30248), at the end of Cashel St., which displays local crafts, a facsimile of the *Book of Kells,* and archaeological exhibits (open daily 9am-6pm; free). Further on is Glencolmcille's folk village, comprised of stone replicas of old buildings with immaculately thatched roofs. Houses date from 1700, 1850, and 1900. The schoolhouse from the 1850s is open to the general public, but only those taking guided tours get to see the insides of the houses while hearing descriptions of furniture and tools from each period of Irish history. A short path through the village leads past various reconstructed remains, including a Mass rock, a sweat house, and a lime kiln. The shop (tel. 30017) stocks homemade heather, fuschia, and seaweed wines (free samples w/tour) along with whiskey and Guinness marmalade, good for those hung-over breakfasts. (Village open Easter-Sept. Mon.-Sat. 10am-6:30pm, Sun. noon-6pm. Tours April-June and Sept. every hr., July-Aug. every ½hr.; £2.50.)

Fine beaches and cliffs make for excellent hiking in all directions. A 5-mi. walk southwest from the village terminates at **Malinbeg,** a winsome hamlet on the edge of a sandy cove. Formerly notorious for its smuggling tunnels (some of which may still be in use), **Silver Strand** is now ideal for those seeking tranquility. From here, you can laboriously walk up and along the Slieve League coastline (see **Carrick and Slieve League,** p. 342). North of Glencolmcille, **Glen Head** is easily identifiable by the Martello tower at its peak. A sandy beach links the cliffs. The head is an hour's walk from town through land rich in prehistoric ruins. The tourist office and hostel in town each have a wall-map showing the locations of the major sites. A third walk from town begins at the Protestant church and ascends a hill to the ghostly "famine village" of Port. Supposedly haunted by crying babies, this eerie village has been empty since all of its inhabitants emigrated during the Famine. The only current resident, according to local rumor, is an eccentric artist who lives by the isolated bay without electricity or water. The visible phallic rock sticking out of the sea is just what it appears to be: the only part of the Devil's anatomy still visible after St. Colmcille banished him to the ocean.

Devilish Imps

While St. Patrick was the savior of much of Ireland, his act of banishing demons to the North endangered the region. The angry demons placed a fiery river around their territory, and surrounded their land with a dense mist so that no one could see their evil works. Colmcille, a religious man, approached the burning stream in the company of his trusted servant, tu Cerc. The devil hurled a holly rod through the mist that struck and fatally wounded tu Cerc. Colmcille, incensed, threw the javelin back through the mist to clear a line of sight for vengeance. The holly javelin stuck in the ground and grew into a holly tree which still grows at the spot. An angel appeared to Colmcille, and instructed him to use his Dub Duaibsech bell to destroy the imps. With this aid, Colmcille changed the demons into fish and cast them into the sea. These fiendish fish were distinguishable from others by being red in color and blind in one eye. Fishermen were, of course, advised to avoid these dastardly fish. Cromwell liked them filleted.

The road east from Glencolmcille to Ardara passes through the spectacular **Glengesh Pass.** Nine hundred feet above sea level itself, the road tackles the surrounding mountains with hairpin turns. Though a more difficult hitch or bike ride than the route through Killybegs, the views make this route worth your while.

■ Ardara

Originally the center of the Donegal tweed industry, Ardara (ar-DRAH), is now a major attraction for tourists with high credit card limits and a need for tweed. Ardara is no longer the cheapest place to buy Aran sweaters in Donegal, however. For better deals, try the smaller "craft centres" outside of town, where prices tend to be at least £20 lower. Souvenirs spill out of the shops and into the L-shaped pair of streets. Ardara has its moment in the sun on the first weekend of June during **Weavers' Fair,** which brings musicians and weavers to town.

The brand-new **Ardara Heritage Centre** (tel. 41704), in the middle of town, tells the story of tweed with live demonstrations, and shows a film about local attractions. Donegal tweeds incorporate dyes made from Ireland's four elements: lichen, blackberries, heather, and soot. The tearoom at the center serves snacks and refreshments daily from 9:30am-6pm. (Centre open March-Oct. daily 10am-6pm. Admission £2, students £1.) **Ulster Bank** (tel 41121 or 41201) is located on the Diamond (open Mon.-Wed. and Fri. 10am-12:30pm and 1:30-4pm, Thurs. 10am-12:30pm and 1:30-5pm). The **bus** stop and information office are at the Spar **supermarket,** Main St. (tel. 41107; open Mon.-Sat. 8:30am-8pm, Sun. 8:30am-1pm). **Bikes** can be rented at **Donald Byrne's,** West End (tel. 41156), beyond town on the Killybegs Rd. (£7/day, £30/week; deposit £40). Pony treks start from Castle View Ranch, 2½ mi. from Ardara town center (tel. 41212; £10/hr., £45/day). **Chemist,** Front St., is the local pharmacy (open Mon.-Sat. 10am-1pm and 2-6pm). The **post office** is opposite the Heritage Centre (tel. 41101, open Mon.-Fri. 9am-1pm and 2-5:30pm, Sat. 9am-1pm). Three numerals are interwoven to create Ardara's **phone code,** 075.

The **Drumbarron Hostel,** the Diamond (tel. 41200), is clean and comfortable, but the bare walls plead for decoration. Dig the flagstone floors in the kitchen (curfew at 1am, 4- to 8-bed dorm £6/person). Next door, **Laburnum House,** the Diamond (tel. 41146), has grand rooms and windows that stretch to the floor (£12/person). **Charlie's West End Café** (tel. 41656) lacks the trendy atmosphere its name suggests, but the service is quick and the prices are cheap for a tourist town (breakfasts £2; open Mon.-Sat. 8:30am-8pm, Sun. noon-5pm). Check out the colorful selection of mugs at **Nancy's,** Front St., while diving into smoked mackerel (£3.50). **The Central Bar,** Main St. (tel. 41311), has traditional music every single night during July and August. Arrive early for breathing space. For a quieter pint, head two doors down to the tiny **Corner Bar,** which hasn't changed much since the 1930s.

To enjoy beautiful walks along the peninsula located east of Ardara, head south through town and turn right at the horse-riding sign towards **Loughros Point** (LOW-crus). At the next horse-riding sign, either turn right for a beautiful view of Ardara Bay or continue straight to Loughros Point to sight the sea. The **Maghera Caves,** located 5 mi. from the town center, make another pleasant excursion from Ardara. The six caves vary in size and depth; all require a flashlight. At low tide you can enter the Dark Cave, once the refuge of *poteen* makers. A rising tide, however, could trap you inside. To reach the caves, follow the main road south past the Loughros turnoff, then follow the signs several miles west on small roads. The road that passes the caves continues through a mountain pass until it reaches Dungloe.

MIDWEST COAST

Coastal N56 from Glenties to Dungloe, on the midwest coast, bumps and bounces along. The expansive, sandy beaches of the midwest are isolated by the eerie stillness of the Derryeagh Mountains. Expect a leisurely pace in this, the largest *gaeltacht* in Ireland. Buses run infrequently, so be sure to plan your schedule—or not, because you may decide to stay.

DUNGLOE (AN CLOCHAN LIATH) & CROHY HEAD

Dungloe (dun-LO), known locally as the Capital of the Rosses, is a busy market town where travelers stock up before hurrying on to Crohy Head or the mountains. Hundreds of party-lovers flock to Dungloe in the last week of July for the **Mary from Dungloe Festival** (tel. 48519), named after a popular old song about the tragic love affair between Mary and a local lad. The population swells to 80,000 during this 10-day celebration, which attracts famous musicians to both trad and modern parties. The highlight of the festival, of course, is the selection of the annual Donegal ambassador, Mary from Dungloe. For festival information and ticket bookings, call the Festival Booking Office (tel. 21254; open Mon.-Sat. 10am-6pm).

Crohy Head, the peninsula to the southwest of Dungloe, collects strangely-shaped rock formations around a jagged coast. **Crohy Head Youth Hostel (An Óige/HI)** (tel. 21950), in an old coast guard station, offers stupendous views over the Atlantic (April-May £4.50, under 18 £3.50; June-Sept. £5.50, under 18 £4). To reach the peninsula and the hostel from Dungloe, turn onto Quay Rd. halfway down Main St. and follow the bumpy road for about 7 mi.

The Dungloe **tourist office** (tel. 21297), close to the shore, finds rooms and sells all sorts of maps (open June-Oct. Mon.-Sat. 10am-1pm and 2-6pm). The Main St. sports a **Bank of Ireland** (tel. 21077) and an **AIB** (tel. 21179; both open Mon.-Wed. and Fri. 10am-12:30pm and 1:30-4pm, Thurs. 10am-12:30pm and 1:30-5pm). Just across from the caravan park (see below), **Green's Launderette** (tel. 21021) cleans up (large load £5, small load £4; open Mon.-Fri. 9am-6pm). The pharmacy works out of **O'Donnell's Chemist,** Main St. (tel. 21386; open Mon.-Sat. 9am-6pm). Philatelists hang out at the **post office** (tel. 21179; open Mon.-Fri. 9am-1pm and 2-5:30pm, Sat. 9am-1pm). The **phone code,** 075, had a tragic love affair with a local lad.

Greene's Independent Holiday Hostel is attached to the **Dungloe Caravan and Camping Park** (tel. 21021), on Carnemore Rd. near the Esso filling station. Four eight-bunk dorms, a family room and a well-equipped kitchen constitute this basic, clean hostel. (Dorm £6. **Camping** £5/tent plus £2/car and 30p/person. **Bikes** £5/day. Sheets 50p; laundry £3.50.) Farther down Main St. across the bridge and up a small hill, the **Hillcrest B&B,** Barrack Brae (tel. 21484), tops a slope with views of the water, gorgeous rooms, and kind proprietors to boot (£13/person, w/bath £15).

At the sinfully red **Riverside Bistro,** Main St. (tel. 21062), snacks and vegetarian meals (vegetable lasagna £5) are affordable (open daily 12:30-3pm and 6-10pm). **Sweeney's Hotel,** Main St. (tel. 21033), supplies basic lunch fare (ham and cheese sandwich £1.85; lunch served 11:30am-3pm). Dinners are much dearer, my dear; you may have to settle for the large starters (mussels in garlic butter £3.50). The **Cope supermarket,** Main St., opens its doors daily 9am-6pm and Fridays until 7pm. Spacious **Beedy's,** Main St. (tel. 21219), pleases all with trad and a bartender whose infectious laughter will set off long-suppressed giggles. Across the street, **The Atlantic Bar** lures hip characters with its folk and trad sessions on the weekends.

BURTONPORT & ARRANMORE ISLAND

About 5 mi. north of Dungloe, the fishing village of **Burtonport** is less a town than a few pubs clustered around a pier. The ferry to Arranmore Island docks here, and the village is also a good base for fishing and boat trips to the many uninhabited islands in the area. **Sea anglers** leave from the cabin on Burtonport Pier (tel. 42077) most summer mornings (10am) and some evenings (4pm; £10). Book a week in advance. The tiny **tourist office** is just past the Ferry Booking Office to the left of the ferryport (tel. 20101; open Mon.-Sat. noon-6pm, Sun. 2-6pm). The **post office** (tel. 42001) is smack in the middle of town (open Mon.-Fri. 9am-1pm and 2-5pm, Sat. 9am-1pm). The **phone code** for Burtonport and Arranmore Island casts its net at 075.

Campbell's Pier House (tel. 42017) presents a happy face, spacious rooms, wonderful carved wooden doors, and a tiny kitchen where you can make tea and coffee (£14/person, w/bath £18). The **Lobster Pot,** Main St. (tel. 42012), is half-bar, half-restaurant with a cozy atmosphere. Soccer jerseys, nautical bric-a-brac, and a green fiddle decorate the burgundy walls (seafood chowder and brown bread £5; open daily 1-10pm). **The Cope,** at the top of the town (tel. 42004), is the largest **grocery** on either side of the water; stock up before boarding the ferry (open Mon.-Sat. 9am-6pm). **Skippers Tavern** (tel. 42234) sings and rings with trad most nights; **O'Donnell's Bar** (tel. 42255) pours a quieter pint. Both serve pub grub.

Just off the coast lies **Arranmore Island** (it appears on some old maps as "Aran" or "Arran Island") where introspection (by day) and excessive partying (by night) seem to go hand-in-hand. The **ferry** from Burtonport (tel. 20532) takes 20 minutes (July-Aug. Mon.-Sat. 8/day, Sun. 7/day; Sept.-June 2-3/day). Dock office opens daily 8:30am-7:30pm (£6 return, students £5). About 700 people (most with some connection to Chicago, IL) live in the sheltered southeast corner of the island. The smaller population on the other side of the island speaks Irish.

A well-marked footpath—**the Arranmore Way**—encircles the island and will lead you to the lighthouse, high above impressive cliffs and rushing water, at the far tip of the island. The **tourist office** by the ferry dock sells a map of trails on the island (50p). A full perambulation of Arranmore Way takes a good five hours, longer if you're searching for Arranmore's pearls. Four priceless pearls were a gift to Red Hugh O'Donnell from Philip II for Red Hugh's help in saving Spanish sailors when Armada ships went down off the coast. The pearls were last seen on Arranmore Island in 1905, and people are still searching.

Along the shore to the left of the ferry port stretches a string of pubs, houses, and the **Arranmore Island Youth Hostel (An Óige/HI)** (tel. 20574), just 100 yd. from the ferry and smack on the water. The hostel is basic, but its beachfront location makes up for the small kitchen and common space (dorm £4 for members; membership £3.50; open June-Sept.). There are plenty of B&Bs. **Ward's B&B** (tel. 20511), promises clean, spacious rooms and great ocean views (£12/person).

O'Donnell's (a.k.a. Atlantic View Bar), Reilly's, Philly's Bar, Phillbhnán, Andrew's Bar, and **Glen Hotel** make Arranmore's list of pubs a long one for a small population. Each Wednesday in summer, the entire island flocks to one of these for traditional music (the location rotates), though there are usually impromptu sessions at one or two others. Local trad guru Daniel O'Donnell plays on the island every year during the second week in August. With 24-hour licenses in order to serve fishermen returning from sea, some pubs provide "refreshments" into the wee hours of the morning. The only **grocery store** on the island is attached to Phillbhnán pub. It closes at 6pm, but the bartender might be convinced to help someone in dire need of supplies. **Bonners Ferryboat Restaurant** (also the Booking Office) sells snacks.

THE DONEGAL GAELTACHT

To the north and west of Burtonport stretch the haunting, untouched, Irish-speaking **Rosses,** an environmentalist's dream. Stony soil dotted with tiny ponds covers crumpled ground of this headland. Locals will tell you that this is the "real" Donegal, where peat cutting and salmon fishing keep the economy alive. But it only marks the beginning of the Donegal *gaeltacht,* known for its unspoiled scenery and intense trad sessions. This area remains the last part of Ireland where Irish culture—language, music, and dance—is practiced, not produced. Locals are proud that their area has not sold out, yet fear that Bloody Foreland may someday become another Ring of Kerry, Tory Island another Inishmor. So far, most visitors are not of the tour bus variety, but far-flung backpackers and students of the Irish language.

North of Burtonport on the Coast Road dwells the little village of **Kincasslagh,** home to the **Viking House** hotel, owned by country singer Daniel O'Donnell, an effective ambassador for Donegal. A minor road heads west to **Cruit Island,** not really an island at all but rather a peninsula with nice beaches and a host of thatched cottages. **Aran Trail Bikes** (tel. (075) 43213) rents cycles, which are an ideal way to see the Rosses (ask for Smith's house; £10/day, £25/4 days, £35/week; deposit £40; open Mon.-Sat. 11am-6pm). Farther north, the magnificent stretch of sand known as **Carrickfinn Strand** is marred only by the presence of tiny **Donegal Airport.** A few miles down the road from Kincasslagh is the village of **Mullaghduff,** home of Bonner's pub (tel. (075) 43368), renowned for its high-quality trad sessions (Christy Moore makes surprise appearances). Musicians from Scotland and Ireland gather here for a three-day trad festival in late October.

In the heart of the Donegal *gaeltacht,* the village of **Annagry** marks the area of **Rannafast,** famous for its Gaelic story-telling tradition. *Seanachies* like the MacGrianna brothers and Mici Shean Neill perpetuate the Irish language and narrative tradition through their stories. Working to keep alive a language that is still in danger of extinction, an Irish school in Annagry recruits teenagers every summer for Gaelic camps (see **The Irish Language,** p. 68). A bit farther, **Leo's Tavern,** where Clannad and Enya raged, has walls lined with silver, gold, and platinum discs. Despite the kitsch, the pub is still a trad institution, with sessions at least twice a week.

At the intersection of the coast road and N56, minuscule **Crolly** is the gateway to northwest Donegal. **Paddy Oig's** pub has everything a body could need: camping, pub grub, great traditional music, and Irish dancing in summer. **Coillín Darach Caravan & Camping Park** (tel. (075) 31306), just behind the pub, sports a craftshop, tennis court, and modern facilities (July-Aug. £5; Sept.-April £3.50; May-June £4).

The postmistress at the Crolly **post office** is a good source of information on the area and can point you toward the youth hostel. The **shop** next to the post office is open Monday through Saturday 9am-10:30pm. A scenic 4-mi. walk through the mountains of Glenveagh National Park ascends into **Tor,** site of the **Screag an Iolair Hill Hostel** (SCRAG an UH-ler; tel. (075) 48593), one of the best hostels in Ireland. With its own neolithic stone circle and a "meditation room" furnished with mats and Indian tapestries, this mystical hostel hosts frequent trad sessions, poetry readings, and art exhibits. Kind owner Eamonn often takes hostelers to local trad sessions (£6/person; laundry £2; open all year, but call ahead in winter). **Feda O'Donnell** provides a daily coach service to and from Donegal Town (£5), Dublin (£7), Belfast (£7), and Galway (£9). Eamonn will pick up travelers in Crolly. Walkers or bikers should take the Tor Road out of Crolly. The road passes a deserted village on the shores of still Lough Keel and then swings right at the old Tor school. Hostel-seekers should continue straight ahead at the school, past the hostel sign.

The road descends past Ashardan Waterfall and Lake and finally into Glen Tor. Crolly and the hostel nearby make a good base for exploring the unspoiled heath lands of the **Derryveagh Mountains,** inhabited by red deer. Trails for hikers of varying abilities, clearly shown on the *Ordnance Survey Discovery Series I,* begin at the hostel in Tor. As the trails are often hard to follow, hikers should inform the hostel warden of their plans in case of emergency.

One mile north of Crolly, N56 and the coastal road diverge. N56 turns inland and reaches R251 after about 5 mi. This road leads east through Dunlewey, past the foot of conical **Errigal Mountain,** Donegal's highest peak, and eventually to Glenveagh National Park. The drive is studded with stunning views. At the foot of Errigal Mountain in Denlewy village, the **An Óige Errigal Youth Hostel** (tel. (075) 31180) is a hiker's haven. (June-Sept. members £6, under 18 £4.50; off-season members £5, under 18 £4.) The marked trail that begins at the east end of Dunlewey leads up the side of the mountain to the 2466-ft. summit. **Dunlewey Lake** and the **Poison Glen** guard the trailhead at the foot of the mountain. In a mythical battle, Lugh slew Balor of the Evil Eye. Poison from the Eye supposedly permeated the ground in the Glen, but most people attribute the name to an abundance of spurge in the Glen. Three strenuous hours to the summit reveals a frightening **One Man's Pass,** similar to that at Slieve League. The less foot-sure or foolhardy will find a number of shortcuts that bypass the pass. The **Ionad Cois Locha Dunlewey** offers boat tours, weaving demos, loads of info, trad sessions with dancing on Tuesdays, and a fire-warmed café. (Center open Mon.-Sat. 10:30am-6pm, Sun. 11am-7pm; café open Mon.-Sat. 10:30am-6pm, Sun. 11am-7pm. Boat trip £2.50, students £2.)

Two Hearts an Ocean Apart

Once upon a time, in the early part of the century, two young lovers in little Ranafass dreamed of emigrating to Boston. When the time came to depart, the young man realized that he couldn't bear to leave his beloved Donegal. In a hasty show of pride, the young woman left anyway, with barely a goodbye. As the days passed, the lad grew sick with longing. Vowing not to rest until he found his love, he left on the next boat.

Meanwhile, the lass, then in Boston, also reconsidered. Forgiving her true love, she set sail for Ireland. The two ships passed one another on the frothy Atlantic. The youth searched for his lover in Boston for 11 years. Back in Donegal, the woman, brokenhearted at his absence, eventually married another. At long last, the man returned. His search ended, he pleaded with his love to run away with him back to Boston. Though she still loved him, the woman thought of her new family and refused to leave them. The man, driven mad by her refusal, moved to a derelict cottage in the mountains, where he lived in misery for two years before dying of starvation. This tale is remembered in a haunting lament still played in the Donegal *gaeltacht.*

BUNBEG & BLOODY FORELAND

Where N56 moves inland, R257 continues along the coast to Bunbeg. The coastal route is one continuous strip of raw scenery—perfect for cyclists, since there's little traffic. Hitchers tend to stay on N56, where cars pass more often. **Bunbeg Harbour,** the smallest enclosed harbor in Ireland, was a main port of exit and entry at the height of Britain's imperialism. Relics from that period line the harbor: military barracks, grain stones, and a Martello tower. The amiable **Hudi Beag's** pub (tel. (075) 31016) hosts intense, almost professional, trad sessions on Monday nights. Lunches for little money are available at **Errigal View Hotel** (tel. (075) 31355), which also caters to vegetarians (open daily, lunch noon-2:15pm, dinner 6-9:15pm). A ferry to **Tory Island** leaves from the harbor daily at 9am (tel. (075) 31991 or 31340; £12). Halfway from town to the harbor, a pair of stone pillars marks a rough path that leads to the gorge through which the Clady River rushes. The coastal strip north of Bunbeg is the most densely populated rural region in Western Europe.

About 7 mi. north of Bunbeg, **Bloody Foreland,** named for the deep-red hue of the sea at sunset, juts into the ocean. Legend holds that the sea is colored with the blood of sailors who perished in the wrecks of old Spanish galleons. The headland at **Magheraroarty** ("place of Roarty"), farther west, offers miles of unspoiled beaches and clear views. A mythical holy well here remains full of fresh water despite the tide's passing over it twice a day. **Ferries** to **Tory Island** leave from Bunbeg (see above) and Magheraroarty. Bloody Foreland is best approached from north to south.

TORY ISLAND

Visible from the Bloody Foreland, barren Tory Island, named for its *tors* ("hills"), sits 13km off the coast. Its age-old reputation as a haven for pirates prompted people to equate the word "Tory" with "pirate" or "rascal." The use of "Tory" to mean "Conservative" derives from this Irish slang. ("Whig" originally meant a Scottish horse thief.) The original Tory Island pirates were the Fomorians, sour-tempered demons of myth who inhabited Ireland since the beginning of the world. They attacked each mythical settlement one after the other until the Túatha de Danann supplanted them on the mainland. The Fomorians then retreated to Tory Island and the northwest ocean. Their leader in their periodical invasions of the mainland was Balor of the Evil Eye. Human pirates continued the tradition and used the island in the glory days of smuggling. Today, if an islander appears particularly difficult to deal with, mainlanders attribute it to a pirate ancestry.

This small, Irish-speaking community has thus far managed to maintain a strong sense of independence, though a recent spurt in the tourist industry threatens the island's uniqueness and isolation. Islanders themselves refer to the mainland as "the country." Ferry service to the island is more regular and reliable than it used to be, but the king of the island—Rí an Oileáin, or Patsy Dan Rodgeres—still greets all visitors. Many of the island's unusual traditions remain intact, including the superstition which deters people from rescuing those drowning after having fallen off of a boat (make sure to spot the life-jackets on any ferry). Another tradition claims that a stone on one of the island's hills has power to fulfill wishes. Islanders have used the stone to wish shipwrecks on invaders, most recently in 1884, when a gunboat coming to collect taxes was wished to the bottom of the Atlantic. The islanders still pay no taxes (though they do pay to maintain a school). **Donegal Coastline Cruises** (tel. (075) 31320) runs boats from Bunbeg (June-Sept. 1/day at 9am, Oct.-May 5/week; 1¼hr); Magheraroarty (June 2/day at 11:30am and 5pm, July-Aug. 3/day at 11:30am, 1:30 and 5pm; 1½hr); and Portnablagh (July-Aug. 1/week on Wed. at 2pm; all crossings £15 return, students £13; bicycles free). Times depend on tides and weather and are subject to change: storms have stranded travelers here for days (in summer) or even weeks (in winter).

The island's 130 people manage to support a surprising number of businesses, including a shop, a new hotel and restaurant, a tea and craft shop, and **Gailearai Dixon** ("the Dixon Gallery"). The gallery showcases the work of local artists well-known for their unique, child-like painting style. The youth hostel, **Brú Thorái, Radharc Na Mara** (tel. (074) 65145) costs £5 and is the best place to stay while exploring the island's bleak, wind-swept scenes. Historical sights are few, but the monastery that St. Colmcille founded in the 6th century is still present in the Round Tower and Tau Cross close to the town center.

NORTHERN DONEGAL

FALCARRAGH & DUNFANAGHY

Northeast of the Bloody Foreland, white beaches stretch along the coast from Falcarragh to Dunfanaghy. The area's only **tourist information** spouts from the Bord Fáilte office in Irish-speaking **Falcarragh,** located at the school (tel. 65070; open Mon.-Sat. 10am-5pm, Sun. noon-5pm). Financial services are available at the **Bank of Ireland** and its **ATM** (tel. 35484; open Mon.-Wed. and Fri. 10am-12:30pm and 1:30-4pm, Thurs. 10am-12:30pm and 1:30-5pm). The town's **post office,** Main St. (tel. 35110), is open Monday to Friday 9am-1pm and 2-5:30pm, Saturday 9am-1pm. The **phone code** is a crimson-colored 074.

At the small but intimate **Shamrock Lodge Hostel (IHH),** Main St. (tel. 35859), guests peek down the stairs at the revelry in the pub below. The rooms are cozy and comfortable, as are the wee kitchen and living room (dorm £6, private room £7/person). Next to the post office, **Patricia McGraddy** offers B&B in a modern abode. Guests are welcome to jam on her piano (£12/person). Eat to the twang of country & western's top hits at **John's Restaurant,** Main St. (fish fingers and "fries" £2; open Mon.-Sat. 10am-10pm, Sun. 2-10pm). The **Gweedore Bar,** Main St. (tel. (075) 35293), curries the town's favor with a reasonable lunch menu (roast chicken, veggies, potatoes £2.90; lunch served 12:30-2:30pm). Falcarragh lives pub life to the fullest. The **Shamrock Lodge,** in the center of town, buzzes with human activity well into the night. The "young room," as owner Mary calls it, has a jukebox, pool table, and comfy leather seats. The Saturday night trad session is thought by many to be the best in the country (rhythm and blues Friday nights).

Along the coast, 5½ mi. north of Falcarragh and 1½ mi. south of Dunfanaghy, is the unique **Corcreggan Mill Cottage Hostel (IHH)** (tel. 36507). Owner Brendan has converted an old wooden railway car into comfortable rooms with mahogany floors and walls. Other rooms are available in the equally cool, attached stone cottage (dorm £6, private room £4; **camping** £4; organic breakfast £2; **bikes** £7/day). Many hostelers team up to hire the services of **John McGinley's Buslines** (to Falcarragh and nearby areas £1 return; to Bunbeg and Dunlewey £2 return). Hitchers find easy rides to the pubs in Falcarragh. Farther on towards Dunfanaghy, Francis Stewart provides comfortable, flowery **B&B** (tel. 36281; £12/person).

In **Dunfanaghy, Danann's Restaurant,** Main St. (tel. 36150), specializes in slightly expensive but praiseworthy seafood. (Entrees from £7; early 3-course dinner £10, 6-7pm only; open June daily 6-9:30pm; July-Sept. daily 6-10pm.) The **Whisky Fly** (tel. 36208), in the Arnold Hotel, has trad Monday and Friday, folk Wednesday, and sing-alongs Saturday nights during the summer. Otherwise, the town is quiet. The **village shop** is open daily from 9am to 11pm for groceries.

GLENVEAGH NATIONAL PARK

Fourteen miles northwest of Letterkenny on the eastern side of the Derryveagh Mountains, **Glenveagh National Park** (tel. (074) 37088) is justly one of the more popular national parks in Ireland. The founder of the Glenveagh estate, John Adair, had a nasty reputation that doesn't suit the beauty of the park. In the cold April of 1861, he evicted 244 tenants on trumped-up charges. Many of them decided to emi-grate to Australia while others were forced into a subsistence lifestyle in the work-house. The park itself features 37 sq. mi. of forest glens and mountains. Glenveagh is so large that hundreds of people can easily lose themselves in isolation (or simply lose themselves—take a good map just in case). In 1991 its air was deemed the cleanest in Europe. Hostels in Crolly and Errigal are most convenient to the park.

Many visitors climb **Mt. Errigal** and **Slieve Snacht** to boast that they have climbed the two highest mountains in Ireland. Large crowds, especially in summer, take the free minibus from the park's entrance to the castle, 2½ mi. away (last trip 1½hr. before park closes). **Glenveagh Castle** is less than 200 years old but looks like a medieval keep with its thick walls, battle-ready rampart, turrets, and round tower. The gardens and greenhouse are clearly more modern. Marked trails head uphill and down from the castle. The ½-mi. walk uphill to a viewpoint behind the castle is defi-nitely worth the sweat. One of the largest herds of red deer in Europe roams the park—some travelers go to Glenveagh specifically to deer-watch (best done at dusk). (Park and castle open April-May daily 10am-6:30pm; June-Sept. Mon.-Sat. 10am-6:30pm, Sun. 10am-7:30pm; Oct. Sat.-Thurs. 10am-6:30pm. Park £2, students £1; same prices for castle. Garden tours July-Aug. Tues. and Thurs. at 2pm leave from the Castle Courtyard.) Guided nature walks leave from the **visitors center** (July-Aug. Wed. 2pm). Park rangers (tel. (074) 37088) lead hill walks on some Saturdays and can always dole out Glenveagh hiking info.

On the other side of the park, quite close to Letterkenny, **Glebe House and Gal-lery,** in Churchill (tel. (074) 37071), displays Donegal folk art and rare international Victorian folk art. The gallery also houses an impressive collection of fine arts: paint-ings (Louis de Brocquy), ceramics (Picasso), and other works by leading 20th-century artists. (Open around Easter and late May to late Sept. Sat.-Thurs. 11am-6:30pm; last tour 5:30pm. Admission £2, students £1.)

ROSGUILL PENINSULA

The Irish-speaking village of **Carrigart** sits at the base of one of the more beautiful drives in Donegal—the **Atlantic Drive** around the Rosguill Peninsula—and provides the shops and services necessary before setting out on the road. Pull your ductas from the **National Irish Bank** (open July-Aug. Mon.-Fri. 10am-noon, Sept.-June Mon.-Tues. and Thurs.-Fri. 10am-noon). Soap and aspirin are available at **Joy's Pharmacy,** Main St. (tel. (074) 55124; open summer Mon.-Sat. 10am-1pm and 2-6:30pm, winter Mon.-Tues. and Thurs.-Sat. 10am-1pm and 2-6pm, Wed. 10am-1pm). The **post office,** Main St. (tel. (074) 55101), performs all the necessary functions (open Mon.-Fri. 9am-1pm and 2-5pm, Sat. 9am-1pm).

In Carrigart, stay with Mary Gallagher at **Cuan-na-long,** or "Ship-haven" (tel. (074) 55597). The rose garden has been known to bewitch guests (£14/person). A friendly staff at **Greim-Blasta,** Main St. (tel. (074) 55188), serves toasted sandwiches (£1.50) and decadent, luscious desserts (open July-Aug. daily 8am-11pm; Sept.-May 8am-8pm). Down the road, the upscale **Weaver's Restaurant** (tel. (074) 55204) specializes in fresh-from-the-ocean seafood. (Trout £9. Open daily July-Aug. 6pm-10pm. May be closed for renovations winter 1996-97, scheduled to reopen for summer '97. Call ahead.) The **North Star** (tel. (074) 55110), across the way, is Carrigart's favorite pub by far, but nightlife is more lively in Downings. Rent your wheels at **C.C. Cycles** (tel. (074) 55427; £1/hr., £5/day; open daily 9am-9pm).

The Atlantic Drive leads from Carrigart to the very tip of the peninsula, where **Trá na Rosann Youth Hostel (An Óige/HI)** (tel. (074) 55374) watches from the top of a hill 4 mi. from the tiny town of **Downings**. The setting is unbeatable (you're almost on top of the whole world) and the rustic design is surprisingly comfortable, with a flag stone kitchen and warm lounge (dorm £5.50, under 18 £4; open April-Sept.). A convenient shop is 50 yd. from the hostel. Drink down a draught where the locals mill around, at **Singing Pub** (2mi. down the road), a thatched bar with low ceilings, great grub, and trad music nearly every night. Downings itself is a prosperous and prim village known for its fishing and tweed industries.

■ Fanad Peninsula

The Fanad Peninsula juts into the Atlantic between Lough Swilly and Mulroy Bay. Overshadowed by its larger neighbor, Inishowen, the Fanad Peninsula's small area comforts cyclists. In summer, the peninsula's lush greenery makes a striking complement to the sandy beaches. Winter brings even better views. The eastern edge, outlined by the villages of **Ramelton, Rathmullan,** and **Portsalon,** is by far the nicest spot, with colorful old houses and sweeping views across Lough Swilly. The Knockalla Mountains are pretty and easy to climb. The route from Kreevykeel to the breathtaking viewpoint at Saldan Ha Head, near Portsalon, provides a thorough impression of the peninsula. The **phone code** for the entire peninsula juts out 074.

RAMELTON

A river runs through the pretty little town of Ramelton at the mouth of the Leannan Estuary, the eastern gateway to the peninsula. Famous in bygone days for its salmon, Ramelton clings to the last fish house in all of Ireland. The building, formerly used for smoking salmon, is now a restaurant and the **Fish House Craft Gallery** (tel. 51316; open May-Sept. daily 10am-7pm). An interior of bare stone and rough-hewn logs echoes some of the original character (chicken and mushroom crepe £2.50). For affordable feasts in a more refined setting, cross the street to the imposing **Mirabeau Steak House,** the Mall (tel. 51138; salmon steak £5). **Whoriskey's/Spar Supermarket** (tel. 51006) sells groceries (open Mon.-Sat. 8:30am-9pm, Sun. 9am-9pm).The **National Irish Bank,** the Mall (tel. 51028), has money, money, money. Mail arrives at the **post office,** Main St. (tel. 51001; open Mon.-Fri. 9am-5:30am, Sat. 9am-1pm). **Bridge Launderette,** the Mall (tel. 51333), can clean your socks (wash and dry £3.90; open Mon.-Sat. 9:30am-6pm). A **pharmacy** (tel. 51080) graces Main St. (open Mon.-Tues. and Thurs.-Sat. 9am-1pm and 2-6pm, Wed. 9am-1pm).

In the town center, **Crammond House,** Market Sq. (tel. 51055), has spacious, pretty rooms intended mostly for families (single £14, double £27; open Easter-Oct.). One mile out of town on the Milford Rd., Mrs. Kathleen Curran provides a mattress and a meal in pleasant **Clooney House** (tel. 51125; £14/person w/bath). Friday night trad sessions, a good pint, and a funky bathroom recommend 200-year-old **Sweeney's. Bridge Bar** (tel. 51119) has music almost every night (trad on Sundays). **Conway's** (tel. 51297) pours proper pints in an old thatched cottage to the beat of trad and ballads every Saturday.

To discover the area's heritage, follow Main St. uphill from the fish house. Past Crammond House, a right at Mary's Bar will bring you to Back Lane, the old **Presbyterian Meetinghouse. Francis Makemie** preached here before founding the first American Presbytery in 1706. The building now houses the town library and the

NORTHWEST IRELAND

humble **Ramelton Heritage Centre** (tel. 51266). As part of Irish Genealogical Project Centres, the center in Ramelton will help you trace your Donegal ancestors for a fee (registration £10; open Mon.-Thurs. 9am-4:30pm, Fri. 9am-4pm). It has info on other national heritage centers as well. Crowds flock to the Leannan **Festival** during the beginning of July for a carnival, parade, pageant, and more fun and games.

RATHMULLAN

Five miles north along the main coastal road is Rathmullan, an ancient town of historical significance and sandy beaches. In 1607, the last powerful Gaelic overlords, Hugh O'Neill and "Red Hugh" O'Donnell, decided to abandon Ireland after a series of military defeats. They set sail from Rathmullan for the continent with 90 of their retinue. The event is known, and lamented, as the Flight of the Earls (see **Feudalism (1200-1607)**, p.59). The tales of O'Neill and O'Donnell are very much alive and present at the **"Flight of the Earls" Heritage Centre** (tel. 58178), on the coast. Helpful staff use artwork, literature, and wax models to explain the entire area's history in detail. The center, housed in a renovated Martello tower, is historic in itself. (Open June-Sept. Mon.-Sat. 10am-6pm, Sun. noon-6:30pm. Admission £1.50, students £1, families £3.) **Tourist info** is also gladly dispensed at the Heritage Centre (tel. 58229). Around the corner, the remains of romantic 16th-century **Rathmullan Priory** loom. Overgrown with weeds, the crumbling priory affords good views across the lough. Also important in more recent republican history, Wolfe Tone, the famous champion of Irish independence, was arrested in Rathmullan in 1798.

Mrs. McFadden's **Martello B&B,** Kerrs Bay Rd. (tel. 58207), across from the Heritage Centre, is an old, low-ceilinged house in the middle of town. Guests can experience a unique old-world feeling in this 1806 house (TV and sink in each room; single £12, double £22). **Deeney's Supermarket,** Kerrs Bay Rd. (tel. 58148), supplies basic gastronomic needs (open Mon.-Sat. 9am-1pm and 2-8pm, Sun. 9am-1pm and 3-6pm). Quiet **Pier Hotel** (tel. 58178) serves cheap pub grub to everyone in town. (Sandwiches £1. Open for lunch mid-June to mid-Aug. Mon.-Sat. 12:30-5:30pm, Sun. 1-2:30pm; dinner Mon.-Sun. 5:30-8:30pm. Reservations required. Line dancing every Thursday.) A romantic wooded lane runs parallel to the beach from behind the hotel. The **Water's Edge Pub and Restaurant** (tel. 58182) is set on the very spot where the Earls set sail. The **Beachcomber Bar** (tel. 58125), across the street from the hotel, offers a panoramic view (occasional trad and disco, no cover).

GLENVAR & PORTSALON

North of Rathmullan, a dozen slow brooks cross the road as the land rises over the **Knockalla Mountains** and **Glenvar.** Beyond this stretch of road, the coast arcs dramatically between mountain and shore. About halfway to Portsalon, a signposted lane leads from the main road to **Bunnaton Hostel,** Glenvar (tel. 50122), high on a hill above the lough. Once an HI hostel, Bunnaton has declared independence. It's a remote and a difficult hitch, but the peace and quiet are rewarding (£5, private room £7.50/person; sheets £1). Continuing north, the main road becomes both mind-bogglingly steep and breathtakingly beautiful. Just before Portsalon, the road crests a hill: **Knockalla Strand** (some British "beach expert" rated it the second best in the world) and the northern peninsula suddenly appear. **Mike's Bikes,** Doaghbeg (tel. 59207), rents bikes for this perfect cycle (£6/day, £30/week; deposit £35).

Descend into **Portsalon,** the source of these beautiful views. It was once a resort town, but the resort hotel burned down three years ago, leaving just 100-year-old **Rita's** (tel. 59135), a triptych of a restaurant, general store, and pub (restaurant and store open daily 10:30am-8:30pm). To reach Rita's, take the first right toward the pier after the golf club. The **Portsalon B&B** (tel. 59101), next to the post office on the main road, attempts to replace the resort hotel with big, new rooms perfumed by the rosebushes outside (£12/person). **Camping** is available next to Knockalla Strand at the **Knockalla Holiday Centre** (tel. 59108), 5 mi. south of Portsalon (kitchen, laundry, shop, TV, and game room; £6/2-person tent; open Easter-Oct.).

About one hour north of Portsalon by bike, the **Great Arch of Doaghbeg,** a mass of rock detached from seaside cliffs, keeps the **Fanad Lighthouse** company. Over 80 ft. wide, the arch is visible from the cliffs, though not from the main road. From Fanad Head, the route down the western side of the peninsula winds in and out of the inlets of **Mulroy Bay.** Mrs. Borland's **Avalon Farmhouse** (tel. 59031), on Main St. in tiny Tamney has homemade jam and an attractive decor (£13.50/person, w/bath £15; open March-Sept.). Farther south at the foot of the Knockalla Hills, **camping** right on Mulroy Bay in **Rockhill Park,** Kerrykeel (tel. 50012), is another option (tents £5; open mid-April to Oct.).

■ Letterkenny (Leitir Ceana Inn)

Letterkenny is Donegal's commercial and ecclesiastical center. The "white-streaked hill face" on the shores of River Swilly was the fastest growing town in Europe in 1992. The only traffic light in Co. Donegal can be found here, at the intersection of Main St. and Port Rd., although a pedestrian light that most people hope is temporary has also been added. Letterkenny is a functioning city, serving tourists best as a practical hub for exploring the surrounding area. **Letterkenny Bus Service (Handy Bus)** extensively services city routes (70p).

PRACTICAL INFORMATION

Tourist Offices: Bord Fáilte (tel. 21160), 1mi. past the bus station on the Derry Rd. Has info on all Donegal. Open Sept.-June Mon.-Sat. 9am-5pm; July-Aug. Mon.-Sat. 9am-5pm, Sun. 10am-2pm. **Chamber of Commerce Visitors Information Centre,** 40 Port Rd. (tel. 24866 or 25505), may look like a china shop, but the pamphlets and friendly advice (regarding Letterkenny) are no bull. Open June-Sept. Mon.-Sat. 9am-5pm; Oct.-May Mon.-Fri. 9am-5pm.

Banks: AIB, 61 Upper Main St. (tel. 22877 or 22807). Open Mon.-Wed. and Fri. 10am-4pm, Thurs. 10am-5pm; **ATM.**

Buses: at the junction of Port Rd. and the Derry Rd. in front of the Quinnsworth Supermarket. **Bus Éireann** (tel. 21309) makes tours of Inishowen Peninsula and Giant's Causeway (from Letterkenny £7; call to book). They also run regular service to Derry (Mon.-Sat. 3/day, Sun. 2/day; 40min.; £3), Dublin (Mon.-Sat. 4/day, Sun. 3/day; 5hr.; £10 return), Galway (Mon.-Sat.4/day, Sun. 3/day; 4hr.; £10), and Sligo via Donegal Town (Mon.-Sat. 4/day, Sun 3/day; 2½hr. to Sligo, 1½hr. to Donegal; £6). **Feda O'Donnell Coaches** (tel. (075) 48114 or (091) 761656) drives to Galway via Donegal Town (1/day) and to Crolly via Dunfanaghy (1/day). They run more extensive services on Fri. and Sun. **Lough Swilly Buses** (tel. 22400) head north towards the Fanad Peninsula (Mon.-Sat. 3/day), to Derry (Mon.-Sat. 10/day), and south to Dungloe (Mon.-Sat. 5/day; fares £3-7). **John McGinley Coaches** (tel. 35201) sends one bus every day to Gweedore via Dunfanaghy and another to Dublin (£8). **McGeehan's Bus** (tel. (075) 46101) goes to Killybegs (2/day; £7) and Glencolmcille (2/day; £6). **Northwest Busways** (tel. (077) 82619) sends buses around Inishowen (Mon.-Sat. 2/day), making stops in Buncrana (£3), Carndonagh (£4) and Moville (£4.30). **Doherty's Travel** (tel. (075) 21105) has buses that leave for Dungloe and Burtonport from Dunnes Supermaket at 5pm (1/day; £4).

Taxi: Letterkenney Cabs, tel. 21373.

Bike Rental: Church St. Cycles (tel. 26204) near the cathedral. £7/day, £30/week; deposit £40. Open Tues.-Sat. 10am-6pm.

Laundry: Peerless Clean-up, High Rd. (tel. 24538). Wash and dry: small load £4, large load £5-6. Open Mon.-Sat. 9am-8pm.

Hotlines: Samaritans: 20 Port Rd. (tel. 27200). **Letterkenny Women's Aid:** Port Rd. (tel. 24985). Open Mon.-Fri. 9am-5pm.

Pharmacy: Kelly's Pharmacy, Main St. (tel. 22354). Open Mon.-Sat. 9:30am-6pm, Sun. noon-2pm.

Post Office: halfway down Main St. (tel. 22454). Open Mon-Tues. and Thurs.-Sat. 9am-5:30pm, Wed. 9:30am-5:30pm.

Phone Code: 074.

ACCOMMODATIONS

The Manse Hostel (IHH), High Rd. (tel. 25238). From the bus station, head up Port Rd. towards town and turn right up the lane marked "Cove House B&B." Continue past the playground, through the parking lot, and 50yd. up the road. The hostel is across the street. The longer way around goes farther down Port Rd. and then makes a sharp right onto High Rd. Kitschy decor in a central location. Well-equipped kitchen with microwave and free coffee. Bunk beds in 3- or 4-bed dorms, some with sinks. Clean and tidy. £5.50.

Rosemount Hostel, 3 Rosemount Terrace (tel. 21181). Rather dark 6- to 8-bed dorms are upstairs; bathrooms are downstairs. Posters of dead rock stars grace the walls. Dorm £5. Open mid-June to Sept.

McClafferty's, 54 Main St. (tel. 21581). Clean, hotel-like rooms hover above a pub, but remain surprisingly quiet even in the evening. £15/person, w/bath £18.

White Gables, Mrs. McConnelogue, Dromore (tel. 22583), just off the Derry Rd. 1½mi. from town. Clean rooms. The upstairs balcony has spectacular views over Letterkenny. Call for pickup from town. £13.50/person, w/bath £14.50.

FOOD

Like all college towns, Letterkenny offers a fair share of cheap meals. **Quinnsworth,** behind the bus station (tel. 22555), is all you could want in a grocery store (open Mon.-Wed. and Sat. 9am-6pm and Thurs.-Fri. 9am-9pm). **The Natural Way,** 55 Port Rd. (tel. 25738), hawks health food (open Mon.-Sat. 9am-6:30pm).

Pat's Too, Main St. (tel. 21761). Hearty, take-away meals for the budget traveler. Always crowded at night. Delivery available. 9" pizza £3-4.50, kebabs £3-3.50. Open Mon.-Fri. noon-2:30pm and 5pm-midnight, Sat.-Sun. 5pm-midnight.

Pat's Pizza, Market Square, is the pricier restaurant version of Pat's Too, with the welcome addition of seafood and daily specials. Open Mon.-Sun. 5pm-midnight.

The Quieter Moment, 94 Upper Main St. (tel. 27401), uses marble tables and mahogany chairs to create a Bewley's aura.

Galfees, in the basement of the Courtyard Shopping Centre, Main St. (tel. 27173), features both a fresh sandwich bar (sandwiches £1-1.50; open 9am-6pm), and a full restaurant with a broad selection of seafood, Italian, and Mexican food. The evening menu (stuffed taco shells £4; served 5-8pm) is cheaper than the later dinner menu (vegetarian pasta special £6.50; served 6:30-10pm).

PUBS

McGinley's, 25 Main St. (tel. 21106). The young singles huddled around the bar gaze somberly at their drinks—and each other. Live trad sessions Thurs.-Sat.

McClafferty's, 54 Main St. (tel. 21581). Another popular spot where stained glass windows lend special lighting effects and set the mood. Music Thurs. and Sun.

Cottage Bar, Main St. (tel. 21338). A kettle on the hearth, quiet conversation in the corner, and nuns drinking Guinness. Trad music on Thurs. and Fri. nights.

The Pub, 50 Main St. (tel. 26032). No bric-a-brac nor fancy names to distract patrons from their pints. Quality trad sessions Fri. and Sat. nights.

Hotel Clanree, 1mi. out on Derry Rd. (tel. 24369), transforms itself into a nightclub for disco lovers on Sat. and Sun. nights (cover £5-6).

SIGHTS

Neo-Gothic **St. Eunan's Cathedral,** perched high above town on Church La., looks like a castle in the sky when floodlit at night. Moving away from the traffic light, Church La. emerges right off Main St. Proposed as a "resurrection of the fallen shrines of Donegal," construction on the cathedral lasted 11 years, all of which were years of economic hardship and depression. A detailed guidebook is available for (£2.50). (Open daily 8am-5pm, except during the five Sunday masses at 8, 9, 10, 11:15am, and 12:30pm. Free.) Although St. Eunan's is not even 100 years old, its burgeoning congregation has already outgrown it. Out of necessity, a second, modern cathedral has

Heads or Tails

Before turning to spiritual affairs, Saint Colmcille was a fearsome swordsman. During these early years, a great monster lurked in the pool up on Meenaroy where the river that runs through Letterkenny rises. Locals called the monster Swileach because it had 200 eyes on each side of its head. The local chief, Feardorocha, begged Colmcille to help him kill the monster.

When both warriors arrived at the pool early one morning, Swileach reared out of the water and attacked them. Cowardly Feardorocha fled, leaving Colmcille to fight the monster single-handedly. The brave young man drew his sword and halved the monster with a mighty blow. Still not dead, the monster's tail wrapped itself around Colmcille, trying to squeeze the life out of him. Miraculously, Colmcille freed himself from its iron grip and proceeded to make *ciolar coit* of the monster, carving it into many pieces (an ancient version of sushi).

Colmcille then caught up with Feardorocha as the latter was trying to ford the river near Conwal. As Colmcille was about to strike the deserter, Feardorocha begged for mercy. He requested that the saint at least wash the monster's blood off his blade before exacting revenge. Colmcille did so and found that his anger abated. The kindly saint pardoned Feardorocha and remarked that this water would wash away the anger of any person who washed his hand in it. He named the river Swilly after the monster he had slain.

recently been built on the edge of town. Opposite the cathedral, the smaller but more historical **Parish Church of Conwal** (Church of Ireland) shelters a number of tombstones with intriguing inscriptions, some of which date from the 17th century (Sunday services at 8 and 10:30am).

Donegal County Museum, High Rd. (tel. 24613), exhibits anything and everything having to do with Co. Donegal. Artifacts date from all periods, including the Iron Age, Medieval Ireland, and the postmodern era (open Tues.-Fri. 11am-12:30pm and 1-4:30pm, Sat. 1-4:30pm; free).

INISHOWEN PENINSULA

It would be a shame to leave Ireland without seeing the Inishowen Peninsula, an untouristed mosaic of mountains, forests, meadows, and beaches. The white sands are deserted, the pubs are filled with traditional music almost nightly, and residents are happy to share their land and laughter. The peninsula is dotted with many villages and two towns (Buncrana and Cardonagh), but it should really be thought of as a whole, since the sights never cease. It takes two to three days to see the whole she-bang properly without a car.

The nearest commercial center to Inishowen is Derry, whose residents, aware of Inishowen's allure, often vacation there. **Lough Swilly** (tel. (08 01504) 262017) runs buses from Derry to points on the Inishowen: Buncrana (Mon.-Fri. 10/day, Sat. 12/day, Sun. 4/day; 35min.; £2.40); Moville (4/day; 50min.; £3.75); Carndonagh (4/day; 1hr.; £4.20); and Malin Head (Mon., Wed., and Fri. 1/day, Sat. 3/day; 1½hr.; £6); Malin Town (Mon., Wed., and Fri. 1/day, Sat. 3/day; 70min.; £4.90). Lough Swilly also connects Buncrana directly to Carndonagh (Mon.-Sat. 3/day; 50min.). **Northwest Buses** (tel. (077) 82619) runs from Moville through Shrove, Culdaff, Carndonagh, Ballyliffen, Clonmany, Fahan, Buncrana, and on to Letterkenny (Mon.-Fri. 2/day, Sat. 1/day), and from Shrove to Derry via Moville (Mon.-Sun. 2/day; 1hr.).

Inishowen's inland landscape is unusual, but the northern and western shores are especially striking. The clearly posted **Inishowen 100** road takes exactly 100 mi. to navigate the peninsula's perimeter. Drivers will find this the best route for seeing Inishowen. Hitchers report having an easy and pleasant time on this road, since drivers tend to stop for people in isolated areas. Cycling can be arduous around Malin Head due to ferocious winds and hilly terrain. In fact, cyclists may want to use the roads that crisscross the peninsula to shorten long distances between sights. Most of the inland roads look exactly alike, so good directions and a good map are an absolute necessity. Available at tourist offices in Buncrana and Cardonagh, the map published by the Inishowen Tourism Society is the most comprehensive (£3). The **phone code** for all of the Inishowen Peninsula is an untouristed mosaic of 077.

■ Grianan of Aileach

Ten miles south of Buncrana at the bottom of the peninsula, the hilltop ringfort Grianan of Aileach (GREEN-ya of ALL-ya) is a logical place to start or finish a tour of Inishowen. This site has been a cultural center for at least 4000 years: first as a temple for sun-worship, then as a seat of power for the northern branch of the Uí Néill clan, and finally as a Mass rock where Catholics worshipped in secret during the time of the Penal Laws. The fort's name translates approximately into "the sun-house of Aileach." The name derives from the fort's pre-Celtic role as a place of sun-worship, the Celtic belief that the sun-goddess Gráine hibernated here in winter, and the legend of a divine Scottish maiden-princess, Aileach, who supposedly lived here. Much of the present stone structure is a 19th-century reconstruction, but the bottom part of the circular wall is original. Away from the carpark beyond the fort, a cross marks the site of a healing well supposedly blessed by St. Patrick.

The fort figures in a number of legends and tales, including the naming of Inishowen (Owen's Island). Owen was the son of **Niall of the Nine Hostages,** the semi-legendary ancestor of the Uí Néill/O'Neill clan. One story claims that Niall slept with an old hag to gain sovereignty over Ireland. As ruler, he captured young St. Patrick and brought him to Ireland as a slave. Having escaped captivity and begun his missionary work, St. Patrick baptized Niall's son Owen at this very same hillfort, consecrating the Uí Néill fortress as a Christian holy site and ensuring its continued significance. The fate of Grianan of Aileach was sealed in the 11th century when Donal McLaughlin, the reigning Prince of Inishowen, was defeated by Brian Ború's grandson, Murtagh O'Brien. Each of O'Brien's men was ordered to carry away one stone from the royal palace of Aileach so that it could never be a challenger's seat of power.

For the fort, turn left 2 mi. along the Letterkenny Road from Bridgend. The turnoff is at the Burt Circular Chapel, a modern-day replica of the ancient fort. The fort is on top of the hill. No public transport comes near here, so the car-less will have to cycle or walk. Travelers who choose to hitch say drivers are particularly nice on the 2-mi. incline. A more pleasant shortcut returns to Buncrana: take the first left at Burt Circular Chapel. The **Grianan of Aileach Interpretive Centre** (tel. 68512) hunches at the foot of the hill in an old stone church of Ireland, just past St. Aengus Church (the circular chapel). (Centre and restaurant open June-Sept. daily 10am-6pm, Oct.-May noon-6pm. Admission £2, students £1.)

■ Buncrana

North of Fahan, Buncrana looms under the long shadows of the mighty 2019-ft. **Slieve Snacht.** Summer tourism and the Fruit of the Loom's sweatshirt and t-shirt factory (underwear is produced in Malin Town) fortify Buncrana. Bord Faílte operates a summertime **tourist office** (tel. 62600) on the shorefront (open late May to mid-Sept. Tues.-Sun. 10am-1pm and 2-6pm). **AIB** (tel. 61087) counts money at 8 Market Sq. (open Mon.-Wed. and Fri. 10am-12:30pm and 1:30-4pm, Thurs. 10am-12:30pm and 1:30-5pm; **ATM**). **Bank of Ireland,** Main St. (tel. 61399), imitates its competition with an **ATM** (open Mon.-Wed. and Fri. 10am-4pm, Thurs. 10am-5pm). **Hugh McGonagle,** 37 Upper Main St. (tel. 61283), rents cars. **E. Tierney Chemist's,** Lower Main St. (tel. 62412), is the friendly local pharmacy (open Mon.-Sat. 9:30am-6pm, Sun. noon-4pm). **Valu-Clean,** Main St. (tel. 62570), is valued for its washing machines (wash and dry £4.50; open Mon.-Sat. 9am-6pm). The **post office** (tel. 61010) crowds onto Main St., too (open Mon.-Fri. 9am-5:30pm, Sat. 9am-1pm).

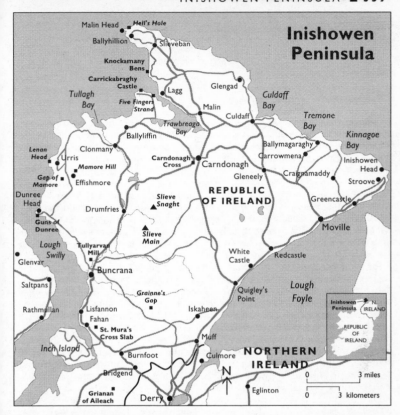

Inishowen Peninsula

Accommodations, Food, & Pubs The bedrooms at **Rattan House,** Swilly Rd. (tel. 61222), give a choice of TV or ocean view. A kitchen is occasionally available; coffee and tea are always accessible (£14/person). **Mill View B&B,** Mill Brae, Lower Main St. (tel. 62043), is closer to the center of town. A chatty proprietor shows guests to clean, spacious rooms and bathrooms (single £15, double £24).

Kitchens rub elbows with banks on Main St. The **Ubiquitous Chip,** 47 Upper Main St. (tel. 62530), scours the world for creative recipes. Happily, chips are not a main theme of the excellent menu. Chicken Bang! Bang! Curry Dip (£6.75) is one of the spicier dishes on the menu. (Vegetarian *tagliatelli* £5.20. Open July-Aug. daily noon-11pm, Sept.-June Mon.-Fri. noon-11pm.) **Dorothy's Kitchen,** 3 Church St. (tel. 62639), combines cultures in a French-bread pizza (£1.80; open daily 11am-1am). **O'Donnell's supermarket,** at the bus depot (tel. 61719), sells staples (open Mon.-Sat. 7:30am-9pm, Sun. 7:30am-8pm). The **West End Bar,** Main St. (tel. 61067), has live music on weekends and karaoke on Sundays. **O'Flaherty's,** Main St. (tel. 61305), has unmistakably Inishowen trad sessions in its large, dark bar. **The Drift Inn,** Main St. (tel. 61999), is also known for good *craic* (occasional trad sessions).

Sights Two castles overlook Swan Park: the stately Queen Anne-era **Buncrana Castle,** in which Wolfe Tone was imprisoned after the French "invasion" of 1798 failed, and the 1430 **O'Doherty Keep,** near Castle Bridge. Not quite Arthurian, the castle looks more like a derelict mansion and is closed to the public anyway. The park itself is peaceful and pleasing. To get to the park, walk up Main St. towards the shorefront. At the cinema crossroads, walk straight down Castle Avenue. The park is beyond the Castle Bridge, which arcs 100 yd. to the right. A **coastal walk** begins at

Castle Bridge, goes past the keep, turns left at the Castle, and then ascends the hill. **Ned Point's Fort,** also along the coast, was built in 1812 but is surprisingly (and not very pleasantly) modern looking. The path reaches Porthaw Bay and culminates in beautiful Dragill Strand. Friar Rogerty's Rock, beyond the beach, witnessed the martyring of a local clergyman in 1632.

■ West Inishowen

DUNREE HEAD & THE GAP OF MAMORE

Six miles northwest of Buncrana, Dunree Head pokes out into Lough Swilly. The **Guns of Dunree** (tel. 61817) stay polished and inactive inside an old fort here, one of six built to defend Lough Swilly against hypothetical Napoleonic invaders. The forts were used through both World Wars. Some of the guns from those wars are on display in **Fort Dunree** ("the fort of the heathen"), the first and only professionally-designed military museum in Ireland, which features the Nazi's original plan for the invasion of Ireland. The fort's coolest feature is its location overlooking Lough Swilly, where it is surrounded by nesting gulls and puffins. The mammoth searchlights used in WWII are still lit at times to search for people lost at sea. (Open June-Sept. Mon.-Sat. 10am-6pm, Sun. 1-6pm. Admission £1.50, students/children 75p.)

Farther north along the Inishowen 100 toward Clonimarry, a sign points left to the edge of the **Gap of Mamore.** This breathtaking pass teeters 800 ft. above sea level between Mamore Hill and Urris. The rocky pass is exhilarating; the otherworldly views over the mountains to the Atlantic can be seen only if you head through the pass from east to west (from inland to coast). The road through the pass rises steeply and proves difficult yet elating for hikers or cyclists. It's easier to drive, though the hairpin turns over the sea are daunting. Mamore Gap was the last point occupied by the British in the Republic of Ireland (they left in 1938). Queen Mebdh of Connacht, Cú Chulainn's archenemy in the Táin (see **Legends and Folktales,** p. 69), is supposedly buried near the Gap of Mamore (and at Knocknarea, Co. Sligo, and in a few other places).

The road descends from the gap onto chilly northern beaches. The Inishowen 100 proceeds to Lenan Head and inviting Lenan Strand. Heading north, the road passes over Dunaff Head, through Rockstown Harbour, and past Tullagh Bay. Two miles from Clonmany, the road arrives at the **Tullagh Bay Caravan and Camping Park** (tel. 76289), between mountains and sea. One of the choicest beaches on the peninsula is just outside your tent. (Laundry; kitchen; shop and café. £4/tent and 50p/person. Showers 20p. Open May 15-Sept. 15.)

CLONMANY & BALLYLIFFIN

North of the gap, two tiny towns, **Clonmany** and **Ballyliffin,** are separated by 1 mi. Clonmany hosts a local trad festival the first week of August. **Keg O'Poteen** (tel. 76415) serves "keg" burgers (£1) and pints of legal alcoholic beverages on Main St. The pub's misleading name probably comes from Inishowen's pride in its old reputation for distilling the best poitín (moonshine) in Éire. Live music ranges from country to Irish ballads (Fri.-Sun.). Traditional singing fills the weekend air in and around **McFeeley's** (tel. 76122), across the street at Corner House.

Apart from its neighbor's festivities, Ballyliffin's own highlights are three long miles of golden sands on Pollan Strand. From the northern end of the beach, ruined **Carrickbrahey Castle** is visible. It has been the seat of both the MacFaul and O'Doherty clans. In the meantime, wanderers can stay at **Castlelawn House** just behind the Strand Hotel in Ballyliffin (tel. 76600; £15/person, all w/bath).

■ North Inishowen

CARNDONAGH

Carndonagh, or "Carn," is Inishowen's main market town. Two miles from the head of Trawbreaga Bay, it's an ideal, if noisy, hub for exploring north Inishowen. **Inishowen Tourism,** Chapel St. (tel. 74933), just off the Diamond, is non-Bord Fáilte (open July-Aug. Mon.-Fri. 9:30am-7:30pm, Sat. 10am-6pm, Sun. noon-6pm; Sept.-June Mon.-Fri. 9:30am-5pm; free accommodation service). In the middle of it all sits an **AIB,** the Diamond (tel. 74388; open Mon. 10am-12:30pm and 1:30-5pm, Tues.-Fri. 10am-12:30pm and 1:30-4pm). For late night jaunts, Carn Cabs provides **taxis** (tel. 74580). **Rent-a-bike,** Pound St. (tel. 74840), rents bikes for further exploration (£6/day; deposit ID; open Mon.-Sat. 9am-6:30pm). **ValuClean,** Bridge St. (tel. 74150), washes and dries (£4.60; open Mon.-Sat. 9am-6pm). **McLaughlin's,** the Diamond (tel. 74120), is the town's pharmacy (open Mon.-Tues. and Thurs.-Sat. 10am-7pm, Wed. 10am-6pm). The **post office,** Bridge St. (tel. 74101), handles mail with care (open Mon.-Fri. 9:30am-1:30pm and 2:30-5:30pm, Sat. 9:30am-1pm).

The rooms sparkle and shine at Mrs. Kathleen Brett's **Dunshenny House,** Millbrae (tel. 74292), ½ mi. down Chapel St. (£13/person w/full breakfast; £11.50 w/continental breakfast; no singles in high season). One mile out of town on the Malin Rd., **Ashdale House B&B** (tel. 74017) takes advantage of its peaceful rural setting (£14/person; double £26, w/bath £30). **Trasbreaga Bay House,** the Diamond (tel. 74352), contents budget travelers (chicken nuggets and chips £2, sandwiches £1; open Mon.-Sat. noon-9pm, Sun. 12:30-2:30pm and 4-10pm). Tiny, modest **Bradley's Bar,** Bridge St. (tel. 74526), has royal bathrooms (Queen Victoria supposedly used the toilet in the men's room). **The Quiet Lady,** the Diamond (tel. 74777), gets noisy at night (trad on Wed., live music Fri. and Sun.).

Commercial Carn has but one sight to offer. The old Church of Ireland hulks ½ mi. down Bridge St. Outside its walls, the 7th-century **Celtic cross** known as Carin Carndonagh is all that remains of the monastery that St. Patrick founded when he brought Christianity to the peninsula. Two ornamented shorter pillars flank the cross. One of them depicts David playing his harp. Another ancient pillar displaying Christ's crucifixion stands in the graveyard of the church.

MALIN, MALIN HEAD, AND CULDAFF

North of Carndonagh, **Malin,** with its perfectly manicured central green, is yet another former winner of the brutally competitive Tidy Town contest. R242 coincides with the Inishowen 100 5 mi. northwest of town as it winds toward Lagg. The sand dunes here are reputedly the highest in Europe, towering 100 ft. high in some places. A little farther on, **Five Fingers Strand,** named for five standing rocks that jut into the bay, looks postcard-perfect with rugged slopes contrasting golden sand and blue water. The turquoise water looks tempting but is icy cold and dangerous for swimming. High above the beach, **Knockamany Bens** provide views of the whole peninsula. Turn left at the little white church to get to the top of this worthwhile detour. Nearby **Malin Ostriches,** Ballylannon (tel. 70661), farms ostriches for their feathers, meat, and leather (open Sat.-Sun. 1-6pm or by appointment; £1).

The northernmost point in Ireland, **Malin Head** is a barren tooth of dark rock jutting up from the ocean spray. Until the 19th century, Malin Head was the site of an annual pilgrimage; young men and women "frisked and played in the water all stark naked" in celebration of the sea god's affair with the goddess of the land. The Head gives today's travelers views of the Paps of Jura in Scotland (on a clear day) and, perhaps, an opportunity to hear the call of the corncrake, one of Ireland's rarest birds. A Lloyds' signal tower built in 1805 by the British Admiralty still stands sentry over the point. The "S. S. EIRE" (*Saor Stát Éire;* "Irish Free State") marked on the cliffs below identified Ireland as neutral territory to Nazi would-be bombers, but less patriotic names spelled out by more recent visitors make this peace signal hard to see. One mile from the head, **Hell's Hole,** a 250-ft. chasm, roars devilishly with the incoming tide. A path to the left of the car park leads here. Further down the coast, naturally formed **Devil's Bridge** arcs over a chasm. The bridge is no longer safe to walk on, so the Devil is stuck where he is. The beaches around Malin Head have a reputation for semi-precious stones: casual walkers sifting through the sands may find jasper, quartz, small opals, or amethysts—the **Malin Pebbles.** The 5-mi. **Atlantic Circle** road, which tours the perimeter of Inishowen's tip, yields arresting views.

Recently refurbished **Malin Head Hostel** (tel. 70309) warms guests with an open fire (£6, private room £8; free showers). Two miles from Malin Head, Mrs. Doyle at **Barracín** (tel. 70184) keeps a friendly, comfortable B&B and tends a beautiful garden. A bulletin board with maps and photos of local sights helps plan the day's agenda (single £16, w/bath £20; double £26, w/bath £28). If you're traveling there by bus, get off at the phone booth that stands a bit past the Malin Head post office. A broader view recommends Mrs. Anne Hawes' **Highview B&B** (tel. 70283), ½ mi. farther down the Malin Rd. The beds are so comfortable that you won't want to get up, but the spacious sitting room has such a great view that you won't want to go to sleep, either (single £18, double £30; all w/bath). Rest and revitalizing brew can be found at **Farren's,** Ireland's northernmost pub, or at **The Cottage** (tel. 70257), which provides tea and scones under a thatched roof (open June-Aug. daily 11:30am-7pm). Back towards Malin Town, **Bree Inn** (tel. 70161) delivers heaping plates of food (fish and chips £2.50; open daily 12:30-11:30pm). In Malin Town itself, all are welcome to eat at the **Malin Hotel** bar (tel. 70645) or to lift a pint at **McLeans'** (tel. 70607) which has trad sessions on weekends.

Anyone interested in music and *craic* should head to **McGrory's** (tel. 79104) in **Culdaff,** where sessions sometimes last until dawn. Attached to McGrory's is **Mac's Backroom Bar,** undoubtedly the best live music venue in the whole northwest of Ireland, which has attracted the likes of Altan and the Waterboys. Chummy owners Neil and John McGrory regularly play in sessions. Wednesday nights are the popular "country jam" where you're likely to hear anything from Garth Brooks to that guy who used to be Prince. Live bands perform on Saturday nights, with trad sessions Tuesday and Friday nights. McGrory's also does B&B so you can roll out of bed and into the pub (or vice versa; £15/person). Glorious **Culdaff Strand,** best seen in the dawn light, is a five-minute walk from McGrory's.

■ East Inishowen

Opposite Malin Head, **Inishowen Head** looks over to the carnival lights of Portrush and gathers sunbathers and swimmers at **Shroove Strand.** Mrs. McCann's warm welcome complements the cozy atmosphere at **Rockall B&B** (tel. 81024), on Culdaff Rd. in Shroove. The smoked salmon she serves for breakfast is a rarity; badger-watching at night is an oddity. Tea facilities; TVs on request (£13/person, w/bath £15). **The Drunken Duck** (tel. 81362) is a friendly, shroving pub named after a local woman whose beer leaked into her ducks' feeding trough—ask the bartender to pour a good pint of Guinness into yours. Charlie McCann will expertly direct you to Port a Doris, a delightful little cove with its share of semi-precious Shroove pebbles. The nimble of limb can hurdle the gate to the cliff walk and find a route to the shore.

GREENCASTLE

The road south from Inishowen Head leads to **Greencastle,** a small fishing village near the misty ruins of a seaside castle and fort. Greencastle's castle, built in 1305, warrants exploration. The Irish government maintains a center for training professional fishing boats in Greencastle. Relics of life on the seas are in the spotlight at the newly-opened **Greencastle Maritime Museum** on the shorefront. Occupying an old coastguard station, the well-organized museum displays an impressive collection of seacraft, including a 19th-century rocket cart, a traditional but newly built Fanad *cur-*

ragh, a wildfowling punt complete with swivel gun, and plenty of ship models and photographs (open Easter-Sept. daily 10am-6pm; admission £1, students 50p).

Fish of all kinds are available at **Kealey's Seafood Bar** (tel. 81010; salmon with anchovy butter £4.50; open Tues.-Sun. 12:30-5pm and 7-9:30pm). **Old Fort Inn** (tel. 81044) was originally a Martello Tower; today it fights off thirst. From its walls, Rathlin Island and Giant's Causeway are visible. The adjoining restaurant, **Cannon's,** specializes in home baking (open daily noon-9:30pm). In a secluded mansion overlooking Lough Foyle, Mrs. Anna Wright warmly welcomes guests to the **Manor House** (tel. 81011). Walk along the beach or on the road to Culdaff to find it (£15/ person). On the other side of town, **Brooklyn Cottage** (tel. 81087) equips all rooms with a TV, but the views of Lough Foyle and Magilligan Point deserve more attention (£16/single, double £30; all w/bath; open Feb.-Nov.).

MOVILLE

A few paces farther south along a coastal path is the grassy seaside promenade of **Moville. Peter Bush** at the Coast Guard Station (tel. 82402; open Mon.-Fri. 9am-5pm) rents boats to any takers. You can rent jet-skis at **Rent-a-Jet,** Quayside (tel. 82052), at the water's edge beside the Hair o' the Dog Saloon (jet-skiing £11-12.50/hr., skiing £7.50/10min.; open Sat.-Sun. 2pm-dusk, Wed. 6pm-dusk). **Hannon's Pharmacy,** Main St. (tel. 82649), cures ills (open Mon.-Sat. 9:30am-1pm and 1:30-6pm, also July and Aug. Sun. noon-2pm). The **post office** functions on Malin Rd. (tel. 82016; open Mon.-Fri. 9am-1pm and 2-5:30pm, Sat. 9am-1pm).

The **Moville Holiday Hostel,** Malin Rd. (tel. 82378), on the edge of town, was converted from old farm buildings. Ireland's oldest bridge is on the hostel grounds. Large four- and eight-bed dorms and a health food shop occupy a wooden interior (dorm £6, w/bath £9; sheets £1). Mrs. B. McGroarty offers B&B in a cute white house at **Naomh Mhuire,** Bath Terrace (tel. 82091; single £14, double £26; open Easter-Sept.). At Mrs. McGuinness's **Dunroman B&B** (tel. 82234) off the Derry Rd., guests can look at Lough Foyle or plop down in front of TVs in comfy rooms (single £13, w/bath £14). **Rosato's,** 7 Malin Rd. (tel. 82247), prepares tasty dishes (prawns in garlic butter £2.25; open daily noon-9pm). On Main St., **Barron's Cafe** (tel. 82472) has cheap snacks and more filling meals of every variety (lamb cutlets w/peas £3.70; open Mon.-Sun. 9:30am-9:30pm). The **Mace Supermarket** deals in edibles on the main street (open daily 7:45am-9pm). Search for fossils in the floor o' the **Hair o' the Dog Saloon,** Lower Pier (tel. 82600; live music weekends).

MUFF

On the southeast coast of the Inishowen Peninsula, just 5 mi. from Derry, the tiny village of Muff boasts one good chipper and the **Muff Hostel (IHH)** (tel. 84188) a *Let's Go* home-away-from-home and the hosteler's best friend. Between Inishowen and Derry, it makes a perfect base for exploring both. Ask the owner about his drinking days with Patrick Kavanagh (dorm £6; open March-Oct.; kitchen and hot showers). The benefits are unending: **Lough Swilly Buses** offers a £3.50 same-day return ticket to Malin Head for guests of the Muff Hostel. Hostelers also get a 15% discount (Mon.-Fri.) at **Ture Inn** down Moville Rd. (tel. 84262; food served after 6pm), where special Sunday brunches cost only £7. Trad jams enliven the atmosphere on Wednesday and Friday nights. (Hostelers can charter a minibus for the return trip, £1/person; otherwise, it's a 25-min. walk.)

NORTHERN IRELAND

The strife that makes the North infamous hides the land's beauty and appeal from international travelers. What they're missing includes the string of seaside villages on the Ards Peninsula; the pockets of green collectively called the Glens of Antrim; the Giant's Causeway, one of the world's strangest geological sights; and the beautiful Fermanagh Lake District. Pub culture and urban neighborhoods show everyday life in a divided (and, most of the time, for most people, peaceful) society.

■ An Introduction

HISTORY & POLITICS

There's a place called "Northern Ireland," but there are no "Northern Irish." The citizens still identify themselves along religious rather than geographic lines—namely as Catholics or as Protestants. The 950,000 Protestants are generally **Unionists** (who want the six counties of Northern Ireland to remain in the U.K.); the 650,000 Catholics tend to identify with the Republic of Ireland, not Britain, and many are **Nationalists** (who want the six counties to be part of the Republic). The 27-year conflict between them has proven to be one of the world's most intractable.

The 17th-century's **Ulster Plantation** systematically set up English and Scottish settlers on what had been Gaelic-Irish land, and gave Derry to the City of London (hence the name "Londonderry"). Over the following two centuries, merchants and working-class emigrants from nearby Scotland settled in northeast Ulster. Their ties to Scotland, proximity to England, and bourgeois leanings meant that Counties Antrim and Down developed an Industrial Revolution economy based on linen and shipbuilding, while the rest of the island remained agricultural. Protestant Unionists in the South made up a small part of the economy; but Ulster Plantation and Scottish settlement, over the course of 300 years, had created a working-class and middle-class population in northeast Ulster who identified with England and the Empire and didn't want Home Rule. The **Orange Order,** widespread by 1830, organized the Protestants and held parades which celebrated their supremacy.

Edward Carson and his ally **James Craig** translated Ulster Unionism into terms the British elite understood. When Home Rule looked likely in 1911, Carson held a mass meeting, and Unionists signed a Covenant promising to resist. When Home Rule appeared imminent in 1914, the Unionist **Ulster Volunteer Force (UVF)** armed itself by smuggling guns in through Larne—an act which inspired Nationalists to smuggle their own guns in through Howth. WWI gave Unionists more time to organize, and gave British leaders time to see that the imposition of Home Rule on all of Ulster would mean havoc as the UVF fought the IRA (Irish Republican Army) who fought the police. The 1920 Government of Ireland Act created two parliaments for North and South. The Act went nowhere in the South and was quickly superseded by the Anglo-Irish Treaty and war, but the measure—intended as a temporary one—became the basis of Northern Ireland's government until 1973. The new Parliament met at **Stormont,** near Belfast.

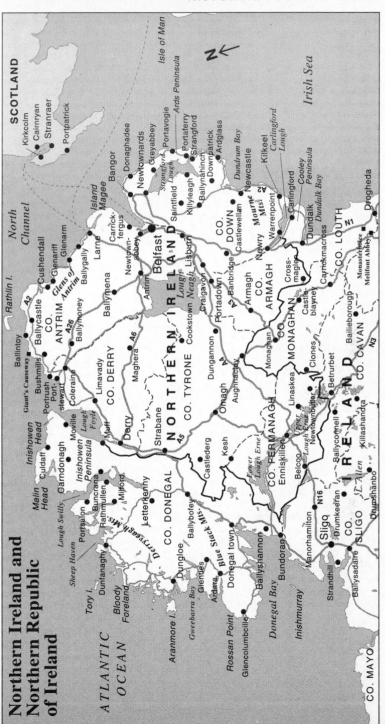

Northern Ireland and
Northern Republic
of Ireland

The new statelet included only six of the nine counties in the province of Ulster. Carson and Craig had approved these odd borders. Their intent was to create the largest possible area which would have a permanent Protestant majority. Craig became the North's first Prime Minister. He, his successor **Sir Basil Brooke,** and most of their Cabinet ministers, thought in terms (as Brooke put it) of "a Protestant state for a Protestant people." Orange lodges and other militant groups continued to control politics, while the Catholic minority boycotted elections. Anti-Catholic discrimination was widespread. The **Royal Ulster Constabulary (RUC),** the new police force in the North, supplemented its ranks with part-time policemen called Bs and **B-Specials,** a major source of Catholic casualties and outrage. The IRA continued sporadic campaigns against the North through the 20s and 30s with little result. The movement was gradually suppressed inside the Irish state.

The depressing 30s sent the Northern economy into the dumps, requiring more and more British subsidies, while the Stormont Cabinet aged and dithered. **WWII** gave Unionists a chance to show their loyalty; the Republic of Ireland stayed neutral and stayed out, but the North welcomed Allied troops, ships, and air force bases. The need to build and repair warships raised employment in Belfast. The Luftwaffe firebombed it towards the end of the war, making Belfast one of the U.K.'s most damaged cities. In May 1945, Churchill thanked the North and attacked Éire's neutrality in a famous speech.

Over the following two decades a grateful British Parliament poured money into Northern Ireland. The North's standard of living stayed higher than the Republic's, but discrimination and joblessness persisted—during the 50s, Ulster unemployment was twice that of Wales. Stormont failed to match social reforms across the water, parliamentary districts were painfully and unequally drawn to favor Protestants, and the working classes' sectarian obsessions frustrated labor activists. Large towns were segregated by religion, perpetuating the cultural separation. After a brief, unsuccessful try at school desegregation, Stormont ended up granting subsidies to Catholic schools. Violence had receded. Barring the occasional border skirmish, the IRA was seen as finished by 1962, and received a formal eulogy-like farewell in the *New York Times.* **Capt. Terence O'Neill** became the third Stormont Prime Minister in 1963. He tried to enlarge the economy and to soften discrimination, meeting in 1965 with the Republic's Prime Minister, **Sean Lemass.** O'Neill may have epitomized the liberal Unionist attitude when he said, "If you treat Roman Catholics with due kindness and consideration, they will live like Protestants."

The economy grew, but the bigotry stayed, as did the Nationalist community's bitterness. The American civil rights movement inspired the 1967 founding of **NICRA** (the **Northern Ireland Civil Rights Association**), which tried to end discrimination in public housing. NICRA tried to distance itself from constitutional concerns, though many Catholics didn't get the message: the Nationalist song "A Nation Once Again" often drowned out "We Shall Overcome" in demonstrations. Protestant extremists included the forceful **Dr. Ian Paisley,** whose **Ulster Protestant Volunteers (UPV)** overlapped in membership with the illegal, paramilitary, resurrected UVF. The first NICRA march was raucous, but nonviolent. The second, in Derry in May, 1968, was a bloody mess disrupted by Unionists and then by the RUC's water cannons. This incident is usually thought of as the culmination of the Troubles.

Catholic **John Hume** and Protestant **Ivan Cooper** formed a new civil rights committee in Derry, but were overshadowed by Bernadette Devlin's student-led, radical **People's Democracy (PD).** The PD encouraged, and NICRA opposed, a four-day march from Belfast to Derry starting on **New Year's Day, 1969.** Paisleyite harassment was nothing compared to the RUC's assault on Derry's Catholic Bogside once the marchers arrived. After that, Derry authorities agreed to keep the RUC out of the Bogside—it became **Free Derry.** O'Neill, granting more civil rights concessions in hopes of calming everyone down, was deserted by more of his hardline Unionist allies. On August 12, 1969, Catholics based in Free Derry threw rocks at the annual Orange parade through the city. The RUC attacked the Catholics, and a two-day siege ensued. Free Derry claimed victory, but the violence showed everyone that the RUC couldn't maintain order. The British Army arrived—it's still there.

O'Neill quit in 1969. Between '70 and '72, Stormont leaders alternated concessions and crackdowns, to little effect. The rejuvenated IRA split in two, with the Marxist "Official" faction fading into insignificance as the new **Provisional IRA** (or **Provos**) took aim at the Protestants. More hopefully, the **Social Democratic and Labor Party (SDLP)** was founded in 1970. By '73, it had become the moderate political voice of Northern Catholics. The British troops became the IRA's main target. British policies of internment without trial outraged Catholics, and led the SDLP to withdraw from government. The pattern was clear: any concessions to the Catholic community might provoke Protestant violence, while anything that seemed to favor the Union risked explosive IRA response.

On January 30, 1972, British troops fired into a crowd of protesters in Derry; the famous event, called **Bloody Sunday,** and the reluctance of the ensuing British investigation increased Catholic outrage. Stormont was finally dissolved in 1973. The **Sunningdale executive,** which split power between Catholics and Protestants, was immediately crippled by a massive Unionist work stoppage, and its lasting replacement was **direct British rule** from Westminster. A 1973 referendum asking "Do you want Northern Ireland to remain part of the United Kingdom?" showed that a majority still supported the Union. The verdict didn't stop the violence.

In 1978, 300 Nationalist prisoners in the Maze Prison in Northern Ireland began a campaign to have their "special category" as political prisoners restored. The campaign's climax of sorts was the H-Block **hunger strike** of '81—ten prisoners fasted themselves to death. Their leader, **Bobby Sands,** was the first to go on hunger strike. He was elected to Parliament from a Catholic district in Tyrone and Fermanagh even as he starved to death. Sands died after 66 days and became a prominent martyr—his face is still seen on murals in the Falls Rd. section of Belfast.

Sands' election to Parliament was no anomaly. The hunger strikes galvanized the Nationalists, and support for **Sinn Féin,** the political arm of the IRA, surged in the early 80s. British Prime Minister Margaret Thatcher and Taoiseach Garret FitzGerald signed the **Anglo-Irish Agreement** at Hillsborough Castle in November 1985. The Agreement grants the Republic of Ireland a "consultative role" but no legal authority in how Northern Ireland is governed. It improved relations between London and Dublin, but infuriated extremists on both sides. Protestant paramilitaries began to attack the British Army, while the IRA continued its bombing campaigns in England. In 1991-92, the Brooke Initiative led to the first multi-party talks in the North in over a decade—Sinn Féin was not included. In December 1994, the **Downing Street Declaration,** issued by John Major and Taoiseach Albert Reynolds, invited the IRA to participate in talks if they refrained from violence for three months.

On August 31, 1994, the IRA announced a "complete" cessation of violence. Wanting a permanent end to terrorism, Unionist leaders bickered over the meaning of this statement. Nonetheless, Sinn Féin leader **Gerry Adams** defended the statement and called for direct talks with the British government. In some sense, Sinn Féin is planning its own end by pursuing these talks. The party has no agenda if the IRA disbands and until 1996, little electoral clout in Northern elections. The SDLP, still led by John Hume, continues to work on behalf of Catholics within a constitutional framework. Paisley still heads the extremist **Democratic Unionist Party,** but the moderate **Official Unionist Party (OUP),** led by **James Molyneaux,** gets more votes. The Irish Constitution retains its paper claim to the six counties, though many young Southerners are sick of Republican platitudes and fear bombs in Dublin if the North ever changes hands. Some speculate that the North's drain on Britain's budget, army, and image might someday make a British withdrawal likely even against the majority's wishes. The Loyalists fear this, too, and have killed more people in the past two years than the IRA.

A flurry of tragic events leaves the future of Northern Ireland as tenable as ever. The IRA ended their ceasefire on February 9, 1996, with the bombing of an office building in London's Docklands. Despite this setback, peace talks, chaired by former U.S. Senator George Mitchell, were finally slated for June 10, 1996. Ian Paisley objected to Mitchell's appointment, calling it a "dastardly deed," but did not boycott the talks. The talks proceed sluggishly and precariously, and without Sinn Féin, which has not yet agreed to the **Mitchell principles,** which include the total disarmament of all paramilitary organizations. The Irish and British governments have resolved to bar Sinn Féin from the talks until the IRA declares a new ceasefire. Unionists argue that the IRA is threatening violence unless Sinn Féin is allowed at the bargaining table. Discussion centers around the decommissioning of IRA arms and a return to some level of Home Rule for the province. In February 1995, John Major issued his **joint framework** proposal. The document suggested the possibility of a new Northern Ireland Assembly, the "harmonizing powers" of the Irish and British governments playing a role in that Assembly, and the right of the people of Northern Ireland to choose their own destiny. A June 15, 1996, blast in a busy Manchester, England, shopping district further tarnished the IRA's image and also cast doubt on the credibility of Gerry Adams.

Violence flared surrounding **Orange Day, 1996,** when the RUC banned an Orange Order march through a Catholic section of Portadown. Protestants reacted by throwing petrol bombs, bricks, and bottles at police, who answered with plastic bullets. After four days of violence, police allowed the marchers to go through, but this time Catholics responded with a hail of debris. Nightly rioting by both sides also took place in Belfast, where three Northern Ireland policemen were wounded, and Derry, where Catholic **Dermot McShane** died after being run over by a jeep. A bomb explosion on July 14, 1996, in Enniskillen is believed to have been the work of the Republican Sinn Féin, a little-known nationalist splinter group.

The 1½ years of ceasefire showed promise and initiative, but few tangible results. In the words of one reporter, "the British government appears snail-like, the Unionist politicians obstructive, and Irish Republicans belligerent." Negotiations are now stalled indefinitely. People hope that a new peace is soon forthcoming, yet many say that the violence of July '96 was the worst the province had seen in 25 years.

Overseas attention to the politics and bombs obscures the weird but often calm tenor of life in the North. Northern Ireland has one of the lowest crime rates in the world—people in England are more likely to be the victims of crime. Unemployment and poor housing are seen as the most pressing problems. Some writers describe the North's conflicts in terms of class. According to these essayists, the moderate middle class wants peace, but the working classes have less to lose and support the extremists. Fringe groups on both sides aren't nearly as visible as the huge division in civil society which sends Protestants and Catholics to separate neighborhoods, separate stores, separate pubs, and often separate schools, with separate (though similar) traditional songs and separate slang. The split can be hard to see on the north Antrim coast (where everyone's on holiday), but the separation is unavoidable in Belfast and Derry.

SECURITY

Terrorists and paramilitaries on both sides want nothing less than to injure a tourist. As long as you stay out of Derry's Bogside and Belfast's Falls, Shankill, and Sandy Row after dark (and South Armagh altogether), you're unlikely to see trouble. Use common sense in conversation, and try not to take a political side or religious bent. Be aware of word choice: "Ireland" can mean the whole island or the Republic of Ireland, depending on who's listening. "Ulster" is a term used almost exclusively by Protestants. It's best to refer to "Northern Ireland" or "the North" and "the Republic" or "the South." "Southern Ireland" is not a viable term.

Since the ceasefire, **border check-points** have been removed and one rarely sees armed soldiers and vehicles in Belfast or Derry. It is still unsafe to hitch in South Armagh. Never take **photographs** of soldiers or of military installations or vehicles; if you do, your film will be confiscated and you may be detained for questioning. Taking pictures of political murals is not considered a crime, though it will blatantly mark you as a "terrorism tourist." Some urban areas have **"control zones,"** where there's no parking due to fear of car bombs. Since **unattended luggage** can also conceal a bomb, it will be viewed with suspicion. **Avoid large cities on July 12** (Orange Day) and on any other day in July or August (the "marching season") when there's a big Orange or Catholic march scheduled. Rural and vacation areas like the Glens and the Causeway Coast are untouched by the parades. As in the Republic, nonpolitical crime is much rarer than it is in America.

MONEY

Money in Northern Ireland is in British pounds (£), called "pounds sterling" to distinguish them from the Irish pound or "punt." Notes printed in Northern Ireland have the same value as the notes printed in England, Scotland, and the Isle of Man, but look different and are *not* accepted in the rest of the U.K. If you're going from the North to England, Scotland, Wales, or to the Isle of Man, remember to swap your Northern Ireland pounds for Bank of England notes before you leave. English, Scottish, and Manx notes *are* accepted in Northern Ireland and near its borders in the Republic; most towns will have shops that take "punt for pound" or the other way around. (The punt has a higher value than the pound in the summer of 1996, but the difference is fractional.)

■ Belfast

Over 400,000 people (¼ of the North's population) live in Belfast, making it the center of Northern Ireland's commercial, artistic, and paramilitary worlds, as well as the second largest city on the island. The student scene fosters the development of pubs, hole-in-the-wall cafés, and urban bustle. Long-term unemployment makes the poorer parts of the city recruiting grounds for extremist groups. **The Troubles** were unforgettable here. Armed British soldiers patrolled the streets, frequent military checkpoints slowed traffic and pedestrians, and stores advertised "Bomb Damage Sales." Although some may have thought that Belfast would be indelibly marked by its part in the 25-year conflict, signs of its dramatic recent history can escape travelers. Except for the numerous murals in the Falls, Shankill, Sandy Row, and East Belfast areas, the heavily protected police stations, the stark peace line and uninhabited nearby houses, and the occasional bombed building, little physical evidence of violent division remains. The Troubles may have had unintended positive results, from the brilliantly grim irony of Belfast's literati, to the black taxi services (started in response to a bus strike), to the ban on cars downtown, which produced a prosperous shopping zone—a lesson for urban planners everywhere. Dockyards, smoke, and architecture look across the ocean to England and Scotland, while the pristine hills behind the small city remind it of its Irish component; it's hard to know in which direction, if any, the people and culture may someday tilt.

Belfast began as a base for "Scots-Irish" Presbyterian settlement and then became a 19th-century industrial center resembling Liverpool and Birmingham, with world-famous shipyards, factories, and exports. Gathering slums, smoke, flax mills, and social theorists as it went, Belfast by 1900 looked much more British than Irish. The Protestant majority that controlled the city felt British, too. Irish fear of Protestant violence (skillfully managed by Unionist leaders like Edward Carson) was instrumental in creating the present divided island. Some combination of Irish tradition and bicultural social angst has arguably made Belfast more important to the arts than Dublin in the last few decades. Actor/director Kenneth Branagh, singer Van Morrison, and a handful of contemporary poets have been influenced by Belfast's mix of excitement and unease.

SECURITY

The working class neighborhoods of West Belfast are sharply divided by the 30-ft. **peace line**—a physical wall that runs halfway between the Catholic Falls Rd. and the Protestant Shankill Rd. The wall was inspired by the violence occurring at the inter-

Central Belfast

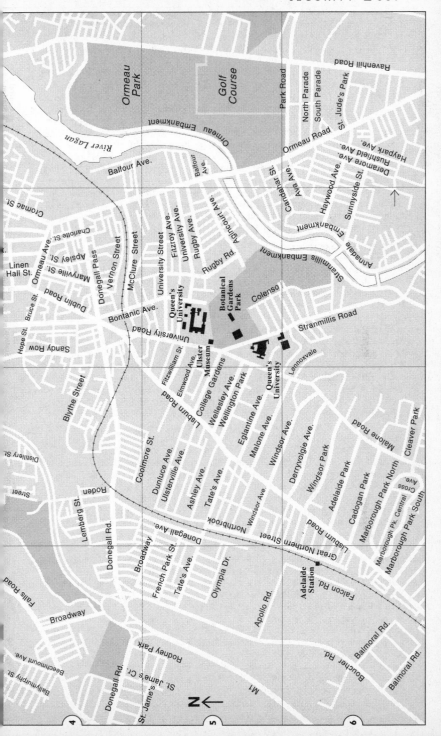

faces, or "no man's land," between Catholic and Protestant areas. Even when sectarian conflict was at its worst, however, Belfast was actually safer for tourists than most American cities. The city center, the "Golden Mile," and the university area to its south rarely see any trouble nowadays. West Belfast, full of joblessness and profound political art, is best seen by day. Those planning to visit the docks for the nightlife should go to and from their chosen destinations in a taxi. Remember that it is against the law to take pictures of soldiers, or of any military item or installation—and that this law is enforced. Many downtown curbs are control zones, where there's no parking permitted due to a well-founded fear of car bombs. For a few days around July 12, when the Protestant Orangemen hold their proud, angry parades, many Catholics leave the city to avoid violence and to get away from street blocks. This time of year, as the 1996 Drumcree riots showed, can be dangerous for visitors; it's best to simply avoid Belfast and Derry. If you ever find yourself inadvertently caught in a riot, don't stick around and gawk (this happened to several hostelers in July '96—they were knocked over the head with glass bottles); either leave the city or stay indoors. No matter how much your sympathies may lean toward one side or the other, this is not your city, or your conflict. The last thing most residents want to discuss is the Troubles—it's best to avoid political discussions altogether.

GETTING THERE

For information on **ferries** and **hovercraft** to Belfast and Larne from England and Scotland, or on flights to Belfast, refer to the Essentials section (p. 32).

From **Belfast International Airport** in Aldee Grove, a **shuttle bus** runs to Belfast's Europa/Glengall St. bus station in the city center and to the central train station (Mon.-Sat. every 2/hr., Sun. 1/hr.; 70min.; £3.70, £6.40 return). An audio-visual stand and an information desk on the ground floor of the airport will fortify you with preliminary orientation. **Avis, Hertz, Europcar,** or **McCausland** all rent cars. The three companies have desks on the ground floor and have similar rates (about £39/day, £185/week). Rows of **taxis** offer to transport you to the city for about £20.

From **Belfast City Airport** (tel. (01232) 457745), **trains** run to Belfast Central Station (Mon.-Sun. 15/day; 6min.; 60p). A **taxi** downtown costs about £5. **Manx Airlines** (tel. (01345) 256256) flies into Belfast City Airport four times per day. Jersey European also lands here. The airport has no currency exchange, but has **ATMs**.

From **Larne ferry terminals,** take a bus or train into Belfast city center. (Buses run Mon.-Fri. 17/day, Sat. 15/day, Sun. 3/day; 1hr.; £2.50, £5.30 return. Trains roll Mon.-Fri. 19/day, Sat. 15/day, Sun. 6/day; 45min.; £3, £4.90 return.) **Flexibus** (tel. 233933) connects the SeaCat hovercraft terminal with Central Station, Laganside Station, Donegall Sq. Station, and the Europa Bus Centre (8/day; 60p, children 25p).

To reach the city center on foot from the **SeaCat terminal** on Donegall Quay, turn left for one block. Turn right just before the Customs House on Albert Sq. and after two blocks turn left onto Victoria St. (not Great Victoria St.). At the Clock Tower, turn right again onto High St., which runs into Donegall Place, where a left will lead to Donegall Sq. at the end of the street.

Trains roll in from **Derry** (Mon.-Fri. 7/day, Sat. 6/day, Sun. 3/day; 2¼hr.; £5.85, £9.50 return); and **Dublin's Connolly Station** (Mon.-Sat. 8/day, Sun. 4/day; 2½hr.; £14.50, £21.75 return). All trains arrive at **Belfast Central Station,** East Bridge St. (tel. 899411). To reach Donegall Square from Central Station, turn left and walk up East Bridge St. to Victoria St. Turn right here, then left onto May St. after two blocks. A free **Rail-Link bus** runs from Central Station to Donegall Square for those encumbered with luggage (Mon.-Sat.). For British rail enquiries, call 230671.

Buses come to Belfast's **Europa/Glengall St. Station** (tel. 320574 or 333000; enquiries open Mon.-Sat. 9am-6pm) from **Dublin's Busáras Station** (Mon.-Sat. 4/day, Sun. 3/day; £10, £12.50 return) and from **Derry's Foyle St. Station** (Mon.-Sat. 6/day, Sun. 4/day; £5.90, £10 return). Buses from Northern Ireland's east coast arrive at **Laganside Station** (tel. 333000 or 232356; enquiries open Mon.-Sat. 8:30am-6pm). All others arrive at Europa/Glengall St. Across the street from the Laganside bus station, Chichester St. leads straight to Donegall Square North. From the Europa/Glengall St. Station, a left at the Great Victoria St. exit leads to Howard St. Donegall Square appears soon after taking a right onto Howard St.

M1 and M2 motorways join to form a backwards "C" through Belfast. A1 branches off from M1 around Lisburn and heads south to Newry, where it changes to N1 before continuing through Dundalk and Drogheda to Dublin. M2 merges into A6, then heads northwest to Derry. Larne is connected to Belfast by the A8. **Hitching** is notoriously hard in and out of Belfast—most people take the bus out as far as Bangor or Larne before they stick out a thumb.

ORIENTATION

Belfast spreads out from **City Hall** in **Donegall Sq.,** six blocks west of the River Lagan and the harbor. A bustling, pedestrianized shopping district extends for four blocks between City Hall and the enormous **Castlecourt Shopping Centre** to the north. **Donegall Place,** which becomes **Royal Ave.,** bisects the pedestrian area as it leaves Donegall Sq. Two blocks west of the center, **Great Victoria St.** runs south until it meets **Dublin Rd.** at **Shaftesbury Sq.** The stretch of Great Victoria between Shaftesbury and the Opera House is known as the **"Golden Mile."** South of the square, Dublin Rd. becomes **University Rd.** and leads to the red bricks of **Queen's University** and a neighborhood of B&Bs, pubs, and cafés.

Divided from the rest of Belfast by the Westlink Motorway, **West Belfast** is poorer and more politically volatile than the city center. There remains a sharp division between sectarian neighborhoods. A Catholic in a Protestant neighborhood would draw looks of suspicion. The Protestant neighborhood stretches along Shankill Rd., just north of the Catholic neighborhood which is centered on Falls Rd. The two are literally separated by a wall. The River Lagan divides industrial **East Belfast** from the rest of the city. The shipyards and docks that brought Belfast fame and fortune extend north on both sides of the river as it grows into **Belfast Lough.**

GETTING AROUND

Public transportation within the city is provided by the red **Citybus Network** (tel. 246485), supplemented by the **Ulsterbus** "blue buses" to the suburbs. Citybuses going south and west leave from Donegall Sq. East; those going north and east leave from Donegall Sq. West (75p). Money-saving four-journey tickets cost £2.50. Travel within the city center costs 45p. Seven-day gold cards allow unlimited travel in the city (£10). Seven-day silver cards permit unlimited travel in either North Belfast, West/South Belfast, or East Belfast (£6). All these transport cards and tickets can be bought from the kiosks in Donegall Sq. and around the city (open Mon.-Sat. 7am-6pm). A free **Rail-Link** bus connects the rail station and the city center, but you must have a train ticket to ride. Citybus services run from 5am to 11pm, though some routes have shorter hours. Late **Nightline** buses cover routes from Shaftesbury Sq. to various parts of the city (maps are posted in Donegall Square; depart Fri.-Sat. midnight, 1, and 2am; £1.50).

PRACTICAL INFORMATION

Tourist Office: St. Anne's Court, 59 North St. (tel. 246609). The usual brochures, plus an excellent map of the city with bus schedules (free). Helpful staff will get you where you need to go and find you a place to stay (in summer, call until 10pm for accommodations). A 24-hr. computerized info point in the outside wall helps travelers arriving at all times. Open Sept.-June Mon.-Sat. 9am-5:15pm; July-Aug. Mon.-Fri. 9am-7pm, Sat. 9am-7pm, Sun. 10am-4pm. The **Northern Ireland Tourist Board,** in the same building, doesn't provide walk-in tourist info.

Irish Tourist Board (Bord Fáilte), 53 Castle St. (tel. 327888). Limited info on the Republic of Ireland. The focus is clearly on Dublin. Open Oct.-Feb. Mon.-Fri. 9am-5pm, March-Sept. Mon.-Fri. 9am-5:30pm, Sat. 9am-noon.

Budget Travel Office: USIT, 13b The Fountain Centre, College St. (tel. 324073), near Royal Ave. Sells ISICs and TravelSave stamps (£5.50) for 50% discount on trains. Books ferries and planes. Open Mon. and Wed.-Fri. 9:30am-5:30, Tues. 10am-5:30pm, Sat. 10am-1pm. **Additional offices:** Queen's University Student Union (tel. 241830), open Mon.-Tues. and Thurs.-Fri. 9:30am-5:30pm, Wed. 10am-5pm. **STA agent:** Arrow Travel, 48 Bradbury Pl. (tel. 232492). Student rates for ferries and planes. Open Mon.-Fri. 9am-5:30pm, Sat. 9:30am-2pm.

Youth Hostel Association of Northern Ireland (YHANI): 22 Donegall Rd. (tel. 324733). Books YHANI hostels free, international hostels for £2. Sells HI membership cards (senior £7, under 18 £3). Open Mon.-Fri. 9am-5pm.

U.S. Consulate General: Queens House, Queen St. (tel. 228239). Open Mon.-Fri. 1-5pm. **Canada, Australia,** and the **Republic of Ireland** are not represented.

Financial Services: Thomas Cook, 22/24 Lombard St. (tel. 236044). Cashes Thomas Cook travelers checks with no commission, others with 2% commission. Open Mon.-Fri. 9am-5:30pm. Belfast International Airport office (tel. (01849) 422536). Open Mon.-Fri. 7am-8pm, Sat.-Sun. 7am-10pm. **American Express** enquiries/service (tel. 242341).

Banks: Ulster Bank, 47 Donegall Pl. (tel. 320222). **First Trust,** 14-16 Donegall Sq. East (tel. 326118). **Bank of Ireland,** 7 Donegall Sq. North (tel. 246241). **Halifax Bank,** 10-11 Shaftesbury Sq. (tel. 247777), also at 41 Arthur St. off Chichester St. near Donegall Sq., and at the Castlecourt Shopping Centre. All have **ATMs;** most close at 3:30pm.

Buses: The **Leaping Leprechaun** bus service (tel. (015047) 42655) takes hostelers to and from IHH hostels on the Antrim coast. Full ticket £18.

Taxis: Huge **black cabs** run set routes to West Belfast, collecting and discharging passengers along the way (standard 55p charge). The cabs heading to Catholic neighborhoods are marked with a Falls Rd., Andersontown, or Irish-language sign; those going to Protestant neighborhoods are painted with a Shankill sign or a red poppy. The cabs are heavily partisan (see **West Belfast,** p. 379). Ordinary 24-hr. metered cabs abound: **City Cab** (tel. 242000; wheelchair accessible); **Diamond Taxi Service** (tel. 646666); **Fona Cab** (tel. 233333).

Car Rental: McCausland's, 21-31 Grosvenor Rd. (tel. 333777). £39/day, £170/week. Ages 21-70 only. Open Mon.-Thurs. 8:30am-6:30pm, Fri. 8:30am-7:30pm, Sat. 8:30am-5pm, Sun. 8:30am-12:30pm. 24-hr. car return at Belfast International Airport Office (tel. (01849) 422022). Belfast City Airport office (tel. 454141). £10 surcharge to drive in the Republic. **Budget,** Great Victoria St. (tel. 230700). £39-59/day, £195-395/week. Ages 23 and over. Open Mon.-Fri. 9am-5:30pm, Sat. 9am-1:30pm. Offices at both airports open 24hr. **Avis,** 69/71 Great Victoria St. (tel. 240404). £42.50/day, £185/week. Fri. afternoon to Mon. morning special £80.50; deposit £35. Ages 23 and over. Open Mon.-Fri. 8am-6pm, Sat. 9am-1pm. Most car rental companies require returns to be made to Northern Ireland offices.

Bike Rental: None in city center. **McConvey Cycles,** 476 Ormeau Rd. (tel. 491163). £7/day, £40/week; deposit £30. Open Mon.-Sat. 9am-5:30pm.

Luggage Storage: Arnie's Hostel will hold bags during the day for those staying there, as will the **YHANI Hostel,** (see **Accommodations,** below).

Camping Equipment: The Scout Shop and Camp Centre, 12/14 College Sq. East (tel. 320580). Vast selection. Ring bell to get in. Open Mon.-Sat. 9:15am-5pm.

Bookstore: Eason's, Castlecourt Shopping Centre, Royal Ave. (tel. 235070). Large Irish section; lots of travel guides. Open Mon.-Wed. and Fri.-Sat. 9am-5:30pm, Thurs. 9am-9pm. **Familia,** Belfast Family History and Cultural Heritage Centre, 64 Wellington Place (tel. 2353952). Big Irish section. Open Mon.-Fri. 9:30am-5:30pm, Sat. 10am-5pm.

Library: Linen Hall Library, 17 Donegall Sq. North (tel. 321707; see **Sights,** p. 376). Open Mon.-Wed. and Fri. 9:30am-5:30pm, Thurs. 9:30am-8:30pm, Sat. 9:30am-4pm. Extensive information on the Troubles, genealogy. Free Irish language courses. Visitor's Pass to the library w/photo ID.

Laundry: Student's Union, Queen's University, University Rd. Wash £1, dry 20p/5min. Open Mon.-Fri. 9am-9pm, Sat. 10am-9pm, Sun. 2-9pm. Students only. **Duds & Suds,** University Rd. (tel. 243956). Popcorn and TV while you wait. Wash £1.50, dry £1.50. 15% discount for students and seniors. Open Mon.-Fri. 8am-9pm, Sat. 8am-6pm, Sun. noon-6pm. Last load 1½hr. before closing.

Bisexual, Gay, and Lesbian Information: Carinated Counseling: (tel. 238668). Open Thurs. 7:30-10pm. Odd name, cool people.
Crisis Lines: Samaritans: (tel. 664422). 24hr. **NI Council on Disability:** (tel. 491011). Open Mon.-Fri. 9am-5pm. **Rape Crisis Centre:** 41 Waring St. (tel. 321830). Open Mon.-Fri. 10am-6pm, Sat. 11am-5pm.
Pharmacy: Boot's, Donegall Place (tel. 242332). Open Mon.-Wed. 9am-5:30pm, Thurs. 9am-8:45 pm, Fri. 9am-8pm, Sat. 9am-6pm.
Hospitals: Belfast City Hospital, Lisburn Rd. (tel. 329241). From Shaftesbury Sq. follow Bradbury Pl. and take the right fork. **Royal Victoria Hospital,** Grosvenor Rd. (tel. 240503). From Donegall Sq., follow Howard St. west into Grosvenor Rd. **Ulster Hospital,** Dundonald St. (tel. 484511).
Emergency: Dial 999; no coins required. **Police:** 65 Knock Rd. (tel. 650222).
Post Office: Central Post Office, 25 Castle Pl. (tel. 323740). Open Mon.-Fri. 9am-5:30pm, Sat. 9am-1pm. *Poste Restante* mail comes here. **Postal code:** BT1 1NB. **Branch offices:** dozens, two of which are **Botanic Garden Post Office,** 95 University Rd. (tel. 381309), across from Queen's University and **Shaftesbury Sq. Post Office,** 7-9 Shaftesbury Sq. (tel. 326177; postal code: BT2 7DA). Open Mon.-Fri. 9am-5:30pm, Sat. 10am-12:30pm.
Telephones: Even in Belfast, fewer than half of public phones accept phonecards (available at most grocery stores). Coins are a necessity when exploring the city.
Phone code: 01232.

ACCOMMODATIONS

Nearly all of Belfast's accommodations are located near Queen's University, south of the city center. Relatively safe and convenient to pubs and restaurants, this area is by far the best place to stay in the city. Bus #59, 69, 70, 71, 84, and 85 run there from Donegall Sq. East. B&Bs multiply between Malone Rd. and Lisburn Rd. south of Queen's, and the YWCA and the independent hostel are in this area. B&Bs are surprisingly busy during the summer; reservations are recommended.

Hostels & University Housing

Arnie's Backpackers (IHH), 63 Fitzwilliam St. (tel. 242867). From Europa bus station (a 10-min. walk), turn right onto Great Victoria St. At Shaftesbury Sq., veer to the right fork on Bradbury Pl., then fork left on University Rd. Fitzwilliam St. is across from the University. Relaxed, friendly atmosphere provides a real respite from tiring travels. Arnie and Rosie the wonderdog provide tea and toast. The **Leaping Leprechaun** stops here (see **Buses,** above). 4- to 6-bed dorm £7.50. Kitchen always open. Luggage storage during the day.
YHANI Belfast Hostel, 22 Donegall Rd. (tel. 315435). Clean, airy, modern rooms with 2-6 beds, some with bath. Note: this hostel is located near Sandy Row, a Loyalist stronghold that saw violence in July '96. No kitchen. They'll return your cycle to Dublin's Rent-a-bike but keep the deposit. Coffee shop open daily 7:30am-8pm. Charge for check-in after 11pm. Dorm £9, w/bath £10.50. Wash and dry £3, powder 50p. Book 2 weeks ahead for weekends. Wheelchair accessible.
YWCA, Queen Mary's Hall, 70 Fitzwilliam St. (tel. 240439). To get here from the bus station, see **Arnie's,** above. Co-ed. Bright, spic 'n' span rooms with sinks. Limited self-service kitchen open 7am-11pm. B&B £14/person. 3-bed dorm w/out sheets £8/person. Dinner £5. £1 wash (no dry). Always full during the school year; in summer, book 1-2 weeks in advance.
Queen's University Accommodations, 78 Malone Rd. (tel. 381608). Bus #70 or 71 from Donegall Sq. East runs here. On foot, Great Victoria Rd. runs into Malone Rd. An undecorated, institutional dorm: spacious single or twin rooms with sinks and desks. Strong, reliable showers; little ventilation. 24-hr. kitchen with toaster and little else; common rooms with TV. Single £8 for U.K. students, £9 for international students, £11-16 for non-students. Double £18. Free laundry. Open mid-June to mid-Sept. and Christmas and Easter vacations.

Bed & Breakfasts

The university-area B&Bs are all similar in price and quality. Though individual houses are often full, you can usually find a bed somewhere in the neighborhood.

Mrs. Davidson's East-Sheen Guest House, 81 Eglantine Ave. (tel. 667149). The best deal in Belfast, if you can get a room. Sweet Mrs. D. serves enormous breakfasts, as well as dinner, at no extra charge. Rooms are bright and clean. £16.50/person (£17.50 as of Jan. 1, 1997).

The George, 9 Eglantine Ave. (tel. 683212). Reassuringly spotless rooms, all with shower and TV. Cushy leather couches by the big picture window in the common room. Single £19. Twin double £36. Double w/bath £42. Family room £48.

Marine House, 30 Eglantine Ave. (tel. 381922). An orderly rose garden out front, high ceilings in the huge common room. Rooms vary in size. Single £18. Double £34, w/bath £40. Triple £45.

Liserin Guest House, 17 Eglantine Ave. (tel. 660769). Comfy beds invite you to flop down in pastel rooms. One single has a skylight. Coffee, tea, and biscuits available all day in the dining room. Single £20. Double £36.

Eglantine Guest House, 21 Eglantine Ave. (tel. 667585). Vinyl headboards shine in tiny singles. Tea, coffee, and fresh bread. Single £20. Double £36. Triple £45.

Camera House, 44 Wellington Park (tel. 660026 or 667856). Nondescript rooms with TVs and phones. Single £20. Twin w/shower £40. Double w/bath £45.

Pearl Court Lodge, 67 Malone Rd. (tel. 662985). Comfortable rooms give ready access to the University. £19/person.

Drumragh House, 647 Antrim Rd. (tel. 773063), several miles north of city center. Citybus #123 and 45 stop in front of this house with large rooms in a more residential neighborhood. Pretty gardens at the foot of Cave Hill. £18/person.

FOOD

Belfast eateries offer alternatives to the bland and greasy frying tradition. Dublin Rd. and the Golden Mile (of Great Victoria St.) have the highest concentration of restaurants. Bakeries and cafés dot the shopping areas, but most close at 5:30pm.

The **Mace Supermarket** on the corner of Castle St. and Queen St. sells cheap groceries (open Mon.-Wed. and Fri.-Sat. 9am-6pm, Thurs. 9am-9pm). For fruits and vegetables, plunder the lively **St. George's Market,** East Bridge St., in the enormous warehouse between May St. and Oxford St. (open Tues. and Fri. 7am-3pm). **The Nutmeg,** 9A Lombard St. (tel. 249984), supplies healthy foods, baked goods, and raw ingredients (open Mon.-Sat. 9:30am-5:30pm).

Queen's University Area

Bookfinders, 47 University Rd. (tel. 328269). Smoky, atmospheric bookstore/café has the lived-in look. Soup and bread (£1.40) amid stacks of old books. Occasional poetry readings. Art gallery upstairs. Open Mon.-Sat. 10am-5:30pm.

Bluebells, 50 Botanic Ave. (tel. 322622). A hangout for the young intellectuals who spend hours here. Great food, homemade ice cream (small cone 35p), and newspapers. Big bowl of soup and homemade bread £1.25. Open Mon.-Sat. 8am-10:30pm, Sun. 9am-8pm.

Cloisters Bistro, in the Queen's University Student Union, University Ave. (tel. 324803). Mediocre but cheap cafeteria food. Open Mon.-Fri. 8:30am-6:30pm, but closes at 3pm during school vacations.

The Tea House, 245 Lisburn Rd. (tel. 611292). Second-hand bookstore upstairs and a dark café with good vegetarian dishes below. Open Mon.-Sat. 10am-4:15pm.

The Attic Restaurant, 54 Stranmillis Rd. (tel. 661074). A tiny second-floor restaurant that practically spills out the windows to the Victorian balcony. Light fare for lunch (homemade soup, chicken sandwich, and tea £2.50). Heartier food at dinner (huge roast and potatoes £7). Open Mon.-Sat. 11:30am-3pm and 5-10:30pm, Sun. 11am-3pm and 5-9pm.

The Greek Shop, 43 University Rd. (tel. 331135). Bring your own wine for a Bacchanalian feast complete with stuffed grape leaves (£2.75). Feast at lunch but fast at the more expensive dinner (*souvlaki* £6). Open Mon. noon-3:30pm, Tues.-Fri. noon-3:30pm and 6-10pm, Sat. 1-2:30pm and 6-10pm.

The Golden Mile & The Dublin Road

Revelations Internet Café, Great Victoria St. Get connected to comfy couches and cool music in this student hangout. Internet access £4/hr., £2/½hr. Veggie sandwiches £2-3. Open Mon.-Fri. 10am-10pm, Sat. 10am-8pm, Sun. noon-10pm.
Café Equinox, 32 Howard St. (tel. 230089), behind the gift store. Sleek black café serves chic double espressos and the best sandwiches in Belfast (£2-3). Open Mon.-Sat. 9:30am-5:30pm.
Banana's, 4 Clarence St. (tel. 339999). Ceiling fans, palm trees, and Caribbean food with an Irish twist (bacon and banana sandwich with salad £3.25). Cheaper food during happy hour (5-7pm). Open Mon-Sat. noon-3pm and 5-11pm.
Harvey's, 95 Great Victoria St. (tel. 233433). A yuppie pizza joint with big wooden booths (margherita pizza £5.75). Open daily 5pm-midnight.
Spuds, 23 Bradbury Pl. For the hungry insomniac and the post-club crowd. Huge baked potatoes laden with curry, chili, and other indigestible delights (£1.10-1.80). Open Mon.-Thurs. and Sat. 11am-3am, Fri. 11am-4am, Sun. 11am-1am.

North of Donegall Square

The Sunflower Café, 90a Castle St. (tel. 246660). Artsy atmosphere; nothing on the menu over £3 (*fettucine carbonara* £2.50). Open Mon.-Sat. 9am-10pm.
The Daily Sandwich, 60 Lower Donegall St. (tel. 240596), across from St. Anne's Cathedral behind the tourist office. Huge, fresh sandwiches for £1.30. Free newspaper perusal. Open Mon.-Fri. 10am-4pm.
Bambrick's, corner of Wellington Pl. and College Sq. (tel. 423203). Many notice the intricate mosaic exterior before seeing the café itself. Unlimited cup of coffee (75p) washes down a full Irish breakfast (£1). Eggplant parmesan w/potato £3. Open Mon.-Fri. 9:30am-4:30pm, Sat. 11am-4pm.
Bewley's, 31 Lombard St. (tel. 232568), in front of the Donegall Arcade. Coffee shop delicacies with that Dublin aura. Open Mon.-Sat. 9am-5:30pm.

PUBS

Pubs were prime targets for sectarian violence at the height of the Troubles in the 60s and 70s. As a result, most of the popular pubs in Belfast are relatively new, though some have recreated a traditional flavor. Ask the student staff at the Queen's University Student Centre about current hip night spots. The *Bushmills Irish Pub Guide,* by Sybil Taylor, relates the history of Belfast's pubs (£7 at tourist office).

Queen's University Area

The Botanic Inn (the "Bot"), 23 Malone Rd. (tel. 660460). Huge and hugely popular student bar. Always packed; sardine-like on weekends. Open til 1am.
The Eglantine Inn (the "Egg"), 32 Malone Rd. (tel. 381994). More students, but less scamming. Locals bands showcase upstairs on the weekends. Open til 1am.
The Queens University Student Union (tel. 324803) hops and bops during termtime: 2 popular bars, discos 6 days/week (cover £2), and occasional live bands. In summer, the bars are quiet, but discos continue on Thurs. and Sat.
The Elms, 36 University Rd. (tel. 322106). A rough-around-the-edges student bar for those who don't want frills. Live bands most nights, trad on Thurs.
The Empire, 42 Botanic Ave. (tel. 328110). Pizza (£2) to go with all that beer. Bigscreen TV. Beergarden. Sept.-June stand-up comedy on Tues. (cover £3.50).

The Golden Mile & The Dublin Road

Lavery's, 12 Bradbury Pl. (tel. 327159). The popular, if rather unattractive, place to be for all (cool) kinds of people—bikers to students to road-hog intellectuals. Young crowd. **Lavery's Off-License,** next door, sells booze until 1am.
Crown Liquor Saloon, 46 Great Victoria St. Famous, convivial place that reminds you that you are now in the U.K. The National Trust was quick to claim this property—with its gilt ceilings, gas lamps, and Victorian booths—as its own.

Robinson's, 38-40 Great Victoria St. (tel. 247447). Recently bombed but none the worse for the wear. Incredibly lively, it offers 4 floors of bars, including a motorcycle-themed "Rock Bottom" sporting a real Harley in the basement and "The Spot" on the top floor, which hosts live rock bands Thurs.-Sat. "Fibber Magee's," at the back of the ground floor, is modelled after traditional Irish pubs, while Robinson's resembles a Victorian British drawing room. Trad sessions on Mon. nights.

Morrisons, 21 Bedford St. (tel. 248458). A new pub with a painstakingly reconstructed "traditional" atmosphere. Always packed.

North of Donegall Square

Queens Bar, 4 Queen's Arcade (tel. 321347). Friendly, low-pressure atmosphere in a tiny alley off Donegall Pl. attracts a broad mixture of people, gay and straight.

The Crow's Nest, 26 Skipper St. (tel. 325491), off High St., across from the Albert Memorial Clock. A jovial gay and lesbian crowd. Popular disco Thurs.-Sat. nights at 9:30pm (cover £1). Ask the helpful staff for other frequented gay hangouts.

Kelly's Cellars, 30 Bank St. (tel. 324835), off Royal Ave. near the Primark building. Favored, smoke-stained, working-class bar. The oldest pub in Belfast that hasn't been renovated. Trad on Thurs., folk or rock Fri.-Sat. (cover £1-2).

The Parliament Bar, Dunbar St., around the corner from the Duke. Gay and lesbian crowd parties at discos on Tues., Fri., and Sat. nights, sways to classical music on Mon. nights, and even swings to golden oldies.

Near the Docks

The pubs by the docks are full of unique character and are also among the few in Belfast that have survived the violence of the past 25 years intact. A cab should be used for transport to and from the dock area, as it can be dangerous at night.

The Liverpool Bar, Donegall Quay, opposite the SeaCat terminal. The best trad venue in the city on Wed. and Sat. nights.

The Front Page, 9 Ballymoney St. (tel. 324924). Packs the locals in nightly. Plays live music on weekends.

SIGHTS

The best way to see Belfast is through the **Citybus** (tel. 458484) "Belfast: A Living History" tour. The tour through the Falls, the Shankill, East Belfast, and Sandy Row is engaging. (June-Sept. tours every Tues., Thurs., and Sun. at 2pm; 2½hr.; £6.50, students £6. Illustrated souvenir booklet, tea, and scone included.) You are unlikely to get such an objective view from a black taxi tour, which charge more anyway. Citybus offers a 3½-hour "Belfast City Tour" of the city's major architectural landmarks (leaves from Castle Place July-Aug. Wed. 1:30pm; £6.50, students £4.50).

The **tourist office** on North St. will arm you with a valuable free map listing bus routes and most major sites and limitless brochures in an attempt to make the city navigable. A more detailed Greater Belfast area map is also available for £3. The *Belfast Civic Festival Trail* pamphlets, self-guided walking tours of various neighborhoods, are detailed and interesting. One-hour **walking tours** focus intensely on Belfast's history; they leave the tourist office daily at 2pm (£2.50, students £2).

Donegall Square

Belfast City Hall, Donegall Sq. (tel. 320202 ext. 2618), is the administrative and geographical center of Belfast, distanced from the crowded streets by a grassy square. Its green copper dome, 173 ft. high, is visible from any point in the city. Neoclassical marble columns and arches figure prominently in A. Brunwell Thomas's 1906 design. Inside, a grand marble staircase ascends under the watchful dome to the second floor. Portraits of the city's Lord Mayors somberly line the halls, and glass and marble shimmer in three elaborate reception rooms. The City Council's oak-paneled chambers, used only once a month, are deceptively austere considering the Council's reputation for rowdy meetings (they sometimes devolve into fist fights). If you want to see the council in action, a councillor can sign you in with 48-hour notice. Otherwise, there is no public access to debates. In the gardens, marble statues of Queen Victoria and Sir Edward Harland (of Harland and Wolff shipyard fame) stand over the crowds. An inconspicuous pale gray stone column commemorates the 1942 arrival of the U.S. Expeditionary Force, whose soldiers were stationed here to defend the North from Germany. The interior of City Hall is accessible by guided tour. (Sept.-June Wed. 10:30am; July-Aug. Mon.-Fri. 10:30am and 2:30pm; 1hr. Free. Due to security, reservations must be made a day in advance.)

Across the street from City Hall, the **Scottish Provident Institution,** built in 1902, is recognizable by its asymmetrical roofline and 16 sculpted lions' heads. Other decorations depicting the loom, ships, and spinning wheel represent the industries which made Belfast prosperous. The northwest corner of Donegall Sq. shelters the wood-paneled **Linen Hall Library,** 17 Donegall Sq. (tel. 321707). The library contains a famous collection of political materials. Devoted librarians scramble for every Christmas card, poster, hand bill, and newspaper article related to the Troubles that they can get their hands on (open Mon.-Wed. and Fri. 9:30am-5:30pm, Thurs. 9:30am-8:30pm, Sat. 9:30am-4pm).

Cornmarket

Just north of the city center, a shopping district envelops eight blocks around Castle St. and Royal Ave. This area, known as Cornmarket after one of the commodities originally sold here, has been a marketplace since Belfast's early days. The barricades which prevent cars from entering fall roughly where the old city walls stood in the 17th century. A McDonald's stands on the site of the old city castle (hence Castle St.). Just across College Sq., **The Old Museum Arts Centre** (tel. 235053) mounts rotating art exhibits and hosts frequent concerts (open Mon.-Fri. 9am-5:30pm, Sat. 10am-5pm; free). Amid the chaos of Rosemary St., the **First Presbyterian Church of Belfast** is the city's oldest church (open Wed. 10:30am-12:30pm).

Although the Cornmarket area is dominated by modern buildings, snapshots of old Belfast remain in the tiny alleys, or **Entries,** which connect some of the major streets. A drink at any of the pubs along these alleys induces feelings of nostalgia. On Ann St., a hand and an umbrella stick out of the wall over an umbrella store. The entrance to Pottinger's Entry, which contains the old **Morning Star Pub** in all its traditional splendor, is right across the street. Farther down Ann St., **Joy's Entry** was the alley where the *Belfast News Letter* was printed for over 100 years. The only establishment in the entry—**Globe Tavern**—is disappointingly modern inside. Off Lombard St., **Winecellar Entry** is the site of Belfast's oldest pub, **White's Tavern,** which has been serving drinks since 1630. It's still an ideal place for an afternoon pint, though you may have to fight with 60-odd women for a spot at the bar. The city's oldest public building, **The Old Stock Exchange,** is here too, on the corner of North and Waring Streets. The tireless Charles Lanyon designed a new facade for the building in 1845 when the original was deemed not grand enough.

St. Anne's Cathedral Area

Belfast's newspapers all set up shop north of the Cornmarket shopping district, around the still active Church of Ireland cathedral (on Donegall St.), which is called the **Belfast Cathedral** or **St. Anne's.** To keep from disturbing regular worship, this cathedral, begun in 1899, was built around the smaller, earlier church already on the site. Upon completion of the cathedral's exterior, the earlier, now enclosed, church was removed brick by brick from inside. The mosaic above the Chapel of the Holy Spirit depicts St. Patrick arriving in southeast Co. Down and bringing Christianity to Ireland. The tops of each of the cathedral's 10 interior pillars depict somebody's idea of the 10 basic professions of Belfast: Science, Industry, Healing, Agriculture, Music, Theology, Shipbuilding, Freemasonry, Art, and Womanhood (a nice enough profession, but the pay stinks). Signs in one section of the cathedral ask you to say a prayer for Northern Ireland between noon and 2pm (open daily 9am-6pm).

North Belfast

At the bottom of the hills that rise outside the city sits **Belfast Castle,** presented to the city by the Earl of Shaftesbury in 1934. Though in perfect condition, the castle is closed to the general public, but anyone can walk through the grounds. At the top of **Cave Hill,** on which the castle was built, **McArt's Fort** is the Fort of Matudan, the ancient Ulster King, where the more modern United Irishmen plotted rebellion in 1795. The summit is nicknamed "Napoleon's Nose." Its breathtaking view over the city and Belfast Lough is certainly nothing to sneeze at. Marked trails lead north of the fort to five caves in the area. Historians believe that the caves are actually ancient mines, of which only the lowest is accessible.

The Docks & East Belfast

Belfast has its own combined version of a leaning tower and Big Ben: the precarious **Albert Memorial Clock Tower.** Designed in 1865 by W. J. Barre, the 115-ft. tower leans at the entryway to the docks area, where Oxford St. briefly parallels the Lagan. The Albert of mention is Prince Albert, Queen Victoria's consort.

Although the docks area was the activity hub of old Belfast, continued commercial development and Belfast's urban revisionism have obliterated anything old enough to remember the city's founding. The stately **Custom House,** built by Charles Lanyon in 1857, stands between Queen Sq. and Albert Sq. on the approach to the river from the clock tower. Designed in an imaginative E-shape, it rests on an elaborate pediment of Britannia, Neptune, and Mercury, the god of trade. This is Belfast's answer to Dublin's famous Custom House (Belfast's is closed to the public).

An organ with port and starboard lights carries the tune at **Sinclair Seamen's Church,** Corporation St. (next to Donegall Quay), the church with a theme. The minister delivers his sermons from a pulpit carved in the shape of a ship's prow; collections are taken in miniature lifeboats (Sun. services 11:30am and 7pm; open Wed. 2-4pm). The exterior was designed by prolific **Charles Lanyon,** the same architect who designed The Custom House and virtually every other notable mid-19th-century Belfast building (except the Albert Memorial Clock Tower, and he was angry about that). Lanyon later became mayor of Belfast.

Farther south along Donegall Quay, **Lagan Lookout** provides a walkway across newly built **Lagan Weir** and offers an interpretive center (tel. 315444) with displays on the history of Belfast and the harbor. The £14-million weir was built to eliminate the Lagan's drastic tides, which used to expose stinking mud flats during ebb. The weir is part of a huge development project for Belfast which includes the **Laganside Trail** along the far side of the river, a road/rail bridge (currently under construction), and a huge hotel and concert hall (also under construction, but scheduled to open in 1997 to seat over 2000). The walkway across the weir provides an unusual perspective on the city. The interpretive center, on the other hand, is of benefit only for those intensely interested in the history of the Lagan and its curbmasters. But the center does mention the thrilling story of Houdini's near brush with death in Donegall Bay (open Mon.-Fri. 11am-5pm, Sat. noon-5pm, Sun. 2-5pm; admission £2).

The twin cranes nicknamed **"Samson and Goliath"** tower over the Harland and Wolff shipyard in East Belfast and are visible from anywhere across the river. During the 19th and early 20th centuries, Harland and Wolff fashioned Belfast into one of the world's premier shipbuilding centers. The builder's most famous single creation was, unfortunately, the *Titanic.* The shipyards figure in numerous poems and novels set in Belfast, notably at the end of Paul Muldoon's "7, Middagh St." Back on the western side of the Lagan, the **One Gallery,** 1 Oxford St. (tel. 310400), exposes the city to the work of contemporary Belfast artists (open Mon.-Fri. 10am-4pm; free).

Queen's University Area

South of city center, the main building of **Queen's University** sits back from the road in its revival Tudor red brick. Designed by Charles Lanyon in 1849, it was modeled after Magdalen College, Oxford. Only the facade was finished properly; the sides are disappointing. The **Visitors Centre** (tel. 335252), with the usual exhibits and memorabilia, is in the Lanyon Room to the left of the main entrance to the building (open Mon.-Sat. 10am-4pm). The University has its own art collection, **Fenderesky Gallery,** inside the Crescent Arts Centre, 2 University Rd. (tel. 242338), which puts up contemporary shows all year (open Tues.-Sat. 11:30am-5:30pm).

On warm days, a majority of the student population suns itself at the **Botanic Gardens** (tel. 324902) down the street. Meticulously groomed, the gardens offer a welcome green respite from the gray Belfast streets. The **Tropical Ravine House** provides a break from the cold Irish weather—it's about 95°F inside. The ornate **Palm House** overflows with greenery at a much more comfortable temperature. (Gardens open daily 8am-dusk; Tropical House and Palm House open Mon.-Fri. 10amnoon and 2-5pm, Sat.-Sun. 2-5pm. Free.) Amid the Botanic Gardens, the **Ulster Museum** (tel. 381251) off Stranmillis Rd. has developed a variety of exhibits for its huge display halls. Irish art, local history, and antiquities are all subjects for investigation. The treasure salvaged from the *Girone,* a Spanish Armada ship that sank off the Causeway Coast in 1588, is on display here. The Mummy of Takabuti and a Maori War canoe add an exotic note. It takes at least 1½ hours to see the museum properly (open Mon.-Fri. 10am-5pm, Sat. 1-5pm, Sun. 2-5pm; free).

South Belfast

No perfume could compete with the 100,000 rose bushes at **Sir Thomas and Lady Dixon Park,** Upper Malone Rd. The gardens were founded in 1836 and include the stud China roses, imported between 1792 and 1824, which provided the foundation for current British roses. New strains of roses are tested at the City of Belfast International Rose Trials held here from late June to early August. The Belfast Parks Department (tel. 320202) excites guests with promises of the red squirrel and the elusive bluebell glade. Buses #70 and 71 from Donegall Sq. East run to the roses. The public search room at the **Public Record Office,** 66 Balmoral Ave. (tel. 661621), allows you to trace your ancestors (open Mon.-Fri. 9am-5pm). Out on the Ballynahatty Rd., a strange earthen ring with a dolmen in the middle goes by the name of **Giant's Ring.** Little is known about the 200-yd.-wide circle.

The Golden Mile

Belfast's pride and joy, the **Grand Opera House** on Great Victoria St., has been cyclically bombed by the Provos, restored to its original splendor at enormous cost, and then bombed again. The **Grand Opera House Ticket Shop,** 17 Wellington Place (tel. 241919; 24-hr. information line tel. 249129), sells tickets for performances (open Mon.-Wed. 8:30am-8pm, Thurs. 8:30am-9pm, Fri. 8:30am-6:30pm, Sat. 8:30am-5:30pm). The Opera House is at its best during performances (musicals, operas, ballets, and concerts), but it is possible to visit during the day. Call the booking office (open Mon.-Sat. 9:45am-5:30pm) to make an appointment, or ask at the stage door on Glengall St. If there's no rehearsal at the moment, they'll give you a tour. Farther down Great Victoria St., the plush **Europa Hotel** has the dubious distinction of being "Europe's most bombed hotel." Across the street, the **Crown Liquor Saloon,** Great Victoria St., is a showcase of carved wood, gilded ceilings, and stained glass, all fully restored by the National Trust. The box-like snugs fit groups of two or 10 comfortably. Just ring the buzzer when you want another round (see **Pubs,** p. 375).

Great Victoria St. proceeds south to **Shaftesbury Square,** where the one neon sign allows tourism officials to compare it to Piccadilly Circus. Nearby, the **Crescent Arts Centre,** 2 University Rd. (tel. 242338), dedicates gallery space to Belfast artists (open Tues.-Sat. 11:30am-5:30pm). The center teaches eight-week courses in yoga, trapeze, writing, trad music, ballet, and drawing (1 class/week; £28 total).

WEST BELFAST

Separated from the rest of the city by the Westlink motorway, the working-class neighborhoods of West Belfast lie at the heart of political tensions in the North. The Catholic area (centered on Falls Rd.) and the Protestant neighborhood (centered on the Shankill) are grimly separated by the **peace line,** a gray wall between the two warring parts of town. Along the wall, abandoned houses with blocked-up or broken windows point to a troubled past and an uncertain future. These two neighborhoods embody both the raw sentiment that drives the Northern Irish conflict and the casual calm with which those closest to the Troubles approach daily life. These epicenters of political violence in Belfast are unique to the city and may intrigue the curious. Not a "sight" in the traditional sense, West Belfast is presented here for anthropological exploration, not consumer tourism. It is polite (and wise) to remember that residents usually object to being scrutinized as social anomalies. Be discreet when photographing murals or you may be dubbed a "terrorist tourist." As the murals in the Falls and Shankill are constantly changing, the sections below describe only a handful. We provide a glossary of their symbols and terms (p. 382).

Practical Information

With care and common sense, the Falls and Shankill can be visited in **safety.** Stay far away after dark. By day, visit in a car, on foot, or in a black cab. The Protestant Orangemen's marching season, around Orange Day on July 12, is a risky time to visit the area, since the proud, angry parades can inspire political violence (as in July '96; see **History and Politics,** p. 362). Other ceremonial occasions, such as the Catholic West Belfast Festival (August 7-15), may also be dangerous times to visit. *Never* take pictures of soldiers, police, or military installations; if you do, your film will be confiscated and you may be detained for questioning. You can freely take pictures of murals and buildings, but if you want snapshots of people, be sure to ask their permission for both courtesy and safety's sake. To see both the Falls and Shankill, the best plan is to visit one, then return to the city center before heading to the other. The area around the peace line is still desolate and the least safe of these areas.

Black cabs are the community shuttles that whisk West Belfast residents to the city center along set routes, picking up and dropping off passengers on the way. For the standard fare (55p), you can ask to be let off anywhere along the route. Black cabs can also reasonably be hired by groups for **tours** of the Falls or Shankill (£15-20/hr.). **Catholic black cabs,** identified by signs which read "Falls Rd.," "Andersontown," or which are written in Irish, leave the city center from Donegall Sq. and the taxi park on Castle St. **Protestant black cabs,** identified by red poppies or "Shankill" signs, head up and down the Shankill Rd. from their base at the top of North St.

The Falls

The Falls is much larger than Shankill and, with a younger population, still growing. Moving west on Divis St., away from the city center, a high-rise apartment building marks the site of the **Divis Tower,** an ill-fated housing development built by optimistic social planners in the 1960s. This project soon became an IRA stronghold and experienced some of the worst of Belfast's Troubles in the 70s. The British army still maintains a small base on the roof.

Continue west as Divis St. turns into the Falls Rd. The **Sinn Féin office** on the right is marked by the wire cage enclosing the building and surveillance camera outside. To get in, ask next door at the Republican bookstore marked *"Sioppa na hEalaine."* (You have to ring a bell to be admitted to the bookstore.) Tell the shopkeeper that you're a tourist interested in seeing the Republican sights of West Belfast, and you will probably be escorted to the office next door. Sinn Féin sometimes gives tours of

---

The Rape of the Falls

The area stretching from Divis Tower to Cavendish Sq. is known as the **Lower Falls.** This area was sealed off by the British Army for 35 hours in July, 1970, in an episode known as the **Rape of the Falls.** Soldiers, acting on a tip that arms were hidden in some of the houses, searched homes at random while residents were forbidden to leave the area, not even for milk or bread. It is estimated that before this event, there were only 50 Republicans in the area. After the incident, however, over 2000 people turned to the IRA. Many regard this to be the biggest mistake ever made by the British army in Northern Ireland.

the neighborhood if they can get a group together. If not, they will give you a map which shows the largest groups of murals and other sites of Republican significance. On the side of the bookstore is a large mural with a portrait of Bobby Sands and an advertisement for the Sinn Féin newspaper, *An Phoblacht*. Continuing down the Falls you will see a number of "cultural" murals characterized by Celtic art and the Irish language. They display scenes of traditional dance and music, or grimmer portraits of Famine victims. One particularly moving mural, on the corner of the Falls and RPG Ave., shows the 10 hunger strikers who died in 1981-82 above a quote from Bobby Sands: "Our revenge will be the laughter of our children." Murals in the Falls, unlike those of the Shankill, are becoming less militant in nature, though there are two left in the Lower Falls which commend violence. One shows women banging bin lids on the ground in the face of British paratroopers (the echoing sound warned neighbors of impending raids). The grim slogan reads: "25 years of resistance—25 more if needs be." Unartistic political graffiti, concerning Sinn Fein, the RUC, and Paddy Kelly, are everywhere.

The Falls Rd. soon splits into Andersontown Rd. and Glen Rd. (the site of Ireland's only urban *gaeltacht*). On the left are the Celtic crosses of **Milltown Cemetery,** the resting place of many Republican dead. Inside the entrance, a memorial to Republican casualties is bordered by a low green fence on the right. Bobby Sands's grave stands here. Another mile along the Andersontown Rd. lies the road's namesake—a housing project (formerly a wealthy Catholic neighborhood)—and several good murals. The Springfield Rd. RUC station is the most attacked police station in Ireland and the U.K.; its charred, paint-splattered defenses are formidable.

Shankill & Sandy Row

North St., to the left of the tourist office, quickly turns into Shankill Rd. as it crosses the Westlink and then arrives in Protestant Shankill, once a thriving shopping district, now a Loyalist stronghold standing firm in the face of the expanding Falls. Streets are wider here than in the Falls; there are fewer houses because of the great migrations out of the area in the 70s. Since Catholics tended not to leave the Falls, a near generation gap between the majority of residents in these two areas has resulted. The **peace line** looms at the end of any of the side roads to the left. Many of the neighborhood's murals have been painted on the sides of the buildings that front the Shankill Rd. The murals in the Shankill tend to glorify the UVF and UFF rather than celebrate any aspect of "Orange" culture. At Canmore St., a significant mural on the left depicts the Apprentice Boys "Shutting the Gates of Derry—1688" as the Catholic invaders try to get through. A little farther, also on the left and across a small park, a big, faded mural labeled "UVF—then and now" depicts a modern, black-garbed "soldier" and a historical soldier side-by-side. The densely decorated **Orange Hall** sits on the left at Brookmount St. McClean's wallpaper, on the right, was formerly Fizzel's fish shop, where 10 people died in an October, 1993, bomb attack. The side streets to the right guide you to the **Shankill Estate,** home of more murals. Through the estate, the **Crumlin Road** heads back to the city center past an army base and the courthouse and jail, which are on opposite sides of the road but linked by a tunnel. The oldest Loyalist murals are to be found here. The intersection of the Crumlin and Shankill roads saw some of the worst rioting in July, 1996.

The Shankill area is shrinking as middle-class Protestants abandon it, but **Sandy Row,** another Protestant area, has more to show. It begins at Donegall Rd. next to the youth hostel at Shaftesbury Sq. An Orange Arch, with King Billy on top, marks the entrance to the Protestant area. Nearby murals show the Red Hand of Ulster, a British bulldog, and King Billy crossing the Boyne. While murals in the more volatile Falls and Shankill areas are often defaced or damaged, better-preserved and more elaborate murals adorn the secure Protestant enclave of East Belfast, across the Lagan. Several line Newtownards Rd. One mural likens the UVF to the ancient hero, Cuchulainn—Ulster's defender. It eerily resembles a mural in Derry which represents the Irish army in these same mythical terms. Ulster's legendary warrior is apparently the only symbolic figure admired by both sides of the struggle.

A Primer of Symbols in the Murals of West Belfast

The Red Hand: the symbol of Ulster (found on Ulster's crest), usually used by Unionists to emphasize the separateness of Ulster from the rest of Ireland.

Blue, White, & Red: the colors of the British flag; often painted on curbs, signposts, etc., to demarcate Unionist murals and neighborhoods.

Bulldog: represents Britain.

King Billy/William of Orange: sometimes depicted on a white horse, crossing the Boyne to beat the Catholic King James II at the 1690 Battle of the Boyne. The Orange Order was later founded in his honor. A major Protestant icon.

The Apprentice Boys: a group of young men who shut the gates of Derry to keep out the besieging troops of James II, beginning the great siege of 1689. They have become Protestant folk heroes, inspiring an honorary association in their name. The slogan **"No Surrender,"** also from the siege, has been appropriated by radical Unionists, especially Rev. Ian Paisley.

Lundy: the name of a Derry leader who advocated surrender during the siege; now a term for anyone who wants to give in to Catholic demands.

Taig: phonetic spelling of an Irish given name, Teague; slang for a Catholic.

Star of David: allies the North with Israel, equating the IRA with the PLO.

Orange & Green: colors of the Irish Republic's flag; often painted on curbs and signposts in Republican neighborhoods.

Landscapes: sometimes imply Republican territorial claims to the North.

The Irish Volunteers: Republican tie to the earlier (nonsectarian) Nationalists.

Éireann go bráth: "Ireland forever"; a popular IRA slogan.

Tiocfaidh ár lá: (CHOCK-ee-ar-LA) "Our day will come." Irish is a sure sign of a Nationalist mural.

Phoenix: symbolizes united Ireland rising from the ashes of British persecution.

Lug: Celtic god, seen as the protector of the "native Irish" (Catholics).

ARTS & ENTERTAINMENT

Belfast's many cultural events and performances are best covered in the free, monthly *Arts Council Artslink* (at the tourist office and all art galleries). Daily listings appear in the daily *Belfast Telegraph* (also a Fri. arts supplement) as well as in Thursday's *Irish News.* The **Crescent Arts Centre,** 2 University Rd. (tel. 242338), supplies general arts info and more specific news about their own exhibits and concerts. Queen's University and the University of Ulster host many arts events during the school year. July is a slow month for the arts in Belfast; around July 12, the whole city shuts down. For more extensive information on pub entertainment (including special guests), pick up the free, biweekly, two-page news bulletin *That's Entertainment,* available at most pubs and the YHANI hostel.

Theater

Belfast's theater season runs from September to June. Some plays are produced in the summer, but most playhouses "go dark" for the tourist season. The truly **Grand Opera House,** Great Victoria St. (tel. 241919; 24-hr. information 249129), boasts an impressive mix of large productions of opera, ballet, musicals, and drama. During the opera season in September, tickets can be purchased by phone. (Tel. 381241. Students get a 50% discount on Tues. and Thurs. if they buy tickets after noon on the day of the performance. Tickets range £8-160.) Tickets for other events are available at the box office, 17 Wellington Pl. (open Mon.-Sat. 9:45am-5:30pm). **The Arts Theatre,** 41 Botanic Ave. (tel. 324936), houses its own company but hosts touring troupes as well. (Open Aug.-June; box office open Mon.-Sat. 10am-7pm. Tickets £3-7.) **The Lyric Theatre,** 30 Ridgeway St. (tel. 381081), mixes Irish plays with international theater. **The Group Theatre,** Bedford St. (tel. 329685), specializes in comedies. (Open Sept.-May; box office open Mon.-Fri. noon-3pm. Tickets £3-5.) **The Ulster Hall** (see below) puts on a few plays.

Music

Ulster Hall, Linenhall St. (tel. 229685), brings music for a wide range of tastes to town (box office open Mon.-Sat. 9am-5pm). **The Grand Opera House** (see above) also resounds with less shrill notes. The only other music in Belfast is that found in pubs. For traditional music, try **Madden's Bar,** 74 Smithfield (tel. 244114), on Wednesday through Saturday nights; **The Liverpool Bar,** Donegal Quay, opposite the SeaCat terminal, on Wednesday and Saturday nights; **Kelly's Cellars,** 30 Bank St. (tel. 324835), on Thursday; **The Parador Hotel,** 473 Ormeau Rd. (tel. 491883), on Thursday; **The Duke of York,** Lower Donegall St. (tel. 241062), on Monday and Thursday; and **The Bot** on Sunday.

The **Elms** has folk/rock bands most nights and trad on Thursday. **The Front Page** plays a wide range of music mostly on weekends. **The Egg** has good local rock on the weekends. **Robinson's** spends a long weekend (Thurs.-Sat.) with rock and dance bands upstairs (see **Pubs,** p. 375). The **Drumkeen Hotel,** Upper Galwally (tel. 491321), can put you in a loose, jazzy mood on Wednesday. More of the same can be found at the **Terrace Restaurant,** 255 Lisburn Rd. (tel. 381655), on Thursday and **The Cutter's Wharf,** Lockview Rd. (tel. 662501), on Sunday.

The **Ulster Orchestra** plays a series of free summer concerts sponsored by the BBC on Friday nights at Ulster Hall. (For info and free tickets, send a stamped, self-addressed envelope to BBC Ticket Unit, Broadcasting House, Ormeau Ave., Belfast BT2 8HQ.)

Dance Clubs

Nightclubs are another way to get up and get down. The **Dome and Limelight** complex, Ormeau Ave. (tel. 325968), is a dance club with a pub attached. Monday is gay and lesbian night (straights also welcome); Friday and Saturday are student-only discos; Tuesday is for everyone; Thursday and sometimes Sunday bring a live band (9pm; cover £1-7). Crowds flock to **Lavery's,** 12 Bradbury Place (see **Pubs,** p. 375), for discos every night except Sundays (Mon.-Wed. cover £1, Thurs. £2, Fri.-Sat. £2.50). **Queen's University Student Centre** (tel. 324803) has student-only discos six nights per week during term time and Thursday and Saturday in summer (cover £2). **The Crow's Nest** (see **Pubs,** p. 375) has dancing for gays and lesbians every night of the week; straights are welcome. **Parliament Bar** (see **Pubs,** p. 375) has a gays and lesbian disco Thursday and Saturday (cover £2); straights are unwelcome.

Events: The Belfast Festival at Queen's

Belfast reigns supreme in the art world for three weeks each November when Queen's University hits the town with its annual festival. Over 300 separate performances of opera, ballet, film, and comedy invade venues across the city, drawing groups like the Royal Shakespeare Theatre. Tickets for the most popular events sell out months ahead of time, although there's almost always something to see if you haven't planned ahead. For advance tickets and schedules, write to: Mailing List, Festival House, 25 College Gardens, Belfast BT9 6BS by August. Ticket sales by mail begin September 15. From October 15 through the festival's end, tickets are available by phone (tel. 667687).

■ Near Belfast

ULSTER FOLK AND TRANSPORT MUSEUM

Five miles east of Belfast on the way to the Ards Peninsula on the Bangor Rd., the **Ulster Folk and Transport Museum** (tel. (01232) 428428) stretches over 60 acres in Cultra. The Folk Museum is the better half of this marriage. More than 25 buildings dating from the past three centuries have been moved from their original locations around Ulster and reconstructed stone by stone on museum property. Each of the buildings has been restored inside and out, and visitors may wander freely. Since this is an *Ulster* museum, all nine of its counties contribute: Monaghan, Cavan, and Donegal plus the six that comprise Northern Ireland. The buildings represent all different regions and social classes: along with the lighter side of life, visitors can enter into the one-room building which an 18th-century family once shared with their livestock. An entire village is slowly materializing near the entrance. The set of old cottages comes complete with an 18th-century church from Kildare, Co. Down, a coal distributer's shop from Belfast, and an 18th-century one-room schoolhouse from Ballycastle, Co. Antrim. In the printer's shop on "Main Street," an original 1844 newspaper press prints posters for upcoming museum events. Little written commentary accompanies the reconstructions, but the buildings' attendants can answer any questions. The museum also hosts many special events, including pipe ban tattoos, flute performances, and textile exhibitions.

The Transport Museum and the Railway Museum are across the road from the Folk Museum. Inside the **Transport Museum,** some horse-drawn coaches, cars, bicycles, and planes trace the history of moving vehicles. A *Titanic* exhibit, which includes original blueprints, details the Belfast-built ship and its fate. The hangar-like **Railway Museum** stuffs in 25 old railway engines. Half a day is just long enough to see the museums here, but spending fewer than two hours would be foolish. Ulsterbuses #1 and 2 from Oxford St. Station run to Cultra. (Open July-Aug. Mon.-Sat. 10:30am-6pm, Sun. noon-6pm; April-June and Sept. Mon.-Fri. 9:30am-5pm, Sat. 10:30am-6pm, Sun. noon-6pm; Oct.-March Mon.-Fri. 9:30am-4pm, Sat.-Sun. 12:30-4:30pm; closed Dec. 24-26. Admission £3.30, HI members £2.20.)

CARRICKFERGUS

Eight miles northeast of Belfast on the Antrim coast, Carrickfergus was thriving when Belfast was but a village. Carrickfergus is now past its heyday, but it can back up its claim to being Ireland's oldest town with massive **Carrickfergus Castle,** the oldest Norman castle in Ireland. This suburb-port's major artistic products are the poet Louis MacNeice and a rock fanzine called *Mos Eiseley.* The rectory on North Rd. was MacNeice's boyhood home. The poem he wrote about his hometown describes "The little boats beneath the Norman castle,/ The pier shining with lumps of crystal salt." The town itself is named after King Fergus, who drowned just offshore in 531 AD. He had come to the town to find a cure for his skin disease.

A well-stocked **tourist office** (tel. 366455) hangs out in the new mall on Antrim St., which also contains the Knight Ride attraction. (Open April-Sept. Mon.-Fri 9am-6pm, Sat. 10am-6pm, Sun. noon-6pm; Oct.-March Mon.-Sat. 10am-5pm, Sun. noon-5pm.) **Ulster Bank** is at 37 High St. (tel. 351309; open Mon. 9:30am-noon and 1:30-5pm, Tues.-Fri. 10am-noon and 1:30-3:30pm; **ATM**). **Trains** chug into the station at the top of North St. (tel. 351286) from Belfast and continue to Larne. (Mon.-Fri. 19/day, Sat. 15/day, Sun. 6/day; 20min. from Belfast, 30min. from Larne.) **Buses** drop you off in the center of town but pick you up at the bus stop on Joymount. Buses to Belfast stop on the main road next to the Harbour Car Park. Buses head to Belfast (Mon.-Fri. 35/day, Sat. 16/day, Sun. 12/day; 1hr.; £1.70, £2.80 return) and rarely to Larne (June-Sept. Mon.-Sat. 1/day; 35min.; £1.15). Pharmacy services are available at **McFarlands,** 10 High St. (tel. 362541). The **post office,** 46 Antrim St. (tel. 351640), has a passport photo booth (open Mon.-Thurs. 9am-5:30pm, Fri. 9:30-5:30pm, Sat. 10am-12:30pm). The **postal code** is BT3 878. The **phone code** is an itchy 01960.

Jean Kernohan's **Marathon House,** 3 Upper Station Rd. (tel. (01232) 862475), in Greenisland, is a picture-perfect B&B set back from the road in a beautiful English garden. Trains from Belfast stop in Greenisland, which is not far at all from Carrickfergus. The B&B is a short five-minute walk up the hill from the station (£15/person). High St. is the most likely place to find sustenance. The **Old Tech Griddle,** 20 High St. (tel. 351914), cuts huge slices of quiche (£1.35) and makes cheap sandwiches (£1; open Mon.-Sat. 9am-5:30pm). **Mauds,** Scotch Quarter (tel. 367428), sells Guinness ice cream (90p) alongside other, more palatable flavors (open daily 9am-9pm). Only for the adventurous, the **Dobbins Inn Hotel,** 6-8 High St. (tel. 351905), sells traditional Ulster food: champ (mashed potatoes mixed with scallions simmered in milk) and black pudding (a type of blood sausage made with oats; fried black pudding w/onions and apples in soda bread £2.75; food served 5:30-8:30pm).

The **castle** (tel. 351273), the seat of English power in Ulster from the 12th to the 17th century, has weathered its tumultuous 800-odd years well, although a brigade of Disneyesque fiberglass figures now inhabits the castle. Cuthbert the Crossbowman & Co. aside, the castle is exciting to explore. Practically every room is open (including the latrines), and you can read as much history as you want from the signs. From the train station, Victoria St. leads to cobbled, pedestrianized North St. The castle rises where the road meets the water (bus drivers will let you off right outside if you ask). (Open April-Sept. Mon.-Sat. 10am-6pm, Sun. 2-6pm; Oct.-March Mon.-Sat. 10am-4pm, Sun. 2-4pm. Admission £2.70.)

Most of the old **town wall** survives. An entry behind town hall gives access to the remaining chunk of wall. The archway at North Gate is still intact, proving or disproving the local tradition that the arch would stand until a wise man joined the Borough Council. The Irish and Scotch parts of town lie outside the walls of this very English town. Excavations of the Irish, or West Gate, area revealed skulls that are believed to have been displayed on pikes following a gruesome execution. **Knight Ride,** Antrim Rd. (tel. 366455), for all its advertisements, doesn't compete with the castle. This theme ride re-enacts the town history which a fictitious older resident of Carrickfergus tells his annoyingly enthusiastic grandson. A life-size mural at the end of High St. depicts a day in 1536. After the ride, a walk-through exhibit fills in the gaps of the story. (Open April-Sept. Mon.-Sat. 10am-6pm, Sun. noon-6pm; Oct.-March Mon.-Sat. 10am-5pm, Sun. noon-5pm. Last admission 30min. before closing. Admission £2.70; joint ticket with castle £4.85.)

Down & Armagh

Those parts of the North that lie south of the Lagan aren't visited as often as the Causeway Coast; the things to see are more subtle and less-hyped. The Ards Peninsula, which points south from Belfast, is sandier than the northern coast of the island, and pleasing and fun in its entirety. The Mourne Mountains, almost directly south of Belfast and near the Republic, slope scenically just inland from the beach party at Newcastle. Co. Armagh is situated inland from Belfast and is seldom visited, except by religious pilgrims. The southern half of Armagh is known as a flashpoint for Troubles (the area around Crossmaglen has been especially dangerous). Although the political situation is still volatile and the county is not free of violence, safety conditions are improving. Armagh Town has a full plate of cultural goodies.

▨ Bangor

Close both to Belfast and to open sea, Bangor was once *the* seaside resort for Belfast residents. The town now caters especially to families and older vacationers. Parks accost visitors from the left and right. As a beach town built for urbanites, Bangor can offer its share of entertainment. Besides, its location makes it an inevitable stop on the way down the Ards Peninsula.

PRACTICAL INFORMATION

Tourist Office: Tower House, 34 Quay St. (tel. 270069). From the bus and train stations, a left down Main St. leads to the Marina. A right along the water leads past the Royal Hotel to Tower House. Open July-Aug. Mon.-Fri. 9am-8pm, Sat. 10am-7pm, Sun. noon-6pm; Sept.-June Mon.-Fri. 9am-5pm, Sat. 10-11am.

Banks: Halifax Bank, 20 Main St. (tel. 270013). Open Mon.-Fri. 9am-5pm, Sat. 9am-noon. **ATM** accepts Plus and Visa. **First Trust,** Main St. (tel. 270628). Open Mon.-Fri. 9:30am-4:30pm. **ATM** takes Visa and MasterCard.

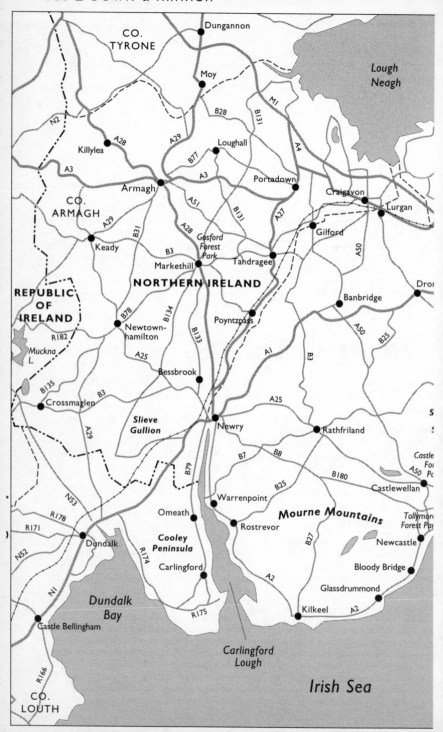

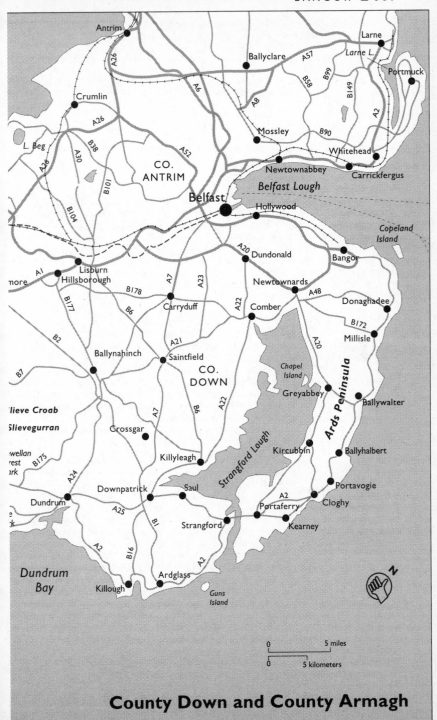

County Down and County Armagh

Train Station: Abbey St. (tel. 270141), next to the bus station. To Belfast (40/day; 20min.; £2.50, £3.70 return) and Carrickfergus (£3.80).

Buses: Abbey St. (tel. 271143). To Belfast (20/day; ¾hr.; £1.80, £2.55 return) and all towns on the Ards Peninsula, including Donaghadee (34/day; ½hr.; £1.10) and Newtownards (34/day; 25min.; £1.10).

Bike Rental: Sampson's Cycles, 109 High St. (tel. 462929). £6/day, £30/week; deposit £60. Open Mon.-Sat. 9am-5:30pm.

Pharmacy: Boot's Pharmacy, Main St. (tel. 271134). Open Mon.-Fri. 9am-5:30pm, Sat. 9am-6pm.

Hotline: Samaritans, 92 Dufferin Ave. (tel. 464646). Open daily 9:15am-10pm.

Emergency: Dial 999; no coins required. **Police:** Castle Park Ave. (tel. 454444).

Post Office: Main St. Open Mon.-Fri. 9am-5:30pm, Sat. 9am-12:30pm. **Postal Code:** BT20 5ED.

Phone Code: 01247.

ACCOMMODATIONS, FOOD, & PUBS

Without hostel or campground, this city teems with B&Bs in the £12-15 range; they're listed in the tourist office window. Coastal Seacliff Rd. and inland Princetown Rd. near the train and bus stations are full of choices. **Tara Guesthouse,** 51 Princetown Rd. (tel. 468925), pampers guests with spacious rooms, all with bath and TV (£17/person). **Pierview House,** 28 Seacliff Rd. (tel. 463381), alters its rates depending on the size of the room, length of stay, and time of year (£14-16/person). **St. Ives,** 58 Seacliff Rd. (tel. 469444), has rooms with TVs (£14/person).

Sandwich Express, 48 Bingham St. (tel. 462131), just off High St., seats its customers at a counter and serves them grilled cheese sandwiches (£1; open Mon.-Sat. 8:30am-4pm). Hearty meals await folks at the **Bungy Jump Café Restaurant,** 99/101 Main St. (tel. 461529). Rubber cords hold up framed photographs of jumpers in action (12" pizza £5-6; open Mon.-Sat. noon-7pm, Sat.-Sun. brunch noon-4pm). **Wosley's,** 24 High St. (tel. 460495), envelops patrons in red velvet. Dinner special for two includes two 9" pizzas and two bottles of beer (£7; open Mon.-Thurs. noon-6pm, Fri.-Sat. noon-7pm, Sun. 12:30-2pm). Pubs gather in the triangle on High St. and along the waterfront. **Jenny Watts,** High St. (tel. 270401), has a Sunday lunch jazz session, folk and trad on Tuesdays, and a nightclub upstairs on Friday and Saturday nights. Across the street, **Wosley's** regulars boogie to disco (Wed.-Sat., cover £2-3). **The Windsor** (tel. 473943) watches over the Marina from 24 Quay St., and the **Steamer Bar,** 30-32 Quay St. (tel. 467699), plunges you deep into a nautical mood.

SIGHTS

North Down Visitors and Heritage Centre, Town Hall, Castle Park (tel. 271200), has a model of obliterated Bangor Abbey and much faded paraphernalia from Bangor's heyday as a seaside resort. The Jordan room displays an unrelated collection of Far Eastern art. Around the Heritage Centre are 129 acres of sometimes wooded, sometimes grassy **Castle Park.** Trail guides will steer you through the grounds and the arboretum (center open Tues.-Sat. 10:30am-4:30pm, Sun. 2-4:30pm; free). Nearby, 37-acre **Ward Park** (up Castle St. or Hamilton Rd. from Main St.) entices with tennis courts, bowling greens, and a cricket pitch. A string of lakes down the middle also harbors a wildlife sanctuary. The **North Down Coastal Path** forays for 15 mi. from Holywood through Bangor and Groomsport to Orlock Point. Along the way are abandoned WWII lookouts, Helen's Bay (a popular bathing spot), Crawfordsbum Country Park, an old fort with a massive gun, and a giant redwood. Bicycles are banned from the path. The region it covers is recognized for its colonies of Black Guillemots, which look like penguins. The Bangor-Holywood portion, more striking than the rest, should take 3½ hours to walk.

The path also passes through the picturesque village of Crawfordsbum, which boasts Ireland's oldest hotel. **The Old Inn** on Main St. dates back to 1614. (Open July-Aug. Tues.-Sat. 10:30am-5:30pm, Sun. 2-5:30pm; Sept.-June Tues.-Sat. 10:30am-4:30pm, Sun. 2-4:30pm. Free. Wheelchair accessible.) The **Crawfordsbum Country**

Park is one of the more popular forest parks in Northern Ireland, as it offers both coastal paths and green forests. The **Visitors Centre** spouts about the park's natural history (tel. 8533621; park open daily 8:30am-dark; center open daily 9am-5pm).

In mid-June, the week-long **Bangor and North Down Festival** brings in gymnasts and bands for events such as a masquerade barbecue. Deep-sea **fishing boats** (B.J. Meharg, Bangor Harbour Boats, tel. 455321) leave the marina for some good sport (June-Aug. Mon.-Sun. 3/day; Sept.-Oct. Sat.-Sun. 1/day; £5). The same boats make trips to Black Head (£8), Carrickfergus (£5), Orlock (£9), Copeland Islands (£5), and Rockport Reef (£5).

ARDS PENINSULA

Bounded on the west by tranquil Strangford Lough, the Ards Peninsula guards the rest of Co. Down from the agitated Irish Sea to its east. The Strangford Lough shore from Newtownards to Portaferry is crowded with wildlife preserves, historic houses, crumbling ruins, and spectacular lake views. On the eastern shore of the Ards, each wee fishing village seems tinier and twice as nice as the one before.

Ulsterbus leaves Laganside Station in Belfast to traverse the peninsula, stopping in almost every town. **Trains** roll no farther than Bangor. From the south, a **ferry** crosses frequently between Strangford and Portaferry (see **Portaferry,** p. 390). The Ards Peninsula can be seen efficiently and attractively by bike.

DONAGHADEE

The fishing villages which line the coast south of Bangor each consist of little more than one harbor and a few pubs each. The largest is **Donaghadee,** famous for its lifeboat and lighthouse. Donaghadee was Ulster's most important passenger port from the 17th century until 1849, when the mail boat began to patronize Larne. The composer Franz Liszt spent several days here waiting for a ship to bring him and his piano back to England. **Ulsterbus** drives to Donaghadee from Bangor (Mon.-Fri. 17/day, Sat.-Sun. 15/day; 20min.; £1.35) and from Belfast (19/day; 1hr.; £2.20).

A well-spent morning would include walks along the waterfront or a stroll to the still-operational first electrical lighthouse in Ireland. Past the lighthouse, the formerly communal potato fields called the **town commons** spread along the shore. An old ruined *motte* (MOTE) towers above the village. It held all the ammunition used to blast stone from the hill for building the harbor. In July and August, Quinton Nelson (tel. (01247) 883403) skips boats out to the **Copeland Islands,** a wildlife sanctuary just offshore (£4, children £2). Everyone in town knows about the **RNLB Sir Samuel Kelly.** In 1953, the *Samuel Kelly* rescued scores of passengers when the ferryboat *Princess Victoria,* sank just offshore on its way from Scotland to Belfast. The spruced-up boat is now displayed on Lemons Wharf. Donaghadee's **summer festival** arrives at the beginning of August. The week-long party includes dancing, kite-flying, abseiling, and lots of music.

A restful night in Donaghadee can be spent at **The Deans,** 52 Northfield Rd. (tel. (01247) 882204; £15/person) or at **Waterside B&B,** 11 New Rd. (tel. (01247) 888305), which isn't on the waterside (£15/person). Locals will entertain you at **The Moat Inn,** 102 Moat St. (tel. (01247) 883297); don't go swimming after their huge burger and chips (£3.20). **Grace Neill's Pub,** 35 High St., has been in business since 1611. This lucky pub has catered to Peter the Great and Oliver Cromwell.

South of Donaghadee, gnat-sized fishing villages buzz along the eastern shoreline. **Millisle, Ballywalter, Ballyhalbert, Portavogie, Cloughey,** and **Kearney** make good stops on an afternoon's drive, but none merit a special visit. **Portavogie** is charming, and **Millisle** is home to the **Ballycopeland Windmill.** A2 runs the length of the shore, where hitching a ride is reportedly easy.

MOUNTSTEWART & GREYABBEY

Five miles south of Newtownards on A20, roving pheasants greet you at **Mountstewart House and Gardens** (tel. (012477) 88387 or 88487). Held by a string of Marquesses of Londonderry, both house and garden are now National Trust property and worth a detour to see, if the Ulster Protestant Ascendancy intrigues you. Many of the trappings of this stately 18th-century manor are faded and tattered, but the regal portraits, gilded ceilings, chandeliers, and china still manage to give the place an air of grandeur. The 22 chairs in the formal dining room, purchased by the 3rd Marquess of Londonderry, once held the arses of Europe's greatest diplomats at the 1814 Congress of Vienna, which divvied up the post-Napoleonic continent. Outside, 85 acres of verdant grounds and manicured shrubbery wait to be explored. Lady Edith's **Dodo Terrace** houses an interesting menagerie of concrete animals. The ornate **Temple of the Winds,** a one-time banquet hall, tops a hill with a super view of Strangford Lough. To reach the temple, go out towards the main road, turn left, and walk about ¼ mi. (House open May-Sept. daily, including bank holidays, except Tuesdays, 1-6pm; April and Oct. Sat.-Sun. 1-6pm. Last tour starts at 5pm. Gardens open April-Sept. daily 10:30am-6pm; Oct. Sat.-Sun. 10:30am-6pm. Temple open same days as house 2-5pm. Admission £3 for house, garden, and temple; £1 for temple only.) To reach Mountstewart from Belfast, take the Portaferry bus from Laganside Station (19/day; 35min.; £1.90) and tell the driver to let you off at Mountstewart. Hitchers report success on the A20.

Two miles farther south on A20 lies miniscule **Greyabbey,** whose Main Street consists of four pubs, several antique stores, two art galleries, and a few other general shops, including the **post office**/news agent/gift shop. The ruins of the eponymous grey **Cistercian abbey** provide views of neighboring Grey Abbey House and the medieval "physick" (emphasis on "sick") herb garden. Only some foundations of the abbey and the walls of the main buildings, including the entire chapel, are left intact. The abbey was built in 1193 with the support of Affreca, wife of John de Couny and daughter of the King of Man, who vowed during a storm at sea to found a monastery if she survived. The abbey is known as the first church in Ireland to have been built in the Gothic rather than the typical Romanesque style. Turn left on the A20 to reach the abbey—it's at the end of the road. (Open April-Sept. Tues.-Sat. 10am-7pm, Sun. 2-7pm. Admission £1, seniors and children 50p. Wheelchair accessible.) The Portaferry bus from Belfast also stops in Greyabbey outside the **police station,** Main St. (tel. (012477) 88222).

PORTAFERRY

A relatively untouristed but expanding fishing village at the tip of the Ards Peninsula, Portaferry grabs its moment in the sun each year during the **Galway Hookers Festival.** Fish nets, not fishnets, characterize these boating beauties, which hail from western Ireland. (Hookers are traditional boats with thick black hulls and billowing maroon sails.) The Galway Yacht Club sails a fleet to Portaferry every year for a big party on the fourth weekend in June. For general info, call the **Ards Borough Council Community Relations/Tourism** (tel. 812215); sailing info can be obtained from Herbie Taylor (tel. (01396) 610800). Book B&Bs months in advance.

The main non-hooker attraction is **Exploris,** The Ropewalk (tel. 28062). Located near the dock next to small, ruined Portaferry Castle, Exploris houses first-rate exhibits on local ocean and seashore ecology. Walk through the meandering, cave-like corridors to find open tanks teaming with friendly sea-rays and nurse sharks (one ray even comes when you call). (Aquarium open Mon.-Fri 10am-6pm, Sat. 11am-6pm, Sun. 1-6pm. Admission £3, students, seniors, and children £2.15.)

The Portaferry **tourist office** trailer parks by the ferry dock (open mid-June to Aug. Mon.-Fri. 10am-5pm, Sat. 11am-5pm, Sun. 1-5pm). **Ferries** (tel. (01396) 86637) leave from the waterfront at 15 and 45 minutes past the hour for a five-minute chug to Strangford. (Boats run Mon.-Fri. 7:45am-10:45pm, Sat. 8:15am-11:15pm, Sun. 9:45am-10:45pm; 60p, seniors and ages 5-12 30p.) **Buses** from Belfast stop at The Square in the center of town (19/day; 1½hr.; £4.10). **Northern Bank,** 1 The Square (tel. 28028; open Mon. 10am-12:30pm and 1:30-5pm, Tues.-Fri. 10am-12:30pm and 1:30-3:30pm; **ATM** accepts only VISA), and the **post office,** 2 The Square (tel. 28201; open Mon.-Tues. and Thurs.-Fri. 9am-1pm and 2-5:30pm, Wed. 9am-1pm, Sat. 9am-12:30pm) are both within spitting distance of the bus stop. The **postal code** is BT22 1LN. The **phone code** is a portly 012477.

A decidedly pleasant stay awaits you at the **Portaferry Barnholm Youth Hostel (YHANI),** 11 The Strand (tel. 29598), across the street from the ferry. Most rooms are private and have views of the Lough. Semiprivate bathrooms, a large kitchen, and a greenhouse-like dining room are pluses; thin walls and large groups of Irish on holiday may be minuses to backpackers. Reservations are recommended, since the hostel is often full (£9/person). Otherwise, skip to the B&Bs in the center of town. Just off The Square, **Home from Home B&B,** 15 High St. (tel. 28580), has enormous beds and poses as a tea house and café during the day (£15/person). The **Tara Caravan Park,** 4 Ballyquentin Rd. (tel. 28459), has space (£2.50/tent; open April-Oct.); campers can also settle across the Lough in **Strangford** (see below).

For cheap food during the day, try the Bewley's wannabe **Cafe Kim** (tel. 29696), just past the Square towards the water, where all meals are £1-4 (open Mon.-Sat. 9am-5pm, Sun. noon-5pm). Across the street, **The Cornstore** (tel. 29779) offers an unheralded combination of Greek, Middle Eastern, and Irish cuisine for those who can't decide between pita and soda bread at the **Spar Market** on High St. (Chicken kebab and rice £3.75; restaurant open Mon.-Thurs. 11am-9:30pm, Fri.-Sat. 11am-10pm, Sun 11am-8:30pm.) At night, everyone stumbles into the **Fiddler's Green,** Church St., where publican Frank leads rowdy traditional sing-alongs and welcomes live folk bands on some evenings. John Wayne paraphernalia mercilessly covers the walls of **The Quiet Man,** across the street. No pilgrim can miss Wayne's letter to the pub's former owner, which hangs in a massive frame. **M.E. Dunnigan's,** Ferry St., has the simple charm of every "smallest pub in Ireland," where everybody knows your name.

ST. PATRICK'S VALE

When St. Patrick's boat was swept into Strangford Lough in 432 AD, the beleaguered saint probably didn't imagine that the surrounding area would be revered. Reminders of the famous saint's footsteps lie all over this verdant coastal region. The towns in St. Patrick's Vale are also famous for sea activities, wildlife, lively festivals, and the mist-shrouded Mourne Mountains.

■ Strangford

This tiny Viking village hovers under screaming seagulls across the Lough from Portaferry, northeast of Downpatrick on A25, and north of Ardglass on A2. Apart from its friendly residents, the best thing about this village is its proximity to the Castle Ward National Trust property. Two miles from Strangford, **Castle Ward House and Estate** (tel. (01396) 881204), resides atop a hill. One wing of the house, built in 1768, is classical, which satisfied Lord Bangor; the other is Gothic, to please Lady Anne. They split up soon after the house was built. The 700-acre estate includes a temple, a tower house, a restored corn mill, and the **Strangford Lough Wildlife Centre.** From Strangford, head up A25 towards Downpatrick. Where the Lough curves to the right, head off the road onto a driveway between two white houses which will take you to a path along the water's edge. To reach Castle Ward House, you can either follow the path (dappled with sunlight on a nice day) or return to the road (only another ¼mi.), from which you approach the estate through its main gates and get a splendid view of the Lough. (House open May-Aug. Sun.-Wed. and Fri.-Sat. 1-6pm, April and Sept.-Oct. Sat.-Sun. 1-6pm. Estate and Grounds open year-round dawn to dusk. Wildlife Centre open July-Aug. Sun.-Wed. and Fri.-Sat., 2-6pm; April-June and Sept. Sat.-Sun. 2-6pm. Admission to House £2.60, to Estate £3.50/car (Nov.-March £1.75/car), free if you walk. Wildlife Centre free with estate admission.) In town, a small 16th-century tower house, with the dubious appellation of "Strangford Castle," stands near the ferry dock (key to gate available from Mr. Seed, 39 Castle St., 10am-7pm).

In Strangford, Peter McErlean welcomes you to red and white **Cuan Bar and Restaurant,** 6 The Square (tel. (01396) 881222), which cooks pub food during the day (lasagna £5; food served Mon.-Sun. 11:30am-11pm). Locals nurse their pints on curved velvet seats at **The Lobster Pot,** 11 The Square (tel. (01396) 881288). Another popular spot is **The Hole in the Wall Bar & Lounge** (tel. (01396) 881301) on the road to Downpatrick, run by a golf fanatic. The **Castle Ward Caravan Park** (tel. (01396) 881680), on the Castle Ward National Trust property, charges £7 per tent (open mid-March to Oct.; free showers). **Ferries** leave Strangford for Portaferry on the hour and half hour (Mon.-Fri. 7:30am-10:30pm, Sat. 8am-11pm, Sun. 9:30am-10:30pm). **Buses** for Downpatrick leave from in front of the ferry dock (9/day, 4/Sat.; 30min.; £1.60).

■ Downpatrick

Bustling pedestrians, loitering schoolchildren, and heavy traffic all merge on the streets of Downpatrick, Down's county seat and supposed burial place of St. Patrick. The country around it shelters religious and archaeological sites related to St. Patrick and links the rolling hills of Ards Peninsula to the more dramatic Mourne Mountains. Although the sights are interesting, the city itself does not have much to offer and merits only a day trip.

PRACTICAL INFORMATION

Tourist office: 74 Market St. (tel. 612233). Grab literature on all of Co. Down, useful maps, and souvenirs from the gift shop. Open Mon.-Sat. 9:30am-5pm, Sun. noon-5pm; July-Aug. open til 6pm daily.
Banks: Northern Banks, 58 Market St. (tel. 614011). Open Mon. 9:30am-5pm, Tues.-Fri. 10am-3:30pm; **ATM. Bank of Ireland,** 80-82 Market St. (tel. 612911). Open Mon.-Fri. 9:30am-4:30pm; **ATM.**
Buses: 83 Market St. (tel. 612384). Frequent buses to: Belfast (Mon.-Fri. 32/day, Sat. 15/day, Sun. 6/day; 45min.; £2.85); Newcastle (Mon.-Fri. 18/day, Sat. 12/day, Sun. 4/day; 20min.; £1.90); Strangford (Mon.-Fri. 9/day, Sat. 5/day; 25min.; £1.60).
Taxis: 96 Market St. (tel. 614515). Fun 10am-3:30am.
Pharmacy: Foy's Chemist, Irish St. (tel. 200321). Open Mon.-Fri. 9am-5:30pm.
Hospital: Downe Hospital (tel. 613311).
Emergency: Dial 999; no coins required. **Police:** Irish St. (tel. 613434 or 615011).
Post office: 65 Market St. (tel. 612061), inside the Supervalu near the meat. Open Mon.-Fri. 9am-5:30pm, Sat. 9am-12:30pm. **Postal code:** BT30 6LZ.
Phone code: 01396.

ACCOMMODATIONS, FOOD, & PUBS

It's preferable to stay the night in Portaferry or Newcastle, but if you find yourself stranded, head to Mrs. Murray's **Hillside,** 62 Scotch St. (tel. 613134), situated in a 200-year-old Georgian house in the town center (£14/person). **Mrs. Coburn,** 47 Roughal Park (tel. 612656), is also in town (open March-Sept.; single £15, double £28; German and French spoken). The closest campground is **Castle Ward,** near Strangford; the nearest hostel is in Newcastle.

Locals rave about **The Pepper Pot** on St. Patrick's Ave., which serves Ulster Frys for a low £1.50 from Monday to Saturday 9:30-11am. (Open Mon.-Tues. 9:30am-5:30pm, Wed. 9:30am-6pm, Thurs. 9:30am-6:30pm, Fri. 9:30am-7pm.) Bewley's coffee and sandwiches fuel discussion of the latest art exhibit at the **Down Arts Café,** Irish St. (tel. 615283). The staff provides info about activities in town (open Mon.-Sat. 10am-4:30pm). The take-away look of **Oakley Fayre's** bakery, 52 Market St. (tel. 612500) disguises a large coffee shop which serves pastries, sandwiches, and filled baked potatoes (open Mon.-Sat. 9am-5:15pm). Chinese food simmers on Scotch St. and English St.

Locals say that some of Downpatrick's pubs "become boxing rings" on the weekends. Turn the other cheek and head for the **De Courcy Arms,** 14 Church St. (tel. 612522), a student hangout with live music at least two nights per week. A stuffed ostrich head adorns the wall. Around the corner on English St., **Denvir's Hotel** (tel. 612012) has a bar that dates from 1642 and has housed the likes of Daniel O'Connell, Jonathan Swift, and the "founder" of Denver, CO. Proud proprietor Lenore Rae will tell you an earful of history and may make the Down delicacy, sloak (cooked seaweed). **Hootenanny,** 21 Irish St. (tel. 612222), has bands on Saturday, trad music on Sunday during meals, and stays open on Sunday until the last person drops.

SIGHTS

Just up the hill from the tourist office, **Down County Museum and Heritage Centre,** The Mall (tel. 615218), does regional history with unusual flair. Housed in the old jail, the museum introduces you to St. Patrick, a wax gang of 19th-century prisoners, and some voracious Vikings. (Open July to mid-Sept. Mon.-Fri. 11am-5pm, Sat.-Sun. 2-5pm; mid-Sept. to June Tues.-Fri. 11am-5pm, Sat. 2-5pm. Free.)

Next door to the museum, **Down Cathedral** (tel. 614922; Church of Ireland) sits atop the idyllic **Hill of Down,** originally a Bronze Age hill fort. The medieval illuminated *Book of Armagh,* now cohabiting with its cousins in the Trinity College library, claims that St. Patrick is buried in the hill. Rebuilt in 1818, the present cathedral incorporates stone carvings from its medieval predecessor into its own walls and houses the only private pew boxes still in use in Ireland. Although the cathedral's location is linked to the patron saint of Catholic Ireland, the church itself is Protestant and a Union Jack hangs in the foyer—a sadly ironic reminder of Ulster's intractable division. (Open Mon.-Fri. 10am-5pm, Sat.-Sun. 2-5pm, except during services. Free.) In the graveyard, a stone commemorates the so-called **grave of St. Patrick**—although Patrick is believed to be buried under the church, the stone has become legend. The **Down Arts Centre,** 2-6 Irish St. (tel. 615283), converted from the old Town Hall, hosts traveling exhibitions (free) and stages musical performances (mostly in autumn). (Open Mon., Fri. and Sat. 10am-4:30pm, Tues. and Thurs. 10am-10pm. Tickets £5, £2.50 for students.)

■ Near Downpatrick

St. Patrick dominates the landscape and mentality here, but 8000 years of continuous occupation has left the area a variety of remains. Most masterful and famous of all is **Saul** (2mi. northeast of Downpatrick on the Strangford Rd.), where St. Patrick is believed to have landed in the 5th century. After being converted to Christianity, the local chief gave Patrick a barn *(sabhal)* which later became the first parish church in Ireland (open daily until 6pm). 1932 replicas of an early Christian church and round tower commemorate the landing. Nearby, **St. Patrick's shrine** consists of a huge granite statue of the saint, bronze panels depicting his life, and an open-air temple. Even nonbelievers will appreciate the 360° view of the lough, the mountains, and, on a clear day, the Isle of Man. Located off Ardglass Rd. from Downpatrick, water in the **Struell Wells** runs through underground channels from one well to the next. Belief in their curative powers originated long before St. Patrick arrived on the scene with Christianity.

One mile from Downpatrick on the Belfast road lie the ruins of the **Cistercian Inch Abbey.** Founded in 1180 by John de Courcy, Down's Norman conqueror, little of the monastery remains. The site itself, on an island in the Quoile River, makes a dreamy backdrop for a picnic. (Open April-Sept. Tues.-Sat. 10am-7pm, Sun. 2-7pm. Admission 75p.) The **Quoile Pondage Nature Reserve,** off the Strangford Rd. (tel. (01396) 615520), offers hiking trails and picnic sites around a lake which was converted from salt to fresh water by human activity. The flood-control barrage also resulted in an unusual collection of vegetation, fish, and insect life. The Quoile Countryside Centre provides a plethora of information (open April-Sept. daily 11am-5pm; Oct.-March Sat.-Sun. 1-4:30pm).

■ Newcastle & the Mournes

On a sunny day with an ocean breeze, Newcastle is an attractive preliminary to Slieve Donard. When the weekend arrives, however, Newcastle becomes as peaceful as the New Jersey Shore as children crowd the streets and vacationers squabble over a place in the lines for waterslides. No one competes for places on the beach any more, since it is quite polluted and unsafe for swimming. Anyone looking for natural beauty heads up into the mountains or north along the untrammeled dunes. Situated at the foot of Slieve Donard, the highest peak in Northern Ireland, Newcastle is by far the best base from which to explore the hypnotic Mourne Mountains.

The 15 rounded peaks of the Mourne Mountains sprawl across the southeastern corner of Northern Ireland. Volcanic activity spewed five different kinds of granite onto the mountains 75 million years ago, resulting today in a rainbow of rocky color. No road penetrates the center of the mountains, leaving walkers a welcome solitude. The 15 peaks form a skewed figure-eight with two large valleys in the middle. The larger of these holds **Ben Crom** and **Silent Valley,** reservoirs built in the early 1900s to supply water to Belfast, and still in use.

ORIENTATION & PRACTICAL INFORMATION

The main road in town stretches along the waterfront, changing names from Main St. to Central Promenade to South Promenade. Those who thumb a ride stand at either end of the main road: south for Kilkeel or north for Downpatrick.

Tourist Office: 10-14 Central Promenade (tel. 22222), about halfway down the street. Free map and visitor's guide of Newcastle's complex street plan. Open June-Aug. Mon.-Sat. 10am-5pm, Sun. 2-6pm; Sept.-May daily 2-6pm.

Banks: AIB/First Trust Bank, 28/32 Main St. (tel. 23476). Open Mon. 9:30am-5pm, Tues.-Fri. 10am-3:30pm; **ATM. Northern Bank,** 60 Main St. Open Mon. 9:30am-5pm, Tues.-Fri. 10am-3:30pm. **Ulster Bank** is also on Main St.

Buses: 5-7 Railway St. (tel. 22296), at the end of Main St., away from the mountains. Buses run to: Belfast (Mon.-Sat. 21/day, Sun. 13/day; 70min.; £3.65), Downpatrick (Mon.-Fri. 19/day, Sat. 14/day, Sun. 5/day; 40min.; £1.90), Kilkeel (Mon.-Fri. 18/day, Sat. 17/day, Sun. 7/day; 40min.; £1.95), Newry (Mon.-Sat. 4/day, Sun. 2/day; 30min.; £3.95).

Taxi: Donard Cabs (tel. 24100 or 22823).

Bike Rental: Wiki Wiki Wheels, 10B Donard St. (tel. 23973). £6.60/day, £30/wk. They also have panniers. Driver's license or credit card deposit. Open Mon.-Sat. 9am-6pm, Sun. 2:15-6pm.

Pharmacy: G. Maginn, 9 Main St. (tel. 22923). Open Mon.-Sat. 9am-6pm. **Chemist,** 49 Central Promenade (tel. 23248). Open Mon.-Sat. 9am-6pm.

Camping Equipment: Hill Trekker, 115 Central Promenade (tel. 23842). Trail maps, tips for hiking in the Mournes, info about guided tours, and hiking boots (£2.50/day, deposit £10). Open daily 10am-5:30pm.

Emergency: Dial 999 (including mountain rescue); no coins required.

Police: South Promenade (tel. 23583).

Post Office: 35 Central Promenade (tel. 22418). Open Mon.-Wed. and Fri. 9am-12:30pm and 1:30-5:30pm, Thurs. and Sat. 9am-12:30pm. **Postal Code:** BT33 ODJ. **Phone code:** 013967.

ACCOMMODATIONS

B&Bs in this summer resort town are relatively expensive; luckily there are two quality hostels. Of the area's numerous **campsites,** the Tollymore Forest Park is probably the most scenic, but the mountains themselves are a free and legal alternative, especially if you like sleeping under the stars without electricity or water.

Newcastle Youth Hostel (YHANI/HI), 30 Downs Rd. (tel. 22133), a scone's throw from the Percy French Bar. Clean, spacious, central, and on the waterfront. The helpful, amiable proprietor will show you the way to the well-furnished kitchen. The only drawbacks are the short beds and scarcity of showers. Lockout 11am-5pm. £6.50/person, under 18 £5.50. Free laundry. MC/Access, Visa.

Glenada YWCA, 29 South Promenade (tel. 22402), at the far end of town. 8-bunk rooms in a posh building with lots of common space and balconies overlooking the sea. No kitchen. Often filled with groups, so call a week in advance. Ask for the backpackers' rate (£8/person, w/breakfast £10/person). Family suite w/kitchen also available for 6 people (£25). Wheelchair accessible.

Castlebridge House, 2 Central Promenade (tel. 23209). Understandably popular, with cozy rooms, an ideal location overlooking the bay, and a fabulous sitting room. Mrs. Lynch will even give you the run of her kitchen at night. £14/person.

Drumrawn House, Central Promenade (tel. 26847), about a 10-min. walk from the bus station. Georgian townhouse on the water for £14/person.

Glenside Farm House, 136 Tullybrannigan Rd. (tel. 22628), a long, if lovely, 1½-mi. walk from town (take Bryansford Rd. and look for signs). Clean, simple rooms. Small single £11. Double £20.

Arundel, 23 Bryansford Rd. (tel. 22232). Just off the southern end of Central Promenade, with a huge lounge, comfy beds, loads of flowers, and a mountain view. £15/person.

Camping: Tollymore Forest Park, 176 Tullybrannigan Rd. (tel. 22428), a 2-mi. walk along A2 (hitchers report it's not hard to get a ride). Excellent facilities include a café with delicious doughnuts, showers, a wildfowl exhibit and arboretum, and 584 hectares of well-marked walks and gardens. Oh, and a well-lit camping area with electricity. May-Sept. £9.50/tent; Oct-April £6.

FOOD & PUBS

The nougat-like density of take-aways, candy stores, and ice cream shops on the waterfront could keep you on a permanent sugar high. **Maud's,** at Castlebridge Court, 139 Main St., flaunts Orgasmic Pooh Bear (honeycomb and vanilla) ice cream. It also serves up soup and sandwiches (open Mon.-Fri. 11am-10:30pm, Sat.-Sun. 11am-11:30pm). Several other bakeries have similarly light fare.

The Strand, 53-55 Central Promenade (tel. 23472). Don't let the ice cream stand/ bakery exterior fool you—inside a proper restaurant serves the usual Irish fare (lasagne and chips £4). Open Mon.-Sat. 9am-5:30pm, Sun. noon-5pm.

Central Park Restaurant/Nite Club (tel. 22487), on the south end of Central Promenade, prepares filling meals at reasonable prices. Live bands perform on weekends, and the night club is open until 1am.

Cygnet Coffee Shop, Savoy Lane (tel. 24758), just off Main St. behind the modern Catholic Church. Coffee shop fare with particularly good taste (croissants or pancakes 75p). Open Mon.-Sat. 10am-5:30pm, Sun. 11:30am-5:30pm.

Newcastle is not the place for a quiet drink. Popular (and packed) spots include the **Anchor Bar,** 9 Bryansford Rd. (tel. 23344), which draws a sociable crowd of mixed ages inside its triangular stained-glass windows, and **Quinn's,** 62 Main St. (tel. 26400), where Wellingtons hang from the ceiling. For a classier and dearer drink, head to **Percy French,** in the Slieve Donard Hotel at the northern end of the beach (tel. 23175). Before he became a bar, Mr. French wrote a popular ballad about the Mourne Mountains. He also wrote the lines, "Remember me is all I ask, and yet, if remembrance prove a task, forget."

SIGHTS: THE MOURNE MOUNTAINS

Before heading for the hills, stop at the **Mourne Countryside Centre,** 91 Central Promenade (tel. (013967) 24059), where the friendly and knowledgeable staff will help you plan your hike. *Mourne Mountain Walks* (£5), which maps 10 good day hikes, is sold here. Those planning to stay in the Mournes overnight ought to buy the

Mourne County Outdoor Pursuits Map (£4), a detailed topographical map. The Mourne Countryside Centre offers guided walks on Mondays in the summer. (Transportation costs £1-2. Meet at 10am sharp at the Centre, but it's best to call ahead.) The center will photocopy parts of maps for day hikes (open Mon.-Fri. 9am-5pm, Sat.-Sun. noon-5pm; winter hours may vary). If the center is closed, ask for maps at the tourist office and advice at **Hill Trekker** (see **Practical Information,** p. 394). Seasoned hikers looking for company might want to join the **Mourne Rambling Group** (tel. (013967) 24315), which sends groups into the Mournes each Sunday. Shuttlebuses run between Silent Valley and Ben Crom (July-Aug. Mon.-Sat. 11:15am-6pm). **Ulsterbus'** *Mourne Rambler* makes three trips through the mountains to drop off hikers (July-Aug. Mon.-Sat. drop-off at 9:30 and 10:45am, pick-up at 3:30pm; £3 return). This bus is the best way to get to the trailheads even if you have a car, because it allows you to begin and end your hike in different places. Ulsterbus also gives one-hour tours of the mountains that leave from Belfast (tel. (01232) 333000).

The **Mourne Wall** encircles the interior of the mountains just short of the peaks. Built from 1904 to 1923 to mark the catchment area for the reservoirs below, the wall is a favored hike. Following the length of the 22-mi. wall takes a strenuous eight hours; many people break it up with a night under the stars. Wilderness **camping** is legal and popular. Common spots include the north end of Ben Crom reservoir and the shores of Lough Shannagh and the Trassy River. Hare's Gap and the shore of Blue Lough at Annalong are also good places to pitch. Remember to bring warm clothing as the mountains get cold and windy at night.

The **Brandy Pad,** an old path running from Bloody Bridge (2mi. south of Newcastle) right across the mountains, is also frequented; it was used in the 1800s to smuggle brandy and tobacco from the Isle of Man. Hiking along the Glen River is an attractive option. Locals swim in the crystal-clear (and cold) tiny pools. The Mourne's highest peak, **Slieve Donard** (1800ft.) towers above Newcastle, challenging those below to a tough but manageable day hike to its summit (5-hr. return). The record for running up and down is fabled to be a hard-to-believe 45 minutes. The peak next door, **Slieve Commedagh,** ("the mountain of watching") is 2500 ft. high. It, too, is best approached from Newcastle. To reach either peak, head to the **Donard Park** on the corner of Central Promenade and Bryansford Rd. Follow the dirt path at the back of the carpark carefully (it crosses 2 bridges) and you will hit the Mourne Wall. At the wall, turn left for Slieve Donard, right for Slieve Commedagh. A Mountain Rescue team stands by for emergencies. Those with cars can follow the road to **Spelga Dam** (marked as you leave Newcastle) for sublime views of the Mournes.

■ Nearby Forest Parks

Two forest parks, managed by the Dept. of Agriculture for timber production and recreation, are just a hop, skip, and a jump from Newcastle. **Tollymore Forest Park** lies just two miles west of town at 176 Tullybrannigan Rd. (tel. (013967) 22428). A network of marked trails and Ireland's rare Strawberry Tree, in the arboretum, are highlights. The Strawberry Tree, also found in Spain, grows wild in Ireland and produces edible but very sour berries which turn from white to red. Trails range from one to nine miles in length; the walks will afford glimpses of diverse wildlife including deer, foxes, badgers, and if you're particularly quiet, otters. The "Rivers Trail" hike (3mi.) encompasses most of the park and is highly recommended, as is Salmon Leap Falls. For those with stamina, the aptly named "Long Haul Trail" (8mi.) encircles the Park's borders. The park is well-equipped with a campground (see **Newcastle: camping,** p. 395), visitors center, café, and arboretum (open year-round daily 10am-sunset; £2.50/car). Take the Bryansford bus and ask to be let off at Tollymore (buses run Mon.-Sat. 6/day, Sun. 2/day). **Murlough National Nature Reserve,** on the Dundrum Rd. (tel. (013967) 51467), has sand dunes, heath, and woodlands (£1.50/car; beach and walks always open). Since Newcastle Bay is now so polluted, Murlough is the closest beach safe for swimming. Take the Downpatrick or Belfast bus and get off at Murlough. (Visitor center open June to mid-Sept. daily 10am-5pm; guided walks for observation of seabirds and seals.)

Farther north, **Castlewellan Forest Park,** The Grange, Castlewellan (tel. (013967) 78664), spreads itself out in the hills just north and east of the Mournes. (From Newcastle, take A50 past its junction with A25.) Inside the park, which claims to house the finest arboretum in Ireland, a Scottish baronial castle overlooks a small lake surrounded by Castlewellan Gold, the park's unique species of cypress. The castle itself is now a Christian Conference Centre and off-limits to the public, but the Park alone is impressive. The tropical birdhouse offers avian thrills. The Sculpture Trail creatively displays sculptures made of natural materials. The lake overflows with trout; fishing permits are available April to mid-October (call the park for info). For £9 you can pitch a tent here too—but only if you've booked at least two weeks in advance. (Oct.-Easter £4.50. Call Mon.-Fri. 8:30am-4:30pm for info and site booking. Park open daily 10am-sunset. £2.20/car, no charge on foot.) **Buses** run from Newcastle to Castlewellan (Mon.-Fri. 26/day, Sat. 20/day, Sun. 6/day; 10min.; 90p).

Those interested in outdoor sessions in canoeing, kayaking, archery, orienteering, or rock-climbing should contact the Glen River YMCA (tel. (013967) 23172) for prices and information. Unfortunately, the center no longer provides accommodation for campers or backpackers. Less avid outdoor enthusiasts might prefer a picnic in Donard Park, just off Central Promenade, at the foot of the Mournes.

■ Carlingford Lough

KILKEEL

Kilkeel holds Northern Ireland's largest fishing fleet but offers little else than fish. For a view of the harbor, avoid the obvious but drab Harbour Drive; instead, walk down Kockchree Ave. (off Greencastle St.), and turn left onto the Cliff Walk. Kilkeel is a staunchly Protestant town; it's best to avoid political discussion altogether. Inland, the Mournes continue to stun travelers with their savage beauty. The **tourist office,** 6 Newcastle St. (tel. (016937) 62525), is open Mon.-Sat. 10am-5pm.

Slieve Binnian and Silent Valley are the area attractions; to reach them, head towards Newcastle on A2. About one mile from Kilkeel, take a left at the Aircraft Furnishings Co. (you'll see British and American flags in front). From here, hike 3 mi. uphill to the park. Hitchers report a good amount of success, and much less exhaustion than walkers, on the hill. The summit of **Slieve Binnian** (2400ft.), a good dayhike, is renowned for its scenic views. **Silent Valley,** a well-managed park with an information center, expensive café, and craft shop, is the site of Belfast's reservoir (center open year-round daily 10am-6:30pm). From Kilkeel, head straight out the Moyadd road to the park. From there, a 3-mi. path runs up the side of Silent Valley to Ben Crom reservoir. In July and August, you can travel this route by shuttle bus (May-June and Sept. weekends only; £1.50). (Reservoir grounds open June-Sept. daily 10am-6:30pm; Oct.-April 10am-4pm. £3/car.)

If you're stuck in Kilkeel for the night, **Heath Hall,** 160 Moyadd Rd. (tel. (016937) 62612), is by far the best choice. Tea, sandwiches, advice on seeing Co. Down, and limitless kindness are some of the benefits of staying in this alluring farmhouse (£15/person). Ms. McGlue will pick up lost or tired travelers in town, but call ahead.

WARRENPOINT

Farther along the coast on the A2, the pretty harbor town of **Warrenpoint** sports both an idyllic, isolated inlet and a bustling waterfront. On a sunny day, you can sit on the sea wall for hours and watch colorful spinnakers float across the horizon. Pick up tourist info and free maps at the **Town Hall** (tel. 52256) on Church St. opposite The Square. The helpful and well-informed staff will be glad to assist you (open Mon.-Fri. 9am-5pm). Get money at **Ulster Bank,** 2 Charlotte St. (tel. 52323; open Mon.-Fri. 9:30am-4:30pm). Warrenpoint has a sporadic summertime ferry service to Omeath on the Cooley Peninsula (in the Republic). **Red Star Passenger Ferry** (tel. 74088) is a great tradition (operates June-Sept. 1:30-6pm from Marine Parade weather permitting; £2 return). Carlingford Lough cruises are also available on the **Maiden of Mourne,** an enclosed water coach, from Easter to mid-September (tel. 72950; weather permitting; £3). **Stewarts Cycles,** 7 Osbourne Mews (tel. 73565), off Marine Parade, has bikes (£6/day, £25/week; open Mon.-Tues. and Thurs.-Fri. 10am-noon and 2-6pm, Sat. 10am-1pm and 2-6pm). The **post office,** 9 Church St. (tel. 52225; open Mon.-Tues. and Thurs. 8:30am-5:30pm, Wed. 8:30am-1pm, Fri. 9am-5:30pm, Sat. 9am-12:30pm), will hold mail if you mark it with the **postal code,** BT34 3HN. Warrenpoint's **phone code** mourns 016937.

   Mrs. Joan O'Hare, 6 St. George's St. (tel. 73265), proffers rooms across the street from the park. Mrs. O'Hare knows the latest on the Warrenpoint pub scene and how to help a hangover (£14/person). A mile out of town, **Firóne,** 74 Upper Dromore Rd. (tel. 74293; Duke St. turns into Upper Dromore Rd.), keeps homemade jam in the kitchen and potted plants in the bathroom (£16/person). **Glen Rosa B&B,** 4 St. George's St. South (tel. 72589), is central but dark (£15; open Feb.-Oct.).

   Diamonds Restaurant, The Square (tel. 52053), offers pasta, burgers (£2.50), seafood, and desserts. Upstairs seats have a good view of the Lough. Chicken Kiev is the house specialty for £5.25 (open Mon.-Thurs. 10am-7pm, Fri.-Sat. 10am-10pm, Sun. 12:30-10pm). The closest you'll get to a diner atmosphere is the **Central Cafe** (tel. 72904), across from the tourist office. Locals talk and read papers at shadowed tables (open Mon.-Fri. 8:30am-5:30pm, Sat. 9am-5pm, Sun. noon-5pm). Warrenpoint's lively nightlife satisfies all ages. On weekend nights, **Mac's Bars,** 1-2 Marine Parade (tel. 52082), caters to the young and the restless. Check out the Ode to Mac's inscribed on the outside wall which promotes the joys of various liquors. Around the corner, **The Crown,** The Square, with its stone floors and Guinness memorabilia, is equally popular. **Club Cherie,** Marine Parade, is the summer disco.

   Warrenpoint and the surrounding area host several lively festivals during the summer. Thousands of people gather here to witness the **Maiden of the Mournes Festival** in August; maidens from Ireland and some parts of the U.S. gather to display their personalities and talents. This event is preceded by the **Fiddler's Green Festival** in **Rostrevor** (3mi. from Warrenpoint along A2). Musicians from Ireland and abroad present original compositions. Rostrevor is also known for Kilbroney Park (more wildlife) and Rostrevor Forest, which rises rapidly to the altitude of 1600 ft.

ARMAGH & AROUND

The best time to visit Armagh is during apple blossom season in May, when the surrounding countryside, known as the "orchard of Ireland," is covered in pink. The **Apple Blossom Festival** brings a number of events to the city and culminates in a lavish May Ball. County Armagh's other population centers, **Craigavon** and **Portadown** (a standoff here sparked intense Orange Day rioting in 1996; see **History and Politics,** p. 366) near Lough Neagh, are industrial centers of little interest to tourists. South Armagh is a Republican stronghold (the IRA men responsible for the February 1996 Canary Wharf bombing in London were from the region), yet locals and tourist officials stress that the area is safe for visitors. Armagh boasts several verdant recreational forest areas, the largest being **Slieve Gullion Forest Park.** Call the Forest Officer (tel. (01693) 38284) for more information.

■ Armagh

According to legend, St. Patrick chose Armagh as his base. Since then, Armagh (pop. 52,000) has been revered as the ecclesiastical capital of Ireland. Deriving from *Ard Macha* ("Macha's Height"), the city was named after the legendary pagan Queen Macha. But the city, with its magnificent cathedrals, has been and remains the administrative center for both the Catholic Church in Ireland and the Protestant Church of Ireland. Armagh's vibrant history, which stretches from prehistoric activity at nearby Navan Fort to associations with Jonathan Swift, has been partially dimmed by sectarian violence in the past decade. Tourism picked up during the ceasefire, but, as this year's riots demonstrated, visitors should be cautious around Orange Day. On March 17, people come from far and near to celebrate St. Patrick's patronage of the city.

ORIENTATION & PRACTICAL INFORMATION

Armagh's street plan is confusing. Head to the clearly signposted **tourist office** on English St. for a free map. English St., Thomas St., and Scotch St. define the city center. Just to the east lies **The Mall,** a long grassy park which used to be a race course, but was converted into an innocent park when betting and racing were deemed inappropriate to the sanctity of an ecclesiastical city. Just west of the city center, the two cathedrals sit on neighboring hills—the Catholic Cathedral lifts two neo-Gothic spires, the Church of Ireland a medieval-looking tower. While **buses** stop along both sides of The Mall, most of them leave from the bus station on Mall West.

Tourist Office: Old Bank Building, 40 English St. (tel. 521800). From the bus station, turn left, and walk past The Mall to the roundabout. Turn left up the hill onto College St. and then take the first left. The tourist office is 15yd. ahead on the right, in the large building with the sign for St. Patrick's Trian. Pick up the *Essential Guide for Visitors to Armagh* and a wealth of other info. Open Mon.-Sat. 9am-5pm, Sun. 1-5pm.

Bank: Northern Bank, 78 Scotch St. (tel. 522004). Open Mon. 9:30am-5pm, Tues.-Fri. 10am-3:30pm.

Buses: Mallview Terrace, Mall West (tel. 522266). To: Belfast (Mon.-Fri. 20/day, Sat. 15/day, Sun. 8/day; 65min; £4.20); Enniskillen (Mon.-Sat. 3/day; 2hr.; £5.10).

Bike Rental: Brown's Bikes, 21A Scotch St. (tel. 522782; £5/day).

Pharmacy: J. W. Gray, corner of Russell and English St. Open Mon.-Sat. 9am-6pm.

Hospital: Tower Hill, off College Hill, tel. 522341.

Emergency: dial 999, no coins required. **Police:** Newry Rd., tel. 523311.

Post Office: 31 Upper English St. (tel. 510313). Mail is held at 46 Upper English St., just across the street (tel. 522856). Open Mon.-Fri. 9am-5:30pm, Sat. 9am-7pm.

Postal Code: BT61 7BA.

Phone Code: 01861.

ACCOMMODATIONS

Armagh has few B&Bs, but they are seldom full. **Padua Guest House,** 63 Cathedral Rd. (tel. 522039) is just past the Catholic Cathedral (#63 is next door to #10). Kind Mrs. O'Hagen and her large doll collection greet guests with a cup of tea. Watch color TV in some rooms; hear the loud cathedral bells in all of them (£12/person). Mrs. McRoberts will kindly welcome you to the large and stately **Desart Guest House,** 99 Cathedral Rd. (tel. 522387). The rooms are floral and clean (£14-16/person). Mrs. Mckenna's **Clonhugh Guest House,** College Hill (tel. 522693), north of the tip of The Mall, is so full of bric-a-brac that you may not be able to sit, but her bedrooms are comfortable (£15/person). **Gosford Forest Park,** off A28 (tel. 551277; ranger tel. 552169), has room for tents 7 mi. southeast of Armagh. The park includes a castle, old walled garden, poultry sheds, and miles of nature trails. The Market Hill bus will drop you within walking distance of the park. (£2/car, £1/person; **camping** £9/2-person tent, Oct.-Easter £5. Park open daily 10am-sunset).

FOOD & PUBS

The lack of restaurants that are open late may be a result of formerly soldier-strewn streets. What little Armagh has for restaurants is scattered across English St. and Scotch St. The best bet may be to pick up supplies at **Emerson's,** 57 Scotch St., or at **Shambles Market** (tel. 528192), across from the Catholic Cathedral (Tues. and Fri. 9:30am-5pm), for a picnic on The Mall or near the old Friary. Sleek **Fat Sam's,** the

Shambles (tel. 525555), offers a dazzling variety of cheap subs (curried chicken with pineapple and sweet corn, £1.60; open Mon.-Fri. 8:45am-6pm, Sat. 9:15am-5pm). **The Basement Cafe** (tel. 52431) sits under the Armagh Film House on English St. and serves el cheapo meals inside its baby blue walls (margherita pizza £3; open Mon.-Sat. 9am-7pm). **Rainbow Restaurant,** 13 Upper English St. (tel. 525391), serves standard lunch fare, buffet style (open Mon.-Sat. 8:30am-5:30pm). At **Hester's Place,** 12a English St. (tel. 522374), the unpretentious enjoy cheap, juicy burgers (£1.60; open Mon.-Sat. 9am-5pm). **The Station Bar,** 3 Lower English St. (tel. 523731), looks like a dive but is one of the most popular pubs in town, with trad on Tuesdays and Thursdays. **Harry Hoots',** on Railway St. (tel. 522103), is another happening hangout. The **Northern Bar,** across the street (tel. 527315 or 527316), provides live entertainment and dancing (3 nights/week), and hoots right back.

SIGHTS

Armagh's twin cathedrals are the city's pride and joy. **The Church of Ireland Cathedral of St. Patrick** (tel. 523142) is a 19th-century restoration of a 17th-century structure that was based on a 13th-century plan. Graves of famous dead people include that of the great Irish King, Brian Ború. (Open April-Sept. daily 10:30am-5pm; Nov.-March daily 10:30am-4pm. Services Sun. at 10, 11am, and 3:15pm. Tours June-Aug. Mon.-Sat. 11:30am and 2:30pm. Free.) Across town, the **Catholic Church of St. Patrick** raises its heady spires from Cathedral Rd. Opened in 1873 to a crowd of 20,000 spectators, the cathedral's imposing exterior and exquisite mosaic interior are marred only by the ultra-modern granite sanctuary, which appears to be a combination of pagan and martian design. (Open daily 9am-5pm. Services Sun. at 9, 10:30am, and noon. Free.)

In the center of town, **St. Patrick's Trian** (tel. 527808) shares a building with the tourist office. Most of the exhibits emphasize St. Patrick's role in Armagh. *The Armagh Story* is a walk-through display and audio-visual presentation in which Vikings, priests, and pagan warriors relate the lengthy history of the town. A smaller, but well-done display recreates Swift's *Land of Lilliput.* (Open April-Sept. Mon.-Sat. 10am-5:30pm, Sun. 1-6pm; Oct.-March Mon.-Sat. 10am-5pm, Sun. 2-5pm. Admission £3.25, students £2.40.) Up College Hill north of The Mall is the **Armagh Observatory,** founded in 1790 by Archbishop Robinson (of Palace Demesne fame). Would-be astronomers can observe the modern weather station and a refractory telescope dating from 1885. The Robinson Dome provides self-guided tours (grounds open Mon.-Fri. 9:30am-4:30pm). Celestial wonders await in the **Planetarium,** College Hill (tel. 523689). Booking ahead is strongly recommended, as seating is limited to 100 people. (Open April-June Mon.-Fri. 10am-5pm, 3pm show, Sat.-Sun. 1:30-5pm, 2 and 3pm shows; July-Aug. Mon.-Fri. 10am-5pm, shows hourly 11am-4pm, Sat.-Sun. 1:30-5pm, 2 and 3pm shows; Sept.-March Mon.-Fri. 10am-5pm, 3pm show, Sat. 1:30-5pm, 2 and 3pm shows. Free.)

At the **Armagh County Museum** (tel. 523070) on the east side of The Mall, undiscriminating historians have stuffed a panoply of 18th-century objects—old wedding dresses, pictures, stuffed birds, jewelry, and militia uniforms—into huge wooden cabinets (open Mon.-Sat. 10am-1pm and 2-5pm; free). On Friary Rd. south of the town center, the ruins of the 13th-century **Franciscan Friary,** the longest-standing friary in Ireland, occupy a peaceful green corner of the **Palace Demesne.** The palace and its chapel and stables were built by the 18th-century Archbishop of Armagh, Richard Robinson, in an effort to rebuild the entire city. Although closed to the public, the palace's stables have been converted into a high-class tourist attraction. **The Palace Stables Heritage Centre** (tel. 529629), puts on a slick multi-media show about "A Day in the Life" of the closed palace—July 23, 1776. (Open April-Sept. Mon.-Sat. 10am-7pm, Sun. 1-7pm; Oct.-March Mon.-Sat. 10am-5pm, Sun. 2-5pm. Admission £3, students £2.50.) Take a peek at an open first edition of *Gulliver's Travels,* covered with Swift's own scrawled marginalia, at the **Armagh Public Library,** Abbey St. (tel. 523142; open Mon.-Fri. 10am-12:30pm and 2-4pm).

Queen Macha

For 800 years, Navan Fort served the Kings of Ulster as their capital. Legend holds that the founding and the name of the fort, *Emain Macha,* are derived from a story concerning the pagan Queen Macha. The queen raced and defeated King Conchobar's horses, after which she collapsed and died while giving birth to twins (*emain,* in Irish). In honor of the tragedy and in respect for the successful and powerful queen, the name of the Ulster king's capital was attributed to the twins of Queen Macha. As retribution for Conchobar's role in her death, his warriors were cursed to suffer Macha's birth pangs in the future. The curse took effect when Queen Medbh of Connacht invaded Ulster in search of King Conchobar's bull (see **Legends and Folktales,** p. 69). The king's soldiers began to suffer Macha's birth pangs, rendering them unable to fight. Fortunately, King Conchobar's one particularly strong and immune warrior, Cú Chulainn, fought and defeated each of Medbh's warriors one by one, thus saving Ulster from ruin.

■ Near Armagh

NAVAN FORT

On the outskirts of Armagh, **Navan Fort,** also called *Emain Macha* (AHM-win maka), was the capital of the Kings of Ulster for 800 years. The whole area is an archaeological site of primary importance to historians of Iron Age Ireland. The legendary founding of the fort is attributed to Queen Macha (see **Queen Macha,** p. 401), though it is also associated with St. Patrick, who probably chose Ard Macha as a base for Christianity because of its relative proximity to this pagan stronghold. The **Navan Centre** (tel. (01861) 525550), built deep into the hill, presents a 70-minute program of films and interactive exhibits on the factual archeological evidence of the hills and the legends associated with the site. The powerful and often violent stories about this, the first capital of Ulster, may prompt you to explore the fort itself (¼mi. from the Centre). Few parts of the earthworks are still visible and the overgrown fort mount may seem disappointingly lacking in evidence of human civilization, but the view is expansive. The center and fort are located on the Killylea Rd. (A28), 2 mi. west of town. (Centre open July-Aug. Mon.-Sat. 10am-7pm, Sun. 11am-7pm; April-June and Sept. Mon.-Sat. 10am-6pm, Sun. 11am-6pm; Oct.-March Mon.-Fri. 10am-6pm, Sat. 11am-6pm, Sun. noon-6pm. Admission £3.75, students £2.50; fort free and always open.) Nearby, artificial ritual pools called the **King's Stables** and **Loughnashade** (Lake of the Treasures) are the receptacles where the ancient Celts dumped everything from gold jewelry to iron weapons to a human head, presumably as offerings to the gods. The grisly remains are no longer visible, however, and the pools themselves aren't spectacular.

LOUGH NEAGH & OXFORD ISLAND

Legend has it that a giant scooped a heap of prime Ulster real estate out of the ground and chucked it into the sea, creating the Isle of Man and Lough Neagh. The U.K.'s largest lake sits smack in the center of Northern Ireland's industrial heartland, touching five of the North's six counties. Birdwatching, water-skiing, and various aquatic activities are just about the only amusements in the towns around the Lough; its shores are best seen as daytrips from Belfast or Armagh.

On the southeast shore of the Lough, the **Lough Neagh Discovery Centre,** Oxford Island National Nature Reserve, Craigavon (tel. (01762) 322205), contains acres of wooded parkland for exploration, with or without a guided tour. Boat rides to the islands run several times daily. Audio-visual displays in the center itself detail the lake's ecosystem and wildlife. (Open April-Sept. daily 10am-7pm; Oct.-March Wed.-Sun. 10am-5pm. Last admission 1hr. before closing. Admission £2.) The lakeshore hosts hundreds of bird species every year. The **Kinnego Caravan Park,** Kinnego Marina, Lurgan (tel. (01762) 327573), receives campers (£6/2-person tent).

Antrim & Derry

North of lively Belfast, smoke stacks cease to obstruct views of the sea as stodgy Larne gives way to the wooded mountains of the nine Glens of Antrim, stomping grounds of the Ulaid dynasty for over a thousand years. Today, tiny, non-dynastic towns nestle into a coastline dotted with beaches. The towns are linked by a flat road that is a cyclist's paradise. Farther west, natural formations become staggering and inspire contemplation of the massive forces that caused the Causeway. The garish lights and lively atmospheres of Portrush and Portstewart, however, will cause light-headedness rather than introspection. The northern coast culminates at Derry, the North's second largest city whose turbulent history matches the dramatic coast. The inland woods and country parks provide a welcome change from the stormy seas and looming rocks. The Sperrin Mountains are worth days of exploration.

■ Larne

The **ferries** that depart for Scotland from here are the only worthwhile reason to pass through industrial Larne, but now that the Hoverspeed SeaCat goes directly to Belfast, few pedestrians will want to use the Larne ferry (see **By Ferry**, p. 31). **P&O Ferries** (tel. (01574) 274321) operates from Larne. Travelers should arrive 45 minutes early, as ferries often leave early and, when they don't, they're often full. **Larne Town** lies 15 minutes down the coast and inland from the harbor. From the harbor, the first right after the ferry port becomes Curran Rd. after the bridge and then turns into Main St. when it reaches town.

Practical Information The **tourist office,** Narrow Gauge Rd. (tel. 260088), has loads of info, a free town map, and a good geological and historical exhibition (open July-Sept. Mon.-Wed. 9am-5pm, Thurs.-Fri. 9am-7:30pm, Sat. 9am-6pm, Sun. 11am-6pm; Oct.-June Mon.-Sat. 9am-5pm). **Halifax Bank** (tel. 270214), on the corner of Broadway and Main St., has an **ATM** that accepts Plus and Visa (open Mon.-Fri. 9am-5pm, Sat. 9am-noon). **Trains** run between Belfast's Central Station and Larne Harbour (Belfast office tel. (01232) 741700, Larne office tel. (01574) 270517; Mon.-Fri. 19/day, Sat. 15/day, Sun. 6/day; 50min.; £3). **Buses** leave frequently from Larne (tel. (01574) 272345) for Belfast's Laganside Station (Mon.-Sat. 17/day, Sun. 3/day; 50-min. express or 1½hr.; £2.50). Those departing on a ferry from Larne should ensure that their train or bus terminates in Larne Harbour, rather than in Larne Town, a 15-minute walk away. Larne's **post office,** 78 Main St. (tel. 272518), feels an affinity for the **postal code**, BT4 01AA. Larne's **phone code** spews 01574.

Accommodations, Food, & Pubs Most people wouldn't choose to stay in Larne, but if you're too weary to move on, there's no shortage of beds. B&Bs most convenient to both the harbor and the bus and train stations lie along Curran Rd. A right turn from the bus station leads to a roundabout. From here, Circular Rd. crosses Curran Rd., the first road on the right. From the harbor, the first right after the ferry port crosses a bridge and turns into Curran Rd. **Mrs. McKane,** 52 Bay Rd. (tel. 274943), just off Curran Rd., stocks her rooms with TVs and hotpots (single £15; double £28, w/bath £30). **The Curran Caravan Park,** 131 Curran Rd. (tel. 273797 or 260088), midway between the harbor and town, has lawn bowling, putting greens, and grubby bathrooms (£4/person, hook-up £1.50; £6.50/caravan).

In the center of town, **Stewart's Supermarket,** on Broadway, has a wide selection of food (open Mon.-Tues. and Sat. 9am-5:30pm, Wed.-Fri. 9am-9pm). The lunch menu is affordable at **Carriages,** 105 Main St. (tel. 275132), as opposed to its expensive dinner menu. Cheap pizza persists all day (seafood flan with salad £3; open daily noon-11pm). The cozy and unique atmosphere at lamp-lit **Bailie,** 111-113 Main St.

(tel. 273947), is perfect for cuddling. Fridays and Sundays feature live music while Thursdays and Saturdays amplify less entertaining karaoke.

GLENS OF ANTRIM

North of Larne, nine lush green valleys, or "glens," slither from the hills and high moors of Co. Antrim down to the seashore. Although there is nothing significant to see in the glen towns, people inexplicably love visiting them. A2 connects the small towns at the foot of each glen to each other. For once, this road along the rocky shore is suitable for any mode of transport: driving, biking, or hitching. The glens themselves (and the mountains and waterfalls) can best be seen by heading inland from one of the base towns. The area's only hostel is in Cushendall.

   Bus service through the glens is scant at best. Two Ulsterbus routes serve the area (Belfast tel. (01232) 320011, Larne tel. (01574) 272345). Bus #162 from Belfast stops in Larne, Ballygally, Glenarm, and Carnlough (Mon.-Fri. 10/day, Sat. 8/day, Sun. 2/day), and sometimes continues to Waterfoot, Cushendall, and Cushendun (Mon.-Fri. 4/day, Sat. 3/day). An infrequent summertime Antrim Coaster follows the coast road from Belfast to Coleraine, stopping at every town (June-Sept. Mon.-Sat. 2/day; left at 9am and 2pm in summer '96). The Ulsterbus Express from Belfast to Portrush doesn't go anywhere near the Glens. Rides in the glens average £2-5.

   Hitching is decent, but the winding, narrow road between cliffs and the sea wall doesn't allow for easy stopping. The photo opportunity points and crossroads are the best places to try your luck. **Cycling** is fabulous. The coast road from Ballygally to Cushendall is both scenic and flat. After the road divides north of Cushendall, the coastal route, which passes the spectacular views of Torr Head, runs through hills that make even motorists groan. The inland route, through Ballypatrick Forest, is more manageable but still far from flat. The Cushendall hostel rents **bikes** (£6/first day, £5/additional day, £30/week; deposit £30; pannier bags £5).

BALLYGALLY

This tiny village stretches along the water's edge, surrounded by a wide sandy beach and gentle hills. Well-preserved **Ballygally Castle** dominates the strip. Also called the **Halfway House Hotel**, it was built in 1625 by a Scotsman who needed a fortified home. Coach travelers in the past used to stop here on their journeys between Larne and Glenam. The Castle's **ghost room** is inhabited by a female spectre who plummeted from the tower window hundreds of years ago. A fortune-teller sometimes reads futures there. The rocky outposts that appear in the sea just before entering the village are rumored to be the submerged ruins of another castle. Bally-gally's **post office,** Coast Rd. (tel. 583229; open Mon.-Tues. and Thurs.-Fri. 9am-1pm and 2-5:30pm, Wed. 9am-1pm, Sat. 9am-12:30pm), knows the difference between the **postal code,** BT40 2QX, and the **phone code,** 01574.

   Fifty yards up the road from the spot where the bus stops as it enters town, B&B with a view can be had at **Té an Téasa,** 4 Coastguard Cottages, Coast Rd. (tel. 583591). The bright, modern house distinguishes itself with a funky staircase (£13/person). Also along the coast road but nearer to Larne, the **Carnfunnock Country Park** (tel. 260088 or 270541) provides **campsites** (£5) and a walled garden, where sundials of all shapes and sizes tell the time and give timely advice, e.g. "Hasten slowly." One sundial points a beam of light, rather than a shadow, at the correct hour. The hedge maze next to the garden is shaped like Northern Ireland; the entrances and exits to the maze are at the major ports. Inquire at the visitors center for entrance to the maze (open daily 8am-8pm). **Lough Restaurant,** 260 Coast Rd. (tel. 583294), serves large sandwiches (£1) and a standard Irish snack menu (£2-2.75; open daily 11am-8:30pm). The adjoining **grocery store** (tel. 274117) has a large stock of food (open Mon.-Sat. 9am-9pm, Sun. noon-5pm). The aptly named **Dungeon Bar** (tel. 583212) has trad on Saturdays.

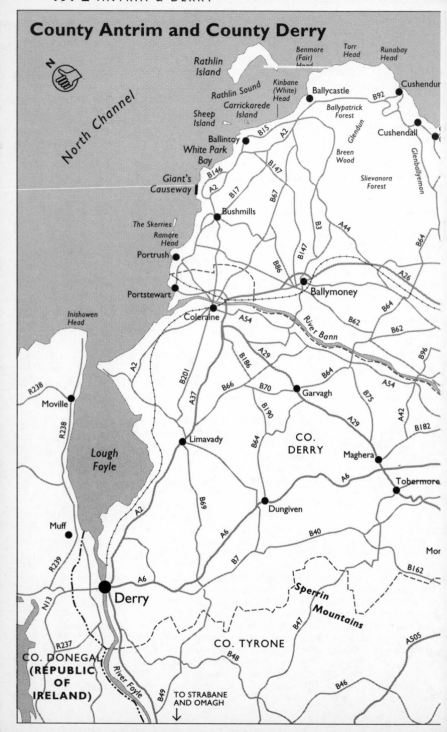

County Antrim and County Derry

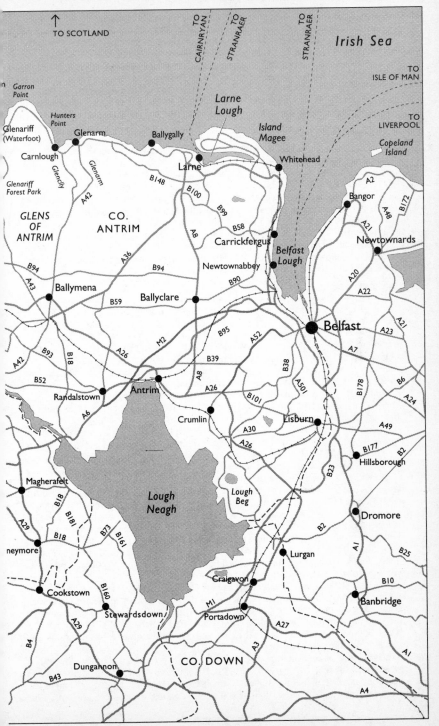

GLENARM

Six flat, winding, coastal miles along A2 lead up to Glenarm ("glen of the army"), the southernmost glen. You can kiss the road goodbye and hike the 6 mi. along the **Ulster Way** trail (a good map is necessary, of course). Just before entering Glenarm, the **madman's window** appears on the right. This huge hole through a gigantic block of chalk is the work of the elements. Small, quiet, and unexciting Glenarm Village is graced with several pubs, a few stray artists, and the grand entrance to **Glenarm Forest,** where trails trace the river's path for miles (open daily 9am-sunset). Nestled at the foot of the glen, the village has been the seat of the MacDonnells, the Earls of Antrim, since they first arrived from Scotland in the 13th century. Today, the 13th Earl of Antrim still resides here in **Glenarm Castle.** Just off the main street, the Castle hides behind the trees north of the river. Only the 17th-century gate is visible from outside. A **festival** shocks this sleepy town during the first week of July.

Margaret's B&B and Café, 10 Altmore St. (tel. (01574) 841307), provides the only alternative to pub grub in town. It doubles the pleasure with large, comfortable rooms with religious messages on the walls. (B&B £14/person. Café open Mon.-Sat. 9am-midnight.) **Heatherdew Tavern,** 1 New Rd. (tel. (01574) 841221), or the **Bridgend Tavern** (tel. (01574) 841247; occasional trad in summer), on Toberwine St., will pour you a pint. Glenarm's **post office** (tel. (01574) 841218) is halfway down Toberwine St. (open Mon.-Tues. and Thurs.-Fri. 9am-1pm and 2-5:30pm, Wed. and Sat. 9am-1pm). The **postal code** is a madman at BT44 0AP.

WATERFOOT & GLENARIFF

Nine miles farther up the coast, the village of Waterfoot guards Antrim's broadest glen, Glenariff, often deemed the most beautiful of the nine. (Waterfoot itself is sometimes called Glenariff—don't get lost.) Thackeray dubbed Glenariff "Switzerland in miniature," presumably because it was steep and pretty, since secretive banks and trilingual skiers are rare. Glenariff's **coastal caves** are worth exploring. They gape on the way to the Red Bay pier from town. Due to the Penal Laws, Catholics learned their catechism in the School Cave under dripping stalactites.

Four miles down the road from the village at **Glenariff Forest Park,** waterfalls splash down shaded hills to feed the **River Glenariff.** If you're starting from south of the park, you can save yourself the 3-mi. uphill hike to the official entrance by taking the downhill road marked with red arrows which branches left towards the Manor Lodge Restaurant. From the north, A2 (Glenariff Rd.) goes past flat-topped **Lurigethan** (1153ft.) on the right. The ruined walls of **Red Bay Castle** are straight ahead just before you pass under Red Arches. The road then veers away from the sea (it doesn't follow signs to Glenariff). After about 4 mi., signs point left to the park. Once inside, paths marked by red arrows begin at the **Manor Lodge** and climb up the **Waterfalls Trail.** Just inside the park entrance, a 1¾-mi. trail veers left to shadow the River Glenariff as it crashes downstream (and downhill) over jagged rocks. Bridges cross streams and sweet-smelling flora up to the **Waterfall Restaurant,** still within the forest park. The café has tasty "quickies" for £3. (Park open March-Oct. Mon.-Sun. 10am-dusk. £3/car, £1/person.) The Cushendun-Ballymena **bus** (Mon.-Sat. 4/day, Sun. 1/day) passes the park entrance. Ask to be dropped off here and wave your arms for the driver's attention to reboard.

You can either camp at **Glenariff Forest Park Camping,** 98 Glenariff Rd. (tel. (012667) 58232; tents £5-7.50), or find one of the many farmers in the area who welcome campers (ask in town). Alternatively, stay in Waterfoot itself, or settle just up the road in Cushendall; at **Glen Vista,** 245 Garcon Rd. (tel. (012667) 71439), near the beach at the foot of the glen after the caravan park, bright, clean rooms overlook the sea (£13/person; open June-Sept.).

Waterfoot may be a one-street town, but it has two charismatic pubs. **The Mariners' Bar,** 7 Main St. (tel. (012667) 71330), has trad every Sunday and some summer weeknights, as well as varied live music on Friday and Saturday nights. **Harvey's,** across the street, has beergarden action and occasional impromptu sessions. **The**

Glens of Antrim Feis, one of Northern Ireland's major music and dance festivals, is held here in late June/early July.

■ Cushendall

The capital of the Glens region, **Cushendall,** 2 mi. north of Waterfoot, is an unpretentious town with no arcades and no neon. The town fosters lively pubs and takes advantage of its lucky location: moors, hills, and the rough seashore form a triangle with the town at its center. Three of the nine glens (Glenballyeamon, Glenaan, and Glencorp) are closer to Cushendall than to any other human habitation.

PRACTICAL INFORMATION

Tourist office, Mill St. (tel. 71180), near the bus stop and opposite the library. A wealth of information. Open Mon.-Fri. 10am-1pm and 2-7:30pm, Sat. 10am-1pm and 2-4:30pm; mid-June to Aug. also open Mon.-Sat. 6-8pm.

Banks: Northern Bank, Shore St. (tel. 71243). Open Mon. 9:30am-5pm, Tues.-Fri. 10am-3:30pm.

Buses: July-Aug. buses stop in Waterfoot, Glenarm, Ballygally, Larne, Carrickfergus, and Belfast (2/day) and Cushendun, Ballycastle, Giant's Causeway, Portrush, Portstewart, and Coleraine (2/day). Call the Ballymena bus station (tel. (01266) 652214) for off-season information.

Bike Rental: Ardclinis Activity Centre, 11 High St. (tel. 71340). Mountain bikes £10/day; deposit credit card, passport, or £50; wetsuits £6/day.

Camping equipment: O'Neill's Country Sports, Mill St. (tel. 72009). They also sell fishing tackle. Open Mon.-Thurs. and Sat. 9:30am-5:30pm, Fri. 9:30am-8pm, Sun. noon-5:30pm.

Pharmacy: Gillan Pharmacy, 2 Mill St. (tel. 71523). Open Mon. and Wed.-Sat. 9:30am-5:30pm, Tues. 9:30am-1:30pm.

Post office, Mill St. (tel. 71201). Open Mon. and Wed.-Fri. 9am-1pm and 2-5:30pm, Tues. and Sat. 9am-12:30pm. The **postal code** is BT44 0RR.

Phone code: 012667.

ACCOMMODATIONS

Cushendall Youth Hostel (YHANI/HI), Layde Rd. (tel. 71344), 1mi. from town. A "YHA" sign appears on a wall along the (uphill) road that forks left from Shore St., but the warden will pick you up if you call ahead. A recent architectural tune-up generated a phenomenal kitchen with color-coordinated cutting boards. Dorm: members £6.50, under 18 £5.50. Bikes £6/day. Open March-Dec.

Glendale, Mrs. O'Neill's, 46 Coast Rd. (tel. 71495). It's hard to imagine a warmer welcome or a better bathtub. £13/person, w/bath £15.

Shramore, 27 Chapel Rd. (tel. 71610). Three quiet, restful rooms and a bathtub for £14/person. Open May-Sept.

Cushendall Caravan Park, 62 Coast Rd. (tel. 71699), adjacent to Red Bay Boatyard. Summer £7.50/tent, winter £4.50/tent.

Glenville Caravan Park, 22 Layde Rd. (tel. 71520). £3/tent.

FOOD & PUBS

After all those trees in the Glens, it's nice to be around people and pubs again. **Spar supermarket,** Bridge St., is open 365 days per year (366 in leap years; 8am-10pm).

Gillian's Home Bakery and Coffee Shop, 6 Mill St. (tel. 71404). Simple food that you could cook yourself, but it's cheap. Hot dog 70p, beans on toast £1.50. Open Mon.-Sat. 9am-8pm, Sun. 11am-8pm.

The Moyle Inn, Bridge St. (tel. 71300). Everything and anything with chips. Open Mon.-Sat. 10am-5pm.

Harry's, Mill St. (tel. 72022). Bar snacks are quick and satisfying (chicken kiev £3; served Mon.-Sat. noon-5pm, Sun. noon-3pm) but evening meals are less pub-like and more expensive and complex (£6-9; served daily 6-9:30pm).

Joe McCollam's, 23 Mill St. (tel. 71330), a.k.a. "Johnny Joe's." A tiny, ancient, and completely traditional barroom that will soothe spirits. Lively trad nights feature impromptu ballads, fiddling, and slurred limericks (summer Thurs. and Sat.-Sun.).

Lurig Inn, 5 Bridge St. (tel. 71527), is right next door. Music plays most nights and much less common *céilí* dancing happens on the first Fri. of every month.

SIGHTS

The sandstone **Curfew Tower** endures in the center of town on the corner of Mill St. The tower was built in 1825 to contain rowdy townspeople after a riot or a revel. Today it is privately owned and closed to the public. The remnants of a Franciscan Friary, **Layde Church,** lie just a short walk from the hostel along the coast road to Cushendun. The church was appropriated for use as a Protestant church until the 1800s. Inland from the church, **Tieveragh Hill,** known locally as Fairy Hill, embodies a gate to the Otherworld that is inhabited by ancient "little people." The tiny folk play haunting music on Halloween, which coincides with the Celtic new year's festival of Samhain. **Lurigethan Hill** would soar above town if its top weren't so remarkably flat.

Ossian's Grave molders on the lower slopes of Tievebulliagh Mountain. In fact a neolithic burial cairn dating from around 2000 BC, it is linked only by tradition with the Ulster warrior-bard Ossian who, according to legend, was buried here in about 300 AD (see **Legends and Folktales,** p. 69). This merry poet, while relating his family's adventures to St. Patrick, allegedly tried to convince the saint that Christianity was far too restrictive for the boisterous Gaels. This episode was later incorporated into young Yeats's first long poem. A2 leads north from Cushendall towards Ballymoney to the lower slopes of Tievebulliagh, where a sign points the way. The steep walk up the southern slope of Glenaan rewards with views of the lush valley. Powerboats for racing on the waves are available at **Red Bay Boats Ltd.,** 21 Dalnade Park (tel. 71331; £8/1hr., £6/hr. for 2-5 hr., and £32/6hr.). Every Friday of the summer, **McMullan's Sea Angling Service** (tel. 71282) sends a fishing boat from the pier at 6:30pm (£7; book ahead).

■ Near Cushendall: Cushendun

Five miles north of Cushendall on A2, the tiny, picturesque seaside village of Cushendun was bought in its entirety by the National Trust in 1954. Since then, Big Brother has protected the town's "olde," quaint, squeaky-clean image from any danger. Cushendun has none of the hustle and little of the bustle which characterizes its larger neighbor to the south. This picture-perfect village has a set of murky **sea caves** that perforate its vast beach. The caves were weathered out of the stone cliffs by the sea when it was much higher than it is now. The largest cave, located just past the Bay Hotel, provides the only entrance to **Cave House,** which was built in 1820. It is currently occupied by the Mercy religious order but closed to the public. From behind the hotel, an excruciatingly steep path leads to the cliff top.

The **National Trust** office, 1 Main St. (tel. (01266) 74506), plays up the town's two attractions with displays on Cushendun's history and the sea caves. They also sell a good map of walks in the area (50p; open daily 1-5pm, Easter-June and Sept. Sat.-Sun. 1-5pm). You can sip tea downstairs in a tourist-priced **tea room** (burgers 90p, big sandwiches £1.20; open daily 11:30am-6:30pm). **The Bay Hotel,** 20 Strandview Park (tel. (01266) 74267), provides simple rooms, breakfast, and nice views (£16/person) as well as bar snacks and pub grub (chicken royal £4.75; open daily 12:30-3pm). Mrs. McKay's **Sleepy Hollow B&B,** 107 Knocknacarry Rd. (tel. (01266) 761513), is cheaper (£15/person). Camping at **Cushendun Caravan Site,** 14 Glendun Rd. (tel. (01266) 761254), is cheapest with a TV/game room (£7.25/tent; wash and dry £1.50; open March-Sept.). The multi-talented **Bay Hotel** has folk music in the bar on Saturdays. **Buses** pause at Cushendun's one grocery shop (open daily 8:30am-10pm) on their way to Waterfoot (Mon.-Sat. 9/day, Sun. 1/day) and Ballycastle (Mon.-Sat. 2/day).

CAUSEWAY COAST

Past Cushendun, the northern coast shifts from lyrical into dramatic mode: 600-ft. cliffs dominate yielding white beaches. The Giant's Causeway, for which the whole region is named, is a honeycomb of black and red hexagonal columns. The rock formations, suited to a science fiction scene, extend off the coast toward Scotland. The Giant's Causeway itself is seldom less crowded than the towns which lead up to it.

A2, which is suitable for cycling, connects the main towns along the Causeway. Ulsterbus #172 runs between Ballycastle and Portrush along the coast (Mon.-Fri. 7/ day, Sat. 6/day; 1hr.; £2.90) and makes frequent connections to Portstewart. In good summer weather, the open-topped **Bushmills Bus** (Coleraine bus station, tel. (01265) 43332) outlines the coast between Coleraine (5mi. south of Portrush) and the Giant's Causeway (July-Aug. Mon.-Sat. 4/day, Sun. 2/day). The summertime **Antrim Coaster** bus (tel. (01232) 333000) runs up the coast from Belfast to Portstewart (June and Sept. Mon.-Sat. 2/day, July-Aug. daily 2/day). Ulsterbus also runs package **tours** in the area that leave from Belfast or elsewhere (£3-6). From points farther south along the coast, many rely on their thumbs or on the express bus from Belfast (June-Sept. 9/day). Those **hitching** along A2 or the inland roads (marginally quicker) find that the lack of cars slows them down.

CUSHENDUN TO BALLYCASTLE

Seven miles north of Cushendun, just south of Ballycastle, **Fair Head** magnetically attracts international hikers. Challenging basalt cliffs plummet straight down to rocky scree. Bikes should be left at home: the hills are so horrific that cyclists will spend more time walking than wheeling. Those in cars should head straight for this stretch of road, though they seldom do. The lack of autos translates into poor hitching conditions. High **Torr Head,** halfway to Fair Head from Cushendun, is the closest spot to Scotland in all Ireland. Just to the south, a steep road from Crockanore runs down to undiscovered **Murlough Bay,** protected by the National Trust.

A2 straight from Cushendun to Ballycastle is more manageable for cyclists, with one long climb but an even longer descent from a boggy plain. Part of the high plain has been drained and planted with evergreens. The result is secluded **Ballypatrick Forest,** which includes a forest drive and several pleasant, pine-scented walks. **Camping** is allowed with a permit from the ranger or the Forest Office (tel. (012657) 62301), 2 mi. toward Ballycastle on A2 (basic facilities; £4/tent). Past the forest, the landscape is even more desolate. A few miles north, a high hollow contains a **vanishing lake** which can appear and disappear into the bog in less than a day. When the lake is full, it has fish in it, but where do they go when it empties?

> ### Save the Last Dance for Me
>
> Legend maintains that a certain Princess Taisie, whose royal presence was often seen along this coast, was so beautiful that suitors came from far and wide to compete for her hand. Two of her most ardent admirers, trying to determine who had the right to wed the Princess (they didn't want to bother her with the question), engaged in a duel. One of the headstrong suitors was mortally wounded. As he lay dying, he called a liegeman to his side. The liegeman swore that he would exact revenge upon the winner of the duel. This dedicated servant appeared as a happy guest at the wedding reception. But when the groom's attention was diverted, the liegeman seized his moment. He waltzed the bride to the edge of the cliffs and threw her over. Her body washed up at Fair Head.

■ Ballycastle

The Glens of Antrim and the Causeway Coast converge upon L-shaped Ballycastle, a bubbly seaside town with a busy beach and great pubs. Weekend discos induce revelers to travel miles to get to town. Weekdays are a little less crowded. Though Ballycastle (not to be confused with the town in Co. Mayo) means "town of the castle," don't look for a castle here. The eponymous castle was demolished in 1856. While Ballycastle is not unpleasant, those desiring to visit the famous sights to its west (Giant's Causeway) or the south (Glens of Antrim) may want to stay closer to them.

ORIENTATION & PRACTICAL INFORMATION

Ballycastle's main street runs perpendicular to the waterfront. It starts at the ocean as Quay Rd., becomes Ann St., and then Castle St. Most restaurants and shops are found along Ann St. and its successor, Castle St. As Quay Rd. meets water, the road takes a sharp left onto North St., where more stores and food await. The amusement grounds and "park" here make it a popular meeting place for young people. Unfortunately, the groovy coastal walk beyond North St. has been closed for safety reasons. Most B&Bs and the hostel perch on Quay Rd.

Tourist Office: Sheskburn House, 7 Mary St. (tel. 62024). 24-hr. computerized information outside. Open July-Aug. Mon.-Fri. 9:30am-7pm, Sat. 10am-6pm, Sun. 2-6pm; Sept.-June Mon.-Fri. 9:30am-5pm, Sat. 10am-4pm.

Banks: First Trust Bank, 32-34 Ann St. (tel. 63326). Open Mon.-Fri. 9:30am-4:30pm; **ATM** accepts Mastercard and Visa.

Ferry: See **Rathlin Island,** p. 411.

Buses: Stop at the Diamond and the Marine Hotel. Get rides to: Cushendall (Mon.-Sat. 3/day; 40min.; £2.40); Portrush (Mon.-Sat. 7/day; 1hr.; £2.90); and Belfast (Mon.-Sat. 6/day, Sun. 4/day; 3hr.; £5.50).

Taxis: tel. 62822 or 62537.

Bike Rental: J. Spence, Castle St. (tel. 62487). £5/day; no deposit. **Northern Auto Factors,** 41 Castle St. (tel. 63748), £6/day.

Pharmacy: McMichael's, 10 Ann St. (tel. 63342), open Mon.-Sat. 9am-6pm.

Post Office: 3 Ann St. (tel. 62519). Open Mon.-Tues. and Thurs.-Fri. 9am-1pm and 2-5:30pm, Wed. 9am-1pm, Sat. 9am-12:30pm. **Postal code:** BT54 60H.

Phone Code: 012657.

ACCOMMODATIONS

Watch out for the Ould Lammas Fair on the last Monday and Tuesday in August. B&Bs fill almost a year in advance, and even hostel beds fill weeks before the big event. The 40-bed **Castle Hostel (IHH),** 62 Quay Rd. (tel. 62337), has a central location, comfortable co-ed bunk rooms, modern showers, and *two* kitchens, but the common space can get crowded (dorm £5; **camping** £3; laundry £1). The new **Ballycastle Backpackers Hostel,** 4 North St. next to the Marine Hotel (tel. 63612 or 69458), is small (15 beds), spacious, and extra-friendly. Most rooms have sea views (dorm £6; free laundry). Just up the road towards town, you can eat or sleep at **Fragrens,** 34 Quay Rd. (tel. 62168). Mrs. Frayne will spoil you with TV, a navigable tub, and free tea and coffee. (Separate smoking and non-smoking rooms. £14/person, w/bath £15. £2 less for continental breakfast instead of Irish; dinner £7.) **Hilsea,** 28 North St. (tel. 62385), is a large, businesslike guest house offering bright rooms overlooking Rathlin Island and the Sea of Moyle (£16/person).

FOOD & PUBS

Brady's Supermarket, 54 Castle St. (tel. 62349), is just 10 minutes from the hostel (open Mon.-Sat. 9am-9pm, Sun. 10:45am-9pm). Closer still, the **Fruit Shop,** the Diamond (tel. 63348), sells greens (and reds and oranges; open Mon.-Sat. 8am-6pm).

Beach House Cafe, Bayview Rd. (tel. 62262), is close to the pier. Romantic views of the bay and Fair Head are marred only by the loud amusement park. Serves sinful but cheap desserts and snacks, as well as full meals (sundaes £1.80-2, lasagna £2.50; open daily 9am-9pm). **The Strand Restaurant,** North St., plays Bryan Adams, but it redeems itself with a large menu that includes several vegetarian dishes (vegetable pie £5) and dandy desserts (crepes £2; open daily 11am-10pm). At the subterranean grotto called **Cellar Pizzeria,** 11a The Diamond (tel. 63037), savory pizzas that will feed at least three (£6-7) slip onto your tables. (Delivery for orders of £5 or more daily 6-11pm. Open Sept.-May daily 5-11pm; June-Aug. Mon.-Sat. 12:30-3pm and 5-11pm, Sun. 5-11pm.)

Though renowned for its nuttiness during the Fair, Ballycastle is lively throughout the entire year. Tourists usually head for tiny, fire-warmed **House of McDonnell,** Castle St. (tel. 62975), which has trad on Fridays in summer. The **Anglers' Arms,** 12 North St. (tel. 62155), promises fun with nightly sing-alongs during the summer; occasional live music adds to the enjoyment. **The Central Bar,** 12 Ann St. (tel. 63877), has all kinds of live music (Wed., Sat., and sometimes Tues. nights). **McCarroll's Pub,** 5 Ann St. (tel. 62123), is the place to be on Thursdays when it spins traditional reels and jigs. Locals fill the **Boyd Arms,** 4 The Diamond (tel. 62364), in appreciation of folk music (Fri.) or trad. **The Harbour Bar,** North St., is the locals' hangout. For the fast-paced, the weekend disco at the **Marine Hotel,** North St. (tel. 62222), provides entertainment (cover Sat. £4, Sun. £5). The hotel also organizes line dancing on Wednesday nights (£3/person).

SIGHTS

Just off the Diamond, **Boyd Church** raises its octagonal spire over a mostly carpeted sandstone interior. The Boyd family ruled Ballycastle through the 17th and 18th centuries. The town's development is largely attributed to Hugh Boyd (landlord 1727-1765). The **Ballycastle Museum** on Castle St. will take you by the hand to guide you through the town's history (open summer Mon.-Sat. noon-6pm; free). Outside town on the road from Cushendall, the **Bonamargy Friary** lies in ruins. Within the MacDonnell vault are the remains of the first Earls of Antrim. Near the main entrance, a flat tombstone marks the **grave of the Black Nun.** As a sign of humility, Julia MacQuillan chose her grave here, where people would be forced to step on her.

Visitors to Ballycastle enjoy doing things rather than just observing objects. **Christopher McCaughan,** 45 Ann St. (tel. 62074), goes fishing on summer nights in the *Lady Moyle* and will be happy to have you on board (£5). You could just **fish** off the pier, where pollock, mackerel, colefish, plaice, and cod abound (inquire at the tourist office about licenses). The old stone harbor, now filled with silt, has been covered with 10 grass **tennis courts** and a **bowling green** near the beach (£1.50/hr., racket and ball rental 70p). **Celtic Journeys,** 111 Whitepark Rd. (tel. 69651), organizes afternoon rambles, day walks, and weekend trips around North Antrim, including Rathlin Island. Guides emphasize local wildlife and myths (prices vary).

On the last Monday and Tuesday of August, Ballycastle hosts Northern Ireland's oldest and most famous fair, the **Ould Lammas Fair.** The fair was originally a week-long fiesta but is now crammed into two frenzied days. Continuing the traditions of the ancient Celtic harvest festival, the fair jams Ballycastle's streets with vendors selling cows, sheep, crafts, and baked goods. Traditional musicians pack the pubs even tighter. *Dulse* (nutritious seaweed dried on local roofs, reputedly good for the brain) and *yellow-man* (sticky toffee made from a secret recipe) are two curiosities associated almost exclusively with the fair. Both are worth a try.

■ Near Ballycastle

RATHLIN ISLAND (FORT OF THE SEA)

Just off the coast at Ballycastle, boomerang-shaped Rathlin Island is the ultimate in escapism for 20,000 puffins, the odd golden eagle, and about 100 human beings, including the famous Mary Black. Its windy surface can support few trees; its perimeter is lined with 200-ft. cliffs. A leaflet, available at the Ballycastle tourist office, describes the island's walks and sights. A new **interpretive center** on Rathlin Island also has maps (10p) of walks to the extreme points of the island: East Lighthouse, West Lighthouse, and Rue (South) Lighthouse. The center gives an interesting display of the small island's interesting history (open daily 11am-5pm; free). While Rathlin makes a beautiful day-trip in nice weather, be warned that there is absolutely nothing to do in bad weather.

The island generates two-thirds of its own electricity with three wind turbines, visible from most parts of the island. Electricity was brought to the island in 1992. The wind machines are named **Conn, Ardh,** and **Fiachra,** who were the three sons of mythical chieftain Lir. He was forced to spend 300 years in the Sea of Moyle after being cursed by the boys' wicked stepmother. Another legend claims that Robert the Bruce, a Scottish national hero, hid in one of the many caves underneath the east lighthouse after his defeat by the English in 1306. He was inspired by a spider who shared the cave. The arachnid enduringly tried to climb up its thread to the roof of the cave. The previously dispirited Robert returned to Scotland with renewed determination and won the Scottish throne.

A **minibus** (call Johnny Curry tel. (012657) 63905) sometimes runs from the pub to the **bird sanctuary** at the tip of the island (£2.50 return). The bus will wait while you take in the lighthouse area. The lighthouse itself is the best point from which to view birds, but it's usually locked. Call the warden (tel. (012657) 63935) in advance to gain entrance. The bus also makes occasional trips to Rue Point. Here, visitors can clamber over (and comb through) the remains of **Smuggler's House,** whose wall cavities supposedly hid contraband. Ironically, the official tax house is just yards away. Rathlin residents were known for their hatred of tax collectors who clogged their harbor (Ushet Port). Fair Head looms a few miles away and seals frolic freely here. No matter how good a swimmer you may be, don't try swimming to Fair Head. The currents are notoriously vile.

The island town has one pub and a few stores, all within 300 yd. of the dock. **Mrs. McCurdy,** the Quay (tel. (012657) 63917), offers B&B from £14 (open March-Sept.). The **Richard Branson Dive/Holiday Centre,** the Harbour (tel. (012657) 63915), brings divers to the island. If there's extra space in their bunkroom, they may let you stay for £10 (B&B £12). The Holiday Centre is named after the hot-balloonist who crashed just short of Rathlin Island. Rumor has it that the island's lads battled strong currents to save him from drowning but refused to complete the rescue until he promised to donate money to Rathlin. **MacCraig's Bar** (tel. (012657) 63974) may also allow camping on its grounds. The bar—the single entertainment center for the entire island—takes care of the snacks (big sandwiches £1.10), pool (20p/game), video games, and on occasion discos and karaoke. The head of **Duncan,** Rathlin's last Highland bull who went loco and had to be shot, graces the wall. Exchange stories with locals and visitors alike while enjoying spectacular views from the outdoor tables.

Two **ferries, Rathlin Venture** (tel. (012657) 63917) and **Iona Isle** (tel. (012657) 63901), run to the island daily from the pier at Ballycastle. (To Rathlin 10:30am, in summer also 12:15, 5, and 6:45pm; from Rathlin 4pm, in summer also 9, 11:45am, and 5pm.) The ferries may leave early (or late), so passengers should arrive a few minutes early (£3.40; £5.70 day return.)

BALLINTOY & CARRICK-A-REDE ISLAND

Five miles west of Ballycastle, the village of Ballintoy inspires smiles with a picturesque church and a tiny, equally attractive, harbor. Just off the coast, **Sheep Island** is home to puffins, razor bills, shag, kittiwakes, and the largest cormorant colony in Ireland. Its name comes from the 11 sheep that used to be taken to the island each year to graze—10 were thought to be too few (the sheep would get too fat) and 12 were thought too many (they would starve). Access to the island is now restricted to protect the nesting birds.

Smaller and better-known **Carrick-a-rede Island** lies offshore to the east of Ballintoy. Carrick-a-rede means "rock in the road," a reminder of the fact that the island presents a barrier to migrating salmon returning to their home rivers. Fishermen have been setting up their nets for 350 years exactly at that point where the fish have to go around the island. To reach the nets, the fishermen have strung a rope bridge between the main road and the island. Crossing the flimsy bridge over the dizzying 80-ft. drop to rocks and sea below is now a popular activity for tourists. Be extremely careful in windy weather, as the bridge has been known to flip over! A sign 1 mi. east of Ballinatoy marks the turnoff for the bridge from the coast road.

The wildlife and walks on the island are just as interesting as the bridge is thrilling. Humans can get quite close to cliff-nesting, black-and-white razor bills (which look like mini-penguins) as well as more mundane gulls. A fishing hut totters on the east side of the island, from which salmon nets stretch out into the sea. On a clear day, you can see the Hebrides. The **National Trust Information Centre** (tel. (012657) 62178) on the mainland has info about the island. For 50p, they'll give you a certificate stating that you successfully crossed the bridge (open May-June daily 11am-6pm, July-Aug. daily 10am-6pm). The center has a convenient carpark (open April-Sept.; £2/car) and allows **camping** for one night only (tel. (012657) 62178 or 31159; £2/person; tent must be down by 10am; no facilities except toilets).

■ Giant's Causeway

Advertised as the eighth natural wonder of the world, the Giant's Causeway is deservedly Northern Ireland's most famous sight. In the absence of weekend crowds, it easily lives up to the reputation. Forty thousand hexagonal columns of basalt form a honeycomb path from the foot of the cliffs far into the sea. Geologists have decided that the Causeway resulted from an unusually steady cooling of lava which stimulated crystallization, but legend disagrees (see **McCool Story,** below).

The **Causeway Visitors Centre** (tel. (012657) 31855), near its head, caters to all needs. It sells an excellent leaflet of walks (50p) that will guide you the 8 mi. back to Whitepark Bay or along several shorter circular walks. Every 15 minutes, it also runs minibuses the ½ mi. to the columns (70p return). An audio-visual show informs about the fact and fiction of the Causeway. (Centre open July-Aug. daily 10am-7pm; Sept.-June 10am-5pm. Causeway always open. Admission £1, students 80p. £2/car to park in the lot, free just outside the center.) There are gift shops and tea rooms aplenty outside the center (tea room closes at 6:15pm). Many paths loop to and from the Causeway. Two leave the visitors center, one along the cliff and another along the coast. They merge after 4 mi. When making a circuit of the two, it's best to go out by the low road and return by the high one, as the lower one is by far more stunning. The well-tended track winds through naturally sculpted amphitheaters and inlets studded with bizarre, creatively named formations (such as the "organ"). Although not essential, the center's trail leaflet contains a helpful map and basic geological and human history. To see the Causeway in its full glory, it's necessary to trek at least the 2½ mi. to **Hamilton's Seat.**

McCool Story

Irish legend states that Finn McCool, the warrior giant, fell in love with a female giant on Staffa Island, off the Scottish coast. The devoted lover built the Causeway to bring her across to Ulster, which explains the existence of similar beehive-esque rock formations on Staffa. McCool also had other interests in Scotland: he desired to fight the Scottish giant Benandonner. But when he realized how big his Scottish rival was, McCool decided to use wit instead of brute force. The wily Irishman, with the help of his wife, disguised himself as an infant. When the Scottish giant saw the size of this Irish "baby," he was terrified by the anticipated proportions of the father. Benandonner quickly fled back to Scotland, destroying the Causeway on his return trip in order to ensure that the huge father McCool would never be able to cross the sea to challenge him.

BUSHMILLS

On its own merits, it's no slouch of a seacoast. Nevertheless, the shores west of Giant's Causeway and Whitepark Bay may seem comparatively tame and unpopular. Two miles west of the National Trust Visitors Centre, the ardently Protestant town of **Bushmills** remains the home of **Bushmills Irish Whiskey.** Distilling since 1609, the family-owned Bushmills is the oldest functioning whiskey producer in the world. The fact that Sir Thomas Phillips issued the distillery license to himself does not detract from the authenticity of the product. Indeed, in the 18th century, when roads were virtually nonexistent, this was the only welcome respite gentlefolk could get on their travels. When the distillery is operating, you get to see actual whiskey being made. Production stops on occasion, but (less interesting) tours are still held. Around Christmas and the second week in October, both distilling and tours cease. For just £3000, you can buy a barrel of the Millennium Whisky scheduled to be opened in the year 2000. (Tel. (012657) 31521. Tours, with free sample, every 15min. Open March-Oct. daily 9:30am-4pm; Nov.-Feb. Mon.-Fri. 9am-5:30pm, last tour 4pm. Admission £2.50, students £2.)

■ Portrush

By day, the merry-go-rounds, water slides, and arcades of Portrush go full-throttle as throngs of Irish vacationers roam the streets and its two beaches. By night, the same roaring hordes produce some of the North's best nightlife, with live music nightly in at least one pub in town. Portstewart's beaches and the Giant's Causeway are within easy cycling distance.

PRACTICAL INFORMATION

Tourist Office: Dunluce Centre (tel. 823333), on the way to town. Dead posh. They won't hold your pack but will answer your questions. 24-hr. computerized info outside. Ulsterbus representative on hand to arrange day tours. Open July-Aug. daily 9am-8pm; Sept.-April Mon.-Sat. 10am-4pm, Sun. noon-5pm; May-June Mon.-Fri. 9am-5pm.

Banks: First Trust, 25 Eglinton St. (tel. 822726). Open Mon.-Fri. 9:30am-4:30pm; **ATM. Ulster Bank,** 33 Eglinton St. (tel. 823730). Open July-Aug. Mon.-Fri. 9:30am-4:30pm; Sept.-June Mon.-Fri. 9:30am-12:30pm and 1:30-4:30pm; **ATM.**

Trains: Station: Eglington St. (tel. 822395), in the center of town. Carriages from Belfast (Mon.-Sat. 8/day, Sun. 2/day; 2hr.; £5.90, £9 return) and Derry (Mon.-Sat. 7/day, Sun. 2/day).

Buses: Dunluce St. (tel. 824065). Regular buses to Portstewart (30/day; 13min.; £1). Ulsterbus #172 (4/day) runs along the coast to Bushmills (20min.), the Giant's Causeway (25min.), and Ballycastle (1hr.). The open-topped Bushmills bus (#177) goes to Portstewart, Bushmills, and the Giant's Causeway in good weather (daily 5/day). **Ulsterbus** also has day tours to Ards Peninsula (£8), Roe Valley (£4), and Silent Valley (£7.50); inquire at tourist office or bus station.

Taxis: tel. 822777 or 824901.

Bike Rental: Causeway Coast Cycles, 6 Bath St. (tel. 824334). £6/day, £30/week; deposit £30.

Surfing Equipment: Atlantic Drive & Surf, 102 Main St. (tel 823273). Rent or buy. Surfboard £8/day, wetsuit £8/day; deposit credit card.

Early closing day: Sept.-June on Wed.; July-Aug. none.

Pharmacy: Heron Chemist, 5-9 Main St. (tel. 822324). Open daily 9am-11pm.

Emergency: Dial 999; no coins required. **Police:** tel. 822721.

Post Office: 23 Eglinton St. (tel. 823700). Open Mon.-Tues. and Thurs.-Fri. 9am-12:30pm and 1:30-5:30pm, Wed. 9am-1pm, Sat. 9am-12:30pm. **Postal code:** BT56 8DX.

Phone Code: 01265.

ACCOMMODATIONS

Portrush is the best place to stay before or after seeing the Giant's Causeway. If anything can, **Ma Cool's Hostel,** 5 Causeway View Terrace (tel. 824845), can make staying in Portrush a pleasure. Friendly hostelers and wardens gather in the common room to exchange travel stories. Owner Joanna's laugh is infectious (microwave; free coffee; dorm £6; wash and dry £2). From the bus stop, turn left onto Dunluce St. and follow it towards the harbor. When you come to a three-pronged fork, take the middle road, which is Mark St. The hostel is a few yards past the intersection of Mark St. and Main St. on Causeway View Terrace. From the train station, Mark St. is the second left after turning left out of the station.

Portrush supports so many B&Bs that tourists seem more plentiful than residents. Nearly every other townhouse along Mark St., Kerr St., and Mount Royal is a B&B. Most are indistinguishable in size, character, and price. **Atlantis,** 10 Ramore Ave. (tel. 824583), offers an ocean view in a comparatively quiet neighborhood. Use of the kitchen and free tea and coffee are added bonuses (in summer £14/person, off season £12). **Avarest,** 64 Mark St. (tel. 823121), has sea views, tea- and coffee-making facilities, and TVs in all rooms, as well as a central location (£13.50/person, off season £12).

FOOD

The proliferation of fast food in Portrush may seem all-encompassing, but a few good restaurants hide amid the neon. If you're not up to the search, stock up on groceries at **Cost-Cutter,** Main St. (tel. 823715; open Mon.-Fri. 9am-7pm, Sat. 9am-6pm, Sun. 10am-5pm).

Dionysus, 53 Eglinton St. (tel. 823855). God-like Greek food. Lots of vegetarian and vegan dishes. Entrees around £5. Open Mon.-Sat. 5:30-10pm, Sun. 5:30-9:30pm.
The Singing Kettle, 315 Atlantic Ave. This small, comfortable coffee shop sells exotic burgers and sandwiches. Garlic mushrooms in homemade roll £1.75. Vegetarian version of Ulster fry £3. Banana milkshake 95p. Charmingly (or maybe frustratingly) vague opening hours, but typically open daily 10am-6pm.
Boogies' Diner, 47 Eglinton St., (tel. 822561). American-style 50s diner. Open Mon., Thurs., and Sat. 11am-2am, Tues.-Wed., Fri., and Sun. 11am-9pm.

PUBS & ENTERTAINMENT

The **Harbour Bar,** 5 Harbour Rd. (tel. 825047), is a spit-in-the-sawdust sailors' pub popular with the locals. The adjacent Harbour Inn also serves good pub grub. At the other end of the social spectrum, **Ramore Wine Bar,** the Harbour (tel. 823444), offers harbor-side elegance (food served 12:30-2 and 5:30-9pm). The Victorian-fronted **Alpha Bar,** 63 Eglinton St. (tel. 823889), the **Atlantic Bar,** and adjacent **McNally's,** Atlantic Ave. (tel. 822727), all have Irish charm and superior *craic*. The **Londonderry Hotel** (more commonly called the **Derry**), Main St. (tel. 823693), next to the Atlantic and McNally's, is the place to be on Saturdays (w/funk, house, and acid jazz), but Tudor-faced **Shunter's,** in the railway station, draws crowds on Tuesdays (July-Aug. live music every night). Partiers make tracks for **Traks Nightclub** at the railway station (tel. 822112; cover charge). Popular **Station Bar** (tel. 823509), next door, pounds the drums.

Finish your evening (or begin your morning) at a Portrush institution, **Beetles Bar and Disco** (everyone calls it **Kelly's;** tel. 823539), just outside Portrush on the Bushmills Rd. Kelly's has *11* bars and *three* discos (from punk to house to 70s funk). Excessive and sometimes downright tacky, every sector of youth culture in Northern Ireland fits in somewhere. Regular rave nights. Boy George DJ-ed here in 1996.

Northern Irish theater companies travel to Portrush to present their acts on the **Summer Theatre** stage (tel. 822500) in the old town hall. (Nightly shows at 8pm. Tickets £4. Box office open in summer Mon.-Sun. 10:30am-12:30pm and 6:30-8pm.)

SIGHTS

The biggest sight around—the Giant's Causeway—isn't even here. The most widely advertised attraction in Portrush is the over-hyped **Dunluce Centre,** Dunluce Arcade (tel. 824444), which tries to capitalize on every fact or story. Moving seats in the Turbo Tours theater make Dino Island that much more real. A multimedia presentation on local folklore will not knock your socks off. For 50p you can climb a squat tower to look at the view. (Open July-Aug. daily 10am-8pm; Sept.-March Sat.-Sun. noon-5pm; April-June Mon.-Fri. noon-5pm, Sat.-Sun. noon-7pm. Turbo Tours £2.20, off-peak £2; whole center £4.50, off-peak £4.) In refreshing contrast, the understated **Countryside Centre,** 8 Bath Rd. (tel. 823600), on the waterfront, is small but lovingly cared for. The assortment of displays includes wildlife exhibits, a tide pool with sea urchins and starfish, and loads of old pictures. A (free) viewing platform outside can help identify the many land masses in the distance. (Open June-Sept. Wed.-Mon. noon-8pm, Tues. noon-5pm. Viewing platform always open.)

■ Near Portrush: Portstewart

Portstewart is by no means less crowded than its larger neighbor, but thoughtful town planning has saved this smaller town from Portrush's garish fate. Carnival lights are the only thing reminiscent of the merry-go-round mentality of Portrush vacationers. A fantastic beach, popular with surfers, and a popular pub bring more hip throngs to Portstewart. At high tide the sea comes right up to the wall of the main street. A path to the beach runs around the convent on the main street.

Portstewart's tiny **tourist office,** Town Hall (tel. 832286), opens only for the summer tourists (open Mon.-Sat. 10am-1pm and 1:30-4pm). **First Trust,** 13 the Promenade (tel. 833723), offers financial services inside and out at the **ATM** (open Mon.-Fri. 9am-5pm, Sat. noon-3:30pm). A pharmacy distributes plasters at **Super Chem,** the Promenade (tel. 833844; open Mon.-Sat. 9am-9pm, Sun. noon-9pm). **Buses** coming into town stop just before the Promenade. The **post office,** 90 the Promenade (tel. 832001), does the usual (open Mon.-Fri. 9:30am-4:30pm). Portstewart's gnarly **phone code** is 01265, dude.

Accommodations, Food, & Pubs The Victoria Terrace area, on the left as you head out of town on the Portrush Rd., is laden with beds. From the bus stop, face the sea, turn right, and follow Main St. around the corner. Victoria Terrace juts out to the left. The **Causeway Coast Independent Hostel,** 4 Victoria Terrace (tel. 833789), is friendly and comfortable, with walls lined with stunning mountain photographs. Free laundry, library-like common room, and immediate access to ice cream (dorm £6, double £15; sheets sometimes 50p). **Wandering Heights,** 12 High Rd. (tel. 833250), provides B&B in rooms with sea views and TVs. Owner Mrs. Robinson says, "good food is guaranteed" (£14/person, off-season £12).

Portstewart cultivates both good cooks and a tradition of superb ice cream. **Mace Supermarket,** on the Promenade, has the usual groceries and tons of cheeses (open Mon.-Sat. 8:30am-11pm). **Good Food and Co.,** 44 the Promenade (tel. 836386), makes quiche (80p), sandwiches, breads, and pastries (mini-pizzas 70p; open Mon.-Sat. 9am-10pm; Sept.-June Mon-Sat. 9am-6pm). **Ashiana Tandoori Restaurant,** 12 the Diamond (tel. 834455), offers exotic evening meals. Curry-starved tourists indulge themselves with inexpensive Indian food (king prawn curry madras £5; open Mon.-Thurs. noon-midnight, Fri-Sat. 5pm-2am, Sun. 5-11pm). Sixty-three steps above the Promenade, **Cassioni's** (tel. 834777) serves its beloved pizza, pasta, and more (open daily 5-11pm). **Morelli's Sundae Garden,** the Promenade (tel. 832150), is infamous for its superb high-calorie and sugar concoctions and their creative names, like the pink panther waffle (Irish beauty sundae £3.10, single scoops available; open daily 9:30am-11:30pm). **Piaf's,** the Promenade (tel. 833377), serves ice cream and "overbaked" French bread (open Mon.-Fri. 9am-11:30pm, Sat.-Sun. 9am-midnight). Most of the town and all of its students head for the **Anchor Pub,** 87 the Promenade (tel. 832003), to put back some pints by the fire. Summer Wednesdays and Saturdays bring live rock, while term-time Mondays see trad night. The upstairs **disco** pounds all year (Mon.-Sat. 10pm-1am; cover Fri.-Sat. £2).

Sights In Portstewart, you either take the high road or the low road (but neither will get you to Scotland). One coastal walk leads to Portrush and one path along the **cliffs** ends up at the convent (the big white building with the cross). **The Strand,** ½ mi. west of town, is owned and preserved in all its long beauty by the National Trust. A small but dedicated group of surfers call the waters around here and Portrush home. For those who dare to try out the Irish waves, **Ocean Warriors** (tel. 836500), located at the intersection of the road to the beach and the Promenade, rents wet-suits (£4/5hr.), surfboards (£10/½day), and bodyboards (£3/½day). According to locals, September brings the best surfing on 8- to 10-foot waves. Kowabunga, dude. The **Flowerfield Arts Centre,** 185 Coleraine Rd. (tel. 833959), shelters traveling art exhibitions, holds frequent lectures on subjects ranging from local history and folk-lore to the royal family, and hosts jazz concerts (£4). Sand sculptures are also dis-played in appropriate weather. About 6 mi. out of town on the road to Portrush is 16th-century Dunluce Castle, with much of its original structure still intact (castle open daily 9am-6:30pm; free).

■ Derry City

Derry's long and troubled history has given rise to powerful popular symbols used by both sides of the sectarian conflict. The siege of Derry in 1689 created Protestant folk heroes out of the "Apprentice Boys" who closed the city gates on the advancing armies of the Catholic King James II. More recently, the violence of the early 70s reached a pinnacle in "Bloody Sunday," so-called by Republicans as a symbol of what they see as continuing British tyranny. Even the city's name has strong political asso-ciations. The Northern and British governments officially call it "Londonderry," as do many Northern Protestants. Catholics and the Catholic-majority City Council call the city "Derry." The shorter name, used colloquially by some Protestants, is less politi-cally charged and is the preferred usage for visitors to the city.

Modern Derry is in the middle of a determined and largely successful effort to cast off the legacy of the Troubles. Even with the end of the 1994-95 ceasefire, it seems that Derry residents still entertain a realistic hope of prosperity and consensus (for more information, see **History and Politics,** p. 362). Most parts of the city, and espe-cially the downtown area, show evidence of Derry's rapid development. Construc-tion and commerce are booming there. The recent success of "Impact '92," a huge festival celebrating cultural diversity, did much to improve the city's image and morale, and to revitalize the tourist industry. Derry's rock scene is thriving; gig post-ers crowd any available wall. While its controversial history is one of Derry's more fas-cinating characteristics, its brilliant rock scene and the improving cultural milieu are attractions in their own right.

ORIENTATION & PRACTICAL INFORMATION

Downtown Derry denotes the old city within the walls plus the pedestrianized shop-ping district around Waterloo St. just northwest of the walls. Derry's inner streets form a geometrical grid. Inside the old city, four main streets connect the four main gates (Bishop's Gate, Ferryquay Gate, Shipquay Gate, and Butcher's Gate) to the cen-tral square: the **Diamond.** The university area can be reached by taking a left off Strand Rd. just past Strand Bar. The **Bogside** neighborhood is west of the walls. The Protestant **Waterside** neighborhood, with the train station, has settled across Craigavon Bridge on the east shore of the River Foyle. Since the renewal of violence in the summer of 1996, it is unsafe to visit these areas at night.

Tourist Office: 8 Bishop St. (tel. 267284). The friendly staff doesn't give recommen-dations but does distribute the truly useful *Derry Tourist Guide* and free maps.

Bord Fáilte keeps a desk here, too (tel. 369501). Open July-Aug. daily 9am-8pm; Sept.-June Mon.-Fri. 9am-5:15pm.

Budget Travel: USIT, Ferryquay St. (tel. 371888). ISICs, YHANI, and HI cards, and Travelsave stamps. Open Mon.-Fri. 9:30am-5:30pm, Sat. 10am-1pm.

Banks: First Trust, Shipquay St. (tel. 363921); open Mon.-Fri. 9:30am-4:30pm. **Bank of Ireland,** Shipquay (tel. 264141); open Mon.-Wed. and Fri. 10am-3:30pm, Thurs. 9:30am-5pm. **Northern Bank,** Guildhall Sq. (tel. 265333); open Mon.-Wed. and Fri. 10am-3:30pm, Thurs. 9:30am-5pm. All have **ATMs.** The **Richmond Centre,** a shopping center next to the Diamond (tel. 260636), has a bureau de change; open Mon.-Wed. 9am-5:30pm, Thurs.-Fri. 9am-9pm, Sat. 9am-6pm.

Eglinton/Derry Airport: Eglinton (tel. 810784). 7mi. from Derry. Flights to Manchester, Glasgow, Jersey, London, Birmingham, Edinburgh, and Dublin.

Trains: Duke St., the Waterside (tel. 42228), on the east bank. Trains from Derry only go east to Coleraine, Ballymena, Lisbum, and Belfast (Mon.-Fri. 7/day, Sat. 6/day, Sun. 4/day; to Belfast 2½hr.; £7). A sideline from Coleraine zips north to Portrush. No rail lines connect Derry to the Republic.

Buses: Foyle St., between the walled city and the river. **Ulsterbus** (tel. 262261) serves all destinations in Northern Ireland and some in the Republic. To: Belfast (Mon.-Fri. 12/day, Sat. 9/day, Sun. 6/day; 1½-3hr.; £5.90); Enniskillen (Mon.-Fri. 5/day, Sat. 3/day, Sun. 1/day; 2½hr.; £5.60); Dublin (Mon.-Sat. 3/day, Sun. 2/day; £10); Galway (Mon.-Sat. 4/day, Sun. 2/day; 5½hr.); Donegal Town (Mon.-Sat. 4/day, Sun. 2/day; 1½hr.; £7.70); and Sligo (Mon.-Sat. 4/day, Sun. 2/day; 2½hr.). **Lough Swilly** private bus service (tel. 262017) heads to Inishowen, Letterkenny, and the Fanad Peninsula. Buses to: Malin Head (Mon.-Fri. 11/day, Sat. 3/day; 1½hr.; £6); Letterkenny (Mon.-Sat. 11/day, Sun. 8/day; 1hr.; £4.20); Buncrana (Mon.-Fri. 10/day, Sat. 12/day, Sun. 4/day; 35min.; £2.40). **Northwest Busways** (tel. (00 353 77) 82619) has offices in the Republic. Buses depart Derry for Inishowen from Patrick St. opposite the Multiplex Cinema.

Taxi: Quick Cabs, Custom House St. (tel. 260515). **Tower Taxis,** Bishop St. (tel. 371944). Derry also has a fleet of **black cabs** (tel. 260247) with set routes, though it's neither as extensive nor as famous as the Belfast black cab system.

Car Rental: Ford Rent-a-Car, Desmond Motors Ltd., 173 Strand Rd. (tel. 360420). £36.75/day, £183.75/week; deposit £180. Must be over 25. Open Mon.-Fri. 9am-1pm and 2-5:30pm. Weekend package: Fri. 4pm-Mon. 9am, £73.50.

Bike Rental: Rent-A-Bike, Magazine St. (tel. 372273), at the YHANI hostel. £6/first day, £5/additional day, £30/week; deposit passport or £50.

Laundry: Duds 'n' Suds, 141 Strand Rd. (tel. 266006). Pool table and big screen TV. Wash £1.65, dry £1.65. Open Mon.-Fri. 8am-9pm, Sat. 8am-8pm.

Women's Centre, 24 Pump St. (tel. 267672). Open Mon.-Fri. 9:30am-5pm.

Bisexual, Gay, and Lesbian Information: Carafriend Counselling (tel. 263120). Open Thurs. 7:30-10pm.

Disabled Services: Foyle Disability Action, 58 Strand Rd. (tel. 360811), serves the physically or mentally disabled.

Hotline: Samaritans, 16 Clarendon St. (tel 265511). Open 10am-8pm. 24-hr. phone service all year.

Pharmacy: Connor's Pharmacy, 3a/b Strand Rd. (tel. 264502). Open Mon.-Wed. 9am-5:30pm, Thurs.-Fri. 9am-9pm, Sat. 9am-6pm.

Hospital: Altnagelvin Hospital, Glenshane Rd. (tel. 45171).

Emergency: Dial 999; no coins required. **Police:** Strand Rd. (tel 367337).

Post Office: 3 Custom House St. (tel. 362274). Open Mon. 8:30am-5:30pm, Tues.-Fri. 9am-5:30pm, Sat. 9am-12:30pm. Unless addressed to 3 Custom House St., *Poste Restante* letters will go to the Postal Sorting Office (tel. 362577) on the corner of Great James St. and Little James St. **Postal Code:** BT48 6AA.

Phone Code: 01504.

ACCOMMODATIONS

Oakgrove Manor (YHANI/HI), Magazine St. (tel. 372273). A colorful mural on the side of the building identifies this modern, spacious, and institutional hostel. Centrally located. Not always well-supervised. Scantily-equipped kitchen looks like McDonald's. Wheelchair accessible. Curfew 2am. Checkout 10am strictly

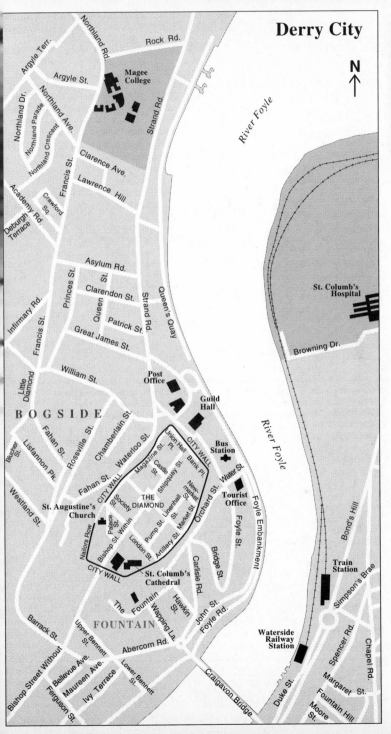

Derry City

N

Northland Rd.

Rock Rd.

Argyle Terr.

Argyle St.

Magee College

Strand Rd.

River Foyle

Northland Dr.

Northland Parade

Northland Ave.

Northland Crescent

Francis St.

Clarence Ave.

Lawrence Hill

Academy Rd.

Crawford Sq.

Deburgh Terrace

Asylum Rd.

St. Columb's Hospital

Infirmary Rd.

Princes St.

Clarendon St.

Queen St.

Patrick St.

Strand Rd.

Queen's Quay

Browning Dr.

Francis St.

Great James St.

Little Diamond

William St.

Post Office

BOGSIDE

Blucher St.

Lisannon Pk.

Fahan St.

Rossville St.

Chamberlain St.

Waterloo St.

Guild Hall

Union Hall Pl.

Magazine St.

Castle St.

Shipquay St.

Bank Pl.

CITY WALL

Bus Station

Water St.

River Foyle

Westland St.

Fahan St.

CITY WALL

Society St.

THE DIAMOND

New-market St.

Orchard St.

Tourist Office

St. Augustine's Church

Palace St.

Bishop St. Within

Pump St.

Linenhall St.

London St.

Artillery St.

Market St.

Foyle St.

Foyle Embankment

Nailors Row

CITY WALL

Carlisle Rd.

Bridge St.

Bond's Hill

St. Columb's Cathedral

The Fountain

Hawkin St.

John St.

Foyle Rd.

Train Station

Simpson's Brae

Barrack St.

FOUNTAIN

Wapping La.

Upper Bennett St.

Abercorn Rd.

Bishop Street Without

Bellevue Ave.

Maureen Ave.

Ivy Terrace

Lower Bennett St.

Craigavon Bridge

Waterside Railway Station

Duke St.

Spencer Rd.

Margaret St.

Fountain Hill

Chapel Rd.

Ferguson St.

Moore St.

enforced. 10-bed dorm £7.50. 6-bed dorm w/bath £8. 4-bed dorm w/bath £9. Single w/shower and breakfast £15. Double w/shower and breakfast £28. Ulster fry £2.50, continental breakfast £1.50. Sheets 50p; towels 50p. Laundry in basement: wash 50p, dry 50p, powder 50p. Pool table 20p.

Aberfoyle Hostel, 29 Aberfoyle Terrace, Strand Rd. (tel. 370011). The hostel is 50yd. past the large, cream building on the left, and is a 10-min. walk from the city center. This small (17 beds), intimate hostel has recently come under new management. Kitchen and common room can get a bit crowded but the young wardens are nice and laid-back. Dorm £7.50.

Muff Hostel, Muff, Co. Donegal, Republic of Ireland (from the North, tel. (00 353 77) 84188). Just 5mi. outside Derry, this friendly hostel combines the best of two worlds: relaxed and solacing accommodation in the country for the evening and easy access to the city during the day. Martin Cooke's invigorating welcome keeps hostelers here for days (£6; open March-Oct.). Lough Swilly buses leave Foyle St. in Derry for Muff (Mon.-Fri. 8/day, Sat. 7/day, last bus 6:10pm; 60p, 75p return).

Magee College, Northland Rd. (tel. 265621, ext. 5233). Take the Ballygoarty or Rosemont bus from Foyle St., or walk ½mi. up Strand Rd. and turn left after the Strand Bar. Truly institutional dorms. Single £6. Double £10. Free showers, kitchens, and laundry available during Easter week and again mid-May to Sept. Mandatory reservations accepted Mon.-Fri. 9am-5pm (rooms are available for weekends, but you must arrive during office hours).

YMCA, 51 Glenshane Rd. (tel. 301662), 3mi. from city center; from Foyle St. take the Tullyalley bus down Glenshane Rd. Not a hostel, but they'll provide you with a mattress if you need it (£2). Accepts both sexes. Open mid-July to mid-Sept.

Florence House, 16 North Land Rd. (tel. 268093). Large, sunny bedrooms in a townhouse around the corner from the university. £15/person.

Joan Pyne, 36 Great James St. (tel. 269691). Small flowery rooms shelter tired souls back from popular Bogside pubs, just minutes away. £16/person, w/bath £17.

Grace McGoldrick, 10 Crawford Sq. (tel. 265000). In the middle of it all and often full of contented guests. £15/person.

FOOD

Restaurants, mostly around the walled city, tend to be expensive. Take-aways and cafés are a better option. Wellsworth **supermarket,** Waterloo Pl., is in the pedestrian shopping district around the corner from the post office (open Mon.-Tues. and Sat. 9am-5:30pm, Wed.-Fri. 9am-9pm). **Scoop-A-Market,** 19 Strand Rd. (tel. 262939), sells health foods and dispenses free recipe hints (open Mon.-Thurs. 9am-6pm, Fri. 9am-9pm, Sat. 9am-6pm).

The Sandwich Co., the Diamond (tel. 372500), corner of Ferryquay St. and Bishop St. A huge assortment of freshly constructed sandwiches (almost all for £1.45). Open Mon.-Sat. 8:30am-5pm.

Boston Tea Party, 13 Craft Village (tel. 264568). Quaint wrought-iron tables and flowered curtains. Every July 4, diners throw the flowered curtains into the River Foyle with relish and war-whoops (Irish stew £1.30). Open daily 9am-5:30pm.

Anne's Hot Bread Shop, William St. (tel. 269236), in the Bogside. A Derry institution. Open late, late, late. Big portions, no frills. How long does bread have to be heated until it becomes toast? Open daily 8am-3am.

Bound for Boston, Waterloo St. (tel. 262375). Mexican and American food. Try the Clintonburger. Open Mon.-Wed. noon-8pm, Thurs.-Sat. noon-10pm.

Kylemore Cafe, Carlisle Rd., inside the Foyleside Shopping Centre (tel. 317776). That exquisite coffee shop aura permeates. Open Mon.-Tues. 8am-8pm, Wed.-Fri. 8am-9pm, Sat. 8am-7pm, Sun. noon-6pm.

Webcrawler Internet Cafe, 52 Strand Rd. (tel. 374773). Drink a cup of joe and e-mail him, too. £2/½hr., £2.50/hr. Open Mon.-Sat. 9am-9pm, Sun. noon-9pm.

PUBS

Derry may not satisfy every craving at dinner, but it compensates with a superb drinking scene, in quality and quantity. Trad and rock music flare up most nights.

The Dungloe, 41-43 Waterloo St. (tel. 267716). Loved all around. Almost nightly trad music downstairs (10pm). Live blues or rock or even "alternative" discos upstairs (cover £1-2; 11pm).

Peadar O'Donnell's, 63 Waterloo St. (tel. 372318). An old-style pub named for the famous Donegal man who organized the Irish Transport and General Workers Union and took an active role in the 1921 Irish Civil War. Bric-a-brac crowds the walls. Bric-a-brac crowd of all ages fills the benches.

The Gweedore Bar, 59-61 Waterloo St. (tel. 263513). Next door to Peadar's, this Victorian pub imitation offers trad, rock, and bluegrass most weekends. The tourist lure extends to an assortment of Guinness memorabilia.

The Carraig Bar, or "Rock," 113-119 Strand Rd. (tel. 267529). Destroyed by a bomb in 1973, no signs of the violence remain in the splendid Victorian bar with stained glass. Lively, friendly students. Discos Wed.-Sat. Look cool, please.

Bound for Boston, Waterloo St. Busy and full of young people. Tues. trad sessions and occasional rock and blues downstairs (no cover); disco Sat. and Sun. and alternative or reggae bands other nights upstairs (cover £2). Their ads advise, "Bring a towel and your dancing slacks."

The River Inn and **Gluepot** (tel. 267463). These two adjoining pubs on Shipquay together occupy the site of "the oldest bar in Ireland." The River Inn often has music, but the Gluepot is stickier.

The Townsman Bar, 33 Shipquay St. (tel. 260820). Hip folk squeeze together to fit into this popular pub. The original interior is from an old chemist shop, complete with ghastly 19th-century medical tools. A low front bar contrasts nicely with the French country house behind.

SIGHTS

Harry Bryson's animation and his love for the city he claims never to have left make for an entertaining (though far from impartial) **walking tour.** Amusing and shocking anecdotes constitute a good part of the tour's substance. (Tour leaves from the tourist office June-Aug. Mon.-Fri. 10:30am and 2:30pm; 1½hr.; £2.50. Sept.-May call tel. 365151 ext. 307 or the tourist office to arrange a tour.) **Foyle Civic Bus Tours,** presented by Ulsterbus, run a circuit of six stops, including the University, Guild Hall, and St. Eugene's Cathedral (July-Aug. Tues. and Thurs. 2pm; £3).

Derry's earliest associations are religious. It was both a Celtic holy place (the name Derry comes from the Old Irish *daire,* meaning "sacred oak grove") and site of a monastery founded by St. Columcille (kol-um-KEEL) in the 6th century. The city itself was built as the crowning achievement of the Ulster Plantations at the beginning of the 17th century. After the "Flight of the Earls" in 1607, much of Ulster was left without local leaders. The English seized the moment and asserted their mastery of the area by taking land from the native Catholic residents and granting it to Protestant settlers from England and Scotland. Derry itself was granted to the London guilds, which built the walled city of "London"-derry. After withstanding several rebellions by the displaced local Catholics, the city experienced the famous 105-day siege of 1689. In addition to the beloved Apprentice Boys, the siege created a villain for present-day Protestants to abhor. **Robert Lundy,** the city's leader who advocated surrender during the siege, is labeled a traitor. His effigy is still burnt every year at an August 12th ceremony commemorating the closing of the gates. A reviled and grotesque caricature can be seen in the Tower Museum (see below).

In the 18th and 19th centuries, Derry became an industrial center for port and linen. As the River Foyle receded, working-class settlements developed outside the walls. Partition made Derry a border city and a Catholic majority made it a headache for Unionist leaders. It became the locus of some of the most blatant religious discrimination. The civil rights marches that sparked off the Troubles originated here in 1968. "Free Derry" (the western, Catholic part of the city, controlled by the IRA and a "no-go area" for the army from 1969-72), "Bloody Sunday" (Jan. 30, 1972, when British troops fired on demonstrators and killed 14), and "Operation Motorman" (the July 1972 army effort to penetrate the "no-go" area and arrest IRA leaders) became powerful logos for Derry Catholics and Republicans everywhere. While the Protestant and Catholic communities are still sharply divided, recent years have seen them coexisting peacefully. Moves to mix religions in the Derry school system may someday unify civil society—when today's five-year-olds are all grown up.

The Walls

Derry's city walls, 18 ft. high and 20 ft. thick, were erected between 1614 and 1619. They've never been breached or attacked, hence the nickname "the Maiden City." The walls are entirely accessible to the public. Wherever there are steps, visitors can freely climb to the top. Seven **cannons** along the northeast wall, between Magazine Gate and Shipquay Gate, were donated by Queen Elizabeth I and the London Guilds who "acquired" the city during the Ulster Plantation. A plaque on the outside of this section of wall marks the water level of the Foyle in the days when it ran right along the walls (it's now 300ft. away). The stone tower along the southeast wall past New Gate was built to protect **St. Columb's Church,** sheltered inside the wall.

Stuck in the center of the southwest wall, **Bishop's Gate** was remodeled in 1689 into an ornate triumphal gate in honor of King William III, the Protestant victor in the battles of 1689. Bishop's Gate is accessible only on foot—its proximity to the courthouse means that cars (possibly carrying carbombs) are prohibited. The **northwest wall** supports a massive cannon, "Roaring Meg," which was donated by London fishmongers in 1642 and used in the 1689 siege. The sound of the cannon alone was rumored to be enough to strike fear into the hearts of enemies. The massive marble platform that stands here now was built to hold a marble statue of the Rev. George Walker, joint-governor of Derry during the siege. The first statue placed here of the joint-governor was blown up in 1973. Its replacement was ready in 1992, but hours before its unveiling an anonymous phone call threatened to blow the new one up if it were placed overlooking the Bogside. The authorities backed down, and the marble Rev. Walker II now stands securely within the city walls. His platform is currently being converted to add to the viewpoints already existing on the city walls. A bit farther, between Royal Bastion and Butcher's Gate, lurks **Memorial Hall** where the modern-day Apprentice Boys have their headquarters. They still maintain the traditions of the 13 Guild apprentices who shut the city gates, thereby launching the Great Siege of Derry.

Within the Walls

The tall spire of **St. Columb's Cathedral,** Bishop St. (tel. 267313), is visible from almost anywhere in Derry. The cathedral shouldn't be confused with less grand St. Columba's Church outside the walls, which commemorates the same saint in different orthography. Built between 1625 and 1633, St. Columb's Cathedral was the first Protestant Cathedral in Britain or Ireland (all the older ones were confiscated Catholic Cathedrals). The original spire is thought to have been made of wood coated with lead. But during the Great Siege the lead was removed and smelted into bullets and cannonballs, resulting in the steeple's present stony appearance. The interior is fashioned of roughly-hewn stone and holds an exquisite Killybegs altar carpet, a bishop's chair dating from 1630, and hand-carved oak pew ends, of which no two are the same. A tiny, museum-like **chapterhouse** at the back of the church displays the original locks and keys for the four main city gates, part of Macaulay's *History of England,* and relics from the 1689 siege. Outside in the graveyard, the tombstones lie flat on the ground. They were leveled in an attempt to protect the graves from defacement by Jacobite cannonballs during the siege. (Open Mon.-Sat. 10am-5pm. Cathedral free, chapterhouse 50p. Call to arrange a free cathedral tour.)

Just outside Shipquay Gate stands the neo-Gothic **Guildhall** (tel. 365151), home to the City Council. First built in 1890, wrecked by fire in 1908, and destroyed by bombs in 1972, today's structure contains replicas of the original stained-glass windows. Those in the main hall depict one version of the history of Derry. Among the bountiful rarities is the Mayor's chain of office, which was officially presented to the city by William III. (Open Mon.-Fri. 9am-5pm. Free tours July-Aug. 9:30am-4:30pm.) The

Guildhall also sponsors various concerts, plays, and exhibitions throughout the year. A more detailed history of Derry is revealed at the award-winning **Tower Museum,** just inside Magazine Gate (tel. 372411), by a series of short videos and life-like tableaux. The last video presents an engaging and unbiased summary of the city's recent turbulent past. The whole museum deserves at least 1½ hours of exploration. (Open Sept.-June Tues.-Sat. 10am-5pm; July-Aug. Mon.-Sat. 10am-5pm, Sun. 2pm-5pm. Last entrance 4:30pm. Admission £3, students £1.)

The **Derry Craft Village** was designed in the medieval style. It was built by entrepreneurial youth from the Bogside in an abandoned lot from cast-away building materials. The village encompasses cafés, craft shops, and **Bridie's Cottage,** which offers an evening of Irish song, dance, and storytelling (June-Sept. Tues., Thurs., and Sat. 8:30pm). **Teach Ceoil (Music House)** hosts informal *céilí* in the same building on Wednesdays and Fridays; the £5 fee includes supper and traditional bread and tea. (To book, call Mary McLaughlin (tel. 269033).)

Outside the Walls

Brilliant **murals** in both Protestant and Catholic neighborhoods remind anyone who cares to look that Derry's recent turbulent history is far from over. The areas which contain this genre of pop art are generally safer than most big American cities, but there is still a watchful, cautious feeling in the streets. Tourists must remember not to photograph police, soldiers, or military installations. The famously Protestant sections of Derry are **Waterside,** to the east of the River Foyle, and the **Fountain Estate,** west of the river. The Fountain is reached from the walled city by exiting through the left side of Bishop's Gate. Though Waterside is more populous, the Fountain holds the better Protestant murals and curb paintings. Some Loyalist murals grace the Waterside along Bond St. and Irish St. Most of the murals convey clear meanings (see **The Falls,** p. 380).

The best-known Catholic neighborhood, the **Bogside,** is easily recognizable. A huge mural, just west of the city walls at the junction of Fahan St. and Rossville Square, declares "You Are Now Entering Free Derry." The politically loaded phrase is sometimes used by activists to describe the Bogside and Creggan areas. Nearby, a stone monument commemorates the 14 protesters shot on Bloody Sunday. Many murals in this neighborhood are also memorials to Bloody Sunday, which became a symbol of the British Army's behavior during the Troubles. They can be found along the street that proceeds from the first right (at the Bogside Inn) past the "Free Derry" mural. The better murals are in the housing projects on either side of the street. On the back of the community center on the left, murals reflect on the role of the "Bothers" in the daily life of Derry. They depict children playing amid murals and memorials. In both Belfast and Derry, peace groups have lately organized children of all religions to paint big, glorious, non-sectarian murals. "The Auld Days" (at the junction of William and Rossville St. in the Bogside across from Pilot's Row Community Centre) is one of several renditions of a formerly peaceful city. One piece of popular art, unveiled in July of 1992, at the end of Craigavon Bridge, also reflects hopes for future peace. The Carlisle Square sculpture shows two men reaching out to each other across a divide in the walls they stand upon.

Magee College, 15 minutes east of city center, has been a part of the University of Ulster since October 1984. Magee has changed allegiances several times. Originally a member of the Royal University of Ireland in 1879, by 1909 it had become part of Trinity College Dublin. A grassy carpet is laid before the main building on a high hill. Built in 1865, the neo-Gothic building shines among its clumsy neighbors.

ENTERTAINMENT

Derry has a limited but active arts scene. Both Irish and international artists get exposure at **Orchard Gallery,** Orchard St. (tel. 269675; open Tues.-Sat. 10am-1pm and 2-6pm). The **Foyle Arts Centre** (tel. 266657 or 363166), on Lawrence Hill off Strand Rd., promotes a broad range of arts, including music, drama, and dance. The **Rialto Entertainment Centre,** Market St. (tel. 262567 or 260516), has all those favorites plus photography. **St. Columb's Hall,** Orchard St. (tel. 267789), welcomes traveling musicians and theater groups to the town's largest playhouse. The hall also houses **Orchard Cinema** in an intimate theater (tel. 262845; box office open Mon.-Fri. 10am-4pm; tickets £5-10). The **Guildhall** (tel. 365151) combines government and artistic functions. Shows include jazz concerts and dance championships. The **Strand Multiplex Quayside Centre,** Strand Rd. (tel. 373900), brings Hollywood movies to town. *Let's Go*'s pub listings of Derry include many trad and rock venues (see **Pubs,** above). Rock gigs also haunt **The Waterloo, Caspers,** and **Legends.** Discos groove upstairs at the **Strand Tavern,** Strand Rd. (tel. 266446; Thurs. techno/house £2-5). The **Squires Night Club** and **Voxbox,** just behind the Townsman, are popular with all kinds of people (Mon. and Thurs.-Sat., cover £3-5).

Tyrone & Fermanagh

■ Omagh

The area surrounding Omagh (OME-ah), draws tourists more than the city itself. Sights of spectacular beauty and museums with masterful exhibits dot the region: a mist-shrouded mountain range, a pine-scented forest park (in a country where trees are as rare as sunshine), the top-notch Ulster American Folk Park and Ulster History Park, not to mention a brilliant hostel. Omagh doesn't have the urban character of Galway or the solitude of Inishbofin, but there are plenty of other reasons to stay here. A5 links Omagh to Derry and Armagh; A32 lumbers toward Enniskillen.

Practical Information Omagh's **tourist office** (tel. 247831, after hours 240774) is in the center of Market St. (open Oct.-March Mon.-Fri. 9am-5pm; April-Sept. Mon.-Sat. 9am-5pm). **Halifax Building Society** (tel. 246931) provides pounds at 22 High St. (open Mon.-Fri. 9:30am-5pm, Sat. 9am-noon; **ATM**), as does **Abbey National Building Society,** 59 High St. (tel. 247121; open Mon.-Tues. and Thurs.-Fri. 9am-5pm, Wed. 9:30am-5pm, Sat. 9am-noon. **ATM** accepts American Express, Visa, and Plus.) **Ulsterbus** runs from the station on Mountjoy Rd. (tel. 242711) to: Belfast (Mon.-Sat. 8-9/day, Sun. 4/day; 2hr.; £5.60, student £4.80); Derry (Mon.-Sat. 11/day, Sun. 4/day; 1hr.; £4, student £3.40); Dublin (Mon.-Sat. 6/day, Sun. 4/day; 3hr.; £9, student £7); and Enniskillen (Mon.-Sat. 5-7/day, Sun. 1/day; 1hr.; £3.70, student £3.20). The station **stores luggage** for 50p per bag (open Mon.-Sat. 9am-5:45pm). **Conway Cycles,** 1 Old Market Pl. (tel. 246195), rents bikes in the alley across from the tourist office (£8/day, £40/week; deposit £30; open Mon.-Sat. 9am-5:30pm). The **post office** is at 7 High St. (tel. 242970; open Mon.-Fri. 9am-5:30pm, Sat. 10am-12:30pm). The **postal code** is BT78 1AB. Oh, Ma, the **phone code** here is 01662.

Accommodations, Food, & Pubs You'll forget you're on a budget at the **Glenhordial Hostel,** 9a Waterworks Rd. (tel. 241973). This new hostel boasts sparkling cleanliness, a conservatory, a wok, hairdryers, and a plethora of other luxuries (even a dartboard). Bill and Marella Fyffe will share a pint with hostelers and ensure a pleasant stay. From the bus station, walk up B48 towards Gortin. Veer right at the first fork (by the car showroom). Follow that road (and the hostel signs) for 2 mi. Call for pick-up; the Fyffes will get you at the bus station if they're home. (£6/person. Sheets included; laundry £1. Bikes £7.50/day. Wheelchair accessible.)

Closer to town, the **4 Winds,** 63 Dromore Rd. (tel. 243554), defines cozy accommodation. Mr. Thomas, a retired chef, provides tea and coffee and a filling Irish breakfast. Call for pick-up or directions for the 10-minute walk. (£15/person. Optional dinner *à la carte* from £6.50, July-Sept. only; packed lunches on request. Discounts for stays over 4 days.) Pitch a tent 8 mi. north of Omagh at **Gortin Glen Caravan and**

Camping Park, Gortin Rd. (tel. (016626) 48108), in a forest park that would make Grizzly Adams feel at home (£4/2-person tent).

At **Expressway** (tel. 243637), opposite the bus station, sit down to lunch with Marilyn Monroe (meat, chips, and veggies, £2.70; served until 5pm) or order from their take-out menu (open Mon.-Sat. 8:30am-6pm). The **Pink Elephant,** 19 High St. (tel. 249805; open daily 8am-5:30pm), offers a similar deal for £2.90, and serves breakfast from 8-11am (£2.50). **O'Doherty's at Sally O'Brien's,** 35 John St. (tel. 242521) has history. The legend of Sally who died of a broken heart will make you weep in your Guinness. Once you've recovered, head next door to **Sally O'Brien's,** a nightclub with live bands (Fri. 18 and over, Sat. 21 and over, Sun. 25 and over).

Sights Five miles north of Omagh on Strabane Rd., the **Ulster American Folk Park** (tel. 243292), attracts tourists, residents, and frogs. Over two million people emigrated from Ulster between 1700 and 1900, and the museum chronicles some of their history and experiences. The indoor exhibition includes life-sized clay figures of such Ulster-American heroes as Davy Crockett and frighteningly accurate, full-scale tableaux of a famine cottage, a New York City Irish tenement, and a big black bear. Outside, a 19th-century rural village educates visitors about life in bygone Ireland. More awesome, however, is the **Ship and Dockside Gallery** in which a 100-ft. brig sits in front of dockside brick buildings, transported from Belfast and Derry. On the ship, visitors can walk through the cramped living quarters of the emigrants, while the sounds of creaking timbers, wind, waves, and seagulls induce seasickness. After disembarking, visitors walk through an "American" town and a 19th-century Pennsylvania backcountry village, complete with log cabin, fancy house, corn crib, and giant barn. Ask one of the guides how soap was made; you won't like what you hear. Watch out for loose, squealing pigs. (Park open Easter-Sept. Mon.-Sat. 11am-6:30pm, Sun. 11:30am-7pm; Oct.-Easter Mon.-Fri. 10:30am-5pm. Admission £3.50, students £1.70. Wheelchair accessible. Last admission to park 1½hr. before closing.) Access to the Emigration Database containing ships' passenger lists is available (Mon.-Fri. 9:30am-4:30pm; fees vary). To get to the park from Omagh, stay on Strabane Rd. for 5 mi., or take the Omagh-Strabane bus (Mon.-Fri. 14/day, Sat. 13/day, Sun. 5/day; 10min.; £1.15, students £1).

Less spectacular than the Folk Park but well worth seeing is the **Ulster History Park** (tel. (016626) 48188), 7 mi. out of town on Gortin Rd. You'll know you're there when you see three round buildings wearing large witch hats. (The Omagh/Gortin bus stops right outside Mon.-Sat. 2/day; £1.30, student £1.10.) Designed to trace settlement in Ireland from the Stone Age, the park contains full-scale reconstructions of neolithic huts, passage tombs, a round tower, a *crannog,* and a castle. Be on the lookout for anachronisms such as a butter churn in a ring fort and a radio in a monk's stone hut. An exhibition explains the history of Ulster (pre-Christian to the Plantations) for those not in the know. (Open April-Sept. Mon.-Sat. 10:30am-6:30pm, Sun. 11:30am-7pm; Oct.-March Mon.-Fri. 10:30am-5pm. Last admission to the park 90min. before closing. Admission £3, students £1.75). The deer-infested, "purely coniferous" **Gortin Glen Forest Park** is just a three-minute walk up from the History Park (exit left). Nature trails and breath-taking views abound. Archaeology enthusiasts should check out Ireland's answer to Stonehenge. Situated between Omagh and Cookstown, **Creggan** overflows with 44 well-preserved monuments dating from the Neolithic Period.

■ Near Omagh: Sperrin Mountains

Less than a half hour northeast of Omagh by car sprout the strikingly beautiful **Sperrin Mountains,** covered with hare and heather. Rollercoaster back roads lead not only to lost sheep, but to tremendous views of the lazy countryside. A few too many tour buses beep through, but the area is beautiful. Walkers and cyclists can pick up the **Ulster Way** 3½ mi. east of Sperrin. This section of the trail is over 25 mi. long: it weaves through the heart of the mountains and then meets the A6 main road 4 mi.

south of **Dungiven.** Those with cars should cruise along the Plumbridge-Sperrin Rd. (B47, commonly known as the Glenelly Rd.). From Omagh's tourist office you can purchase a copy of *The Ulster Way: Accommodation for Walkers* (30p) for places to stay, or *The Ulster Way* (£1) which maps the best trails through the mountains (5 trails, 10-36mi. long). These trails are country lanes that lead past farmhouses, go up and down hills, and get more use from rabbits and sheep than humans. The **Sperrin Heritage Centre** (tel. (016626) 48142) is on Glenelly Rd. between Cranagh and Sperrin. Glaciation, bootlegging in the Poteen Mountains, and the discovery of gold are all hot topics. For 65p you get to try your own luck with a pan (open May-Oct. Mon.-Fri. 11am-6pm, Sat. 11:30am-6pm, Sun. 2-7pm; admission £1.80).

Just north of the Sperrins in Dungiven, the **Flax Mill Hostel (IHH)** (tel. (015047) 42655) charms residents with stone walls, antique but spacious bathrooms, and a rustic lack of electricity. Never fear; there are open hearth fires in the rooms and trad sessions in the cozy lounge to warm things up. To get there, either call for pick-up or take Derry Rd. out of Dungiven and take the first right after the bridge pointing you towards Limavady and Roe Valley Country Park. Proceed along the third road to your left called Altmover Rd. and the Flax Mill is about ¾ mi. down the first lane to your right (dorm £5; **camping** £3; continental breakfast £1.50).

■ Dungannon

Fourteen miles northwest of Armagh, the busy but uninteresting town of **Dungannon** sits at the beginning of M1 to Belfast. Buses scurry between Armagh and Dungannon (Mon.-Fri. 6/day, Sat. 5/day, Sun. 1/day; 30min.; £1.95, students £1.70). The **Killymaddy Tourist Information Centre** on Ballygawley Rd. (tel. (01868) 767259) can help you plan a visit to the area (open July-Aug. Mon.-Thurs. 9am-6pm, Fri. 9am-6pm). Local bus #80 covers the 3 mi. between the town center and the **Tyrone Crystal Factory** (tel. (01868) 725335), where tours show you each intricate step involved in the crystal-making process. (Tours run Mon.-Thurs. 9:30am-3:30pm, Fri. 9:30am-12:30pm, Sat. 9:30am-2pm; £2.) A few miles away (also on bus route #80), the town of **Coalisland** has turned an old cornmill in the center of town into its own **heritage center** (tel. (01868) 748532). Its exhibits teach visitors about the area's industrial history. (Open June-Sept. Mon.-Fri. 10am-8pm, Sat. 11am-6pm, Sun. 2-6pm; Jan.-May, Oct.-Dec. Mon.-Fri. 10am-6pm.)

Just off M1, 6 mi. east of Dungannon, **Peatlands Park** (tel. (01762) 851102) contains native reserves, an interpretive center with interactive displays on the natural and human history of peat bogs, and a small railroad which was originally used to carry turf out of the bogs. Turf-cutting demonstrations on busy days. (Park open June-Sept. daily 9am-9pm; Oct.-May 9am-dusk; visitor center open June-Sept. daily 2-6pm. Both free; railroad 70p.)

FERMANAGH LAKE DISTRICT

Upper and Lower Lough Erne extend on either side of Enniskillen like the two blades of a propeller. They lure vacationers to a lake district several times larger and far less trampled than England's. Lower Lough Erne is north of Upper Lough Erne. The upper lough (which flows down into the other, and hence lower, lough) extends south into Co. Cavan, in the Republic. Hiking, biking, canoeing, windsurfing, and orienteering provide the action in the area. Everything worth seeing is within 20 mi. of Enniskillen, the county's only sizable town.

■ Enniskillen

Busy Enniskillen (pop. 14,000) lies on an island between Upper and Lower Lough Erne. It is a true city, with shops and services that aid in touring the accessible Lake

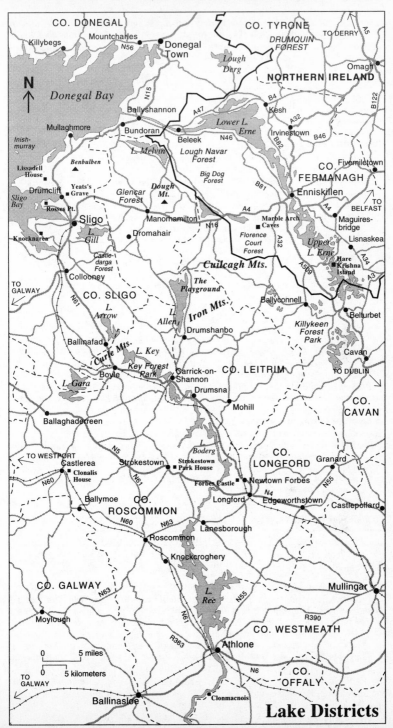

Lake Districts

428 ■ TYRONE & FERMANAGH

District. Enniskillen is lovely and friendly, but it will never forget the 1987 Remembrance Day bombing that killed 11 people, injured 61, and shocked millions. In 1996, just as people were getting used to the idea of peace, another bomb exploded outside a hotel in the town, killing no one but adding to this town's pain.

ORIENTATION & PRACTICAL INFORMATION

Enniskillen's main street is actually five smaller ones. From west to east they run: Darling St., Church St., High St., Townhall St., and East Bridge St. Queen Elizabeth Rd. parallels the main street to the north; Wellington Rd. parallels it to the south. Sligo Rd. and Derrygonnelly Rd. lie across the bridges on the west side of the town center (cross the bridge by Enniskillen castle—Derrygonnelly Rd. is straight ahead, Sligo Rd. to your left). The Dublin/Belfast Rd. is at the other end of the city center.

Tourist Office: Fermanagh Tourist Information Centre, Wellington Rd. (tel. 323110), is across the street from the bus station, with plenty of information and a well-informed staff. Ask about guided town walks in the summer. Open June and Sept. Mon.-Fri. 9am-5:30pm, Sat. 10am-6pm, Sun. 11am-5pm; July-Aug. Mon.-Fri. 9am-6:30pm, Sat. 10am-6pm, Sun. 11am-5pm; Oct.-May Mon.-Fri. 9am-5pm.

Banks: First Trust Savings Bank, 8 East Bridge St. (tel. 322464). Open Mon.-Fri. 9:30am-4:30pm; **ATM** accepts Visa and MasterCard. **Halifax Building Society,** 20 High St. (tel. 327072). Open Mon.-Fri. 9am-5pm, Sat. 9am-noon; **ATM** accepts Plus and Visa.

Bus Station: Wellington Rd. (tel. 322633), across from the tourist office. Clean and swanky. Open Mon.-Sat. 9am-5:30pm. Bus service to: Belfast (Mon.-Fri. 10/day, Sat. 8/day, Sun. 5/day; 2¼hr.; £5.90, students £4.90); Derry (Mon.-Fri. 7/day, Sat. 4/day, Sun. 3/day; 3hr.; £5.60, students £4.80); Dublin (Mon.-Sat. 4/day, Sat. 5/day, Sun. 3/day; 3hr.; £9.70, students £6.50); Sligo (Mon.-Sat. 3/day; 1hr.; £7.30, students £3.80); and Galway (Mon.-Sat. 1/day; 5hr.; £12.40, students £8.10).

Taxis: Call-a-Cab, tel. 324848; **Diamond Taxis,** tel. (0800) 123444 (free call).

Luggage Storage: Ulsterbus Parcel-link (tel. 322633), at the bus station. Open daily 9am-5:30pm; 50p/bag.

Bike Rental: Erne Tours, Round 'O' Quay, Derrygonnelly Rd. (tel. 322882). £7/day, £35/week. **Spokes and Sports,** Church St. (tel. 325251). £6/day, £25/week; deposit £35.

Laundry: Paragon Cleaners, 12 East St. (tel. 325230). £4-6/load, varies by weight. Open Mon.-Sun. 9am-1pm and 1:30-5:30pm.

Hospital: Erne Hospital, Cornagrade (tel. 324711). "Good Samaritan" policy: those who fall ill while on vacation in Enniskillen receive free treatment.

Emergency: Dial 999; no coins required. **Police:** tel. 322823.

Post Office: East Bridge St. (tel. 324525). Open Mon.-Fri. 9am-5:30pm, Sat. 9am-12:30pm. **Postal code:** BT74 7BW.

Phone code: 01365.

ACCOMMODATIONS

Backpackers are limited to a remote hostel 11 mi. from town, or B&Bs which are almost always full in high season. Call ahead for a room or you'll be sleeping in the bus station (although it *is* a swanky bus station).

Castle Archdale Youth Hostel (YHANI/HI) (tel. (013656) 28118), take the Pettigo bus from the station and ask the driver to let you off at Lisarrick. Walk 1mi. left down Kesh-Enniskillen Rd., then turn right into the park at a small church, and walk 1mi. Hitchers report little luck. The hostel occupies one corner of a stately 19th-century home—the hostel is neither in, nor identical with, the castle, but they share the surrounding forest and lakeside trails, overflowing with odd-looking turkeys and multi-colored rabbits. The dorms are large, the kitchen small, and the showers hot. £6.50/person. Laundry £2.

Curraig Aonrai, 19 Sligo Rd. (tel. 324889). Look for the sign on Sligo Rd. Mrs. Mulhern charges £12.50 a night for her aqua and pink rooms. Closest B&B to town center (5-min. walk). Aqua bathtub!

Abbeyville, 1 Willoughby Ct. (tel. 327033). Well-marked 10-min. walk down the Derrygonnelly Rd. Mrs. McMahon's flowery rooms are stocked with TVs and piles of tourist info (from £15/person). Pink bathtub!

Rossole House, 85 Sligo Rd. (tel. 323462). The expensive but spiffy option—£15/person. Double w/bath £32 (no singles). Located in a gorgeous stone Georgian house on the Lough shore. TVs in all rooms.

Lough Melvin Holiday Centre, Garrison (tel. 58142), 25mi. out of Enniskillen on A4/B52 Rd. A convenient stopover on the way from Enniskillen to Sligo Town. Spelunking, sailing, and pony-trekking (£8/½day, £15/day). Caters mostly to groups, so the hostel will either be jam-packed or empty. May-Sept. dorm £9, single £13, double £24. Oct.-April £7.50, £11, £20 respectively. Continental breakfast £1.80, fisherman's breakfast £4.50. **Camping** March-Sept. £5/tent.

Lakeland Canoe Centre, Castle Island (tel. 324250, evenings 322411), is within walking distance of town with a free ferry service (8am-12pm) and sports equipment for hire. Dorm £9. B&B £10.50. **Camping** £4/person.

FOOD & PUBS

Franco's, Queen Elizabeth Rd. (tel. 324424). Cozy nooks, wooden tables, candles in bottles, and red napkins inhabit this popular bistro. Heavenly pizza from £4.75, pasta from £7, and seafood. Opens at noon, closes late.

The Crowe's Nest, High St. (tel. 325252). Gas masks, swords, and other aids to digestion are exhibited around this pub/grill. Central location. Live music Mon.-Thurs. nights. Lasagna and salad £4.50, huge all-day breakfast £3.90.

Barbizon Café, 5 East Bridge St. (tel. 324556). A totem pole, miniature palm tree, and surreal paintings keep company with Enniskillen's falafel-chomping crowd. Chicken kebab sandwich £2.50. Open Mon.-Sat. 8:30am-6pm.

Aisling Centre, 37 Darling St. (tel. 325811), serves light lunches and snacks. Great afternoon tea special (3-5pm): £1 buys you tea, a scone and pastry.

White Star Bar, 1 Church St. (tel. 325303). Barmaids scuttle between beseeching drinkers. Well-stocked bar (more than just beer), middle-aged crowd, and dark room. Music Fri.-Sun. nights. "Home-cooked" roast beef £3.25.

Bush Bar, 26 Townhall St. (tel. 325210). Narrow, woody bar greets you. "Rave" bar in back—rave music, luminescent lights, black walls—merriment and fun.

Blakes of the Hollow, 6 Church St. (tel. 322143). Reads "William Blake" on the front. So old and red that they put it on a postcard; so brightly lit inside that the young crowd can find their drinks even with blurred vision.

SIGHTS

Inside Enniskillen's grand castle, the **Fermanagh County Museum** (tel. 325050 or 325000) presents a comprehensive look at rural Fermanagh, beginning with a wildflower exhibition and culminating in a large-scale tableau of a 1930s country kitchen. The Museum of the Royal Inniskilling Fusiliers and Dragoons is a military historian's playground. (Open July-Aug. Sat.-Mon. 2-5pm, Tues.-Fri. 10am-5pm; May-June and Sept. Mon. and Sat. 2-5pm, Tues.-Fri. 10am-5pm; Oct.-April Mon. 2-5pm, Tues.-Fri. 10am-5pm. Last admission 4:30pm. Admission £2, students £1.50.)

One and a half miles south of Enniskillen on A4, **Castle Coole** (tel. 322690) rears up in neoclassical *hauteur*. The National Trust spent £7 million restoring it for tourists. The acres of landscaped grounds are covered by buttercups and wild daisies (and the occasional unicorn). The castle grounds are 10 minutes along on the Dublin Rd.; the castle itself appears at the end of a 20-minute hike up the driveway. (Open April and Sept. Sat.-Sun. 1-6pm; May-Aug. Fri.-Wed. 1-6pm. Last tour 5:15pm. Tours £2.50.) Diagonally across the street from the castle entrance, the **Ardhowen Theatre** (tel. 325440) poses by the lake shore, satisfying dance, drama, music, and film enthusiasts. (Tickets available from the box office Mon.-Sat. 9am-5pm, and until 9pm on the night of a performance; £5-8.)

If you don't have time to explore the surrounding Lake District, Erne Tours Ltd. offers a quickie (1¾-hr.) **tour** of upper Lough Erne, including a half-hour stop at the very cool Devenish Island (see below). Tours on the **MV Kestrel** (tel. 322882) leave from the Round 'O' Jetty in Brook Park, two minutes down the Derrygonnelly Rd. (May-June Sun. 2:30pm.; July-Aug. daily 10:30am, 2:15, and 4:15pm, also Tues., Thurs., and Sun. 7:15pm.; Sept. Tues., Sat., and Sun. 2:30pm. £4; 50p discount on morning trips.)

■ Near Enniskillen: Florence Court & The Marble Arch Caves

Ten miles southwest of Enniskillen, Florence Court and the Marble Arch Caves can be combined into a daytrip. **Florence Court** (tel. (01365) 348249), an 18th-century Georgian mansion, was completed 20 years before Castle Coole. The building is surrounded by the **Florence Court Forest Park,** which also includes an impressive walled garden. The Rococo Court once housed the Earls of Enniskillen; the third Earl left behind his fossil collection for visitors' delectation. To get there take Sligo Rd. out of Enniskillen, then turn left onto the A32 (Swanlinbar Rd.) and follow the signs. (Estate open all year 10am to 1hr. before dusk. Florence Court open April-May and Sept. Sat.-Sun. noon-6pm; June-Aug. Wed.-Mon. noon-6pm. Admission £2.60.)

Four miles farther on the road from Florence Court to Belcoo (take the Sligo bus to Belcoo and walk 3 mi. following the signposts; the indirect route makes this a fairly difficult hitch) are the **Marble Arch Caves** (tel. (01365) 348855), a subterranean labyrinth of hidden rivers and weirdly sculpted limestone. An underground boat trip begins the tour which leads to impressive creations sculpted by nature's imaginative hand over thousands of years. Especially pleasing are the reflections of stalactites in the river. (Open late March to June and Sept. daily 10am-4:30pm; July-Aug. daily 10am-5pm. Admission £5, students £3.)

▓ Lower Lough Erne

DEVENISH ISLAND

The ruins on tiny Devenish Island are a worthwhile destination for anyone with an interest in Irish medieval history and archeology. St. Molaise founded a monastic center here in the 6th century. Viking raids and Plantation reforms finally put an end to the long monastic life by the 17th century, when the whole congregation moved to Monea, on the mainland. **St. Molaise's House,** an old oratory, an 81-ft. round tower (dating from the 12th century), and an Augustinian priory (from the 15th century) are all that remain today. The **round tower** is completely intact—you can even climb to the top. From Enniskillen, sail on the **M.V. Kestrel's** tour of the lakes (see above). If you want to see only the island, the **Devenish Ferry** leaves from **Trory Point.** (April-Sept. Tues.-Sat. 10am-7pm, Sun. 2-7pm; £2.25, includes ticket to small museum on island.) Ask the driver of the Pettigo bus to let you off at Trory ferry station, or drive 4 mi. out of Enniskillen on the Irvinestown Rd. to the ferry terminal sign, at a gas station. However you travel the 10 minutes to the island, dress warmly, because strong winds howl. **Boa Island** and **White Island** are also of interest for their many brilliant examples of both pagan and Christian carvings. You can drive across Boa Island on the Kesh-Belleek Rd., while a ferry service based at the Castle Archdale Marina runs an hourly boat to White Island. (Tel. (01365) 631850. Open June to early Sept. Tues.-Sat. 10am-7pm, Sun. 2-7pm. £2.25.)

BELLEEK

At the tip of Lower Lough Erne, on the national border, tiny Belleek is famous for its delicate, lace-like china. Tours of the **Belleek Pottery** factory feature the tradesmen in action. The **Visitors Centre** (tel. (013656) 58501) is both museum (with originals like "Crouching Venus") and shop—nothing at discount prices, though, since all flawed pieces are destroyed. (Tours available Mon.-Fri. 9:30am-12:15pm and 2:15-4:15pm, last tour on Fri. at 3:30pm; £1. Visitors center open March-June and Sept. Mon.-Fri. 9am-6pm, Sat. 10am-6pm, Sun. 2-6pm; July-Aug. Mon.-Fri. 9am-8pm, Sat. 10am-6pm, Sun. 11am-8pm; Oct. Mon.-Fri. 9am-5:30pm, Sat. 10am-5:30pm; Nov.-Feb. Mon.-Fri. 9am-5:30pm.) Also in Belleek, **ExplorErne** (tel. (013656) 58866), chronicles the history and heritage of the Lough Erne region. (Open March-Easter Mon. and Thurs.-Fri. 11am-5pm; Easter-June Thurs.-Mon. 11am-5pm; July-Aug. Tues.-Fri. 11am-8pm, Sat.-Mon. 11am-5pm; Sept. Tues.-Fri. 11am-5:30pm, Sat.-Mon. 11am-5pm. £1.) Belleek is 25 mi. from Enniskillen on the Derrygonnelly Rd. (A46).

ULSTER WAY

Serious hikers should consider tackling the Fermanagh stretch of the Ulster Way. These 23 mi. of forested paths are marked by wooden posts with yellow arrows and stenciled hikers. Leading from Belcoo to Lough Navar, the path is neither smooth nor level, so those on bikes or in wheelbarrows should think again. Take a detailed map and food—shops and transport are scarce. The tourist office's *Ulster Way* pamphlet and the Fermanagh section of *The Ulster Way* (both 75p) contain detailed descriptions of the route, its sights, and its history.

ISLE OF MAN

The Isle of Man (or "Mann") is a pint-sized anomaly floating in the middle of the Irish Sea. The 70,000 Manx are British and swear allegiance to Queen Elizabeth, but they aren't part of the United Kingdom. Mann has its own legislature (the world's oldest), flag (a pinwheel with feet), currency, and post office, which complement its unique fauna (weird cats and sheep and extinct ponies, cows, and pigs) and language.

The Manx relish their eccentricities, though nowadays they worry that they are becoming too mainstream. Manx home rule has spawned the lax tax laws that created the island's huge offshore finance industry and lured hundreds of tycoons too rich to live in high-tax Britain; these "tax exiles" now zip around Douglas in expensive cars, leaving the young Irish immigrants who work for them to suck down their cigar fumes. The *Manx Independent* has big debates over a perceived dilution of Manx culture; 50% of the population was born off-island, pulling the Isle of Man closer to Ireland, Britain, and the rest of the world. The EU has also had a big effect: it pressured the Manx government to de-criminalize homosexuality in 1992 and to abolish capital and corporal punishment in 1993.

The island is beautiful, ringed by cliffs, sliced by deep valleys, criss-crossed by lovable antique trains, and small enough to be thoroughly explored in a week. The **Manx language,** a close cousin to Irish and Scots Gaelic, is taught in schools, and is still heard when the Manx legislature's laws are proclaimed on July 5 on **Tynwald Hill. Manx cats** (both rumpies and stumpies) are still bred on the island, as are the terrifying, four-horned Manx Loghtan sheep. Mann's most famous delicacy is its **kippers,** smoked herring which are usually eaten at breakfast. Manx kippers, caught and smoked locally (especially in Peel), are said to be tastier and more oily (that's a good thing) than the typical English variety. The three-legs-of-Mann emblem appears on every available surface, asserting the Manx identity with the slogan "Quocunque Jeceris Stabit": whichever way you throw me, I stand. The Isle of Man has weathered the political and cultural changes on either side of the Irish Sea without losing its independence or its moxie: visitors will come to cherish the fierce and indomitable Manx spirit.

HISTORY

Farming settlements on the Isle of Man date back to at least 4000 BC. Legend has it that St. Patrick brought Christianity to Mann circa 450 AD, leaving real-life reminders like round towers and Celtic crosses. The Vikings landed on Mann in the 800s and established the **Tynwald**—the world's oldest legislature. Scottish and English domination of the island began in 1265. Direct rule ended in 1405 when Henry IV gave Mann to the **Earls of Derby,** who were succeeded by the **Atholls.** But, in 1765, the **Isle of Man Purchase Act** granted the island to the Crown, for a fee. Then, as now, the island's tax status had enriched it and nearly ruined it: smugglers would import goods to the Isle and then float them by night to England and Ireland, thereby avoiding the high British tariffs. The Atholls collected a modest customs duty, the Manx merchants prospered, and the Crown lost revenue. England responded by forcing the Isle of Man into its customs union. Deprived of tax revenue, the island fell into poverty. The Manx language fell out of favor among the upper classes—by 1900, every islander would be able to speak English. **Henry Loch,** chosen by the Crown to be Governor of the Island in 1863, raised tax revenue, began public works projects such as breakwater construction, and strengthened the House of Keys. Today the Isle controls its own internal affairs and finances. Its continuing customs union with the U.K. remains a bone of contention among the Manx—many want to lower Manx duties, stimulating

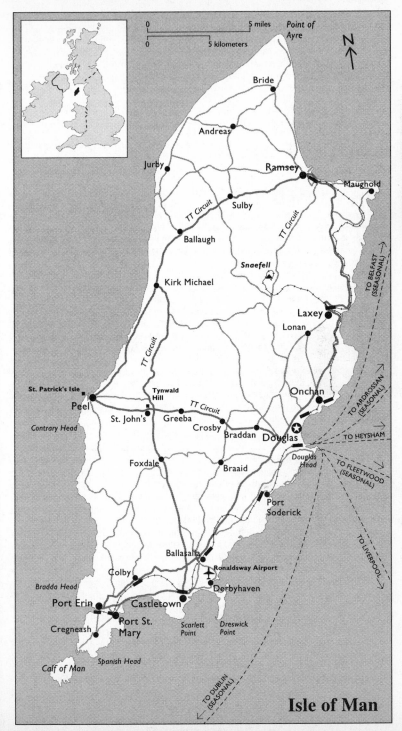

Isle of Man

The Isle of Man shares an international phone code with Britain of 44 (see **Essentials,** p. 44 for dialing instructions). All British pounds (from England, Scotland, or Northern Ireland) are accepted in the Isle of Man; however, Manx bills and coins are not accepted outside the Isle. Exchange before you leave, or save your interesting Manx currency for souvenirs. The Isle of Man issues its own stamps; British stamps are not valid.

tourism and trade just as the low taxes have stimulated the financial industry. Today, 14% of the population is involved in finance.

■ Getting There

The Isle of Man is a logical stopover between England or Scotland and the Republic or Northern Ireland. It's also possible to travel from Belfast or Dublin to Douglas, then to return to the Irish city from which you did not depart.

BY FERRY

The **Isle of Man Steam Packet Company** runs the only ferries to the island. Sailings to and from **Belfast** (May-Sept. 2-4/week, usually Mon., Fri., and Sun.; 4½hr.); **Dublin** (May-Sept. 2-4/week, usually Thurs. and Sun.; 4½hr.); **Heysham** (June-Sept. 1-2/day, Jan.-March Mon-Fri. 1/day; 3¾hr.); **Liverpool** (July-Aug. Mon., Wed., and Fri.-Sat.; Oct.-May only Sat.; 4½hr.); **Fleetwood** (June-Sept. 1/week; 3½hr.); and **Ardrossan,** Scotland (in cooperation with Caledonian MacBrayne; June-Aug. 1/week on Sat. or Sun.; 8hr.). Heysham and Liverpool are the only routes covered all winter.

Fares are highest on summer weekends and lowest in winter. 1996 one-way fares ranged from £20 to £28, students and seniors £15 to £28. Bikes are free. Return tickets are about 10% cheaper than two singles, but only if you return within five days. Thus, it's nearly as cheap to go from England to the Isle of Man to Ireland as to do a roundtrip. Sailings may fill up weeks in advance in summer. For **reservations,** call the Douglas office of the Isle of Man Steam Packet Co. (tel. (01624) 661661; fax 661065; open Mon.-Sat. 7am-7pm, Sun. 6am-11:30am and 12:30-7:30pm) or the Belfast office: W.E. Williames, Northern Rd. (tel. (01232) 351009; open Mon.-Fri. 9am-5:15pm). Bookings can also be made through travel agents.

BY TRAIN/FERRY COMBINATION

Combination Sea/Rail tickets are available from any British Rail station to Douglas and will save you money if you're planning to return to the same city. The ferry crossing is by ship from Heysham. From **London,** the whole trip takes about eight hours and costs £77 to £97 return; from **Edinburgh,** nine hours and £75-92. Fares are higher on weekends and from June to September. Combination tickets are available from some travel agents, but many in Douglas don't sell them. It's best to reserve your space on the ferry directly with the Isle of Man Steam Packet Co., especially since advance reservations (on rail and ferry) save quite a bit of money. British Rail passes qualify for discounts on combined Sea/Rail tickets.

BY AIR

Manx Airlines (U.K. tel. (01345) 626629 or (01624) 824313, Dublin tel. (01) 260 1588) flies from Ronaldsway Airport (tel. (01624) 823311) in the south of the island to Belfast, Cork, Dublin, London, Manchester, Glasgow, and seven other British destinations. **Jersey European** (tel. (01345) 676676) flies between Ronaldsway, Blackpool, and Belfast daily. USIT offers a student flight from Belfast to Ronaldsway (£78 return). **Knight Air** (tel. (01345) 626489) flies from Leeds.

■ Once There

GETTING AROUND

The Isle of Man has an extensive system of public transportation managed by **Isle of Man Transport,** Strathallan Crescent, Douglas (train info tel. 663 3666, bus info tel. 662525; open Mon.-Sat. 7:30am-10pm, Sun. 8am-4pm). The seven-day **Freedom Ticket** gives free passage on any public transport on the island (buses, railways, and horse trams) for £25.20. Discount tickets and a comprehensive bus/train timetable (50p) are available from the major bus and train stations, newsagents, some B&Bs, and the Discovery Guides Visitors Centre in Douglas.

Buses

Frequent buses connect the four major towns and every tiny hamlet on the island. While they lack the romance of the railroads, buses, particularly the double-decker ones, offer prime vantage points from which to view the island. Return tickets on buses are usually 15-20% cheaper than two singles. A **three-day Bus Rover** discount ticket allows unlimited bus travel on three days out of seven (£10.20), a good deal if riding trains (which are less extensive) doesn't interest you. It's more difficult to make the **one-day Bus Rover** ticket (£4.40) worth its price.

The **Tours (Isle of Man) Bus Tour Company** (tel. 676105) provides transportation from Douglas to events such as concerts and parades, and makes daytrips to towns and sights (£1.50-3.70 return). Schedules are posted at the Douglas tourist office and the Crescent Leisure Centre in Douglas. Tickets can also be bought at the Discovery Guides Centre and the Booking Office at Villa Marina, Loch Promenade. Full-day "Round the Island" tours leave at 10:15am, stop in Peel, Ramsey, and Port Erin, and arrive back in Douglas by 5pm. The schedule of other tours (including local tours, tours in a 40s bus, and mystery tours) changes weekly. (Full-day tours £7.50-8, ½-day and evening tours £3.50-3.70.)

Trains

Thousands of "railway enthusiasts" come from Britain each year to experience the shaky, clackety rides in the original Victorian cars of the electric and steam trains. Most of these dedicated people have been on all the steam trains in Britain and compare notes when they get together. A subset enjoy taking pictures of the trains, for whom the Manx bus company runs a special service known as the "chasing bus." Its sole purpose is to follow the route of a particular train and reach each stop before the train. The term **trainspotting** has weaseled its way into British slang to mean something that is boring and pointless. Inquire at bus station for details.

The unique Isle of Man Railways run along the east coast from Port Erin in the south to Ramsey in the north. A separate line of the electric railway, the **Snaefell Line** (opened to the public on August 21, 1895), branches off 6 mi. north of Douglas at Laxey to head to the top of Snaefell, the island's highest peak. The **Steam Railway,** dating from 1873, used to cover much of the island, but only the line south from Douglas to Port Erin is still running. The **Electric Railway,** dating from 1893, runs north from Douglas to Ramsey. The #1 and 2 trains of the M.E.R. (Manx Electric Railway) are the two oldest trains in the world. The 2 mi. of Douglas between the Steam and Electric Railway Stations is covered by bus or by **horse-drawn trams.**

The Electric Railway runs from 10am to 6:15pm (April-June and Sept.-Oct. 5/day; July-Aug. 14/day). The Steam Railway runs from 10am to 5:30pm (July-Aug. Mon.-Thurs. 6/day, Fri.-Sun. 4/day; April-June, Sept. and the last week of Oct. 4/day). The **three-day Rail Rover** ticket includes unlimited travel on the Steam, Electric, and Snaefell Mountain Railways. (3 out of 7 days, £13.70. 1-day £9.20. Children ½-price.)

By Bike or Thumb

The island's small size makes it easy to get around by bike. The southern three-fourths of the island are covered in rolling hills which present a manageable challenge to cyclists. Bike rental is available but expensive in Douglas and Ramsey. Since the ferry carries bikes for free, it's wiser to import them. Some of the walking trails described below are open to bikes, but many are not. Back roads are fairly quiet.

For tired walkers, hitching provides a legal, socially acceptable alternative to public transport. The scarcity of hitchhikers on the island probably relates more to the lack of budget travelers and the ease of public transport than to any difficulty in getting lifts. Locals claim that the Isle of Man is one of the safer places for hitching. Nonetheless, *Let's Go* does not recommend hitching (see **By Thumb,** p. 38).

By Foot

The short distances between towns and sights make walking feasible. Three long-distance, marked **hiking trails** are maintained by the Manx government. **Raad ny Foillan,** or "The Road of the Gull," is a 90-mi. path marked with seagull signs, which traces the island's perimeter. **Bayr ny Skeddan,** or "The Herring Road," marked by herring signs, covers the less spectacular 14 mi. between Peel in the west and Castletown in the east. (Walking east to west allows you to see the sunset at Peel.) The end of this trail overlaps the **Millennium Way,** which begins in Castletown and goes north to Ramsey, following the course of an ancient highway for 28 mi. The tourist office in Douglas has a free sheet which describes Raad ny Foillan and Bayr ny Skeddan and lists places to stay along Raad ny Foillan. *The Walks of Man Natural History* is the best pamphlet at tourist offices. The **Venture Centre** (tel. 814240), the **Isle of Man Rambling Association** (tel. 624095), and the **Manx Discovery Guides** (tel. 673444) also have info.

ACCOMMODATIONS

Although the Isle of Man has no youth hostels, competition for the declining tourist trade has produced plenty of inexpensive guesthouses, most of them in Douglas. The *Isle of Man Holiday Guide,* available from the tourist office, lists all of the approved accommodations on the island, including some campgrounds. B&Bs or guesthouses which aren't on this list aren't necessarily bad, but they may not be up to official standards. Though many B&Bs often fill up, it should still be possible to find a cheap place to stay, except during **T.T. races** (the first two weeks in June; see **Events,** below). B&Bs raise their rates but still fill up a year in advance for the races.

The other cheap option is **camping,** made more pleasant by the island-wide ban on trailer caravans (campers). Camping on the island must be done on a campsite, unless you find the "common land," where you can pitch your tent for free. It's located near the remote northern tip of the island. Ask in the Douglas tourist office.

EVENTS

These are as much reasons to avoid Mann as they are reasons to visit. During the motorcycle races, crowds are huge and raucous. A calendar of events is listed in detail in the *Official Guide to the Isle of Man: What's On.*

T.T. (Tourist Trophy) Race Weeks. First 2 weeks in June. All kinds of crazy events, and huge crowds, jazz, music, and theater. Islanders often give directions in relation to the "T.T. Circuit," marked on the Isle of Man map.

Manx Heritage Festival. Week of July 5. Music recitals and flower displays in the island's churches. Tynwald Fair sees the pronouncement of new laws on July 5, which is the Isle of Man Bank Holiday and Manx National Day.

Southern "100" Motorcycle Races. Mid-July. Call 822546 for info.

International Football Festival. Last week in July. Gangs of large, noisy, beer-drinking men from across Britain (*very* international) play ball. Info tel. 661930.

Manx Grand Prix Motorcycle Races and Vintage Motorcycle Rally. Last weekend in August. Race info tel. 627979.

■ Douglas

The capital of a none-too-large country, Douglas really is a grape-sized metropolis. There's culture (the famed Gaiety Theatre and the remarkable Manx Museum), diversity (rich old Brits, struggling young Irish, and a spattering of "others"), restaurants (some serve banana milkshakes), and commercialism. Douglas bloomed in the Victorian era after it was named the capital of the island, replacing smaller Castletown Harbour. Douglas's heyday was at the turn of the 20th century—the Victorian railway and horse tram network and promenades continue to define Douglas.

GETTING THERE

From the **airport,** the main coast road heads 8 mi. northeast to Douglas. The Port St. Mary/Douglas bus drives this route (Mon.-Sat. 28/day, Sun. 12/day; 25min.; £1.25; open Mon.-Sat. 6:20am-10:50pm). The steam train will stop at Ronaldsway Airport if you notify the guard first. The **ferry terminal,** designed to look like the three legs of Mann, lies at the southern end of Douglas near the bus station and shopping area.

GETTING AROUND

During the summer, **horse-drawn trams** (streetcars; tel. 675522) run along tracks up and down the Promenade every few minutes between 9am and 8-10pm (April-Sept.). The service is slow but inexpensive (£1.30) and quaint. Stops are posted every 200 yd. or so, so you can get on or off almost anywhere you want. **Buses** also run along the Promenade every few minutes, connecting the Bus and Steam Railway stations with the Electric Railway and Onchan (bus station to Electric Railway 60p). Local buses are covered by the Bus Rover **passes,** and both buses and horse trams are covered by the seven-day Freedom Ticket. A seven-day ticket covering local buses within Douglas and Onchan (£7) probably won't do most tourists much good. Another ticket costs £4.40 for 10 journeys, and may be a better value. The £1.30 "Ride-A-Day" ticket for horse trams is probably a safer buy. The one-day or three-day Rail Rovers also include the #30 bus service running between the Electric Railway Station and the Steam Railway Station, including stops on the Promenade and embarkation at Villa Marina, Loch Peninsula.

ORIENTATION & PRACTICAL INFORMATION

Douglas stretches for 2 mi. along the seafront, from Douglas Head in the south to the Electric Railway terminal in the north. **Douglas Head** is separated from the rest of town by the River Douglas, which flows into the harbor. Just north of the river, the shopping district spreads around **Victoria St.,** and turns into Duke St. and pedestrianized Strand St. **The Promenade,** which changes its name frequently, is a wide street that runs between the long crescent of beach and a row of grand but slightly tattered Victorian terrace houses. **Summer Hill** branches inland, just before the Electric Railway station. The neighborhood village of Onchan is north and east. At the point where Harris turns into Central Promenade, Broadway leads up a steep hill to **Nobles Park,** site of recreation facilities and the start of the T.T. course.

Tourist Office: Sea Terminal Building (tel. 686766). Helpful leaflets and lists of everything from nice views to ballroom dance venues. Bus and rail timetables and passes for sale here. Free map of Douglas (with all street names) available. The *Isle of Man: What's On* guide is most valuable. Open May-Aug. daily 9am-7:30pm; Sept.-April Mon.-Thurs. 9am-5:30pm, Fri. 9am-5pm, Sat. 9am-1pm.
Travel Agent: There are no budget travel agencies, but **Lunn Poly Holiday Shop,** 83 Strand St. (tel. 612848), offers cheap flights. Open Mon.-Sat. 9am-5:30pm.
Financial Services: American Express: Palace Travel, Central Promenade (tel. 662662), in the Palace Hotel. **Thomas Cook,** Strand St. (tel. 626288). Open Mon.-Sat. 9am-5:30pm. **A.T. Mays Travel Agents,** 1 Regent St. (tel. 623330). Bureau de

change is convenient to the ferry terminal for trading Manx money into English bills before you leave. Open Mon.-Fri. 9am-5:30pm, Sat. 9am-5pm.

Banks: Isle of Man Bank, (tel. 637100), corner of Regent and Strand St. Open Mon.-Fri. 9:30am-5pm, Sat. 9:30am-12:30pm; all branches on the island charge a £5 commission for changing travelers cheques; **ATM. TSB,** 78 Strand St. (tel. 673755). Open Mon.-Thurs. 9:30am-4pm, Fri. 9:30am-6pm; **ATM.**

Transportation: Isle of Man Transport, Strathallan Crescent (trains tel. 663366, buses tel. 662525). Open Mon.-Sat. 7:30am-10pm, Sun. 8am-4pm. See **Getting There,** p. 434 and **Getting Around,** p. 435.

Taxis: A-I Taxis (tel. 674488). 24-hr. service to the whole island.

Car Rental: Athol Car Hire, Hill St. (tel. 623232; fax 620782; Ronaldsway Airport tel. 822481). Nissans. Ages 23-75. **E.B. Christian and Co.,** Bridge Garage (tel. 673211; fax 677250). Fords. Ages 21-75. **Cleveland Self-Drive Car Hire,** 30a Esplanade Lane (tel. 621844; fax 628833). Nissans and Fords. Ages 23-70.

Bike Rental: Eurocycles, 8a Victoria Rd. (tel. 624909), off Broadway. 18-speed mountain bikes £7/day, £35/week; deposit ID. **HSS Hire Shops,** 32 South Quay (tel. 622987). Mountain bikes £12.50/day, £6.50/additional day for 3 days, £25/week; deposit £100. Open Mon.-Fri. 8am-5:30pm, Sat. 8:30am-noon.

Library: Manx Museum Library. Every book relating to Manx studies, genealogical information, and history (see **Sights,** p. 440). Open Mon.-Sat. 10am-5pm.

Launderette: Broadway Launderette, 24 Broadway (tel. 621511). £2.50 wash, 20p/5min. dry. Open Mon.-Wed. and Fri.-Sat. 8:30am-5:30pm, Sun. 9am-2pm.

Weather: for info call (01696) 888300. 24hr.

Bisexual, Gay, and Lesbian Info: Carrey-Friend (tel. 611600), Thurs. 7-10pm. **Ellan Vannin Gay Group,** P.O. Box 195, Douglas IM99 1QP (no phone).

Crisis Hotline: Samaritans, 5 Victoria Pl. (tel. 663399), near Broadway. Drop-ins 10am-10pm; hotline 24hr.

Pharmacy: Flynn's Pharmacy, 44 Duke St. (tel. 674014). Mon.-Sat. 9am-6pm.

Hospital: Nobles Hospital, Westmoreland Rd. (tel. 663322).

Emergency: Dial 999, no coins required. **Police:** tel. 631212.

Post Office: Regent St. (tel. 686114). Wide range of interesting Manx stamps. For free info pack on Manx stamps, call 686132 or write: Philatelic Bureau, Circular Rd., Douglas, IOM, IM99 1PB. Open Mon.-Fri. 9am-5:30pm, Sat. 9am-12:30pm.

Phones: Strand St.; Villa Marina Arcade; Harris Promenade, Broadway. Cardphones are common, cards are sold in any post office or newsagent. British or Northern Irish BT cards do not work on Isle of Man phones.

Phone Code: 01624 for the whole island.

ACCOMMODATIONS

Inexpensive guesthouses (in the £10-13 range) can be found on the promenades, but the majority of them cluster on Church Rd., around Broadway, on Castle Mona Ave. (off Central Promenade), and around Mona Drive (halfway up Central Promenade). The Mona Drive area is quietest but farthest from the center of town.

Merridale Guest House, 30 Castlemona Ave. (tel. 673040). Large, squeaky-clean bedrooms with sinks and coffee/tea facilities. Sells rover and freedom tickets, stamps, phonecards, and postcards. Fran and Ken are encyclopedia of info on IOM. No vacancies for T.T. '97. £15/person, £13 if you mention *Let's Go;* £12/person for more than 1 night. Open May-Sept.

Glen Villa, Broadway (tel. 673394), 2 doors down from the Ranch Café. Attractive Victorian exterior houses comfortable rooms and a private bar where Pauline and "Big" Al will entertain late into the evening. £13/person.

Sea Nook, 10 Empire Terrace (tel. 676830). Turn off Central Promenade next to the Imperial Hotel, turn right after 50yd. onto Empire Terrace. A well-groomed rose garden leads to small but pleasant rooms with views of Douglas Bay. All have sinks and teapots. Single £14. Double £25. Open May-Sept.

Nobles Park Grandstand Campsite, on the site of the T.T. races' start and finish line. Only campground in Douglas. £4.50/site. Showers £1, toilets free. Open June-Sept. except during the races (first 2 weeks in June). For info and reservations, call the Douglas Corporation (tel. 621132) Mon.-Fri. 9am-5pm.

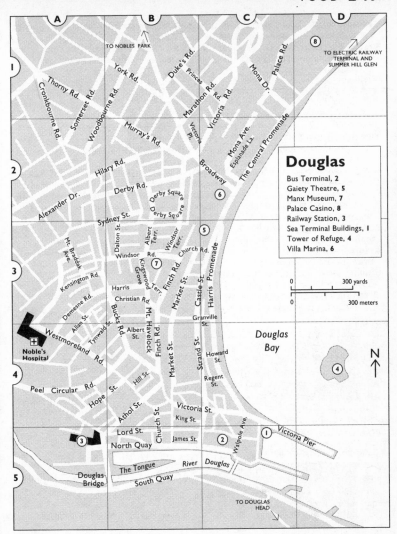

Douglas

Bus Terminal, **2**
Gaiety Theatre, **5**
Manx Museum, **7**
Palace Casino, **8**
Railway Station, **3**
Sea Terminal Buildings, **1**
Tower of Refuge, **4**
Villa Marina, **6**

ISLE OF MAN

FOOD

Groceries can be found at the enormous **Safeway,** Chester St. (tel. 673039), near the Manx Museum (open Mon.-Thurs. and Sat. 8:30am-8pm, Fri. 8:30am-9pm). Fresh and cheap fruits and vegetables tempt the palate at **Robinson's,** Strand St. (open daily 8am-6pm). **Holland and Barrett Health Food Store,** Strand St., sells things that crunch (open Mon.-Tues. and Thurs.-Sat. 9am-5:30pm, Wed. 9:30am-5:30pm).

Victoria's, Castle St. (tel. 626003). Tasty coffee shop fare served on a balcony overlooking the street. The owner is endearingly cheeky. Open Mon.-Sat. 9am-6pm.
L'Experience, Summer Hill (tel. 623103), near the Electric Railway station. Good French cooking at reasonable lunchtime prices (French ploughman's lunch w/Brie £2.75). Expensive dinners. Lunch Mon. and Wed.-Sat. noon-2pm, dinner Mon. and Wed.-Sat. 7-11pm.

Green's, North Quay (tel. 629129). Douglas's only vegetarian restaurant. Quiche and salad £3. Open Mon.-Sat. 9am-5pm, Sun. 10am-4pm.

Saagar Tandoori, 1 South View, Summerhill (tel. 674939). Good Indian food with a lovely bay view (vegetable rice £2.75). Open noon-2:30pm and 6pm-midnight.

PUBS

Manx pubs are not known for their music. While pubs are busy and fun every night of the week, entertainment generally falls into either the disco or country-singer category. Irish music and jazz appear only for special events. In summer, hordes of young people roam the streets until the wee hours of the morning, while the hotel bars generally fill with older people. Women tend to dress up for nights out.

Bushy's Bar (tel. 675139) at the intersection of Loch Promenade and Victoria St. One of the island's most popular pubs has live rock bands on weekends (cover £3-5), and tasty Bushy's beer to recommend it. A stumbling crowd spills out into the square in front of the bar on summer evenings.

Brendann O'Donnell's, 16-18 Strand St. This popular pub displays its Irish origins with a lengthy story written outside its door. Look for traditional cobbler's tools and a few old shoes in the windows.

Cul-de-Sac Bar and Pizzeria, 3 Market Hill (tel. 623737). The largest selection of beer on the island, including Hell Lager and Elephant Beer. Youthful crowds munch pizza and snacks. Cheap lunch specials served Mon.-Fri. noon-2pm, Sat. noon-6pm. Other food available Mon.-Sat. 5:30pm-late. Closed Sun. in winter.

Quids Inn, 56 Loch Promenade (tel. 611769). A money-saver for serious drinkers: pay £1 to get in and £1/drink. Closed during the day in winter.

SIGHTS

Trainspotters arise! The Victorian Steam Railway, Electric Railway, and Horse Trams are a living transportation museum. The **Electric Railway and Horse Tram terminal** marks the northeastern boundary of Douglas (look for the enormous "Electric Railway" sign). See **Ramsey** (p. 441) for one of the terminal's uses.

Just 100 yd. toward town, Summer Hill, on its way to neighboring Onchan, runs past the entrance to **Summer Hill Glen,** a peaceful green corridor of forest that follows a stream for ½ mi. up a narrow river valley. On summer evenings the glen is transformed into Mother Goose's worst nightmare, as blinking colored lights depict familiar nursery rhymes and dinosaurs. A half mile left down Glencrutchery Rd. lies huge **Nobles Park,** where the T.T. races begin and end. The park contains a campground, tennis courts, lawn bowling, and mini-golf.

Just past the Villa Marina on Harris Promenade sits one of the more impressive reminders of the island's Victorian heyday, the **Gaiety Theatre** (tel. 625001). The remarkable, newly restored stained-glass awning of the theater tickles Victorian fancy, and the gilded and cherubic interior is even better. Frequent performances offer a glimpse of the theater in action, but to see the fascinating antique machinery under the stage you'll have to take a guided tour. A little old lady sitting in seat D-14 is one of the theater's three ghosts. (Tours every Sat. at 10:30am, July-Aug. also Thurs. 2:30pm; 1½hr. Tea and scones afterwards. Free, but donation encouraged.)

Just south of the Gaiety Theatre, signs lead from the shopping district to a parking garage with an elevator to the **Manx Museum** (tel. 675522). The museum, which takes about three hours to see properly, chronicles the natural and human history of the island from the Ice Age to the present. A 12,000-year-old Irish Elk skeleton, a reconstruction of the "Pagan Lady's Grave" discovered at Peel Castle, and displays on the wartime internment of resident aliens on the island vie for visitors' attention. The **National Art Gallery** and a library stocked with books on Manx subjects are also inside. (Museum and library open Mon.-Sat. 10am-5pm. Free.)

The thing that looks like a little castle sitting on a rock in Douglas Bay is the **Tower of Refuge.** It sits on treacherous Conister Rock, which has caused many shipwrecks. The tower was built in 1832 to provide a shelter in which shipwreck survivors could wait out the storm before being rescued. The southern end of Douglas is marked by **Douglas Head,** which has lovely views back onto Douglas town.

ENTERTAINMENT

Most visitors to the Isle of Man want to participate in, rather than watch, their entertainment. As a result, the arts and entertainment scene here tends to be heavy on hypnotists and country crooners, but low on theater and concerts. Jazz and trad are usually available to those who keep their eyes open.

The splendid **Gaiety Theatre** (tel. 625001) is the only theater of note on the island, but it does its best to fill the hole in the Manx arts scene with a complete range of musical and theatrical productions. The theater's season runs from March through December, but its busiest period is from July to October, when there are plays most nights. (Box office open Mon.-Sat. 10am-4:30pm and performance nights. Tickets £4-12; discounts for seniors and children.) The Royal Hall at the **Villa Marina,** Harris Promenade (tel. 628855), has a variety of tacky entertainment, from Ron Ricco the Hypnotist to professional wrestling. Occasionally a pearl like the Chinese State Circus appears among the seaweed of 70s tribute bands. The **Summerland Complex** (tel. 625511), next to the Electric Railway terminal, provides similar cheesy fun as well as popular first-run films.

Douglas pubs like **Bushy's Bar** often have live rock and folk in summer. **Smuggler's** (tel. 629551) in the Admiral Hotel, Loch Promenade, hosts folk bands (April-Sept. Thurs. 8:40pm; cover £1.50) and the **Ridgeway Hotel,** Ridgeway St. (tel. 675612), has live music (Thurs.-Sat.). The Summerland Complex hosts the **Manx Youth Orchestra** every Sunday night (free) and a summer cabaret (Mon.-Sat. 8pm).

The **Stakis Hotel Complex** has a popular nightclub and a casino, both open until 3:30am. **Paramount City,** Queens Promenade (tel. 622447), turns into a nightclub called **The Dark Room** on Wednesdays, Fridays, and Saturdays (9pm-2am; Wed. free; Fri. and Sat. free before 10pm, £3 after 10pm; over 21). It also contains the **Director's Bar,** which serves until 2am. **Jimmy B's,** Central Promenade, in the Castle Mona Hotel, has karaoke on Thursdays (Mon.-Sat. 8pm-2am; over 21 only). **The Tardis,** Barrack St. (tel. 661547), is a reminder of the frightening number of Doctor Who fans on Mann (open Mon.-Sat. 10pm-2am; Mon.-Thurs. free, Fri.-Sat. cover £3).

■ Near Douglas

On the western edge of Douglas, about 2 mi. from the Douglas bus station on the Peel Rd., the village of **Braddan** offers two sights of interest to visitors. The old church next to the old cemetery on the Peel Rd. houses a major collection of Viking-era **Manx crosses** along with a few Celtic-period crosses. Also in Braddan, **Bushy's Brewery,** Mount Murray, offers tours by appointment (tel. 661244).

Three miles south on the Castletown Rd. from Douglas lies the **Isle of Man Home of Rest for Old Horses** (tel. 674594), **Bulhrenny.** Most of the venerable horses once pulled Douglas trams (open late May to mid-Sept. Mon.-Wed. 10am-4:50pm). For younger equine action, the **Manx Equestrian Centre** (tel. 621852 or 675901) offers pony trekking through the countryside. They will pick you up from town (£5/hr., £10/half-day, £20/day includes lunch).

Northeast of Douglas, the neighboring village of **Onchan** holds several well-preserved Celtic-era **cross slabs** in the village church on Church Rd. Take any Onchan bus to Avondale Rd., continue in the bus's direction, and turn right onto Church Rd. **Molly Carrooin's Cottage** presents the preserved cottage of a 19th-century washerwoman (open June to mid-Sept. Tues. and Sun. 2:30-4:30pm; free).

■ Ramsey

The second-largest town on the island, Ramsey lies on the northwest coast where the Electric Railway line ends and the low northern plain begins. The town retains its Victorian feel in the harbor area (though the harbor is quite ugly) and offers few sights of interest to tourists. But it is convenient to points north and west, like Maughold, the Point of Ayre, and Jurby.

The **tourist office** (tel. 812228) is in the library in the town hall (open Mon.-Sat. 9:30am-5:30pm). **ATMs** are found at the **Isle of Man Bank** (tel. 812829) and **Barclays** (tel. 813596), both on Parliament St. (both open Mon.-Wed. and Fri. 9:30am-3:30pm, Thurs. 9:30am-5:30pm). The **Electric Railway** runs to Ramsey from Douglas via Laxey (May-Sept. 14/day; 1¼hr.; £5 return). **Buses** arrive from Douglas (23/day; 50min.; £1.85). **Ramsey Cycles,** Bowring Rd. (tel. 814076), rents three-speed bikes (£5/day, £20/week) and mountain bikes (£7/day, £40/week; no deposit; open Mon.-Sat. 9am-5:30pm). The Ramsey **post office** (tel. 812248) is on Court Row.

Accommodations in town are rather upscale. It would be cheaper and more relaxing to stay at Maughold (p. 442). The only affordable B&B in town is flower-strewn **Stanleyville Guest House,** Stanley Mount West (tel. 814420), around the corner from the beach (£16/person).

There are scarcely any restaurants open for dinner. Stock up at **Safeway's,** Christian St. (tel. 813228; open Mon. 8:30am-7pm, Tues.-Thurs. until 8pm, Fri. until 9pm, Sat. 8am-7pm). Popular **Francesco's** (tel. 814692) right next to the Viking Hotel is a real treat. Cheery Italian atmosphere accompanies good food (*tortellini al formaggio* £3.50; open Tues.-Sat. noon-1:45pm, and 7-9:45pm). The **Mitre Hotel,** Parliament St. (tel. 813045), serves ocean views with the pints.

On the edge of town lies 40-acre **Mooragh Park,** complete with lake, gardens, and bowling and putting greens all built on land reclaimed from a marsh. You can rent rowboats, canoes, or sailing dinghies here from 11am (tel. 813375). Sailing and wind-surfing lessons also available (£15/2 people; open Easter to June weekends only, June-Sept. daily). The **Grove Rural Life Museum** (tel. 675522), has been restored to its original condition as an upper-class Victorian country house. It is less engaging than its counterpart, the Cregneash Folk Museum (p. 445), but has resident Manx cats. The Museum is 1 mi. out of town, on A9 to Andreas. (Open Easter-Sept. daily 10am-5pm. Admission £2.) Ramsey hosts **Yn Chruinnaght** (tel. 815705) in the last week in July. The festival features music, dance, art, and literature from all the Celtic nations: Mann, Scotland, Ireland, Wales, Cornwall, and Brittany.

■ Near Ramsey

MAUGHOLD

Three miles southeast of Ramsey, Maughold makes a terrific excursion from Ramsey by bus or by bike along the coast road. The **Maughold Churchyard** contains the best collection of Celtic and Norse Manx crosses on the island, as well as the remains of three early Christian chapels, or *keeills,* dating from as early as 800. Manx crosses, which date from early Christian times, are Celtic crosses, similar to those found in Ireland (a cross with a circle), that show a Norse influence. The church itself, parts of which date from the 11th century, was named after St. Maughold. Legend holds that he was an Irish sinner who was tied up and cast adrift in the Irish Sea by St. Patrick as punishment. When he washed up on Maughold Head, he was so grateful to have survived that he founded an abbey on the site of the present church. A road leads from the churchyard to the lighthouse on **Maughold Head,** where a nice cliff walk known as the **Maughold Brooghs** begins. **Cardle Vooar Farm** (tel. 812160) provides accommodation in a rural setting (£14/person; open April-Oct.). The **Venture Centre** at Maughold (tel. 814240) offers a number of unique outdoor activities, including grass-skiing, abseiling, clay pigeon shooting and archery.

POINT OF AYRE

From Ramsey, the main coastal road leads north through **Bride** and, 7 mi. later, to the **Point of Ayre,** the northern tip of the island. A walk along the coast affords spectacular views of the mountains of Scotland, only 17 mi. away. To the west lie **The Ayres,** a region of elevated sand dunes rich in plant and bird life. **Ayres Visitors Centre** (tel.

801985) has displays on wildlife inside and sandy nature trails outside (open mid-May to Sept. Wed.-Sun. 2-5pm; free). **Buses** run from Ramsey to Bride (Mon.-Sat. 3/day, Sun. 2/day; 15min; £1). From there, the center is 2 mi. down the road west from Bride. The north road leads to the Point of Ayre. Buses also run from Ramsey directly to the Point of Ayre (Mon.-Sat. 1/day; 20min.; £1).

■ Castletown

Nine miles south of Douglas, Castletown retains much of its energy and all of its history from its stint as the old capital of the island. (The town was "de-throned" because its harbor was too small.) The **tourist office** is located at the Town Commissioner's office at the Civic Centre (tel. 825005). The Square and the narrow streets to its north and west contain most of the town's history and businesses, including the **IOM Bank,** 3 Market Sq. (tel. 822503; open Mon.-Wed. and Fri. 9:30am-3:30pm, Thurs. 9:30am-5:30pm; **ATM**) and the **post office,** Arbory St. (tel. 822516; open Mon.-Fri. 9am-12:30pm and 1:30-5:30pm, Sat. 9am-12:30pm). **Buses** from Port Erin/Port St. Mary (21/day; 25min.; £1.10) and Douglas (29/day; 35min.; £1.45) stop next to the castle. The **Steam Railway** station is a five-minute walk out of town toward Ballasalla (4-6/day; to Douglas, 40min.; to Port Erin, 20min.).

Accommodations, Food, & Pubs The most inexpensive place to stay in town is **Sandymount,** Bowling Green Rd. (tel. 822521), an imposing house near the beach. From the Castle, cross the footbridge, walk right along the sea to Bowling Green Rd., and head to its other end. From the railway station, turn left (away from town center), go 200 yd. to the rotary, and turn right. The house is on the left (£15/person; open April-Sept.). The only year-round option is **The Rowans,** Douglas St. (tel. 823210), facing the beach (£16.50/person).

Simple meals, omelettes (£2.85-3.40), baked potatoes (£2-3), and sandwiches (£1.30-2.30) are available at **Ye Olde Bakery Café,** 31 Malew St. (tel. 823092). The **G-Q bistro,** 5 Malew St. (tel. 822937), offers large pasta dishes for £3-4 (mediterranean *paella* £3.75; open Mon.-Sat. 9am-10pm, Sun. noon-9pm). The **George Hotel,** Market Sq. (tel. 822533), offers a historic atmosphere and a wide bar menu (chili *con carne* £3.50; food served Mon.-Sat. noon-2pm). The lively, friendly **Glue Pot,** at the Hotel, overlooking the harbor, sticks to drinkers from all over the island.

Sights In summer, guided **walking tours** of Castletown leave from the tourist office on Tuesdays at 11am (£1.50 for 1¼-hr. tour; for info, call 823209). Otherwise, call guide Hugh Jackson (tel. 824412). The former seat of the Lords of Man, **Castle Rushen** (tel. 825761), dominates the center of town. The castle, which had its origins with the last Viking king, Magnus, around 1250, is one of the best preserved castles in the British Isles. Practically every room in the castle is open for exploration, and plaques explain the uses of each room during each period of the castle's history. The banquet hall, castle kitchens, and workmens' sheds have all been reconstructed to resemble their appearances in the 1400s. A "high-ranking" officer sits on the garderobe (toilet), with appropriate sound effects. Several rooms are given over to exhibits which chronicle the history of the island and the castle through its use as an 18th-century prison. You can purchase a pamphlet on the history of the castle at reception for 50p, or just get the story from the friendly staff. (Open Easter-Sept. daily 10am-5pm. Admission £3, students £2.50.)

From the castle, a short walk toward the pier across the footbridge and around the corner leads to the small **Nautical Museum** (tel. 675522), with its 18th-century yacht and replica ship's cabin (open Easter-Sept. daily 10am-5pm; admission £2). Across from King William College, ¼ mi. down the road, rises a small hill with a ruin at the top. Probably originally a prehistoric burial mound, this site, know as **Hango Hill,** is where the Manx patriot Illiam Dhone (William Christian) was executed for treason after he supported greater Manx independence from Britain.

ISLE OF MAN

Two miles north on the main Douglas Rd., the village of **Ballasalla** houses the ruins of the medieval Cistercian **Rushen Abbey.** Ballasalla also holds a rare opportunity to pet or purchase a **Manx cat,** characterized by their absent tail, long hind legs, awkward walk, and intestinal problems. These cats appeared on the island only 300 years ago; some surmise that they are a cat/rabbit crossbreed. **Mr. F. J. Wadsworth,** The Sycamores, Airport Rd. (tel. 824 345), breeds and sells Manx cats. Completely tailless "rumpies" cost £100, while tiny-tailed "stumpies" go for £50.

■ Port Erin

Near the southern tip of the island, Port Erin, where grassy knolls rise above the sea, is perhaps the prettiest town on Mann. Port Erin has remained small and quiet despite the preponderance of tourist accommodations. While B&Bs here are slightly more expensive than those in Douglas, the town's saner atmosphere and beautiful setting make it a tempting place to stay.

Practical Information The **tourist office,** Commissioners Office, Station Rd. (tel. 832298), dishes a few pamphlets and advice on accommodations (no bookings; open May to late Sept. Mon.-Thurs. 9am-5pm, Fri. 9am-4:30pm, Sat. 9am-noon). The **IOM Bank** on Station Rd. processes pounds (tel. 822503; open Mon.-Wed. and Fri. 9:30am-3:30pm, Thurs. 9:30am-5:30pm). **Trains** chug to Douglas (4-6/day; 65min.; £3.75). **Buses** zoom to Douglas (23/day; 55min.; £1.75); and Peel (3/day; 50min.; £1.80). From the bus stop, turn right, then right again at the Haven Bar. This street goes past the train station and down to the Upper Promenade. **Sea Sports,** Strand Rd., rents rods for **fishing** from the Port Erin pier (£4.50/day; open daily 10am-6pm). **Port Erin Stables,** (tel. 621852 or 675901) welcomes beginners (½-day pony trek £10; free pickup from town). **Woodworth's Chemist,** Orchard Rd. (tel. 832139), is the local pharmacy (open daily 9am-6pm, except Sat. open 9am-5:30pm). The **post office** posts up on Church Rd. (tel. 833119; open Mon.-Wed. and Fri. 9am-1pm and 2-5:30pm, Thurs. 9am-1pm, Sat. 9am-12:30pm).

Accommodations, Food, & Pubs **York House,** The Promenade (tel. 832440), gives a friendly welcome, clean rooms overlooking the beach, and huge breakfasts (vegetarian option; £13/person). **Epworth,** Church Rd. (tel. 832431), off the Promenade near the center of town is popular and comfortable with sinks in the rooms (£15/person; open May-Sept.). **Grosvenor House,** The Promenade (tel. 832369), showcases outstanding breakfasts and a view of the beach that can't be beat. TVs in all rooms—catch up on *Doctor Who* (from £15/person, w/bath £18; winter £13/person, w/bath £16/person).

Port Erin can keep you well fed. If you tire of inexpensive restaurants, try the **Shop-rite Supermarket,** Orchard Rd., behind the bus stop (open Mon.-Tues. 9am-5:30pm, Wed.-Fri. 9am-8pm, Sat. 8:30am-5pm). **Cozy Nook Café,** Lower Promenade (tel. 835020), has an incredible setting on the beach with views of the bay and Mourne Mountains on a clear day. (Sandwiches £1.30-1.50 and salads £2.50-3.25.) Summer evenings (6:30-9pm) are chef's night off: cook-your-own-barbecues (£3-5.50; open April-Sept. Mon.-Sat. 10:30am-5pm, 6:30-9pm, Sun. 10:30am-9pm (early closing in bad weather); Oct.-March Fri.-Sun. 10am-6pm). **DaVinci's Grosvenor House,** The Promenade (tel. 832369), offers interesting pasta dishes, pizza, steaks, and seafood (7" pizzas from £2.50, pasta £4-5; open Mon. and Wed.-Sat. 7-10pm, Sun. noon-3pm and 7-10pm). **The Falcon's Nest Hotel Coffee Shop,** corner of Station Rd. and Strand Rd., is a classy joint with cheap meals (baked potato with cheese, tuna, and salad £2.25; open Mon.-Sat. 8:30am-6pm, Sun. noon-5pm).

Sights Cruises to the **Calf of Man,** the small island and bird sanctuary off the southern tip of Man, leave from the Port Erin pier during the summer daily in good weather. Visitors can choose between a 1¼-hour cruise around the Calf, with good views of the cliffs, seals, the odd basking shark, and countless sea birds, or a ferry service. The ferry gives anywhere from an hour to a whole day to explore the island and its herds of four-horned Loghtan sheep. (Tel. 832339; April-Sept. Cruises leave 10:15am daily. Ferries leave 10:15, 11:30am, and 1:30pm daily, last return at 3:30pm. £6 return.) You can also charter a boat from Port St. Mary. Bob Taylor at **Gemini Fishing Charter and Sightseeing** (tel. 832761) can arrange wildlife watching or sea angling trips.

The **Railway Museum** in the railway station is free and contains two antique trains (open April-Oct. 9am-noon and 1-4pm). The **Marine Interpretation Centre** (tel. 832027) is in the University of Liverpool's Department of Marine Biology. A small room houses displays and a video on the ecology of the Calf and surrounding waters (open April-Oct. Mon.-Fri. 10am-5pm; free). To reach the University Centre from Port Erin, face the sea, turn left, and walk as far as you can. A pleasant path begins across from the Port Erin Royal Hotel, leading north along the cliffs past sandy coves to **Bradda Head,** which is capped by a key-shaped tower built to honor local philanthropist and safe-maker William Milner. This short walk, especially peaceful and beautiful at sunset, offers views across to the Mourne Mountains of Northern Ireland. On some days, the Mournes seem to "come right into the bay," a sure sign that the next day will be rainy. Erosion makes it dangerous to leave the path.

The 1½-mi. road to Cregneash past the strange Neolithic **Meayll Circle** (a chambered burial mound) makes a nice walk. The **Cregneash Village Folk Museum** (tel. 675522) is a fascinating preservation of 19th-century life in a farming village. Farmers and craftspeople in traditional dress demonstrate their skills for the visitors. You can also read about how Manx ponies, cattle, and pigs (referred to as "purrs") became extinct, and gaze at the still existing Loghtan sheep and an occasional Manx cat. Be sure to watch the 10-minute video at the shop. (Open Easter-Sept. 10am-5pm; last admittance 4pm. Admission £2.) The 6-mi. portion of the coastal walking path *(Raad ny Foillan)* between Port Erin and the fishing village of **Port St. Mary** to the east is a manageable walk with stunning views of cliffs and sea. (Buses run back to Port Erin frequently.) The *Southern Walks* pamphlet, free from tourist offices, describes these walks.

The **Erin Arts Centre,** Victoria Sq. (tel. 832662), hosts several events. The **Mannanan International Festival of Music and the Arts** features all kinds of classical music, dance, drama, and lectures in late June and early July. **Sundays at Eight** is a monthly happening (first Sun. of the month) of classical recitals. Contact the Arts Centre for more info. At Port St. Mary, Wednesday is **Craft and Heritage Day** during the summer. The fair is held at Town Hall, the Promenade (open 10am-4pm).

■ Peel

The "most Manx of all towns" or "the Sunset City," Peel is a beautiful fishing town on the west coast of the island. Narrow streets and small stone buildings have hardly changed since the days when its fishers sailed from here to the Hebrides. The town is the headquarters of the big-time Manx kipper industry; except for connoisseurs of brine, visitors to Peel will more likely enjoy its cathedrals and coastal walks.

Practical Information The **tourist office,** Town Hall, Derby Rd. (tel. 842341), has pamphlets with self-guided walking tours (open Mon.-Thurs. 9am-5:15pm, Fri. 9am-4:30pm. **IOM Bank** counts change on Atholl St. (tel. 842122; open Mon.-Wed. and Fri. 9:30am-3:30pm, Thurs. 9:30am-5:30pm; **ATM**). **Buses** from the station is on Atholl St., next to the IOM bank, go to: Douglas (23/day; 40min.); Ramsey (10/day; 40min.); and Port Erin (1-2/day; 55min.). The **post office** licks stamps on Market Pl. (tel. 842282; open Mon.-Wed. and Fri. 9am-12:30pm and 1:30-5:30pm, Thurs. and Sat. 9am-12:30pm.

Accommodations, Food, & Pubs The **Haven Guest House,** 10 Peveril Ave. (tel. 842585), off Peveril Rd. offers non-smoking rooms with teapots, TVs, radios, and bathrooms, and delightful mountain views (£17/person; open all year). **Seabourne House,** Mount Morrison (tel. 842571), offers vegetarian breakfasts (an easy escape

ISLE OF MAN

from kippers) and tea-making facilities (£15/person). **Peel Camping Park,** Derby Rd., past the school (tel. 842341), has laundry, a game room, a TV room, and a wheel-chair-accessible bathroom (£4/person; open May-Sept.).

There aren't many food options in Peel—everyone's too focused on the yummy kippers. **Peel Wholefoods,** 5 Douglas St., sells health food to crafty eaters (open Fri.-Wed. 9:30am-5pm, Thurs. 9:30am-7pm). The best bet for food is the **Creek Inn Pub,** The Quay (tel. 842216; crab salad £5; food served Mon.-Sat. 11am-11pm, Sun. noon-1:30pm and 8-10pm), and the best place to drink is the **White House Hotel,** a former farmhouse on the Tynwald Rd. The **Harbor Lights Café** (tel. 843196), sits in front of the beach on Shore Rd. (kippers and brown bread £3; outside seating).

Sights **Peel Town Walks** (tel. 842852) start from Point Odin's Raven, The Quay, with a special focus on the town's architecture and personalities (Wed. 2:30pm; 1½hr.; £1.50). Alternatively, the free *Peel on Foot* self-guided walking tours (there are 3 in the series) are available at the tourist office.

Romantic **Peel Castle** is located on **St. Patrick's Isle,** now connected to the main-land by a causeway, where the first Christian missionaries (followers of St. Patrick) landed around 450. A second wave of missionaries from Iona (St. Columba's crew) came around 550; many Manx churches are still named for them. In the 800s, Viking raids forced the Christians to build churches out of stone instead of timber and sod. In the 10th century, the clever monks added round towers, the better to see you with, my dear Viking. The castle's name derives from an earlier fort made of timber, or "piles," built by the Viking King Magnus Barefoot. The castle has a ghost, in the form of a black dog, the **Moddey Dhoo,** which supposedly scared a soldier to death in the 17th century. A mark on the ground in front of the castle's entrance shows a medieval system of timekeeping: when the shadow of the castle's corner hit the mark at noon, it was time to change the guard. Peel Castle was the site of a major archaeo-logical excavation which uncovered the "Pagan Lady's Grave," now on display at the Manx Museum (see p. 440). Inside the castle are a 10th-century Irish-style round tower and the 13th-century **Cathedral of St. German.** The damp, eerie **Bishop's Dungeon** under the cathedral was used for hundreds of years to punish sinners for terrible offenses such as missing church. The path over the rocks around the castle offers views of the sea and the **seals.**

The two **kipper factories** on the island are in Peel. They don't give factory tours, but you can buy fresh kippers there: try **Devereau,** Mill Rd., the largest curer of Manx kippers in the known universe. You can even write them for mail-order, vacuum-sealed kippers. Peel Castle hosts the **Theatre Set Up** (tel. 842104), an open-air Shakespeare festival held every mid-July. **Viking Boat Races** (tel. 843640), held in August, pit teams of 20 rowers in Viking-style boats against the unforgiving bay.

LONDON

Tourists heading towards Ireland may consider London a mere waystop—a point of view which would shock many Londoners, who have a hard time viewing their city as anything but the center of the world. Heathrow Airport and Victoria Station are the points of entry for immigrants from every continent and isle. The Victorian doorway inscribed with an Anglican piety may belong to a Sikh or a Muslim in a city internalizing its imperial past. The most fascinating aspects of London derive from this—the tension between the rigid past and riotous present, the "foreign" and the traditional. If you can squeeze an extra couple of days into your journey, London is a superb place to get to know.

Many flights to Ireland from both the States and the continent connect in London (see **Getting There,** p. 26). Remember that London travel agents offer some economical train-and-ferry or bus-and-ferry connections to Ireland, Northern Ireland, and the Isle of Man—see **Getting There** for details, or stop in at one of the budget travel offices listed below in **Practical Information.** For an absolutely dapper little book packed with first-rate info on this city, grab a copy of *Let's Go: London,* or its trusty glossy, mappy sidekick *Let's Go Map Guide: London*

ORIENTATION & PRACTICAL INFORMATION

London is divided into boroughs and postal code areas, and into informal districts. Both the borough name and postal code prefix appear at the bottom of most street signs. The city has grown by absorbing nearby towns, which is reflected in borough names such as "City of Westminster" and "City of London" (or simply "The City").

Central London, on the north side of the Thames and bounded roughly by the Underground's Circle Line, contains most of the major sights. Within central London, the vaguely defined **West End** incorporates the understated elegance of Mayfair, the shopping streets around Oxford Circus, the theaters and tourist traps of Piccadilly Circus and Leicester Square, the exotic labyrinth of Soho, chic Covent Garden, and London's unofficial center, **Trafalgar Square.** East of the West End lies **Holborn,** center of legal activity, and **Fleet Street,** the traditional journalists' haunt.

Around the southeastern corner of the Circle Line is **The City:** London's financial district, with the Tower of London at its eastern edge and St. Paul's Cathedral nearby. Farther east is the ethnically diverse and working-class **East End** and the epic construction site of **Docklands.** Moving back west along the river and the southern part of the Circle Line, is the district of **Westminster,** the royal, political, and ecclesiastical center of England, where you'll find Buckingham Palace, the Houses of Parliament, and Westminster Abbey. In the southwest corner of the Circle Line, below the expanse of **Hyde Park,** are gracious **Chelsea,** embassy-laden **Belgravia,** and **Kensington,** adorned with London's posher shops and restaurants.

Around the northwest corner of the Circle Line, tidy terraces border **Regent's Park;** nearby are the faded squares of **Paddington** and **Notting Hill Gate,** home to large Indian and West Indian communities. Moving east towards the Circle Line's northeast corner leads to **Bloomsbury,** which harbors the British Museum, London University colleges, art galleries, and specialty bookshops. Trendy residential districts stretch to the north, including **Hampstead** and **Highgate,** with the enormous Hampstead Heath and fabulous views of the city.

Trying to reach a **specific destination** in London can be frustrating. Numbers often go up one side of a street and down the other. One road may change names four times in fewer miles, and a single name may designate a street, lane, square, and row. A good map is key. For a day's walk, London Transport's free map will do, but those

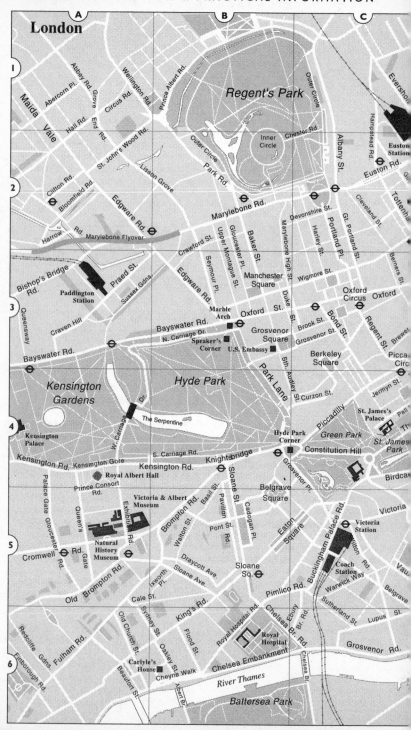

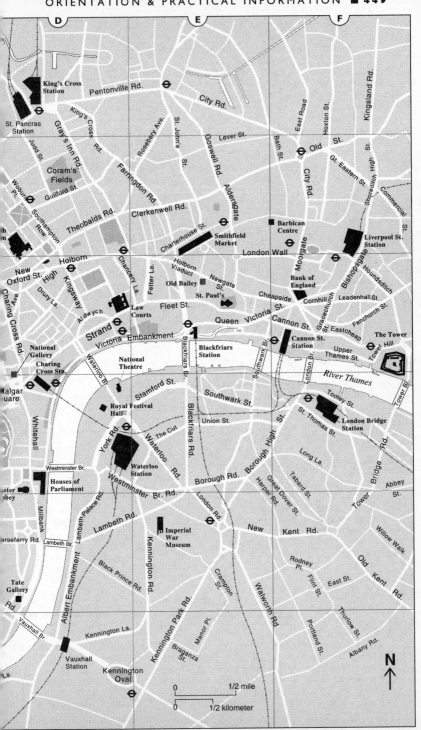

staying longer ought to buy a London street index. *London A to Z* (that's "ay to *zed*," by the way) and *Nicholson's Streetfinder* (both around £4) are excellent.

For the most part, London is a tourist-friendly city. It's hard to unwittingly wander into unnerving neighborhoods; these areas, in parts of Hackney, Tottenham, and South London, lie well away from central London. The areas around King's Cross/St. Pancras and Notting Hill Gate tube stations are a bit seedy at night. Avoid parks, heaths, and the riverbanks in all areas after dark. Late trains on the tube out of central London are usually crowded and noisy, but waiting late at night at less central stations can be unsettling. In general, unattended packages will be taken either by thieves or by the police, who are remarkably anxious (and rightly so) about terrorist bombs. Leave nothing unattended.

Tourist Offices: London Tourist Board Information Centre: Victoria Station Forecourt, SW1 (tel. (0839) 123 432; recorded message only; 39-49p/min.). Tube: Victoria. Info on London and England and an accommodations service (£5 booking fee, plus 15% refundable deposit). Expect long waits. Open April.-Nov. daily 8am-7pm; Dec.-March Mon.-Sat. 8am-7pm, Sun. 8am-5pm. Additional tourist offices located at **Heathrow Airport** (open April-Nov. daily 9am-6pm; Dec.-March 9am-5pm) and **Liverpool St. Underground Station** (open Mon. 8:15am-7pm, Tues.-Sat. 8:15am-6pm, Sun 8:30am-4:45pm). **British Travel Centre:** 12 Regent St. Tube: Piccadilly Circus. Down Regent St. from the Lower Regent St. tube exit. Ideal for travelers bound for destinations outside of London. Combines the services of the BTA, British Rail, and a Traveller's Exchange with an accommodations service. Open May-Oct. Mon.-Fri. 9am-6:30pm, Sat. 9am-5pm, Sun. 10am-4pm; Nov.-April Mon.-Fri. 9am-6:30pm, Sat.-Sun. 10am-4pm. **City of London Information Centre:** St. Paul's Churchyard, EC4 (tel. 606 3030). Tube: St. Paul's. Info on the City of London. Open April-Oct. daily 9:15am-5pm; Nov.-March Mon.-Fri. 9:15am-5pm, Sat. 9:15am-12:30pm.

Budget Travel: London is *the* place to shop for cheap bus, plane, and train tickets to North America, Africa, Asia, and Australia. Browse the ads in *Time Out* or the *Evening Standard.*

Embassies and High Commissions: United States Embassy: 24 Grosvenor Sq., W1 (tel. 499 9000). Tube: Bond St. **Australian High Commission:** Australia House, The Strand, WC2 (tel. 379 4334; in emergency, tel. 438 8181). Tube: Aldwych or Temple. Visa info (0891) 600 333. Passport info dial main line between 2-4pm. Open Mon.-Fri. 9:30am-3:30pm. **Canadian High Commission:** MacDonald House, 1 Grosvenor Sq., W1 (tel. 258 6600). Tube: Bond St. or Oxford Circus. Visas Mon.-Fri. 8-11am. **Irish Embassy:** 17 Grosvenor Pl., SW1 (tel. 235 2171). Tube: Hyde Park Corner. Open Mon.-Fri. 9:30am-1pm and 2:15-5pm. **New Zealand High Commission:** New Zealand House, 80 Haymarket, SW1 (tel. 930 8422). Tube: Charing Cross. Open Mon.-Fri. 10am-noon and 2-4pm. **South African High Commission:** South Africa House, Trafalgar Sq., WC2 (tel. 451 7299). Tube: Charing Cross. Open 10am-noon and 2-4pm.

Flights: Heathrow Airport (tel. (0181) 759 4321) is the world's busiest airport. From Heathrow, take the **Underground** to central London (45min.; about £3). London Transport's **Airbus** (tel. 222 1234) zips from Heathrow to central points, including hotels (1hr.; £6). Many flights land at **Gatwick Airport** (tel. (0293) 535353). From there, take the BR Gatwick Express train to Victoria Station (daily 5:30am-11pm every 15min., 11pm-1am and 4-5:30am every 30min., 1-4am every hr. on the hr.; 35min.; day return £8.50-10). **National Express** (tel. (0990) 808080) buses run from Victoria Station to Gatwick (5:30am-10pm every hr.; 1hr.; £7.50, return £11). Taxis take twice as long and cost 5 times as much. British Rail's Stansted Express runs to **Stansted Airport** (tel. (01223) 311 999) from Liverpool St. station (£10).

Trains: 8 major stations: Charing Cross, Euston, King's Cross, Liverpool St., Paddington, St. Pancras, Victoria, and Waterloo. All stations linked by Underground. For train info stop by ticket offices at the stations or any LTB or BTA tourist office.

Buses: Victoria Coach Station (tube: Victoria), located on Buckingham Palace Rd., is the hub of Britain's denationalized coach network. **National Express coaches** (tel. (0990) 808080) service an expansive network. The Greater London area is served by **Green Line** (tel. (0181) 668 7261) coaches, which leave frequently from Eccleston Bridge behind Victoria Station. Purchase tickets from the driver. Discounts include the one-day **Rover** ticket (£7, valid on almost every Green Line coach and London Country bus Mon.-Fri. after 9am, Sat.-Sun. all day).

Public Transportation: Call the 24-hr. help line (222 1234) for a live operator who will help you plan subway and bus travel. The **Underground** (or **Tube**) is fast, efficient, and crowded. It opens about 6am; the last train runs around midnight. Buy your ticket before you board and pass it through automatic gates at both ends of your journey. On-the-spot £10 fine if you're caught without a valid ticket. The **Travelcard** is a must for budget travelers. One-day Travelcards cannot be used before 9:30am Mon.-Fri., and are not valid on night buses (adult one-day Travelcard, zones 1 & 2, £3). Travelcards can be used on the Underground, regular buses, British Rail (Network SouthEast), and the Docklands Light Railway. The one-week and one-month Travelcards can be used at any time, and are valid for Night Bus travel. (1-wk. Travelcard, zones 1&2, £14.80; 1-mo. Travelcard, zones 1&2, £56.90. Bring a passport-sized photo). **Night buses** (the "N" routes) run frequently throughout London 11pm-6am. All pass through Trafalgar Sq. Pick up a free brochure about night buses, which includes times of the last BritRail and Underground trains. The **bus** network is divided into 4 zones. In and around central London, one-way fares cost 50p-£1.20, depending on the number of zones you cross. Pick up free maps and guides at **London Transport's Information Centres** (look for the lowercase "i" logo on signs) at the following major tube stops: King's Cross, Piccadilly Circus, Oxford Circus, St. James's Park, Liverpool St., Hammersmith, and Heathrow Terminals 1, 2, 3 station (most open Mon.-Fri. 8am-6pm; central London stations also have weekend hours).

Taxis: Hail taxis with a light signifying that they're empty. London fares are steep, and 10% tip is standard. In addition to licensed black cabs, there are tons of unregulated "minicabs" in the Yellow Pages.

Hitchhiking: Anyone who values safety will take a train or bus out of London. Hitchers check the University of London Union's **ride board** on the ground floor of 1 Malet St., WC1 (tube: Russell Sq.), or ask at youth hostels. **Freewheelers** is a rideshare agency. £10 annual membership required. Each match-up costs £3. Single-sex matching available. Call (0191) 222 0090, e-mail freewheelers@freewheelers.co.uk, http://www.freewheelers.co.uk/freewheelers, or write Freewheelers, Ltd., 25 Low Friar St., Newcastle upon Tyne, NE1 5UE.

Bisexual, Gay, and Lesbian Information: London Lesbian and Gay Switchboard (tel. 837 7324). 24-hr. advice and support service. **Bisexual Helpline** (tel. (0181) 569 7500). **Lesbian Line** (tel. 251 6911).

Hotlines: Samaritans: 46 Marshall St., W1 (tel. 734 2800). Tube: Oxford Circus. Highly respected 24-hr. crisis hotline provides an ear (rather than advice) for suicidal depression and other problems. **The London Rape Crisis Centre's Rape Crisis Hotline,** P.O. Box 69, WC1 (tel. 837 1600). Phones answered Mon.-Fri. 6-10pm, Sat.-Sun. 10am-10pm.

Pharmacies: Every police station keeps a list of emergency doctors and chemists in its area. Listings under "Chemists" in the Yellow Pages. **Bliss Chemists** at Marble Arch (5 Marble Arch, W1; tel. 723 6116) is open daily, including public holidays, 9am-midnight.

Medical Assistance: In an emergency, you can be treated at no charge in the A&E ward of a hospital. You have to pay for routine medical care unless you work legally in Britain, in which case NHS tax will be deducted from your wages and you will not be charged. Socialized medicine has lowered fees here, so don't ignore any health problem merely because you are low on cash. The following have 24-hr. walk-in A&E (also known as casualty) departments: **Chelsea & Westminster Hospital,** 369 Fulham Rd., SW10 (tel. 746 8000; tube: South Kensington or Fulham Broadway); **Charing Cross Hospital,** Fulham Palace Rd. (entrance St. Dunstan's Rd.), W6 (tel. (0181) 846 1234; tube: Baron's Ct. or Hammersmith); **St. Thomas' Hospital,** Lambeth Palace Rd., SE1 (tel. 928 9292; tube: Westminster); **University College Hospital,** Gower St. (entrance on Grafton Way), WC1 (tel. 380 9857; tube: Euston or Warren St.). For others, look under "Hospitals" in the gray Businesses and Services phone book.

Emergency: Dial 999; no coins required.

Post Office: Save hassle and have mail sent to **Trafalgar Sq.,** 24-28 William IV St., London WC2N 4DL (tel. 930 9580). Tube: Charing Cross. Open Mon.-Thurs. and Sat. 8am-8pm, Fri. 8:30am-8pm.

Telephones: Most phones accept change and phonecards, some accept only phonecards. London has 2 **city codes:** 0171 (central London) and 0181 (outer London). Use the code only if you are calling from one area to the other. **All London numbers listed in Let's Go are (0171) unless otherwise indicated.**

ACCOMMODATIONS

Write well in advance to reserve rooms for summer—landing in London without reservations is like landing on a bicycle that has no seat. B&Bs are a bargain for groups of two or more, while hostels are the cheapest (and most social) option for small groups and single travelers. Check for reduced weekly rates in hotels.

YHA/HI Hostels

Cheap, cheery, and full of the young, London's YHA hostels can be a welcome relief from dreary urban B&Bs. Reserve ahead for July and August; if not, it's still worth calling (central tel. 248 6547). Bring a padlock to secure your personal locker.

Oxford Street, 14-18 Noel St., W1 (tel. 734 1618; fax 734 1657). Tube: Oxford Circus. Spacious TV lounge with plenty of comfortable chairs, fully equipped kitchen with microwave, and currency exchange. 24-hr. security. Small, clean rooms of 2-4 with pink walls. £17.30, under 18 £14.10. Continental breakfast £2.70. Book at least 3-4 weeks in advance, very few walk-ins accepted.

City of London, 36 Carter La., EC4 (tel. 236 4965; fax 236 7681). Tube: St. Paul's. Antiseptic cleanliness and a full range of services, including secure luggage storage, currency exchange, laundry facilities, theater box office, and 24-hr. security. Reception open 7am-11pm. Single-sex rooms only. 5- to 8-bed dorm £19.75, under 18 £16.55. 10- to 15-bed dorm £16, under 18 £12.50. Single or double £22.75, under 18 £19.15. Triple or quad £20.15, under 18 £17.10. Special weekly rates available Sept.-Feb.

Earl's Court, 38 Bolton Gdns., SW5 (tel. 373 7083; fax 835 2034). Tube: Earl's Ct. A converted townhouse in a leafy residential neighborhood. Rooms of 4-16. Continental breakfast. Reception open 7am-11pm. 24-hr. security. Meals available in the large, well-designed cafeteria 5-8pm. Kitchen and laundry access. All rooms single-sex. £17.70, under 18 £15.55.

Holland House, Holland Walk, W8 (tel. 937 0748; fax 376 0667). Tube: High St. Kensington. This handsome Jacobean mansion and fairly nondescript modern addition house some 200 beds. The reception is large and drearily functional, but the rooms are clean and spacious. Laundry and kitchen facilities. 24-hr. access. £17.50, under 18 £15.55. The restaurant offers a set dinner for £4.15 from 5-8pm.

Highgate, 84 Highgate West Hill, N6 (tel. (0181) 340 1831; fax 341 0376). Tube: Archway. About 35min. from central London. An unassuming Georgian house set along a residential street. Smallest and cheapest HI hostel in London YHA. 4-16 beds/room. Clean bathrooms have flowered curtains and pink floors. TV lounge, kitchen facilities. Midnight curfew; no lockout. Reception open 8:45-10am, 1-7pm, and 8-11:30pm, but small staff sometimes closes it throughout the day, particularly in winter. £12.55, under 18 £8.80. Breakfast, served early, £2.80.

Private Hostels

Private hostels, which do not require an HI card, generally have a youthful clientele and often sport a vaguely bohemian atmosphere. Some have kitchen facilities and there are rarely curfews.

Palace Hotel, 31 Palace Ct., W2 (tel. 221 5628; fax 243 8157). Tube: Notting Hill Gate or Queensway. Young community atmosphere and bright dorm rooms make this great deal an excellent social space for enthusiastic hostelers. Airy rooms with tall windows all house 8 beds. Shower facilities are immaculate. Single-sex rooms often available. £12. Cash only.

Quest Hotel, 45 Queensborough Terr., W2 (tel. 229 7782). Tube: Queensway. Communal, clean, and sociable; staff throws one theme party a month. 2-bed dorm (one available) £17, 4- to 8-bed dorms (coed and 1 women-only) £12-14. Key deposit £3. Continental breakfast included, English breakfast £2.

Albert Hotel, 191 Queens Gate, SW7 (tel. 584 3019; fax 823 8520). Tube: Gloucester Rd. Elegant, wood-paneled hostel with sweeping staircases. Located in one of London's most elegant districts. Backpackers lounge on sunny balconies. Rooms range from large dorms to intimate twins, most with bath. Continental breakfast. 24-hr. reception. 4- to 6-bed dorm £12.50-13. Larger dorm (single-sex or coed) £10. Single £26. Twin £35.

Victoria Hotel, 71 Belgrave Rd., SW1 (tel. 834 3077; fax 932 0693). Tube: Pimlico. Clean, bohemian hostel. 70 beds. Bright red bunk beds brighten the standard rooms. Lots of long term guests make this hostel feel like a home. Reception open 24hr. 5-bed dorm (coed) £14; 6-bed dorm (coed) £13.50; 6-bed dorm (women only, 1 available) £14; 8-bed dorm (coed) £12.50-14.

Curzon House Hotel, 58 Courtfield Gdns., SW5 (tel. 581 2116; fax 835 1319). Tube: Gloucester Rd. Tidy and cool; recently installed showers. Most rooms have tall ceilings and mammoth windows that overlook a gracious park; no bunkbeds here. Continental breakfast. Kitchen. Luggage storage. 4-bed dorm (single-sex only) £15. Single £28. Double £18. Triple £18. Quad £17, w/bath £18.

Central University of Iowa Hostel, 7 Bedford Pl., WC1 (tel. 580 1121; fax 580 5638). Tube: Holborn or Russell Sq. Bright, spartan rooms with bunk beds, new wood furniture, and bookshelves. Clientele, like the hostel, is bright and clean. Reception open 8am-10pm. Continental breakfast. Single £20. Double £18. Triple/quad £16. Open mid-May to Aug. MC, Visa.

Astor's Museum Inn, 27 Montague St., WC1 (tel. 580 5360; fax 636 7948). Tube: Holborn, Tottenham Ct. Rd., or Russell Sq. If they're full, they'll direct you to 1 of 3 other Astor's hostels and pay for your tube or cab fare. Bathrooms feature "London's only glowing toilet." Reception open 24hr. No curfew; coed dorms. 4-bed dorm £15. 6- to 8-bed dorm £14. 10-bed dorm £13.

Tonbridge School Clubs, Ltd., corner of Judd and Cromer St., WC1 (tel. 837 4406). Tube: King's Cross/St. Pancras. Students with non-British passports only. No frills and no privacy, but dirt cheap. Men sleep in basement gym, women in karate-club hall. Blankets and foam pads provided. Lockout 9:30am-10pm; use caution when walking in the area at night. Midnight curfew. £5.

University Halls of Residence

London's university residences often accommodate visitors for limited periods during the summer break and during Easter vacations. Many of these halls are characterized by box-like rooms and institutional furniture. Most charge around £20 and contain all singles, offering more privacy than a hostel. Call well in advance (by April for July reservations), as conference groups tend to snatch up rooms early. Rooms are generally available from early June to mid-September.

High Holborn Residence, 178 High Holborn, WC1 (tel. 379 5589; fax 379 5640). This 2-year-old London School of Economics hall provides an amazing combination of comfort and affordability. Singles are spacious and immaculately furnished. Usually booked far in advance, but they keep some singles available for walk-in customers. Continental breakfast, lounge and bar, laundry facilities. Reception open daily 7am-11pm. Single £25. Twin £43, w/bath £47. Discounts for longer stays. Open July to mid-September.

Carr Saunders Hall, 18-24 Fitzroy St., W1 (tel. 323 9712; fax 580 4718). Tube: Warren St. Newer London School of Economics building. Reception open 8:30am-11:30pm. English breakfast. Single £22. Double £42. Under 12 half-price.

John Adams Hall, 15-23 Endsleigh St., WC1 (tel. 387 4086; fax 383 0164). Tube: Euston. Elegant Georgian building belongs to London University. Singles are small and simple. Reception open Mon.-Fri. 8am-1pm and 2-10pm, Sat. 8am-1:30pm and

5:30-10pm, Sun. 9am-1:30pm and 5:30-10pm. English breakfast. Laundry facilities, TV lounge. Single £21.40, 5 or more days £19. Double £37, 5 or more days £33.

Wellington Hall, 71 Vincent Sq., Westminster, SW1 (tel. 834 4740; fax 233 7709). Tube: Victoria. Charming Edwardian hall on pleasant, quiet square. Memorable oak panels and stained-glass windows in dining room. Spacious rooms come with desks. English breakfast. Single £23. Twin £35.

Lightfoot Hall, Manresa Rd. at King's Rd., SW3 (tel. 333 4898 or 351 6011 for booking; fax 333 4901). Tube: Sloane Sq. or South Kensington. Prime location between Chelsea and Kensington. Rooms in a modern, institutional block. Continental breakfast. Satellite TV. Bar. Single £21. Double £33.

Queen Alexandra's House, Kensington Gore, SW7 (tel. 589 3635 or fax 589-3177). Tube: South Kensington. Women only. Magnificent Victorian building with ornate bars and staircases running through the lobby. Continental breakfast. Kitchen and sitting room. Cozy rooms, mostly singles, £23. Although the hall is officially only open to guests from mid-July to mid-Aug., a few beds may be open during the off season; call ahead. Write weeks in advance for a booking form.

Connaught Hall, 36-45 Tavistock Sq., WC1 (tel. 387 6181; fax 383 4109). Tube: Russell Sq. Graceful London University Hall with a quiet atmosphere. 200 small, single study bedrooms on long, typical college dorm hallways with sinks, wardrobes, desks, and tea-making facilities. Reception open daily 8am-11pm. English breakfast. Single £20. Reservations recommended. Open July-Aug. and Easter.

Bed & Breakfasts

The number of B&Bs boggles the mind. While some are about as indistinct as blades of grass, many feature distinctive furnishings and a warm, welcoming atmosphere.

Near Victoria Station

Although accommodations can be fairly expensive, guests at B&Bs around Victoria Station are close to London's attractions as well as transportation connections. In the summer, prudent visitors make reservations at least two weeks in advance.

Melbourne House, 79 Belgrave Rd., SW1 (tel. 828 3516; fax 828 7120). Tube: Pimlico. Modern, private custom-designed showers have smashing water pressure and glass doors. Sparkling bedrooms, all of which come with TV and phone. English breakfast with cereal option. Singles £22-28, w/bath £40-45. Doubles w/bath £58-65. Triple w/bath £75-80. 2-room quad w/bath £80-90.

Oxford House, 92-94 Cambridge St., SW1 (tel. 834 6467; fax 834 0225). Tube: Victoria. Commodious rooms with flowered wallpaper. Firm beds, new pastel double-lined shower curtains. Fabulously well prepared English breakfast. Single £30-32. Double £40-42. Triple £51-54. Quad £68-72. Reserve 3-4 weeks ahead.

Georgian House Hotel, 35 St. George's Dr., SW1 (tel. 834 1438; fax 976 6085). Terrific discounts on "student rooms" on the 3rd and 4th floors (you don't even need to be a student, just be willing to walk up the long flights of stairs). Clean, well-appointed rooms. Ask about older, but slightly cheaper, rooms in the annex. Single £28, students £18, w/bath £32-39. Double w/bath £47-53, students £31. Triples w/bath £56-65, students £42. Quad £70, students £50. MC, Visa.

Luna and Simone Hotel, 47-49 Belgrave Rd., SW1 (tel. 834 5897; fax 828 2474). Tube: Pimlico. Immaculate and well-maintained, the building is constantly being refurbished. The rooms, decorated in shades of blue, all come with TV, phones, hairdryers, and firm mattresses. English breakfast. Luggage storage. Single £28, w/bath £42. Double £40, w/bath £54. Triple £54, w/bath £65.

Earl's Court

The area feeds on the tourist trade—beware the hustlers. Travel agencies, take-away eateries, currency exchanges, and souvenir shops dominate. The area also has a vibrant gay and lesbian population.

York House Hotel, 27-29 Philbeach Gdns., SW5 (tel. 373 7519; fax 370 4641). Special features include a modish 60s-style TV lounge and a lovely garden. Hallway facilities are extraordinarily clean, as are the rooms. English breakfast. Single £26. Double £42, w/bath £58. Triple £52, w/bath £68. Quad £59.

Half Moon Hotel, 10 Earl's Ct. Sq., SW5 (tel. 373 9956; fax 373 8456). Graceful mirrors on every landing and inexpensive, adequate rooms. Telephone and TV (w/Sky and CNN) in every room. Continental breakfast. Single £20-25, w/shower £30-35. Double £30-35, w/shower £45. Triple £42, w/shower £60.

Kensington & Chelsea

These hotels prove convenient for those who wish to visit the stunning array of museums that line the southwest side of Hyde Park. Prices are a bit higher, but hotels here tend to be significantly more sober and comfortable than many at Earl's Court.

Abbey House Hotel, 11 Vicarage Gate, W8 (tel. 727 2594). Tube: Notting Hill Gate. Hotel has achieved a level of comfort that can't be rivaled at these prices. Palatial rooms with color TV, washbasin, and fresh towels. Bedrooms (none w/bath) are spotless and elegant. English breakfast. Single £34. Double £55. Triple £66. Quad £76. Quint £86. Book ahead 1 month. No credit cards.

Vicarage Hotel, 10 Vicarage Gate, W8 (tel. 229 4030; fax 792 5989). Tube: Notting Hill Gate. Sweeping staircase surrounded by classy red velvet striped wallpaper and gold framing. The stately breakfast room is only surpassed by the small, comfortable, and immaculate bedrooms, which contain fancy wooden wardrobes and antique mirrors. Ample English breakfast. Single £36. Double £58. Triple £70. Quad £80. Negotiable winter rates. Reserve 1 month ahead. No credit cards.

Bloomsbury

Despite its proximity to the West End, Bloomsbury maintains a fairly residential demeanor. Gracious, tree-filled squares and a prime location (within Zone 1 on the tube) make hotel prices a pound or two higher here.

Arosfa Hotel, 83 Gower St., WC1 (tel./fax 636 2115). Tube: Goodge St. Nearly new furnishings and fixtures, spacious rooms, and immaculate facilities. Single £27. Double £40, w/bath £50. Triple £53, w/bath £63. Quad £63, w/bath £73.

Arran House, 77-79 Gower St., WC1 (tel. 636 2186 or 637 1140; fax 436 5328). Tube: Goodge St. Relatively large rooms with TV and hot pot. Spotless bathrooms. Show *Let's Go 1997* for these prices. Single £31, w/shower £36, w/bath £41. Double £46, w/shower £51, w/bath £61. Triple £61, w/shower £66, w/bath £70. Quad £67, w/shower £72, w/bath £82. Quint £76.

Alhambra Hotel, 17-19 Argyle St., WC1 (tel. 837 9575; fax 916 2476). Tube: King's Cross. Singles in the main building are clean and modest. Rooms w/bath in the newly refurbished annex are pricier and posher. Singles from £25, w/bath £30. Doubles from £35, w/shower £40, w/bath £45.

Ridgemount Hotel, 65-67 Gower St., WC1 (tel. 636 1141 or 580 7060). Tube: Russell Sq. Bright rooms with cheery pink bedspreads on firm beds. Radiantly clean throughout. Single £28, w/bath £38. Double £40, w/bath £51. Triple £50, w/bath £66. Quad £64, w/bath £74. Call well in advance. No credit cards.

Celtic Hotel, 62 Guilford St., WC1 (tel. 837 9258 or 837 6737). Tube: Russell Sq. Basic, clean, sparsely furnished rooms. For safety's sake, they don't give room keys but will open the door for guests 24hr. Front rooms can be noisy. English breakfast. Single £32.50. Double £44.50. Triple £63. Quad £72. Quint £90.

Paddington & Bayswater

These neighborhoods are located on the northern edge of Hyde Park/Kensington Gardens. (Tube: Paddington.)

Hyde Park Rooms Hotel, 137 Sussex Gdns., W2 (tel. 723 0225 or 723 0965). Recently renovated rooms are bright and airy. An astounding value. Single £20-24, w/bath £30-36. Double £30-36, w/bath £45. Triple £45, w/bath £54.

Dean's Court Hotel, 57 Inverness, W2 (tel. 229 2961; fax 727 1190). Clean, functional rooms with firm mattresses, a filling breakfast, full-pressure showers, and a friendly atmosphere. Well over half the beds are in the dorms (an unbeatable bargain). All rooms without facilities. English breakfast. Twin/double £36-48. Triple £48. Share rooms £12.50.

Compton House Hotel and Millard's Hotel, 148-152 Sussex Gdns., W2 (tel. 723 2939; fax 723 6225). Not quite what comes to mind when one normally thinks "Compton"—a clean, if careworn, establishment. Single £22-25, w/bath £35-38. Double £35, w/bath £44-48. Triple £51, w/bath £63.

Barry House Hotel, 12 Sussex Pl., W2 (tel. 723 7340; fax 723 9775; http://www.traveling.com/london/barry.htm). One of the UK's first on-line B&Bs—visit their website. Bright, smallish cyber-rooms with TVs and phones. Single £30, w/bath £38. Double w/bath £55-62. Triple w/bath £72-75. Quad £88.

FOOD

London presents a tantalizing range of foreign and English specialties. With Indian, Lebanese, Greek, Chinese, Thai, Italian, West Indian, and African food inexpensive and readily available, the city has few rivals when it comes to diversity. If you eat but one meal in London, let it be Indian—London's Indian food is rivaled only by India's. Meals are cheaper on Westbourne Grove (Tube: Bayswater), or near Euston Station (Tube: Euston) than in the West End.

The West End

Mandeer, 21 Hanway Place, W1 (tel. 323 0660 or 580 3470). Tube: Tottenham Ct. Road. Food is exceedingly fresh, primarily organic, and all vegetarian. The best deal in the house is the lunch buffet; for under £4 you get 3 heaping portions and rice. Open Mon.-Sat. for lunch (self-service) noon-3pm, dinner 5:30-10pm.

The Stockpot, 18 Old Compton St., W1 (tel. 287 1066). Tube: Leicester Sq. or Piccadilly. Beloved by locals, who pack the sidewalk tables, it's the cheapest place in Soho to soak up some style. Entrees £2.10-4.85. Open Mon.-Tues. 11:30am-11:30pm, Wed.-Sat. 11:30am-11:45pm, Sun. noon-11pm. Also at 40 Panton St.

The Wren Café at St. James's, 35 Jermyn St., SW1 (tel. 437 9419). Tube: Piccadilly Circus or Green Park. Wholefood/vegetarian delights served in the shadow of a Christopher Wren church. Tranquil and gorgeous for lunch. Casserole of the day with brown rice £3.50. Open Mon.-Sat. 8am-7pm, Sun. 10am-5pm.

Neal's Yard Bakery Co-op, 6 Neal's Yard, WC2 (tel. 836 5199). Tube: Covent Garden. Only organic flour and filtered water are used in the delicious breads here. A small, open-air counter offers baked goods, sandwiches, and salads—all vegetarian with many vegan options. Large 3-seed loaf £2. Bean burger £1.90. 50% discount on day-olds. No smoking. Open Mon.-Sat. 10:30am-5pm.

Sofra, 36 Tavistock St., WC2 (tel. 240 3773). Tube: Covent Garden. This Turkish restaurant serves the freshest of foods in a cool, swanky Mediterranean atmosphere. £5 set dinner includes your choice of hummus, tabouleh, or a soup and salad, and a main course of chicken, lamb, or *kofa*. Open daily noon-midnight.

Lorelei, 21 Bateman St., W1 (tel. 734 0954). Tube: Tottenham Ct. Rd., Leicester Sq., or Piccadilly Circus. Unassuming bistro works its magic on the food, keeping it affordable and delicious. The *Poorman* (tomato, garlic, and oregano pizza) was designed with the budget diner in mind (£2.90). Open Mon.-Sat. noon-11pm.

Lok Ho Fook, 4-5 Gerrard St., W1 (tel. 437 2001).Tube: Leicester Sq. A busy place with good prices. Noodles, fried or in soup, £2.80. Helpful staff will aid the novice. Open daily noon-11:45pm. Major credit cards.

Kowloon Restaurant, 21-22 Gerrard St., W1 (tel. 437 0148). Leicester Sq. Meal-sized portions of vermicelli, wheat, or Ho-fun rice noodles (£2.50-5) served steaming and cheap in this Chinatown institution. Open daily noon-11:45pm.

City of London & East End

The Place Below, in St. Mary-le-Bow Church crypt, Cheapside, EC2 (tel. 329 0789). Tube: St. Paul's. Attractive and generous vegetarian dishes served in the unexpectedly light atmosphere of a stone church basement. Makes for a religious dining experience, so to speak. Second dining room moonlights as an ecclesiastical court, where the Archbishop of Canterbury still settles cases pertaining to Anglican law and swears in new bishops a few times a year. Quiche and salad £5.55. Open Mon.-Fri. 7:30am-2:30pm.

Bengal Cuisine, 12 Brick La., E1 (tel. 377 8405). Tube: Aldgate East. First among a string of many, this restaurant distinguishes itself through quick service and tasty dishes. Chicken curries £3.35-4.45. 10% student discount on weekends. Open daily noon-midnight.

The Cherry Orchard Café, 247 Globe Rd., E2 (tel. (0181) 980 6678). Tube: Bethnal Green. A lovely un-Chekhovian restaurant run by Buddhists. The strictly vegetarian menu changes daily. Delicious hot entrees around £3.50. Open Mon. 11am-3pm, Tues.-Fri. 11am-7pm.

Kensington, Knightsbridge, Chelsea, & Victoria

Ciaccio, 5 Warwick Way, SW1 (tel. 828 1342). Tube: Victoria. An intimate Italian eatery whose prices and spices make it a giant for budget eaters. Pick a container of pasta and one of about 10 sauces (pesto, veggie, tomato, and meat), and they'll heat it up for £1.39-2.50. Open Mon.-Fri. 10am-6pm, Sat. 9:30am-5pm.

Chelsea Kitchen, 98 King's Rd., SW3 (tel. 589 1330). Tube: Sloane Sq. Locals rave about the eclectic menu of cheap, filling, tasty food: turkey and mushroom pie, *spaghetti bolognese,* and a Spanish omelette are each £2.60 or less. Breakfast served 8-11:25am. Open Mon.-Sat. 8am-midight, Sun. 9am-11:30pm.

Entre Nous, 488 King's Rd., SW3 (tel. 352 4227). Tube: Sloane Sq. Portions of tremendous size despite the chic café atmosphere. Huge sandwiches on crusty bread £1.20-3. Specials (around £3) are a phenomenal value—mounds and mounds of delicious food. Open Mon.-Fri. 8am-6pm, Sat. 10am-6pm.

Parson's Restaurant, 311 Fulham Rd., SW10 (tel. 352 0651). Tube: South Ken. Lovely wood floors and tables give an airy open feel. In the summer the ceiling opens like a sun-roof and you can pretend that you're in a convertible. Huge pasta specials (£4.25-4.65) come with a free second helping and free refills on coffee. Open daily noon-1am, last orders at 12:30am (midnight on Sun.).

Bloomsbury & North London

Wagamama, 4A Streatham St., WC1 (tel. 323 9223). Tube: Tottenham Ct. Rd. Fast food with a high-tech twist: waitstaff take your orders on hand-held electronic radios that transmit directly to the kitchen. Noodles in various combinations and permutations £3.80-5.70. Not the place for a long, quiet meal: average turnover time is 20min. No smoking. Open Mon.-Fri. noon-2:30pm and 6-11pm, Sat. 12:30-3pm and 6-11pm, Sun. 12:30-3pm and 6-11pm. Cash only.

Rhavi Shankar Bhel Poori House, 133-135 Drummond St., NW1 (tel. 338 6458). Tube: Euston Sq. Indian vegetarian cuisine. Most entrees £2.50-3.80. Daily specials (£2-3) are an absolute godsend to hungry travelers who crave good Indian vegetarian grub. Open daily noon-10:45pm.

Chutney's, 124 Drummond St., NW1 (tel. 338 0604). Tube: Warren St. Cheerful café serving vegetarian dishes from Western and Southern India. All-you-can-eat lunch buffet Mon.-Sat. noon-2:45pm and Sun. noon-10:30pm (£5). Open Mon.-Sat. noon-2:45pm and 6-11:30pm, Sun. noon-10:30pm. Visa, MC, Access.

Café Olé, 119 Upper St., N1 (tel. 226 6991). Tube: Angel. A hip Italian/Spanish bar/café bustling with Islington trendies of all ages. Lunch menu offers pasta (£4-4.50) and salads (£3.50), in addition to sandwiches (£1-2.50). The selection of pastas and salads expands at dinner; all are around £5. Open Mon.-Sat. 8am-11pm.

LeMercury, 140a Upper St., N1 (tel. 354 4088). Tube: Angel or Highbury and Islington. Outstanding French food at low prices. Main courses £5.45. Lunch is a super value at £4. Open Mon.-Sat. 11am-11pm, Sun. noon-11:30pm.

Le Petit Prince, 5 Holmes Rd., NW5 (tel. 267 0752). Tube: Kentish Town. French/Algerian cuisine served in café/restaurant adorned with illustrations from Saint-Exupéry's *Le Petit Prince.* Vegetarian couscous £5. Lamb, chicken, and fish dishes are slightly more expensive, but come with unlimited couscous and vegetable broth. Lunch menu includes crepes (£4.25-4.40) and a coriander, guacamole, and melted goat cheese sandwich (£4). Open daily noon-3pm and 7-11:30pm.

Nontas, 14-16 Camden High St., NW1 (tel. 387 4579). Tube: Mornington Crescent or Camden Town. This wonderfully intimate restaurant is one of the best Greek venues in the city. The incomparable *meze* (£8.75) offers a seemingly endless selection of dips, meats, and cheeses. Other Hellenic fare includes kebabs (£5.40-

5.70). Don't take a vegetarian here unless you can placate them with 95p spirits (rum, whiskey, etc...). Open Mon.-Sat. noon-3pm and 6-11:30pm.

Captain Nemo, 171 Kentish Town Rd., NW1 (tel. 485 3658). Tube: Kentish Town. Seemingly unassuming Chinese/chippie take-away combo rocks your world with their tangy, delicious chips in curry sauce (£1.20). We'd travel 10,000 leagues under the sea for a crack at these heavenly spuds. Open Mon.-Fri. noon-3pm and 5:30pm-midnight, Sat.-Sun. 5:30pm-midnight.

Paddington, Notting Hill, & Bayswater

Manzara, 24 Pembridge Rd., W11 (tel. 727 3062). Tube: Notting Hill Gate. A wonderfully cheap place to get your grub on after a stroll through the Portobello market. In the afternoon, pizzas are £3, and sandwiches are £1. In the evenings, they offer a £6 all-you-can-eat array of Greek and Turkish specialties. Chomp! Take-away discount. Open daily 8am-midnight.

The Grain Shop, 269a Portobello Rd., W11 (tel. 229 5571). Tube: Ladbroke Grove. Direct the staff to fill various-sized take-away containers with any combination of the 6 hot vegetarian dishes—large £4.10, medium £3, small £2. Groceries also available, many organic. Open Mon.-Sat. 10am-6pm.

Khan's, 13-15 Westbourne Grove, W2 (tel. 727 5240). Tube: Bayswater. Cavernous, noisy, and crowded, Khan's persists as the best bargain around for delicious Indian cuisine. The chicken *saag* (chicken cooked with spinach £3) contains piquant spices that are well complemented by flat *nan* bread (£1.10) or rice (£1.35). Open daily noon-3pm and 6pm-midnight. Major credit cards.

PUBS

London's 7000 pubs are as colorful as their country counterparts, but in London the clientele varies widely from one neighborhood to the next. Avoid pubs near train stations; many prey on naïve tourists. For the best pub prices head to the East End. Stylish, lively pubs cluster around the fringes of the West End. Many historic alehouses lend an ancient air to areas recently swallowed up by the urban sprawl, such as Highgate and Hampstead.

The Dog and Duck, 8 Bateman St., W1 (tel. 437 4447). Tube: Tottenham Ct. Rd. Frequent winner of the Best Pub in Soho award, its size keeps the crowd down. Inexpensive pints (£1.85-2.10). Evenings bring locals, theater-goers, and, yes, some tourists. Open Mon.-Fri. noon-11pm, Sat. 6-11pm, Sun. 7-10:30pm.

The Three Greyhounds, 25 Greek St., W1 (tel. 287 0754). Tube: Leicester Sq. This tiny, medieval-style pub provides welcome respite from the endless cafés and posturing of Soho. 1996 winner of the Best Pub in Soho award. Open Mon.-Sat. 11am-11pm, Sun. noon-3pm and 7-10:30pm.

Riki Tik, 23-24 Bateman St., W1 (tel. 437 1977). Tube: Leicester Square, Tottenham Ct. Rd., or Piccadilly Circus. A hyped, hip, and tremendously swinging bar specializing in orgasmic flavored vodka shots (try the white chocolate, £2.40). The decor is George Jetson on acid, the crowd is swish, and the drink prices are exorbitant. Come during happy hour (5:30-7:30pm) when the deliciously fruity cocktails are a near-bargain at £6.50/pitcher. Open Mon.-Sat. noon-1am. Get there before the pubs close, or you'll be asked to pay a £3 cover. MC, Visa.

Lamb and Flag, 33 Rose St., WC2, off Garrick St. (tel. 497 9504). Tube: Covent Garden or Leicester Sq. A traditional old English pub, with no music and still separated into 2 sections—the public bar for the working class, and the saloon bar for the businessmen, though today the classes mix. Open Mon.-Thurs. 11am-11pm, Fri.-Sat. 11am-10:45pm, Sun. noon-10:30pm.

World's End Distillery, 459 King's Rd. near World's End Pass before Edith Grove (tel. 376 8946). Tube: Sloane Sq. Cavernous, imposing one-room pub in Chelsea. Open Mon.-Sat. 11am-11pm, Sun. noon-3pm and 7-10:30pm.

The Old Crown, 33 New Oxford St., WC1 (tel. 836 9121). Tube: Tottenham Ct. Rd. A thoroughly untraditional pub. Cream-colored walls, faded pine-green bar, green plants, and funky brass crowns which suspend light fixtures from the ceiling. The lively crowd spills out onto the outdoor seating, creating a babble of voices above the cool jazz playing in the background; quieter seating upstairs. Open Mon.-Sat. noon-11pm. Major credit cards.

The Blind Beggar, 337 Whitechapel Rd., E1 (tel. 247 3798). Tube: Whitechapel. You may be sitting where George Cornell sat when he was gunned down by rival Bethnal Green gangster Ronnie Kray in 1966. Keep your head low. Spacious pub with conservatory and garden. Open Mon.-Sat. 11am-11pm, Sun. noon-10:30pm.

The Engineer, 65 Gloucester Ave., NW (tel. 722 0950). Tube: Chalk Farm. Classic pub design with bright, flowery atmosphere that makes everybody feel relaxed. The Primrose Hill crowd does not object to the pricey menu, but one beer in such a cheery joint won't kill you. Beer £2. Open daily noon-11pm. Major credit cards. Wheelchair accessible.

Filthy MacNasty's Whiskey Café, 68 Amwell St. (tel. 837 6067). Tube: Angel. "In drink you're mine all the time...In drink, in drink" bellow the patrons of this famously small Irish pub. Celtic drawings line the fire-colored walls; former Pogues singer Shane MacGowan frequently appears for last call. Renowned location for traditional Irish music. Live shows Thurs.-Sun. all day. Open daily 11am-11pm. Wheelchair accessible.

Prospect of Whitby, 57 Wapping Wall, E1, London Docks (tel. 481 1095). Tube: Wapping. 600-year-old pub with sweet riverside terrace. Open ceilings and a rustic flagstone bar pale next to glorious Thamescape. Riverside terrace and prohibitive upstairs restaurant. Very touristy. Open daily 11am-3pm and 6:30-11pm.

SIGHTS

London is best explored on foot. But if you have only one day in London, a tour may be a good way to intensify your sightseeing experience. The **Original London Sightseeing Tour** (tel. (0181) 877 1722) provides a convenient, albeit cursory, overview of London's attractions from a double-decker bus. Tours lasting two hours depart from Baker St., Haymarket (near Piccadilly Circus), Marble Arch, Embankment, and near Victoria Station. Route includes views of Buckingham Palace, the Houses of Parliament, Westminster Abbey, the Tower of London, St. Paul's, and Piccadilly Circus. A ticket allows you to ride the buses for a 24-hour period—permitting visitors to hop off at major sights and hop on a later bus to finish the tour. (Tours daily 9am-5:30pm, buses come every 5-10min.; £10, under 16 £5.)

Mayfair to Parliament

An auspicious beginning to a day's wander is **Piccadilly Circus** and its towering neon bluffs (Tube: Piccadilly Circus). At the center of the Nash's swirling hub stands a fountain topped by a statue everyone calls Eros but is actually supposed to be the Angel of Christian Charity. North are the tiny shops of Regent St. and the renovated seediness of **Soho,** a region which sports a vibrant sidewalk café culture where pornography once reigned supreme. Outdoor cafés, upscale shops, and slick crowds huddle in **Covent Garden,** to the northeast. Paths across **Green Park** lead to **Buckingham Palace** (Tube: Victoria or Green Park), now open to tourists. The **Changing of the Guard** occurs daily (April to late-Aug.) or every other day (Sept.-March) at 11:30am unless it's raining. Arrive early or you won't see a thing.

The Mall, a wide processional, leads from the palace to **Admiralty Arch** and Trafalgar Square. **St. James' Park,** south of the Mall, shelters a duck preserve and a flock of lawn chairs (70p/4hr.). The center of a vicious traffic roundabout, **Trafalgar Square** (Tube: Charing Cross), centers on Nelson's Column, a 40-ft.-high statue astride a 132-ft. column. Political Britain branches off **Whitehall,** just south of Trafalgar. Draped in black velvet, Charles I was led out of the **Banqueting House** (corner of Horse Guards Ave. and Whitehall) and beheaded. The building now hosts less lethal state dinners. (Open Mon.-Sat. 10am-5pm but closed for government functions. Admission £3, seniors and students £2.25.) The Prime Minister resides off Whitehall at **10 Downing Street,** now closed to tourists. In the middle of Whitehall is the **Cenotaph,** a monument to Britain's war dead. Whitehall ends by the sprawling **Houses of Parliament** (Tube: Westminster). Access to the House of Commons and the House of Lords is extremely restricted since a member was killed in a bomb blast in

1979. You may sit in the upper galleries of the Lords or Commons if you queue up outside when either are in session. **Big Ben** is like Charlie from *Charlie's Angels;* you can hear him but you can't see him. Big Ben is neither the tower nor the clock, but the 14-ton bell, cast when a similarly proportioned Sir Benjamin Hall served as Commissioner of Works. Church and state tie the knot in **Westminster Abbey,** coronation chamber to English monarchs for the past 684 years. The **Poet's Corner,** the **Grave of the Unknown Warrior,** and the elegantly perpendicular **Chapel of Henry VII** all reside here. Britain bestows no greater honor than burial within these walls. The abbey plumber is buried here among such greats as Elizabeth I, Darwin, Dickens, and Newton. Ask about the story surrounding the Stone of Scone. (Abbey open Mon.-Sat. 7:30am-6pm, Wed. 6-7:45pm, Sun. in-between services. Free. Chapels and transepts open Mon.-Fri. 9am-4:45pm, also Wed. 6-7:45pm, Sat. 9am-2:45pm and 3:45-5:45pm. Admission £4, students £2; all parts of the abbey £2 Wed. 6-7:45pm. Photography permitted Wed. evenings only.)

Hyde Park & Kensington to Chelsea

Hyde Park shows its best face on Sundays from 11am to dusk, when soapbox orators take freedom of speech to the limit at **Speaker's Corner** (Tube: Marble Arch, *not* Hyde Park Corner). To the west, **Kensington Gardens,** an elegant relic of Edwardian England, celebrates the glories of model yacht racing in the squarish Round Pound. From the gardens you can catch a glimpse of Kensington Palace. The **Royal Albert Hall,** on the south edge of Hyde Park, hosts the Proms, a gloriously British festival of music. Up Brompton Rd. near Knightsbridge, **Harrods** (Tube: Knightsbridge) vends under their humble motto, *Omnia Omnibus Ubique* ("All things for all people, everywhere"). (Open Mon.-Tues. and Sat. 10am-6pm, Wed.-Fri. 10am-7pm.) Still-fashionable **King's Road** (Tube: Sloane Sq.), to the south in **Chelsea,** attempts to do justice to its bohemian past; the area has sheltered both Oscar Wilde and the Sex Pistols.

Regent's Park to Fleet Street

Take a picnic from Harrods to the expanse of **Regent's Park,** northeast from Hyde Park across Marylebone (Tube: Regent's Park). The **London Zoo,** in the north end, has mambos, Asian lions, and piranhas. (Open daily 10am-5:30pm; Oct.-March 10am-4pm. Admission £7.50, students £6.50.) **Camden Town** (Tube: Camden Town), bordering the park to the northeast, sports rollicking street markets.

Bloomsbury—eccentric, erudite and disorganized—is known for its literary and scholarly connections, including the **British Museum. Fleet Street** is the traditional den of the British press, though nearly all the papers have moved to cheaper real estate. Close by are the **Inns of Court,** which have controlled access to the English Bar since the 13th century.

City of London & the East End

Once upon a time, "London" meant the square-mile enclave of the **City of London;** the rest of today's metropolis were far-flung towns and villages. The **Tower of London** was the grandest fortress in medieval Europe and the palace and prison of English monarchs for over 500 years. Its best-known edifice, the **White Tower,** is also the oldest, begun by William the Conqueror. In 1483, the "Princes in the Tower" (Edward V and his brother) were murdered in the **Bloody Tower** in one of the great unsolved mysteries of history. Two of the wives of jolly King Henry VIII were beheaded in the courtyard, and in 1941 Rudolf Hess was sent to the Tower after his parachute dumped him in Scotland. The **Crown Jewels** include the Stars of Africa, cut from the enormous Cullinan Diamond, which was mailed third-class from the Transvaal in an unmarked brown paper package. (Tube: Tower Hill. Open March-Oct. Mon.-Sat. 9am-6pm, Sun. 10am-6pm; Nov.-Feb. Mon.-Sat. 9am-5pm, Sun. 10am-5pm. Admission £8.30, students and seniors £6.25.) Next to the Tower is **Tower Bridge,** one of London's best-known landmarks. Other shrapnel of history are scattered throughout the City, among them 24 Christopher Wren churches interspersed with the soaring steel of modern skyscrapers. Peruse smaller churches, such as the

Strand's **St. Clement Danes** of "Oranges and Lemons" fame, or the superb **St. Stephen Walbrook** near the Bank of England (Tube: Bank). True-blue cockney Londoners are born within earshot of the famous bells of **St. Mary-le-Bow,** Cheapside. In the German Blitz in 1940, **St. Paul's Cathedral** stood firm in a sea of fire. Climb above the graves of Wren, Nelson, and Wellington in the crypt to the dizzying top of the dome; the view is unparalleled. (Tube: St. Paul's. Open Mon.-Sat. 8:30am-4pm; ambulatory and crypt open Mon.-Sat. 8:30am-4pm; galleries open Mon.-Sat. 8:45am-4:15pm. Cathedral, ambulatory, and crypt £3.50, students £3. Cathedral, ambulatory, crypt, and galleries £6, students £5.) The immense **Barbican Centre** (tube: Barbican or Moorgate) is one of the most impressive and controversial post-Blitz rebuilding projects.

The **East End** is a relatively poor section of London with a history of racial conflict. A large working-class population moved into the district during the Industrial Revolution, soon followed by a wave of Jewish immigrants fleeing persecution in Eastern Europe who settled around **Whitechapel.** Notable remnants of the former East End community include the city's oldest standing synagogue, **Bevis Marks Synagogue,** Bevis Marks and Heneage La., EC3 (tel. 626 1274; tube: Aldgate). From Aldgate High St. turn right onto Houndsditch; Creechurch Lane on the left leads to Bevis Marks. In 1978, the latest immigration wave brought a large Muslim Bangladeshi community to the East End. At the heart of this community is **Brick Lane** (tube: Aldgate East), a street lined with Indian and Bangladeshi restaurants, colorful textile shops, and grocers stocking ethnic foods. (To reach Brick Lane, head left up Whitechapel as you exit the tube station; turn left onto Osbourne St., which turns into Brick Lane.) On Sundays, vibrant market stalls selling books, bric-a-brac, leather jackets, and salt beef sandwiches flank this street and Middlesex St., better known as **Petticoat Lane.**

The South & Outskirts

Lesser-known but equally rewarding treasures lie south of the river, the area currently experiencing a heartening cultural and economic renewal. **Southwark Cathedral,** a smallish, quiet church, boasts London's second-best Gothic structure and a chapel dedicated to **John Harvard** (Tube: London Bridge). West along the riverbank, a reconstruction of Shakespeare's Globe Theatre is underway; first fall season is slated for the summer of '97. South London's entertainment history lives on in the festive **South Bank Arts Centre** (Tube: Waterloo).

The genteel Victorian shopping and residential district of Brixton (tube: Brixton) became the locus of a Caribbean and African community who followed large-scale Commonwealth immigration in the 1950s and 60s. Most of the activity in Brixton centers around the **Brixton Market** at Electric Ave., Popes Rd., and Brixton Station Rd. Choose from among the stalls of fresh fish, vegetables, and West Indian cuisine, or browse through the stalls of African crafts and discount clothing. Nearby, on the corner of Coldharbor and Atlantic, the **Black Cultural Archives,** 378 Coldharbor Lane (tel. 738 4591), mounts small but informative exhibits on black history.

The transport system that encouraged London's urban sprawl blurs the line between the city and its surroundings. If Hyde Park seemed but a small bit of green, **Highgate** and **Hampstead Heath** will prove that there is an English countryside. To the east, Karl Marx and George Eliot repose in the gothic tangle of **Highgate Cemetery,** Swains Lane. (Tube: Archway. **Eastern Cemetery** open Mon.-Fri. 10am-4:45pm, Sat.-Sun. 11am-4:45pm. Admission £2, but varies nominally. **Western Cemetery** access by guided tour only Mon.-Fri. at noon, 2, and 4pm, Sat.-Sun. every hr. 11am-4pm. Admission around £3. Camera permit £1, valid in both sections.)

London **Docklands,** the largest commercial development in Europe, has utterly changed the face of East London within the space of 10 years. As part of the Thatcher government's privatization program, redevelopment of the area was handed over to the private sector—in the form of the **London Docklands Development Corporation (LDDC)**—along with a generous helping of public funds. Since then, the LDDC has been at the helm of what it calls "the most significant urban regeration program in the world." The best way to see the region is via the **Docklands Light Railway**

(DLR) (tel. 918 4000), a futuristic, totally automatic, driverless elevated rail system. All tickets, Travelcards, and passes issued by London Transport, London Underground, and British Rail are valid on the DLR provided they cover the correct zones. The first stop for any Docklands tour should be the **Docklands Visitors Centre** (tel. 512 1111; DLR: Crossharbor, then left up the road; open Mon.-Fri. 8:30am-6pm, Sat.-Sun. 9:30am-5pm).

Head by train or boat to red-brick **Hampton Court Palace** (tel. (0181) 781 9500) for a quirky change of pace. (Open March to late Oct. Mon. 10:15am-6pm, Tues.-Sun. 9:30am-6pm; late Oct. to March Mon. 10:15am-4:30pm, Tues.-Sun. 9:30am-4:30pm. Last admission 45min. before closing. Gardens open at the same time, but close at 9pm or dusk, whichever comes first (free). All-encompassing admission £8, students £5.75, under 16 £4.90, under 5 free, families £19.50. Admission to maze or Privy Garden only £1.70, under 16 £1.) Its grounds contain the famous hedgerow maze (British Rail: Hampton Court). From the first Monday before Easter until the end of September, a boat runs from Westminster Pier to Hampton Court, leaving in the morning at 10:30, 11:15am, and noon, and returning from Hampton Court at 3, 4, and 5pm (the trip takes 3-4hr. one way; adult one-way £7, return £10).

Windsor Castle (tel. (01753) 868286 or 831118 for 24-hr. information line) is the Queen's spectacular country retreat. British Rail serves Windsor and Eton Central station and Windsor and Eton Riverside station, both of which are near Windsor Castle (street signs point the way; open April-Oct. daily 10am-5:30pm, last admission at 4pm; Nov.-March daily 10am-4pm, last admission at 3pm; admission £8.50).

Just west of central London on the Thames lie the serene and exotic **Kew Gardens.** Lose yourself in the controlled wilderness of the grounds, or explore the Victorian and modern glasshouses containing thousands of plant species. (Tube or British Rail: Kew Gardens. Gardens open Mon.-Fri. 9:30am-6:30pm, last admission 6pm; Sat.-Sun. and bank holidays 9:30am-7:30pm, last admission 7pm. Conservatories close at 5:30pm. Call to confirm closing times as they may vary by season. Admission £5, students and seniors £3; late admission from 4:45pm £3. Tours leave Victoria Gate daily at 11am and 2pm, £1.)

Museums

British Museum, Great Russell St. (tel. 323 8299 or 580 1788 for recorded info), Tube: Tottenham Ct. Rd. or Holborn. The closest thing this planet has to a complete record of the rise and ruin of world cultures. Among the plunder on display are the Rosetta Stone (whose inscriptions allowed French scholar Champollion to decipher hieroglyphics) and the Elgin Marbles. Also hoards an early manuscript of *Beowulf* and 2 of 4 surviving copies of the *Magna Carta.* Open Mon.-Sat. 10am-5pm, Sun. 2:30-6pm. Free. Special exhibits £3, students £2.

National Gallery, Trafalgar Sq. (tel. 839 3321 or 747 2885 for recorded info), Tube: Charing Cross. One of the world's finest collections of European painting; heavyweight works by da Vinci, Turner, and Velázquez. The new Micro Gallery, a computerized, illustrated catalogue, will print out a free personalized tour. Open Mon.-Sat. 10am-6pm, Wed. 6-8pm, Sun. noon-6pm. Free.

National Portrait Gallery, St. Martin's Pl. (tel. 306 0055), opposite St. Martin's in the Fields. Tube: Charing Cross. Doubles as *Who's Who in Britain.* Open Mon.-Sat. 10am-6pm, Sun. noon-6pm. Free.

Tate Gallery, Millbank (tel. 887 8000), up the Thames from Parliament Sq. Tube: Pimlico. The best of British artists such as Gainsborough, Reynolds, and Constable, along with works by Monet, Dalí, and Matisse. Simply put, the best place for contemporary art fans in London. The vast J.M.W. Turner collection rests in the Clore Gallery, an extension of the main building. Both open Mon.-Sat. 10am-5:50pm, Sun. 2-5:50pm. Free.

Victoria and Albert Museum, Cromwell Rd. (tel. 938 8500 or 938 8441 24-hr. recorded info or 938 8349 current exhibits). Tube: South Kensington. A mind-boggling array of fine and applied arts from all periods and places. Open Mon. noon-5:50pm, Tues.-Sun. 10am-5:50pm. Admission about £5, students free.

Madame Tussaud's, Marylebone Rd., NW1 (tel. 935 6861). Tube: Baker St. The classic waxwork museum. Open Mon.-Fri. 10am-5:30pm, Sat.-Sun. 9:30am-5:30pm. Admission £8.75, seniors £6.60, children £5.75.

Museum of London, 150 London Wall, EC2 (tel. 600 3699 or 600 0807 for 24-hr. info). Tube: St. Paul's or Barbican. From Londinium to the Docklands. Free lectures Wed.-Fri. 1:10pm. Open Tues.-Sat. 10am-6pm, Sun. noon-6pm, bank holidays 10am-6pm, last entry 5:30pm. Admission £3.50, students £1.75. Free after 4:30pm.

Museum of the Moving Image (MOMI), South Bank Centre, SE1 (tel. 928 3232 or 401 2636 for 24-hr. information). Tube: Waterloo. The entertaining museum charts the development of image-making with light, from shadow puppets to film and telly. Open daily 10am-6pm; last entry 5pm, but allow around 2hr. Admission £6, students £4.85, handicapped, seniors, children £4, family £16.

Science Museum, Exhibition Rd., SW7 (tel. 938 8008 or 938 8080). Tube: South Kensington. Closet science geeks will be outed by their orgasmic cries as they enter this wonderland of diagrammed motors, springs, and spaceships. This superbly arranged 5-story collection rivals the best science museums around. Open daily 10am-6pm. Admission £5, students £2.90, under 5 and people with disabilities free. Free daily 4:30-6pm.

Sir John Soane's Museum, 13 Lincoln's Inn Fields, WC2 (tel. 405 2107). Tube: Holborn. Soane was an architect's architect, but the idiosyncratic home he designed for himself will intrigue lay-persons. Famous artifacts on display include Hogarth paintings, the massive sarcophagus of Seti I, and casts of famous buildings and sculptures from around the world. Open Tues.-Sat. 10am-5pm. Free.

The Wallace Collection, Hertford House, Manchester Sq., W1 (tel. 935 0687). Tube: Bond St. Owned by various Marquises of Hertford and the illegitimate son of the fourth Marquis, Sir Richard Wallace, this mansion defines the adjective "sumptuous." Wonderful collection of Dutch art—though those indifferent to Dutch masterpieces will love the largest armor and weaponry collection outside of the Tower of London. Open Mon.-Sat. 10am-5pm, Sun. 2-5pm. Free.

ENTERTAINMENT

At any given time, Londoners and visitors can choose from a fantastic array of entertainment options. For guidance consult *Time Out* (£1.70), or *What's On* (£1.20).

Theater, Music, & Film

London **theater** is unrivalled. Seats cost about £8-30 and up, and student/senior standby (with an "S" or "concessions" in listings) puts even the best seats within reach—around £7 shortly before curtain (come 2hr. early to get a seat). **Day seats** are sold cheaply (9-10am, the day of performance) to all; queue up earlier to snag one. The **Leicester Square Ticket Booth** sells half-price tickets on the day of major plays (open Mon.-Sat. noon-6:30pm; long wait. £1.50-2 fee; cash only). Standby tickets for the **Royal National Theatre,** on the South Bank (tel. 928 2252; tube: Waterloo) sell two hours beforehand (£8-12). Students and seniors standby 45 minutes before hand (£6.50). The **Barbican Theatre** (tel. 628 2295 or 638 8891; tube: Barbican or Moorgate), London home of the Royal Shakespeare Co., student and senior standbys for £6.50 from 9am on the day of performance. Often, more exciting performances for significantly less cash are to be found on the **Fringe,** smaller less commercial theaters.

Most major **classical music** is staged at the acoustically superb **Royal Festival Hall** (tel. 960 4242; tube: Waterloo) and the **Barbican Hall.** Hampstead Heath's **Kenwood House** and the **Marble Hill House** have low-priced outdoor concerts on summer weekends (tel. (0181) 973 3427 and (0171) 413 1443). Opera and ballet embellish the **Royal Opera House** (tel. 304 4000; tube: Covent Garden) and the **London Coliseum** (tel. 632 8300; tube: Charing Cross or Leicester Sq.). Londoners have been lining up for standing room in the **Royal Albert Hall's "Proms"** (BBC Henry Wood Promenade Concerts), the most popular and endearing feature of the London music scene, for nearly a century.

Every **pop music** phenomenon that didn't take off in London came here at some point. Ticket offices and record shops list concerts. **Brixton Academy** (tel. 924 9999; tube: Brixton), is a large, rowdy venue for a variety of music including rock and reggae (advance tickets £8-25). **Ronnie Scott's,** 47 Frith St., W1 (tel. 439 0747; tube: Leicester Sq. or Piccadilly Circus), has London's greatest jazz (cover from £12).

The Prince Charles, Leicester Pl., WC2 (tel. 437 8181; tube: Leicester Sq.) is a Soho institution: four shows per day (cheerily deconstructed on the recorded phone message), generally second runs and a sprinkling of classics for only £1.75-2.25. **Everyman Cinema,** Hollybush Vale, Hampstead, NW3 (tel. 435 1525; tube: Hampstead), has double and triple bills based on either a theme or a classic celluloid figure. Special seasonal runs; membership 60p per year. (Mon.-Fri. £4.50, Sat.-Sun. £5, students Mon.-Fri. £3.50.) **Gate Cinema,** Notting Hill Gate Rd. (tel. 727 4043; tube: Notting Hill Gate), is London's last full-time smoking cinema (£5.75).

Dance Clubs

London pounds to 100% Groovy Liverpool tunes, ecstatic Manchester rave, hometown soul and house, imported U.S. hip-hop, and Jamaican reggae. Many clubs host a variety of provocative one-night stands (like "Get Up and Use Me") throughout the week. If you're looking for a truly underground dance experience, keep your ear to the ground. While news of serious raves travels exclusively by word of mouth, they can attract thousands of revelers "in the know," who congregate in abandoned warehouses or in open fields outside the city. Check listings in *Time Out* for the latest—their picks tend to be on target.

Iceni, 11 White Horse St., W1 (tel. 495 5333). Tube: Green Park. Off Curzon Street. Three beautiful floors of deep funk in this stylish Mayfair hotspot. Those who can't keep the beat appreciate the board games. Cover £5-8. Open Wed.-Sat. 10pm-3am.

The Fridge, Town Hall Parade, Brixton Hill, SW2 (tel. 326 5100). Tube: Brixton. Night bus N2. A serious dance dive with a stylish multi-ethnic crowd. Telly psychedelia, twisting dance cages, and Saturday's "Love Muscle," the ultimate London one-nighter, pack in a beautiful and shocking mixed-gay clientele. Every Fri. is a different theme night—call for the latest update. Cover £10, with flyer £8. Open Fri.-Sat. 10pm-6am.

Ministry of Sound, 103 Gaunt St., SE1 (tel. 378 6528). Tube: Elephant & Castle. Night Bus N12, N62, N65, N72, N77, or N78. Another south of the Thames megaclub, with the long queues, beefy covers, beautiful people, and pumping house tunes. An excellent way to while away a Sunday morning. Cover Fri. £10, Sat. £15. Open Fri. 11pm-8am, Sat. 11pm-9am.

Jazz Bistro, 340 Farringdon St., EC1 (tel. 236 8112). Tube: Farringdon. With a handle like "Jazz Bistro" it's amazing how unpretentious this place is. A refreshing enclave of Farringdon bohemian on the fringe of the decidedly un-boho City. Cover never tops £4. Open nightly 10pm-3am.

Offbeat Entertainment

Old Bailey, corner of Old Bailey and Newgate St. (tel. 248 3277). Tube: St. Paul's. Trial-watching persists as a favorite occupation, and the Old Bailey fills up whenever a gruesome or scandalous case is in progress. You can enter the public Visitors' Gallery and watch bewigged barristers at work. Even women wear the wigs so that they too may look like wise old men. Cameras, large bags, and backpacks may not be taken inside. Open Mon.-Fri. 10am-1pm and 2-4pm; entrance in Warwick Passage off of Old Bailey.

Porchester Spa, Queensway, W2 (tel. 792 3980). Tube: Bayswater or Royal Oak. In the Porchester Centre. A Turkish bath with steam and dry heat rooms and a swimming pool. Built in 1929, the baths are a newly refurbished Art Deco masterpiece of gold and marble. Rates are high (3hr. £17.50), but devoted fans keep taking the plunge. Open daily 10am-10pm. Men bathe Mon., Wed., and Sat.; women bathe Tues., Thurs., and Fri. On Sun. women may bathe from 10am-4pm, and couples may bathe together from 4-10pm at the special rate of £23.50/couple for 3hr. Swimwear required for mixed couples night.

Speakers' Corner, in the northeast corner of Hyde Park. Tube: Marble Arch. Crackpots, evangelists, political activists, and more crackpots speak their minds every Sun. 11am-dusk.

The Rocky Horror Picture Show, at the Prince Charles Cinema (see p. 464). This ain't *Cats* anymore, boys. Witness the legend in its hometown, complete with a live troupe and biscuit throwing. Fri. 11:30pm. Admission £6, concessions £3.

Vidal Sassoon School of Hairdressing, 56 Davies Mews, W1 (tel. 318 5205). Tube: Bond St. Become your own offbeat entertainment. Cuts, perms, and colorings at the hand of *un petit* Sassoony. Cut and blow dry £11 (concessions £5.50), which includes lengthy consultations with an experienced stylist before the students do their worst. Most "students" have spent time styling at lesser studios before even being allowed to study with the maestro. Make sure you have about 2-2½hr. to spare. Appointment recommended. Open Mon.-Fri. 9:30am-4pm.

BISEXUAL, GAY, & LESBIAN LONDON

Travelers coming to London will be delighted by the range of London's very visible gay scene, which covers everything from the flamboyant to the cruisy to the mainstream. For further info contact the gay, lesbian, and bisexual helplines (p. 451).

The Box, Seven Dials, 32-34 Monmouth St., WC2 (tel. 240 5828). Tube: Covent Garden. Small, intimate, stylish gay bar off of Covent Garden. Women-only "Girl Bar" every Sunday attracts nice girls, entice girls, shock girls, frock girls, cute girls, and boot girls. Cover £1. Open Mon.-Sat. 11am-11pm, Sun. 7pm-midnight.

Balans, 60 Old Compton St., W1 (tel. 437 5212). Tube: Leicester Square. Fiery flower arrangements and feral zebra-print lampshades create a ruthlessly glamorous ambience for the mostly gay, male clientele in this brasserie/bar. Lots of veggie options, and it never closes.

Comptons of Soho, 53 Old Compton St., W1 (tel. 437 4445). Tube: Leicester Sq. or Piccadilly Circus. Soho's "official" gay pub, always busy with a large crowd of all ages. Horseshoe-shaped bar encourages the exchange of meaningful glances. The upstairs offers a mellower scene, where patrons can gaze at a big screen TV instead of each other. Open Mon.-Sat. noon-11pm, Sun. noon-10:30pm.

Drill Hall Women-Only Bar, 16 Chenies St., WC1 (tel. 631 1353). Tube: Goodge St. A much anticipated one-nighter located in the lobby of one of London's biggest alternative theatres. Dim lighting and red walls. Crowded and laid back. Open Mon. 6-11pm.

Old Compton Café, 35 Old Compton St., W1 (tel. 439 3309). Tube: Leicester Sq. Open 24hr. in the geographic epicenter of Soho, this is *the* gay café. Tables and people (mostly 20- and 30-something males) overflow onto the street.

Substation Soho, Falconberg Ct., W1 (tel. 287 9608). Tube: Tottenham Ct. Rd. For gay men who find the Old Compton St. scene too tame, a cruisy, late-night testosterone fest—one popular one-nighter is the underwear-only grope-a-thon "Y Front" (changing rooms provided). Open Mon.-Thurs. 10pm-3am, Fri. 10pm-4am, Sat. 10:30pm-6am. If it's Sunday, you can't wait for 10pm, or you live south of the Thames, **Substation South,** 9 Brighton Terr., SW9 (tel. 732 2095; tube: Brixton) provides a similar scene in Brixton, but is open at 6pm, and on Sun. 6pm-1am. Cover for either £2-4.

Wilde About Oscar, 30-31 Philbeach Gdns., SW5 (tel. 373 1244 before 5pm or 835 1858 after 5pm). Tube: Earl's Ct. A definite splurge (entrees about £10), but it's worth it—dine in the manicured garden of a gay B&B. Candles, flowers, and few tables make for an intimate dining encounter. Main courses are mostly French dishes. Open daily 7pm-midnight.

"Wow Bar," Saturdays from 8-11pm at Glasshouse St., Piccadilly (tel. (0956) 514574 for info and free membership). Tube: Piccadilly Circus. Newly transplanted "lipstick lesbian" haunt whose former guests include Martina Navratilova. Cover before 9pm and for members £2; otherwise £3.

Heaven, Villiers St., WC2 (tel. 839 3852), underneath The Arches. Tube: Embankment or Charing Cross (Villiers is off the Strand). Still the oldest and biggest gay disco in Europe. Three dance floors, high-tech lighting, pool tables, and a capacity of nearly 4000 mean big fun. Bumping garage music Fri. 10pm-3:30am, Sat. 10pm-4am. Cover Fri. £6, after 11:30pm £7.50. Sat. £7; after 11:30pm £8.

"G.A.Y.," at London Astoria 1 (Sat.), and 2 (Thurs. and Mon.), 157 Charing Cross Rd., WC2 (tel. 734 6963). Tube: Tottenham Ct. Rd. A 3-nights-a-week pop extravaganza amidst chrome and mirrored disco balls. Emphatically unpretentious clientele (very mixed, in both gender and orientation). Mon. 10:30pm-3am, Thurs. 10:30pm-4am, Sat. 10:30pm-5am. Cover Mon. £3, £1 if student or with flyer; Thurs. £3, free with flyer; Sat. £6, with flyer £5.

SHOPPING

Books

Dillons, Trafalgar Sq., Grand Building, WC2 (tel. 839 4411). Tube: Charing Cross or Leicester Sq. One of London's best chains. Strong on academic subjects, particularly history and politics. Fair selection of reduced-price and secondhand books, plus classical CDs and tapes. Open Mon.-Sat. 10am-9pm, Sun. noon-6pm.

Bell, Book and Radmall, 4 Cecil Ct., WC2 (tel. 240 2161). Tube: Leicester Sq. A small antiquarian bookstore with a zippy staff, an exceptional selection of American and British first editions, and an impressive supply of sci-fi and detective novels. Open Mon.-Fri. 10am-5:30pm, Sat. 11am-4:30pm.

Clothing & Shoes

Fortnum & Mason, 181 Piccadilly, W1 (tel. 734 8040). Tube: Green Park or Piccadilly Circus. Liveried clerks vend expensive foods in red-carpeted and chandeliered halls at this renowned establishment. Look out for rare free samples of the food court's exquisite wares. Open Mon.-Sat. 9:30am-6pm.

Harrods, 87-135 Brompton Rd., SW3 (tel. 730 1234). Tube: Knightsbridge. Simply put, this is *the* store in London, perhaps the world. They can do everything from finding you a live rhinoceros to arranging your funeral. Shorts, ripped clothing, and backpacks are forbidden in this quasi-museum of luxury—nevertheless, the downstairs seems like a tourist convention at times. Luxury washrooms (£1) offer fluffy towels and an almost unimaginable selection of fragrant washes and wipes. Open Mon.-Tues. and Sat. 10am-6pm, Wed.-Fri. 10am-7pm.

Top Shop/Top Man, 214 Oxford St., W1 (tel. 636 7700). Tube: Oxford Circus. Multi-story megastore right at Oxford Circus with the trendiest of inexpensive fashions for men and women, with something to suit one's flamboyant side. Open Mon.-Wed. and Fri.-Sat. 10am-7pm, Thurs. 10am-8pm, Sun. noon-6pm.

Shelly's, 159 Oxford St., W1 (tel. 437 5842). Tube: Oxford Circus. Shelly's reverses the preppie ethic of sensible shoes at outrageous prices—they offer outrageous shoes at sensible prices. Always displaying the most current styles. Open Mon.-Wed. and Fri.-Sat. 9:15am-6:15pm, Thurs. 9:15am-7:15pm, Sun. noon-6pm.

Specialty Shops

Honour, 86 Lower Marsh, SE1 (tel. 401 8220). Tube: Waterloo. One of the few places in England where rubber isn't just another word for an eraser. The first floor stocks wigs and all sorts of rubber and PVC gear for fetish trendies, the second floor features the sort of bondage gear you wouldn't wear to a club. Open Mon.-Fri. 10:30am-7pm, Sat. 11:30am-5pm.

Into You, 144 St. John St., EC1 (tel. 253 5085). Tattooing, body-piercing, and related literature and items. If pain is pleasure and permanency doesn't bother you, then take the plunge. Open Tues.-Fri. noon-7pm, Sat. noon-6pm.

APPENDIX

■ Climate

The following chart gives the average high and low temperatures in degrees centigrade (Celsius) and the average yearly rainfall in centimeters during four months of the year. Dublin is on the southeast coast, Cork is on the south coast, Mullingar is in the center of Ireland, and Belfast is on the northeast coast, in Northern Ireland.

| Temp in °C | January | | April | | July | | October | |
Rain in cm	Temp	Rain	Temp	Rain	Temp	Rain	Temp	Rain
Dublin	8/1	6.7	13/4	4.5	20/11	7.0	14/6	7.0
Cork	9/2	11.9	13/5	5.7	20/12	7.0	14/7	9.9
Mullingar	7/1	8.8	13/4	5.5	19/11	8.9	13/6	9.4
Belfast	6/2	8.0	12/4	4.8	18/11	9.4	13/7	8.3

■ Telephone Codes

COUNTRY CODES

The following are the international telephone codes for calling *to* a particular country. These codes must be entered after the international access code of the country you are calling *from*. For example, if calling the Republic of Ireland from the United States, one would first dial 011 (the U.S. international access code), and then 353 (Ireland's country code).

Republic of Ireland: 353.
Northern Ireland: from the Republic 08; from other countries 44.
Britain & Isle of Man: 44.
USA and Canada: 1.
Australia: 61.
New Zealand: 64.
South Africa: 27.

CALLING CARD CALLS

The following services will allow you to place collect calls (expensive) or charge them to a calling card (less so).

	Republic of Ireland	Northern Ireland, Isle of Man, London
Australia Direct	1800 550 061	0800 890 061
British Telecom	1800 550 144	
Ireland Direct		0800 890 353
New Zealand Direct	1800 799 964	0800 799 964
Telekom South Africa	1800 990 353	0800 990 044
AT&T Direct	1800 550 000	0800 890 303
MCI WorldPhone	1800 551 001	0800 890 222

■ Weights & Measures

1 millimeter (mm) = 0.04 inches (in.)	1 inch = 25mm
1 meter (m) = 1.09 yards (yd.)	1 yard = 0.92m
1 kilometer (km) = 0.621 miles (mi.)	1 mile = 1.61km
1 gram (g) = 0.04 ounces (oz.)	1 ounce = 25g
1 kilogram (kg) = 2.2 pounds (lbs.)	1 pound = .45kg
1 "stone" (weight) = 14 pounds	1 pound = .71 stone
1 liter = 1.057 U.S quarts (qt.)	1 U.S quart = 0.94 liters
1 liter = 0.88 Imperial quarts	1 Imperial quart = 1.14 liters
1 Imperial gallon = 1.19 U.S. gallons (ga.)	1 U.S. gallon = .84 Imperial gallons
1 British pint = 1.19 U.S. pints (pt.)	1 U.S. pint = .84 British pints

To convert from °C to °F, multiply by 1.8 and add 32.
To convert from °F to °C, subtract 32 and multiply by 5/9.

°C	30	26	22	18	14	10	6	2	-1	-5
°F	86	79	72	64	57	50	43	36	34	23

■ Holidays

Government agencies, post offices, and banks are closed on these days, and businesses may have special (shorter) hours. Transportation, in particular, practically grinds to a halt; check schedules carefully.

January 1		New Year's Day
March 17	*Republic of Ireland and Northern Ireland*	St. Patrick's Day
April 4, 1997		Good Friday
April 7, 1997		Easter Monday
May 6, 1997	*Northern Ireland, Isle of Man, London*	May Day Holiday
May 27, 1997	*Northern Ireland, Isle of Man, London*	Spring or Whitsun Holiday
June 3, 1997	*Republic of Ireland*	First Monday in June
July 5	*Isle of Man*	Tynwald Fair Day
July 12	*Northern Ireland*	Orange Day
August 5, 1997	*Republic of Ireland*	First Monday in August
August 26, 1997	*Northern Ireland, Isle of Man, London*	Late Summer Holiday
October 30, 1997	*Republic of Ireland*	Last Monday in October
December 25		Christmas Day
December 26		St. Stephen's Day/Boxing Day

APPENDIX

■ Events

late February	*Dublin*	**Dublin Film Festival.**
March 17	*Ireland*	**St. Patrick's Day.** A source of merriment.
late April	*Carlingford, Co. Louth*	**Leprechaun Hunt.** A treasure hunt with five stone leprechauns hidden on the Cooley Mountains and monetary rewards for finders.
early June	*Douglas*	**T.T. (Tourist Trophy) Motorcycle Races.**
early June	*Rathdrum*	**International Cartoon Festival.**
mid-June	*Ballycastle*	**Fleadh Amhrán agus Rince.** Big festival of song and dance.
June 16	*Dublin*	**Bloomsday.** Dublin loves *Ulysses.*
late June	*The Curragh*	**Irish Derby.** Ireland's Super Bowl.
late June	*Portaferry*	**Galway Hookers' Regatta.** Traditional Irish vessels sail up Strangford Lough.
early July	*Miltown Malbay*	**Willy Clancy Summer School.** Big summer gathering of Irish musicians.
July 5	*St. John's*	**Tynwald Fair.** The Isle of Man's national holiday—big processions and pomp.
July 12 (Orange Day)	*Belfast, Derry*	**Ancient Order of Hibernians' Parades.** The Feast of the Assumption is marked by processions and open-air meetings.
late July	*Sligo*	**Irish National Sheepdog Trials.**
late July–early August	*Dungloe*	**Mary from Dungloe International Festival.** Select the Mary from Dungloe. Contact Charlie "the Yank" Boyle (tel. (075) 48519).
late July–early August	*Youghal*	**Youghal Premier Busking Festival.** Buskers compete for valuable prizes.
early August	*Kinsale*	**Kinsale Regatta.**
early August	*Thurles, Co. Tipperary*	**Féile.** Three day rock/pop/trad event with endless big names and a Woodstock-like atmosphere. Also known as the "Trip to Tipp."
mid-August	*Miltown Malbay*	**International "Darlin' Girl from Clare" Festival.** Fashion extravaganza with "Darlin' Girls" as models: Pat Kenny interviews each.
late August	*Clonmel*	**Fleadh Ceoil na hÉireann.** Ireland's premier cultural festival.
late August	*Tralee*	**Rose of Tralee International Festival.** A Rose of Tralee is chosen from girls of Irish descent from all over the world. Televised nationwide.
late August	*Ballycastle*	**Oul' Lammas Fair.** Horse and sheep market, edible seaweed for sale.
September	*Dublin*	**All-Ireland Hurling Final.**
September	*Lisdoonvarna*	**Lisdoonvarna Matchmaking Festival.**
September	*Dublin*	**All-Ireland Football Finals.**
late September	*Waterford*	**Waterford Festival of Light Opera.**
early October	*Kildare*	**Irish National Yearling Sales.**
early October	*Dublin*	**Dublin Theater Festival.**
mid-October	*Kinsale*	**Kinsale Gourmet Festival.**
mid-October	*Wexford*	**Wexford Opera Festival.**
November	*Queen's University, Belfast*	**Belfast Festival at Queen's.** Huge: drama, ballet, cinema, music from classical to folk.

■ Glossary

IRISH-ENGLISH WORDS

Many Irish-English words and usages duplicate those in England; some don't. Words derived from Irish are listed separately below.

bangers and mash	sausage and mashed potatoes
bap	a soft bun, like a hamburger bun
bedsit	one-room apartment, sometimes with kitchen
bill	check (in restaurants)
biro	ball point pen
busker	street musician
candy-floss	cotton candy
caravan	trailer, mobile home
cheap	inexpensive (not "shoddy")
chemist	pharmacist
chips	french fries
chipper/chippy	fish and chips vendor
coach	bus (long-distance)
concession	discount on admission (for students, OAPs, etc.)
crisps	potato chips
dear	expensive
dole, on the dole	welfare or unemployment benefits
dolmen	chamber formed by huge stones
drumlin	small hill
DUP	Democratic Unionist Party; led by Ian Paisley
dustbin	trash can
en suite	with bathroom (and usually shower)
fag	cigarette
first floor	first floor up (second floor)
fiver, tenner	£5 note, £10 note
flat	apartment
fook	emphasis
football	Gaelic football in South, soccer in North
fortnight	two weeks
gaol	pronounced (and means) "jail"
ground floor	first floor
hire	rental
hoover	vacuum cleaner
INLA	Irish National Liberation Army, an IRA splinter group
IRA	Irish Republican Army (Nationalist paramilitary group)
lavatory, lav	bathroom
left luggage	luggage storage
to let	to rent
loo	bathroom
lorry	truck
Loyalist	pro-British
mate	pal
motorway	highway
nappies	diapers
Nationalists	those who want Northern Ireland to be a part of the Republic of Ireland
the North	relatively neutral term for Northern Ireland

OAP	old age pensioner; a senior citizen
off-license	retail liquor store
Orangemen	A widespread Protestant Unionist group
OUP	Official Unionist Party; the largest party in Northern Ireland
pants	underwear
petrol	gasoline
pissed	drunk
pub grub	quality bar food (see **Pubs & Food,** p. 80)
publican	barkeeper
punt	Irish pound
quay	"key"; a waterside street
queue up, "Q"	line up
quid	pounds
rashers	little sausages
redundancies	job layoffs
Republican	see *Nationalist*
return ticket	roundtrip ticket
roundabout	rotary road interchange
rubber	eraser
RUC	Royal Ulster Constabulary, the Northern Ireland police force
SDLP	Social Democratic and Labor Party; moderate Nationalist party in Northern Ireland
self-catering	accommodation with kitchen facilities
self-drive	car rental
to shift	to chat with the intention of hooking up
single ticket	one-way ticket
to slag	to tease and ridicule in the inimitable Irish fashion
to snog	to kiss
snooker	a game like pool
snug	enclosed booth within a pub
sterling	British pound
stone	14 pounds (in body weight)
strand	beach
subway	underground walkway
sultanas	similar to raisins or currants
take-away	take-out food
The Troubles	Northern Ireland's Protestant/Catholic conflict
toilet	bathroom
torch	flashlight
trad	traditional Irish music
trainers	sneakers
traveller	an ethnic group (see p. 67)
UDA	Ulster Defence Association (Unionist paramilitary group)
UDR	Ulster Defence Regiment, the British Army unit in Northern Ireland
UFF	Ulster Freedom Fighters (Unionist paramilitary group)
Unionists	those who want Northern Ireland to remain part of the U.K.
UVF and UDF	Ulster Volunteer/Defence Force (Unionist paramilitary groups)
way out	exit
zed	letter "Z"

APPENDIX

IRISH WORDS & PHRASES

The following bits of the Irish language are either used often in Irish English or are common in Irish place names. Spelling conventions do not always match English pronunciations: for example, "mh" sounds like "v," and "dh" sounds like "g."

aerphort	AYR-fort	airport
aisling	ASH-ling	vision or dream, or a poem or story thereof
An Lár	on lahr	city center
Ar aghaidh linn: Éire	uhr EYE linn: AIR-ah	*Let's Go: Ireland*
Baile Átha Cliath	BALL-yah AW-hah CLEE-ah	Dublin
bodhrán	BOUR-ohn	traditional drum
Bord Fáilte	bored FAHL-tshuh	Irish Tourist Board
Conas tá tú?	CUNN-us thaw too?	How are you?
céilí	KAY-lee	Irish dance
craic	krak	good cheer, good pub conversation, a good time
Dáil	DOY-il	House of Representatives
dia dhuit	JEE-a dich	good day, hello
dia's muire dhuit	JEE-as MWUR-a dich	reply to "good day"
dún	doon	fort
Éire	AIR-uh	Ireland; official name of the Republic of Ireland
fáilte	FAHL-tshuh	welcome
feis	fesh	an assembly, Irish festival
Fianna Fáil	FEE-in-ah foil	"Soldiers of Destiny," political party
Fine Gael	FINN-eh gayl	"Family of Ireland," political party
fir	fear	men
fleadh	flah	a musical festival
gaeltacht	GAYL-tokt	a district where Irish is the everyday language
garda, Garda Siochána	GAR-da SHE-och-ANA	police
go raibh maith agat	guh roh moh UG-ut	thank you
inch, innis, ennis	inch, innis, ennis	island; river meadow
kil	kill	church; cell
knock	nok	hill
lei thras	LEH-hrass	toilets
lough	lohk	lake
mná	min-AW	women
mór	more	big, great
ní hea	nee hah	no (sort of; it's tricky)
oíche mhaith dhuit	EE-ha woh dich	good night
ogham	O-um	early Irish, written on stones
Oifig an Phoist	UFF-ig un fwisht	Post Office
poitín	po-CHEEN	moonshine; sometimes-toxic homemade liquor
rath	rath *or* rah	earthen fort
sea	shah	yes (sort of; it's tricky)
seanachaí	SHAN-ukh-ee	storyteller
Seanad	SHAN-ud	Senate

Sinn Féin	shin fayn	"Ourselves Alone," the political wing of the IRA
sláinte	SLAWN-che	cheers, to your health
slán agat	slawn UG-ut	goodbye
slieve *or* **sliabh**	shleev	mountain
sraid	shrawd	street
Taoiseach	TEE-shukh	Prime Minister
teachta dála (TD)	TAKH-ta DAH-lah	member of Irish parliament
telefón	TEL-eh-fone	telephone
Tír na nÓg	cheer na nohg	Land of Youth
trá	thraw	beach
uilleann	ILL-in	"elbow," bagpipes played with the elbow

USEFUL PHRASES

It's said that Eskimos have 40 different words for snow.

How 's the weather today?	*Conas atá an aimsir inniú?*	CUNN-us a thaw un AM-shir in-YOU?
It is…	*Tá sé*…	thaw shay
cloudy	*scamallach*	SCOM-ull-uckh
cold	*fuar*	FOO-ur
cool	*finuar*	fin-OOR
wet	*fliuch*	flukh
frosty	*ag cur sioc*	egg cur shuk
Tomorrow it will be…	*Amárach, beidh sé*…	um-AW-ruckh beg-shay
raining	*ag cur báistí* or *fearthaine*	egg cur BAWSH-tee or FAR-han-a
snowing	*ag cur sneachta*	egg cur SHNOKH-ta
windy	*gaofar*	GWEE-fur
showery	*ceathach*	KYAH-ukh
foggy	*ceombar*	KYO-wur
damp	*tais*	tash
I am…	*táim*…	thaw im
tipsy	*súgach*	SOO-gakh
drunk	*ar meisce*	uhr MEH-shka
very drunk	*ar dearg mheisce*	uhr jar-eg-VEH-shka
quite drunk	*ólta*	OLE-ta
blind drunk	*caoch ólta*	KWEE-ukh OLE-ta

APPENDIX

Index

INDEX

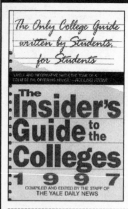

★Let's Go 1997 Reader Questionnaire ★

Please fill this out and return it to **Let's Go, St. Martin's Press,**
175 5th Ave. NY, NY 10010

Name: _____ **What book did you use?**_____

Address: _____

City: _____ **State:** _____ **Zip Code:** _____

How old are you? under 19   19-24   25-34   35-44   45-54   55 or over

Are you (circle one)   in high school   in college   in grad school
employed   retired   between jobs

Have you used Let's Go before? yes no

Would you use Let's Go again? yes no

How did you first hear about Let's Go? friend   store clerk   CNN
bookstore display   advertisement/promotion   review   other

Why did you choose Let's Go (circle up to two)? annual updating
reputation   budget focus   price   writing style
other: _____

Which other guides have you used, if any? Frommer's $-a-day Fodor's
Rough Guides   Lonely Planet   Berkeley   Rick Steves
other: _____

Is Let's Go the best guidebook? yes no

If not, which do you prefer? _____

**Which part of Let's Go do you feel needs most to be improved, if any
(circle up to two)?** packaging/cover   practical information
accommodations   food   cultural introduction   sights
practical introduction ("Essentials")   directions   entertainment
gay/lesbian information   maps   other: _____

How would you like to see these things improved?

_____

_____

How long was your trip?   one week   two weeks   three weeks
one month   two months or more

Have you traveled extensively before? yes no

Do you buy a separate map when you visit a foreign city? yes no

Have you seen the Let's Go Map Guides? yes no

Have you used a Let's Go Map Guide? yes no

If you have, would you recommend them to others? yes no

Did you use the internet to plan your trip? yes no

Would you buy a Let's Go phrasebook adventure/trekking guide
gay/lesbian guide

**Which of the following destinations do you hope to visit in the next three
to five years (circle one)?** Australia China South America Russia
other: _____

Where did you buy your guidebook?   internet   chain bookstore
independent bookstore   college bookstore   travel store
other: _____